INTERMEDIATE ACCOUNTING

The Willard J. Graham Series in Accounting

consulting editor

Robert N. Anthony Harvard University

INTERMEDIATE ACCOUNTING

Glenn A. Welsch, Ph.D., C.P.A.
Professor of Accounting

Charles T. Zlatkovich, Ph.D., C.P.A.
Professor of Accounting

John Arch White, Ph.D.
Professor of Accounting, Emeritus

all of the
Graduate School of Business
University of Texas at Austin

Fourth Edition **1976**

RICHARD D. IRWIN, INC. Homewood, Illinois 60430
Irwin-Dorsey Limited Georgetown, Ontario L7G 4B3

Fourth Edition

First Printing, May 1976
Second Printing, August 1976

ISBN 0-256-01817-0
Library of Congress Catalog Card No. 75-39360

Printed in the United States of America

Preface

This fourth edition of our textbook is designed, as were the three previous editions, for students who have completed the study of two semesters or quarters of accounting principles. It is planned for a two-semester sequence, but with judicious selection of and emphasis on material the text is readily adaptable to shorter courses or to the needs of schools using the quarter plan. It is designed to complement a principles text having one of the same coauthors,[1] but may be used following any reasonably complete first-year text in accounting.

Accounting theory and concepts are emphasized throughout. Students are provided reasons for the various accounting practices and procedures presented; they will learn the more important "why" along with the "how" of current accounting practice. This edition continues the comprehensive features which gained wide recognition for the prior editions. Upon completion, the student should be well prepared for the theory and practice sections of the Uniform CPA Examination and for advanced courses in accounting. A salient feature of this book is that, rather than avoiding troublesome complexities, by omission or oversimplified exposition, it deals with them comprehensively and, where appropriate, alternative viewpoints are presented. Examination of the chapter contents will reveal that all important aspects of each topic are considered, consistent with the objectives of the book, despite the fact that this imposes on the text a comparatively high level of sophistication.

At the outset this edition provides a carefully designed review of the fundamentals. Next it introduces the concepts of present value and utilizes them throughout the remaining discussions. This feature is in line with the significant trend in the official pronouncements of the accounting profession to require application of these concepts in a wide range of accounting practices such as those dealing with debt and receivable transactions, amortization of discounts and premiums, leases, pensions, investments, and certain other related transactions. Experience by the authors and many others has confirmed that these

---

[1] Glenn A. Welsch and Robert N. Anthony, *Fundamentals of Financial Accounting* (Homewood, Ill.: Richard D. Irwin, Inc., 1974); or William W. Pyle and John Arch White, *Fundamental Accounting Principles* (Homewood, Ill.: Richard D. Irwin, Inc., 1975).

concepts are not particularly troublesome to accounting students if introduced early in intermediate accounting and then applied throughout the course. Rather than using a less sophisticated (and inadequate) instructional content, this textbook reflects the increasing accounting sophistication in this area currently found in *APB Opinions*, FASB *Statements*, and the Uniform CPA Examinations.

Preferred accounting terminology is used throughout on a consistent basis. Citations and references to pronouncements of the APB, FASB, American Institute of Certified Public Accountants, the American Accounting Association, and the Securities and Exchange Commission permeate the 25 chapters. As a new and useful feature, this fourth edition includes an Appendix after the last chapter which lists all of the *Accounting Research Bulletins* (ARBs), *APB Opinions* and FASB *Statements* to date. The Appendix also indicates their current status and the chapters in which each is cited.

Recognizing that students learn much of their accounting at this point in their study by solving relevant assignment materials, the authors have supplied a wealth of questions, exercises, and problems for each chapter. The former policy of including both short exercises and longer comprehensive problems that are both relevant and challenging has been continued. Approximately 90 percent of these materials have been revised. An appropriate selection of materials from Uniform CPA Examinations is to be found in the assignment material. The professor is provided an unusually wide range of assignment materials of varying difficulty so that selections can be made that are suited to the student group.

This edition provides a unique variety of supplementary materials for the instructor and student. They include, in addition to the textbook, the following:

For the instructor:

1. A comprehensive teacher's manual including teaching suggestions and step-by-step computations.
2. An examination booklet classified by chapter.
3. A list of key figures.

For the student:

4. A study guide that incorporates for each chapter (*a*) study suggestions, (*b*) a study summary of important points with illustrations, (*c*) questions for self-evaluation and (*d*) answers to the questions for self-checkup.
5. A comprehensive *review* practice set designed to be used during the early part of the first semester. This practice set is included in the Study Guide (4 above); transaction narrative, forms, and selected key figures are provided therein. The complete solution is given in the Teacher's Manual (1 above).
6. A complete set of working papers that provides forms (with certain captions provided) for working the exercises and problems.

In addition, the prior policy of providing supplementary booklets, upon request and without cost, covering future FASB *Statements* will be continued by the authors and publisher.

Chapters are arranged in a teachable and logical sequence. They are grouped to facilitate rearrangement to suit individual preferences. The first two chapters set the stage for all that follows by presenting an integrating overview of the foundations of accounting theory. Following are three chapters that comprehensively review the principles of financial accounting and which carry the student somewhat beyond equivalent coverage in the traditional elementary accounting course.

Chapter 6 presents the concepts of present-value and actuarial mathematics and indicates their primary applications in financial accounting. This location significantly simplifies explanations, illustrations, and understandings in numerous instances throughout the course of intermediate instruction (and advanced courses as well). The authors also recognized the trend to include some instruction in present-value concepts in the better elementary accounting textbooks; the instruction should be continued on a higher level of sophistication at the intermediate level.

Chapters 1 through 14 are usually viewed as the first course in intermediate accounting. These chapters present a comprehensive treatment of assets and liabilities. Chapters 15 through 17 are devoted to corporations. Long-term investments in equity and debt securities are discussed in Chapters 18 and 19. The last six chapters are devoted, in order, to: special reporting problems, the Statement of Changes in Financial Position, pension plans, leases, statement analysis, and price-level accounting. Each of these chapters (as well as certain others) may be omitted in part or in whole, without significantly affecting the continuity of the course.

We are indebted to numerous colleagues and students from universities throughout the nation whose comments and suggestions led to many valuable improvements in this fourth edition. We appreciate the permission granted by the Financial Accounting Standards Board, the American Accounting Association and the American Institute of CPAs to quote from their various pronouncements. The latter organization also permitted us to make liberal use of materials adapted from the Uniform CPA Examinations.

We are especially appreciative of the many valuable suggestions provided by our colleagues and friends: David L. Wilson, Kermit D. Larson, Edward L. Summers, Fred Streuling, Larry A. Tomassini, Allen Bizzell, Lewis L. Davidson, and Charles H. Griffin. We also express thanks to graduate students at the University of Texas at Austin: Morley Lemon, Dewey Ward, Patti Smith, Scott Ikenberry, Richard Ratliff, Kathy Anderson, Charles Inman, Robert Sharp, Jacqueline Well, and Don Jones. Special gratitude is due Margaret Whatley, MPA candidate, for critiques, proofing, typing, and a host of other most helpful activities. Particularly valuable was a comprehensive critique of the textual and assignment materials provided by Phyllis Barker, Indiana State University, and many substantive suggestions by Kathryn C. Buckner, Georgia State University. We also express our thanks to numerous users of the prior editions for valuable suggestions in respect to content and arrangement.

Austin, Texas
April 1976

GLENN A. WELSCH
CHARLES T. ZLATKOVICH
JOHN A. WHITE

Contents

Chapter 1

Introduction

OBJECTIVES OF THE BOOK

This book focuses on financial accounting which provides financial information primarily for decision-makers outside the entity. This financial information is provided to external decision-makers primarily by means of general-purpose statements of operating results (i.e., the income statement), financial position (i.e., the balance sheet), and changes in financial position (i.e., statement of changes in financial position). Consistent with the broad objective of reporting to external parties, this book concentrates on the application of accounting theory, standards, principles, and procedures to accounting problems. The fundamental rationale for the various aspects of financial accounting are stressed. This book is designed especially for accounting majors, regardless of specialized interests in public, industrial, governmental, tax, or social accounting. Another objective is to prepare students for early entry into the real world of accounting; consequently, current financial accounting practices and trends are emphasized.

This book presumes that the student has studied a course in fundamentals of financial accounting.[1] Satisfactory completion of this text should prepare students for all advanced accounting courses. Emphasis throughout on theory, standards, and principles—the "why" of accounting—enables students to cope with new and complex accounting problems on a conceptual rather than a procedural (or memory) level.

ACCOUNTING DEFINED

Accounting can be broadly defined as an information processing system designed to *capture* and *measure* the economic essence of events that affect an entity and to report their economic effects on that entity to

[1] Refer to books such as: G. A. Welsch and R. N. Anthony, *Fundamentals of Financial Accounting* (Homewood, Ill.: Richard D. Irwin, Inc., 1974).

decision-makers.[2] This broad definition serves the two broad groups of decision-makers: internal decision-makers and external decision-makers. These two groups have different information needs resulting from different relationships with the entity. *Internal* decision-makers are the managers responsible for planning the future of the entity, implementing the plans, and controlling operations on a day-to-day basis. Because of their internal relationship to the entity, they can command whatever financial data they may need or desire at dates of their choice. Further, the information is for their sole use and generally is not intended to be communicated to outsiders. The process of developing and reporting financial information to internal users is usually called *management accounting,* and the reports are referred to as internal management reports. Because of the confidential nature of internal management reports, and their focus on internal decision making, there is no requirement (other than as specified by the management) that they conform to generally accepted accounting standards. Clearly, internal management reports should be structured to conform to the particular decision-making needs of the management.

In contrast, the external decision-makers (i.e., the external users of financial information) make distinctly different types of decisions regarding the entity, such as, to invest or disinvest, to loan funds, and so on. External decision-makers comprise present and potential investors and creditors, investment analysts, governmental units, and the public at large. In view of the diverse range of external users of financial data, the accounting profession has developed *general-purpose financial statements* designed to meet their decision-making needs. These statements are developed in a phase of accounting known as *financial accounting.* Financial accounting may be broadly defined as information processing, beginning with transactions and other events affecting the entity, progressing through its accounting system, and reporting of their economic impact to external decision-makers. The external users, because of their detachment from the entity, cannot directly command specific financial information from the entity; therefore, they must rely primarily on general-purpose financial statements. The accounting profession, in order to serve external users, has developed a network of accounting theory, standards, principles, and procedures designed to assure that external financial reports are: (1) service oriented – basically they are designed to serve the decision-making needs of the external users; (2) credible – they are intended to be fair representations of the economic circumstances of the entity; and (3) accurate and free of bias – they must conform to specified standards of accounting and reporting.

---

[2] Another useful definition is: Accounting is a service activity. Its function is to provide quantitative information, primarily financial in nature, about economic entities that is intended to be useful in making economic decisions – in making reasoned choices among alternative courses of action. Accounting includes several branches, for example, financial accounting, managerial accounting, and governmental accounting (AICPA, *Statement of the Accounting Principles Board No. 4* [New York, October 1970], p. 17).

OBJECTIVES OF EXTERNAL FINANCIAL STATEMENTS

Measurement of the economic effect of transactions and other events on an entity, and the communication of those economic effects, is the essence of financial accounting. Communication of the economic effect, by means of general-purpose financial statements, encompasses, as a minimum, the following:

1. Income statement—a periodic statement of the results of operations that reports revenues, expenses, extraordinary items, net income, and earnings per share.
2. Balance sheet—a periodic statement of financial position that reports assets, liabilities, and owners' equity.
3. Statement of changes in financial position—a periodic statement of the inflow of funds, outflow of funds, and net change in funds. This statement measures funds, in terms of either cash or working capital.
4. Supplementary information to assure full disclosure.

Because of the dynamic nature of the environment, general-purpose financial statements are in a constant state of evolution. The environment consists of the various aspects of a society: social, political, and economic. As the environment changes, the needs of external decision-makers change. Consequently, accounting measurements and reporting must evolve to meet those needs. Fundamentally, the basic objectives of external financial statements are:

> (1) To provide information useful for making economic decisions.
> (2) To serve primarily those users who have limited authority, ability, or resources to obtain information and who rely on financial statements as their principal source of information about an enterprise's economic activities.
> (3) To provide information useful to investors and creditors for predicting, comparing, and evaluating potential cash flows in terms of amount, timing, and related uncertainty.
> (4) To provide users with information for predicting, comparing, and evaluating enterprise earning power.
> (5) To supply information useful in judging management's ability to use enterprise resources effectively in achieving the primary enterprise goal.
> (6) To provide factual and interpretative information about transactions and other events which is useful for predicting, comparing, and evaluating enterprise earning power. Basic underlying assumptions with respect to matters subject to interpretation, evaluation, prediction, or estimation should be disclosed.[3]

We stress that the focus of financial accounting is on the *measurement* of economic effects and *communication* of the results to external decision-makers. The complexities of measurement, and the volume of

---

[3] AICPA, *Objectives of Financial Statements, Report of the Study Group on the Objectives of Financial Statements* (New York, October 1973), pp. 61–66 (adapted).

data processing encountered in an accounting system, are necessary to serve the end result—communication. We strongly emphasize this point because it is easy for the student to become immersed in the system and its procedures and to lose sight of the primary objective—reporting to the decision-maker.

PROFESSIONAL ACCOUNTANTS

Accounting has a long and interesting history. Today professional accountants fulfill an important and unique role in society.[4] The professional accountant is usually a *certified public accountant* (CPA). As with lawyers, physicians, and engineers, accountants are engaged in a wide variety of endeavors. The primary endeavors are:

1. Public accounting—The independent certified public accountant offers services to the public in a manner similar to the doctor, lawyer, or architect. These services include: *(a)* auditing (the attest function), *(b)* tax planning and determination of tax liability, and *(c)* management advisory services (consulting). Certified public accountants in public practice have a unique relationship with their clients as an *independent* and impartial reviewer of the financial statements. Although *independent accountants* are paid by the client, the independence concept extends their responsibilities to third parties; that is, to users of the financial statements.

The primary service rendered by the independent certified public accountant is the audit or attest function. The result of this function is to provide the client with *audited* financial statements including an "auditors report" (see page 137). The auditor's report (1) states the scope of the audit examination of the accounts, and (2) expresses an "opinion" whether the financial report "presents fairly" in accordance with generally accepted accounting standards. The attest function is particularly important to external statement users because it is intended to protect them against outright misrepresentation and bias on the part of the reporting entity. The attest function lends credibility to the financial statements because the auditor must be independent of the client and responsive to the needs of the external users of the financial statements.

2. Industrial accounting—A large number of certified public accountants work in businesses where they serve as accountants, internal auditors, tax specialists, systems experts, controllers, financial vice presidents, and chief executives. In these capacities, their specialized interests typically focus on management, tax, and financial accounting. As an employee, they are not in the role of *independent* certified public accountants.

---

[4] A careful distinction should be made between an accountant and a bookkeeper. A bookkeeper is involved in the routine clerical phase of the accounting process, whereas an accountant is competent in transaction analysis, measurement of economic events, systems design, analytical and interpretative processes, financial evaluation, and the management process. (See Welsch and Anthony, *Fundamentals of Financial Accounting,* chap. 1.)

3. Governmental and nonprofit accounting—Certified public accountants serve at all levels of government and not-for-profit entities: local, state, national, and international. In these capacities they are not in the role of *independent* certified public accountants.

Since this is a book on financial accounting, it focuses on generally accepted accounting principles and standards. These are the standards that the *independent* certified public accountant must carefully interpret, apply, and enforce.

ACCOUNTING ORGANIZATIONS AND LITERATURE

Because of the importance of external financial reports to investors, creditors, government, and the public at large, there is widespread interest in generally accepted accounting standards and the way in which they are established. In recent years interest in how the accounting profession answers its public-interest responsibility has increased dramatically. Various aspects of the financial reports of major companies and industries are reported by the news media almost every day.

The development of accounting theory and generally accepted accounting standards has been influenced by the financial community, governmental regulations, laws, professional accounting organizations, and accounting literature. Primary among the organizations are the American Institute of Certified Public Accountants, Financial Accounting Standards Board, Securities and Exchange Commission, and the American Accounting Association. The role of these organizations is important in understanding the objectives, evolution, and complexities of financial accounting.

Similarly, in your study of financial accounting, the accounting literature is important. Most of the organizations cited above support publications which are influential since they report the results of research, real-life problems, and suggested changes in accounting standards. They are rich sources for discussions of the major issues in accounting. Throughout this book numerous citations from the literature are provided. Early in your study of accounting you should become familiar with the primary accounting publications and use them to expand and enrich your comprehension of the major issues and the relevant alternatives being discussed for their resolution.

AMERICAN INSTITUTE OF CERTIFIED PUBLIC ACCOUNTANTS (AICPA)

This is the professional organization of certified public accountants. It is controlled by the CPAs in public practice; consequently, its primary efforts and publications have focused on the practice of public accounting. Its primary publications relating to financial accounting are:

1. *The Journal of Accountancy*—a monthly magazine containing pronouncements, articles, and special sections of direct interest to the independent CPA.

2. *Accountants' Index*—an annual publication containing an index of the accounting literature published during the year.
3. *Accounting Trends and Techniques*—an annual publication containing a survey of the characteristics of the annual financial reports of 600 corporations. It presents tabulations, explanations, and illustrations of reporting procedures, policies, terminology, disclosures, and so on.
4. *Accounting Research Studies*—a series of monograms that focused on specific accounting problems. These studies provide background information, discussion of alternative solutions, and often recommendations.
5. *Statements on Auditing Procedures*—These statements are issued at various times and focus on specific auditing procedures to be followed by the independent CPA. These statements usually are studied comprehensively in the auditing courses offered at most colleges.
6. Statements that deal with specific accounting principles, standards, and procedures:[5]
   a. *Accounting Research Bulletins*—During the period 1938 through 1958, the AICPA had a *Committee on Accounting Procedure* which was responsible for "narrowing the areas of differences and inconsistencies" in accounting practice. To this end the Committee issued pronouncements dealing with accounting principles and procedures. The first 42 pronouncements were restated and revised as:

      Accounting Research Bulletin (ARB) *43*, "Restatement and Revision of Accounting Research Bulletins," June 1953.

      From 1953 to 1958, eight additional bulletins were issued; the last *Accounting Research Bulletin* was *No. 51*. In addition, during this period the AICPA Committee on Terminology issued eight terminology bulletins recommending improvements in accounting terminology. These were combined as *Accounting Terminology Bulletin No. 1*, "Review and Resumé, August 1953." Since they have been reaffirmed in many respects, they continue to exert some influence as recommendations.
   b. *Opinions of the Accounting Principles Board*—To provide more emphasis on the formulation of accounting principles, the AICPA established the *Accounting Principles Board* (APB) to replace the Committee on Accounting Procedure. The APB designated its pronouncements as *Opinions*. The *Opinions* prescribe specific accounting principles and procedures for designated types of trans-

---

[5] The contents of these statements, opinions, and bulletins are listed in the Appendix to this book with chapter citations used by your authors. Refer to the following sources for details:

(*a*) AICPA Professional Standards, vol. 3, *Accounting—Current Text*, as of September 1, 1975, AICPA.

(*b*) Original Pronouncements—*Opinions of the Accounting Principles Board* (Nos. 1–31 inclusive) and *Statements of the Financial Accounting Standards Board* (Nos. 1–12) as cited in the chapters to follow.

actions and other events. During its period of existence from 1959 to 1973, the Board issued 31 *Opinions*. In addition, the Board issued four *Statements*. In contrast to the *Opinions*, the *Statements* present recommendations, rather than requirements, which it was hoped would be followed with a consequent improvement in financial accounting and reporting to external decision-makers.

The *Accounting Research Bulletins* (ARBs), *Accounting Terminology Bulletins*, and the *Opinions of the Accounting Principles Board* are still in effect, as amended; therefore, they often will be cited in the chapters to follow.[6]

FINANCIAL ACCOUNTING STANDARDS BOARD (FASB)

In the 1960s and early 1970s there were many complaints, within and outside the accounting profession, with respect to the establishment of accounting standards. These complaints focused on *(a)* lack of participation by organizations other than the AICPA, *(b)* "quality" of the opinions, *(c)* failure to develop a "broad statement of the objectives and principles" underlying external financial reports, and *(d)* insufficient output. Consequently, a committee was appointed to "study the issues and problems involved in setting accounting principles, and to make recommendations for improving the process and to make it more responsive to the needs of those who rely on financial statements." The "Wheat" Committee presented its report in March 1972.[7] Basically, the report recommended the following:

1. A Financial Accounting Foundation—composed of nine trustees appointed by the Board of Directors of the AICPA. Responsibilities: to appoint members of the Financial Accounting Standards Board; to appoint a Financial Accounting Standards Advisory Council; to raise funds to support the new structure; and to periodically review and revise the basic structure.
2. A Financial Accounting Standards Board (FASB)—composed of seven full-time members to establish standards of financial accounting and reporting. Four members would be CPAs drawn from public practice. The other three would not need to hold a CPA certificate but should possess extensive experience in the financial reporting field.
3. A Financial Accounting Standards Advisory Council—approximately 20 members; to work closely with the FASB, in an *advisory* capacity; to establish priorities, establish task forces, react to proposed standards; and whenever called upon.
4. Structure research activities with its objectives and needs clearly in mind.

The recommendations of the Committee were accepted by the AICPA.

---

[6] AICPA, *APB Accounting Principles*, vols. 1 and 2.

[7] *Establishing Financial Accounting Standards, Report of the Study on Establishment of Accounting Principles, American Institute of Certified Public Accountants*, March 1972, pp. 105 (chairman of the Committee, Francis M. Wheat).

Consequently, the APB was discontinued and the FASB became operational July 1, 1973. The first action of the FASB was a decision that the previous *Accounting Research Bulletins* approved by the APB, and the *Opinions* of the APB (as amended), would continue in force. To date the FASB has issued a number of pronouncements designated as:

1. Statements of Financial Accounting Standards—The FASB decided to issue *Statements of Standards* rather than *Opinions* used by the APB. They specify accounting principles and procedures (now called standards) on specific accounting issues. They have the same "force" as the *APB Opinions*.
2. Interpretations—These interpret prior *ARB*s, *APB Opinions*, and FASB *Statements of Financial Accounting Standards*.

Prior to issuing a *Statement* the FASB typically: (1) prepares and distributes a *Discussion Memorandum* which provides an analysis of the issue under consideration; (2) holds a *public hearing* on the issue; and (3) issues an *exposure draft* of the proposed statement. This process was designed to gain wide participation and full consideration of all relevant aspects of each accounting issue considered. After the process is completed, the FASB then makes a decision *(a)* whether to issue a statement, and *(b)*, in case of issue, the standards of financial accounting and reporting to be prescribed. The FASB *Statements* and interpretations of the *Opinions* are cited in the text.

The Appendix after Chapter 25 lists the *ARB*s, *APB Opinions* and FASB *Statements* issued to date; chapter citations in this book also are cited.

SECURITIES AND EXCHANGE COMMISSION (SEC)

A number of governmental regulatory agencies exert a continuing influence on accounting and reporting by businesses. Among these agencies are: Internal Revenue Service, Federal Power Commission, Interstate Commerce Commission, and the Securities and Exchange Commission. The SEC exerts a powerful influence on the development of accounting standards.

Because of the conditions reflected in the securities market at the beginning of the depression of the 1930s, Congress passed the Securities Act of 1933, the Securities Exchange Act of 1934, and the Public Utility Holding Company Act of 1935. The 1934 Act created the Securities and Exchange Commission and gave it broad authority to regulate the issuance and sale of securities in interstate commerce; that is, securities sold to the general public, including those listed on the stock exchanges. The Commission was given the authority to prescribe external financial reporting requirements for those companies under its jurisdiction. To obtain permission to sell an issue of securities, a company must obtain SEC approval of a *prospectus* which becomes a public record. The prospectus reports extensive information about the company, its officers, securities, and financial condition. The financial part of the prospectus must be audited by an independent CPA. After receiving permission to sell securities, the company must file with the Commission, as a matter of public record, audited financial statements each subsequent year and unaudited quarterly statements. The Commission requires more information in these annual financial statements than is typically included in the "published financial statements" furnished to the shareholders.

The SEC filing and reporting requirements are published as:

1. *Regulation S-X*—This is the original document issued by the Commission which prescribed the reporting requirement, including instructions and forms.
2. *Accounting Series Releases*—These releases are amendments, extensions, and additions to *Regulation S-X*. Over 159 *ASR*s have been issued to date.
3. Special SEC Releases.
4. Decisions on cases that come to the SEC.

Although the SEC has wide statutory authority to prescribe financial accounting and external reporting requirements, the Commission generally has relied on the accounting profession to set accounting standards, to enforce them, and to regulate the profession. The working relationship between the SEC and the accounting profession has been a positive one, and accounting regulation has remained largely in the private sector. However, there have been numerous occasions where the SEC has forced the accounting profession to move forward in tackling critical problems. These situations generally have been in areas where the SEC concluded that the public interest was not being fully served on a timely basis. In a few instances, the SEC has imposed certain accounting and reporting practices without waiting for the profession to act. Clearly, the SEC has exerted a significant influence on the establishment of accounting and reporting standards. This influence has increased in the last few years and is reflected in this book.

PERSUASION VERSUS COMPULSION

Until 1964 the accounting profession, through the AICPA, followed a policy of persuasion. The pronouncements of the Accounting Procedures Committee and the Accounting Principles Board were viewed as recommendations of generally accepted accounting principles. They were not binding on the profession; there was no strict requirement for adherence.

Their force depended upon their "general acceptance" by the accounting profession. Acceptance was encouraged by persuasion; that is, by convincing the independent CPA that they represented the preferred solution to given accounting problems. By 1964, many leaders of the profession were convinced that persuasion alone was insufficient to reduce the wide range of differences and inconsistencies evident in accounting and reporting to external decision-makers. There were numerous instances where identical transactions could be accounted for by any one of several significantly different methods. Net income could be readily "doctored" by selecting a particular accounting approach from among several deemed "generally accepted."

Consequently, a particularly significant milestone in the development of accounting practice occurred in October 1964, when the Council of the AICPA adopted recommendations requiring that for fiscal periods beginning after December 31, 1965, *departures from accounting principles specified in APB Opinions and the preceding Accounting Research Bulletins be disclosed in footnotes to financial statements or in independent auditor's reports when the effects of any such departure on the financial statements was material.* This statement forced the independent CPA to follow the pronouncements or to assume the burden of proof that other principles applied were "generally accepted" and "fairly presented" the financial results. Because of this burden of proof, and the risk of liability to statement users, the pronouncements have been followed. Thus, the policy of persuasion gave way to *compulsion.* Most observers agree that the new policy has been more effective.

AMERICAN ACCOUNTING ASSOCIATION (AAA)

The American Accounting Association is an organization dominated by accounting educators; however, its membership is open to practicing, industrial, and governmental accountants. Its broad objectives are the developing of accounting theory, encouraging and sponsoring accounting research, and improving education in accounting. The Association operates primarily through a series of committees and publishes monograms, committee reports, and a quarterly periodical, *The Accounting Review.* This periodical contains articles and sections that cover a wide range of subjects largely oriented toward research and accounting education.

Since 1936 the American Accounting Association, through its committees, has issued a series of statements on accounting theory. Starting in June 1936 with "A Tentative Statement of Accounting Principles Underlying Corporate Financial Statements," the Association carried on an active research program on accounting theory. These statements were issued as pamphlets and as articles in the *Accounting Review.* The 1936 statement was revised and supplemented three times; the latest revision was called "Accounting and Reporting Standards for Corporate Financial Statements, 1957 Revision." This statement, along with the preceding statements and nine supplements, was published in a single pamphlet by the Association in 1957. The latest statement, prepared by a special AAA committee, was published in 1966 and was entitled *A Statement of Basic Accounting Theory.* Like prior AAA statements, it dealt primarily with accounting theory, as opposed to accounting practice and procedures. The committee was more concerned with "what should be, as opposed to what was, or what is."[8] The statements relating to account-

[8] AAA, *A Statement of Basic Accounting Theory* (Evanston, Ill., 1966).

ing principles issued by the Association were *normative* rather than descriptive. That is, they tended to be more general, theoretical, and oriented toward future practice, whereas those issued by the AICPA primarily dealt with problems arising in current practice. Numerous references to these statements will be made throughout the discussions in this book.

INCOME TAX LEGISLATION AND FINANCIAL ACCOUNTING

Income tax legislation and administration has a significant impact on financial accounting. The financial effects of income tax legislation must be recorded in the accounting system and reported on the financial statements. From another point of view, accounting maintains a careful distinction between financial accounting standards and practices and the legal provisions for determining tax liability. A primary objective of financial accounting is to measure and report net income (as defined by accounting standards), whereas the objective of income tax legislation is to assess a tax. The Congress, in devising tax legislation to generate revenue for the government, also seeks to encourage particular actions on the part of the taxpayers to serve certain social and fiscal policy ends. For example, accelerated depreciation, investment credit, exclusion from tax on the interest received on municipal bonds, deductibility of contributions to charitable organizations, statutory depletion, and so on, are favorable "tax breaks" to encourage the taxpayer to make certain choices that are believed to be in the public interest. Thus, tax legislation defines taxable income as something quite different than the amount designated as "accrual net income" by the accounting profession. Typically, taxable income and net income are two different amounts for a business.

Throughout your study of accounting, remember that the "income tax way" often is not in accord with the accounting way (see Chapter 20, Income Tax Allocation). Nevertheless, although income tax legislation and administration do not establish accounting principles and reporting standards, their indirect influence is substantial. For example, the inventory *Lifo* method often was frowned on by the accounting profession until it became an acceptable method for income tax purposes; the same was true for accelerated depreciation.

The accounting profession has vigorously opposed tax legislation and administration to limit tax alternatives (such as a choice among several acceptable depreciation methods) to the one used for financial accounting purposes. This policy is considered counterproductive by the accounting profession because it tends to encourage businesses to use, in the accounting system, the method most favorable for tax purposes with no regard as to whether it best measures accrual net income.

CONCLUDING COMMENT

This chapter introduces the nature and objectives of financial accounting and reporting to external decision-makers. It presents a broad view of the accounting environment, the influential organizations affecting accounting, and the scope of the literature. It emphasizes that accounting must be responsive to the evolving needs of society; consequently, accounting principles and practices also are continually evolving. There are many forces in society that bear on, and determine, the general direction of the changes. In the next chapter, we will turn our attention to the foundations of financial accounting theory.

QUESTIONS

1. Define accounting in a broad sense.
2. Explain the distinction between financial and management accounting. Does this distinction mean that a company should have two accounting systems? Explain.
3. What is meant by general purpose financial statements? What are their basic components?
4. What are the basic objectives of external financial statements?
5. Explain why the emphasis in financial accounting is on *measurement* and *communication.*
6. What are the primary endeavors of certified public accountants?
7. The independent certified public accountant fulfills a unique professional role. Explain the concept of independence and why it is important to society in general.
8. The following statements deal specifically with accounting principles, standards and procedures. For each, you are to explain their development and their current status generally:

   a. *Accounting Research Bulletins*
   b. *Accounting Terminology Bulletins*
   c. *Opinions* of the APB
   d. FASB *Statements of Financial Accounting Standards*
   e. FASB Interpretations

9. Explain the developments that led to the establishment of the FASB.
10. Briefly explain the role that the SEC has fulfilled in the establishment of accounting standards. What has been its relationship to the accounting profession in this role?
11. What is the AAA? What role has it fulfilled in the development of accounting theory and standards?
12. Briefly explain the relationship of income tax legislation to financial accounting standards.
13. Is an approach that is permitted for income tax purposes necessarily "generally accepted" for financial accounting purposes? Explain.
14. Why does the accounting profession oppose *conformity* between taxable income provisions and accrual accounting standards?

Chapter 2

Theoretical Foundations of Financial Accounting and Reporting

The study of accounting can be approached on a theoretical or procedural basis, or a combination of the two. In this book, consistent with our objectives stated in Chapter 1, a combination approach is presented. At this level, the student interested in accounting should learn the basic accounting principles and procedures used to classify, analyze, and record transactions, and to report the summarized results to decision-makers. The procedural aspect of financial accounting involves the preparation of accounting entries, maintenance of accounts, and preparation of financial statements. However, of more importance, is a comprehension of the theoretical foundation that underlies financial accounting and reporting. This provides the rationale for the procedural aspects of accounting. We emphasize the conceptual foundation throughout this book.

A definition of theory, appropriate for accounting, is "a coherent set of hypothetical, conceptual, and pragmatic principles forming the general frame of reference for a field of inquiry."[1] Accounting theory is man-made to respond to the changing broad social and economic environment within which the accounting function operates.

Accounting theory is in a continuous process of evolution. The organizations, discussed in Chapter 1, have been influential in this continuing evolution. Accounting theory, as we know it today, is based upon both inductive and deductive reasoning, economic theory, experience, pragmatism, and general acceptability. Since accounting theory is pragmatic, it cannot be derived from, or proven by, the laws of nature as can be done in mathematics and the natural sciences.

At the present time, there is no single, agreed upon, statement of the broad structure of financial accounting theory. However, there does

---

[1] For those who desire to pursue in depth the subject of financial accounting theory, the authors recommend the following: Eldon S. Hendriksen, *Accounting Theory*, rev. ed. (Homewood, Ill.: Richard D. Irwin, Inc., 1970).

appear to be general agreement with respect to the basic theoretical foundations that underly financial accounting. The purpose of this chapter is to discuss those foundations.

BROAD THEORETICAL STRUCTURE

In discussing accounting theory, one is confronted with a problem of terminology. Accounting literature makes numerous references to theory, assumptions, concepts, postulates, principles, standards, rules, procedures, and practices. Although each of these terms may be precisely defined, general usage by the profession has served to give them loose and overlapping meanings. To establish a basis for consistent terminology throughout this book we have designed the broad structure, and selected the terminology, presented in Exhibits 2–1 and 2–2. It is *descriptive,* since it describes present accounting, not prescriptive or normative (i.e., what accounting should be in the future). It represents *current* accounting theory and practice classified into the six basic components shown in Exhibit 2–1.

This frame of reference is easily understood and conforms to current usage. It will serve as a consistent and integrated theoretical structure

EXHIBIT 2–1
Hierarchy of a Broad Structure of Financial Accounting and Reporting

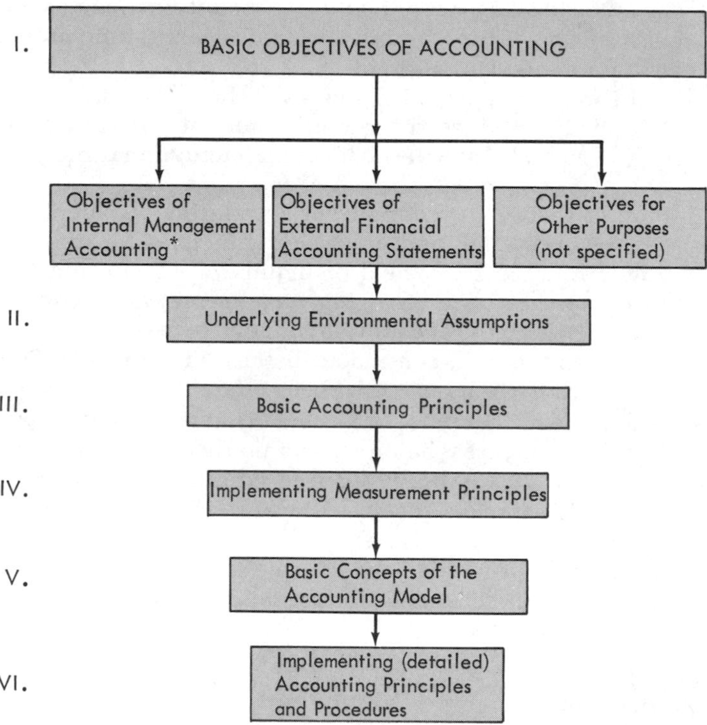

* Not focused on in this book; see books on management accounting.

for the readership of this textbook. Although not complete in every respect, it will serve as a valuable reference when later chapters discuss the rationale for the accounting and reporting treatment accorded the various accounting issues.

The structure outlined in Exhibits 2–1 and 2–2 is explained below. This structure is presented at the outset in order to provide the reader

EXHIBIT 2–2
A Broad Structure of Financial Accounting and Reporting

I. Basic Objectives of Accounting
  1. Objectives of internal management accounting
  2. Objectives of external financial accounting statements
  3. Objectives for other purposes (not yet specified)

II. Underlying Environmental Assumptions
  1. Separate-entity assumption
  2. Continuity assumption
  3. Unit-of-measure assumption
  4. Time-period assumption

III. Basic Accounting Principles
  1. Cost principle
  2. Revenue principle
  3. Matching principle
  4. Objectivity principle
  5. Consistency principle
  6. Financial reporting principle
  7. Modifying (or exception) principle
    a. Materiality
    b. Conservatism
    c. Industry peculiarities

IV. Implementing Measurement Principles
  1. Selection of the objects, activities, and events to be measured
  2. Identification and classification of the attributes of each object, activity, and event to be measured
  3. Assignment of quantitative amounts to the attributes
    a. Monetary
    b. Nonmonetary
  4. Modifying measurement principle
    a. Uncertainty
    b. Objectivity
    c. Limitations of monetary unit
    d. Cost effectiveness

V. Basic Concepts of the Accounting Model
  1. Financial position model: Assets = Liabilities + Owners' Equity
  2. Results of operations model: Revenues − Expenses = Net Income
  3. Changes in financial position model: Resource Inflows − Resource Outflows = Net Change in Resources

VI. Implementing (Detailed) Accounting Principles and Procedures
  1. Those related to determination of net income
  2. Those related to measurement of assets and liabilities
  3. Those related to presentation of accounting information
  4. Those related to how transactions and other events should be recorded, classified, and summarized
  5. Other accounting procedures

with a broad conceptual view that will be especially useful in understanding the subsequent chapters. In each chapter, we will refer explicitly to one or more of these concepts. Therefore, the student should return to this chapter often so that upon completion of the text there will be a keen understanding of the structure of current accounting theory and practice. An in-depth understanding of this foundation will *(a)* minimize the need to memorize procedures; and *(b)* help to resolve, on a logical basis, complex accounting issues not previously encountered.

Exhibit 2–1 presents the six basic components of the broad structure. The exhibit presents the *basic objectives of accounting* as the highest level in the hierarchy. As we move down the hierarchy, the theoretical focus shifts to the practices of *implementing* principles and procedures (the rules – how it is done!). Most of the *ARBs, APB Opinions,* and FASB *Standards* and interpretations are at this lower level.

Exhibit 2–2 presents an outline of the six basic components of the broad structure of financial accounting including the specific concepts. The remainder of this chapter will discuss, in order, each of the items listed in Exhibit 2–2.

BASIC OBJECTIVES OF ACCOUNTING

The broad structure of accounting and reporting of financial information is based upon objectives. The basic objective of accounting is to provide relevant information to decision-makers. These decision-makers can be broadly classified as internal (i.e., the management of the entity) and external (i.e., the equity investors, creditors, government, and the general public).

Financial accounting focuses on *external* decision-makers. Governmental units have special requirements which are specified by law or by regulatory decree. Therefore, financial accounting objectives currently focus on reporting to equity investors, creditors, and the general public. Consequently, the broad objective of external financial accounting statements is to provide relevant information to equity investors, creditors, and the general public.

One of the major issues currently facing the accounting profession is whether the financial reporting objective should relate to the three groups, or to two of them, or only to one – the equity investors. A related issue is the problem of specifying in the objective *(a)* the assumed sophistication of the decision-maker (i.e., the statement user), and *(b)* the decision models the user should utilize. These issues remain unsettled. Clearly, greater specificity of the objectives of external financial accounting reports would significantly influence the broad structure of financial accounting.

UNDERLYING ENVIRONMENTAL ASSUMPTIONS

The underlying environmental assumptions are broad aspects of the total *environment* in which accounting normally operates, and they directly affect the objectives of accounting. The underlying assumptions do not include all aspects of the environment but only those that directly affect the way in which a business entity operates. Accounting must conform to these environmental influences on the business entity. The underlying environmental assumptions—*separate entity, continuity, unit of measure,* and *time period*—suggest pervasive and accepted characteristics of the business environment that are broader even than accounting.

Separate-Entity Assumption

Accounting is concerned with specific and separate entities. Thus each enterprise is considered as an *accounting unit* separate and apart from the owner or owners and from other entities. A corporation and the shareholders are separable entities for accounting purposes. Also partnerships and sole proprietorships are treated as separate and apart from the owners despite the fact that this distinction is not made in the legal sense.

Under the separate-entity concept the business entity is considered to own all resources committed to its purpose, subject to the rights and interests of creditors. The separate-entity assumption recognizes the fact that transactions of the business and those of the owners should be accounted for and reported separately. All records and reports are developed from the viewpoint of the particular entity. This viewpoint affects the analysis of transactions, accumulation and classification of data, and the resultant financial reporting. It provides a basis for clear-cut distinction in analyzing transactions between the enterprise and the owners. As an example, the personal residence of an individual owning an unincorporated business is not considered to be an appropriate item to report for the business, although there is a common owner. In this example the accounting entity makes a distinction that is not made in the legal sense; creditors may look to both the personal residence and the business assets for satisfaction of claims against the common owner. The accountant would be in an untenable situation from time to time if he or she did not have this basic concept to rely on in making distinctions between personal and business transactions. Pressures to overlook this distinction are encountered by accountants occasionally.

Continuity Assumption

The continuity assumption is frequently referred to as the "going-concern" concept. It assumes indefinite continuance of the accounting entity; that is, the business is not expected to liquidate in the foreseeable future. The assumption does not imply that accountancy assumes permanent continuance; rather there is a presumption of stability and continuity for a period of time sufficient to carry out contemplated operations, contracts, and commitments. This concept establishes the rationale of acccounting on a *nonliquidation basis,* and thus provides the theoretical foundation for many of the valuations and allocations common in accounting. For example, depreciation and amortization procedures rely upon this concept. The estimates of remaining useful life and residual value are based upon the asset itself rather than upon an expectation of early liquidation of the entity.

This assumption generally underlies the decisions of investors to commit capital to the enterprise. Therefore, accounting for these commitments and the resulting incomes and losses must be based upon the assumption that the enterprise will continue to function in the contemplated manner, performing the business activities consistent with prior objectives including earning a return for the entrepreneur. The concept, as applied to accounting, holds that continuity of business activity is a reasonable expectation. If the particular entity should face serious loss and probable liquidation, conventional accounting based on the continuity assumption would not be appropriate for determining and reporting the true conditions. In such cases *liquidation* accounting is appropriate wherein all valuations immediately are accounted for at estimated realizable amounts.

Accountants are aware that no business entity will continue forever. To satisfy the continuity assumption, it is essential only that on the basis of *present facts* it appears that the business will continue so that its present resources are utilized according to plan without serious loss of capital investment. Only on the basis of this assumption can the accounting process remain stable and attain the objective of accurately recording and reporting on the capital commitments, the efficiency of management, and the financial status of the enterprise as a going concern.

Unit-of-Measure Assumption

Some unit of exchange is essential to raise the level of commerce above that of barter. Similarly, some unit of measurement is necessary in accounting. With so many diverse assets and equities that must be recorded, analyzed, and reported, there must be a common denominator. Obviously, to be of maximum usefulness, accounting ideally should employ the same unit of measure as employed by the business community, that is, the monetary unit. Accounting may deal with some data in nonmonetary units; however the monetary unit predominates. Thus money is the common denominator—the yardstick—in the accounting process.

The unit-of-measure assumption asserts that accounting will measure and report the results of the economic activities of the entity in terms of money. It recognizes, as does society generally, that the monetary unit is the most effective means of communicating financial information. At this point we encounter a critical problem in accounting: unlike the yardstick which is always 36 inches long, the monetary unit (dollar) changes in value or purchasing power. Consequently, when there is inflation or deflation, dollars of different size (real value) are entered in the accounts over a period of time and dollars of cost are intermingled in the accounts as if they were of equal purchasing power. Because of this practice it is said that accounting either "assumes a stable monetary unit" or "changes in the value of money are not significant." However, in view of the relatively recent high rate of inflation, accounting has begun to reflect price-level effects. Accounting during periods of inflation and deflation is discussed in Chapter 25.

The unit-of-measure assumption has exerted a significant impact on the development of accounting. The basic theoretical concepts discussed in the next section of this chapter in part rest upon this assumption. Adherence to the cost principle (discussed below) and cost apportionments are related to this assumption. It is the basis in terms of *original* dollars of inflow and outflow. A subsequent section discusses the modifying measurement principle.

Time-Period Assumption

Although the results of operations of a specific business enterprise cannot be known precisely until it has completed its life-span (i.e., final liquidation), short-term financial reports are necessary. Thus the environment—the business community and government—has imposed upon accounting a calendar constraint; that is, the necessity for assigning changes in wealth of a firm to a series of short time periods. These time periods vary; however, the year is the most common interval as a result of established business practice, tradition, and governmental requirements. For example, income tax laws require determination of income on an annual basis. Some firms adhere to the calendar year; however, more and more firms are changing to the fiscal or "natural" business year, the end of which is marked by the lowest point of business activity in each 12-month period. During the last few years, a number of leading companies have issued *interim* financial statements each quarter (a three-month period) which report summary information. Interim financial information "is essential to provide investors and others with timely information as to the progress of the enterprise."[2] Many companies also prepare *internal management* reports on a daily, weekly, or monthly basis.

The time-period assumption recognizes the need by the business community, and society in general, for short-term periodic financial statements. This assumption underlies the whole area of *accruals* and *deferrals* that distinguishes accrual basis accounting from cash basis accounting. If there were no need for periodic reports during the life-span of a business, accruals and deferrals of revenues and costs would be unnecessary. To illustrate, assume Company X was organized and $100,000 cash was invested in it. Assets were acquired, liabilities assumed, revenues earned, and costs paid for a five-year period at which time the business was liquidated (everything converted to cash) and the resulting cash of $175,000 returned to the investors. Assuming no return to the

---

[2] AICPA, *APB Opinion No. 28* (New York, May 1973), par. 9.

investors during the five-year period, we can report with certainty that the company earned $75,000 cash income. No accruals or deferrals (adjusting entries to the accountant) are necessary to determine the net income for the business. However, if the investors required a financial statement each year, accruals and deferrals for items such as unpaid wages, uncollected revenues, depreciation expense, and prepaid expenses would have to be made each period.

The continuity in business operations tends to obscure the results of the short-term "test readings" which accounting renders in the form of periodic financial statements. Many continuous and interrelated streams of data are arbitrarily severed in the preparation of annual financial statements. Despite these difficulties, short-term financial reports are of such significance to decision-makers that the accounting process must be designed to produce them. The time-period assumption recognizes this need despite the fact that precision is difficult to attain.

BASIC ACCOUNTING PRINCIPLES

Seven basic accounting principles are listed in Exhibit 2–2. For our purposes, basic accounting principles are defined as broad standards or guidelines that rest upon the four fundamental underlying assumptions discussed above. These principles have evolved through experience to fulfill the primary objective of accounting – to provide relevant information to decision-makers (refer to page 3). They have been developed by the accounting profession and have stood the test of general acceptability. These basic principles do not include *detailed* principles and procedures.

Cost Principle

This basic principle permeates the entire accounting process. It often is referred to as the "historical cost principle" as opposed to the fair market value or replacement cost theories. The cost principle holds that *cost* is the appropriate basis for initial accounting recognition (at date of the transaction) of all asset acquisitions, service acquisitions, expenses, liabilities, and owners' equity. It also holds that subsequent to acquisition, cost values are retained throughout the accounting process. The cost principle recognizes the basic subject matter of accounting as completed transactions which are to be translated into their financial effect on the entity in terms of the exchange price established at the date of the completed transaction. In applying the cost principle, the accountant frequently faces a serious problem of *measuring* cost, that is, where noncash considerations are involved. In determining cost the "cash bargained price" is utilized. Where considerations other than cash are involved, the cost measure is the cash equivalent of the consideration given up in the transaction or the cash equivalent of the asset or service acquired, whichever is the more clearly evident. Thus, where capital stock is issued to pay for land, the asset is recorded at the fair market value of the stock if that value is determinable; otherwise the fair market value of the land must be determined as objectively as possible. Another problem arises when noninterest-bearing debt is given for an asset. Cost is the *present value* of the future amount of cash to be paid (*APB Opinion No. 21*). These two problems are discussed in detail in subsequent chapters.

The cost principle indicates that compared with other alternatives, the exchange price derived in an arm's-length transaction is the most useful for accounting and reporting. It is determinable, definite, and objective; it is not a matter of conjecture, opinion, or estimation. It is the basis used by the business community, taxing authorities, and society in general. As a result, users of financial statements know that a good portion of the information is based on objectively determined amounts. To illustrate the importance of these reasons, assume that instead of the cost principle, a "fair market value principle" is used. This principle would require that at each financial statement date (i.e., each year-end), all of the assets on the balance sheet be stated at their then fair market value. Appraisals and estimates would have to be made annually for receivables, investments, inventories, plant, equipment, land, patents, liabilities, and so on. The accountants may have one opinion, the management another opinion, and both may disagree with outside appraisers. The external statement user may have little confidence in these subjective judgments. The question would arise as to what should be included in net income. Assume a plant that cost $100,000 at the beginning of the year is appraised at $125,000 at year-end. Should the $25,000 increase in reported assets be reflected as an increase in net income for the year? Critics counter that the cost principle seriously distorts the financial statements in periods of significant inflation or deflation. Also some people believe that current market value, rather than original cost, better serves the external decision-maker. These issues are discussed in Chapter 25.

Revenue Principle

The revenue principle (*a*) defines revenue, (*b*) specifies how revenue should be measured, and (*c*) pinpoints the timing of revenue recognition. Each of the three facets of the revenue principle presents difficult conceptual and operational problems.

Revenue Defined. Revenue can be defined as "the creation of goods or services by an enterprise during a specific interval of time." Note that this definition does not dictate either the measurement (amount) or timing (date of recognition) of the revenue but is neutral in respect to them.[3] Another useful definition, from a different viewpoint, is: "Revenue . . . is the monetary expression of the aggregate of products or services transferred by an enterprise to its customers during a period of time."[4] The

---

[3] Adapted from Hendriksen, *Accounting Theory*, p. 161.

[4] AAA Committee on Accounting Concepts and Standards, *Accounting and Reporting Standards for Corporate Financial Statements and Preceding Statements and Supplements* (Columbus, Ohio, 1957), p. 5.

revenue principle holds that revenue should include all changes in the net assets of the firm other than those arising from owners' equity transactions. That is, revenue is the measure of new assets received for *(a)* the sale of goods and services; *(b)* interest, rents, royalties, and so on; *(c)* net gain on the sale of assets other than stock-in-trade; and *(d)* gain from advantageous settlement of liabilities. In applying the broad principle we will see in later chapters that adequate reporting (under the reporting principle) requires that revenue be reported in segments such as operating revenue and extraordinary gains.

Measurement of Revenue. The revenue principle dictates that revenue should be measured as the net cash equivalent price derived in an arm's-length exchange transaction. Thus, revenue is best measured by the net cash exchange value of the product, service, or other asset. This concept requires that all discounts be viewed as adjustments made to reach the true cash exchange value (i.e., sales and cash discounts should be deducted from sales revenues) and that in noncash transactions the fair market value of the consideration given or received, whichever is the more clearly determinable, should determine the revenue value.

Timing Revenue Recognition. This subprinciple generally is referred to as the revenue *realization* concept. The basic concept is that revenue is realized, and should be recorded as earned, when *(a)* there has been an exchange transaction involving a transfer of goods or services, and *(b)* the earning process is essentially complete. The realization concept is a pragmatic test for timing revenue recognition since it is characterized more by operational rather than by strict theoretical content. The primary test of revenue recognition is the point of sale. The point of sale generally is viewed as the time when ownership to the goods passes. For example, in the case of goods shipped f.o.b. shipping point, ownership passes at the time they are turned over to the shipper, hence revenue would be recognized at this point; whereas goods shipped f.o.b. destination give rise to revenue only upon delivery at destination.

Where services rather than goods are involved, revenue is considered realized, or earned, when the services are rendered. As a practical matter, the realization of revenue frequently is recognized when the service is completed and billed.

The timing of revenue recognition described above is often called the *sales basis.* It requires *accrual basis accounting* rather than cash basis accounting. For example, transactions for sales of goods or services on credit are recorded and reported in the period in which they occurred rather than in the period in which the cash is collected. The sales basis should be used where the following conditions exist: *(a)* the ultimate collection of the sales or service price in full is reasonably certain; and *(b)* the expenses related to the particular transaction appear to be determinable, with reasonable accuracy, in the period of sale or service. These conditions are essential to completion of the earning process.

Because of special circumstances in application of the realization concept there are four exceptions to its application. The exceptions are known as the cash, percentage-of-completion, production, and cost recovery approaches.

Cash Approach. Under this approach revenue is recognized on a cash basis. To illustrate, assume an installment sale of $600 that cost $360, and credit terms of $20 per month for 30 months. There is a potential gross margin of $240 or $8 per installment. Under the cash approach no revenue would be recognized at the date of sale; instead, $8 of revenue would be recognized as each collection is made. This is also known as the *installment method* of recognizing revenue. This method should be used where the sales basis is not appropriate due to the absence of reasonable assurance that ultimate collection will be made, or where the related and significant expenses and costs cannot yet be determined with a reasonable degree of accuracy. The existence of these conditions indicate that the earning process is not essentially completed at point of sale. The installment method has very limited application.

Percentage-of-Completion Approach. This approach is appropriate for certain long-term construction contracts. Revenue is recognized on the basis of progress of construction, although the earning process is not fully completed until delivery at the completion date. To illustrate, assume a construction company receives a $6,000,000 contract to construct a building that will require three years to build. Assume the estimated construction cost to the contractor is $5,700,000; therefore, a $300,000 profit over the three-year period is expected. At the end of the first year the building is one-third completed. Under this approach, the contractor may recognize $100,000 profit at the end of the first year. Contractors may, at their option, elect to use the percentage-of-completion approach or apply the revenue principle in the usual way and recognize no revenue until completion of the contract. Both approaches are widely used (see Chapter 10).

Production Approach. This approach is similar to percentage-of-completion approach. It is often applied in the case of cost-plus-fixed-fee contracts. Revenue is recognized as production progresses with a portion of the fixed fee recorded as earned.

Cost Recovery Approach. This approach is sometimes called the *sunk cost* approach. Under this approach all of the related costs incurred (i.e., the sunk costs) are recovered before any revenue is recognized. The cost recovery approach should be used for highly speculative transactions where the ultimate outcome is completely unpredictable. For example, an investor may have purchased bonds where the interest was in default for a number of years. The purchase price was at a fraction of the maturity value of the bonds because of the improbability of final collection. The transaction was highly speculative. Under the cost recovery approach, collections of interest would not be taken up as revenue until the original investment was recovered; collections subsequent to this point would be recognized as revenue.

Clearly the problem of determining when revenue should be recognized is a critical one. Due to diverse transactions involving revenue, no single theoretical concept can apply to all situations; therefore, accountants necessarily have developed the realistic guidelines explained above to determine when revenue should be recognized.

The Matching Principle

The matching principle holds that for any period for which net income is to be reported, the revenues to be recognized should be determined according to the revenue principle; then the expenses incurred in generating that revenue should be determined and reported for that period. If revenue is carried over from a prior period or deferred to a future period in accordance with the revenue principle, all elements of expense related to that revenue likewise should be carried over from the prior period or deferred, as the case may be. This matching of expenses with revenue frequently is a difficult problem; however, careful matching is an essential function of accounting if there is to be a proper determination of periodic net income.

Many costs are deferred to the future by reporting them as assets because they have a future benefit or will aid in the generation of future revenues. Examples are inventories, prepaid expenses, and depreciable assets. Subsequently, they are recorded and reported as periodic expenses to *match* them with the future revenues. The deferral as assets, and subsequent write-off as periodic expenses in accordance with the matching principle, is generally based on *cause and effect*. Some are written off as expenses based on physical association (such as inventories and supplies used); some on a time basis (such as rent, interest, insurance, and depreciation); and some because there is no identifiable or measurable future benefit (such as advertising, donations to worthy causes, and research and development).

The matching principle requires that *accrual basis accounting*, as opposed to cash basis accounting, be used to record and report expenses. Thus, *adjusting entries* must be used to update expenses for the period. Examples are depreciation expense, supplies used, expired insurance, accrued (i.e., unpaid) expenses such as wages, warranty costs, and estimated bad debt expense. These often require the use of estimates. To illustrate, assume a home appliance is sold for cash during the last month of the current accounting period and it is guaranteed for a period of 12 months from date of sale. The sales revenue will be recognized as earned during the current accounting period. The expense of honoring the warranty also should be recognized in the current accounting period, although the actual warranty cost will not be known until the next year. Therefore, at the end of the current year, the amount of the warranty expense must be estimated, recorded, and reported. In this way the warranty expense is matched with the revenue of the period to which it is related.

Objectivity Principle

This principle holds that to the fullest extent possible, accounting and reporting should be based on data that are *(a)* objectively determined, and *(b)* verifiable. *Objective determination* means that accounting should be based on completed arms'-length exchange transactions. An arms'-length transaction is characterized by an agreement between two or more parties that have adverse interests – the interest of the seller is a high price, whereas the interest of the buyer is a low price. Accountants recognize that many aspects of accounting are not based on factual data but necessarily involve estimates. For example, depreciation expense is based on *(a)* factual data – the cost of the asset, and *(b)* two estimates – useful life and residual value. The objectivity principle specifies that when estimates are necessary, they should be objectively determined by rational and systematic approaches including consideration of past experience and realistic expectations for the future.

Verifiability means that to the fullest extent possible, accounting data should be supported by verifiable business documents originating outside the business entity. Events recognized that do not result from transactions (such as periodic depreciation) must be supported by internally prepared documents that can be verified by the independent CPA. Thus, verifiability focuses on the adequacy of evidence to support the data processed in the accounting system and reported on the financial statements.

Consistency Principle

This principle states that in recording and reporting economic events, there must be consistent application of accounting concepts, standards, and procedures from one accounting period to the next. Consistent application in accounting for an entity is essential so that the resulting financial statements for successive periods are comparable. Financial reports are more useful when prepared on a consistent basis because trends and other important relations are revealed. Inconsistent application of accounting standards often will materially affect reported net income and balance sheet amounts. For example, if a company used *Fifo* one year and *Lifo* the next year for inventory costing, and straight-line depreciation followed by accelerated depreciation, net income and asset amounts reported on the financial statements would become capricious. Inconsistency, if allowed, would open the door to manipulation of financial statements.

The consistency principle does not preclude an entity from changing to a different principle or procedure if it better measures economic reality. "Accounting Changes," *APB Opinion No. 20* (issued July 1971), specifies the conditions under which a change in accounting can be made and the disclosure requirements necessary to adequately explain the effect. The consistency principle, as implemented by *APB Opinion No. 20,* prevents repetitive and manipulative changes. This *Opinion* is discussed in a subsequent chapter.

The standard opinion given by the independent CPA, as a part of the audited financial statements, specifically recognizes the consistency principle as follows:

In our opinion the aforementioned financial statements present fairly the financial position of XYZ Company at December 31, 19–, and the results of its operations and the changes in its financial position for the year then ended, in conformity with generally accepted accounting principles applied on a basis *consistent with that of the preceding year.*[5]

Financial Reporting Principle

This principle often is called the *full-disclosure* principle; however, it is a broader concept. The financial reporting principle maintains that financial statements should be designed and prepared to reasonably assure complete and understandable reporting of all significant information relating to the economic affairs of the accounting entity. The financial statements must be complete in the sense that all information reported is necessary for a "fair" presentation so that a "reasonably prudent investor" would not be misled; that is, sufficient information must be presented to permit a "knowledgeable" user to reach an informed decision. The principle is especially important for unusual events, major changes in expectations, and poststatement findings.

The financial reporting principle focuses on presentation of adequate and understandable information in the financial statements. It relates to the nature of the statements, information to be shown, classification of information on the statements, parenthetical information in the statements, and explanatory notes appended to the statements. *Full disclosure* emphasizes the necessity to include explanatory notes and parenthetical information to supplement the basic amounts reported in the financial statements. The standards of financial statement preparation developed by the accounting profession to implement the financial reporting principle are summarized in Exhibit 2–3. Application of these reporting standards will be discussed and illustrated throughout the remaining chapters.

Modifying (or Exception) Principle

In a prior discussion the point was made that accounting principles are not principles of nature but are man-made. Further, accounting principles are subject to change when there is a change in the environment in which they operate, or in the related needs of financial statement users. Accounting principles are pragmatic and must be applied to a diverse set of facts and conditions. In view of these considerations some exceptions are to be expected. The modifying principle encompasses three fairly specific concepts which have been widely recognized and accepted in accounting as essential to accomplish the broad objectives of accounting. The three concepts that comprise the modifying principle are discussed below.

Materiality. Although accounting rests upon a solid theoretical

---

[5] AICPA, "Codification of Auditing Standards and Procedures," *Statement on Auditing Standards No. 1* (New York, 1972), p. 81.

foundation, it must be pragmatic. Therefore, theory is applied realistically taking into account the nature of the economic event – the transaction – and the overall economic environment. Thus, the concept of materiality asserts that transactions and other events involving insignificant economic effects need not be accorded strict theoretical treatment because the economic effect is not *material* enough to affect the decision-maker. A less costly and timesaving approach may be used to account

EXHIBIT 2–3
Financial Reporting Principle
Standards of Financial Statement Presentation

1. Basic financial statements required:
   a. Balance sheet – statement of financial position.
   b. Income statement – statement of operations.
   c. Statement of changes in financial position – statement of inflows and outflows of funds.
   d. Supporting schedules essential for full disclosure.
2. Complete balance sheet – include all assets, liabilities, and classes of owners' equity (clearly identified).
3. Complete income statement – include all revenues, expenses, net income, infrequently occurring or unusual items, and earnings per share (clearly identified).
4. Classification and segregation – separate disclosure of the important components of the financial statements to make the information more useful.
5. Gains and losses – revenues and expenses other than sales of products, merchandise, or services should be separated from other revenue and expenses and the net effect disclosed as gains and losses.
6. Extraordinary items – extraordinary gains and losses (net of tax) should be presented separately from other revenue and expenses in the income statement.
7. Working capital – disclosure of components of working capital (current assets less current liabilities) is presumed to be useful in most enterprises.
8. Offsetting – assets and liabilities in the balance sheet should not be offset unless a legal right of setoff exists.
9. Consolidated statements – when one entity owns more than 50% of the outstanding voting stock of another entity consolidated statements are more meaningful.
10. Accounting period – basic time period for financial statements is one year; interim financial statements recommended for each quarter.
11. Foreign balances – financial information about foreign operations should be translated into U.S. dollars.
12. Accounting policies – accounting policies should be separately disclosed and explained.
13. Full disclosure – in addition to informative classifications and segregation of information, financial statements should disclose all additional information necessary for fair presentation. Notes and parenthetical information necessary for adequate disclosure are an integral part of the financial statements.

Adapted from: AICPA, "Basic Concepts and Accounting Principles Underlying Financial Statements," *Statement of the Accounting Principles Board No. 4* (New York, October 1970), pars. 188–201.

for *immaterial amounts.* In applying this modifying, or exception, concept, the accountant must weigh the worth of strict accuracy and compliance with accounting principles against the cost and time consumed in recordkeeping. Strict adherence to principles is not required when the accuracy of the financial report is not materially affected.

At the present time, the accounting profession has been unable to precisely define the line between a material and an immaterial amount. Materiality is a question of the effect on the user of the statements. Generally it is related to the more important financial amounts such as sales dollars, net income, total assets, total liabilities, and owners' equity. The *CPA Handbook* states:

> An item in relation to a financial statement would be considered material only if it would have a significant effect upon an important judgment based on that statement. Whether a particular item is material or significant cannot be determined by consideration only of the item itself. Its relationship to other items and to the surrounding circumstances have to be known before that judgment can be made.[6]

To illustrate, assume X Corporation purchased a pencil sharpener costing $5.98 that has an estimated useful life of three years. The assets on the balance sheet total approximately $100,000, and net income approximates $30,000. Theoretically, the pencil sharpener should be debited to an asset account and depreciated over three years at $2 per year. Clearly the $5.98 is immaterial to total assets, and the $2 is immaterial to net income. Under the materiality concept the rational accounting approach would be to debit the $5.98 to expense in the year of acquisition. No rational decision-maker would be influenced by these amounts in this particular situation. Observe that the materiality concept does not permit nonrecording and nonreporting of a transaction; it simply permits a pragmatic approach for handling immaterial amounts.

Some people assume that an amount that is 10% or less of a selected base amount is not material. This tendency should be avoided. The nature of the amount and its relative importance to other important amounts must be considered. For example, because of its size, 5% of revenue of $600 million probably should be considered material. It is important that each accounting entity establish uniform policies for implementing the materiality concept.

Conservatism. The concept of conservatism holds that where acceptable alternatives for an accounting determination are available, the alternative having the *least favorable immediate influence* on owners' equity should be selected. In recognizing assets where alternative valuations are acceptable, the lower should be selected, and the higher of two alternative liability amounts should be recorded. In recording expenses and revenues where there is reasonable doubt as to the appropriateness of alternative amounts, the one having the least favorable effect on net income should be chosen. Thus, where there is a choice among alternative valuations, accounting seeks to avoid favorable ex-

---

[6] *CPA Handbook,* vol. II, chap. 17, p. 24.

aggeration by relying on rational conservatism. Conservatism in accounting frequently results in an exception from theoretical treatment. For example, "lower of cost or market" as used in costing inventories is a departure from the cost principle.

Although the accounting profession has generally accepted the concept that profits should not be anticipated and that probable losses should be recognized as soon as the amounts are reasonably determinable, overconservatism usually results in misrepresentation. Reliance on conservatism should never be used to avoid the more laborious procedures to attain reasonable accuracy. Many errors in accounting have been committed under the guise of conservatism. A modified view of conservatism currently exerts an impact on accounting thought and practices.

The concept of conservatism is often misunderstood and criticized. It is essential because it is thought that when the "correct" amount is not determinable, the investment community usually is better served by understatement rather than overstatement of net income and assets. Accountants must make many accounting decisions based on judgment in selecting alternatives, making estimates, and applying accounting principles. These choices often affect net income, assets, and owners' equity; and they do not have a single answer that can be proven "correct." The concept of conservatism (a better word would be realism) provides a time-tested guideline for making these choices. Examples of the application of conservatism are: selecting an estimated useful life and residual value for depreciation purposes, the write-off of an asset of doubtful value, the write-off of an uncollectible account, application of the lower-of-cost-or-market rule in valuing marketable equity securities and inventories, accruing anticipated losses, and using an accelerated depreciation method.

Industry Peculiarities. Because accounting focuses on usefulness, feasibility, and pragmatism, the peculiarities of an industry (such as the extractive industry) may warrant certain exceptions to accounting principles and practices. The modifying principle permits special accounting for specific items where there is a clear precedent in the industry based on uniqueness, rationale, and feasibility. It is appropriate also to note that some differences in accounting occur in response to legal requirements; this is especially true with respect to companies subject to regulatory controls.

IMPLEMENTING MEASUREMENT PRINCIPLES

The information presented in external financial reports results from a wide range of accounting measurements. These measurements necessarily depend upon measurement principles, approaches, and techniques from other quantitative disciplines. The implementing measurement principles are those that have special application in accounting. Accounting measurement approaches and techniques generally rest upon the four broad implementing principles discussed below.

Selection of the Objects, Activities, and Events to Be Measured

The first step in measurement is to determine what is to be measured. Fundamentally, accounting measures assets, liabilities, owners' equity, revenues, expenses, net income, resource inflows, and resource outflows. In measuring these broad classifications, *objects* must be selected and measured, such as inventory, plant and equipment, land, receivables, and obligations. Similarly, *activities* such as sales of goods and services, payment of dividends, and sale and issuance of equity securities must be identified for measurement. In addition, selected *events*, other than transactions, often must be measured. Examples of these events are casualty losses, price-level changes, depreciation, and certain "unrealized" gains and losses.

Identification and Classification of Attributes

When an object, activity, or event has been selected for measurement, its specific attributes to be measured must be identified. For example, if goods held for resale (i.e., inventory) are selected for measurement, attributes such as units, description, condition, cost, net realizable value, replacement cost, and so on, can be measured. For measurement purposes, a choice must be made of the attributes to be measured that are relevant to the objectives of financial reports. As another example, assume an advertising *activity* is to be measured. Attributes such as description, number of ads, media used, cost, and effectiveness can be considered for measurement, and choices must be made. Measurement of the attributes of depreciation, such as cost basis depreciation, economic depreciation, and types of assets depreciated, are examples of *other events*. Because of relevance, time, and cost, the number of attributes measured generally are limited with respect to each object, activity, and other event. The attributes to be measured, to the extent feasible, must be classified to facilitate measurement and data processing. For example, one attribute classification pervading accounting is *historical cost*.

Assignment of Quantitative Amounts

Accounting measurements of the selected attributes (of the things to be measured) are quantitative. Numerical values that can be aggregated must be assigned to the attributes of the objects, activities, and other events. For example, numerical values (such as number of units and dollar cost) must be assigned to each asset so that aggregate total asset amounts can be derived. The assignment of quantitative amounts for accounting purposes generally is in monetary terms. However, many numerical accounting measurements are not monetary, such as units of inventory, trends (i.e., indexes), shares of stock, and the number of employees, plants, and products.

Modifying Measurement Principle

Since accounting measurements are made in an uncertain environment with limited data available, some adaptation of the basic measurement principle is necessary. This pragmatic aspect of accounting measurement not only affects the measurement process itself but influences accounting principles, procedures, and reports. For example, the inherent difficulties in measuring the "fair market value" of the multitudinous "parts" of a large complex business has been a significant argument for retaining the concept of historical cost as the valuation basis in accounting.

The modifying measurement principle has numerous facets; however, the major constraints are *(a)* uncertainty, *(b)* objectivity, *(c)* limitations of the monetary unit, and *(d)* cost effectiveness. *Uncertainty* arises because many measurements in accounting depend upon predictions. Primarily, these arise from the necessity to allocate values between past and future periods. Examples are depreciation expense, bad debt expense, warranty expense, deferred taxes, amortization of intangibles, and deferred revenue. The higher the degree of uncertainty, often the more complex the measurement.

Because of the importance attached to *objectivity* in accounting and financial reporting (see objectivity principle previously discussed), measurement adaptations are necessary to minimize bias. In addition, measurements must be based on verifiable and objective evidence. This constraint has had a strong influence on the selection and adaptation of measurement approaches and techniques used in accounting.

The *unit-of-measure assumption* (previously discussed) imposes a constraint on accounting measurements. There is general agreement that accounting measurements must use the monetary unit, although, over time, it is not a stable measuring unit. The instability of money as a measurement unit has been the basis for numerous proposals to modify both accounting principles and the selection of measurement approaches and techniques.

Cost effectiveness relates the value of information to the decisionmaker to the cost of measuring and reporting that information. Measurement often is a costly effort; consequently, it must be adapted to meet the constraint of cost effectiveness. This often means that some accuracy and completeness in measurement are sacrificed.

BASIC CONCEPTS OF THE ACCOUNTING MODEL

The accounting process broadly encompasses *(a)* collection of economic data affecting an accounting entity; *(b)* analysis of the economic effects of transactions and other events affecting the entity; *(c)* measuring, recording, and classifying the economic effects; and *(d)* reporting the summarized effects in periodic financial statements. This integrated process is built upon the fundamental assumptions, basic accounting principles and measurement principles, and the *accounting model.* This model comprises three submodels which parallel the three financial statements, viz:[7]

1. Financial position model—This is an economic model, expressed in algebraic format, that reflects the status of the resources (assets), obligations (liabilities), and residual equity (owners' equity) of the entity at specific points in time. Coupled with it, to facilitate data processing, is an arithmetical technique referred to as the debit-credit concept. This model, which reflects the basic content of a balance sheet (more appropriately, a statement of financial position), is:

	Assets		=	Liabilities		+	Owners' Equity	
Basic Model →								
	(Debit)	(Credit)		(Debit)	(Credit)		(Debit)	(Credit)
Debit-Credit Concept →	Increase			Decrease			Decrease	
		Decrease			Increase			Increase
	+	−		−	+		−	+

2. Results of operations model—This model is reflected by the income statement, or more appropriately, the statement of operating results. The model is:

   Revenue − Expenses = Net Income

3. Changes in financial position model—This model is reflected by the statement of changes in financial position. The model is:

   Funds Inflows − Funds Outflows = Net Change in Funds

DETAILED PRINCIPLES AND PROCEDURES

The fundamental underlying assumptions and the basic accounting principles, discussed in the preceding paragraphs, provide the broad foundation for the *detailed* principles and procedures that have been developed and accepted for financial accounting and reporting purposes. The detailed principles and procedures prescribe how transactions and other events should be recorded, classified, summarized, and reported. They are the means of implementing the underlying assumptions and the basic principles. Exhibits 2–1 and 2–2 present six categories of detailed principles and procedures; those relating to the financial reporting principle are summarized in Exhibit 2–3. The detailed principles and procedures are discussed and illustrated throughout the chapters to follow.

The term *generally accepted accounting principles* (often abbreviated as GAAP) is widely used in accounting. Although it is used in several contexts, it generally is used as defined in APB *Statement No. 4* (October 1970), par. 138:

---

[7] For a review of these basic concepts, see G. A. Welsch and R. N. Anthony, *Fundamentals of Financial Accounting* (Homewood, Ill.: Richard D. Irwin, Inc., 1974).

> Generally accepted accounting principles therefore is a technical term in financial accounting. Generally accepted accounting principles encompass the conventions, rules, and procedures necessary to define accepted accounting practice at a particular time. The standard of "generally accepted accounting principles" includes not only broad guidelines of general application, but also detailed practices and procedures.

Therefore, it is consistent with the structure outlined in Exhibit 2–2.

ACCOUNTING ON THE ACCRUAL BASIS VERSUS THE CASH BASIS

In the preceding discussion, we explained that generally accepted accounting principles require the accrual basis for accounting and reporting purposes. Nevertheless, some small sole proprietorships and partnerships use the cash basis because of its simplicity and because the financial reports are constructed only for the owners and perhaps the local banker. However, the banker may well have trouble in interpreting them, and they cannot be "certified" by an independent CPA.

When cash basis accounting is used, revenue is not recognized when the exchange transaction occurs, but rather only when the cash is collected. Similarly, expenses are not recognized when they are incurred as a result of an exchange transaction, but rather only when the cash payment is made. Therefore, net income (or loss) is essentially a cash concept. Cash basis accounting, since it is not in conformity with generally accepted accounting principles, is only briefly reviewed here to emphasize the characteristics of accrual basis accounting.

Accrual basis accounting is specified by the revenue and matching principles and is implicit in most of the other principles. Under the revenue principle, revenue is considered realized (i.e., earned), and is recognized in the accounts and reports, in the period in which the transaction occurs, regardless of the periods in which the related cash is collected. Similarly, under the matching principle, an expense is recognized, and matched with the revenue of the period to which it relates, regardless of when the related cash is expended. Therefore, net income determined in accordance with generally accepted accounting principles is not a cash concept; it is an approximation of income in the economic sense.

To illustrate the basic difference between accounting on the accrual basis versus on the cash basis, assume the following summarized data:

	Year 19A	*Year 19B*	*Year 19C*
Cash collections for sales:			
On 19A sales	$80,000	$15,000	$ 5,000
On 19B sales		90,000	30,000
Cash payments for expenses:			
On 19A expenses	50,000	7,000	3,000
On 19B expenses	6,000*	50,000	14,000

* Prepayments of 19B expense.

The income statements would reflect the following:

	Year 19A	Year 19B
Cash basis:		
Revenue	$ 80,000	$105,000
Expenses	56,000	57,000
Net income—cash basis	$ 24,000	$ 48,000
Accrual basis:		
Revenue	$100,000	$120,000
Expenses	60,000	70,000
Net income—accrual basis	$ 40,000	$ 50,000

The misstatement of income on the cash basis is material in amount when there is a lag between the exchange transactions and the related cash-flow transactions.

CONCLUSION

The discussion of the broad structure of financial accounting and reporting in this chapter is intended to provide the student with a frame of reference for study of subsequent chapters. Rather than presenting these concepts piecemeal throughout the text, the authors have chosen to present them briefly in this chapter. In studying the subject matter in subsequent chapters, these concepts will be reconsidered and related to the problem or practice at hand.

After studying this book we strongly recommend that the student return to this chapter for more critical study. Such an approach will help insure comprehension of a firm foundation of theory. We cannot overemphasize the importance of an understanding and appreciation of the foundations of accounting theory as opposed to a mere memorization of procedures and techniques. The accountant, whether in public practice or in industry, is faced continually with accounting problems that do not fit precisely what may have been encountered or considered previously; somehow many of them do not fit neatly into specific accounting practice and procedures. Consequently, many very practical judgments and decisions must be made by the accountant, and they should be resolved on the basis of sound theoretical analysis. For this approach there must be a logical and internally consistent structure of accounting theory. An accountant must have a deep understanding of the meaning and relevance of accounting theory to be successful as a professional. In this connection, we might repeat the hope, expressed earlier in this chapter, that there will emerge in the relatively near future an improved formulation of the foundations of accounting theory as contrasted with the implementing principles, procedures, and practices.

QUESTIONS

1. Define theory with special emphasis on accounting.
2. Explain briefly the characteristics of each of the following categories of the broad structure of financial accounting theory:
   a. Basic accounting objectives.
   b. Underlying environmental assumptions.
   c. Basic accounting principles.
   d. Implementing measurement principles.
   e. Basic concepts of the accounting model.
   f. Detailed principles and procedures.
3. Give the four underlying environmental assumptions and briefly explain each.
4. Complete the following:

Example	*Underlying Environmental Assumptions*
a. The presentation of annual financial reports.	________________
b. Measurement of assets, liabilities, and owners' equity in dollars.	________________
c. Exclusion from the balance sheet of the personal assets of the owner.	________________
d. Depreciation of a recently acquired fixed asset over an estimated life of 25 years when the youngest shareholder is 86 years of age.	________________

5. What is the basic problem created by the unit-of-measure assumption when there is significant inflation?
6. Explain why the time-period assumption gives rise to accruals and deferrals in accounting.
7. List the seven basic accounting principles. How are they different from the detailed principles and procedures?
8. Explain the cost principle. Why is it used in preference to fair market value or replacement cost?
9. How is cost measured in noncash transactions?
10. Define the revenue principle and explain each of its three aspects: *(a)* definition, *(b)* measurement, and *(c)* realization.
11. How is revenue measured in transactions involving noncash items (exclude credit situations)?
12. There are four exceptions to the revenue principle, briefly explain each: *(a)* cash, *(b)* percentage-of-completion, *(c)* production, and *(d)* cost recovery.

13. Explain the matching principle. What is meant by "the expense should follow the revenue"?

14. Explain why the matching principle usually necessitates the use of adjusting entries. Use depreciation expense, unpaid wages, and expired insurance as examples.

15. Relate the matching principle to the revenue and cost principles.

16. Explain the objectivity principle; focus on objectivity and verifiability.

17. Explain the consistency principle. Why is it important to the statement user?

18. Explain the financial reporting principle and relate it to the standards of financial statement presentation presented in Exhibit 2–3.

19. Why is a modifying, or exception, principle essential? Briefly explain each of the following: (*a*) materiality, (*b*) conservatism, and (*c*) industry peculiarities.

20. Complete the following:

Example	*Concepts of the Modifying Principle Applied*
a. Banks do not separately report working capital.	________________
b. An asset costs $100,000, the estimated residual value is $400 which was disregarded in computing depreciation.	________________
c. Marketable securities that cost $75,000 were reported on the balance sheet at $62,000 which was the fair market value at balance sheet date.	________________

21. List and explain the four implementing measurement principles.

22. What are the four basic phases of the accounting process?

23. Give and briefly explain the three basic concepts of the accounting model.

24. Explain the nature of, and the need for, implementing (detailed) principles and procedures.

25. Briefly explain the technical term "generally accepted accounting principles" as used by the accounting profession.

DECISION CASE 2–1

ABC Corporation, at the end of 1975, reported the following (summarized):

Balance Sheet		*Income Statement*	
Total assets	$400,000	Sales revenue	$800,000
Total liabilities	100,000	Expenses	760,000
Total owners' equity	300,000	Net income	40,000

Required:

a. This problem focuses on the concept of materiality. For this particular company you are to present your own definition of what would be material. Make it as specific and precise as you can. Do not feel constrained by the definition in the chapter.

b. On the basis of *your definition,* use your best judgment to respond to each of the following examples. For each example make a choice as to materiality, then justify it.

1. At the end of the accounting year accrued wages are material if the amount is (check for "yes" response):

______	$ 100	______	$ 10,000
______	500	______	20,000
______	1,000	______	50,000
______	5,000	______	100,000

2. At the end of the accounting year unearned revenues (cash has been collected) are material if the amount is (check for "yes" response):

______	$ 100	______	$ 10,000
______	500	______	20,000
______	1,000	______	50,000
______	5,000	______	100,000

3. At the beginning of the accounting year a fixed asset, with an estimated useful life of five years and no residual value, was purchased. The transaction is material if the amount is (check for "yes" response):

______	$ 100	______	$ 10,000
______	500	______	20,000
______	1,000	______	50,000
______	5,000	______	100,000

EXERCISES

Exercise 2–1

Give the generally accepted principle(s) that establishes the dollar valuation in the balance sheet for each of the following items:

a. Accounts receivable.
b. Short-term (temporary) investments.
c. Inventory.
d. Plant and equipment.
e. Plant site (land).
f. Patent.

Exercise 2–2

Explain how each of the following violates (if it does) the financial reporting principle.

a. Owners' equity reports only two amounts: capital stock, $100,000; and retained earnings, $80,000. The capital stock has a par value of $100,000 and originally sold for $150,000 cash.
b. Although sales amounted to $900,000 and cost of goods sold, $500,000, the first line on the income statement was revenues, $400,000.
c. No earnings per share amounts were reported.

d. Although current assets amounted to $200,000 and current liabilities $180,000, the balance sheet reported, under assets, the following: working capital, $20,000.

e. The income statement showed only the following classifications:

Gross revenues
Costs
Net profit

f. There was no comment or explanation of the fact that the company changed its inventory method from *Fifo* to *Lifo*.

Exercise 2–3

On December 31, 1975, the balance sheet for ABC Corporation showed the following (summarized):

Current assets*	$ 60,000	Current liabilities		$ 30,000
Fixed assets	135,000	Long-term liabilities		20,000
Patent	5,000	Contributed capital	$100,000	
		Retained earnings	50,000	150,000
	$200,000			$200,000

* No cash

On this date the business (including all assets and liabilities) was sold to John Doe who paid $225,000 cash which included $35,000 for "goodwill." Assume generally accepted accounting principles were followed. Explain in terms of these principles why the selling price was still $40,000 higher than the sum of owners' equity shown on the balance sheet plus the goodwill.

Exercise 2–4

Present accounting theory is based on the assumption that the "value of money" is relatively stable. If there is a significant change in the price level, or in the purchasing power of the dollar, problems arise in interpreting income data as determined under conventional accounting procedures.

Required:

State and explain briefly the nature of such problems as related to inventories and fixed assets. You need not attempt to offer specific solutions to these problems.

(AICPA adapted)

Exercise 2–5

In making an audit of a corporation you find certain liabilities, such as taxes, which appear to be overstated. Also some semiobsolete inventory items seem to be undervalued, and the tendency is to expense rather than to capitalize as many items as possible.

In talking with the management about the policies, you are told that "the company has always taken a very conservative view of the business and its future prospects." Management suggests that they do not wish to weaken the company by reporting any more earnings or paying any more dividends than are absolutely necessary, since they do not expect business to continue to be good. They point out that the undervaluation of assets, and so on, does not lose anything for the company and creates reserves for "hard times."

Required:

You are to discuss fully whether the policies followed by the company are appropriate and comment on each of the arguments presented by management.

(AICPA adapted)

Exercise 2–6

What is your understanding of the meaning of *consistency* in the application of accounting principles—for example, as used in the standard form of an independent public accountant's report?

(AICPA adapted)

Exercise 2–7

Accountants frequently refer to a concept of "conservatism." Explain what is meant by conservatism in accounting. Discuss the question of the extent to which it is possible to follow accounting procedures which will result in consistently conservative financial statements over a considerable number of years. Give an example of an application of conservatism in accounting.

(AICPA adapted)

Exercise 2–8

A financial statement included the following note: "During the current year, plant assets were written down by $2,000,000 because of economic conditions. This resulted in substantial savings to the company. Depreciation and other charges in the future years will be lower as a result; this will benefit the profits of future years." Appraise this statement in terms of (1) economic soundness, and (2) generally accepted accounting principles.

Exercise 2–9

The following summarized data were taken from the records of XY Company at December 31, 1975, end of the accounting year:

1. Sales: 1975 cash sales, $300,000; 1975 credit sales, $100,000.
2. Cash collections during 1975: On 1974 credit sales, $30,000; on 1975 credit sales, $80,000; on 1976 sales (collected in advance), $20,000.
3. Expenses: 1975 cash expenses, $180,000; 1975 credit expenses, $70,000.
4. Cash payments during 1975: For 1974, credit expenses, $10,000; for 1975, credit expenses, $40,000; for 1976, expenses (paid in advance), $5,000.

Required:

Complete the following statements for 1975 as a basis for evaluating the difference between cash and accrual accounting.

	Cash Basis	*Accrual Basis*
Sales revenue	$__________	$__________
Expenses	__________	__________
Net Income	__________	__________

Exercise 2–10

The general manager of the Cumberland Manufacturing Company received an income statement from the controller. The statement covered the calendar year. The general manager said to the controller, "This statement indicates that a net income of only $100,000 was earned last year. You know the value of the company is much more than it was this time last year."

"You're probably right," replied the controller. "You see, there are factors in accounting which sometimes keep reported operating results from reflecting the change in the fair market value of the company."

Required:

Present a detailed explanation of the accounting theories and principles to which the controller referred.

(AICPA adapted)

PROBLEMS

Problem 2–1

This problem focuses on the revenue principle. Respond to each of the following:

a. Define revenue in accordance with the revenue principle.
b. What should be the dollar amount of revenue recognized under the revenue principle in the case of (1) sales and services for cash, and (2) sales and services rendered in exchange for noncash considerations?
c. When should revenue be recognized in the case of long-term, low down payment sales and when collectibility is very uncertain.
d. When should revenue be recognized for long-term construction contracts?
e. When should revenue be recognized when there is a highly speculative transaction involving potential revenue?

Problem 2–2

AD Corporation has been involved in a number of transactions necessitating careful interpretation of the revenue principle. For each of the following 1975 transactions specify *(a)* the amount of revenue that should be recognized during 1975, and *(b)* explain the basis for your determination.

a. Regular credit sales amounted to $600,000 of which two thirds was collected by the end of 1975; the balance will be collected in 1976.
b. Regular services were rendered on credit amounting to $100,000 of which three fourths will be collected in 1976.
c. A special item, that had been repossessed from the first purchaser, was sold again for $20,000. A $1,000 cash down payment was received in 1975; the balance is to be paid on a quarterly basis during 1976 and 1977. Repossession again would not be a surprise! The item has a cost of $14,000.
d. On January 1, 1974, the company purchased a $10,000 note. Because it was highly speculative whether the note was collectible, the company was able to acquire it for $1,000 cash. The note specifies 8% simple interest payable each year (disregard interest prior to 1974). The first collection on the note was $2,000 cash on December 31, 1975. Further collections are highly speculative.

Problem 2–3

Appraise each of the following statements in terms of accounting principles and assumptions.

a. Lower of cost or market should be used in costing inventories.
b. The cost principle relates only to the income statement.
c. Revenue should be recognized when the cash is received.
d. Accruals and deferrals are necessary because of the separate-entity assumption.
e. Revenue should be recognized as early as possible and expenses as late as possible.
f. The accounting entity is considered to be separate and apart from the owners.
g. A transaction involving a very small amount may be disregarded because of materiality.
h. The monetary unit is not stable over time.
i. Revenues should be recognized sooner rather than later, and expenses should be recognized later rather than sooner.
j. Full disclosure requires the use of notes to the financial statements.

Problem 2–4

Appraise the following items in financial statements in terms of generally accepted accounting principles. Indicate what principle(s) is violated and how it is violated with respect to each item.

a. Inventory is overstated by $8,000.
b. One old plant has been idle for six years; there is little likelihood that it will ever be opened. It has been depreciated at the regular amount, $10,000, each of the six years. It is reported on the current balance sheet at a book value of $140,000; estimated scrap value is $10,000.
c. The company sustained a $20,000 loss due to storm damage during the current year. The loss was reported as follows:
   Income statement: storm loss, $2,000.
   Balance sheet: deferred charge (under assets), $18,000.
d. Accounts receivable of $60,000 included amounts due from the company president amounting to $50,000.
e. Usual and ordinary repairs on fixed assets were recorded as follows: Debit: Fixed Assets, $8,000. Credit: Cash, $8,000.
f. Treasury stock (i.e., stock of the company that was sold and subsequently bought back from the shareholders) was reported on the balance sheet as an asset.
g. Depreciation expense was deducted directly from retained earnings.
h. Income tax expense was deducted directly from retained earnings.

Problem 2–5

Cheatum Corporation was experiencing a bad year because they were operating at a loss. In order to minimize the loss they recorded certain transactions as indicated below. Determine for each transaction, what accounting principle was violated (if any) and explain the nature of the violation. Also in each instance indicate the correct accounting treatment.

a. Goods for resale (inventory) were being acquired for $1 per unit. However, the company located a good deal and acquired 10,000 units for $7,500 cash. They recorded the purchase as follows:

Inventory	10,000	
Cash		7,500
Revenue		2,500

b. At the beginning of the year a new machine costing $24,000 was purchased for cash for use in the business. The estimated useful life was ten years and a residual value of $4,000. The following depreciation entry was made at the end of the year:

Depreciation expense	1,000	
Accumulated depreciation (based on 20-year life)		1,000

c. A patent was being amortized over a 17-year useful life. The amortization entry made at the end of the current year was:

Retained earnings	800	
Patent		800

d. Two delivery trucks were repaired (motor tune-up, new tires, brakes relined, front end realigned) at a cost of $350. The following entry was made:

Fixed asset – trucks	350	
Cash		350

e. Although the bad debt loss rate did not change, no adjusting entry was made for the estimate of $450.

Problem 2–6

The transactions summarized below were recorded as indicated during the current year. Determine, for each transaction, what accounting principle was violated (if any) and explain the nature of the violation. Also in each instance indicate how the transaction should have been recorded.

a. The company owns a plant that is located on a river that floods every few years. As a result, the company suffers a flood loss regularly. During the current year the flood was severe causing an uninsured loss of $4,800. The following entry was made for repair of the loss:

Retained earnings	4,800	
Cash		4,800

b. The company originally sold and issued 50,000 shares of $100 par value common stock. During the current year 45,000 of these shares were outstanding and 5,000 were held by the company as treasury stock (they had been bought back from the shareholders in prior years). Near the end of the current year the board of directors declared and paid a cash dividend of $2 per share. The dividend was recorded as follows:

Retained earnings	100,000	
Cash		90,000
Investment income		10,000

c. The company needed a small structure for temporary storage. A contractor quoted a price of $60,000. The company decided to build it themselves. The cost was $50,000. The following entry was made:

Fixed assets—warehouse	60,000	
Cash		50,000
Revenue		10,000

d. To construct the structure in (*c*) above the company borrowed $50,000 cash from the bank at 10% per annum. The loan was paid at the end of the year, and the following entry was made (12 months interest):

Note payable	50,000	
Fixed assets—warehouse	5,000	
Cash		55,000

Problem 2–7

Following is a series of transactions during 1976 for RS Corporation. Analyze each of them and then answer the questions.

a. The company engaged a local attorney to represent it in a dispute with respect to an accident involving a company vehicle. The attorney presented a bill for services for $1,500. Since the company was short of cash, the attorney agreed to accept ten shares of RS Corporation common stock (par $10 per share). The last sale of stock was for $17 per share three years earlier. The transaction to record settlement of the attorney's fee is under consideration.
(1) What accounting principle should govern? Explain.
(2) When should the fee be recognized as an expense? Explain.
(3) What amount should be recorded as legal expense? Explain.

b. The corporation sold a large item of equipment which it stocked for sale. The sale was made on December 31, 1976, for $10,000 cash. It is estimated that because of a one-year guarantee on the equipment, during the following year $300 cash will be spent on the warranty. Recognition of the warranty expense is under consideration.
(1) What accounting principle should govern? Explain.
(2) When should the warranty expense be recognized? Explain.
(3) What amount should be recorded as warranty expense in 1976? In 1977? Explain.

c. At December 31, 1976, there was an item in the inventory of goods for resale that cost $200. Because it had become obsolete it is estimated that it can be sold for $50 cash. Accounting for the obsolete item is under consideration.
(1) What accounting principle should govern? Explain.
(2) What amount should be used by the company for this item in the December 31, 1976, inventory? Explain.

d. The corporation acquired a special item of equipment that would be used in operations (a fixed asset). The suppliers catalog listed the item at $15,000. Since the corporation was short of cash it exchanged a small parcel of land that it had acquired ten years earlier at a cost of $8,000. The land was assessed for tax purposes at $12,000, and a recent appraisal by an independent appraiser showed a fair market value of $14,000. Accounting for the equipment is under consideration.
(1) What accounting principle should govern at the date of acquisition? Explain.
(2) What amount should be debited to the fixed asset account? Explain.
(3) What accounting principle governs the recognition of depreciation on the asset? Explain.

Problem 2–8

The following summarized data were taken from the records of AC Corporation at the end of the annual accounting period, December 31, 1976:

Sales for cash	$246,000
Sales on account	84,000
Cash purchases of merchandise for resale	170,000
Credit purchases of merchandise for resale	40,000
Expenses paid in cash	71,000
Accounts receivable:	
Balance in the account on January 1, 1976	23,000
Balance in the account on December 31, 1976	30,000
Accounts payable:	
Balance in the account on January 1, 1976	14,000
Balance in the account on December 31, 1976	16,000
Merchandise inventory account:	
Beginning inventory, January 1, 1976	50,000
Ending inventory, December 31, 1976	60,000
Accrued (unpaid) wages at December 31, 1976 (none at January 1, 1976)	2,000
Prepaid expenses at December 31, 1976 (none at January 1, 1976)	3,000
Fixed assets—equipment:	
Cost when acquired	100,000
Annual depreciation	10,000

Required:

Based on the above data complete the following income statements for 1975 in order to evaluate the difference between cash and accrual basis:

	Cash Basis		Accrual Basis	
Sales revenue		$____		$____
Less expenses:				
Cost of goods sold	$____		$____	
Depreciation expense	____		____	
Remaining expenses	____		____	
Total Expenses		____		____
Pretax Income		$____		$____

Problem 2–9

The general ledger of Enter-tane, Inc., a corporation engaged in the development and production of television programs for commercial sponsorship, contains the following accounts before amortization at the end of the current year:

Account	*Balance (debit)*
Sealing Wax and Kings	$51,000
The Messenger	36,000
The Desperado	17,500
Shin Bone	8,000
Studio Rearrangement	5,000

An examination of contracts and records revealed the following information:

a. The first two accounts listed above represent the total cost of completed programs that were televised during the accounting period just ended. Under the terms of an existing contract, Sealing Wax and Kings will be rerun during the next accounting period at a fee equal to 50% of the fee for the first televising of the program. The contract for the first run produced $300,000 of revenue. The contract with the sponsor of The Messenger provides that at the sponsor's option, the program can be rerun during the next season at a fee of 75% of the fee on the first televising of the program.

b. The balance in The Desperado account is the cost of a new program which has just been completed and is being considered by several companies for commercial sponsorship.

c. The balance in the Shin Bone account represents the cost of a partially completed program for a projected series that has been abandoned.

d. The balance of the Studio Rearrangement account consists of payments made to a firm of engineers which prepared a report relative to the more efficient utilization of existing studio space and equipment.

Required:

1. State the general principle (or principles) of accounting that are applicable to the first *four* accounts.
2. How would you report each of the first *four* accounts in the financial statements of Enter-tane, Inc.? Explain.
3. In what way, if at all, does the Studio Rearrangement account differ from the first four? Explain.

(AICPA adapted)

Chapter 3

Review—The Accounting Model and Information Processing

The broad objective of financial accounting is to provide relevant financial information to external decision makers. The information reported on periodic financial statements summarizes the economic impacts of a multitude of transactions and other events on an entity. Identification, analysis, recording, and classification of the impacts of transactions and other events require an efficient and sophisticated accounting information processing system. The larger the entity, the greater the number of transactions, and, consequently, the more complex the information processing system. The information processing system (i.e., the accounting system) must be designed effectively and economically to (1) collect and measure economic data, (2) classify and process the data, and (3) report the summarized economic effects to decision-makers. An accounting system must be tailored to the entity's characteristics such as size, nature of operations, organizational structure, management approaches, and the impact of government regulations. However, there is a fundamental structure, based upon the accounting model, that is common to most accounting systems.

We assume in this book that the reader has a sound knowledge of the *fundamentals* of financial accounting. Nevertheless, in this and the next two chapters, we shall review those fundamentals.[1] The purpose of this chapter is to review and illustrate the *sequential* accounting information processing cycle that is repeated each accounting period.

THE ACCOUNTING MODEL

In Chapter 2 we outlined the fundamental accounting model on which accounting systems are based. This model is composed of three submodels, each of which represents one basic component of the peri-

[1] For a more comprehensive introductory discussion see: G. A. Welsch and R. N. Anthony, *Fundamentals of Financial Accounting* (Homewood, Ill.: Richard D. Irwin, Inc., 1974).

odic financial statement designed for external decision-makers. The three submodels are:

1. Financial position model: Assets = Liabilities + Owners' Equity (A = L + OE).
2. Results of operations model: Revenues − Expenses = Net Income (R − E = NI).
3. Funds flow model: Funds Inflow − Funds Outflow = Net Change in Funds (FI − FO = NCF).

Coupled with the accounting model is the debit-credit concept. This is a mathematical technique used to record increases and decreases in specific variables in the model—assets, liabilities, owners' equity, revenues, and expenses.

Fundamentally, all recognized accounting events are recorded in the accounting system in terms of the *financial position model:* A = L + OE. The debit-credit concept is superimposed on this basic model as follows:

	Assets		=	Liabilities		+	Owners' Equity	
Basic Model								
Debit-Credit Concept	Debit for Increases	Credit for Decreases		Debit for Decreases	Credit for Increases		Debit for Decreases	Credit for Increases

Since investments by owners and revenues *increase* owners' equity and since withdrawals by owners and expenses *decrease* owners' equity, the model can be expanded to include them as follows:

Assets		=	Liabilities		+	Owners' Equity	
Debit for increases	Credit for decreases		Debit for decreases	Credit for increases		Debit for decreases: *a.* Withdrawals by owners'. *b.* Expenses.	Credit for increases: *a.* Investments by owners'. *b.* Revenues.

Observe in the above diagram, that although the debits are *always* on the left and the credits on the right, the increases and decreases are opposite on each side of the equation. That is, debits represent increases to assets and decreases to liabilities and owners' equity; whereas credits represent decreases to assets and increases to liabilities and owners' equity. Expenses are recorded as debits and revenues as credits. This algebraic arrangement forces debits always to equal credits. Thus, the fundamental accounting model always maintains a dual balancing feature, viz:

1. Assets = Liabilities + Owners' Equity.
2. Debits = Credits.

Because of this dual feature, the accounting model is often referred to as a *double-entry system.* These two balancing features, in addition to

EXHIBIT 3–1
Information Inputs in an Accounting System

Typical Transaction	*Transaction Analysis*	*Entry into the Accounting System*			*Basic Accounting Model (cumulative balances)*		
		Accounts	*Debit*	*Credit*	*A* =	*L* +	*OE*
1. Service Corporation was organized; owners invested $100,000 cash and received nopar common stock.	Asset increased—cash, $100,000. Owners' equity increased—common stock, $100,000. Liabilities—no effect.	Cash .... Common stock ...	100,000	 100,000	+100,000 100,000	 —0—	 +100,000 100,000
2. Borrowed $50,000 on a note.	Asset increased—cash, $50,000. Liabilities increased—note payable, $50,000. Owners' equity—no effect.	Cash .... Notes payable......	50,000	 50,000	+ 50,000 150,000	 +50,000 50,000	 100,000
3. Purchased equipment for use in the business, $40,000; paid cash.	Asset increased—equipment, $40,000. Asset decreased—cash, $40,000. Liabilities—no effect. Owners' equity—no effect.	Equipment .... Cash	40,000	 40,000	+ 40,000 − 40,000 150,000	 50,000	 100,000

4. Services rendered to clients, \$20,000; of which \$15,000 was collected in cash.	Assets increased—cash, \$15,000; accounts receivable, \$5,000. Revenue (owners' equity) increased \$20,000. Liabilities—no effect.	Cash .... Accounts receivable .... Service revenue...	15,000 5,000	20,000	+ 15,000 + 5,000 170,000	50,000	+ 20,000 120,000
5. Incurred operating expenses, \$11,000; of which \$8,000 was paid in cash.	Asset decreased—cash, \$8,000. Liability increased—accounts payable, \$3,000. Owners' equity (expense) decreased, \$11,000.	Expenses................. Cash .... Accounts payable...........	11,000	8,000 3,000	− 8,000 162,000	+ 3,000 53,000	− 11,000 109,000
6. Paid \$2,000 on accounts payable (5 above).	Asset decreased—cash, \$2,000. Liability decreased—accounts payable, \$2,000. Owners' equity—no effect.	Accounts payable................. Cash	2,000	2,000	− 2,000 160,000	− 2,000 51,000	109,000
7. Depreciation for one year on equipment, estimated life ten years, no residual value. (3 above).	Asset decreased—accumulated depreciation, \$4,000. Owners' equity decreased—depreciation expense, \$4,000. Liabilities—no effect.	Depreciation expense .... Accumulated depreciation, equipment	4,000	4,000	− 4,000 156,000	51,000	− 4,000 105,000

other purposes, automatically call attention to many types of errors and add considerable reliability to the output of an accounting system.

Whether an accounting system is maintained manually, mechanically, or electronically, each entry is recorded in the basic accounting model. Thus, each entry entered in an accounting system, continuously maintains the dual-balancing feature. The fundamental information processing approach is reviewed in Exhibit 3–1. In particular, note the following: (1) transaction analysis in terms of the basic accounting model, (2) method of recording the increases and decreases, (3) A = L + OE for each entry and cumulatively, and (4) debits equal credits for each entry and cumulatively.

THE ACCOUNTING INFORMATION PROCESSING CYCLE

The accounting system provides a systematic approach for processing information from the capture of raw economic data that affect the entity to the end result, the periodic financial statements. Therefore, an accounting system incorporates an information processing cycle, often called the accounting cycle, that is repeated each accounting period. This cycle is common to all double-entry accounting systems; however, the larger the enterprise, the more complex its application. The accounting information processing cycle, diagrammed in Exhibit 3–2, reflects the primary phases in the *sequential order* in which they are usually accomplished. Each of these phases will be discussed and illustrated in order.

COLLECTION OF RAW ECONOMIC DATA (PHASE 1)

The accounting system collects raw economic data about events affecting the entity that are to be recorded. There are two types of events that are recognized in an accounting system: (1) exchange transactions between the entity and one or more outside parties, such as the sale of goods, purchase of assets, sale of securities, and payment of wages; and (2) other events that are not transactions but which exert an economic impact on the enterprise and must be recorded. These events may be external such as casualties (i.e., floods, fires, hurricanes, etc.) and changes in currency exchange rates. Also they may be internal, which involves the conversion or use of resources such as depreciation of fixed assets and amortization of intangibles.[2]

Raw economic data are collected by means of *source documents*. Exchange transactions, since they involve external parties, almost always generate their own source documents – sale invoices, credit bills, freight bills, notes signed by debtors, purchase orders, deposit slips, checks, and so on. For recognized events that are not transactions, the entity itself must prepare the source documents. Examples are: depreciation computations, schedules of assets lost due to casualty, amorti-

[2] For convenience in exposition, the term *transactions* will be used broadly to include both transactions and the other events to be recognized.

EXHIBIT 3–2
Diagram of the Accounting Information Processing Cycle

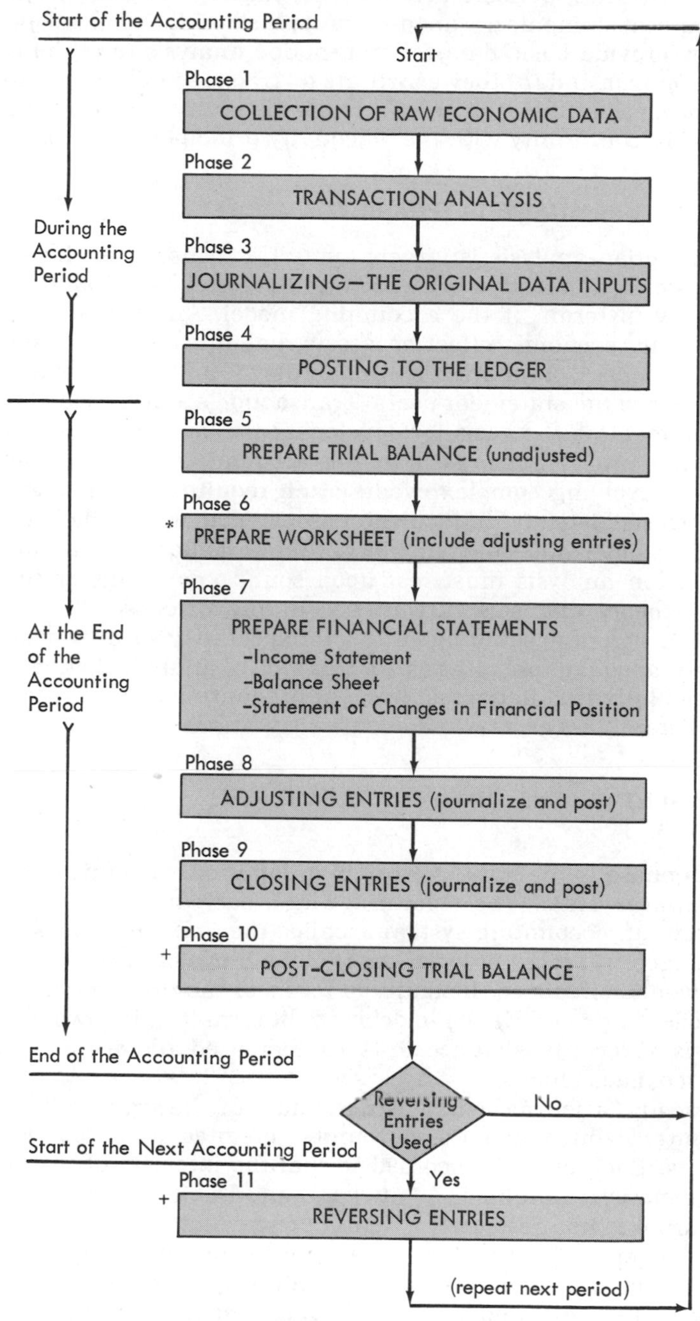

Note: See Exhibit 3–12 for complete summary.

* Worksheet is optional. If not used, prepare an *adjusted* trial balance after Phase 8 as a basis for preparing the financial statements.

\+ Optional.

zation schedules, periodic inventory schedules, and issue requisitions. The source documents are an important phase of data collection because *(a)* they provide basic data for transaction analysis (and the resulting journal entry), and *(b)* they constitute a "track record" so that the event and the measurement of its effects on the entity can be subsequently *verified* in conformity with the objectivity principle (see Chapter 2).

TRANSACTION ANALYSIS (PHASE 2)

Transaction analysis is largely mental. It constitutes the study and analysis of a transaction to identify and assess its economic impact on the entity in terms of the accounting model. An analysis is made to measure its economic effect on assets, liabilities, owners' equity, revenues, expenses, fund inflows, fund outflows, and other measurements of interest to the statement users. Transaction analysis, which includes measurement, is the basis for developing the *accounting entry,* or entries, that must be recorded in the accounting system. Transaction analysis involving complex events often requires a high degree of accounting sophistication since the competence with which it is done ultimately determines the reliability of the periodic financial statements. Transaction analysis must rest upon sound knowledge of the fundamental theory and structure of accounting discussed in Chapter 2. Memorization of accounting entries for specific types of transactions is wholly inadequate preparation for this type of analytical endeavor. This is particularly true in the real world of accounting because the accountant constantly faces new and complex situations.

JOURNALIZING—THE ORIGINAL DATA INPUT (PHASE 3)

This phase is the initial, or original, input of economic data into an accounting system. The record in which each transaction is first recorded in an accounting system is called the *journal.* This is a chronological record (i.e., by order of date) of each transaction that expresses its economic effects on the entity in terms of the fundamental accounting model (A = L + OE) and in debit-credit format; it follows transaction analysis. It records what accounts are increased and decreased and the amount of each change.

Basically, a journal entry lists the date of the transaction, and the account(s) debited and the account(s) credited and their respective amounts. Each entry is recorded so that the integrity of the duality of the system is maintained: A = L + OE and Debits = Credits. Although the journal is not absolutely essential (one could skip it and go directly to the ledger), it is important because it *(a)* maintains a chronological record of the transactions recognized in the system, which is useful for subsequent tracing; and *(b)* shows in one place all aspects of each transaction (i.e., all accounts affected and the amounts).

In an accounting system usually there are two types of journals:

(1) the general journal, and (2) several special journals. Each special journal is designed to accommodate like-kind transactions. The commonly used special journals are: credit sales, credit purchases, cash receipts, cash payments, and the voucher journal. Special journals are discussed and illustrated in Appendix A of this chapter. Most accounting systems use at least a general journal. A general journal will be used in the chapters to follow because of its value for instructional purposes. The general journal format, with a typical entry, is shown in Exhibit 3–3.

EXHIBIT 3–3
General Journal and General Ledger Illustrated

General Journal

Page J-16

Date 1976	Accounts and Explanation	Ledger Folio*	Amount Debit	Amount Credit
Jan. 2	Equipment	150	15,000	
	Cash	101		5,000
	Notes payable	215		10,000
	Purchased equipment for use in the business. Paid $5,000 cash and gave a $10,000, one-year, 9% interest-bearing note.			

* The figures in this column indicate ,a. that the amount has been posted to the ledger, and ,b. the account number in the ledger to which posted.

General Ledger

Cash — Acct. 101

Date	Item	Amount	Date	Item	Amount
1976 Jan. 1	Balance	18,700	1976 Jan. 2	J-16†	5,000

Equipment — Acct. 150

Date	Item	Amount	Date	Item	Amount
1976 Jan. 1	Balance	62,000			
2	J-16	15,000			

Notes Payable — Acct. 215

Date	Item	Amount	Date	Item	Amount
			1976 Jan. 2	J-16	10,000

† This figure indicates the journal page from which the amount was posted.

POSTING TO THE LEDGER (PHASE 4)

After the initial recording in the journal, the next step is to transfer the information to the ledger. The transfer process is called *posting* and is done at various times for all transactions. This transfer has the effect of reclassifying the information from a chronological format to an account classifications format in the *ledger*. Posting from the journal to the ledger is illustrated in Exhibit 3–3.

Recall that the ledger consists of a large number of separate accounts. There are accounts for each kind of asset (such as cash, accounts receivable, investments, fixed assets, and intangible assets), liability (such as accounts payable and bonds payable), owners' equity (such as capital stock and retained earnings), and the revenue and expense accounts. Posting amounts from the journal to the ledger results in reclassification of the data in ledger accounts which are compatible with the classifications of information in the financial statements.

Real and Nominal Accounts

The accounts in the ledger often are classified as follows:

1. Real accounts—These are the balance sheet accounts; they are *permanent*, or real, in the sense that they are not closed at the end of the accounting period. They are the asset, liability, and owners' equity accounts.
2. Nominal accounts—These are the income statement accounts; they are *temporary*, or nominal, in the sense that they are closed at the end of the accounting period. They are the revenue and expense accounts.

Frequently an account, either real or nominal, will be *mixed* in the sense that its balance has both a real (i.e., balance sheet) component and a nominal (i.e., income statement) component. To illustrate, assume that on January 1 of the current year, a three-year insurance premium of $600 was paid and debited to an asset account, Prepaid Insurance. On December 31 of the current year, of the $600, the nominal component, Insurance Expense, is $200 and the real component, Prepaid Insurance, is $400 (an asset). An adjusting entry on December 31, debiting Insurance Expense and crediting Prepaid Insurance for $200, is necessary to "unmix" the Prepaid Insurance asset account by removing the expense component of $200.

Subsidiary Ledgers and Control Accounts

Most companies use both a *general ledger* and one or more *subsidiary ledgers*. For each subsidiary ledger there is a related *control account* in the general ledger. The control account reflects summary information only whereas the subsidiary ledger reflects the details that support the control account. The general ledger contains the complete account structure for all assets, liabilities, owners' equity, revenues, and expenses.

Each subsidiary ledger is a device for keeping track of a multitude of details that relate to a particular *control account* in the general ledger. To illustrate, a department store may have 10,000 credit customers. A separate account receivable must be kept for each customer. Rather than 10,000 separate accounts receivable in the general ledger, one controlling account, Accounts Receivable Control, should be used. A separate accounts receivable subsidiary ledger composed of a separate account for each customer should also be maintained. Each credit sale would *(a)* be posted directly to the customer's account in the subsidiary ledger, and *(b)* the total of all credit sales would be posted to the Accounts Receivable Control account in the general ledger. Thus, at any time when posting is complete, the sum of the balances in the customer accounts in the subsidiary ledger would agree with the single balance in the Accounts Receivable Control account.

Subsidiary ledgers often are used for cash (when there are numerous cash accounts), accounts receivable, accounts payable, fixed assets, capital stock (the subsidiary ledger for this account is a record for each shareholder), revenue, and expense. Subsidiary ledgers and control accounts are discussed and illustrated in Appendix A to this chapter.

PREPARE A TRIAL BALANCE—UNADJUSTED (PHASE 5)

At the end of the period after all of the regular entries have been journalized and posted to the ledger, a trial balance should be prepared. Since this trial balance is prepared before the adjusting entries are made, it is often called the *unadjusted trial balance.* A trial balance is simply a list of the accounts in the general ledger and their respective debit or credit balances. A trial balance, prepared after all of the regular entries, but before the adjusting entries, serves the following purposes:

1. It verifies that debits equal the credits.
2. It provides important information for the development of—
   a. A worksheet, and
   b. The end-of-the-period adjusting entries.

An unadjusted trial balance for Canby Retailers, Inc., is shown in Exhibit 3–4. This trial balance will be used to illustrate the discussions to follow.

PREPARE WORKSHEET (PHASE 6)

As soon as the unadjusted trial balance is available, the following end-of-the-period procedures can be completed:

1. Develop the adjusting entries.
2. Journalize and post the adjusting and closing entries.

3. Develop an adjusted trial balance.
4. Develop the financial statements.

These procedures can be completed in the order listed above. Remember that the adjusting entries must be taken into consideration before the financial statements can be developed. However, accountants usually insert another step, preparation of two worksheets, viz: (1) one to facilitate development of the adjusting entries, the income statement, and the balance sheet; and (2) one to facilitate preparation of the statement of changes in financial position. These worksheets are simply *facilitating techniques.* They constitute an orderly and systematic approach to completing *(a)* the financial statements on a timely basis, and *(b)* the adjusting and closing entries. This is the only reason for using these worksheets.

A worksheet based on the trial balance given in Exhibit 3–4 is pre-

EXHIBIT 3–4

CANBY RETAILERS, INC.
Unadjusted Trial Balance
December 31, 1976

Account	*Debit*	*Credit*
Cash	$ 55,300	
Marketable securities (bonds)	20,000	
Accounts receivable	45,000	
Allowance for doubtful accounts		$ 1,000
Inventory of merchandise (periodic system)	75,000	
Prepaid insurance	600	
Accrued investment revenue receivable		
Land	8,000	
Building	160,000	
Accumulated depreciation, building		90,000
Equipment	91,000	
Accumulated depreciation, equipment		27,000
Accounts payable		29,000
Income taxes payable		
Accrued bond interest payable		
Prepaid rent revenue		
Bonds payable, 6%		50,000
Common stock, par $100		150,000
Contributed capital in excess of par		20,000
Retained earnings		31,500
Sales revenue		325,200
Investment revenue		500
Rent revenue		1,800
Purchases	130,000	
Freight on purchases	4,000	
Purchase returns		2,000
Selling expenses*	104,000	
General and administrative expenses*	23,600	
Interest expense	2,500	
Extraordinary loss	9,000	
Income tax expense		
Totals	$728,000	$728,000

* These broad categories of expense are used to conserve space.

sented in Exhibit 3–5. This worksheet provides data for the income statement and balance sheet.[3]

Worksheet Techniques

The worksheet shown in Exhibit 3–5 was prepared as follows:

1. Enter the unadjusted trial balance (Exhibit 3–4) on the worksheet using the first pair of amount columns.
2. Develop the adjusting entries and record them in the second pair of columns.
3. Extend the unadjusted balances, plus and minus the adjustments, to the adjusted trial balance columns and check for balance.
4. Extend the adjusted amounts to the right, line by line, to the pair of columns under the financial statement on which they should be reported: income statement, statement of retained earnings (optional), and balance sheet.
5. Check each pair of columns for equality of debits and credits.

Development of Adjusting Entries

Because of accrual basis accounting, numerous adjustments must be made to the account balances (as reflected in the unadjusted trial balance) at the end of each accounting period. These adjustments are necessary to restate (i.e., adjust) certain income statement and balance sheet accounts because (1) some accounts have a "mixed" balance which includes both real and nominal components, and (2) certain transactions have not yet been entered in the accounts. These adjustments may be classified as follows:

Prepaid (Deferred) Items:

1. Prepaid expense—an expense paid but not yet incurred (i.e., not yet recognized).
2. Prepaid revenue—a revenue collected but not yet earned (i.e., not yet realized); frequently called unearned rent revenue.

Accrued Items:

3. Accrued expense—an expense incurred but not yet paid.
4. Accrued revenue—a revenue earned but not yet collected.

Other Items:

5. Estimated items.

Prepaid Expenses. A prepaid expense occurs when a company has paid for services or supplies that are not used, or consumed, by the end of the accounting period. To illustrate, Canby Retailers, Inc., on January 1,

[3] Preparation of a worksheet for the statement of changes in financial position is discussed and illustrated in Chapter 21. It is more complex than one for the income statement and balance sheet. If you are not interested in the worksheet technique, study only the material captioned "Developing Adjusting Entries," and then move directly to the caption "Prepare Financial Statements."

EXHIBIT 3–5

CANBY RETAILERS, INC.
Worksheet for the Year Ended December 31, 1976

Accounts	Unadjusted Trial Balance		Adjusting Entries		Adjusted Trial Balance		Income Statement		Retained Earnings		Balance Sheet	
	Debit	Credit	Debit	Credit	Debit	Credit	Debit	Credit	Debit	Credit	Debit	Credit
Cash	55,300				55,300						55,300	
Marketable securities (bonds)	20,000				20,000						20,000	
Accounts receivable	45,000				45,000						45,000	
Allowance for doubtful accounts		1,000		(e) 1,200		2,200						2,200
Inventory (periodic system)	75,000				75,000		75,000	90,000*			90,000	
Prepaid insurance	600			(a) 200	400						400	
Accrued investment revenue receivable			(d) 100		100						100	
Land	8,000				8,000						8,000	
Building	160,000				160,000						160,000	
Accumulated depreciation, building		90,000		(e) 10,000		100,000						100,000
Equipment	91,000				91,000						91,000	
Accumulated depreciation, equipment		27,000		(e) 9,000		36,000						36,000
Accounts payable		29,000				29,000						29,000
Income taxes payable				(g) 20,000		20,000						20,000

Accumulated bond interest payable				(c) 500		500						500
Prepaid rent revenue				(b) 600		600						600
Bonds payable, 6%		50,000				50,000						50,000
Common stock, par $10		150,000				150,000						150,000
Contributed capital in excess of par		20,000				20,000						20,000
Retained earnings		31,500				31,500				31,500		
Sales revenue		325,200				325,200		325,200				
Investment revenue		500		(d) 100		600		600				
Rent revenue		1,800	(b) 600			1,200		1,200				
Purchases	130,000				130,000		130,000					
Freight on purchases	4,000				4,000		4,000					
Purchase returns		2,000				2,000		2,000				
Selling expenses	104,000		(e) 8,200 (f) 1,200		113,400		113,400					
General and administrative expenses	23,600		(a) 200 (e) 10,800		34,600		34,600					
Interest expense	2,500		(c) 500		3,000		3,000					
Extraordinary loss	9,000				9,000		9,000					
Income tax expense			(g) 20,000		20,000		20,000					
Net Income							30,000			30,000		
Retained Earnings									61,500			61,500
Totals	728,000	728,000	41,600	41,600	768,800	768,800	419,000	419,000	61,500	61,500	469,800	469,800

* This is only one of several techniques for entering the ending inventory on a worksheet.

1976, paid a three-year insurance premium in advance amounting to $600. At that date, the $600 payment was recorded as a debit to Prepaid Insurance and a credit to Cash. On the unadjusted trial balance of the worksheet, the $600 is reflected as the debit balance of an asset account, Prepaid Insurance. Since $200 of this service was "used" in 1976, there remains a $400 prepaid expense. Therefore, on December 31, 1976, an adjusting entry must be made as follows (the letter code to the left is used on the worksheet, Exhibit 3–5, for reference in study):

a. December 31, 1976:

Insurance expense (general and administrative expense)	200	
Prepaid insurance		200

The effects of this entry, which may be easily observed on the worksheet, are (1) to adjust the asset account to $400 on the balance sheet, and (2) to record the $200 expense component on the income statement.[4]

Prepaid Revenues. A prepaid revenue occurs when a company collects a revenue in advance and at the end of the accounting period some of it is not yet earned. Therefore, one account has a balance that must be separated into its income statement (nominal) and balance sheet (real) components by means of an adjusting entry. To illustrate, Canby Retailers, Inc., on January 1, 1976, leased to J. R. Jones a small office in their building that was not needed. At the start they collected, in advance, $1,800 cash for 18 months rent. At that time, the collection was recorded as a debit to Cash and a credit to Rent Revenue. On December 31, 1976, the $1,800 balance in the Rent Revenue account included $600 prepaid rent revenue. Therefore, the following adjusting entry was made (see Exhibit 3–5):

b. December 31, 1976:

Rent revenue...	600	
Prepaid rent revenue		600

This entry leaves $1,200 in the Rent Revenue account and separates as a liability, the $600 prepaid rent revenue. The $600 is a liability on December 31, 1976, because Canby owes that amount of "occupancy" to Jones. In 1977 the $600 will be transferred to the Rent Revenue account.

Accrued Expenses. An accrued expense is an unpaid expense that has not been recorded in the accounts at the end of the accounting period. Therefore, at the end of the accounting period, an adjusting entry must be made to recognize it. To illustrate, Canby Retailers, Inc., has a liability for bonds payable of $50,000. These bonds require payment of 6% annual interest each October 30. Therefore, on December 31, 1976, there was accrued interest of $50,000 × .06 × 2/12 = $500.

---

[4] Sometimes a prepaid expense is initially debited to an expense account instead of an asset account. In this case, an adjusting entry also is required. To illustrate, assume the $600 was initially debited to *Insurance Expense;* the adjusting entry would be: debit, Prepaid Insurance, $400; credit, Insurance Expense, $400. In either case the net effect on the statements is the same.

This accrued interest must be recognized by the following adjusting entry (see Exhibit 3–5):

c. December 31, 1976:

Interest expense	500	
Accrued bond interest expense payable		500

This adjusting entry records (1) the expense for income statement purposes, and (2) the liability for balance sheet purposes.

Accrued Revenues. An accrued revenue is one that, although not yet recorded in the accounts, has been earned but not collected at the end of the accounting period. Therefore, an adjusting entry must be made to recognize it. To illustrate, Canby Retailers, Inc., owns marketable securities (bonds) that cost $20,000 (at par value). These bonds earn 6% annual interest which is received each November 30. Since there is accrued investment revenue earned for the month of December, an adjusting entry must be made as follows (see Exhibit 3–5):

d. December 31, 1976:

Accrued investment revenue receivable	100	
Investment revenue ($20,000 × .06 × 1/12)		100

This entry records (1) an asset, accrued investment revenue receivable, for balance sheet purposes; and (2) a revenue, for income statement purposes.

Adjusting Entries for Estimated Items

Some adjusting entries must be based on *estimated amounts* because they depend upon future conditions and events. This means that some revenues and expenses for the current period will be determined by estimates. For example, depreciation expense, bad debt expense, and warranty (guarantee) expense must be based on estimates of future useful life, future collectibility, and future expenditures respectively.

Depreciation Expense. When certain assets, such as a machine, are acquired for use in operating a business (i.e., not for sale), they are "used up" over time through wear and obsolescence. The amount of this *use cost* is measured each accounting period and recorded as depreciation expense. Depreciation expense is always an estimate because the amount depends upon a known amount, the cost of the asset, and two estimates, useful life and residual (or scrap) value. To illustrate, Canby Retailers, Inc., has two assets on which depreciation is computed, viz:

$$\text{Building: } \frac{\text{Cost, \$160,000} - \text{Residual Value, \$10,000}}{\text{Estimated Useful Life, 15 Years}} = \$10,000$$

$$\text{Equipment: } \frac{\text{Cost, \$91,000} - \text{Residual Value, \$1,000}}{\text{Estimated Useful Life, Ten Years}} = 9,000$$

Total Depreciation Expense for the Year $19,000

Based on these computations, an adjusting entry is necessary as follows (see Exhibit 3–5):

e. December 31, 1976:

Depreciation expense (selling)	8,000	
Depreciation expense (general and administrative)	11,000	
Accumulated depreciation, building		10,000
Accumulated depreciation, equipment		9,000

Depreciation expense was debited to two accounts because the company follows the policy of *allocating* it to the two categories of expense based upon the relative floor space used and the relative cost of the equipment used in operations and administration.

Bad Debt Expense. Credit sales and services almost always cause some losses due to uncollectible accounts receivable (i.e., bad debts). The fact that an account is uncollectible may be determined several periods subsequent to the period in which the credit was extended and the sale or service recognized as revenue in accordance with the revenue principle (see Chapter 2). The matching principle (see Chapter 2) requires that all *expenses* associated with sales and service revenue be recognized in the period in which the revenue was recorded. Since the actual amount of the revenue is recorded as earned for the period and the bad debt loss may not be known for several periods in the future, an estimation of bad debt expense must be recorded by means of an adjusting entry. To illustrate, Canby Retailers, Inc., extended credit on sales during 1976 amounting to $120,000. Experience by the company indicates an expected average bad debt loss rate of 1% of credit sales. Therefore, the following adjusting entry was needed (see Exhibit 3–5):

f. December 31, 1976:

Bad debt expense (selling)	1,200	
Allowance for doubtful accounts		1,200

The credit is made to an "allowance" account rather than directly to accounts receivable, because the identity of specific customers involved is not presently known. The allowance account is reported on the balance sheet as a deduction from accounts receivable (i.e., it is a contra asset account). When an account is subsequently determined to be bad, it is written off as a debit to the allowance account and a credit to Accounts Receivable; this will have no effect on expenses or on the book value of accounts receivable.

Completion of the Worksheet

After the adjusting entries are entered on the worksheet (in the second pair of columns), it is completed by extending each account balance (i.e., the trial balance amount plus or minus any adjustments) to the next columns as illustrated in Exhibit 3–5. Two pairs of the columns shown on this exhibit are not essential: (1) the Adjusted Trial Balance columns, which are used to insure accuracy (i.e., a debits = credits check *after* the adjusting entries); and (2) the Retained Earnings column, which can be merged with the balance sheet. Observe in the extending that debits are always extended as debits and credits as credits.

There are three additional aspects of the worksheet that warrant some explanation:

1. Note that the *beginning* inventory amount, $75,000, is extended to the income statement as a debit and that the *ending* inventory is entered as a credit to the income statement and as a debit to the balance sheet.[5] This procedure results from the company's *periodic inventory system* (see Chapter 8). When a company uses the periodic inventory system, a Purchases account is used and the inventory account is unchanged during the period; it reflects the *beginning inventory* amount. Therefore, at the end of the accounting period, this balance must be closed out and the *ending* inventory amount, determined by physical count and valued at cost, must be recorded. In contrast, when a *perpetual inventory system* is used, purchases and issues are recorded directly in the inventory account on a continuing basis. Therefore, the inventory amount in the trial balance will reflect the ending inventory amount and no closing (or adjusting) entries will be needed for it on the worksheet. The inventory balance is extended directly to the Balance Sheet debit column. When the perpetual inventory system is used, there will be no purchases account; however, there will be a Cost of Goods Sold account on the worksheet. The Cost of Goods Sold account is extended directly to the Income Statement debit column as an expense.
2. When all of the amounts have been extended, the difference between the debits and credits under income statement will represent *pretax income*. This amount must be determined to compute income tax expense, for which an adjusting entry must be made. To illustrate, for Canby Retailers, Inc., the computation would be as follows, assuming an average 40% income tax rate:

Income Statement column totals (pretax):	
Credit total	$419,000
Debit total (before income taxes)	369,000
Pretax income	50,000
Income tax expense ($50,000 × .40)	20,000
Net Income	$ 30,000

The adjusting entry would be:

g. December 31, 1976:

Income tax expense	20,000	
Income taxes payable		20,000

3. After the above adjusting entry is made, the extensions can be com-

---

[5] This approach views the two entries for the beginning and ending inventories as *closing* entries (see page 66). Another approach is to view them as *adjusting* entries. The technique used on the worksheet for inventories represents only one way; several other ways are widely used. The final result is precisely the same.

pleted. The amount of net income, $30,000, is entered on the worksheet as a debit to Income Statement and a credit to Retained Earnings. The ending balance of Retained Earnings is then extended to the balance sheet and the last two pairs of columns summed; in the absence of errors each pair of columns on the worksheet will balance. The worksheet can be used as a guide for the remaining phases in the cycle.

A worksheet for a manufacturing company, with explanatory comments, is shown in Appendix B to this chapter.

PREPARE FINANCIAL STATEMENTS (PHASE 7)

The income statement, statement of retained earnings, and balance sheet can be prepared directly from the completed worksheet. An income statement and balance sheet, taken directly from the worksheet (Exhibit 3–5), are presented in Exhibits 3–6 and 3–7, respectively. Financial statements are discussed in Chapters 4 and 5.

EXHIBIT 3–6

CANBY RETAILERS, INC.
Income Statement*
For the Year Ended December 31, 1976

Revenues:		
Sales		$325,200
Investments		600
Rent		1,200
Total Revenue		327,000
Expenses:		
Cost of goods sold†	$117,000	
Selling	113,400	
General and administrative	34,600	
Interest	3,000	
Total Expenses (excluding income taxes)		268,000
Pretax operating income		59,000
Income taxes ($59,000 × .40)		23,600
Income before extraordinary items		35,400
Extraordinary loss	9,000	
Less tax saving ($9,000 × .40)	3,600	5,400
Net Income		$ 30,000

Earnings per share:	
Income before extraordinary items ($35,400 ÷ 15,000 shares)	$2.36
Extraordinary loss ($5,400 ÷ 15,000 shares)	(.36)
Net Income ($30,000 ÷ 15,000 shares)	2.00

* This is a single-step income statement; various formats are discussed in Chapter 4.

† Computation of cost of goods sold:

Beginning inventory	$ 75,000
Purchases	130,000
Freight-in	4,000
Purchase returns	(2,000)
Total Goods Available for Sale	207,000
Less ending inventory	90,000
Cost of Goods Sold	$117,000

EXHIBIT 3–7

CANBY RETAILERS, INC.
Balance Sheet*
At December 31, 1976

Assets

Current Assets:		
Cash		$ 55,300
Marketable securities		20,000
Accounts receivable	$ 45,000	
Allowance for doubtful accounts	2,200	42,800
Inventory		90,000
Prepaid insurance		400
Investment revenue receivable		100
Total Current Assets		208,600
Operational Assets:		
Land		8,000
Building	160,000	
Accumulated depreciation, building	100,000	60,000
Equipment	91,000	
Accumulated depreciation, equipment	36,000	55,000
Total Operational Assets		123,000
Total Assets		$331,600

Liabilities

Current Liabilities:		
Accounts payable		$ 29,000
Income taxes payable		20,000
Bond interest payable		500
Prepaid rent revenue		600
Total Current Liabilities		50,100
Long-Term Liabilities:		
Bonds payable, 6%		50,000
Total Liabilities		100,100
Stockholders' Equity		
Contributed Capital:		
Common stock, par $10, 15,000 shares outstanding	$150,000	
Contributed capital in excess of par	20,000	
Retained earnings	61,500	
Total Stockholders' Equity		231,500
Total Liabilities and Stockholders' Equity		$331,600

* Balance sheets and appropriate supplementary information are discussed in Chapter 5.

If a worksheet is not used, adjusting entries should be entered in the journal, posted to the ledger, and then an *adjusted trial balance,* taken from the ledger, will provide information for these statements.

The statement of changes in financial position requires a separate analysis, usually on a specially designed worksheet similar to those illustrated in Chapter 21.

JOURNALIZING AND POSTING ADJUSTING ENTRIES (PHASE 8)

The adjusting entries should be entered in the general journal and posted to the general ledger, dated the last day of the accounting period. The adjusting entries *update* the ledger accounts by separating the "mixed" accounts into their real (i.e., balance sheet) and nominal (i.e., income statement) components. The adjusted nominal accounts are then ready to close.

If a worksheet, such as Exhibit 3–5, is developed, the adjusting entries can be taken directly from it. They are identical to those illustrated earlier. Recall that after the adjusting entries are posted to the general ledger, each account will then reflect the account balances shown in Exhibit 3–5, under the caption *Adjusted Trial Balance.*

CLOSING ENTRIES (PHASE 9)

Recall that the balance sheet accounts are called *real* or *permanent accounts* in the sense that they are not closed out to a zero balance at the end of the accounting period. In contrast, the income statement accounts are called *nominal* or *temporary accounts* because at the end of each accounting period they are closed out to a zero balance. The income statement accounts are the *revenue* and *expense* accounts and are *subaccounts* to owners' equity. Revenues increase owners' equity, and expenses decrease owners' equity. These subaccounts are used each period to *classify* and *accumulate* revenue and expense information. At the end of the period, when they have served this information *classification* and *accumulation* purpose, each account is closed to Income Summary and in turn the net effect of their balances (i.e., net income or net loss) is transferred from Income Summary to Retained Earnings. The transferring process is called closing entries. The purpose is to close the nominal accounts to a zero balance so they will be ready for reuse the next period. A closing entry simply transfers a credit balance to another account as a credit, or it transfers a debit balance to another account. Generally, two *clearing,* or *suspense, accounts* called Cost of Goods Sold and Income Summary are used for convenience, although they are not essential. The nominal accounts are reopened the next period to record the revenues and expenses for that period.

The closing entries can be taken directly from the *adjusted trial balance;* or if a worksheet such as the one in Exhibit 3–5 is used, they can be taken directly from the Income Statement columns. To illustrate, the closing entries for Canby Retailers, Inc., would be as follows:[6]

December 31, 1976:

1. To close the revenue accounts to Income Summary:

Sales revenue	325,200	
Investment revenue	600	
Rent revenue	1,200	
Income summary		327,000

2. To close the purchases and beginning inventory accounts, to record the ending inventory, and to record cost of goods sold:[7]

Ending inventory (December 31, 1976)	90,000	
Purchase returns	2,000	
Cost of goods sold	117,000	
Purchases		130,000
Freight on purchases		4,000
Beginning inventory (January 1, 1976)		75,000

3. To close the expense accounts, including cost of goods sold, to Income Summary:

Income summary	297,000	
Cost of goods sold		117,000
Selling expenses		113,400
General and administrative expenses		34,600
Interest expense		3,000
Extraordinary loss		9,000
Income tax expense		20,000

4. To close Income Summary account to Retained Earnings:

Income summary	30,000	
Retained earnings		30,000

For review purposes, the closing process is diagrammed in T-account form in Exhibit 3–8. Observe that after the closing process, each income

[6] The closing entries can be grouped in various ways, one of which is illustrated here. Alternatively, a separate closing entry can be made for each nominal account. Obviously, the net effect of the closing process would be the same.

[7] The Cost of Goods Sold account often is not used with a periodic inventory system. In this case, these accounts are closed directly to Income Summary. Also recall that when the periodic inventory system is used, the inventory accounts may be handled in the adjusting entries, in which case they would not be included in the closing entries; in either approach, the *beginning* inventory balance must be closed out and the *ending* inventory balance recorded. The net effect is the same.

To illustrate using the same data:

Adjusting entries (inventory):

Cost of goods sold	75,000	
Inventory (beginning)		75,000
Inventory (ending)	90,000	
Cost of goods sold		90,000

Closing entry for purchase accounts:

Purchase returns	2,000	
Cost of goods sold	132,000	
Purchases		130,000
Freight on purchases		4,000

EXHIBIT 3–8
Closing Process Diagramed

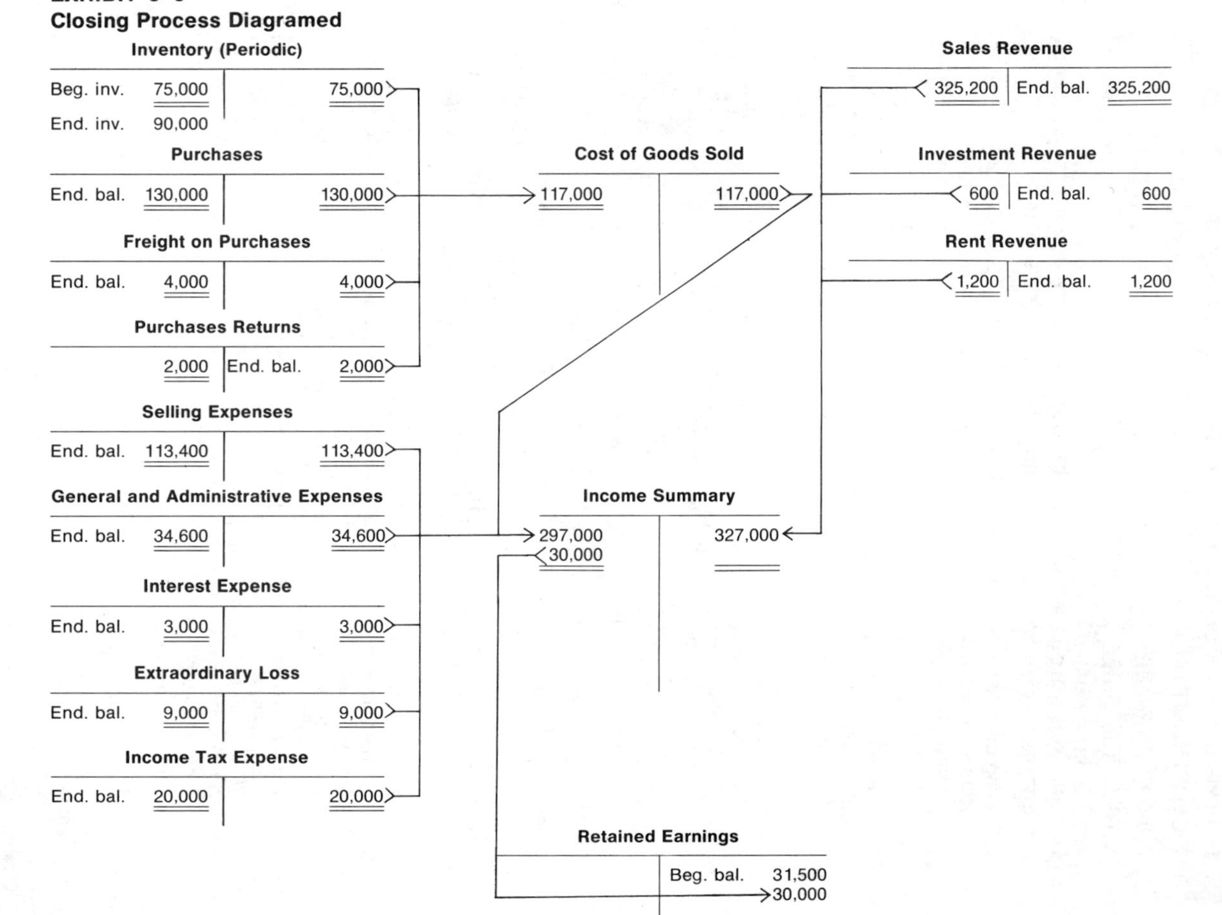
Inventory (Periodic)
Beg. inv. 75,000 | 75,000
End. inv. 90,000
Purchases
End. bal. 130,000 | 130,000
Freight on Purchases
End. bal. 4,000 | 4,000
Purchases Returns
2,000 | End. bal. 2,000
Selling Expenses
End. bal. 113,400 | 113,400
General and Administrative Expenses
End. bal. 34,600 | 34,600
Interest Expense
End. bal. 3,000 | 3,000
Extraordinary Loss
End. bal. 9,000 | 9,000
Income Tax Expense
End. bal. 20,000 | 20,000
Cost of Goods Sold
117,000 | 117,000
Income Summary
297,000 | 327,000
30,000
Retained Earnings
| Beg. bal. 31,500
| 30,000
Sales Revenue
325,200 | End. bal. 325,200
Investment Revenue
600 | End. bal. 600
Rent Revenue
1,200 | End. bal. 1,200

statement (i.e., nominal) account reflects a zero balance; therefore, they are ready to be used again during the next accounting period.

POST-CLOSING TRIAL BALANCE (PHASE 10)

In a preceding paragraph, we defined a trial balance as a listing of the accounts in the general ledger along with their balances. The purposes of a trial balance usually are *(a)* to verify the equality of the debits and credits, and *(b)* to have the account balances handy for other uses. We have discussed two different trial balances up to this point: the *unadjusted* trial balance, taken immediately after the current entries are completed for the accounting period, but before the adjusting entries, and the *adjusted* trial balance which reflects the account balances after the adjusting entries. A third trial balance generally is taken after the closing entries have been posted. It is called the *post-closing trial balance* and is used to verify that the debits and credits are equal at the start of the next accounting period. It is usually done on an adding machine (or by computer) rather than by preparing a formal listing.

REVERSING ENTRIES (PHASE 11)

After the adjusting and closing entries are journalized and posted to the general ledger, the accounts are ready for information inputs of the next period. Prior to starting the new information inputs, many companies make *reversing entries.* A reversing entry is dated the first day of the next period and simply reverses or "backs out" an adjusting entry that was made at the end of the period just ended. Reversing entries serve only one purpose; that is, to facilitate (i.e., simplify) a subsequent entry. Reversing entries are always optional; the same end results are attained whether or not they are used. If used, only a few of the adjusting entries usually are reversed.

The purpose and application of reversing entries are illustrated in Exhibit 3–9. In the exhibit, a series of entries related to accrued wages are analyzed under two options: (1) with a reversing entry, and (2) without a reversing entry. The exhibit demonstrates the *facilitating* feature of reversing entries. It also suggests the kinds of adjusting entries that are candidates for reversal. Although it is impossible to provide rigid rules for selecting adjusting entries to be reversed, some guidelines can be given.

1. Adjusting entries usually reversed—As a general rule, *only adjusting entries for accrued expenses and accrued revenues* should be reversed. Examples of accrued expenses are unpaid wages, interest, utilities, and other regularly recurring expenses that require subsequent cash disbursements. Examples of accrued revenues are uncollected interest, rent, and other recurring revenues that result in subsequent cash collections.
2. Adjusting entries not reversed—As a general rule, adjusting entries

EXHIBIT 3–9
Reversing Entries Illustrated

BOX CORPORATION
Annual Accounting Period Ends, December 31, 1976

With Reversing Entry			*Without Reversing Entry*		
a. Adjusting entry—The last payroll was paid on December 28, 1976; the next payroll will be on January 5, 1977. Therefore, at December 31, 1976, accrued (unpaid) wages for three days amounted to $15,000. The following adjusting entry is required:					
December 31, 1976:			December 31, 1976:		
Wage expense	15,000		Wage expense	15,000	
Accrued wages payable		15,000	Accrued wages payable		15,000
b. Closing entry—The revenue and expense accounts are closed to Income Summary.					
December 31, 1976:			December 31, 1976:		
Income summary*	215,000		Income summary*	215,000	
Wage expense		215,000	Wage expense		215,000
c. At this point the adjusting and closing entries have been journalized and posted to the ledger. The information processing cycle for 1976 has been completed. At this point in time, January 1, 1977, the accountant must decide what adjusting entries are to be *reversed* (if any). *Question:* Would a reversing entry for accrued wages on January 1, 1977, simplify, or facilitate, making the next payroll entry on January 5, 1977?					
Decision-reversing entry, January 1, 1977:			*Decision—no reversing entry to be made.*		
Accured wages payable	15,000				
Wage expense		15,000			
(Note this reverses the adjusting entry made above on December 31, 1976.)					
Effect: Accrued Wages Payable account now reflects a zero balance; Wage Expense reflects a *credit* balance of $15,000.			Effect: Accrued Wages Payable account continues to reflect a credit balance; Wage Expense reflects a zero balance.		
d. Subsequent payroll entry—Payment of $36,000 payroll on January 5, 1977. This amount includes the $15,000 liability (accrued wages) carried over from December 1976.					
January 5, 1977, payroll entry (disregarding payroll taxes):					
Wage expense	36,000		Accrued wages payable	15,000	
Cash		36,000	Wage expense	21,000	
			Cash		36,000
Did the reversing entry simplify this subsequent entry? The answer is yes; the last entry, on the left, required only one debit. However, after the last entry, under both methods, the Wage Expense account reflects a debit balance of $21,000 and Accrued Wages Payable reflects a zero balance. Without the reversing entry, the amount of unpaid wages must be identified which is troublesome when a number of such situations exist. Also when the payroll processing is computerized, a special routine must be written for the first payment entry which is different from the remaining 51 payroll entries during the year when no reversing entry is made.					

* Includes $200,000 paid during the period.

for deferred expenses and deferred revenues are not reversed. Examples of deferred (i.e., prepaid) expenses are insurance premiums and unused supplies. Examples of deferred revenues are interest collected in advance, rent collected in advance, and subscriptions collected in advance.

3. Estimated adjusting entries not reversed—Adjusting entries based on estimates, where there is no subsequent cash inflow or outflow, are not reversed. Examples are depreciation and bad debt expense.

Alternatively, a guideline may be expressed as follows: adjusting entries should be reversed when they create or add to balances in *real* accounts. They should not be reversed when they create or add to balances in *nominal* accounts. There is an exception to the first sentence:

if the real account balance augmented is a valuation contra account (e.g., accumulated depreciation or allowance for doubtful accounts), then the adjusting entry ought not be reversed because to do so would undo the effects of having made it.

Although these guidelines may be helpful in deciding whether the reversal of a particular adjusting entry would be useful, one must consider *(a)* the original entry, *(b)* the adjusting entry, and *(c)* most important, the subsequent entry. The above rules cannot substitute for judgment.

INFORMATION PROCESSING PROCEDURES

Information processing involves the ways and order of accomplishing the tasks necessary to collect raw economic data, record their economic

EXHIBIT 3–10
Summary of the Accounting Information Processing Cycle

Phase (order)	*Identification*	*Objective*	*Text Page*
1	Collection of raw economic data.	To gather inputs to the accounting system. The inputs are supported by source documents as a basis for *(a)* transaction analysis, and *(b)* subsequent verifiability.	50
2	Transaction analysis.	To identify, assess, and measure the economic impact on the enterprise of each transaction recognized. To provide the basis for developing the accounting entry to be made in the journal.	52
3	Journalizing.	To provide a chronological record (i.e., by date) of the entries in the accounting system which reflect the increases and decreases in each account.	52
4	Posting.	To transfer the economic effects from the journal to the ledger; to reclassify and accumulate the economic effects for each asset, liability, owners' equity, revenue, and expense.	54
5	Prepare unadjusted trial balance.	To provide, in a convenient form, a listing of the accounts and their balances in the general ledger after all current entries have been posted. It serves to *(a)* check the debit-credit equality, and *(b)* provide data for use in developing the worksheet and the adjusting entries.	55
6*	Prepare worksheets.	To provide an organized and systematic approach at the end of the accounting period for developing *(a)* the adjusting entries, *(b)* the financial statements, and *(c)* the closing entries. One worksheet suffices for the income statement and balance sheet. Another worksheet is needed to develop the statement of changes in financial position.	55
7	Prepare financial statements.	To provide a vehicle for communicating summarized financial information to external decision-makers.	64
8	Journalize and post adjusting entries.	To update the general ledger by separating the "mixed" accounts into their real (i.e., balance sheet) and nominal (i.e., income statement) components so they will be ready for the closing process.	66
9	Journalize and post closing entries.	To close the nominal accounts to retained earnings so they will be ready for reuse during the next period for accumulating and classifying revenues and expenses.	66
10*	Prepare post-closing trial balance.	To verify the debit-credit accuracy of the general ledger after the closing entries are posted.	69
11*	Reversing entries.	To facilitate subsequent entries by reversing certain adjusting entries. They are journalized and posted on the first day of the new period.	69

* Optional.

effects on the entity, classify the information, and, finally, prepare the financial statements and supporting information. In most companies, a large amount of information must be processed daily. This work can be both time consuming and costly. Therefore, a well-designed information processing system is needed to provide a smooth, uninterrupted, and efficient flow of information from point of incurrence to the end result, the financial statements. Information processing may be done (1) manually, where the work is performed by hand; (2) mechanically, where the information is processed by the use of sorting equipment, tabulating machines, and so on; and (3) electronically, where electronic computers are used. Typically, an accounting system will use each of these approaches in varying degrees depending upon its complexity.

Consideration of these information approaches is not within the objectives of this book. For instructional purposes, the manual approach is used.

SUMMARY OF THE INFORMATION PROCESSING CYCLE

An understanding of the information processing cycle will assist you in comprehending the chapters to follow. Each chapter considers various accounting problems, each of which is related to one or more steps in the cycle. It is especially helpful if you clearly understand how those problems relate to the broad area of information collection, transaction analysis, recording, classifying, and reporting. The sequence of the cycle is both logical and efficient. Exhibit 3–10 lists the major sequential phases of the cycle, summarizes the objective of each, and provides a cross-reference to the chapter.

Appendix A. Control Accounts, Subsidiary Ledgers, and Special Journals

An accounting system usually includes application of the information processing techniques known as special journals, subsidiary ledgers, and control accounts. This Appendix discusses and illustrates these elements of the system.

CONTROL ACCOUNTS AND SUBSIDIARY LEDGERS

The general ledger is the main ledger; it includes an account for each asset, liability, owners' equity, revenue, and expense. To facilitate recordkeeping for accounts that involve a large amount of detail, selected general ledger accounts are designated as *control accounts* to which only summary information is posted. The details related to each control account are maintained in a separate subsidiary ledger (one for each control account). Thus, each control account is supplemented by its specially designated subsidiary ledger. To illustrate, accounts receivable, because of the large number of credit customers, usually is designated as *accounts receivable control* in the general ledger and is supported by a separate *accounts receivable subsidiary ledger* which is composed of individual customer accounts. This arrangement will be illustrated below.

JOURNALS

Both general and special journals are used in most accounting systems. Even when extensive use is made of special journals, there will be a need for a general journal in which to record those transactions that should not be recorded in the special journals. Exhibit 3–11 illustrates such an entry. These include nonrepetitive current transactions and the adjusting and closing journal entries. Occasionally there will be a complex entry with characteristics that would, in part, qualify for entry in a special journal, and in part in the general journal. Such entries may be entered only in the general journal or, alternatively, "split" between the general journal and a special journal.

Special Journals

A special journal serves the same purpose as a general journal except that it is designed to handle *only* one type of transaction because of the large volume of transactions of a particular type. Each special journal, therefore, is designed specifically to simplify the data processing tasks involved in journalizing and posting a particular type of transaction. The format of each special journal and the number used depend upon the types of frequent transactions recorded by the entity. Commonly used special journals are:

EXHIBIT 3–11

General Journal
Page J-14

Date 1976	Accounts and Explanation	Ledger Folio	Amounts Debit	Amounts Credit
Jan. 2	Equipment—trucks	140	9,000	
	Notes payable	214		9,000
	Purchased truck for use in			
	the business. Gave $9,000,			
	60-day, 10% interest-bearing			
	note.			

1. Credit sales journal – designed for credit sales entries only.
2. Credit purchases journal – designed for credit purchases only.
3. Cash receipts journal – designed for all cash receipts.
4. Cash payments journal – designed for all cash payments.
5. Voucher system journals (replaces No. 4 when the voucher system is used) –
   a. Voucher register – designed to record payment vouchers only.
   b. Check register – designed to record all checks written in payment of vouchers.

Special Journal for Credit Sales. This journal is designed to accommodate entries for credit sales only. Therefore, it would handle only the following type of entry (cash sales would not be entered in this journal)[8]:

January 1, 1976:

	If Recorded at Net		*If Recorded at Gross*	
Accounts receivable	980		1,000	
Sales revenue		980		1,000
Credit sale to Adams Company; invoice price, $1,000; terms, 2/10, n/30.				

Credit sales may be recorded at net of discount or gross of discount as illustrated above. Theoretically, net of discount is preferable; however for practical reasons they often are recorded at gross of discount. To illustrate, in each approach the subsequent collection entry would be as follows:

Case A – Collection within the discount period:

	If Recorded at Net		*If Recorded at Gross*	
Cash	980		980	
Sales discount			20	
Accounts receivable		980		1,000

Case B – Collection after the discount period:

Cash	1,000		1,000	
Accounts receivable		980		1,000
Interest revenue		20		

The theoretical basis for recording net of discount is *(a)* because of the high implicit interest rate (2% in 10 days), most customers pay within the discount period; *(b)* the net amount represents the cash equivalent sales price of the goods, hence the receivable should be measured at the net amount; *(c)* if a customer is extended credit and fails to pay within the discount period there is a charge (2% in this case) for use of the vendor's money, hence the vendor has earned interest revenue;

[8] Terms, 2/10, n/30, mean that if the account is paid within ten days after date of sale, a 2% discount is permitted to encourage early payment. If not paid within the 10-day discount period, the full amount is due at the end of 30 days.

EXHIBIT 3–12

Special Journal — Credit Sales Page S-23

Date 1976	Sales Invoice No.	Accounts Receivable (name)	Terms	Ledger Folio	Receivable and Sale Amount	Dept. Sales	
						Dept. A	Dept. B
Jan. 2	93	Adams Co.	2/10, n/30	112.13	980		
3	94	Sayre Corp.	2/10, n/30	112.80	490		
11	95	Cope & Day Co.	net	112.27	5,734	(Not illustrated — the two totals below would be posted to a sales subsidiary ledger.)	
27	96	XY Mfg. Co.	2/10, n/30	112.91	1,960		
30	97	Miller, J. B.	2/10, n/30	112.42	196		
31	–	Totals	–	–	9,360		
31	–	Posting	–	–	(112/500)		

and (*d*) the $20 is revenue not a deduction from sales. The practical basis for recording gross is (*a*) precedent, (*b*) the amount of discount is not material in relation to total sales, (*c*) many customers do not pay within the discount period, and (*d*) sales discount is a reduction in sales price. However, on this latter point it often happens that the sale is in one period and the collection in a later period; this tends to mismatch the discount with the sale that caused it. On the other hand, the net method tends to record the interest revenue in the period earned. Either method is generally acceptable, primarily because the difference is not material (also see Chapter 8).

Exhibit 3–12 shows a typical special journal for credit sales for a business that has two sales departments. The general ledger contains an Accounts Receivable Control account. Observe that this special journal provides a convenient format to record all of the relevant data on each credit sale. Also, it can be designed to differentiate sales by department. Clearly, it is easier to enter a credit sale in this format than in the general journal. Sales can be entered at either net or gross of discount in the sales journal.

The mechanics of posting amounts from the special sales journal to the general and subsidiary ledgers also are simplified. There are two phases of posting a special journal, viz:

1. *Daily posting*—Daily the amount for each customer is posted to the individual account in the accounts receivable *subsidiary ledger*. Daily posting is essential so that each customer's account will be up-to-date when the customer pays. Posting is indicated by entering the account number in the folio column. For example, the number 112.13 entered in the folio column in Exhibit 3–12 is the account number assigned to Adams Company and signifies that $980 was posted as a debit to that account.
2. *Monthly posting*—At the end of each month, the amount column is summed. This total is posted to two accounts in the general ledger; that is, Account No. 112 denotes that $9,360 was posted (1) as a debit to Account No. 112 (Accounts Receivable Control), and (2) as a credit

EXHIBIT 3–13

Purchases Journal — Page S-19

Date 1976	Purchase Order No.	Account Payable (name)	Terms	Ledger Folio	Amount
Jan. 3	41	P. T. Mfg. Co.	1/20, n/30	210.61	990
7	42	Able Suppliers, Inc.	net	210.12	150
31	–	Totals	–	–	2,760
31	–	Posting	–	–	(612/210)

to Account No. 500 (Sales Revenue). The T-accounts shown in Exhibit 3–16 illustrate how these postings are reflected in the general ledger and the subsidiary ledger. Observe that the two ledgers show the *journal page* from which each amount was posted.

Special Journal for Credit Purchases. In situations where there are a large number of credit purchases, data processing may be facilitated by using a special journal designed only for this type of transaction, viz:

January 4, 1976:

Purchases	990	
Accounts payable (PT Mfg. Co.)		990
Purchased merchandise for resale; invoice price, $1,000; terms, 1/20, n/60.		

This transaction, rather than being entered in the general journal, would be entered in the purchases journal as in Exhibit 3–13. In this illustration the purchases are recorded at net of discount which is the theoretically correct approach. For practical reasons purchases also are recorded at gross of discount. Basically, the same practical and theoretical considerations apply that were discussed above for sales discount (see Chapter 8 for further discussion of this issue). During the month, each amount would be credited to the individual creditors' accounts in the *accounts payable subsidiary ledger*.

At the end of the month, the total of the amount column (i.e., $2,760) would be posted to the general ledger as *(a)* a debit to the Purchases account (No. 612), and *(b)* a credit to the Accounts Payable *Control* account (No. 210).

Special Journal for Cash Receipts. Since a large volume of transactions for cash receipts is typical, a special cash receipts journal is often used. This special journal is designed to accommodate *all* cash receipts. Therefore, it must have a column for *cash debit* and several credit columns, including a credit column for *sundry accounts*. Credit columns are designated for recurring credits, and a Sundry column accommodates infrequent credits. A typical special cash receipts journal is shown in Exhibit 3–14.

During the month, each amount in the Accounts Receivable column is posted as a credit to the individual customer accounts in the *accounts receivable subsidiary ledger*. At the end of the month, *(a)* the individual amounts in the Sundry column are posted as credits to the appropriate general ledger accounts, and *(b)* the totals are posted to the general ledger as indicated by the folio numbers, viz: Cash, debit; Accounts Receivable, credit; and Sales, credit. The total of the sundry accounts is not posted since the individual amounts have already been posted.

Special Journal for Cash Payments. Because of the large volume of cash disbursements, most companies use a special journal designed to accommodate *all* cash payments. The special journal must have a column for *cash credits* and a number of debit columns including one for sundry accounts. Debit columns are set up for frequently recurring

EXHIBIT 3–14

Cash Receipts Journal — Page CR-19

Date 1976	Explanation	Debits: Cash	Credits: Account Title	Ledger Folio	Accounts Receivable	Sundry Accounts	Sales
Jan. 4	Cash sales	11,200		—			11,200
7	On acct.	4,490	Sayre Corp.	112.80	4,490		
8	Sale of land	10,000	Land	123		4,000	
			Gain on sale land	510		6,000	
10	On acct.	1,000	Adams Co.	112.13	1,000		
19	Cash sales	43,600		—			43,600
20	On acct.	5,734	Cope & Day Co.	112.27	5,734		
31	Totals	116,224		—	11,224	34,000	71,000
31	Posting	(101)		—	(112)	(NP)*	(500)

* NP—Not posted.

EXHIBIT 3–15

Cash Payments Journal — Page CP-31

Date 1976	Check No.	Explanation	Credits: Cash	Debits: Account Name	Ledger Folio	Accounts Payable	Sundry Accounts	Cash Purchases
Jan. 2	141	Pur. mdse.	3,000		—			3,000
10	142	On acct.	990	P.Q. Mfg. Co.	210.61	990		
15	143	Jan. rent	600	Rent exp.	612		600	
16	144	Pur. mdse.	1,810		—			1,810
31	–	Totals	98,400		—	5,820	1,600	34,700
31	–	Posting	(101)		—	(210)	(NP)	(612)

debits, and the Sundry column for infrequent debits. A typical special cash payments journal, with some common entries, is shown in Exhibit 3–15. Posting follows the same procedures explained above for the cash receipts special journal.

Reconciling a Subsidiary Ledger

The sum of all accounts in a subsidiary ledger must agree with the overall balance reflected in the control account in the general ledger. To

EXHIBIT 3–16
General Ledger and Subsidiary Ledger Illustrated

General Ledger (partial)

Cash — No. 101

Date	Item	Ref.	Debit	Date	Ref.	Credit
1976 Jan. 1	Balance		18,000	1976 Jan. 31	CP-31	98,400
31		CR-19	116,224			

Accounts Receivable Control — No. 112

Date	Item	Ref.	Debit	Date	Ref.	Credit
1976 Jan. 1	Balance		5,000	1976 Jan. 31	CR-19	11,224
31		S-23	9,360			

Equipment — No. 140

Date	Item	Ref.	Debit	Date	Ref.	Credit
1976 Jan. 2		J-14	9,000			

Notes Payable — No. 214

Date	Item	Ref.	Debit	Date	Ref.	Credit
				1976 Jan. 2	J-14	9,000

Sales Revenue

Date	Item	Ref.	Debit	Date	Ref.	Credit
				1976 Jan. 31	S-23	9,360
				31	CR-19	71,000

Subsidiary Ledger – Accounts Receivable (Acct. No. 112)

Adams Company — No. 112.13

Date	Item	Ref.	Debit	Date	Ref.	Credit
1976 Jan. 1	Balance		1,000	1976 Jan. 10	CR-19	1,000
11		S-23	980			

Cope & Day Company — No. 112.27

Date	Item	Ref.	Debit	Date	Ref.	Credit
1976 Jan. 11		S-23	5,734	1976 Jan. 20	CR-19	5,734

Miller, J. B. — No. 112.42

Date	Item	Ref.	Debit	Date	Ref.	Credit
1976 Jan. 31		S-23	196			

Sayre Corporation — No. 112.80

Date	Item	Ref.	Debit	Date	Ref.	Credit
1976 Jan. 1	Balance		4,000	1976 Jan. 7	CR-19	4,490
3		S-23	490			

XY Manufacturing Company — No. 112.91

Date	Item	Ref.	Debit	Date	Ref.	Credit
1976 Jan. 27		S-23	1,960			

assure that this correspondence exists, frequent reconcilations should be made. Clearly, a reconciliation cannot be accomplished unless all posting is complete, both to the control account and to the subsidiary ledger. To illustrate, a reconciliation based upon the information in Exhibit 3–16 for *Accounts Receivable Control* and the *accounts receivable subsidiary ledger* would be as follows:

Reconciliation of Accounts Receivable Subsidiary Ledger
(at January 31, 1976)

		Amount
Subsidiary ledger balances:		
112.13	Adams Company	$ 980
112.42	Miller, J. B.	196
112.91	XY Manufacturing Company	1,960
	Total—per Balance in Accounts Receivable Control ($14,360 − $11,224)	$3,136

The above discussion was intended to review the concepts underlying special journals, control accounts, and subsidiary ledgers. Their design and use depend upon the characteristics of the company. They do not require new accounting principles since they are only data processing techniques. The above discussion also serves to emphasize the four primary efficiencies that may result from their use, viz: (1) journalizing is simplified, (2) posting is simplified, (3) subdivision of work is simplified, and (4) a highly trained person is not needed to maintain a special journal or a subsidiary ledger that involves only one type of transaction.[9]

Appendix B. Worksheet for a Manufacturing Company

A worksheet for a manufacturing company is somewhat different from that illustrated in Exhibit 3–5 for a merchandising company. Because of the cost accounting procedures generally used for the manufacturing activity, the worksheet should include a pair of columns for *manufacturing*. All of the manufacturing costs, including the raw materials and work in process inventories, are extended to manufacturing. A worksheet for a manufacturing situation is illustrated in Exhibit 3–17. The following information will be helpful in studying this worksheet:

[9] Voucher system journals are not discussed since they involve essentially the same procedures as illustrated. The voucher system journals are known as *(a)* the voucher register, and *(b)* the check register.

EXHIBIT 3–17

DUNCAN MANUFACTURING COMPANY
Worksheet for the Year Ended December 31, 1976

Accounts	Unadjusted Trial Balance		Adjustments		Manufacturing		Income Statement		Balance Sheet	
	Debit	Credit	Debit	Credit	Debit	Credit	Debit	Credit	Debit	Credit
Cash	32,000								32,000	
Inventory, January 1 (periodic system):										
Raw materials	55,000				55,000	62,000			62,000	
Work in process	76,000				76,000	81,000			81,000	
Finished goods	54,000						54,000	52,000	52,000	
Equipment (ten-year life)	300,000								300,000	
Accumulated depreciation – equipment		90,000		*(a)* 10,000						100,000
Remaining assets	13,000								13,000	
Accounts payable		15,000								15,000
Accumulated interest expense				*(b)* 800						800
Income taxes payable				*(c)* 36,000						36,000
Mortgage payable (8% each Nov. 1)		60,000								60,000
Common stock, par $10		200,000								200,000
Retained earnings		74,200								74,200
Sales revenue		474,800						474,800		
Manufacturing costs:										
Raw material purchases	70,000				70,000					
Direct labor	100,000				100,000					
Factory overhead	75,000		*(a)* 7,000		82,000					
Distribution expenses	70,000		*(a)* 2,000				72,000			
General and administrative expenses	65,000		*(a)* 1,000				66,000			
Interest expense	4,000		*(b)* 800				4,800			
Income tax expense			*(c)* 36,000				36,000			
Cost of goods manufactured						240,000	240,000			
Net Income							54,000			54,000
Totals	914,000	914,000	46,800	46,800	383,000	383,000	526,800	526,800	540,000	540,000

a. Only representative accounts and adjusting entries are included.

b. There are columns for manufacturing; however, the columns for adjusted trial balance sheet and retained earnings have been omitted to demonstrate these simplifications. They were noted as optional in in the chapter.

c. Only three typical adjusting entries are included. Depreciation expense was allocated on a reasonable basis as follows: factory, 70%; distribution, 20%; and general, 10%. Interest was accrued for two months.

d. The current cost accounting entries for factory costs were:

	Debit	Credit
Raw material purchases	70,000	
Direct labor	100,000	
Cash		170,000
Factory overhead	65,000	
Various accounts		65,000

e. The ending inventories at December 31, 1976, were:

Raw materials	62,000
Work in process	81,000
Finished goods	52,000

f. An average corporate income tax rate of 40% is assumed.

A cost of goods manufactured statement, taken directly from the manufacturing columns in the worksheet, would be as follows:

DUNCAN MANUFACTURING COMPANY
Statement of Cost of Goods Manufactured
For the Year Ended December 31, 1976

Materials:		
Beginning inventory	$ 55,000	
Purchases	70,000	
Total Materials Available	125,000	
Less: Ending inventory	62,000	
Cost of materials used		$ 63,000
Direct labor		100,000
Factory overhead		82,000
Total Factory Costs		245,000
Add: Beginning work in process inventory		76,000
		321,000
Less: Ending work in process inventory		81,000
Cost of Goods Manufactured		$240,000

Observe on the worksheet that the last amount ($240,000) was transferred from the Manufacturing columns to the Income Statement columns (a debit since it is a cost). In other respects the amounts are extended to the last four columns as explained and illustrated in the chapter (Exhibit 3–5).

QUESTIONS

1. Explain why an accounting information processing system must be tailored to the characteristics of the entity.

2. What is the accounting model? Give the three submodels and briefly explain each.

3. Complete the following matrix by entering debit or credit in each cell.

Item	Increase	Decrease
Liabilities		
Revenues		
Assets		
Expenses		
Owners' equity		

4. Explain the dual feature of the fundamental accounting model.

5. Broadly explain the purpose of the accounting information processing model.

6. With respect to the collection of raw economic data for the accounting system, why are source documents important? Give some examples of source documents.

7. Explain the nature and purpose of transaction analysis.

8. What kind of events are recorded in the accounting system? Explain.

9. What is meant by journalizing? What purpose does it serve?

10. What is meant by posting? What purpose does it serve?

11. Distinguish between mixed, real, and nominal accounts.

12. Classify the following accounts, before the adjusting entries, as mixed, real, or nominal (explain any assumptions you make):

Accounts receivable	Prepaid insurance
Supplies inventory	Notes payable
Retained earnings	Interest revenue
Patents	Common stock
Interest expense	Property tax expense

13. Distinguish between the general ledger, control accounts, and subsidiary ledgers. What is the basic purpose of each?

14. Explain the difference between the general journal and special journals. What is the basic purpose of each?

15. What is a trial balance? What are the two purposes of a trial balance? Distinguish between unadjusted, adjusted, and post-closing trial balances.

16. Why is a worksheet a facilitating technique? What does it facilitate? If a worksheet is strictly optional, as it is, why is it usually used?

17. What is the purpose and nature of an adjusting entry? Explain why they generally must be made. Explain why the adjusting entries must be considered prior to developing the financial statements.

18. Match the following:

a. An expense incurred but not yet paid.	______Prepaid expense
b. A revenue collected but not yet earned.	______Accrued expense
c. A revenue earned but not yet collected.	______Accrued revenue
d. An expense paid but not yet incurred.	______Prepaid revenue

19. Why are the adjusting entries journalized and posted?

20. What is the purpose and nature of the closing entries? Why are they journalized and posted?

21. What is the purpose and nature of reversing entries? Why are they journalized and posted?

22. X Company owes a $4,000, 9%, three-year, interest-bearing note payable. Interest is paid each November 30. Therefore, at the end of the accounting period, December 31, the following adjusting entry was made:

Interest expense	30	
Accrued interest payable		30

Would you recommend that a reversing entry be used in this situation? Explain.

23. Number the following phases in the accounting information processing cycle to indicate their normal sequence of completion:

_____ Reversing entries.
_____ Posting.
_____ Transaction analysis.
_____ Collection of raw data.
_____ Journalize and post adjusting entries.
_____ Journalize and post closing entries.
_____ Prepare financial statements.
_____ Journalize current transactions.
_____ Prepare post-closing trial balance.
_____ Prepare worksheet.
_____ Prepare unadjusted trial balance.

24. In posting a special journal, there are two phases: daily posting and periodic posting. Explain the purpose and nature of each.

25. What circumstances would suggest the need for special journals? Why?

26. What kind of entries are made in the following special journals?
    a. Purchases journal.
    b. Cash receipts journal.
    c. Sales journal.
    d. Cash payments journal.

EXERCISES

Exercise 3–1

Develop a diagram that shows that manner in which transactions are recorded in the accounting system in terms of the financial position model. Include the concept of debits and credits. Explain why expenses are increased with a debit and revenues are increased with a credit. Also explain the basis for the designation double-entry system.

Exercise 3–2

The following selected transactions were completed during the current year by Clay Corporation:

a. Clay Corporation sold 50,000 shares of its own common stock, par $1 per share, for $60,000 cash.
b. Borrowed $30,000 cash on a one-year, 9%, interest-bearing note.
c. Purchased real estate for use in the business at a cash cost of $40,000, which consisted of a small building ($35,000) and the lot on which it was located ($5,000).
d. Purchased merchandise for resale at a cash cost of $8,600. Assume periodic inventory system.
e. Purchased merchandise for resale on credit; terms, 2/10, n/30. If paid within the ten days, the cash payment would be $490; however, if paid after ten days,

the payment would be $500. Since the company takes all discounts, credit purchases are recorded at net.

f. Sold merchandise for $9,600; collected one half in cash and the balance is due in 30 days.

g. Paid the balance due on the purchase in *(e)* within the ten day period.

Required:

Enter each of the above transactions in a general journal. Use the letter to the left to indicate the date.

Exercise 3–3

The 11 phases that compose the accounting information processing cycle are listed to the left in scrambled order. To the right is a brief statement of the objective of each phase, also in scrambled order. You are to present two responses.

Required:

(Use a separate sheet of paper.)

1. In the blanks to the left, number the phases in the usual sequence of completion.
2. In the blanks to the right, use the letters to match each phase with its objective.

Sequence (order)	*Phases*	*Matching (with objective)*	*Objective*
______	Journalizing.	______	*a.* Verification after closing entries.
______	Reversing entries.	______	*b.* Communication to decision-makers.
______	Transaction analysis.	______	*c.* Verification before adjusting entries.
______	Prepare financial statements.	______	*d.* Transfer from journal to ledger.
______	Journalize and post closing entries.	______	*e.* Based on source documents.
______	Collection of raw data.	______	*f.* Update general ledger by separating "mixed" accounts.
______	Posting.		*g.* Assess economic impact on each transaction.
______	Journalize and post adjusting entries.	______	*h.* Original input into the accounting system.
______	Prepare worksheets.	______	*i.* To facilitate subsequent entries.
______	Prepare unadjusted trial balance.	______	*j.* To obtain a zero balance in the revenue and expense accounts.
______	Prepare post-closing trial balance.	______	*k.* A logical and systematic technique for completing the end-of-the-period procedures.

Exercise 3–4

Frank Corporation completed the three transactions given below:

a. January 1, 1976—sold 10,000 shares of its own unissued common stock, par $1 per share, for $18,000 cash.
b. January 3, 1976—purchased a large machine costing $50,000. Payment was $10,000 cash down payment, a $15,000, one-year, 10% interest-bearing note payable, and a $25,000, three-year, 8%, interest-bearing note payable.
c. February 1, 1976—sold two lots for $7,500, that would not be needed. Received $2,500 cash down payment and a $5,000, 90-day, 10% interest-bearing note. The two lots had a book value of $6,000.

Required:

1. Give the general journal entry to record each of the three transactions.
2. Set up T-accounts and post the entries in 1. Use a systematic numbering system for posting purposes.

Exercise 3–5

A clerk for Searls Company prepared the following unadjusted trial balance which the clerk was unable to balance:

	Debits	*Credits*
Cash	$ 33,563	
Accounts receivable	31,000	
Allowance for doubtful accounts	(2,000)	
Inventory		$ 18,000
Equipment	81,500	
Accumulated depreciation		12,000
Accounts payable	18,000	
Notes payable		25,000
Common stock, par $10		80,000
Retained earnings		14,000
Revenues		75,000
Expenses	60,000	
Totals (out of balance by $1,937)	$222,063	$224,000

Assume you are examining the accounts and have found the following errors:

a. Equipment purchased for $7,500 at year-end was debited to Expense.
b. Sales on account for $829 were debited to Accounts Receivable for $892 and credited to Revenues for $829.
c. A $6,000 collection on accounts receivable was debited to Cash and credited to Revenues.
d. The inventory amount is understated by $2,000.

Required:

Prepare a corrected trial balance. Show computations.

Exercise 3–6

Lyle Company adjusts and closes its accounts each December 31. The following are situations that require an adjusting entry at year-end. You are requested to prepare the adjusting entry in the general journal for each of the situations. Show computations.

a. A machine is to be depreciated for the full year. It cost $71,000, and the estimated useful life is 15 years with an estimated residual value of $11,000. Assume straight-line depreciation.
b. Credit sales for the current year amounted to $120,000. The estimated bad debt loss rate on credit sales is one half of 1%.
c. Property taxes for the current year have not been recorded or paid. A statement, for the calendar year, was received near the end of December for $2,400. The taxes are due and will be paid February 1 in the next year.
d. Supplies costing $800 were purchased for use in the offices during the year and debited to Office Supplies Expense. An inventory of these supplies at the end of the year reflected $150 on hand (unused).
e. Lyle rented an office in its building to an outsider for one year, starting on September 1. Rent for one year amounting to $1,800 was collected at that date. The total amount was credited to Rent Revenue.
f. Lyle holds a note receivable received from a customer dated November 1 of the current year. It is a $1,000, 9%, interest-bearing note, due in one year. At the maturity date, Lyle will collect the face value of the note plus interest for one year.

Exercise 3–7

For each of the following situations, you are to give, in general journal form, the adjusting entry required at the end of the annual accounting period, December 31. Show computations.

a. At the end of the year, unpaid and unrecorded salaries amounted to $2,500.
b. The company owns a building which is to be depreciated for the full year. It cost $254,000, has an estimated useful life of 20 years, and a residual value of $54,000. Accumulated depreciation at the beginning of the current year was $60,000.
c. The company rented some space in its building to an outsider on August 1 of the current year and collected $2,400 cash which was rent for one year in advance. Rent Revenue was credited for $2,400 on August 1.
d. The company paid a two-year insurance premium in advance on July 1 of the current year amounting to $900. The $900 was debited to Prepaid Insurance when paid.
e. Credit sales for the current year amounted to $90,000. The estimated bad debt loss rate is one half of 1% of credit sales.
f. On July 1 of the current year, the company received a $10,000, one-year, 8% interest-bearing note from a customer. At maturity date, the company will collect the face amount of $10,000 plus interest for one year.

Exercise 3–8

Piper Company adjusts and closes its accounts each December 31. Below are two typical situations involving adjusting entries.

a. During the current year, office supplies were purchased for cash, $650. At the end of the current year, an inventory showed $200 unused supplies still on hand.

Required:

Give the adjusting entry assuming at the time of the purchase that: Case A, the $650 was debited to Office Supplies Expense; Case B, the $650 was debited to Office Supplies Inventory.

b. On June 1, the company collected cash, $2,400, which was for rent collected in advance for the next 12 months.

Give the adjusting journal entry assuming at the time of the collection that: Case A, the $2,400 was credited to Rent Revenue; Case B, the $2,400 was credited to Rent Collected in Advance (i.e., Prepaid Rent Revenue).

Exercise 3–9

1. On January 1, 1976, the Office Supplies Inventory account showed a balance on hand amounting to $350. During 1976, purchases of office supplies amounted to $800, which was debited to Office Supplies Inventory account. An inventory of office supplies on hand at December 31, 1976 reflected unused supplies amounting to $125. Give the adjusting journal entry that should be made on December 31, 1976.
2. On January 1, 1976, the Prepaid Insurance account showed a debit balance of $300, which was for coverage for the three months, January–March. On April 1, 1976, the company took out another policy covering a two-year period from that date. A two-year premium amounting to $3,600 was paid and debited to Prepaid Insurance. Give the adjusting journal entry that should be made on December 31, 1976.

Exercise 3–10

Write a suitable explanation for each of the following journal entries:

a. Wage expense	1,400	
Accrued wages payable		1,400
b. Warranty (guarantee) expense	950	
Estimated warranty liability		950
c. Insurance expense	600	
Prepaid insurance		600
d. Interest expense	1,200	
Accrued bond interest expense		1,200
e. Interest receivable	900	
Interest revenue		900
f. Income summary	5,000	
Retained earnings		5,000
g. Rent revenue	750	
Deferred rent revenue		750

Exercise 3–11

The adjusted trial balance for Joy Company showed the following on December 31, 1976, which is the end of the annual accounting period:

Sales revenue	$82,000	Selling expenses	$23,000
Interest revenue	1,000	Administrative expenses	13,000
Purchases	44,000	Interest expense	400
Purchase returns	500	Income tax expense	1,000
Freight-in	1,500		
Beginning inventory (periodic)	17,800	Additional data: Ending inventory	19,000

Required:

1. Set up T-accounts for each of the above items; enter the balances and diagram the closing entries. Use Cost of Goods Sold and Income Summary accounts.
2. Explain the manner in which you handled the inventory amounts. Explain an alternate approach.

Exercise 3–12

At the end of the annual accounting period, Jester Corporation made the following adjusting entries:

December 31, 1976:

a. Depreciation expense	5,000	
Accumulated depreciation		5,000
b. Wage expense	2,000	
Accrued wages payable		2,000
c. Bad debt expense	400	
Allowance for doubtful accounts		400
d. Income tax expense	6,000	
Income tax payable		6,000

Required:
1. Journalize the reversing entries that you think should be made on January 1, 1977.
2. Explain for each adjusting entry, the analysis you used to decide whether to reverse it.

Exercise 3–13

At the end of the annual accounting period, AB Corporation made the following adjusting entries:

December 31, 1976:

a. Property tax expense	800	
Property taxes payable		800
(These are paid once each year.)		
b. Rent receivable	2,000	
Rent revenue		2,000
(Rent revenue is collected each month.)		
c. Patent amortization expense	1,000	
Patents		1,000
d. Warranty expense	600	
Estimated warranty liability		600
e. Salary expense	2,000	
Accrued salaries payable		2,000

Required:

1. Journalize the reversing entries that you think should be made on January 1, 1977.
2. Explain, for each adjusting entry, the analysis you used to determine whether to reverse it.

Exercise 3–14

Complete the following tabulations by entering the appropriate amount in each blank space:

1.

	Owners' Equity at Start of Period	*Additional Investment by Owner*	*Withdrawals by Owner*	*Owners' Equity at End of Period*	*Net Income or (Loss)*
a.	$10,000	$2,000	$1,000	$16,400	$____
b.	18,000	3,000	____	22,000	4,700
c.	____	1,200	800	30,000	(2,200)
d.	15,500	600	____	12,950	(2,000)
e.	18,000	____	2,700	22,000	4,700

2.

	Sales	*Finished Goods Initial Inventory*	*Cost of Goods Manu- factured*	*Finished Goods Ending Inventory*	*Cost of Goods Sold*	*Gross Margin*	*Expenses*	*Net Income*
a.	$____	$15,000	$60,000	$____	$67,000	$23,000	$____	$1,000
b.	80,000	____	48,000	2,000	____	23,000	18,000	____
c.	____	20,000	____	36,000	59,000	18,000	____	8,000

Exercise 3–15 (based on Appendix A)

Dow Company uses special journals for credit sales, credit purchases, cash receipts, and cash payments. For each of the following transactions, you are to indicate the appropriate journal.

Transactions	*Appropriate Journal*
a. Sold common stock of Dow for cash.	______
b. Purchased merchandise for resale; terms, 2/10, n/60.	______
c. Borrowed $5,000 on 8% note.	______
d. Recorded depreciation expense.	______
e. Sold merchandise for cash.	______
f. Purchased merchandise for cash.	______
g. Purchased equipment for cash.	______
h. Sold fixed asset for cash.	______
i. Purchased machinery on credit.	______
j. Collected an account receivable.	______
k. Paid a note payable.	______
l. Recorded accrued wages.	______
m. Paid cash dividend on common stock.	______
n. Recorded estimated bad debt expense.	______
o. Recorded amortization expense on patent.	______

Exercise 3–16 (based on Appendix A)

Brown Retailers use special journals. Below is the special credit sales journal with several representative transactions:

Special Journal – Credit Sales						Page S-9	
						Dept. Sales	
Date 1976	Sales Invoice No.	Account Receivable	Terms	Folio	Amount	A	B
1	21	Fly Corporation	2/10, n/30		98	40	58
5	22	B. T. Company	"		490	290	200
7	23	Easton Company	"		294	104	190
11	24	Fly Corporation	"		588	288	300
13	25	Wells Company	"		686	300	386
18	26	Fly Corporation	"		147	100	47
21	27	Easton Company	"		784	554	230
28	28	B. T. Company	"		245	200	45
31	29	Wells Company	"		637	407	230

Required:

1. Sum the above special journal and post it to the appropriate accounts in the general ledger and the two subsidiary ledgers. Use control accounts and subsidiary ledgers for sales and accounts receivable; assign systematic numbers to the accounts.
2. Prove the correctness of the two subsidiary ledgers.

Exercise 3–17 (based on Appendix A)

Sorensen Retailers use special journals. Below is a special cash receipts journal with several selected transactions.

Cash Receipts Journal							Page CR-8
		Debits	Credits				
Date 1976	Explanation	Cash	Account Title	Folio	Accounts Receivables	Sundry Accounts	Sales
1	Cash sales	30,000					30,000
2	On account	4,200	Riley Corporation		4,200		
5	Cash sales	10,000					10,000
6	On account	1,240	Brown, Inc.		1,240		
8	Sale of temporary		Temporary investments			4,000	
	investment	7,000	Gain			3,000	
11	Cash sales	41,000					41,000
12	Borrowed cash	10,000	Notes payable			10,000	
15	On account	5,500	Watson Company		5,500		
18	Collected interest	600	Interest revenue			600	
31	Cash sales	52,000					52,000

Required:

1. Sum the above special journal and post it to the appropriate accounts in the general ledger and subsidiary ledger. Use control account and subsidiary ledger for accounts receivable. Assign systematic numbers to the accounts. Assume beginning balances of Riley Corporation, $8,400; Brown, Inc., $1,240; and Watson, $10,000.
2. Prove the correctness of the subsidiary ledger.

PROBLEMS

Problem 3–1

The following selected transactions were completed during the current year by Botts Corporation:

a. Botts sold 10,000 shares of its own common stock, par $10 per share, for $12 per share and received cash in full.
b. Borrowed $40,000 cash on an 8%, one-year, interest-bearing note.
c. Purchased equipment for use in operating the business at a net cash cost of $35,000; paid in full.
d. Purchased merchandise for resale at a cash net cost of $20,500; paid cash. Assume a periodic inventory system.
e. Purchased merchandise for resale on credit terms 2/10, n/60. The merchandise will cost $9,800 if paid within ten days, after ten days, the payment will be $10,000. The company always takes the discount; therefore, such purchases are recorded at net.
f. Sold merchandise for $38,000; collected $30,000 cash, and the balance is due in one month.
g. Paid $9,000 cash for operating expenses.
h. Paid the balance for the merchandise purchased in *(e)*, within the ten days.
i. Collected the balance due on the sales in *(f)*.
j. Paid cash for an insurance premium, $500; the premium was for two years' coverage.

Required:

1. Enter each of the above transactions in a general journal. Use the letter to the left to indicate the date.
2. Post each entry to appropriate T-accounts (number them consecutively).
3. Prepare an unadjusted trial balance.

Problem 3–2

The following selected transactions were completed during the current year by Grogan Corporation:

a. At date of organization, sold and issued 50,000 shares of its common stock, par $1 per share, for $75,000 cash.
b. Purchased a plant site for $100,000. The site included a building worth $82,000 and the land worth $18,000. Payment was made; $70,000 cash and a $30,000 one-year, 9%, interest-bearing note.
c. Borrowed $50,000 cash from the local bank; signed a 9% interest-bearing note due in six months.
d. Purchased equipment for use in the business for $12,000; paid cash.
e. Purchased goods for resale at a net cost of $80,000; paid $70,000 cash, balance on open account. Assume perpetual inventory system.
f. Sold goods for cash, $62,000.
g. Paid operating expenses, $31,000.
h. Sold goods for cash, $48,000.
i. Purchased goods for cash, $21,000.
j. Paid the $10,000 due from transaction *(e)*.
k. Sold and issued 30,000 shares of its common stock for $60,000.
l. On due date, paid the local bank the note given in entry *(c)* in the amount of $50,000 plus the interest to maturity date.
m. Purchased a two-year insurance policy on the building and equipment. Paid the two-year premium amounting to $1,400.

Required:

1. Journalize the above transactions in a general journal. Use the letters to the left to indicate dates.
2. Set up T-accounts (number them starting with 101) as needed and post the entries from the journal. Use folio notations.
3. Prepare an unadjusted trial balance.

Problem 3–3

Ring Company adjusts and closes its books each December 31. It is now December 31, 1976, and the adjusting entries are to be made. You are requested to prepare, in general journal format, the adjusting entry that should be made for each of the following items. Show computations.

a. Credit sales for the year amounted to $200,000. The estimated loss rate on bad debts is one fourth of 1%.
b. Unpaid and unrecorded wages at December 31 amounted to $1,950.
c. The company paid a two-year insurance premium in advance on April 1, 1976, amounting to $3,000 which was debited to Prepaid Insurance.
d. The worksheet is being completed, and pretax income has been computed to be $40,000. The applicable corporate tax rate is 22% on the first $25,000 income, plus 48% on all income above $25,000.

e. A machine that cost $33,700 is to be depreciated for the full year. The estimated useful life is ten years; and the residual value, $2,000. Assume straight-line depreciation.

f. The company rented a warehouse on June 1, 1976, for one year. They had to pay the full amount of rent one year in advance on June 1 amounting to $4,800, which was debited to Rent Expense.

g. The company received a 10%, interest-bearing note from a customer with a face amount of $6,000. The note was dated September 1, 1976; the principal plus the interest is payable one year later. Notes Receivable was debited, and Sales credited on September 1, 1976.

h. On December 30, 1976, the property tax bill was received in the amount of $1,700. This amount applied only to 1976 and had not been previously recorded. The taxes are due, and will be paid, on January 15, 1977.

i. On April 1, 1976, the company signed a $30,000, 8% interest-bearing note payable. On that date, Cash was debited and Notes Payable credited for $30,000. The note is payable on March 30, 1977, for the face amount plus interest for one year.

j. The company purchased a patent on January 1, 1976, at a cost of $5,950. On that date, Patent was debited and Cash credited for $5,950. The patent has an estimated useful life of 17 years and no residual value.

Problem 3–4

Tracy Company adjusts and closes its accounts each December 31. It is December 31, 1976. You are requested to prepare, in general journal format, the adjusting entry that should be made for each of the following items. Show computations.

a. The company owns a building and the site on which it is situated. The Building account reflects a cost of $267,000, and the site, $20,000. The estimated useful life of the building is 20 years, and the residual value, $17,000. Accumulated depreciation to January 1, 1976, was $66,000. Assume straight-line depreciation.

b. Property taxes for the current year have not been recorded or paid. A tax statement was received near the end of December for $6,000. The taxes are due, and will be paid, on February 15, 1977.

c. The company received a $6,000, 10%, interest-bearing note from a customer on June 1, 1976. On this date, Notes Receivable was debited and Sales credited for $6,000. The face of the note plus interest for one year is payable on May 30, 1977.

d. At December 31, 1976, the Supplies Inventory account showed a debit balance of $1,350. An inventory of unused supplies taken at year-end reflected $380.

e. Sales for the year amounted to $1,500,000, of which $300,000 was on credit. The estimated bad debt loss rate, based on credit sales, was one third of 1% for the year.

f. On August 1, 1976, the company rented some space in its building to an outsider and collected $4,200 cash rent in advance. This was for the 12 months starting August 1, 1976, and was credited to Rent Revenue.

g. At December 31, 1976, unrecorded and unpaid salaries amounted to $8,000.

h. On April 1, 1976, the company borrowed $20,000 on a one-year, 9%, interest-bearing note. On that date, Cash was debited and Notes Payable credited for $20,000. On maturity date, the face amount plus interest for one year must be paid.

i. On January 1, 1976, the company purchased, with cash, a patent for use in the business at a cost of $2,550, which was debited to Patent. The patent has an estimated remaining economic life of 15 years and no residual value.

j. The company uses the periodic inventory system whereby the inventory is physically counted, then valued at unit cost at each year-end. The company prefers to consider the inventory amounts as adjusting entries. The beginning inventory amount was $38,000, and the ending inventory (December 31, 1976) was $44,500. You are to give the adjusting entry for each inventory amount assuming a Cost of Goods Sold account is used.

k. The worksheet is being completed; all of the above adjusting entries have been recorded on it. Pretax income has been computed to be $60,000. The applicable corporate tax rates are 22% on the first $25,000 income plus 48% on all income above $25,000.

Problem 3–5

The following situations relate to the XY Corporation. The fiscal (accounting year) ends December 31. The situations relate to the year 1976. XY Corporation is a manufacturer rather than a retailer. The books are adjusted and closed each December 31.

In each instance, you are to give *only* the adjusting entry (or entries) that would be made on December 31, 1976, incident to adjusting and closing the books and preparation of the annual financial statements. State clearly any assumptions that you make. Give each adjusting entry in general journal format.

Situation 1: The company owns a machine that cost $87,000; it was purchased on July 1, 1973. It has an estimated useful life of 15 years and a residual value of $12,000. Straight-line depreciation is used. The machine is still being used.

Situation 2: Sales for 1976 amounted to $800,000, including $300,000 credit sales. It is estimated, based on past experience of the company, that bad debt losses will be one half of 1% of credit sales.

Situation 3: On January 1, 1975, the company purchased a patent that cost $15,300; at that time the estimated useful life remaining was 17 years. The patent is used in operations.

Situation 4: At the beginning of 1976, Office Supplies Inventory amounted to $200. During 1976, office supplies amounting to $4,100 were purchased which was debited to Office Supplies Expense. An inventory of office supplies at the end of 1976 showed $250 on the shelves. The January 1 balance of $200 is still reflected in the Office Supplies Inventory account.

Situation 5: On July 1, 1976, the company paid a three-year insurance premium amounting to $900; this amount was debited to Prepaid Insurance.

Situation 6: On October 1, 1976, the company paid rent on some leased office space. The payment of $3,000 cash was for the following 12 months. At the time of payment, Rent Expense was debited for the $3,000.

Situation 7: On July 1, 1976, the company borrowed $60,000 from the Sharpstown bank; the loan was for 12 months at 7% interest on the face of the note. Since it was a noninterest-bearing note, the interest was taken out of the proceeds at the date of the loan; hence, Cash was debited for $55,800; Interest Expense debited for $4,200, and Notes Payable was credited for $60,000.

Situation 8: Finished goods inventory on January 1, 1976, was $120,000; and on December 31, 1976, it was $135,000. Assume periodic inventory procedures and that inventory entries are viewed as adjusting entries.

Situation 9: The company owned some property (land) that was rented to Jack Joske on April 1, 1976, for 12 months for $3,600. On April 1, the entire annual rental of $3,600 was credited to Rent Revenue Collected in Advance and Cash was debited.

Situation 10: On December 31, 1976, wages earned by employees but not yet paid (nor recorded in the accounts) amounted to $7,500. Disregard payroll taxes.

Situation 11: On December 31, 1976, it was discovered that some raw material purchased on the preceding day, although not paid for, was included in the final inventory. A purchase had not been recorded. The cost was $950.

Situation 12: On September 1, 1976, the company loaned $12,000 to an outside party; the loan was at 9% per annum and was due in six months; interest is to be paid at maturity, as a consequence, Cash was credited for $12,000 and Notes Receivable debited for the same amount on September 1.

Situation 13: On January 1, 1976, factory supplies on hand amounted to $100. During 1976, factory supplies costing $1,800 were purchased and debited to Factory Supplies Inventory. At the end of 1976, a physical inventory count revealed that factory supplies on hand amounted to $300.

Situation 14: The company purchased a gravel pit on January 1, 1974, at a cost of $30,000; it was estimated that approximately 60,000 tons of gravel could be removed prior to exhaustion. It was also estimated that the company would utilize five years to exploit this natural resource. Tons of gravel removed were: 1974–2,000; 1975–7,000; 1976–5,000.

Situation 15: At the end of 1976, it was found that there were postage stamps costing $90 still on hand (in a "postage" box in the office). When the stamps were purchased, Miscellaneous Expense was debited and Cash credited.

Situation 16: At the end of 1976, property taxes for 1976 amounting to $2,300 had been assessed on property owned by the company. The taxes are due no later than February 1, 1977. The taxes had not been recorded on the books since payment had not been made.

Situation 17: The company borrowed $30,000 from the bank on December 1, 1976. A 60-day note payable was signed that called for 8% interest payable on the due date. As a consequence, on December 1, 1976, Cash was debited and Notes Payable credited for $30,000.

Situation 18: On July 1, 1976, the company paid the city a $500 license charge for the next 12 months. On that date, Cash was credited and License Expense debited for $500.

Situation 19: On March 1, 1976, the company made a loan to the company president and received a $12,000 noninterest-bearing note receivable. The loan was due in one year and called for 6% annual interest (or discount) with interest taken out in advance. As a consequence, Cash was credited for $11,280, Interest Revenue credited for $720, and Notes Receivable debited for $12,000.

Situation 20: The company owns three "company cars" used by the executives. A six-month maintenance contract on them was signed on October 1, 1976, whereby a local garage agreed to do "all the required maintenance." The payment was made for the following six months in advance. On October 1, 1976, Cash was credited and Maintenance Expense was debited for $1,800.

Problem 3–6

The post-closing trial balance of the general ledger of Watkins Corporation at December 31, 1975, reflected the following:

Account No.	*Account*	*Debit*	*Credit*
101	Cash	$28,000	
102	Accounts receivable	18,000	
103	Allowance for doubtful accounts		$ 400
104	*Inventory (periodic)	10,000	
105	Equipment (20-year life; no residual value)	20,000	
106	Accumulated depreciation		6,000
200	Accounts payable		9,000
201	Accrued wages payable		
202	Income taxes payable		
300	Common stock, par $1		50,000
301	Retained earnings		10,600
302	Income summary		
400	Revenues		
500	Operating expenses		
501	Purchases		
600	Income tax expense		
		$76,000	$76,000

*Ending inventory, $15,000 (at December 31, 1976).

The following is a summary of the transactions during 1976 (use the number to the left to indicate the date):

Date

1. Sold goods, $90,000, of which $20,000 was on credit.
2. Purchased goods, $40,000, of which $10,000 was on credit; assume periodic inventory.
3. Collected accounts receivable, $35,000.
4. Paid accounts payable, $17,000.
5. Paid operating expenses, $23,800.
6. Sold common stock of the company, 2,000 shares at par, collected cash in full.
7. On the last day of the year, purchased a new machine at a cost of $12,000, paid cash. Estimated useful life, ten years; residual value, $10,000.

Required:

1. Set up T-accounts in the general ledger for the accounts listed above; they are all you will need. Enter the beginning balances.
2. Journalize each of the above transactions in the general journal.
3. Post the journal entries; use folio notations.
4. Prepare an unadjusted trial balance.
5. Journalize and post the adjusting entries. Accrued (unpaid) wages at year-end amounted to $800. Bad debt expense is estimated to be 1% of credit sales for the period. Assume straight-line depreciation. Assume a flat 22% corporate income tax rate.
6. Prepare an adjusted trial balance.
7. Prepare an unclassified income statement and balance sheet.
8. Journalize and post the closing entries.
9. Prepare a post-closing trial balance.

Problem 3–7

The post-closing trial balance of the general ledger of Voss Corporation at December 31, 1975, reflected the following:

Account No.	Accounts	Debit	Credit
101	Cash	$ 27,000	
102	Accounts receivable	21,000	
103	Allowance for doubtful accounts		$ 1,000
104	Inventory (periodic system)*	35,000	
105	Prepaid insurance (20 months remaining)	900	
200	Equipment (20-year estimated life; no residual value)	50,000	
201	Accumulated depreciation		22,500
300	Accounts payable		7,500
301	Accrued wages payable		
302	Income taxes payable (for 1975)		4,000
400	Common stock, par $1		80,000
401	Retained earnings		18,900
500	Sales revenue		
600	Purchases		
601	Operating expenses		
602	Income tax expense		
700	Income summary		
		$133,900	$133,900

* Ending inventory, $45,000 (at December 31, 1976).

The following transactions occurred during 1976 in the order given (use the number at the left to indicate the date):

Date

1. Sold goods for $30,000 of which $10,000 was on credit.
2. Collected $17,000 on accounts receivable.
3. Paid income taxes payable (1975), $4,000.
4. Purchased merchandise $40,000, of which $8,000 was on credit.
5. Paid accounts payable, $6,000.
6. Sold goods for cash, $72,000.
7. Paid operating expenses, $19,000.
8. Sold and issued 1,000 shares of common stock, par $1, for $1,000 cash.
9. Purchased merchandise, $100,000, of which $27,000 was on credit.
10. Sold goods for $98,000, of which $30,000 was on credit.
11. Collected cash on accounts receivable, $26,000.
12. Paid cash on accounts payable, $28,000.
13. Paid various operating expenses in cash, $18,000.

Required:

1. Set up T-accounts in the general ledger for each of the accounts listed in the beginning trial balance and enter the beginning balances.
2. Journalize each of the transactions listed above for 1976. Use general journal only.
3. Post the journal entries; use folio notations.
4. Prepare an unadjusted trial balance.
5. Journalize the adjusting entries and post them to the ledger. Assume the bad debt rate is ½% of credit sales for the period and an average 40% corporate income tax rate. At December 31, 1976, accrued wages, $300. Assume straight-line depreciation.
6. Prepare an adjusted trial balance.
7. Prepare an unclassified income statement and balance sheet.
8. Journalize and post the closing entries. Do not use a Cost of Goods Sold account.
9. Prepare a post-closing trial balance.

Problem 3–8

Young Corporation adjusts and closes its books each December 31. At December 31, 1976, the following unadjusted trial balance has been developed from the general ledger:

Accounts	Balances (Unadjusted) Debits	Credits
Cash	$132,830	
Accounts receivable	34,000	
Allowance for doubtful accounts		$ 5,400
Inventory (periodic system)	62,000	
Prepaid insurance (15 months remaining as of January 1, 1976)	600	
Long-term note receivable (7%)	12,000	
Investment revenue receivable		
Land	27,000	
Building	240,000	
Accumulated depreciation, building		130,000
Equipment	90,000	
Accumulated depreciation, equipment		50,000
Accounts payable		23,000
Accrued salaries payable		
Income taxes payable		
Accrued interest payable		
Prepaid rent revenue		
Bonds payable, 5%		120,000
Common stock, par $10		200,000
Contributed capital in excess of par		10,000
Retained earnings		27,900
Sales revenue		290,000
Investment revenue		630
Rent revenue		6,000
Purchases	164,000	
Purchase returns		4,000
Selling expenses	51,000	
General and administrative expenses	35,000	
Interest expense	3,500	
Extraordinary loss (pretax)	15,000	
Income tax expense		
	$866,930	$866,930

Additional data for adjustments and other purposes:

a. Estimated bad debt loss rate is one half of 1% of credit sales. Ten percent of 1976 sales were on credit. Classify as a selling expense.

b. Ending inventory (December 31, 1976), $70,000.

c. Interest on the long-term note receivable was last collected on September 30, 1976.

d. Estimated useful life on the building was 20 years; residual value, $40,000. Allocate 10% to administrative. Assume straight-line depreciation.

e. Estimated useful life on the equipment was ten years; residual value, zero. Allocate 10% to administrative. Assume straight-line depreciation.

f. Unrecorded and unpaid sales salaries payable at December 31, 1976, was $7,500.

g. Interest on the bonds payable was paid last on July 31, 1976.
h. On August 1, 1976, the company rented some space in its building to an outsider and collected $6,000 for 12 months rent in advance which was credited to Rent Revenue.
i. Adjust for expired insurance. Assume selling expense.
j. Assume an average 40% corporate income tax rate on all items including the extraordinary loss.

Required:

1. Enter the above unadjusted trial balance on a worksheet similar to Exhibit 3–5.
2. Enter the adjusting entries on the worksheet and complete it (round to nearest dollar).
3. Prepare an unclassified income statement and a balance sheet.
4. Journalize the closing entries.

Problem 3–9

Astro Corporation currently is completing the end-of-the-period accounting process. At December 31, 1976, and the following unadjusted trial balance has been developed from the general ledger:

	Balances (Unadjusted)	
Accounts	*Debits*	*Credits*
Cash	$ 61,900	
Accounts receivable	38,000	
Allowance for doubtful accounts		$ 2,000
Inventory (periodic system)	80,000	
Office supplies inventory	900	
Long-term note receivable (7%)	12,000	
Equipment	180,000	
Accumulated depreciation, equipment		64,000
Patent	8,400	
Accrued interest receivable		
Accounts payable		23,000
Accrued interest payable		
Income taxes payable		
Property taxes payable		
Prepaid rent revenue		
Mortgage payable, 8%		60,000
Common stock, par $100		100,000
Contributed capital in excess of par		15,000
Retained earnings		32,440
Sales revenue		700,000
Investment revenue		560
Rent revenue		3,000
Purchases	400,000	
Freight-in	7,000	
Purchase returns		2,000
Selling expenses	164,400	
General and administrative expenses	55,000	
Interest expense	4,400	
Income tax expense		
Extraordinary gain (pretax)		10,000
	$1,012,000	$1,012,000

Additional data for adjustments and other purposes:

a. Estimated bad debt loss rate is one fourth of 1% of credit sales. Credit sales for the year amounted to $200,000. This is a selling expense.
b. Ending inventory, December 31, 1976, $95,000.
c. Interest on the long-term note receivable was last collected August 31, 1976.
d. Estimated useful life of the equipment is ten years; residual value, $20,000. Allocate 10% to administrative expenses. Assume straight-line depreciation.
e. Estimated remaining economic life of the patent is 14 years (from January 1, 1976) and no residual value. Assume straight-line amortization to selling expense (used in sales promotion).
f. Interest on the mortgage payable was last paid on November 30, 1976.
g. On June 1, 1976, the company rented some office space to an outsider for one year and collected $3,000 rent in advance for the year which was credited to Rent Revenue.
h. On December 31, 1976, received a statement for calendar year 1976 unrecorded property taxes amounting to $1,300. The amount is due February 15, 1977. Assume it will be paid on that date and that it is a selling expense.
i. Office supplies on hand at December 31, 1976, amounted to $300 (selling expense).
j. Assume an average 40% corporate income tax rate on all items including the extraordinary gain.

Required:

1. Enter the above adjusted trial balance on a worksheet similar to Exhibit 3–5.
2. Enter the adjusting entries and complete the worksheet.
3. Prepare an unclassified income statement and balance sheet.
4. Journalize the closing entries.

Problem 3–10

Write a suitable explanation for each of the following journals entries:

	Debit	Credit
a. Sales revenue	50,000	
Rent revenue	2,000	
Interest revenue	1,000	
Sales returns		1,500
Income summary		51,500
b. Salary expense	7,000	
Accrued salaries payable		7,000
c. Rent revenue	800	
Deferred rent revenue		800
d. Income summary	10,000	
Inventory		10,000
e. Inventory	12,000	
Income summary		12,000
f. Interest receivable	900	
Interest revenue		900
g. Supplies used expense	400	
Supplies inventory		400

h. Income summary	39,000	
Operating expenses		21,000
Administrative expenses		16,000
Interest expense		2,000
i. Interest expense	750	
Accrued interest expense payable		750
j. Income summary	8,800	
Retained earnings		8,800
k. Investment revenue	600	
Deferred (unearned) investment revenue		600
l. Warranty (guarantee) expense	500	
Estimated warranty liability		500
m. Income tax expense	3,700	
Income taxes payable		3,700
n. Property tax expense	360	
Property taxes payable		360
o. Supplies inventory	440	
Supplies expense		440

Problem 3–11

The adjusted trial balance for Ransom Corporation reflected the following on December 31, 1976, end of the annual accounting period:

Cash	$ 27,900	
Inventory (periodic system)	18,000	
Accounts receivable	32,000	
Allowance for doubtful accounts		$ 500
Prepaid insurance	600	
Equipment	100,000	
Accumulated depreciation, equipment		20,000
Accounts payable		13,400
Accrued wages		800
Income taxes payable		5,000
Bonds payable		20,000
Common stock, par $10		100,000
Retained earnings		12,400
Sales revenue		126,000
Interest revenue		1,000
Sales returns	3,000	
Purchases	70,000	
Freight-in	2,500	
Purchase returns		900
Operating expenses	28,000	
General expenses (including interest)	13,000	
Income tax expense	5,000	
	$300,000	$300,000

Inventory, December 31, 1976, $23,000.

Required:

1. Set up T-accounts only for the accounts to be closed and Retained Earnings.

Enter the balances. Diagram the closing entries. Use Cost of Goods Sold and Income Summary accounts.

2. Journalize the closing entries to agree with your diagram.
3. Explain the manner in which you handled the inventory amounts.
4. Did you use a Cost of Goods Sold account? Explain the alternate approach.

Problem 3–12

The summarized adjusted trial balance for Exter Corporation reflected the following on December 31, 1976, end of the annual accounting period:

Cash	$ 60,700	
Inventory (periodic system)	12,000	
Accounts receivable	21,000	
Allowance for doubtful accounts		$ 400
Prepaid insurance	300	
Accounts payable		17,600
Accrued wages payable		1,000
Income taxes payable		2,000
Common stock, par $10		50,000
Retained earnings		17,300
Sales revenue		88,000
Sales returns	2,000	
Purchases	45,000	
Freight-in	1,000	
Purchase returns		700
Operating expenses	18,400	
General expenses (including interest)	14,600	
Income tax expense	2,000	
	$177,000	$177,000

Inventory (ending), December 31, 1976, $18,800.

Required:

1. Set up T-accounts for Retained Earnings and those accounts that are to be closed. Enter the balances. Diagram the closing entries. Use an Income Summary account.
2. Journalize the closing entries to agree with your diagram.
3. Explain the manner in which you handled the inventory amounts. Explain an alternate approach.
4. Did you use a Cost of Goods Sold account? Explain an alternate approach to the one you used.

Problem 3–13

At the end of the accounting period, Burke Corporation made the following adjusting entries:

December 31, 1976:

a. Depreciation expense	7,000	
Accumulated depreciation		7,000
b. Bad debt expense	1,000	
Allowance for doubtful accounts		1,000
c. Insurance expense	600	
Prepaid insurance		600

	Debit	Credit
d. Supplies used expense	2,000	
Supplies inventory		2,000
e. Wage expense	5,000	
Accrued wages payable		5,000
f. Rent receivable	3,000	
Rent revenue		3,000
g. Utilities (electric) expense	4,000	
Estimated utilities payable		4,000
h. Interest expense	900	
Accrued interest payable		900

Required:

1. The first four adjusting entries given above generally are not viewed as candidates for reversal on January 1, 1977. Explain why each one is generally not a candidate.
2. The last four adjusting entries shown above generally are viewed as candidates for reversal on January 1, 1977. Give the reversing entry for each and explain why it may be desirable to reverse.
3. The last entry may, or may not, be reversed. In either event, the net effect is the same. Assume the next interest payment is March 31, 1977, for $1,200 (interest for the past 12 months). Prepare entries side by side under the captions "With Reversing Entry" and "Without Reversing Entry" and demonstrate that the net effects are the same.

Problem 3–14 (based on Appendix A)

Boley Company uses special journals for credit sales and credit purchases. Below are listed some selected transactions involving purchases and sales. Amounts given for credit transactions are before any deduction of discount unless otherwise stated. Sales and purchases on credit are recorded net of discount. Assume periodic inventory.

a. Purchased merchandise for cash, $9,800, from X Corporation.
b. Sold merchandise on credit terms 2/10, n/30, $1,000, to AD Company.
c. Purchased merchandise, $3,000, terms, 2/10, n/30, from Benson Company.
d. Purchased equipment from Roy Company for use in the business for $10,000; paid cash.
e. Collected for merchandise sold in (*b*) within ten days.
f. Sold merchandise on credit terms 2/10, n/30, $2,000, to Z Company.
g. Purchased merchandise for cash, $15,000, from AK Company.
h. Sold merchandise for cash, $41,800, to AD Company.
i. Sold merchandise on credit terms 2/10, n/30, $4,000, BT Corporation.
j. Purchased merchandise from X Corporation, $1,500, credit terms 2/10, n/30.
k. Paid for merchandise purchased in (*c*) above within the discount period.
l. Sold merchandise to VEE Company, $3,300, credit terms 2/10, n/60.
m. Purchased merchandise from Benson Company, $4,000; terms, 2/10, n/30.

Required:

1. Design special journals for credit sales and credit purchases similar to those illustrated in the chapter.

2. Enter in the two special journals appropriate transactions from the above list. Enter the remaining entries in the general journal.
3. Set up ledger accounts for Sales, Purchases, Accounts Receivable Control, and Accounts Payable Control in the general ledger, and appropriate subsidiary ledgers for the two latter control accounts. Use T-account format. Post appropriate amounts to these records. Systematically number the accounts for posting purposes.
4. Prove the accuracy of the accounts receivable and accounts payable records.

Problem 3–15 (based on Appendix A)

Thomas Company is a small department store. The accounting system is manually maintained. Control accounts and subsidiary ledgers are used. The following information was selected from the accounting system at January 1, 1976:

Journals	*Page No. to Be Used*
General journal	J-27
Special journals:	
Credit sales	S-13
Credit purchases	P-9
Cash receipts	CR-22
Cash payments	CP-34

General Ledger Accounts	*Balance Jan. 1, 1977*	*Account No.*
Cash	$ 72,000	101
Accounts receivable	38,000	105
Inventory (periodic system)	45,000	110
Equipment	25,000	204
Accounts payable	21,000	303
Notes payable	10,000	305
Common stock, par $10	100,000	400
Contributed capital in excess of par		401
Retained earnings	49,000	410
Sales revenue		500
Sales returns		501
Purchases		600
Purchase returns		601
Expenses		700
Subsidiary Ledgers		
Accounts receivable (No. 105):		
Ames, C. P.	7,000	105.1
Graves Company	16,000	105.2
Mason Corporation	5,000	105.3
White Company	10,000	105.4
Accounts payable (No. 303):		
Buford Wholesale Company	11,000	303.1
Dawn Suppliers, Inc.	7,000	303.2
Paul Wholesale Company	3,000	303.3

The following transactions were completed during the month of January 1976:

Date

1. Purchased merchandise for cash, $18,000.
2. Paid $11,000 owed to Buford Wholesale Company within the discount period.

3. Sold merchandise for cash, $26,000.
4. Purchased a new truck for use in the business; paid cash, $4,200.
5. Sold merchandise to XY Corporation on credit; terms, 2/10, n/60; $9,800 if paid within ten days, otherwise $10,000 (record at net of discount).
6. Paid expenses $4,500.
7. Purchased merchandise on credit from Sauls Company; credit terms, 2/10, n/60; $20,000, if paid within ten days; otherwise add 2% charge.
8. Sold merchandise for cash, $37,000.
8. Collected on accounts receivable within the discount period as follows: Ames, $7,000; Graves, $16,000; and White, $10,000.
9. Purchased merchandise for cash, $21,000.
9. Collected in full from XY Corporation for the sale of January 5.
9. Paid accounts payable within the discount period: Dawn, $7,000; Paul $2,000.
10. Collected accounts receivable from Mason Corporation, $5,000, within the discount period.
10. Returned merchandise purchased from Paul Wholesale Company because its specifications were incorrect; received a credit for $1,000.
14. Paid expenses, $9,600.
15. Sold merchandise for cash, $11,400.
16. Paid balance due to Sauls within the discount period.
19. Borrowed $30,000 cash on a one-year, 8%, interest-bearing note.
22. Sold merchandise on credit terms, 2/10, n/30, as follows (net amount): Ames, $6,000; Graves, $13,000; Mason, $9,000; and White, $4,000.
23. A customer returned merchandise, purchased a few days earlier; since the correct size was unavailable, customer was given a cash refund of $175.
24. Collected the balance due from White Company within the discount period.
25. Returned damaged merchandise to a wholesale supplier and received a cash refund of $450.
26. Purchased merchandise on credit from Buford Wholesale Company; terms, 2/10, n/60; net amount, $35,000.
27. Purchased merchandise on credit from Dawn Suppliers, Inc.; terms, 2/10, n/60; net amount, $12,000.
28. Cash sales, $47,000.
29. Sold merchandise on credit to XY Corporation on the usual terms, net amount, $16,500.
30. Collected in full for the credit sale to Mason on January 22.
31. Sold common stock of Thomas Company to a new shareholder, 1,000 shares for $20,000 cash.

Required:

1. Set up a general journal and special journals for credit sales, credit purchases, cash receipts, and cash payments, similar to those illustrated in Appendix A. Sales and purchases on credit are recorded at net of discount.
2. Set up T-accounts for the general ledger and two subsidiary ledgers, accounts receivable and accounts payable. Enter the beginning balances in the T-accounts.
3. Journalize the above transactions in the appropriate journals.
4. Post to the subsidiary and general ledgers; use folio numbers.
5. Prepare reconciliation of the subsidiary ledgers.
6. Prepare a trial balance from the general ledger.

Problem 3–16 (based on Appendix B)

Rose Manufacturing Corporation is in the process of completing the end-of-the-period accounting process. It is now December 31, 1976, and the following unadjusted trial balance has been developed from the general ledger:

Accounts	Balance (Unadjusted) Debits	Credits
Cash	$ 171,300	
Inventory, January 1 (periodic system):		
Raw materials	42,000	
Work in process	60,000	
Finished goods	38,000	
Accounts receivable	18,000	
Allowance for doubtful accounts		$ 450
Factory supplies inventory	6,300	
Plant and equipment	430,000	
Accumulated depreciation		180,000
Remaining assets (not subject to depreciation)	102,000	
Accounts payable		37,000
Accrued wages payable		
Accrued interest payable		
Income taxes payable		
Mortgage payable (9%, each August 31)		40,000
Common stock, par $100		500,000
Retained earnings		42,550
Sales revenue		800,000
Manufacturing costs:		
Raw materials purchases	180,000	
Direct labor	200,000	
Factory overhead	100,000	
Distribution expenses	160,000	
Administrative expenses	90,000	
Interest expense	2,400	
Cost of goods manufactured		
Income tax expense		
	$1,600,000	$1,600,000

Additional data for adjustments and other purposes:

a. Ending inventories: raw materials, $45,000; work in process, $54,000; finished goods, $40,000.
b. Estimated bad debt loss rate is one third of 1% of credit sales. Credit sales for the period were $150,000 (distribution expense).
c. An inventory of factory supplies taken on December 31, 1976, showed unused supplies amounting to $4,800 (factory overhead).
d. Plant and equipment is depreciated over a 20-year life (estimated); residual value is $30,000 (debit Factory Overhead for depreciation).
e. Unrecorded and unpaid administrative wages at December 31 amounted to $3,500.
f. The last interest payment on the mortgage was on August 31, 1976.
g. Assume 40% corporate income tax rate.

Required:

1. Enter the above unadjusted trial balance on a worksheet similar to Exhibit 3–17.
2. Enter the adjusting entries on the worksheet and complete it; assume straight-line depreciation.
3. Prepare a manufacturing statement, single-step income statement, and an unclassified balance sheet.
4. Journalize the closing entries.

Chapter 4

Review—The Income Statement and Retained Earnings

Periodic financial statements are the means by which information collected, recorded, and summarized in the accounting system is communicated to external decision-makers. Financial statements and the supplementary statements generally necessary for full disclosure are:

1. Income statement
   Supplementary—statement of retained earnings
2. Balance sheet
   Supplementary—statement of changes in stockholders' equity
3. Statement of changes in financial position
   Supplementary—changes in elements of working capital

The periodic financial statements present primarily *historical* information. They are *general-purpose* statements because they are designed primarily to serve several groups of decision-makers—investors, creditors, and the public at large. Also, they are summary in nature and are fundamentally related; that is, each statement is interrelated with the other statements. These relationships are illustrated in Exhibit 4–1.

In Exhibit 4–1, the income statement and the statement of changes in financial position are shown as the connecting links between the beginning and ending balance sheets. They are designed to explain, to the decision-maker, the causes of the changes in financial position during the period. The income statement explains the changes from *operations* (i.e., revenues and expenses), whereas the statement of changes in financial position explains the changes in financial position in terms of *fund* inflows and outflows during the period. The three statements are viewed by the accounting profession as the minimum requirement for reporting to external decision-makers.

This chapter discusses the income statement and the statement of retained earnings.

EXHIBIT 4–1
Relationships between Financial Statements

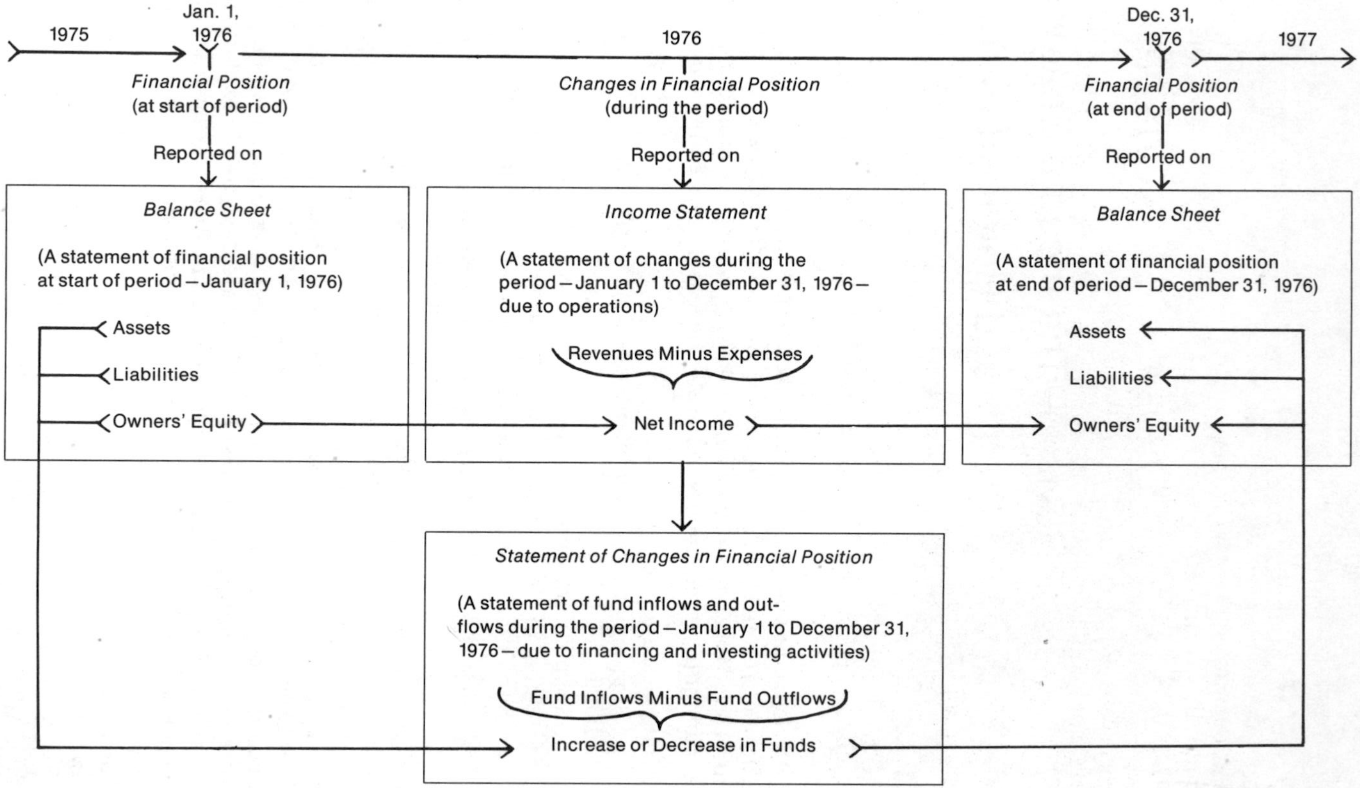

1975 — Jan. 1, 1976 — 1976 — Dec. 31, 1976 — 1977

Financial Position
(at start of period)

Reported on

Balance Sheet

(A statement of financial position at start of period – January 1, 1976)

Assets

Liabilities

Owners' Equity

Changes in Financial Position
(during the period)

Reported on

Income Statement

(A statement of changes during the period – January 1 to December 31, 1976 – due to operations)

Revenues Minus Expenses

Net Income

Financial Position
(at end of period)

Reported on

Balance Sheet

(A statement of financial position at end of period – December 31, 1976)

Assets

Liabilities

Owners' Equity

Statement of Changes in Financial Position

(A statement of fund inflows and outflows during the period – January 1 to December 31, 1976 – due to financing and investing activities)

Fund Inflows Minus Fund Outflows

Increase or Decrease in Funds

CONCEPT OF INCOME

Income is defined differently by economists and accountants. The economist broadly defines income as the change in real wealth between the beginning and end of a specified period; to state it another way, income is the net increase in real wealth that could be distributed to the owners of a business at the end of the period without reducing the real wealth of the entity from that at the start of the period. This concept requires careful measurement of the wealth at the beginning and end of each period. It provides no specific details for the causes of net income. Conceptually, wealth at each point in time should be measured as the *present value* of all expected future cash flows. Because of the difficulties in applying this concept, other ways of measuring wealth have been suggested, such as the current cash equivalent market value.

In contrast, the *accountant* defines net income on the basis of completed transactions that cause revenues and expenses. Income is defined as the difference between revenues and expenses arising from completed transactions. The economist's concept of income is impractical to apply; it is based upon subjective information and does not provide details required. Consequently, the accounting profession has evolved the *transactions approach* to define and measure net income. The transactions approach is pragmatic, provides details for continuous accounting, focuses on the stewardship function, and maintains a relatively high degree of objectivity.

The transactions approach used in accounting collects detailed data on each transaction and records the effects in terms of changes in assets, liabilities, and owners' equity (i.e., in terms of the basic accounting model). Basically, changes in assets, liabilities, and owners' equity are recognized if they are evidenced by *completed exchange transactions*. Changes in value generally are not recognized when they occur if they arise from changes in market valuations and changes in expectations; instead, they are recognized when exchange transactions occur. To illustrate, if an asset is acquired for $1,000 and subsequently increases in value to $1,200, the $200 accretion is not recognized as revenue. Should the asset later be sold for $1,300, a $300 gain would be recognized in the period of sale. The broad structure of accounting discussed in Chapter 2 explicitly requires the transactions approach. Since accounting defines income as the difference between total revenue and total expense, these two concepts require careful definition.

Revenue may be conceptually defined as the inflow of assets for the aggregate of products or services transferred (i.e., sold) by an enterprise during a specified period.[1] A pragmatic, though conceptually deficient, definition that more nearly expresses current practice is given in APB *Statement No. 4* as follows:

[1] Adapted from AAA Committee on Accounting Concepts and Standards, *Accounting and Reporting Standards for Corporate Financial Statements and Preceding Statements and Supplements* (Columbus, Ohio, 1957), p. 5.

> Revenue is a gross increase in assets or a gross decrease in liabilities recognized and measured in conformity with generally accepted accounting principles that results from those types of profit-directed activities of an enterprise that can change owners' equity. Revenue under present generally accepted accounting principles is derived from three general activities: *(a)* selling products, *(b)* rendering services and permitting others to use enterprise resources, which result in interest, rent, royalties, fees, and the like, and *(c)* disposing of resources other than products—for example, plant and equipment or investments in other entities. Revenue does not include receipt of assets purchased, proceeds of borrowing, investments by owners, or adjustments of revenue of prior periods.[2]

At this point it may be advisable to return to Chapter 2 for a review of the *revenue principle,* paying particular attention to when revenue is considered realized.

Expense may be defined conceptually as the use and consumption of goods and services in the process of obtaining revenues.[3] A pragmatic, though conceptually deficient, definition that more nearly expresses current practice is given in APB *Statement No. 4* as follows:

> Expenses are gross decreases in assets or gross increases in liabilities recognized and measured in conformity with generally accepted accounting principles that result from those types of profit-directed activities of an enterprise that can change owners' equity. Important classes of expenses are (1) cost of assets used to produce revenue (for example, cost of goods sold, selling and administrative expenses, and interest expense), (2) expense from nonreciprocal transfers and casualties (for example, taxes, fires and theft), (3) costs of other assets other than products (for example, plant and equipment or investments in other companies), disposed of, (4) costs incurred in unsuccessful efforts, and (5) declines in market prices of inventories held for sale. Expenses do not include repayments of borrowing, expenditures to acquire assets, distributions to owners (including acquisition of treasury stock), or adjustments of expenses of prior periods.[4]

At this point you should return to Chapter 2 and restudy the discussion of the cost principle (page 20).

Terminology Problems

The terms revenue, income, gain, and earnings are often used rather loosely. The following distinctions will aid later discussions:

1. Revenue—resources received for goods sold (such as sales revenue) and services provided (such as services, rent, and interest revenue).
2. Income—a difference; that is, revenue minus expense.
3. Earnings—another term for income.

---

[2] AICPA, "Basic Concepts and Accounting Principles Underlying Financial Statements of Business Enterprises," *Statement of the Accounting Principles Board No. 4* (New York, 1960), pp. 58–60. This definition is conceptually deficient primarily because of circularity.

[3] Adapted from Eldon S. Hendrickson, *Accounting Theory,* rev. ed. (Homewood, Ill.: Richard D. Irwin, Inc., 1970), p. 177.

[4] AICPA, *Statement No. 4,* pp. 58–60.

4. Gain—a net revenue amount derived from transactions that are indirectly related to normal operations such as "gain from sale of fixed assets." In practice, gains generally are broadly classified as a revenue.

Similarly, the terms cost, expense, and loss are troublesome; the following distinctions are widely recognized:

1. Cost—the amount of resources given up to acquire goods and services which, at point of acquisition, are assets, such as prepaid insurance and fixed assets.
2. Expense—the use of assets and services in the creation of revenue; that is, an expired asset. Thus, most costs subsequently become expense. Cost and expense may be the same as in the case where office supplies are acquired and immediately used. In most instances, expense flows from cost, as in the case of office supplies acquired and subsequently used over two or more periods.
3. Loss—an unfavorable effect (asset reduction) not directly related to normal operations such as storm loss, loss on sale of fixed assets, and loss due to theft. In practice, losses are broadly classified as an expense.

FORM OF INCOME STATEMENT

The accounting profession has not specified a particular format that must be used for the income statement because reasonable flexibility to fit various situations is considered more important than a standard format. A complete income statement is required that adequately reports all revenues and expenses. In addition, a number of *ARBs*, *APB Opinions*, and FASB *Statements* specify certain disclosure requirements that influence income statement presentation. Examples are presentation of extraordinary items, income tax expense, earnings per share, and items that are *either* unusual or occur infrequently.

Two different formats are widely used for the income statement, although there are numerous variations of each. These are generally referred to as the single-step and the multiple-step formats. A recent study of 600 major companies reported that 65% use the single-step and 35% use the multiple-step format.[5]

Single-Step Format

The single-step format focuses on two classifications: revenues and expenses. These two classifications are viewed broadly as defined in APB *Statement No. 4* (see definitions on pages 109 and 110). A single-step income statement is illustrated in Exhibit 4–2. Observe the three basic categories: revenues, expenses, and extraordinary items. It is aptly

[5] AICPA, *Accounting Trends and Techniques, 1975* (New York, 1975), p. 247. This is an excellent reference for learning how various companies handle the multitude of different items on financial statements.

EXHIBIT 4–2
Single-Step Income Statement

ILLUSTRATIVE COMPANY
Income Statement
For the Year Ended December 31, 1976

Revenues:		
Sales (less returns and allowances of $10,000)		$540,000
Services		130,000
Rent		1,200
Interest and dividends		4,800
Gain on sale of fixed assets		6,000
Total Revenues		682,000
Expenses:		
*Cost of goods sold	$314,000	
*Distribution	153,500	
*Administrative	73,500	
Depreciation	54,000	
Interest	6,000	
Loss on sale of investments	5,000	
Income taxes	29,500	
Total Expenses		635,500
Income before extraordinary item		46,500
Extraordinary item:		
Loss (specified)	10,000	
Less: Tax savings	4,800	5,200
Net Income		$ 41,300

Earnings per share on common stock (20,000 shares outstanding):	
Income before extraordinary item	$2.33
Extraordinary loss	.26
Net Income	$2.07

* These items may be detailed in the statement, or separately in the notes to the financial statements, or as separate schedules.

called a single-step statement because there is only one step—income before extraordinary items—involving revenues and expenses. Exhibit 4–2 shows a "pure" single-step format; therefore, all revenues are grouped under one classification. This includes gains (other than extraordinary) such as the one illustrated. A gain is distinctly different from the other revenue items illustrated in that it reflects a net difference. That is, the $6,000 gain is the result of a transaction such as:

Cash received from sale of fixed asset	$15,000
Less book value of the asset sold	9,000
Gain from sale of fixed asset	$ 6,000

In contrast, all other revenues are gross in the sense that the related expenses are deducted separately.

Consistent with the broad classification of revenues, all expenses are included under one broad category consistent with the definition quoted above from APB *Statement No. 4*. Included in the expenses illustrated is a *loss* which is distinctly different from the other expenses because it is a net difference as illustrated above for the gain.

There are numerous variations of the single-step format, such as:

1. Reporting income taxes separate from expenses (as a separate item immediately preceding income before extraordinary items).
2. Reporting one or more separate captions for certain revenues and expenses (such as, *financial items*—interest revenue and interest expense; *other revenues and expenses*—interest, dividends, gains and losses; and *other charges and credits*). When one of these three captions is used, it is located immediately above the caption, "income before extraordinary items."

The single-step format enjoys wide use because the broad classifications make it very flexible. Classification problems are minimized, and the presentation is simplified. On the other hand, some accountants feel that more intermediary differences, such as *gross margin on sales*, should be reported for the convenience of the decision-maker.

Multiple-Step Format

This format focuses on multiple classifications, multiple intermediary differences, and relatively more detail. The multiple-step format is illustrated in Exhibit 4–3. Observe that the first major intermediary difference is gross margin on sales followed by income from operations, income before taxes and extraordinary items, income before extraordinary items, and finally, net income. There are no broad classifications for revenues and expenses; rather they are reported under several different classifications. Those who prefer the multiple-step format believe that the multiple classifications communicate better information to the user. Disadvantages often cited focus on relative inflexibility, as evidenced by these common complaints: (1) difficulty in naming and defining appropriate subcategories of revenues and expenses, (2) separation of revenues and expenses into several categories implies a priority that is hard to defend, and (3) difficulty of reporting service revenue when there is also sales revenue—inclusion of service revenue with sales revenue distorts the intermediary amount, gross margin on sales.

Like the single step format, the multiple-step format has many variations. However, the differences are above the caption, "income before extraordinary items."

The diversity in income statement formats reflects the efforts of the entity to tailor the statement to the particular situation and reflects, in part, their conception of what should be communicated and how it should be communicated to the user. Income statements are presented in the Appendixes to this and the following chapter for your study.

Manufacturing Situation. An income statement of a manufacturing company differs from others in the presentation of manufacturing

EXHIBIT 4–3
Multiple-Step Income Statement

MELON COMPANY
Income Statement
For the Year Ended December 31, 1976

Sales revenue			$600,000
Less: Sales returns and allowances			18,600
Net Sales			581,400
Cost of goods sold:			
Beginning merchandise inventory		$152,000	
Merchandise purchases	$376,500		
Freight-in	1,200		
Cost of purchases	377,700		
Less: Purchase returns and allowances	12,200	365,500	
Total Goods Available for Sale		517,500	
Less: Ending merchandise inventory		159,500	
Cost of Goods Sold			358,000
Gross margin on sales			223,400
*Operating expenses:			
Distribution expenses		110,000	
General and administrative expenses		43,000	
Total Operating Expenses			153,000
Income from primary operations			70,400
Other revenues:			
Rent	1,200		
Interest and dividends	4,800		
Gain on sale of fixed assets	12,000	18,000	
Other expenses:			
Interest	4,500		
Loss on sale of investments	3,500	8,000	10,000
Income before income taxes and extraordinary item			80,400
Income taxes			32,090
Income before extraordinary item			48,310
Extraordinary item:			
Loss due to earthquake		10,000	
Less: Tax saving		4,800	5,200
Net Income			$ 43,110

Earnings per share on common stock (20,000 shares outstanding):

Income before extraordinary item	$2.42
Extraordinary loss	.26
Net Income	$2.16

* These may be detailed on the statement or separately in the notes to the financial statements as separate schedules.

costs. In a trading company, goods are purchased ready for sale, but a manufacturing company makes its own goods for sale. In the latter case, "merchandise purchases" is replaced by "cost of goods manufactured," and a statement of cost of goods manufactured is often prepared as a supporting schedule to the income statement.

If the Melon Company manufactured the goods sold, the cost of goods sold section of the income statement in Exhibit 4–3 would appear as follows:

Cost of goods sold (for a manufacturing firm):		
Finished goods inventory, January 1, 1976	$152,000	
Cost of goods manufactured (see manufacturing schedule)	365,500	
Total Goods Available for Sale	517,500	
Less: Finished goods inventory, December 31, 1976	159,500	
Cost of Goods Sold		$358,000

A supporting schedule of cost of goods manufactured details the costs of production generally as follows:

Manufacturing Schedule

MELON COMPANY
Cost of Goods Manufactured
For the Year Ended December 31, 1976

Raw material:			
Inventory, January 1, 1976		$ 28,000	
Purchases	$196,400		
Less: Returned purchases	800	195,600	
Freight-in		900	
Material available for issue		224,500	
Inventory, December 31, 1976		31,000	
Cost of material consumed			$193,500
Direct labor			106,200
Manufacturing expenses (factory overhead):			
Depreciation – buildings		2,200	
Depreciation – machinery		15,100	
Fuel		20,900	
Insurance – buildings and machinery		480	
Indirect labor		16,100	
Repairs – buildings		1,920	
Repairs – machinery		2,800	
Taxes – plant and equipment		1,600	
			61,100
Goods in process:			
Inventory, January 1, 1976		26,800	
Inventory, December 31, 1976		22,100	
Decrease			4,700
Cost of Goods Manufactured			$365,500

Supporting Expense Schedules. Occasionally, it is desirable to provide detailed information with respect to the summarized amounts shown on an income statement. Generally, this is best done with one or more supplementary schedules. One such schedule was illustrated above for manufacturing costs. A detailed schedule of operating expenses to supplement the income statement given in Exhibit 4–3 could be as follows:

MELON COMPANY
Schedule of Operating Expenses
For the Year Ended December 31, 1976

Operating expenses:		
Distribution expenses:		
Advertising	$32,000	
Salaries	35,000	
Commissions	31,000	
Freight-out	3,000	
Insurance on inventory	1,000	
Other selling expenses	8,000	$110,000
General and administrative expenses:		
Office expenses	4,800	
Office payroll	32,100	
Depreciation of office equipment	1,100	
Rent	2,000	
Bad debt expense	3,000	43,000
Total Operating Expenses		$153,000

SPECIAL PROBLEMS AFFECTING THE INCOME STATEMENT

Until the 1930s the balance sheet, as a statement of financial position, was viewed by the business community as dominant because the assets owned and the liabilities owed were considered to be the most important indicator of the future potential of an enterprise. However, there was a gradual shift to recognizing the ability of the enterprise to generate income and cash which is more significant. Consequently, the income statement assumed a dominant role. Although the importance of cash flow has been largely overlooked in financial reporting, currently it is coming to the forefront.[6]

Because of the importance attached to the income statement for several decades, the accounting profession has focused on refining the concepts and accounting procedures for the measurement and reporting of net income. Consequently, the pronouncements by the several accounting groups, particularly the FASB, AICPA and the AAA, tend to focus on the income statement. In the remainder of this chapter, we will review the important income reporting issues on which the profession has taken a definite position.

DISCLOSURE PROBLEMS

Recall the discussions of full disclosure under the reporting principle in Chapter 2. This broad principle encompasses all external financial reporting. With respect to the income statement, full disclosure is par-

[6] AICPA, *Objectives of Financial Statements* (New York, October 1973). This report, often referred to as the Trueblood Report, states on page 62: "Creditors and investors are concerned with the ability of the enterprise to generate cash flows to them and with their ability to predict, compare, and evaluate the amount, timing, and related uncertainty of these future cash flows. An objective of financial statements is to provide information to investors and creditors for predicting, comparing, and evaluating potential cash flows to them in terms of amount, timing, and related uncertainty." Cash flow is discussed in Chapter 21, Statement of Changes in Financial Position.

ticularly critical. There is a limit to the extent of disclosure possible in the income statement itself by way of titles, amounts, and parenthetical information. Therefore, the typical income statement refers to a number of *notes to the financial statements*. Typically, these notes include elaborations such as amounts, schedules, and written explanations. Their objective is a presentation of information, essential to full disclosure, that cannot be effectively communicated in another manner. Therefore, they must be viewed as an important supplement to the financial statements. Generally, pronouncements of the profession on reporting specific items specify that they may, or in some cases must, be disclosed in footnotes when it is impractical to adequately present the information in the statement itself.

DEPRECIATION

APB Opinion No. 12, paragraph five, requires that *(a)* the amount of depreciation expense for the period, and *(b)* the method or methods of depreciation used, be disclosed either in the financial statements or in the notes thereto. This requirement was instituted because depreciation is a noncash expense; therefore, it must be considered in assessing the amount of cash outflow that was needed to meet expenses. Also, since the amount of depreciation expense reported depends upon internal decisions of management rather than on external transactions, it is subject to considerable latitude. Statement users need to know both the amount of depreciation expense and how it was determined (i.e., the method of depreciation used) in order to evaluate its impact on net income, assets, and cash flows.

Since 1967 all financial statements have reported depreciation expense. *Accounting Trends and Techniques, 1974* (AICPA), shows that of 600 major companies, 42% reported it in the income statement and 58% disclosed it in a footnote to the statement. In a manufacturing enterprise, one must remember that much of the depreciation expense may be included in the inventory and cost of goods sold amounts; therefore, reporting by footnote is characteristic of these kinds of companies.

INCOME TAXES

Income taxes are assessed on profit-making corporations but not on sole proprietorships or partnerships. In contrast, the income of a sole proprietorship and partnership must be reported as income to the owners.[7] In turn, the stockholder must pay income taxes on dividends received; consequently, it is sometimes argued that corporate income is subject to double taxation.

Income taxes paid by corporations are viewed as an expense (as

[7] There are certain exceptions. For example, a corporation that qualifies under Subchapter S, Internal Revenue Code, is viewed, for income tax purposes, the same as a partnership. These are generally referred to as "Subchapter S Corporations."

opposed to a partial distribution of profits to the government); and because of their amount, they must meet the requirements of the full-disclosure principle. To meet these requirements, *APB Opinion No. 11* (1967) prescribed two types of income tax allocation procedures:

1. Intraperiod Tax Allocation – This requires that the income tax for the year be allocated within and between the income statement and the statement of retained earnings. It is an allocation of income tax expense within a single period.
2. Interperiod Tax Allocation – This requires that income tax *expense* for the period (for income statement purposes) and income taxes *payable* (for balance sheet purposes) be separately computed. Any difference is recorded as deferred income taxes. These situations arise when there is a revenue or expense on the income statement for the current year that appears on the income tax return either before or after the current year. This comes about because accounting principles and tax laws do not always agree as to the year in which the revenue or expense should fall. It is an allocation of income tax expense between periods. This type of allocation is discussed in Chapter 11 (liabilities).

Intraperiod Tax Allocation

The need for allocation of income tax expense within and between the income statement, statement of retained earnings, and balance sheet is explained in *APB Opinion No. 11* as follows:

> The need for tax allocation within a period arises because items included in the determination of taxable income may be presented for accounting purposes as *(a)* extraordinary items, *(b)* adjustments of prior periods (or of the opening balance of retained earnings) or *(c)* as direct entries to other stockholders' accounts.[8]

The concept underlying intraperiod tax allocation is that on the financial statements for the period, *the income tax consequences should be reported along with the transaction that caused the tax expense.* Thus, total income tax expense for the period must be allocated to (1) income before extraordinary items, (2) extraordinary items, (3) prior period adjustments (retained earnings), and (4) direct entries to other stockholders' accounts to the extent that there are items in each category that affected total income tax expense for the period. Clearly, in most cases income tax expense for the period will be directly related to the first two categories – income before extraordinary items and extraordinary items. Seldom do the last two categories (prior period adjustments and other owners' equity accounts) affect income taxes.

Intraperiod tax allocation (sometimes called interstatement allocation) is not complicated or controversial. Exhibits 4–4, 4–5, and 4–6 illustrate application of the concept in three different situations. Note in

---

[8] AICPA, "Accounting for Income Taxes," *Accounting Principles Board Opinion No. 11*, (New York, 1967).

EXHIBIT 4–4
Intraperiod Tax Allocation – with Extraordinary Gain

Situation

A Corporation accounts for the period reflected the following:

1. Income before income taxes and before extraordinary items, $100,000.
2. Extraordinary gain (specified), $40,000.
3. Income tax expense, $60,700.*

A CORPORATION
Partial Income Statement

Income before income taxes and extraordinary items.........		$100,000
Less: Applicable income taxes		41,500
Income before extraordinary items		58,500
Extraordinary items:		
Gain on extraordinary item (designated)........................	$40,000	
Less: Applicable income tax	19,200	
Extraordinary gain, net of applicable income tax......		20,800
Net Income		$ 79,300

* Computation of tax allocation:
Tax on ordinary income:
$25,000 × 22% = $ 5,500
$75,000 × 48% = 36,000 ..... $41,500

Tax on extraordinary item
$40,000 × 48% = ... 19,200
Total Income Tax Allocated $60,700

Entry for income taxes:

Income tax expense	60,700	
Income taxes payable		60,700

EXHIBIT 4–5
Intraperiod Tax Allocation – with Extraordinary Loss

Situation

B Corporation accounts for the period reflected the following:

1. Income before income taxes and before extraordinary items, $100,000.
2. Loss on earthquake damage, $40,000.
3. Income tax expense, $22,300.*

B CORPORATION
Partial Income Statement

Income before income taxes and extraordinary items.........		$100,000
Less: Applicable income taxes		41,500
Income before extraordinary items		58,500
Extraordinary items:		
Extraordinary loss	$40,000	
Less: Applicable tax saving	19,200	
Extraordinary loss, net of applicable income tax		20,800
Net Income		$ 37,700

* Computation of tax allocation:
Tax on ordinary income:
$25,000 × 22% = $ 5,500
$75,000 × 48% = 36,000 ..... $41,500

Tax saving on extraordinary loss:
$40,000 × 48% = ... (19,200)
Total Income Tax Allocated.........$22,300

Entry for income taxes:

Income tax expense	22,300	
Income taxes payable		22,300

EXHIBIT 4–6
Intraperiod Tax Allocation—Retained Earnings Affected

Situation

C Corporation records for the period reflected the following:

1. Income before income taxes and before extraordinary items, $100,000.
2. Loss on earthquake damage, $40,000.
3. Income tax expense, $118,300.*
4. Claim for damages settled and collected (lawsuit), $200,000 (a prior period adjustment).
5. Balance retained earnings, beginning of period, $140,000.
6. Dividends paid during year, $20,000.

C CORPORATION
Partial Income Statement

Income before income taxes and extraordinary items......		$100,000
Less: Applicable income tax......................................		41,500
Income before extraordinary items................................		58,500
Extraordinary items:		
Extraordinary loss	$ 40,000	
Less: Applicable income tax saving	19,200	
Extraordinary loss, net of applicable income tax ...		(20,800)
Net Income...		$ 37,700

C CORPORATION
Statement of Retained Earnings

Retained earnings at beginning of period:		
As previously reported		$140,000
Add: Damages collected (lawsuit settled)	$200,000	
Less: Applicable income tax	96,000	104,000
Beginning balance restated		244,000
Add: Net income for period		37,700
		281,700
Deduct: Dividends paid during period		20,000
Retained earnings, end of period		$261,700

* Computation of tax allocation:

Tax on ordinary loss:	
$25,000 × 22% = $ 5,500	
$75,000 × 48% = 36,000	$ 41,500
Tax saving on extraordinary item:	
$40,000 × 48% =	(19,200)
Tax on retained earnings item:	
$200,000 × 48% =	96,000
Total Taxes Allocated	$118,300

Entry for income taxes:

Income tax expense	22,300	
Prior period adjustment (income taxes)	96,000	
Income taxes payable......		118,300

each exhibit that total income tax expense for the period is simply allocated to each of the four categories (listed above) so that the tax consequence follows the item that gives rise to the tax. You should particularly be aware in each illustration of the several amounts that would be incorrectly reported without intraperiod allocation of income tax expense. For example, in Exhibit 4–6, if one were to report total tax expense ($118,300) as a direct reduction from pretax income ($100,000) at least four amounts would be misstated: income before extraordinary items, net extraordinary loss, net income, and restated balance of retained earnings.

In computing the amount of income tax expense for each separate category, the assumption was made that the tax applies first to normal operations and then to the other items. Thus, in Exhibit 4–6, extraordinary items and prior period adjustments were taxed at the 48% rate. Another method of computing the interstatement tax allocation that has been widely used is based on an "average" tax rate for the period. Essentially this method involves computation of the average tax rate for the period then allocating income taxes to each classification on a proportional basis by utilizing this average. Since the issuance of *APB Opinion No. 11* in 1967 the averaging method has been used less frequently.

EARNINGS PER SHARE

Earnings per share (EPS) is the relationship between reported income and outstanding shares of common stock (i.e., income ÷ average number shares of common stock outstanding). EPS is not computed on preferred stock. The reporting of EPS amounts has long been common in various information and press releases directed at investors and the financial community. Also, PE ratios are now reported daily in the news media. The practice has grown and, for accountants, has recently undergone a rapid evolution which has now proceeded to the point that reporting earnings per share on the face of the income statement, on which the accountant is expressing professional opinion, is mandatory.

Historically, reporting earnings per share on statements appearing in annual reports was optional prior to the issuance of *APB Opinion No. 9* in December 1966. In that *Opinion* the Accounting Principles Board stated "that earnings per share data are most useful when furnished in conjunction with a statement of income." Accordingly, the Board *strongly recommends* that earnings per share be disclosed in the statement of income. It is the Board's opinion that the reporting of per share data should disclose amounts for *(a)* income before extraordinary items; *(b)* extraordinary items, if any (less applicable income tax); and *(c)* net income—the total of *(a)* and *(b)*. *APB Opinion No. 15* issued in May 1969 changed the recommendation to a *requirement*. The latter *Opinion* calls for two presentations of earnings per share on the income statement: *(a)* primary earnings per share, and *(b)* fully diluted earnings per share. These terms are explained and discussed later in this section.

APB Opinion No. 15 is a lengthy, complex document. Only its highlights will be presented here; it is not feasible to attempt a discussion of all of the details covered in its more than 60 pages of text and ex-

EXHIBIT 4–7
Calculation of Earnings per Share under Increasingly Complex Cases

<table>
<tr><th>Assumptions</th><th>Calculation and Reporting EPS</th></tr>
<tr><td>Case A
Assumptions: 30,000 common shares outstanding throughout the year; net income for the year $96,000.</td><td>Net income $96,000
Earnings per common share ($96,000 ÷ 30,000 shares) .... $3.20</td></tr>
<tr><td>Case B
Assumptions: 30,000 common shares outstanding throughout the year; income before extraordinary items, $96,000, extraordinary loss less applicable tax saving $21,000; net income for year $75,000.</td><td>Income before extraordinary item $96,000
Extraordinary loss less applicable tax saving 21,000
Net Income $75,000
Earnings per common share:
Income before extraordinary item $3.20
Extraordinary loss .... .70
Net Income $2.50

$96,000 ÷ 30,000 shares = $3.20
21,000 ÷ " = .70
75,000 ÷ " = 2.50</td></tr>
<tr><td>Case C
Assumptions: 30,000 common shares outstanding from January 1 through April 1, on which date an additional 10,000 common shares were sold; other data as in Case B.</td><td>Income before extraordinary item $96,000
Extraordinary loss less applicable tax saving 21,000
Net Income $75,000
Earnings per common share:
Income before extraordinary item $2.56
Extraordinary loss .... .56
Net Income $2.00

Calculation of weighted average number of shares:
Inclusive dates | Months | Shares | Product
Jan. 1–Apr. 1 | 3 | 30,000 | 90,000
Apr. 1–Dec. 31 | 9 | 40,000 | 360,000
| 12 | | 450,000

Average: 450,000 ÷ 12 = 37,500

$96,000 ÷ 37,500 shares = $2.56
21,000 ÷ " = .56
75,000 ÷ " = $2.00</td></tr>
<tr><td>Case D
Assumptions: 30,000 common shares outstanding from January 1 through April 1, on which date an additional 10,000 common shares were issued as a stock dividend; other data as in Case B (no additional shares were sold).</td><td>Income before extraordinary item $96,000
Extraordinary loss less applicable tax saving 21,000
Net Income $75,000
Earnings per common share:
Income before extraordinary item $2.40
Extraordinary loss .... .53
Net Income $1.87

As provided in APB Opinion No. 9, when there is a stock dividend the divisor is the number of shares outstanding at year-end (in this case 40,000).

$96,000 ÷ 40,000 shares = $2.40
21,000 ÷ " = .53
75,000 ÷ " = 1.87</td></tr>
</table>

hibits. Further, approximately a year after its publication *Opinion No. 15* was supplemented by an interpretive booklet of well over 100 pages.[9]

The simplest possible calculation of earnings per share in compliance with *Opinion No. 15* would involve a company with only common stock authorized, all of which had remained outstanding throughout its fiscal year. If such a company had only ordinary income, that is, no extraordinary items, calculation of its earnings per share for the year would merely involve dividing the net income by the number of shares. See Exhibit 4–7, Case A.

A slight advance in complexity would have the company experience an extraordinary gain or loss in arriving at its net income. In this case, earnings per share figures would be reported for income before extraordinary items and for net income. See Exhibit 4–7, Case B.

The next advance in complexity would involve a company with only common stock and had experienced an increase in the number of shares outstanding during the period due to the sale of common stock or the purchase of treasury shares. A material increase due to the sale of additional shares would call for the calculation of the weighted average of the number of shares outstanding. See Exhibit 4–7, Case C. However, a material increase due to a stock dividend or stock split would call for simply dividing by the number of shares outstanding at year-end.[10] See Exhibit 4–7, Case D.

The next level of complexity involve situations where there is both common and preferred stock; beyond those are situations where there are convertible securities (i.e., convertible preferred stock and convertible bonds) that may be converted into common stock. These complexities involve the concepts of common stock equivalents and fully diluted earnings per share. These situations are discussed in Chapter 17.

EXTRAORDINARY ITEMS AND PRIOR PERIOD ADJUSTMENTS

Recall that extraordinary items are reported in a separate category on the income statement and prior period adjustments are reported on the statement of retained earnings (*APB Opinions No. 9* and *No. 30*). These two types of items have been controversial for a number of years because they are (*a*) difficult to define precisely, and (*b*) of different concepts of net income.

---

[9] AICPA, "Reporting the Results of Operations," *APB Opinion No. 9* (New York, 1966), p. 119 (emphasis supplied) *Opinion No. 15* requires EPS for (*a*) income before extraordinary items, and (*b*) net income. EPS on extraordinary items is recommended but not mandatory. Also, J T. Ball, *Computing Earnings per Share, Unofficial Interpretations of APB Opinion No. 15* (New York AICPA, 1970).

[10] If the common shares change as a result of a stock dividend or split (or reverse split), the computations should give retroactive recognition to an appropriate equivalent change in capital structure for all periods presented in the case of comparative statements. Where such changes occur after the close of a fiscal period but before statements are issued, per share computations should be based on the new number of shares since readers' primary interests are presumably related to current capitalization. Disclosure should reflect the number of shares in the calculation.

Concepts of Net Income

For a number of years, two different concepts of net income were prominent in accounting practice and literature. These concepts usually are referred to as the *current operating concept* and the *all-inclusive concept*.[11] Fundamentally, they differed with respect to whether unusual and infrequently occurring gains and losses should be included in net income and, consequently, reported on the income statement.

The *current operating concept* holds that in the measurement and reporting of net income, *only* the operating revenues and expenses should be included. Thus, the unusual, or nonoperating, and infrequently recurring gains and losses should be viewed as direct debits (decreases) and credits (increases) to Retained Earnings and reported on the statement of retained earnings. In contrast, the *all-inclusive concept* holds that in measuring and reporting net income, all operating revenues and expenses and all unusual and infrequently recurring gains and losses should be included. Under this concept, the statement of retained earnings would report only the net income, or loss, and dividends declared for the period. The two concepts in their pure form are compared in Exhibit 4–8. This exhibit emphasizes the point at issue—*what* should be included in net income? Observe that the current operating concept in this case shows a net income of $100,000 compared with $160,000 under the all-inclusive concept. From this, it is not difficult to perceive that it is an important issue.

It is generally correct to say that historically the AICPA favored the current operating concept whereas the AAA tended to favor the all-inclusive concept. With the issuance of *Opinion No. 9* in December 1966, the APB took a compromise position which leaned strongly toward the all-inclusive concept. That *Opinion* requires that all of the unusual, nonoperating, and infrequently recurring items be included in the computation of net income and reported separately on the income statement, except for a very limited range of items called prior period adjustments. The *Opinion* specified that the prior period adjustments should be reported on the statement of retained earnings and accounted for as direct debits and credits to Retained Earnings. *APB Opinion No. 9* set forth the basic principle as follows:

> Net income should reflect all items of profit and loss recognized during the period with the sole exception of the prior period adjustments described below. *Extraordinary items* should, however, be segregated from the results of ordinary operations and shown separately in the income statement, with disclosure of the nature and amounts thereof.
>
> Under this approach, the income statement should disclose the following elements:
>
> Income before extraordinary items
> Extraordinary items (less applicable income tax)
> Net Income[12]

---

[11] Some synonyms for *current operating performance* include "earnings power" and for *all-inclusive* "clean surplus" and "historical."

[12] AICPA, *APB Opinion No. 9*, pars. 17 and 20.

EXHIBIT 4–8
Operating and All-Inclusive Concepts Compared

Income Statement

Operating Concept		*All-Inclusive Concept*	
Operating revenues	$980,000	Operating revenues	$980,000
Operating expenses	(880,000)	Operating expenses	(880,000)
		Unusual and infrequently occurring items:	
		Gain—expropriation of plant by foreign government	30,000
		Loss—earthquake damages	(10,000)
		Gain—damages received in lawsuit	80,000
		Loss—additional assessment of income taxes, prior years	(40,000)
Net Income	$100,000	Net Income	$160,000

Statement of Retained Earnings

Operating Concept		*All-Inclusive Concept*	
Beginning balance	$ 75,000	Beginning balance	$ 75,000
Add net income	100,000	Add net income	160,000
Total	175,000	Total	235,000
Deduct:		Deduct:	
Dividends	(50,000)	Dividends	(50,000)
Unusual and infrequently occurring items:			
Gain—expropriation of plant by foreign government	30,000		
Loss—earthquake damages	(10,000)		
Gain—damages received in lawsuit	80,000		
Loss—additional assessment of income taxes, prior years	(40,000)		
Ending Balance	$185,000	Ending Balance	$185,000

Extraordinary Items

Extraordinary items were defined in *APB Opinion No. 9;* however, the definition was imprecise, resulting in wide variation in application. It became a favorite way to "doctor" income before extraordinary items. Since investors are interested in a representative income amount useful for projecting future income potentials, the caption, "extraordinary items," became especially critical. Because of the dollar amount of the items under this caption, net income was often primarily composed of items which would not recur in the reasonable future and were not directly related to ongoing operations.

As a consequence, the APB issued *Opinion No. 30,* in June 1973. It was hoped that a redefinition of extraordinary items would correct the abuses. The definition of extraordinary items provided by *Opinion No. 30* is very restrictive, viz:

> Criteria for Extraordinary Items:
>
> Judgment is required to segregate in the income statement the effects of events or transactions that are extraordinary. . . . an event or transaction should be presumed to be an ordinary and usual activity of the reporting entity . . . unless the evidence clearly supports its classification as an extraordinary item as defined in this opinion.
>
> Extraordinary items are events and transactions that are distinguished by their unusual nature *and* by the infrequency of their occurrence. Thus, *both* of the following criteria should be met to classify an event or transaction as an extraordinary item:
>
> *a. Unusual nature*—The underlying event or transaction should possess a high degree of abnormality and be of a type clearly unrelated to, or only incidentally related to, the ordinary and typical activities of the entity, taking into account the environment in which the entity operates.
> *b. Infrequency of occurrence*—The underlying event or transaction should be of a type that would not reasonably be expected to recur in the foreseeable future, taking into account the environment in which the entity operates.[13]

There are two aspects of the above definitions that should be emphasized. First, both criteria must be met. Thus, an item that meets *either,* but not both, does not qualify as an extraordinary item. Obviously, there are not many such items. Secondly, in applying the two criteria, the *environment* in which the entity operates is often controlling. For example, earthquake damage usually would be extraordinary—it is certainly unusual and occurs infrequently in most parts of the world. However, if one were to locate a plant on a fault where earthquakes occur regularly, earthquake damage would be an ordinary item in that *particular environment;* the damage would be neither unusual nor

---

[13] AICPA, "Reporting the Results of Operations," *APB Opinion No. 30* (New York, 1973), pars. 19–20.

infrequent. Thus, whether an event or transaction is extraordinary ordinarily depends not on the type of event but rather *on the environment in which it occurs* (i.e., the situation). This basic point is overlooked in most discussions of extraordinary items; however, it is fully discussed in *Opinion No. 30*. The *Opinion* list only three different kinds of events that usually would be classified as extraordinary: (1) a major casualty, such as an earthquake; (2) expropriation by a foreign government; and (3) prohibition under a newly enacted law or regulation.

The *Opinion* specifically states that the following should not be considered as extraordinary items because they result from customary and continuing business activities:

a. Write-down or write-off of receivables, inventories, equipment leased to others, or other intangible assets.
b. Gains or losses from exchange or translation of foreign currencies, including those related to major devaluations or revaluations.
c. Gains or losses on disposal of a segment of a business.
d. Other gains or losses from sale of abandonment of property, plant, or equipment used in the business.
e. Effects of a strike, including those against competitors and major suppliers.
f. Adjustments of accruals on long-term contracts.

Because of the widespread misunderstanding of extraordinary items, as defined in *Opinion No. 30*, we have included some specific examples in Appendix A to this chapter.[14]

Reporting Unusual or Infrequent Items

In the discussion above, we referred to items that are *either* unusual or infrequent, but not both. They do not qualify as extraordinary items; however, they should be called to the attention of the statement user to fulfill the *full-disclosure* requirement. Therefore, *APB Opinion No. 30* requires that they be reported separately on the income statement, viz:

> A material event or transaction that is unusual in nature or occurs infrequently, but not both, and therefore does not meet both criteria for classification as an extraordinary item, should be reported as a separate component of income from continuing operations. The nature and financial effects of each event and transaction should be disclosed on the face of the income statement, or alternatively, in notes to the financial statement.[15]

To illustrate, items that are *either* unusual or infrequent, but not both, should be reported along the following lines to meet the full-disclosure requirement:

---

[14] AICPA, "Accounting Interpretations, APB Opinion No. 30," *The Journal of Accountancy,* November 1973, pp. 82–84.

[15] AICPA, *APB Opinion No. 30,* par. 26.

Income Statement (Partial)

Pretax income from continuing operations		$112,000
Unusual or infrequent items (see Note X):		
Loss from disposal of long-term investment	$43,000	
Gain on disposal of machinery	31,000	12,000
Total		100,000
Income tax on operations and unusual or infrequent items		41,500
Income before extraordinary item		58,500
Extraordinary item:		
Loss due to hurricane damage (less applicable tax saving); see Note Y		26,500
Net Income		$ 32,000
Earnings per share of common stock (20,000 shares outstanding):		
Income before extraordinary item		$2.93
Extraordinary loss		1.33
Net Income		$1.60

Other formats can be devised to display the unusual or infrequent items in ways that meet the spirit of the above quotation from *Opinion No. 30.*

Prior Period Adjustments

Since prior period adjustments never flow through the income statement but are direct debits or credits to Retained Earnings, they were defined very restrictively in *APB Opinion No. 9.* They are further removed from continuing operations than are extraordinary items. The *Opinion* specifies four criteria, all of which must be met, for an item to qualify for treatment as a prior period adjustment, viz:

1. Can be specifically identified with and directly related to the business activities of a particular prior period.
2. Are not attributable to economic events occurring subsequent to the date of the financial statement for the prior period.
3. Depend primarily on determinations by persons other than the management.
4. Were not susceptible to reasonable estimation prior to the current period.

This restrictive definition means that prior period adjustments are rare. Three examples, that often qualify, cited in the *Opinion* are: (1) nonrecurring adjustments or settlements of income taxes from prior years, (2) public utility settlements with regulatory bodies, and (3) settlement of court litigations. Reporting of prior period adjustments is illustrated in Exhibit 4–9.

A prior period adjustment is best recorded in the accounts in a special adjustment account, appropriately titled, rather than as a direct entry to Retained Earnings. Special adjustment accounts are closed to Retained

Earnings at the end of the period. Recall that this is the procedure usually used for dividends to shareholders; a *dividends* account is debited which is then closed to Retained Earnings at the end of the period. It is helpful to think of the accounts that are set up for closing to Retained Earnings as the same amounts that are reported on the statement of retained earnings. The same kind of correspondence can be attained with respect to the revenue and expense accounts. They are closed to Income Summary and are the accounts and amounts reported on the income statement.

ACCOUNTING CHANGES

Accounting changes are discussed in detail in Chapter 20; however, it is necessary at this point to review some aspects of them. Accounting changes involve four distinctly different types of situations; and each requires a different accounting treatment. The four types of accounting changes specified in *APB Opinion No. 20* are:[16]

1. *Accounting errors.* The use of inappropriate accounting principles (including procedures) and unsupportable estimates, outright mathematical mistakes, oversights, and failure to properly reflect the economic essence of a transaction all constitute accounting errors.
2. *Changes in estimates.* The use of estimates (such as in determining depreciation or bad debt expense) is a natural consequence of the accounting process. From time to time, experience and additional information make it possible for estimates to be improved. For example, a fixed asset, after having been used (and depreciated) for 6 years, may realistically be changed from the original 10-year estimated life to a 15-year estimated life. Changes of this type are referred to as "changes in estimates" and are to be distinguished from an error or change in accounting principle.
3. *Changes in accounting principle.* Because of a change in circumstances, or the development of a new accounting principle, a change in the recordkeeping and financial reporting approach to one or more types of transactions may be desirable or necessary. For example, a change in circumstances may make it desirable, from the accounting point of view, to change from straight-line depreciation to sum-of-the-years'-digits depreciation. This would be a change in accounting principle, that is, a change from one acceptable principle to another acceptable principle.
4. *Change in the accounting entity* (see Chapter 20).

Now let's review briefly the accounting and reporting approach that is appropriate for the first two of these accounting changes. Type 3 and 4 changes will be discussed in subsequent chapters. You should observe in this brief discussion that each type of accounting change calls for a different approach to accommodate it appropriately.

---

[16] AICPA, "Accounting Changes," *APB Opinion No. 20* (New York, 1971).

Treatment of Accounting Errors

Clearly, when an error in the accounting process is identified it should be corrected immediately in such a way as to reflect what the results would have been had the error not been committed. Thus, when an error is found that was committed in the *current year*, the accounts (and related schedules) should be corrected prior to preparation of the current financial reports. This normally can be best effected by reversing the incorrect entry and reentering the transaction correctly.

When an error is located during the current accounting period that was committed during some *prior period*, correction is more complex, especially where two or more past periods are affected. In this kind of situation a *correcting entry* must be made to reflect the correct current balances in the *real* accounts (i.e., the balance sheet accounts) and the *nominal* accounts (i.e., the income statement accounts). *APB Opinion No. 20* specifies the approach that should be used to correct this type of error. Often the correcting entry must include an "adjustment" amount; and the issue is whether this amount is to be treated as a normal operating item, an unusual or infrequent item, an extraordinary item, or a prior period adjustment. *Opinion No. 20* states: "The Board concludes that correction of an error in the financial statements of a prior period discovered subsequent to their issuance should be reported as a prior period adjustment." Thus, this type of error often requires recognition of a prior period adjustment in the accounts and on the statement of retained earnings.

To illustrate, assume a machine cost $10,000 (with a ten-year estimated useful life and no residual value), when purchased on January 1, 19A, was debited in full to an expense account. The error was discovered December 29, 19D. The following correcting entry would be required in 19D:

December 29, 19D:

Machinery	10,000	
Depreciation expense (for 19D)	1,000	
Accumulated depreciation (A through D)		4,000
Prior period adjustment, error correction		7,000

The Prior Period Adjustment, Error Correction account would be closed to Retained Earnings on December 31, 19D.

Treatment of Changes in Estimates

These kind of changes are not considered errors; they are changes in estimates such as the useful life, residual value, loss rate on bad debts, and estimated warranty costs. As a company attains more experience in these areas, there is often a sound basis for revising a prior estimate. *APB Opinion No. 20* specifies that in such instances the *prior* accounting results are not to be disturbed; simply, the new estimate is to be used over the remaining periods including the current period. Thus, a change in estimate is made on a *prospective* basis.

To illustrate, assume a machine that cost $24,000 is being depreciated on a straight-line basis over a ten-year estimated useful life with no residual value. Near the end of the seventh year, on the basis of more experience with the machine, it is estimated that the useful life should have been 14 years. Thus, the remaining life is now eight years. This is a change in estimate and at the end of the current year would require the following *adjusting entry* only:

December 31, current year:

Depreciation expense	1,200	
Accumulated depreciation, machinery		1,200

Computations:

Original cost	$24,000
Accumulated depreciation to date ($24,000 × 6/10)	14,440
Difference—to be depreciated over 8 years remaining life	$ 9,600
Annual depreciation over remaining life: $9,600 ÷ 8 years =	$ 1,200

Treatment of Changes in Accounting Principles

These kinds of changes are the result of decisions by the management because the newly selected principle is more appropriate in reflecting net income and financial position. When an accounting principle is changed a "correction" is required to reflect the effect of the change over. For example a company had depreciated a machine $2,200 to date using the straight-line method. A change was made to sum-of-the-years'-digits depreciation; the amount of depreciation would have been $3,400, indicating a "correction" of $1,200. The entry for the change would be:

Change in accounting principle (closed to income summary)	1,200	
Accumulated depreciation		1,200

This topic is discussed comprehensively in Chapter 20.

STATEMENT OF RETAINED EARNINGS

A statement of retained earnings usually is presented as a supplement to the income statement and balance sheet because it is needed to comply with the full-disclosure requirement. However, many companies are presenting a *statement of owners' equity* instead, which details all changes in owners' equity, not just retained earnings. The latter statement is discussed in Chapter 5 (see Exhibit 5–3).

The purpose of the statement of retained earnings is to report all changes in retained earnings during the year, to reconcile the beginning and ending balance of retained earnings, and to provide a connecting link between the income statement and the balance sheet. The ending balance of retained earnings is reported on the balance sheet as one element of owners' equity (see Exhibit 4–1) In accordance with *APB Opinion No. 9*, the major segments of a statement of retained earnings are (1) prior period adjustments, (2) net income or loss for the period, and

EXHIBIT 4–9
Statement of Retained Earnings Illustrated

ILLUSTRATIVE COMPANY
Statement of Retained Earnings
For the Year Ended December 31, 1976

Retained earnings, balance January 1, 1976	$ 77,400
Prior period adjustments:	
Additional income taxes assessed on income of prior years	(28,000)
Damages collected from settlement of lawsuit (net of tax)	15,000
Balance as adjusted	64,400
Add: Net income, 1976 (per income statement, Exhibit 4–2)	41,300
	105,700
Deduct: Cash dividends paid in 1976 ($1.50 per share)	30,000
Retained Earnings, Balance December 31, 1976 (Note 7)	$ 75,700

Note 7: Retained earnings—Of the $75,700 ending balance in retained earnings, $50,000 is restricted from dividend availability under the terms of the bond indenture. When the bonds are retired the restriction will be removed.

(3) dividends to stockholders. A typical statement of retained earnings is shown in Exhibit 4–9.

Restrictions on Retained Earnings

Restrictions on retained earnings serve to limit retained earnings' availability for dividends to the unrestricted balance. Restrictions may arise because of *legal requirements,* as in the case of treasury stock held (in some states); by *contract,* as in the case of a bond indenture; or by *management decision,* as in the case of "retained earnings appropriated for future plant expansion." When a restriction is removed the amount then returns to dividend availability. *Accounting Trends and Techniques, 1975* (AICPA) revealed that 71% of the 600 companies surveyed reported restrictions imposed by debt agreements, capital expenditures, treasury stock purchases, or contracts with outside parties. In years past, restrictions sometimes were reported as separate items on the statement of retained earnings (or balance sheet); however, in recent years they generally are reported in notes to the financial statements as illustrated in Exhibit 4–9. Retained earnings is discussed in depth in Chapter 16.

Combined Income Statement and Retained Earnings

The income statement and statement of retained earnings may be presented together in the form of a combined statement. *Accounting Trends and Techniques, 1975* (AICPA), reported that approximately 31% of the 600 leading companies studied followed this format. The primary advantage is that it brings together related and relevant information for the statement user. The following is a typical format at the bottom of the income statement:

Net income	$41,300
Retained earnings, January 1, 1976	77,400
Prior period adjustments (Note 6)	(13,000)
Cash dividends during 1976 ($1.50 per share)	(30,000)
Retained Earnings, December 31, 1976 (Note 7)	$75,700

Note 6: Prior period adjustments—During the year, the company was assessed additional income taxes from prior years in the amount of $28,000. Also during the year, a lawsuit, arising from an accident, was settled in favor of the company; damages amounting to $15,000 were collected (net of taxes).

Note 7: Restrictions—Of the $75,700 ending balance in retained earnings, $50,000 is restricted from dividend availability under the terms of the bond indenture. When the bonds are retired, the restriction will be removed.

ACTUAL FINANCIAL STATEMENTS

Throughout this chapter, we have used illustrative examples for instructional purposes. To enable you to move easily to real-life financial statements, we have included Appendixes at the end of this and the following chapter which present recent financial statements for two well-known companies. We have selected representative statements that use typical format and terminology. One set uses a modified single-step format for income statements, and the other a modified multiple-step format. We suggest that you constructively, but critically, examine these examples and relate them to what you have learned at this point in your study.

Appendix A. Characteristics and Examples of Extraordinary Items*

If it has been determined that the particular event or transaction is not a disposal of a segment of a business, then the criteria for extraordinary items classification should be considered. That is: Does the event or transaction meet both criteria of *unusual nature* and *infrequency of occurrence*?

Discussion. Paragraphs 19–22 of the *Opinion* discuss the criteria of unusual nature and infrequency of occurrence of events or transactions taking into account the environment in which the entity operates. Paragraph 23 specifies certain gains or losses which should not be reported as extraordinary unless they are the direct result of a major casualty, an

* Source: Excerpts from "Accounting Interpretations—APB Opinion 30," *Journal of Accountancy*, November 1973, pp. 82–84.

expropriation or a prohibition under a newly enacted law or regulation that clearly meets both criteria for extraordinary classification. Events or transactions which would meet both criteria in the circumstances described are:

10. A large portion of a tobacco manufacturer's crops are destroyed by a hail storm. Severe damage from hail storms in the locality where the manufacturer grows tobacco is rare.
11. A steel fabricating company sells the only land it owns. The land was acquired 10 years ago for future expansion, but shortly thereafter the company abandoned all plans for expansion and held the land for appreciation.
12. A company sells a block of common stock of a publicly traded company. The block of shares, which represents less than 10 percent of the publicly held company, is the only security investment the company has ever owned.
13. An earthquake destroys one of the oil refineries owned by a large multinational oil company.

The following are illustrative of events or transactions which do not meet both criteria in the circumstances described and thus should not be reported as extraordinary items:

14. A citrus grower's Florida crop is damaged by frost. Frost damage is normally experienced every three or four years. The criterion of infrequency of occurrence taking into account the environment in which the company operates would not be met since the history of losses caused by frost damage provides evidence that such damage may reasonably be expected to recur in the foreseeable future.
15. A company which operates a chain of warehouses sells the excess land surrounding one of its warehouses. When the company buys property to establish a new warehouse, it usually buys more land than it expects to use for the warehouse with the expectation that the land will appreciate in value. In the past five years, there have been two instances in which the company sold such excess land. The criterion of infrequency of occurrence has not been met since past experience indicates that such sales may reasonably be expected to recur in the foreseeable future.
16. A large diversified company sells a block of shares from its portfolio of securities which it has acquired for investment purposes. This is the first sale from its portfolio of securities. Since the company owns several securities for investment purposes, it should be concluded that sales of such securities are related to its ordinary and typical activities in the environment in which it operates, and thus the criterion of unusual nature would not be met.
17. A textile manufacturer with only one plant moves to another location. It has not relocated a plant in 20 years and has no plans to do so in the foreseeable future. Notwithstanding the infrequency of occurrence of the event as it relates to this particular company, moving

from one location to another is an occurrence which is a consequence of customary and continuing business activities, some of which are finding more favorable labor markets, more modern facilities and proximity to customers or suppliers. Therefore, the criterion of unusual nature has not been met and the moving expenses (and related gains and losses) should not be reported as an extraordinary item. Another example of an event which is a consequence of customary and typical business activities (namely financing) is an unsuccessful public registration, the cost of which should not be reported as an extraordinary item. (For additional examples, see Paragraph 23 of the *Opinion.*)

Disposals of part of a line of business, such as examples 5–9 of this interpretation, should not be classified as extraordinary items. As discussed in Paragraph 13 of the *Opinion,* such disposals are incident to the evolution of the entity's business, and therefore the criterion of unusual nature would not be met.

Question. Paragraph 27 of the *Opinion* states that events and transactions that were reported as extraordinary items in statements of income for fiscal years ending before October 1, 1973, should not be restated except that a statement of income including operations of discontinued segments of a business that meet the Paragraph 13 criteria may be reclassified in comparative statements to conform with the provisions of Paragraphs 8 and 9 of the *Opinion.* If a gain or loss on such a disposal in a prior year had been classified as an extraordinary item but was not computed in the *manner* specified in Paragraphs 15–17 of the *Opinion,* may the prior year income statements be reclassified and the gain or loss adjusted to comply with the provisions of the *Opinion?*

Interpretation. The *Opinion* specifically uses the term "reclassified" in Paragraph 27 and makes direct reference to Paragraphs 8 and 9, which describe the manner of reporting disposals of a segment of a business as defined in Paragraph 13. While such reclassification is optional under the *Opinion,* there should not be a redetermination (restatement) of net income using the measurement principles specified in Paragraphs 15–17. Since *Opinions* of the Board are not intended to be retroactive unless otherwise stated, the method of computing the gain or loss on disposals of a segment should not be retroactively applied if it results in a change in net income of a prior year.

Question. Events or transactions which are not disposals of a segment of a business and are not extraordinary items may nevertheless be required to be reported as a separate component of income from continuing operations under the provisions of Paragraph 26 of the *Opinion.* If a company sells a portion of a line of business which does not meet the definition of a segment of a business as defined in Paragraph 13 of the *Opinion,* should the gain or loss be calculated using the measurement principles for determination of gain or loss on disposal of a segment of a business as prescribed in Paragraphs 15–17 of the *Opinion,* and how should the financial effects of such sale be reported?

Interpretation. The gain or loss on a sale of a portion of a line of business which is not a segment of a business as defined in Paragraph 13 should be calculated using the same measurement principles as if it were a segment of a business (Paragraphs 15–17 of the *Opinion*). Under the provisions of Paragraph 26 of the *Opinion,* the amount of such gain or loss should be reported as a separate component of income from continuing operations. However, the gain or loss should not be reported on the face of the income statement net of income taxes or in any manner inconsistent with the provisions of Paragraphs 8 and 11 of the *Opinion* which may imply that it is a disposal of a segment of the business. In addition, the earnings per share effect should not be disclosed on the face of the income statement. Revenues and related costs and expenses of the portion of the line of business prior to the measurement date should not be segregated on the face of the income statement but may be disclosed in the notes to the financial statements, and such disclosure is encouraged. In addition, the notes to the financial statements should disclose, if known, those items specified in Paragraph 18 of the *Opinion.*

The foregoing examples are illustrative. It should be recognized that all attendant circumstances, which can vary from those above, need to be considered in making the judgments required by *APB Opinion No. 30.*

Appendix B. Specimen Statements

KOPPERS

Report of Certified Public Accountants

ARTHUR YOUNG & COMPANY
CERTIFIED PUBLIC ACCOUNTANTS

The Board of Directors and Shareholders
Koppers Company, Inc.

We have examined the accompanying consolidated balance sheet of Koppers Company, Inc. and subsidiaries at December 31, 1974 and 1973 and the related consolidated statements of income, changes in financial position and shareholders' equity for the years then ended. Our examination was made in accordance with generally accepted auditing standards, and accordingly included such tests of the accounting records and such other auditing procedures as we considered necessary in the circumstances.

In our opinion, the statements mentioned above present fairly the consolidated financial position of Koppers Company, Inc. and subsidiaries at December 31, 1974 and 1973, the consolidated results of their operations and the consolidated changes in their financial position for the years then ended in conformity with generally accepted accounting principles applied on a consistent basis during the period except for the change in the method of valuing inventories in 1974, with which we concur, as described in the statement of accounting policies.

Arthur Young & Company

Pittsburgh, Pennsylvania
January 27, 1975

Consolidated Statement of Income

Koppers Company, Inc. and Subsidiaries

Years ended December 31, 1974 and 1973
(See accompanying statement of accounting policies and notes to financial statements.)

	1974	1973
Net sales	**$914,184,752**	$723,933,402
Operating expenses (Notes 5 and 8):		
Cost of sales	**725,654,818**	552,393,829
Depreciation and depletion	**27,808,950**	28,740,943
Taxes, other than income taxes	**16,502,384**	14,898,696
Selling, research, general and administrative expenses	**71,219,080**	69,948,274
	841,185,232	665,981,742
Operating profit	**72,999,520**	57,951,660
Other income (expense):		
Dividends:		
Affiliated company (Note 1)	**12,961,985**	—
Other	**616,526**	520,561
Interest income	**1,098,121**	1,018,412
Provision for possible decline in value of investments	**(1,626,000)**	(1,000,000)
Profit on sales of capital assets	**870,599**	1,193,426
Equity in earnings of affiliates (dividends received: 1974—$335,366; 1973—$542,212)	**1,701,023**	1,382,023
Miscellaneous	**162,403**	161,359
	15,784,657	3,275,781
Interest expense:		
Term debt (Note 6)	**10,045,097**	7,989,756
Other	**2,600,984**	2,121,722
	12,646,081	10,111,478
Income before provision for income taxes	**76,138,096**	51,115,963
Provision for income taxes (Note 7)	**28,356,976**	21,580,619
Net income for the year	**$ 47,781,120**	$ 29,535,344
Average number of shares of common stock outstanding during year	**5,785,334**	5,632,733
Net earnings per share of common stock	**$8.16**	$5.14

Consolidated Balance Sheet

ASSETS

Koppers Company, Inc. and Subsidiaries

December 31, 1974 and 1973
(See accompanying statement of accounting policies and notes to financial statements.)

	1974	1973
Current assets:		
Cash	**$ 16,103,463**	$ 15,165,561
Accounts receivable:		
Due from affiliate (Note 1)	**11,899,000**	—
Trade, less allowance for doubtful accounts of $1,996,766 in 1974 and $1,836,173 in 1973 (Note 2)	**158,557,672**	129,450,232
Inventories:		
Product inventories	**58,912,408**	49,143,522
Work in process	**51,116,772**	28,692,899
Raw materials and supplies	**35,909,807**	26,637,611
Prepaid expenses	**6,597,963**	5,978,997
Total current assets	**339,097,085**	255,068,822
Investments:		
Common and preferred stock of affiliate, at cost (Note 1)	**55,265,264**	—
Affiliated companies, at equity (Note 3)	**12,197,647**	10,181,448
Other, at cost	**10,399,799**	10,995,588
	77,862,710	21,177,036
Less allowance for possible decline in value	**4,150,000**	2,524,000
	73,712,710	18,653,036
Notes and accounts receivable due after one year	**3,839,590**	2,443,640
Fixed assets, at cost:		
Buildings	**45,496,798**	52,768,643
Machinery and equipment	**355,366,260**	411,018,395
	400,863,058	463,787,038
Less accumulated depreciation	**206,235,617**	247,167,689
	194,627,441	216,619,349
Depletable properties, less accumulated depletion	**19,363,244**	12,629,091
Land	**12,719,951**	11,055,477
	226,710,636	240,303,917
Intangible assets, net of amortization	**3,619,311**	3,092,007
Deferred charges	**925,866**	667,045
	$647,905,198	$520,228,467

LIABILITIES AND SHAREHOLDERS' EQUITY

	1974	1973
Current liabilities:		
Federal income tax	**$ 13,483,408**	$ 12,950,500
Other taxes	**7,680,047**	6,729,639
Accounts payable, principally trade	**48,605,005**	40,344,857
Accrued pensions (Note 5)	**9,331,222**	7,647,000
Other accruals	**29,553,334**	19,980,552
Advance payments received on contracts	**30,337,549**	16,844,015
Debt due within one year including short-term borrowings of $2,401,000 in 1974 (Note 6)	**5,032,202**	2,540,589
Total current liabilities	**144,022,767**	107,037,152
Term debt due after one year (Note 6):		
6% notes due $3,000,000 annually commencing August 1, 1977	**50,000,000**	50,000,000
Term loan payable to banks	**60,000,000**	30,000,000
Notes payable to banks	**33,000,000**	10,000,000
5.8% promissory notes due $670,000 annually	**7,320,000**	7,990,000
Pollution control notes	**10,600,000**	10,600,000
Other	**5,725,960**	4,167,568
	166,645,960	112,757,568
Deferred compensation	**5,464,629**	4,982,295
Deferred income taxes	**18,765,718**	20,565,869
Deferred foreign exchange gain	**855,160**	629,000
Minority shareholders' interest in subsidiaries	**46,281**	214,804
Total liabilities	**335,800,515**	246,186,688
SHAREHOLDERS' EQUITY		
Cumulative preferred stock, $100 par value:		
Authorized 300,000 shares, issued 150,000 shares, 4% series	**15,000,000**	15,000,000
Preferred stock, no par value:		
Authorized 1,000,000 shares, issued-none	**—**	—
Common stock, $5 par value, authorized 8,000,000 shares, issued and outstanding 5,799,955 in 1974 and 5,687,916 in 1973	**28,999,775**	28,439,580
Capital in excess of par value	**62,933,097**	61,289,033
Earnings retained in the business (Notes 3 and 6)	**205,171,811**	169,313,166
Common shareholders' equity	**297,104,683**	259,041,779
Total preferred and common shareholders' equity	**312,104,683**	274,041,779
	$647,905,198	$520,228,467

Consolidated Statement of Changes in Financial Position

Koppers Company, Inc. and Subsidiaries

Years ended December 31, 1974 and 1973
(See accompanying statement of accounting policies and notes to financial statements.)

	1974	1973
Source of funds:		
Operations:		
Net income	$ 47,781,120	$ 29,535,344
Depreciation and depletion	27,808,950	28,740,943
Deferred income taxes and other expenses	(1,133,812)	3,105,161
Provision for possible decline in value of investments	1,626,000	1,000,000
Equity in earnings of affiliated companies, less dividends received	(1,365,657)	(839,811)
Funds provided from operations	74,716,601	61,541,637
Proceeds from term debt issued	66,524,162	36,347,536
Conversion of Sinclair-Koppers partnership fixed assets to investment in an affiliated company	62,660,057	—
Redemption of investment in an affiliated company	25,219,200	—
Common stock issued	3,216,607	2,158,913
Book value of fixed assets and other noncurrent assets disposed of or sold	3,436,587	2,861,168
	235,773,214	102,909,254
Disposition of funds:		
Fixed assets purchased	80,271,479	61,719,216
Term debt retired	12,635,770	44,386,760
Dividends paid	12,934,823	10,730,640
Investment in an affiliated company	80,668,057	—
Other	2,220,437	3,617,729
	188,730,566	120,454,345
Increase (decrease) in working capital	$ 47,042,648	$(17,545,091)
Changes in components of working capital:		
Increase (decrease) in current assets:		
Cash	$ 937,902	$ 1,450,405
Accounts receivable	41,006,440	6,924,725
Inventories	41,464,955	11,294,978
Prepaid expenses	618,966	(612,526)
	84,028,263	19,057,582
Increase (decrease) in current liabilities:		
Federal income tax	532,908	11,613,338
Other taxes	950,408	883,620
Accounts payable	8,260,148	3,882,896
Accrued pensions	1,684,222	2,782,278
Other accruals	9,572,782	8,175,715
Advance payments received on contracts	13,493,534	10,217,459
Term debt due within one year, including short-term borrowings	2,491,613	(952,633)
	36,985,615	36,602,673
Increase (decrease) in working capital	$ 47,042,648	$(17,545,091)

Consolidated Statement of Shareholders' Equity

Koppers Company, Inc. and Subsidiaries

Years ended December 31, 1974 and 1973
(See accompanying statement of accounting policies and notes to financial statements.)

	Cumulative Preferred Stock	Common Stock	Capital In Excess of Par Value	Earnings Retained in the Business	Total Preferred and Common Shareholders' Equity
Balance at January 1, 1973	$15,000,000	$28,140,725	$59,428,975	$150,508,462	$253,078,162
Net income for the year 1973	—	—	—	29,535,344	29,535,344
Cash dividends paid:					
On preferred stock, $4.00 per share	—	—	—	(600,000)	(600,000)
On common stock, $1.80 per share	—	—	—	(10,130,640)	(10,130,640)
Common stock issued (59,771 shares) for acquisitions	—	298,855	1,860,058	—	2,158,913
Balance at December 31, 1973	15,000,000	28,439,580	61,289,033	169,313,166	274,041,779
Net income for the year 1974	—	—	—	47,781,120	47,781,120
Cash dividends paid:					
On preferred stock, $4.00 per share	—	—	—	(600,000)	(600,000)
On common stock, $2.14 per share	—	—	—	(12,334,823)	(12,334,823)
Common stock issued during 1974:					
102,039 shares for acquisitions	—	510,195	1,299,064	1,012,348	2,821,607
10,000 shares for stock options exercised at $39.50 per share	—	50,000	345,000	—	395,000
Balance at December 31, 1974	$15,000,000	$28,999,775	$62,933,097	$205,171,811	$312,104,683

Statement of Accounting Policies

Koppers Company, Inc. and Subsidiaries

The Company employs generally accepted accounting principles on a consistent basis to present fairly its financial position, results of operations and changes in financial position. The major accounting policies of the Company are set forth below. The word "Company" as used in this report includes consolidated entities as well as Koppers Company, Inc.

Principles of Consolidation

The consolidated statements include the accounts of the Company and all of its subsidiaries. All intercompany transactions have been eliminated.

Foreign Currency

The accounts of foreign subsidiaries maintained in foreign currencies have been converted to U.S. dollars on the following bases: current assets and current liabilities at year-end exchange rates; noncurrent assets, noncurrent liabilities and equity at rates of exchange in effect when acquired; and revenue and expense accounts at average rates of exchange in effect during the period, except for depreciation which is converted at rates of exchange which were in effect when the respective assets were acquired. Unrealized exchange gains are not recognized as income but are credited to unrealized exchange gain reserves. Unrealized exchange losses are charged against income to the extent that they exceed any unrealized exchange gain reserves established in prior years.

Inventories

Inventories are valued at the lower of cost or market. Effective January 1, 1974, the Company adopted the LIFO (last-in, first-out) method of determining cost for substantially all domestic inventories of Koppers Company, Inc. This was done because the rapid increase in prices during the year would result in an overstatement of profits if use of the FIFO (first-in, first-out) method were continued, since inventories sold were replaced at substantially higher prices. This accounting change increased 1974 cost of goods sold by $34,038,000 and, accordingly, decreased net income by $16,638,000 ($2.88 per share). It is not possible under the LIFO method to determine the effect of this change on prior years. Cost for the remainder of the inventories represents average costs or standard costs which approximate actual on the first-in, first-out basis. Market is replacement cost for raw materials and net realizable value for work in process and finished goods.

Investments

Companies owned 50% or less but more than 20% are accounted for on the equity method except for certain foreign investments, which are valued at cost because of repatriation regulations. Note 1 explains the accounting for a major investment in an affiliate.

Fixed Assets

Buildings, machinery and equipment are depreciated on the straight-line method over their useful lives. All ordinary maintenance and repair expenses are charged to operations. Extraordinary repairs, which materially extend the life of property, are generally charged to accumulated depreciation. Timber and mineral properties are depleted on the basis of units produced.

When land, standing timber or property units are sold, the difference between selling price and cost, after recognition of accumulated depreciation and depletion, is reflected in Other Income.

Intangible Assets

Patent costs are amortized over the lives of the patents. The excess of purchase price over net asset value of businesses acquired is amortized over the estimated useful lives of such assets not exceeding 40 years.

Long-Term Contracts

Sales and income on long-term construction contracts are accounted for on the percentage-of-completion basis; losses are recognized as soon as they are determined.

Research and Development

Research and development costs are expensed as incurred.

Pension Plans

The Company has pension plans covering substantially all employees. The Company provides for amortization of unfunded prior service costs over periods up to 40 years and pays provisions for pension expense into trust funds.

Income Taxes

Deferred income taxes are provided for timing differences between financial and tax reporting. Benefits from investment tax credits are reflected currently in income.

Notes to Financial Statements

Koppers Company, Inc. and Subsidiaries

1. Reorganization of Sinclair-Koppers Company

The Company entered into an agreement effective January 1, 1974 with Atlantic Richfield Company to reorganize their Sinclair-Koppers partnership.

The business and net assets of the partnership were transferred to a new corporation (ARCO/Polymers, Inc.) in exchange for $100 (one hundred dollar) par value 12½% preferred stock and $1 (one dollar) par value common stock Class A and B. The Class A common stock was distributed to Atlantic Richfield, and all the 12½% nonvoting preferred stock and all of Class B common stock, which constitutes approximately 20% voting interest, was distributed to the Company. The securities received by the Company can be redeemed for cash at the option of ARCO/Polymers. Either the Company or ARCO/Polymers may cause to be redeemed by ARCO/Polymers in 1981 all the outstanding shares then held by the Company at contributed value.

All earnings of ARCO/Polymers are required to be distributed as dividends currently on its outstanding stock, first on the preferred stock and the balance on the common stock. Such dividends are declared and paid quarterly.

Prior to 1974, the Company's 50% interest in the income, expenses, assets and liabilities of the partnership had been included in the financial statements, while in 1974 the Company's interest is shown as an investment, and income is reported as dividends are earned. Therefore, the following important components of the Company's share of Sinclair-Koppers partnership included in the Company's consolidated financial statements at December 31, 1973 are furnished to facilitate comparison of 1974 and 1973:

Net working capital	$18,008,000
Net fixed assets	$62,660,000
Net sales	$81,066,000
Depreciation	$ 6,185,000
Operating profit	$12,052,000

2. Accounts Receivable

Receivables include the following amounts applicable to long-term construction contracts:

	1974	1973
Billed	$29,027,000	$22,131,000
Retainage	10,084,000	9,146,000

3. Investments in Affiliated Companies, at Equity

Consolidated earnings retained in the business include $9,080,000 in 1974 and $7,804,000 in 1973, representing the Company's equity in undistributed retained earnings of the affiliated companies less deferred taxes.

4. Foreign Operations

The Company's financial statements include the following amounts related to consolidated subsidiaries (all wholly owned) located outside of the United States at December 31, 1974 and 1973 and for the years then ended:

	1974	1973
Assets	$49,825,000	$44,352,000
Liabilities	$26,350,000	$12,855,000
Sales	$56,638,000	$48,143,000
Net income	$ 1,390,000	$ 4,677,000

5. Pensions

Total pension expense in 1974 was $9,754,000 as compared with $7,647,000 in 1973. In 1974, pension expense was increased as a result of recognition of a portion of the unrealized depreciation of investments held by the pension trusts. The market value of these investments in 1973 did not necessitate the recognition of unrealized depreciation. The unfunded prior service costs under all plans at December 31, 1974 amounted to $28,332,000.

6. Debt

On April 1, 1974, the Company obtained an 8½%, $30,000,000 bank term loan of ten years with no repayments during the first seven years. Repayment provisions specify that 25% of the principal amount is to be paid in each of the eighth and ninth years, with 50% to be repaid in the tenth year. The $30,000,000 loan obtained February 1, 1973 has the same terms except that the interest rate is ¾ of 1% over the prime rate, with a maximum average annual interest cost during the first seven years of 7½%. Any interest payments in excess of this maximum will be refunded to the Company at the end of the seven-year period. The interest rate during the eighth, ninth and tenth years will be ¾ of 1% over the prime rate.

A bank credit agreement providing for up to $75,000,000 of 90-day renewable revolving credit loans became effective August 1, 1974. Interest on the loans is at the prime rate until July 31, 1977, at which time the notes are convertible at the option of the Company into term notes payable in eight equal semiannual installments commencing January 31, 1978 with interest at the prime rate plus ¼ of 1% through August 1, 1979 and at the prime rate plus ½ of 1% thereafter. During the renewable period, the Company is required to pay a commitment fee of ½ of 1% per annum on the unborrowed amount.

The Company has issued notes to provide funds for the construction of pollution control facilities at Company

Koppers Company, Inc. and Subsidiaries

plants. The notes bear interest at approximately 6%, payable semi-annually with principal payments commencing June 1, 1983 in annual installments over 16 years.

The aggregate term-debt maturity amounts for the years 1975 through 1979, respectively are $2.629.000; $2.394.000; $4,614.000; $12.533.000; and $12.352.000

The Company's term-debt agreements contain various restrictions as to dividend payments and incurrence of additional indebtedness. Under the most restrictive provisions at December 31, 1974, $54.846.000 of consolidated earnings retained in the business was available for cash dividends, and the Company could incur additional indebtedness of approximately $30.346.000.

The Company has additional agreements which make available $18.000.000 in short-term borrowings. The Company is not required to pay a commitment fee on the unborrowed funds under these agreements. At December 31, 1974, the Company had $2.401.000 of borrowings under these agreements.

The Company issues short-term promissory notes (commercial paper) to cover peak working capital requirements. The average amount of commercial paper outstanding during the year was $17,286,000 with a daily weighted averaged annual interest rate of 11.3%. The maximum amount of the commercial paper outstanding during the year was $30,000,000. No amounts were outstanding at the end of the year.

7. Income Taxes

Income tax expense has the following components:

	Years ended December 31, 1974	1973
Federal:		
Current	$25,487,482	$13,839,707
Deferred ...	(1,788,043)	1,498,785
	23,699,439	15,338,492
State	3,821,089	2,041,469
Foreign:		
Current	1,548,294	3,534,658
Deferred ...	(711,846)	666,000
	836,448	4,200,658
Total	$28,356,976	$21,580,619

Deferred taxes resulted from the following:

	1974	1973
Excess of tax over book depreciation	$ (365,000)	$3,171,000
Items charged to expense on the books but not currently deductible for tax:		
Incentive payments ...	33,000	(537,000)
Investment reserve	(487,800)	(300,000)
Loss on foreign purchase commitments ..	(945,000)	—
Other—net	(735,089)	(169,215)
	$(2,499,889)	$2,164,785

The difference between the statutory and effective income tax rates is as follows:

	Years ended December 31 1974	1973
Statutory tax rate:		
Federal	48.0%	48.0%
State net of Federal tax benefit	2.6%	2.5%
Foreign	(0.1%)	(1.3%)
Investment tax credit ..	(2.9%)	(3.7%)
Effect of lower statutory tax rate applicable to dividends received from an affiliated company	(8.5%)	—
Other—net	(1.9%)	(3.3%)
	37.2%	42.2%

The current provisions for Federal income taxes have been reduced by $2,201,000 and $1,909,000 in 1974 and 1973, respectively, for the investment tax credit.

8. Commitments and Contingencies

The total rental expense amounted to $10,622,000 in 1974 as compared with $9,927,000 in 1973.

At December 31, 1974, the minimum rental commitments under noncancelable leases with remaining terms of more than one year are as follows:

	Financing Leases	Other Leases	Total
1975...	$ 3,251,000	$ 4,727,000	$ 7,978,000
1976...	2,985,000	2,925,000	5,910,000
1977...	2,755,000	1,805,000	4,560,000
1978...	2,145,000	1,279,000	3,424,000
1979...	1,955,000	764,000	2,719,000
1980-1984..	2,689,000	930,000	3,619,000
1985-1989..	1,124,000	40,000	1,164,000
1990-1994..	422,000	1,000	423,000
	$17,326,000	$12,471,000	$29,797,000

The Company has guaranteed $8,373,000 indebtedness of affiliated and other corporations.

QUESTIONS

1. The income statement is a *general-purpose* statement. What does this mean?
2. Explain briefly how the income statement is a connecting link between the beginning and ending balance sheets.
3. Briefly explain the economist's definition of income. How does the accountant define income as reflected by the completed transactions approach?
4. Define revenue. Compare the conceptual view with the pragmatic definition provided by APB *Statement No. 4.*
5. Define expense. Compare the conceptual view with the pragmatic definition provided by APB *Statement No. 4.*
6. Distinguish between cost and expense. What is a loss?
7. Briefly explain the two "pure" formats used for income statements. Explain why actual income statements are usually somewhere between these two formats.
8. What is the basic difference between an income statement for a trading company and a manufacturing company?
9. Explain the reporting principle, including its full-disclosure aspect. (Refer to Chapter 2.)
10. Explain why the total amount of depreciation expense must be disclosed in the financial statement.
11. Briefly distinguish between intraperiod and interperiod tax allocation.
12. Define earnings per share. Why it is required as an integral part of the income statement? What amounts must be reported on the income statement?
13. Explain the difference between the all-inclusive and the operating concepts of income. Which concept do you prefer? Why?
14. Define an extraordinaly item. How should extraordinary items be reported on a *(a)* single-step, and *(b)* multiple-step income statement?
15. How are items that are either unusual or infrequent, but not both, reported on the income statement?
16. Define prior period adjustments; give the four criteria. How are prior period adjustments reported on the financial statements? Do you agree with this approach? Explain why.
17. What are the four types of accounting changes identified in *APB Opinion No. 20*? Define what is meant by a change due to *(a)* accounting error, and *(b)* change in estimate.
18. Explain the basic approach in accounting and reporting *(a)* accounting errors, and *(b)* changes in estimates.
19. What items are reported on a statement of retained earnings? Explain how it provides a link between the current income statement and the balance sheet.
20. What is meant by restrictions on retained earnings? How are they usually reported?

21. Explain why many companies prefer a combined statement of income and retained earnings.

DECISION CASE 4–1

The president of Taylor School Supply Company, a wholesaler, presents you with a comparison of distribution costs for two salespersons and wants to know if you think their compensation plan is working to the detriment of the company. The president supplies you with the following data:

	Salesperson	
	McKinney	*Sim*
Gross sales	$247,000	$142,000
Sales returns	17,000	2,000
Cost of goods sold	180,000	100,000
Reimbursed expenses (e.g., entertainment)	5,500	2,100
Other direct charges (e.g., samples distributed)	4,000	450
Commission rate on gross sales dollars	5%	5%

Required:

1. A salesperson's compensation plan encourages one to work to increase the measure of performance to which compensation is related. List the questionable sales practices by a salesperson that might be encouraged by basing commissions on gross sales.
2. *a.* What evidence that the compensation plan may be working to the detriment of the company can be found in the data?
   b. What other information should the president obtain before reaching definite conclusions about this particular situation? Why?

(AICPA adapted)

DECISION CASE 4–2

J. B. Jacobson opened a small retail cash-and-carry grocery business with an investment of $1,000 cash, $5,000 merchandise, and a lot and building valued at $18,000. Fixtures were obtained by signing a note payable in equal installments over a 36-month period. Cash is paid for all merchandise purchases, and Jacobson maintains no formal accounting records. When asked how one knew how well one was doing and where one stood, Jacobson made the following statement: "As long as I do not buy or sell anything except merchandise and that remains fairly constant, I can judge my profit or loss by the increase or decrease in my bank balance."

Required:

Evaluate Jacobson's statement in the light of the facts known.

DECISION CASE 4–3

Generally accepted accounting principles define income as Revenue minus Expense equals Income. This model requires that revenue and expense be identified and carefully measured. Also, it requires a careful correspondence between revenue and expense.

Required:

1. What principle, or principles, govern identification and measurement of revenues?

2. What principle, or principles, govern identification and measurement of expenses?
3. Identify and explain some of the troublesome problems in applying the principles identified in 1 and 2.
4. What guidelines govern identification and measurement of extraordinary items? Do you agree with these guidelines? Explain.
5. What guidelines govern identification and measurement of prior period adjustments? Do you agree with these guidelines? Explain.
6. What guidelines govern reporting of items that are either unusual or infrequent, but not both? Do you agree with these guidelines? Explain.

EXERCISES

Exercise 4–1

For each of the following transactions, state when revenue and/or expense should be recognized; explain the basis for your decision. Assume the accounting period ends December 31.

a. On December 21, 1976, merchandise was sold for $3,000 cash. The buyer took possession of two thirds of the merchandise on that date. The balance will be picked up on January 3, 1977.
b. Services were rendered to a customer starting on December 27, 1976. The services will be completed around January 5, 1977, at which time cash in full will be collected. Assume eight working days are involved.
c. During 1976 the company sold ten TV sets and collected $4,000 cash in full. The company gives a one-year guarantee. It is estimated that the average cost per set under the guarantee is $15. Assume by the end of 1976, one half of the guarantees on the ten sets have been satisfied.
d. On December 31, 1976, a used truck was sold by the company that had been used in operating the business and had a book value of $300. The sales price was $500 which was payable six months from date of the sale plus 8% interest per annum.
e. On December 27, 1976, the company received an income tax refund of $1,000 after four years of negotiations with the Internal Revenue Service.

(*Hint:* Restudy the revenue, cost, and matching principles in Chapter 2.)

Exercise 4–2

For each of the following transactions, state when revenue and/or expense should be recognized; explain the basis for your decision. Assume the accounting period ends December 31, 1976.

a. On December 30, 1976, sold $2,000 merchandise; terms, 2/10, n/30.
b. On December 29, 1976, paid $15,000 for advertising in the local paper. The ads related only to a clearance sale that would run from January 1–31, 1976.
c. Performed services each working day for a customer that extended from December 27, 1976, through January 5, 1977. Assume ten working days are involved. Cash collected was $2,000 (in full) on December 27, 1976.
d. Sold a used TV set for $100 on December 28, 1976, and collected $75 cash. The balance is due in six months; however, collection of the balance is very doubtful, and the set will not be worth repossessing again. It is now carried in the books at $60.

e. On December 1, 1976, borrowed $6,600 cash and gave a noninterest-bearing note payable; received cash, $6,000 (the face of the note less interest for one year deducted in advance).

(*Hint:* Restudy the revenue, cost, and matching principles in Chapter 2.)

Exercise 4–3

The following items were taken from the adjusted trial balance of Blue Trading Corporation on December 31, 1976. Assume a flat 40% corporate tax rate on all items (including the casualty loss).

Sales	$640,000
Rent collected	2,400
Interest revenue	900
Gain on sale of fixed assets (assume not qualified as a capital gain)	1,000
Distribution expenses	136,000
General and administrative expenses	110,000
Interest expense	1,500
Depreciation for the period	6,000
Extraordinary item: Major casualty loss (pretax)	20,000
Common stock (par $10)	100,000
Cost of goods sold	350,000

Required:

1. Prepare a single-step income statement (include EPS).
2. Prepare a multiple-step income statement (include EPS).
3. Which format do you prefer? Why?

Exercise 4–4

The following items were taken from the adjusted trial balance of Slim Manufacturing Corporation at December 31, 1976:

Sales	$900,000
Cost of goods manufactured	550,000
Dividends received on investment in stocks	6,500
Finished goods inventory, January 1, 1976	45,000
Interest expense	4,200
Extraordinary item: Major fire loss (already reduced for tax savings)	33,000
Distribution expenses	135,300
Common stock, par $20	200,000
Administrative and general expenses	113,000
Interest revenue	2,300
Finished goods inventory, December 31, 1976	51,300
Income taxes (excluding the extraordinary item); assume a flat 40% corporate tax rate	?

Required:

1. Prepare a single-step income statement (include EPS).
2. Prepare a multiple-step income statement (include EPS).
3. Which format do you prefer? Why?

Exercise 4–5

The following items were taken from the adjusted trial balance of Swenson Trading Corporation at December 31, 1976:

Sales revenue	$ 96,000
Distribution expenses	24,000
Interest revenue	600
Cost of goods sold	54,000
Extraordinary item: Major casualty loss (already reduced for income tax savings)	9,000
Interest expense	1,000
Gain on sale of fixed assets (assume not taxed as a capital gain)	3,000
Common stock, par $10	100,000
Income tax expense (excluding extraordinary item); assume a flat 22% corporate tax rate	?
General and administrative expenses	10,600

Required:

1. Prepare a single-step income statement (include EPS).
2. Prepare a multiple-step income statement (include EPS).
3. Which format do you prefer? Explain.

Exercise 4–6

The following pretax amounts were taken from the adjusted trial balance of Howe Company at December 31, 1976:

Balance, retained earnings, January 1, 1976	$ 33,000
Sales revenue	120,000
Cost of goods sold	51,000
Distribution expenses	32,000
Administrative expenses	23,000
Extraordinary loss (pretax)	10,000
Prior period adjustment, a gain (pretax)	8,000
Dividends paid	6,000

Assume a flat 30% corporate tax rate on all items, including the extraordinary loss and prior period adjustment. Also assume common stock outstanding is 5,000 shares.

Required:

1. Prepare a single-step income statement and a statement of retained earnings including intraperiod tax allocation (include EPS).
2. Give the entry to record income taxes payable (assume none yet paid).

Exercise 4–7

The following pretax amounts were taken from the adjusted trial balance of White Corporation on December 31, 1976:

Balance, retained earnings, January 1, 1976	$ 38,000
Sales revenue	200,000
Cost of goods sold	100,000
Distribution expenses	31,000

Administrative expenses	29,000
Extraordinary gain (pretax)	10,000
Prior period adjustment, a loss (pretax)	20,000
Dividends paid	8,000

Assume the corporate income tax rates are 22% on the first $25,000 of net income and 48% on all income above that amount, including the extraordinary item and the prior period adjustment.

Common shares outstanding during the year were 10,000.

Required:

1. Prepare a multiple-step income statement with intraperiod tax allocation and EPS.
2. Prepare a statement of retained earnings with intraperiod tax allocation and EPS.
3. Give the entry to record income taxes payable (assume none yet paid).

Exercise 4–8

The following pretax amounts were taken from the adjusted trial balance of Vinson Corporation at December 31, 1976:

Dividends paid	$ 30,000
Sales revenue	190,000
Cost of goods sold	100,000
Operating expenses	60,000
Extraordinary loss (pretax)	15,000
Prior period adjustment, a gain (pretax)	10,000
Common stock (par $10)	150,000
Beginning retained earnings, January 1, 1976	45,000

Required:

1. Preparc a complete single-step income statement. Assume 22% rate for the first $25,000 of income and 48% on all amounts above $25,000. Show computations of earnings per share information.
2. Prepare a statement of retained earnings.
3. Give the entry to record income taxes payable (assume none yet paid).

Exercise 4–9

The following pretax amounts were taken from the adjusted trial balance of Asher Corporation at December 31, 1976:

Sales revenue		$240,000
Cost of goods sold		110,000
Operating expenses		80,000
Extraordinary gain (pretax)		10,000
Prior period adjustment, a loss (pretax)		20,000
Common stock (par $10):	*Shares*	
Outstanding January 1, 1976	15,000	
Sold and issued April 1, 1976	5,000	
Sold and issued October 1, 1976	8,000	
Outstanding December 31, 1976	28,000	

Required:

Prepare a complete single-step income statement. Assume an average 30% corporate tax rate on all items. Show computations of earnings per share.

Exercise 4–10

On December 31, 1976, the following pretax amounts were taken from the adjusted trial balance of Jackson Corporation:

Sales revenue	$190,000
Cost of goods sold	100,000
Operating expenses	45,000
Extraordinary loss (pretax)	20,000
Prior period adjustment, loss (pretax)	10,000

Assume an average 40% corporate tax rate on all items.

Common stock (par $10):	
Shares outstanding, January 1, 1976	15,000
Stock dividend, shares issued on July 1, 1976	5,000

Required:

Prepare a single-step income statement. Show computations for earnings per share.

Exercise 4–11

The following pretax amounts were taken from the adjusted trial balance of Searles Corporation at December 31, 1976:

Revenues	$400,000
Cost of goods sold	220,000
Operating expenses	100,000
Infrequent item, loss on disposal of long-term investment (pretax)	10,000
Extraordinary item, gain on expropriation of plant by foreign government (pretax)	20,000
Common stock (par $10), 10,000 shares outstanding.	

Assume an average 40% corporate tax rate on all items.

Required:

Prepare a single-step income statement that meets the full-disclosure requirements with respect to infrequent items, extraordinary items, tax allocation, and earnings per share.

Exercise 4–12

The following pretax amounts were taken from the adjusted trial balance of Youngblood Corporation at December 31, 1976:

Sales and service revenues	$200,000
Cost of goods sold	105,000
Operating expenses	65,000
Unusual item, gain on sale of major fixed asset (pretax)	10,000
Extraordinary item, loss on major flood (pretax)	25,000
Prior period adjustment, damages paid from lawsuit (pretax)	5,000
Common stock (par $1), 50,000 shares outstanding.	

Assume an average 40% corporate tax rate on all items.

Required:

Prepare a single-step income statement that meets the full-disclosure requirements with respect to unusual items, extraordinary items, tax allocation, and earnings per share.

Exercise 4–13

AB Company has a machine that cost $34,000 when acquired on January 1, 1971. The estimated useful life was 15 years and a residual value of $4,000. Straight-line depreciation is used. On December 31, 1976, prior to the adjusting entry, it was decided that the machine should have been depreciated over a 21-year useful life, with no change in the residual value.

Required:

1. Give the adjusting entry at the end of 1976 for depreciation expense. Show computations.
2. Give the correcting entry required at the end of 1976. If none is required, so state and give the reasons.

Exercise 4–14

It is December 31, 1976, and the SY Company is preparing adjusting entries at the end of the year. The company owns two trucks of different types. The following situations confront the company accountant:

a. Truck No. 1 cost $6,500 on January 1, 1974. It is being depreciated on a straight-line basis over an estimated useful life of ten years with a $500 residual value. At December 31, 1976, it has been determined that the useful life should have been eight years instead of ten, with no changes in the residual value.

b. Truck No. 2 cost $4,550 on January 1, 1973. It is being depreciated on a straight-line basis over an estimated useful life of seven years with a $350 residual value. At December 31, 1976, it was discovered that no depreciation had been recorded on this truck for 1973 and 1974.

Required:

1. For each truck, give the correct adjusting entry for depreciation expense at December 31, 1976. Show computations.
2. For each truck, if a correcting entry is required, provide it and show computations. If no correcting entry is needed, give the reasons.

Exercise 4–15

The following pretax amounts were taken from the accounts of Sauls Corporation at December 31, 1976:

Cost of goods sold	$60,000
Sales revenue	95,000
Operating expenses	20,000
Extraordinary item, loss due to expropriation of plant by a foreign government (pretax)	10,000
Prior period adjustment, damages collected on lawsuit (pretax)	6,000
Cash dividends	4,000
Retained earnings balance, January 1, 1976	25,000
Common stock (par $10) outstanding, 10,000 shares.	

Assume an average 30% corporate income tax rate on all items. Assume the expropriation and the damages collected are subject to tax.

Required:

Prepare a combined single-step income statement and statement of retained earnings including income tax allocation and earnings per share. Show computations.

Exercise 4–16

The following pretax amounts were taken from the accounts of Rawls Corporation at December 31, 1976:

Sales revenue	$140,000
Cost of goods sold	80,000
Distribution and administrative expenses	45,000
Extraordinary item (gain from expropriation of foreign plant)	15,000
Prior period adjustment (additional tax assessment on 1972 return)	8,000
Interest expense	600
Cash dividends	5,000
Retained earnings balance, January 1, 1976	30,000
Common stock (par $5), 20,000 shares outstanding.	

Assume an average 40% corporate tax rate on all items. Assume the expropriation is subject to tax.

Required:

Prepare a combined multiple-step income statement and statement of retained earnings, including income tax allocation and earnings per share. Show computations.

PROBLEMS

Problem 4–1

Below is listed a number of transactions and amounts that are reported on the annual financial statement. For each item, you are to indicate how it should be reported. A list of responses is given so you can indicate your response by *code letter*. Enter only one letter for each item. You should comment on doubtful items.

Code	Classification
A.	Balance sheet, appropriately classified
	Income statement:
B.	Revenue
C.	Expense
D.	Unusual or infrequent, but not both
E.	Extraordinary item
	Statement of retained earnings:
F.	Prior period adjustment (as an addition or deduction)
G.	Addition to retained earnings
H.	Deduction to retained earnings
I.	Note to the financial statement only

1. ____ Total amount of cash and credit sales for the period.
2. ____ Allowance for doubtful accounts.
3. ____ Gain on sale of fixed asset.
4. ____ Hurricane damages.
5. ____ Depreciation expense for manufacturing company.
6. ____ Payment of $30,000 additional income tax assessment (on prior year's income).
7. ____ Earthquake damages.
8. ____ Distribution expenses.
9. ____ Estimated warranties payable.
10. ____ Gain on disposal of long-term investments in stocks.
11. ____ Net income for the period.
12. ____ Insurance gain on major casualty (fire) – insurance proceeds exceeded the book value of the assets destroyed.
13. ____ Cash dividends declared and paid.
14. ____ Rent collected on office space rented temporarily.
15. ____ Interest paid and interest accrued on liabilities.
16. ____ Dividends received on stocks held as an investment.
17. ____ Damages paid as a result of a lawsuit by an individual injured while shopping in the store; the litigation covered three years.
18. ____ Loss due to expropriation of a plant in a foreign country.
19. ____ A $10,000 bad debt – the receivable had been outstanding for five years and the party cannot be located.
20. ____ Adjustment due to correction of an error made two years earlier.
21. ____ On December 31, of current year, paid rent expense in advance for the next two years.
22. ____ Cost of goods sold.
23. ____ Interest collected from a customer on a one-year note receivable.
24. ____ Installment payment on a large machine, which included $1,000 interest for the current year.
25. ____ Year-end bonus of $50,000 paid to employees for performance during the year.

Problem 4–2

During the current year, 1976, Ayr Company completed a number of transactions that posed questions as to when revenue and/or expense should be recognized. The end of the accounting period is December 31. For each of the following selected transactions, state when revenue and/or expense should be recognized and give the basis for your decision:

a. Merchandise was sold on the credit basis during the year. The terms were 25% down payment plus six monthly payments. The collection experience on such sales, although not as good as on regular credit sales (due at end of month of sale), has been quite satisfactory.

b. On December 24, 1976, the company sold a used TV set that had been repossessed and was set up in used goods inventory at $60. The sales price was $110. At the date of sale, $70 cash was collected; the balance due in six months. There is a high probability that collection will not be made and the TV set probably will not be worth repossessing again.

c. During 1976 the company sold 30 TV sets for a total of $6,000 and collected cash in full. The sets are guaranteed for 12 months from date of sale. It is estimated that the guarantee will cost the company, on the average, $15 per set. At year-end, it was estimated that one half of the guarantees were still outstanding.

d. On December 14, 1976, received a $20,000 income tax refund from prior years. The negotiations extended over a three-year period.

e. Services were rendered to a customer starting on December 28, 1976, and will be completed January 4, 1977. Cash in full ($3,000) will be collected at date of completion of the services. Assume eight working days.

f. On July 1, 1976, paid a two-year insurance premium in advance, $600.

g. On December 30, 1976, sold merchandise for $5,000; terms, 2/10, n/30.

h. On December 1, 1976, sold a customer merchandise for $1,000. Collected $600 cash and received a $400, 8%, interest-bearing note for the remainder, due in three months.

i. On November 15, 1976, the court assessed the company damages amounting to $25,000 cash. The suit was filed in 1974 as a result of an accident in the company store. Payment will be made on January 10, 1977.

j. On December 23, 1976, purchased merchandise for resale, $18,000; terms, 2/10, n/30.

(*Hint:* Restudy the revenue, cost, and matching principles in Chapter 2.)

Problem 4–3

The following information was taken from the adjusted trial balance of Wonder Trading Corporation at December 31, 1976:

Merchandise inventory, January 1, 1976	$ 70,000
Purchases	121,400
Sales	394,600
Purchase returns	3,400
Sales returns	5,200
Common stock (par $10)	200,000
Depreciation expense (70% administrative; 30% distribution)	50,000
Rent revenue	3,600
Interest expense	6,400
Investment revenue	2,500
Distribution expenses (exclusive of depreciation)	105,500
General and administrative expenses (exclusive of depreciation)	46,000
Gain on sale of fixed assets (ordinary)	5,000
Loss on sale of long-term investments (ordinary)	3,600
Income tax expense (not including extraordinary item)	?
Extraordinary item: Major flood loss (tax savings already deducted)	20,000
Freight paid on purchases	1,000
Merchandise inventory, December 31, 1976	90,000

Assume an average 40% corporate income tax rate on all items (including capital gains and losses and extraordinary items).

Required:

1. Prepare a single-step income statement and a schedule of cost of goods sold to support it.
2. Prepare a multiple-step income statement including EPS.
3. Explain the relative merits and disadvantages of each format.

Problem 4–4

The following information was taken from the adjusted trial balance of Cox Manufacturing Corporation at December 31, 1976.

Sales	$980,000
Purchases	150,000
Raw materials inventory, January 1, 1976	30,000
Work in process inventory, January 1, 1976	40,000
Finished goods inventory, January 1, 1976	20,000
Sales returns	5,000
Purchase returns	4,000
Freight on purchases	7,500
Distribution expenses	140,000
General and administrative expenses	92,300
Rent revenue	4,800
Investment revenue	3,000
Gain on sale of fixed assets (ordinary)	8,000
Interest expense	9,000
Extraordinary gain (expropriation of plant by foreign government; income tax effect already deducted)	40,000
Loss on sale of long-term investments (ordinary)	10,000
Manufacturing expenses:	
Direct labor	230,000
Factory overhead	190,000
Raw materials inventory, December 31, 1976	24,000
Work in process inventory, December 31, 1976	38,000
Finished goods inventory, December 31, 1976	22,000
Income tax expense (not including extraordinary item)	?

Assume an average 40% corporate income tax rate on all items.

Required:

1. Prepare a schedule of cost of goods manufactured to supplement the income statement.
2. Prepare a single-step income statement including EPS. Assume 20,000 shares of common stock outstanding.
3. Prepare a multiple-step income statement including EPS.
4. Discuss the relative merits and disadvantages of each format.

Problem 4–5

The following pretax amounts were taken from the adjusted trial balance of Mason Company at December 31, 1976:

Revenues	$600,000
Expenses	480,000
Extraordinary item, loss (pretax)	30,000
Prior period adjustment, gain (pretax)	15,000
Beginning balance, retained earnings	55,000
Dividends paid	10,000

Common stock outstanding, 5,000 shares.

Required:

1. Prepare a single-step income statement and a statement of retained earnings with intraperiod tax allocation and EPS. Assume an average corporate income tax rate of 41.81% on all items.
2. Use the same data to complete the above requirement except assume a tax rate of 22% on the first $25,000 of income and 48% on all income above that amount (for all items). Compute intraperiod tax allocation in the following order: operating income, extraordinary items, and prior period adjustments (including EPS).
3. Give the entry to record income tax expense and income taxes payable under both requirements 1 and 2.
4. Assess the different results between 1 and 2.

Problem 4–6

The following pretax amounts were taken from the adjusted trial balance of Thyme Corporation at December 31, 1976:

Balance retained earnings, January 1, 1976	$ 48,000
Sales revenue (net of return sales)	200,000
Cost of goods sold	110,000
Distribution expenses	75,000
Administration expenses	25,000
Extraordinary item, gain (pretax)	30,000
Prior period adjustment, gain (pretax)	5,000
Dividends	6,000

Common stock outstanding, 10,000 shares.

Assume an average 30% corporate income tax rate on all items.

Required:

1. Prepare a single-step income statement and a statement of retained earnings with intraperiod tax allocation and EPS.
2. Assume net sales were $220,000 and that the prior period adjustment was a loss; all other amounts are the same as given. Prepare a single-step income statement and statement of retained earnings with intraperiod tax allocation and EPS.
3. Give the entry to record income taxes payable (assume none yet paid) for 1 and 2.

Problem 4–7

The following pretax amounts were taken from the adjusted trial balances of Walden Corporation at December 31, 1975, and 1976:

	1976	1975
Sales and service revenue	$200,000	$170,000
Cost of goods sold	80,000	70,000
Operating expenses	67,000	58,000
Extraordinary item, major casualty loss (pretax)	15,000	-0-
Prior period adjustment, refund from 1971 income taxes		10,000
Prior period adjustment, a loss (pretax)	20,000	
Cash dividends	36,000	4,000
Stock dividends (July 1, 1975, see below)		120,000*
Balance, retained earnings, January 1, 1975		160,000

Common stock (par $10) shares outstanding:

January 1, 1975	15,000
Stock dividends, July 1, 1975	5,000
December 31, 1975	20,000
October 1, 1976 sold and issued	10,000
December 31, 1976	30,000

* Amount debited to retained earnings.

Assume an average 40% corporate income tax rate on all items; including the casualty and prior period adjustment losses.

Required:

1. Prepare a comparative income statement, using single-step format, with columns for 1976 and 1975. Include earnings per share and intraperiod tax allocation. Show computations.
2. Prepare a comparative statement of retained earnings with columns for 1976 and 1975.
3. Give the entry for income taxes at the end of 1976; assume all 1975 taxes have been paid.

Problem 4–8

The following pretax amounts were taken from the adjusted trial balances of Myers Corporation at December 31, 1975, and 1976:

	1976	1975
Sales revenue	$360,000	$340,000
Cost of goods sold	190,000	175,000
Distribution expenses	70,000	64,000
Administrative expenses	54,000	51,000
Extraordinary items (pretax):		
Loss from major casualty	20,000	
Gain from expropriation of plant by foreign government		16,000
Prior period adjustments (pretax):		
Damages collected from lawsuit	38,000	
Additional income taxes assessed on 1970 return		9,000
Dividends:		
Common stock dividend (10,000 shares)		150,000*
Cash	5,000	4,000
Balance retained earnings, January 1, 1975		275,000

Common stock outstanding (par $10):	Shares
January 1, 1975	20,000
July 1, 1975, common stock dividend	10,000
December 31, 1975	30,000
July 1, 1976, sold and issued	6,000
December 31, 1976	36,000

*Amount debited to retained earnings.

Assume an average 40% corporate income tax rate on all items (including the casualty loss, expropriation, and damages).

Required:

1. Prepare a comparative income statement, using single-step format, with columns for 1976 and 1975. Include earnings per share and intraperiod tax allocation. Show computations.
2. Prepare a comparative statement of retained earnings with columns for 1976 and 1975.
3. Give the entry for income taxes at the end of 1976; assume all 1975 taxes and the 1970 assessment have been paid.

Problem 4–9

Presented below are the comparative statements of consolidated income and retained earnings of the Sureal Corporation for the years ended December 31, 1975, and 1976, as prepared by the corporation's president.

SUREAL CORPORATION
Statements of Consolidated Income and Retained Earnings
Years Ended December 31

	1976	1975
Revenues:		
Sales	$275,000	$233,000
Investment revenue	10,000	7,500
Gain on sale of fixed assets (ordinary)		10,000
Refund of income taxes from 1973	13,750	
Total Revenues	298,750	250,500
Expenses:		
Cost of goods sold	115,000	102,000
Depreciation	17,000	15,000
Distribution expenses	45,000	49,000
General and administrative expenses	57,000	54,000
Loss on destruction of plant (assume extraordinary)	12,000	
Interest expense	8,000	
Federal income tax expense	15,500	13,250
Total Expenses	269,500	233,250
Net Income	$ 29,250	$ 17,250
Retained earnings, January 1	$ 14,225	$ 4,975
Add net income	29,250	17,250
Total	43,475	22,225
Deduct cash dividends	12,000	8,000
Retained Earnings, December 31	$ 31,475	$ 14,225

Assume the income tax amount is correct; the loss on destruction of plant is given net of tax. Assume the average number of shares of common stock outstanding were: 1975, 15,000; 1976, 18,000.

Required:

Recast the above combined statement of income (use a modified single-step format) and retained earnings. Make it complete in every respect. Comment on any doubtful items as well as preferred alternatives you selected. Include earnings per share.

Problem 4–10

Brown Corporation is undergoing the annual audit by the independent CPA at December 31, 1976. During the audit, the following situations were found that needed attention:

a. Near the end of 1974, an asset that cost $1,200 was debited to operating expenses. The asset has a six-year estimated life and no residual value. The company uses straight-line depreciation.

b. During 1976 the company constructed a small warehouse using their own employees. The cost was $10,000. However, before the decision to build it themselves was made, they solicited a bid from a contractor; the bid was $15,000. Upon completion of the warehouse, they made the following entry in the accounts:

Warehouse (a fixed asset)	15,000	
Cash		10,000
Miscellaneous revenue		5,000

c. Prior to recording depreciation expense for 1976, the management decided that a large machine that cost $128,000 should have been depreciated over a useful life of 16 years instead of 20 years. The machine was acquired January 2, 1971. Assume the residual value of $8,000 was not changed.

d. During December 1976 the company disposed of an old machine for $6,000 cash. Annual depreciation was $2,000 per year; at the beginning of 1976 the accounts reflect the following:

Machine (cost)	$18,000
Accumulated depreciation	13,000

At date of disposal, the following entry was made:

Cash	6,000	
Machine		6,000

e. A patent that cost $3,400 is being amortized over its legal life of 17 years at $200 per year. At the end of 1975, it had been amortized down to $800. At the end of 1976, it was determined, realistically, in view of a competitor's patent, that it will have no economic value to the company by the end of 1977. Straight-line amortization is used.

Required:

For each of the above situations, explain what should be done in the accounts. If a journal entry is needed to implement your decision in each case, provide it along with supporting computations.

Problem 4–11

The following pretax amounts were taken from the accounts of Heinz Corporation at December 31, 1976:

Sales revenue	$540,000
Cost of goods sold	280,000
Distribution expenses	105,000
Administration expenses	70,000
Interest revenue	1,000
Interest expense	3,000
Unusual item – gain on sale of major fixed asset	19,000
Extraordinary item – loss on expropriation of foreign plant (pretax)	30,000
Balance retained earnings, January 1, 1976	93,000
Cash dividends	15,000
Prior period adjustment – additional taxes assessed on 1973 return	8,000

Common stock (par $1), 50,000 shares outstanding.

Restriction on retained earnings amounting to $25,000 per indenture agreement on bonds payable.

Assume an average 45% corporate income tax rate on all items.

Required:

Prepare a combined multiple-step income statement and statement of retained earnings including tax allocation and earnings per share. Show computations.

Problem 4–12

The following amounts were taken from the accounting records of Frumer Corporation at December 31, 1976:

Sales revenue	$240,000
Service revenue	60,000
Cost of goods sold	130,000
Distribution and administrative expenses	125,000
Investment revenue	6,000
Interest expense	4,000
Infrequent item – loss on sale of long-term investment	10,000
Extraordinary item – earthquake loss (pretax)	27,000
Cash dividends	8,000
Prior period adjustment – tax refund on 1971 tax return	12,000
Balance retained earnings, January 1, 1976	78,000

Common stock (par $5), 30,000 shares outstanding.

Restriction on retained earnings, $50,000 per bond payable indenture.

Assume an average 45% corporate income tax rate on all items.

Required:

Prepare a combined single-step income statement and statement of retained earnings including tax allocation and earnings per share. Show computations.

Problem 4–13

The following financial statements have come to you for review:

BROWN PRODUCTION COMPANY
Profit and Loss Statement
December 31, 1976

Incomes:			
Gross sales		$256,800	
Less: Sales returns		5,120	
Net sales			$251,680
Costs and expenses:			
Cost of goods sold:			
Inventory, January 1		98,500	
Purchases	$132,600		
Less: Purchase returns	2,780	129,820	
		228,320	
Inventory, December 31		102,300	
Cost of goods sold			126,020
Gross profit			125,660
Operating costs:			
Selling expenses		38,000	
General and administrative expenses:			
General expenses	20,000		
Depreciation	8,800		
Bad debt expense	1,080	29,880	
Total Operating Costs			67,880
Income from operations			57,780
Other income:			
Interest income			970
Profit before federal income taxes			58,750
Less: Federal income taxes			28,720
Net Profit			$ 30,030

BROWN PRODUCTION COMPANY
Statement of Earned Surplus
December 31, 1976

Balance, January 1		$267,600
Corrections:		
Additions:		
Depreciation overstated		3,400
Adjusted balance		271,000
Additions during current year:		
Profit	$30,030	
Gain on sale of land	8,200	38,230
		309,230
Deductions:		
Dividends	30,000	
Loss on sale of machinery	9,650	39,650
Earned Surplus Balance, December 31, 1976 (carried to the balance sheet)		$269,580

Required:

Critically evaluate the above statements. What reporting concept appears to have been applied? Cite items to support your response. List and explain all of the aspects of the above statements that you would change in order to conform to appropriate reporting and terminology currently.

Problem 4–14

The following income statement and statement of retained earnings were prepared by the bookkeeper for the Snow Corporation:

SNOW CORPORATION
Profit and Loss Statement
December 31, 1976

Sales income (net)		$ 85,000
Service income		46,000
Total		131,000
Cost of sales:		
Inventory	$ 34,000	
Purchases (net)	71,000	
Total	105,000	
Inventory	40,000	65,000
Gross profit on sales		66,000
Expenses:		
Salaries, wages etc.	36,000	
Depreciation and write-offs	7,000	
Rent	3,000	
Taxes	500	
Utilities	2,100	
Promotion	900	
Sundry	6,700	(55,200)
Special items:		
Gain on asset sold		6,000
Inventory theft		(2,800)
Net Profit		$ 14,000

SNOW CORPORATION
Earned Surplus Statement
December 31, 1976

Balance, December 31, 1975, earned surplus		$27,000
Add: Profit		14,000
Correction of inventory error		5,000
Total		46,000
Deduct: Fire loss	$13,000	
Dividends	10,000	
Earned surplus transferred to capital	5,000	28,000
Balance, December 31, 1976, Earned Surplus		$18,000

Required:

List all aspects of the above statements that you consider to be wrong. Give your recommendations on each item.

Problem 4–15

The Appendix to this chapter gives an actual income statement and a statement of retained earnings. Examine them carefully and respond to the following questions:

a. Are they comparative statements? Explain.
b. Are they consolidated statements? What do you understand this to mean?
c. Is the income statement in single-step or multiple-step format? Explain any variations in format from those illustrated in this chapter. What title was used for the income statement?
d. Is the combined income statement and statement of retained earnings used?
e. How many different kinds of revenue are reported? How many different kinds of expenses are reported?
f. Is this a trading or a manufacturing company? Explain.
g. How is interest expense and interest revenue reported?
h. Is the total amount of depreciation expense reported? How?
i. Are there any unusual or infrequently occurring (but not both) items reported? How?
j. Is a discontinuance of a segment of the business reported? How? Is it net of tax?
k. Are any extraordinary items reported? What are they? Are they net of tax?
l. How are the expenses classified?
m. How are the revenues classified?
n. Was income taxes allocated? Explain.
o. How many earnings per share amounts were reported for the last year? Was there any explanation of the computation of EPS?
p. What "differences" were reported? Gross margin? Income from continuing operations? Income before extraordinary items? Net income? Others (list)?
q. What was the profit margin (net income divided by sales) for the last year?
r. List all unusual features of the income statement. What aspects of it would you criticize? Explain.
s. What title was used on the statement of retained earnings?
t. Were any prior period adjustments reported? Explain each. Were they net of tax?
u. Do you agree with their classification as prior period adjustments? Explain.
v. Were any dividends reported? What kind?
w. Did the auditor's report express any reservations about the income statement? Explain.
x. How many notes to the financial statements referred to the income statement? List the principal point at issue in each note. Overall, did the notes satisfy your full-disclosure expectations? Explain.
y. Were there any unusual features in the statement of retained earnings? Explain. What aspects of it would you criticize? Explain.
z. Overall, do you believe these two statements could be improved with respect to format and terminology? Explain each change that you would suggest for consideration.

Problem 4–16

The Appendix to Chapter 5 gives an actual income statement and statement of retained earnings. Examine them carefully and respond to the questions posed in Problem 4–15.

Problem 4–17

Obtain an audited financial statement for the latest year for a company of your choice (from the library or other source) and use it as a basis for responding to each of the questions posed in Problem 4–15.

Problem 4–18

The following income statement was developed by Hypothetical Company. It is unusual because all of the subclassifications of items are included.

HYPOTHETICAL COMPANY
Income Statement
For the Year Ended December 31, 1976

Sales			$980,000
Cost of goods sold			420,000
Gross margin			560,000
Operating expenses:			
Distribution	$252,000		
General and administrative	78,000	$330,000	
Other revenue and expenses:			
Interest expense	7,000		
Interest revenue	3,000	4,000	
Unusual or infrequent gains and losses:			
Gain on sale of investment	21,500		
Losses from storm damage	7,500	(14,000)	
Total Operating Expenses and Unusual or Infrequent Items			320,000
Pretax income from continuing operations and other items			240,000
Income taxes (46% average rate)			110,400
Income from continuing operations and other items			129,600
Discontinuance of a segment of the business (loss)		60,000	
Less: Income tax savings (46%)		27,600	32,400
Income before extraordinary item			97,200
Extraordinary item:			
Loss from earthquake		40,000	
Less: Income tax savings (46%)		18,400	21,600
Net Income			$ 75,600

Earnings per share (50,000 shares common stock outstanding):

Income before extraordinary item ($97,200 ÷ 50,000 shares)	$1.94
Extraordinary item (loss) ($21,600 ÷ 50,000 shares)	(0.43)
Net income ($75,600 ÷ 50,000 shares)	$1.51

Entry for income taxes:

Income tax expense	64,400	
Income taxes payable ($110,400 − $27,600 − $18,400 = $64,400)		64,400

Required:

Critically review the format and captions used from the viewpoint of the statement user. Redraft the statement using the format and captions you believe should be used. Comment on any particular items you encounter.

Chapter 5

Review—The Balance Sheet and Statement of Changes in Financial Position

The preceding chapter reviewed the income statement and statement of retained earnings. This chapter will review the two remaining statements required by generally accepted accounting principles—the balance sheet and the statement of changes in financial position. The relationships between the required statements were graphically presented in Exhibit 4–1. In Part A, we will discuss the balance sheet; and in Part B, the statement of changes in financial position.

PART A—BALANCE SHEET

A balance sheet presents the assets, liabilities, and owners' equity of an enterprise, at a specific date, measured in conformity with generally accepted accounting principles. Because it is a presentation of the current *financial position* of an entity, it is often referred to as the *statement of financial position*. The designation, balance sheet, was adopted during the period when accounting first evolved; it refers to the fact that it balances in terms of the fundamental accounting model: Assets = Liabilities + Owners' Equity. It is unfortunate that this nondescriptive designation continues to be widely used today. Because of wide usage, we use it in this text, although reluctantly.

CHARACTERISTICS OF THE BALANCE SHEET

The financial position of an enterprise is represented by the various assets owned, obligations owed, and claims of the owners at a designated date. For example, a balance sheet should be dated "At December 31, 19XX," in contrast with an income statement, which is dated "For the Year Ended December 31, 19XX." In APB *Statement No. 4*, financial position is defined as:

> The *financial position* of an enterprise at a particular time comprises its assets, liabilities, and owners' equity and the relationship among them, plus contingencies, commitments, and other financial matters that pertain to the enterprise at that time. The financial position of an enterprise is presented in the *balance sheet* and in notes to the financial statements.[1]

Fundamentally a balance sheet reports *(a)* a listing of the assets, liabilities, and components of owners' equity; and *(b)* a quantitative measurement (valuation) of each item listed. First, let's look at the definitions of the three categories reported.

Assets Defined

Assets can be defined at both a conceptual and a pragmatic level. At the conceptual level, two representative definitions are:

> Assets are economic resources devoted to business purposes within a specific accounting entity; they are aggregates of service-potentials available for or beneficial to expected operations.[2]
>
> Assets represent expected future economic benefits, rights to which have been acquired by the enterprise as a result of some current or past transaction.[3]

Hendricksen observes that these basic definitions require the following characteristics:

1. There must exist some specific right to future benefits or service potentials.
2. The rights must accrue to a specific individual or firm.
3. There must be a legally enforceable claim to the rights or services.[4]

In contrast, APB *Statement No. 4* provides a pragmatic definition that focuses on current accounting practice, viz:[5]

> *Assets*—economic resources of an enterprise that are recognized and measured in conformity with generally accepted accounting principles. Assets also include certain deferred charges that are not resources but that are recognized and measured in conformity with generally accepted accounting principles.[6]

This definition defines assets in terms of generally accepted accounting principles; this approach has been subjected to criticism because of the implicit circularity.

---

[1] AICPA, "Basic Concepts and Accounting Principles Underlying Financial Statements," *Statement of the Accounting Principles Board No. 4* (New York, October 1970), pp. 49–50.

[2] AAA Committee on Accounting Concepts and Standards, *Accounting and Reporting Standards for Corporate Financial Statements and Preceding Statements and Supplements* (Columbus, Ohio, 1957), p. 3.

[3] Robert T Sprouse and Maurice Moonitz, "A Tentative Set of Broad Accounting Principles for Business Enterprises," *Accounting Research Study No. 3* (New York: AICPA, 1962), p. 20.

[4] Eldon S. Hendricksen, *Accounting Theory* (Homewood, Ill.: Richard D. Irwin, Inc., 1970), p. 253.

[5] AICPA, APB *Statement No. 4*, pp. 49–50.

[6] Deferred charges that are not resources include items such as "charges from income tax allocation." See also Chapter 11.

Liabilities Defined

Liabilities may be conceptually defined as "obligations to convey assets or perform services, obligations resulting from past or current transactions and requiring settlement in the future."[7] APB *Statement No. 4* provides the following pragmatic definition that reflects current practice:

> *Liabilities*—economic obligations of an enterprise that are recognized and measured in conformity with generally accepted accounting principles. Liabilities also include certain deferred credits that are not obligations but that are recognized and measured in conformity with generally accepted accounting principles.[8]

Owners' Equity Defined

Owners' equity is defined as the amount of the interest of the owners of an enterprise; it is the excess of the assets over the liabilities. It is also referred to as the *residual interest*. The owners' equity section of the balance sheet reports the various *sources* of capital provided by owners; that is, the amount of resources provided by owners (contributed capital) and the amount of internally generated resources retained by the entity (retained earnings).

MEASUREMENTS (VALUATIONS) ON THE BALANCE SHEET

Assets as measured on the balance sheet rarely represent their market value at the date of the balance sheet. Rather, the assets are measured at what is often called *book value*. Book value is the result of applying the cost and matching principles (with certain exceptions); generally, it is acquisition cost less accumulated write-offs to date. Cash is reported at its current value, accounts receivable at expected net realizable value (amount of the receivables less the allowance for doubtful accounts), inventories and marketable equity securities usually are reported at lower of cost or market, and plant and equipment are reported at cost less accumulated depreciation.

Liabilities as measured on the balance sheet usually represent their current cash equivalent or discounted present value (which is generally the maturity amount of the debt).

Since *owners' equity* is a residual amount, it does not report the current fair market value of the business; rather, it is a measurement of the owners' interest that reflects the measurements used for the assets and liabilities, as determined in accordance with generally accepted accounting principles.

Throughout the remaining chapters of this book, we will identify and apply the accounting concepts, standards, and procedures used to derive the measurements that are reported on the financial statements of an enterprise.

---

[7] Sprouse and Moonitz, *Accounting Research Study No. 3*, p. 37.

[8] AICPA, APB *Statement No. 4*, pp. 49–50.

IMPORTANCE OF THE BALANCE SHEET

The balance sheet generally is viewed as of less significance to decision-makers than the income statement. Nevertheless, sophisticated decision-makers consider each part of the overall financial statement essential to gaining a balanced view. This includes the income statement, balance sheet, statement of changes in financial position, supporting schedules, notes to the statements, and the auditor's report. To single out one of these parts for exclusive use often results in inadequate information and serious oversights. Regardless of what may be reported on a single statement, the *opinion* of the independent CPA (i.e., the auditor) is overriding. Similarly, the notes may report the single most important issue with respect to a particular decision. Because of the complexity of most enterprises and the varied economic ramifications, users of financial statements should focus on the totality of the financial statements rather than upon a single amount (such as EPS) or a single report, such as the income statement.

The balance sheet, as a part of the total financial statement, is important because it tells, at a specific date, the different assets held, the obligations by type and amount, and the sources and amounts of owners' equity. The balance sheet also provides subclassifications intended to aid the user. Various balance sheet amounts often are used in conjunction with amounts from other sources (such as the income statement) to analyze relationships, trends, and so on. Examples of relevant relationships are asset turnover, ratio of debt to owners' equity, earnings per share, and return on investment. Classification of liabilities as long term and short term often aids creditors and others in assessing the ability of the entity to meet its future obligations. All decision makers are interested in these issues as well as the composition of the assets and the capital structure.

Some decision-makers believe that the balance sheet has limited usefulness because the assets are not reported at their *current fair market value*. This is a basic problem facing the accounting profession because it poses critical measurement problems. Criticism is also directed to the fact that some balance sheet amounts (and other reported amounts) involve estimates, such as accumulated depreciation. Assuming the estimates are realistic, this criticism is not well founded. Of necessity, all decision making is surrounded by uncertainty; therefore it requires extensive use of estimates. Actual historical data provide the decision-maker only with a base from which to make realistic estimates or predictions.

BALANCE SHEET FORMAT

The reporting principle requires that a full and complete balance sheet be presented as an integral part of the periodic financial statement. Although the format of the balance sheet is not specified, one of two different formats is almost always used. The *account form* was used by approximately 71% of the 600 companies reported in the *Accounting Trends and Techniques, 1975* (AICPA). The three major categories may be positioned either horizontally or vertically (the usual arrangement), viz:[9]

1. Account Form—Horizontal Arrangement

Assets		*Liabilities*	
Details		Details	
		Total Liabilities	$300,000
		Owners' Equity	
		Details	
		Total Owners' Equity.	600,000
Total Assets	$900,000	Total Liabilities and Owners' Equity..............	$900,000

2. Report Forms—Vertical Arrangement

Assets		Or: *Assets*	
Details		Details	
Total Assets	$900,000	Total Assets	$900,000
Liabilities		*Less Liabilities*	
Details		Details	
Total Liabilities	$300,000	Total Liabilities	300,000
Owners' Equity		*Owners' Equity*	
Details		Details	
Total Owners' Equity.	600,000	Total Owners' Equity.	$600,000
Total Liabilities and Owners' Equity..............	$900,000		

CLASSIFICATIONS IN THE BALANCE SHEET

To help the decision-maker in analysis, interpretation, and evaluation of the wide range of financial information reported on a balance sheet, items are usually grouped according to common characteristics. The assets tend to be grouped in decreasing order of liquidity (i.e., nearness to cash), and the liabilities by time to due date, and owners' equity in decreasing order of permanency. Classifications of information used in a balance sheet, and the array of items under each classification, are influenced by the industry and type and size of the enterprise. For example, the balance sheet of a financial institution, such as a bank, will reflect quite different classifications than those for a manufacturing company. Variations in format and classification observed in actual statements generally are designed to comply with the reporting principle

[9] Another, the financial position format, is sometimes used. It is a vertical arrangement that shows noncurrent assets added to and noncurrent liabilities deducted from working capital to equal owners' equity.

since it specifies that reporting must be informative, fair, and not misleading. Therefore, flexibility in format and classifications is generally viewed as desirable. Nevertheless, there is a reasonable degree of uniformity. Insofar as it is feasible to generalize on balance sheet classifications, and in view of the variety of captions often used, the following classifications are representative of sound reporting practices:

Assets

1. Current assets (including prepaid expenses).
2. Investments and funds.
3. Operational (or fixed) assets – tangible.
4. Operational assets – intangible.
5. Other assets.
6. Deferred charges.

Liabilities

1. Current liabilities (including short-term deferred credits).
2. Long-term liabilities (including long-term deferred credits).

Owners' Equity

1. Contributed capital:
   a. Capital stock.
   b. Contributed capital in excess of capital stock.
2. Retained earnings.
3. Unrealized capital increment.

Observe that the above classifications provide for the three major captions: assets, liabilities, and owners' equity. Under each major caption are several subclassifications, the designations of which tend to vary as explained above. Observe that we have included *deferred credits* in liabilities (some are current; others long term); however, a separate caption, "Deferred Credits," sometimes is reported between long-term liabilities and owners' equity. This poses an inconsistency since the fundamental accounting model represented by the balance sheet (Assets = Liabilities + Owners' Equity) does not include a separate category for deferred credits. Observe that *deferred charges* (i.e., long-term prepaid expenses) are included in the asset category. Following the same logic, deferred credits are properly classified as liabilities.

An illustrative balance sheet is shown in Exhibit 5–1 to supplement the discussions to follow.

CURRENT ASSETS

Current assets are cash and other assets commonly identified as those which are *reasonably expected* to be realized in cash, or to be sold, or consumed during the *normal operating cycle* of the business or within one year from the balance sheet date, whichever is the longer. The normal operating cycle is defined as the average period of time between the expenditure of cash for goods and services and the date that those goods and services are reconverted to cash. It is the average length of time from cash expenditure, to inventory, to sale, to accounts receivable, and back to cash. For many businesses, the operating cycle is shorter than one year. However, there are certain businesses, particularly those manufacturing businesses with extended production processes, where the operating cycle extends beyond one year; examples include shipbuilding, distilleries, and logging. The length of the normal operating cycle is important to the classification of current assets when it extends beyond one year.

Current assets usually are presented on the balance sheet in order of decreasing liquidity (i.e., nearness to cash conversion). The major items comprising current assets, in order of liquidity, are: cash, short-term investments, receivables, inventories, and prepaid expenses. Items that are not current assets include: cash and claims to cash which are restricted for uses other than current operations, long-term investments, receivables which have an extended maturity date, land and natural resources, depreciable assets, and long-term prepayments of expenses.

Although the definition of current assets is reasonably clear-cut, problems are often encountered in implementation. In applying the definition of current assets, the phases "normal operating cycle" and "reasonably expected to be realized in cash" both involve judgment in application. Consequently, there is a tendency to incorrectly classify certain items as current assets because of their favorable effect on working capital. Recall that working capital is the difference between current assets and current liabilities. For example, marketable securities may be classified as a current or noncurrent asset depending upon the *stated intention* of the management as to the planned holding period. By a simple change in *intention* by the management, classification of the securities can be changed. Prepaid expenses is another area where there is considerable variation in classification. A short-term prepayment should be classified as a current asset (i.e., a prepaid expense), whereas a long-term prepayment should be classified as noncurrent (i.e., a deferred charge). Nevertheless, a three-year prepayment of an insurance premium usually is classified as a current asset, a procedure that can be justified only on the basis of materiality.

In some companies and industries, there is no basis for using a current asset category. For example, financial institutions, such as banks, do not report current assets because it would be pointless in view of the nature of their asset structure. Exhibit 5–1 illustrates how current assets should be reported. Observe the parenthetical information provided to satisfy the full-disclosure requirement.

CURRENT LIABILITIES

The definition of current liabilities parallels the definition of current assets; that is, current liabilities are short-term liabilities "whose liquidation is reasonably expected to require the use of existing resources properly classified as current assets, or the creation of other liabilities."[10]

[10] AICPA, *Accounting Research and Terminology Bulletins, Final Edition*, (New York, 1961), p. 21.

EXHIBIT 5–1

AB CORPORATION
Statement of Financial Position (i.e., Balance Sheet)
At December 31, 1976

Assets

Current Assets:			
Cash			$ 34,000
Short-term investments (current market value $21,000)			20,000
Accounts receivable (trade)		$ 43,100	
Less: Allowance for doubtful accounts		1,300	41,800
Merchandise inventory (*Fifo,* lower of cost or market)			120,000
Prepaid expenses:			
Supplies inventory			1,200
Prepaid insurance			3,000
Total Current Assets			220,000
Investments and Funds:			
Investment in bonds of X Corporation (at cost)		30,000	
Investment in stock of Y Corporation (equity basis)		70,000	
Plant expansion fund		50,000	
Total Investments and Funds			150,000
Land, Building, and Equipment:			
Land		24,000	
Building	$200,000		
Less: Accumulated depreciation (straight line)	80,000	120,000	
Equipment and fixtures	140,000		
Less: Accumulated depreciation (straight line)	56,000	84,000	
Total Land, Building and Equipment			228,000
Intangible Assets:			
Patent (cost, $17,000, less accumulated amortization, $8,000)		9,000	
Franchise (cost, $30,000, less accumulated amortization, $14,000)		16,000	
Total Intangible Assets			25,000
Other Assets:			
Land held for future building site			37,000
Deferred Charges:			
Rearrangement costs			8,000
Total Assets			$668,000

Current liabilities include the following short-term items:

1. Accounts payable for goods and services that enter into the operating cycle of the business.
2. Special payables for nonoperating items and services.
3. Short-term notes payable.
4. Collections in advance for unearned revenue (such as rent revenue collected in advance).
5. Accrued expenses for wages, salaries, commissions, rentals, royalties, income, and other taxes.
6. Other obligations to be paid out of current assets such as serial maturities of long-term debts.

EXHIBIT 5–1 *(continued)*

Liabilities			
Current Liabilities:			
Accounts payable (trade)			$ 43,700
Notes payable			20,000
Rent revenue collected in advance			1,800
Accrued wages payable			2,000
Current payment on long-term note			20,000
Income taxes payable			12,500
Total Current Liabilities			100,000
Long-Term Liabilities:			
Note payable, 9%, due 1977–78	$ 40,000		
Less 1977 current payment	20,000	$ 20,000	
Bonds payable, 6%, due 1985	150,000		
Less unamortized discount	4,000	146,000	
Total Long-Term Liabilities			166,000
Total Liabilities			266,000
Stockholders' Equity			
Contributed Capital:			
Preferred stock, 6% cumulative, nonparticipating, authorized 20,000 shares, par $10, issued and outstanding 5,000 shares		50,000	
Common stock, nopar, authorized 100,000 shares, issued and outstanding 75,000 shares		225,000	
Total Stated Capital		275,000	
Additional contributed capital:			
In excess of par value of preferred stock		45,000	
Total Contributed Capital		320,000	
Retained earnings (Note A)		82,000	
Total Stockholders' Equity			402,000
Total Liabilities and Stockholders' Equity			$668,000

Note A. Under the terms of the bond indenture, an amount of retained earnings, determined by a formula, is restricted from dividend availability. The formula, computed for 1976, restricts retained earnings in the amount of $56,000. This amount will be increased each year as provided by the bond indenture formula. When the bonds are retired, the restriction will be automatically removed.

Items not properly classified as current liabilities include long-term notes, bonds, and obligations that will not be paid out of current assets. For example, a bond issue due during the coming year would not be classified as a current liability if it is to be paid out of a special cash fund classified under the caption "Investments and Funds." Similarly, a currently maturing bond issue that is to be refunded (i.e., paid off by issuing a new series of bonds) should not be classified as a current liability as specified in FASB *Statement Nos. 6* and *12.*

WORKING CAPITAL

Working capital is defined as current assets minus current liabilities. Because it is an abstract concept, this does not define working capital; it simply tells how it is computed. If all of the current assets were converted to cash at their *book value* and all of the current liabilities paid, it would be the amount of cash remaining. Although the concept of working capital is widely used by accountants and security analysts, many investors have problems with it because of the abstraction. They understand cash, as it is definable and circulates freely; in contrast, no one ever handles, receives, or pays "working capital" as such. It is for this reason that many investors are more concerned with the items that comprise current assets and current liabilities than with the abstract difference between two opposites. A company may well report an excellent working capital position and at the same time have a serious cash deficiency. For these and other reasons, many accountants believe that cash flow statements are significantly more informative than are working capital statements (see Part B in this Chapter).

Nevertheless, the amount of working capital and the working capital ratio is widely viewed as a measure of liquidity; that is, the ability of the enterprise to meet its short-term obligations. To illustrate, AB Corporation, Exhibit 5-1, reported the following:

Current assets	$220,000
Current liabilities	100,000
Difference—Working Capital	$120,000

The amount of working capital is $120,000; and the working capital, or current, ratio is: $220,000 ÷ $100,000 = 2.2. The ratio indicates that the current assets are 2.2 times the current liabilities, or that for each $1 of current liabilities there is $2.20 in current assets. Because of the tendency of creditors and security analysts to view working capital as an index of liquidity, the independent auditor sometimes encounters attempts to misclassify some assets as current and some liabilities as noncurrent in order to report a better working capital position than actually exists.

Offsetting of current assets and liabilities is improper because this practice avoids full-disclosure and would permit a business to show a more favorable current ratio than actually exists. For example, a business whose current assets consist of cash of $20,000 and receivables of $25,000 and currently owing notes payable of $10,000 and accounts payable of $5,000 has a current ratio of 3 to 1. If the intent to use $10,000 of the cash to pay the notes is reflected in the balance sheet by offsetting, the current ratio would rise to 7 to 1. Offsetting is permissible only where a legal right of offset exists; thus, it would be proper to offset a $5,000 overdraft in one account with a bank against another account reflecting $8,000 on deposit in that same bank. Offsetting the two amounts where two different banks are involved is unacceptable.

INVESTMENTS AND FUNDS

This caption is often labeled "Investments." It includes noncurrent assets, other than the operating assets, acquired for their financial or investment advantage, and funds set aside for future purposes. Items reported under this caption are long-term commitments; they include:

1. Long-term investments in securities, such as stocks, bonds, and long-term notes.
2. Investments in subsidiaries including long-term advances.
3. Long-term investments in tangible assets such as land and buildings which are not used in current operations.
4. Funds set aside for long-term future use such as bond sinking funds (to retire bonds payable), expansion funds, stock retirement funds, and long-term savings deposits.
5. Cash surrender value of life insurance policies.

The important distinctions are that the items *(a)* are nonoperational, and *(b)* management plans their long-term retention. The fact that an investment is currently marketable does not prevent its inclusion under this caption. Exhibit 5–1 illustrates typical reporting of this category of assets.

OPERATIONAL ASSETS

Operational assets are defined as those assets used in carrying out the operations of the entity. Operational assets are distinguished from stock in trade (i.e., inventories of raw materials, work in process, finished goods, merchandise, and supplies). Historically, operational assets have been labeled as *fixed assets* because of their relative permanence or long-term nature. Operational assets are subclassified as follows:

1. Tangible—Those characterized by physical existence such as land, buildings, machinery, equipment, furniture, fixtures, tools, containers, and natural resources.
2. Intangible—Those having no physical existence but having value because of the rights their ownership confers. Examples are patents, copyrights, trademarks, brand names, leaseholds, formulas, processes, and goodwill.

Operational Assets—Tangible

This group of operational assets is separately reported on the balance sheet under various captions depending upon the type of business. Manufacturing enterprises generally use captions such as *property, plant, and equipment;* and other enterprises use captions such as *property and equipment,* or simply *property.* Companies seldom use the older caption, *fixed assets.*

Tangible operational assets include items that are not subject to depreciation (land) and depreciable items, such as buildings, machinery, and fixtures. Land should be reported separately from depreciable assets. *APB Opinion No. 12* requires that the balance sheet report *(a)* balances of major classes of depreciable assets by nature or function; *(b)* accumulated depreciation, either by major classes of depreciable assets or in total; and *(c)* a general description of the methods used in computing depreciation for the major classes of operational assets. The word "reserve" should not be used to refer to accumulated depreciation. Exhibit 5-1 illustrates appropriate reporting of tangible operational assets.

Operational Assets – Intangible

This classification (assets having no physical existence) is separately reported on the balance sheet under the title *intangible assets*. Major items should be separately listed; and the accumulated amount of amortization, if material in amount, should be disclosed. Seldom is the contra account, accumulated amortization, separately listed; this contrasts with the usual treatment given tangible operational assets (see Exhibit 5-1).

OTHER ASSETS

"Other assets" are those which cannot be reasonably categorized under the usual asset classifications. Examples include cash in closed banks, stock subscriptions receivable (when demand for payment will not be made in the near future), and idle operational assets. Items should be analyzed carefully before being reported as other assets because often there is a logical basis for classifying them elsewhere. Items such as deferred strike losses and flood losses intended to be written off in time are sometimes reported as other assets. This treatment is unsupportable inasmuch as there is no element of future benefit associated with such losses; hence, there is no asset value.

DEFERRED CHARGES

Deferred charges represent debit balances derived from expenditures not recognized as costs of operations of current or prior periods but involving a future benefit, and hence they are carried forward to be matched with future revenues. The everyday meaning of deferred is *delayed*, and charge is synonymous with *debit;* hence, these "delayed debits" have been held for matching against future revenues. Deferred charges are distinguished from prepaid expenses on the basis of the *time* over which they will be amortized; that is, they involve a longer period of time than do prepaid expenses. The following accounts typify those found under the "Deferred Charges" caption: Machinery Rearrangement Costs, Taxes (especially in connection with tax deferments such as discussed in Chapter 11), Organization Costs (alternatively shown under "intangibles"), Pension Costs Paid in Advance and Insurance Prepayments (long-term prepayments not classed as current), and start-up costs.

LONG-TERM LIABILITIES

A long-term liability is an obligation that will not require the use of current assets during the upcoming normal operating cycle or during the next year, whichever is longer. All liabilities not appropriately classified as current liabilities are reported under this caption. Typical long-term liabilities are bonds payable, long-term notes payable, long-term lease obligations, and the noncurrent portion of deferred income taxes.

Bonds payable should be reported at their current debt equivalent, or their present value, at the date of the balance sheet. Therefore, when reporting bonds payable, any unamortized premium should be added to the amount of the bonds and any discount should be subtracted. To illustrate:

Bonds sold at a discount:

Long-Term Liabilities:		
Bonds payable, 6%, due 19XX	$100,000	
Less: Unamortized bond discount	7,000	$ 93,000

Bonds sold at a premium:

Long-Term Liabilities:		
Bonds payable, 6%, due 19XX	$100,000	
Add: Unamortized bond premium	7,000	$107,000

DEFERRED CREDITS

Occasionally a company will include the caption "Deferred Credits," between long-term liabilities and owners' equity. Typical deferred credits are: long-term deferred income taxes, deferred revenues (i.e., revenues collected in advance), deferred investment tax credit, and deferred foreign currency translation gains. Admittedly, these items are difficult to classify, yet use of this caption is generally discouraged because these items are liabilities or an indication of a future liability. Practically all companies report them under the liability captions. More detailed discussion of deferred credits appears in Chapter 11 (also refer to footnote 6 of this chapter).

OWNERS' EQUITY

Owners' equity represents the residual interests in a business; it is the difference between total assets and total liabilities. For a sole proprietorship, it usually is called proprietor's equity; for a partnership, partners' equity; and for a corporation, stockholders' or shareholders' equity. Owners' equity is subclassified to reflect sources; therefore, for a corporation, the following sources are reported:

1. Contributed capital:
   a. Capital stock.
   b. Contributed capital in excess of capital stock.
2. Retained earnings.
3. Unrealized capital.

Capital Stock

This caption reports the *source* of owners' equity as represented by the stated or legal capital of the corporation as specified legally and in the Articles of Incorporation (i.e., the Charter) of the company. This source is the amount of legal capital provided by the stockholders. Each class of stock, common and preferred, must be reported at the par, or stated amount; or in the case of nopar stock, the total amount paid in (these matters vary depending on the law of the state of incorporation). Details of each class of capital stock should be set out separately, including title of each issue; number of shares authorized, issued, outstanding, and subscribed; conversion features; callability; preferences; and any other special features.

Contributed Capital in Excess of Capital Stock

This is often called *additional paid in capital.* It reports the amounts received by the corporation in excess of the par or stated value of the capital stock outstanding. These amounts are received when the corporation sells its stock at a premium (sometimes called premium on capital stock) and from treasury stock transactions. This topic is discussed in detail in Chapters 15–17.

Retained Earnings

Retained earnings (formerly called earned surplus) is the accumulated earnings of a corporation less losses and dividends to date. It reports the amount of resources (from undistributed earnings) that the corporation has retained for use in operations, expansion, and growth. In most corporations, in the long term, it is the major *source* of capital. In the long term, corporations tend to distribute dividends to the stockholders equivalent to considerably less than 50% of the earnings, thus establishing a continuing source of funds for internal use. Indirectly, retained earnings represent additional investments by the stockholders since they forego dividends equal to the balance of retained earnings. A negative balance in retained earnings is usually called a *deficit.*

Not infrequently, a portion of the total amount of retained earnings is *restricted* or *appropriated.* This means that during the period of restriction, the specified amount is not available for dividends. For example, AB Corporation (Exhibit 5–1) has total retained earnings of $82,000; however, $56,000 of that amount is restricted for a specific period of time. After the restriction is removed, the $56,000 again becomes available for dividends, subject to declaration by the board of directors of the corporation. A restriction may result from a legal requirement, as in the case where state law (in which the corporation is organized) imposes a restriction equal to the cost of any treasury stock held. Such laws are designed to protect the creditors of the corporation. Or, a restriction may be contractual, as in the case where the bond indenture carries such a stipulation. This situation is illustrated in Exhibit 5–1. Finally, the board of directors may decide to arbitrarily "appropriate" a portion of retained earnings, as in the case of "retained earnings appropriated for future plant expansion."

Restrictions or appropriations may be reflected in either of two ways. A few companies make an entry in the accounts to reflect the restriction or appropriation. For example, the $56,000 restriction on retained earnings reported by AB Corporation (Exhibit 5–1) could be recorded and reported as follows:

Entry in the accounts:

Retained earnings	56,000	
Retained earnings restricted by bond indenture		56,000

Reporting on the balance sheet then could be as follows:

Retained earnings, unappropriated	$26,000	
Retained earnings, restricted by bond indenture	56,000	
Total Retained Earnings		$82,000

In recent years, the above approach has practically disappeared. Instead, no formal entry is made in the accounts. Restrictions and appropriations are usually disclosed in the notes to the financial statements as illustrated in Exhibit 5–1.[11] Accounting for, and reporting of, retained earnings is discussed in detail in Chapter 16.

UNREALIZED CAPITAL

This component of owners' equity has seldom been used in the past because of some unsettled accounting issues related to fair market valuations. However, the recent issuance of FASB *Statement No. 12* (December 31, 1975) will cause it to be used more often because the statement requires recognition of the "unrealized loss or gain" resulting from the application of the concept of lower of cost or market to long-term equity investments in capital stock (not bonds) accounted for on the cost basis (see Chapter 18 for the equity basis and consolidated statements). *Statement No. 12* requires the accumulated unrealized loss be accounted for and reported separately as an unrealized element of owners' equity.

To illustrate the use of unrealized capital, we will present an application of FASB *Statement No. 12*. The statement requires that long-term (i.e., noncurrent) investments in capital stock of another company be carried and reported at lower of cost or market. An "allowance" account must be used to accomplish this effect. The statement provides that, upon sale of a long-term investment, the difference between selling price and cost is a *realized* gain or loss. In contrast, at the end of the accounting period, an adjusting entry must be made to write down the portfolio to market (if it is lower than cost) and the recognition of an *unrealized* loss or gain. The following sequence of entries are illustrative:

---

[11] AICPA, *Accounting Trends and Techniques, 1975* (New York, 1975), pp. 212, 229–34.

January 1, 19A – Acquired as a long-term investment, 1,000 shares of X Corporation common stock @ $20.

Long-term investment, common stock, X Corp., (1,000 shares)	20,000	
Cash		20,000

December 31, 19A – Adjusting entry to lower of cost or market ($15).

Unrealized loss on long-term investments in equity securities [1,000 × ($20 – $15)]	5,000	
Allowance to reduce long-term investments in equity securities to market		5,000

September 1, 19B – Sold 100 shares of X Corporation @ $18.

Cash (100 × $18)	1,800	
Realized loss on sale of long-term investment	200	
Long-term investment, common stock, X Corp. (100 shares @ $20)		2,000

December 31, 19B – Adjusting entry to lower of cost or market ($19).

Allowance to reduce long-term investments in equity securities to market $5,000 – [900 shares × ($20 – $19)]	4,100	
Unrealized gain on long-term investments in equity securities		4,100

The financial statements for 19A and 19B would reflect the following:

	19A		*19B*	
Income Statement:				
Realized loss on sale of long-term investments				$ 200
Balance Sheet:				
Funds and investments:				
Investment, Common stock, X Corp., at cost	$20,000		$18,000	
Less: Allowance to reduce to lower of cost or market	5,000	$15,000	900	$17,100
Stockholders' Equity:				
Unrealized capital:				
Unrealized loss on long-term investments in equity securities		($ 5,000)		($ 900)

Statement No. 12 specifies that should an investment in the capital stock of another company be changed from a short-term to a long-term investment or vice versa, the investment shall be transferred "at the lower of its cost or market value at date of transfer and the difference shall be accounted for as if it were a realized loss and included in the determination of net income." FASB *Statement No. 12* is discussed in greater detail in Chapters 7 and 18.

Unrealized capital has been used in some situations to accomodate the capital arising from the writing up of fixed assets (see Chapter 13). The above discussion should not be understood to imply that writeups of assets to fair market value are currently in accordance with generally accepted accounting principles. However, there are a few exceptions as explained in Chapters 7, 13 and 25.

PART B—STATEMENT OF CHANGES IN FINANCIAL POSITION

Since the issuance of *APB Opinion No. 19* (effective September 30, 1971), a statement of changes in financial position, in addition to the income statement and balance sheet, must be included in the annual financial statement. Although it evolved from the old funds statement (which was optional), it is significantly different in a number of respects. The statement of changes in financial position reports the *financing* and *investing* activities of a business enterprise during a specified period.

It is a *change statement,* as diagrammed in Exhibit 4–1, because the financing and investing activities serve to explain the causes of the changes between the beginning and ending balance sheets other than those explained by the income statement (which is also a change statement). Thus, it is dated the same as the income statement, "For the Year Ended (date)" Exhibit 5–2 presents a statement specially designed for instructional purposes.

The financing activities are represented as *inflows of funds* into the enterprise primarily from *(a)* operations (i.e., revenues less expenses), *(b)* issuance of capital stock, *(c)* borrowing, and *(d)* sale of assets owned by the entity (such as investments and operational assets). The investing activities are *outflows of funds* from the enterprise primarily for *(a)* acquisition of assets, *(b)* retirement of debt, and *(c)* payment of dividends. Thus, the statement reports all inflows and outflows of funds.

For purposes of the statement of changes in financial position, funds usually are defined as either (1) cash equivalents (cash plus short-term or temporary investments), or (2) working capital (current assets minus current liabilities). Consequently, when a statement of changes in financial position is used, the user should be alert to identify which of these two measures of funds was used in its preparation. *APB Opinion No. 19* permits either measure but requires that the identity be specified.

The statement of changes in financial position also must be based on an *all-resources concept*. This means that *all* financing and investing activities must be incorporated in it regardless of whether funds were directly affected. The word *all* is particularly important because it requires that direct exchanges (i.e., trades) be included even though neither cash nor working capital was affected. Examples of direct exchanges are the acquisition of property and paying for it by issuing capital stock, the conversion of bonds payable to common stock, and the trading of one asset, such as a tract of land, for a machine. In direct exchanges, there often is neither an inflow nor outflow of funds (of course, some exchanges do involve a cash difference). Nevertheless, transactions of this type must be included "as if" funds equal to the fair market value actually flowed in and out. This type of transaction is illustrated in Exhibit 5–2, as it should be reported in the statement and explained in a note. At the start of the period, the company had out-

EXHIBIT 5–2

ILLUSTRATIVE CORPORATION
Statement of Changes in Financial Position—Cash Equivalent Basis
For the Year Ended December 31, 1976

Sources of Cash (Inflow of Funds):		
From operations:		
Revenues (accrual basis)	$850,000	
Add (deduct) adjustments to derive cash basis:		
Increase in accounts receivable (trade)	(10,000)	
Cash generated from revenues		$840,000
Expenses (accrual basis)	740,000	
Add (deduct) adjustments to convert to cash basis:		
Depreciation expense	(30,000)	
Amortization of intangibles	(1,000)	
Inventory increase	28,000	
Accounts payable decrease (trade)	12,000	
Income taxes payable increase	(14,000)	
Loss on sale of operational assets	(5,000)	
Cash disbursed for expenses		730,000
Total Cash Generated by Operations		110,000
From extraordinary item net of income tax		20,000
From other sources:		
Sale of unissued preferred stock	45,000	
Sale of operational assets	25,000	
Common stock issued to retire convertible bonds (Note A)	100,000	
Total Cash Generated from Other Sources		170,000
Total Cash Generated from All Sources		300,000
Uses of Cash (Outflow of Funds):		
Payment of cash dividends	40,000	
Payment of long-term note payable	50,000	
Acquisition of operational assets	120,000	
Purchase of long-term investment, stock of X Corporation	30,000	
Retirement of 5%, convertible bonds payable (Note A)	100,000	
Total Cash Expended for All Purposes		340,000
Net Increase (Decrease) in Cash and Cash Equivalents during the Period		$ (40,000)

Notes to the financial statements:

Note A. All of the outstanding 5% convertible bonds payable tendered to the Company for conversion to nopar common stock in accordance with the conversion provision in the bond indenture. Conversion required the issuance of 10,000 shares of nopar common stock; no cash was paid or received incidental to the conversion.

standing 5% convertible bonds payable with a maturity amount of $100,000. The bonds carried a conversion agreement which permitted the bondholders to turn them in during 1975 or 1976 and receive, in return, a specified number of shares of the nopar common stock of the company. During 1976, all of the bondholders tendered their bonds and received the requisite number of shares of stock. Thus, debt was retired by the issuance of common stock (a direct exchange of noncash items). Although no cash flowed in either direction, the transaction must be reported on the statement of changes in financial position "as if" cash was received for the stock and was then disbursed to retire the bonds. Therefore, the noncash exchange is reflected both as a source of cash and a use of cash, supplemented with an explanatory note to assure full disclosure. Without the all-resources requirement, direct exchanges would not be reported in the statement, thus often omitting significant financing and investing activities.

Observe in Exhibit 5–2 that cash flows related to operations are shown separately for revenues and expenses. In contrast, actual statements usually start with the difference, net income, and then report "adjustments" to derive "total cash generated by operations." The approach illustrated in Exhibit 5–2 generally is favored for instructional purposes (and often for communication purposes) because it does not imply that depreciation and amortization is a source of cash; rather, it emphasizes that they are adjustments to derive total cash outflows required for the expenses. Also, in this format, the "adjustments" are more easily understood. The net effect is the same regardless of the approach used.

The statement of changes in financial position is not difficult to understand and interpret, especially when prepared on a cash equivalent basis as in Exhibit 5–2. However, the adjustments in the section "from operations" sometimes are not readily understood. Exhibit 5–2 reports that sales recognized, on an accrual basis, amounted to $850,000; however, since $10,000 of that amount was not collected by the end of the year, the cash inflow from sales was $840,000. Alternatively, had accounts receivables *decreased,* the $10,000 would have been added, giving a cash inflow from sales of $860,000. In a similar manner, total expenses, determined on an accrual basis, must be adjusted to a strict cash basis. Depreciation expense and amortization expense of intangibles, since they were included in total expense but did not require cash expenditure, must be *deducted* from expenses. The inventory increase is added since additional cash (above cost of goods sold) was expended for this increase. Similarly, the *decrease* in accounts payable required the expenditure of additional cash above the amount of expenses recognized on the accrual basis. The increase in income taxes payable means that less cash (i.e., $14,000) was expended for this item than the amount of income tax expense reported. The loss on sale of operational assets, although included in total expenses, does not represent cash. The amount of cash from the sale of operational assets is reported under "other sources" as $25,000.[12]

Preparation and interpretation of the statement of changes in financial position on both the cash equivalent and the working capital basis are discussed in detail in Chapter 21.

---

[12] The entry to record the disposal of the operational assets was:

Cash (sales price)	25,000	
Loss on sale of operational assets	5,000	
Operational assets (book value)		30,000

SOME SPECIAL REPORTING ISSUES

We will conclude the review of information processing and the financial statements with a brief discussion of several special reporting issues that are commonly encountered.

Terminology

As in all professions, accounting has its own jargon. Often the same word or phrase is used to mean different things. We commented on some of these terminology problems in Chapter 2—concepts, assumptions, principles, standards, and procedures. In preparing reports, accountants should refrain, as much as possible, from using vague and complex terminology. Generally, less technical terms can be used to better convey the message. Captions in statements and titles of items listed should be carefully selected, particularly since the statements will be used by a wide range of decision-makers, few of whom are trained in accounting. From time to time, pronouncements, such as the *ARBs, APB Opinions,* and FASB *Statements,* specifically recommend improved terminology.

For example, some years ago, the term "reserve" was used by accountants to refer to *(a)* a contra asset account for accumulated depreciation, such as "reserve for depreciation"; *(b)* an estimated liability for estimated warranty liability, such as "reserve for warranties"; and *(c)* an appropriation of retained earnings, such as "reserve for future expansion." *Accounting Terminology Bulletin No. 1* recommended that the term be restricted to the latter usage. However, many accountants do not use it even in that context. Similarly, the terminology bulletin recommended use of the terms *retained earnings* instead of earned surplus and *net income* instead of net profit. *APB Statement No. 19* recommended use of the title, *statement of changes in financial position,* instead of the older title, funds flow statement. Confusion of the terms cost and expense, discussed in Chapter 4, is another example of careless terminology. Throughout later chapters we will often discuss preferred terminology since effective communication is a primary objective of accounting.

Comparative Statements

To evaluate the financial potentials of an enterprise, one should have available financial information for two or more periods. For prediction purposes, trends are usually much more revealing than information for only one period. In recognition of this fact, *ARB No. 43* states:

> The presentation of comparative financial statements in annual and other reports enhances the usefulness of such reports and brings out more clearly the nature and trends of current changes affecting the enterprise. Such presentation emphasizes the fact that statements for a series of periods are far more significant than those for a single period and that the accounts

for one period are but an installment of what is essentially a continuous history.[13]

Comparative statements for the current and prior year are now considered essential to meet the full-disclosure requirement. Of the 600 companies analyzed in *Accounting Trends and Techniques, 1974* (AICPA), all but one presented comparative statements. The actual statements shown in the appendixes at the end of Chapters 4 and 5 display comparative amounts. In addition to comparative statements, many companies present a special tabulation of especially relevant financial items for time spans of 5 to 20 or more years. Items often included are: total revenues, income before extraordinary items, net income, depreciation expense, earnings per share, dividends, total assets, total owners' equity, number of shares outstanding, and average stock price. These long-term summaries are particularly useful to external decision-makers.

Rounding of Amounts

All major companies round amounts in their financial statements. According to *Accounting Trends and Techniques, 1975* (AICPA), of the 600 companies surveyed, 41% rounded to the nearest dollar, 57% to the nearest thousand dollars, and 2% to the nearest million dollars; none reported cents. Amounts not rounded often suggest greater accuracy than actually exists.

Subsequent Events

Certain important events or transactions which occur subsequent to the balance sheet date but prior to the actual issuance of the financial statements (ordinarily one to three months) and which have a material affect on the financial statements are called *subsequent events*. Subsequent events must be reported because they involve important information that would influence the statement users' interpretation and evaluation of the future potentials of the enterprise. Auditing standards define these events and specify that they must be either *(a)* reflected in the statements, or *(b)* disclosed in notes to the statements, depending upon their nature.[14]

Subsequent events should be reflected *in the statements* if they (1) provide additional evidence about conditions that existed at balance sheet date, (2) affect estimates inherent in the process of preparing the financial statements, and *(c)* require adjustments to the financial statements resulting from the estimates. An example would be a material loss on an uncollectible receivable because of a customer's deteriorating financial condition. The deteriorating financial condition presumably

---

[13] AICPA, "Restatement and Revision of Accounting Research Bulletins," *Accounting Research Bulletin No. 43* (New York, 1953), chap. 2, sec. A.

[14] AICPA, *Statement on Auditing Standards No. 1* (New York, 1973), pp. 123–31.

was occurring at balance sheet date but recent information made it more evident.

Those subsequent events that should be *disclosed in notes* to the statements are characterized as *(a)* conditions that did not exist at balance sheet date but *(b)* arose subsequent to the balance sheet date and do not result in adjustment to the financial statements. Examples listed in *Auditing Standard No. 47* are: sale of a bond or capital stock issue, litigation based on an event subsequent to the balance sheet date, inventory losses due to casualty, and losses on receivables due to a condition that arose subsequent to balance sheet date (such as a fire or flood). The fire or flood did not "exist" at the balance sheet date.

This topic is considered in depth in auditing texts and courses (see also footnote 5).

Full Disclosure

Full disclosure is a particularly important concept in the *reporting principle* discussed in Chapter 2. Full disclosure requires that there be complete and understandable reporting of all significant information relating to the economic affairs of the enterprise so that the financial statements will not be misleading. Full disclosure requires, in addition to the financial information reported in the body of the financial statements, additional information in notes to the financial statements, supporting schedules, cross-references, contra items, and parenthetical explanations. The accountant must exercise judgment in deciding the way in which each significant event or transaction should be reported to meet the full-disclosure requirement.

Notes to the financial statements is a singularly important part of the financial report because a note is often the only feasible way of adequately explaining and elaborating on certain critical events and situations. A particular note may refer to a single amount on one of the three basic statements or to several amounts on two or more of them, or to a situation that is not directly reflected on any of them. The guideline for deciding when a note is required, other than where specifically required, is simply judgmental within the framework of complete reporting, or alternatively, misleading inferences. Notes typically are a combination of narrative elaboration, additional amounts, and supplementary tables.

A number of *APB Opinions* and FASB *Statements* specifically require certain disclosures in the notes to the financial statements. For example, FASB *Statement of Accounting Standards No. 2*, "Accounting for Research and Development Costs" (October 1974) states:

> A government-regulated enterprise that defers research and development costs for financial accounting purposes in accordance with Addendum to APB Opinion No. 2, "Accounting for the Investment Credit," shall disclose the following additional information about its research and development costs:
>
> *a.* Accounting policy, including basis for amortization.

b. Total research and development costs incurred each period for which an income statement is present and the amount of those costs that has been capitalized or deferred in each period.

Moreover, "Disclosure of Accounting Policies," *APB Opinion No. 22* (April 1972), specifically requires that information about *important* accounting policies adopted by the enterprise, including their identification and description must be disclosed "in a separate *Summary of Significant Accounting Policies* preceding the notes to the financial statements or as the initial note." At a minimum, the summary should include policies that involve *(a)* a selection from existing acceptable alternatives, *(b)* principles and methods peculiar to the industry, and *(c)* unusual or innovative applications of generally accepted accounting principles.

The actual statements presented in the Appendixes to Chapters 4 and 5 include typical notes.

Supporting schedules may be incorporated in the notes or presented separately. Supporting schedules are typical for large and complex companies, and in situations where a particular item involves a number of complex changes during the period. We mentioned in Chapter 4 that when there have been numerous changes in owners' equity, the statement of retained earnings often is replaced with a more comprehensive schedule. As an example, Exhibit 5–3 presents an actual supplementary schedule, *statement of stockholders' equity,* that often is used to disclose the detailed changes and balances of all elements of owners' equity.

Parenthetical notes are widely used to disclose information such as the method of inventory costing—Inventory (*Lifo;* applied on lower-of-cost-or-market basis). *Contra items,* such as accumulated depreciation and allowance for doubtful accounts, are reported as separate line deductions or parenthetically. *Cross-references* may provide expeditious and useful disclosures as in the case of mortgaged assets. Assets pledged as security for a loan may be identified parenthetically, and the related liability is cross-referenced to the pledged assets.

Auditors' Report

The auditors' report is also called the accountants' report and the independent accountants' report. It usually follows the financial statements and the notes; however, many believe that it should be the first item because of the importance attached to it by some statement users and the heavy responsibility auditors assume in expressing their opinion on the credibility of the statements. The independent auditors' primary function is to express an *opinion* on the financial statements. Although the auditor has sole responsibility for his or her opinion expressed in the auditor's report, the primary responsibility for the statements and the supporting notes rests with the management of the enterprise. The statements are those of the management; the auditor affirms or disaffirms them in the *opinion.*

EXHIBIT 5–3
Statement of Stockholders' Equity

EMERSON ELECTRIC CO. (SEP)
Consolidated Statement of Stockholders' Equity

	Preferred Stock	*Common Stock*	*Additional Paid-in Capital*	*Retained Earnings*	*Treasury Stock*	*Total*
			($ Thousands)			
Year ended September 30, 1973:						
Balance at beginning of year	$8,275	47,283	12,637	337,134	(5,241)	400,088
Add (deduct):						
Net earnings	–	–	–	75,873	–	75,873
Stock options exercised	–	99	2,453	–	128	2,680
Preferred stock conversions	(4,789)	2,682	2,107	–	–	–
Expenses of common stock split	–	–	(153)	–	–	(153)
Stock issued by pooled companies prior to combination	–	66	574	–	–	640
Cash dividends:						
Preferred stock – $.90 per share	–	–	–	(2,572)	–	(2,572)
Common stock – $.62½ per share	–	–	–	(29,498)	–	(29,498)
By pooled companies prior to combination	–	–	–	(379)	–	(379)
Balance at End of Year	$3,486	50,130	17,618	380,558	(5,113)	446,679
Year ended September 30, 1972						
Balance at beginning of year:						
As previously reported	8,584	22,963	33,741	291,324	(5,288)	351,324
Adjustments:						
Common stock split	–	22,963	(22,963)	–	–	–
Poolings of interests	–	1,119	174	9,676	–	10,969
As restated	8,584	47,045	10,952	301,000	(5,288)	362,293
Add (deduct):						
Net earnings	–	–	–	66,867	–	66,867
Stock options exercised	–	65	1,549	–	55	1,669
Preferred stock conversions	(309)	173	136	–	–	–
Cash dividends:						
Preferred stock – $.90 per share	–	–	–	(3,014)	–	(3,014)
Common stock – $.59½ per share	–	–	–	(26,975)	–	(26,975)
By pooled companies prior to combination	–	–	–	(744)	–	(744)
Treasury stock acquired	–	–	–	–	(8)	(8)
Balance at End of Year	$8,275	47,283	12,637	337,134	(5,241)	400,088

Source: AICPA, *Accounting Trends and Techniques, 1974* (New York, 1974), p. 325.

The auditor's report includes (1) a *scope* paragraph, and (2) an *opinion* paragraph. The standard format of the auditors' report is as follows:

(Scope paragraph)

> We have examined the balance sheet of X Company as of (at) December 31, 19XX, and the related statements of income, retained earnings and changes in financial position for the year then ended. Our examination was made in accordance with generally accepted auditing standards, and accordingly, included such tests of the accounting records and such other auditing procedures as we considered necessary in the circumstances.

(Opinion paragraph)

> In our opinion, the financial statements referred to above present fairly the financial position of X Company as of (at) December 31, 19XX, and the results of its operations and the changes in its financial position for the year then ended, in conformity with generally accepted accounting principles applied on a basis consistent with that of the preceding year.[15]

There are eight key elements in the report that have special significance:

1. Date
2. Salutation
3. Identification of the statements examined
4. Statement of scope of the examination
5. Opinion introduction
6. Reference to fair presentation in conformity with generally accepted accounting principles
7. Reference to consistency
8. Signature[16]

Upon completion of the audit, the independent CPA is required to draft the opinion paragraph to clearly communicate his or her judgment for giving one of the following:

1. Unqualified opinion—An unqualified opinion is given when the CPA has formed the opinion that the statements (1) "fairly present" results of operations, financial position, and changes in financial position; (2) conform to generally accepted accounting principles, applied on a consistent basis; and (3) full-disclosure requirements are met so that the statements are not misleading.
2. Qualified opinion—A qualified opinion is given when there is an "exception" or "subject to" clause because all of the key requirements for an unqualified opinion are not fully met. A qualified opinion must clearly explain the nature of the "exception" or "subject to" and its effect on the financial statements.
3. Adverse opinion—An adverse opinion is given when the financial statements do not "fairly present" (see above). Also, material exceptions require an adverse opinion on the statements as a whole.
4. Disclaimer of opinion—When the auditor has not been able to obtain

---

[15] AICPA, *Statement on Auditing Standards No. 2* (New York, 1973), pp. 2–3.

[16] AICPA, *The Auditor's Report—Its Meaning and Significance* (New York, 1967), p. 2.

sufficient competent evidential matter to form an opinion, the auditor must state that he or she is unable to express an opinion (i.e., a disclaimer). The auditor must explain the reasons for not giving an opinion.

A comprehensive discussion of the responsibilities of the independent auditor is beyond the scope of this book. The above summary is provided to indicate the importance of the auditor's representations when an opinion is provided on whether the representations of the management in the financial statements fairly present, to all users of the statements, the company's financial position, statement of income, and changes in financial position. It is reasonable, therefore, to suggest that the auditors' report should be read prior to spending much time on the financial statements. If it is other than unqualified, one should proceed with caution.

Appendix—Specimen Statements

BETZ

FINANCIAL REPORT Betz Laboratories, Inc. and Subsidiaries

DESIGN, TREATMENT AND CONTROL OF INDUSTRIAL, COMMERCIAL AND MUNICIPAL WATER, WASTEWATER AND PROCESS SYSTEMS. Betz produces and sells a wide range of specialty chemical products and associated feeding and control equipment used in the treatment of industrial water and industrial processes utilizing water, including the technical and laboratory services necessary to utilize Betz products effectively. Betz and its subsidiaries also manufacture control instruments for water and process systems and design water and waste distribution, waste treatment and water filtration plants for municipalities and industry.

Operations are conducted primarily in the United States and Canada and also in Mexico, Europe, Southeast Asia and the Caribbean. The Company employs approximately 2,100 persons.

Sales of Products and Services

By Company Groupings

	1974	1973	Increase
U.S. SPECIALTY CHEMICAL OPERATIONS Betz Laboratories, Inc. and Betz Entec, Inc.	$ 71,758,000	$51,112,000	40%
INTERNATIONAL OPERATIONS Betz International, Inc. and its foreign subsidiaries and regions	9,200,000	6,100,000	51
CANADIAN OPERATIONS Betz Laboratories, Ltd.	6,128,000	4,385,000	40
CONSULTING ENGINEERING Betz Environmental Engineers, Inc. and its affiliates—Johnson and Williams, Inc., William J. Murdoch Engineers, Inc. and J.B. Converse & Co., Inc.	10,510,000	6,624,000	59
INSTRUMENTATION Uniloc, Inc., Micro Sensors, Inc. and Kay-Ray, Inc.	9,620,000	6,713,000	43
	107,216,000	74,934,000	
Less: sales to affiliated marketing companies for subsequent resale to customers	(4,206,000)	(3,092,000)	
CONSOLIDATED SALES OF PRODUCTS AND SERVICES	$103,010,000	$71,842,000	43%

By Classes of Products and Services

	Percentage of Consolidated Net Sales and Revenues				
	1970	1971	1972	1973	1974
Specialty Chemicals and Associated Products	85.7	83.2	82.4	81.5	80.5
Electronic systems and instruments*	7.3	8.2	9.1	9.3	9.3
Consulting engineering and design*	7.0	8.6	8.5	9.2	10.2

*Includes sales of companies acquired in pooling of interests transactions.

Accountants' Report

To the Shareholders and Board of Directors
Betz Laboratories, Inc.
Trevose, Pennsylvania

We have examined the consolidated balance sheets of Betz Laboratories, Inc. and subsidiaries as of December 31, 1974, and December 31, 1973, and the related consolidated statements of operations, shareholders' equity, and changes in financial position for the years then ended. Our examinations were made in accordance with generally accepted auditing standards and, accordingly, included such tests of the accounting records and such other auditing procedures as we considered necessary in the circumstances.

In our opinion, the financial statements referred to above present fairly the consolidated financial position of Betz Laboratories, Inc. and subsidiaries at December 31, 1974, and December 31, 1973, and the consolidated results of their operations and changes in their financial position for the years then ended, in conformity with generally accepted accounting principles consistently applied during the period except for the change, with which we concur, in the method of valuing inventories as described in Note 4 to the consolidated financial statements.

Philadelphia, Pennsylvania
January 31, 1975

Ernst & Ernst

Consolidated Statements of Operations

BETZ LABORATORIES, INC. AND SUBSIDIARIES
Years ended December 31, 1974 and 1973

	1974	1973
Net sales and revenues	$103,009,768	$71,841,501
Other income	369,686	514,651
	103,379,454	72,356,152
Costs and expenses:		
Cost of products sold and services rendered	48,859,158	32,870,406
Selling, engineering, research, and administrative expenses	37,641,151	27,939,686
Interest expense	330,340	147,262
	86,830,649	60,957,354
EARNINGS BEFORE INCOME TAXES	16,548,805	11,398,798
Income taxes—Note 7	8,202,000	5,461,000
NET EARNINGS	$ 8,346,805	$ 5,937,798
Net earnings per share (after pooling of interests adjustment—Note 2—Acquisitions)	$ 1.04	$ .74
Average number of shares	8,017,102 shares	7,971,681 shares

See notes to consolidated financial statements.

Consolidated Balance Sheets

BETZ LABORATORIES, INC. AND SUBSIDIARIES

December 31, 1974 and 1973	1974	1973
ASSETS		
CURRENT ASSETS		
Cash	$ 2,295,294	$ 2,251,973
Short-term investments—at cost (approximating market)	127,500	2,226,922
Accounts receivable, less allowances: 1974—$274,043: 1973—$123,500:		
Trade	14,823,497	10,256,270
Consulting engineering contracts—Note 3	7,037,517	6,058,853
	21,861,014	16,315,123
Inventories—Note 4:		
Finished products and goods purchased for resale	4,439,269	2,911,209
Raw materials	8,563,792	4,877,857
Consulting engineering contracts in process	4,116,341	3,011,448
	17,119,402	10,800,514
Prepaid expenses and sundry	922,748	771,762
TOTAL CURRENT ASSETS	42,325,958	32,366,294
PROPERTY, PLANT, AND EQUIPMENT—on the basis of cost		
Buildings	11,867,121	10,708,567
Machinery and equipment	16,036,928	13,241,202
Allowance for depreciation (deduction)	(8,795,805)	(7,171,692)
	19,108,244	16,778,077
Land	1,487,243	1,497,903
Construction in progress (estimated cost to complete—$3,200,000)	4,362,234	576,454
	24,957,721	18,852,434
INTANGIBLE ASSETS—at cost, net of amortization		
Cost in excess of net assets of businesses acquired	821,985	738,750
Deferred charges and patents	717,565	519,169
	1,539,550	1,257,919
	$68,823,229	$52,476,647
LIABILITIES AND SHAREHOLDERS' EQUITY		
CURRENT LIABILITIES		
Notes payable to banks	$ 1,303,869	$ 76,685
Trade accounts payable	5,709,651	4,253,569
Payroll and related taxes	2,683,117	1,335,598
Accrued vacation pay	624,454	510,825
Contributions due retirement plans	947,916	134,405
Other accrued expenses	1,912,208	1,091,809
Due seller of acquired company	—	353,537
Federal, foreign, and state income taxes—Note 7	5,583,525	2,984,334
Current portion of long-term debt	170,635	164,466
TOTAL CURRENT LIABILITIES	18,935,375	10,905,228
LONG-TERM DEBT—Note 5	2,596,558	1,828,388
OTHER LIABILITIES		
Deferred compensation	208,000	414,000
Deferred federal income taxes—Note 7	1,482,998	1,293,515
	1,690,998	1,707,515
SHAREHOLDERS' EQUITY—Note 6		
Preferred Shares, par value $.10 a share: Authorized 1,000,000 shares; issued—none		
Common Shares, par value $.10 a share:		
Authorized—35,000,000 shares		
Issued and outstanding: 1974—8,034,479 shares; 1973—7,991,679 shares	803,448	799,168
Capital in excess of par value	13,551,441	11,922,890
Retained earnings	31,993,949	25,313,458
Unearned compensation (deduction)	(748,540)	—
TOTAL SHAREHOLDERS' EQUITY	45,600,298	38,035,516
COMMITMENTS AND CONTINGENT LIABILITY—Notes 8 and 9		
	$68,823,229	$52,476,647

See notes to consolidated financial statements.

Consolidated Statements of Changes in Financial Position

BETZ LABORATORIES, INC. AND SUBSIDIARIES
Years ended December 31, 1974 and 1973

	1974	1973
SOURCE OF FUNDS		
From operations:		
Net earnings	$ 8,346,805	$ 5,937,798
Expenses not requiring outlay of funds:		
Depreciation and amortization	1,896,160	1,470,510
Deferred compensation	203,813	82,000
Deferred income taxes	524,826	475,572
TOTAL FROM OPERATIONS	10,971,604	7,965,880
From financing activities:		
Borrowings of long-term debt	1,011,515	1,509,741
Borrowings of short-term debt	1,352,184	52,257
Common Stock issued relating to stock options and acquisition of minority interests	332,365	786,225
Capital transaction of pooled company prior to acquisition	290,000	(144,000)
Other:		
Accounts payable and accrued expenses	6,461,451	2,194,426
Tax benefit relating to employees' early disposition of stock acquired under stock options	154,113	152,428
TOTAL SOURCE OF FUNDS	20,573,232	12,516,957
DISPOSITION OF FUNDS		
Invested in operations:		
Accounts receivable	5,545,891	2,329,701
Inventories	6,318,888	4,122,688
Prepaid expenses and sundry	150,986	250,858
Property, plant, and equipment	7,904,524	4,638,309
Purchased companies:		
Property, plant, and equipment	—	68,405
Cost in excess of net assets	—	745,000
Deferred charges	—	369,741
Deferred income taxes	—	(763,599)
TOTAL INVESTED IN OPERATIONS	19,920,289	11,761,103
Other:		
Repayments of long-term debt	237,176	111,290
Repayments of short-term debt	125,000	—
Cash dividends paid	1,666,314	1,539,678
Deferred compensation paid	302,000	12,000
Acquisition of intangible assets	378,554	2,958
TOTAL DISPOSITION OF FUNDS	22,629,333	13,427,029
DECREASE IN CASH AND SHORT-TERM INVESTMENTS	(2,056,101)	(910,072)
Cash and short-term investments at beginning of period	4,478,895	5,388,967
CASH AND SHORT-TERM INVESTMENTS AT END OF PERIOD	$ 2,422,794	$ 4,478,895

See notes to consolidated financial statements.

Consolidated Statements of Shareholders' Equity

BETZ LABORATORIES, INC. AND SUBSIDIARIES

Years ended December 31, 1974 and 1973

	1974	1973
COMMON SHARES		
Balance at beginning of year	$ 799,168	$ 794,837
Par value of shares sold under stock options—Note 6	1,190	4,331
Par value of shares issued under Stock Incentive Plan—Note 6	2,389	—
Par value of shares issued in connection with the purchase of minority interest—Note 2	701	—
BALANCE AT END OF YEAR	$ 803,448	$ 799,168
CAPITAL IN EXCESS OF PAR VALUE		
Balance at beginning of year	$11,922,890	$10,992,886
Tax benefit relating to employees' early disposition of stock acquired under stock options	154,113	152,428
Capital transaction of pooled companies prior to acquisition	290,000	(4,318)
Proceeds in excess of par value of shares sold under stock options—Note 6	175,397	781,894
Capital in excess of par value of shares issued under Stock Incentive Plan—Note 6	853,964	—
Capital in excess of par value of shares issued in connection with the purchase of minority interest—Note 2	155,077	—
BALANCE AT END OF YEAR	$13,551,441	$11,922,890
RETAINED EARNINGS		
Balance at beginning of year	$25,313,458	$21,055,020
Net earnings for the year	8,346,805	5,937,798
Capital transaction of pooled company prior to acquisition	—	(139,682)
Cash dividends paid (per share: 1974—$.21; 1973—$.195) (including $16,483 in 1974 and $28,899 in 1973 for pooled company prior to acquisition)	(1,666,314)	(1,539,678)
BALANCE AT END OF YEAR	$31,993,949	$25,313,458

See notes to consolidated financial statements.

Notes to Consolidated Financial Statements

Note 1—Summary of Significant Accounting Policies

Principles of Consolidation—The consolidated financial statements include the accounts of the Company and all subsidiaries. All significant intercompany items and transactions are eliminated from the consolidated statements.

Foreign Operations—Current assets and liabilities of foreign subsidiaries are translated at year-end rates of exchange. Long-term assets and liabilities are translated at rates in effect in the year of acquisition. Operations are translated at average rates prevailing during each year. Unrealized gains (losses) of approximately $81,000 for 1974 and ($29,000) for 1973, respectively, are included in net earnings. If long-term debt had been translated at the year-end rates of exchange, the amount of that debt would have increased by approximately $49,000 and $43,000 for 1974 and 1973, respectively. The assets, liabilities, net sales, and net earnings of foreign subsidiaries are:

	1974	1973
Total assets at end of year	$11,386,619	$6,827,132
Total liabilities at end of year	6,509,790	3,281,131
Net sales for the year	12,971,348	9,091,279
Net earnings for the year	1,187,036	864,486

Inventories—Finished products, goods purchased for resale, and raw materials inventories are stated at the lower of cost or market, cost being substantially determined by the last-in, first-out method in 1974, and by the first-in, first-out method in 1973 (see Note 4); Consulting engineering contracts in process represent the accumulated costs of engineers' time and expenses less costs billable, generally at the completion of significant phases of such contracts, and less allowances for estimated losses. The Company includes currently in income the excess of such billings over related accumulated contract cost.

Depreciation—For financial reporting purposes, depreciation is computed principally by the straight-line method over the estimated useful lives of the assets as follows: buildings—17 to 45 years; machinery and equipment—8 to 15 years; furniture and fixtures—10 years; automobiles and trucks—3 to 6 years.

Research and Development—All research and development costs are charged to expense as incurred. Total research and development costs amounted to $2,500,000 in 1974 and $2,000,000 in 1973.

Patents—The costs of patents purchased by the Company are amortized over their remaining lives.

Income Taxes—The Company files a consolidated federal return and provides for current taxes on that basis. Deferred taxes are provided on timing differences between financial and tax reporting (see Note 7). Investment tax credits are accounted for by the flow-through method as a reduction of the provision for federal income taxes. No provisions have been made for United States income taxes on the unremitted earnings of foreign subsidiaries because the Company plans to continue to finance foreign expansion and operating requirements by reinvestment of such undistributed earnings. Presently, no increase in income taxes would result from remittance of such earnings because of the foreign tax credits available.

Retirement Plans—The Company and its subsidiaries have pension plans covering substantially all of their employees. The policy is to fund pension costs accrued. The past service cost of the Company's plan is fully funded. Past service cost of one subsidiary's plan is being amortized over 30 years.

Cost in Excess of Net Assets of Businesses Acquired—These costs are being amortized ratably over ten and forty years according to the Company's estimate of the period benefited.

Note 2—Acquisitions

In November 1974 the Company acquired J. B. Converse & Co., Inc. in exchange for 157,460 shares of Common Stock in a pooling of interests transaction. The revenues and net earnings of Converse in 1974 for the period prior to the acquisition amounted to $1,538,000 and $205,000, respectively. As previously reported, the consolidated revenues and net earnings for 1973 were $70,430,054 and $5,790,827 ($.74 per share), respectively.

In 1974 the Company acquired certain minority interests in subsidiary companies for $177,000, represented by 7,012 shares of Common Stock and $20,000 in cash. Of this amount, $116,000 was assigned to cost in excess of net assets acquired.

In August 1973 the Company acquired Kay-Ray, Inc. in exchange for 100,007 shares of Common Stock in a pooling of interests transaction. The sales and net earnings of Kay-Ray, Inc. in 1973 for the period prior to the acquisition amounted to $931,269 and $163,174, respectively.

In the latter half of 1973 a subsidiary purchased the assets and businesses of two consulting engineering companies for $1,522,318 in cash and notes, of which $745,000 was assigned to cost in excess of net assets acquired. Additionally, a noncompete agreement, having a present value of $369,741, was entered into with the owner of one of these companies. The revenues and earnings of these companies are not material in relation to the accompanying consolidated statement of operations.

Note 3—Accounts Receivable

The components of accounts receivable from consulting engineering contracts are as follows:

	1974	1973
Fees billed (1)	$2,431,532	$1,580,602
Fees earned but unbilled (2)	4,605,985	4,478,251
	$7,037,517	$6,058,853

(1) Fees billed include insignificant amounts of retainage which will be due upon completion of the contract and acceptance by the owners.

(2) These fees were unbilled because of the billing practices of J. B. Converse & Co., Inc., which, prior to the acquisition in a pooling of interests transaction in 1974, used the cash method of accounting. The Company intends to conform such billing practices to those followed by its other consulting engineering companies.

Note 4—Change in Accounting Method

In 1974, the Company changed its method of determining cost for substantially all of its chemical inventories from the first-in, first-out (FIFO) method to the last-in, first-out (LIFO) method. In adopting LIFO, management believes this method will more fairly present its results of operations by reducing the effect of inflationary cost increases in its chemical inventories and thus better match current costs with current revenues. It was not practical for international subsidiaries to change their method of valuing chemical inventories. The Company did not change to LIFO for other than chemical inventories because management does not believe LIFO provides an improved matching of costs and revenues for products and services whose results of operations are not significantly affected by inflationary cost increases in inventories. The effect of the change in 1974 was to reduce inventories by approximately $2,500,000 and net earnings by approximately $1,250,000 ($.16 per share). Inventories aggregating $7,200,000 at December 31, 1974, were stated at LIFO cost.

Note 5—Long-Term Debt

The Company obtained loans or issued long-term notes as follows:

	1974	1973
Loans with foreign banks	$ 676,167	$ 838,515
Mortgage payable, 7¾%, payable in installments of principal and interest aggregating $988 per month	81,301	86,630
Notes payable to individuals, at ½% above prime rate, payable in monthly installments of $3,869	603,564	649,992
Note payable relating to noncompete agreement (net of imputed interest at 8½% of $209,972 in 1974, and $239,576 in 1973) payable through 1987	355,478	370,524
Construction financing arrangement with industrial development authority—interest at 70% of prime rate. Construction may be financed to a maximum of $2,600,000. The loan is payable in 120 equal monthly installments beginning no later than August, 1976.	1,011,515	—
Mortgage payable, 9%, payable in installments of principal and interest aggregating $996 per month	39,168	47,193
	2,767,193	1,992,854
Amount due within one year	170,635	164,466
	$2,596,558	$1,828,388

Certain foreign subsidiaries are financing the construction of new plants with foreign bank loans which are guaranteed by the Company. One bank loan for $263,314 bears interest at 8.7 percent per annum and is repayable in eight annual installments approximating $38,000 which commenced in 1974. In connection with this loan, the Belgian Government has agreed to subsidize the subsidiary to the extent of 4 percent per annum of interest payable to 1976. Two other bank loans are payable in varying installments with $45,329 due by December 31, 1975. The larger loan ($365,775) bears interest at 2½ percent per annum above the Bank's base lending rate, but not less than 7%.

Note 6—Stock Option and Stock Incentive Plans

At December 31, 1974, the Company had reserved an aggregate of 300,292 shares of its Common Stock for issuance under its Qualified Stock Option and Employee Stock Incentive Plans. No effect is given to outstanding options in the computation of earnings per share, since the effect would be immaterial.

Options granted under the Qualified Stock Option plans are at the fair value at the date of grant and are exercisable at the time of the grant and for five years thereafter. No person may receive an option if he owns (or would own if his option were exercised) stock possessing 5 percent of the voting power or value of all classes of stock of the Company. Option activity is summarized as follows:

	Number of Shares	Option Price Per Share
Outstanding at January 1, 1973	131,580	$12.25 -$43.25
Granted	58,000	37.25 - 37.75
Exercised	(29,300)	12.25 - 33.50
Outstanding at December 31, 1973	160,280	12.25 - 43.25
Granted	220,480 (1)	22.625- 34.625
Cancelled	(169,180) (1)	18.125- 43.25
Exercised	(11,900)	12.25 - 23.00
Outstanding at December 31, 1974	199,680	18.125- 37.75

(1) Includes options for 165,480 shares which were terminated and a like number of new options granted at $22.625 a share. These new options become exercisable 5 years after the date of grant of the original terminated options. At December 31, 1974, options for 32,800 shares were exercisable, and options for 21,500 shares were available for future grants.

In addition, apart from the Qualified Plan, options for 3,000 shares are outstanding at $22.625 and become exercisable in 1975. In 1973, 14,000 options were exercised at prices ranging from $18.125 to $21.875 apart from the Qualified Plan.

In 1974, the shareholders of the Company approved an Employee Stock Incentive Plan which provides that up to 100,000 shares of Common Stock may be granted to April 30, 1984, at the discretion of the Board to key employees. The Company granted 23,888 shares during 1974. Key employees receiving grants are entitled to receive dividends, but assumption of full beneficial ownership is contingent upon continuous employment for the period, usually four or five years, stipulated at the time of grant. In the event the employee does not remain in continuous employment for the periods stipulated, the shares are cancelled and revert to the Company for reissuance under the Plan.

The aggregate fair market value of the shares granted under this plan is considered unearned compensation at the time of grant and compensation is earned ratably over the stipulated period.

Note 7—Provision for Income Taxes

The provision for income taxes includes deferred taxes on timing differences as follows:

	1974	1973
Depreciation	$444.210	$298.572
Deferred compensation	(104.976)	(35,000)
Accrued revenues	135.117	142,000
DISC income	50.475	70,000
	$524.826	$475.572

Current taxes payable have been reduced in 1974 and 1973 by investment tax credits of $111,000 and $149,000, respectively. Federal income tax returns have been settled by the IRS through 1970.

A reconciliation of the effective income tax rate for 1974 and 1973 with the statutory federal income tax rate of 48% is as follows:

	1974	1973
Federal tax rate	48.0%	48.0%
State and local taxes, net of federal income taxes	2.1	2.4
Investment tax credits	(.7)	(1.3)
Foreign tax credit	(.9)	(1.0)
Other items	1.1	(.2)
Effective income tax rate	49.6%	47.9%

Note 8—Commitments

Employee Retirement Plans—Aggregate contributions to employee retirement plans of the Company and its subsidiaries were $554,124 in 1974 and $324,929 in 1973. The unfunded past service cost at July 1, 1974, of one subsidiary company's plan is $457,000. Aggregate amounts in the pension funds exceeded the actuarially computed value of the plans' vested benefits as of December 31, 1973, the latest valuation date. The Company does not anticipate any material changes in its pension costs as a result of the 1974 Pension Reform Act. In addition, the provision for the Stock Bonus Profit Sharing Plan amounted to $530,586 in 1974 and $179,404 in 1973. Contributions to this plan are determined at the discretion of the Board of Directors, and may be in cash or Common Stock of the Company at the equivalent fair market value.

Other Plans—The Company has a discretionary bonus plan for officers. The Board of Directors determines whether or not a bonus will be paid and sets the amount using the increase in consolidated earnings before income taxes as a guide. The amounts provided aggregated $298,662 and $91,996 for 1974 and 1973, respectively.

Long-Term Leases—Total rental expense for all leases amounted to $1,881,025 in 1974 and $1,294,537 in 1973.

The future rental commitments as of December 31, 1974 for all noncancelable leases are as follows:

	Total	Building Space	Equipment	Automobiles
1975	$957,651	$479,959	$34,070	$443,622
1976	577,680	274,901	48,816	253,963
1977	136,353	64,778	47,835	23,740
1978	94,502	49,150	45,352	
1979	42,133	90	42,043	
1980-1984	79,726	—	79,726	

As of December 31, 1974, there are no future commitments on present noncancelable leases after 1984.

Leases for substantially all of the building space may be renewed for periods varying from one to four years upon expiration of present leases.

Note 9—Contingent Liability

Prior to acquisition, action had been brought against J. B. Converse & Co., Inc. as an additional third-party defendant in which plaintiff is seeking aggregate damages of $2,300,000. No provision has been made for possible loss since management denies liability, and the Company's counsel believes that the claim is unreasonable and that there is no supportable legal basis for the subsidiary's liability.

QUESTIONS

1. What is a balance sheet? Why is it dated differently than an income statement and a statement of changes in financial position?
2. Define assets. Contrast the conceptual and pragmatic definitions. Why are they different?
3. Define liabilities. Contrast the conceptual and pragmatic definitions. Why are they different?
4. Explain, in general terms, why the balance sheet is important to the decision-maker.
5. Explain why the balance sheet does not report the fair market value of a business.
6. Contrast the two balance sheet formats. Which one do you prefer? Explain.
7. Define current assets and current liabilities emphasizing their interrelationship.
8. Define working capital. What is the current ratio?
9. Distinguish between short-term investments and the investments classified as investments and funds. Under what conditions could an investment be moved from current assets to investments and funds and vice versa?
10. What are operational assets? Distinguish between tangible and intangible operational assets.
11. Why is it often necessary to use a caption "Other Assets?" Give two examples of items that might be reported under this classification.
12. Explain a deferred charge and contrast it with a prepaid expense.
13. Distinguish between current and noncurrent liabilities. Under what conditions would a noncurrent liability amount be reclassified as a current liability?
14. What is a deferred credit? Explain why this classification on a balance sheet is difficult to defend conceptually.
15. What is owners' equity? What are the main components of owners' equity?
16. What is a restriction on retained earnings? How are restrictions reported?
17. What is the purpose of the statement of changes in financial position? What is meant by all-resources concept?
18. Distinguish between a statement of changes in financial position prepared on *(a)* a cash equivalent basis, and *(b)* a working capital basis.
19. Explain the position of the accounting profession with respect to use of the terms reserves, surplus, and net profit. Why is care in selection of terminology used in financial statements important?
20. What is a comparative statement? Why are they important?

21. What is meant by subsequent events? Why are they reported? How are they reported?
22. In general, why are notes to the financial statements important? How does the accountant determine when a note should be included?
23. What is the auditors' report? Basically, what does it include? Why is it especially important to the statement user?
24. Are the financial statements representations of the management of the enterprise, the independent accountant, or both? Explain.

DECISION CASE 5–1

A. McDougald & Sons is a family corporation operating a chain of seven retail clothing stores in the Southwest. The total owners' equity of $5 million (all shares are outstanding) is owned by A. McDougald, president and founder, and eight men and women in the McDougald family. Except for accounts payable, modest amounts of short-term bank credit, and the usual short-term liabilities, the entire resources of the enterprise came from contributed capital and retained earnings. The general reputation of the company is excellent, and there have never been complaints about slowness in paying its liabilities. The family now has an opportunity to undertake a profitable expansion from seven to ten stores and estimates that upwards of $2,500,000 would be required for the purpose. It will be necessary to borrow this sum, and the issuance of five- to eight-year mortgage notes is contemplated.

Because the business is closely held and has never borrowed to an extent that made issuance of financial statements to outsiders necessary, the only persons who have seen the corporation's statements are members of the family, a few top employees, and some governmental officials, chiefly tax agents. When A. McDougald was told by a prospective lender that detailed financial statements for the past five years and audited statements for the most recent year as a basis for considering the loan would have to be provided, McDougald's initial reaction was to "hit the ceiling." After consideration, however, McDougald became willing to have the audit made and to release balance sheets as of the end of the most recent five years. McDougald was, as yet, unwilling to release statements of income and changes in financial position, and a majority of the other owners agreed with this stand.

Required:

1. If these five balance sheets are quite detailed, what can prospective lenders ascertain from them?
2. In your opinion would the five balance sheets give enough information to warrant granting a $2,500,000 secured intermediate-term loan? Explain the basis for your response.
3. If you were the lending officer of the prospective creditor and sought a compromise in the form of getting some added financial facts without receiving the other statements, what added information would be most useful to you? Explain your reasons.

EXERCISES

Exercise 5–1

To the left is a list of several different items from a typical balance sheet for a corporation. To the right is a list of brief statements of the valuations usually reported on the balance sheet for the different items.

Required:

Use the code letters to the right to indicate, for each balance sheet item listed, the *usual* valuation reported on the balance sheet. Feel free to comment on any doubtful items. Some code letters may be used more than once or not at all.

Balance Sheet Items

______Accounts receivable (trade).
______Marketable (short-term) investments.
______Inventories (merchandise for sale).
______Long-term investment in bonds of another company (purchased at a discount).
______Plant site (in use).
______Plant and equipment (in use).
______Patent (in use).
______Accounts payable (trade).
______Bonds payable (sold at a premium).
______Common stock (par $10 per share).
______Contributed capital in excess of par.
______Retained earnings.
______Land (future plant site).
______Idle plant (awaiting disposal).
______Natural resource.

Valuations Reported

a. Amount payable when due (usually no interest because short term).
b. Lower of cost or market.
c. Original cost when acquired.
d. Fair market value at date of the balance sheet whether it is above or below cost.
e. Original cost less accumulated amortization over estimated economic life.
f. Par value of the outstanding shares.
g. Face amount of the obligation plus unamortized premium.
h. Realizable value expected.
i. Cost to acquire the asset plus discount amortization.
j. Cost when acquired less accumulated depreciation.
k. Accumulated income less accumulated dividends.
l. Excess of issue price over par value.
m. No valuation reported (explain).
n. Expected net disposal proceeds.
o. Cost less depletion.
p. None of the above (when this response is used, explain the valuation usually used).

Exercise 5–2

Following are listed, in scrambled order, the major and minor captions for a balance sheet and a statement of changes in financial position (cash equivalent basis). Terminology given in the chapter is used.

1. Owners' equity.
2. Sources of cash (inflows).
3. Contributed capital.
4. Add (deduct) adjustments to revenue to derive cash basis.
5. Retained earnings.
6. Expenses (accrual basis).
7. Current liabilities.
8. From extraordinary items (net of tax).
9. Uses of cash.
10. Unrealized capital increment.
11. Assets.
12. Total cash expended for all purposes.
13. Operational assets – tangible.
14. Cash generated from revenues.
15. Total cash generated from other sources.
16. Long-term liabilities.
17. Total assets.
18. Current assets.
19. Capital stock.
20. Cash from other sources.
21. Other assets.
22. From operations (cash inflow).
23. Revenues (accrual basis).
24. Contributed capital in excess of par.
25. Deferred charges.
26. Total cash generated by operations.
27. Total cash generated from all sources.
28. Liabilities.
29. Investments and funds.
30. Net increase (decrease) in cash equivalents during the period.
31. Operational assets – intangible.
32. Cash disbursed for expenses.
33. Total liabilities.
34. Total liabilities and owners' equity.
35. Total owners' equity.
36. Add (deduct) adjustments to expenses to derive cash basis.

Required:

Set up two captions: *(a)* Balance Sheet; *(b)* Statement of Changes in Financial Position. For each caption, list the numbers given above in the order that they normally would be reported on the statement (do not renumber). Example:

a. Balance Sheet: 11, 18, and so on.
b. Statement of Changes in Financial Position: 2, 22, and so on.

Comment on any doubtful items.

Exercise 5–3

Indicate the best answer for each of the following (explain any qualifications):

1. Working capital means –
   a. Excess of current assets over current liabilities.
   b. Current assets.
   c. Capital contributed by stockholders.
   d. Capital contributed by stockholders plus retained earnings.
2. The distinction between current and noncurrent assets and liabilities is now based primarily on –
   a. One year; no exceptions.
   b. One year or operating cycle, whichever is shorter.
   c. One year or operating cycle, whichever is longer.
   d. Operating cycle; no exceptions.
3. Under current generally accepted accounting principles unexpired insurance is a –

a. Noncurrent asset.
b. Deferred charge.
c. Prepaid expense.
d. Short-term investment.

4. Which of the following is not a current asset?
   a. Office supplies inventory.
   b. Short-term investment.
   c. Petty cash (undeposited cash).
   d. Cash surrender value of life insurance policy.
5. Which of the following is not a current liability?
   a. Accrued interest on notes payable.
   b. Accrued interest on bonds payable.
   c. Rent revenue collected in advance.
   d. Premium on bonds payable (unamortized).
6. A deficit is synonymous with—
   a. A net loss for the current period.
   b. A cash overdraft at the bank.
   c. Negative working capital at the end of the period.
   d. A debit balance in retained earnings at the end of the period.
7. A balance sheet is an expression of the model—
   a. Assets = Liabilities + Owners' Equity.
   b. Assets = Liabilities − Owners' Equity.
   c. Assets + Liabilities = Owners' Equity.
   d. Working Capital + Operational Assets − Long-Term Liabilities = Contributed Capital.
8. Acceptable usage of the term *reserve* is reflected by—
   a. Deduction from an asset to reflect accumulated depreciation.
   b. Description of a known liability for which the amount is estimated.
   c. Restriction on retained earnings.
   d. Deduction on the income statement for an expected loss.
9. Which terminology essentially is synonymous with "balance sheet"?
   a. Operating statement.
   b. Statement of changes in financial position.
   c. Statement of financial value of the business.
   d. Statement of resources, obligations, and residual equity.
10. The "operating cycle concept"—
    a. Causes the distinction between current and noncurrent items to depend on whether they will affect cash within one year.
    b. Permits some assets to be classed as current even though they are more than one year removed from becoming cash.
    c. Is becoming obsolete.
    d. Affects the income statement but not the balance sheet.

Exercise 5–4

A typical balance sheet has the following captions:

A. Current assets.
B. Investments and funds.
C. Operational assets (land, buildings, and equipment).

D. Intangible assets.
E. Other assets.
F. Deferred charges.
G. Current liabilities.
H. Long-term liabilities.
I. Capital stock.
J. Additional contributed capital.
K. Retained earnings.

Indicate by use of the above letters (use capitals and print) how each of the following items would be classified. When an item is a contra amount (i.e., a deduction) in a caption, place a minus before it.

1. Accounts payable (trade).
2. Prepaid interest revenue (on a note receivable).
3. Accumulated depreciation.
4. Investment in stock of X Company (long term).
5. Plant site (in use).
6. Restriction on retained earnings.
7. Office supplies inventory.
8. Loan to company president (collection not expected for two years).
9. Accumulated income less accumulated dividends.
10. Bond discount unamortized (on bonds payable).
11. Bond sinking fund (to retire long-term bonds).
12. Prepaid insurance.
13. Accounts receivable (trade).
14. Short-term investment.
15. Allowance for doubtful accounts.
16. Building (in use).
17. Common stock (par $10).
18. Accrued interest revenue.
19. Patent.
20. Land (speculative).

Exercise 5–5

Typical balance sheet captions are listed in Exercise 5–4. Indicate, by use of the letters given there (use capitals and print), how each of the following items would be classified. When an item is a contra amount (i.e., a deduction) in a caption, place a minus before it.

1. Short-term investments.
2. Premium unamortized (on bonds payable).
3. Bonds payable (long term).
4. Cash dividends payable (within six months).
5. Prepaid rent revenue.
6. Accumulated depreciation.
7. Premium on common stock issued.
8. Idle plant held for final disposal.
9. Deferred costs being amortized over five years.
10. Inventory of supplies.
11. Preferred stock.
12. Discount unamortized on long-term investment in bonds of another company.
13. Installment payment due in six months on long-term note payable.
14. Accrued interest on note payable.
15. Rent revenue receivable.
16. Allowance for doubtful accounts.
17. Investment in bonds of another company (long term).
18. Undeposited cash (for making change).
19. Accounts receivable (trade).
20. Deficit.

Exercise 5–6

The following trial balance was prepared by Lowe Company as of December 31, 1976:

Cash	$ 7,200	
Accounts receivable	14,000	
Merchandise inventories	13,000	
Equipment	28,000	
Land	6,000	
Building	8,000	
Deferred charges	1,100	
Accounts payable		$ 5,500
Note payable—6%		8,000
Capital stock (par $10)		43,000
Earned surplus		20,800
	$77,300	$77,300

You ascertain that certain errors and omissions are reflected in the above, including the following:

1. The $14,000 balance in accounts receivable represents the entire amount owed to the company; of this sum, $12,500 is from trade customers, and 5% of that amount is estimated to be uncollectible. The remaining sum owed to the company represents a long-term advance to its president.
2. Inventories include $2,000 of goods incorrectly inventoried at double their cost (i.e., at $4,000). No correction has been recorded. Office supplies on hand of $400 are also included in the balance of inventories.
3. When the equipment and building were purchased new on January 1, 1972, they had, respectively, estimated lives of 10 and 25 years. They have been depreciated by the straight-line method on the assumption of zero salvage values, and depreciation has been credited directly to the asset accounts.
4. The balance of the Land account includes a $1,000 payment made as a deposit of earnest money on the purchase of an adjoining tract. The option to buy it has not yet been exercised and probably will not be exercised during the coming year.
5. The note matures March 31, 1977, having been drawn July 1, 1976. Interest on it has been ignored.
6. Common stock shares outstanding, 4,000.

Required:

Prepare a correct classified balance sheet using preferred terminology. Use whichever form is specified by your instructor; if not specified, use the format you prefer. Show computation of retained earnings.

Exercise 5–7

The following balance sheet has come to your attention:

DYER CORPORATION
Balance Sheet Statement
For Year Ended December 31, 1976

Assets

Liquid Assets:			
Cash		$ 31,000	
Receivables	$ 29,000		
Less: Reserve for bad debts	700	28,300	
Inventories		42,000	
			$101,300
Investments and Funds:			
Petty cash fund		200	
Sinking fund		70,000	
			70,200
Permanent Assets:			
Land and buildings	140,000		
Less: Reserve for depreciation	9,000	131,000	
Equipment	84,000		
Less: Reserve for depreciation	29,000	55,000	
			186,000
Deferred Charges:			
Prepaid expenses		2,700	
Accrued sinking fund income		600	
			3,300
Total			$360,800

Obligations

Short term:			
Accrued interest on mortgage		$ 700	
Accounts payable		36,500	
Reserve for income taxes	$ 13,000		
Less: U.S. government bonds	8,000	5,000	
			$ 42,200
Long term:			
Mortgage payable*			74,000

Net Worth

Capital stock		150,000	
Earned surplus		52,400	
Reserve for contingencies		66,400	
		268,800	
Less: Treasury stock		24,200	
			244,600
Total			$360,800

* The mortgage payable matures April 18, 1977, and is funded by the sinking fund.

Required:

Constructively criticize the above balance sheet. Set up your responses in the following format:

Specific Criticism (list)	*Explanation of Criticism*	*Correct Treatment*
1.		
Etc.		

Exercise 5–8

The ledger of May Manufacturing Company reflects obsolete terminology but you find its books have been, on the whole, accurately kept. After the most recent closing of the books at December 31, 1976, the following accounts are submitted to you for the preparation of a balance sheet.

Accounts payable	$ 2,700	Raw materials	$ 9,600
Accounts receivable	9,800	Reserve for bad debts	500
Accrued expenses	800	Reserve for depreciation	9,000
Bonds payable—7%	25,000	Rent paid in advance (a debit)	4,000
Capital stock ($100 par)	100,000	Sinking fund	8,000
Cash	18,200	Land	15,000
Earned surplus	xx,xxx	Note receivable	6,600
Factory equipment	31,200	Work in process	18,300
Finished goods	11,100		
Investments	13,700		
Office equipment	9,500		

You ascertain that two thirds of the depreciation relates to factory and one third to office equipment and that $4,000 of the balance in the Investments account will be converted to cash during the coming year; the remainder represents a long-term investment. Rent paid in advance is for the next year. The land was acquired as a future plant site. The note receivable is signed by the company president and is due in 1978. The sinking fund is being accumulated to retire the bonds at maturity.

Required:

1. Prepare a classified balance sheet using preferred terminology.
2. Compute *(a)* the amount of working capital, and *(b)* the current ratio.

Exercise 5–9

Reed Corporation is preparing the balance sheet at December 31, 1976. The following items are at issue:

a. Notes payable, long term, $60,000. This note will be paid in installments. The first installment of $20,000 will be paid August 1, 1977.
b. Bonds payable, 6%, $200,000; at December 31, 1976, unamortized premium amounted to $6,000.
c. Bond sinking fund, $40,000; this fund is being accumulated to retire the bonds at maturity. There is a restriction on retained earnings required by the bond indenture equal to the balance in the bond sinking fund.
d. Rent revenue collected in advance for the first quarter of 1977, $6,000.
e. After the balance sheet date, but prior to issuance of the 1976 balance sheet, one third of the merchandise inventory was destroyed by flood (date January 13, 1977), estimated loss $150,000.

Required:

Show, by illustration, how each of these items should be reported, and disclosed, on the December 31, 1976, balance sheet.

Exercise 5–10

Based upon the following information, prepare the stockholders' equity section of the balance sheet for Short Corporation, at December 31, 1976:

Retained earnings	$ 80,000
Preferred stock, par $10, authorized 15,000 shares	100,000
Restriction on retained earnings as required by a special contract	30,000
Cash received above par of preferred stock	15,000
Common stock, nopar, 50,000 shares issued (75,000 shares authorized)	175,000

Exercise 5–11

The following adjusted trial balance was prepared by Cotton Corporation at December 31, 1976:

Debits		*Credits*	
Cost of goods sold	$270,000	Sales revenue	$500,000
Distribution and administrative expenses	130,000	Accumulated depreciation, plant and equipment	40,000
Income tax expense	41,500	Accounts payable	10,000
Cash	39,000	Income taxes payable	11,000
Short-term investments	12,000	Bonds payable	50,000
Accounts receivable	70,000	Allowance for doubtful accounts	3,000
Merchandise inventory	90,000	Premium on bonds payable (unamortized)	1,000
Office supplies inventory	2,000	Common stock, par $10 (authorized 50,000 shares)	200,000
Investment in bonds of X Corporation (long term), cost	35,000	Excess of issue price over par on common stock	18,000
Land (plant site in use)	10,000	Retained earnings, balance January 1, 1976	37,000
Plant and equipment	100,000		
Franchise (less amortization	8,000		
Rearrangement costs*	15,000		
Idle equipment held for disposal	7,500		
Dividends paid during 1976	40,000		
	$870,000		$870,000

* Amortization period three years; this is the unamortized balance.

Required:

1. Prepare a single-step income statement.
2. Prepare a classified balance sheet.

Exercise 5–12

The following statement has just been prepared by Wilkerson Corporation:

WILKERSON CORPORATION
Statement of Changes in Financial Position
For the Year Ended December 31, 1976

Sources of Funds:		
From operations:		
Revenues	$260,000	
Decrease in trade accounts receivable	8,000	
Total Funds from Revenues		$268,000
Expenses	220,000	
Add (deduct) noncash expenses:		
Depreciation	(17,000)	
Amortization of patent	(1,000)	
Inventory increase	7,000	
Accounts payable decrease	2,000	
Income taxes payable increase	(1,000)	
Loss on sale of machinery	(4,000)	
Total Funds for Expenses		206,000
Funds generated by operations		62,000
From other sources:		
Sale of machinery	12,000	
Long-term note payable	25,000	
Issuance of capital stock for future plant site (Note A)	30,000	
Total Funds from Other Sources		67,000
Total Funds Generated during the Year		129,000
Uses of Funds:		
Retirement of mortgage note	20,000	
Cash dividends	24,000	
Purchase of long-term investment (stock, X Corporation)	15,000	
Acquisition of machinery (operational asset)	11,000	
Acquisition of land for future plant site (Note A)	30,000	
Total Funds Used during the Year		100,000
Net Increase (Decrease) in Cash and Short-Term Investments during the Year		$ 29,000

Required:

1. How are funds measured in this statement? Explain.
2. What was the net income for the year? How much did cash increase from operations? How did management generate more cash from operations than profit?
3. Explain the transaction "sale of machinery." Note that it is referred to twice.
4. Write footnote A with respect to the future plant site. Note that it is referred to twice.
5. Explain why depreciation expense and amortization of patent were deducted from total expenses. Why was the inventory change added to expenses?
6. Some changes in terminology are needed. Identify them and suggest preferable terminology.

PROBLEMS

Problem 5–1

To the left are typical items from a balance sheet for a corporation. To the right is a list of brief statements of *valuations* usually reported on a balance sheet for different items.

Required:

Use the code letters to the right to indicate for each balance sheet item listed, the *usual* valuation reported on the balance sheet. Provide explanatory comments for each doubtful item. Some code letters may be used more than once or not at all.

Balance Sheet Item

____ Cash.
____ Marketable investments (short term).
____ Accounts receivable (trade).
____ Notes receivable (short term).
____ Inventories (merchandise for sale).
____ Prepaid expenses (such as insurance).
____ Long-term investment in bonds of another company (purchased at a premium).
____ Long-term investment in stock of another company (less than 20% of the outstanding shares).
____ Plant site (in use).
____ Plant equipment (in use).
____ Patent (used in operations).
____ Deferred charge.
____ Accounts payable (trade).
____ Income taxes payable.
____ Notes payable (short term).
____ Bonds payable (sold at a discount).
____ Common stock (nopar).
____ Preferred stock (par $10 per share).
____ Contributed capital in excess of par.
____ Retained earnings.
____ Land held for speculation.
____ Land held for a future plant site.
____ Damaged merchandise (goods held for sale).

Valuation Reported

a. Total amount paid in by stockholders when issued.
b. Face amount collectible at maturity.
c. Lower of cost or market.
d. Cost to acquire the asset.
e. Excess of issue price over par value.
f. Accumulated income less accumulated dividends.
g. Cost to acquire less amortization to date.
h. Estimated realizable value (amount billed less estimated loss due to uncollectibility).
i. Par value of shares outstanding.
j. Cost less expired or used portion.
k. Cost at date of investment.
l. Par value.
m. Cost at date of investment less unamortized premium.
n. Current market value.
o. Amount payable when due (short term).
p. Face amount of the obligation less unamortized discount.
q. Cost to acquire less accumulated depreciation.
r. Fair market value at the date of the balance sheet whether it is above or below cost.
s. No valuation reported (explain).
t. Current value.
u. None of the above (when this response is used, explain the valuation usually used).

Problem 5–2

Typical balance sheet classifications are as follows:

A. Current assets.
B. Investments and funds.
C. Operational assets (land, buildings, and equipment).
D. Intangible assets.
E. Other assets.
F. Deferred charges.
G. Current liabilities.
H. Long-term liabilities.
I. Capital stock.
J. Additional contributed capital.
K. Retained earnings.

Indicate by use of the above letters (use capitals and print), how each of the following items would be classified. When it is a contra item (i.e., a deduction) in a caption, place a minus before it. Comment on doubtful items; and if an item is not reported on the balance sheet, write *none*.

1. Cash.
2. Cash set aside to meet long-term purchase commitment.
3. Land (used as plant site).
4. Accrued salaries.
5. Investment in subsidiary (long term; not a controlling interest).
6. Inventory of damaged goods.
7. Idle plant being held for disposal.
8. Investment in bonds of another company.
9. Cash surrender value of life insurance policy.
10. Goodwill.
11. Natural resource (timber track).
12. Allowance for doubtful accounts.
13. Stock subscriptions receivable (no plans to collect in near future).
14. Organization costs.
15. Discount on bonds payable.
16. Interest revenue collected in advance.
17. Accrued interest payable.
18. Accumulated amortization on patent.
19. Prepaid rent expense.
20. Short-term investment (common stock).
21. Rent revenue collected in advance.
22. Net of accumulated earnings and dividends.
23. Trade accounts payable.
24. Current maturity of long-term debt.
25. Land (held for speculation).
26. Notes payable (short term).
27. Special cash fund accumulated to build plant five years hence.
28. Bonds issued – to be paid within six months out of bond sinking fund.
29. Long-term investment in rental building.
30. Copyright.
31. Accumulated depreciation.
32. Deferred plant rearrangement costs.
33. Franchise.
34. Discount on long-term investment costs.
35. Premium on bonds payable (unamortized).
36. Common stock (at par value).
37. Petty cash fund.
38. Deficit.
39. Contributed capital in excess of par.
40. Earnings retained in the business.

(AICPA adapted)

Problem 5–3

The president of Hill Manufacturing Company is a personal friend of yours and he tells you the company has never had an audit and is contemplating having one principally because it is suspected that the financial statements are not well prepared. As an example the president hands you the following balance sheet for review:

HILL MANUFACTURING CO., INC.
Balance Sheet
For the Year Ended December 31, 1976

Assets

Liquid Assets:		
Cash in banks		$12,000
Receivables from various sources net of reserve for bad debts		5,000
Inventories		6,000
Cash for daily use		500
Total		23,500
Permanent Assets:		
Treasury stock		5,000
Fixed assets (net)		26,000
Grand Total		$54,500

Obligations and Net Worth

Short Term:		
Trade payables		$ 3,000
Salaries accrued		1,000
Total		4,000
Long Term:		
Mortgage		7,000
Net Worth:		
Capital stock	$30,000	
Earned surplus	13,500	
Total		43,500
Grand Total		$54,500

Required:

1. List and explain your criticisms of the above balance sheet; focus on all aspects of it.
2. Using the above data prepare a classified balance sheet that meets your specifications. Where amounts needed are missing use assumed, but realistic, amounts. *Hint:* Treasury stock is a reduction of stockholders' equity since it is the company's own stock reacquired by purchase.

Problem 5–4

The most recent balance sheet of Ray Corporation appears below.

RAY CORPORATION
Balance Sheet
For the Year Ended December 31, 1976

Assets

Current:			
Cash		$ 5,000	
Marketable securities		10,000	
Accounts receivable		30,000	
Merchandise		25,000	
Supplies		5,000	
Stock of subsidiary company (not a controlling interest)		17,000	$ 92,000
Investments:			
Cash surrender value of life insurance		20,000	
Treasury stock		25,000	45,000
Tangible:			
Buildings and land	$56,000		
Less: Reserve for depreciation	10,000	46,000	
Equipment	15,000		
Less: Reserve for depreciation	10,000	5,000	51,000
Deferred:			
Prepaid expenses		2,000	
Discount on bonds payable		10,000	12,000
Total			$200,000

Liabilities and Capital

Current:		
Accounts payable	$16,000	
Reserve for income taxes	17,000	
Customers' accounts with credit balance	100	$ 33,100
Long Term:		
Bonds payable	45,000	
Mortgage	12,000	57,000
Reserve for bad debts		900
Capital:		
Capital stock, par $10	75,000	
Earned surplus	25,000	
Capital surplus	9,000	109,000
Total		$200,000

Required:

1. List and explain your criticisms of the above balance sheet.
2. Prepare a correct classified balance sheet. *Hint:* The capital stock was sold above par. Deduct treasury stock from shareholders' equity.

Problem 5–5

The balance sheet shown below, which was submitted to you for review, has been prepared for inclusion in the published annual report of the XYZ Company for the year ended December 31, 1976:

XYZ COMPANY
Balance Sheet
December 31, 1976

Assets

Current Assets:			
Cash			$ 1,900,000
Accounts receivable		$3,900,000	
Less: Reserve for bad debts		50,000	3,850,000
Inventories—at the lower of cost (determined by the first-in, first-out method) or market			3,500,000
Total Current Assets			9,250,000
Fixed Assets:			
Land—at cost		200,000	
Buildings, machinery and equipment, furniture and fixtures—at cost	$4,200,000		
Less: Reserves for depreciation	1,490,000	2,710,000	2,910,000
Deferred Charges and Other Assets:			
Cash surrender value of life insurance		15,000	
Unamortized discount on first-mortgage note		42,000	
Prepaid expenses		40,000	97,000
Total Assets			$12,257,000

Liabilities

Current Liabilities:			
Notes payable to bank			$ 750,000
Current maturities of first-mortgage note			600,000
Accounts payable—trade			1,900,000
Reserve for income taxes for the year ended December 31, 1976			700,000
Accrued expenses			550,000
			4,500,000
Funded Debt:			
4% first-mortgage note payable in quarterly installments of $150,000		$4,200,000	
Less: Current maturities		600,000	3,600,000
Reserves:			
Reserve for damages		50,000	
Reserve for possible future inventory losses		300,000	
Reserve for contingencies		500,000	
Reserve for additional federal income taxes		100,000	950,000
Capital:			
Capital stock—authorized, issued and outstanding 100,000 shares of $10 par value		1,000,000	
Capital surplus		300,000	
Earned surplus		1,907,000	3,207,000
Total Liabilities			$12,257,000

Additional data:

1. Reserve for damages was set up by a charge against current fiscal year's income to cover damages possibly payable by the company as a defendant in a lawsuit in progress at the balance sheet date. Suit was subsequently compromised for $50,000 prior to issuance of the statement.
2. Reserve for possible future inventory losses was set up in prior years, by action of board of directors, by charges against earned surplus. No change occurred in the account during the current fiscal year.
3. Reserve for contingencies was set up by charges against earned surplus over a period of several years by the board of directors to provide for a possible future recession in general business conditions.
4. Reserve for federal income taxes was set up in a prior year and relates to additional taxes which the Internal Revenue Service contended that the company owed. The company has good evidence that settlement will be effected for the $100,000.
5. Capital surplus consists of the difference between the par value of $10 per share of capital stock and the price at which the stock was actually issued.

Required:

State what changes in classification or terminology you would advocate in the presentation of this balance sheet to make it conform with generally accepted accounting principles and with present-day terminology. State your reasons for your suggested changes.

(AICPA adapted)

Problem 5–6

The adjusted trial balance for Rollins Corporation, and other related data, at December 31, 1976, are given below in scrambled order. Although the company uses obsolete terminology, the amounts are correct. Assume perpetual inventory.

Additional information:

a. Market value of the short-term marketable securities is $47,300.
b. Merchandise inventory is based on *Fifo;* lower of cost or market.
c. Goodwill is being amortized (i.e., written off) over a 20-year period. The amortization for 1976 has already been recorded (as a direct credit to the Goodwill account). Amortization of other intangibles are recorded in this manner except for the patent (a contra-account is used for it).
d. Reserve for income taxes represents the estimated taxes payable at the end of 1976. Reserve for estimated damages was set up by debiting retained earnings during 1975. The $10,000 was the estimated amount of damages that would have to be paid as a result of a damage suit against the company; at December 31, 1976, the appeal was still pending. The $10,000 is an appropriation, or restriction, placed on retained earnings by management.

e. The cash advance from customer was for a special order that will not be completed and shipped until March 1977; the sales price has not been definitely established since it will be based on cost (no revenue should be recognized for 1976).

Cash	$ 44,100
Land (used for building site)	29,000
Cost of goods sold	108,000
Marketable securities (stock of S Company, short term)	44,000
Goodwill (unamortized cost)	12,000
Merchandise inventory	30,000
Office supplies inventory	1,000
Patent	7,000
Operating expenses	42,000
Income tax expense	17,500
Bond discount (unamortized)	7,500
Prepaid insurance	900
Building (at cost)	150,000
Land (held for speculation)	31,000
Accrued interest income	300
Accounts receivable (trade)	15,700
Note receivable, 10% (long-term investment)	20,000
Cash surrender value of life insurance policy	9,000
Deferred store rearrangement costs (assume a deferred charge)	6,000
Dividends paid during 1976	10,000
Prior period adjustment (tax assessment from prior year)	16,000
	$601,000

Reserve for bad debts	$ 1,100
Accounts payable (trade)	15,000
Revenues	200,000
Reserve for income taxes	7,500
Note payable (short term)	12,000
Common stock, par $10, authorized 50,000 shares	100,000
Reserve for depreciation, building	90,000
Retained earnings, January 1, 1976	48,000
Accrued wages	2,100
Reserve for estimated damages	10,000
Premium on common stock	15,000
Reserve for patent amortization	4,000
Cash advance from customer	3,000
Accrued property taxes	1,300
Note payable (long term)	16,000
Precollected interest income	1,000
Bonds payable, 6% ($25,000 due June 1, 1977)	75,000
	$601,000

Required:

1. Prepare a single-step income statement and a statement of retained earnings.
2. Prepare a classified balance sheet including appropriate disclosures. Use preferred terminology and format.

Problem 5–7

The adjusted trial balance for Nashville Manufacturing Corporation at December 31, 1976, is given below in scrambled order. Debits and credits are not indicated; all amounts are correct. Assume a normal balance situation in each account. Assume perpetual inventory system.

Work in process inventory	$ 24,000
Accrued interest on notes payable	1,000
Accrued interest receivable	1,200
Accrued income on short-term investments	1,000
Common stock, nopar, authorized 20,000 shares, issued 10,000	150,000
Cash in bank	40,000
Trademarks (unamortized cost)	1,400
Land held for speculation	17,000
Supplies inventory	600
Goodwill (unamortized cost)	20,000
Raw material inventory	13,000
Bond sinking fund	10,000
Accrued property taxes	1,200
Accounts receivable (trade)	19,000
Accrued wages	2,300
Mortgage payable (due in three years)	10,000
Building	130,000
Prepaid interest expense	1,700
Organization expenses (unamortized cost—assume deferred charge)	7,800
Deposits (cash by cus-tomers on sales orders to be delivered next quarter; no revenue yet recognized)	1,000
Long-term investment in bonds of K Corporation (at cost)	60,000
Patents (unamortized cost)	$ 12,000
Reserve for bond sinking fund*	10,000
Reserve for depreciation, office equipment	1,600
Reserve for depreciation, building	5,000
Premium on preferred stock	8,000
Cash on hand for change	400
Preferred stock, par $100, authorized 5,000 shares, 5% noncumulative	60,000
Precollected rent income	900
Finished goods inventory	42,000
Note receivable (short term)	4,000
Bonds payable, 6%, (due in 15 years)	50,000
Accounts payable (trade)	11,000
Reserve for bad debts	1,400
Notes payable (short term)	7,000
Office equipment	25,000
Land (used as building site)	8,000
Short-term investments (at cost)	15,500
Retained earnings, unappropriated (balance January 1, 1976)	13,200
Cash dividends paid during 1976	20,000
Revenues during 1976	400,000
Cost of goods sold for 1976	210,000
Expenses for 1976 (including income taxes)	90,000
Income taxes payable	40,000

* This is a restriction on retained earnings required by the bond indenture equal to the bond sinking fund which is being accumulated to retire the bonds.

Additional information:
Inventories are based on *Fifo;* lower of cost or market.

Required:

1. Prepare a single-step income statement. To compute earnings per share, deduct $3,000 of net income as an allocation to preferred stock.
2. Prepare a classified balance sheet; use preferred terminology and format. Comment on any items you consider doubtful with respect to classification.
3. Assume between December 31, 1976, and completion date, that a flood damaged the finished goods inventory in an amount estimated to be $17,000. Prepare an appropriate disclosure note to the balance sheet.

Problem 5–8

The following statement has just been prepared by Sutton Corporation:

SUTTON CORPORATION
Statement of Changes in Financial Position

Sources of Funds:		
From operations:		
Revenues	$630,000	
Adjustments for nonfund items:		
Accounts receivable decrease	15,000	
Total Funds from Revenues		$645,000
Expenses	550,000	
Adjustments for nonfund items (deductions):		
Depreciation	(30,000)	
Inventory increase	17,000	
Accounts payable increase	(11,000)	
Income taxes payable decrease	4,000	
Loss on sale of long-term investment	(3,000)	
Total Funds Required for Expenses		527,000
Funds generated by operations		118,000
From other sources:		
Sale of long-term investment	21,000	
Disposal of land (Note A)	50,000	
Sale of unissued common stock	15,000	
Long-term note payable	20,000	
Total Funds from Other Sources		106,000
Total Funds Generated		224,000
Uses of Funds:		
Dividends	40,000	
Acquisition of machinery (Note A)	50,000	
Payment on bonds payable	100,000	
Total Funds Used		190,000
Increase in Cash and Temporary Investments during the Year		$ 34,000

Required:

1. How are funds measured in this statement? Explain.
2. What was the net income for the year? How much cash was generated from operations? Explain how management generated more cash than profits.
3. What was the primary source of funds? What was the primary uses of funds? What sources and uses would you rely on for future predictions of funds flow in this company? Explain.
4. Explain the long-term investment transaction. Why is it reflected in two places?
5. Write Note A with respect to the machinery and land.
6. Explain why the accounts receivable decrease was added to revenues.
7. Explain the reason for the addition or deduction of each adjustment to total expenses.
8. Some changes in terminology would be helpful. Identify them and suggest preferable terminology.

Problem 5–9

The following information was taken from the records of Adamson Corporation for the year ended December 31, 1976:

Net income (Revenues, $560,000 – Expenses, $500,000)	$60,000
Depreciation expense	12,000
Accounts receivable increase	3,000
Accounts payable decrease	4,000
Purchase of operational assets (cash)	23,000
Merchandise inventory increase	5,000
Cash dividends paid	23,000
Loss on sale of operational asset (Cash, $18,000 – Book Value, $20,000)	2,000
Sold unissued common stock (cash)	35,000
Acquired future plant site; payment by issuance of 5,000 shares of common stock (fair market value)	24,000
Payment on bonds payable	25,000
Borrowed on long-term mortgage note	40,000

Required:

1. Use the above information to prepare a statement of changes in financial position, cash equivalent basis.
2. Write the disclosure note with respect to the future plant site.

Problem 5–10

The Appendix to this chapter gives an actual income statement and statement of changes in financial position. Examine them carefully and respond to the following questions. Respond for the latest year unless directed otherwise.

a. Are they comparative statements? Explain.
b. Are they consolidated statements? What do you understand this to mean?
c. What format was used for the balance sheet? Explain variations in format from those outlined in the chapter.
d. What title was used for the balance sheet and how was the statement dated?
e. How may different subclassifications were used for assets? For liabilities? For owners' equity? Explain variations from those suggested in the chapter.
f. What was total current assets? Total current liabilities? Amount of working capital? What was the current ratio?
g. How were short-term investments valued? Explain
h. How were inventories costed? Explain.
i. What was the percent of the allowance for doubtful accounts to accounts receivable?
j. Were there any investments and funds? Explain the nature of each.
k. How were operational assets labeled and valued? Explain. What was the average percent of accumulated depreciation on each category of operational assets? From this, how would you characterize the operational assets as to remaining life?
l. Were any intangibles reported? Explain them.
m. Were any prepaid expenses reported? Were any deferred charges reported?

What were the deferred charges? Do you agree with the classification on this item? Explain.

n. Were any "other or miscellaneous" assets reported? List them.

o. How were liabilities classified? Do you agree with the classification of each liability? Explain why.

p. Was any unamortized bond premium or discount reported? If yes, how was it reported? Do you agree with the method of reporting? Explain.

q. Were there any convertible debt securities? What were the terms of conversion?

r. Do you agree with the subclassifications of stockholders' equity? Explain.

s. How many different classes of stock were there? What was the par per share of each? For each class, how many shares were (1) authorized, (2) issued, (3) held as treasury stock, and (4) outstanding?

t. Were there any restrictions on retained earnings? How were they reported?

u. What percent of total assets were provided by (1) creditors, and (2) owners?

v. What title and date was used on the statement of changes in financial position?

w. Was the statement of changes in financial position prepared on a working capital basis or a cash equivalent basis? How was this made known to you in the statement?

x. What percent of total fund inflows came from (1) operations, (2) extraordinary items, and (3) other sources?

y. How many notes to the statements referred to the balance sheet? The statement of changes in financial position? What was the important issue in each?

z. What was the scope of the independent auditors' examination? What kind of opinion did the auditor give? Explain.

aa. Were there any unusual features of the balance sheet and the statement of changes in financial position? What kind?

bb. Overall, do you believe these two statements could be improved with respect to format and terminology? Explain each change that you would recommend for consideration.

Problem 5–11

The Appendix to Chapter 4 gives an actual income statement and statement of changes in financial position. Examine them carefully and respond to the questions posed in Problem 5–10. Respond for the latest year unless directed otherwise.

Problem 5–12

Obtain an audited financial statement for the latest year for a company of your choice (from the library or other source) and use it as a basis for responding to each of the questions posed in Problem 5–10.

Problem 5–13 (Review of Chapters 3, 4, and 5)

On January 1, 1976, Hays Company had the following trial balance:

No.	Account	Debit	Credit
101	Cash	$ 96,000	
102	Accounts receivable	45,000	
103	Allowance for doubtful accounts		$ 670
104	Office supplies inventory	800	
105	Inventory (periodic system)*	60,000	
106	Short-term investments		
107	Investment revenue receivable		
108	Fund to construct future plant	30,000	
109	Machinery	120,000	
110	Accumulated depreciation, machinery		72,000
111	Land (future plant site)	15,000	
112	Patent	4,000	
113	Other assets	55,000	
201	Accounts payable		35,000
202	Accrued interest payable		
203	Income taxes payable (1975)		12,330
204	Long-term mortgage note		
301	Common stock (par $10)		150,000
302	Contributed capital in excess of par		30,000
303	Retained earnings		125,800
400	Income summary		
500	Sales revenue		
501	Investment revenue		
600	Purchases		
601	Freight on purchases		
602	Purchase returns		
700	Selling expenses		
701	General and administrative expenses		
702	Interest expense		
703	Depreciation expense		
704	Income tax expense		
801	Extraordinary items		
802	Prior period adjustments		
		$425,800	$425,800

* Depending on the worksheet technique used, additional account for the ending inventory could be used.

1976 entries (use number to left for date notations):

1. Paid 1975 income taxes payable on March 3, 1976, in full.
2. Purchases ....$350,000 (of which $50,000 was on credit)
   Purchase returns .... 1,000 (on account)
   Freight on purchases .... 2,000 (cash)
3. The following selling expenses were incurred and paid during 1976:
   - Advertising ....$ 10,000
   - Salaries 130,000
   - Other selling 15,000
4. The following general and administrative expenses were incurred and paid during 1976:
   - Salaries $100,000
   - Office supplies .... 500 (debit Acct. #104)
   - Rent expense 24,000
5. A mortgage note was dated and signed on March 1, 1976, for $75,000; this amount of cash was received. Interest will be paid annually on this date; 8% interest.
6. A short-term investment was acquired for cash on June 1, 1976, at par, $20,000, 6%. The interest will be received annually thereafter on this date.

7. Suffered severe flood loss amounting to $40,000 (assume extraordinary item). (Credit cash because this was spent to restore the damages.)
8. Received damages (cash) of $30,000 from a court case which began in 1973.
9. At December 31, 1976, interest on the building fund amounting to $1,500 was added to the fund balance.
10. Cash collections on accounts receivable, $85,000.
11. Cash payments on accounts payable, $65,000.
12. Cash paid for dividends amounting to $2 per share (debit retained earnings).
13. Sales were $700,000 of which 15% was on credit.
14. Ending inventory was $70,000.

Required:

1. Set up a general journal and T-accounts (with account numbers). Enter beginning balances in the ledger accounts. All of the ledger accounts needed are listed in the above trial balance.
2. Journalize and post the current entries. Use posting notations.
3. Set up a worksheet with a minimum of eight columns (or more if you prefer). Develop the unadjusted trial balance from the ledger and enter it in the first two money columns of the worksheet.
4. Enter the following adjusting entries on the worksheet and complete it (label the adjusting entries with the letters to the left).
   a. Bad debt expense is 1% of total credit sales.
   b. Office supplies inventory at December 31, 1976, was determined by count to be $600.
   c. Accrue the investment revenue at 6% per year.
   d. The machinery had an estimated life of ten years, no salvage value; assume straight-line depreciation and a full year's depreciation for 1976.
   e. On January 1, 1976, the patent had eight years remaining life; assume straight-line amortization. General and administrative expense.
   f. Accrue interest on the mortgage note.
   g. Assume an average income tax rate of 40% on all items.
5. Prepare a single-step income statement and statement of retained earnings.
6. Prepare a classified balance sheet.
7. Journalize and post the adjusting entries.
8. Journalize and post the closing entries.
9. Prepare a post-closing trial balance.
10. Which adjusting entries would you reverse?

(Note: Unless directed otherwise by your instructor, to conserve time, you may substitute *account numbers* for account titles on completing any, or all, of the following requirements: 2, 3, 5, 6, 7, 8, and/or 9.)

Chapter 6

Concepts of Future and Present Value

PURPOSE OF THE CHAPTER

This chapter focuses on the time value of money, commonly called interest. It is the cost of using money over time. Outflows for the time value of money are identified as interest expense, whereas inflows for the time value of money are identified as interest revenue. Entities at various times make decisions that involve either *(a)* receiving funds, goods, or services currently with a promise to make payments over one or more future periods; or *(b)* committing funds currently as an investment to obtain returns over one or more future periods. In both situations the time value of money is fundamental and important to the decision-making process and in subsequently measuring and reporting the financial effects of earlier decisions. Federal law now requires that the *true annual* rate of interest be specified on installment contracts and consumer loans. This often requires application of present value concepts.

Because of the time value of money (aside from inflation or deflation), a dollar has a different value today (often referred to as time zero) than at future or past dates. Therefore, dollar inflows and outflows that occur at significantly different dates cannot simply be aggregated in a meaningful way; rather they must be restated at a common date to reflect the time value of money by applying the concepts of present and/or future value. Restatement for the interest factor is essential in many situations: *(a)* when preparing information inputs for decision making (such as capital budgeting), and *(b)* for accounting measurement and reporting. Therefore, the accountant's knowledge necessarily must include an understanding of the concepts to be discussed in this chapter. Discussion of these concepts is presented early in this book because of their widespread use in accounting measurements, recording, and reporting as discussed and illustrated in later chapters. Some applications of future and present value concepts in accounting are:

1. Notes receivable and payable – Measuring and reporting those notes that either carry no stated rate of interest or a rate of interest that is not realistic in comparison with the "going" rates.

2. Leases–Measuring and reporting long-term leases.
3. Pensions–Measuring and reporting numerous aspects of pension plans.
4. Assets–Measuring and reporting assets acquired with long-term debt when the interest rate is unspecified or unrealistic.
5. Installment contracts–Measuring and reporting the effects of assets acquired or sold on long-term installment terms.
6. Sinking funds–Measuring and reporting resources (funds) set aside for specific uses in the future.
7. Depreciation–Measuring depreciation charges when the sinking fund or annuity methods are used.
8. Capital additions–Evaluation of the probable effects of alternative investments in capital assets.
9. Business combinations–Measuring and reporting of such items as receivables, debts, and accruals in a combination by purchase.
10. Premium and discount on certain receivables and payables–Measuring the amortization of bond premium and discount for both investments in bonds and bonds payable.
11. Future commitments of goods and/or services–Measuring and reporting future commitments to furnish or receive goods or services when the interest rate is unspecified or unrealistic.

The purpose of this chapter is to present the concepts of future and present value in a way that emphasizes their application in the accounting process–measuring, recording, and reporting. The basic concepts are presented and illustrated in a way that builds a solid foundation for their applications in subsequent chapters (and in more advanced accounting courses). The use of prepared tables, which are available from many sources, is emphasized. Part A discusses the amount and present value of 1, and Part B discusses annuities.

CONCEPT OF INTEREST

Interest (i.e., the time value of money) represents the excess of resources (usually cash) received or paid over the amount of resources lent or borrowed at an earlier date. To illustrate, assume Entity A loaned Entity B $6,000 cash for one year with the stipulation that $6,600 cash would be repaid. The time value of money for this contract would be:

Beginning of year, amount of resources committed		$6,000
End of year, amount of resources returned		6,600
Difference–time value of money per contract........................		$ 600
Analysis:		
Actual interest in dollars	$600	
Actual interest as a rate ($600 ÷ $6,000)	10%	

Simple Interest

In the above example the interest was based on the principal amount ($6,000), which would be the usual case in a loan covering one period only. However, had the loan covered two or more periods, a question would arise about the interest assumption.

Simple versus Compound Interest

When a loan covers two or more periods, interest may be computed on either a simple or a compound interest basis. *Simple interest* is computed only on the principal amount. For example, assume the above loan contract was for two years with specified simple interest of 10% per year on the principal amount of $6,000. The amount of interest would be $600 × 2 = $1,200 (i.e., the simple interest amount). In contrast, *compound interest* is computed on the principal amount plus all interest that has accumulated on the principal. For example, assume the above loan contract was for two years with specified compound interest of 10% per year. The amount of compound interest would be computed as follows:

		Interest	Interest Basis	Resource Flows
Year 1:	Principal (resources committed)		$6,000	$6,000
	Interest ($6,000 × .10)	$ 600		
Year 2:	Amount subject to interest..................		6,600	
	Interest ($6,600 × .10)	660		
	Amount of resources returned			7,260
	Interest amount	$1,260		$1,260

Clearly, when a choice is available, the investor would always opt for compound interest. In the above example the investor would receive $60 ($1,260 − $1,200) more interest on a compound interest basis than on a simple interest basis. In contrast, the borrower would have to pay $60 more interest. Simple interest usually is applicable to short-term receivables and payables, and compound interest is used for long-term contracts.

Interest Periods

Contracts which call for compound interest usually specify the interest rate on an *annual* basis. The interest periods—those intervals at which interest is accrued and added to the principal—may or may not be as much as one year apart. For example, a contract may call for "interest at 8% compounded annually," or for "interest at 8% compounded semiannually." In the first instance the rate is 8% for one interest period of a year; in the second instance the rate is 4% for each interest period of six months. If interest of 8% is compounded quarterly, the rate per period (quarter) is 2%, and there would be four interest periods per year. If an annual rate is stated and there is no mention of the frequency of compounding, interest is assumed to be compounded annually.[1]

Summary of Concepts

The concepts of future and present value involve four basic values. These four concepts, discussed in the order listed below, may be briefly identified as:

Part A—Amount and Present Value of 1:

1. *Amount of 1*—the future value of $1 at the end of n periods at i compound interest rate.

$$a = (1 + i)^n \text{ (see Table 6–1)}$$

2. *Present value of 1*—the present value of $1 due n periods hence, discounted at i compound interest rate:

$$p = \frac{1}{(1 + i)^n} \text{ (see Table 6–2)}$$

Part B—Annuities:

3. *Amount of annuity of 1*—the future value of n periodic contributions (rents) of $1 each plus accumulated compound interest at i rate.

$$A_o = \frac{(1 + i)^n - 1}{i} \text{ (see Table 6–3)}$$

4. *Present value of annuity of 1*—the present value of n periodic contributions (rents) of $1 each to be received, or paid, each period discounted at i compound interest rate. Stated another way: The amount that must be invested today at i compounded interest rate in order to receive n periodic receipts in the future of $1 each.[2]

$$P_o = \frac{1 - \frac{1}{(1 + i)^n}}{i} \text{ (see Table 6–4)}$$

PART A—AMOUNT AND PRESENT VALUE OF 1

In order to understand these two concepts, a clear distinction between an "amount" and "present value" is essential. Fundamentally, the difference is in the time assumption. "Amount" is a concept of *future* amounts, whereas "present value" is a concept of *present* amounts. This

---

[1] Throughout this chapter and in the problem materials, short-term periods and even interest rates usually are used to facilitate comprehension. Also amounts usually are rounded to even dollars. Obviously, in the real world these simplifications generally cannot be used.

[2] These are for *ordinary* annuities, not annuities due. Also the notations used vary considerably. For example, the symbol for an amount of annuity of 1 often used is $S_{\overline{n}|i}$, and for present value of annuity of 1, $A_{\overline{n}|i}$.

distinction can be graphically displayed. Note in particular the time direction indicated by the arrows.

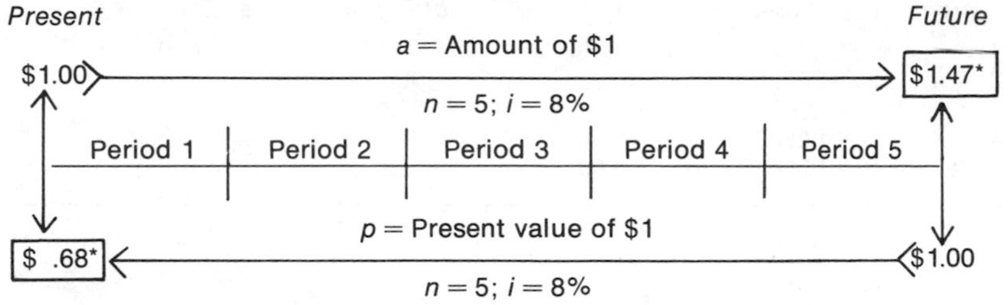

AMOUNT OF 1

The concept of amount of 1 (the symbol is a) is often called compound interest. The future amount is the principal at the start plus accumulated compound interest. For example, $1,000 deposited in a savings account at 8% interest per year on January 1, 1976, would amount (accumulate) to $1,469 at the end of the fifth year (December 31, 1980) assuming annual compounding. The increase of $469 would be accumulated compound interest during the five years.

Calculation of Amount of 1

It is convenient and customary to use a base figure of 1 in compound interest calculations. In the United States it would be natural to think of 1 as $1. The figure 1 could just as readily stand for one peso or one of some other unit of currency.

We can determine how much an investment of $1 would be worth after being left for a specified number of periods at a specified compounding rate per period by any one of several methods. To illustrate, assume $1 is invested for five years at 8% compounded annually. The total of principal and compound interest at the end of the five years may be determined by any one of the following methods:

1. *By successive interest computations* – multiply the principal ($1) by the interest rate (.08) and add the $.08 interest thus obtained for the first period, and the sum ($1.08) is the amount (a) at the end of the first period. This amount becomes the interest-bearing principal for the second period. This sum is principal plus interest $(1 + i)$, which may then be used as the multiplier in each succeeding period to secure the compound amount. Exhibit 6–1 uses this multiplier to secure the amount (a) at the end of each of the five periods.

2. *By formula* – substitute in a formula which states that for n interest periods at i rate of interest the amount of 1 is, $a = (1 + i)^n$. Substituting, we would say $1 invested at 8% annual compound interest for 5 years = $(\$1 + .08)^5$, or $1.47+. (Verifiable in Table 6–1.) Fifth-power

EXHIBIT 6–1

Period	Balance at Start of Period	Multiplier $(1+i)$	Amount at End of Period	Alternate Computation at End $(1+i)^n$
1	$1	1.08	$1.08	$(1.08)^1$
2	1.08	1.08	1.1664	$(1.08)^2$
3	1.1664	1.08	1.25971	$(1.08)^3$
4	1.25971	1.08	1.36049	$(1.08)^4$
5	1.36049	1.08	1.46933	$(1.08)^5$

multiplication is a laborious process and would be especially so where the exponent is large. If a calculator is not available, one could employ logarithms to simplify the calculations. Exhibit 6–1 demonstrates that the formula for amount of 1 is: $a = (1 + i)^n$.

3. *By table*—Standard tables of the various future and present values may be obtained from numerous sources. Partial tables are presented in this chapter for your convenience. Table 6–1 is based on the formula $a = (1 + i)^n$; therefore it presents the amount of 1 values (for a limited number of periods and interest rates). Reference to Table 6–1, down the 8% column, and across on the five-period line, shows the amount of 1 to be 1.46933 (i.e., $1.47+, as computed above in Exhibit 6–1). Obviously, tables facilitate computation of future and present values. However, a word of caution is in order. Observe that Table 6–1 is entitled *Amount of 1* and the underlying formula is $a = (1 + i)^n$. The heading of the table (including the formula on which it is based) must be considered carefully since it is very easy to take an amount from the wrong table. Also, not infrequently tables show values carried to only two, three, or four decimal places. When the table value is to be applied to a large amount, rounding to this extent can cause a material error in the resulting amount computed. Observe that the tables presented in this chapter are carried to five places.

Future Amount of a Specified Principal

Since the standard tables are based on $1 (for example, as in Table 6–1), amounts other than $1 are simply multiplied by appropriate table value. To illustrate, assume a company deposits $10,000 cash in a fund (or a savings account) that will earn 8% compounded annually for six years. How much will be in the fund at the end of the sixth year from the deposit date? We can readily compute this future amount by referring to Table 6–1, Amount of 1, as follows: $10,000 $\times\ a_{\substack{n=6\\i=8\%}}$; that is, $10,000 $\times$ 1.58687 = $15,869. The interest revenue earned would be $5,869.

As another example, assume another company deposits $50,000 cash in a building fund which will be needed at the end of ten years and that the fund will earn 8% interest per annum compounded semiannually. Since the interest periods are one-half year, there are 20 interest periods and the compound interest rate is 4% per period. By reference to Table 6–1, the computation of the future amount is $50,000 × $a_{\substack{n=20\\i=4\%}}$; that is, $50,000 × 2.19112 = $109,556. Interest revenue earned over the ten-year period would be $59,556.

Determination of Other Values Related to Amount of 1

In each of the two examples given above, *three* values were provided. To restate the first example: *(a)* principal, $10,000; *(b)* interest rate, 8%; and *(c)* periods, 6. A fourth value, the future amount $15,869, was computed. Obviously, if *any* three of these four values are known, the other one can be derived. Thus, there are three types of problems that may be encountered; viz:

1. To determine the future amount (discussed above—compound amount of a specified principal).
2. To determine the required interest rate (discussed below—determination of compound interest rate).
3. To determine the required number of interest periods (discussed below—determination of number of periods).

Determination of the Compound Interest Rate

If the amount to which a given principal sum will accumulate (or is desired to accumulate) is known, and the number of periods is known, the required rate of compound interest can be calculated.

As an example, if it is desired to invest $5,000 at interest compounded annually for ten years so as to accumulate $10,795, what rate of interest is required? To find the rate the following steps may be taken:

1. $10,795 ÷ $5,000 = $2.159, the amount to which $1 would accumulate at the unknown interest rate by the end of the ten-year period.
2. Referring to an amount of 1 table (Table 6–1) and reading across the ten-period line we find the amount of 2.15892 under the 8% column; thus, this is the required interest rate.

Often it is necessary to interpolate to derive the required rate. Suppose once again $5,000 is to be invested for ten years. In this case it is desired to accumulate $11,000. Here the rate of increase is the same as if $1 had grown to $11,000 ÷ $5,000 = 2.20. Referring to the ten-period line, we find the value under 8% is 2.15892; under the next higher rate, 9%, it is 2.36736. Therefore, the rate is between 8% and 9%—somewhat closer to the former—not quite one half of the way between them. We can conclude that the interest earned must be about 8¼%. Or more precisely,[3]

$$\left[8\% + \frac{2.20 - 2.15892}{2.36736 - 2.15892}(9 - 8)\right] = 8.20 + \%$$

[3] *Linear* interpolation was illustrated; calculus or methods of finite differences could have been used to give a more precise answer.

Determination of Number of Periods

If the amount to which a given sum will accumulate is known, and the interest rate is known, the required number of periods can be calculated. To use the above example again, assume the following is known: *(a)* investment to be made \$5,000; *(b)* accumulation desired \$10,795; and *(c)* the desired interest rate to be 8%. To compute the required number of interest periods, the following steps may be taken:

1. \$10,795 ÷ \$5,000 = \$2,159, the amount \$1 would accumulate at 8% for the unknown number of interest periods.
2. Referring to an amount of 1 table (Table 6–1) and reading down the 8% column we find 2.159 (rounded) on the ten-year line, thus the required (implied) number of interest periods is ten.

An Accounting Application of Amount of 1

Sonora Corporation, in order to assure funds for a planned future expansion, deposited \$50,000 cash in a plant expansion fund on January 1, 1976. The bank, serving as trustee, will pay 7% interest compounded annually. The funds will be needed on January 1, 1979.

Required:

1. Compute the fund balance at December 31, 1978.
2. Prepare an accumulation table for the fund.
3. Give the accounting entries for the entire period including withdrawal on January 1, 1979.

Solution:

1. Fund balance at December 31, 1978:

$$\$50{,}000 \times a_{\substack{n=3\\ i=7\%}} = \$50{,}000 \times 1.22504 = \underline{\underline{\$61{,}252}}$$

2. Accumulation table, plant expansion fund:

Date	Interest Revenue	Fund Balance
1-1-76 deposit		\$50,000
12-31-76	\$50,000 × .07 = \$3,500	53,500
12-31-77	53,500 × .07 = 3,745	57,245
12-31-78	57,245 × .07 = 4,007	61,252

3. Entries:

1-1-76 deposit of cash:

	Debit	Credit
Plant expansion fund	50,000	
Cash		50,000

Each December 31 interest revenue earned:

	12-31-76		12-31-77		12-31-78	
Plant expansion fund	3,500		3,745		4,007	
Investment revenue		3,500		3,745		4,007

1-1-79 withdrawal of fund:

Cash	61,252	
Plant expansion fund		61,252

PRESENT VALUE OF 1

Present value is the present, or time zero, value of a sum of future dollars discounted back from a specified future date to the present date at a given rate of compound interest. It is a present, rather than a future, concept. Present value involves compound discounting, thus it can be said to be the inverse of the amount-of-1 concept of compound interest. Since a future amount is discounted, the present value will always be less than the future amount. For example, $1 discounted at 8% per annum for one year has a present value of $.9259, and discounted for two years has a present value of $.8573. The symbol usually used for present value of 1 is p.

We have seen that $1 invested at i interest rate per period has a future value (amount of 1) of $(1 + i)^n$ dollars. It follows that $(1 + i)^n$ dollars has a present value that is less than $(1 + i)^n$ by an inverse or reciprocal relationship. To illustrate, assume $1, an interest rate of 8%, and 1 period:

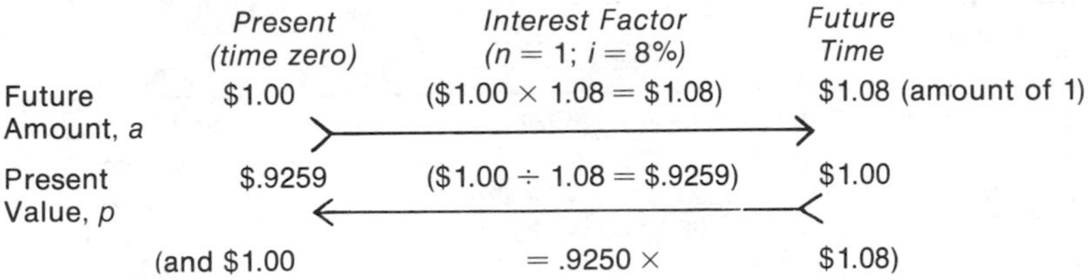

The reciprocal relationship between the amount of 1 and the present value of 1 provides a symbolic expression of the computation of present value amounts, viz:

$$\text{Amount of 1, } a = (1 + i)^n$$

Therefore; the reciprocal relationship is

$$\text{Present value of 1, } p = \frac{1}{(1 + i)^n}$$

This is the formula for computation of all present value of 1 amounts.

Computation of Present Value of 1

Present value of 1 amounts can be laboriously computed through compound discounting inversely to that shown on Exhibit 6–1 for future amounts. Also, present value amounts can be computed by dividing the values given in Table 6–1, Amount of 1, into 1.00. For example, $p_{\substack{n=5 \\ i=8\%}}$ can be computed as follows: 1.00 ÷ 1.46933 (from Table 6–1) = .68058. However, a much more convenient approach is to use a standard table that discounts $1 at various "$n$" and "$i$" values. A *present value of 1* table for various interest rates and periods is shown as Table 6–2. (Carefully observe the table heading and the underlying formula.) Each value in this table is a reciprocal of the corresponding value in the amount of 1 table.

An Accounting Application of Present Value of 1

To compute the present value of a future amount, the appropriate present value amount from Table 6–2 is multiplied by the specified future amount. To illustrate, assume Blue Corporation acquired a new machine on January 1, 1976. Because of a shortage of cash, the vendor agreed to let Blue Corporation pay for the machine at the end of the third year after purchase, that is, on December 31, 1978. The amount to be paid at that date is $50,000, which includes all interest charges. Assume the going compound interest rate is 8% per year. Question: Taking into account the interest, what was the cost of the machine, when acquired, in conformity with the cost principle? We must compute the present value of the future amount of $50,000 as follows: $\$50{,}000 \times p_{\substack{n=3\\i=8\%}} = \$50{,}000 \times .79383$ (from Table 6–2) = $39,691. A *debt schedule* for this situation would be:

Date	*Interest Expense Incurred*	*Liability Balance*
1-1-76		$39,691
12-31-76	$39,691 × .08 = $3,175	42,866
12-31-77	42,866 × .08 = 3,429	46,295
12-31-78	46,295 × .08 = 3,705*	50,000

* Adjusted for rounding error from using a five-place table.

It follows that the sequence of entries for this situation would be:

1-1-76 Acquisition of the machine:

Machine	39,691	
Liability		39,691

Each December 31, to record interest expense incurred:

	12-31-76		*12-31-77*		*12-31-78*	
Interest expense	3,175		3,429		3,705	
Liability		3,175		3,429		3,705

12-31-78 payment of the liability:

Liability	50,000	
Cash		50,000

Other values can be computed for present value of 1 as illustrated above for amount of 1.

PART B—ANNUITIES

Annuities involve the same concepts of future value and present value discussed in Part A. Annuities are identical to the amount of 1 and present value of 1 concepts except for one addition, concept of an *annuity*. The term annuity means a series of payments, or receipts, of *equal amounts* for a series of *equal time periods*. There is one equal amount (often called a rent) for each equal time period. In contrast, amount of 1 and present value of 1 involves a single amount only at the beginning (present) or at a future specified date. The monthly payments on an auto loan, for example, constitute an annuity; there is an equal cash payment each month by one party and an equal cash receipt each month by the other party. The future and present value of an annuity may be graphically displayed on a *time scale* as follows:

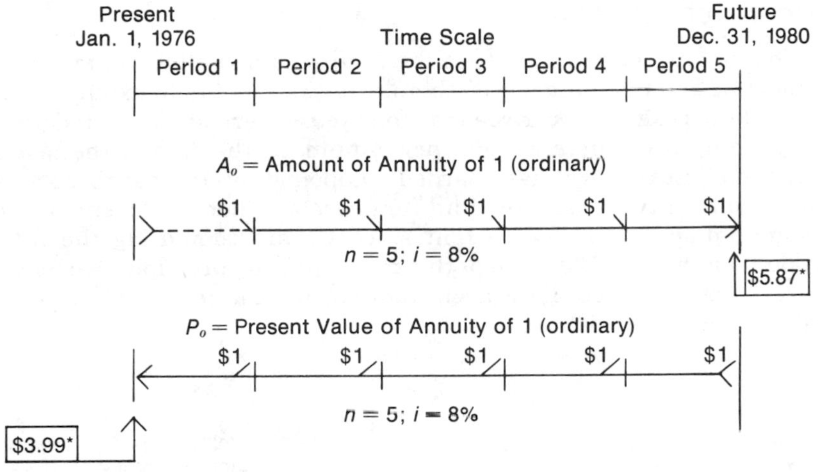

* Rounded to even cents.

The subscript "o" in A_o and P_o denotes an ordinary annuity.

In the above illustration observe that there are five *equal* rents in each instance (since $n = 5$) and the rents are at the *end* of each period. The *amount of annuity of 1* is a future concept, and the future amount of the five rents of $1 is $5.87. The future value will always be greater than the sum of the rents by the amount of the compound interest accumulation. Since the rents are assumed to be on the last day of each period, observe that for the amount of an annuity of 1, the future amount is calculated at the date of the last rent. This means that since there is no interest after the last rent, there is one more rent than *interest* periods.[4]

[4] The above illustration, and the discussion, assumes an *ordinary annuity* in each instance. The primary characteristic is that the rents are assumed to be at the *end* of each period as reflected in the graphic depiction. In contrast, an *annuity due* assumes the rents are at the *beginning* of each period. Annuities due will be discussed in a subsequent section.

The *present value of annuity of 1* is a present (i.e., time zero) concept. As shown in the above illustration, the present value of the five rents of \$1 each is \$3.99. The present value will always be less than the sum of the rents by the amount of the compound interest discounting. Note that the present value of annuity of 1, as shown above, is assumed to be at the *beginning* of the first period (i.e., time zero), or to state it another way, the rents are assumed to be at the end of each period. This means that there are the same number of interest discount periods as rents.

While the term annuity may imply equal *annual* rents to some people, we should note that equal rents over any series of equal time intervals, such as monthly, quarterly, semiannually, or annually, constitute an annuity. The accountant commonly encounters a variety of transactions involving annuities.

AMOUNT OF AN ANNUITY

The *amount of an annuity* is the *future* sum of all its rents plus the compound interest on each of them. Consider a simple example. Suppose you deposit \$100 per year for four years (periods) in a fund which earns compound interest at 6% per annum. At the date of the last deposit, the first rent will have earned compound interest for three years, the second for two years, the third for one year. There will be no interest accumulation on the fourth rent since we are computing the future amount on the date of deposit of this rent. Applying principles we learned in Part A on amount of 1, the accumulation at the *date of the last deposit* will be seen to consist of—

Date of Deposit		
Year 1	$\$100 \times (1.06)^3 =$	\$119.10
Year 2	$\$100 \times (1.06)^2 =$	112.36
Year 3	$\$100 \times (1.06)^1 =$	106.00
Year 4	\$100	100.00
Amount of Annuity (Ordinary)		\$437.46

The symbol often used to denote the amount of an annuity of 1 is A. The underlying formula to compute the amount of an annuity of 1 is based upon the formula for an amount of 1 (Table 6–1) since the amount of an annuity of 1, as illustrated above, is the sum of a series of computations of the amount of 1. Therefore, the underlying formula is:

$$A_o = \frac{(1 + i)^n - 1}{i}$$

Notice in the heading of Table 6–3 that this is the indicated formula for those table values. Observe that the notation "n" refers to the number of *periodic rents* and *not* to the number of interest periods; "i" refers to the interest rate per period (and not to the annual rate except when the periods are one year in length). The values given in Table 6–3 are at the *date of the last rent* (i.e., the rents are at the end of each period); therefore, it is called an ordinary annuity as is indicated in the title of the table.

Use of Table of Amount of Annuity of 1

Tables of amount of annuity of 1 are commonly used to calculate the future amount of a series of rents at a specific rate of compound interest. In most situations the following are known: (1) the amount of the equal rents; (2) the number of rents, "n"; and (3) the interest rate per period, "i." To determine the future amount of a specific situation, the appropriate value from Table 6–3 is multiplied by the amount of the periodic rent.

To illustrate an accounting application, assume Hill Corporation plans to expand the office building three years from now. To assure sufficient cash for this purpose the company has decided to set up a building fund by making three equal annual contributions of $60,000 cash on each December 31, starting in 1976. The funds will be needed on December 31, 1978, the date of the last deposit. The fund will be deposited with a trustee and will earn 7% per year compounded annually.

Required:

1. What will be the balance of the fund on December 31, 1978; that is, immediately after the last deposit?
2. Prepare a fund accumulation table for this situation.
3. Prepare the accounting entries for the entire period.

Solution:

1. Balance in the fund on December 31, 1978 (ordinary annuity basis):

$$\$60{,}000 \times A_{o\,\substack{n=3\\i=7\%}} = \$60{,}000 \times 3.2149 \text{ (from Table 6–3)} = \underline{\underline{\$192{,}894}}$$

2. Accumulation table—building fund, through December 31, 1978:

Date	Cash Deposits	Interest Revenue Earned	Fund Increases	Fund Balance
12-31-76......	$60,000		$60,000	$ 60,000
12-30-77......		$ 60,000 × .07 = $4,200	4,200	64,200
12-31-77......	60,000		60,000	124,200
12-30-78......		124,200 × .07 = 8,694	8,694	132,894
12-31-78......	60,000		60,000	192,894*

* Balance on date of last deposit (i.e., an ordinary annuity). Assume that interest is credited to the fund each December 30.

3. Required journal entries:

Deposits in the fund:

	12-31-76		12-31-77		12-31-78	
Building fund	60,000		60,000		60,000	
Cash		60,000		60,000		60,000

Interest revenue earned on the fund:

	12-30-77		12-30-78	
Building fund...	4,200		8,694	
Interest revenue		4,200		8,694

Determination of Other Values Related to Amount of Annuity

In the immediately preceding example, *three* values were given as follows: (1) periodic rents, \$60,000; (2) number of rents, 3; and (3) the periodic interest rate, 7%. A fourth value, the future accumulation in a sinking fund, \$192,894, was computed. Obviously, if any three of these four values are known, the other one can be derived. Thus, as was illustrated with respect to the amount of 1, there are four types of potential problems involving amount of an annuity of 1 that may be encountered; viz:

1. To determine the future annuity accumulation (value); discussed immediately above.
2. To determine an unknown interest rate.[5]
   Example (based on above data):
   Given:
   a. Periodic rents, \$60,000.
   b. Rents, 3.
   c. Future accumulation desired, \$192,894.
   To derive the required interest rate:
   a. \$192,894 ÷ \$60,000 = 3.2149 (table value for 3 rents at unknown interest rate).
   b. Reference to Table 6–3, *line* for 3 rents indicates the required interest rate to be 7%.
3. To determine an unknown number of periodic rents.
   Example (based on above data):
   Given:
   a. Periodic rents, \$60,000.
   b. Future accumulation desired, \$192,894.
   c. Interest rate, 7% per period.
   To derive the required number of rents:
   a. \$192,894 ÷ \$60,000 = 3.2149 (table value for \$1 at 7% for unknown number of rents).
   b. Reference to Table 6–3, *column* for 7% interest indicates the required number of rents to be 3.

---

[5] In the following example, the data used above, with one "given" changed in each instance, is used in order to clearly demonstrate the correctness of the answer and the reasons for the computational approach.

4. To determine the unknown amount of each rent.
   Example (based on above data):
   Given:
   a. Number of rents, 3.
   b. Interest rate per period, 7%.
   c. Future accumulation desired, $192,894.
   To derive the unknown amount of each rent:
   a. Reference to Table 6–3, *column* for 7% and *line* for 3 rents gives the value 3.2149.
   b. $192,894 ÷ 3.2149 = $60,000 (the period rent required).

PRESENT VALUE OF AN ANNUITY

The *present value of an annuity* is the equivalent value *now* (i.e., the present) of a series of future dollars (i.e., periodic rents) discounted back from a series of specific future dates (i.e., periods) to the present date at a specified rate of compound interest (i.e., compound discounting). Since it involves compound discounting instead of compound interest, it can be said to be the inverse of the amount of an annuity explained above. For example, $1 (the periodic rent) due at the end of each of three periods in the future (total sum due $3), when discounted back at 8% compound interest, has a present value of $2.58. Alternatively, $2.58 deposited today at 8% compound interest per period would pay back $1 at the end of each of the three future periods. Significantly, it should be noted that the rents on the present value of an ordinary annuity are assumed to be at the *end* of each period; hence, in contrast to the amount of an annuity of 1, there are the same number of interest periods as rents.[6]

The symbol often used to denote the present value of annuity of 1 is P. As before, "n" indicates the number of periodic rents, and "i" the rate of discounting each period. Table 6–4 gives the present values of annuity of 1 for a number of periods and interest rates. Observe the heading of the statement and the underlying formula, viz:

$$\frac{1 - \frac{1}{(1+i)^n}}{i}$$

The values in Table 6–4 represent an *ordinary* annuity; therefore, they are at the *beginning of the period* of the first rent (see page 253). To illustrate a typical accounting application, assume Delphi Corporation is negotiating the purchase of a certain natural resource. It is estimated that the resource will produce a net cash inflow of $200,000 per year for the next three years. Assume the "going" rate of compound interest is 8% per year. *Question:* What is the maximum amount that should be paid today (i.e., at the present time) for the mine?

---

[6] In both instances an *ordinary* annuity is assumed; annuities due are discussed in the next section. The above amounts are rounded.

Solution:

This requires computation of the present value of the three future rents as follows:

$$\$200{,}000 \times P_{o_{\substack{n=3\\ i=8\%}}} = \$200{,}000 \times 2.577 \text{ (from Table 6–4)} = \underline{\underline{\$515{,}420}}$$

If purchased at this price the acquisition entry would be:

Natural resource (identified)	515,420	
Cash (and/or debt)		515,420

Determination of Other Values Related to Present Value of Annuity

In the immediately preceding example, *three* values were given as follows: (1) the periodic rent or contribution, r; (2) the number of periodic contributions, n; and (3) the periodic discounting rate, i. A fourth value, the present value, P ($515,420) was computed. Obviously, if *any* three of these four values are known, the other one can be derived. Thus, as illustrated for the amount of an annuity of 1, there are four types of potential problems related to the present value of an annuity that may be encountered, viz:

1. To determine the present value of a series of future rents; discussed and illustrated immediately above.
2. To determine an unknown interest rate.
   Example (based on above data):
   Given:
   a. Periodic rents, $200,000.
   b. Number of periodic rents, 3.
   c. Present value of the future rents, $515,420.
   To derive the required interest rate:
   a. $515,420 ÷ $200,000 = 2.5771 (approximate table value for 3 rents at unknown interest rate).
   b. Reference to Table 6–4, *line* for 3 rents, indicates the required interest rate to be 8%.
3. To determine an unknown number of periodic rents.
   Example (based on above data):
   Given:
   a. Periodic rents, $200,000.
   b. Interest rate, 8%.
   c. Present value of the future rents, $515,420.
   To derive the unknown number of periodic rents:
   a. $515,420 ÷ $200,000 = 2.5771 (approximate table value at 8% at unknown number of rents).
   b. Reference to Table 6–4, *column* for 8%, indicates that 3 periodic rents are required.
4. To determine the unknown amount of each rent.
   Example (based on above data):
   Given:
   a. Number of periodic rents, 3.

b. Interest rate per period, 8%.
c. Present value of the future rents, $515,420.

To derive the amount of each rent:
a. Table 6–4 value at 8%, 3 rents = 2.5771.
b. $515,420 ÷ 2.5771 = $200,000 (the periodic rent).

To illustrate an accounting application similar to the last illustration, assume Voss Corporation purchased a fixed asset resulting in the incurrence of a $50,000 debt on January 1, 1976. The liability is to be paid in three equal installments on each December 31, starting at the end of 1976. The interest rate is 9 percent, and each installment is to include both interest and principal.

Required:

1. Compute the amount of each equal annual installment.
2. Prepare a debt amortization schedule for this situation.
3. Give the journal entries covering the period of the debt.

Solution:

1. $\$50{,}000 \div P_{o_{\substack{n=3\\i=9\%}}}$ = $50,000 ÷ 2.53129 (from Table 6–4) = $19,753 (the periodic rent)

2. A debt amortization schedule is a decumulation table that shows the reduction of the debt from $50,000 to zero over the three-year period. The debt amortization schedule showing interest expense and reduction of principal each period would be as follows:

Debt Amortization Schedule

Date	Cash Payment	Interest Expense	Payment on Principal	Unpaid Principal
1-1-76				$50,000
12-31-76	$19,753[a]	$4,500[b]	$15,253[c]	34,747[d]
12-31-77	19,753	3,127	16,626	18,121
12-31-78	19,753	1,632*	18,121	-0-

[a] Computed above.
Successive computations:
[b] $50,000 × .09 = $4,500.
[c] $19,753 − $4,500 = $15,253.
[d] $50,000 − $15,253 = $34,747.

* Adjusted for rounding error.

3. Journal entries:

1-1-76 to record the debt:

	Debit	Credit
Fixed asset......................	50,000	
Liability		50,000

Each December 31 to record payment (per above schedule):

	12-31-76		12-31-77		12-31-78	
Interest expense	4,500		3,127		1,632	
Liability	15,253		16,626		18,121	
Cash		19,753		19,753		19,753

ANNUITIES DUE

Discussion of annuities to this point has been confined to *ordinary annuities* since they represent the more or less "normal" situation encountered. It will be recalled that with respect to ordinary annuities, specific assumptions were noted in the preceding discussions relative to the *timing* of the rents and the interest periods. *Annuities due* involve different assumptions with respect to the timing of rents. The timing distinction is: For ordinary annuities, the rents are assumed to be paid or received at the *end* of each period; in contrast, for annuities due, the rents are assumed to be paid or received at the *beginning* of each period.

Amount of Annuity Due

In the case of the amount of an ordinary annuity, the future amount is calculated as of the date of the last rent since the rents are assumed to be at the end of each period. In contrast, the amount of an annuity due is calculated at the end of the period of the last rent since the rents are assumed to be at the beginning of each period. The contrast between the two timing assumptions can be graphically shown as follows ($n = 4$; $i = 8\%$):[7]

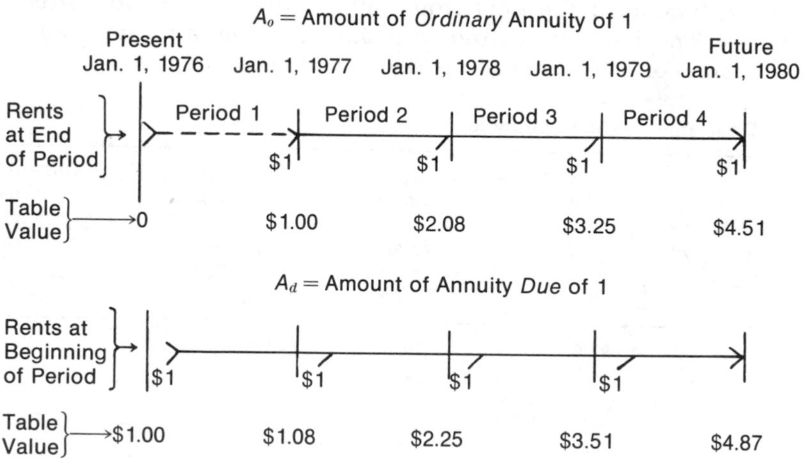

In the above diagram the following differences may be observed:

---

[7] The subscript "*o*" is an ordinary annuity and "*d*" an annuity due. The terms "ordinary" and "due" were coined by mathematicians; many accountants prefer more descriptive terminology:

1. Instead of "ordinary"—"end-of-the-period annuities."
2. Instead of "due"—"beginning-of-the-period annuities."

Characteristic	Type of Annuity	
	A_o – Ordinary	A_d – Due
1. Timing of each rent.	End of each period	Beginning of each period
2. Number of rents.	Four	Four
3. Number of interest periods.	Three	Four
4. Point in time of the future amount (i.e., the table amount).	On date of last rent	At end of period following last rent

The differences reflected in (3) and (4) are due solely to the different timing assumption for the rents. An understanding of the difference between an ordinary annuity and an annuity due is important in solving annuity problems. Care must be exercised to select the one that fits the specifications of the problem or situation. Ordinary annuity tables are found in various sources more often than annuity due tables. In situations where only an ordinary annuity table is available and an annuity due amount is needed, the conversion is simple and straightforward. Conversion from an ordinary annuity to an annuity due amount can be accomplished easily in either of two ways, viz:

1. Multiply the ordinary annuity amount by $(1 + i)$. That is, $A_d = A_o \times (1 + i)$. For example, the annuity due amounts shown in the graphic illustration on the previous page were computed as follows:

Interest	Rents	Amount of Ordinary Annuity (Table 6–3)	Multiplier × (1 + i)	–	Amount of Annuity Due
8%	1	1.00000	(1.08)	=	1.08000
8%	2	2.08000	(1.08)	=	2.24640
8%	3	3.24640	(1.08)	=	3.50611
8%	4	4.50611	(1.08)	=	4.86660

Conversely, one could convert from an annuity due to an ordinary annuity by reversing the computations; that is, amount of annuity due, $n = 4$, $i = 8\%$, $4.86660 \div 1.08 = 4.50611$ (ordinary annuity).

2. Read the amount from an ordinary annuity table for *one greater* than the number of rents, then *subtract* the numeral 1 from it.[8] This has the effect of adding interest to the ordinary annuity amount for one period. To illustrate for $n = 3$; $i = 8\%$:

From Table 6–3 (amount of ordinary annuity), $n = 4$; $i = 8\%$	4.50611
Subtract the numeral 1	−1.00000
Difference–Amount of Annuity Due, $n = 3$; $i = 8\%$	3.50611

[8] Frequently expressed as $(n + 1 \text{ rents}) - 1$. Each method serves to increase the interest period by 1 for an annuity due and maintains the same number of rents.

In applying the concepts of future and present value, it is generally helpful to graphically analyze the situation, or problem, in a manner similar to the graphic illustrations in this chapter. This initial step will indicate the appropriate future or present value concept to apply. To illustrate, two examples are given below with explanation of the solution approaches. These focus on different situations requiring an amount of ordinary annuity and amount of annuity due.

Situation A: On January 1, 1976, Dawson Corporation entered into a contract with a foreign company that required Dawson to pay $50,000 cash on December 31, 1978. Because of disagreement over credit terms, it was agreed that Dawson would deposit three equal annual amounts in a Swiss bank starting December 31, 1976, so that the $50,000 would be available on December 31, 1978. On that date the bank will pay the foreign company in full. The bank agreed to add 6% annual compound interest to the fund each December 31.

Required:

1. Diagram the annuity required by the agreement to establish the debt payment fund with the bank.
2. What kind of annuity is indicated? Explain.
3. Compute the amount of the equal annual payments.

Solution:

1. Diagram of the annuity ($n=3$; $i=6\%$):

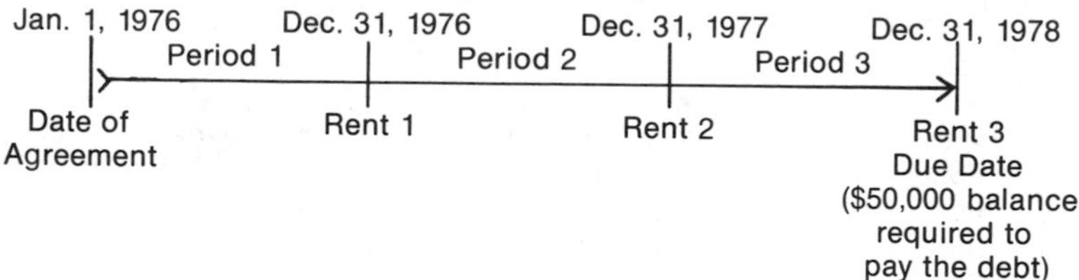

2. Since the rents are at the end of the period this is an *ordinary* annuity; that is, the future amount is at the date of the last rent.

3. $\text{Rent} = \dfrac{\text{Future Amount}}{A_{o\,\substack{n=3\\i=6\%}}} = \dfrac{\$50{,}000}{3.1836 \text{ (Table 6–3)}} = \underline{\underline{\$15{,}705}}$

Situation B: On January 1, 1976, Cotter Corporation decided to create a plant expansion fund by making three annual deposits of $60,000 each on January 1, 1976, 1977, and 1978. The fund will be held by a trustee who will increase the fund on a 7% annual compound interest basis. The fund will be needed on December 31, 1978.

Required:

1. Diagram the annuity created in this situation. Identify dates.

2. What kind of annuity is indicated? Explain.
3. Compute the balance in the fund on December 31, 1978, and prepare a fund accumulation table.

Solution:

1. Diagram of the annuity ($n = 3$; $i = 7\%$):

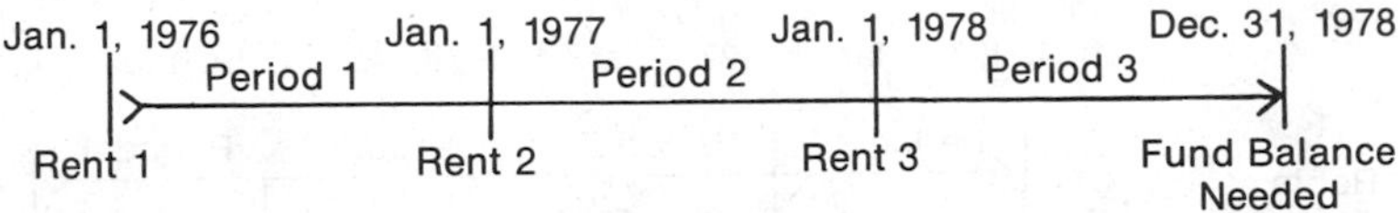

2. Since the rents are at the beginning of each period this is an annuity *due;* the amount desired in the fund is at the end of the period in which the last rent is contributed. Since the rents build a future amount it is an *amount of annuity due of 1.*
3. Fund balance at December 31, 1978:

Conversion:

$A_{d_{\substack{n=3\\i=7\%}}} = 3.2149$ (Table 6–3) $\times 1.07 = 3.43994$

Fund balance = $60,000 × 3.43994
= $206,396

The fund accumulation table for this amount of annuity due, $n = 3$; $i = 7\%$ would be:

Date	Cash Deposits	Interest Revenue Earned	Fund Increases	Fund Balance
1-1-76	......$60,000		$60,000	$ 60,000
12-31-76......		$ 60,000 × .07 = $ 4,200	4,200	64,200
1-1-77	 60,000		60,000	124,200
12-31-77......		124,200 × .07 = 8,694	8,694	132,894
1-1-78	 60,000		60,000	192,894
12-31-78......		192,894 × .07 = 13,502	13,502	206,396

This accumulation table, prepared on an annuity due basis, may be compared with a similar set of facts, on an ordinary annuity basis, illustrated on page 237. Compare the timing difference for the rents and the resultant effects on the interest accumulations and fund balances.

Present Value of Annuity Due

In the case of present value of an ordinary annuity the rents are assumed to be at the end of the period; therefore, the discount as calculated as of one period back from the first rent. In contrast, present value of an annuity due assumes the rents are at the beginning of each period; therefore, there is no discounting on the first rent. The contrast between the two timing assumptions for present value can be graphically shown as follows ($n = 4$; $i = 6\%$):

P_o = Present Value of *Ordinary* Annuity of 1

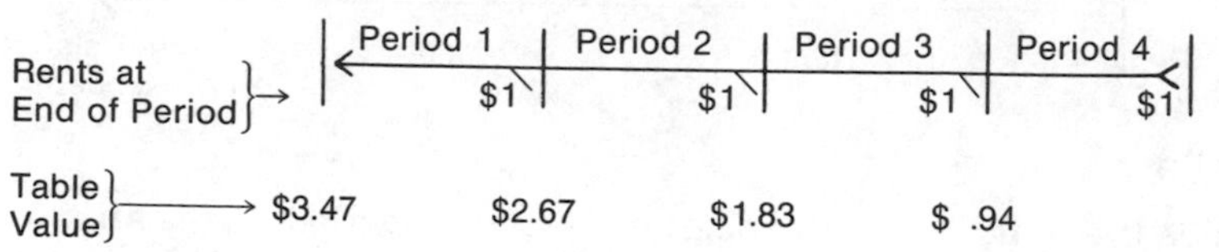

P_d = Present Value of Annuity *Due* of 1

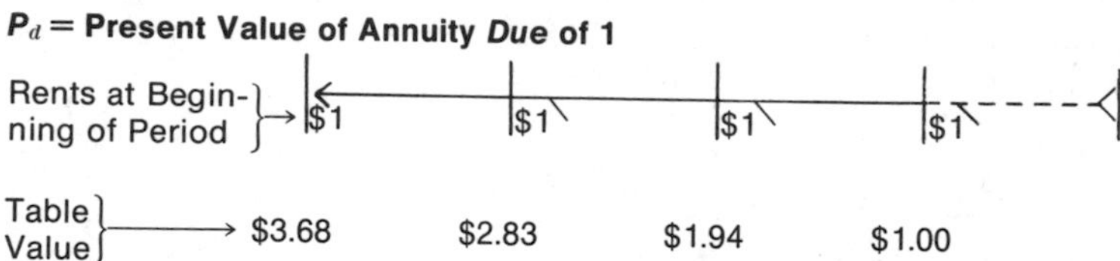

The above diagram shows that the *present value* of an ordinary annuity is calculated as of the beginning of the period even though the rents are at the end of each period (there are the same number of interest discount periods as rents). In contrast, the present value of an annuity due is computed at the date of the first rent (there is one less interest discount period than rents). Often an ordinary annuity table is available, but not an annuity due table. In such situations the present value of an ordinary annuity may be converted to the present value of an annuity due by either of two approaches, viz:

1. Multiply the present value ordinary annuity by $(1 + i)$. That is, $P_d = P_o \times (1 + i)$. For example, the present value of ordinary annuity for $n = 4$; $i = 6\%$ is 3.46511. The present value of an annuity due of 1 for $n = 4$; $i = 6\%$ is: $3.46511 \times 1.06 = 3.67301$.
2. Read the present value of an ordinary annuity of 1 table for *one less* than the number of rents, then *add* the numeral 1 to it.[9] To illustrate for $n = 4$; $i = 6\%$:

From Table 6–4 (present value of ordinary annuity) $n = 3$; $i = 6\%$ ...	2.67301
Add the numeral 1	1.00000
Summation—Present Value of Annuity Due, $n = 4$; $i = 6\%$........	3.67301

[9] Frequently expressed as $(n - 1 \text{ rents}) + 1$. Either method serves to reduce the discount period by one for an annuity due and maintains the same number of rents.

Two situations presented below, with solutions, illustrate the different characteristics of present value of an ordinary annuity and annuity due. Careful attention to the timing of the rents is necessary in order to determine which type of annuity should be applied to each situation or problem.

Situation C: On January 1, 1976, Brown Corporation owes a $30,000 debt which is due. The creditor agreed to let Brown pay the debt in four equal annual payments on December 31, 1976, 1977, 1978, and 1979. Interest at 8% per year is to be paid on the unpaid principal. Each equal payment is to include interest and principal.

Required:

1. Diagram the annuity represented by the annual payments. Identify dates.
2. What kind of annuity is represented? Explain.
3. Compute the amount of the equal annual payments on the debt.

Solution:

1. Diagram of the annuity ($n = 4$; $i = 8\%$):

Jan. 1, 1976	Dec. 31, 1976	Dec. 31, 1977	Dec. 31, 1978	Dec. 31, 1979
	Period 1	Period 2	Period 3	Period 4
Debt $30,000	Payment No. 1	Payment No. 2	Payment No. 3	Payment No. 4

2. Since the payments are to be made at the end of each period, this is an ordinary annuity and the present value (i.e., the debt) is computed at the beginning of the first period.
3. The amount of each equal annual payment is computed as follows:

$$\text{Rent} = \frac{\text{Present Value}}{P_{o\,\substack{n=4\\ i=8\%}}} = \frac{\$30{,}000}{3.31213 \text{ (Table 6–4)}} = \$9{,}058$$

Situation D: John Doe was seriously injured while working for X Corporation. On January 1, 1976, an agreement was reached whereby X Corporation would deposit $100,000 with the City Bank, as trustee. The bank agreed to pay 6% compound interest per year on the unused principal while making five equal annual payments to Doe. The payments are to be made on each January 1, starting immediately, until the fund, including all interest accumulations is fully expended.

Required:

1. Diagram the annuity represented by the payments. Identify dates.
2. What kind of annuity is represented? Explain.
3. Compute the amount of each equal annual payment.

Solution:

1. Diagram of annuity ($n = 5$; $i = 6\%$):

Jan. 1, 1976	Jan. 1, 1977	Jan. 1, 1978	Jan. 1, 1979	Jan. 1, 1980
Period 1	Period 2	Period 3	Period 4	Period 5
Rent 1	Rent 2	Rent 3	Rent 4	Rent 5

Present Value $100,000

2. Since the rents are at the beginning of the period (the first one starts immediately), this is an annuity due. Since the $100,000 is deposited at the start, that amount represents the present value of the annuity on which the amount of the equal rents is based. The computation is:

3. $$\text{Rent} = \frac{\text{Present Value}}{P_{d\,\substack{n=5\\i=6\%}}} = \frac{\$100{,}000}{4.46511^*} = \underline{\underline{\$22{,}396}}.$$

* Conversion:
From Table 6–4, 4.21236 × 1.06 = 4.46511.

USING MULTIPLE TABLE VALUES

Often situations are encountered where the analysis will require the use of two or more tables. These situations often involve annuities with uneven contributions (i.e., rents). Problems with these characteristics can be resolved readily if one understands the concepts underlying future amount and present value.

To illustrate, assume ST Construction Company is negotiating to purchase 40 acres of land with a deposit of gravel suitable for exploitation. The two parties are negotiating the price. ST Company has completed an extensive study that provided the following estimates:

Expected net cash revenues over the life of the resource:	
Year 1	$ 5,000
Years 2–5 (per year)	30,000
Years 6–9 (per year)	40,000
Year 10 (last year—resource exhausted)	10,000
Estimated sales value of the 40 acres, after exploitation and net of land-leveling costs (end of tenth year)	2,000

Required:

Assuming the above estimates are realistic, compute how much ST Construction Company should offer for the land assuming they expect a 12% return on their investment. Assume all amounts are at year-end. Disregard income taxes.

Solution:

This requires computation of the present value of the future expected cash inflows as follows:

Year 1: $\$5{,}000 \times p_{\substack{n=1\\i=12\%}} = \$5{,}000 \times .89286 =$	$ 4,464
Years 2–5: $\$30{,}000 \times P_{\substack{n=5-1\\i=12\%}} = \$30{,}000 \times (3.60478 - .89286) =$	81,358
Years 6–9: $\$40{,}000 \times P_{\substack{n=9-5\\i=12\%}} = \$40{,}000 \times (5.32825 - 3.60478) =$	68,939
Year 10: $(\$10{,}000 + \$2{,}000) \times p_{\substack{n=10\\i=12\%}} = \$12{,}000 \times .32197 =$	3,864
Offering Price	$158,625

The solution involved the use of the two present value tables: present value of $1, and present value of ordinary annuity of $1. Alternatively, it can be solved by using only the former table in which case the discounting would have to be computed for each of the ten years separately and then summed. By using the annuity table for the periods 2–5 and 6–9, computational time was shortened; the results are the same.

SUMMARY

This chapter has presented the concepts of compound interest and focuses on their relevance to certain accounting problems. At the beginning of the chapter the primary accounting applications were listed. These applications are required to conform to GAAP (generally accepted accounting principles). Because of the wide range of accounting applications accountants need a thorough understanding of them. In a related activity, they also have considerable relevance in financial analyses, capital budgeting, and alternative choice problems which accountants often encounter whether in public, private, or governmental accounting. Throughout the later chapters, and in subsequent advanced accounting courses, the concepts of compound interest will be used.

TABLE 6–1
Amount of 1, $a = (1 + i)^n$

Periods	2%	2½%	3%	4%	5%	6%
1	1.02000	1.02500	1.03000	1.04000	1.05000	1.06000
2	1.04040	1.05062	1.06090	1.08160	1.10250	1.12360
3	1.06121	1.07689	1.09273	1.12486	1.15762	1.19102
4	1.08243	1.10381	1.12551	1.16986	1.21551	1.26248
5	1.10408	1.13141	1.15927	1.21665	1.27628	1.33823
6	1.12616	1.15969	1.19405	1.26532	1.34010	1.41852
7	1.14869	1.18869	1.22987	1.31593	1.40710	1.50363
8	1.17166	1.21840	1.26677	1.36857	1.47746	1.59385
9	1.19509	1.24886	1.30477	1.42331	1.55133	1.68948
10	1.21899	1.28008	1.34392	1.48024	1.62889	1.79085
11	1.24337	1.31209	1.38423	1.53945	1.71034	1.89830
12	1.26824	1.34489	1.42576	1.60103	1.79586	2.01220
13	1.29361	1.37851	1.46853	1.66507	1.88565	2.13293
14	1.31948	1.41297	1.51259	1.73168	1.97993	2.26090
15	1.34587	1.44830	1.55797	1.80094	2.07893	2.39656
16	1.37279	1.48451	1.60471	1.87298	2.18287	2.54035
17	1.40024	1.52162	1.65285	1.94790	2.29202	2.69277
18	1.42825	1.55966	1.70243	2.02582	2.40662	2.85434
19	1.45681	1.59865	1.75351	2.10685	2.52695	3.02560
20	1.48595	1.63862	1.80611	2.19112	2.65330	3.20714
21	1.51567	1.67958	1.86029	2.27877	2.78596	3.39956
22	1.54598	1.72157	1.91610	2.36992	2.92526	3.60354
23	1.57690	1.76461	1.97359	2.46472	3.07152	3.81975
24	1.60844	1.80873	2.03279	2.56330	3.22510	4.04893
25	1.64061	1.85394	2.09378	2.66584	3.38635	4.29187

Periods	7%	8%	9%	10%	11%	12%
1	1.07000	1.08000	1.09000	1.10000	1.11000	1.12000
2	1.14490	1.16640	1.18810	1.21000	1.23210	1.25440
3	1.22504	1.25971	1.29503	1.33100	1.36763	1.40493
4	1.31080	1.36049	1.41158	1.46410	1.51807	1.57352
5	1.40255	1.46933	1.53862	1.61051	1.68506	1.76234
6	1.50073	1.58687	1.67710	1.77156	1.87041	1.97382
7	1.60578	1.71382	1.82804	1.94872	2.07616	2.21068
8	1.71819	1.85093	1.99256	2.14359	2.30454	2.47596
9	1.83846	1.99900	2.17189	2.35795	2.55804	2.77308
10	1.96715	2.15892	2.36736	2.59374	2.83942	3.10585
11	2.10485	2.33164	2.58043	2.85312	3.15176	3.47855
12	2.25219	2.51817	2.81266	3.13843	3.49845	3.89598
13	2.40985	2.71962	3.06580	3.45227	3.88328	4.36349
14	2.57853	2.93719	3.34173	3.79750	4.31044	4.88711
15	2.75903	3.17217	3.64248	4.17725	4.78459	5.47357
16	2.95216	3.42594	3.97031	4.59497	5.31089	6.13039
17	3.15882	3.70002	4.32763	5.05447	5.89509	6.86604
18	3.37993	3.99602	4.71712	5.55992	6.54355	7.68997
19	3.61653	4.31570	5.14166	6.11591	7.26334	8.61276
20	3.86968	4.66096	5.60441	6.72750	8.06231	9.64629
21	4.14056	5.03383	6.10881	7.40025	8.94917	10.80385
22	4.43040	5.43654	6.65860	8.14027	9.93357	12.10031
23	4.74053	5.87146	7.25787	8.95430	11.02627	13.55235
24	5.07237	6.34118	7.91108	9.84973	12.23916	15.17863
25	5.42743	6.84848	8.62308	10.83471	13.58546	17.00006

TABLE 6–2

Present Value of 1, $p = \frac{1}{(1+i)^n}$

Periods	2%	2½%	3%	4%	5%	6%
1	.98039	.97561	.97087	.96154	.95238	.94340
2	.96117	.95181	.94260	.92456	.90703	.89000
3	.94232	.92860	.91514	.88900	.86384	.83962
4	.92385	.90595	.88849	.85480	.82270	.79209
5	.90573	.88385	.86261	.82193	.78353	.74726
6	.88797	.86230	.83748	.79031	.74622	.70496
7	.87056	.84127	.81309	.75992	.71068	.66506
8	.85349	.82075	.78941	.73069	.67684	.62741
9	.83676	.80073	.76642	.70259	.64461	.59190
10	.82035	.78120	.74409	.67556	.61391	.55839
11	.80426	.76214	.72242	.64958	.58468	.52679
12	.78849	.74356	.70138	.62460	.55684	.49697
13	.77303	.72542	.68095	.60057	.53032	.46884
14	.75788	.70773	.66112	.57748	.50507	.44230
15	.74301	.69047	.64186	.55526	.48102	.41727
16	.72845	.67362	.62317	.53391	.45811	.39365
17	.71416	.65720	.60502	.51337	.43630	.37136
18	.70016	.64117	.58739	.49363	.41552	.35034
19	.68643	.62553	.57029	.47464	.39573	.33051
20	.67297	.61027	.55368	.45639	.37689	.31180
21	.65978	.59539	.53755	.43883	.35894	.29416
22	.64684	.58086	.52189	.42196	.34185	.27751
23	.63416	.56670	.50669	.40573	.32557	.26180
24	.62172	.55288	.49193	.39012	.31007	.24698
25	.60953	.53939	.47761	.37512	.29530	.23300

Periods	7%	8%	9%	10%	11%	12%
1	.93458	.92593	.91743	.90909	.90090	.89286
2	.87344	.85734	.84168	.82645	.81162	.79719
3	.81630	.79383	.77218	.75131	.73119	.71178
4	.76290	.73503	.70843	.68301	.65873	.63552
5	.71299	.68058	.64993	.62092	.59345	.56743
6	.66634	.63017	.59627	.56447	.53464	.50663
7	.62275	.58349	.54703	.51316	.48166	.45235
8	.58201	.54027	.50187	.46651	.43393	.40388
9	.54393	.50025	.46043	.42410	.39092	.36061
10	.50835	.46319	.42241	.38554	.35218	.32197
11	.47509	.42888	.38753	.35049	.31728	.28748
12	.44401	.39711	.35553	.31863	.28584	.25668
13	.41496	.36770	.32618	.28900	.25751	.22917
14	.38782	.34046	.29925	.26333	.23199	.20462
15	.36245	.31524	.27454	.23939	.20900	.18270
16	.33873	.29189	.25187	.21763	.18829	.16312
17	.31657	.27027	.23107	.19784	.16963	.14564
18	.29586	.25025	.21199	.17986	.15282	.13004
19	.27651	.23171	.19449	.16351	.13768	.11611
20	.25842	.21455	.17843	.14864	.12403	.10367
21	.24151	.19866	.16370	.13513	.11174	.09256
22	.22571	.18394	.15018	.12285	.10067	.08264
23	.21095	.17032	.13778	.11168	.09069	.07379
24	.19715	.15770	.12640	.10153	.08170	.06588
25	.18425	.14602	.11597	.09230	.07361	.05882

TABLE 6–3

Amount of Annuity of 1 (Ordinary), $A_o = \dfrac{(1+i)^n - 1}{i}$

Periodic Rents	2%	2½%	3%	4%	5%	6%
1	1.00000	1.00000	1.00000	1.00000	1.00000	1.00000
2	2.02000	2.02500	2.03000	2.04000	2.05000	2.06000
3	3.06040	3.07562	3.09090	3.12160	3.15250	3.18360
4	4.12161	4.15252	4.18363	4.24646	4.31012	4.37462
5	5.20404	5.25633	5.30914	5.41632	5.52563	5.63709
6	6.30812	6.38774	6.46841	6.63298	6.80191	6.97532
7	7.43428	7.54743	7.66246	7.89829	8.14201	8.39384
8	8.58297	8.73612	8.89234	9.21423	9.54911	9.89747
9	9.75463	9.95452	10.15911	10.58280	11.02656	11.49132
10	10.94972	11.20338	11.46388	12.00611	12.57789	13.18079
11	12.16872	12.48347	12.80780	13.48635	14.20679	14.97164
12	13.41209	13.79555	14.19203	15.02581	15.91713	16.86994
13	14.68033	15.14044	15.61779	16.62684	17.71298	18.88214
14	15.97394	16.51895	17.08632	18.29191	19.59863	21.01507
15	17.29342	17.93193	18.59891	20.02359	21.57856	23.27597
16	18.63929	19.38022	20.15688	21.82453	23.65749	25.67253
17	20.01207	20.86473	21.76159	23.69751	25.84037	28.21288
18	21.41231	22.38635	23.41444	25.64541	28.13238	30.90565
19	22.84056	23.94601	25.11687	27.67123	30.53900	33.75999
20	24.29737	25.54466	26.87037	29.77808	33.06595	36.78559
21	25.78332	27.18327	28.67649	31.96920	35.71925	39.99273
22	27.29898	28.86286	30.53678	34.24797	38.50521	43.39229
23	28.84496	30.58443	32.45288	36.61789	41.43048	46.99583
24	30.42186	32.34904	34.42647	39.08260	44.50200	50.81558
25	32.03030	34.15776	36.45926	41.64591	47.72710	54.86451

Periodic Rents	7%	8%	9%	10%	11%	12%
1	1.00000	1.00000	1.00000	1.00000	1.00000	1.00000
2	2.07000	2.08000	2.09000	2.10000	2.11000	2.12000
3	3.21490	3.24640	3.27810	3.31000	3.34210	3.37440
4	4.43994	4.50611	4.57313	4.64100	4.70973	4.77933
5	5.75074	5.86660	5.98471	6.10510	6.22780	6.35285
6	7.15329	7.33593	7.52333	7.71561	7.91286	8.11519
7	8.65402	8.92280	9.20043	9.48717	9.78327	10.08901
8	10.25980	10.63663	11.02847	11.43589	11.85943	12.29969
9	11.97799	12.48756	13.02104	13.57948	14.16397	14.77566
10	13.81645	14.48656	15.19293	15.93742	16.72201	17.54874
11	15.78360	16.64549	17.56029	18.53117	19.56143	20.65458
12	17.88845	18.97713	20.14072	21.38428	22.71319	24.13313
13	20.14064	21.49530	22.95338	24.52271	26.21164	28.02911
14	22.55049	24.21492	26.01919	27.97498	30.09492	32.39260
15	25.12902	27.15211	29.36092	31.77248	34.40536	37.27971
16	27.88805	30.32428	33.00340	35.94973	39.18995	42.75328
17	30.84022	33.75023	36.97370	40.54470	44.50084	48.88367
18	33.99903	37.45024	41.30134	45.59917	50.39594	55.74971
19	37.37896	41.44626	46.01846	51.15909	56.93949	63.43968
20	40.99549	45.76196	51.16012	57.27500	64.20283	72.05244
21	44.86518	50.42292	56.76453	64.00250	72.26514	81.69874
22	49.00574	55.45676	62.87334	71.40275	81.21431	92.50258
23	53.43614	60.89330	69.53194	79.54302	91.14788	104.60289
24	58.17667	66.76476	76.78981	88.49733	102.17415	118.15524
25	63.24904	73.10594	84.70090	98.34706	114.41331	133.33387

TABLE 6–4

Present Value of Annuity of 1 (Ordinary), $P_o = \dfrac{1 - \dfrac{1}{(1+i)^n}}{i}$

Periodic Rents	2%	2½%	3%	4%	5%	6%
1	.98039	.97561	.97087	.96154	.95238	.94340
2	1.94156	1.92742	1.91347	1.88609	1.85941	1.83339
3	2.88388	2.85602	2.82861	2.77509	2.72325	2.67301
4	3.80773	3.76197	3.71710	3.62990	3.54595	3.46511
5	4.71346	4.64583	4.57971	4.45182	4.32948	4.21236
6	5.60143	5.50813	5.41719	5.24214	5.07569	4.91732
7	6.47199	6.34939	6.23028	6.00205	5.78637	5.58238
8	7.32548	7.17014	7.01969	6.73274	6.46321	6.20979
9	8.16224	7.97087	7.78611	7.43533	7.10782	6.80169
10	8.98259	8.75206	8.53020	8.11090	7.72173	7.36009
11	9.78685	9.51421	9.25262	8.76048	8.30641	7.88687
12	10.57534	10.25776	9.95400	9.38507	8.86325	8.38384
13	11.34837	10.98318	10.63496	9.98565	9.39357	8.85268
14	12.10625	11.69091	11.29607	10.56312	9.89864	9.29498
15	12.84926	12.38138	11.93794	11.11839	10.37966	9.71225
16	13.57771	13.05500	12.56110	11.65230	10.83777	10.10590
17	14.29187	13.71220	13.16612	12.16567	11.27407	10.47726
18	14.99203	14.35336	13.75351	12.65930	11.68959	10.82760
19	15.67846	14.97889	14.32380	13.13394	12.08532	11.15812
20	16.35143	15.58916	14.87747	13.59033	12.46221	11.46992
21	17.01121	16.18455	15.41502	14.02916	12.82115	11.76408
22	17.65805	16.76541	15.93692	14.45112	13.16300	12.04158
23	18.29220	17.33211	16.44361	14.85684	13.48857	12.30338
24	18.91393	17.88499	16.93554	15.24696	13.79864	12.55036
25	19.52346	18.42438	17.41315	15.62208	14.09394	12.78336

Periodic Rents	7%	8%	9%	10%	11%	12%
1	.93458	.92593	.91743	.90909	.90090	.89286
2	1.80802	1.78326	1.75911	1.73554	1.71252	1.69005
3	2.62432	2.57710	2.53129	2.48685	2.44371	2.40183
4	3.38721	3.31213	3.23972	3.16987	3.10245	3.03735
5	4.10020	3.99271	3.88965	3.79079	3.69590	3.60478
6	4.76654	4.62288	4.48592	4.35526	4.23054	4.11141
7	5.38929	5.20637	5.03295	4.86842	4.71220	4.56376
8	5.97130	5.74664	5.53482	5.33493	5.14612	4.96764
9	6.51523	6.24689	5.99525	5.75902	5.53705	5.32825
10	7.02358	6.71008	6.41766	6.14457	5.88923	5.65022
11	7.49867	7.13896	6.80519	6.49506	6.20652	5.93770
12	7.94269	7.53608	7.16073	6.81369	6.49236	6.19437
13	8.35765	7.90378	7.48690	7.10336	6.74987	6.42355
14	8.74547	8.24424	7.78615	7.36669	6.98187	6.62817
15	9.10791	8.55948	8.06069	7.60608	7.19087	6.81086
16	9.44665	8.85137	8.31256	7.82371	7.37916	6.97399
17	9.76322	9.12164	8.54363	8.02155	7.54879	7.11963
18	10.05909	9.37189	8.75563	8.20141	7.70162	7.24967
19	10.33560	9.60360	8.95011	8.36492	7.83929	7.36578
20	10.59401	9.81815	9.12855	8.51356	7.96333	7.46944
21	10.83553	10.01680	9.29224	8.64869	8.07507	7.56200
22	11.06124	10.20074	9.44243	8.77154	8.17574	7.64465
23	11.27219	10.37106	9.58021	8.88322	8.26643	7.71843
24	11.46933	10.52876	9.70661	8.98474	8.34814	7.78432
25	11.65358	10.67478	9.82258	9.07704	8.42174	7.84314

QUESTIONS

1. Explain what is meant by the time value of money.
2. Fundamentally what is the difference between simple interest and compound interest?
3. Briefly explain each of the following:
   a. Amount of 1.
   b. Present value of 1.
   c. Amount of annuity of 1.
   d. Present value of annuity of 1.
4. Give the numerical values of n and of i in determining the compound amount of a sum for ten years for each of the following:
   a. 5% compounded annually.
   b. 5% compounded semiannually.
   c. 8% compounded quarterly.
   d. 6% compounded monthly.
5. Explain what is meant by the amount of 1. Relate it to the present value of 1.
6. If the table value for amount of 1 is known, how may it be converted to the table value for present value of 1?
7. Define an annuity in general terms. Explain rents and relate them to time periods and interest rates.
8. The table for amount of an annuity provides the value 3.09 (rounded) at 3% for three periods; explain the meaning of the table value.
9. What is meant by the present value of an annuity? Contrast it with the amount of an annuity.
10. Explain the fundamental difference between *(a)* amount of an ordinary annuity, and *(b)* amount of an annuity due.
11. Explain the fundamental difference between *(a)* present value of an ordinary annuity, and *(b)* present value of an annuity due.
12. Complete the following table of values assuming $n = 11$; $i = 10\%$:

	Annual Compounding	*Semiannual Compounding*
a. Amount of 1.	________	________
b. Present value of 1.	________	________
c. Amount of ordinary annuity of 1.	________	________
d. Amount of annuity due of 1.	________	________
e. Present value of ordinary annuity of 1.	________	________
f. Present value of annuity due of 1.	________	________

EXERCISES

Exercise 6–1

Dowd Company plans to deposit $55,000 today in a special building fund which will be needed at the end of six years. They are looking for a financial institution (as trustee) that will pay them 8% interest on the fund balance.

Required:

How much will the fund total assuming (show computations):

Case A – Annual compounding?
Case B – Semiannual compounding?
Case C – Quarterly compounding?

Exercise 6–2

Dustin Company, at the present date, has $33,000 which will be deposited in a savings account until needed. It is anticipated that $84,415 will be needed at the end of nine years to expand some manufacturing facilities. What rate of interest would be required to accumulate the $84,415 assuming compounding on an annual basis? Show computations.

Exercise 6–3

Franklin Corporation is planning an addition to the office building as soon as adequate funds can be accumulated. The corporation has estimated that the addition will cost approximately $95,212. At the present time $60,000 cash is on hand that will not be needed in the near future. A local savings institution will pay 8% interest (compounded annually). How many periods would be required for the $60,000 to accumulate to $95,212? Show computations.

Exercise 6–4

North Company has on hand $75,000 cash that will not be needed in the near future. However, the company will expand operations within the next three to five years. At the present date, the company has decided to establish a savings account locally which will earn 6% interest compounded annually. The interest will be added to the fund each year. Assuming the deposit of $75,000 is made on January 1, 1977, *(a)* compute the balance that will be in the fund at the end of the third year, and *(b)* prepare an accumulation table for the fund.

Exercise 6–5

Samson Company will need $150,000 cash to renovate an old plant five years from now. Assume a financial institution will increase a fund at 6% interest. Compute the amount of cash that must be deposited now to meet this need assuming (show computations):

Case A – Annual compounding?
Case B – Semiannual compounding?

Exercise 6–6

Brush Corporation has planned a plant expansion which will require approximately $160,000 at December 31, 1978. Since they have some idle cash on hand now, January 1, 1976, they desire to know how much they would have to invest as a lump sum now to accumulate the required amount assuming 6% annual compound interest is added to the fund each December 31.

Required:

1. Compute the amount that must be invested on January 1, 1976.
2. Prepare an accumulation table for plant expansion fund.

Exercise 6–7

Dowdy Company purchased some additional equipment that was needed because of a new contract. The equipment was purchased on January 1, 1976. Because the contract would require three years to complete and Dowdy was short of cash, the vendor agreed to accept a down payment of $5,000 and a two-year noninterest-bearing note for $45,000 (this amount includes all interest charges) due December 31, 1977. Assume a 10% annual rate of interest.

Required:

1. Compute the cost of the equipment. Show computations.
2. Give the entry at date of acquisition of the equipment.
3. Prepare a debt schedule.

Exercise 6–8

Storm Company, on January 1, 1976, has a contract whereby the company is due to receive $24,000 cash on December 31, 1981. The company is short of cash and desires to discount (sell) this claim. They are willing to accept a 12% annual discount (annual discounting). Under these conditions how much cash would Storm receive on January 1, 1976? What would be the amount of interest paid by Storm? Show computations.

Exercise 6–9

On January 1, 1976, Fawn Corporation, signed a $300,000 noninterest-bearing note which is due on December 31, 1980. According to the agreement they have the option to pay the $300,000 at maturity date or to pay the obligation in full on January 1, 1976, on an 8% compound interest discount basis. What would be the single amount of cash required on January 1, 1976, to settle the debt in full? Show computations. Assume this debt was incurred to purchase a fixed asset. What should be recorded as the cost of the asset? Explain.

Exercise 6–10

S. Rath has a two-year-old child. Rath has decided to set up a fund to provide for the child's college education. A local financial institution will handle the fund and increase it each year on a 6% annual compound interest basis. Rath desires to make a single deposit on January 1, 1976, and specifies that the fund must have a $30,000 balance at the end of the 17th year. What amount of cash must be deposited on January 1, 1976. Show computations. Set up an accumulation table to cover the first two years

Exercise 6–11

Strawn Company desires to accumulate a plant expansion fund over the next five years. The company will make equal deposits in the fund of $5,000 starting on December 31, 1976. The fund will be increased by the trustee by 8% interest. What will be the balance in the fund on December 31, 1980 (immediately after the last deposit), assuming:

1. Annual contributions and compounding?

2. Semiannual contributions and compounding?
3. Quarterly contributions and compounding?

Exercise 6–12

Foster Corporation has decided to accumulate a debt retirement fund over the next three years by making equal annual deposits of $22,000 on December 31, starting at the end of 1976. Assume the fund will accumulate annual compound interest at 7% per year which will be added to the fund balance.

Required:

1. What will be the balance in the fund on December 31, 1978 (that is, immediately after the last deposit)?
2. Prepare an accumulation table for this fund.

Exercise 6–13

Based upon the situation described in Exercise 6–12, prepare the journal entries for the period January 1, 1976, through December 31, 1978.

Exercise 6–14

Stevens Company desires to accumulate a fund to retire a debt of $40,000. The debt is due on January 1, 1983. Equal annual contributions will be made to the fund by Stevens on each December 31, starting in 1976 and ending in 1982. The fund will be increased each year by 6% annual compound interest. Compute the amount of the equal annual contributions.

Exercise 6–15

Eagle Corporation plans to establish a debt retirement fund, beginning December 31, 1976, amounting to $8,750 by making contributions of $2,000 to a trustec each December 31, so that the desired amount will be available on December 31, 1979, the date of the last rent. Compute the interest rate that must be applied to the fund on an annual compound basis to satisfy these requirements. Show your computations.

Exercise 6–16

Sperry Corporation has decided to create a plant expansion fund by making equal annual deposits on each December 31 of $3,000. Interest at 7% compounded annually will be added to the fund balance. The company wants to know how many deposits will be required to build a fund of $75,390 (at the date of the last rent). Show your computations.

Exercise 6–17

Alcan Company is considering purchasing a large used machine that is in excellent mechanical condition. The company plans to keep the machine for ten years at which time the residual value will be minimal. An analysis of the capacity of the machine and the costs of operating it (including materials used in production) provided an estimate that the machine would increase net revenue by approximately $8,500 per year. Compute the approximate amount that should be paid now for the machine assuming a 10% compound interest expectation. Assume also that the revenue is realized at each year-end. Show your computations and disregard income tax considerations.

Exercise 6–18

On January 1, 1976, Dustin Corporation purchased a machine at a cost of $60,000. They paid $26,791 cash and incurred a debt for the difference. This debt is to be paid off in equal annual installments of $6,000 payable each December 31. The interest rate on the unpaid balance each period is 9% per annum. How many annual payments must be made? Show your computations.

Exercise 6–19

On January 1, 1976, the Caster Company decided to create an expansion fund by making equal annual deposits of $66,000. The fund is required on December 31, 1980. Interest at 6% compounded annually will be added to the fund. Five deposits are planned. Two alternative dates are under consideration, viz:

Alternative A – Make the deposits on each December 31 starting in 1976.
Alternative B – Make the deposits on each January 1 starting in 1976.

Required:

Complete the following table:

Alternative	Type of Annuity	Balance in the Fund at End of 1980	
		Computations	Amount
A			
B			

Exercise 6–20

Stans Company agreed on January 1, 1976, to deposit $120,000 cash with a trustee. The trustee will increase the fund on a 5% compound interest basis on the fund balance each successive year. The trustee is required to pay out the fund in equal annual installments to a former employee of Stans over a ten-year period so that the fund is completely exhausted at the end of that time. Two alternative payment dates are under consideration, viz:

Alternative A – Make the annual payments to the former employee each December 31 starting in 1976.
Alternative B – Make the annual payments to the former employee each January 1 starting in 1976.

Required:

Complete the following table:

		Amount of the Equal Annual Payments	
Alternative	*Type of Annuity*	*Computations*	*Amount*
A			
B			

PROBLEMS

Problem 6–1

Gardner Company plans to deposit $20,000 in a special fund for future use as needed. The fund will accumulate 8% interest. The fund will be initiated on January 1, 1976.

Required:

a. Complete the following table by entering, in each cell, the balance in the fund:

	Number of Years		
Compounding Assumption	2	4	6
Annual			
Semiannual			
Quarterly			

b. Prepare an accumulation table based on the first cell (annual only).

c. Give journal entries for the fund based on the first cell (annual only).

Problem 6–2

a. An investor planned to deposit $5,000 in a savings account that would accumulate at 7% annual compound interest for three years. Compute the balance that would be in the savings account at the end of the third year. Prepare an accumulation table for this situation and verify the fund balance.

b. Another investor planned to deposit $5,000 in a savings account that would accumulate to $5,955 at the end of three years assuming annual compound interest. Compute the interest rate that would be necessary. Show computations. Prepare an accumulation table for this situation and verify the interest rate computed.

c. Another investor planned to deposit $5,000 in a savings account that would accumulate to $6,475 assuming 9% annual compound interest. Compute the number of periods that would be necessary. Show computations. Prepare an accumulation table for this situation and verify the number of periods computed.

Problem 6–3

a. An investor planned to deposit $40,000 in a savings account that would accumulate to $42,400 at the end of year 1. Assume the deposit was made at the beginning of year 1. What would be the balance in the fund at the end of the fifth year? The tenth year? The 20th year? Show computations.

b. Another investor planned to deposit $50,000 in a savings account that would accumulate to $89,542 at the end of the tenth year. What rate of annual compound interest would have to be earned on the fund to meet these specifications? Show computations.

c. Another investor planned to deposit $10,000 at annual compound interest. The investor desires to accumulate $20,000 over a ten-year period. What rate of interest would be required to meet these specifications? Show computations. Interpolation is required.

Problem 6–4

Constance Corporation decided to place $90,000 in a special expansion fund for use in the future as needed. The fund will accumulate at 6% annual compound interest. The fund will be established on March 1, 1976, and the interest will be added to the fund balance on an annual compound interest basis.

Required:

a. Compute the balance that will be in the fund at the end of three years, five years, and ten years respectively.

b. Prepare an accumulation table for three years (verify your first computation in [*a*]).

c. Give the journal entries for Constance Corporation for *(b)* the first three years. Disregard adjusting and closing entries.

d. What adjusting entry would be made on December 31, 1976 for *(b)* assuming this is the end of the accounting period for Constance Corporation.

Problem 6–5

Bennett Company anticipates that it will need $200,000 cash for an expansion in the next few years. Assume an interest rate of 8%. The company desires to set up a fund now, January 1, 1976, so $200,000 will be available when needed.

Required:

a. Complete the following table by entering, in each cell, the amount that must be deposited now to meet the above specifications:

	Number of Years		
Compounding Assumption	2	3	5
Annual			
Semiannual			

b. Prepare an accumulation table based on the first cell.

c. Give journal entries for the fund based on the first cell.

Problem 6–6

Sord Construction Company has just won a bid on a major contract. The contract will require the purchase of new equipment costing approximately $200,000. The vendor, X Company, requires $50,000 cash down payment and will accept a two-year $150,000 noninterest-bearing note (assume an interest rate on this type of note to be 9% per annum). The $150,000 includes all interest charges.

Required:

a. Compute the cost of the equipment on January 1, 1976. Show computations.
b. Give the entry by Sord on date of purchase to record the equipment and the related financing.
c. Prepare a debt schedule for the note that reflects the annual interest expense and the principal.
d. Give journal entries by Sord each year while the note is outstanding and for final payment of the note.
e. Assume that Sord is short of cash on the date of the purchase. To raise cash for the down payment Sord is considering the sale (discounting) of a $60,000 receivable owed to them by John Doe that is due on December 31, 1978 (i.e., three years hence). The receivable is evidenced by a noninterest-bearing note. Sord has located an individual that will buy this future claim at a 12% compound annual discount.

Compute the amount that Sord would receive on January 1, 1976, the date of the sale of the future claim against John Doe. Show computations.

Problem 6–7

Morley Company is trying to "clean up" some of its debts. On January 1, 1976, the company has savings accounts as follows:

Date Established	*Amount Deposited (a single deposit for each)*	*Annual Compound Interest Rate*
Jan. 1, 1965	$20,000	4%
Jan. 1, 1971	90,000	5

The outstanding debts to be paid off are as follows:

Due Date	*Type of Note*	*Face of Note*
Dec. 31, 1978	Noninterest bearing	$ 60,000
Dec. 31, 1985	Noninterest bearing	200,000

Required:

a. Compute the amount of cash that can be obtained from the two savings accounts on January 1, 1976.
b. Compute the amount for which the two debts can be settled on January 1, 1976, assuming a going rate of interest of 9%.
c. How much extra cash additional to the savings accounts will be needed to settle the two debts on January 1, 1976 (in addition to the cash available from the savings accounts)?

Problem 6–8

a. Complete the following table assuming $n = 7$; $i = 9\%$:

Concept	Usual Symbol	Table Formula	"Value" Based on $1	Source
1. Amount of 1.	______	______	______	______
2. Present value of 1.	______	______	______	______
3. Amount of ordinary annuity of 1.	______	______	______	______
4. Present value of ordinary annuity of 1.	______	______	______	______
5. Amount of annuity due of 1.	______	______	______	______
6. Present value of annuity due of 1.	______	______	______	______

b. Present a time scale similar to the illustrations in the chapter for each of the above concepts. Identify dates, periods, and amounts.

Problem 6–9

Bell Corporation is contemplating the accumulation of a special fund to be used for expanding sales activities into the western part of the country. It is January 1, 1976, and the fund will be needed at the beginning of 1979 according to present plans. The fund will earn 6% interest compounded annually. The company is considering two plans for accumulating the fund by December 31, 1978, viz:

Plan A – Make three annual deposits of $50,000 each, starting on December 31, 1976.

Plan B – Make three annual deposits of $50,000 each, starting on January 1, 1976.

Required:

a. What kind of annuity is involved for each plan? Compute the balance that will be in the special fund on December 31, 1978, under each plan. Show computations.

b. Prepare an accumulation table for each plan.

c. Tabulate the entries for each plan. Set up a tabulation with the following captions:

Date	*Fund, Debit*	*Cash, Credit*	*Interest Revenue, Credit*

d. Explain why the fund has a different balance under each plan.

Problem 6–10

Freedom Company desires to build a special fund for future use in expanding into a foreign country by depositing an equal annual amount in the fund. The fund will be increased each year at 6% annual compounding. The company is considering two alternatives as follows:

Alternative A – Deposit $50,000 annually December 31, 1976, through December 31, 1980.

Alternative B – Deposit $50,000 annually on January 1, 1976, through January 1, 1980.

Required:

a. Compute the balance that will be in the fund for each alternative at December 30, 1980.
b. Prepare an accumulation table for Alternative B.
c. Give the entries indicated for Alternative B through December 31, 1980.

Problem 6–11

Ross Corporation desires to build a special debt retirement fund amounting to $50,000. A trustee has agreed to handle the fund and to increase it on a 5% annual compound interest basis. Ross will make equal annual contributions of $11,600 at the end of each year, starting on December 31, 1976. Assume an ordinary annuity situation.

Required:

a. Determine the number of contributions that Ross must make to meet these specifications. Show computations.
b. Prepare an accumulation table for the fund.
c. Give the journal entries during the period the fund is being accumulated.

Problem 6–12

Stickney Company agreed with its president, Jonas Smith, to set up a fund with a trustee that will pay Mr. Smith $40,000 per year for the three years following his retirement. Smith will retire on January 1, 1976, and the equal annual payments are to be made by the trustee each December 31 starting in 1976. The trustee will add to the fund, 5% annual compound interest on the fund balance each year-end. The fund is to have a zero balance on December 31, 1978, the date of the last payment.

Required:

a. Compute the single sum that must be deposited with the trustee on January 1, 1976, to meet these specifications.
b. Prepare a decumulation table through December 31, 1978. Set up table cap tions as follows: Date; Cash Payments; Interest Revenue Earned; Fund Decreases; and Fund Balance.

Problem 6–13

Roller Construction Company can purchase a used crane that will be needed on a new job that will continue for approximately three years. It is January 1, 1976, and the crane is needed immediately. Because of a shortage of cash Roller has asked the vendor for credit terms with no down payment. The vendor expects 11% annual compound interest. The crane can be purchased under these terms by making three payments of $6,400 each on December 31, 1976, 1977, and 1978.

Required:

a. What should be the cash price of the crane on January 1, 1976?
b. Give the entry to record the purchase of the crane on the credit terms.
c. Prepare a debt amortization schedule using the following format:

Date	*Cash Payment*	*Interest Expense*	*Reduction on Principal*	*Liability Balance*

Problem 6–14

Ronnie Student is considering the purchase of a Super Sail Boat which has a cash price of $6,500. Terms can be arranged for a $2,000 cash down payment and payment of the remaining $4,500, plus interest at 11% per annum, in three equal annual payments. Assume purchase on January 1, 1976, and each payment on each December 31 thereafter.

Required:

a. Compute the amount of each annual payment assuming annual compound interest.
b. What did the boat cost including interest? What was the interest amount?
c. Prepare a debt amortization schedule using the following format:

Date	*Cash Payment*	*Interest Expense*	*Reduction on Principal*	*Liability Balance*

Problem 6–15

Complete the following table of future and present values based on $1, assuming 6 years and 12% interest:

		Value Based on $1, Assuming Compounding		
Concept	*Symbol*	*Annual*	*Semiannual*	*Quarterly*
1. Amount of 1.	______	______	______	______
2. Present value of 1.	______	______	______	______
3. Amount of ordinary annuity of 1.*	______	______	______	______
4. Amount of annuity due of 1.*	______	______	______	______
5. Present value of ordinary annuity of 1.*	______	______	______	______
6. Present value of annuity due of 1.*	______	______	______	______

* Assume one rent in each compound interest period.

Indicate sources, or show computations, of each value.

Problem 6–16

Carson Company rents a warehouse for an annual rental of $2,000. They have some idle cash and have approached the owner with a proposal to pay three years' rent in advance. The owner has agreed to a compound discount rate of 10%.

Required:

a. Assume it is January 1, 1976, and that the three rents are due on January 1, 1976, 1977, and 1978. Compute the amount that Carson Company would have to pay as a single sum on January 1, 1976. What kind of annuity is this? Explain.
b. Assume it is January 1, 1976, and that the three rents are due on December

31, 1976, 1977, and 1978. Compute the amount that Carson Company would have to pay as a single sum on January 1, 1976. What kind of annuity is this? Explain.

c. Explain why the single sums to be paid computed under (1) and (2) are different.

Problem 6–17

On January 1, 1976, Larson Company signed a three-year contract to rent some space that they needed immediately. The lease provided that Larson could pay annual rentals on each January 1 of $17,000, beginning in 1976, or alternatively, they can pay rent in advance at a 7% annual compound discount.

Required:

a. What sum would have to be paid by Larson on January 1, 1976, for the three annual rentals? What amount would be saved by advance payment?

b. What kind of annuity is this? Explain.

Problem 6–18

On January 1, 1976, Cunard Company owes an $80,000 debt which is due. Since the company is short of cash they have reached an agreement with the creditor whereby the debt and interest is to be paid in equal annual installments on January 1, 1976, 1977, and 1978. Interest is 9% annual compounding.

Required:

a. What kind of annuity is this? Explain.

b. Compute the amount of the equal annual payments.

c. Prepare a debt amortization schedule, using the following format:

Date	*Cash Payment*	*Interest Expense*	*Reduction of Principal*	*Liability Balance*
1/1/76				$80,000

Problem 6–19

Shakey Corporation is negotiating to purchase a plant from another company that will complement Shakey's operations. They have just completed a careful study of the plant and have developed the following estimates:

Expected net cash revenues:	
Years 1–5 (per year)	$44,000
Years 6–10 (per year)	34,000
Year 11	20,000
Year 12	10,000
Expected net residual value at end of year 12	3,000

Required:

a. Compute the amount that Shakey should be willing to pay for the plant assuming an 11% return on the investment. Assume all amounts are at year-end; disregard income taxes.

Because Shakey is short of cash assume the down payment is $150,000. The bank will lend Shakey the balance at 9% per annum payable in equal annual payments (including interest and principal) over the first five years. The payments will be at each year-end, starting one year after the date of purchase.

b. Compute the amount of the equal annual payments on the loan. Compute the total interest that will be paid.

c. Give the entries (or entry) to record the purchase in *(a)* and the loan in *(b)* using the amounts you computed.

Chapter 7

Cash, Short-Term Investments, and Receivables

This chapter focuses on cash and near-cash items, often called quick assets. The three most liquid assets are cash, short-term investments, and current receivables (including short-term notes receivable). Their interchangeability and other similarities make it desirable to discuss them in a single integrated chapter. Planning, control, and accounting for this particular group of current assets involve common problems, concepts, and procedures. To facilitate discussion the chapter is divided into three parts.

PART A—CASH

Cash is the medium of exchange and is used for most of the measurements in accounting. Because of its pervasive use by society the concept of cash is understood by most people; however, accounting for and reporting cash inflows and outflows presents some special problems. This part focuses on accounting for cash, including control; reporting cash flows is discussed in Chapter 21, Statement of Changes in Financial Position.

COMPOSITION OF CASH

Two principal characteristics of cash are (1) its availability as a medium of exchange, and (2) its use as a measurement in accounting for the other items. Although its purchasing power may change, accountants make no effort to revalue cash. Some special measures which can be taken in conjunction with the effects of price-level changes on certain other financial statement items are discussed in Chapter 25. Cash includes coins, currency, and certain types of formal negotiable paper which are accepted by banks for deposit; but it excludes some items commonly intermingled with cash. Examples of *exclusions* include postage stamps and cash-due memos. Cash-due memos or IOU's from officers, owners, or employees should be classified as special receivables, not as cash. Formal *negotiable* paper (i.e., transferable by endorsement) which is due on demand is classified as cash. Thus, bank drafts, cashier's checks, money orders, certified checks, and ordinary checks constitute cash for accounting purposes. Balances on deposit in commercial banks should be considered as cash if subject to immediate use. Balances in savings accounts generally are classed as short-term investments because the bank usually has a right to advance notice of withdrawal. Certificates of deposit are classed as cash; time certificates of deposit, depending on maturity dates and managerial intent, are classed as either short-term or long-term investments.

Deposits in foreign banks create two special problems, viz: (1) foreign currency units, such as pounds or pesos, first must be translated to dollars; and (2) it is not uncommon for the foreign deposits to be subject to restricted conversion and transfer to other countries. Discussion of conversion of deposits in foreign banks is beyond the scope of this book. Even when spendable immediately or in the near future, cash in foreign banks should be set out separately on the balance sheet.

Current assets were discussed in Chapter 5. The AICPA Committee on Accounting Procedure, in *Accounting Research Bulletin No. 43*, stated that such resources as "cash and claims to cash which are restricted as to withdrawal or use for other than current operations, are designated for expenditure in the acquisition or construction of noncurrent assets, or are segregated for the liquidation of long-term debts" should be excluded from current assets. The committee then added:

> Even though not actually set aside in special accounts, funds that are clearly to be used in the near future for the liquidation of long-term debts, payments to sinking funds, or for similar purposes should also, under this concept, be excluded from current assets. However, where such funds are considered to offset maturing debt which has properly been set up as a current liability, they may be included within the current asset classification.[1]

Petty cash funds and cash in the hands of branches or divisions should be included as cash because these ordinarily are used to meet current operating expenses and to liquidate current liabilities.

Checks drawn against a bank balance which have not been mailed or otherwise delivered to the payees by the end of the accounting period should not be deducted from the cash balance. The entry already made to record the check should be reversed before preparing the financial statements. An overdraft in a bank account should be shown as a current liability. However, where a depositor has overdrawn one account with Bank A but has positive balances in other accounts in that bank, it is appropriate to offset and show the net asset or liability on the

---

[1] AICPA, "Restatement and Revision of Accounting Research Bulletins," *Accounting Research Bulletin No. 43* (New York, 1961), p. 21.

balance sheet. It is improper to offset an overdraft in Bank A against a balance on deposit in Bank B.

CONTROL OF CASH

The control of cash is critical in many businesses because *(a)* it is usually in short supply, or in some cases there is idle cash; and *(b)* it is easy to conceal and transport, and it is desired by everyone.

The control of cash involves careful planning of cash needs and control of expenditures and careful recordkeeping to assure that all cash is properly accounted for. Thus, control of cash generally requires the following:

1. A detailed cash budget that specifies planned cash inflows and outflows (not considered in this book).
2. Detailed cash control reports for internal management use to assure that cash is controlled as planned and as a basis for revising cash plans.
3. A system of internal control that incorporates careful delegation of authority for handling cash receipts, cash payments, and the related recordkeeping. The essential details of a system of internal control were discussed in Chapter 3.
4. Proper accounting for all cash receipts and cash disbursements including assurances that there are no unauthorized uses of cash receipts or improper cash disbursements. Chapter 3, Appendix A, discussed and illustrated the use of control and subsidiary accounts and special journals. These are important procedures in attaining adequate control of cash.
5. Adequate disclosure of cash inflows and outflows in the external financial statements provided to stockholders and others. This subject is discussed in Chapter 21, Statement of Changes in Financial Position, Cash Basis.

Control of Cash Receipts

Cash inflows in most businesses come from numerous sources; therefore, the procedures that should be used to attain adequate control are varied. However, the following procedures are important in all situations:

1. Assign responsibilities and develop a system so there is a continuous and uninterrupted flow of cash from initial receipt to deposit in an authorized bank account. This requires *(a)* immediate counting of all cash received, *(b)* immediate recording of all cash received, and *(c)* timely deposit of all cash received.
2. Separation of all responsibilities for the cash-handling and cash-recording functions. In this manner an effective system of internal checks is implemented.
3. Continuous and close supervision of all cash-handling and recordkeeping functions, including daily cash reports for internal use.

Control over Cash Disbursements

The cash outflows in most businesses are for many purposes. Many of the cash defalcations happen in the disbursements process because they are relatively easy to cover up unless there is an effective system to control cash payments. In such situations, one or more of the fundamentals of internal control are missing. Although each control system should be tailored to the situation, there are several fundamentals that are indispensable; these are:

1. Make all cash disbursements by check. An exception can be made for small miscellaneous payments by use of a petty cash system.
2. Establish a petty cash system with tight controls and close supervision.
3. Prepare checks and sign them only when supported by adequate documentation and verification.
4. Separate responsibilities for cash disbursement documentation, check writing, check signing (and in some cases check mailing), and recordkeeping.
5. Supervise continuously and closely all cash-disbursement and recordkeeping functions including periodic internal reports.

Petty Cash

The term petty cash, or *imprest cash,* refers to a systematic approach often used for making small expenditures that would be too impractical (too costly and time consuming) to make by check. Examples of typical payments are for the daily paper delivered to the office, express payments, local taxi fares, special postage charges on delivery, and minor office supplies. A petty cash system operates as follows:

1. A reliable employee is designated as the petty cash custodian. This person receives a single amount of cash for specified petty cash purposes, disburses the funds as needed, receives adequate documentation for each disbursement, maintains a running record of the cash on hand, and periodically reports the total amount spent supported by the documentation received for each disbursement. The record maintained, in addition to the documentation, often is referred to as the petty cash book.
2. When the petty cash held by the custodian runs low, a request for a resupply, supported by the documentation of prior expenditures, is submitted to the designated supervisor of company cash.
3. The initial amount to establish the petty cash fund, and resupply to the custodian, are provided by separate checks, made payable to petty cash, and processed in the normal manner.
4. Accounting—the initial check establishing the petty cash fund is recorded as a debit to Petty Cash and a credit to Cash. Checks to resupply the fund are recorded by debiting the expense accounts (or other accounts) for the expenditures reported by the custodian and by crediting Cash.

5. There should be close supervision and surprise audits of cash on hand and supporting documentation for expenditures.

To illustrate, assume a petty cash fund is established in the amount of $100 and employee X is designated as the custodian. At the end of the first two weeks the custodian requested a resupply of the $87 spent, supported by adequate documentation that reflected the following: postage, $18.50; office supplies bought, $23.60; taxi fares (local), $31; meals for employees, $10; and daily paper, $3.90. The indicated entries would be as follows:

To establish the petty cash fund:

Petty cash	100.00	
Cash		100.00

To replenish the fund (at end of second week):

Postage expense	18.50	
Office supplies expense	23.60	
Administrative expense	44.90	
Cash		87.00

The effect of the last entry is to increase the amount of cash held by the custodian to $100, the amount reflected in the Petty Cash account.

CASH OVERAGE AND SHORTAGE

Cash is susceptible to theft, and it is inevitable that errors will be made in counting cash; therefore, cash overages and shortages must be expected. Cash overages and shortages, usually determined on a daily basis, should be recorded in an account entitled Cash Overages and Shortages with an offset to the regular Cash account. A debit balance in this account represents an operating expense and a credit represents a miscellaneous revenue. In the abscncc of theft, cash overages and shortages tend to balance out to zero over a period of time. In contrast, theft, when discovered and if material in amount, should be recorded as a credit to the regular Cash account and as a debit to *(a)* a receivable if recovery is expected from the individual involved or an insurance or bonding company, or *(b)* an extraordinary loss (on the presumption that it is unusual and infrequent), if there is no recovery probable.

RECONCILIATION OF BANK WITH BOOK BALANCE

At the end of each month, the ending cash balance on deposit reported in the bank statement should be reconciled with the ending cash balance on deposit and on hand as reflected in the cash accounts of the business. Reconciliation of bank with book balances serves two important purposes: (1) control – it serves to check the accuracy of the records of both the bank and the company; and (2) accounting entries – it provides information for entries on the books of the company for items reflected on the bank statement that have not been recorded by the company (e.g., a bank service charge).

Reconciliation of the bank balance with the balance of the Cash account requires an analysis of the *monthly bank statement* and the cash records maintained by the company. Generally there will be a difference between the two cash balances. The usual causes of differences between the cash balance per the bank statement and the cash balance on the books of the company may be classified as follows:

A. Items already recorded as cash receipts in the books of the company but not yet added to the bank balance on the bank statement.

   Examples:

   1. Unrecorded deposits – deposits made up and deposited in the bank by the company but not reported by the bank on the current bank statement.
   2. Cash on hand including petty cash (i.e., not deposited).

B. Items already added to the bank balance but not recorded in the company books.

   Examples:

   1. Interest allowed the depositor by the bank but not yet recorded in the company books.
   2. Collections (and deposits) of notes and drafts by the bank for the depositor but not yet recorded on the company books.

C. Items already recorded as cash disbursements on the company books but not deducted by the bank from the bank balance.

   Example:

   1. Outstanding checks – checks written and properly recorded in the company books but not yet cleared through the bank.

D. Items already subtracted from the bank balance but not recorded in the company books:

   Example:

   1. Bank service charge.

It is possible to reconcile the bank and book balances by working from the bank balance to the book balance, or the opposite, or to reconcile both the book balance and bank balance to a common amount known as the correct or *true cash balance*. The "true balance" method is generally used.[2] The method is illustrated in Exhibit 7–1 based on the following data:

---

[2] The "true balance" method is preferable for the following reasons:

1. The reconciliation naturally falls into two parts (Books and Bank), and all the reconciling entries to be made in the books are grouped in the section devoted to the *book balance*.

2. It is less confusing. After the correctness of each item has been verified, the reconciliation merely involves placing such items under the appropriate part as an addition or deduction.

3. The reconciliation can be used as a schedule supporting the cash balance reported on the balance sheet; the last line on the reconciliation is reported on the balance sheet.

1. Bank statement, March 19A:

Balance carried forward from February		$1,800
Deposits	$6,550	
Interest collected by the bank on a note for the company	20	6,570
Total		8,370
Charges:		
Checks cashed	6,962	
Service charge by bank	4	6,966
Balance, March 31		$1,404

2. Company records:

Cash account, March 19A:

Debits:		
Balance from February	$1,600	
Cash receipts	7,000	
Total		$8,600
Credits:		
Checks written		7,065
Balance, March 31		$1,535

3. An analysis of the bank statement compared with the company records revealed the following:
   a. A deposit made on March 31 for $450 was not included on the bank statement.
   b. Cash on hand in the company (hence, not deposited), $100.
   c. Checks written by the company and recorded in the accounts but not cleared (i.e., not deducted on the bank statement) by March 31:

No. 401	$150	
No. 403	200	
No. 412	53	$403

Using these data, the bank balance of $1,404 and the book balance of $1,535 are reconciled to the true cash balance, as computed on the reconciliation, $1,551 (Exhibit 7–1). The true balance would be reported as the cash balance on the balance sheet at March 31, 19A.

EXHIBIT 7–1
Bank Reconciliation

Bank Balance			*Book Balance*	
Balance per bank		$1,404	Balance per books	$1,535
Additions:			Additions:	
Unrecorded deposit	$450		Interest collected by bank	20
				1,555
Cash on hand	100	550		
		1,954		
Deductions:			Deductions:	
Outstanding checks:			Bank charges	4
No. 401	150			
No. 410	200			
No. 412	53	403		
True Cash Balance		$1,551	True Cash Balance	$1,551

Entries to record items on the bank reconciliation which have not been recognized on the books previously may be taken directly from the bank reconciliation. If the method of reconciliation illustrated above is used, those items listed under the caption "book balance" constitute the amounts to be recognized. The entries necessary to reflect the correct cash balance in the books ($1,551 in the illustration) are as follows:

Cash	20	
Interest revenue		20
Expense—bank charges	4	
Cash		4

COMPREHENSIVE RECONCILIATION

Comprehensive reconciliation or reconciliation of receipts and disbursements for a month (or an entire fiscal period) is usually undertaken by auditors and frequently by accountants. A comprehensive reconciliation has the advantages of *(a)* providing a complete reconciliation of the differences between the beginning and ending balances, *(b)* reflecting the detailed differences separately for the bank statement and the accounts, and *(c)* facilitating reconciliation in complex situations. Thus, comprehensive reconciliation is akin to a true balance reconciliation; however, it differs in that it also reconciles receipts and payments for the period under consideration and begins with a true balance type reconciliation (made as of the end of the prior period).

To illustrate the procedure, refer to the true balance reconciliation in Exhibit 7-1 completed on March 31, and assume the necessary entries to correct cash were reflected in the company's account as of that date. April transactions reflected on the bank statement and the company's Cash account are shown below. The reconciliation is shown in Exhibit 7-2.

Bank Statement, April 19A:*

Date	Item	Amount
Mar. 31	Balance forward	$ 1,404
Apr. 1	Deposit *The $450 unrecorded deposit + $100 undeposited cash as of March 31.*	550
2–29	Deposits *Other April receipts deposited.*	10,800
30	Note collected *$500 note + $15 interest collected by bank in behalf of company.*	515
	Total Receipts	11,865
	Initial balance + receipts	13,269
Apr. 1	Check Nos. 401 and 410 *March checks cleared in April.*	350
2–29	Check Nos. 413–430 *April checks cleared in April.*	10,700
30	April service charge	10
	Total April charges	11,060
30	Balance, April 30	$ 2,209

Cash Account (per books), April 19A:

Mar. 31	Cash balance	$ 1,551
	Reflects entries called for by March 31 reconciliation.	
Apr. 2–29	Receipts	10,800
	Receipts which were also deposited during April.	
30	Receipts	400
	Deposit in transit at April 30.	
30	Receipts	200
	Cash on hand at April 30.	
	Total Receipts	11,400
	Initial balance + receipts	12,951
Apr. 2–29	Check Nos. 413–430	10,700
	April checks cleared in April.	
30	Check No. 431	100
	April check outstanding April 30.	
		10,800
30	Balance, April 30	$ 2,151

* Explanation in italics not part of the bank statement and Cash account.

EXHIBIT 7–2
Comprehensive Reconciliation

	Balance March 31	*April Receipts*	*April Payments*	*Balance April 30*
Balances per bank	$1,404	$11,865	$11,060	$2,209
Unrecorded deposits:				
March 31........	450	(450)		
April 30		400		400
Undeposited cash:				
March 31........	100	(100)		
April 30		200		200
Outstanding checks:				
March 31, No. 401	(150)		(150)	
No. 410	(200)		(200)	
No. 412	(53)			(53)
April 30, No. 431			100	(100)
Correct Balances	$1,551	$11,915	$10,810	$2,656
Balances per company's books...	$1,551	$11,400	$10,800	$2,151
April service charge........			10	(10)
Note and interest collected		515		515
Correct Balances	$1,551	$11,915	$10,810	$2,656

Observe that Check No. 412 for $53 which was outstanding at March 31 is still outstanding at April 30 and that payment on it has not been stopped.

Entries needed to record the correct cash balance as of April 30 are as follows:

Cash	515	
Note receivable		500
Interest revenue		15
Expense—bank charges	10	
Cash		10

The company should report a cash balance of $2,656 on its April 30 balance sheet.

PART B—SHORT-TERM INVESTMENTS

Prior to a discussion of accounting for short-term investments, it is appropriate to describe briefly the nature and types of investments. Investments generally are classified for balance sheet purposes as either short-term investments (often called temporary investments) or long-term investments (often called permanent investments). This distinction is entirely one of accounting and not of law and arises out of the nature of the security and the purpose of the investment. Investment purposes may be outlined as follows:

A. Short-term investments:
   1. Funds set aside for emergency use on a current basis and invested in marketable securities.
   2. Investment of short-term excess cash.

B. Long-term investments:[3]
   1. Stocks, bonds, and similar securities of another company held on a long-term basis.
   2. Advances to affiliates or subsidiaries.
   3. Funds earmarked for a designated purpose such as retirement of a funded debt, replacement of plant and equipment, or payment of pensions.
   4. Cash value of life insurance on company executives.
   5. Major expenditures for certain types of memberships in associations and exchanges, such as a broker's "seat" on a stock exchange.
   6. Assets, other than investment securities, such as land not used in regular business operations.
   7. Funds invested in long-term assets not directly related to the primary operations of the company. For example, the National Laundry Machinery Company purchased a patent on a special pressing device, developed it for use in a field not in competition with its own operations, and secured regular royalties from its licensing. The cost of this patent should be accounted for as a long-term investment rather than as an intangible fixed asset.

SHORT-TERM INVESTMENTS DEFINED

Short-term investments are reported on the balance sheet under the current asset caption. To be classified as a current asset a short-term investment must meet the following twofold test:

[3] Discussed in Chapters 18 and 19.

1. The security must be *readily marketable*. It must be a security which is regularly traded on a security exchange or for which there is an established market.
2. It must be the *intention* of the company's management to convert the security into cash in the short run and hence back into the normal operations for which working capital is used. This criterion has proven somewhat troublesome to auditors in practice. "Intentions" are elusive and prone to change from one period to the next.

VALUATION OF SHORT-TERM INVESTMENTS

Short-term investments are recorded initially at cost in conformance with the cost principle. Subsequent to acquisition they may be accounted for at–

1. Lower of cost or market.
2. Cost.
3. Market.

Lower of Cost or Market

FASB *Statement No. 12, Accounting for Certain Marketable Securities* (effective December 31, 1975), requires that investments in marketable equity securities be valued at each balance sheet date on a lower of cost or market basis.[4] The statement also applies to long-term investments in marketable equity securities. Long-term investments are discussed in Chapter 18; therefore, this chapter will focus only on short-term investments. Equity securities, as used in *Statement No. 12*, encompass all capital stock (including warrants, rights, and stock options) except preferred stock that, by its terms, must be redeemed either at the option of the issuer or the investor. Equity securities do not include bonds and other debt instruments since they are debt securities.

To apply lower of cost or market to investments in marketable equity securities, *Statement No. 12* specifies: "The carrying amount of a marketable equity securities portfolio shall be the lower of its aggregate cost or market value, determined at balance sheet date. The amount by which aggregate cost of the portfolio exceeds market value shall be accounted for as the valuation allowance."

In applying the concept of lower of cost or market, *Statement No. 12* makes a careful distinction between realized and unrealized gains and losses. A *realized* gain or loss is defined as the difference between the net proceeds received at sale and the cost of an equity security. In contrast, an *unrealized* gain or loss is defined as the difference between the aggregate market value and aggregate cost of the investment portfolio

---

[4] The provisions of FASB *Statement No. 12* do not apply to debt securities, to redeemable preferred stock (since it is similar to debt), or to long-term investments accounted for by the equity method (see Chapter 18). Also, that statement does not apply to industries having specialized practices with respect to marketable securities, including such financial organizations as insurance companies, investment companies, mutual funds, and securities dealers.

of marketable equity securities on a given date. Thus, realized gains and losses are recognized only when a security is disposed of. However, unrealized losses are recognized at the end of the accounting period when an adjusting entry is made to reflect lower of cost or market. In the accounts, an "allowance" account (a contra asset) is used to record the amount of the difference between aggregate market and aggregate cost when market is lower. On the other side of the entry, an unrealized gain/loss account is used. On the income statement, the unrealized gain or loss on short-term investments (but not long-term investments) is reported along with investment revenue. On the balance sheet, the allowance account balance is subtracted from the investment cost, thus reporting the portfolio at lower of cost or market. Dividends received on equity securities are credited to investment revenue.

To illustrate the accounting and reporting of short-term investments in marketable equity securities, the following transactions and responses are given.

January 5, 19A—D Company acquired the following short-term investments:

Company E—Common stock (par $10), 5,000 shares at $20 per share.
Company F—Common stock (nopar), 3,000 shares at $30 per share.
Company G—Preferred stock (nonredeemable, par $20), 2,000 shares at $40 per share.

Short-term investments in equity securities	270,000	
Cash		270,000

December 31, 19A—Adjusting entry to record lower of cost or market valuation. Market values: E stock, $16; F stock, $31; G stock, $39.

Unrealized loss on short-term investments in equity securities*	19,000	
Allowance to reduce short-term investments in equity securities to market		19,000

* Closed to income summary.

Computation:

Company	Shares	Cost	Market	Unrealized Gain (loss)
E	5,000	@ $20 = $100,000	@ $16 = $ 80,000	($20,000)
F	3,000	@ $30 = 90,000	@ $31 = 93,000	3,000
G	2,000	@ $40 = 80,000	@ $39 = 78,000	(2,000)
Total		$270,000	$251,000	($19,000)

March 1, 19B—Received cash dividends as follows: E stock, $1.00 per share; F stock, $.50 per share; G stock, none.

Cash	6,500	
Investment revenue		6,500

December 31, 19B—Adjusting entry to record lower of cost or market valuation. Market values: E stock, $18; F stock, $31; G stock, $42.

Allowance to reduce short-term investments in equity securities to market	16,000	
Unrealized gain on short-term investments in equity securities (closed to income summary)		16,000

Computation:

Company	Shares	Cost	Market	Unrealized Gain (loss)
E	5,000	@ $20 = $100,000	@ $18 = $ 90,000	($10,000)
F	3,000	@ $30 = 90,000	@ $31 = 93,000	3,000
G	2,000	@ $40 = 80,000	@ $42 = 84,000	4,000
Total		$270,000	$267,000	($ 3,000)

Balance in allowance account	$19,000
Balance need in allowance account..............	3,000
Decrease in account (debit)	$16,000

Under the provisions of *Statement No. 12,* recoveries such as the $16,000 are permitted to be reflected in the accounts and reported on the income statement to the extent unrealized losses have previously been reported but the unrealized gains cannot exceed the previously recognized unrealized losses. Of course, *Statement No. 12* explicitly applies only to certain stocks; by inference, the same principle can be extended to other types of securities held as short-term investments.

October 10, 19C – Sale of the G Company stock at $44 per share.

Cash (2,000 shares × $44)	88,000	
Short-term investments in equity securities (2,000 shares × $40)		80,000
Realized gain on sale of short-term investments*		8,000

* Closed to income summary.

Observe in the last entry that no cognizance was taken of the allowance account and the realized gain or loss is calculated in terms of recorded original cost.[5] The allowance account is adjusted only at the end of the period.

The financial statements at the end of 19A and 19B would reflect the following:

	19A		19B	
Income Statement:				
Investment revenue				$ 6,500
Unrealized loss on equity securities..................		$ 19,000		
Unrealized gain on equity securities..................				16,000
Balance Sheet:				
Current Assets:				
Short-term investments in equity securities at cost..	$270,000		$270,000	
Less: Allowance to reduce equity securities to market...	19,000		3,000	
Marketable equity securities portfolio at lower of cost or market.....................................		$251,000		$267,000

[5] Paragraph 23 of FASB *Statement No. 12* provides that unrealized gains and losses on marketable securities shall be considered as timing differences for income tax allocation purposes; however, that tax effects should be recognized on unrealized capital losses only when there exists assurance beyond a reasonable doubt that the benefit will be realized by an offset of the loss against capital gains. In the opinion of the authors; conservatism would normally mitigate against such tax allocation recognition (see Chapter 11).

Alternatively, the balance sheet may be as follows:

Current Assets:
Short-term investments in equity securities (cost
$270,000), at lower of cost or market $251,000

Disclosure requirements specified by FASB *Statement No. 12* are:

> The following information with respect to marketable equity securities owned shall be disclosed either in the body of the financial statements or in the accompaning notes:
>
> *a.* As of the date of each balance sheet presented, aggregate cost and market value (each segregated between current and noncurrent portfolios when a classified balance sheet is presented) with identification as to which is the carrying amount.
>
> *b.* As of the date of the latest balance sheet presented, the following, segregated between current and noncurrent portfolios when a classified balance sheet is presented:
>
> i. Gross unrealized gains representing the excess of market value over cost for all marketable equity securities in the portfolio having such an excess.
>
> ii. Gross unrealized losses representing the excess of cost over market value for all marketable equity securities in the portfolio having such an excess.
>
> *c.* For each period for which an income statement is presented:
>
> i. Net realized gain or loss included in the determination of net income.
>
> ii. The basis on which cost was determined in computing realized gain or loss (i.e., average cost or other method used).
>
> iii. The change in the valuation allowance(s) that has been included in the equity section of the balance sheet during the period and, when a classified balance sheet is presented, the amount of such change included in the determination of net income.

Valuation at Cost

Short-term investments that are not covered by the provisions of FASB *Statement No. 12* (i.e., redeemable preferred stock and debt securities) are accounted for under the prior provisions of *ARB No. 43*, Chapter 3A which states: "In the case of maketable securities where market value is less than cost by a substantial amount and it is evident that the decline in market value is not due to a mere temporary condition, the amount to be included as a current asset should not exceed market value." Although lower of cost or market is specified, in actual practice short-term investments generally have been carried at cost in view of the "substantial" and "mere temporary condition" qualifiers. (Reference: *Accounting Trends and Techniques*, 1975, AICPA, p. 99).

When this basis of valuation is used, the short-term investment account remains unchanged except for acquisitions and dispositions. In view of the issuance of FASB *Statement No. 12*, the cost method is appropriate for nonstock short-term investments when the price change is "temporary" and when there has been no material drop in the market value of the securities compared to their cost. Cost includes brokerage costs, taxes, and all other legitimate and reasonable costs incurred in acquisition, as well as the agreed upon purchase price. In the case of bonds bought between interest dates, it does not include accrued interest purchased, which should be charged to Interest revenue.

To illustrate application of the cost method to *debt securities* acquired as a short-term investment, the following transactions and responses are given.

November 1, 19A—Purchased six $1,000 Baxter Company bonds at 104. Interest at 5% per annum is payable each March 1 and September 1. Accrued interest for September 1 to November 1 had to be purchased:

Short-term investments, bonds ($6,000 × 1.04)	6,240	
Investment revenue ($6,000 × 5% × 2/12)	50	
Cash		6,290

December 31, 19A—End of the accounting period. Adjusting entry for accured interest on Baxter bonds (September 1 to December 31):

Interest receivable	100	
Investment revenue ($6,000 × 5% × 4/12)		100

December 31, 19A—To close investment revenue account:

Investment revenue ($100 − $50)	50	
Income summary		50

March 1, 19B—Collection of semiannual interest on Baxter bonds (assuming no reversing entry was made on January 1, 19B):

Cash	150	
Interest receivable		100
Investment revenue		50

April 30, 19B—Sold the Baxter bonds at 103¾ plus accrued interest March 1 to April 30):

Cash [($6,000 × 103¾) + ($6,000 × 5% × 2/12)]	6,275	
Loss on sale of short-term investments	15	
Short-term investments, bonds		6,240
Investment revenue ($6,000 × 5% × 2/12)		50

December 31, 19B—To close investment revenue and loss on sale of investments:

Investment revenue ($50 + $50)	100	
Loss on sale of short-term investments		15
Income summary		85

Market Value

As rising prices have accelerated and inflation has become a worldwide phenomenon, there has been an increasing clamor to depart from historical cost (i.e., the cost principle) as the basis for asset valuation.

The movement toward current or "fair value" has proceeded farther in other developed countries than in the United States.[6] This is partly because laws of some countries have permitted use of values other than cost for tax and other purposes, and also because in some instances their inflation rate has been extremely high by all standards. It seems safe to say that if the same certainty could attend the valuation of other assets as would apply to marketable securities, there would probably have been a greater impetus toward fair market values in accounting. Mutual funds and certain other types of financial entities often value and report their relatively vast investment portfolios at current market.

As to short-term investments, the primary arguments usually cited favoring current market as a valuation basis include:

1. Eliminating the present inconsistency inherent in use of lower of cost or market, wherein unrealized losses are recognized but unrealized gains are ignored.
2. Assigning to each period such gains or losses from holding investments which actually did occur during the period. Under the historical cost approach, much of the gain or loss that is finally recognized when the short-term investments are sold may have occurred in one or more earlier periods.
3. Reporting short-term investments at current market value is more informative to statement users than reporting at cost (which may be materially lower).
4. Eliminating the manipulation of periodic net income. For example, income can be artificially generated near the end of the period by selling securities from the portfolio that had a low cost and now have a high price. In the next period, the securities, or similar securities, are repurchased to maintain the portfolio. There have been occasional examples of this manipulation that changed a material loss to a net income amount.

Arguments against current market as a valuation basis are:

1. Market values often cannot be determined with reasonable certainty. A problem often arises because of a "thin market" with large blocks of securities and with securities that trade infrequently.
2. Market value at the balance sheet date may not be especially significant, particularly if there are no plans to sell them in the reasonably near future.
3. Recording market values will cause unrealized gains to be reported on the income statement.
4. Except for certain financial entities, market values are not permitted for income tax purposes.

Accounting and reporting marketable securities on the basis of market prices, instead of cost, poses two problems, viz: (1) determination of

---

[6] Fair value accounting is discussed in Chapter 25.

the appropriate fair market value of the securities at the end of each period, and (2) the method of recognizing the resulting market gain or loss (often called holding gains or losses). In accordance with present GAAP, the revenue realization principle does not permit the recognization of holding gains; however, holding losses are recognized by using the lower-of-cost-or-market approach.

To illustrate the issue of recognizing holding gains, assume a short-term investment in common stock is acquired at a cost of $10,000 at the beginning of 19A. Assume the fair market value of the stock at the end of 19A is $11,000. The indicated entries, assuming accounting on the basis of fair market value, would be:

At date of acquisition (record at cost):

Investments, short term	10,000	
Cash		10,000

At end of period (market $11,000); to record market gain:

Investments, short term	1,000	
Market gain on investments (or unrealized market gain on investments)		1,000

Some accountants feel strongly that the market gain of $1,000 should be reflected on the income statement for 19A; others feel equally strong that the gain is unrealized in 19A and should be reported on the balance sheet at the end of 19A as unrealized. They believe that it should be recognized on the income statement when the investment is finally sold. Of course, this latter approach inconsistently reports the investment on the balance sheet at market value, but reports net income on the basis of cost. To illustrate, assume the investment is sold during 19B for $11,500. The indicated entry would be:

a. Assuming market gain was considered as realized in 19A:

Cash	11,500	
Investments, short term		11,000
Gain on sale of investments		500

b. Assuming the market gain was considered as unrealized in 19A:

Cash	11,500	
Unrealized market gain on investments	1,000	
Investment, short term		11,000
Gain on sale of investment		1,500

A balance in the Unrealized Market Gain on Investments account (if used) would be classified, on the balance sheet, under owners' equity as "unrealized capital."

At this date, no definitive position for all businesses has been developed by the accounting profession in accounting for short-term investments on the basis of fair values (also see Chapter 25). Currently, generally accepted accounting principles require the use of cost or lower of cost or market as explained above.

IDENTIFICATION OF UNITS

When short-term investments are sold, or otherwise disposed of, a question frequently is posed in respect to identification of unit cost. For example, assume three purchases of stock in XY Corporation as follows: purchase No. 1, 200 shares @ $80; purchase No. 2, 300 shares @ $100; and purchase No. 3, 100 shares @ $110. Now assume 100 shares are sold at $120; what is cost? For accounting purposes, *specific identification* of the particular shares sold is preferable; however, in cases where such identification is not feasible, *Fifo* or *average cost* flow may be assumed; the former appears to be more generally used. The Internal Revenue Service requires specific identification for tax purposes, and when it cannot be applied *Fifo* must be used.

INVESTMENT REVENUE ON SHORT-TERM INVESTMENTS

Investment revenue from *capital stock* of other companies held as a short-term investment is recorded upon notification of the declaration of a cash dividend. Stock dividends received on such stock do not represent revenue, rather they serve to reduce the cost per share of the investment. Cash dividends on capital stock (common or preferred) held as an investment are not accrued prior to declaration.

Bonds purchased at a price above par are acquired at a premium; and if acquired below par, at a discount. In the case of short-term investments in bonds, the investment account is debited at cost and no premium or discount accounts are used. Any premium or discount on a bond held as a short-term investment is not amortized because, by definition, the investment will be converted to cash in the near future and the disposal date and price are unknown. This is in contrast to the accounting for bonds held as a long-term investment where amortization of premium and discount is required (see Chapter 19). Interest receivable on short-term investments in bonds is accrued at the end of the accounting period by means of an adjusting entry.

PART C—RECEIVABLES

This section focuses on the classification, measurement, and accounting for receivables. Broadly speaking, the term *receivables* encompasses the entity's claims for money, goods, and services from other entities. For the most part, receivables consist of amounts due from customers and clients arising from normal operations; however, a variety of other receivables are encountered from time to time. The following aspects of receivables are discussed:

1. Trade receivables:
   a. Accounts receivable.
   b. Notes receivable.

2. Special receivables:
   a. Deposits.
   b. Claims against various parties.
   c. Advances to employees, officers, and stockholders.
3. Collection expectations:
   a. Current.
   b. Noncurrent.
4. Receivables used for borrowing:
   a. Accounts receivable assignment, factoring, sale, and pledging.
   b. Notes receivable discounting.

TRADE RECEIVABLES

Trade receivables usually mark the first point in the sequence of merchandising and service transactions. The amounts *billed* as receivables are established by exchange credit transactions and usually are billed at the gross amount that can be realized in cash. The two principal classes of trade receivables are accounts receivable and notes receivable.

ACCOUNTS RECEIVABLE

The term *accounts receivable* is commonly used to designate trade debtors' accounts. Other receivables are separately designated and recorded as special receivables. Considerable objection may be raised against the unqualified title "Accounts receivable." Strictly speaking, any claim for which no written statement of the obligation (such as a note) has been received by the creditor is an account receivable. The careless use of a title so broadly inclusive is not sufficiently descriptive to convey the true nature of the various assets included. It is preferable to employ more descriptive titles for the various classes of accounts receivable, such as "Accounts receivable – trade debtors" for accounts due for regular sales to customers. Such usage facilitates classification and interpretation of these assets on the balance sheet. Ordinarily accounts receivable are classified under the "Current asset" caption on the balance sheet, yet there are some special accounts receivable which should not be classified as current.

Measurement of Bad Debt Expense and Accounts Receivable. Valuation of accounts receivable poses the problem of estimating the amount which will be actually realized from the accounts through collection.[7] When credit is extended on a continuing basis, there are some inevitable losses due to uncollectibility. These losses are considered to be a normal expense of business. In accordance with the matching principle, this expense must be matched with the revenue of the period in which the

---

[7] Receivables arising from sales and services should be recorded at net of any trade discounts; see Chapter 8 for a complete discussion of accounting for cash discounts on receivables.

sales and service transactions occurred, rather than in later periods when the specific accounts receivable are found to be uncollectible. However, since these bad accounts cannot be known until future periods the expense must be estimated in advance, recorded in the accounts, and reported on the current financial statements.

The Accounts Receivable account reflects the amount collectible and a special valuation, or contra asset account, Allowance for Doubtful Accounts (or Allowance for Bad Debts), is used to record the estimates.

There are two common approaches used to estimate the loss due to uncollectible accounts; each approach has two adaptations as follows:

1. Estimating bad debt expense:
   a. On the basis of past experience the average percentage or ratio relationship for the company between actual losses from bad debts and *net credit sales* is ascertained. This percentage, adjusted for anticipated conditions, is then applied to the actual net credit sales of the period to determine both the current expense and concurrent addition to the allowance for doubtful accounts.
   b. Use the same procedure as in *(a)* except the percentage of bad debts to cash plus credit sales is used.
2. Estimating the net value of present receivables:
   a. Determine from past experience the average ratio or percentage of the amount uncollectible in accounts receivable to the total amount of outstanding accounts receivable. This percentage, adjusted for expected conditions, is then applied each period to the balance in accounts receivable. The balance in the allowance account is then adjusted so that its balance equals the total of the estimated uncollectible accounts.
   b. Age the accounts receivable and from the resulting analysis and other available information estimate the total uncollectible accounts. The balance in the allowance account is then adjusted so that its balance equals the total of the estimated uncollectible accounts.

The use of any of these approaches to estimate bad debts must take cognizance of changes in credit policy, changes in economic conditions, and any other external factors which might have a bearing upon the ability of customers to pay their debts. After a method is selected, it should be subjected to a more or less continuous review on the part of the accountant and the officers of the company so that rates may be revised or the approach changed to secure reliable results.

Accounting for Bad Debt Expense. The two methods of measuring bad debt expense outlined above affect the way in which the amount is determined for the adjusting entry to record estimated bad debt expense at the end of the period. In the first approach, estimation of bad debt expense, the amount estimated is recorded. In contrast, in the second approach, the allowance account is adjusted to the estimated balance needed.

To illustrate accounting for bad debt expense and uncollectible receivables, assume the following data for X Company:

Beginning balances:	
Accounts receivable (debit)	$100,000
Allowance for doubtful accounts (credit)	2,000
Transactions during the period:	
Credit sales	500,000
Cash sales	700,000
Collections on accounts receivable	420,000
Accounts written off as uncollectible	2,500

The indicated entries relating to bad debts are:

a. To write off the bad accounts:

Allowance for doubtful accounts	2,500	
Accounts receivable (specific accounts)		2,500

The write-off of uncollectible accounts as bad normally would occur during the period and would precede the end-of-the-period adjusting entries. In some cases, as in this one, the allowance account has a temporary debit balance of $500.

The two different approaches for estimating the amount for the adjusting entry for bad debt expense are as follows:

b. Adjustment of the allowance by estimating bad debt expense (Method 1 above): Assume past experience has indicated that 1% of credit sales normally will not be collected and that this pattern is expected to continue.

Bad debt expense ($500,000 × 1%)	5,000	
Allowance for doubtful accounts		5,000

After posting this entry the allowance account will reflect a credit balance of $4,500.

c. Adjustment of allowance by estimating the net value of present receivables (Method 2 above): Assume it is estimated that 1.1% of the balance of accounts receivable eventually will be uncollectible.

Bad debt expense	2,453	
Allowance for doubtful accounts		2,453

Computation:
To adjust to the desired credit balance as follows:

Desired balance (1.1% of $177,500)	$1,953
Debit balance in allowance before adjustment	500
Amount of Credit Needed	$2,453

A debit balance in the allowance account, should it occur after the adjusting entry, means that inadequate provision has been made in the past. If it is determined that the estimates have been too high or too low, the current and future rates should be adjusted accordingly. This would be a *change in estimate* as prescribed in "Accounting Changes," *APB Opinion No. 20* (see Chapters 2 and 20).

Evaluation of Methods

Both methods of estimating bad debts are acceptable under generally accepted accounting principles. Each method has certain strengths and weaknesses. The first method discussed, *estimation of bad debt expense,* is generally preferable because it focuses on the matching principle by measuring current bad debt expense in relationship to the revenues of the current period that caused the bad accounts. Thus, it focuses on matching current expense with current revenue and emphasizes the income statement rather than the balance sheet. In respect to the use of credit sales or total sales, clearly the former is preferable because cash sales cannot cause credit losses.

The second method discussed, *estimation of net value of present receivables,* focuses on the balance sheet because it is essentially an evaluation of the net realizable value of all accounts receivable reflected in the accounts at the end of the current period. It only incidentally measures bad debt expense. It suffers from the probability that the bad debt expense reported on the income statement for the period may not be particularly related to the credit sales of the current period, thus violating the matching principle. It favors the balance sheet over the income statement. In applying this method, aging the accounts receivable (discussed below) at the end of each period is preferable to the use of a simple estimate as illustrated above.

Aging Accounts Receivable. Aging accounts receivables involves an analysis of each individual account to determine the amounts not yet due, moderately past due, and considerably past due. Classification of amounts by age (i.e., length of time uncollected) is deemed important because experience shows that the older an account the higher the probability of uncollectibility. Aging requires the preparation of an *aging schedule* similar to the illustration in Exhibit 7–3. In the absence

EXHIBIT 7–3

Aging Schedule for Accounts Receivable (at December 31, 19XX)

			Past Due		
Customer	*Receivable Balance Dec. 31, 19XX*	*Not Past Due*	*1–30 Days*	*31–60 Days*	*Over 60 Days*
Davis	$ 500	$ 400	$ 100		
Evans	900	900			
Field	1,650		1,350	$ 300	
Harris	90			30	$ 60
King	800	700	60	40	
Zilch	250	250			
Total	$32,500	$26,000	$4,200	$2,000	$300

of specific identification of collections, as related to several charges to an account, *Fifo* order is used in the aging schedule.

Upon completion of the aging schedule each past-due amount should be reviewed by credit department personnel to determine its probable collectibility. Sometimes such a procedure is prohibitively time consuming; therefore, the general approach used is to develop estimated loss percentages for each *age category* based on previous loss experience of the company. This approach to the aging schedule is shown in Exhibit 7–4.

EXHIBIT 7–4
Estimating Allowance for Doubtful Accounts, Aging Approach (at December 31, 19XX)

Status	*Total Balances*	*Loss Experience Percentage*	*Estimated Amount to Be Lost*
Not due	$26,000	1%	$ 260
1–30 days past due	4,200	8	336
31–60 days past due	2,000	25	500
Over 60 days past due	300	50	150
	$32,500		$1,246

At December 31, 19XX, the allowance for doubtful accounts would be adjusted to a credit balance of $1,246.

Bad Debts Collected. When an amount is collected from a customer whose account was previously written off as uncollectible, the customer's account should be recharged with that amount (or with the entire balance previously written off if it now appears collectible) and the allowance account should be credited for the same amount. This entry will cause the debtor's account to reflect a detailed record of the credit and related collections. Such information may be useful in future dealings with the customer.

Customers' Credit Balances. When individual customers' accounts have credit balances (from prepayments or overpayments), the amount may be deducted from the debit balances of the customers' accounts if immaterial in amount. If they are material in amount, separate disclosure as liabilities is preferable; "Credit balance of customers' accounts" is a suitable title.

Notes Receivable

Notes receivable may consist of trade notes receivable, which arise from regular operations, and special notes receivable. Trade notes receivable are by far the most common. When material amounts are involved, trade notes and special notes should be accounted for and reported separately.

Notes receivable are unconditional written promises to pay the payee or holder of the note (i.e., a holder in due course) a specified sum. The payee ordinarily would be in possession of the note unless it has been endorsed to a subsequent holder in due course. Not all notes are negotiable (i.e., transferable by endorsement); hence separate classification of negotiable and nonnegotiable notes is required. Requisites for negotiability are a matter of law.

Notes may be designated as *(a)* interest-bearing or *(b)* noninterest-bearing; theoretically, however, all commercial notes are interest bearing. Interest-bearing notes require payment of the *face* amount of the note at maturity plus interest. In contrast, a noninterest-bearing note includes the interest in the face amount. Thus the present value of an interest-bearing note is the same as its maturity amount (i.e., its face value). In contrast, the present value of a noninterest-bearing note is less than its maturity amount.

Conceptually, a note receivable is recorded in the accounts and reported at its current present value (refer to Chapter 6). An interest-bearing note that specifies the going rate of interest will always have a current present value that is the same as its face amount.[8] However, when a note is noninterest-bearing or when the specified interest rate on an interest-bearing note is different from the going rate, the current present value and the maturity amounts will be different. In these two situations the current present value should be computed and reported as discussed and illustrated in Chapter 11 in respect to notes payable.

For purposes of this chapter a note receivable under two different assumptions (Case A, interest-bearing; and Case B, noninterest-bearing) will be illustrated.

Assume K Company sold merchandise for $2,000 on July 1, 19A, on credit and received a note receivable due in one year. The going rate of interest is 8%, and the accounting period ends on December 31. Assume two different situations, viz:

Case A – Interest-bearing note, face amount $2,000. Payable at maturity, face amount plus interest at 8%, $160; total, $2,160.

Case B – Noninterest-bearing note, face amount, $2,160, which includes 8% interest on the net amount of the sales price (rather than on the face amount of the note). The amount of the sale can be verified as: $2,160 ÷ 1.08 = $2,000.[9]

The entries for each separate case are:

---

[8] This can be demonstrated readily by using the appropriate table values given in Chapter 6 to discount from maturity to the present *(a)* the maturity amount, and *(b)* the interest payments required. These two discounted amounts when summed will always equal the face amount of the interest-bearing note.

[9] See Chapter 11, Liabilities, for discussion of the situation where the interest rate is applied to the face amount of the note.

	Case A Interest-Bearing Note		*Case B Noninterest-Bearing Note*	
July 1, 19A—to record note and sale:				
Notes receivable	2,000		2,160	
Unearned discount on notes receivable*				160
Sales revenue		2,000		2,000
December 31, 19A—adjusting entry at end of accounting period:				
Interest receivable ($2,000 × 8% × 6/12)	80			
Unearned discount on notes receivable			80	
Interest revenue		80		80
June 30, 19B—collection of note (assuming no reversing entry on January 1, 19B):				
Cash	2,160		2,160	
Unearned discount on notes receivable			80	
Interest receivable		80		
Interest revenue		80		80
Notes receivable		2,000		2,160

* Alternative title, unearned interest revenue.

On the December 31, 19A balance sheet, the balance in "Unearned discount on notes receivable" should be deducted from "Notes receivable" to reflect the then present value of the note.[10]

Though not all of the documents reported under the caption "notes receivable" technically are notes, the distinctions between them are seldom deemed vital enough to warrant the use of separate accounts for each type. For example, bills of exchange and trade acceptances usually are included in notes receivable. Drafts, trade acceptances, and other bills of exchange are written orders drawn by one party on a second party to pay a third party an amount of money under specified conditions.

The Notes Receivable account should include only commercial paper with trade debtors which is related to the operating cycle and not past due. All other notes, including those between the entity and its officers, employees, or stockholders, should be reported separately. Notes of affiliated companies also should be shown separately.

Balance sheet classification of notes receivable may be either current or noncurrent depending upon collection expectations.

Provision for Losses on Notes. Provision for uncollectible notes

[10] Alternatively, the noninterest-bearing note could have been recorded net of the discount (i.e., at $2,000) and the discount amortization entered in the note account so that the balance would be $2,160 at maturity date. The results are precisely the same.

from trade customers normally should be included in the provision credited to Allowance for Doubtful Accounts.

Discounting of Notes Receivable. If a note receivable is endorsed to another payee before maturity, the original payee receives money (through the discounting) before maturity, but may become *contingently liable* for payment of the note. This is generally called discounting a note receivable, and the contingent liability depends on whether or not the note was endorsed with or without recourse. Since the bank or other endorsee normally is unwilling to accept the note without recourse, most notes give rise to a contingent liability when discounted.

The interest cost of discounting a note receivable is computed as follows:

$$\frac{\text{Interest Cost}}{\text{(or discount)}} = \frac{\text{Maturity Value}}{\text{of the Note}} \times \frac{\text{Discount}}{\text{Rate}} \times \frac{\text{Time to Be Held}}{\text{by the New Payee}}$$

To illustrate, assume Company X has a 90-day, 10% interest-bearing note receivable, face amount, $3,000. It is discounted at the bank at 9% after being held 30 days from issue date. The proceeds and interest cost would be calculated as follows:

Maturity amount:		
Face amount	$3,000	
Interest to maturity ($3,000 × 10% × 3/12)	75	$3,075.00
Interest cost (discount):		
$3,075 × 9% × 2/12		46.13
Proceeds (Cash Received) upon Discounting		$3,028.87

Company X, the endorser, would record the discounting transaction in either of the following ways:

	Interest Expense and Revenue Recognized Separately		*Interest Expense and Revenue Recognized at Net*	
Cash	3,028.87		3,028.87	
Interest expense	46.13			
Notes receivable		3,000.00		3,000.00
Interest revenue		75.00		28.87

The first entry is preferable theoretically because it separately recognizes the expense and revenue elements. Also some accountants prefer to credit Notes Receivable Discounted for the face amount of the note; this account would be a contra account to Notes Receivable. It is one method of recording the contingent liability (also see Chapter 11).[11]

---

[11] A less conventional, though theoretically defensible, recording of the transaction would be:

Cash	3,028.87	
Interest revenue (for 1 month)		25.00
Gain on discount of notes		3.87
Notes receivable		3,000.00

Often the refinements in recording discounted notes involve amounts (such as the $3.87) that are not material.

Disclosure of the Contingent Liability on Discounted Notes. Reporting contingencies, as specified in FASB *Statement No. 6*, is discussed and illustrated in Chapter 11. When a note receivable is discounted, the transfer by endorsement creates a contingent liability for the endorser, as defined in FASB *Statement No. 6*. Such a contingent liability usually is disclosed by a note to the financial statements such as the following: "The company is contingently liable for notes receivable discounted amounting to $3,000 should the maker default on due date. There is no reason to expect default at that date." Other methods sometimes used are:

1. Current Assets:

Notes receivable (contingent liability for notes discounted, $3,000)		$7,000

2. Current Assets:

Notes receivable	$10,000	
Less: Notes receivable discounted	3,000	7,000

Dishonored Notes Receivable. When a note receivable is not paid or renewed at maturity it is said to be dishonored. The accounting procedure for a dishonored note depends on whether or not the note has been discounted. If a dishonored note has been discounted, ordinarily it will be necessary for the original payee to pay it (unless he or she endorsed it without recourse).

To illustrate, assume the $3,000 interest-bearing note discounted by Company X was defaulted by the maker. Company X paid the bank the face amount of the note plus interest and a protest fee of $15. Company X would record the default as follows:

Special receivable—dishonored note	3,090	
Cash		3,090

On the other hand, if this same note had not been discounted, upon dishonor the required entry by Company X would have been:

Special receivable—dishonored note	3,075	
Notes receivable		3,000
Interest revenue		75
To charge dishonored note to account of maker together with accrued interest to maturity date.		

After dishonor, interest accrues on the maturity amount plus accrued interest and any protest fees at the *legal* rate of interest. However, if the note is uncollectible, the total claim should be written off as a bad debt.

Balance sheet presentation of dishonored notes would list a special receivable with adequate provision for the uncollectibility expectations. Footnote disclosure would be necessary for large notes in default.

SPECIAL RECEIVABLES

Receivables, other than trade receivables, generally are classified as special receivables. They may be represented by open accounts or notes and may be current or noncurrent. Some of the usual types of special receivables are:

1. Deposits made to other parties to cover potential damages, and deposits as a guarantee of performance of a contract or payment of an expense.
2. Prepayments to others on contingent purchases and expense contracts.
3. Claims against creditors for damaged or lost or returned goods.
4. Claims against common carriers for lost or damaged goods.
5. Claims against the government for rebates.
6. Claims against officers and employees.
7. Claims against customers for return of containers (no deposit).
8. Advances to subsidiaries.
9. Advances to officers and employees.
10. Dividends receivable (declared but not yet paid by the issuing corporation).
11. Unexpended balances of working funds in the hands of agents.
12. Claims against insurance companies for losses sustained.
13. Claims in litigation.
14. Unpaid calls on stock subscriptions (subscriptions receivable).

Special receivables that are related to the operating cycle or are collectible within one year should be appropriately designated and reported in the current asset section of the balance sheet. Other special receivables normally are reported on the balance sheet under a noncurrent caption such as "Other assets." Thus, receivables from officers, employees, or affiliates, whether arising from cash advances or from sales, would be classed as noncurrent if not collectible on a current basis.

Special receivables should be evaluated independently, and a special allowance for doubtful accounts for this class of receivables should be established when warranted by the prevailing circumstances.

USE OF RECEIVABLES TO SECURE IMMEDIATE CASH

Companies frequently utilize receivables to secure immediate cash prior to the regular collection date. The common methods of obtaining immediate cash on receivables are: (1) discounting of notes receivable (discussed above), (2) assignment of accounts receivable, (3) factoring of accounts receivable, (4) outright sale of accounts receivable, and (5) pledging accounts receivable. While detailed contractual arrangements vary, the following brief description generally typifies these transactions and their accounting.[12]

---

[12] Some of the following added details may be of interest. Accounts financed are commonly owed by other businesses rather than consumers. The volume and popularity of this kind of financing have increased markedly, especially since World War II. Contrary to popular belief, many very solvent businesses with excellent credit ratings use accounts receivable financing.

Assignment

Accounts receivable financing frequently involves the assignment to a financing institution of receivables arising on open-account sales. Frequently, these assignments are made on a "with recourse, nonnotification" basis. "With recourse" means that accounts becoming excessively delinquent or uncollectible must be repurchased by the seller or replaced with other accounts receivable of equivalent value. "Nonnotification" means debtors are not informed of the assignment, and hence remit to the seller in the usual way. As the seller collects on the invoices that have been assigned, the cash is transmitted to the finance company.

The cash advanced may range from 70% to 95% of the amount in the accounts. Annual interest rates charged may range as high as 18% to 20% where risks are greater and the low dollar volume per account causes high costs.

Assignment of receivables with recourse is akin to the discounting of notes receivable, and the accounting procedure is essentially parallel. An illustrative problem is presented to demonstrate the essential accounting for the assignment of accounts receivable.

Illustrative Problem. W Company assigned $40,000 of its receivables to Z Finance Company under a contract, including a promissory note, whereby the latter agreed to advance 85% of their amount.

Debtors remit directly to W since the assignment was "with recourse, nonnotification." The series of transactions and related entries are shown in Exhibit 7–5.

EXHIBIT 7–5
Assignment of Accounts Receivable

Transaction	*Entries on W's Books*		
Jan. 2: Assigned $40,000 accounts receivable; advance received 85%; gave note payable.	Accounts receivable assigned	40,000	
	Accounts receivable		40,000
	Cash ($40,000 × 85%)	34,000	
	Notes payable (Z Finance Co.)		34,000
Jan: Collected $30,000 of assigned accounts less cash discounts $300. Sales returns $500.	Cash	29,700	
	Sales discounts	300	
	Sales returns	500	
	Accounts receivable assigned		30,500
Jan. 31: Remitted collections to finance company plus $350 interest.	Financing expense	350	
	Notes payable (Z Finance Co.)	29,700	
	Cash		30,050
Feb: Collected balance of assigned accounts except $200 written off as uncollectible.	Cash	9,300	
	Allowance for doubtful accounts	200	
	Accounts receivable assigned		9,500
Feb. 28: Remitted balance due to finance company plus $100 interest.	Financing expense	100	
	Notes payable (Z Finance Co.)	4,300	
	Cash		4,400

On January 31, the balance sheet would reflect the following:

Current Assets:		
Accounts receivable		$150,000
Accounts receivable assigned............................	$9,500	
Less: Note payable on assigned accounts	4,300	
Equity in accounts receivable assigned		5,200
Total Accounts Receivable			$155,200

Obviously, the details of a contract, such as the one illustrated above, will determine the appropriate accounting entries.

Factoring

Accounts receivable may be sold on a *without recourse* basis to factors.[13] Customers whose accounts are sold are notified to pay directly to the factor who assumes the functions of billing, collecting, and so on.

Under a factoring contract, the factor controls the granting of credit for the client. As the latter sells to customers, copies of the sales invoices and supporting documents are sent to the factor. The client usually obtains cash immediately upon transferring the invoices. Gross amounts of the invoices less any discounts and allowances and less the factor's commission and a margin or reserve (factor's margin or reserve) to cover expected returns and claims is the measure of cash available. Interest (above the factor's commission) is charged only on cash drawn *prior* to the average due date of the factored invoices. Available money not drawn plus the amount reserved becomes available without interest cost on the average due date.

In addition to interest, factors charge commissions to compensate for their credit and collection services and the credit losses they must bear. Since cash needs are often seasonal, proportions of available cash drawn probably will vary throughout the term of the factoring contract.

Outright Sale of Accounts Receivable

Occasionally accounts receivable are sold outright to a third party, usually without recourse. Outright sale involves a prohibitively high discount rate, varying from 15% to 50%, depending upon the circumstances. Outright sale occurs most frequently when a business is in serious financial difficulty. No unique accounting problems are involved; Cash is debited, the receivables sold and the related amount of the allowance for doubtful accounts are closed out, and the difference is recorded as the finance charge.

Pledging

Loans are sometimes obtained from banks and other lenders by pledging accounts receivable as security. The borrower continues to collect

[13] Factors are financing organizations which buy trade receivables. Factoring is encountered in many lines of industry but is especially widespread in the textile industry.

the receivables and usually is required to apply collections to reduction of the loan. This method of lending on receivables is sometimes used because commercial banks may lack express or implied power to purchase accounts receivable. Disclosure of the fact that portions of the accounts receivable balance have been pledged should be accomplished by balance sheet footnotes or appropriate parenthetical notations. The accounting by the borrower is essentially the same as that illustrated above for assignment.

QUESTIONS

1. Define cash in the accounting sense.
2. In what circumstances, if any, is it permissible to offset a bank overdraft against a positive balance in another bank account?
3. If you were called upon to establish a petty cash system that would be particularly effective from the standpoint of internal control, what important features would you incorporate in it?
4. Where (if at all) do items *(a)* through *(g)* belong in the following reconciliation?

Balance per bank statement, June 30	$x,xxx.xx
Plus	________
Minus	________
June 30 True Balance	$9,600.00
Balance per our ledger, June 30	$x,xxx.xx
Plus	________
Minus	________
June 30 True Balance	$9,600.00

a. Note collected by bank for depositor on June 29; notification was received July 2 when the June 30 bank statement was delivered by the mail carrier.
b. Checks drawn in June which had not cleared bank by June 30.
c. Chock of a depositor with a similar name which was returned with checks accompanying June 30 bank statement and which was charged to our account.
d. Bank service charge for which notification was received upon receipt of bank statement.
e. Deposit mailed June 30 which reached bank July 1.
f. Notification of charge for imprinting our name on blank checks was received with the June 30 bank statement.
g. Upon refooting cash receipts book, we discovered that one receipt was omitted in arriving at the total which was posted to the Cash account in the ledger.

5. Briefly describe a "comprehensive" bank reconciliation.
6. What criteria must a security meet to qualify as a short-term investment?
7. What is properly included in the cost of short-term investments?

8. In what ways, if any, does the accounting for investments in bonds differ if the securities are held as long-term investments instead of as short-term investments?
9. An investor bought 100 shares of PQ Company stock in January for $6,700 and another 100 in March for $7,000. In October, the investor sold 150 shares at 77. What is the amount of the gain or loss? Discuss briefly.
10. The account, Allowance to Reduce Short-Term Investments in Equity Securities to Market, may properly be debited or credited. Under what circumstances would this account be credited? Debited?
11. Briefly describe the basic approaches to estimating allowance for doubtful accounts in connection with trade receivables. Evaluate each approach.
12. It sometimes happens that a receivable which has been written off as uncollectible is subsequently collected. Describe the accounting procedures in such an event.
13. How should customer accounts that have credit balances be reported in the financial statements?
14. T Company received a $1,000 note from a customer which bore interest at 8% and matured in three months. After holding it one month, the note was discounted by T at the bank at 9%. Compute T's proceeds.
15. How should special receivables be reported on the balance sheet?
16. Aside from discounting notes receivable, by what other means can receivables be used to secure immediate cash?

EXERCISES

PART A: EXERCISES 1–7

Exercise 7–1

The following items are on hand at the end of the period:

	Exclude from Cash Balance		
	Yes	*No*	*Explanation*
a. Postdated checks.	____	____	____________
b. Time deposits.	____	____	____________
c. Money advanced to officers.	____	____	____________
d. Postage stamps in cash drawer.	____	____	____________
e. Sight draft left with bank for collection.	____	____	____________
f. Deposit in foreign bank.	____	____	____________
g. Money orders.	____	____	____________
h. Cashiers' checks.	____	____	____________
i. Note receivable left with bank for collection.	____	____	____________
j. Time draft left with bank for collection.	____	____	____________
k. Check returned by bank, insufficient funds.	____	____	____________

Required:

1. Complete the above tabulation to indicate what items should be excluded from the cash balance.
2. Provide an explanation of the basis for exclusion.

Exercise 7–2

Indicate the amount (and how derived) which could be prcperly reported as Cash for each of the following independent cases:

a. Balance in general checking account, Bank H, $5,000; overdraft in special checking account, Bank H, $800; check held from company president for $400 received six weeks ago in settlement of advance to the president.
b. Balance in Bank P, $20,000; refundable deposit with state treasurer to guarantee performance of highway contract in progress, $10,000; balance in Banco de Sur America, $2,000 (foreign and restricted).
c. Cash on hand, $500; cash in Bank C, $9,000; cash held by salespersons as advances on expense accounts, $800; postage stamps on hand received from mail-order customers, $50.
d. Balance in checking account, $10,000; demand certificates of deposits, $5,000; deposit with bond sinking fund trustee, $15,000; cash on hand, $1,000.
e. Negotiable instruments in cash drawer on December 31:

From	*Date of Check*	*Other Data*	
Customer W	Dec. 29	On past-due account.	$500
Customer X	Dec. 30	In payment of $1,000 invoice of December 23.	700
Customer Y	Dec. 24	Previously deposited and returned; insufficient funds.	300
Customer Z	Jan. 2 (next year)	In full payment of account.	400
J. T. Brown	Dec. 29	American Express traveler check.	100

Exercise 7–3

As a part of their newly designed internal control system, the Mark Corporation established a petty cash fund. Operations for the first month were:

a. Wrote a check for $500 on August 1 and turned the cash over to the custodian.
b. Summary of the petty cash expenditures:

	Aug. 1–15	*Aug. 16–31*
Postage	$ 48	$ 46
Supplies used	230	220
Delivery expense	90	150
Miscellaneous expenses	20	30
Total	$388	$446

c. Fund replenished on August 16.
d. Fund replenished on August 31 and increased by $100.

Required:

Give all entries indicated through August.

Exercise 7–4

Foster Company, as a matter of policy, deposits all receipts and makes all payments by check. The following data were taken from the cash records:

Reconciliation at May 31

Balance per bank	$7,000
Add: Outstanding deposits	1,200
	8,200
Deduct: Outstanding checks	1,500
Balance per Books	$6,700

June Results

	Per Bank	*Per Books*
Balance, June 30	$ 4,090	$ 5,100
June deposits	10,600	12,300
June checks	14,500	13,900
June note collected	1,000	–
June bank charges	10	–

Required (for June):

1. Compute the unrecorded deposits and outstanding checks.
2. Reconcile the bank account.
3. Give any correcting entries indicated.

Exercise 7–5

Reconciliation of Darden Company's bank account at May 31 was as follows:

Balance per bank statement	$14,000
Deposits outstanding	800
Checks outstanding	150*
	$14,650
Balance per books	$14,664
Unrecorded service charge	14*
	$14,650

* Denotes deduction.

June data are as follows:

	Bank	*Books*
Checks recorded	$11,500	$11,800
Deposits recorded	10,100	11,000
Service charges recorded	12	14
Collection by bank ($800 note plus interest)	820	–
NSF check returned with June 30 statement (will be redeposited; assumed to be good)	50	–
Balances June 30	13,358	13,850

Required:

1. Compute unrecorded deposits and outstanding checks at June 30.
2. Prepare a reconciliation for June.
3. Prepare entries needed at June 30.

Exercise 7–6

Kay Company's cash transactions were made through its accounts at First National Bank. On April 30 the company reconciled its bank and book balances as follows:

Balance per bank statement		$7,900
Deduct outstanding checks:		
No. 698	$ 30	
No. 699	80	
No. 702	25	135
		7,765
Add:		
Outstanding deposit	150	
April service charge	3	
May Company check charged to our account	40	193
April 30 Book Balance		$7,958

In summary form, the Cash account on Kay Company's books for May is as below:

Cash

April 30, balance	7,958	April service charge	3
May collections	14,210	Checks drawn	13,812

At May 31 the following checks were outstanding: No. 702, $25; No. 735, $100; No. 738, $60; and No. 740, $20. The May 31 receipts amounting to $420 were mailed to the bank at the close of business that day. The May service charge of $5 was recorded by the bank only. The $40 item shown on the April 30 reconciliation was corrected by the bank during May. Assuming no errors by either the bank or Kay Company, the bank's records can be inferred on the basis of the foregoing.

Required:

Prepare a comprehensive reconciliation for May.

Exercise 7–7

Wilson Company deposits all its receipts in the bank and makes all disbursements by check. Its February 28 bank reconciliation was as follows:

Balance, per bank		$5,414
Add: Outstanding deposits	$170	
Unrecorded bank service charge	6	176
		5,590
Deduct: Outstanding checks		390
Balance per Books		$5,200

March data are as follows:

	Per Bank	Per Books
Balance, March 31	$6,024	$3,994
March deposits reflected	4,760	4,900
March checks reflected	6,170*	6,100
Note collected (including $20 interest)	2,020	–
Service charge recorded	–	6

* Includes a check drawn by Dilson Company for $150.

Required:

1. Determine apparent outstanding deposits and checks as of March 31.
2. Prepare a comprehensive reconciliation for March.
3. If March 31 were the end of Dilson's fiscal year, what entries would be needed on its books? Draft them.

PART B: EXERCISES 8–11

Exercise 7–8

At January 1, the short-term investments of Whitearch Company were:

Number Held	Description	Par Value Each	Total Cost
6	Bonds, Day Co., 5% per annum (paid each April 1 and October 1)*	$1,000	$5,850
100	Shares, Knight Company, common stock ...	50	8,300

* Assume accrued interest reversed January 1.

The transactions below relate to the above short-term investments and those bought and sold during the year. All transactions are cash.

Feb. 2	Received $150 dividend from Knight Company.
Mar. 1	Sold four (4) Day Company bonds for a total consideration (including accrued interest) of $4,100.
Apr. 1	Collected semiannual interest on Day Company bonds.
May 1	Bought three bonds of King, Ltd. These 4%, $1,000 bonds pay interest each March 1 and September 1. Total consideration paid, $3,050.
June 1	For $2,100 sold the remaining Day Company bonds.
Aug. 2	Received $150 dividend from Knight Company.
Sept. 1	Collected semiannual interest on King, Ltd. bonds.
Dec. 31	Adjust and close books; recognize all accruals. At January 1, market value of marketable securities exceeded cost. However, at December 31, market prices on a per security basis were:

	Market Price
Knight Company common shares	72¼
King, Ltd. bonds	102*

* Does not include accrued interest.

Required:

Journalize the foregoing transactions assuming lower-of-cost-or-market valuation on all short-term investments.

Exercise 7–9

Case A. At December 31, 19A, the portfolio of short-term investments of Margo Company were comprised of the following items:

Description	Quantity	Cost	Unit Market Prices
Hygro Corp. bonds, 7%, $1,000	5	$5,200	101½
Damon common stock	50 shares	2,300	40⅝
Martin common stock	100 shares	2,100	24

Assuming lower of cost or market is applied to all short-term investments:

a. At what value should the aggregate of short-term investments be reported on the December 31, 19A, balance sheet of Margo Company? Show computations.

b. One year later, the short-term investment portfolio of Margo consisted of–

Description	Quantity	Cost	Unit Market Prices
Damon common stock	20 shares	$ 920	37¼
Martin common stock	30 shares	630	23
Dries Corporation bonds, 8%, $1,000	4	4,040	100½

During 19B, Margo had sold the 30 Damon shares at a gain of $200 and the 70 Martin shares at a gain of $140. At what value should the aggregate of short-term investments be reported on the December 31, 19B, balance sheet of Margo Company assuming lower of cost or market for all securities? Show computations.

Case B. Davis Company bought, as a short-term investment, seven of the $1,000 bonds of Massengill Corporation on April 1, 19A, at 102 plus accrued interest. These 9% bonds pay interest semiannually each May 1 and November 1. On December 1, 19A, four (4) of the bonds were sold at 101¼ plus accrued interest. Davis Company adjusts and closes books on December 31.

a. Journalize all events relating to the bonds for 19A, assuming the cost method.

b. If the bonds had been bought as a long-term or permanent investment, what added information would have been needed and why?

Exercise 7–10

Prepare journal entries to record the following transactions relating to 8% bonds of Dial Corporation purchased as a short-term investment. These bonds pay interest each May 1 and November 1.

Aug. 1 Cash of $39,800 is disbursed for $40,000 par value bonds including interest.

Nov. 1 Collected interest.
Dec. 31 Adjust and close books for the year. The market value of the bonds is 98 excluding interest (assume LCM and use the cost method).
Jan. 1 Make any necessary reversing entries.
Feb. 1 Sold half of the bonds, receiving a check for $19,600, including accrued interest.
May 1 Collected interest.

Exercise 7–11

On January 20, 19A, K Corporation acquired the following short-term investments in marketable equity securities:

Company L—500 shares common stock (nopar) at $60 per share.
Company M—300 shares preferred stock (par $10, nonredeemable) at $20 per share.

Additional data:

December 31, 19A Market values: L stock, $52; M stock, $24.
March 2, 19B Received cash dividends per share as follows: L stock, $1.00; M stock, $.50.
October 1, 19B Sold 100 of the Company M shares at $26 per share.
December 31, 19B Market values: L stock, $56; M stock, $25.

Required:

1. Give all entries indicated for K Corporation for the above short-term investments in marketable equity securities.
2. Show how the investments and related gains and losses would be reflected on the financial statements for K Corporation for 19A and 19B.

PART C: EXERCISES 12–18

Exercise 7–12

When examining the accounts of Hampton Company, you ascertain that balances relating to both receivables and payables are included in a single controlling account (called Receivables) which has a $44,100 debit balance. An analysis of the details of this account revealed the following:

	Debits	*Credits*
Accounts receivable—customers	$75,000	
Accounts receivable—officers	4,000	
Debit balances—creditors	900	
Expense advances to salespersons	2,000	
Capital stock subscriptions receivable	9,200	
Accounts payable for merchandise		$38,500
Unpaid salaries		6,600
Credit balances in customer accounts		1,000
Payments received in advance for shipments not yet made		900

Required:

1. Give entry to reflect correct treatment of the above items and to clear the old receivables account.
2. How should the items be reported on Hampton Company's balance sheet?

Exercise 7–13

An analysis of the receivables control account (debit balance, $81,600) of Elba Corporation at December 31 revealed the following:

a. Accounts from regular sales (current)	$60,000
b. Accounts known to be uncollectible	2,000
c. Dishonored notes charged back to customers	8,000
d. Credit balances in customer accounts	400
e. Accounts of customers past due	6,000
f. Due from employees	6,000

The Allowance for Doubtful Accounts is adjusted each December 31. Its balance before adjustment on December 31 was a $1,600 debit. It was estimated that losses on receivables amounts at December would average as follows:

Item	*Loss %*
a	1
c	20
e	5

Required:

1. Give journal entries (*a*) to close the old receivables account, and (*b*) to reflect bad debt expense.
2. Indicate proper reporting on Elba Corporation's December 31 balance sheet. Assume all amounts to be material.

Exercise 7–14

The following data are available concerning a company whose fiscal year is the calendar year:

Sales (of which $100,000 are on credit)	$120,000
Accounts receivable, January 1	70,000
Accounts receivable, December 31	80,000
Allowance for doubtful accounts, January 1	2,000 (credit)
Allowance for doubtful accounts, December 31*	1,000 (debit)

* Before making year-end adjusting entry for bad debt expense.

Required:

1. Assuming there were no recoveries of doubtful accounts previously charged off, what was the amount of receivables charged off as uncollectible during the year?
2. What was the amount of cash inflow from receivables during the year?
3. Give the year-end adjusting entry for bad debts under each of the following independent assumptions:
   a. Bad debts estimated to be 4% of credit sales.
   b. Bad debts estimated to be 3% of total sales.
   c. Bad debts estimated to be 5% of uncollected receivables.
   d. Bad debts estimated on basis of aging; the estimate is:
      (1) On receivables less than 60 days old ($20,000), 1%.
      (2) On receivables 60 to 120 days old ($50,000), 3½%.
      (3) On remaining receivables, 6%.

Exercise 7–15

Prasit Company has been in business three years and is being audited for the first time. Concerning accounts receivable, the auditor ascertained that the company has been charging off receivables as they finally proved uncollectible and treated them as expenses at the time of write-off. (Put another way, receivables were valued at 100 cents on the dollar.)

It is determined that receivables losses have approximated (and can be expected to approximate) 1½% of net sales. Down to the time of the audit, the company's sales and receivable write-off experience were as below:

Year of Sales	Amount of Sales	Accounts Written Off in—		
		19A	*19B*	*19C*
19A	$ 800,000	$2,000	$7,500	$1,000
19B	700,000	—	3,000	6,500
19C	1,000,000	—	—	3,500

Required:

1. Indicate the amount by which net income was understated or overstated (ignoring income tax effects) each year under the company's policy. Assume for purpose of this requirement that the old policy is to be in effect for 19C.
2. If Prasit Company were to switch over to a more acceptable basis of accounting for bad debts, assuming books were still open for 19C, what entry should be made at year-end, 19C?

Exercise 7–16

Eugenia Company accepted an interest-bearing note receivable for $3,000 from a customer whose account receivable had become due. In respect to the note, give the indicated journal entry for each of the following events; show computations. (Use months, not days.)

1. Received the note which matures in four months and bears interest at 8%.
2. Discounted the above note after two months at 9% interest. Make the entry under the two methods of recording.
3. The customer paid the note at maturity.
4. The customer defaulted on the note, and Eugenia Company paid the holder including a $15 protest fee.

Exercise 7–17

On November 1, 19A, Philip Company received from two customers two notes for merchandise sold to them. Each note was in settlement for a sale of goods for $9,000. Customer A gave an 8%, three-month, interest-bearing note. Customer B gave a three-month, noninterest-bearing note with an implied interest rate of 8% (i.e., 8% interest on the sales price was included in the face of the note).

Required:

1. Give all entries pertaining to the two notes on Philip Company's books from

date of receipt through time of payment assuming the company adjusts and closes its books at December 31, 19A.

2. Show how the notes should be reflected on the December 31, 19A, balance sheet.

Exercise 7–18

A, Inc., assigned $50,000 of its receivables to Z Finance Company. The contract provided that Z would advance 80% of their gross value. A's debtors continued to remit directly to it with the checks being endorsed to Z immediately.

During the first month, customers owing $35,000 remitted $34,600 taking advantage of $400 cash discounts. Sales returns totaled $1,000. The finance charge paid after the first month was $300.

During the second month, remaining receivables were collected in full except for $200 written off as uncollectible. Final settlement was effected with the finance company, including payment of $100 added interest.

Required:

Give the journal entries needed to record the above assignment of accounts receivable. Closing entries are not necessary.

PROBLEMS

PART A: PROBLEMS 1–5

Problem 7–1

The cash records for Voss Company provided the following data for the month of March:

	March 1	March 31
Balances per bank statement	$15,600.09	$14,459.91
Balances per company books	14,375.00	13,409.00

Relevant items:

a. Outstanding checks March 31 (verified as correct)	$1,400
b. Deposits in transit March 31 (verified as correct)	800
c. Interest earned on bank balance (reported on bank statement)	18
d. NSF check (customer check returned with bank statement)	50
e. Service charge by bank (reported on bank statement)	7
f. Error in deposit for cash sales (deposit slip showed overage, corrected by bank)	10
g. Error by bank (check for $10.89 cleared at $10.98)	
h. Note collected by bank for us (including $30 interest)	1,030
i. Deduction for church (per signed bank deduction form)	20
j. Cash on hand	500

Required:

1. Prepare a bank reconciliation in good form showing correct balance for the balance sheet. *Hint:* Be alert for a cash overage or shortage.
2. Prepare necessary entries at March 31.

Problem 7–2

The records pertaining to cash for High Company provided the following data for May:

Bank statement:	
a. Balance, May 31	$34,500
b. Service charges for May	5
c. NSF check returned with May statement; customer gave this check, will redeposit next week, assumed to be good	50
d. Note receivable ($5,000) collected for High by the bank and added to balance	5,200
e. Error from previous month in interest collected on another note receivable; bank credited High account in May for the amount	100
Books:	
f. Balance, May 31	30,700
g. Cash on hand	400
h. Unrecorded deposit	3,700
i. Outstanding checks	2,665

Required:

1. Prepare a bank reconciliation in good form. Assume all amounts provided above are correct. *Hint:* Be alert for a cash overage or shortage.
2. Give required entries for May 31.

Problem 7–3

Tetzlaff Corporation began doing business with Fidelity Bank on October 1. On that date, the true cash balance was $4,000. All cash transactions are cleared through the bank account. Subsequent transactions during October and November relating to the Tetzlaff and Fidelity accounts are summarized below:

	Tetzlaff Company Books	*Fidelity Bank Books*
October deposits	$7,360	$7,110
October checks	6,290	6,130
October service charge	–	10
October 31 balance	5,070	4,970
November deposits (regular)	8,220	8,280
November checks	9,410	9,220
November service charge	–	15
Note collected by bank (includes $15 interest)		1,015
October service charge	10	–
November 30 balance	3,870	5,030

Required:

1. On the basis of the foregoing data, prepare a comprehensive bank reconciliation for November.
2. Assuming November 30 is the end of Tetzlaff's fiscal year, give entries that would be required by the bank reconciliation.

Problem 7–4

You are examining the records of a client where internal control is found to be weak. Part of your work includes reconciliation of cash for December 19A. You have determined that the client's reconciliation as of November 30, 19A, is correct. The following information is available to you:

Client's Reconciliation, November 30, 19A

Cash per general ledger	$2,631.74
Less: Cash on hand	210.89
	2,420.85
Less: Bank service charge for November	9.00
	2,411.85
Add: Outstanding checks	991.00
Balance per Bank	$3,402.85

Cash receipts are summarized weekly; the cash receipts books for December appears below:

Dec.	1	Balance from Nov. 30	$ 2,631.74
	8	Received on accounts	25,774.80
	15	Received on accounts	27,447.56
	22	Received on accounts	4,659.82
	29	Received on accounts	5,886.85
			$65,300.77

The cash payments record for December was as follows:

Dec.	1	November service charge	$ 9.00
	3	Checks	5,236.50
	5	Checks	3,645.21
	8	Checks	16,394.89
	10	Checks	15,873.42
	12	Checks	4,848.89
	19	Checks	3,622.83
	22	Checks	3,692.09
	31	Checks	7,657.70
Balance – December 31			4,311.24
			$65,300.77

Cash on hand December 31 amounted to $100. The transactions per the December bank statement, which are correctly recorded by the bank, show that deposits amounting to $62,870.92; checks paid amounted to $57,952.03; service charges for the month were $10; and a charge of $100 was made against the account because of the return unpaid of a customer's check. Neither the service charge nor the returned check were recorded on the client's books. The total of outstanding checks as of December 31 was found to be $4,110.50.

Required:

Prepare a comprehensive reconciliation for December together with a brief explanation of any items not self evident.

(AICPA adapted)

Problem 7–5

In connection with an audit of cash of Distributors, Inc., as at December 31, 19A, the following information has been obtained:

a. Balance per bank:

11/30/19A	$ 185,700
12/31/19A	193,674

b. Balance per books:

11/30/19A	154,826
12/31/19A	167,598

c. Receipts for the month of December, 19A:

Per bank	1,350,450
Per books	2,335,445

d. Outstanding checks:

11/30/19A	63,524
12/31/19A	75,046

e. Dishonored checks are recorded as a reduction of cash receipts. Dishonored checks which are later redeposited are then recorded as a regular cash receipt. Dishonored checks returned by the bank and recorded by Distributors, Inc., amounted to $6,250 during the month of December 19A; according to the books, $5,000 were redeposited. Dishonored checks recorded on the bank statement but not on the books until the following months amounted to $250 at November 30, 19A, and $2,300 at December 31, 19A.

f. On December 31, 19A, a $2,323 check of the ABC Company was charged to the Distributors, Inc., account by the bank in error.

g. Proceeds of a note of the Able Company collected by the bank on December 10, 19A, were not entered on the books:

Principal	$2,000
Interest	20
	2,020
Less: Collection charge	5
	$2,015

h. The company has hypothecated (assigned) its accounts receivable with the bank under an agreement whereby the bank lends the company 80% on the hypothecated accounts receivable. Accounting for and collection of the accounts are performed by the company, and adjustments of the loan are made from daily sales reports and daily deposits.

The bank credits the Distributors, Inc., account and increases the amount of the loan for 80% of the reported sales. The loan agreement states specifically that the sales report must be accepted by the bank before Distributors, Inc., is credited. Sales reports are forwarded by Distributors, Inc., to the bank on the first day following the date of sales.

The bank allocates each deposit 80% to the payment of the loan and 20% to the Distributors, Inc., account.

Thus, only 80% of each day's sales and 20% of each collection are entered on the bank statement.

The Distributors, Inc., accountant records the hypothecation of new accounts receivable (80% of sales) as a debit to Cash and a credit to the bank loan as of the date of sales. One hundred percent of the collections on accounts receivable is recorded as a cash receipt; 80% of the collections is recorded in the cash disbursements book as a payment on the loan.

In connection with the hypothecation, the following facts were determined:

1. Included in the deposits in transit is cash from the hypothecation of accounts receivable. Sales were $40,500 on November 30, 19A, and $42,250 on December 31, 19A. The balance of the deposit in transit at December 31, 19A, was made up from collections of $32,110 which were entered on the books in the manner indicated above.
2. Collections on accounts receivable deposited in December other than deposits in transit totaled $1,200,000.
3. Sales for December totaled $1,450,000.

i. Interest on the bank loan for the month of December, charged by the bank but not recorded on the books, amounted to $6,140.

Required:

1. Prepare bank reconciliations as of November 30, 19A, and December 31, 19A, and reconciliations of cash receipts and disbursements per bank with cash receipts and disbursements per books for the month of December 19A. (Assume that you have satisfied yourself as to the propriety of the above information.) Show computations where applicable.
2. Prepare adjusting journal entries as required to correct the Cash account at December 31, 19A.

(AICPA adapted)

PART B: PROBLEMS 6–9

Problem 7–6

On January 1, 19A Scott Company acquired the following short-term investments in marketable equity securities:

Company	*Stock*	*Number of Shares*	*Cost per Share*
T	Common (nopar)	1,000	$20
U	Common (par $10)	600	15
V	Preferred (par $20, nonredeemable)	400	30

Data subsequent to the acquisition is as follows:

December 31, 19A	Market values: T stock, $16; U stock, $15; V stock, $34.
February 10, 19B	Cash dividends received per share: T stock, $1.50; U stock, $1.00; V stock, $.50.
November 1, 19B	Sold the share of V stock at $38 per share.
December 31, 19B	Market values: T stock, $18; U stock, $17; V stock, $33.

Required:

1. Give all entries indicated for Scott Company for 19A and 19B.
2. Show how the income statement and balance sheet for Scott Company would reflect the short-term investments for 19A and 19B.

Problem 7–7

Walsh Manufacturing Company's short-term investment portfolio included the following at December 31, 19A:

	Cost
AB Company, nine 8% bonds (face, $9,000)	$9,300
BC Corporation common, 50 shares, nopar	1,800
CD Corporation, 4% preferred, 150 shares (par, $40)	8,000

Transactions relating to the securities during 19B were as follows:

Jan. 25 Received semiannual dividend check on CD shares.
Mar. 1 Collected semiannual interest on AB bonds.
Apr. 15 Sold 30 shares of BC Corporation stock for $1,020.
May 1 Sold six of the AB bonds for a total consideration (including accrued interest) of $6,350.
June 20 Purchased 50 shares of EF Corporation, common at 47 plus $30 brokerage fees.
July 25 Received semiannual dividend check on CD shares.
Sept. 1 Collected semiannual interest on AB bonds.
Oct. 1 Purchased a $1,000 9% bond of DE, Inc., for total consideration of $1,100. Interest payment dates on this bond are February 1 and August 1.
Nov. 17 Sold remaining BC Corporation shares for $700.
Dec. 2 Received $60 dividend check from EF Corporation.
Dec. 31 Preparatory to adjusting and closing the books for the year the following data as to current market values of securities held were obtained:

Security	*Market*
AB bonds (ex-interest)	103
CD preferred	54
DE, Inc., bond (ex-interest)	104
EF common	45

Required:

Journalize the foregoing transactions; adjust and close the books at December 31, 19B. Value the total portfolio of securities at market by means of an Allowance to Reduce Short-Term Investments to LCM account.

Hint: Do not overlook reversal of accrued interest adjustment on AB bonds on January 1, 19B.

Problem 7–8

The DEF Manufacturing Company has followed the practice of valuing their short-term investments in marketable securities at the lower of cost or market. At December 31, 19B, their account, Investment in Marketable Securities, had a balance of $40,000; and the account, Allowance to Reduce Investments from Cost to Market, had a balance of $2,000. Analysis disclosed that on December 31, 19A, the facts relating to the securities were as follows:

Security	*Cost*	*Market*	*Allowance Required*
X Company bonds	$20,000	$19,000	$1,000
Y Company bonds	10,000	9,000	1,000
Z Company bonds	20,000	20,300	0
	$50,000		$2,000

During 19B, the Y Company bonds were sold for $9,200; the difference between the $9,200 and the cost of $10,000 being charged to "Loss on Sale of Securities." The market price of the bonds on December 31, 19B, was X Company bonds, $19,200; Z Company bonds, $20,400.

Required:

1. What justification is there for the use of the lower of cost or market in valuing marketable securities?
2. Did the DEF Company properly apply this rule on December 31, 19A? Explain, including any alternative methods of application.
3. Are there any additional entries necessary for the DEF Company at December 31, 19B, to reflect the facts on the balance sheet and income statement in accordance with generally accepted accounting principles? Explain.

(AICPA adapted)

Problem 7–9

Check the best answer in each of the following and provide the basis (including computations where appropriate) to support your choice.

1. The June bank statement of Lucas Company showed a June 30 ending balance of $187,387. During June, the bank charged back NSF (i.e., insufficient funds) checks totaling $3,056, of which $1,856 had been redeposited by June 30. Deposits in transit on June 30 were $20,400. Outstanding checks on June 30 were $60,645, including a $10,000 check which the bank had certified on June 28. On June 14 the bank charged Lucas' account for a $2,300 item which should have been charged against the account of Luby Company; the bank did not detect the error. During June the bank collected foreign items for Lucas; the proceeds were $8,684, and bank charges for this service were $19. On June 30 the adjusted cash in bank of Lucas Company is:
   a. $149,442.
   b. $159,442.
   c. $147,142.
   d. $158,242.
   e. None of the above.
2. Which of the following items should never be included in the current sections of the balance sheet?
   a. Premium paid on short-term bond investment.
   b. Receivable from customer not collectible during coming year.
   c. Deferred income taxes resulting from interperiod income tax allocation.
   d. Funded serial bonds.
3. The test or marketability must be met before securities owned can be properly classified as—
   a. Debentures.
   b. Treasury stock.
   c. Long-term investments.
   d. Current assets.
4. How is the premium or discount on bonds purchased as a short-term investment generally reported in published financial statements?
   a. As an integral part of the cost of the asset acquired (investment) and amortized over a period of not less than 60 months.
   b. As an integral part of the cost of the asset acquired (investment) until such time as the investment is sold.
   c. As expense or revenue in the period the bonds are purchased.

d. As an integral part of the cost of the asset acquired (investment) and amortized over the period the bonds are expected to be held.

5. Postage stamps and IOUs found in cash drawers should be reported as–
   a. Prepaid expense and receivables.
   b. Cash because they represent the equivalent of money.
   c. Petty cash.
   d. Investments.
6. George Company maintains two checking accounts. A special checking account is used for the weekly payroll only, and the general checking account is used for all other disbursements. Each week, a check for the aggregate amount of the payrolls is drawn on the general account and deposited in the Payroll account. Individual checks are drawn on the Payroll account. The company maintains a $5,000 minimum balance in the Payroll account. On a monthly bank reconciliation, the Payroll account should:
   a. Show a zero balance per the bank statement.
   b. Show a $5,000 balance per the bank statement.
   c. Reconcile to $5,000.
   d. Be reconciled jointly with the general account in a single reconciliation.
7. Which of the following is a current asset?
   a. Cash surrender value of a life insurance policy of which the company is the beneficiary.
   b. Investment in marketable securities for the purpose of continuing control of the issuing company.
   c. Cash designated for the purchase of tangible fixed assets.
   d. Trade installment receivables normally collectible in 18 months.
8. Which of the following should not be considered as a current asset?
   a. Installment notes receivable due over 18 months in accordance with normal trade practice.
   b. Prepaid property taxes.
   c. Marketable securities purchased as a short-term investment with cash provided by current operations.
   d. Cash surrender value of a life insurance policy carried by a corporation, the beneficiary, on its president.

(AICPA adapted)

PART C: PROBLEMS 10–14

Problem 7–10

Records for Zarb Trading Company concerning receivables and recent sales history provided the following:

Cash sales for the period	$1,600,000	
Credit sales for the period	1,000,000	
Balance in trade receivables, start of period	200,000	
Balance in trade receivables, end of period	240,000	
Balance in allowance for doubtful accounts, start of period	4,000	(credit)
Accounts written off as uncollectible during period	6,000	

Recently Zarb's management has become concerned about various estimates used in their accounting process, including those relating to receivables and bad debts. The company is reviewing the various alternatives with a view to selecting the most appropriate one.

Assume the following simplified estimates:

1. Bad debt expense approximates three fifths of 1% of credit sales.
2. Bad debt expense approximates one fourth of 1% of net sales (cash plus credit sales).
3. As a rough estimate, 5% of the uncollected receivables will be bad at any one time.
4. Aging of the accounts at month-end indicated that three fourths of them would incur a 3% loss while the other one fourth would incur an 8% loss.

Required:

Four different approaches are being considered. Identify and briefly explain and give the advantages of each approach. After each explanation, give the adjusting entry based on the period data available.

Problem 7–11

The Installment Jewelry Company has been in business for five years but has never had an audit made of its financial statements. Engaged to make an audit for 19E, you find that the company's balance sheet carries no allowance for doubtful accounts, uncollectible accounts having been expensed as written off, and recoveries credited to income as collected. The company's policy is to write off at December 31 of each year those accounts on which no collections have been received for three months. The installment contracts generally provide for uniform monthly collections over a time span of two years from date of sale.

Upon your recommendation the company agrees to revise its accounts for 19E in order to account for bad debts on the allowance basis. The allowance is to be based on a percentage of sales which is derived from the experience of prior years.

Statistics for the past five years are as follows:

Year	*Charge Sales*	*Accounts Written Off and Year of Sale*			*Recoveries and Year of Sale*
19A	$100,000	(19A) $ 550			
19B	250,000	(19A) 1,500	(19B) $1,000		(19A) $100
19C	300,000	(19A) 500	(19B) 4,000	(19C) $1,300	(19B) 400
19D	325,000	(19B) 1,200	(19C) 4,500	(19D) 1,500	(19C) 500
19E	275,000	(19C) 2,700	(19D) 5,000	(19E) 1,400	(19D) 600

Accounts receivable at December 31, 19E, were as follows:

19D sales	$ 15,000
19E sales	135,000
	$150,000

Required:

Prepare the adjusting journal entry or entries with appropriate explanations to set up the Allowance for Doubtful Accounts. (Support each item with organized computations; income tax implications should be ignored. The books have been adjusted but not closed at December 31, 19E.)

(AICPA adapted)

Problem 7–12

Albert Company sold a building and the land on which it is located on January 1, 19A, receiving, as its consideration, a $100,000 note receivable payable in three years without interest. The sale was recorded as follows by Albert Company:

Note receivable	100,000	
Accumulated depreciation – building	100,000	
Building		150,000
Land		25,000
Gain on sale of building		25,000

It has been determined that 8% is a reasonable interest rate to impute to the note. You are recommending adjusting and correcting entries as of December 31, 19A (end of Albert Company's fiscal year). The books have not been adjusted or closed for 19A.

Required:

1. Give an entry to correct the sale entry and the adjustment for interest as of December 31, 19A. (Round to nearest dollar.)
2. Give entry to recognize interest earned at December 31, 19B.
3. Make entries at end of third year to *(a)* recognize interest earned, and *(b)* record collection of the note.
4. Aside from the correction in Requirement 1 for interest, do you see any other problem in the sale entry as originally made? Explain.

Problem 7–13

Nabors Company has experienced a critical cash-flow problem largely occasioned by collection problems with certain customers. Consequently, it has become involved in a number of transactions relating to notes receivable. The following transactions occurred during a period ending December 31 (end of the accounting period):

May	1	Received a $10,000, 90-day, 9% interest-bearing note from E. M. Smith, a customer, in settlement of an account receivable for that amount.
May	1	Received a $15,000, six-month, 9% interest-bearing note from M. Johnson, a customer, in settlement of an account receivable for that amount.
Aug.	1	Discounted the Johnson note at the bank at 10%.
Aug.	2	Smith defaulted on the $10,000 note.
Sept.	1	Received a one-year, noninterest-bearing note from D. Karnes, a customer, in settlement of a $6,000 account receivable. The face of the note was $6,600, and the going rate of interest 10% (on the amount of the receivable).
Oct.	1	Received a $25,000, 90-day note from R. M. Cates, a customer. The note was in payment for goods purchased and was interest-bearing at 8%.

Oct. 1 Collected the defaulted Smith note plus accrued interest to September 30 (10% per annum on the total amount due for three months).
Nov. 1 Johnson defaulted on the $15,000 note. Nabors Company paid the bank to total amount due plus a $25 protest fee.
Dec. 30 Collected Cates note in full. Collected from Johnson in full including interest on the full amount at 10% since default date.
Dec. 31 Accrued interest on outstanding notes.

Required:

1. Give the entry to record each of the above transactions. Show computations.
2. Show how the outstanding notes at December 31 would be reported on the balance sheet.

Problem 7–14

Doe Company finances some of its current operations by assigning accounts receivable to a finance company. On July 1, 19A, it assigned, under guarantee, accounts amounting to $40,000, the finance company advancing to them 80% of the accounts assigned (20% of the total to be withheld until the finance company has made full recovery), less a commission charge of one half of 1% the total accounts assigned.

On July 31 the Doe Company received a statement that the finance company had collected $21,000 of these accounts, and had made an additional charge of one half of 1% of the total accounts outstanding as of July 31 – this charge to be deducted at the time of the first remittance due Doe Company from the finance company. On August 31 the Doe Company received a second statement from the finance company, together with a check for the amount due. The statement indicated that the finance company had collected an additional $16,000 and had made a further charge of one half of 1% of the balance outstanding as of August 31.

Required (on books of Doe Company):

1. Give the entry to record the assignment of the accounts on a notification basis (July 1).
2. Give entry to record the data from the first report from the finance company (July 31).
3. Reconstruct the report submitted by the finance company on August 31; show details to explain cash remitted and the uncollected accounts still held by the finance company.
4. Give the entry to record the data in the report of August 31.
5. Explain how the items should be reported on the financial statements of Doe Company at July 31 and August 31.

(AICPA adapted)

Chapter 8

Inventories – General Problems

The basic purpose in accounting for inventories is to aid in the determination of net income by matching appropriate inventory cost with revenue; a secondary purpose is to provide an inventory amount for the balance sheet. Inventories present problems of considerable magnitude for both the accountant and management. Both must seriously consider such inventory problems as measurement, control, safeguarding, and cost allocation. These problems are especially critical in view of the materiality of inventories in the typical business and the fact that inventories directly affect both the income statement and the balance sheet. These factors have caused the accounting profession to give particular attention to the problems related to inventories. This and the two following chapters present the principal accounting concepts and procedures relating to inventories.

THE NATURE OF INVENTORIES

As an accounting category, *inventories* is an asset represented by goods owned by the business at a particular point in time and held for the purpose of future sale or for utilization in the manufacture of goods for sale. No other asset includes so great a variety of properties under a single heading, for practically all kinds of tangible goods and properties are found in the inventories of one business or another. Machinery and equipment are fixed assets of the business using them, but constituted at one time a part of the inventory of the manufacturer of such equipment. Even a building until finished and turned over to a buyer is an inventory item, a "contract in process," among the assets of the builder.

In many companies, inventories represent a significant portion of current assets or even total assets. Inventories generally represent an active asset in that there is constant usage and replacement. Although many inventory items are small, they frequently have considerable value; therefore, the problem of safeguarding inventories ranks next to protecting for cash. The advisability of adequate stocking of items for sale, coupled with the risk of loss and cost of overstocking, creates critical management planning and control problems. Failure to control inventories adequately and to account for inventory quantities and costs might well lead to business failure.[1]

CLASSIFICATION OF INVENTORIES

The major classifications of inventories relate to the types of business. A trading entity (i.e., wholesale and retail) acquires merchandise for resale, whereas a manufacturing concern acquires raw materials and component parts and manufactures finished products. The flow of inventory costs through these two types of entities may be diagrammed as follows:

Trading entity:

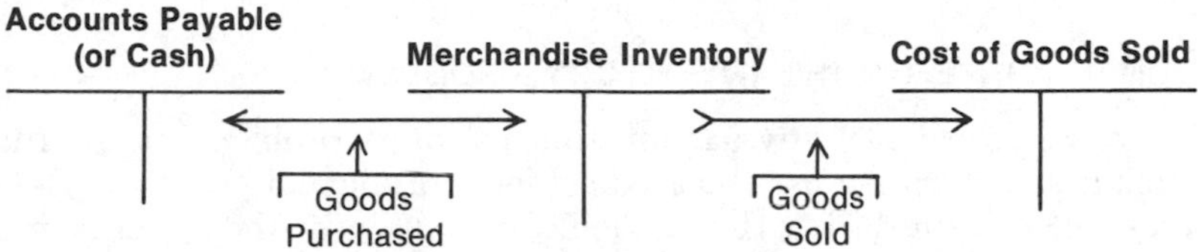

Manufacturing entity:

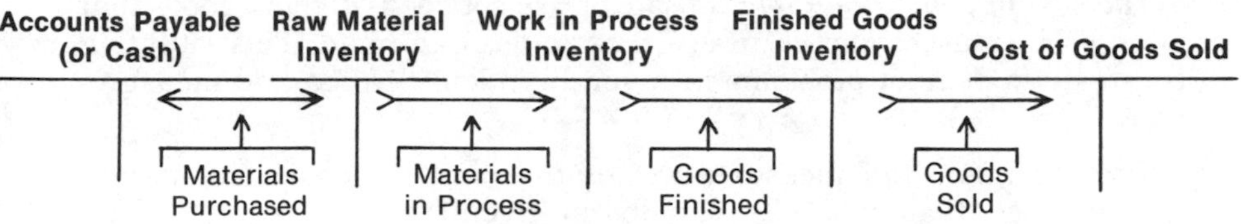

Inventories may be defined as follows:

1. Merchandise inventory—goods on hand purchased by a trading entity for resale. The physical form of the goods is not altered prior to resale.
2. Manufacturing inventory—the combined inventories of a manufacturing entity consisting of—
   a. Raw materials inventory—tangible goods purchased or obtained from natural sources and on hand principally for direct use in the manufacture of goods for resale. Parts or subassemblies manufactured prior to use are sometimes classified as raw materials; however, a preferable classification is *parts inventory.*
   b. Work in process inventory—goods partly processed and requiring further processing before sale. Work (goods) in process inventory normally is valued at the sum of *direct material, direct labor,* and *allocated manufacturing overhead costs* incurred to date of the inventory.

[1] For an introductory discussion of accounting for inventories refer to: G. A. Welsch and R. N. Anthony, *Fundamentals of Financial Accounting* (Homewood, Ill.: Richard D. Irwin, Inc., 1974), chap. 7.

c. Finished goods inventory – manufactured articles completed and being held for sale. Finished goods inventory normally is valued at the sum of *direct material, direct labor,* and *allocated manufacturing overhead costs* related to their manufacture.
d. Manufacturing supplies inventory – items on hand such as lube oils for the machinery, cleaning materials, and supply items which comprise an insignificant part of the finished product as, for example, the thread and glue used in binding this book.

3. Miscellaneous inventories – items such as office supplies, janitorial supplies, and shipping supplies. Inventories of this type normally are used in the near future and usually are charged to selling or general expense when used; consequently, these inventory amounts generally are reported as a prepaid expense (supplies inventory).

THE DUAL PHASE OF THE INVENTORY PROBLEM

The basic cause of many accounting inventory problems is the fact that goods sold during a fiscal period seldom correspond exactly to those produced or bought during that period. Consequently, the typical situation is one where physical inventory increases or decreases. This increase or decrease in physical inventory necessitates a corresponding *allocation of the cost of goods available* for sale or use between *(a)* those goods that were sold or used, and *(b)* those that remain on hand. This situation creates two distinct problems in inventory identification and measurement, viz:

1. Identification and measurement of the *physical goods* (items and quantities) that should be included in inventory.
2. Measurement of the *accounting values* assigned to the physical goods included in inventory.

IDENTIFICATION OF GOODS (ITEMS) THAT SHOULD BE INCLUDED IN INVENTORY

In identifying the physical goods to be included in inventory, accountants apply the general rule that all goods to which the concern has *ownership* at inventory date should be included, regardless of their location. The seller should include in inventory goods under contract for sale but not yet segregated and applied to the contract. Further, mere segregation does not create a "passage of ownership" – the terms of the contract itself must be determining. Since at the close of an accounting period, a business may *(a)* hold goods which it does not own or *(b)* own goods which it does not hold, care must be exercised in identifying the goods properly included in inventory.

Goods purchased, though not received, should be included in the inventory of the purchaser provided ownership to such goods has passed. Application of the "passage of ownership" rule requires the following: if the goods are shipped *f.o.b. destination,* ownership does not pass until the purchaser receives the goods from the common carrier; if the goods are shipped *f.o.b. shipping point,* ownership passes when the seller delivers them to the common carrier.[2]

Goods *out* on consignment, those held by agents, and those located at branches should be included in inventory. On the other hand, goods *held* (but owned by someone else) for sale on commission or consignment and those received from vendors but rejected and awaiting return for credit should be excluded from the inventory.[3]

In identifying items that should be included in inventory where there is a question as to whether ownership has passed, the accountant must exercise judgment in the light of the particular situation. Obviously the legal position should be followed; however, the accountant will face many situations where a strict legal determination is impractical. In such cases the intent of the sales agreement, policies of the parties involved, industry practices, and other available evidence of intent must be considered.

MEASUREMENT OF PHYSICAL QUANTITIES IN INVENTORY

The physical quantities in inventory may be determined by means of *(a)* a *periodic (physical) inventory,* or *(b)* a *perpetual inventory.*

Periodic Inventory System

When this system is used, an actual count of the goods on hand is taken at the end of each period for which financial statements are to be prepared. The goods are counted, weighed, or otherwise measured, then extended at *unit costs* to derive the inventory valuation. When a periodic inventory system is used, end-of-the-period entries are required for *(a)* adjusting or closing the beginning inventory, and *(b)* recording the ending inventory.

Under the periodic system cost of goods sold is a *residual amount* and cannot be independently verified. To illustrate:

Cost of goods sold:		
Beginning inventory (carried forward from last period)...	$ 50,000	
Merchandise purchases (accumulated in the accounts)........	200,000	
Goods available for sale............	250,000	
Less: Ending inventory (determined by count)	60,000	
Cost of Goods Sold (a residual amount)		$190,000

The accounting entries and external financial reporting, when the peri-

[2] Refer to Chapter 2, discussion of the revenue principle.

[3] Consignment is a special marketing arrangement whereby the consignor (the owner of the goods) ships merchandise to another party, known as a consignee, who is to act as a sales agent only. The consignee does not purchase the goods, but assumes responsibility for their care, and upon sale remits the proceeds (less expenses and a commission). Goods out on consignment, since they are owned by the consignor until sold, should be excluded from the inventory of the consignee and included in the inventory of the consignor.

odic inventory system is used, were discussed and illustrated in Chapters 3 and 4.

Perpetual Inventory System

When this system is used, detailed subsidiary records are maintained for each item of inventory. An Inventory Control account is maintained on a current basis; consequently, the detailed inventory records for each different item will provide for recording *(a)* receipts, *(b)* issues, and *(c)* balances on hand, usually in both quantities and dollar amounts. Thus, the physical amount and valuation of goods on hand at any time are readily available from the accounting records; consequently, a physical inventory count is unnecessary except to check on the accuracy of the inventory records from time to time. Such checks (physical counts) are usually made at least annually or on a continuous rotation basis when large inventories are involved. When a discrepancy is found, the perpetual inventory records must be adjusted to the physical count. In such cases the inventory account is debited or credited as necessary for correction and an inventory adjustment account such as "Inventory Overages or Shortages" is used for the contra amount. The inventory adjustment account is closed to the Income Summary account at the end of the period.

A perpetual inventory system is particularly useful *(a)* to control and safeguard inventory, and *(b)* when monthly statements are prepared. A perpetual inventory is generally considered to be one of the essential characteristics of a good cost accounting system.

To briefly review and compare the accounting procedures for the periodic and the perpetual inventory systems, the following simplified data are used:

	Units	*Unit Amount*
Merchandise inventory, beginning	500	$4.00
Merchandise purchases during the period	1,000	4.00
Total Goods Available for Sale	1,500	
Merchandise sold during the period	900	6.00 (sales price)
Merchandise Inventory, Ending	600	

Comparative Entries

Periodic Inventory System			*Perpetual Inventory System*		
a. Merchandise purchased for resale:					
Purchases (1,000 @ $4)	4,000		Merchandise inventory	4,000	
Cash		4,000	Cash		4,000
b. Merchandise sold;					
Cash (900 @ $6)	5,400		Cash	5,400	
Sales revenue		5,400	Sales revenue		5,400
			Cost of goods sold	3,600	
			Merchandise inventory (900 @ $4)		3,600

c. Entries at end of the accounting period:

To close purchases account:			None required since inventory and cost of goods sold account balances already up to date.
Income summary 4,000			
Purchases	4,000		
To close beginning inventory account:			
Income summary 2,000			
Inventory (beginning)...	2,000		
To record ending inventory:			
Inventory (ending) 2,400			
Income summary.........	2,400		
Income Statement (Partial):			
Sales revenue ...	$5,400	Sales revenue	$5,400
Cost of goods sold:			
Beginning inventory...$2,000			
Purchases 4,000			
Goods available for sale 6,000			
Ending inventory... 2,400			
Cost of goods sold	3,600	Cost of goods sold..............	3,600
Gross margin ...	$1,800		$1,800
Balance Sheet (Partial):			
Current Assets:			
Merchandise inventory......	$2,400	Merchandise inventory	$2,400

A typical subsidiary inventory record (for Raw Material X) that would be maintained under the perpetual inventory system (but not under the periodic system) is shown in Exhibit 8–1.

EFFECT OF INVENTORY ERRORS

Recall the effect of inventory errors on income, viz: The overstatement of final inventory overstates pretax income by the same amount, and an understatement of final inventory understates pretax income. Conversely, an overstatement of the beginning inventory understates pretax income by the same amount, and an understatement of the beginning inventory overstates pretax income. An overstatement of purchases alone, overstates cost of goods sold and understates pretax income.

Incorrect inclusion or exclusion of physical units for inventory purposes will result in errors in the financial statements. The following errors are not uncommon:[4]

Inclusion of items that should not be in final inventory:

[4] Some of the effects of these errors will differ depending on the inventory flow method used, that is, *Fifo, Lifo,* and so on.

EXHIBIT 8–1
Perpetual Inventory Record

SUBSIDIARY LEDGER

PERPETUAL INVENTORY RECORD

Article *Raw Material X* Unit *lbs.* Maximum *1,600*

Location *L-15* Bin No. *32* Minimum *800*

Verification Dates

Date	Ordered		Received or Completed					Issued or Sold				Balance on Hand		
	Order No.	Units	Order No.	Ref.	Units	Unit Cost	Total Cost	Ref.	Units	Unit Cost	Total Cost	Units	Unit Cost	Total Cost
Jan. 1												*1,000*	*$.40*	*$400*
10			*17*		*500*	*$.40*	*$200*					*1,500*	*.40*	*600*
18									*600*	*$.40*	*$240*	*900*	*.40*	*360*
19	*18*	*700*												

1. *Incorrect inclusion of items in inventory, and the purchase recorded.* These two errors result in an overstatement of inventory, purchases, and accounts payable. In this case pretax income will be correctly stated, since the errors in inventory and purchases will offset; however, the assets and liabilities on the balance sheet each will be overstated by the same amount.
2. *Incorrect inclusion of items in inventory, but purchase not recorded.* This error results in an overstatement of the final inventory, hence both pretax income and assets are overstated by the same amounts.

Exclusion of items that should be admitted to final inventory:

3. *Incorrect exclusion of items from inventory, but the purchase correctly recorded.* This error results in an understatement of the final inventory, hence an understatement of both pretax income and assets by the same amounts.
4. *Incorrect exclusion of items from inventory, and the purchase not recorded.* These two errors result in an understatement of inventory, purchases, and accounts payable. In this case pretax income will be correctly stated, since the errors in inventory and purchases will offset; however, the assets and liabilities on the balance sheet each will be understated by the same amount.

The effects of each situation are demonstrated in Exhibit 8–2.

Errors similar to those discussed above, which relate to purchases, may also arise when goods are sold. These errors not only cause the financial statements for the current period to be in error but also frequently cause future amounts to be wrong.

MEASURING OF THE ACCOUNTING VALUE OF INVENTORY

At date of acquisition, inventory items are recorded at cost in harmony with the *cost principle;* subsequently when sold the cost is matched with revenue in accordance with the *matching principle.* Inventory items remaining on hand at the end of an accounting period are valued on the basis of the cost principle except when their value has been eroded through damage, obsolescence, erosion of replacement cost, and similar factors, in which case they are "valued" in accordance with the concept of *conservatism* (for example, by the lower-of-cost-or-market procedure). The discussions to follow in this and the next two chapters consider special inventory problems and procedures within the context of these broad theoretical requirements.

The *accounting value* of inventories represents an *acceptable* allocation of the total cost of goods or materials *available* between that portion used or sold (cost of goods sold) and that portion held as an asset for subsequent use or sale (inventory). The nature of the allocation is indicated in the following diagram (based on the example given on pages 322 and 323):

EXHIBIT 8–2
Effects of Inventory Errors (pretax)

		(1)	(2)	(3)	(4)
		Inventory Error Incorrectly Included $1,000 in Final Inventory		*Inventory Error Incorrectly Excluded $1,000 from Final Inventory*	
	Correct Amounts	*Purchases in Error (was recorded)*	*Purchases Are Correct (was not recorded)*	*Purchases Are Correct (was recorded)*	*Purchases in Error (was not recorded)*
Income Statement:					
Sales	$10,000	$10,000	$10,000	$10,000	$10,000
Initial inventory	3,000	3,000	3,000	3,000	3,000
Purchases	12,000	13,000†	12,000	12,000	11,000*
Total	15,000	16,000	15,000	15,000	14,000
Final inventory	8,000	9,000†	9,000†	7,000*	7,000*
Cost of goods sold	7,000	7,000	6,000	8,000	7,000
Gross margin	3,000	3,000	4,000	2,000	3,000
Expenses	1,000	1,000	1,000	1,000	1,000
Income	$ 2,000	$ 2,000	$ 3,000†	$ 1,000*	$ 2,000
Balance Sheet:					
Assets (inventory)	$ 8,000	$ 9,000†	$ 9,000†	$ 7,000*	$ 7,000*
Liabilities (payables)	12,000	13,000†	12,000	12,000	11,000*
Retained earnings	20,000	20,000	21,000†	19,000*	20,000

* Under
† Over.

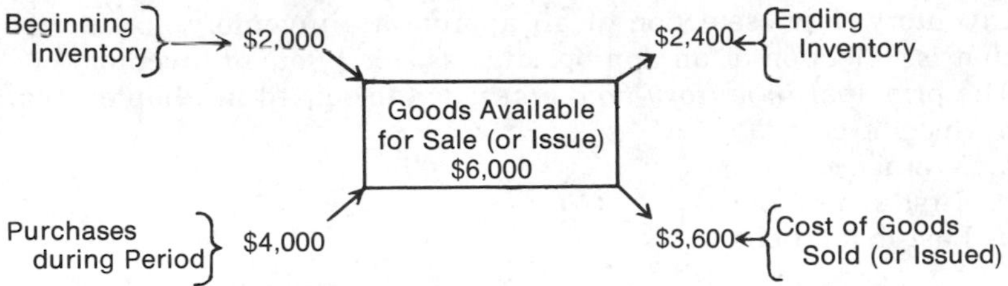

There are a number of procedures used for measuring the accounting value of inventories that satisfy the theoretical requirements. The acceptability of a number of procedures, as opposed to a single one, suggests the wide variation in inventory characteristics and conditions as related to particular situations and purposes. Basically the accounting values for inventories serve two somewhat opposing purposes. One purpose implies procedures that may not appear to be entirely appropriate for the other purpose. One is to develop a monetary value for the inventory reported on the *balance sheet*. There it is desirable to report this resource at cost or at its future utility to the business, whichever is lower. The other purpose, directed toward the *income statement*, is to measure the inventory value so there is a proper measurement of income between accounting periods. Conservatism with respect to inventory values in terms of one objective may not be conservative in terms of the other objective. In recent years the income measurement objective has predominated as indicated by the following quotation from *Accounting Research Bulletin No. 43:*

> In accounting for the goods in the inventory at any point of time, the major objective is the matching of appropriate costs against revenues in order that there may be a proper determination of the realized income. Thus, the inventory at any given date is the balance of costs applicable to goods on hand remaining after the matching of absorbed costs with concurrent revenues. This balance is appropriately carried to future periods provided it does not exceed an amount properly chargeable against the revenues expected to be obtained from ultimate disposition of the goods carried forward.[5]

Measurement of acceptable values for (1) inventory and (2) cost of goods sold, involves two distinct problems, viz:

1. Inventory unit cost – selection of an appropriate *unit cost* for valuation of the items in inventory. The principal bases or *inventory valuation methods* are:
   a. Cost basis.
   b. Departure from cost basis:
      1. Lower of cost or market.
      2. Net realizable value.
      3. Replacement cost.
      4. Selling price.

---

[5] AICPA, "Restatement and Revision of Accounting Research Bulletins," *Accounting Research Bulletin No. 43* (New York, 1961).

2. Inventory flow—selection of an appropriate inventory flow method, that is, selection of an appropriate *assumed flow* of inventory costs. The principal *inventory flow methods* (discussed in Chapter 9) are:
   a. Specific cost.
   b. Average cost.
   c. First-in, first-out.
   d. Last-in, first-out.

CONTENT OF UNIT COST

The cost principle provides the theoretical foundation for measurement of unit cost for inventory and cost of goods sold purposes, viz:

> The primary basis of accounting for inventories is cost, which has been defined generally as the price paid or consideration given to acquire an asset. As applied to inventories, cost means in principle the sum of the applicable expenditures and charges directly or indirectly incurred in bringing an article to its existing condition and location.[6]

Thus unit inventory cost is measured by the total outlay made to acquire the goods in question and to prepare them for the market. These costs include not only the purchase price but also those incidental costs such as excise and sales taxes, duties, freight, storage, insurance on the merchandise while in transit or in storage, and all other costs incurred on the goods up to the time they are ready for use or for sale to the customer. Some incidental costs, such as freight-in, frequently can be identified directly with specific goods, while other incidental costs may require a reasonable allocation to specific goods. As a practical matter many incidental costs, although theoretically a cost of goods purchased, frequently are not included in inventory valuation but reported as a separate expense; the cost of allocating may not be warranted by the slight increase in accuracy. In such cases *consistency* in application is particularly important.

General administrative and distribution expenses, often called *period expenses,* are not included in determining unit inventory costs because they are not directly related to the purchase or manufacture of goods for sale. They are called period expenses because they are deducted on the income statement for the period in which incurred.

Freight-In

Freight and other incidental costs paid in connection with purchase of materials for use or merchandise for resale are additions to unit cost. Where such charges can be identified with specific goods, they should be charged to such goods. However, in some cases identification is impractical. Consequently, it is sometimes best to record transportation costs in a special account such as Freight-In and to report it as an addition to cost of goods sold in the case of a trading concern and to cost of

---

[6] Ibid., p. 28.

materials used in a manufacturing entity. However, in this case failure to add freight costs to the purchase price directly causes cost of goods sold to be overstated and inventory to be understated. Theoretically, freight-in should be apportioned to cost of goods sold and final inventory in proportion to the quantity of goods involved in each.

Purchase Discounts

Cash discounts sometimes are given, as an element of credit purchases, to encourage early payment. Under the cost principle, the net cash equivalent paid is cost. Payments made for the extension of credit are accounted for as expenses. Theoretically, all cash discounts permitted, whether taken or not, should be omitted from cost upon payment of invoices. Discounts not taken constitute a financing expense. Since cash discounts are reductions in the cost of specific goods, they reduce both cost of purchases and inventory valuation. Therefore, credit purchases should be recorded at *net of discount* to reflect the *correct cost.* Alternatively, for practical reasons and because the cash discount often is immaterial, purchases may be recorded at the *gross amount.*

To illustrate each approach, assume merchandise is purchased for $1,000 on credit terms of 2/10, n/30. Assume further that three fourths of the charge is paid within the ten-day discount period.

Net of Discount Approach			*Gross Amount Approach*		
To record the purchase (perpetual inventory system):					
Merchandise inventory	980		Merchandise inventory	1,000	
Accounts payable (net)		980	Accounts payable (gross)		1,000
To record payment of three fourths of the liability within discount period:					
Accounts payable (net)	735		Accounts payable (gross)	750	
Cash		735	Cash		735
(980 × .75 = $735)			Discount on purchases		15
To record payment of one fourth of the liability after the discount period:					
Accounts payable (net)	245		Accounts payable (gross)	250	
Interest expense*	5		Cash		250
Cash		250			

* Alternative title: Purchase discounts lost.

The net-of-discount approach correctly reflects the cost of the merchandise in conformity with the cost principle and also correctly states the amount of the liability since most companies take all discounts and pay only the net amount. Remember that 2% interest saved by paying within ten days is a significantly higher rate on an annual basis. This method also correctly allocates the discount effect between inventory and cost of goods sold. It follows the cost principle because the true costs of purchases, cost of goods sold, and inventory are recorded and reported. Similarly, accounts payable is recorded and reported at the amount that is usually paid. It does not violate the revenue principle by recording and reporting purchase discounts as "other income"; rather, it considers purchase discounts lost as expense.

When the gross method is used, purchase discounts taken are recorded separately in the Discount on Purchases account (as a credit). The amount often then is reported as financial revenue (similar to interest revenue). This violates the revenue principle; clearly, there is no financial revenue because there has been no earning process. The buyer is not lending money to the seller and thereby generating revenue; rather the buyer is paying a bill on time. To avoid this effect, the amount of discount taken sometimes is deducted in full from cost of goods sold. Of course, this understates cost of goods sold and overstates the ending inventory because all of the discount is deducted from cost of goods sold for the period. Thus, it is theoretically deficient. It has the advantage of simplicity, and the misstatement of amounts are often not material in relation to total purchases.[7]

DEPARTURES FROM THE COST PRINCIPLE IN COSTING INVENTORY

Under certain prescribed conditions generally accepted accounting principles require departure from the cost principle in measuring the unit cost of inventory items. In most of these situations conservatism overrides the cost principle. The exceptions may be classified as follows:

1. Lower of cost or market.
2. Net realizable value.
3. Replacement cost.
4. Selling price.

Lower of Cost or Market

Under the concept of conservatism, known losses, although not actually evidenced by a specific transaction, are recognized in the period of occurrence. In contrast, known gains not evidenced by a specific transaction are not recognized until realized. Therefore, under the lower-of-

---

[7] A variation of these two approaches sometimes is used; it attempts to attain the advantages of the net approach and avoid recording the liability at net. It is called the net-gross approach. To illustrate, the above transactions would be recorded as follows:

To record purchases at net and liability at gross:

	Debit	Credit
Merchandise inventory (net)	980	
Allowance for purchase discounts	20	
Accounts payable		1,000

To record payment within the discount period:

	Debit	Credit
Accounts payable	750	
Allowance for purchase discounts		15
Cash		735

To record payment after discount period:

	Debit	Credit
Accounts payable	250	
Interest expense (or discounts lost)	5	
Cash		250
Allowance for purchase discounts		5

Any balance in the allowance account is reported as contra to the Accounts Payable account. Theoretically, this method is sound; due to its complexity, however, it is seldom used.

cost-or-market rule the unit cost used is the lower of *(a)* cost or *(b)* market at the end of the period. This position of conservatism has been accepted by the accounting profession on the basis of *(a)* the matching principle, that is, the utility of the goods on hand is less than original cost, hence there has been a loss which should be recognized for the period in which the decline in utility took place, and revenue should be matched with the replacement cost of goods sold; and *(b)* from the point of view of balance sheet conservatism the asset inventory should be reported at the lower figure. It is particularly important to realize also that there is an implicit assumption in the lower-of-cost-or-market rule that selling prices decrease in direct proportion to decreases in replacement cost. The position of the Committee on Accounting Procedure of the AICPA is expressed in *Accounting Research Bulletin No. 43* as:

> A departure from the cost basis of pricing the inventory is required when the utility of the goods is no longer as great as its cost. Where there is evidence that the utility of goods, in their disposal in the ordinary course of business, will be less than cost, whether due to physical deterioration, obsolescence, changes in price levels, or other causes, the difference should be recognized as a loss of the current period. This is generally accomplished by stating such goods at a lower level commonly designated as *market*.[8]

Cost, as used in this context, refers to the actual unit cost as defined in the preceding paragraphs and through application of an acceptable inventory flow method such as average, *Fifo,* or *Lifo* (see Chapter 9).

Market, as used in this context, by accountants and by the Treasury Department for income tax purposes, is defined as follows: "Under ordinary circumstances 'market' means the current bid price prevailing at the date of the inventory for the particular merchandise in the volume in which usually purchased by the taxpayer." In applying this definition the type of firm and the nature and condition of the items in inventory must be taken into account as follows:

1. For stock-in-trade, raw materials, and purchased parts, use purchase or replacement basis—*market* for the stock-in-trade of a trading concern is the current bid prices from the normal suppliers for the volume normally purchased, adjusted for regular transportation costs and other necessary expenses to secure the goods from the usual outlets.

2. For goods in process and finished goods, use reproduction basis—*market* for the goods in process and finished goods inventories for the manufacturer is based on the cost of manufacturing the items at the prevailing market prices for raw materials, labor, and other factory costs.

3. For damaged and deteriorated items use realization basis—*market* frequently must be interpreted in terms of the *condition* of the items in inventory. Damaged, obsolete, depreciated, used, and otherwise deteriorated items in inventory seldom will have a determinable replacement value in their current condition; therefore, accountants generally agree that such items should be valued for inventory purposes at their *net realizable value*. However, some accountants prefer net realizable value

---

[8]*Accounting Research Bulletin No. 43.*

less an allowance for normal profit. For example, the inventory under each of these concepts would be calculated as follows:

Final inventory, 1,000 units at estimated sales price	$1,000
Less: Estimated distribution cost at $.40 per unit	400
Inventory at *net realizable value*	600
Less: Allowance for normal profit (10% on sales)	100
Inventory at *Net Realizable Value Less Normal Profit*	$ 500

The deduction of distribution cost is necessary to prevent capitalization of the item at more than its current fair market value. In applying the lower-of-cost-or-market procedure, certain *exceptions* were recognized by the Committee on Accounting Procedure of the AICPA. "Judgment must always be exercised and no loss should be recognized unless the evidence indicates clearly that a loss has been sustained. There are, therefore, exceptions to such a standard." These exceptions were described as follows:

> As used in the phrase *lower of cost or market* the term *market* means current replacement cost (by purchase or by reproduction, as the case may be) except that:
>
> (1) Market should not exceed the net realizable value (i.e., estimated selling price in the ordinary course of business less reasonably predictable costs of completion and disposal); and
> (2) Market should not be less than net realizable value reduced by an allowance for an approximately normal profit margin.[9]

These exceptions in effect establish a "ceiling" and a "floor" for *market* in the comparison with original *cost* in applying the procedure. Exhibit 8–3 gives several independent situations under which the lower-of-cost-or-market rule is applied. The cost and other values are those of a single unit. Observe in the illustration that "market" results from a choice among current replacement cost, the ceiling (net realizable value), and the floor (net realizable value less normal profit). The "market" thus derived is compared with "cost" in order to determine the appropriate inventory valuation.

The limits (ceiling and floor) are necessary to measure properly the economic utility of the items in inventory. For example, in Case II in Exhibit 8–3, current replacement cost is $.65 and the net realizable value (ceiling) is $.60. To carry the $.65 forward in inventory, which is more than the net realizable value, would result in a charge against future sales greater than the economic utility of the goods, and a charge against current income for an amount less than the anticipated loss; hence the reported profit and inventory value of each period would be incorrect. In Case III, Exhibit 8–3, the net realizable value less normal profit (floor) is greater than current replacement cost, hence the floor value ($.50) should be carried forward in inventory. To carry forward a market value of $.45 would result in an understatement of the inventory since at $.50 a normal profit margin will be earned when the item is

[9] *Accounting Research Bulletin No. 43,* p. 31.

EXHIBIT 8–3
Exceptions – Computation of Lower of Cost or Market

	Case			
	I	*II*	*III*	*IV*
a. Cost (per unit)	$1.00	$1.00	$1.00	$.45
b. Current replacement cost (per unit)	.55	.65	.45	.40
c. Ceiling (net realizable value–estimated sales price less predictable cost of completion and disposal)*	.60	.60	.60	.60
d. Floor (net realizable value less a normal profit margin)*	.50	.50	.50	.50
e. Market (selected from *b, c,* and *d* values)	.55	.60	.50	.50
f. Inventory valuation under lower-of-cost-or-market rule (selected from *a* and *e*)	.55	.60	.50	.45

* Additional data to verify ceiling and floor:

	I	*II*	*III*	*IV*
Estimated selling price	$.85	$.90	$.80	$.75
Less: Estimated cost to complete and sell	.25	.30	.20	.15
Net realizable value (ceiling)	$.60	$.60	$.60	$.60
Less: Estimated normal profit	.10	.10	.10	.10
Net Realizable Value Less Profit (Floor)	$.50	$.50	$.50	$.50

sold. Therefore, if current replacement cost as the market value ($.45) were carried forward in this case, future profits on the inventory items would be overstated, and current period profits understated.

In applying the exceptions *Bulletin No. 43* states: "Because of the many variations of circumstances encountered in inventory pricing, Statement 6 (see above quotation) is intended as a guide rather than a literal rule. It should be applied realistically in light of the objectives expressed in this chapter and with due regard to the form, content, and composition of the inventory."

ACCOUNTING PROBLEMS IN APPLYING LOWER OF COST OR MARKET

In applying the lower-of-cost-or-market procedure two primary accounting problems arise, viz:

1. How will the procedure be applied to determine the overall inventory valuation?
2. How will the resulting inventory valuation be recorded in the accounts?

Determination of Overall Inventory Valuation

In applying the lower-of-cost-or-market procedure in determining the overall inventory valuation, three approaches have been suggested: (1) by comparison of cost and market separately for each item of inventory, (2) by comparison of cost and market separately for each *classification*

EXHIBIT 8–4
Applying Lower of Cost or Market

			Lower of Cost or Market Applied by—		
Commodity	*Cost*	*Market*	*Individual Items*	*Classification*	*Total*
Classification A:					
Item 1	$10,000	$ 9,500	$ 9,500		
Item 2	8,000	9,000	8,000		
	18,000	18,500		$18,000	
Classification B:					
Item 3	21,000	22,000	21,000		
Item 4	32,000	29,000	29,000		
	53,000	51,000		51,000	
Total............	$71,000	$69,500			$69,500
Inventory Valuation...			$67,500	$69,000	$69,500

of inventory, and (3) by comparison of *total* cost with *total* market for the inventory. Exhibit 8–4 shows the application of each approach.

Generally, the lower-of-cost-or-market procedure applied to is by *individual items.* However, under certain circumstances, application of the procedure to classifications or totals may have greater significance for accounting purposes. For example, in applying the procedure to the raw materials inventory of a manufacturer producing only one major product and using several raw materials having common characteristics, the utility of the total stock of raw material may have more significance than the individual market prices of each raw material. Consistency in application is essential.

A particular problem arises when there are several unit costs with respect to a particular commodity to be compared with a single unit *market* price. This situation frequently arises when first-in, first-out (discussed in next chapter) and similar inventory flow procedures are used. In such cases the aggregate cost for the commodity should be compared with the aggregate market (see Exhibit 8–5).

With respect to departures from cost in inventory valuation, once an inventory item has been reduced to a value lower than cost, *subsequent*

EXHIBIT 8–5
Lower of Cost or Market and *Fifo*

		Unit Prices				Inventory Valuation	
Commodity	*Units on Hand*	*Actual Cost*	*Current Market*	*Aggregate Cost*	*Aggregate Market*	*Unit*	*Total*
A	10,000 10,000	$4.00 3.85	$3.90	$ 78,500	$ 78,000	$3.90	$78,000
B	10,000 10,000	7.70 8.00	7.90	157,000	158,000	7.70 8.00	77,000 80,000

accounting would consider the reduced value as "cost" for that particular item. Items once reduced for inventory valuation purposes should not be subsequently restored to their original cost.

Recording Lower of Cost or Market in the Accounts

Recall that purchases are initially recorded at cost; therefore, if the inventories subsequently are reduced to *less than cost* (i.e., market when lower), two different *items* must be recognized: *(a)* the actual *cost* of goods used or sold, and *(b)* the *loss* due to decline in utility of the inventory (i.e., the difference between cost and market), frequently referred to as a *holding loss*. Proper accounting requires that these two different items—cost and loss—be accounted for and reported separately. Two methods of recording the results of the lower-of-cost-or-market rule in the accounts generally are found in practice:

1. Direct inventory reduction method wherein the actual cost of goods sold or used and the holding loss in inventory utility are *not* separately accounted for and reported.
2. Inventory allowance method wherein the cost and holding loss are separately accounted for and reported for *both* the beginning and ending inventories.

Recording in the accounts is further complicated by the fact that some firms employ a *periodic* inventory system, whereas other firms employ a *perpetual* inventory system.

In order to illustrate and compare the two methods outlined above, assume the following inventories for the years 19A and 19B:

Inventory Date	*At Original Cost*	*At Lower of Cost or Market*	*Difference (loss)*
January 1, 19A	$75,000	$75,000	$ -0-
December 31, 19A	80,000	70,000	(10,000)
December 31, 19B	60,000	56,000	(4,000)

The two methods are illustrated in Exhibit 8–6 for both perpetual and periodic inventory assumptions. The related income statements are compared in Exhibit 8–7 to show the effect of each method on the statement.

Evaluation of the Two Approaches. The effects on the income statement of each of the two methods of recording lower of cost or market are reflected in Exhibit 8–7. The two methods derive the same periodic net income amount and inventory valuation on the balance sheet each period. The difference is the manner in which the details are reported. The first approach includes the holding loss in cost of goods sold, whereas the second approach reports the holding loss separately. The first approach can be viewed as minimal disclosure, whereas the second approach represents maximum reporting. Regardless of the method

EXHIBIT 8–6
Comparison of Methods of Recording Lower of Cost or Market in the Accounts

	Periodic Inventory System				Perpetual Inventory System			
	19A		19B		19A		19B	
1. Direct inventory reduction method—holding loss not recognized separately:								
a. To close beginning inventory:								
Income summary	75,000		70,000		No comparable entry			
Inventory		75,000		70,000				
b. To record (or reduce) ending inventory to LCM basis:								
Inventory	70,000		56,000					
Cost of goods sold					10,000		4,000	
Income summary		70,000		56,000				
Inventory ($80,000 – $70,000) and ($60,000 – $56,000)						10,000		4,000
2. Inventory allowance method—holding loss recognized separately for both beginning and ending inventory:								
a. To close beginning inventory:								
Income summary	75,000		80,000		No comparable entry			
Inventory		75,000		80,000				
b. To record (or reduce) ending inventory and holding loss:								
Inventory	80,000		60,000					
*Holding loss (gain—credit) on inventory........	10,000			6,000	10,000			6,000
Income summary		80,000		60,000				
Allowance to reduce inventory to market ($10,000 credit – $4,000 debit = $6,000 debit adjustment needed)		10,000	6,000			10,000	6,000	

* Closed to Income Summary.

EXHIBIT 8–7 Lower of Cost or Market – Reporting Inventory Holding Losses

	(1) Direct Inventory Reduction Method – Holding Loss Not Recognized Separately		(2) Inventory Allowance Method – Holding Loss Recognized Separately for Both Beginning and Ending Inventory	
Income Statement – Year Ended December 31, 19A:				
Sales		$200,000		$200,000
Cost of goods sold:				
Beginning inventory	(cost) $ 75,000		(cost) $ 75,000	
Purchases	115,000		115,000	
Goods available for sale	190,000		190,000	
Less: Ending inventory	(LCM) 70,000	120,000	(cost) 80,000	110,000
Gross margin		80,000		90,000
Less: Expenses		60,000		60,000
		20,000		30,000
Less: Loss on inventory reduction to market				10,000
Add: Gain on inventory adjustment to market				
Net income		$ 20,000		$ 20,000
Balance Sheet – December 31, 19A:				
Inventory		$ 70,000	80,000	
Less: Allowance for inventory reduction to market			10,000	$ 70,000
Income Statement – Year Ended December 31, 19B:				
Sales		$220,000		$220,000
Cost of goods sold:				
Beginning inventory	(LCM) $ 70,000		(cost) $ 80,000	
Purchases	118,000		118,000	
Goods available for sale	188,000		198,000	
Less: Ending inventory	(LCM) 56,000	132,000	(cost) 60,000	138,000
Gross margin		88,000		82,000
Less: Expenses		66,000		66,000
		22,000		16,000
Less: Loss on inventory reduction to market				
Add: Gain on inventory adjustment to market				6,000
Net Income		$ 22,000		$ 22,000
Balance Sheet – December 31, 19B:				
Inventory		$ 56,000	$ 60,000	
Less: Allowance for inventory reduction to market			4,000	$ 56,000

used, "when substantial and unusual losses result from the application of this rule it will frequently be desirable to disclose the amount of the loss in the income statement as a charge separately identified from the consumed inventory costs described as *cost of goods sold*."[10]

In the second method illustrated, the credit balance in Allowance for Inventory Reduction should be shown on the balance sheet as a deduction from the related inventory, thus stating the inventory at market. This method is generally referred to as the allowance method, although it is sometimes inappropriately referred to as the "reserve" method.

The direct inventory reduction method (where the market loss is not recognized separately) has the practical advantage of simplicity. The primary disadvantages of this method are: *(a)* there is no distinction on the income statement between actual cost and market (holding) loss with a consequent overstatement of cost of goods sold and understatement of gross margin; and *(b)* the perpetual inventory subsidiary records must be adjusted to the reduced value.

With respect to balance sheet presentation when lower of cost or market is used, it is desirable that original cost be shown parenthetically or in some similar manner. Because of practical considerations, the parenthetical method is frequently used.

The allowance method is theoretically preferable because there is a distinction between actual cost and market loss on the income statement and balance sheet. Provision is made for reporting the inventory on the balance sheet at cost and subtracting the balance in the Allowance for Inventory Reduction to Market account. It is maintained that the effect of market fluctuations are correctly reported even though a *gain* may be recognized. For example, in Exhibit 8–7 the $6,000 *gain* for 19B is comprised of the $10,000 *loss* relating to the beginning inventory (recognized as a loss in the prior period), offset by the $4,000 *loss* relating to the 19B ending inventory. These two amounts offset to a *gain*, since the beginning inventory is *added* to cost and the ending inventory is *subtracted* as a cost in view of the computation of cost of goods sold in terms of original cost. In view of the current market value of $4,000 below cost, the position is taken that in terms of original cost and in recognition of the $10,000 loss previously recorded, there is a $6,000 gain that should be recognized in the current period.

The nature of the *gain* that frequently is reported may be seen more clearly by assuming that market is below cost at the end of one period and that there is no ending inventory at the end of the next period. The write-down in the prior period shifts cost (or rather a loss) from one period to the other. For example, assume the ending inventories are: Period 1—cost, $20,000, and market, $19,000; Period 2—no ending inventory (see Exhibit 8–8). The $1,000 market loss in Period 1 appears reasonable. The $1,000 market gain in Period 2 is in effect an adjustment of the initial inventory figure to $19,000. On the basis of actual cost the $1,000 must be added as income in the second period.

Another advantage frequently cited for the allowance method is that

[10] Ibid., p. 33.

when a company maintains a perpetual inventory system, the subsidiary inventory records need not be adjusted to a reduced value since the inventory control accounts remain at original cost. The position appears sound for a trading concern; however, there is a serious question as to whether it is equally sound for a manufacturing company, since failure to adjust the raw material inventory values to the reduced value might result in questionable costs for goods in process and finished goods inventories when the materials are issued. The primary disadvantages of the allowance method are *(a)* complexity, and *(b)* reporting a gain such as discussed above is impractical. However, this effect is implicit in the other methods, although not explicitly reported.[11]

EXHIBIT 8–8
Effect of Inventory Holding Losses on Net Income

	Period 1—Final Inventory at Market Is $1,000 below Cost		*Period 2—No Final Inventory*	
	At Actual Cost	*At Lower of Cost or Market (allowance method)*	*At Actual Cost*	*At Lower of Cost or Market (allowance method)*
Sales	$100,000	$100,000	$200,000	$200,000
Beginning inventory	10,000	10,000	20,000	20,000
Purchases	70,000	70,000	100,000	100,000
Total	80,000	80,000	120,000	120,000
Ending inventory	20,000	20,000	–	–
Cost of sales	60,000	60,000	120,000	120,000
Gross margin	40,000	40,000	80,000	80,000
Market loss (gain)		1,000		(1,000)
Net	$ 40,000	$ 39,000	$ 80,000	$ 81,000

NET REALIZABLE VALUE AND REPLACEMENT COST

Many accountants believe that inventories should be reported at either net realizable value or replacement cost rather than at actual cost. They believe that inventories should be reported at these values whether they are *above* or below actual cost because "fair value" better serves the decision-maker using the financial statements.

Current generally accepted accounting principles limit the use of net

---

[11] A variation of the allowance method is sometimes used. It derives the same results; however, the allowance account is not used. To illustrate, the entries would be as follows (based on the data used in Exhibits 8–6 and 8–7):

	19A		*19B*	
To close beginning inventory:				
Income summary	75,000		70,000	
Inventory		75,000		70,000
To record ending inventory and holding loss:				
Inventory	70,000		56,000	
Holding loss on inventory (gain)	10,000		4,000	
Income summary		80,000		60,000

realizable value and replacement cost to situations where specific inventory items were used or have become damaged, obsolete, or repossessed. Alternatively, the loss in value that is due to normal business operations, such as style changes, shop wear, change in local demand, and similar operational expectations, should be accounted for under the lower-of-cost-or-market procedure.

Goods subject to unusual changes in value and repossessed items should be valued at current replacement cost in their present condition. For example, assume X Appliance Store has on hand a repossessed TV set that cost $300. It was sold for $500 and was repossessed when $350 was owed on it by the customer. Assume further that similar used TV sets could be purchased for $290. The repossession should be recorded as follows:

Inventory—repossessed merchandise (replacement cost)	290	
Loss on repossession*	60	
Accounts receivable		350

* If repossessions are normal in the situation, the allowance for doubtful accounts should be debited because the estimated rate would anticipate such losses.

Often replacement cost for used or damaged merchandise cannot be realistically or objectively determined. In this situation net realizable value may be used. To illustrate, assume the facts for X Appliance Store as above with the added assumptions that no replacement cost is available, the used TV set can be sold for $300, and that disposal (resale) costs will approximate 15% of the sales price. The repossession would be recorded as follows:

Inventory—repossessed merchandise (net realizable value)	255	
Loss on repossession	95	
Accounts receivable		350

Computation of inventory value:

Estimated sales value	$300
Less: Estimated disposal costs (15%)	45
Net Realizable Value	$255

Assume further that the TV set is subsequently sold for $310 cash. The entry would be:

Cash	310	
Inventory—repossessed merchandise		255
Selling costs		45
Gain on sale of repossessed merchandise		10

When repossessions are a recurring feature of operations, estimates of future losses should be made and recorded in the year of sale as a debit to expense and as a credit to an allowance account similar to Allowance for Doubtful Accounts. In this situation, when there is a repossession any loss determined at that subsequent date should be charged to the allowance account.

Damaged and obsolete goods should be reported at current replacement cost in their present condition, or alternatively, at net realizable value.

Inventory losses resulting from storm, fire, flood, and other unusual events, if material in amount, should be reported separately *(a)* as extraordinary items or *(b)* as a line item listed above income before extraordinary items in conformity with the criteria set forth in "Reporting the Results of Operations," *APB Opinion No. 30* (see Chapter 4).

INVENTORIES VALUED ABOVE COST AT SELLING PRICE

Under certain unusual circumstances an inventory item may be valued at selling price. The circumstances, to conform to generally accepted accounting principles are:

> It is generally recognized that income accrues only at the time of sale, and that gains may not be anticipated by reflecting assets at their current sales prices. For certain articles, however, exceptions are permissible. Inventories of gold and silver, when there is an effective government-controlled market at a fixed monetary value, are ordinarily reflected at selling prices. A similar treatment is not uncommon for inventories representing agricultural, mineral, and other products, units of which are interchangeable and have an immediate marketability at quoted prices and for which appropriate costs may be difficult to obtain. Where such inventories are stated at sales prices, they should of course be reduced by expenditures to be incurred in disposal, and the use of such basis should be fully disclosed in the financial statements.[12]

Under this method, when there is a decrease in selling price, a holding loss would be reported; conversely, when there is an increase in selling price, a holding gain would be reported. Thus, net income would include gross margin and the holding gain or loss for the period. This effect can be attained by valuing the inventory at selling price (also see Chapter 25 on fair value accounting). To illustrate, assume the following simplified data:

Year	*Sales*	*Purchases at Cost*	*Ending Inventory at Selling Price*	*Expenses*
19A.........	$ -0-	$1,000	$1,750	$300
19B.........	1,700	-0-	-0-	300

The comparative results would be:

	Cost Basis		*Selling Price Basis*	
	19A	*19B*	*19A*	*19B*
Income Statement:				
Revenue..........................	$ -0-	$1,700	$750	$1,700
Cost of goods sold...........	-0-	(1,000)	-0-	(1,750)
Expenses	(300)	(300)	(300)	(300)
Gain (loss)........................	$(300)	$ 400	$450	$ (350)
Balance Sheet:				
Inventory	$1,000	$ -0-	$1,750	$ -0-

Illustrative of several pricing methods, a published financial statement recently reported the following inventory items:

[12] *Accounting Research Bulletin No. 43.*

Inventories:
At market:
Wheat and other grains, flour and meal .... $xxxx
At lower of cost (first-in, first-out) or market:
Soybeans and other raw materials xxxx
Supplies xxxx
At cost (last-in, first-out):
Soybean, linseed, sperm, and crude fish oil xxxx

RELATIVE SALES VALUE METHOD

When two or more items having different characteristics are purchased for a lump sum and a separate cost for each item is required for accounting purposes, some method of apportioning the *joint cost* must be used. The apportionment of the lump cost logically should be related to the economic utility of each item and the quantities involved. Since the *sales value* of a particular item may be a reasonable indication of its relative utility, apportionment of the joint cost of "basket purchases" is usually made on the basis of the *relative sales value* of the several items. Also, when joint costs are incurred subsequent to purchase, such costs frequently are allocated on the basis of relative sales value.

To illustrate, assume a packing plant purchases 1,000 bushels of orchard-run apples (ungraded) for $1,000, and that after purchase the apples are sorted into three grades at a cost of $35 with the following results: Grade A, 200 bushels; Grade B, 300 bushels; and Grade C, 500 bushels. Assume further that sorted apples are selling at the following prices: Grade A, $2; Grade B, $1.50; and Grade C, $.60. The cost apportionment may be made as shown in Exhibit 8–9.

EXHIBIT 8–9
Relative Sales Value Method

					Apportioned Cost	
Grade	*Quantity (bushels)*	*Unit Sales Price*	*Total Sales Value*	*Multi-plier**	*Total†*	*Per Bushel‡*
A	200	$2.00	$ 400	.90	$ 360	$1.80
B	300	1.50	450	.90	405	1.35
C	500	.60	300	.90	270	.54
	1,000		$1,150		$1,035	

* Total cost divided by total sales value, that is, $1,035 ÷ $1,150 = .90.
† Total sales value times multiplier.
‡ Unit sales price times multiplier.

Assuming a perpetual inventory system, the purchase would be recorded as follows:

Raw material inventory—apples Grade A (200 @ $1.80)	360	
Raw material inventory—apples Grade B (300 @ $1.35)	405	
Raw material inventory—apples Grade C (500 @ $.54)	270	
Cash		1,035

In cost allocations such as illustrated above, quantities lost due to shrinkage or spoilage should be ignored thereby resulting in a greater unit cost for the remaining units. In the case of real estate developments, improvements such as streets and parks may be apportioned in this manner to the cost of the salable areas. While the relative sales value method is frequently used, other bases, such as Btu's in petroleum products, are sometimes used.

LOSSES ON PURCHASE COMMITMENTS

Occasionally a company will contract with a supplier for a specific *quantity* of materials during a specified future *period* at an agreed *unit cost.* Basically, such purchase commitments (contracts) may be *(a)* subject to revision or cancellation before the end of the specified period, or *(b)* not subject to revision or cancellation. Each of these situations requires different accounting and reporting procedures.

In the case of purchase contracts *subject to revision or cancellation,* where a future loss is possible, and if the amount of the commitment is material, full-disclosure requires a footnote. To illustrate, assume XY Company entered into a purchase contract during October 1976 that: "During 1977, 50,000 units of Material X will be purchased at $5 each. Upon 60 days notice, this contract is subject to revision or cancellation by either party." The following footnote should be included in the financial statements for 1976:

> Note 1. At the end of 1976 a purchase contract for a maximum of $250,000 for raw materials during 1977 was in effect. The contract can be revised or canceled upon 60 days notice by either party. At the end of 1976, the materials had a market price of $240,000.

Where purchase contracts are *not subject to revision or cancellation,* and when there is a high probability of loss which can be realistically measured, the loss should be recorded in the accounts and reported in the financial statements. In the above example, assume the $240,000 market price is realistically measured and does not appear to be a temporary situation. Therefore, the loss on the purchase commitment should be recorded as follows:

Estimated loss on purchase commitment	10,000	
Liability – noncancellable purchase commitment		10,000

The estimated loss is reported on the 1976 income statement and the liability is reported on the balance sheet. When the goods are received in 1977, they are debited to merchandise inventory (or purchases) at their then current market value and the liability account is debited for the $10,000 estimated in 1976. To illustrate, assume the above raw materials have a market value at date of delivery of $235,000. The purchase entry would be:

Raw materials (or purchases)	235,000	
Liability – noncancellable purchase commitment	10,000	
Loss on purchase contract	5,000	
Cash		250,000

This is in accordance with *ARB No. 43*, Chapter 4, Statement 10 which reads: "Accrued net losses on firm purchase commitments for goods for inventory, measured in the same way as are inventory losses, should, if material, be recognized in the accounts and the amounts thereof separately disclosed in the income statement." FASB *Statement No. 5*, March 1975, requires this treatment.

QUESTIONS

1. In general, why should the accountant and the management be concerned with inventories?
2. List and briefly explain the usual inventory classifications.
3. Why are inventories such as office supplies, janitorial supplies, and shipping supplies frequently reported as prepaid expenses rather than as inventory?
4. What general rule is applied by accountants in determining what goods should be included in inventory?
5. Assume you are in the process of adjusting and closing the books at the end of the fiscal year (for the purchaser), what treatment, for inventory purposes, would you accord the following goods in transit? *(a)* invoice received for $5,000, shipped f.o.b. shipping point; *(b)* invoice received for $10,000 shipped f.o.b. destination; and *(c)* invoice received for $1,000, shipped f.o.b. shipping point and delivery refused on the last day of the period due to damaged condition.
6. Complete the following:

	Include in Inventory	
	Yes	*No*
a. Goods out on consignment.	____	____
b. Goods held on consignment.	____	____
c. Merchandise at our branch for sale.	____	____
d. Merchandise at conventions for display purposes.	____	____
e. Goods held by our agents for us.	____	____
f. Goods held by us for sale on commission.	____	____
g. Goods held by us but awaiting return to vendor due to damaged condition.	____	____
h. Goods returned to us from buyer, reason unknown to date.	____	____

7. Explain the principal aspects of a periodic inventory system.
8. Why is cost of goods sold often a residual amount?
9. Explain the effect of each of the following errors in the final inventory of a trading business:
   a. Incorrectly included 100 units of Commodity A, valued at $1 per unit, in the final inventory; the purchase was recorded.
   b. Incorrectly included 200 units of Commodity B, valued at $2 per unit, in the final inventory; the purchase was not recorded.
   c. Incorrectly excluded 300 units of Commodity C, valued at $3 per unit, from the final inventory; the purchase was recorded.

d. Incorrectly excluded 400 units of Commodity D, valued at $4 per unit, from the final inventory; the purchase was not recorded.

10. What is meant by the "accounting value" of inventory? What accounting principles predominate in measuring this value?

11. In determining *unit cost* for inventory purposes, how should the following items be treated?
    a. Freight on goods and materials purchased.
    b. Purchase returns.
    c. Purchase discounts.

12. Should purchase discounts be *(a)* deducted in total in the income statement for the period in which the discounts arose, or *(b)* deducted in part in the income statement and in part from inventory on the balance sheet? Explain.

13. Cost is the primary basis for inventory valuation. List the four exceptions to cost discussed in the chapter. Under what specified conditions is each generally acceptable?

14. Why is the concept of lower of cost or market applied to inventory valuation?

15. What is the nature and purpose of the Allowance for Inventory Reduction to Market account?

16. In what specific situations may inventories be valued at selling price even though it is above cost?

17. How should damaged, obsolete, and depreciated merchandise on hand at the end of the period be valued for inventory purposes?

18. What are the basic assumptions underlying the relative sales value method when used in allocating costs for inventory purposes?

19. Briefly outline the accounting and reporting of losses on purchase commitments when *(a)* the purchase contract is subject to revision or cancellation, and *(b)* it is noncancellable.

DECISION CASE 8–1

Ward Manufacturing Company has been in operation since 1952 and has experienced satisfactory growth since that time. L. Ward, the organizer, was an experienced and skilled machinist having operated a small custom machine shop for years. In 1952, with the financial assistance of a friend, Ward organized the company to manufacture specially designed trailers for the transportation of horses. Most of the trailers manufactured were designed to haul one horse; consequently, they were built to meet the particular desires of each customer. These trailers varied from a standard type to super deluxe models in keeping with the horse-show tradition.

In 1960 the company started making trailers for boats. Two standard models were developed for sale to sporting goods stores, and in addition trailers were made to meet the specifications of individual buyers. The company recently experienced an unexpected demand for boat trailers which was attributed to their quality, competitive price, and design. Ward is having considerable difficulty keeping up with this demand and hesitates to add capacity, workers, and materials needed, on the basis of expectations, rather than on the basis of firm orders.

As a consequence, the firm has lost some business. Customarily a 50% deposit is required on all custom-made trailers.

Ward has been particularly interested in the manufacturing side of the business, although the financial and management aspects appear to be a problem. Ward is not inclined to be the executive type. As a result of some income tax difficulties Ward engaged an outside CPA to set up records and help with the financial management of the company. One employee spends part time on the present recordkeeping which involves minimum records on cash, salaries, receivables, and wages.

The company regularly stocks 23 different items of raw materials and numerous small supplies such as bolts, screws, welding materials, and paint. The Company loses about two thirds of the available cash discounts on purchases through oversight. Customarily the company pays freight on the purchases. Finished goods, on the lot, usually consist of 8 to 15 horse trailers, 20 to 35 boat trailers, plus small quantities of eight other small items generally manufactured. Frequently, customers leave trailers on the lot a week or more before picking them up. Several kinds of raw material currently on hand are of such a nature that the replacement cost is less than the original cost. The company has always had difficulty with raw materials and supplies; frequently shortages hold up work on jobs for days. Frequently, substitutions of higher cost materials are necessary due to items out of stock. The raw materials are stored both outside and inside, and individual workmen select the material as they need it on a help-yourself basis. Ward feels that the company cannot afford an inventory clerk. Items are reordered from a notebook kept on Ward's desk where individual workers are instructed to write down any items that are low or out of stock. When raw materials are received they are moved to the storage area and placed wherever space is available. Space is a problem. No inventory records are maintained. No payments are made for raw materials unless the invoice is signed by the employee that checked in the goods. Theft is no problem for the company.

The CPA has decided to install a job-order cost system so that costs will be accumulated by job for direct material, direct labor, and manufacturing overhead; and it is recognized that in view of the smallness of the company, the overall system must be simple and easy to operate.

The CPA is concerned about the raw material and finished goods inventory situations in particular and has asked you to make recommendations relative to the inventory problem. The CPA has decided to employ *Fifo* and lower of cost or market. Specifically, the CPA wants your suggestions for the company relative to (1) determination of quantities in inventory, (2) treatment of freight-in and purchase discount, (3) the accounting treatment of lower of cost or market, and (4) recommendations for better control of inventory. Sound reasons are expected to support your suggestions.

Required:

Narrate your recommendations to the company giving particular attention to the raw materials and finished goods inventories. Give supporting reasons.

EXERCISES

Exercise 8–1

Listed below for the Adams Sales Company are items of inventory that are in question. The company stores a good portion of the merchandise in a separate warehouse and transfers damaged goods to a special inventory account. The company policy is "satisfied customers."

a. Items counted in warehouse by inventory crew	$30,000
b. Invoice received for goods ordered, goods shipped but not received (Adams pays the freight)	400
c. Items shipped today, f.o.b. destination, invoice mailed to customer	60
d. Items currently being used for window displays	600
e. Items on counters for sale per inventory count (not in [*a*])	6,000
f. Items in shipping department, invoice not mailed to customer	140
g. Items in receiving department, refused by Adams because of damage	80
h. Items shipped today, f.o.b. shipping point, invoice mailed to customer	300
i. Items included in warehouse count, damaged, not returnable	120
j. Items included in warehouse count, specifically segregated for shipment to customer next period per sales contract	200
k. Items in receiving department, returned by customer, no communication received from the customer	100
l. Items ordered and in the receiving department, invoice not received	500

Required:

Complete the following tabulation to reflect the correct inventory:

Item	*Exclude or Include in Inventory*	*Amount*	*Explanation*
a. Items counted in warehouse	Include	$30,000	Items on hand
b. Etc.			
Total Inventory Valuation		$	

Exercise 8–2

The records of X Company reflected the following data: sales revenue, $60,000; purchases, $45,900; net income to sales revenue, 4%; one inventory amount was $12,500; and expenses, $10,200.

Required:

1. Reconstruct the income statement. Assume a periodic inventory system.
2. Give entries at the end of the period for the inventories assuming: Case A, a periodic inventory system; and Case B, a perpetual inventory system.

Exercise 8–3

The records for K Company at December 31, 19A, reflected the following:

	Units	*Unit Amount*
Sales during the period	10,000	$11
Inventory at beginning of period	2,000	5
Merchandise purchased during the period (for cash)	18,400	5
Purchase returns during the period (cash refund)	100	5
Inventory at end of the period	?	

Required:

In parallel columns, give entries for the above transactions, including entries at the end of the period assuming:

Case A – Periodic inventory system.
Case B – Perpetual inventory system.

Use the following format:

Accounts	*Case A*	*Case B*

Exercise 8–4

The independent CPA for Brown Company found the following errors in the records of the company:

a. Incorrect exclusion from the final inventory of items costing $3,000 for which the purchase was not recorded.
b. Inclusion in the final inventory of goods costing $5,000, although a purchase was not recorded. The goods in question were being held on consignment from Conley Company.
c. Incorrect exclusion of $2,000 from the inventory count at the end of the period. The goods were in transit (f.o.b. shipping point); the invoice had been received, and the purchase recorded.
d. Inclusion of items on the receiving dock that were being held for return to the vendor because of damage. In counting the goods in the receiving department, these items were incorrectly included. With respect to these goods, a purchase of $4,000 had been recorded.

The records (uncorrected) showed the following amounts: *(a)* purchases, $170,000; *(b)* pretax income, $15,000; *(c)* accounts payable, $20,000; and *(d)* inventory at the end of the period, $40,000.

Required:

Set up a table to reflect the uncorrected balances, changes occasioned by the errors, and the corrected balances for (1) purchases, (2) pretax income, (3) accounts payable, and (4) inventory.

Exercise 8–5

The records of Smith Company reflected the following:

Sales revenue		$160,000
Cost of goods sold:........................		
Beginning inventory	$10,000	
Purchases	85,000	
Goods available for sale..............	95,000	
Ending inventory	25,000	70,000
Gross margin		90,000
Expenses..................................		60,000
Net Income (pretax)......................		$ 30,000

The following errors were found that had not been corrected:

a. Accrued expenses not recognized, $6,000.
b. Prepaid revenues amounting to $4,000 are included in the sales revenue amount.

c. Goods costing $10,000 were incorrectly included in the ending inventory (they were being held on consignment from Blue Company). No purchase was recorded.

d. Goods costing $3,000 were correctly included in the ending inventory; however, no purchase was recorded (assume a credit purchase).

Required:

1. Recast the income statement on a correct basis.
2. What amounts would be incorrect on the balance sheet if the errors are not corrected?

Exercise 8–6

Milam Company uses a perpetual inventory system. The items on hand are inventoried on a rotation basis throughout the year so that all items are checked twice each year. At the end of the year, the following data relating to goods on hand are available:

	Per Perpetual Inventory		
Product	*Units*	*Unit Cost*	*Per Physical Count (units)*
A	200	$ 1	180
B	1,500	2	1,520
C	2,000	3	1,900
D	8,000	1	8,000
E	13,000	2	12,800
F	500	20	480
G	9,400	5	9,495
H	11,000	2	11,200
I	4,000	21	3,990
J	5,000	10	4,995

Required:

Determine the amount of the inventory overage or shortage and give the indicated entry. Indicate the final disposition of any discrepancy that is recorded.

Exercise 8–7

The recapitulation of inventory taken on December 31 was as follows for Noonan Company:

a. Merchandise in the store at 10% above cost	$330,000
b. Merchandise out on consignment at sales price (including markup of 60% on selling price)	9,600
c. Goods held on consignment from the Brown Electrical Company at sales price (sales commission, 20% of sales price included)	2,400
d. Goods purchased, in transit (shipped f.o.b. shipping point; estimated freight, not included, $600), invoice price	5,000
e. Goods out on approval, sales price, $1,500, cost, $1,000	1,500
Total Inventory	$348,500

Required:

Compute the correct final inventory. Show computations.

Exercise 8–8

Rose Company purchased 6,000 pounds of Commodity X at $5 per pound. In addition, the company paid $230 freight on the purchase. The company also purchased 20,000 pounds of Commodity Y at $2 per pound and 4,000 pounds of Commodity Z at $8 per pound. In connection with the two latter purchases, which were delivered simultaneously by the trucking line, a freight charge (not detailed by product) was paid amounting to $432. The company uses a perpetual inventory system.

Required:

1. Give the combined entry to record the purchases from a theoretical point of view.
2. From a practical point of view, how could the purchases be recorded?
3. If you suggested a different entry from the practical point of view, indicate the basis for your suggestion.

Exercise 8–9

Roberts Trading Company purchased merchandise on credit for $20,000; terms, 2/15, n/30. Payment for $15,000 of this amount was made during the discount period; the balance was paid after the discount period. The company uses a perpetual inventory system.

Required:

Give entries in parallel columns to record the purchase and payments on the liability assuming:

a. Net of discount approach is used for purchase discounts.
b. Gross amount approach is used for purchase discounts.

Which approach is preferable? Why?

Exercise 8–10

Economy Trading Company purchased merchandise on credit for $40,000; terms, 2/10, n/30. Payment was made within the discount period. At the end of the fiscal period, one fourth of this merchandise was unsold. Determine (1) the cost of goods sold that would be reported on the income statement, and (2) the final inventory valuation as regards this particular lot of merchandise assuming:

a. Purchases and accounts payable are recorded at gross, and purchase discounts are reported on the income statement as other income.
b. Purchases and accounts payable are recorded at gross, and purchase discounts are deducted in total from purchases on the income statement.
c. Purchases and accounts payable both are recorded at net.

Evaluate the several approaches. Which approach do you prefer? Why?

Exercise 8–11

HiFi Company, a large dealer in radio and television sets, buys large quantities of a television model which costs $400. The contract reads that if 100 or more are purchased during the year, a bonus or rebate of $15 per set will be made. On December 15, the records showed that 150 sets had been purchased and that 10 remained on hand in inventory. A claim for the rebate was made to the jobber, and a check was received on January 20 after the books were closed.

Required:

1. At what valuation should the inventory be shown on December 31? Why?
2. What entry should be made relative to the rebate on December 31? Why?
3. What entry would be made on January 20? Why?

Exercise 8–12

Small Company had 1,000 units of Product A in inventory at the end of the fiscal period. The unit cost was $60; estimated distribution costs $3 per unit; and the "normal" profit is $4 per unit. Compute the unit valuation of the inventory under each separate case listed below. Apply the lower-of-cost-or-market procedure in accordance with the "exceptions" specified by the Committee on Accounting Procedure of the AICPA.

Case	*Anticipated Sales Price*	*Current Replacement Cost*	*Case*	*Anticipated Sales Price*	*Current Replacement Cost*
a)	$65	$61	*f)*	$68	$61
b)	70	62	*g)*	50	44
c)	60	58	*h)*	59	57
d)	58	50	*i)*	61	53
e)	66	57	*j)*	73	59

Exercise 8–13

In the process of auditing the records of Ace Company, your client takes the position that under the lower-of-cost-or-market procedure the two items listed below should be reported in the final inventory at $12,000 (total). Do you agree? If not, indicate the correct inventory valuation by item. Show computations.

"Handyman" hedge clippers: 300 on hand; cost, $22 each; reproduction cost, $16; estimated sales price, $30; estimated distribution cost, $9 each; and normal profit, 10% on the sales price.

"Handyman" edgers: 200 on hand; cost, $40 each; reproduction cost, $36 each; estimated sales price, $90; estimated distribution cost, $28; and normal profit, 20% of sales.

Exercise 8–14

The inventory records of the M Company showed the following data:

		Unit Basis	
Product	*Units*	*Cost*	*Market*
A	200	$1.50	$1.60
B	500	1.00	.90
C	300	3.00	3.20
D	100	4.00	4.20

Required:

Determine the value of the inventory assuming the lower-of-cost-or-market procedure is applied –

a. To individual items.
b. To groups assuming A and B are in one group and C and D are in another group.
c. To totals.

Exercise 8–15

The inventories for the years 19A and 19B are shown below for Ryan Retailers, Inc.:

Inventory Date	*Original Cost*	*Lower of Cost or Market*	*Difference*
January 1, 19A	$6,000	$6,000	$-0-
December 31, 19A	7,000	6,500	500
December 31, 19B	9,000	9,000	-0-

Required:

1. Give, in parallel columns, the journal entries to apply the lower-of-cost-or-market procedure to the inventories for 19A and 19B, assuming the company uses the direct inventory reduction method (where the holding loss is not separately recognized) under *(a)* periodic inventory procedures, and *(b)* perpetual inventory procedures.
2. What are the primary advantages and disadvantages of the direct inventory reduction method compared with other methods that could be used?

Exercise 8–16

Utilizing the data given in Exercise 8–15, give, in parallel columns, the journal entries to apply the lower-of-cost-or-market procedure to the inventories for 19A and 19B, assuming the company utilizes the inventory allowance method where the holding losses in the beginning and ending inventories are separately recognized under *(a)* periodic inventory procedures, and *(b)* perpetual inventory procedures. What are the primary advantages and disadvantages of this method?

Exercise 8–17

Snappy Canning Company purchased 1,910 bushels of ungraded apricots at $2 per bushel. The apricots were sorted as follows: Grade One, 600 bushels; Grade Two, 400 bushels; Grade Three, 900 bushels. Handling and sorting costs amounted to $500. The current market prices for graded apricots were: Grade One, $4 per bushel; Grade Two, $3 per bushel; and Grade Three, $1 per bushel. The company utilizes a perpetual inventory system. What entry would be made to record the purchase? Show computations of total and unit costs for each grade assuming the relative sales value method of cost allocation is used.

Exercise 8–18

Community Development Corporation purchased a tract of land for development purposes. The tract was subdivided as follows: 30 lots to sell at $6,000 per lot, and 80 lots to sell at $9,000 per lot. The tract cost $200,000 and an additional $25,000 was spent in general development costs. Assuming cost allocation is based on the relative sales value method, give entries for *(a)* purchase of the tract and payment of the development costs, *(b)* sale of one $6,000 lot, and *(c)* sale of one $9,000 lot. Assume a perpetual inventory system.

Exercise 8–19

Swift Realty Company purchased and subdivided a tract of land at a cost of $440,000. The subdivision was on the following basis:

20% used for streets, alleys, and parks.
30% divided into 100 lots to sell for $4,000 each.
40% divided into 200 lots to sell for $3,000 each.
10% divided into 50 lots to sell for $2,000 each.

Required:

1. Assuming the relative sales value method is used, compute the valuation of the inventory of lots at the end of the first year assuming 20, $4,000 lots; 50, $3,000 lots; and 10, $2,000 lots are on hand. (Ignore paving costs and other deferrable costs.) Assume a perpetual inventory system.
2. Record the purchase of the lots, reflect the cost allocation.
3. Record the sale of one $4,000 lot.

Exercise 8–20

Sweet Candy Company purchased 1,000 bags of orchard-run pecans at a cost of $3,460. In addition, the company incurred $50 for transportation and grading. The pecans graded out as follows:

Grade	*Quantity*	*Current Market Price per Bag*
A	300	$7.00
B	500	6.00
C	150	5.00
Waste	50	

Required:

Assuming the relative sales value method is used to allocate joint costs, give:

a. The entry for purchase assuming a perpetual inventory system (show computations).
b. Valuation of final inventory assuming the following quantities are on hand: Grade A, 100 bags; Grade B, 80 bags; and Grade C, 20 bags.
c. Sale of 20 bags of the Grade A pecans.

Exercise 8–21

A fire damaged some of the merchandise held for sale by Thomas Appliance Company. Five television sets and six stereo sets were damaged. They will be repaired and sold as used sets. Data are as follows:

	Per Set	
	Television	Stereo
Inventory (at cost)	$300	$200
Estimated cost to repair	40	30
Estimated cost to sell	20	20
Estimated sales price	120	90
Insurance recovery (cash)	25	20

Required:

1. Compute the appropriate inventory value for each set.
2. Give the separate entries to record the damaged goods inventory for the television and stereo sets. Assume a perpetual inventory system.
3. Give the entries to record the subsequent repair of the television sets and the stereo sets. (Credit Cash.)
4. Give the entry to record sale for cash of one television set and one stereo set. (Credit Distribution Costs.)

Exercise 8–22

Zakin Corporation, during 1975, signed a contract with Young Company to "purchase 20,000 subassemblies, at $30 each during 1976."

Required:

1. On December 31, 1975, end of the annual accounting period, the financial statements are to be prepared. Under what additional contractual and economic conditions should disclosure of the contract terms be made only by means of a note in the financial statements? Prepare an appropriate note. Assume the cost is dropping.
2. What additional contractual and economic conditions would require accrual of a loss? Give the accrual entry. Assume the cost has dropped.
3. Assume the subassemblies are received in 1976 when their cost was at the estimate you used in Requirement 2. The contract was paid in full. Give the required entry.

PROBLEMS

Problem 8–1

As the auditor for the year ended December 31, 19A, you found the following transactions occurred near the closing date for Adkins Company:

a. Merchandise received on January 6, 19B costing $800 was recorded on January 6, 19B. An invoice on hand showed the shipment was made f.o.b. supplier's warehouse on December 31, 19A. Since the merchandise was not on hand at December 31, 19A, it was not included in the inventory.

b. A sealed packing case containing a product costing $900 was in Adkins shipping room when the physical inventory was taken. It was not included in the inventory because it was marked *"Hold for customer's shipping instructions."* Investigation revealed that the customer's order was dated December 18, 19A, but that the case was shipped and the customer billed on January 10, 19B. The product was a regular stock item.

c. A special machine, fabricated to order for a customer, was finished and in the shipping room on December 31, 19A. The customer had inspected it and was satisfied with it. The customer was billed in full for $1,000 on that date. The machine was excluded from inventory because it was shipped on January 1, 19B.

d. Merchandise costing $700 was received on December 28, 19A, and a purchase was not recorded. You located the related papers in the hands of the purchasing agent; they indicated *"on consignment from Baker Company."*

e. Merchandise costing $2,000 was received on January 3, 19B, and the related purchase invoice recorded January 5. The invoice showed the shipment was made on December 29, 19A, f.o.b. *destination.*

Required:

For each situation, state whether the merchandise should be included in the client's inventory. Give your reason for the decision on each item.

(AICPA adapted)

Problem 8–2

Assume you are the independent auditor for the Cline Manufacturing Corporation. The final inventory for the year ended December 31, 19A, is under consideration. The following problems related to the final inventory have arisen, and the company accountant requests your advice on them:

	Material A @ $3	*Material B @ $5*
Raw material inventory data on December 31, 19A (in units):		
a. Items counted in bins Nos. 1–5	12,000	2,000
b. Purchase invoice received, items not received (f.o.b. shipping point)		200
c. Items counted in bin No. 2, set aside for return to vendor next period per agreement December 20, 19A; not up to specifications, shipped January 2, 19B		100
d. Items counted in bin No. 3 that had been issued to factory and returned by them in damaged condition, not returnable to vendor		50
e. Items counted in bin No. 4 from a shipment partly damaged when received, returnable to vendor per agreement; shipped January 3, 19B		40
f. Items purchased, on receiving dock, refused because of damage	50	
g. Items purchased, on receiving dock, invoice not received	100	300
h. Items counted in bin No. 5, to be returned to vendor, rejected for incorrect specs	200	
i. Purchase invoice received, items not received (f.o.b. destination)	20	100

	Product X @ $10	Product Y @ $20
Finished goods inventory data on December 31, 19A (in units):		
j. Items counted in warehouse (excluding the items below)	15,000	10,000
k. Items shipped to customer on January 1, 19B, invoice mailed December 31, 19A (f.o.b. shipping point)		500
l. Items completed by factory, counted in the work in process inventory; not transported to warehouse	800	
m. Items on receiving dock, returned by customer because of damage, notification from customer received		50
n. Items on trucking company dock, invoice mailed to customer, buyer pays freight	500	
o. Items in damaged condition	20	10
p. Items in shipping department, invoice not mailed to customer	80	
q. Items shipped December 31, 19A, f.o.b. destination; invoice mailed January 2, 19B	100	
r. Items on consignment to Brady Distributing Company	400	700
s. Items specifically segregated and crated for shipment to Cline Branch X	100	100
t. Items used for display purposes	10	30
u. Items specifically segregated and crated for shipment to customer early next period per signed sales contract		500
v. Items on receiving dock, returned by customer, no notification received (not damaged)	20	

Required:

Compute the valuation of the final inventory of raw materials and finished goods indicating specifically what items you would include and exclude. Give reasons you would present to the company relative to any doubtful items. The following format is recommended:

		Material A		Material B		
Item	*Inventory Include/Exclude*	*Units*	*Amounts*	*Units*	*Amounts*	*Explanation*

Problem 8–3

Foster Company's fiscal period ends on December 31, 19A. The company uses a periodic inventory system. An independent CPA was engaged after the end of the year to perform an audit. Therefore, the CPA did not observe the taking of the inventory. As a result, an examination was made of the inventory records, purchases, and sales.

The financial statements prepared by the company (uncorrected) showed the following: final inventory, $60,000; accounts receivable, $60,000; accounts payable, $20,000; sales, $400,000; purchases, $160,000; and pretax net income, $30,000.

The following data were found during the audit:

a. Merchandise that cost $10,000 and sold on December 31, 19A, for $14,000 was included in the final inventory. The sale was recorded. The goods were in transit; however, a clerk failed to note that the goods were shipped f.o.b. shipping point.

b. Merchandise that cost $6,000 was excluded from the final inventory and not recorded as a sale for $7,500 on December 26, 19A. The goods had been specifically segregated. According to the terms of the contract of sale, ownership did not pass until actual delivery.

c. Merchandise that cost $15,000 was included in the final inventory. The related purchase was not recorded. The goods had been shipped by the vendor f.o.b. destination; and the invoice, but not the goods, was received on December 30, 19A.

d. Merchandise in transit that cost $7,000 was excluded from inventory because it was not on hand. The shipment from the vendor was f.o.b. shipping point. The purchase was recorded on December 29, 19A, when the invoice was received.

e. Merchandise in transit that cost $11,000 was excluded from inventory because it had not arrived. The related purchase was not recorded by December 30, 19A. The merchandise was shipped by the vendor f.o.b. shipping point.

f. Merchandise that cost $8,000 was included in the final inventory since it was on hand. The merchandise had been rejected because of incorrect specifications and was being held for return to the vendor. The merchandise was recorded as a purchase on December 26, 19A.

g. Merchandise that cost $18,000 was excluded from the inventory, and the related sale for $23,000 was recorded. The goods had been segregated in the warehouse for shipment; there was no contract for sale; however, there was a purchase order from the customer.

h. Merchandise that cost $10,000 was out on consignment to the Goode Distributing Company and was excluded from the final inventory. The merchandise was recorded as a sale of $25,000 when shipped on December 2, 19A.

Required:

Prepare a schedule with one column for each of the six financial statement accounts (starting with the uncorrected balances) plus any other columns, deemed useful. Show the specific corrections to each balance and the corrected balances. Explain the basis for your decision on questionable items.

Problem 8–4

Hiam Company completed the following selected transactions during 19A for Product A:

	Units	Unit Amount
Beginning inventory	5,000	$18
Purchases	20,000	18
Purchase returns	1,000	18
Sales	18,000	35
Sales returns	100	35
Ending inventory per physical count	5,800	
Inventory shortage	?	
Expenses (excluding income taxes), $258,900		

Required:

1. In parallel columns, give entries for the above transactions including entries

at the end of the accounting period, December 31, 19A, for (assume cash transactions):

Case A – A periodic inventory system.
Case B – A perpetual inventory system.

2. Prepare a multiple-step income statement assuming a periodic inventory system, 10,000 shares of common stock outstanding, and a 40% income tax rate.
3. What amounts, if any, would be different on the income statement assuming a perpetual inventory system is used? Explain.

Problem 8–5

Harris Company has completed the income statement and balance sheet (summarized and uncorrected shown below) at December 31, 19A. Subsequently, during the audit, the following items were discovered:

a. Expenses amounting to $3,000 were not accrued.
b. A conditional sale on credit for $9,000 was recorded on December 31, 19A. The goods, which cost $5,000, were included in the final inventory because they had not been shipped since the customer's address was not known and the credit had not been approved. Ownership had not passed.
c. Merchandise purchased on December 31, 19A, on credit for $6,000, was included in the final inventory because the goods were on hand. A purchase was not recorded because the accounting department had not received the invoice from the vendor.
d. The final inventory was overstated by $10,000 due to an addition error on the inventory sheet.
e. A sale return (on account) on December 31, 19A, was not recorded: sales amount, $15,000; cost, $8,000. The ending inventory did not include the goods returned.

	Uncorrected Amounts	Items for Correction (a)	(b)	(c)	(d)	(e)	Corrected Amounts
Income Statement:							
Sales revenue	$90,000						
Cost of goods sold	50,000						
Gross margin	40,000						
Expenses	30,000						
Pretax income	$10,000						
Balance Sheet:							
Accounts receivable	$32,000						
Inventory	20,000						
Remaining assets	40,000						
Accounts payable	11,000						
Remaining liabilities	6,000						
Common stock	60,000						
Retained earnings	15,000						

Required:

Set up a schedule similar to the one above and derive the corrections. Indicate increases and decreases for each transaction. Explain any assumptions made with respect to doubtful items. Disregard income taxes.

Problem 8–6

Pope Company purchased merchandise during 19A on credit for $63,000 (includes $3,000 freight charges paid in cash); terms, 2/10, n/30. All of the gross liability, except $10,000, was paid within the discount period; the remainder was paid within the 30-day term. At the end of the annual accounting period, December 31, 19A, 90% of the merchandise had been sold and 10% remained in inventory. The company uses a perpetual system.

Required:

1. Give entries, in parallel columns, for the purchase and the two payments on the liability assuming *(a)* purchases and accounts payable are recorded at gross, and *(b)* purchases and accounts payable are recorded at net.
2. What amounts would be reported for the final inventory and cost of goods sold under each method. Assume purchase discounts, under the gross method are reported as a deduction from cost of goods sold. Explain why the amounts are different between the two methods.
3. Which method do you prefer? Why?

Problem 8–7

The information shown below relating to the final inventory was taken from the records of the Morris Publishing Company:

		Per Unit	
Inventory Classification	*Quantity*	*Cost*	*Market*
Newsprint:			
Stock A	200	$300	$330
B	60	250	230
Special stock (white):			
Stock H	20	70	65
I	10	60	62
Special stock (colored):			
Stock S	8	75	70
T	4	90	80
U	7	100	110

Required:

1. Determine the valuation of the above inventory at cost and at lower of cost or market assuming application by *(a)* item by item, *(b)* classifications, and *(c)* total inventory.
2. Give the entry to record the ending inventory for each approach assuming periodic inventory and—
   a. Direct inventory reduction method.
   b. Allowance method.
3. Which method do you prefer? Why?

Problem 8–8

The records of Waters Company provide the following data relating to inventories for the years 19A and 19B:

Inventory Date	*Original Cost*	*At Lower of Cost or Market*
January 1, 19A	$40,000	$40,000
December 31, 19A	50,000	46,000
December 31, 19B	40,000	37,000

Other data available are:

	19A	*19B*
Sales	$220,000	$250,000
Purchases	135,000	150,000
Administrative and selling expenses	51,000	61,000

The company values inventories on the basis of lower of cost or market and uses the periodic inventory system. For problem purposes use only pretax amounts.

Required:

1. Give, in parallel columns, for 19A and 19B, the entries to apply the lower-of-cost-or-market procedure under each of the two methods: Case A – direct inventory reduction where the holding loss is not separately reported; and Case B – the allowance method. Set up a format similar to the following:

Accounts	*Amounts* 19A	19B
Case A:		
Entries		
Case B:		
Entries		

2. Prepare an income statement and show the inventory amounts for the balance sheet for each case. Follow the format illustrated in the chapter.
3. Which method do you prefer? Why?

Problem 8–9

The summarized income statements for the Ashton Company are shown below as developed by the company. The inventories are valued at cost.

	19A	*19B*
Sales	$104,000	$97,000
Cost of goods sold:		
Beginning inventory	25,000	20,000
Purchases	75,000	73,000
Total	100,000	93,000
Ending inventory	20,000	15,000
Cost of goods sold	80,000	78,000
Gross margin	24,000	19,000
Less: Operating expenses	14,000	12,000
Pretax Income	$ 10,000	$ 7,000

The inventories valued at lower of cost or market would have been at the beginning of 19A, $24,000; end of 19A, $17,000; and end of 19B, $13,000.

Required:

1. Restate the 19A and 19B income statements applying the lower-of-cost-or-market rule for each of the following procedures (use a format similar to that illustrated in the text). Disregard income taxes.
   a. Direct inventory reduction method where the inventory holding loss is not reported separately.
   b. Allowance method where the inventory holding losses in both beginning and ending inventories are reported separately.
2. Which procedure is preferable? Why?

Problem 8–10

Fresh Fruit Company purchased a large quantity of mixed grapefruit for $34,300, which is sorted at a cost of $900 as indicated below. Sales (at the sales price indicated) and losses (frozen, theft, rotten, etc.) are also listed.

Grade	*Baskets Bought*	*Sales Price per Basket*	*Baskets Sold*	*Baskets Lost*
A	3,000	$4.00	2,000	50
B	4,000	3.00	3,000	60
C	10,000	1.50	8,000	80
D	6,000	.75	4,000	
Culls	1,000	.50	900	
Loss	55			

Required:

1. Give entry for purchase assuming a perpetual inventory system. Show computations.
2. Give entries to record the sales and cost of goods sold.
3. Give entry relative to the losses assuming the losses are recorded separately from cost of sales.
4. Determine the valuation of the final inventory.
5. Compute the direct contribution for each grade of grapefruit. (Disregard operating, administrative, and selling expenses.)

Problem 8–11

On May 1, 19A, Box and Carr invested $90,000 cash each for the purpose of purchasing and subdividing a tract of land for residential building purposes.

On June 1, they purchased 30 acres comprising the subdivision, at $5,000 per acre, paying $50,000 in cash and giving a one-year, 8% interest-bearing note (with mortgage) for the balance. Development costs amounted to $92,000.

The property was subdivided into 300 lots of equal size, 100 of which were to sell at $3,000 each and the balance at $4,000 each.

During June to December 19A the following sales were made for one-half cash and the balance on 9% interest-bearing notes, due in six months from date of sale.

	Lots
Group A (sold at $4,000 each)	30
Group B (sold at $3,000 each)	20

Cash collections on the notes receivables up to December 31, 19A, amounted to $50,000 principal and $4,000 interest. Accrued interest recorded at December 31, 19A, amounted to $3,000.

Operating and selling expenses amounted to $95,000 by the end of December 19A. No payment was made on the note payable.

Required:

1. Journal entries for all of the above transactions. Disregard income taxes.
2. Statement of income for the months of June through December.
3. Compute the inventory of unsold lots on December 31, 19A.

Problem 8–12

Broome Appliance Company completed the following selected (and summarized) transactions during 19A:

a. Purchased merchandise for resale, quoted at $150,000, on credit terms, 2/10, n/30; immediately paid 80% of the cash cost.
b. Paid freight charges on purchases amounting to $6,000 cash.
c. Paid 60% of the accounts payable within the discount period. The remaining amount was unpaid at year-end; however, at year-end none was beyond the discount period.
d. Returned merchandise to a vendor because of damage in shipment and received a $1,980 cash refund.
e. Sold merchandise for $300,000, of which 10% was on end-of-the-month credit terms.
f. Repossessed a refrigerator abandoned by a customer who left town. The sales price was $400 of which $300 was unpaid. The refrigerator cost $320. Estimates are that the used refrigerator can be sold for $250 and that cost of repairs will be $30 and selling costs will be $10.
g. Operating expenses paid in cash, $90,000.
h. Paid $30 to repair the repossessed refrigerator.
i. The purchases amount given in *(a)* included a shipment, on credit, that had a quoted cost of $8,000 (terms, 2/10, n/30). The liability had not been paid. The shipment was in transit, f.o.b. destination, at December 31, 19A. The invoice had been received. It was not included in the ending inventory amount.
j. The beginning inventory was $70,000.
k. The ending inventory (excluding the repossessed refrigerator) was $78,000 at cost; at lower of cost or market, $73,000.

Accounting policies followed by the company are: *(a)* annual accounting period ends December 31; *(b)* purchases and accounts payable are recorded at net of cash discounts; *(c)* freight charges are allocated to the merchandise when purchased; *(d)* all cash discounts allowed are taken; *(e)* used and damaged merchandise carried in a separate inventory account; *(f)* inventories are reported at lower of cost or market and the loss on the ending inventory separately recognized (i.e., the allowance method).

Required:

1. Give entries for transactions *(a)* through *(h)* assuming periodic inventory system.
2. Give the end of the period entries (adjusting and closing).
3. Prepare a multiple-step income statement (19A). Assume 10,000 shares of common stock outstanding. Assume an income tax rate of 40%.
4. Show how the final inventory should be reported on the balance sheet at December 31, 19A.

Problem 8–13

Quillen Distributing Company completed the following selected (and summarized) transactions during 19A:

a. Merchandise inventory on hand January 1, 19A: $100,000 (already recorded).
b. Purchased merchandise for resale at quoted price of $200,000 on credit terms, 2/10, n/30. Immediately paid 85% of the cash cost.
c. Paid freight on merchandise purchased, $9,000 cash.
d. Paid 40% of the accounts payable within the discount period. The remaining payables were unpaid at the end of 19A and were still within the discount period.
e. Merchandise was returned to a supplier that had a quoted price of $3,000. A cash refund of $2,940 was received since the items were unsatisfactory.
f. Sold merchandise for $370,000 of which 10% was on credit terms, n/30.
g. A television set caught fire and was damaged internally; it was returned by the customer since it was guaranteed. The set was sold for $600 of which $200 remained unpaid. The set cost $420. Estimates are that the set, when repaired, can be sold for $240. Estimated repair costs are $50, and selling costs are estimated to be $10.
h. Operating expenses (administrative and distribution) paid in cash, $115,000.
i. Excluded from the purchase given in *(b)* and from the final inventory was a shipment for $7,000 (net of discount). This shipment was in transit, f.o.b. shipping point at December 31, 19A. The invoice was in hand.
j. Paid $50 cash to repair the damaged television set (see [*g*] above).
k. Sold the damaged television set for $245; selling costs allocated, $10.
l. The ending inventory was $110,000 at cost, and $102,000 at lower of cost or market. Assume an average income tax rate of 40%.

Accounting policies followed by the company are: *(a)* annual accounting period ends December 31; *(b)* purchases and accounts payable are recorded at net of cash discounts; *(c)* freight charges are allocated to merchandise when purchased; *(d)* all cash discounts are taken; *(e)* used and damaged merchandise carried in a separate inventory account; and *(f)* inventories are reported at lower of cost or market and the allowance method is used.

Required:

1. Give entries for transactions *(b)* through *(k)* assuming periodic inventory system.
2. Give the end of the period entries (adjusting and closing).
3. Prepare a multiple-step income statement (19A). Assume 10,000 shares of common stock outstanding.
4. Show how the final inventory should be reported on the balance sheet at December 31, 19A.

Chapter 9

Inventories—Flow and Matching Procedures

In Chapter 8 two pervasive inventory problems were identified—measurement of inventory *unit cost* and selection of an appropriate flow method. This chapter focuses on the latter problem; that is, the selection of an assumed inventory cost flow such as average cost, *Fifo*, or *Lifo*. To facilitate discussion and provide flexibility in the choice of materials, this chapter is divided into two parts: Part A—Inventory Flow Methods and Part B—Complexities in Application of *Lifo*.

PART A—INVENTORY FLOW METHODS

When goods are purchased or manufactured there is an inflow of cost; when the goods are later sold or issued there is an outflow of cost. The net difference between these cost flows is represented by the amount remaining in inventory. During a period of time such as a month or year, items typically are manufactured or purchased at different unit costs. Upon issue or sale of the items where more than one unit cost is involved, the accountant is faced with the problem of selecting an appropriate unit cost for accounting purposes. Alternatively, the problem can be viewed as one of costing the units remaining on hand in inventory and of measuring the amount of cost of goods sold or used.

A definite policy on the assumed flow of costs for inventory and cost of goods sold (or cost of issues) is established when a particular inventory flow method is selected. Although some inventory flow methods may be essentially consistent with the physical flow of goods in a specific case, the methods focus on the flow of *costs* rather than on the flow of physical goods. *ARB No. 43* states:

> Cost for inventory purposes may be determined under any one of several assumptions as to the flow of cost factors (such as first-in first-out, average, and last-in first-out); the major objective in selecting a method should be to choose the one which, under the circumstances, most clearly reflects periodic income.[1]

Each inventory flow method discussed in this chapter conforms to the *cost principle;* they do not involve departures from cost. The concept of *unit cost* discussed in Chapter 8 is applied; the central issue is the order in which these actual unit costs are assigned to inventory and cost of goods sold. Fundamentally, the selection of an inventory flow method reflects the manner in which the *matching principle* is to be applied to determine the cost of goods sold amount that is deducted from sales revenue for the period. Clearly, this affects net income and income taxes (a cash outflow). Generally accepted accounting principles state that the method selected should be the one that "most clearly reflects periodic income" in each particular situation. Of course, all of the methods give the same results if costs do not change, which is seldom the case.

The inventory flow methods discussed in this chapter are:

1. Specific cost identification.
2. Average cost.
3. First-in, first-out *(Fifo).*
4. Last-in, first-out *(Lifo).*
5. Miscellaneous methods.

For purposes of illustrating the various methods, the simplified data given in Exhibit 9-1 are used.

EXHIBIT 9–1

Transactions		Received			
		Units	Unit Cost	Units Issued	Units on Hand
Jan. 1	Inventory (@ $1)				200
9	Purchase	300	$1.10		500
10	Sale			400	100
15	Purchase	400	1.16		500
18	Sale			300	200
24	Purchase	100	1.26		300

Using the data given in Exhibit 9–1, we can pinpoint, by diagram, the problem of selecting an assumed cost flow method for inventory and cost of goods sold purposes, viz:

[1] AICPA, "Restatement and Revision of Accounting Research Bulletins," *Accounting Research Bulletin No.* 43 (New York, 1961), p. 29.

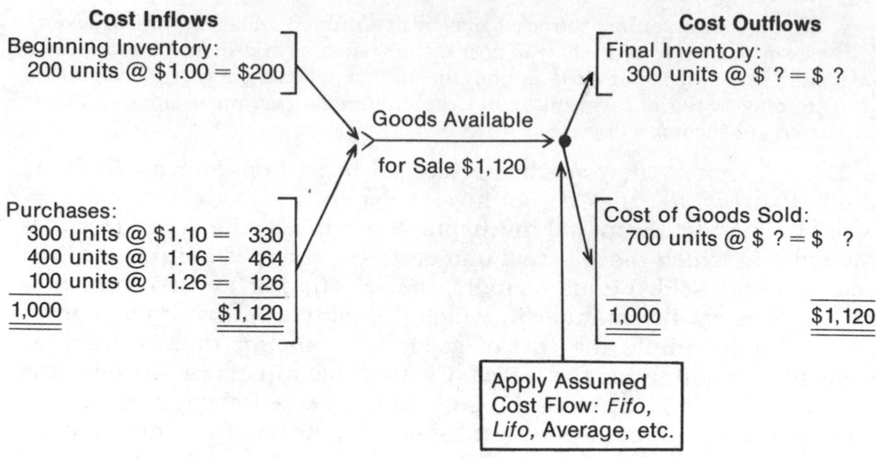

The application of the several inventory flow methods will usually vary somewhat depending on whether *periodic* or *perpetual* inventory procedures are utilized. The discussions to follow will distinguish between these procedures as they affect the application of the inventory flow method.

Recall that under periodic inventory procedures, the ending inventory is determined by a physical unit count; the unit costs (as defined in Chapter 8) are then applied by using one of the flow methods discussed in this chapter. Cost of goods sold (or used) is determined by subtracting the final inventory cost from the *goods available* amount. In contrast, under perpetual inventory procedures, all receipts and issues of inventory items are recorded so that an up-to-date or running inventory balance is continuously maintained directly in the records. As a consequence, the inventory records provide the amounts for inventory and cost of goods sold.

SPECIFIC COST IDENTIFICATION

When the goods involved are relatively large or expensive and small quantities are handled, it may be feasible to tag or number each item when purchased or manufactured, as the case may be, so that the actual unit cost can be indicated on each item by code. This procedure makes it possible to easily identify the *unit cost* for each issue or sale and also for each item in inventory. The specific cost identification method identifies the *cost flow* with the specific flow of physical goods and may be applied with either periodic or perpetual inventory procedures. The specific cost method requires careful identification of each item; consequently, it is seldom used because of the practical limitation created by the detailed records involved, and because specific items remaining (as opposed to specific items issued) frequently are there more or less by accident. There is the possibility of profit manipulation by arbitrary selection of items. To illustrate, assume there are three identical stereo sets on the floor available for sale that cost $400, $420, and $426. One is sold for $600. In this instance, reported cost of goods sold (and gross margin) would depend upon the arbitrary selection between the three unit costs. The method lacks objectivity in application in many situations. However, the method is essential in certain situations such as dealers in automobiles and rare gems.

AVERAGE COST

The average cost method is based on the concept that the best measure of inventory on the balance sheet and of cost of goods sold on the income statement is a representative unit cost for the period. The concept of average cost is applied in two ways depending upon the inventory system, viz: *(a)* periodic inventory system – weighted average unit cost for the period, and *(b)* perpetual inventory system – moving average unit cost.

Weighted Average

Under this method, a weighted average unit cost is computed at the end of the period by using the unit purchase prices and the number of units in the beginning inventory and purchases for the period. The weighted unit price, thus computed, is applied to *(a)* the units in the final inventory, and *(b)* the units sold (to derive cost of goods sold). Exhibit 9–2 illustrates application of the weighted average method using the data given in Exhibit 9–1. Observe that the weighted average unit cost is derived by dividing the total amount for goods available for sale by the total number of units available.

EXHIBIT 9–2
Inventory – Weighted Average Illustrated

	Units	*Unit Price*	*Total Cost*
Goods available:			
Jan. 1 Inventory	200	$1.00	$ 200
9 Purchase	300	1.10	330
15 Purchase	400	1.16	464
24 Purchase	100	1.26	126
Total	1,000	1.12*	1,120
Cost of goods sold at weighted average cost:			
Jan. 10	400	1.12	448
18	300	1.12	336
	700		784
Final inventory at weighted average cost:			
Jan. 31	300	1.12	$ 336

* Weighted average unit cost ($1,120 ÷ 1,000 = $1.12).

The weighted average method is used frequently because it is theoretically and mathematically sound and is relatively easy to apply. Average cost minimizes the effect of extreme variations in purchase prices; on a rising market, weighted average cost will be lower than current cost, and on a declining market, it will be higher than current cost. The method is particularly sound because it is rational and systematic and it is not subject to manipulation. It is appropriate for periodic inventory procedures because *(a)* the inventory of physical units is not determined (counted) until the end of the period, and *(b)* the weighted average unit cost can be determined at that time. Thus, the measurements necessary to compute the amount of the final inventory and the amount of cost of goods sold are determined at the same point in time.

Moving Average

When a perpetual inventory system is used, the weighted average approach cannot be used because the unit cost cannot be calculated until the end of the period. To overcome this problem, a moving weighted average unit cost may be used because it provides a new unit cost *after each purchase*. Thus, when goods are sold, or issued, the moving average unit cost is used at that point in time. Application of the moving average concept in a perpetual inventory system is shown in Exhibit 9–3 (based on data from Exhibit 9–1).

Note that the moving average unit cost is computed directly on the inventory card *after each purchase,* thus facilitating the current costing of issues during the period. On January 9 the $1.06 moving average cost was derived by dividing the total cost $530 by the total units 500; on January 15 the $1.14 moving average was derived by dividing $570

EXHIBIT 9–3
Perpetual Inventory Record (moving average illustrated)

	Received			*Issued*			*Balance*		
Date	*Units*	*Unit Cost*	*Total Cost*	*Units*	*Unit Cost*	*Total Cost*	*Units*	*Unit Cost*	*Total Cost*
Jan. 1							200	$1.00	$200
9	300	$1.10	$330				500	1.06*	530
10				400	$1.06	$424	100	1.06	106
15	400	1.16	464				500	1.14*	570
18				300	1.14	342	200	1.14	228
24	100	1.26	126				300	1.18*	354

* New average computed.

by 500 units; and on January 24, $354 divided by 300 units gave the $1.18 moving average. The ending inventory of 300 units is costed at the latest moving average unit cost of $1.18 (total $354). Cost of goods sold is the sum of the "Issued, Total Cost" column, $766.

The moving average is conceptually, mathematically, and practically sound. It is rational, consistent, not subject to manipulation, and is a representative average that is more current than the weighted average.

A practical problem with both the weighted and moving average methods is that the unit costs may not be even amounts. This problem usually is resolved by pricing the issues (cost of goods sold) so that the inventory unit costs are even.

In matching costs with revenues, the averaging methods do not match the latest unit cost with sales revenue. Rather, they generally provide inventory and cost of goods sold amounts between the *Lifo* and *Fifo* extremes. However, the amounts on the balance sheet (ending inventory) and on the income statement (cost of goods sold) are consistent as to valuation.

FIRST-IN, FIRST-OUT

The first-in, first-out method *(Fifo)* is based upon the assumption that the first goods purchased, or manufactured, are the first costed out upon sale or issuance. Since the costs are "flowed out" in the same order that they flowed in, cost of goods sold (or issued) are costed at the *oldest* unit cost and the goods remaining in inventory are costed at the *newer* unit cost amounts. Application of *Fifo* requires the use of *inventory layers* for the different unit costs. The method may be used, without complexity, with either periodic or perpetual inventory systems.

Using the illustrative data in Exhibit 9–1, and a physical inventory count at the end of the period, *Fifo* results would be determined as follows:

***Fifo*—Periodic Inventory System**

	Beginning inventory (200 units @ $1)		$ 200
	Add purchases during the period (computed above)		920
	Goods available		1,120
Inventory Computation	Deduct final inventory (300 units per physical inventory count):		
	100 units @ $1.26 (most recent purchase)	$126	
	200 units @ $1.16 (next most recent purchase)	232	
	Total Inventory		358
	Cost of Goods Sold (or Issues)		$ 762

The same data are used in Exhibit 9–4 to illustrate the application of *Fifo* with a perpetual inventory system. Note the maintenance of inventory layers throughout the period. This is necessary to cost out each issue.

EXHIBIT 9–4
Perpetual Inventory Record (*Fifo* illustrated)

	Received			Issued			Balance		
Date	Units	Unit Cost	Total Cost	Units	Unit Cost	Total Cost	Units	Unit Cost	Total Cost
Jan. 1							200	$1.00	$200
9	300	$1.10	$330				200 300	1.00 1.10	200 330
10				200 200	$1.00 1.10	$200 220	100	1.10	110
15	400	1.16	464				100 400	1.10 1.16	110 464
18				100 200	1.10 1.16	110 232	200	1.16	232
24	100	1.26	126				200 100	1.16 1.26	232 126 $358

In contrast with *Lifo*, discussed in the next section, *Fifo* gives the same results for the ending inventory and cost of goods sold (or issued) under the periodic and perpetual inventory systems. Also, under the perpetual inventory system, the issues on the inventory record may be costed out either *(a)* currently throughout the period (i.e., each time there is a withdrawal), or *(b)* all at the end of the period, with the same results. Again this is not the case with *Lifo*, as is illustrated in the next section. Because of the internal consistencies of *Fifo*, the final inventory derived under perpetual inventory procedures may be readily verified as follows (refer to Exhibit 9–4):

Most recent purchase (January 24)	100 @ $1.26	$126
Next most recent purchase (January 15)...............	200 @ 1.16	232
Total Inventory (January 31)	300	$358

Fifo is widely used for inventory costing purposes because *(a)* it is easy to apply, *(b)* it is adaptable to either periodic or perpetual inventory procedures, *(c)* it produces an inventory amount for the balance sheet that approximates current replacement cost, *(d)* the flow of cost tends to be consistent with the physical flow of goods, *(e)* it is systematic and rational, and *(f)* it is not subject to manipulation. The fundamental weakness of *Fifo* is that it does not match *current cost* of goods sold with current revenues; rather the oldest unit costs are matched with the current sales revenue (also see Chapter 25). This means that when costs are rising (as is the case with inflation) reported net income will tend to be overstated; and, conversely, when prices are falling reported net income will tend to be understated. Some critics have said this tendency indirectly contributes to the severity of boom and bust conditions. The income tax implications also are serious—when prices are rising, pretax income tends to be overstated; and as a result, there is overassessment of income taxes and a negative effect on cash flow. On a downswing the opposite prevails.

LAST-IN, FIRST-OUT

The last-in, first-out *(Lifo)* method of inventory cost flow is based on the concept that the latest unit acquisition cost should be matched with current sales revenue. Consequently, under this method the cost outflows are inverse to the cost inflows. The units remaining in the ending inventory are costed at the oldest unit costs available, and the units in cost of goods sold, or issued, are costed at the newest unit costs available. *Lifo* application requires the use of inventory layers for the different unit costs.

Although the *Lifo* concept is simple, its application often is quite complex, because of the detailed recordkeeping required, the discipline (rules) necessary to prevent inconsistent results and manipulation, and a formidable array of tax regulations that must be followed.

This section will present the *Lifo* concept assuming a specific goods, single product situation.[2] Of course, this simple situation seldom exists in the real world of accounting; and to look at it alone, without consideration of the implementation problems, would give an oversimplified view of this complex subject. Therefore, Part B presents the primary complexities encountered in *Lifo* application.

Lifo may be applied with either a periodic or perpetual inventory system. Assuming a *periodic inventory system*, and a physical inventory of units at the end of the period, *Lifo* results would be determined as follows:

***Lifo*— Periodic Inventory System**

Periodic Inventory Computation *(Lifo)*	Goods available (per above)		$1,120
	Deduct final inventory (300 units per physical inventory count):		
	200 units @ $1 (oldest costs available; from January 1 inventory)	$200	
	100 units @ $1.10 (next oldest costs available; from January 9 purchase)	110	
	Total Inventory		310
	Cost of Goods Sold (or Issues)		$ 810

When *Lifo* is applied with *perpetual* inventory procedures, the *issues*

[2] This is variously called the *quantity, specific goods,* or *unit Lifo* method of applying the *Lifo* concept; see Part B.

may be costed on the inventory card *(a)* currently throughout the period (i.e., each time there is a withdrawal), or *(b)* only at the end of the period. With respect to *Lifo* the timing of the costing of issues becomes important, since costing currently results in a different inventory valuation and cost of goods sold amount than costing at the end of a period. Costing at the end of the period will give the same results as periodic inventory procedures. The applications of *Lifo* under *perpetual inventory* procedures are shown in Exhibit 9–5 when the issues are costed currently throughout the period; and Exhibit 9–6 shows the issues costed at the end of the period. Note the maintenance of inventory layers for each different unit cost in the Balance column.

The items shown in italics in Exhibit 9–6 were entered at the end of the period. Note that Exhibit 9–6 (costed at end of period) provides the same inventory valuation ($310) as the previous periodic inventory computation. On the other hand, Exhibit 9–5 (costed currently) provides an inventory valuation of $342. The $32 difference occurs because the issues on January 10 and 18 were out of different inventory layers as a result of the difference in the timing in costing issues. The difference between the *cost of issues* on the two records is also $32. From this illustration it is apparent that the *Lifo* inventory valuation costed at the end of the period (but not when costed currently) may be verified readily by pricing the number of units in inventory out of the oldest unit costs.

Lifo Inventory Liquidation

A serious problem under *Lifo* procedures occurs when a company fails to maintain the base year, or "normal" inventory position. This erosion of the base year inventory occurs when usage exceeds acquisitions of an inventory item subsequent to adoption of *Lifo* (i.e., the base year). To illustrate, assume the following:

	Units	Unit Cost	Total Cost
Beginning inventory (assumed to be the base year inventory)	10,000	$1.00	$10,000
Purchases	40,000	1.50	60,000
Total Available for Sale	50,000		70,000
Sales (44,000 units, issues on *Lifo* basis)	40,000	1.50	60,000
	4,000	1.00	4,000
	44,000		64,000
Final Inventory	6,000	1.00	$ 6,000

In the above example the company failed to maintain the base year inventory position by 4,000 units. This failure may have been due to—

a. Voluntary inventory liquidation. Management may have decided to reduce normal inventory quantity for some reason, such as shortage

EXHIBIT 9–5
Perpetual Inventory Record (*Lifo* illustrated – costed currently)

	Received			Issued or Sold			Balance		
Date	Units	Unit Cost	Total Cost	Units	Unit Cost	Total Cost	Units	Unit Cost	Total Cost
Jan. 1							200	$1.00	$200
9	300	$1.10	$330				200 300	1.00 1.10	200 330
10				300 100	$1.10 1.00	$330 100	100	1.00	100
15	400	1.16	464				100 400	1.00 1.16	100 464
18				300	1.16	348	100 100	1.00 1.16	100 116
24	100	1.26	126				100 100 100	1.00 1.16 1.26	100 116 126 $342

EXHIBIT 9–6
Perpetual Inventory Record (*Lifo* illustrated – costed at end of period)

	Received			Issued or Sold			Balance		
Date	Units	Unit Cost	Total Cost	Units	Unit Cost	Total Cost	Units	Unit Cost	Total Cost
Jan. 1							200	$1.00	$200
9	300	$1.10	$330				500		
10				400* *Detail:* *100* *300*	 *$1.26* *1.16*	 *$126* *348*	100		
15	400	1.16	464				500		
18				300 *Detail:* *100* *200*	 *1.16* *1.10*	 *116* *220*	200		
24	100	1.26	126				300 *Detail:* *200* *100*	 *1.00* *1.10*	 *200* *110* *$310*

* Since pricing of issues is delayed until the end of the period, the first issue (400 units) is priced out of the last purchase (100 units at $1.26), and so on.

of liquid funds, anticipation of a decline in prices, or anticipation of an improvement in the product.[3]

b. Involuntary inventory liquidation. Noncontrollable causes such as shortages, strikes, delayed delivery dates, or unexpected demands may have forced the inventory reduction.

As a result of the liquidation of a part of the base inventory, cost of goods sold includes 4,000 units costed at an old cost ($1 per unit) which is matched against current revenue causing a distortion of reported net income. Assuming the inventory liquidation is temporary, should the 4,000 units be costed out at $1 per unit or at some other cost? The problem is further complicated if the 4,000 units are replaced in the next period, say at $1.60 per unit. Should the restoration of the base inventory position be at $1 per unit or at $1.60 per unit? One approach used, when the inventory liquidation is temporary, involves charging Cost of Goods Sold with the replacement cost, crediting Inventory at *Lifo* cost, and crediting the difference to a special account as follows (assuming perpetual inventory procedures):

Cost of goods sold (40,000 @ $1.50) + (4,000 @ $1.60)	66,400	
Inventory (40,000 @ $1.50) + (4,000 @ $1)		64,000
Excess of replacement cost of *Lifo* inventory temporarily liquidated (4,000 @ $.60)		2,400

When the liquidated inventory is replaced (base position restored) the following entry is made:

Inventory (4,000 @ $1)	4,000	
Excess of replacement cost of *Lifo* inventory temporarily liquidated (4,000 @ $.60)	2,400	
Accounts payable (4,000 @ $1.60)		6,400

If the replacement occurs at a price other than $1.60, the inventory amount is affected by the difference. A balance (credit) in the Excess of Replacement Cost of *Lifo* Inventory Temporarily Liquidated should be reported as a special liability because it represents an amount which will have to be spent without a corresponding increase in inventory. There is disagreement on the theoretical validity of this procedure. Some accountants believe it is necessary to protect the integrity of the *Lifo* concept; others view it as income manipulation. As a practical matter, erosion of the base inventory seldom occurs because the IRS usually will disallow *Lifo* for tax purposes if it does occur.

Few companies use *Lifo* for *internal* accounting and control purposes. Most companies using *Lifo* have changed to it from another method for tax and external reporting purposes. Generally, for internal purposes they prefer to continue the method used in the past. For internal purposes, and in the accounts, most companies use either *Fifo*,

[3] A major criticism of *Lifo* is that it is subject to profit manipulation, for example, year-end purchasing policy can be used (1) to reduce reported profits by heavy buying, if prices have increased; and (2) to overstate profits by permitting inventories to decline and "old" low prices to be charged to cost of goods sold.

average, standard costs, or variable costing. These results are converted to *Lifo* for income tax purposes and for *external financial reporting,* external to the accounts. In some cases the results of the conversion to *Lifo* are entered in the accounts as a single amount by using an inventory allowance account (Allowance to Reduce Inventory to *Lifo* Basis). Unfortunately, this account is sometimes referred to as a "*Lifo* Reserve."

In those cases where *Lifo* is used for internal purposes and entered in the accounts throughout the period, the issues are almost always costed *currently* because the management cannot await until year-end for internal financial and control reports. Current costing minimizes the *Lifo* impact on inventory and cost of goods sold, whereas costing at the end of the year maximizes its impact. Consequently, the internal results generally are adjusted to an annual *Lifo* effect to attain the maximum tax benefit.

The Internal Revenue Code permits a company to use *Lifo* on the income tax return only if it is also used for its *external financial reports.* However, this does not require that *Lifo* must be used for internal purposes or entered into the accounts.

Comparison of *Lifo* with *Fifo*

The significant effects of *Lifo* may be emphasized by comparing it with *Fifo.* As long as unit cost prices remain constant, the two methods give the same results; when unit cost prices change materially, the two methods provide significantly different effects on assets (inventories and cash) and net income (costs). Note that the comparative effect will depend upon the direction of the change in unit cost prices. With *rising* prices *Fifo* matches low costs (oldest costs) with increased sales revenue (inflated dollars) and provides an inventory valuation approximating higher current replacement cost, whereas *Lifo* matches high costs (newer costs) with increased sales revenue and provides an inventory valuation on a low-cost (oldest cost) basis. Conversely, with *declining* prices *Fifo* matches high costs (oldest costs) with decreased sales revenue and provides an inventory valuation approximating lower current replacement cost, whereas *Lifo* matches low costs (newer costs) with decreased sales revenue and provides an inventory valuation on a high-cost (oldest cost) basis.

With respect to the *cash flow* effects, when prices are rising *Lifo* results in a lower pretax net income amount and, consequently, less income tax; therefore, cash flow is greater than when *Fifo* is used. These effects can be observed in Exhibit 9–7. The data given in that exhibit assumes rising prices; note in particular the impact of *Lifo* on net income (a negative effect) and on cash inflow (a positive effect).

Because of a continuing worldwide inflationary trend and the pervasiveness of income taxes, an increasing number of companies are shifting to *Lifo.* The primary advantages of *Lifo* generally cited are: (1) it provides a better matching of current costs with current revenue;

EXHIBIT 9–7
***Lifo* Compared with *Fifo*—Prices Rising**

Basic Data Assumed

Beginning cash balance		$ 2,000
Beginning inventory balance,	5,000 units @	5 (base inventory)
Purchases during period,	5,000 units @	7
Sales,	5,000 units @	18
Expenses (excluding income taxes)		35,000
Income tax rate, 40%		

Comparative Results

	First-In, First-Out			*Last-In, First-Out*			*Increase (Decrease) from Fifo to Lifo*
	Units	*@*	*Amount*	*Units*	*@*	*Amount*	
Income Statement:							
Sales	5,000	$18	$90,000	5,000	$18	$90,000	$ -0-
Cost of goods sold	5,000	5	25,000	5,000	7	35,000	10,000
Gross margin			65,000			55,000	(10,000)
Expenses			35,000			35,000	-0-
Pretax income			30,000			20,000	(10,000)
Income taxes (@ 40%)			12,000			8,000	(4,000)
Net Income			$18,000			$12,000	$ (6,000)
Balance Sheet (limited to above transactions):							
Cash (assuming all transactions were cash)			$10,000			$14,000	$ 4,000
Inventory			35,000			25,000	(10,000)
Net Effect (same as difference in net income)							$ (6,000)

(2) in periods of inflation, it results in lower income taxes, hence greater cash inflows; (3) it reflects the usual pricing policy of an enterprise to raise selling prices when replacement cost increases even though the goods already on hand are not yet sold; and (4) it is systematic.

The primary arguments generally cited against *Lifo* are: (1) it understates assets—the inventory on the balance sheet is costed at old, out-of-date cost; (2) it does not correctly match replacement cost with revenue; (3) it is subject to manipulation—profits can be manipulated by changing the usual purchasing patterns (voluntary inventory liquidation); (4) it is subject to involuntary inventory liquidation; (5) cost flows do not correspond to the physical flow of goods; and (6) it presents too many complexities and variations in application.

MISCELLANEOUS INVENTORY FLOW METHODS

Numerous methods for determining the cost of inventory, in addition to those discussed above, have been proposed. Except in a few unique situations, none of these has been accepted under generally accepted accounting principles for external financial reporting purposes. However, some of them are used for *internal cost accounting* purposes. As background, several miscellaneous methods are briefly reviewed in this section.

Next-In, First-Out

Nifo refers to the concept that cost of goods sold should be costed at the unit cost anticipated for the next purchase of a like volume. The concept attempts to precisely match cost of goods sold with the actual cost of replacing the goods sold. It is maintained that *Lifo* fails to precisely match replacement cost with current revenues since the method employs the cost of the latest purchase *prior* to the actual sale. *Nifo* has not received even limited general acceptance.

Cost-of-Last-Purchase

Colp, as a method of inventory costing, has been proposed as a way to overcome the inherent lag in the usual *Lifo* procedures. Under this method *all issues* are priced at the last actual purchase price regardless of the number of units involved. Under certain conditions relating to price change and quantities, this method conceivably could produce a negative inventory value. For this and other obvious reasons it has received little attention.

Base Stock Method

The base stock (or normal stock) method is generally viewed as the predecessor of the *Lifo* method. The method assumes that there is a normal or base stock of goods that should be maintained at all times. The base stock represents a permanent commitment of resources, similar to a fixed asset, that is costed at a normal price which is viewed as the original cost—usually the lowest cost experienced by the company. Maintenance of the base inventory at a constant amount is intended to avoid the problem of inventory profits. Goods must be acquired above the minimum base stock for operational purposes. These goods are viewed as temporary increments and are recorded at cost; issues should be costed out of the increment on a *Lifo* basis, although *Fifo* or average sometimes is used for practical reasons. The base stock method is illustrated in Exhibit 9–8.

The purpose of the base stock method is similar to that of last-in, first-out, that is, the matching of current costs with current revenues. The permanency assumed with respect to the base stock provides another avenue for justification. The method is not generally used because of the arbitrary nature of both the quantity and unit values of the assumed base stock; essentially similar results may be obtained under *Lifo;* it is subject to manipulation through selective purchasing; and it is not permitted for income tax purposes.

EXHIBIT 9–8
Base Stock Inventory Method

	Units	Unit Cost	Amount
Base stock	10,000	$1.00	$10,000
Extra stock	2,000	1.20	2,400
Total Beginning Inventory	12,000		12,400
Purchases:			
First	2,000	1.30	2,600
Second	6,000	1.40	8,400
Total Available	20,000		23,400
Ending inventory (11,000 units per count):			
Base stock	10,000	1.00	10,000
Extra stock	1,000	1.20	1,200
Total	11,000		11,200
Cost of Goods Sold	9,000		$12,200

STANDARD COSTS FOR INVENTORY

In manufacturing entities using a standard cost system, the inventories are valued, recorded, and reported for internal purposes on the basis of a standard unit cost. The standard cost approximates an ideal or expected cost; and its use prevents the inflation of inventory values by excluding losses and expenses due to inefficiency, waste, and abnormal conditions. Under this method the *differences* between actual cost and standard cost are recorded in separate variance accounts which are written off in the current period as a loss or *period cost* rather than being capitalized in inventory. Standard costs may be applied to raw materials, work in process, and finished goods inventories. To illustrate the utilization of standard costs for raw materials, assume a particular company has just adopted standard cost procedures and that the initial inventory is zero. During the current period the company makes two purchases and one issue and records them as follows:

1. To record the purchase of 10,000 units of raw material at $1.10 actual cost; standard cost has been established at $1:

Raw materials (10,000 units @ $1)	10,000	
Raw materials purchase price variation (10,000 units @ $.10)	1,000	
Accounts payable (10,000 units @ $1.10)		11,000

2. To record issuance of 8,000 units of raw material to factory for processing:

Material in process	8,000	
Raw materials (8,000 units @ $1)		8,000

3. To record the purchase of 2,000 units of raw material at $.95:

Raw materials (2,000 units @ $1)	2,000	
Raw materials purchase price variation (2,000 units @ $.05)		100
Accounts payable (2,000 units @ $.95)		1,900

Results for the period:

Purchases at actual cost:		
10,000 units @ $1.10	$11,000	
2,000 units @ .95	1,900	
Total		$12,900
Issues at standard cost:		
8,000 units @ $1	$ 8,000	
Final inventory at standard cost:		
4,000 units @ $1	4,000	12,000
Raw Materials Purchase Price Variation (debit – charged against current income as a *loss*)		$ 900

Under the procedures illustrated above for raw material there would be no need to consider inventory flow methods such as *Lifo, Fifo,* and average, since only one cost – the standard cost – appears in the records. In addition, perpetual inventory records could be maintained in *units only,* since all issues and inventory valuations are at the constant standard price. Clearly standard cost represents a departure from the cost principle as currently interpreted. We have included this brief discussion because for external reporting purposes, standard cost results generally are not used except in special circumstances. Therefore, the inventory is restated for external reports according to one of the generally accepted methods discussed above. Standard costs are widely used for *internal management* planning and control. A detailed discussion of standard cost procedures is beyond the scope of this book and can be found in any complete cost accounting textbook.

Variable or Direct Cost for Inventory

For *internal management* planning and control purposes, the concept of variable or direct costing is often used in manufacturing companies. Under this concept, the fixed and variable costs are distinctly segregated. This separation is especially useful for internal management planning and control, particularly in manufacturing situations. One important aspect of this concept is that the cost of goods manufactured is measured as the sum of the variable costs only; that is, the sum of direct materials, direct labor, and variable manufacturing overhead. All fixed costs, including fixed manufacturing overhead, are treated as period costs; that is, they are deducted from revenues of the period rather than being capitalized and carried forward in inventory (and later reported as a part of cost of goods sold).

Valuation of inventories at only variable production costs, although highly useful for internal management purposes, is not generally acceptable for external financial reporting purposes nor can it be used for tax purposes except in special circumstances. Consequently, for external reporting and tax purposes, companies using variable costing for internal purposes convert the inventory and cost of goods sold to "actual" by using methods such as dollar-value *Lifo* (see Part B).

SELECTION OF A FLOW METHOD

The trend in use of the several inventory cost flow methods, for external reporting and tax purposes, is indicated in the following tabulation taken from AICPA, *Accounting Trends and Techniques, 1975* (p. 114):

Inventory Flow Methods (based on 600 companies)

	1974	*1973*	*1972*	*1971*	*1970*
First-in, first-out	375	394	377	333	292
Average cost	236	235	242	220	203
Last-in, first-out	303	150	150	144	146
Standard costs	49	52	54	36	30
Retail method	35	39	35	31	27
Specific or "actual" cost	24	23	26	15	17
Accumulated production cost	19	18	25	24	23
Replacement or current cost	9	10	8	13	16
Other	4	6	3	6	11
Totals*	1054	927	920	822	765

* Some companies use more than one method.

Selection of an inventory flow method, or whether to change from one method to another, presents a complex problem. Although income measurement should be the primary consideration, it is difficult to realistically avoid considering income tax effects. With respect to income measurement, it is also unrealistic to disregard the problem of inventory profits. In periods of rising prices, *Lifo* tends to minimize inventory profits whereas *Fifo* tends to maximize them. The tendency to emphasize the income statement, the relatively high inflation trend, and tax effects have prompted a number of companies in recent years to switch to *Lifo*. With respect to the favorable income tax effect of *Lifo* during periods of inflation, one must recognize that it would reverse with deflation. Because of the complexities involved and the potentials for manipulation, the Internal Revenue Code and Regulations pose a formidable array of rules governing *Lifo* for income tax purposes. On the other hand, the diverse economic impacts in the long run versus the short run and the negative impact of *Lifo* during periods of inflation on income, EPS, and certain other ratios, which may cause the price/earnings multiple to be less favorable than otherwise, has caused many companies to consider a switch to *Lifo* to be undesirable for them.

PART B—COMPLEXITIES IN APPLYING *LIFO*

Lifo adheres to the cost principle. Major accounting firms consistently report that *Lifo* is generally viewed as a cost method for income tax and external reporting purposes and that most companies use either *Fifo* or average in their accounts for internal cost accounting and management purposes. The Internal Revenue Code (Section 472 c) dictates that any company using *Lifo* for tax purposes must also use it for *ex-*

ternal reports. This means that companies using other methods in the accounting system must convert those results to *Lifo* external to the accounts.[4] Application of *Lifo* often poses relatively complex conversion problems when there are diverse operations and numerous items in inventory. Particular problems also are encountered when a company decides to change to *Lifo* from another method for tax and financial reporting purposes.

Lifo application problems are discussed in the following order:

1. Initial adoption of *Lifo*.
2. Continuing application of *Lifo* after adoption.
   a. Quantity of goods method–
      (1) By single items.
      (2) By multiple inventory pools.
   b. Dollar-value method (for either single or multiple inventory pools).
      (1) Double extension.
      (2) Link chain.
   c. Indexing.
3. *Lifo* applied to interim statements.
4. *Lifo* reserves.

INITIAL ADOPTION OF *LIFO*

Income tax regulations permit taxpayers to use *Lifo* for all or part of the total inventory of goods (i.e., for manufacturers and processors – raw materials, work in process, finished goods; for retailers and wholesalers – merchandise for sale). In the typical *Lifo* situation, the company has changed from some other method to *Lifo* for tax and external reporting purposes, although a few companies have changed in the opposite direction. The switch to *Lifo* involves a change in accounting method as described in *APB Opinion No. 20* ("Accounting Changes"). Paragraph 20 of that *Opinion* requires that the *cumulative* effect of a change in accounting principle be shown between the captions extraordinary items and net income. However, paragraph 26 of that *Opinion* specifically rules out measurement of the cumulative effect when the change is *to Lifo* (but not the reverse) because the prior period differences are almost always not determinable. The total effect of adopting *Lifo* is reported as an addition to *cost of goods sold* in the year of change. The following is a typical footnote for the year of change:

> At the beginning of the current year, the company changed its inventory measurement basis to cost applied on the last-in, first-out method. In prior years, inventories were measured on the first-in, first-out method, and stated at lower of cost or market. Had the *Fifo* method been used during the current year, inventory would have been $10,000,000 higher than reported in the attached statements for 1975. The net effect of the change in 1975 was to reduce net income (after tax) by approximately $4,800,000 ($.30 per

[4] Since *Lifo* at year-end is different than *Lifo* priced currently, conversion even in this case is usually done.

share). Proforma effects of retroactive application are not realistically determinable.

The management believes that the newly adopted inventory method will attain a better matching of current expenses with current revenues.[5]

When there is a change to *Lifo*, the *base year* is the year in which the change is made; and the *Lifo base cost* for the initial inventory, that is, the *base inventory,* at the start of the base year is the ending inventory (adjusted to cost regardless of the prior method used) carried over from the prior year (Reg. 1.472–2). This means that adjustments to the prior ending inventory, to lower of cost or market, must be restored (LCM is not applicable to *Lifo*) as well as any other write-downs.

For illustrative purposes throughout Part B, the inventory data for Tye Company given in Exhibit 9–9 will be used. In this example, the base year would be 19B and the base inventory amount would be $6,100 at the start of 19B. For the above reasons, no "adjustment" for this accounting change would be made in the accounts or reported on the financial statements for 19B.

EXHIBIT 9–9
Tye Company – Illustrative Data (inventory change to *Lifo*)

Situation: *a. Fifo* was used in prior years and through 19A for all purposes.
b. Lifo was adopted at start of 19B for (1) income tax purposes and (2) external financial purposes.
c. Fifo continued in the accounts and for internal management purposes.

Inventory Data per Accounts (*Fifo* basis)

	Item A			*Item B*			
	Units	*Cost*	*Total*	*Units*	*Cost*	*Total*	*Total Amount*
Year 19A:							
Ending inventory:							
Layer 1	1,000	$1.00	$1,000	2,000	$2.00	$ 4,000	
Layer 2				500	2.20	1,100	
	1,000	$1.00	$1,000	2,500	$2.04	$ 5,100	$6,100
Year 19B:							
Purchases	3,000	$1.20	$3,600	4,000	$2.50	$10,000	
Sales	(2,800)			(3,500)			
Ending inventory:							
Fifo	1,200	1.20	1,440	3,000	2.50	7,500	$8,940
Year 19C:							
Purchases	3,300	1.30	4,290	4,200	2.60	10,920	
Sales	(3,200)			(4,200)			
Ending inventory:							
Fifo	1,300	1.30	1,690	3,000	2.60	7,800	$9,490

[5] "Accounting Changes Related to the Cost of Inventory," FASB *Interpretation No. 1,* "In applying *APB Opinion No. 20,* preferability among accounting principles shall be determined on the basis of whether the new principle constitutes an improvement in financial reporting and not on the basis of the income tax effect alone."

Full-disclosure requirements, and limitations, in respect to the *initial adoption* of *Lifo* include:

1. Explanation of the change and the basis for the change.
2. Basis used for determining the inventory amounts.
3. Beginning and ending inventory amounts.
4. Excess of replacement or current cost over the *Lifo* amount.
5. For the base year *only*, and only by footnote, the dollar inventory difference between *Lifo* and the alternative method previously used and proforma income and earnings per share amounts for the method.

The IRS specified the last as a *constraint* because some companies, while taking the tax benefit, attempt to mitigate the adverse impact of *Lifo* on net income and earnings per share, by publishing and announcing results of the alternative inventory basis with a view to influencing investors. Violation of this constraint will result in disallowance of *Lifo* by the IRS; the objection is to the inconsistency in reporting on one inventory basis *(Lifo)* to the IRS and on another basis *(Fifo)* to the public.

CONTINUING APPLICATION OF *LIFO*

After adopting *Lifo* for income tax and external reporting purposes, several methods of *Lifo* application are acceptable. These several methods make *Lifo* feasible for practically all taxpayers. Fundamentally, there are three *Lifo* application methods: (1) quantity of goods *Lifo*, (2) dollar-value *Lifo*, and (3) retail *Lifo* (discussed in Chapter 10).

Quantity of Goods *Lifo*

This method (often called specific goods *Lifo* or unit *Lifo*) has two approaches known as (1) the single-item approach, and (2) the multiple pools approach.

Single-Item Approach. The single-item approach was illustrated in Part A of this chapter. It requires that the *quantity* of each item or product in the ending inventory be determined either by physical inventory count or from perpetual inventory records; then unit costs are applied in *Lifo* order, in the manner shown in Exhibit 9–6, to derive the *Lifo* inventory amount. Normally, the *Lifo* inventory amount will consist of a *base Lifo inventory* amount plus subsequent incremental *Lifo* layers for each new price. To illustrate, the *Lifo* ending inventories for Tye Company (data given in Exhibit 9–9) are shown in Exhibit 9–10.

The single-item approach is used in small businesses and in situations where there are a small number of different inventory items or products. In larger and more complex situations, the detailed recordkeeping usually is considered to be too burdensome, except in cases where only a few major items of inventory are on the *Lifo* basis.

Multiple Pools Approach. The multiple pools approach involves grouping of "substantially identical" items into inventory pools. Each

EXHIBIT 9–10
***Lifo*—Quantity of Goods Method, Single-Item Approach**

	Ending Inventory (*Lifo* basis)						
	Item A			*Item B*			
	Units	*Cost*	*Amount*	*Units*	*Cost*	*Amount*	*Total Amount*
Year 19B:							
Layer 1	1,000	$1.00	$1,000	2,000	$2.00	$4,000	
Layer 2	200	1.20	240	500	2.20	1,100	
Layer 3				500	2.50	1,250	
Total	1,200		$1,240	3,000		$6,350	$7,590
Year 19C:							
Layer 1	1,000	1.00	$1,000	2,000	2.00	$4,000	
Layer 2	200	1.20	240	500	2.20	1,100	
Layer 3	100	1.30	130	500	2.50	1,250	
Total	1,300		$1,370	3,000		$6,350	$7,720

pool then is treated as if it were a single inventory item. For the beginning inventory (the base layer when *Lifo* was adopted), the units in a pool are assumed to have been acquired at the same time so that the unit cost for the beginning inventory can be obtained by dividing the total number of units into the total inventory cost. The *ending Lifo inventory* each period, to the extent that the number of units do not exceed the beginning inventory, is obtained by multiplying the number of units remaining in inventory by the average unit cost at the start of the current period. The number of units in the ending inventory in excess of the number at the start (an inventory increment or layer) is valued by multiplying the excess number by (1) the average cost of purchases during the period; or (2) if the purchases during the current year are less than units sold, by price layers related to the units in order of acquisition (i.e., *Lifo* order). The ending inventory then is the base layer plus the incremental layers.

To illustrate, assume for Tye Company, Exhibit 9–9, that the two products are *substantially identical.* Therefore, under this assumption, the two items can be treated as an individual inventory pool. The ending inventories for this pool (let's call it Pool No. 1) would be computed as shown in Exhibit 9–11. Any remaining pools (such as Pool Nos. 2, 3, etc.) comprising the inventory, computed in this same manner, would be summed to determine the total amount of the ending *Lifo* inventory. Compared with the single-item approach, the multiple pools approach reduces the computations by approximately one half. This demonstrates the primary advantage of the multiple pools approach.

The multiple pools approach, although less burdensome clerically than the single-item approach, is not widely used because generally there are a number of pools with a consequent heavy clerical burden. Also, it does not resolve the problems of changes in the *mix* of items and products in the inventory.

EXHIBIT 9–11
***Lifo*–Quantity of Goods Method, Multiple Pools Approach**

	Ending Inventory (*Lifo* basis)					
	Year 19B			Year 19C		
Base layer	*a.* 3,500	@ $1.74 =	$6,100	*c.* 3,500	@ $1.74 =	$6,100
Incremental layer	*b.* 700	1.94 =	1,360	700	1.94 =	1,360
				d. 100	2.03 =	203
Total Inventory...........	4,200		$7,460	4,300		$7,663

Computations:

a. $6,100 ÷ 3,500 = $1.7429 (average).

b. 3,000 units @ $1.20 = $ 3,600
4,000 units @ 2.50 = 10,000
7,000 $13,600

$13,600 ÷ 7,000 = $1.9429 (average)

c. From 19A ending inventory.

d. 3,300 units @ $1.30 = $ 4,290
4,200 units @ 2.60 = 10,920
7,500 $15,210

$15,210 ÷ 7,500 = $2.03 (average)

Changes in Items (Product Lines) in *Lifo* Inventory

Some industries commonly experience a constant change in the inventory mix—some products are dropped, others are added, and technological changes cause a continuing change in item or product mix content of the inventory over a period of years. In the quantity of goods method, the change in mix would cause the old *Lifo* inventory costs (usually low relative to current costs) to be moved out to cost of goods sold and replaced with later inventory costs which are usually much higher. To illustrate, a company may experience the following *Lifo* inventory situation over a five-year period:

	Lifo Inventory Unit Costs				
Product	*19A*	*19B*	*19C*	*19D*	*19E*
A..............	$1.00	$1.20	Discontinued		
B..............	3.50	3.75	$4.00	Discontinued	
C..............	2.80	2.90	3.00	$3.15	$3.30
D..............		*4.00	4.18	4.30	4.40
E..............			*5.50	5.60	5.80

* New products.

Clearly, with no change in quantity of goods, the *Lifo* inventory in dollars would have changed and the old (low) costs converted to more current (high) costs. The *quantity method* gives this result; however, the dollar-value method tends to overcome this problem, as explained later.

The quantity of goods *Lifo* method (including the single items and multiple pools approaches) is not widely used because *(a)* it is burdensome in complex situations, *(b)* the impact of change in technology and product mix is great, and *(c)* it lacks flexibility in avoiding the drastic impact of inventory invasions, particularly the base inventory.

Dollar-Value *Lifo*

This method was developed to overcome, as much as possible, the basic deficiencies of the quantity of goods method discussed above. Originally, only the quantity of goods method, single-item approach, was used for *Lifo;* however, because of its great clerical burden, the multiple pools approach evolved. Following that, dollar-value *Lifo* developed. Fundamentally, in the dollar-value *Lifo* method, the base inventory and any subsequent incremental layers are measured directly in terms of *dollars* rather than in quantities of *units.*

The dollar-value *Lifo* method uses the concepts of inventory pools and *index numbers.* This method has two approaches generally identified as (1) double-extension and (2) link-chain. These two approaches have common characteristics; their differences reflect adaptations to accommodate peculiarities in different situations. IRS regulations require that the double-extension approach be used in all cases except where it is clearly unrealistic. Use of the link-chain approach must be clearly preferable in the particular situation before it can be used. Consequently, dollar-value, double-extension *Lifo* is used in most situations.

Significantly, the dollar-value method enlarges the concept of an *inventory pool.* Recall that under the quantity of goods, multiple pools approach, an inventory pool could encompass *only* items that are *substantially identical.* In contrast, the dollar-value method permits an inventory pool to encompass all items that are characterized by *similarity.* Similarity is defined as a "natural business unit" pool which would consist of a product line, or related product lines, where raw materials, manufacturing, and sales distributions are integrated or related. Separate plants manufacturing similar products would constitute a natural business unit. A pool would include the raw materials, work in process, and finished goods inventories. Thus, the degree of inventory aggregation under the dollar-value method is very broad compared with the quantity of goods method. This aggregation of inventory pools significantly reduces the clerical burdens involved and, in addition, better copes with the disturbing impacts of changing product mix and technology. The level of aggregation thus provides a significant advantage of dollar-value *Lifo.*

Other than for computation of the index, the dollar-value method does not focus on inventory quantities of physical goods, but rather on inventory dollars; therefore, the computations require that each *Lifo* inventory pool be costed at both *base year dollar costs* and *current period dollar costs.* When the dollar total of the ending inventory at base year costs exceeds the dollar total of the beginning inventory at base costs, an inventory increment or layer has been added. If the difference is less, inventory *liquidation* has occurred. The inventory increment, stated at base year cost, must be converted, by using *appropriate index numbers,* to current year cost. If inventory is later decreased, the reductions are taken from the most recent increments or layers.

The index numbers used in dollar-value *Lifo* computations are critical because they materially affect the results. Tax regulations and generally accepted accounting principles require that a price index be used that is specific to the inventory pool as opposed to an external index or a general price index.[6] This means that an internal price index must be computed each period based upon the change in costs as reflected in the inventory and purchase records of the company. The internal price index is computed as follows:

$$\frac{\text{Ending Inventory for the Period at Current Year Costs}}{\text{Ending Inventory for the Period at Base Year Costs}} = \text{Price Index for the Current Year}$$

This index number and the internal index numbers for prior years are used to convert the ending inventory to the *Lifo* basis.

Dollar-value *Lifo* computations are complicated because they involve two distinct phases that may be summarized as follows:

Phase A—Computation of an internal index for the current year that is specific to the inventory pool:

- Step 1. Determine the base year inventory in dollars; that is, the inventory value at the date of adoption of *Lifo*. This base inventory is maintained permanently if at all possible.
- Step 2. As the denominator for the index calculation, cost the ending inventory for the current period *at base year costs.*
- Step 3. As the numerator for the index calculation, cost the ending inventory for the current period at *current year costs.*
- Step 4. Compute the internal price index for the current year by dividing the results of step 3 by step 2.

Phase B—Computation of *Lifo* inventory by application of index numbers:

- Step 5. Convert the ending inventory layers, priced at base year costs, to the ending inventory layers at *Lifo* cost by applying the index number applicable to each layer.

These two phases are illustrated subsequently. They are applied with both the double-extension approach and the link-chain approach, on the basis of either:

a. A single pool—A single pool is used for the entire company when (1) the company is a manufacturer or processor, and (2) overall operations constitute a "natural business unit." Thus, an automobile manufacturer may use a single pool that would encompass raw materials, component parts, work in process, and finished goods (as if it were one big inventory item).

b. Multiple pools—Each pool encompasses a group of inventory items that are *similar* in respect to raw materials, manufacturing, and distribution. A separate inventory pool is formed which corresponds

[6] Two exceptions to this requirement are explained in a subsequent section—Indexing.

to the "natural business" *subunits* of the company. Manufacturers may use either single pool or multiple pools; however, retailers, wholesalers, and jobbers must use multiple pools. For example, a large department store may have separate inventory pools for mens clothing, ladies clothing, home appliances, and so on.

Obviously, single pool, because of the higher degree of aggregation, generally is preferred to multiple pools where there is a choice.

Dollar-Value Method, Double-Extension Lifo Approach. Double extension, as a designation, is based upon the fact that under dollar-value *Lifo*

EXHIBIT 9–12

***Lifo* Inventory—Dollar-Value Method, Double-Extension Approach**

Phase A—Computation of Internal Index for Current Year

Step 1. Base inventory when *Lifo* adopted (at base year costs):

Beginning of base year (19B):			
Item A	1,000 @	$1.00	$1,000
Item B	2,500	2.04	5,100
Total Base Inventory			$6,100

Step 2. Ending inventory at base year costs:

	Year End 19B			Year End 19C		
Item A	1,200 @	$1.00	$1,200	1,300 @	$1.00	$1,300
Item B	3,000	2.04	6,120	3,000	2.04	6,120
Total Ending Inventory at Base Year Costs			$7,320			$7,420

Step 3. Ending inventory at current year costs:

Item A ($3,600 ÷ 3,000 = $1.20)	1,200 @	$1.20	$1,440			
Item B ($10,000 ÷ 4,000 = $2.50)	3,000	2.50	7,500			
19B—Total Ending Inventory at Current Costs			$8,940			
Item A ($4,290 ÷ 3,300 = $1.30)				1,300 @	$1.30	$1,690
Item B ($10,920 ÷ 4,200 = $2.60)				3,000	2.60	7,800
19C—Total Ending Inventory at Current Costs						$9,490

Step 4. Current year index:

Current Year Costs ÷ Base Year Costs ......$8,940 ÷ $7,320 = 1.2213
$9,490 ÷ $7,420 = 1.278976

Phase B—Computation of Ending *Lifo* Inventory Amount

Step 5.	Ending Inventory at Base Year Costs	Index (from Step 4)	Ending Inventory at Lifo Cost
End of 19B:			
Base year beginning inventory	$6,100	1.0000	$6,100
Incremental layer: 19B ($7,320 − $6,100)	1,220	1.2213	1,490
Ending inventory at *Lifo*	$7,320		$7,590
End of 19C:			
Base year beginning inventory	$6,100	1.0000	$6,100
Incremental layers: 19B (from 19B)	1,220	1.2213	1,490
19C ($7,420 − $7,320)	100	1.278976	128
Ending Inventory at *Lifo*	$7,420		$7,718

the ending inventory is double costed (or double priced); that is, in base year dollars and in current year dollars. This requires that an internal price index specific to the inventory be computed (Phase A computation in Exhibit 9–12). Double extension is the basic dollar-value approach; the link-chain approach is a short-cut adaptation suitable only for special situations.

Double extension, for a single pool, is illustrated and explained in Exhibit 9–12 for Tye Company (basic data given in Exhibit 9–9).

In Exhibit 9–12, an inventory incremental layer was added each year. The annual increment to the ending *Lifo* inventory was valued on the basis of the most recent purchase cost as reflected by the current year index. Alternatively, use of the earliest purchase or the average purchase cost during the current year is permitted for tax purposes.

Inventory Liquidation

Frequently there will be full or partial *inventory liquidation* (or invasion) of one or more of the incremental layers. Liquidation should come from the most recent incremental layers. To illustrate, let's adapt the above illustration with the assumption that 19C sales for Item A were 3,500 units; this would leave 1,000 units of Item A in the 19C ending inventory—a liquidation of the inventory of the prior year by 200 units of Product A. In this situation, steps 2 through 4 for 19C would be as follows:

Steps 2, 3, and 4:

	Step 2—At Base Year Cost		*Step 3—At Current Period Cost*	
Item A	1,000 @ $1.00 =	$1,000	1,000 @ $1.30 =	$1,300
Item B	3,000 2.04 =	6,120	3,000 2.60 =	7,800
Total		$7,120		$9,100

Step 4—indcx: $9,100 ÷ $7,120 = 1.278.

Step 5. Calculation of the ending *Lifo* inventory using the following indexes:

	Ending Inventory at Base Year Cost	*Index*	*Ending Inventory at Lifo Value*
Year 19C:			
Base cost (at base date)...............	$6,100	1.0000	$6,100
19B increment ($1,220 − $200*)	1,020	1.2213	1,246
	$7,120		$7,346

* Liquidation: 19B............... $7,320
19C............... 7,120
$ 200

Observe that the liquidation is taken from the most recent layer and the index is applied for the year that the increment was added to inventory rather than the 19C index.

Change in Product Mix

This problem was discussed previously (page 385). With the dollar-value method, when a new item is added to the product line (and hence to inventory), a *reconstructed* cost for it is established as the base cost at *(a)* what the item would have cost at the base date (based upon base year price lists, etc.); or *(b)* if the item did not exist at that date, the first cost after the base date that can be reconstructed; or *(c)* if no prior cost can be determined, then the cost at the date that the item was first stocked for use or sale. To illustrate, let's adapt the data for Tye Company for 19C. Assume Item A was completely sold and discontinued during 19C, that Item C was added to the line, and the following additional information:

Ending inventory, 19C:

Item	*Units*	*Current Unit Cost*	*Base Year Cost*
A (discontinued)	-0-	-0-	$1.00
B (continued)	3,000	$2.60	2.04 (as before)
C (new product)	2,000	1.10	.80 (Reconstructed to base date)

Steps 2 through 4, for this situation, would be (disregard the inventory liquidation example):

Item	*Step 2—At Base Year Cost*	*Step 3—At Current Period Cost*
A (discontinued)...		
B	3,000 @ $2.04 = $6,120	3,000 @ $2.60 = $ 7,800
C	2,000 @ .80 = 1,600	2,000 @ 1.10 = 2,200
	$7,720	$10,000

Step 4. Index for 19C: $10,000 ÷ $7,720 = 1.295.

Step 5. Calculation of ending *Lifo* inventory using the indexes:

	Ending Inventory at Base Year Cost	*Index*	*Ending Inventory at Lifo Value*
Year 19C:			
Base cost (at base date)	$6,100	1.000	$6,100
19B increment (as before)	1,220	1.2213	1,490
19C increment ($7,720 − $7,320)............................	400	1.295	518
Total	$7,720		$8,108

The reconstructed base year cost prevents the adverse product-mix impact on the *Lifo* inventory amount. This is a distinct, and significant, advantage of the dollar-value method (for both the double-extension and link-chain approaches).

There are other problems such as damaged or obsolete goods and erosion of the base year inventory (which usually causes disallowance of the *Lifo* method by the IRS). However, the preceding discussions are intended to cover the basic application procedures. The dollar-value, double-extension approach, applied on a single-pool basis is extremely flexible and tends to maximize the *Lifo* impact.

Application of the dollar-value, multiple pools approach is identical with that illustrated above. The same procedures are applied to each separate pool, and the results of the separate computations are summed to derive the total *Lifo* inventory.

Dollar-Value Method, Link-Chain Approach. The link-chain approach was developed to better cope with the dual problems of (1) changes in items or product mix, and (2) rapid technological changes. These changes may exert a significant negative impact on *Lifo* inventory results. Although the double-extension approach partially adjusts for these changes, the link-chain approach goes farther in that direction. Application of the link-chain approach is illustrated in Exhibit 9–13.[7]

The link-chain approach involves the same two phases as illustrated above for the double-extension approach. However, the current year index is computed differently and a *cumulative index* is computed. The current year index is computed as follows:

$$\frac{\text{Ending Inventory for the Period at Current Year Costs}}{\text{Ending Inventory for the Period at Beginning of the Year Costs}} = \text{Index for the Current year}$$

Thus, rather than being an index from the base year costs to current year costs (as is the case with the double-extension method) the index represents the change in costs for the current year only.

A cumulative index is used for converting the inventory to *Lifo;* the cumulative index is computed for each year by multiplying the index for the current year (above) by the cumulative index for the prior year. This linking together of the two ratios is the basis for the designation "link chain." Computation of the index for the current year and the cumulative index for the year is illustrated in Exhibit 9–13.

The ending inventory at current year prices is then divided by the cumulative index to convert that amount to *base cost* (Column E, Exhibit 9–13). The ending inventory for the current period, at base cost, is used in Phase B to calculate the incremental layer (or liquidation) of inventory during the current period (at base cost). The incremental layer, at base cost, is then multiplied by the cumulative index to derive the *Lifo amount.*

---

[7] This schedule could have been designed to parallel Exhibit 9–12; however, it has been rearranged to demonstrate variations that may attain greater efficiency in particular circumstances. The schedules are not unique.

EXHIBIT 9–13
***Lifo* Inventory–Dollar-Value, Method, Link-Chain Approach**

Phase A–Computation of Internal Index

	(Step 2) Beginning of Year Cost (A) Note (a)	(Step 3) Current Year Cost (B) Note (b)	(Step 4) Current Year Index (C) (B ÷ A)	Cumulative Index (D) (prior D × current C)	Ending Inventory at Total Base Cost (E) (B ÷ D)
(Step 1) Beginning of base year (19B)	$6,100	$6,100	1.0000	1.0000	$6,100
End of 19B	7,320	8,940	1.2213	1.2213	7,320
End of 19C	9,060	9,490	1.0475	1.2793	7,418

Note (a)–beginning cost:		Note (b) current cost:
19B: Item A–1,200 @ $1.00 =	$1,200	1,200 @ $1.20 = $1,440
Item B–3,000 @ 2.04 =	6,120	3,000 @ 2.50 = 7,500
	$7,320	$8,940
19C: Item A–1,300 @ 1.20 =	$1,560	1,300 @ 1.30 = $1,690
Item B–3,000 @ 2.50 =	7,500	3,000 @ 2.60 = 7,800
	$9,060	$9,490

Phase B–Computation of *Lifo* Inventory Amount

Step 5.	Ending Inventory at Total Base Cost (Col. E)	Cumulative Index (Col. D)	Ending Inventory at *Lifo* Cost
End of year 19B:			
Base year beginning inventory	$6,100	1.0000	$6,100
Increment 19B ($7,320 – $6,100)	1,220	1.2213	1,490
	$7,320		
Ending Inventory at *Lifo*			$7,590
End of year 19C:			
Base year beginning inventory	$6,100	1.0000	$6,100
Increment 19B..	1,220	1.2213	1,490
Increment 19C ($7,418 – $7,320)	98	1.2793	125
	$7,418		
Ending Inventory at *Lifo*			$7,715

For study convenience and for comparative analysis, the two phases, and five computational steps, summarized on page 387, were prominently identified in Exhibits 9–12 and 9–13.

The double-extension and link-chain methods will give the same results for the first year of application (19B in the illustration); in the periods following the results will be different, often by significant amounts. Link chain tends to give a lower ending inventory amount; however, this is not always the case.

The link-chain method represents a short-cut approach in applying the dollar-value method and is preferred where there are numerous changes in inventory items. For tax purposes, it is limited to those situations where the double-extension method can be shown to be impracticable or unsuitable to the situation because of product mix and technological impacts. The link-chain method provides maximum flexibility in application of the *Lifo* concept.

Indexing

In the preceding discussions and illustrations of dollar-value *Lifo*, the indexes used were *internal indexes* since they were computed from the internal inventory data of the company; no externally computed indexes were used. Recall that computation of the internal index each period, under both methods (double extension and link chain), required that *(a)* unit cost data and *(b)* physical unit data for the ending inventory be available for each item in the inventory pool. In complex situations, this requirement for detailed data often poses a critical problem. As a consequence, there are two situations where the index might be derived in another way, viz:

1. Internal index derived on sampling basis – In situations where detailed unit and cost data for each item in the *entire* inventory pool is impractical (because of technological changes, extensive variety of items, or extreme fluctuations in the variety of items), the tax regulations state that an internal index may be computed by using a "representative portion of the inventory pool or by use, of other sound and consistent statistical methods." When this internal sampling approach is used, computation of the internal index is precisely the same as illustrated for the *(a)* double-extension approach in Exhibit 9–12, and *(b)* link-chain approach in Exhibit 9–13, except sampling data rather than total data are used.
2. External index – In situations where *neither* the entire ending inventory pool nor statistical sampling of the pool is feasible for computing an internal index, an *appropriate external price index* may be used. This is a rare situation because it is very difficult to justify in light of the IRS tax regulations. The selection of an external price index avoids the detailed index computations illustrated above (i.e., Phase A). Therefore, only Phase B computations are necessary. This phase simply involves costing the ending inventory base layer and incremental layers.[8] To illustrate the simplification, assume the following data for Tye Company:

Inventory data:

Base year inventory, end of 19A at 19A costs..................	$6,100
19B ending inventory, at 19B costs (*Fifo* basis)................	8,940

External price index selected:

19A..............	1.0000
19B..............	1.2213

[8] This is a widely used assumption in accounting literature for *Lifo* problems. It oversimplifies the dollar-value *Lifo* and gives no flavor of the real-life complexities encountered by all accountants. As explained earlier, the use of an external index is rarely permissible.

Required:

Compute the 19B ending inventory at *Lifo* value assuming the dollar-value, double-extension approach.

Solution:[9]

Computation of *Lifo* inventory amount (only Phase B needed):

	Ending Inventory Base Year Cost	*Selected Index*	*Ending Inventory at Lifo Value*
End of 19B:			
Base year beginning inventory	$6,100	1.0000	$6,100
Increment, 19B....................	1,220[b]	1.2213	1,490
Total Inventory at Base Year Cost	$7,320[a]		$7,590

Computations:

[a] 19B ending inventory at 19A cost, $8,940 ÷ 1.2213 = $7,320
Less: Base inventory (19A ending inventory at 19A cost)... 6,100

[b] Difference: Inventory Increase in 19B at 19A Cost... $1,220

LIFO APPLIED TO INTERIM STATEMENTS

We have consistently stated that most companies using *Lifo* continue to maintain their accounts on *Fifo,* or some other basis, and make a conversion to *Lifo* inventory at year-end. This means that interim statements (quarterly) unless converted in some way, would be inconsistent with the annual report. *APB Opinion No. 28,* "Interim Reporting" (and the SEC as well), specifies that the consistency principle similarly applies to interim statements and the annual statements. Therefore, a company using *Lifo* for annual statements must also use it for interim statements. This often poses a critical problem because certain *Lifo* effects during the year may be changed before year-end. For example, there may be a liquidation of incremental layers, or even invasion of the base layer during the year, that may be replaced before year-end. Therefore, the company must forecast, at the end of the interim period, whether there will be replacement by the end of the year. Basically, the company must make a first quarter estimate of the inventory *quantity* expected to be on hand at year-end. This quantity is then used to compute the estimated dollar difference expected at year-end between *Lifo* and the inventory method used for operating purposes. This difference should be allocated to each interim period on some rational basis, such as the ratio of quarterly sales to estimated annual sales. *Fifo,* average, and specific identification costing methods do not pose this interim problem.

---

[9] We assumed an external index identical to the internal index computed in Exhibits 9–12 and 9–13 to demonstrate that there is no difference in application between the use of an internal index versus an external index except to the extent that the index values are different (and the index does not have to be computed which is the complex and burdensome phase).

LIFO RESERVES

Companies using *Lifo* for tax and external reporting purposes and some other method, such as *Fifo,* for internal management and record-keeping purposes, sometimes employ a *Lifo* allowance account (often inappropriately called a *Lifo* reserve account) to reflect the difference between the two inventory amounts.

To illustrate, one company reported inventories as follows:

	1975	*1974*
Current Assets:		
Finished goods, work in process, and raw materials, *Lifo* basis (net of *Lifo* reserve of $3,200,000 in 1975 and $2,900,000 in 1974)	$8,000,000	$6,500,000

Clearly, this reflects that the inventory method used for internal management purposes *(Fifo)* reflected ending inventory balances of $11,200,000 in 1975 and $9,400,000 in 1974. Although seldom formally entered in the accounts, the difference could be recognized in the accounts as follows:

1974 (first *Lifo* year):

Cost of goods sold	2,900,000	
Allowance to reduce inventory to *Lifo* basis		2,900,000

1975:

Cost of goods sold	300,000	
Allowance to reduce inventory to *Lifo* basis ($3,200,000 – $2,900,000)		300,000

SUMMARY

The discussions in Part B have pinpointed the primary problems in *Lifo* application. Since the quantity, or specific unit, method of applying *Lifo* illustrated in Part A is seldom applied, for external purposes, its study alone imparts an oversimplification of the *Lifo* issue. In application, *Lifo* is comparatively complex and involves considerable clerical effort. Because of the wide range of opportunities for differences, and because it is subject to inventory manipulation, it has been accorded intensive attention by governmental regulatory agencies such as the SEC and the IRS. Similarly, the major accounting firms have devoted much research and study to *Lifo* because they generally view it as a conceptually and economically sound approach to the measurement of income. Also, accountants insist that the concept be applied in a conceptually sound, consistent, and realistic way in each diverse situation. *Lifo* is generally recommended in situations where:

1. Continuing price changes (inflation) can be projected realistically.
2. Income taxes will increase or remain high.
3. Inventory quantities (volume) will not decrease materially.
4. Shortages of items stocked are not expected.
5. Long-run trends in the business can be projected realistically.

QUESTIONS

PART A

1. What are the primary purposes to be served in selecting a particular inventory flow method? Why is the selection particularly important?
2. Briefly explain the differences between periodic and perpetual inventory procedures. Under what circumstances are each generally used?
3. Does the adoption of perpetual inventory procedures eliminate the need for physical count or measurement of inventories? Explain.
4. Explain the specific cost method and indicate the objections to it.
5. Distinguish between a weighted average and a moving average in determining unit cost. When is each generally used? Explain.
6. Explain the essential features of first-in, first-out. What are the primary advantages and disadvantages of *Fifo*? Explain the difference in the application of *Fifo* under *(a)* periodic inventory procedures, and *(b)* perpetual inventory procedures. In contrast with *Lifo*, how does it affect cash flow?
7. Explain the essential features of last-in, first-out. What are the primary advantages and disadvantages of *Lifo*? Explain the difference in application of *Lifo* under *(a)* periodic inventory procedures, and *(b)* perpetual inventory procedures.
8. Explain why *Lifo* costed currently and *Lifo* costed at the end of the month may give different results.
9. What is meant by inventory layers? Why are they significant with respect to the *Fifo*, *Lifo*, and base stock methods?
10. Assuming the *Lifo* method, what is meant by inventory liquidation? Why is it a serious problem for *Lifo* but not *Fifo*?
11. How is *Lifo* usually applied *(a)* in the accounts, *(b)* on the income tax return, and *(c)* the external financial reports.
12. Compare the balance sheet and income statement effects of *Fifo* versus *Lifo* *(a)* when prices are rising, and *(b)* when prices are declining.

PART B

13. Why do the IRS regulations limit reporting to a footnote, for the base year only, of the impact on net income of two different inventory methods (and one of the methods is used for tax purposes)?
14. What is meant by the quantity of goods *Lifo* method? Identify and distinguish between the two approaches used to implement this method.
15. Explain how changes in the item or product mix of *Lifo* ending inventories over a period of several years will adversely affect the results of the quantity of goods approach.
16. What are the primary differences and limitations of the *Lifo* quantity method versus the dollar-value method?

17. Contrast the concept of a *Lifo* inventory pool as between the quantity method and the dollar-value method.

18. What are the basic features of the dollar-value *Lifo* method?

19. Contrast the dollar-value method, double-extension approach with the dollar-value method, link-chain approach, and indicate when each is appropriate.

20. What is indexing? When can an external price index be used?

21. Explain the problem that *Lifo* poses when interim statements are prepared. Why is this problem unique to *Lifo*?

DECISION CASE 9–1

As a member of the controller's department of XYZ Corporation, you have been involved in an initial discussion with some other company executives concerning the merits of *Lifo* versus *Fifo* inventory procedures for the company. The following items were listed during the initial discussion:

	Characteristic of—		
Items	*Fifo*	*Lifo*	*Brief Explanation*
1. Matches the actual physical flow of goods.	Yes		
2. Levels income.			
3. Tends to cause income to vary with prices.			
4. Matches old costs with new prices.			
5. Costs inventory at approximate replacement cost.			
6. Matches new costs with new prices.			
7. Emphasizes the balance sheet.			
8. Emphasizes the income statement.			
9. Subject to profit manipulation.			
10. Gives higher profits when prices rise.			
11. Gives lower profits when prices fall.			
12. Processes costs same order as incurred.			
13. Matches current costs with current revenue.			
14. Acceptable for income tax purposes.			
15. Income figure more accurately reflects profits that are available to owners.			

Required:

1. Complete the above tabulation.
2. Be prepared to discuss each item in detail.
3. Be prepared to explain and illustrate item 15.

EXERCISES

PART A: Exercises 1–9

Exercise 9–1

The perpetual inventory records of the North Company provided the following data for one item of merchandise for sale (assume the transactions in order of the number given).

	Units	*Unit Cost*	*Amount*
Goods available for sale:			
Beginning inventory..............	500	$6.00	$ 3,000
Purchases: (1)	600	6.10	3,660
(3)	600	6.20	3,720
(5)	400	6.30	2,520
	2,100		$12,900
Sales: (2)	900		
(4)	500		
(6)	300		

Required:

1. Complete the following (round unit costs to even cents and amounts to even dollars).

Costing Method	*Valuation* — *Final Inventory*	*Cost of Goods Sold*
a. Fifo	$________	$________
b. Lifo (unit basis costed at end of period and assume base inventory is 400 units) ...	$________	$________
c. Weighted average	$________	$________
d. Base stock (base 300 units @ $1)...........	$________	$________

2. Compute the amount of pretax net income and rank the methods in order of the amount of pretax net income (highest first) assuming *Fifo* net income is $30,000.
3. Which method would you prefer in this instance? Why?

Exercise 9–2

The raw material records of the Star Manufacturing Corporation showed the following data relative to raw material K (assume the transactions occurred in the order given):

	Units	*Unit Cost*
1. Inventory..............	300	$2.00
2. Purchase..............	400	2.10
3. Issue....................	600	
4. Purchase..............	500	2.20
5. Issue....................	400	
6. Purchase..............	600	2.30

Required:

1. Compute the cost of issues for the period and the final inventory assuming (round unit costs to even cents):

   a. Weighted average method.

b. Moving average method.
c. *Fifo.*
d. *Lifo* (unit basis; costed at end; 300 units in base layer).

2. Under what general circumstances would each be preferable?

Exercise 9–3

The inventory records of Goldstein Retailers showed the following data relative to a particular unit sold regularly (assume transactions in the order given):

	Units	*Unit Cost*
1. Inventory	2,000	$4.00
2. Purchases	18,000	4.50
3. Sales (@ $13 per unit)	7,000	
4. Purchases	6,000	4.60
5. Sales (@ $13.50 per unit)	16,000	
6. Purchases	4,000	4.70

Required:

1. Complete the following tabulation (round unit costs to even cents and keep unit costs of inventory even):

	Ending Inventory	*Cost of Goods Sold*	*Gross Margin*
a. *Fifo*	______	______	______
b. Weighted average	______	______	______
c. *Lifo* (unit basis, costed at end, 2,000 units in base layer)	______	______	______
d. Moving average (show computations)	______	______	______

2. What method would be your first choice? Explain the basis for your choice.

Exercise 9–4

Stockton Corporation manufactures three different products which are stocked for regular sale. The principal product is referred to as "Benders." The records of the company for the month of January provided the following data relative to Benders. The company maintains perpetual inventory records for finished goods. Assume the transactions in the order given.

1. In stock	30 units @ $5.00
2. Received from factory	10 units @ 5.30
3. Shipments	20 units
4. Received from factory	40 units @ 5.20
5. Shipments	50 units
6. Received from factory	20 units @ 5.40
7. Shipments	12 units

The company is using the weighted average method and periodic inventory procedures and is considering a change to *Fifo* or moving average for internal purposes because a perpetual inventory system will be used.

Required:

1. Which method would you prefer? Why?
2. Construct the perpetual inventory record for Benders using the method you

preferred in Requirement 1. (Round unit costs to even cents and keep inventory at even cents per unit.)

Exercise 9–5

Simpson Company produced 40,000 units during the year. Sales were 50,000 units, and the beginning inventory was 30,000 units (base inventory, 10,000 units @ $5 = $50,000). The unit cost of production for the year was $10, and the initial inventory was carried at $210,000. Complete the following (round inventory unit costs to even cents):

	Ending Inventory		
	Computations	*Amount*	*Pretax Income*
a. First-in, first-out..............		$______	$90,000
b. Last-in, first-out (unit basis, costed at end).................		$______	$______
c. Weighted average		$______	$______

Exercise 9–6

Noonan Company uses *Lifo* (unit basis). The following data were available relative to the primary raw material for period 19A:

	Units	*Unit Cost*
Beginning inventory (base inventory)..............	5,000	$3.00
Beginning inventory (excess)	1,000	3.10
Purchases	19,000	3.40
Issues	22,000	

The first purchase in period 19B was 10,000 units at $3.70 per unit.

Required:

1. Compute the ending *Lifo* inventory and the cost of issues for period 19A.
2. Give the journal entries for purchases and issues, record the period 19A inventory invasion in the accounts (debit purchases to Inventory and issues to Work in Process).
3. Give the journal entry for the purchase in period 19B.
4. How should the inventory and any related accounts be reported on the balance sheet at the end of period 19A?

Exercise 9–7

Lilly Company currently uses *Fifo* for all purposes. The inventory records for the period reflected the following for one major item sold regularly:

Beginning inventory	10,000 units @ $ 8
Purchases during the period	40,000 units @ 10
Sales during the period (@ $30)	35,000 units
Expenses (excluding income taxes)..............	$40,000
Beginning cash balance	$20,000
Income tax average rate	45%

The company is considering a change to *Lifo* for all purposes. Assume the beginning inventory given above will be the *Lifo* base inventory.

Required:

1. Assuming all transactions are cash basis, compare *Lifo* and *Fifo* results by preparing for each: *(a)* an income statement, and *(b)* a partial balance sheet (limited to the above transactions). Include a column for *differences* and show computations of cash balances. Assume 100,000 shares of common stock outstanding.
2. In this situation, based on the data at hand, which inventory method would you recommend? Why?
3. Under what conditions would you recommend the other method?

Exercise 9–8

Fisher Company records standard costs in the accounts. The finished goods inventory records are maintained at standard. When raw material is purchased, the difference between standard cost and actual cost is recorded in a separate variance account and reported as a *loss or gain* for the period in which the goods were purchased. The records relating to one item of raw material showed the following: standard cost per unit, $5; beginning inventory, 1,000 units; purchases during the period were No. 1–2,000 units at $5.10, No. 2–800 units at $4.95, and No. 3–1,200 units at $5; sales were 3,500 units at $12; expenses paid were $20,000.

Required:

1. Give journal entries for the purchases, sales, and expenses.
2. Prepare an income statement (disregard income taxes). Assume 3,000 shares of common stock outstanding.

Exercise 9–9

Barber Manufacturing Company produces a single product in one plant that is distributed nationally. The plant is highly mechanized; therefore, fixed costs are relatively high. Full manufacturing cost and *Lifo* has been used for internal, external, and tax purposes. Because there is only one plant and wide distribution, a large inventory of finished goods is maintained. The controller is considering a variable (direct) costing system for internal purposes. *Lifo* (unit basis) will continue to be used for income tax purposes. The following year-end amounts were determined on a *Lifo* (full-cost) basis:

Sales (8,000 units @ $91)	$728,000
Cost of goods sold (@ $46)	368,000
Gross margin	360,000
Expenses (fixed)	160,000
Pretax income	200,000
Income taxes (@ 40%)	80,000
Net income	$120,000

Beginning inventory, finished goods	None
Manufacturing costs (10,000 units):	
Direct material used	$ 55,000
Direct labor incurred	175,000
Factory overhead – fixed	150,000
Factory overhead – variable	80,000
Ending inventory, finished goods (2,000 units)	(92,000)
Cost of Goods Sold	$368,000

Required:

1. Recast the above statements for internal purposes on a direct cost basis. Use the beginning inventory as given.

2. Which basis should be used for external reporting purposes? Explain.
3. Explain why net income is different between *Lifo* and direct costing? Use computations to demonstrate the difference.

PART B: Exercises 10–14

Exercise 9–10

On January 1, 19B, Foster Company changed from *Fifo* to *Lifo* for income tax and external reporting purposes. The ending inventory for 19A (*Fifo* basis) was $155,000 (this will be the base inventory amount for *Lifo*). At the end of 19B, the *Lifo* inventory amount, computed using the dollar-value, double-extension approach was $160,000; had the company continued using *Fifo,* this amount would have been $184,000. The average income tax rate is 46%.

Required:

1. Compute the difference in net income for 19B attributable to the change from *Fifo* to *Lifo*. Show computations.
2. Prepare an appropriate note to the financial statements for 19B.

Exercise 9–11

Baker Wholesale Grocery Company uses the *Lifo* method for income tax and external reporting purposes. The ending inventory for 19A (*Lifo* basis) amounted to $260,000 (at base cost). The physical inventory taken at the end of 19B, at 19B costs, amounted to $336,000 (*Fifo* basis). An external price index indicated a 12% increase in prices during 19B. Assume this is a rare situation where an external price index can be used.

Required:

1. Use the external index to compute the *Lifo* inventory amount, assuming dollar-value, double-extension method.
2. Under what special conditions is the external index approach appropriate?

Exercise 9–12

Stonewall Company uses *Lifo* for income tax and external reporting purposes. The *Lifo* base inventory (at end of 19A) for inventory Pool No. 1 amounted to $70,000. The periodic inventory of Pool No. 1 taken at the end of 19B, priced at 19B costs, amounted to $92,000. Analysis of a statistical sample of the inventory and related computations showed a price index for 19A of 100 and for 19B, 115.

Required:

1. Use the period internal indexes already derived to compute the 19B ending *Lifo* inventory amount assuming the dollar-value, double-extension method.
2. Under what conditions is the sampling index approach appropriate?

Exercise 9–13

Kashin Company distributes quarterly interim reports to all shareholders. The annual accounting period ends on December 31. The first quarter interim report, dated March 31, 19B, is being prepared. The company uses *Lifo* for income tax and financial reporting purposes and *Fifo* for internal purposes.

The following data are available:

Actual amounts:	
Base year *Lifo* inventory, January 1, 19B..............	$100,000
Lifo inventory, March 31, 19B..............................	110,000
Estimated amounts:	
Fifo inventory, December 31, 19B	96,000
Lifo inventory, December 31, 19B	78,000

Sales for the first quarter were approximately 30% of the total sales budgeted for the year.

Required:

1. What should be the amount of the *Lifo* ending inventory at the end of the first quarter? Show computations.
2. Justify your answer.

Exercise 9–14

At the end of the annual accounting period, the inventory records of Adams Company reflected the following:

	19A	*19B*
Ending inventory at *Fifo*..............	$350,000	$390,000
Ending inventory at *Lifo*..............	340,000	320,000

The company uses *Fifo* for internal purposes and *Lifo* for income tax and external reporting purposes.

Required:

1. Assume the inventory difference is recognized in the accounts. Give the appropriate journal entry for each year.
2. Show how the inventories should be shown on the 19B comparative balance sheet.

PROBLEMS

PART A: Problems 1–10

Problem 9–1

Stiles Company records showed the following transactions, in order of occurrence, relative to raw material W:

	Units	*Unit Cost*
1. Inventory..............	400	$5.00
2. Purchase..............	600	5.50
3. Issue.....................	700	
4. Purchase..............	900	5.60
5. Issue.....................	800	
6. Purchase..............	200	5.80

Required:

Compute the cost of the issues and final inventory in each of the following completely independent situations (round unit costs to even cents and keep unit inventory cost at even cents; show computations):

Assumption	Units and Amount	
	Final Inventory	Issues
a. Weighted average.		
b. Moving average.		
c. *Fifo.*		
d. *Lifo* costed currently (base inventory, 200 units).		
e. *Lifo* costed at end of period.		
f. Base stock (base stock, 100 units).		
g. Standard cost (standard cost, $4.75).		

Problem 9–2

The records of Smith Trading Company showed the following transactions, in the order given, relating to the major item sold:

	Units	Unit Cost
1. Inventory	3,000	$7.00
2. Purchase	5,000	7.20
3. Sales (@ $15)	4,000	
4. Purchase	7,000	7.50
5. Sales (@ $15)	9,000	
6. Purchase	8,000	7.60
7. Sales (@ $16)	9,000	
8. Purchase	6,000	7.90

Required:

Complete the following tabulation for each independent assumption (round unit costs to even cents and keep inventory at even unit cost; show computations):

Assumption	Units and Amount		
	Ending Inventory	Cost of Goods Sold	Gross Margin
a. *Fifo.*			
b. *Lifo* costed at end of period (base inventory, 1,000 units).			
c. *Lifo* costed currently (base inventory, 1,000 units)—support with a perpetual inventory record.			
d. Weighted average.			
e. Moving average—support with a perpetual inventory record.			

Problem 9–3

The following purchases and sales of a major item, in the order given, were made by the Hoosier Company (beginning inventory was 800 units valued at $600):

	Purchases		Units Sold
	Units	Unit Cost	@ $3 Each
(1)..............	500	$.90	
(2)..............			800
(3)..............	1,600	.85	
(4)..............			1,200
(5)..............	900	.95	
(6)..............	600	.90	
(7)..............			1,700
(8)..............	300	.80	

Required:

Complete the following tabulation for each independent assumption (round to even unit costs and keep unit inventory cost to even cents). Show computations.

	Units and Amount		
Assumption	Ending Inventory	Cost of Goods Sold	Gross Margin
a. Fifo.			
b. Weighted average cost (round unit costs to three places).			
c. Lifo, costed currently (base inventory, 500 units).			
d. Lifo, costed at end of period.			

Problem 9–4

The records of Damon Company showed the following data relative to one of the major items being sold. Assume the transactions occurred in the order given.

	Units	Unit Cost
Beginning inventory...............	7,000	$4.00
Purchase No. 1	6,000	4.20
Sale No. 1 (@ $10)	9,000	
Purchase No. 2	8,000	4.50
Sale No. 2 (@ $11)	4,000	

Required:

1. Compute the cost of goods sold, the valuation of the final inventory, and gross margin under each of the following independent assumptions (round unit costs to nearest cent):

	Amount		
	Inventory	Cost of Goods Sold	Gross Margin
a. Weighted average cost with periodic inventory procedures.			
b. Fifo with perpetual inventory procedures.			
c. Lifo costed at end of period (base inventory, 7,000 units).			
d. Standard cost assuming the standard cost is $4.			

2. Give all entries indicated by the above data assuming:

   Case A – Weighted average cost ([*a*] above).
   Case B – *Fifo* ([*b*] above).
   Case C – Standard cost ([*d*] above).

Problem 9–5

The records of Thomas Company showed the following data with respect to one raw material used in the manufacturing process. Assume the transactions occurred in the order given.

	Units	*Unit Cost*
Inventory	4,000	$7.00
Purchase No. 1	3,000	7.60
Issue No. 1	5,000	
Purchase No. 2	8,000	8.00
Issue No. 2	7,000	
Purchase No. 3	3,000	8.20

Required:

1. Compute cost of goods issued (to work in process) and the valuation of the ending inventory for each of the following independent transactions (round unit costs to even cents and keep unit inventory costs to even cents; show computations):
   a. *Fifo.*
   b. *Lifo,* costed at end of period (base inventory, 4,000 units).
   c. Weighted average.
   d. Moving average.
   e. Standard cost (assuming a standard unit cost of $8).
2. In parallel columns, give all entries indicated for *Fifo* assuming –

   Case A – A Perpetual inventory system.
   Case B – A Periodic inventory system.

Problem 9–6

Wilson Manufacturing Company manufactures one main product. Two raw materials are used in the manufacture of this product. The company uses standard costs in the accounts and carries the raw material, work in process, and finished goods inventories at standard. The records of the company showed the following:

	Material A	*Material B*
Beginning inventory (units)	8,000	5,000
Standard cost per unit	$2.00	$7.00
Purchases during the period:		
No. 1	10,000 @ $2.00	7,000 @ $7.00
No. 2	20,000 @ 1.90	8,000 @ 7.20
Issues during the period (units)	28,000	16,000
Final inventory per physical count (units)	10,000	3,900

Required:

1. Give all entries indicated relative to raw materials assuming standard costs.
2. Determine the value of the final inventory and cost issues for each raw material.
3. Accumulate the amount of the variations from standard for each raw material and explain or illustrate the reporting and accounting disposition of these amounts.

Problem 9–7

Robins Corporation maintains perpetual inventory records on a *Fifo* basis for the three main products distributed by the company. A physical inventory is taken at the end of each six months in order to check the perpetual inventory records.

The following information relating to one of the products for the year was taken from the records of the company:

	Product A
Beginning inventory	9,000 units @ $8.10
Purchases and sales (in the order given):	
Purchase No. 11	5,000 units @ 8.15
Sale No. 1	10,000 units
Purchase No. 12	16,000 units @ 8.20
Sale No. 2	11,000 units
Purchase No. 13	4,000 units @ 8.30
Purchase No. 14	7,000 units @ 8.20
Sale No. 3	14,000 units
Purchase No. 15	5,000 units @ 8.10
Ending inventory (per count)	10,000
Replacement cost (per unit)	$8.00

Required:

1. Reconstruct the perpetual inventory record for Product A.
2. Give all entries indicated by the above data assuming selling price is $18 per unit and that the company employs the direct inventory reduction method (holding losses not separately identified) in recognizing lower of cost or market.
3. Prepare the income statement for this product through gross margin.

Problem 9–8

Watson Trading Company sells three main products. In the past, periodic inventory procedures have been employed on a *Fifo* basis. The records of the company showed the following information relating to one of the products:

Beginning inventory	500 units @ $3.00
Purchases and sales (in the order given):	
Purchase No. 1	400 units @ 3.10
Purchase No. 2	600 units @ 3.15
Sale No. 1	1,000 units
Purchase No. 3	800 units @ 3.25
Sale No. 2	700 units
Sale No. 3	500 units
Purchase No. 4	700 units @ 3.30

In considering a change in inventory policy, the following summary was prepared:

	Illustration			
	(1)	(2)	(3)	(4)
Sales	$15,400	$15,400	$15,400	$15,400
Cost of goods sold	6,911	7,110	6,996	6,905
Gross margin	$ 8,489	$ 8,290	$ 8,404	$ 8,495

Required:

1. Identify the inventory flow method used for each illustration assuming the ending inventory only was affected.
2. What method would you recommend? Give its advantages and disadvantages.

Problem 9–9

Stamford Company uses *Fifo* in costing the raw material inventory. During the first three years of operation, the inventory at the end of each year computed by different methods for comparative purposes was as follows:

	Final Inventory		
	19A	19B	19C
Fifo	$180,000	$200,000	$160,000
Lifo	150,000	160,000	140,000
Average cost (weighted)	170,000	210,000	150,000

Required:

Compute net income under each method. Results under *Fifo* method are given.

	Net Income		
	19A	19B	19C
Fifo	$40,000	$70,000	$30,000
Lifo			
Average cost (weighted)			

Problem 9–10

Foster Company uses *Fifo* for internal accounting and management purposes and *Lifo* for external reporting and income tax purposes. During a recent period, the *Fifo* inventory records reflected the following transactions, in the order given, for the main product:

	Units	Fifo Unit Cost
1. Beginning inventory	5,000	$8.00
2. Purchase	4,000	8.20
3. Sales (@ $20)	7,000	
4. Purchase	8,000	8.30
5. Sales (@ $21)	6,000	

The purchasing officer has determined that the next purchase will cost $8.50 per unit.

Required:

1. Assume the *Lifo* base inventory is 5,000 units at $8. Complete a tabulation as follows:

	Fifo	*Lifo*
Sales revenue		
Cost of goods sold		
Gross margin		

2. Give entries relating to the inventory invasion.
3. Explain and justify the way you handled the invasion of the *Lifo* base inventory.

PART B: Problems 11–19

Problem 9–11

Astro Company decided at the beginning of 19A to change from *Fifo* to *Lifo*. The records of the company showed the following data for 19A relative to one major item distributed:

	Units	*Unit Cost*
Beginning inventory (base inventory layers averaged)	10,000	$3.00
Purchases and sales (in the order given):		
1 Purchase...	8,000	3.20
2 Sold (@ $8.00)	9,000	
3 Sold (@ $8.25)	5,000	
4 Purchase...	7,000	3.20
5 Purchase...	6,000	3.40
6 Sold (@ $8.75)	8,000	
7 Purchase...	3,000	3.50

Expenses (excluding income taxes), $40,000.

Average income tax rate, 40%.

Required:

1. Prepare an income statement for 19A, unit *Lifo* basis. Assume 10,000 shares of common stock outstanding.
2. Prepare an appropriate footnote, and any other required supporting data for the change in 19A from *Fifo* to *Lifo*.
3. What would be disclosed in 19B relative to the change? Why?

Problem 9–12

Young Company changed from *Fifo* to *Lifo* for 19A and future periods. The records of the company pertaining to the main product provided the following data for 19A:

	Units	Unit Cost
Beginning inventory (base inventory) ...	5,000	$6.00
Purchases and sales (in order given):		
First quarter:		
a. Purchase	4,000	6.20
b. Sale (@ $15.00)	6,000	
Second quarter:		
a. Purchase	8,000	6.50
b. Sale (@ $15.60)	6,000	
Third quarter:		
a. Purchase	9,000	6.60
b. Sale (@ $15.60)	8,000	
Fourth quarter:		
a. Purchase	3,000	6.80
b. Sale (@ $16.00)	2,000	
Expenses:		
Year	$146,200	
First quarter	40,000	
Income tax rate, 40%.		

Required:

1. Prepare an income statement for 19A, unit *Lifo* basis. Assume 10,000 shares of common stock outstanding.
2. Prepare a note suitable for the 19A financial statements in view of the change from *Fifo* to *Lifo*.
3. Prepare an income statement for the first quarter of 19A only. Explain how you handled the invasion of the base inventory.
4. Prepare a note suitable for the first quarter financial statement.

Problem 9–13

Storm Company uses *Lifo*, unit basis, to cost the ending inventory for income tax and external reporting purposes. Near the end of 19A, the records, and related estimates, provided the following annual data for one item sold regularly:

	Units	Unit Cost
Beginning inventory:		
Base inventory	10,000	$20
Increment No. 1	5,000	30
Purchases (actual)	60,000	35
* Sales (@ $50 per unit)	65,000	
* Expenses (excluding income taxes) $1,000,000		
Average income tax rate, 48%.		

* Including estimates for remainder of 19A.

On December 26 the company has an opportunity to purchase 30,000 units of the above item at $33 (a special price). Delivery is immediate, and the offer will expire January 3, 19B. The question has been posed whether the purchase (and delivery) should be consummated in 19A or 19B.

Required:

1. What is your recommendation on the purchase date? Support your recommendation with reasons and proforma (as if) income statement and balance sheet data. Include computations suitable for presentation to the company president.

2. Explain why each of the following amounts are different: (*a*) purchases, (*b*) ending inventory, (*c*) gross margin, and (*d*) net income.
3. Would you suspect profit manipulation in this situation? Explain.

Problem 9–14

Milliken Retailers, Incorporated, sells two main products regularly. The products are considered to be "substantially identical" for inventory purposes. The company used *Fifo* through 19A for all purposes. Starting in 19B, *Lifo* was adopted for external reporting and income tax purposes. The inventory pool at *Fifo* (the two products combined) records reflected the following:

	Purchases			*Issues*			*Balance*		
19A: Ending inventory ...							400	1.00	400
19B: Purchase...............	700	1.20	840				400	1.00	400
							700	1.20	840
Sale (@ $3.00)				400	1.00	400			
				100	1.20	120	600	1.20	720
19C: Purchase...............	600	1.35	810				600	1.20	720
							600	1.35	810
Sale (@ $3.40)				600	1.20	720			
				200	1.35	270	400	1.35	540
19D: Purchase...............	500	1.50	750				400	1.35	540
							500	1.50	750
Sale (@ $3.75)				400	1.35	540	500	1.50	750

Required:

1. Compute the ending inventory for years 19B, 19C, and 19D assuming the dollar-value method, double-extension approach is used.
2. Prepare a listing that compares the results for *Fifo* and *Lifo*. Which method should be used? Why?
3. Prepare a suitable footnote for the financial statements for 19B assuming *Lifo* is used.

Problem 9–15

Use the data given in Problem 9–14 to complete the following requirements.

Required:

1. Compute the ending inventory for the years 19B, 19C, and 19D assuming the dollar-value method, link-chain approach is used.
2. Prepare a listing that compares *Fifo* and *Lifo* results. Which method should be used? Why?

Problem 9–16

Stoey Distributing Company sells three main products regularly. The products are considered to be "substantially identical" for inventory purposes. The company used *Fifo* through 19A for all purposes. After 19A, *Fifo* was continued for internal management and accounting purposes; however, at the start of 19B,

Lifo was adopted for income tax and external reporting purposes. The following data, for the three products combined, from the records are for the three years after adoption of *Lifo:*

	Fifo Basis per Accounts		
	Units	*Cost*	*Total*
19A:			
Ending inventory	2,000	$3.00	$ 6,000
19B:			
Purchases	6,000	3.30	19,800
Sales (@ $8)	5,000		
Ending inventory	3,000	3.30	9,900
19C:			
Purchases	10,000	3.50	35,000
Sales (@ $9)	6,000		
Ending inventory	7,000	3.50	24,500
19D:			
Purchases	3,000	4.00	12,000
Sales (@ $9)	6,000		
Ending inventory			
Layer 1	1,000	3.50	3,500
Layer 2	3,000	4.00	12,000
Total	4,000		$15,500

Required:

1. Compute the ending inventory for the years 19B, 19C, and 19D assuming the dollar-value method, double-extension approach is used.
2. Prepare a listing that compares the results of the methods, *Fifo* and *Lifo*. Which method should be used? Why?
3. Prepare an appropriate footnote to the financial statements for 19B assuming double extension is used.

Problem 9–17

Use the data given in Problem 9–16 to complete the following requirements.

Required:

1. Compute the ending inventory for the years 19B, 19C, and 19D assuming the dollar-value, link-chain approach is used.
2. Prepare a listing that compares the results of *Fifo* and *Lifo*. Which method should be used? Why?

Problem 9–18

Thames Company sells two main products that have low volume but high cost. *Fifo,* with a perpetual inventory system, is used for internal cost accounting and management purposes. On January 1, 19B, the company adopted *Lifo* for external reporting and income tax purposes. The *Fifo* inventory records reflected the following:

	Purchases			Issues			Balance		
Product X									
December 31, 19A							200	100	20,000
19B: Purchases	400	130	52,000				400	130	52,000
Sales (@ $300)......				200	100	20,000			
				200	130	26,000	200	130	26,000
							200	130	26,000
19C: Purchases	500	140	70,000				500	140	70,000
Sales (@ $300)......				200	130	26,000	500	140	70,000
							500	140	70,000
19D: Purchases	100	150	15,000				100	150	15,000
Sales (@ $325)......				300	140	42,000	200	140	28,000
							100	150	15,000
Product Y									
December 31, 19A							300	90	27,000
19B: Purchases	400	92	36,800				400	92	36,800
Sales (@ $275)......				300	90	27,000	400	92	36,800
							400	92	36,800
19C: Purchases	100	95	9,500				100	95	9,500
Sales (@ $275)......				400	92	36,800	100	95	9,500
							100	95	9,500
19D: Purchases	400	96	38,400				400	96	38,400
Sales (@ $295)......				100	95	9,500	400	96	38,400

Required:

1. Assume the two products are "substantially identical" for inventory purposes. Compute the ending *Lifo* inventory assuming (show computations):

   Case A – Dollar-value method, double-extension approach.
   Case B – Dollar-value method, link-chain approach.

2. Prepare a listing that compares the results of *Fifo* and *Lifo* for Cases A and B. Which method should be used? Why?
3. Prepare a suitable footnote to the financial statements for 19B assuming double extension is used.

Problem 9–19

Wendt Company has been using *Fifo* for all internal and external reporting purposes. At the start of 19B, it adopted *Lifo* for external financial statement and income tax purposes. The *Fifo* inventory records reported the following for one inventory pool:

	Fifo Basis
19A ending inventory	$100,000
19B ending inventory	120,000
19C ending inventory	130,000
19D ending inventory	135,000

External price index selected: 19A – 1.00; 19B – 1.10; 19C – 1.15; and 19D – 1.21.

Required:

1. Compute the ending *Lifo* inventory amounts for 19B, 19C, and 19D assuming the dollar-value method, using an external price index. The external index selected is given above. Apply the index assuming double extension.
2. Prepare a tabulation comparing inventory amounts under *Fifo* and *Lifo* for 19B, 19C, and 19D. What method should be used? Why?
3. Prepare an appropriate footnote for the 19B financial statements assuming double-extension approach is used.

Chapter 10

Inventories—Special Valuation Procedures

There are numerous situations where the accountants must make estimates relating to inventories. As a result certain inventory estimating procedures have gained wide acceptance. Because of the technical complexities involved in applying the *Lifo* concept when the retail method of inventory is used, this chapter is divided into two parts as follows:

Part A—Estimating Procedures for Inventories
1. Gross margin method
2. Retail method of inventory

Part B—Dollar-Value, *Lifo*-Retail Method

PART A—ESTIMATING PROCEDURES FOR INVENTORIES

GROSS MARGIN METHOD

The gross margin[1] method represents an approach frequently used to approximate the valuation of an inventory independently of a physical count of the goods and as a check on the detailed inventory records in the case of perpetual inventory procedures. The method is based on the assumption that the short-run *rate of gross margin* (gross margin divided by sales) is approximately the same from one period to the next. The method involves computation of total goods *available* for sale in the normal manner based on data provided by the accounts. Next the estimated cost of goods sold is determined by applying the estimated gross margin rate to net sales and deducting this amount from sales to derive estimated cost of goods sold. Deduction of the estimated cost of goods sold from the cost of goods available for sale gives the ending inventory at estimated cost. For example, if the rate of gross margin for a business

[1] The method traditionally has been referred to as the gross profit method, nevertheless the descriptive modern terminology *gross margin* is used throughout these discussions. (Ref. AICPA *Terminology Bulletin No. 2.*)

has been uniformly 40% of sales, the final inventory may be approximated as follows:

	Known Data		Computations	Order of Computations
Net sales		$10,000*		
Cost of goods sold:				
Initial inventory	$ 5,000†			
Add: Purchases	8,000*			
Goods available for sale	13,000			
Less: Final inventory	?		($13,000 − $6,000) = $7,000	3
Cost of goods sold		?	($10,000 − $4,000) = $6,000	2
Gross Margin	40%‡	?	($10,000 × .40) = $4,000	1

* From company records.

† Final inventory from prior period.

‡ Based on recent past performance.

A more comprehensive example where the data are rearranged to facilitate computation follows.

Cost of goods available for sale:		
Beginning inventory		$ 50,000*
Purchases during period	$160,400*	
Freight-in	9,800*	
Total Purchases	170,200	
Less: Purchase returns and allowances	200*	
Net purchases		170,000
Cost of goods available for sale		220,000
Deduct estimated cost of goods sold:		
Sales	201,000*	
Less: Sales returns and allowances	1,000*	
Net sales	200,000	
Less: Estimated gross margin ($200,000 × .20†)	40,000	
Estimated cost of goods sold		160,000
Estimated Cost of Ending Inventory		$ 60,000

* Data available from the records.

† Based on recent past performance.

In some problems relating to the gross margin method, a *cost* percentage (cost of goods sold divided by sales) is given rather than the gross margin percentage (gross margin divided by sales). If either percentage is known the other percentage may be readily determined, since the two percentages must sum to 100%. In the above example, since the rate of gross margin is 20%, the cost percentage is 80% (100% − 20%). In the above example the gross margin rate, or markup, was given as a percent of sales (20% markup on sales); however, it could have been stated as 25% of the *cost of goods sold* (markup on cost). In the latter case a conversion of the rate on cost to a rate on sales would be desirable. Conversion of a rate on cost to a rate on sales or vice versa may be accomplished algebraically as follows:[2]

Symbols: C = Cost
SP = Selling price

1. The markup on cost is 25%; determine the markup (gross margin rate) on sales:

$$C + .25C = SP;\text{ therefore, } C = \frac{1}{1.25}SP,\text{ or } C = .80SP$$

$$\text{Markup on } SP = SP - .80SP;\text{ therefore, } \underline{\underline{\text{Markup on } SP = .20}}$$

2. The markup on sales is 20%; determine the markup on cost:

$$SP - .20SP = C;\text{ therefore, } C = .80SP,\text{ and } SP = 1.25C$$

$$\text{Markup on } C = 1.25C - C;\text{ therefore, } \underline{\underline{\text{Markup on } C = .25}}$$

A more direct approach involves the use of fractions as illustrated below. Note that in all cases the numerator is the same; whereas when converting to a markup on sales, the denominator is the sum of the numerator and denominator of the cost fraction, and when converting to a markup on cost, the denominator is the difference between the numerator and the denominator of the sales fraction. Obviously the fraction or rate on sales must be smaller than the comparable fraction or rate on cost. Observe the relationship between the fractions on each line in the following example:

	Markup	
	On Cost	*On Sales*
a. Markup is 25% on cost; determine the markup on sales	1/4(25%)	1/5(20%)
b. Markup is 33 1/3% on sales; determine the markup on cost	1/2(50%)	1/3(33 1/3%)
c. Markup is 66 2/3% on cost; determine the markup on sales	2/3(66 2/3%)	2/5(40%)

The gross margin method frequently is employed in four different situations as follows:

1. By the auditor or others to test the reasonableness of an inventory valuation provided by some other person or determined by some other means, such as physical inventory, or perpetual inventory. To illustrate, assume the bookkeeper for the company referred to above

[2] An alternative computation (where markup is known on cost) giving the same results without a conversion to markup on sales could be made as follows:

Cost of goods available for sale (per above)..........................	$220,000
Deduct estimated cost of goods sold:	
Sales reduced to estimated cost ($200,000 ÷ 1.25)..............	160,000
Estimated Cost of Ending Inventory	$ 60,000

submitted to the auditor an inventory valuation of $85,000. The gross margin method provides an approximation of $60,000, which would alert the auditor to investigate the inventory situation thoroughly.

2. To estimate the final inventory for internal financial statements (monthly statements for example) prepared during the year where the taking of interim physical inventories is impractical. The method finds fairly wide application for internal reporting purposes.

3. To estimate an inventory destroyed by a casualty such as fire or storm. Obviously, this application would be limited to those situations where the books of accounts are not destroyed since certain basic data from the accounts are essential. Valuation of inventory lost through casualty is necessary *(a)* to estimate the amount of loss, and *(b)* as a basis for settlement of insurance claims related to the inventory loss.

4. To develop budget estimates of cost of goods sold, gross margin, and inventory after a sales budget is developed.

In applying the gross margin method the accountant must bear in mind that a possibility of error exists because of *(a)* the assumption that the gross margin rate used from the past period(s) is realistic and reasonably accurate, and *(b)* the effect of using an *average* rate. In the usual situation a company will carry a number of different lines of merchandise each having a different markup or gross margin. Obviously, a change in markup on one or more lines, or a shift in the relative quantities of each line sold, will change the average gross margin rate (markup) thereby distorting the validity of the results derived by the method.

When the gross margin method is applied where significantly different markup rates are involved, computations should be developed for each separate class of merchandise if practicable.

RETAIL INVENTORY METHOD

The retail method of inventory valuation is widely employed by retail stores, particularly department stores, which sell a great diversity of items. In such situations perpetual inventory procedures generally are impractical, and taking a complete physical inventory more often than annually is uncommon. Several features of department store operation make possible utilization of the retail inventory method. Particular features are *(a)* the departments are frequently homogeneous with respect to the markup on items sold within the departments, and *(b)* articles purchased are immediately priced for resale and displayed. The effect of this latter feature may be observed in the tendency by retailing establishments to relate markups, analyses, budgets, estimates, markdowns, and so on, to *sales price* rather than to cost price. Whereas those in nonretailing endeavors tend to think of markup as being on cost, the retailer traditionally thinks of markup on selling price. The retail inventory method provides a special approach to measure the ending inventory on a (1) *Fifo* basis, (2) average cost basis, (3) lower-of-cost-or-market basis, or (4) *Lifo* basis, depending on how the calculations are made.

The retail inventory method has been actively sponsored by the National Retail Merchants Association and approved by the Internal Revenue Service; consequently, it has become an important method of inventory determination. The accounting profession has accepted the method on its own merits as fundamentally sound where properly administered. It must be realized that the retail inventory method represents an approach in *estimating* the amount of the ending inventory to be used in computing cost of goods sold on the income statement and for reporting on the balance sheet.

Application of the retail method requires that records be kept which show the following data:

1. Beginning inventory valued at both cost and retail.
2. Purchases during the period valued at both cost and retail.
3. Adjustments to the original marked retail price such as additional markups, markup cancellations, markdowns, employee discounts, and markdown cancellations.
4. Data relating to other adjustments such as interdepartmental transfers, returns, breakage, and damaged goods.
5. Sales.

This method is similar to the gross margin method in that the inventory valuation is based on the ratio of cost to selling price. In contrast, the gross margin method uses a historical ratio, whereas the retail inventory method uses a ratio based on the current period relationships. Under the retail method records are maintained so that the ratio may be developed for the current period.

The retail method involves computation of the goods available for sale at both *cost* and *retail*. Total cost is divided by total retail to obtain the *cost ratio*. Sales are then deducted from goods available for sale (at retail); the result is the inventory at retail. Multiplication of the inventory at retail by the cost ratio provides the estimated inventory valuation at cost. Determination of the final inventory valuation employing the retail method is illustrated below with simplified data:

	At Cost	*At Retail*
Goods available for sale:		
Beginning inventory (January 1)	$ 15,000*	$ 25,000*
Purchases during January	195,000*	275,000*
Cost of goods available for sale	$210,000	300,000
Cost ratio: $210,000 ÷ $300,000 = .70		
Deduct January sales at retail		260,000*
Ending inventory (January 31):		
At retail		$ 40,000
At cost ($40,000 × .70)	$ 28,000	

* Data available from the records.

Since the retail inventory method provides only an estimate of the final inventory, a physical inventory should be taken at least annually as a check on the accuracy of the estimates. Significant differences between the physical inventory and the retail inventory estimate should be carefully analyzed. Investigation may indicate *(a)* inventory shortages due to breakage, loss, or theft; *(b)* incorrect application of the retail method; *(c)* failure of departmental managers to report correctly markdowns, additional markups, or cancellations; *(d)* errors in the records; *(e)* errors in the physical inventory; or *(f)* inventory manipulation.

The primary uses of the retail method are as follows:

1. To provide estimated inventory valuations for interim periods (usually monthly) when physical inventories are impracticable. The method provides inventory valuations needed for monthly statements, analyses, and purchasing policy considerations.
2. To provide a means of converting a physical inventory, priced at retail, to a cost basis. To eliminate the necessity of marking the cost (in code) on the merchandise, or referring to invoices, many retail establishments, after physically counting the stock on hand, extend the inventory sheets at retail. The retail value is then converted to cost by applying the retail inventory method without reference to individual cost prices.
3. To provide a basis for interim control of inventory, purchases, theft, markdowns, and additional markups. Many department stores utilize the results of the retail inventory calculation by department for such interim control requirements.
4. To provide a basis for external financial reports.
5. To provide data for income tax purposes.

MARKUPS AND MARKDOWNS

The preceding illustration assumed that there were no changes in the *original* marked selling price. The original selling price is frequently raised or lowered, particularly at the end of the selling season or when replacement costs are changing. The retail method requires that a careful record be kept of all adjustments to the *original* marked selling price since these adjustments must be taken into account in the computation. In order to apply this rule it is important to distinguish between the following terms:

Original sales price – the amount at which the merchandise is first marked for sale.

Markup – the original or initial amount that merchandise is marked up. Thus, it is the difference between cost and the original sales price. It may be expressed as a dollar amount or a percent of either cost or selling price. It is sometimes referred to as initial markup or markon.

Additional markup – an increase in the sales price above the original sales price. Note that the original sales price is the base from which additional markup is measured.

Additional markup cancellations – cancellation of an *additional* markup.

Additional markups less additional markup cancellations is usually called net additional markup.

Markdown—a reduction in selling price below the original sales price.

Markdown cancellation—after a reduction in the original selling price an increase in the selling price which does not exceed the original sales price (after that point an increase is an additional markup).

The definitions may be illustrated by assuming an item, that cost $8, is originally marked to sell at $10; subsequently marked to sell at $11, then finally reduced to sell at $7, viz:

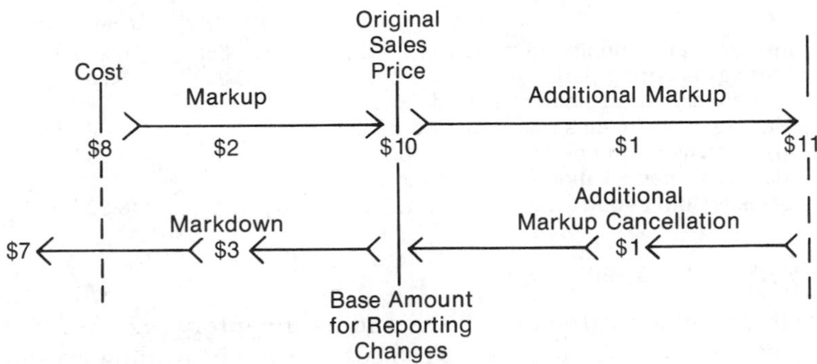

The validity of an inventory amount determined by using the retail inventory method depends largely upon the accuracy with which changes in the original selling price are reported by the merchandising personnel to the accounting department. To illustrate the reporting problem, assume the following additional data relating to the item illustrated immediately above:

Price Changes and Transactions				*Price Change Information Reported to Accounting Department*	
Units acquired..............	100	@	$ 8		
Units sold.....................	60	@	10		
Increase in sales price ...	40	@	1	⟶ Additional markups	$40
Units sold.....................	30	@	11		
Decrease in sales price...	10	@	1	⟶ Additional markup cancellations	10
Units sold.....................	2	@	10		
Decrease in sales price...	8	@	3	⟶ Markdowns	24
Units sold.....................	8	@	7		

APPLICATION OF THE RETAIL INVENTORY METHOD

The basic concept and computations underlying the retail inventory method were illustrated above. However, the way in which the calculations are made determine the approximate valuations. The difference in calculations to derive a particular basis may be outlined as follows:

Basis Desired	Computation of Cost Ratio
1. *Fifo* cost.	Exclude beginning inventory from the computation of the cost ratio.
2. Average cost.	Include beginning inventory in the computation of the cost ratio.
3. Lower of cost or market.	Exclude net markdowns from the computation of the cost ratio; include them after the cost ratio is computed.
4. *Lifo* cost.	Must use dollar-value approach (discussed in Part B).

To illustrate the first three, the following data are assumed from the accounting records of KM Company at the end of the accounting period:

	At Cost	At Retail
Inventory at beginning of period	$ 550	$ 900
Purchases during period	6,290	8,900
Additional markups during period		225
Markup cancellations during period		25
Markdowns during period		600
Markdown cancellations during period		100
Sales for the period		8,500

Retail Method, *Fifo* Cost

Recall that when *Fifo* is used, the ending inventory is costed at the latest unit costs which means that the costs in the beginning inventory will be included in cost of goods sold for the period. Therefore, if the beginning inventory is excluded from the computation of the cost ratio, the result will approximate *Fifo*. The computations for KM Company would be:

Retail Method—Approximate *Fifo* Cost

		At Cost	At Retail
Goods available for sale:			
Beginning inventory		$ 550	$ 900
Purchases during the period		6,290	8,900
Additional markups during the period	$225		
Less: Markup cancellations	25		
Net additional markups			200
Deduct:			
Markdowns during the period	600		
Less: Markdown cancellations	100		
Net markdowns			(500)
Total Excluding Beginning Inventory		6,290	8,600
Cost ratio: $6,290 ÷ $8,600 = .73			
Total Including Beginning Inventory		$6,840	9,500
Deduct:			
Sales			8,500
Ending inventory:			
At retail			$1,000
At approximate *Fifo* cost ($1,000 × .73)		$ 730	

The markups and markdowns must be included as adjustments to the retail amounts because they represent changes in the marked selling prices. The cost ratio must express the relationship between sales value and cost.

Retail Method, Average Cost

Recall that average cost is derived by dividing total goods available for sale in dollars of cost by total units available for sale; both totals include the beginning inventory. Therefore, if we calculate the cost ratio on the basis of totals, including the beginning inventory, the retail method derives approximate average cost. The computation for KM Company would be:

Retail Method—Approximate Average Cost Basis

	At Cost	*At Retail*
Total Including Beginning Inventory (from above)	$6,840	$9,500
Cost ratio: $6,840 ÷ $9,500 = .72		
Deduct:		
Sales		8,500
Ending inventory:		
At retail		$1,000
At approximate average cost ($1,000 × .72)	$ 720	

Retail Method, Lower of Cost or Market (LCM)

Lower of cost or market is a conservative valuation method; it derives an inventory valuation that is less than *Fifo* or average. By excluding net markdowns from the computation of the cost ratio an approximate LCM valuation is derived. The LCM approach may be applied to either the *Fifo* or average computations illustrated above. To illustrate, it is applied to the *average* basis as follows:

Retail Method—Average Cost Basis, Lower of Cost or Market

		At Cost	*At Retail*
Goods available for sale:			
Beginning inventory		$ 550	$ 900
Purchases during period		6,290	8,900
Additional markups	$225		
Less: Markup cancellations	25		
Net additional markups			200
Goods available for sale (Including Beginning Inventory)		$6,840	10.000
Cost ratio: $6,840 ÷ $10,000 = .684			
Deduct:			
Sales			8,500
Remainder			1,500
Markdowns	$600		
Less: Markdown cancellations	100		
Net markdowns			500
Ending inventory:			
At retail			$ 1,000
Average cost basis, lower of cost or market ($1,000 × .684)		$ 684	

Special Items

Special discounts to employees and preferred customers, and known or estimated normal losses from spoilage or breakage, should be included in the computations in a manner similar to markdowns. Return purchases are deducted from purchases at both cost and retail; return sales are deducted from gross sales. Freight-in is added to purchase cost. These items are included in the illustration below:

Retail Method—*Fifo* Basis, Lower of Cost or Market

		At Cost	*At Retail*
Goods available for sale:			
Initial inventory		$ 5,000	$ 7,500
Purchases		23,100	32,800
Freight-in		500	
Purchase returns		(600)	(840)
Net additional markups			540
Total Excluding Beginning Inventory		23,000	32,500
Cost ratio: $23,000 ÷ $32,500 = .71			
Total Including Beginning Inventory		$28,000	40,000
Deduct:			
Sales (net of sales returns)	$30,000		
Net markdowns	3,000		
Employee discounts	2,000		35,000
Final inventory:			
At retail			$ 5,000
Fifo cost basis, lower of cost or market ($5,000 × .71)		$ 3,550	

The ending inventory is valued on the *Fifo* cost basis because the beginning inventory was excluded from the computation of the cost ratio. It is also at lower of cost or market because net markdowns were excluded from the cost ratio computation.

The preceding discussions of the retail inventory method presumed that the merchandise is similar in that *(a)* the markup was essentially the same for each kind of merchandise included, and *(b)* the relative proportion of the various kinds of merchandise in the ending inventory and in sales for the period was essentially the same. In individual departments, this is generally the case; however, on a storewide basis it often is not. Consequently, the essential data are accumulated in the accounting system, and the computations are made, on a departmental basis. The departmental inventories then are summed to derive the total inventory.

INVENTORIES FOR LONG-TERM CONSTRUCTION CONTRACTS

A special inventory valuation problem arises for long-term construction contracts which are typical when buildings, bridges, ships, and dams are built. They are unique because the construction period often extends over two or more accounting periods. Directly related to the inventory valuation problem is one of *income recognition* during the construction period. For example, assume a 2½-year construction period;

should income be recognized as construction progresses (i.e., each period) or should income be recognized only at the end of the 2½ years?

The accounting profession and the income tax laws have recognized two distinctly different methods of accounting for long-term contracts. A business may select either; however, consistency is required once a selection is made. The two methods are generally identified as:

1. The completed-contract method—income recognized only upon completion.
2. The percentage-of-completion method—income recognized each period based upon progress; that is, on the basis of production (see discussion of the revenue principle in Chapter 2).

To illustrate the accounting for long-term construction contracts we will use the following data:

1. Ace Construction Company received a contract to erect a building for $1,500,000. Construction is to start February 1, 19A, and is to be completed in 2½ years from that date.
2. Progress billings are to be submitted at the end of each month based upon percentage-of-completion estimates developed by the independent architect as of the 15th of each month. The billings are payable to the contractor within ten days after the billing.
3. Data covering the entire construction period:

	Year 19A	*Year 19B*	*Year 19C*	*Total*
Contract price				$1,500,000
Costs incurred	$ 350,000	$550,000	$465,000	1,365,000
Estimated costs to complete (at year-end)	1,000,000	460,000	-0-	-0-
Income				$ 135,000
Progress billings	300,000	575,000	625,000	$1,500,000
Collections on billings	270,000	555,000	675,000	1,500,000

Completed-Contract Method

All costs incurred on the long-term construction contract are accumulated in a *Construction in Process Inventory* account. Since long-term construction contracts almost always provide for the contractor to bill the other party for progress payments (determined as agreed upon in the contract), the progress billings, as made, are debited to Accounts Receivable (construction contract billings) and credited to Billings on Contracts (long-term construction). The latter account is not a revenue account; it is an offset to the Construction in Process Inventory account on the balance sheet. If the net difference is a debit, it is usually reported as a current asset; if a credit, as a current liability. When the contract is completed, the income reported is the difference between the accumulated balances in the Billings on Contracts and the Construction in Process Inventory accounts. Under the completed-contract method, therefore, (1) the construction in process inventory is reported at the total cumulated costs to date, less the total progress billings to date; and (2) income on construction contracts ($135,000 in the example) is reported in the year of completion (19C). The entries in the accounts of Ace Construction Company, for this method, are illustrated in Exhibit 10–2, and the financial statement presentation for each year is shown in Exhibit 10–3.

Percentage-of-Completion Method

Under this method, accounting for a long-term construction contract is the same as the completed-contract method explained above except that income is recognized each period during the construction time. Since the income on the contract will not be known until completion, an estimate must be made each period. The estimated amount of income is then apportioned to each period on the basis of percentage of completion of the contract represented by the work done during the period. Since progress billings usually are tied to percentage of completion, this can also be used at the end of the period to apportion the estimated amount of income to each period. Percentage of completion is usually derived as either *(a)* engineering and/or architectural estimates of the work performed to date to the total work necessary to complete the contract, or *(b)* the ratio of total costs incurred to date on the contract to the estimated total costs to be incurred on the contract. The estimated amount of income to be recognized each period is recorded by debiting Construction in Process and crediting Income on Construction (long-term contracts). The latter account is closed to Income Summary each period and reported on the income statement.

Computation of the amount of estimated income to be recognized each year by the Ace Construction Company is illustrated in Exhibit 10–1. Observe that the estimated total income of $135,000 is apportioned to each period on the basis of costs incurred to date to total costs to be incurred. The resulting entries in the accounts of Ace Construction Company are reflected in Exhibit 10–2, and the financial statement presentation for each period is shown in Exhibit 10–3.

Comparative Results

The completed-contract and percentage-of-completion methods of accounting for long-term construction contracts are different approaches of measuring and reporting *(a)* periodic income from construction, and *(b)* the ending inventory (construction in process) during the period of construction. Exhibit 10–2 shows that the entries are identical each period under both methods except entry No. 4 (recognition of income from construction). Over the life of the construction period both methods recognize the same amount of total income. In this respect, the percentage of completion is deficient in that periodic income is recognized on the basis of estimates of remaining costs to complete; however, the total amount of income recognized over the life of a contract is the same for both methods. Alternatively, the completed-contract method, although more objective and more conservative, is generally viewed as deficient because recognition does not reflect current performance. Although most of the work may be completed prior to the last year, all of the income is recognized in the last year.

In respect to reporting on the balance sheet during the construction period, Exhibit 10–3 reflects that both methods derive the same results except for the amount of the ending inventory and retained earnings. Under the percentage-of-completion method the inventory is greater in amount by the accumulated amount of pretax income recognized in the current and prior periods. Thus, for Ace Manufacturing Company the ending inventory (i.e., costs in excess of billings) is greater by $38,889 at the end of 19A, and by $38,889 + $53,758 = $92,647 at the end of 19B. Recall that the estimated income recognized each year was debited to Construction in Process in the percentage of completion method.

Under either method, when there is a projected loss at any time, it must be recognized in the period in which a loss on the contract appears reasonably certain. The loss should be recognized by means of a debit to Loss on Construction Contract and a credit to Construction in Process. The credit removes from the inventory account the amount of costs in excess of expected recovery.

The accounting profession sanctioned the use of either method as follows:

> The committee believes that in general when estimates of costs to complete and extent of progress toward completion of long-term contracts are reasonably dependable, the percentage-of-completion method is preferable. When lack of dependable estimates or inherent hazards cause forecasts to be doubtful, the completed-contract method is preferable. Disclosure of the method followed should be made.[3]

EXHIBIT 10–1

Apportionment of Estimated Income—Percentage-of-Completion Method

	Year 19A	*Year 19B*	*Year 19C*
Contract price	$1,500,000	$1,500,000	$1,500,000
Less costs:			
Actual cost to date	350,000	900,000	1,365,000
Estimated cost to complete	1,000,000	460,000	
Estimated total costs	1,350,000	1,360,000	1,365,000
Estimated Total Income	$ 150,000	$ 140,000	$ 135,000
Apportionment of total income:			
19A:			
$350,000/$1,350,000 × $150,000	$ 38,889		
19B:			
$900,000/$1,360,000 × $140,000		$ 92,647	
Less income recognized to date		38,889	
Income Recognized in 19B		$ 53,758	
19C:			
Total income to be recognized (actual)			$ 135,000
Less income recognized to date			92,647
Income Recognized in 19C			$ 42,353

[3] AICPA, "Long-Term Construction-Type Contracts," *Accounting Research Bulletin No. 45* (New York, 1955), par. 15.

EXHIBIT 10–2
Long-Term Construction Contracts
Completed-Contract and Percentage-of-Completion Methods Compared

Journal Entries

	Completed Contract		*Percentage of Completion*	
Year 19A:				
1. Costs of construction:				
Construction in process ...	350,000		350,000	
Cash, payables, etc. ...		350,000		350,000
2. Progress billings:				
Accounts receivable	300,000		300,000	
Billings on contracts...		300,000		300,000
3. Collections on billings:				
Cash	270,000		270,000	
Accounts receivable ...		270,000		270,000
4. Recognition of income:				
Construction in process ...	(No income recognized until completion)		38,889	
Income on construction*				38,889
Year 19B:				
1. Costs of construction:				
Construction in process ...	550,000		550,000	
Cash, payables, etc. ...		550,000		550,000
2. Progress billings:				
Accounts receivable	575,000		575,000	
Billings on contracts...		575,000		575,000
3. Collections on billings:				
Cash	555,000		555,000	
Accounts receivable ...		555,000		555,000
4. Recognition of income:				
Construction in process ...	(No income recognized until completion)		53,758	
Income on construction				53,758
Year 19C:				
1. Costs of construction:				
Construction in process ...	465,000		465,000	
Cash, payables, etc. ...		465,000		465,000
2. Progress billings (final billing):				

* Closed to income summary.

EXHIBIT 10–2 (continued)

Journal Entries

	Method			
	Completed Contract		*Percentage of Completion*	
Year 19C (continued)				
Accounts receivable	625,000		625,000	
Billings on contracts...		625,000		625,000
3. Collections on billings (in full):				
Cash	675,000		675,000	
Accounts receivable ...		675,000		675,000
4. Recognition of income (and to close the accumulated account balances):				
Construction in process ...			42,353	
Billings on contracts.........	1,500,000		1,500,000	
Construction in process		1,365,000		1,500,000
Income on construction		135,000		42,353

EXHIBIT 10–3
Long-Term Construction Contracts
Completed-Contract and Percentage-of-Completion Methods Compared

Financial Statements

	Year 19A		*Year 19B*		*Year 19C*	
	*C.C.**	*P.C.**	*C.C.*	*P.C.*	*C.C.*	*P.C.*
Balance Sheet						
Current Assets:						
Accounts receivable...	$ 30,000	$ 30,000	$ 50,000	$ 50,000		
Inventory:						
Construction in process	350,000	388,889	900,000	992,647		
Less: Billings on contracts.........	300,000	300,000	875,000	875,000		
Costs in excess of billings	50,000	88,889	25,000	117,647		
Income Statement						
Income on construction	-0-	38,889	-0-	53,758	$135,000	$ 42,353

* C.C.—Completed-contract method.
P.C.—Percentage-of-completion method.

PART B—DOLLAR-VALUE, *LIFO*-RETAIL METHOD

Because of the income tax advantage of using *Lifo,* and the view of many accountants that *Lifo* provides a better matching of current costs with revenue, many retail and wholesale businesses have adopted dollar-value, *Lifo*-retail. When the retail method of inventory is used, *Lifo* results can be attained only by applying the dollar-value concept discussed in Chapter 9, Part B. Along with double extension, and link chain, *Lifo* retail is a variation of dollar-value *Lifo.* It meets the requirements of generally accepted accounting principles and can be used for income tax purposes (Reg. 1.471-8, 1.472-1). When *Lifo* results are desired, the retail inventory and the dollar-value concepts must be combined.

The *Lifo*-retail method requires that *(a)* a distinction be maintained between the base year inventory and subsequent incremental layers, and *(b)* the subsequent layers be measured by applying a price-level index to the results derived from the retail inventory approach. That is, at the end of each period, the retail inventory approach is used and the results are then converted to a *Lifo* basis using a price index.

Tax regulations specify that variety stores using the *Lifo*-retail method must use an *internally computed index* developed as discussed in Chapter 9, Part B. On the other hand, retailers that qualify as department stores (as defined for tax purposes) may use a published external index instead of an internally computed index. The published index used must be one prepared by the Bureau of Labor Statistics. In the discussions and illustrations to follow, we will assume a published index is used.

APPLICATION OF THE DOLLAR-VALUE, *LIFO*-RETAIL METHOD

The dollar-value, *Lifo*-retail method, although conceptually simple, is somewhat complex in application. Basically, it involves an understanding of the use of price-level index numbers. Application of the dollar-value, *Lifo*-retail method involves three distinct phases, viz:

Phase 1—Computation or selection of an appropriate price index.
Phase 2—Computation of the ending inventory using the retail inventory method, *Fifo* basis (not lower of cost or market).
Phase 3—Computation of the ending inventory at *Lifo* cost by applying the index (Phase 1) to the results of Phase 2.

In Phases 2 and 3, a careful distinction must be maintained between the various inventory layers. Each period, the increase or decrease in ending inventory over the beginning inventory is computed; if there is an increase, a new incremental layer has been added during the period; if there is a decrease, there has been a partial or total liquidation of prior layers. A liquidation requires that the prior layers be liquidated in *Lifo* order; that is, the most recent layers must be liquidated first.

For dollar-value *Lifo,* two situations must be considered: (1) computation of the ending inventory on a *Lifo* cost basis at the end of each period (this is repeated each period), and (2) computation of the base inventory amount at the beginning of the base year (a one-time computation when *Lifo* is adopted). Each situation will be discussed and illustrated in this order.

Computation of Ending Inventory at *Lifo* Cost

This process, accomplished at the end of each period, will be illustrated using the following data:

WZ Company – Data from Company Records

	1977		*1978*		*1979*	
	At Cost	*At Retail*	*At Cost*	*At Retail*	*At Cost*	*At Retail*
Beginning (base) inventory	$17,400	$ 30,000				
Purchases	90,480	147,000	$101,500	$172,000	$109,800	$177,000
Net additional markups		8,800		9,000		7,000
Net markdowns...		5,000		6,000		4,000
Sales.................		140,000		162,800		197,800
Applicable price index (1976 = 100)		102		106		110

Assume the company has been using the dollar-value, *Lifo*-retail method for external reporting and income tax purposes. The company uses a published index selected from an external source. A three-year period is used because a lesser span does not adequately illustrate the complexities.

Required:

Computation of the ending inventories for 1977, 1978, and 1979 on the *Lifo* cost basis. Show details of the computations.

Solution with Explanatory Notes:

The computations are shown in Exhibit 10–4 identified by Phase 1 (index), Phase 2 (retail inventory computation, *Fifo* basis), and Phase 3 (computation of the ending inventory at *Lifo* cost). We will focus on 1977 and explain the computations, viz:

Phase 1 – The computed, or selected index, is listed for convenience. These values are used *only* in the Phase 3 computations.[4]

Phase 2 – The ending inventory, on a *Fifo* basis, is computed exactly as illustrated in Part A. Lower of cost or market is not permitted when *Lifo* cost is used. The *Fifo* basis must be used in Phase 2

[4] When the index at the beginning of the base year is not 100, the current year index must be divided by the base index value to obtain the percentage or ratio index. To illustrate, assume the index value at the beginning of the base year is 1.05 and the index at the end of the year is 1.071. The index value to use at the end of 1977 would be: 1.071 ÷ 1.05 = 1.02 as above.

EXHIBIT 10–4 Dollar-Value, *Lifo*-Retail Method

Phase		1977			1978			1979		
1	Price index computed or selected (1976 = 100) ...		102			106			110	
2	Computation of ending inventory at *Fifo* cost:	*At Cost*	*At Retail*	*Cost Ratio*	*At Cost*	*At Retail*	*Cost Ratio*	*At Cost*	*At Retail*	*Cost Ratio*
	Inventory, January 1	$ 17,400	$ 30,000		$ 24,480	$ 40,800		$ 30,740	$ 53,000	
	Purchases	90,480	147,000		101,500	172,000		109,800	177,000	
	Net additional markups		8,800			9,000			7,000	
	Net markdowns		(5,000)			(6,000)			(4,000)	
	Total (excluding beginning inventory) ...	90,480	150,800	.60	101,500	175,000	.58	109,800	180,000	.61
	Total (including beginning inventory)	$107,880	180,800		$125,980	215,800		$140,540	233,000	
	Sales		140,000			162,800			197,800	
	Ending Inventory	$ 24,480	$ 40,800		$ 30,740	$ 53,000		$ 21,472	$ 35,200	
3	Computation of ending inventory at *Lifo* cost:									
	Ending inventory at retail deflated to base year retail prices:									
	1977: $40,800 ÷ 1.02		$ 40,000							
	1978: 53,000 ÷ 1.06					$ 50,000				
	1979: 35,200 ÷ 1.10								$ 32,000	
	Base layer: At base year costs	$ 17,400			$ 17,400			$ 17,400		
	At base year retail prices		(30,000)			(30,000)			(30,000)	
	Incremental layers from prior years: 1977				6,120	(10,000)		*(b)*	(10,000)	
	1978							*(b)*	(10,000)	
	Excess, new increments (or liquidations) at base year retail prices*(a)*		$ 10,000			$ 10,000			$ (18,000)	
	Increment (or liquidation) at current year retail prices:									
	1977: $10,000 × 1.02		$ 10,200							
	1978: 10,000 × 1.06					$ 10,600				
	1979: ($10,000 + $10,000) − $18,000 × 1.02*(b)* ...								$ 2,040	
	Increment (or liquidation) at current year costs:									
	1977: $10,200 × .60	6,120								
	1978: 10,600 × .58				6,148					
	1979: 2,040 × .60 (1977 layer) *(b)*							1,224		
	Total Ending Inventory at *Lifo* Cost	$ 23,520			$ 29,668			$ 18,624		

(a) When this difference is positive there is a new incremental layer; when it is negative there has been a partial liquidation of one or more prior layers. In 1979 there is a liquidation of the 1978 layer and part of the 1977 layer.

(b) The liquidation in 1979 must be taken from the most recent layers, in order, at the price index and cost ratio for the year in which the layers were added. In 1979 the liquidation left the base layer and $2,000 of the 1977 layer (at retail); that is, $2,000 × 1.02 × .60 = $1,224 at *Lifo* cost.

because separation of the "new costs" is necessary for the Phase 3 computations—the *cost ratio* must exclude the beginning inventory.

Phase 3—In Phase 3, the distinction between cost and retail must be maintained by layers. The inventory increase (increment) or decrease (liquidation) during the period is first measured at *base year* retail prices. First the *Fifo* inventory amount from Phase 2 is converted to base year retail prices by dividing that amount by the related price index given in Phase 1 (i.e., 1977: $40,800 ÷ 1.02 = $40,000). The difference between the ending inventory ($40,000) and the beginning inventory ($30,000), both at base year retail prices, gives the new increment or liquidation ($10,000 increment). This increment then is converted *(a)* to current year *retail* prices ($10,000 × 1.02 = $10,200); and then *(b)* to *current year costs* ($10,200 × .60 = $6,120). This is the *Lifo* cost for the new increment.

At the end of 1979, there is a slight complication because the ending inventory is less than the beginning inventory by $50,000 − $32,000 = $18,000 at base year retail prices. This means that there was a partial liquidation of prior layers. The prior incremental layers must be used up in *Lifo* order; that is, in inverse chronological order. Also, the liquidation must be figured at the price index and cost ratio for the layers liquidated. The computations may be analyzed as follows:

Total inventory liquidated at base year retail prices	$18,000
1978 inventory layer liquidated at base year retail prices	10,000
Remainder at base year retail prices	8,000
1977 inventory layer at base year retail prices	10,000
Difference—Remaining 1977 Inventory Layer	$ 2,000
Conversion to *Lifo* Cost: $2,000 × 1.02 × .60 =	$ 1,224

CHANGING TO DOLLAR-VALUE, *LIFO*-RETAIL—COMPUTATION OF BASE INVENTORY

In the discussions and illustrations above for WZ Company, the base inventory (at the beginning of the base year, 1977) was given as follows: at cost, $17,400; at retail, $30,000. These base year beginning inventory values would have been carried forward from the ending inventory of 1976 assuming the company was already on dollar-value, *Lifo* retail. However, *if the company had been on a method other than* Fifo *(such as average, or lower of cost or market), the ending inventory for 1976 would have to be restated at a* Fifo *cost basis*. The restatement usually is relatively simple.

To illustrate, assume WZ Company had been using the retail inventory method, average basis, and lower of cost or market. At the start of 1977, the company decided to change to the dollar-value, *Lifo*-retail method for tax and external reporting purposes. The retail method computation previously developed at the end of December 1976 (at *Fifo*, LCM) was:

	At Cost	At Retail
Inventory, January 1, 1976	$ 5,700	$ 10,000
Purchases	78,300	138,000
Net additional markups		2,000
Total	$84,000	150,000
Cost ratio: $84,000 ÷ $150,000 = .56		
Net markdowns		5,000
Remainder		145,000
Sales		115,000
Ending inventory, December 31, 1976:		
At retail		$ 30,000
At average cost, lower of cost or market ($30,000 × .56)	$16,800	

The computation to restate the beginning base year inventory (January 1, 1977) to a *Fifo* cost basis would be as shown below. Note the exclusion of the January 1, 1976, inventory and inclusion of both markups and markdowns to determine the cost ratio.

	At Cost	At Retail
Beginning inventory	$ 5,700	$ 10,000
Purchases	78,300	138,000
Net additional markups		2,000
Net markdowns		(5,000)
Total (excluding beginning inventory)	78,300	135,000
Total (including beginning inventory)	$84,000	145,000
Cost ratio: *Fifo* cost basis: $78,300 ÷ $135,000 = .58		
Less: Sales		115,000
Beginning base inventory, January 1, 1977:		
At retail		$ 30,000
At cost ($30,000 × .58)	$17,400	

The two values, $30,000 and $17,400, represent the beginning base year inventory. Observe that they were used in Exhibit 10–4.

The entry to restate the January 1, 1977, inventory to base cost would be as follows:

Beginning inventory ($17,400 – $16,800)	600	
Inventory adjustment due to adoption of *Lifo*-retail		600

The inventory adjustment account would be closed to Income Summary and reported on the income statement as a gain during 1977.

This computation is needed only at the date of the change from some other method to dollar-value, *Lifo*-retail.

Because of the increasing use of dollar-value, *Lifo*-retail in the last few years, it has received increasing attention by public and industrial accountants. In applying the concept in the real world, a number of judgments must be made; and if used for tax purposes, the IRS Regulations and rulings must be carefully observed. Neither the accounting profession nor the taxing authorities have deemed it desirable to frame detailed and inflexible rules in this area because of the wide range of situations where it is used. Accounting students should be familiar with the method because of its increasing use.

QUESTIONS

PART A

1. What is the basic assumption implicit in the gross margin method?
2. Approximate the valuation of the ending inventory assuming the following data are available:

Cost of goods available for sale	$100,000
Net sales	150,000
Gross margin rate (on sales)	40%

3. Distinguish between *(a)* gross margin rate on sales, *(b)* gross margin percentage on cost of goods sold, *(c)* cost percentage, *(d)* markup on cost, and *(e)* markup on sales.
4. List the four principal uses of the gross margin method.
5. Why is it frequently desirable to apply the gross margin method by classes of merchandise?
6. Explain the basic approach in the retail method of estimating inventories. What data must be accumulated in order to apply the retail method?
7. The final inventory estimated by the retail inventory method was $40,000. A physical inventory of the merchandise on hand extended at retail showed $35,000. Suggest possible reasons for the discrepancy.
8. What are the primary uses of the retail method of estimating inventories?
9. Why are markdowns and markdown cancellations excluded in computing the cost ratio in the retail inventory method?
10. Explain the essential differences between *(a)* the completed-contract method and *(b)* the percentage-of-completion method of accounting for long-term construction contracts.
11. Why is the ending inventory of construction in process larger when the percentage-of-completion method is used compared with the completed-contract method? How much larger will the amount be?
12. As between the percentage-of-completion method and the completed-contract method, which would you usually prefer? Why? Do you believe that the accounting profession should continue to sanction the two alternative methods for the same set of facts? Why?

PART B

13. Under what circumstances is the dollar-value, *Lifo*-retail method used?
14. Fundamentally, what is the basic distinction between the conventional retail inventory method and the dollar-value, *Lifo*-retail method?

15. Explain why the conventional retail inventory method must be slightly adapted when used in conjunction with the dollar-value, *Lifo*-retail method.

16. Explain why the conventional retail inventory method, as adapted, and the dollar-value, *Lifo*-retail method must be used in conbination to attain *Lifo*-retail results.

17. When *Lifo*-retail is adopted why must the ending inventory of the period prior to the base year be recomputed?

EXERCISES

PART A: EXERCISES 1–12

Exercise 10–1

Income statement data for Bowen Company follows:

Beginning inventory..............	$ 50,000
Purchases	475,000
Sales..................................	725,000

Required:

Determine the ending inventory for each of the following independent assumptions:

a. Estimated gross margin on sales, 40%.
b. Estimated gross margin on cost, 120%.

Exercise 10–2

Assume the following data for Taylor Company for a particular period:

Sales.............................	$120,000
Initial inventory	16,000
Purchases	80,000

For each of the separate situations below, estimate the final inventory:

a. Markup is 40% on sales.
b. Markup is one fourth on cost.
c. Markup is 60% on sales.
d. Markup is 50% on cost.
e. Markup is 57% on cost.

Exercise 10–3

The books of Sutton Company provided the following information:

Inventory, January 1	$ 6,000
Purchases to May 10..............	80,000
Net sales to May 10	98,000

On May 11, the assets of the company were totally destroyed by fire. The insurance company adjuster found that the average rate of gross margin for the past few years had been 33⅓%.

Required:

What was the approximate value of the inventory destroyed assuming the gross margin percentage given was based on (*a*) sales, and (*b*) cost of goods sold?

Exercise 10–4

You are engaged in the audit of the records of Storm Company. A physical inventory has been taken by the company under your observation, although the extensions have not been completed to determine the valuation of the inventory. The records of the company provide the following data: sales, $300,000; return sales, $4,000; purchases (gross), $155,000; beginning inventory, $50,000; freight-in, $5,000; and purchase returns and allowances, $2,000. The gross margin last period was 34% of net sales; you anticipate that it will be 35% for the year under audit. Estimate the value of the ending inventory. Show computations.

Exercise 10–5

The records of Keller Company provided the following data for January for two products sold:

	Product A	*Product B*
Beginning inventory, January 1	$ 40,000	$ 60,000
Purchases during January	147,000	186,000
Freight on purchases	3,000	4,000
Sales during January	300,000	400,000

The gross margin rates on sales for the prior year were: company overall, 44%; Product A, 42%; and Product B, 49%.

Required:

1. Estimate the value of the ending inventory.
2. Under what conditions would your response to Requirement 1 be suspect?

Exercise 10–6

Foster Retail Store uses the retail method of inventory. At the end of June, the records of the company reflected the following:

Purchases during June: at cost, $265,000; at retail, $430,000.
Sales during June: $380,000.
Inventory, June 1: at cost, $40,000; at retail, $70,000.

Estimate the ending inventory for June assuming (*a*) average cost basis, and (*b*) *Fifo* cost basis. Show all computations.

Exercise 10–7

The records of Popular Department Store showed the following data for Department 20 for January: beginning inventory at cost, $15,000, and $26,000 at selling price; purchases at cost, $160,000, and $297,000 at selling price; sales, $303,000; return sales, $6,000; purchase returns at cost, $4,000, and $7,000 at selling price and freight in $5,960. Determine the approximate valuation of the final inventory using the retail inventory method (*a*) at average cost, and (*b*) at *Fifo*. Show all computations.

Exercise 10–8

Use the retail inventory method(lower-of-cost-or-market basis) to estimate the ending inventory *(a)* at average cost and lower of cost or market, and *(b) Fifo* cost and lower of cost or market for Allan Retailers based on the following data:

	At Cost	*At Retail*
Beginning inventory	$ 84,000	$142,000
Purchases	330,000	561,000
Purchases returned	6,000	10,000
Freight-in	5,000	
Additional markups		12,000
Additional markup cancellations		5,000
Markdowns		9,000
Markdown cancellations		2,000
Sales		560,000
Sales returned		4,000

Exercise 10–9

Waters Retail Store has just completed the annual physical inventory, which involved counting the goods on hand then pricing them at selling prices. The inventory valuation derived in this manner amounted to $96,000. The records of the company provide the following data: beginning inventory, $80,000 at retail and $52,120 at cost; purchases (including freight-in and returns), $750,000 at retail and $469,920 at cost; additional markups, $20,000; additional markup cancellations, $8,000; sales, $703,000; return sales, $9,000; and markdowns, $6,000.

Required:

1. Estimate the cost of the ending inventory assuming average cost and lower of cost or market.
2. Note any discrepancies and give possible reasons for them.

Exercise 10–10

The following data were available from the records of Swain's Retail Store with respect to a particular item sold:

	At Cost	*At Retail*
Purchases	$3,310	$5,250
Additional markups		800
Additional markup cancellations		50
Sales		5,000
Markdowns		850
Markdown cancellations		300
Initial inventory	320	

Required:

1. Estimate the ending inventory valuations valued at *(a)* average cost and lower of cost or market, and *(b) Fifo* and lower of cost or market.
2. What conclusions can you draw from your answers to Requirement 1?

Exercise 10–11

Hood Construction Company contracted to build a plant for $500,000. Construction started in January 19A and was completed in November 19B. Data relating to the contract are summarized below:

	19A	*19B*
Cost incurred during the year	$290,000	$135,000
Estimated costs to complete	145,000	
Billings during the year	230,000	270,000
Cash collections during the year	200,000	300,000

Required:

Give the journal entries for Hood, in parallel columns, assuming (*a*) the completed-contract method, and (*b*) the percentage-of-completion method (apportion on cost basis).

Exercise 10–12

Use the data given in Exercise 10–11 to complete a tabulation as follows:

	Completed-Contract Method	*Percentage-Completion Method**
Income Statement		
Income:		
19A	$______	$______
19B	______	______
Balance Sheet		
Receivables:		
19A	______	______
19B	______	______
Inventory—construction in process, net of billings:		
19A	______	______
19B	______	______

* Apportion on a cost basis.

PART B: EXERCISE 13–14

Exercise 10–13

Super Retailer's, Incorporated, uses the *Lifo*-retail inventory method for reporting and income tax purposes. The following data relates to 1977:

	At Cost	*At Retail*	*Cost Ratio*
January 1, 1977, base inventory (carried over from 1976)	$ 6,000	$10,000	.60
Data during 1977:			
Sales		80,000	
Purchases....................................	55,800	85,000	
Net additional markups..................		7,000	
Net markdowns		2,000	

Required:

Assume the index at January 1, 1977, was 100 and at December 31, 1977, 105. Prepare computations for 1977 to derive *(a)* the 1977 ending inventory at *Fifo* cost and *(b)* the 1977 ending inventory at *Lifo* cost. Use a format similar to Exhibit 10–4.

Exercise 10–14

Finley's Retail Store has been using the traditional retail inventory method (lower-of-cost-or-market basis) for a number of years. On January 1, 1976, the management decided to use the *Lifo*-retail method. At the end of 1975, the traditional retail inventory method (LCM) computation was made:

	December 31, 1975	
	At Cost	*At Retail*
Beginning inventory	$ 17,000	$ 30,000
Purchases (net)	151,000	268,000
Net additional markups		2,000
Total	$168,000	300,000
Cost ratio: $168,000 ÷ $300,000 = .56		
Sales (net)		(275,000)
Net markdowns		(5,000)
Inventory, December 31, 1975:		
At retail		$ 20,000
At cost ($20,000 × .56)	$ 11,200	

Required:

1. Compute the values that should be used for the base year beginning inventory (January 1, 1976).
2. Explain why the December 31, 1975, inventory and the base inventory (January 1, 1976) are different.
3. Give the entry required on January 1, 1976, to restate the ending inventory of 1975 to the base inventory amount. Why is the entry made?

PROBLEMS

PART A: PROBLEMS 1–12

Problem 10–1

The records of White Company revealed the following information on August 13, 19A:

Inventory, January 1, 19A	$ 50,000
Purchases, January 1 to August 13	300,000
Sales, January 1 to August 13	400,000
Purchase returns and allowances	3,000
Sales returns	1,000
Freight-in	4,000

A fire completely destroyed the inventory on August 12, 19A, except for goods marked to sell at $6,000 which had an estimated salvage value of $4,000, and for goods in transit to which White Company had ownership; the purchase had been recorded. Invoices recorded on the latter show: merchandise cost, $2,000; and freight-in, $100. The average rate of gross margin on sales in recent years has been 25%.

Required:

1. Compute the inventory fire loss.
2. Under what conditions would your response to Requirement 1 be suspect? Explain.

Problem 10–2

Amber Retail Company is developing a profit plan. The following planned data were developed for a three-month future period.

a. January 1 planned inventory, $90,000.
b. Planned average rate of gross margin on sales, 30%.

Complete the following profit plan:

	Profit Plan Estimates			
	January	*February*	*March*	*Total*
Sales planned	$160,000	$180,000	$190,000	$530,000
Cost of goods sold:				
Beginning inventory	?	?	?	?
Purchases budget	110,000	130,000	160,000	400,000
Total Goods Available	?	?	?	?
Less: Final inventory	?	?	?	?
Cost of goods sold	?	?	?	?
Gross Margin Planned	?	?	?	?

Problem 10–3

Davis Retail Store burned on March 19, 19D. The following information (up to the date of the fire) was taken from the records of the company which were stored in a safe: inventory, January 1, $28,000; sales, $140,000; purchases, $90,000; return sales, $3,000; purchase returns and allowances, $2,000; and freight-in, $4,000. The cost of goods sold and gross margins for the past three years were:

	Cost of Goods Sold	*Gross Margin*
19A	$468,000	$122,000
19B	435,000	130,000
19C	472,000	127,000

Required:

1. Estimate the value of the inventory destroyed in the fire.
2. Under what conditions would your response to Requirement 1 be suspect?

3. The insurance company pays indemnity on "fair market value" at date of the fire. What amount would you recommend that Davis submit as an insurance claim? Explain.

Problem 10–4

Dawson Company in the past valued inventories at cost. At the end of the current period, the inventory was valued at 45% of selling price as a matter of convenience. The current financial statements have been prepared and the inventory sheets destroyed; consequently, you find it impossible to reconstruct the final inventory at actual cost. The following data are available:

Sales	$300,000
Final inventory (at 45% of selling price)	22,500
Cost of goods sold	180,000
Pretax income	32,000
Beginning inventory (at cost)	20,000

Required:

Prepare a corrected multiple-step income statement. Show computations.

Problem 10–5

The records of Stanford Department Store provided the following data for June:

Sales	$730,000	Purchase returns:	
Return sales	2,000	At retail	$ 4,000
Additional markups	9,000	At cost	3,900
Additional markup cancellations	5,000	Freight on purchases	6,000
Markdowns	7,000	Beginning inventory:	
Purchases:		At cost	51,000
At retail	749,000	At retail	95,000
At cost	419,540	Employee discounts	1,000
		Markdown cancellations	3,000

Required:

Estimate the valuation of the ending inventory using the retail inventory method assuming *(a)* average cost, and *(b) Fifo* cost (not lower of cost or market). Show computations.

Problem 10–6

Snowden's Department Store uses the retail inventory method (LCM basis). Data for the year ended January 31, 1976, for one department appear below:

Inventory, January 31, 1975:	
Cost	$ 31,850
Sales price	54,000
Purchases for the year ended January 31, 1976 (gross):	
Cost	137,300
Sales price	245,000
Sales for year (gross)	250,000
Freight on merchandise purchased	6,000

Returns:	
Purchases:	
Cost	1,150
Sales price	2,000
Sales	5,000
Additional markups	4,000
Additional markup cancellations	1,000
Markdowns	12,000
Markdown cancellations	2,000
Employee discounts	500

Required:

Estimate the January 31, 1976, inventory valuation using the retail inventory method assuming:

a. Average cost and lower of cost or market.
b. *Fifo* cost and lower of cost or market.
c. Average cost.
d. *Fifo* cost.

Problem 10–7

The records of Austin Retailers provided the following data for the year:

	At Retail	*At Cost*
Inventory, January 1	$ 220,000	$145,500
Net purchases	1,573,000	973,500
Freight-in		15,000
Additional markups	16,000	
Additional markup cancellations	9,000	
Markdowns	8,000	
Employee discounts	2,000	
Sales	1,400,000	
Inventory December 31 (per physical count valued at retail)	370,000	

Required:

1. Compute the final inventory at average cost and lower of cost or market.
2. Note any discrepancies that are indicated and suggest the possible reasons for them.
3. What accounting treatment should be accorded the discrepancy (if any)?

Problem 10–8

The following monthly data relating to Department 5 were taken from the records of Dottie's, a ladies' ready-to-wear store: inventory March 1 at retail, $70,000, at cost, $47,600; sales, $768,900; return sales, $5,000; purchases at retail, $790,000, at cost, $520,600; freight on purchases, $12,000; special discounts on goods purchased by employees, $1,000; purchase returns at retail, $6,000, at cost, $4,000; additional markups, $14,000; additional markup cancellations, $8,000; markdowns, $7,000; markdown cancellations, $3,000; and loss of merchandise through spoilage and breakage, $1,100 (at retail). Estimate the cost of the final inventory for the department assuming average cost and lower of cost or market.

Problem 10–9

Master Builders, Incorporated, contracted to construct an office building for the Carson Company for $900,000. Construction began on January 15, 19A, and was completed on December 7, 19B. Master Builders' fiscal year ends December 31. Transactions by Master Builders relating to the contract are summarized below:

	19A	*19B*
Costs incurred to date	$500,000	$800,000
Estimated costs to complete..............	320,000	
Progress billings to date	400,000	900,000
Progress collections to date	375,000	900,000

Required:

1. In parallel columns, give the entries on the contractor's books assuming (*a*) the completed-contract method, and (*b*) the percentage-of-completion method allocated on the basis of cost.
2. For each method, prepare the income statement and balance sheet presentations for this contract by year.
3. Which method would you recommend the contractor use? Why?

Problem 10–10

Chicago Construction Company contracted to build a dam for the city of Danville for $975,000. The contract provided for progress payments. Chicago Company closes the books each December 31. Work commenced under the contract on July 15, 19A, and was completed on September 30, 19C. Construction activities are summarized below by year:

19A—Construction costs incurred during the year, $180,000; estimated costs to complete, $630,000; progress billings to the city during the year, $153,000, and collections, $150,000.

19B—Construction costs incurred during the year, $450,000; estimated costs to complete, $190,000; progress billings to the city during the year, $382,500, and collections, $380,000.

19C—Construction costs incurred during the year, $195,000. Since the contract was completed, the remaining balance was billed and later collected in full per the contract.

Required:

1. Give the entries on the contractor's books assuming the percentage-of-completion method is used. Show computation of income apportionment on cost basis.
2. Prepare income statement and balance sheet presentations for this contract by year (percentage-of-completion basis).
3. Prepare income statement and balance sheet presentations by year assuming completed-contract method. For each amount that is different, explain the reason.
4. Which method would you recommend to this contractor? Why?

Problem 10–11

Richards Engineering Company contracted to build a bridge for $750,000. Payments were to be received on the basis of approved engineering estimates of costs as a basis for percentage of completion. The contract specified that 10% of each progress billing would be retained until final completion of the contract. Payment of a billing (less the 10%) is to be within five days after submission.

Transactions relating to the contract are summarized below:

19A—Construction costs incurred during the year, $200,000; estimated costs to complete, $400,000; progress billings, $190,000; and collections per the contract.

19B—Construction costs incurred during the year, $300,000; estimated costs to complete, $115,000; progress billings, $280,000; and collections per the contract.

19C—Construction costs incurred during the year, $110,000. The remaining billings were submitted by October 1 and final collections completed on November 30.

Required:

1. Complete a tabulation as follows:

Date	*Method*	*Income Recognized*	*Receivable Ending Balance*	*Construction in Process Ending Balance*	*Contracts in Excess of Billings Ending Balance*
19A	Completed contract				
	Percentage completion*				
19B	Completed contract				
	Percentage completion				
19C	Completed contract				
	Percentage completion				

* Apportion on basis of costs.

2. Explain what causes the ending balance in construction in process to be different for the two methods.
3. Which method would you recommend for this contractor? Why?

Problem 10–12

Superior Construction Company contracted to construct a building for $300,000. Construction commenced in 19A and was completed in 19C. Data relating to the contract are summarized below:

	19A	*19B*	*19C*
Cost incurred during the year...............	$ 80,000	$120,000	$ 40,000
Estimated costs to complete	158,000	39,000	
Billings during year............................	65,000	130,000	105,000
Collections during year.......................	60,000	128,000	110,000

Required:

Complete a tabulation as follows:

Year	Method	Income Recognized	Receivable Ending Balance	Construction in Process Ending Balance	Contracts in Excess of Billings Ending Balance
19A	Completed contract				
	Percentage completion*				
19B	Completed contract				
	Percentage completion				
19C	Completed contract				
	Percentage completion				

* Apportion on basis of costs.

PART B: PROBLEMS 13–15

Problem 10–13

Midwest Retailers, Incorporated, uses the *Lifo*-retail inventory method. The base inventory at the start of 1976 was:

	At Cost	At Retail	Cost Ratio
January 1, 1976, base inventory (carried over from 1975)	$31,000	$50,000	.62

Data for 1976–78:

	1976		1977		1978	
	At Cost	At Retail	At Cost	At Retail	At Cost	At Retail
Sales (net)		$130,000		$140,000		$155,000
Purchases (net)	$100,800	153,000	$112,000	167,000	$121,600	182,000
Net markdowns		2,000		3,000		2,000
Net additional markups......		9,000		11,000		10,000
Applicable price index (1975 = 100)		104		107		111

Required:

Prepare computations for 1976–78 to derive, for each year, *(a)* the ending inventory at *Fifo* cost, and *(b)* the ending inventory at *Lifo* cost. Use a format similar to Exhibit 10–4.

Problem 10–14

Goode Department Store had been using the conventional retail inventory method (lower of cost or market) for some years. The management decided to continue the retail inventory method but on a last-in, first-out basis. After some investigation the decision was made to change as of January 1, 1976.

a. The 1975 retail records showed the following computations:

	At Cost	At Retail
Inventory, January 1, 1975	$ 32,000	$ 54,000
Purchases (net)	493,400	680,000
Net additional markups		6,000
Total	$525,400	740,000
Cost ratio: $525,400 ÷ $740,000 = .71		
Sales (net)..		(670,000)
Net markdowns		(10,000)
Inventory, December 31, 1975:		
At retail		$ 60,000
At LCM cost ($60,000 × .71)	$ 42,600	

b. Data for 1976–78:

	1976		1977		1978	
	At Cost	At Retail	At Cost	At Retail	At Cost	At Retail
Purchases (net) ...	$501,120	$689,000	$497,000	$711,000	$529,250	$722,000
Net additional markups		16,000		10,000		10,000
Net markdowns ...		9,000		11,000		7,000
Sales (net)		683,900		703,350		732,470
Applicable price index (1975 = 100)..................		103		105		108

Required:

1. Restate the December 31, 1975, inventory to base year cost for January 1, 1976. Give the entry to record the restatement on January 1, 1976 (include an explanation).
2. Prepare computations for 1976–78 to derive, for each year, *(a)* the ending inventory at *Fifo* cost, and *(b)* the ending inventory at *Lifo* cost. Use a format similar to Exhibit 10–4.

Problem 10–15

Sewanee Department Store has used the conventional retail inventory method (LCM basis) for many years. The management decided to change to a *Lifo* cost basis effective January 1, 1976. Relevant data subject to the change follows:

a. Computation of retail inventory (LCM basis):

	At Cost	At Retail
Inventory, January 1, 1975	$ 37,000	$ 60,000
Purchases, net..	227,000	413,000
Net additional markups		7,000
Total	$264,000	480,000
Cost ratio: $264,000 ÷ $480,000 = .55		
Sales, net		(416,000)
Net markdowns		(14,000)
Inventory, December 31, 1975:		
At retail		$ 50,000
At LCM cost ($50,000 × .55)	$ 27,500	

b. Data for 1976–78:

	1976		*1977*		*1978*	
	At Cost	*At Retail*	*At Cost*	*At Retail*	*At Cost*	*At Retail*
Purchases (net) ...	$231,000	$400,000	$262,200	$450,000	$271,600	$470,000
Net additional markups		30,000		17,000		20,000
Net markdowns ...		10,000		7,000		5,000
Sales (net)		380,000		410,000		485,000
Applicable price index 1975 = 110		116.6		122.1		132.0

Required:

1. Restate the 1975 ending inventory to base year cost at January 1, 1976. Give the entry to record the restatement on January 1, 1976, and provide an explanation.
2. Prepare computations for 1976–78 to derive, for each year, *(a)* the ending inventory at *Fifo* cost, and *(b)* the ending inventory at *Lifo* cost. Use a format similar to Exhibit 10–4.

Chapter 11

Liabilities and Income Taxes— Measuring, Recording, and Reporting

This chapter focuses on liabilities of various types and accounting for income taxes. To facilitate discussion and study, Part A considers liabilities in general and Part B discusses accounting for income taxes.

PART A—MEASURING, RECORDING, AND REPORTING LIABILITIES

In general, liabilities are obligations that result from past transactions to pay assets or render services in the future which are definite in amount, or subject to reasonable estimation, as stated or implied in oral or written contracts. The problems of identification and measurement are not as complex as those encountered with respect to assets.

Broadly, liabilities may be classified as *(a)* current and *(b)* long term. In accounting for liabilities, the primary problem is to make certain that no liabilities are omitted from the records and reports. The presence of an asset generally can be determined, whereas the existence of certain liabilities may be hard to ascertain. Accountants frequently see situations where it is to the advantage of management to overstate assets and understate liabilities. In particular, the accountant on occasion may find it almost impossible to learn of all liabilities, such as those owed to obscure parties in other states or regions. Once all liabilities are identified, there remains an important problem of *measurement* or *valuation*.

Conceptually, a liability is the *present value* of the future outlays it requires. Accounting practice generally measures, records, and reports current liabilities at their current cash equivalent amount which in most cases is substantially the same as their discounted present value.

Most liabilities are measured and reported at the maturity amount because *(a)* in the case of current liabilities, the difference between the maturity amount and the present value of the maturity amount is not *material;* and *(b)* long-term debt that specifies the "going-rate" of interest will have identical maturity and present value amounts (see Chapters 6 and 19). Measurement of liabilities is in accordance with the *cost principle.* The amount of a liability usually is determined in an exchange transaction involving the acquisition of goods or services; the value of those goods and services, measured in accordance with the cost principle, in turn determines the amount of the liability.[1]

Although exchange transactions generally establish the definite amount and due date for a liability, there are situations where a definite liability is known to exist although the exact amount and/or the payment date are not known precisely. A section of the chapter is devoted to estimated liabilities.

CURRENT LIABILITIES

Accounting for current liabilities involves the identification of certain types of items, such as short-term debts; accrued liabilities; deposits and advances received from customers, clients, and others; deferred credits; and implied contractual obligations. A particular problem of measurement arises because some of these liabilities are seldom shown in full in the accounts before some adjustment. For example, liabilities, such as wages payable, requiring periodic payments for services rendered continuously are seldom fully recorded in the accounts prior to end-of-the-period adjustments. Such liabilities frequently are not recorded in full except after an analysis has been made of certain financial facts preliminary to adjustments and other procedures have been performed preliminary to preparation of the financial statements. The identification, measurement, and reporting of these more or less fugitive liabilities often is of considerable significance. A primary objective of accounting for liabilities is to identify and measure them so that reporting will be in conformity with the *full-disclosure principle.* The amount and all other pertinent facts relative to liabilities must be identified and reported so that a company's financial condition may be evaluated.

Current Liabilities Defined

Current liabilities for many years were defined as those obligations due within one year of balance sheet date. This definition was related to the older definition of current assets (liquidation within one year). It was recognized that these definitions were unrealistic for many concerns. As a consequence, the Committee on Accounting Procedure of the AICPA defined current liabilities as follows:

> The term *current liabilities* is used principally to designate obligations whose liquidation is reasonably expected to require the use of existing resources properly classifiable as current assets, or the creation of other current liabilities.

---

[1] These concepts are in conformity with *Statement of the Accounting Principles Board No. 4* and *APB Opinion Nos. 21 and 26,* and FASB *Statement No. 6.*

The committee further elaborated as follows:

> As a balance-sheet category, the classification is intended to include obligations for items which have entered into the operating cycle, such as payables incurred in the acquisition of materials and supplies to be used in the production of goods or in providing services to be offered for sale; collections received in advance of the delivery of goods or performance of services; and debts which arise from operations directly related to the operating cycle, such as accruals for wages, salaries, commissions, rentals, royalties, and income and other taxes. Other liabilities whose regular and ordinary liquidation is expected to occur within a relatively short period of time, usually 12 months, are also intended for inclusion, such as short-term debts arising from the acquisition of capital assets, serial maturities of long-term obligations, amounts required to be expended within one year under sinking fund provisions, and agency obligations arising from the collection or acceptance of cash or other assets for the account of third persons.
>
> This concept of current liabilities would include estimated or accrued amounts which are expected to be required to cover expenditures within the year for known obligations *(a)* the amount of which can be determined only approximately (as in the case of provisions for accruing bonus payments) or *(b)* where the specific person or persons to whom payment will be made cannot as yet be designated (as in the case of estimated costs to be incurred in connection with guaranteed servicing or repair of products already sold).[2]

This definition has gained wide acceptance particularly since it recognizes *operating cycles* of varying lengths in different industries.

The principal types of current liabilities are:

1. Known liabilities of a definite amount:
   a. Accounts payable.
   b. Short-term notes payable.
   c. Cash dividends payable.
   d. Advances and funds held as short-term deposits.
   e. Accrued liabilities.
   f. Deferred revenues (revenues collected in advance).
2. Known liabilities, amount dependent on operations:
   g. Taxes (income, sales, and social security).
   h. Bonus obligations.
   i. Accrued liabilities.
3. Known liabilities of an estimated amount:
   j. Guarantee and warranty obligations.
   k. Premium obligations.

Special accounting problems related to these types of current liabilities are discussed in the following sections. Normally each of the current liabilities listed above should be separately accounted for and separately reported on the balance sheet.

---

[2] AICPA, "Restatement and Revision of Accounting Research Bulletins," *Accounting Research Bulletin No. 43* (New York, 1961), pp. 21–22.

Accounts and Notes Payable

Accounts payable and notes payable generally constitute the largest portion of current liabilities. Accounts payable as a designation is usually reserved for the recurring trade obligations of the business. This division in recording and reporting indicates the *source* of short-term funds and the *nature* of the obligation.

In determining the amount of accounts payable for goods purchased near the end of a specific period, careful attention should be given to goods that might be in transit. The purchase and liability should be recorded when *ownership passes*. In view of the fact that it is frequently difficult to determine precisely what goods are in transit, it is customary, for practical reasons, to record the liability for purchases when the goods are received. Frequently, goods are received during the last few days of the period; hence, there is a delay in checking the merchandise and the invoice may not be entered in the records. If the purchase is not recorded, liabilities are understated. Preferably the liability for goods purchased should be recorded net of cash discount allowed because that is the amount of liability that usually will be paid (see Chapter 8).

Short-term notes payable may be secured by collateral (pledged or mortgaged assets), or they may be unsecured. Secured notes should be reported separately, and the nature of the collateral should be reported both with respect to the notes and to the specific assets involved. One method is to report pledged assets in a footnote which refers both to the assets involved and the specific obligation. The preferable method is to report pledged assets parenthetically under both the asset and liability captions. To illustrate:

Investment:		Current Liabilities:	
Stock in X Corporation at cost (pledged for $1,000 note to "Y" Bank)	$5,000	Notes payable (secured by stock in X Corporation) ...	$3,000

Discounted Notes Payable

A note payable may be either *(a)* interest bearing or *(b)* noninterest bearing (often called a discounted note). Despite these designations, all commercial notes require the borrower to pay interest. In theory, interest free loans do not exist because there is always a time cost of using money.

In the case of an *interest-bearing note* payable the borrower receives cash, or equivalent assets or services, for the *face amount* of the note; interest (in addition to the face of the note) is paid at one or more subsequent dates. To illustrate, assume X Company borrowed $3,000 cash and signed a one-year, 8% interest-bearing note, dated October 1, 19A. The borrowing transaction, accrual of interest at the end of the period, December 31, 19A, and repayment on September 30, 19B, would be recorded as follows:

October 1, 19A:

Cash	3,000	
Notes payable, short term		3,000

December 31, 19A:

Interest expense	60	
Accrued interest payable ($3,000 × .08 × 3/12)		60

September 30, 19B: (assuming no reversing entry on January 1):

Accrued interest payable	60	
Interest expense	180	
Notes payable, short term	3,000	
Cash		3,240

In the case of a *noninterest-bearing note,* assuming the interest is based on the face amount of the note, the borrower would receive the face amount of the note less the interest deducted in advance (in the above example $3,000 – $240 = $2,760). In this situation the three entries would be as follows:

October 1, 19A:

Cash	2,760	
Discount on note payable	240	
Notes payable, short term*		3,000

December 31, 19A:

Interest expense	60	
Discount on note payable		60

September 30, 19B:

Interest expense	180	
Notes payable, short term	3,000	
Discount on note payable		180
Cash		3,000

* Alternatively, the note could be recorded at $2,760 and amortized up to $3,000 by the due date; see Chapter 19. The net results are the same.

At the end of 19A notes payable would be reported as follows:

Current Liabilities:		
Notes payable	$3,000	
Less: Discount on notes payable	180	$2,820

Observe that in the case of the interest-bearing note, the *effective* rate of interest was the same as the stated rate of interest, 8% per year. In the case of the noninterest-bearing note, the stated rate of interest was 8%; however, the effective rate of interest was $240 ÷ $2,760 = 8.6957%.

Alternatively, the interest terms may have specified that the 8% interest rate is to be applied to *cash proceeds.* The cash proceeds would be: $3,000 ÷ 1.08 = $2,778 (or $3,000 × .925926, from Table 6–2, = $2,778). On this basis the effective interest rate would be 8%, the same as the interest-bearing rate, and the entries would be the same as above for the discounted note except for the cash inflow and the interest amounts.

Dividends Payable

Cash (or property) dividends payable (i.e., declared but not yet paid) should be reported as a current liability if there is an intention to pay them in the coming year or operating cycle. Stock dividends issuable are not reported as a current liability but as an element of stockholders' equity as explained in Chapter 16. Cash dividends payable are reported as a liability between date of declaration and date of payment on the legal basis that declaration is an enforceable contract that the corporation has assumed by virtue of formal authorization.

Liabilities are not recognized for undeclared dividends in arrears on preferred stock nor for any other dividends not yet declared formally by the board of directors. Scrip dividends payable (liability dividends) are reported as a current liability unless there is no intention to make payment within the near future.

Advances and Returnable Deposits

A special type of liability arises when a company receives deposits from customers and employees. Deposits may be received from customers as guaranties to cover payment of obligations that may arise in the future or to guarantee performance of a contract or service. For example, when an order is taken, a company may require an advance payment to cover losses that would be incurred should the order be canceled. Such advances are liabilities of the company receiving the order until the underlying transaction is completed.

Deposits are frequently received from customers as guaranties for noncollection or for possible damage to property left with the customer. For example, deposits taken from customers by gas, water, light, and other public utilities are liabilities of such companies to their customers. Employees may make deposits for the return of keys and other company property, for locker privileges, and for club memberships. Some of the deposits are fairly permanent; others are current. Deposits should be reported as current or long-term liabilities depending upon the time involved between date of deposit and expected termination of the relationships. In cases where the advances or deposits are interest bearing, accrual of such interest costs is required.

Accrued Liabilities

Accrued liabilities arise because accounting recognition must be given to expenses that have been incurred but not yet paid. Accrued liabilities usually are recognized in the accounts with adjusting entries at the end of the period. For example, property taxes usually are assessed near the end of the calendar year and are payable in the following year. The *matching principle* requires that such expenses and the related liabilities be estimated in advance, recognized in the accounts, and reported on the financial statements on an accrual basis. Determination of expense accruals may be made from an examination of the historical expense accounts and other supplementary records. In recording accrued liabilities it is especially important that appropriate account titles be used such as Wages Payable, Estimated Property Taxes Payable, and Interest Payable.

In respect to the accrual of property taxes the Committee on Accounting Procedure of the AICPA stated:

> Generally, the most acceptable basis of providing for property taxes is monthly accrual on the taxpayer's books during the fiscal period of the taxing authority for which the taxes are levied. The books will then show, at any closing date, the appropriate accrual or prepayment.[3]

For some liabilities established on an accrual basis, such as Property Taxes Payable, the amount actually paid and the amount accrued sometimes will differ. Such differences should be accounted for as an adjustment at the end of the period.

Deferred Credits

A caption "deferred credits" or "deferred revenues" positioned after liabilities and before owners' equity sometimes is shown on published balance sheets. Usually one finds under this caption four types of items, viz:

1. Revenues collected in advance such as interest, rent, and advances received for services yet to be rendered. These items require that obligations, benefits, or services be rendered in the future before the revenue is realized.
2. Credits arising through certain external transactions that are difficult to classify. Examples are: premium on bonds payable, unearned deposit on royalties, discount on reacquired securities, and deferred income on installment sales.
3. Credits arising through certain internal transactions. Examples are: deferred repairs, allowance for rearrangement costs, and equities of minority interests (on consolidated statements).
4. Credits arising from income tax allocation procedures (deferred income taxes).

Rent collected in advance of being earned creates an obligation to render future occupancy (services). Such items are properly reported as liabilities until the services are furnished or there is a transfer of ownership to goods, as the case may be. For example, subscriptions collected in advance on magazines represent a liability to deliver a certain number of issues to the subscriber in the future. As the issues are delivered the liability, Subscriptions Collected in Advance, is reduced by a transfer to a revenue account, such as Subscription Revenue.

---

[3] Ibid., pp. 83–84.

Some of the items listed above are difficult to classify on the balance sheet. This reason underlies the wide usage of the vague balance sheet classification, Deferred credits. Observe that the classification, reported below liabilities and above owners' equity, is not consistent with the basic accounting model Assets = Liabilities + Owners' Equity, and it fails to identify clearly the true nature of the various items reported. Certain of these items are clearly in the nature of liabilities; others represent offsets or additions to related items. It is for these reasons that modern accounting theory and practice consider the deferred classification on the balance sheet to be objectionable. A sound basis for classification of the various items listed above is:

1. Classify as *current liabilities (a)* those items that represent a future claim against current assets whether or not there is an obligation to a specific individual or entity, and *(b)*, those items that will represent revenue when the obligations for goods and services are met.
2. Classify as long-term or *other liabilities* all items that are consistent with (1) above, except that they are not *current*, that is, extended periods of time are involved.
3. Classify all other items according to their characteristics as asset offsets, owners' equity, or additions to regular liabilities.

On the above basis the following classifications are suggested:

Item	*Classification*
Interest revenue collected in advance	Current liability
Rent revenue collected in advance	Current liability
Advances received for services to be rendered in the future	Current liability
Customer deposits, short term	Current liability
Magazine subscriptions collected in advance	Current liability
Deferred repairs	Current liability (represents a "claim" against current assets—may be long-term liability if related to several future periods)
Allowance for rearrangement costs	Current liability
Premium on bonds payable	Long-term liability (add to related bonds payable, see Chapter 19)
Equities of minority interests	Owners' equity (special caption separate from controlling interest; see Chapter 18)
Long-term refundable deposits	Long-term liability
Leasehold advances (leaseholds)	Current or long-term liability
Deferred income taxes	Current or long-term liability depending upon the element of time involved.

Funds Collected for Third Parties

Numerous state and federal laws require businesses to collect taxes from customers and employees for remission to certain governmental agencies. Taxes collected, but not yet remitted, represent current liabilities. To illustrate, assume there is a 5% sales tax and that sales for the period were $400,000. The indicated entries are:

Cash and accounts receivable	420,000	
Sales		400,000
Sales taxes payable		20,000
Sales taxes payable	20,000	
Cash		20,000

Payroll Taxes

Federal income tax laws require the employer to withhold from the pay of each employee an amount representing anticipated income taxes payable by the employee. The amount withheld depends upon the number of dependents and the level of income of the employee. Employers compute the amounts withheld according to a government-prescribed formula, or read them directly from withholding tax tables provided by the government. Income taxes withheld must be remitted to the Treasury through local depositaries (banks), and such amounts are current liabilities of the employer until remittance.

Social security legislation requires that the employer deduct a tax from the pay of each employee under specified conditions. In addition, the employer must match the contribution of the employee and remit the sum of both taxes to the Treasury along with income taxes withheld. Currently (1976–77) the tax amounts to 11.7%, one half of which is paid by the employee (5.85%) and one half by the employer.[4] The tax applies to the first $14,100 (subject to annual change by Congress) paid to each employee during the calendar year. Such taxes are referred to as F.I.C.A. taxes since the enabling act is the Federal Insurance Contributions Act. This tax is to provide survivor benefits, retirement pay, and so on.

Another social security tax levied by the federal government is to provide for *unemployment* insurance. This tax is required by the Federal Unemployment Tax Act and is generally referred to as F.U.T.A. taxes. This tax is paid wholly by the employer (of one or more persons) and amounts to a maximum of 3.2% on the first $4,200 in wages paid each employee. The law provides that 2.7% is payable to the state and .5% is payable to the federal Treasury.

Accounting for withholding taxes, F.I.C.A. taxes, and F.U.T.A. taxes may be illustrated simply. Assume salaries of $10,000 for the month of January and income tax withholdings of $1,100.

1. To record salaries and employee payroll taxes:

Salaries	10,000	
Withholding taxes payable		1,100
F.I.C.A. taxes payable—employees ($10,000 × 5.85%)		585
Cash		8,315

---

[4] The rate schedule for 1978–80 is 6.05%. These rates are changed by Congress from time to time.

2. To record employer payroll taxes:

Expense—payroll taxes	905	
F.I.C.A. taxes payable—employer ($10,000 × 5.85%)		585
F.U.T.A. taxes payable—federal ($10,000 × .5%)		50
F.U.T.A. taxes payable—state ($10,000 × 2.7%)		270

When the taxes are remitted, Cash is credited and the current liability accounts established in the preceding entries are debited.

Tax and Bonus Problems

It is not unusual to find employment contracts providing for the payment of a *bonus* to an officer, branch manager, or other employees of a corporation. A bonus should be treated as an operating expense and set up as a current liability when earned and pending payment. Bonus payments generally are deductible in computing taxable income under federal tax laws. Bonus contracts relating to income earned are usually one of two classes, viz:

1. The bonus is computed on the net income after deducting income taxes, but before deducting the bonus.
2. The bonus is computed after deducting both the bonus and the income taxes.

Since the tax is not determinable before the bonus is computed or vice versa, a special computation is required, based on simultaneous equations. To illustrate a typical situation, assume the Bryan Company reported income of $100,000 before deducting income taxes and before the bonus to the general manager. Assume the tax rate T is 52%, and the bonus rate B is 10%. Two situations are illustrated:

Situation 1: The bonus is based on income after deducting income taxes but before deducting the bonus.

$$B = .10(\$100{,}000 - T) \qquad (1)$$
$$T = .52(\$100{,}000 - B) \qquad (2)$$

Substitute value of T in (2) for T in (1):

$$B = .10[\$100{,}000 - .52(\$100{,}000 - B)] \qquad (3)$$
$$B = .10[\$100{,}000 - \$52{,}000 + .52B]$$
$$B = \$10{,}000 - \$5{,}200 + .052B$$
$$B - .052B = \$4{,}800$$
$$.948B = \$4{,}800$$
$$B = \underline{\underline{\$5{,}063}}$$

Substitute value of B in (2):

$$T = .52(\$100{,}000 - \$5{,}063)$$
$$T = \underline{\underline{\$49{,}367}}$$

Situation 2: The bonus is based on net income after deducting both income taxes and the bonus.

$$B = .10(\$100{,}000 - B - T) \quad (1)$$
$$T = .52(\$100{,}000 - B) \quad (2)$$

Substitute value of T in (2) for T in (1):

$$B = .10[\$100{,}000 - B - .52(\$100{,}000 - B)] \quad (3)$$
$$B = .10[\$100{,}000 - B - \$52{,}000 + .52B]$$
$$B = \$10{,}000 - .10B - \$5{,}200 + .052B$$
$$B + .10B - .052B = \$4{,}800$$
$$1.048B = \$4{,}800$$
$$B = \underline{\underline{\$4{,}580}}$$

Substitute value of B in (2):

$$T = .52(\$100{,}000 - \$4{,}580)$$
$$T = \underline{\underline{\$49{,}618}}$$

Proof of Computations

	Situation 1	*Situation 2*
Computation of taxes:		
Income before tax and bonus	$100,000	$100,000
Deduct bonus (as computed)	5,063	4,580
Taxable income	94,937	95,420
Multiply by tax rate	.52	.62
Tax	$ 49,367	$ 49,618
Computation of bonus:		
Income before taxes and bonus	$100,000	$100,000
Taxes	49,367	49,618
	50,633	50,382
Bonus (as computed)		4,580
Income subject to bonus	50,633	45,802
Multiply by bonus rate	.10	.10
Bonus	$ 5,063	$ 4,580

The entries to record the bonus and income taxes in Situation 2 would be as follows:

1. To record bonus:

Expense–manager's bonus	4,580	
Bonus payable		4,580

2. To record income taxes:

Expense–income taxes	49,618	
Income taxes payable		49,618

3. To record payment of bonus:

Bonus payable	4,580	
Cash		4,580

LONG-TERM LIABILITIES

All liabilities, not classified as current (as defined in the preceding section), usually are classified as long-term liabilities; however, some financial statements carry a second noncurrent category, *other liabilities.* Bonds payable and long-term notes and mortgages are often reported under long-term liabilities, and all other long-term obligations may be reported under the other liabilities category. Bonds payable are reported each period at their maturity amount plus any unamortized premium, or less any unamortized discount (also see Chapter 19).

Unrealistic Interest Rates

A special measurement problem arises when long-term debt either *(a)* specifies an interest rate that is significantly below the going rate of interest, or *(b)* does not specify an interest rate. These situations complicate measurement of *(a)* the amount of the debt that should be reported on the balance sheet, and *(b)* the amount of interest expense that should be reported on the income statement. Prior to *APB Opinion No. 21,* "Interest on Receivables and Payables" (1971), this measurement problem tended to be overlooked in the accounting and reporting processes. The *Opinion* states:

> When a note is received or issued solely for cash and no other right or privilege is exchanged, it is presumed to have a present value at issuance measured by the cash proceeds exchanged. If cash and some other rights or privileges are exchanged for a note, the value of the rights or privileges should be given accounting recognition. . . .
>
> When a note is exchanged for property, goods, or services in a bargained transaction entered into at arm's length, there should be a general presumption that the rate of interest stipulated by the parties to the transaction represents fair and adequate compensation to the supplier for the use of the related funds. That presumption, however, must not permit the form of the transaction to prevail over its economic substance and thus would not apply when (1) interest is not stated, or (2) the stated interest rate is unreasonable, or (3) the stated face amount of the note is materially different from the current cash sales price for the same or similar items or from the market value of the note at the date of the transaction. In these circumstances, the note, the sales price, and the cost of the property, goods, or service exchanged for the note should be recorded at the fair value of the property, goods, or service or at an amount that reasonably approximates the market value of the note, whichever is the more clearly determinable. That amount may, or may not, be the same as its face amount, and any resulting discount or premium should be accounted for as an element of interest over the life of the note.

The two different situations will be illustrated.

Situation 1: Assume Company X acquires an asset (other than cash) and signs a three-year note for $10,000; the note does not specify interest. Assume the going rate of interest for this type of borrowing for this company is 9% payable annually. No fair market value for the asset is determinable.

a. The note and the asset, measured at the present value of the debt, would be recorded as follows:[5]

Asset acquired	7,722	
Discount on note payable	2,278	
Note payable, long term		10,000

Computation: Since there are no periodic cash interest payments, only the maturity amount is discounted for "n" periods, at "i" interest rate to derive the present value of the note, viz: \$10,000 $\times p_{n=3;\, i=9\%}$ = \$10,000 × .772 (Table 6–2) = \$7.722 (see Chapter 6).

b. At the end of the first year, the following adjusting entry for interest expense and discount amortization would be made assuming straight-line amortization (see footnote 6):

Interest expense	759	
Discount on note payable		759

Computation:
Straight-line method (discussed below), \$2,278 ÷ 3 years = \$759.

At the end of the first year, the note would be reported on the balance sheet as follows:

Long-Term Liabilities:		
Note payable, maturity amount	\$10,000	
Less: Unamortized discount (\$2,278 -- \$759)	1,519	\$8,481

Situation 2: Assume the same facts as Situation 1 above except that the note specifies an interest rate of 5%, payable at the end of each 12-month period. In this situation, the stated rate of interest is unreasonable; it is too low by 4%.

a. To measure and record the transaction at the present value of the debt:

Asset acquired	8,988	
Discount on note payable	1,012	
Note payable		10,000

Computation—Since there are periodic cash interest payments, the maturity amounts and the amounts of the three interest payments must be discounted for "n" periods at "i" interest rate to derive the present value of the note, viz:

\$10,000 $\times p_{n=3,\, i=9\%}$ = (as in Situation 1)	\$7,722
(\$10,000 × .05) $\times P_{n=3,\, i=9\%}$ = \$500 × 2.5313 (Table 6–4)	1,266
Total Present Value	\$8,988

b. To record straight-line amortization of discount and interest expense at end of the first year:

Interest expense	837	
Discount on note payable (\$1,012 ÷ 3 years)		337
Cash (\$10,000 × .05)		500

The discount on note payable, Situations 1 and 2, was amortized using the straight-line method. This method, although not theoreti-

[5] Alternatively, some accountants prefer to record the note at its present value of \$7,722. Amortization of the discount would reflect a credit to Note Payable so that a maturity date the liability account would reflect \$10,000. Both methods derive the same results.

cally sound, may be used when the amount is not material (see below).[6]

APB Opinion No. 21, par. 6, requires the interest method of amortization; however, if the difference in results between that method and the straight-line method is not material, the latter method may be used (see Chapter 19). Amortization each year using the interest method would be as follows:

Year	Periodic Cash Interest Payments	Effective Interest	Amortization Amount	Debt Carrying Value
Situation 1:				$ 7,722
1..............	$ 0	$7,722 × .09 = $695	$695	8,417
2..............	0	8,417 × .09 = 757	757	9,174
3..............	0	9,174 × .09 = 826	826	10,000
Situation 2:				8,988
1..............	500	8,988 × .09 = 809	309	9,297
2..............	500	9,297 × .09 = 837	337	9,634
3..............	500	9,634 × .09 = 866	366	10,000

Observe in Situation 2 that the asset is recorded at a higher cost ($8,988 − $7,722 = $1,266) than in Situation 1 because there was a different cash cost; in Situation 1 cash disbursed totaled $10,000 (at the end of the third year) whereas in Situation 2 cash disbursed was ($500 × 3) + $10,000 = $11,500. The difference in asset cost ($1,266) is not the same as the difference in total cash paid ($1,500) because the cash flows in Situation 2 were at different times (i.e., the time value of money caused the difference).

Current Maturities of Long-Term Debt

On the balance sheet for the year preceding the maturity of a long-term debt, the amount to be paid during the upcoming current period, if payable out of current assets, should be reported as a current liability. FASB *Statement No. 7*, "Classification of Short-Term Obligations," specifies that this classification should not be used if the payment is to be made from a sinking fund, or the cash is to be derived from other noncurrent sources. To illustrate, the current payment of a *serial bond issue* would be reported as follows:

Current Liabilities:		
Current payment on bond issue..............		$100,000
Long-Term Liabilities:		
Bonds payable......................................	$500,000	
Less: Current payment	100,000	400,000

[6] AICPA, "Interest on Receivables and Payables," *Accounting Principles Board Opinion No. 21* (New York 1971), par. 15.

Bonds payable are discussed in depth in Chapter 19 in conjunction with long-term investments in bonds.

ESTIMATED LIABILITIES

Estimated liabilities are *known* liabilities that are *uncertain* in amount, and often as to due date at the time the financial statements are prepared. Estimated liabilities should be reported on the balance sheet as either current or long term rather than by footnote. The amount of each such liability should be estimated realistically on the basis of all available information. The account title should clearly indicate that the amount reported is an estimate. For example, appropriate titles are Estimated Income Taxes Payable and Estimated Warranty Liability. The term *reserve* should not be used in account titles for estimated liabilities, although this was common in the past.

There are numerous situations where known liabilities must be estimated as to amount at the balance sheet date. Several typical situations are discussed in the paragraphs to follow.

Liability from Warranties

A warranty or guarantee is a promise by the seller to make good deficiencies in merchandise over a specified period after the sale. Sometimes they involve a formal written agreement; in other cases, only a verbal or implied promise. Since the expenditure of cash or other resources in the future is generally required, a liability exists from the date of sale to the end of the warranty period. This known liability, estimated in amount, should be recognized in the accounts by an accrual entry in the period that the merchandise was sold so that the expense is matched with the revenue of the period in accordance with the matching principle. The estimated amount of the expense is recorded as a debit to operating expense and as a credit to a liability (usually current). When actual resources are expended on the warranty, cash or other assets are credited and the warranty liability debited.

To illustrate, assume Company R sold merchandise for $200,000 cash during the period. Experience has indicated that warranty and guarantee costs will approximate one half of 1% of sales. The indicated entries are:

In year of sale:

Cash	200,000	
Sales revenue		200,000
Estimated warranty expense	1,000	
Estimated warranty liability		1,000

Subsequently during warranty period for actual expenditures:

Estimated warranty liability	987	
Cash (or other resources)		987

Clearly when warranty expense is immaterial in amount, a company would not accrue it as illustrated above; instead, they would account for it on a cash basis because, for practical reasons, the materiality concept is permitted to override the theoretical matching principle.

Liability from Premiums, Coupons, and Trading Stamps

As a promotional device, many companies offer premiums of one kind or another to customers who turn in coupons, trading stamps, labels, box tops, wrappers, and so on, received when merchandise is purchased. At the end of each accounting period, a portion of these will be outstanding (unredeemed by the customers), some of which ultimately will be turned in for redemption. These outstanding claims for premiums represent a liability that must be recognized in the period of sale of the merchandise. The estimated cost of the premiums that will be given should be recorded as an estimated expense of the period of sale and an estimated liability credited.

To illustrate a typical situation, assume Baker Coffee Company offered to customers a premium—a silver coffee spoon (cost to Baker 75 cents each) upon the return of 20 coupons. One coupon is placed in each can of coffee when packed. The company estimated, on the basis of past experience, that only 70% of the coupons would ever be redeemed. The following additional data for two years are available:

	First Year	*Second Year*
Number of coffee spoons purchased @ $.75	6,000	4,000
Number of coupons redeemed	40,000	120,000
Number of cans of coffee sold	100,000	200,000

The indicated entries are as follows:

1. To record purchases of spoons:

	First Year		*Second Year*	
Premiums—silverware	4,500		3,000	
Cash		4,500		3,000

2. To record estimated liability and premium expense on sales:

Premium expense*	2,625		5,250	
Estimated premium claims outstanding		2,625		5,250

* Computations:
Year 1: (100,000 ÷ 20) × $.75 × .70 = $2,625.
Year 2: (200,000 ÷ 20) × $.75 × .70 = $5,250.

3. To record redemption of coupons:

Estimated premium claims outstanding*	1,500		4,500	
Premiums—silverware		1,500		4,500

* Computations:

$\frac{40,000}{20} \times \$.75 = \underline{\underline{\$1,500}}.$

$\frac{120,000}{20} \times \$.75 = \underline{\underline{\$4,500}}.$

4. To close:

Income summary	2,625		5,250	
Premium expense		2,625		5,250

Balances (ending) for financial statements:

Balance Sheet:		
Premiums – silverware (inventory):		
($4,500 – $1,500)	$3,000	
($3,000 + $3,000 – $4,500)		$1,500
Estimated premium claims outstanding (liability):		
($2,625 – $1,500)	1,125	
($1,125 + $5,250 – $4,500)		1,875
Income Statement:		
Premium expense (distribution expenses)	2,625	5,250

The Premiums – Silverware account balance should be reported as a current asset. The balance in the Estimated Premium Claims Outstanding should be reported as a current liability.

In accounting for estimated expenses and liabilities, as illustrated above, not infrequently the actual amount often will vary from the estimate. In this situation, when the actual amount becomes known, an adjustment to the estimated liability account is necessary. Recall that under *APB Opinion No. 20,* this is a change in an estimate, and should be treated as a current item in the period of change; that is, on a prospective rather than on a retroactive basis (see Chapters 4 and 20).

CONTINGENCIES

Prior to the issuance of FASB, *Statement of Financial Standards No. 5* "Accounting for Contingencies," (March 1975), as amended by FASB *Statement No. 11* (December 31, 1975), the reporting of contingencies was quite varied and most of the attention was focused only on *contingent liabilities. Statement No. 5* is much broader; it defines a contingency as:

> . . . an existing condition, situation or set of circumstances involving uncertainty as to possible gain (a gain contingency) or loss (a loss contingency) to an enterprise that will ultimately be resolved when one or more future events occur or fail to occur. Resolution of the uncertainty may confirm the acquisition of an asset or the reduction of a liability or the loss or impairment of an asset or the incurrence of a liability.

Thus, a contingency is characterized by *(a)* an existing condition, *(b)* uncertainty as to the ultimate effect, and *(c)* its resolution depending on one or more future events. Examples of loss contingencies are: collectibility of receivables, warranty obligations, threatened or actual litigation, potential claims for damages, assessments, and guarantees of the debts of others.

The accounting and reporting requirements specified by FASB *State-*

ment No. 5 depend upon the seriousness of a contingency and hence the degree of certainty of loss or gain. To assess the range of certainty versus uncertainty, three terms are used in the *Statement* as follows:

a. Probable—The future event or events are or are not likely to occur.
b. Reasonably possible—The chance of the future event or events occurring (or not occurring) is more than remote but less than likely.
c. Remote—The chance of the future event or events occurring (or not occurring) is slight.

An estimated loss from a contingency may be *(a)* accrued in the accounts and reported in the financial statements and/or *(b)* disclosed in the notes to the financial statements.

A loss contingency *must be accrued* in the accounts and reported in the financial statements (as opposed to footnote only) if two conditions are met:

1. Information prior to issuance of the financial statements indicate that it is *probable* that an asset has been impaired or a liability has been incurred at the date of the financial statements. It is implicit in this condition that it must be probable that one or more future events will occur confirming the fact of the loss.
2. The amount of the loss can be reasonably estimated.

Accrual of Estimated Contingency Losses

A contingency loss that meets both of the above criteria usually involves either *(a)* the reduction of an asset, or *(b)* the incurrence of a liability. Such losses must be accrued in the accounts and reported in the financial statements. A recurring and typical contingency loss arising from the *reduction of an asset* for bad debts (uncollectible receivables). Accounting for this type of contingency loss was explained in detail in Chapter 7. The loss is accrued since it clearly meets both of the above criteria. Recall that Bad Debt Expense is debited and the Allowance for Doubtful Accounts (a contra asset account) is credited for the estimated bad debt losses related to sales for the period. Accrual of this contingency loss has the effect of reducing income and assets by the amount of the estimated loss. It conforms to the matching principle.

A typical contingency loss arising from the *incurrence of a liability* is the obligation for product warranties and guarantees previously discussed. The estimated loss and related liability were accrued because both of the above criteria were met. Similar conditions may exist in the case of injury or damage caused by product defects (such as in drugs, toys, and automobiles).

In contrast, neither the absence of insurance on the assets of an enterprise, or the possibility of future injury to others meets both conditions for accrual of a contingency loss. In these situations, there is an existing condition, the absence of insurance. However, mere exposure to risk does not mean that an asset has been impaired nor that a liability has been incurred.

A contingency loss that is occurring with ever greater frequency is lawsuits for damages. In recent years, these suits have been particularly successful for the plaintiffs. These situations often fall into the *probable* category and, consequently, require *accrual* before the trials are terminated and the court decision rendered. To illustrate, assume XY Company is sued for $500,000 damages for a personal injury suffered by the plaintiff in a truck-auto accident. The truck was owned by XY Company. Although the trial has not been scheduled, the company counsel believes it is probable that the plaintiff will be successful against the company for approximately $100,000 (clearly, this often cannot be reasonably estimated). Therefore, XY Company is required by FASB *Statement No.* 5 to make the following accrual entry prior to preparation of the financial statements:

Extraordinary loss—estimated damages from injury (Note A)	100,000	
Estimated liability—injury claim		100,000

This contingency loss, reported on the income statement, created a contingent liability which is reported as a liability on the balance sheet.

In the case of a contingency loss which must be accrued, resulting in an asset reduction, the credit should be made to an "allowance" account which would be reported as a contra account to the asset involved.

Disclosure of Estimated Contingency Losses

If a contingency loss meets one, but not both, of the criteria listed above, and as a result is not accrued, *disclosure by footnote* must be made when it is at least *reasonably possible* that there has been an impairment of assets or that a liability has been incurred. Disclosure must indicate the nature of the contingency and give an estimate of the *possible* loss, or it must state that a reasonable estimate cannot be made.

In the past this type of contingency loss generally was referred to as a *contingent liability*. For many years, the disclosure of contingent liabilities has been a part of generally accepted accounting principles. Some of the common contingent liabilities are: accommodation endorsements (cosigning a note for another party), purchase commitments, and lawsuit pending. *Statement No.* 5 concludes that disclosure of contingent liabilities shall continue as before under generally accepted accounting principles.

However, all contingency losses, including contingent liabilities, now must be accounted for and reported in accordance with FASB *Statement No.* 5 cited above. One particularly difficult area is determination of the appropriate accounting and reporting with respect to legal litigation, claims, and assessments, whether they are potential, pending, or in process. This area is complicated because many lawyers feel that presettlement disclosure may prejudice the outcome of the case. In these situations, FASB *Statement No.* 5 states that "the opinions of legal counsel and other advisers, the experience of the enterprise in similar cases, the experience of other enterprises, and any decision of the enterprise's management as to how the enterprise intends to respond to the lawsuit, claim or assessment." It has been said that if the enterprise plans to forcefully contest the lawsuit, claim, or assessment, this is evidence that in their opinion a contingency loss is not *probable* (no accrual required) and may not even be *reasonably possible* (no accrual or disclosure required).

Contingency Gains

A contingent gain exists when the three characteristics of a contingency exist (as defined above) and there is apt to be an increase in assets or a decrease in liabilities if the conditions materialize. Consistent with the concept of conservatism, contingency gains usually are not accrued; however, disclosure by footnote is permitted with certain constraints. FASB *Statement No. 5* reads:

a. Contingencies that might result in gains usually are not reflected in the accounts since to do so might be to recognize revenue prior to its realization.
b. Adequate disclosure shall be made of contingencies that might result in gains, but care shall be exercised to avoid misleading implications as to the likelihood of realization.

An example of a contingency gain would be the case where the company has sued another party for damages. Another case would be where expropriation (by a foreign government) of assets is probable and reimbursement will exceed book value.

Appropriations and Reserves of Retained Earnings

The use of "reserves for general contingencies" and appropriations of retained earnings to record the *accrual of contingent losses* is not permitted by FASB *Statement No. 5*. The statement also asserts that if appropriations or reserves of retained earnings are recorded, the debit to create them must be to Retained Earnings, not to loss or expense, and the balances in these accounts must not be reported outside the stockholders' equity section of the balance sheet (also see Chapter 16).

PART B—ACCOUNTING FOR INCOME TAXES

Chapter 4 briefly discussed income tax allocation. In that discussion, the concepts of intraperiod (i.e., interstatement) and interperiod income tax allocation were briefly introduced; here the topic is considered in more depth. *Intraperiod* refers to the allocation of income tax expense within the current period between certain subclassifications on the income statement and sometimes on the statement of retained earnings. *Interperiod* refers to the allocation of income tax expense as between two or more periods. Both types of income tax allocation have the primary purpose of reporting (or matching) income tax expense with operating income, extraordinary items, and prior period adjustments when they have a tax impact. First, interperiod tax allocation will be discussed, then intraperiod allocation.

INTERPERIOD INCOME TAX ALLOCATION

Interperiod income tax allocation between accounting periods is necessary when some transactions (or items) affect the determination of *pretax accounting income* in one accounting period and affect the determination of *taxable income* in a different period. Fundamentally, this is due to differences between (1) the application of generally accepted accounting principles in recognizing revenues and expenses, and (2) the provisions of the income tax laws and related treasury regulations.

The first major pronouncement on income tax allocation was made in 1961 by the AICPA Committee on Accounting Procedure and stated:

> Income taxes are an expense that should be allocated, when necessary and practicable, to income and other accounts, as other expenses are allocated. What the income statements should reflect under this head, as under any other head, is the expense properly allocable to the income included in the income statement for the year.[7]

The next major pronouncement, and the one currently effective, was "Accounting for Income Taxes," *APB Opinion No. 11*, (December 1967). The discussions to follow conform with *Opinion No. 11*.

Federal income taxes are by far the most significant tax levied on the corporation both in respect to complexity and to the impact on decisions of management and on the resultant financial reports. In their early days, income taxes were levied primarily on a cash basis; since 1918 this approach has been modified to more generally conform to accrual accounting as reflected on the periodic financial reports. Despite this trend there are today many divergencies between *pretax accounting income* and *taxable income* for any given period. Clearly, the objectives of income taxation, in addition to raising revenues (presumably according to ability to pay), include: to control the economy, to promote full employment, to stimulate capital expenditures, and to attain certain social ends (i.e., tax deductibility of contributions to certain types of institutions).

Tax Differences

The numerous differences between pretax accounting income and taxable income give rise to *differences;* for some, but not all, of these differences, the tax effect must be recognized in the accounts and in the financial statements. To illustrate, assume for the current year,

---

[7] AICPA, "Restatement and Revision of Accounting Research Bulletins," *Accounting Research Bulletin No. 43* (New York, 1961), p. 88.

19A, pretax accounting income of $40,000; taxable income, $35,000; and an average tax rate of 40%. There would be a difference of $5,000 and a *tax difference* of $5,000 × .40 = $2,000. The central question is the extent to which accounting recognition and reporting should be given to income tax differences. Accounting recognition of tax differences depends on the *type* of underlying difference; there are two distinct types: permanent differences and timing differences.

A number of *APB Opinions* and FASB *Statements* provide instructions on the tax allocation effects. For example, FASB *Statement No. 9* states: "interperiod tax allocation is required for intangible drilling costs and other costs associated with the exploration for and development of oil and gas reserves that enter into the determination of taxable income and pretax accounting income in different periods."

Permanent Differences. Income tax allocation is *never* applied to permanent differences because they will not be offset or reversed in the future; that is, they never "turn around" in the future. Permanent differences arise from *(a)* items that affect determination of pretax accounting income but never affect taxable income, and *(b)* items that affect determination of taxable income but never affect pretax accounting income. Common examples of the two categories are: tax exempt revenue on municipal bonds; the expense portion of premiums paid on life insurance policies carried by an enterprise on its officers; fines and expenses resulting from violations of the law; statutory depletion on natural resources; and amortization of goodwill. Since permanent differences are not subject to tax allocation procedures, our attention in the discussions to follow will focus only on timing differences.

Timing Differences. Income tax allocation procedures *always* are applied to timing differences because the tax effect will offset, reverse, or "turn around" in one or more periods in the future. They will turn around or reverse in the future because items that cause them will be included in the determination of both pretax accounting income and taxable income but in different periods. Four types of transactions cause timing differences, viz:

a. Revenues or gains which are included in taxable income one or more periods after they are included in pretax accounting income; for example, gross profit on installment sales.
b. Expenses or losses which are deducted in determining taxable income one or more periods after they are deducted in determining pretax accounting income; for example, estimated (accrued) warranty costs.
c. Revenues or gains which are included in taxable income before they are included in pretax accounting income; for example, rent revenue collected in advance.
d. Expenses or losses which are deducted in determining taxable income before they are deducted in determining pretax accounting income; for example, depreciation on an accelerated basis for tax purposes, but on a straight-line basis for accounting purposes.

Fundamental Concepts and Procedures

The fundamental concepts and procedures of interperiod income tax allocation are not complex; however, the related recordkeeping can be somewhat burdensome in a complex situation. To illustrate tax allocation in a direct way, assume XY Corporation reported pretax accounting income of $40,000 in Year A and also in Year B and an average tax rate of 40%. Assume further that in Year A a $5,000 expense item was included on the income statement but was not allowable as a deduction on the income tax return until Year B. Thus, there was a timing tax difference of $5,000 × .40 = $2,000. The results for the two years would be as follows:

	Year A	*Year B*
Income taxes payable (per tax return):		
Year A: ($40,000 + $5,000) × .40	$18,000	
Year B: ($40,000 − $5,000) × .40		$14,000
Income Statement:		
Case A—with interperiod tax allocation (correct):		
Pretax operating income	$40,000	$40,000
Less: Income tax expense (allocated):		
$40,000 × .40	16,000	16,000
Net Income	$24,000	$24,000
Case B—without interperiod tax allocation (incorrect):		
Pretax operating income	$40,000	$40,000
Less: Income tax expense (not allocated):		
Same as taxes payable	18,000	14,000
Net Income	$22,000	$26,000

Observe that both total income tax expense and total income taxes payable are the same for the two years combined; however, each is different by year by the amount of the timing tax difference of $5,000 × .40 = $2,000.

Interperiod tax allocation has, as its purpose, the reporting of income tax expense on an accrual basis rather than on the tax return basis. Note that the timing difference in Year A reversed or turned around in Year B. Many accountants believe that failure to allocate tax differences between periods would cause net income to be incorrectly reported because expenses are not properly matched with revenues for the period.

The interperiod tax allocation reflected in the above example would be *accrued in the accounts* at each year-end as follows:

Year 19A:

Income tax expense (per income statement)	16,000	
Deferred income taxes	2,000	
Income taxes payable (per tax return)		18,000

Year 19B:

Income tax expense (per income statement)	16,000	
Deferred income taxes		2,000
Income taxes payable (per tax return)		14,000

A more comprehensive example is shown in Exhibit 11–1. At the end of the year the balance in the deferred income tax account is reported on the balance sheet *(a)* if a debit, as a deferred charge; and *(b)* if a credit, as a liability. The current portion is reported as a current item, and the remainder is reported as a noncurrent item. "Accounting for Income Taxes," *APB Opinion No. 11,* reads:

> Deferred charges and deferred credits relating to timing differences represent the cumulative recognition given to their tax effects and as such do not represent receivables or payables in the usual sense. They should be classified in two categories—one for the net current amount and the other for the net noncurrent amount. This presentation is consistent with the customary distinction between current and noncurrent categories and also recognizes the close relationship among the various deferred tax accounts, all of which bear on the determination of income tax expense. The current portions of such deferred charges and credits should be those amounts which relate to assets and liabilities classified as current. Thus, if installment receivables are a current asset, the deferred credits representing the tax effects of uncollected installment sales should be a current item; if an estimated provision for warranties is a current liability, the deferred charge representing the tax effect of such provision should be a current item.[8]

INTRAPERIOD TAX ALLOCATION

Intraperiod tax allocation sometimes called interstatement allocation, requires the allocation of income tax expense (as derived by application of interperiod tax allocation) within a period to certain subclassifications on the financial statements. The concept of intraperiod tax allocation is that the tax effect should be reported with the item that affected the tax. This means that income tax expense for the period must be allocated to *(a)* income from operations, *(b)* extraordinary items, and *(c)* prior period adjustments to the extent that each of these classifications reports items that affected total income tax expense for the period. This is strictly a *reporting allocation;* no entries are made in the accounts for the intraperiod allocation. The various items are reported *net of tax*. Exhibit 11–1 presents a rare situation where intraperiod tax allocation affects the balance sheet as well as the income statement and statement of retained earnings. The results are illustrated with and without allocation to demonstrate the misleading implications if intraperiod allocation is not followed. Observe that without intraperiod allocation net income is overstated by $12,000 (over 21%).

---

[8] AICPA, "Accounting for Income Taxes," *APB Opinion No. 11* (New York, December 1967), par. 57.

A COMPREHENSIVE ILLUSTRATION

Interperiod and intraperiod tax allocation procedures were discussed separately above; however, they are interrelated. Interperiod allocation is accomplished first (and the effects recorded in the accounts); next income tax expense for the current period is allocated within the period for reporting purposes only. A comprehensive illustration is given in Exhibit 11–2.

DISCLOSURE OF TAX ALLOCATION

Full disclosure of the components of income tax expense (including deferred income taxes) is required. In respect to the income statement *APB Opinion No. 11* states that "the components of income tax expense should be disclosed" on the income statement; that is, in addition to *intraperiod* allocation, taxes estimated to be payable and the tax effects of timing differences should be reported. The *Opinion* states that these amounts "may be presented as separate items in the income statement or, alternatively, as combined amounts with disclosure of the components parenthetically or in a note to the financial statements." An example of the footnote approach is shown in Exhibit 11–3.

EXHIBIT 11–1
Intraperiod Tax Allocation

1. Assumed income tax rate of 40% on all items.
2. Items subject to income taxes:
   a. Pretax operating income, $100,000.
   b. Extraordinary loss, $5,000.
   c. Prior period adjustment (decrease in retained earnings), $20,000 (example, damages paid).
   d. Decrease in owners' equity, $10,000 (example, effect of certain stock option plans).
3. Income tax expense, $26,000.

	Without Intraperiod Tax Allocation (incorrect)	*With Intraperiod Tax Allocation (correct)*	
Income Statement:			
Pretax operating income	$100,000		$100,000
Less: Income tax expense	26,000		40,000
Income before extraordinary item	74,000		60,000
Extraordinary loss	(5,000)	$ 5,000	
Less: Applicable tax saving		2,000	(3,000)
Net Income	$ 69,000		$ 57,000
Statement of Retained Earnings:			
Prior period adjustment (decrease)	$ 20,000	20,000	
Less: Applicable tax saving		8,000	$ 12,000
Balance Sheet:			
Owners' equity (decrease)	$ 10,000	10,000	
Less: Applicable tax saving		4,000	$ 6,000

EXHIBIT 11–2

Comprehensive Illustration – Interperiod and Intraperiod Tax Allocation

Assumptions:

1. Income tax rates: first $25,000, 22%; above $25,000, 48%; capital gains, 25%.
2. Income on installment sales is included in the income tax return in period of collection rather than in period of sale. Collections on installment sales assumed to be in year following sale.
3. Data per accounts:

	19A	*19B*
Income on regular sales	$100,000	$140,000
Income on installment sales..............	40,000	-0-
Extraordinary gain	9,600	9,600

Computations on income tax return:

	19A	*19B*
On regular sales:	$25,000 × 22% = $ 5,500	$ 25,000 × 22% = $ 5,500
	75,000 × 48% = 36,000	115,000 × 48% = 55,200
On installment sales:*		40,000 × 48% = 19,200
On extraordinary gain:	9,600 × 25% = 2,400	9,600 × 25% = 2,400
	$43,900	$82,300

* Other assumptions are acceptable in respect of "order" of regular and installment sales. Also, the tax rates used are for illustrative purposes only.

Partial Income Statement – with Interperiod and Intraperiod Tax Allocation

		19A		*19B*
Income on regular sales		$100,000		$140,000
Income on installment sales		40,000		
Total income before tax and extraordinary items		140,000		140,000
Less: Applicable income taxes*..............		60,700		60,700
Income before extraordinary items		79,300		79,300
Extraordinary items:				
Gain	$9,600		$9,600	
Less: Applicable income tax*.................	2,400	7,200	2,400	7,200
Net Income		$ 86,500		$ 86,500

* Computation of income tax expense (accrual or allocation basis): Same for each year:

$ 25,000 × 22% =	$ 5,500	
115,000 × 48% =	55,200	$60,700
9,600 × 25% =		2,400
Total Tax Expense ...		$63,100

Entries in the accounts to reflect the tax allocation

	19A	
Income tax expense (per income statement)	63,100	
Deferred income taxes		19,200
Income taxes payable (per tax return)		43,900

	19B	
Income tax expense (per income statement)	63,100	
Deferred income taxes	19,200	
Income taxes payable (per tax return)		82,300

Note: For comparative purposes observe that, without income tax allocation, reported net income for 19A would have been $149,600 − $43,900 = $105,700 and for 19B, $149,600 − $82,300 = $67,300; each amount is materially different than that reported under allocation procedures.

Balance sheet disclosure requires *(a)* that income taxes payable be set out separately from deferred tax amounts, and *(b)* that deferred tax balances be reported in two amounts – a net *current* amount and a net *noncurrent* amount. The classification of the deferred amounts as current or noncurrent is made on the basis of the related assets and liabilities. For example, if a deferred tax credit arises as a result of installment receivables that are classified as current assets, then the tax credit would be classified as current. Reporting in this manner is reflected in Exhibit 11–3.

Disclosure of income taxes and the related interperiod and intraperiod tax allocations are illustrated in Exhibit 11–3.

EXHIBIT 11–3
Disclosure of Income Tax Allocation

B CORPORATION
Income Statement (partial)
For the Year Ended December 31, 19B

Income from operations		$120,000
Less: Income tax expense (Note A)		48,000*
Income before extraordinary items		72,000
Extraordinary items:		
Loss	$30,000	
Less: Applicable income tax	12,000	18,000
Net Income		$ 54,000

* An average tax rate of 40% is assumed on all items for illustrative purposes.

B CORPORATION
Balance Sheet (partial)
At December 31, 19B

Current Liabilities:	
Income taxes payable (Note A)	$35,000
Deferred income taxes (Note B)	11,000
Long-Term Liabilities:	
Deferred income taxes (Note B)	19,000

Notes to Financial Statement

A. Income tax payable was computed as follows:

Income tax expense on current operations	$48,000
Add decrease in current deferred tax credit	2,000
Deduct increase in noncurrent deferred tax credit	(3,000)
Income taxes payable on current operations	47,000
Deduct tax saving on extraordinary loss	12,000
Income Taxes Currently Payable	$35,000

B. The current portion of deferred income taxes is for gross profit on installment sales not yet taxed; the net decrease for the current year was $2,000. The noncurrent portion was for the excess tax credit for accelerated depreciation on the tax return over straight-line depreciation reflected on the income statement; the net increase for the year was $3,000.

OPERATING LOSSES AND TAX ALLOCATION

Federal tax laws allow corporations which sustain losses to carry back and carry forward such losses under certain conditions. A corporation may secure refunds of income taxes paid in the three prior years, and if the loss is so large that after adjustment it is not absorbed fully when offset against the profitable years to which it is carried back, it can be carried forward for as many as five years, during which it may reduce taxes that would otherwise be owed on income in those years. The tax provision may be diagrammed as follows:

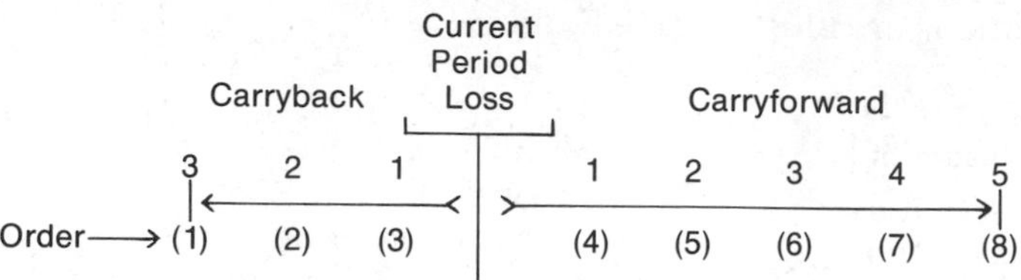

Loss Carryback

In a period where an operating loss follows a period of net income sufficient to offset the loss, the resultant tax carryback will give rise to a refund of income taxes paid in the prior period. Since the refund is virtually certain, the *tax effect* should be recorded in the accounts and reflected in the financial statement for the loss period. *APB Opinion No. 11* states the following:

> The tax effects of any realizable loss carry*backs* should be recognized in the determination of net income (loss) of the loss periods. The tax loss gives rise to a refund (or claim for refund) of past taxes, which is both measurable and currently realizable; therefore the tax effect of the loss is properly recognizable in the determination of net income (loss) for the loss period. Appropriate adjustments of existing net deferred tax credits may also be necessary in the loss period.

To illustrate, assume AB Corporation reported net income before taxes of $80,000 in 19A, its first year of operations. Since the average tax rate was 40% (for illustrative purposes) and pretax accounting income and taxable income coincided, the corporation paid $32,000 in income tax. In 19B, due to a recession, the books showed a net pretax loss of $20,000, after certain technical adjustments. Under the carryback provision this entitled the company to an $8,000 refund of the taxes paid in 19A. Therefore, at the end of 19B the following entry would be made:

19B:

Receivable for refund of 19A income taxes	8,000	
Income tax refund, loss carryback		8,000

The bottom portion of the 19B income statement would show:

Net loss before recognition of tax effect..............	$20,000
Deduct estimated refund of prior year income tax due to loss carryback..................................	8,000
Net Loss..	$12,000

The above entry and the manner of reporting reflects the tax refund which has a high degree of certainty of materializing; its effect is to reduce the loss that otherwise would be reported for 19B. It should be reported in 19B because that is the year in which the refund was "earned."

Loss Carryforward

In the situation where a company has experienced a net operating loss which cannot be offset through a carryback, it may be realized as a carryforward up to five years in the future. Where the years preceding a loss year have been profitable there can be little doubt that a carry*back* equal to or less than the profits of the years to which it can be applied will be fully realized. On the other hand, *uncertainty* necessarily attends the realizability of a carry*forward* since future profits are uncertain. On this point APB in *Opinion No. 11* stated:

> The tax effects of loss carry*forwards* also relate to the determination of net income (loss) of the loss periods. However, a significant question generally exists as to realization of the tax effects of the carry*forwards,* since realization is dependent upon future taxable income. Accordingly, the Board has concluded that the tax benefits of loss carry*forwards* should not be recognized until they are actually realized, except in unusual circumstances when realization is *assured beyond any reasonable doubt* at the time of the loss carry*forwards* arise. When the tax benefits of loss carry*forwards* are not recognized until realized in full or in part in subsequent periods, the tax benefits should be reported in the results of those periods as extraordinary items.

To illustrate the carryforward case, assume that Z Corporation sustained a $50,000 net operating loss during the first year of operations. Also assume for illustrative purposes, a 40% corporate average tax rate and that a potential loss carryforward of $20,000 arises. Whether or not Z Corporation will be able to avail itself of this as a *future* tax saving depends upon whether or not future income is earned. In view of the uncertainty of future income, appropriate accounting for the potential carryforward in the year of the loss is somewhat troublesome. Fundamentally, two alternative accounting approaches are available:

Alternative 1: Assured beyond any reasonable doubt—Recognize the tax carryforward as an asset (receivable for tax refund) and reduce the current operating loss by the amount of the tax carryforward. To illustrate:

Year of loss:

Receivable for tax refund (loss carryforward)	20,000	
Income summary (income tax expense)		20,000

Income Statement:

Pretax operating loss	$50,000
Less: Tax loss carryforward ($50,000 × .40)	20,000
Net Loss	$30,000

Succeeding year, assuming a pretax net operating profit of $80,000:

Income tax expense	32,000	
Receivable for tax refund (loss carryforward)		20,000
Income taxes payable		12,000

Income Statement:

Pretax operating income	$80,000
Less: Income tax expense	32,000
Net Income	$48,000

Alternative 2: Not reasonably certain—Do not recognize the tax carryforward in the period of the loss; report the tax saving in the future period(s) when realized as an extraordinary item (correction of prior period loss). To illustrate:

Year of loss: no entry.

Income Statement:

Pretax operating loss	$50,000
Income tax expense (loss carryforward)	-0-
Net Loss	$50,000

Succeeding year, assuming pretax operating income of $80,000:

Income tax expense	32,000	
Extraordinary item, tax loss carryforward		20,000
Income taxes payable		12,000

Income Statement:

Pretax operating income	$80,000
Less: Income tax expense	32,000
Income before extraordinary items	48,000
Extraordinary item:	
Tax carryforward	20,000
Net Income	$68,000

Selection of the appropriate alternative depends upon the circumstances. Clearly, in the absence of *uncertainty*, Alternative 1 is used. Since the tax saving in the succeeding year was due solely to the loss in Year 1, the benefit should be reflected in the loss period. Seldom is the degree of certainty sufficient to justify Alternative 1.

The APB in *Opinion No. 11* stated that Alternative 1 was appropriate only when realization is assured, viz:

> Realization of the tax benefit of a loss carry*forward* would appear to be assured beyond any reasonable doubt when both of the following conditions exist: *(a)* the loss results from an identifiable, isolated and nonrecurring cause and the company either has been continuously profitable over a long period or has suffered occasional losses which were more than offset by taxable income in subsequent years, and *(b)* future taxable income is virtually certain to be large enough to offset the loss carry*forward* and will occur soon enough to provide realization during the carry*forward* period.

Since Alternative 1 is appropriate *only* when realization of the tax benefit of the loss carry*forward* is assured beyond reasonable doubt, Alternative 2 must be utilized for all other circumstances.

QUESTIONS

PART A

1. In evaluating a balance sheet for their purposes, bankers consistently report that the liability section is the most important part. What is the primary reason for their position on this point?
2. Most liabilities are reported at their maturity amount. In general, when should liabilities, prior to due date, be reported at less than their maturity amount?
3. How is the "cost principle" involved in accounting for current liabilities?
4. Define current liabilities.
5. Differentiate between secured and unsecured liabilities. Explain proper reporting procedures for each.
6. How are dividends declared, but not yet paid, classified on the balance sheet? Explain.
7. What are deferred revenues? What is the basis for classifying them as current liabilities?
8. Define a long-term liability.
9. When goods or services are acquired and a long-term note is given that either *(a)* specifies no interest, or *(b)* specifies an unrealistically low interest rate, how should the note be measured?
10. Basically, what is the accounting definition of a contingency? Why is the concept important?
11. How does the accountant measure the seriousness of a contingency? In general, how does this affect the accounting and reporting of contingencies?
12. Explain why loss contingencies are accounted for and reported differently than a gain contingency.
13. Under what circumstances would you consider appropriation of retained earnings with respect to a loss contingency?

14. How would each of the following items be reported on the balance sheet? Justify doubtful items.

a. Cash dividends payable.
b. Bonds payable.
c. Accommodation endorsement.
d. Lawsuit pending.
e. Stock dividend issuable.
f. Estimated taxes payable.
g. Unearned rent revenue.
h. Deferred interest revenue.
i. Customer deposits on containers.
j. Current payment on bonds payable.
k. Accounts payable.
l. Loans from officers.
m. Accrued wages.
n. Deferred repairs.

PART B

15. Why is *(a)* interperiod, and *(b)* intraperiod tax allocation desirable?

16. In general terms, under what circumstances is income tax allocation appropriate on *(a)* an interperiod basis, and *(b)* an intraperiod basis?

17. Give four specific examples of *timing* differences. Under what circumstances is tax allocation required for each?

18. Interperiod income tax procedures are not appropriate when (check best answer):

a. An extraordinary loss will cause the amount of income tax expense to be less than the tax on ordinary net income.
b. An extraordinary gain will cause the amount of income tax expense to be greater than the tax on ordinary net income.
c. Differences between net income for tax purposes and financial reporting occur because tax laws and financial accounting principles do not concur on the items to be recognized as revenue and expense.
d. Differences between income for tax purposes and financial reporting occur because, even though financial accounting principles and tax laws concur on the items to be recognized as revenues and expenses, they do not concur on the timing of the recognition.

(AICPA adapted)

19. Briefly explain how deferred taxes should be reported on the financial statements.

20. Explain why interperiod tax allocation is both an accounting and reporting procedure, whereas intraperiod tax allocation is strictly a reporting procedure.

21. Explain the distinction between a loss carryback and a loss carryforward. In general, when does each apply?

22. Why is the accounting for a loss carryback different than for a loss carryforward?

EXERCISES

PART A: EXERCISES 1–11

Exercise 11–1

On September 1, 19A, B Company borrowed cash on a $4,000 note payable due in one year. Assume the going rate of interest was 9% per year on this type of note for this company. The accounting period ends December 31.

Required:

Complete a tabulation as follows (show computations):

	Assuming the Note Was—	
	Interest Bearing	*Noninterest Bearing*
a. Cash received (assuming interest is computed on the face amount of the note)	$____	$____
b. Cash paid at due date	$____	$____
c. Total interest paid (cash)	$____	$____
d. Interest expense in 19A	$____	$____
e. Interest expense in 19B	$____	$____
f. Amount of liability to report on balance sheet at December 31, 19A (including any accrued interest)	$____	$____
g. Effective rate of interest (%)	$____	$____

Exercise 11–2

For each of the following, indicate the balance sheet classifications and preferred title; include comments on doubtful items.

a. Accounts payable.
b. Deposits received from customer—trade.
c. Deferred interest revenue.
d. Accrued wages.
e. Accommodation endorsement.
f. Allowance for rearrangement costs.
g. Customer advances on orders received.
h. Sales taxes collected.
i. Bonds payable, one-third paid each year.
j. Advance on rent revenue.
k. Stock dividend declared.
l. Accrued property taxes.
m. Scrip dividends declared.
n. IOU to company president.
o. Accrued interest on note payable.
p. Prepaid interest revenue.
q. Cash dividends payable.

Exercise 11–3

The records of the Rayburn Corporation provided the following information at December 31, 19A:

a. Notes payable trade, short term (included a $4,000 note given on the purchase of equipment that cost $20,000; the assets were mortgaged in connection with the purchase)	$30,000
b. Bonds payable ($10,000 due each April 1)	80,000
c. Accounts payable (including $10,000 owed to the president of the company)	40,000
d. Accrued property taxes	1,000
e. Stock dividends issuable on March 1, 19B (at par value)	12,000
f. Cash dividends payable, payable March 1, 19B	20,000
g. Long-term note payable, maturity amount	15,000
h. Discount on the note (unamortized)	500

Required:

Assuming the fiscal year ends December 31, show how each of the above should be reported on the balance sheet at December 31, 19A.

Exercise 11–4

Stopper Company paid salaries for the month amounting to $60,000. Of this amount, $10,000 was received by employees who had already been paid $14,100 (F.I.C.A.). In addition to the $10,000, another $4,000 was paid to employees who had already been paid $4,200 (F.U.T.A.). Withholding taxes amounted to $5,000, and $1,200 was withheld for investment in company stock per an agreement with certain employees. Use the rates given in the chapter.

Required:

Give entries to record *(a)* the salary payment including the deductions, *(b)* the employer payroll costs, and *(c)* remittance of the taxes.

Exercise 11–5

Baker Company gives the general manager a bonus equal to 20% of net income after tax. The bonus is deductible for tax purposes. Assume an average tax rate of 40%. Net income prior to taxes and bonus was $80,000.

Required:

1. Compute the tax and the bonus.
2. Prove your computations.
3. Give entries to record the tax and the bonus.

Exercise 11–6

Blue Company has an agreement to pay the president a bonus of 10% of net income, after deducting federal income taxes and after deducting an amount equal to 6% on the invested capital. Invested capital amounted to $300,000. Income before deductions for bonus and income taxes was $50,000. The bonus is deductible for tax purposes; assume an average income tax rate of 25%.

Required:

1. Compute the bonus, tax, and net income after deducting both bonus and tax.
2. Prove the computations.

Exercise 11–7

On April 1, 19A, Garrison Company purchased a heavy machine for use in operations by paying $5,000 cash and signing a $24,000 (face amount) non-interest-bearing note due in two years (on March 31, 19C). The going rate of interest for Garrison on this type of note was 8½% payable annually. The company uses straight-line depreciation. The accounting period ends on December 31. Assume a five-year life for the machine and no residual value. The present value of 1 for 2 periods at 8½% is .849455.

Required:

1. Give the entries indicated on April 1, 19A, and December 31, 19A (assume straight-line amortization of the discount). Show computations of the cost of the machine.
2. Complete a tabulation as follows (show computations):
   a. Income Statement, 19A:

      Depreciation expense.. $________
      Interest expense .... $________

b. Balance Sheet, 19A:

Fixed asset—machine .... $______

Accumulated depreciation (disregard residual value).......... $______

Current liability—accrued interest .... $______

Note payable.......... $______

3. When should the interest method, rather than the straight-line method, be used to amortize the discount on the note?

Exercise 11–8

Stroble Company purchased a heavy-duty used truck (a fixed asset), on April 1, 19A, for $2,000 cash plus a $6,000, two-year note payable. The $6,000 face value was due on March 31, 19C, and specified 4% interest payable each March 31. Assume the going rate of interest for this type of debt for this company was 10%. The accounting period ends December 31.

Required:

1. Give the entry to record the purchase on April 1, 19A. Show computations.
2. Complete a tabulation as follows, include computations:
   a. Amount of cash interest payable each March 31 .... $______
   b. Total interest expense for the two-year period .... $______
   c. Amount of interest reported on income statement for 19A ...... $______
   d. Amount of liability reported on balance sheet at December 31, 19A (excluding accrued interest).......... $______
   e. Depreciation expense for 19A assuming straight-line, even months, no residual value, and a four-year life .... $______

Exercise 11–9

Davis Corporation sells a line of products that carry a three-year warranty against defects. Based on past experience, the estimated warranty costs related to dollar sales are: first year after sale—1% of sales; second year after sale—3% of sales; and third year after sale—5%. Sales and actual warranty expenditures for a three-year period were:

	Cash Sales	*Actual Warranty Expenditures*
19A	$ 90,000	$ 900
19B	110,000	4,100
19C	130,000	9,800

Required:

1. Give entries for the three years for the *(a)* sales, *(b)* estimated warranty costs, and *(c)* the actual expenditures.
2. What amount should be reported as a liability on the balance sheet at the end of each year?

Exercise 11–10

Local Grocery has initiated a promotion program whereby customers are given coupons redeemable in U.S. savings bonds. One coupon is issued for each dollar of sales. On the surrender of 750 coupons, one $25 savings bond (cost $18.75) is given. It is estimated that 20% of the coupons issued will never be presented for redemption. Sales for the first period were $400,000, and the number of coupons redeemed totaled 225,000. Sales for the second period were $440,000, and the number of coupons redeemed totaled 405,000. The savings bonds are acquired as needed.

Required:

Prepare journal entries relative to the premium cost for the two periods including closing entries. Show ending balances and computations.

Exercise 11–11

Sampson Company is preparing the annual financial statements at December 31, 19A. A customer fell on the escalator and has filed a lawsuit for $25,000 because of a claimed back injury. The lawyer employed by the company has carefully assessed all of the implications. If the suit is lost, the lawyer's opinion is that the $25,000 will be assessed by the court.

Required:

1. Assume the lawyer, the independent accountant, and the management have reluctantly concluded that it is probable that the suit will be successful. Show how this contingency should be reported on the financial statements for 19A. Also, give any entries that should be made in the accounts in 19A.
2. Assume instead that the conclusion is that it is reasonably possible that the company will be successful. In what way would your response to Requirement 1 be changed?

PART B: EXERCISES 12–17

Exercise 11–12

Income tax returns of Hill Corporation reflected the following:

	Years Ended Dec. 31		
	19A	19B	19C
Royalties	$ 50,000	$ 70,000	$ 40,000
Investments	30,000	10,000	20,000
Rent	60,000		
Total revenues	140,000	80,000	60,000
Deductible expenses	80,000	60,000	50,000
Taxable Income	$ 60,000	$ 20,000	$ 10,000

Assume the average income tax rate for each year was 40%.

The only differences between taxable income on the tax returns and the pretax accounting income relate to rent. On the tax return, the $60,000 rent collected October 1, 19A, relating to a 24-month period ending September 30, 19C, must be included in 19A taxable income. For accounting purposes, this rent revenue was recognized ratably over the period it covered.

Required:

1. Prepare income statements for each year reflecting tax allocation.

2. Give journal entries such as would appear at the end of each year to reflect income tax accrual and allocation.

Exercise 11–13

Jackson Retailers, Inc., would have had identical net income before taxes on both its income tax returns and income statements for the years 19A through 19D were it not for the fact that for tax purposes fixed assets that cost $120,000 were depreciated by the sum-of-the-years'-digits method, whereas for accounting purposes, the straight-line method was used. These fixed assets have a four-year estimated life and zero residual value. Excess of revenue over expenses other than depreciation and income taxes for the years concerned were as follows:

	19A	*19B*	*19C*	*19D*
Pretax accounting income (excluding depreciation)..............	$60,000	$80,000	$70,000	$70,000

Assume the average income tax rate for each year was 40%.

Required:

1. Prepare a partial income statement for each year to reflect tax allocation.
2. Give journal entries at the end of each year to record income taxes.

Exercise 11–14

The actual tax liability of Z Corporation for each of three years was as follows: 19A, $60,000; 19B, $40,000; and 19C, $30,000.

Due to differences in timing of reporting of income for accounting purposes and tax purposes, the following variations existed in these three years:

19A – Pretax accounting income exceeded taxable income by $10,000.
19B – Taxable income exceeded pretax accounting income by 8,000.
19C – Pretax accounting income exceeded taxable income by 15,000.

Required:

Assuming these are timing differences, prepare the journal entry to record income taxes each year assuming an average tax rate of 40%.

Exercise 11–15

The pretax income statements for R Corporation for two years (summarized) were:

	19A	*19B*
Revenues	$180,000	$200,000
Expenses	150,000	165,000
Pretax income..............	$ 30,000	$ 35,000

For tax purposes, the following differences existed:

a. An expense of $10,000 on above income statement for 19B will never be deductible for income tax purposes (it was goodwill amortization).
b. A revenue of $6,000 reported on the above income statement for 19B is taxable in 19A (it was unearned rent revenue).

c. An expense of $8,000 on the above income statement for 19A is not deductible for income tax purposes until 19B (it was estimated warranty costs).

Required:

1. Compute *(a)* income tax expense, and *(b)* income taxes payable for each period. Assume an average tax rate of 40%.
2. Give the entry to record income taxes for each period.
3. Recast the above income statements to include income taxes as allocated.

Exercise 11–16

Larson Corporation reported pretax operating profit in 19A amounting to $80,000, the first year of operations. In 19B, the corporation experienced a $60,000 pretax operating loss. Assume an average income tax rate of 45%.

Required:

1. Compute the income tax consequences for each year.
2. Show how the tax consequences for each year would be reflected in the income statements for each year.
3. Give appropriate entries to record income tax effects for each year.

Exercise 11–17

Wells Corporation experienced a $100,000 pretax operating loss for 19A, the first year of operations. Assume an average 40% tax rate.

Required:

1. Assume the loss resulted from an identifiable cause and that future taxable income over the next five years is virtually certain to be sufficient to offset the loss.
   a. Give entry and a partial income statement for 19A to reflect appropriate tax allocation consequences.
   b. Assume it is now the end of 19B and that a pretax operating profit in 19B is reported amounting to $150,000. Give entry and a partial income statement for 19B to reflect appropriate tax allocation consequences.
2. Assume that at the time of the loss there was no realistic basis to conclude that profits in the next five years would be sufficient to absorb the loss.
   a. Give entry and a partial income statement for 19A to reflect appropriate tax allocation consequences.
   b. Assume pretax operating incomes, following the year of loss, as follows: 19B, break even; 19C, $40,000; and 19D, $90,000. Give entry and a partial income statement for each of these three years to reflect appropriate tax allocation consequences.

PROBLEMS

PART A: PROBLEMS 1–11

Problem 11–1

For each of the situations below indicate (1) correct title, (2) the correct balance sheet classification, (3) the amount to report, and (4) comment on classification. (Suggestion: Set up four columns for your response.)

a. Accounts payable (including $2,000 owed to the company president)	$30,000
b. Trade notes payable (including $9,000 for equipment note)	29,000
c. Long-term note payable (secured by stock in X Company)	10,000
d. Cash dividends payable	12,000
e. Deposits by customers	4,000
f. Prepaid rent revenue	3,000
g. Premium on bonds payable	2,800
h. Bonds payable (annual payment $30,000)	90,000
i. Deferred repairs	1,000
j. Prepaid lease revenue	2,000
k. Estimated taxes payable	7,000
l. Reserve for future contingencies	15,000
m. Estimated future warranty liability	4,500
n. Accommodation endorsement	2,000

Problem 11–2

Mason Corporation borrowed cash on August 1, 19A, and signed a $12,000 (face amount), one year, note payable, due on July 31, 19B. The accounting period ends December 31. Assume a going rate of interest of 10% for this company for this type of borrowing. Assume the interest rate is applied to the face amount of the note.

Required:

1. How much cash would Mason receive on the note assuming: Case A, an interest-bearing note; and, Case B, a noninterest-bearing note. What would be the effective rate of interest in each case? Show computations.
2. Give the following entries for each case:
   a. August 1, 19A, date of the loan.
   b. December 31, 19A, adjusting entry.
   c. July 31, 19B, payment of the note.
3. What liability amounts should be shown in each case on the December 31, 19A, balance sheet?
4. Compute the cash proceeds assuming the 10% interest rate is applied to the cash proceeds.

Problem 11–3

On October 1, 19A, Wilson Company borrowed cash and signed a $27,000, 10%, one-year note payable, due on September 30, 19B. The accounting period ends on December 31.

Required:

1. Compute the amount of cash received on the note assuming (show computations):

   Case A – An interest-bearing note.
   Case B – A noninterest-bearing note, and the interest is based on the face amount of the note.

2. Give entries indicated for each case at October 1, 19A, December 31, 19A, and September 30, 19B.

3. Complete a tabulation as follows:

	Case A Interest Bearing	Case B Noninterest Bearing
a. Total cash received	$_____	$_____
b. Total cash paid	$_____	$_____
c. Total interest paid	$_____	$_____
d. Interest expense in 19A	$_____	$_____
e. Interest expense in 19B	$_____	$_____
f. Liability amounts on balance sheet, December 31, 19A:		
(1) Note	$_____	$_____
(2) Accrued interest	$_____	$_____
g. Effective rate of interest (%)	_____	_____

4. What would the cash received have been assuming the interest is based on the cash proceeds?

Problem 11–4

Thomas Corporation was formed for the purpose of constructing buildings. The first contract involved the construction of an office building. Since the corporation was short of ready cash, an agreement was made with the supervising engineer whereby compensation would be a share of the profits. The agreement provided that the supervising engineer would receive 20% of the profits on the contract after providing for federal income tax and after deducting the bonus.

Upon completion of the construction, the records of the corporation showed the following:

Income before tax and before payment to the supervising engineer (assume a 40% tax rate)	$450,000
Costs already deducted from the net income, not allowable as deductions in computing income taxes but allowed as a deduction before computing the profit to be paid the supervising engineer	10,000

Assume the compensation to the supervising engineer is deductible for income tax purposes.

Required:

1. Compute the amount of the compensation to the supervising engineer and the income taxes assuming the compensation is an expense in determining the basis for the compensation. Show proof of computations.
2. Give entries to record the compensation and taxes.

Problem 11–5

For the purpose of stimulating sales, Black Coffee Company places a coupon in each can of coffee sold, the coupons being redeemable in chinaware. Each premium costs the company $.80. Ten coupons must be presented by the customers to receive one premium. The following data are available:

Month	Cans of Coffee Sold	Premiums Purchased	Coupons Redeemed
January	650,000	25,000	220,000
February...............	500,000	40,000	410,000
March	560,000	35,000	300,000

It is estimated that only 70% of the coupons will be presented for redemption.

Required:

Compute the amount of the premium inventory, liability for premiums outstanding, and premium expense at the end of each month and give the related entries. *Hint:* Set up parallel columns for each period.

Problem 11–6

Crunch Cereal Company gives a premium costing $.50 each for "five box tops received plus $.15 mailing costs." Actual mailing costs average $.10 per premium. Data covering three periods are as follows:

	Period		
	First	Second	Third
Premiums purchased	15,000	25,000	24,000
Tops redeemed for premiums	50,000	100,000	120,000
Boxes of cereal sold at $.80 per box...	220,000	250,000	280,000

It is estimated that 60% of the tops distributed will never be returned.

Required:

1. Give entries for each period to record sales, premium purchases, redemptions, adjustments, and closing entries. *Hint:* Set up parallel columns for the three periods.
2. Indicate how premiums and any related liabilities would be reported on the balance sheet at the end of each period.

Problem 11–7

The following transactions were completed during the year (19A) just ended by Kelso Corporation:

a. Bonds payable dated February 1 with a maturity value of $100,000 were sold at par plus three months accrued interest on May 1. The bonds mature in ten years and bear 6% interest per annum payable on December 31.

b. Merchandise purchased on account amounted to $400,000. Cash payments were $340,000, a $3,000 one-year, 9% interest-bearing note, dated September 1, given to one creditor. Accounts carried over from the preceding year were $30,000.

c. Cosigned a $5,000 note payable for another party.

d. On June 1, the company borrowed cash and a $10,000, one-year, noninterest-bearing note was signed. Assume a going rate of interest of 9% and that interest is based on the face amount of the note.

e. Payroll records showed the following (assume amounts given are correct):

	Employee			Employer		
Gross Wages	With-holding	F.I.C.A.	Union Dues	F.I.C.A.	F.U.T.A. State	F.U.T.A. Federal
$30,000.........	$2,500	$500	$300	$500	$480	$50
20,000.........	1,800	470	200	470	450	45

Remittances were: union, $280; withholding taxes, $4,000; F.I.C.A., $1,900; F.U.T.A.–state, $750; and F.U.T.A.–federal, $95.

f. The company was sued for $25,000 damages. It appears a judgment against the company of about $10,000 is probable.

g. The company accrued $250 per month for "special repairs." At the end of the year only $2,000 had been spent for this purpose. It was decided to put off certain repairs until January, although they were definitely scheduled for December. The basic reason was that certain parts, although purchased, had not arrived by year-end.

h. Cash dividends declared, but not paid, $14,000.

i. On December 31, accrued interest on the bonds.

j. Accrue interest on notes.

Required:

1. Give the entry or entries for each of the above items.
2. Prepare a list (title and amount) of the resulting liabilities at December 31, 19A, assuming it is the end of the period. For each liability, indicate its appropriate classification on the balance sheet. *Hint:* Set up tabulations with three columns: title, amount, and classification.

Problem 11–8

Handy Appliance Company provides a product warranty for defects on two lines of items sold. Line A carries a two-year warranty for all labor and service (but not parts). The company contracts with a local service establishment to provide the requirements of the warranty. The local service establishment charges a flat fee of $50 per unit payable at date of sale.

Line B carries a three-year warranty for labor and parts on service. Handy purchases the parts needed under the warranty and has service personnel who perform the work. On the basis of past experience, it is estimated that for Line B, the three-year warranty costs are 3% of dollar sales for parts and 7% for labor and overhead. Additional data available are:

	Period		
	1	2	3
Sales in units, Line A	700	1,000	
Sales price per unit, Line A	$ 610	$ 660	
Sales in units, Line B	600	800	
Sales price per unit, Line B	$ 700	$ 750	
Actual warranty costs on Line B:			
Parts..	$3,000	$ 9,600	$12,000
Labor and overhead..............................	$7,000	$22,000	$30,000

Required:

1. Give entries for period sales and costs identified by product. *Hint:* Set up parallel columns for the three periods.

2. Complete a tabulation as follows:

	Year End Amounts		
	Period 1	Period 2	Period 3
a. Warranty expense (on the income statement)	$______	$______	$______
b. Estimated warranty liability (on the balance sheet)	$______	$______	$______

Problem 11–9

On September 1, 19A, Robbins Company acquired a badly needed machine (a fixed asset) by paying $5,000 cash and signing a two-year note that carried a face amount of $15,000 due at the end of the two years; the note did not specify interest. Assume the going rate of interest for this company for this type of loan was 8%. The accounting period ends December 31. Base interest calculations on the face of the note.

Required:

1. Give entries on September 1 and December 31, 19A, under *(a)* straight-line amortization of discount, and *(b)* the interest method of amortization.
2. Complete a tabulation as follows and show computations:

	Straight-Line Method	Interest Method
a. Cash paid at maturity	$______	$______
b. Total interest expense	$______	$______
c. Interest expense on income statement for 19A	$______	$______
d. Amount of the liability reported on balance sheet at end of 19A	$______	$______
e. Depreciation expense for 19A (assume straight-line, even months, no residual value, and a useful life of four years)	$______	$______

Problem 11–10

On August 1, 19A, Massie Company purchased a large used machine for operations. Payment was made by cash $6,000 and a $30,000 (face amount), two-year note payable (due on July 31, 19C). The note did not specify interest; however, for Massie, the going rate for this type of transaction was 8½%. Assume straight-line depreciation, a five-year life, and no residual value. The accounting period ends on December 31. The present value of 1 for two periods at 8½% is .84945.

Required:

1. Compute the cost of the machine.
2. Give entries indicated on August 1, 19A, and December 31, 19A. Assume straight-line amortization of note discount.
3. What items and amounts should be reported on the income statement and balance sheet for 19A (include the machine and depreciation).
4. Prepare an amortization schedule for the note assuming the interest method is used.
5. When should the interest method, rather than the straight-line method, be used to amortize the discount for the note?

Problem 11–11

Dollins Company is preparing the annual financial statements at December 31, 19A, and is concerned about application of FASB *Statement No. 5*, "Accounting for Contingencies." Four particular situations are under consideration, viz:

1. The company owns a small plant in a foreign country that has a book value of $3,000,000 and an estimated fair market value of $4,000,000. The foreign government has clearly indicated its intention to expropriate the plant during the coming year and to reimburse Dollins for 50% of the estimated fair market value.
2. An outside party has filed a claim against Dollins for $25,000 claiming that certain actions by Dollins caused them to lose a contract on which the estimated profit was this amount. In the opinion of the attorney hired by Dollins, the probability of the claim being successful is remote. They do not believe it will ever be brought to trial. If necessary, Dollins will defend itself in court.
3. During 19B, a third party (a potential customer) sued Dollins for $150,000 for a claimed injury that occurred on the premises owned by Dollins. No date for the trial has been set; however, the lawyer employed by Dollins has completed a thorough investigation. Although it can be proven that the third party did fall on the premises, the company lawyer believes it will be difficult for the plaintiff to prove injury and there is evidence that it was due to negligence by the plaintiff. Therefore, the attorney believes that it is not probable although it is reasonably possible that the suit will be successful (i.e., for the plaintiff).
4. Dollins had a $10,000, 8%, one-year note receivable from a customer. Dollins discounted the note, with recourse, at the bank to obtain cash before its due date (due on June 1, 19B). If the maker does not pay the bank on the note by due date, Dollins will have to pay it. The customer has an excellent credit rating (having never defaulted on a debt).

Required:

For each situation, respond to the following:

a. What accounting recognition (i.e., journal entries), if any, should be accorded each situation at the end of 19A? Explain why.
b. What should be reported on the income statement, balance sheet, and by footnote in each situation? Explain why.

PART B: PROBLEMS 12–18

Problem 11–12

Speedy Construction Company has contracts for construction of three major projects. The percentage-of-completion method of accounting is used for accounting purposes while the completed contract method is used for the income tax returns. Data pertaining to these contracts are as follows:

	Year			*Percentage Completion*			
Project	*Started*	*Completed*	*Total Profit*	*19A*	*19B*	*19C*	*19D*
A	19A	19C	$ 70,000	40%	50%	10%	
B	19B	19C	90,000		20	80	
C	19B	19D	100,000		10	70	20%

Required:

1. For each year, compute (*a*) income tax expense, and (*b*) income taxes payable; assume an average tax rate of 45%.
2. Give the entry to record income taxes for each year.
3. Complete a tabulation as follows:

	19A	*19B*	*19C*	*19D*
Income Statement:				
Pretax income	$______	$______	$______	$______
Income taxes	$______	$______	$______	$______
Net income.................	$______	$______	$______	$______
Balance Sheet:				
Income taxes payable ...	$______	$______	$______	$______
Deferred taxes (credit)...	$______	$______	$______	$______

Problem 11–13

Parson Company financial statements for a four-year period reflected the following pretax amounts:

	19A	*19B*	*19C*	*19D*
Income Statement (summarized):				
Revenues..............................	$120,000	$130,000	$140,000	$160,000
Expenses..............................	(90,000)	(92,000)	(95,000)	(108,000)
Depreciation (straight line)	?	?	?	?
Pretax income	$?	$?	$?	$?
Balance Sheet (partial):				
Machine (four-year life, no residual value)	$ 40,000	$ 40,000	$ 40,000	$ 40,000
Income taxes payable	?	?	?	?
Deferred taxes	?	?	?	?

The company has an average tax rate of 40% and uses sum-of-the-years'-digits depreciation (no residual value) on the income tax return (for problem purposes, assume this method is acceptable for tax purposes in this situation) and straight line for accounting purposes.

Required:

1. Complete the above income statements incorporating income taxes appropriately allocated.
2. Compute income taxes payable for each year.
3. Give the entry for each year to record income taxes. Prove the deferred tax amount for each year.
4. Explain why tax allocation provides better financial statement amounts in this situation.

Problem 11–14

Uvalde Company financial statements for a three-year period reflected the following pretax amounts:

	19A	19B	19C
Income Statement (summarized):			
Revenues	$190,000	$200,000	$215,000
Expenses	(130,000)	(148,000)	(160,000)
Depreciation expense (straight line)	?	?	?
Income before extraordinary items	?	?	?
Extraordinary items, pretax (loss)	(20,000)		6,000
Net Income, Pretax	$?	$?	$?
Statement of Retained Earnings (partial):			
Prior period adjustment, pretax (loss)			(30,000)
Balance Sheet (partial):			
Machine (three-year life, no residual value)	$ 60,000	$ 60,000	$ 60,000
Income taxes payable	?	?	?
Deferred taxes	?	?	?

Assume a 40% average tax rate on all items and double-declining depreciation (no residual value) for tax purposes (for problem purposes, assume this method is acceptable in this situation for tax purposes).

Required:

1. Restate the above financial statement amounts incorporating income taxes appropriately allocated.
2. Compute taxes payable for each year.
3. Give the entry each year to record income taxes. Prove the deferred tax amounts.
4. Explain why tax allocation derives better financial statement amounts in this situation.

Problem 11–15

Assume the following data for X Corporation are available for a two-year period:

	19A	19B
Operating income, pretax	$100,000	$120,000
Extraordinary losses, pretax	(15,000)	(17,000)
Prior period adjustment, gains, pretax	7,000	8,000
Timing differences included in above amounts:		
a. Revenue on income statement, taxable following period	5,000	
b. Revenue on tax return, on income statement following period	7,000	
c. Expense on income statement, taxable following period	9,000	
d. Expense on tax return, on income statement following period	6,000	
e. Extraordinary loss on income statement, taxable following period	10,000	
f. Prior period gain on statement of retained earnings, taxable next period	4,000	

Assume an average income tax rate of 40% on all items.

Required:

1. Compute income tax expense for each year that should be reflected on the income statement. Show operating income, extraordinary items, and prior period adjustments separately.
2. Compute income taxes payable for each year that should be reflected on the tax return. Show operating income, extraordinary items, and prior period adjustments separately.
3. Give the entry to record income taxes for each year.
4. Prepare a partial income statement and partial statement of retained earnings for each year to show how income tax expense should be reported. Include both interperiod and intraperiod allocation.

Problem 11–16

Noonan Corporation pretax income statements for the first two years of operations reflected the following summarized amounts:

	19A	*19B*
Revenues	$250,000	$280,000
Expenses	220,000	285,000
Pretax Income (Loss)	$ 30,000	$ (5,000)

Assume an average tax rate of 30%.

Required:

1. Restate the income statements incorporating income tax effects and give the entries for each year in respect to income taxes. Show computations.
2. Assume the loss in year 19B was $35,000 instead of $5,000. Restate the income statements incorporating income tax effects and give the entries for each year in respect to income taxes. Explain the basis for your response. Show computations.

Problem 11–17

Petty Corporation pretax financial statements for the first two years of operations reflected the following amounts:

	19A	*19B*
Revenues	$300,000	$330,000
Expenses	320,000	315,000
Pretax Income (Loss)	$ (20,000)	$ 15,000

Assume an average tax rate of 40%.

Required:

1. Assume future income during the next five years is unpredictable (i.e., uncertain):
   a. Restate the above financial statements incorporating the income tax effects appropriately allocated. Show computations.
   b. Give entries to record the income tax effects for each year. Explain the basis for your entries.

2. Assume future income is reasonably certain during the next five years. Complete Requirements 1 *(a)* and *(b)* above.

Problem 11–18

Young Corporation's pretax financial statements for the first four years of operations reflected the following pretax amounts:

	19A	*19B*	*19C*	*19D*
Income Statement (summarized):				
Revenue	$125,000	$155,000	$180,000	$230,000
Expenses	120,000	195,000	170,000	200,000
Pretax Income (Loss)	$ 5,000	$ (40,000)	$ 10,000	$ 30,000

Assume an average income tax rate of 30% and that future incomes are uncertain at the end of each year.

Required:

1. Recast the above statement to incorporate the income tax effects appropriately allocated. Show computations.
2. Give entries to record the income tax effects for each year.

Chapter 12

Operational Assets: Property, Plant, and Equipment — Acquisition, Use, and Retirement

This chapter and the next two chapters focus on a broad category of assets that may be thought of as operational assets because they are used in the operations of the business and are not held for resale. Operational assets, also referred to as fixed assets, may be classified as follows for accounting purposes:

1. Tangible property, plant, and equipment—These operational assets are variously described by the terms *property, plant, and equipment; plant assets; capital assets;* or *tangible fixed assets*. The three classes of this group of assets are:
   a. Those subject to depreciation such as buildings, equipment, tools, and furniture.
   b. Those subject to depletion such as mineral deposits and timber tracts.
   c. Those not subject to depreciation or depletion such as land for plant site, farms, and ranches.
2. Intangibles—Those assets properly classified as fixed assets having no bodily substance; the value is represented by grants and business rights which confer some operating, financial, or income-producing advantages on the owner. They are amortized over their useful life in a manner that accords with the expiration of their economic value to the enterprise.

This chapter discusses property, plant, and equipment; Chapter 13 considers depreciation and depletion; and Chapter 14 focuses on intangibles.

Tangible property, plant, and equipment has five major characteristics: (1) actively used in operations, (2) not held as an investment or for resale, (3) relatively long lived, (4) have physical substance, and (5) provide measurable future benefits to the entity.

CAPITAL AND REVENUE EXPENDITURES

Accounting for expenditures and obligations incident to the acquirement of property, plant, and equipment (tangible or intangible) necessitates classification of such outlays as either *capital expenditures* or as *revenue expenditures*. Capital expenditures relate to the acquirement of an asset, the benefit of which extends over one or more accounting periods beyond the current period; hence, they are recorded in appropriate asset accounts. Capital expenditures made for assets having a limited life are subsequently allocated to the periods benefitted through depreciation, amortization, or depletion. An expenditure that is debited to an asset account or to accumulated depreciation is said to be capitalized.

Revenue expenditures relate to the acquirement of property or benefits that do not extend beyond the current accounting period; hence, they are recorded in appropriate expense accounts for the current period.

In cases where *(a)* a capital expenditure is relatively small, or *(b)* the future benefit is insignificant, or *(c)* reasonable measurement of the future benefit is practically impossible, practical reasons suggest classification of the outlay as a revenue expenditure. Many companies have adopted a practical accounting policy in this respect to the effect that, for example, "expenditures under $50 will be classed as revenue expenditures; expenditures above this amount will be classified as capital expenditures only where there is clearly a significant and measurable benefit accruing to a future period."

PRINCIPLES UNDERLYING ACCOUNTING FOR PROPERTY, PLANT, AND EQUIPMENT

The accounting for property, plant, and equipment fundamentally rests on the *cost and matching principles*. At date of acquisition, these assets are recorded in the accounts at cost. The acquisition cost of these assets is measured by the cash outlay made to acquire such assets; or if considerations other than cash are exchanged for the assets, the fair market value of such consideration at the time of the transaction is the measure of the cost of the assets so acquired. In the absence of a determinable fair market value for the consideration given, the asset is recorded at its fair market value. An asset is not "acquired" until it has been placed in the position where it is to be used and is ready for productivity in the broad business sense; thus all reasonable and legitimate costs incurred in placing an asset in this status are additions to the cost of the asset.

Subsequent to acquisition, items of property, plant, and equipment are carried in the accounts and reported at *(a)* cost (if unlimited life) or (*b*) in the case of a limited life, at cost less accumulated depreciation, amortization, or depletion (reflecting continuing application of the matching principle.)

The following is an outline of the principal aspects influencing the accounting for property, plant, and equipment:

1. Acquisition cost of property, plant, and equipment when acquired:
   a. For cash.
   b. On a deferred payment plan.
   c. For stock or other securities.
   d. Through exchanges.
   e. Through mixed acquisitions at a lump cost.
2. Outlays subsequent to acquisition but before operational use:
   a. Installation costs.
   b. Reinstallation costs.
   c. Repairs and improvements prior to use.
   d. Razing old structures.
   e. Other incidental costs.
3. Assets constructed for own use.
4. Interest during the construction period.
5. Outlays subsequent to the beginning of operational use:
   a. Repairs and maintenance.
   b. Replacements and renewals.
   c. Betterments and improvements.
   d. Additions.
   e. Rearrangements of assets.

At this point we note that in accounting for these assets there are special circumstances where departure from the cost principle has been sanctioned by the accounting profession. These exceptions are discussed subsequently in this chapter.

ASSETS ACQUIRED FOR CASH

If an operational asset is purchased for cash, any outlay that a prudent buyer would make for the asset in an arm's-length transaction, including costs of installation and making ready to use, should be capitalized. The capitalizable costs include the invoice price (less discounts), plus incidental costs such as insurance during transit, freight, duties, ownership searching, ownership registration, installation, and breaking-in costs. All available discounts, *whether taken or not*, should be deducted from the invoice cost. Discounts not taken should be recorded as discounts lost and treated as a current financial expense.

ASSETS ACQUIRED ON DEFERRED PAYMENT PLAN

Assets acquired on a deferred or long-term payment plan (on credit) should be recorded at the cash equivalent price excluding all interest and financing charges. Actual and implied interest and other finance charges should be charged to financing expense and not to the fixed asset account. If the contract of purchase does not specify interest and financing charges, such charges, nevertheless, should be deducted in determining the cost of the asset. If a current cash price for the asset is determinable, the excess charged under the deferred payment contract should be treated as expense apportioned over the period covered by the purchase contract. If no cash price is determinable for the asset, a realistic interest charge should be recognized in recording the purchase. Although sound in theory these latter distinctions are not always observed in practice, since the amounts involved may not be *material*.

To illustrate the purchase of an asset on credit, assume a machine was purchased under a contract that required equal payments of $3,951 at the end of each of three years when the going interest rate was 9% per annum. To record the asset purchased at $11,853 (i.e., $3,951 × 3) would include in the asset account the interest cost implicit in the contract. Rather the asset account should be debited for the *present value* of the three payments discounted at 9% as follows:

$$\begin{aligned} PV &= \text{Annual Payment} \times P \text{ (Table 6–4)} \\ &= \$3{,}951 \times 2.53129 \text{ (present value of annuity of 1 at 9\% for 3 periods)} \\ &= \$10{,}000 \text{ (rounded)} \end{aligned}$$

Therefore, the indicated entries are as follows.

At date of purchase:[1]

Asset – machinery	10,000	
Installments payable – machinery contract		10,000

At payment dates (amounts rounded):

	1st Year		2d Year		3d Year	
Interest expense	900		625		328	
Installments payable – machinery contract	3,051		3,326		3,623	
Cash		3,951		3,951		3,951

A table of debt amortization and interest expense follows (see Chapters 6 and 11):

---

[1] Alternatively this entry could be made as follows:

Asset – machinery	10,000	
Deferred interest cost	1,853	
Installments payable – machinery contract		11,853

The payment entries would be revised accordingly; the net effect would be the same in all respects. The first payment entry would be:

Interest expense	900	
Installments payable – machinery contract	3,951	
Deferred interest cost		900
Cash		3,951

Period	Annual Payment (cash credit)	Interest Expense (debit)		Payment on Liability (debit)	Unpaid Principal
Start............					$10,000
1...............	$ 3,951	$10,000 × 9%	$ 900	$ 3,051	6,949
2...............	3,951	6,949 × 9%	625	3,326	3,623
3...............	3,951	3,623 × 9%	328	3,623*	-0-
	$11,853		$1,853	$10,000	

* Rounding error $2.

ASSETS ACQUIRED IN EXCHANGE FOR SECURITIES

The proper valuation of operational assets received in exchange for bonds and stocks of the acquiring company frequently is difficult to determine for numerous reasons, some of which are:

1. There may be no readily determinable fair market value for the securities or the assets involved.
2. The absence of an arm's-length bargaining with respect to the exchange.
3. The nature of the assets generally involved, such as unexplored or unproven mineral deposits, manufacturing rights, patents, chemical formulas, mining claims, and the like, may make value estimates difficult.
4. The current quoted market price of the security may be based upon a market volume far below the volume of shares involved in the exchange (i.e., a thin market).
5. The vagaries of the stock market, involving as it does wide fluctuations in stock prices over short periods of time, generally casts significant doubt on the relevance of the price per share at a specific time.

The general principle is that assets acquired should be recorded at their then current cash equivalent cost. Lacking this amount, the cost of assets acquired through exchange of securities should be measured as follows:

1. Determine the current fair market value of the consideration given, that is, the securities. Where the securities have an established market price, it should be used assuming there are sound reasons for the presumption that the current price is indicative that the market would absorb the volume of securities involved at that price.
2. If the fair market value of the securities in the volume exchanged cannot be determined, the current fair market value of the assets acquired should be estimated. In the absence of an actual cash-basis sale of the assets involved in the immediate past, an independent appraisal of them by a professionally recognized appraiser may be recorded as the cost of the assets acquired.
3. If a fair market value for either the securities or the assets received cannot be determined objectively, values established by the directors

of the corporation may be used. The law generally allows the directors considerable discretion in establishing values in this situation, except in cases where fraudulent intent on the part of the directors can be shown.

When assets are acquired by exchange of securities, any actual or implied discounts or premiums on the securities should be accounted for in the normal manner. Since bonds have a definite and legally enforceable maturity value and interest charge, problems of valuation of assets received in exchange for them generally are not as critical as in the case where capital stock is involved. Assets acquired in exchange for bonds payable should be recorded at the current cash value of the bonds. If there is no currently established market price for the bonds, the cost of the asset can be computed as the *present value* of the bond principal plus the present value of the interest payments, at the going rate of interest (see Chapters 6 and 19).

Operational assets acquired for cash *and* securities combined should be capitalized at the sum of the cash, and the fair market value of the securities determined in accordance with the standards discussed above. When property is financed through notes, care should be taken so that financing expenses are not charged as a part of the cost of the fixed asset.

ASSETS ACQUIRED THROUGH EXCHANGES

Items of property, plant, and equipment frequently are acquired by trading in an old asset in full, or part payment, for another asset. In some transactions, there is an exchange of two or more noncash assets; in other cases, an asset is acquired by exchanging another asset plus a payment or receipt of cash (often referred to as boot). Prior to the issuance of *APB Opinion No. 29*, "Accounting for Nonmonetary Transactions," (effective September 30, 1973), exchanges were recorded by debiting the asset account for the item acquired at either (1) its quoted list price, (2) the cash paid plus the book value of the old asset exchanged, or (3) at its current fair market value. These three alternatives were widely used in financial accounting.

APB Opinion No. 29 specifies the accounting approach for a wide range of nonmonetary transactions, including those involving the acquisition of operational assets through exchanges. The basic principle established in the *Opinion* is:

> Accounting for nonmonetary transactions should be based on the fair values of the assets (or services) involved which is the same as that used in monetary transactions. This is a *fair market value concept* because realization is assumed to have occurred (i.e., a purchase/sales transaction).

Thus, under the basic principle, the cost of an operational asset acquired in exchange for another nonmonetary asset is the fair market value of the asset surrendered to obtain it, and a gain or loss on the disposition of the old asset should be recognized in accounting for the exchange. The fair market value of the asset acquired should be used to measure its cost only if it is more clearly determinable than the fair market value of the asset surrendered. However, the *Opinion* specifies several exceptions to the basic principle and also covers exchanges where cash (i.e., boot) is paid or received in the exchange.

Similar versus Dissimilar Assets

In respect to the exchange of operational assets, the *Opinion* specifies that the accounting will depend on whether the assets exchanged are *similar* or *dissimilar*. Similar productive assets are defined as "assets that are of the same general type, that perform the same function, or that are employed in the same line of business." All other productive assets would be classified as dissimilar. For example, the trading in of an old truck on a new truck would involve similar assets; however, the trading in of a tract of land on a new truck would involve dissimilar assets.

Accounting Procedures for Exchanges

In exchanges of dissimilar assets, whether or not there is a cash difference (boot) paid or received, both parties record the transaction on a *fair market value* basis. Fair market value, when there is no cash difference, is the fair market value of the asset surrendered (if this is not determinable the fair market value of the asset received is used). When there is a cash difference, fair market value is the cash paid plus the fair market value of the asset surrendered. If the latter is not determinable the fair market value of the asset received is used.

In contrast, when similar assets are exchanged, and no cash difference (boot) is paid or received, both parties reflect a *book value* basis. When a cash difference is received or paid, and the assets are similar, the latter guideline is altered as illustrated in *(c)* below. Therefore, the accounting prescribed by the *Opinion* for the exchange of similar and dissimilar operational assets is as follows:

1. Dissimilar assets—Use the fair market value concept; record the asset acquired at the fair market value of the asset surrendered and recognize a gain or loss on the old asset.

   Example: Company A has an old crane that cost $50,000; accumulated depreciation to date of $45,000 (i.e., a carrying value of $5,000). It is exchanged with Company B for a tract of land; cash boot of $12,000 was paid. The fair market value for the old crane is determined to be $13,000.

   To record the exchange by Company A:

Land ($13,000 + $12,000)	25,000	
Accumulated depreciation (old crane)	45,000	
Machinery—old crane		50,000
Cash		12,000
Gain on disposal of machinery*		8,000

* Fair market value recognized, $13,000 − book value, $5,000 = $8,000.

2. Similar assets—In this situation, a book value concept is prescribed by *APB Opinion No. 29* because it is assumed that nonmonetary exchange transactions are not essentially the culmination of an earnings process.

   The procedure for recording an exchange of similar assets depends on whether a monetary consideration (usually cash boot) was also paid or received in the exchange. Accounting for the three situations is prescribed as follows:

   a. Similar assets exchanged and *no* monetary consideration (boot) paid or received—the cost of the asset acquired is recorded at the carrying (book) value of the asset surrendered.

   Example: Company A exchanged an old crane that cost $50,000, accumulated depreciation to date, $45,000, for another much smaller crane having a current cash price of $8,000. No cash difference was paid or received by Company A in this exchange of similar assets. The exchange would be recorded as follows:

Machinery, new crane (at book value of old crane)......	5,000*	
Accumulated depreciation, old crane	45,000	
Machinery, old crane..		50,000

* Cannot exceed fair market value.

   b. Similar assets exchanged and a monetary consideration (boot) is paid—In this situation, the asset acquired is recorded at the sum of the cash paid plus the book value of the old asset surrendered. As in all cases, the asset acquired cannot be recorded at more than its current fair market value. Therefore, no gain can be recorded; however, if the fair market value of the asset received is less than the sum of the cash paid plus the book value of the old asset, a loss must be recorded.

   Example: Company A exchanged the old crane that cost $50,000, accumulated depreciation, $45,000, for the new smaller crane having a current cash price of $8,000, and *paid* $1,000 cash boot. The transaction would be recorded as follows:

Machinery, new crane ($1,000 + $5,000)....................	6,000	
Accumulated depreciation, old crane	45,000	
Machinery, old crane..		50,000
Cash		1,000

   c. Similar assets exchanged and a monetary consideration (boot) is received—In this situation, *APB Opinion No. 29* specifies that a gain shall be recognized on the asset given up "to the extent that the amount of the monetary receipt exceeds a proportionate share of the recorded amount of the asset surrendered." Thus, when a cash difference is *received,* the assumption is a part sale and a part exchange of the asset surrendered. In this case, a gain on that part sold for cash may be recognized. The asset acquired is recorded as a proportionate part of the book value of the asset surrendered. Thus, this transaction is treated in part at fair market value and in part at book value.

Example: Company A exchanged the old crane that cost $50,000, accumulated depreciation, $45,000, for a new smaller crane having a current cash price of $8,000, and *received* a cash difference of $2,000. The transaction would be recorded as follows:

Cash	2,000	
Machinery, new crane[1]	4,000	
Accumulated depreciation, old crane	45,000	
Machinery, old crane		50,000
Gain on disposal of old machinery[2]		1,000

Computations:

1. Cost of new crane—Book value of old crane less the proportion of book value sold:

Book value, old crane ($50,000 − $45,000)	$5,000
Proportion of book value sold for cash:	
Book value, old $\times \frac{\text{Cash}}{\text{Cash + FMV of asset acquired}}$	
$\$5{,}000 \times \frac{\$2{,}000}{\$2{,}000 + \$8{,}000} =$	1,000
Difference—cost of asset acquired	$4,000

2. Gain on disposal of asset surrendered—Cash received less portion sold of book value of asset surrendered:

Cash received	$2,000
Proportion of book value sold (per above)	1,000
Difference—gain on asset surrendered	$1,000

Alternatively, in case of a loss, the *Opinion* requires that the full amount of such loss be recognized. To illustrate, assume in the preceding example that the accumulated depreciation was $39,000. The transaction would be recorded as follows:

Cash	2,000	
Accumulated depreciation, old crane	39,000	
Loss on disposal of old machinery	1,000	
Machinery, new crane	8,000	
Machinery, old crane		50,000

Observe that the full loss is recognized because the asset acquired cannot be recorded in excess of its fair market value. Thus, there is no calculation of the proportionate part sold. A loss is reported because the book or carrying value of the asset is greater than its fair market value as reflected in the exchange transaction. Under generally accepted accounting principles, the carrying value of the asset is rarely greater than is fair market value.

The *Opinion* does not recognize the quoted list price as the cost of an operational asset in any situation unless that price is the actual cash equivalent price (current market value). List prices often are merely a basis for bargaining rather than a genuine cash cost. To determine fair value in exchanges of operational assets, *Opinion No. 29* states that fair values should be determined by referring to "quoted market prices, independent appraisals, estimated fair values of assets or services received in exchange and other available evidence."[2]

---

[2] Under generally accepted accounting principles, no asset, irrespective of its characteristics, should be recorded at acquisition at more than its then fair market value. This is the definition of cost under the cost principle.

DEPARTURES FROM COST IN ACCOUNTING FOR TANGIBLE ASSETS

Although accounting for assets fundamentally is based upon the cost principle, there are special circumstances where departure from that principle is sanctioned. These exceptions are:

1. Write-up to appraisal value above cost.
2. Write-up due to donation of assets to the company.
3. Write-up due to high and unexpected discovery value.
4. Write-down due to significant and permanent decrease in use value to the company.
5. Revaluations due to quasi-reorganization (discussed in Chapter 16).

Items 2, 3, and 4 are discussed in the paragraphs to follow.

DONATED ASSETS AND DISCOVERY VALUE

Donated Assets

Assets occasionally are donated to a corporation by stockholders for various reasons, and by municipalities, or local nonprofit organizations, as an inducement to locate a plant or other facilities in the area. Frequently, such gifts are conditional upon some particular performance on the part of the corporation such as the employment of a certain number of individuals by a given date.

Strict adherence to the cost principle would involve recording donated assets at the amount of incidental costs incurred in acceptance of the gift and in fulfilling the related agreements. Accountability for the resources of an enterprise and measurement of enterprise earning power require that every economic facility employed, regardless of origin, be entered on the books at acquisition at the current cash equivalent price or some other equivalent value. In the case of donated assets, an independent and realistic appraisal of the current market value of the donated asset should be recorded, provided the donation is unconditional. Should the donor impose restrictions, however, any "negative values" arising from such conditions should be considered in determination of the valuation to be recorded. *APB Opinion No. 29* states that "a nonmonetary asset received in a *nonreciprocal transfer* should be recorded at the fair market value of the asset received." A donated asset would represent a nonreciprocal (one-way) transfer. To illustrate, assume a building, including the land on which it is located, is given by a city to the XYZ Corporation as an inducement to establish a plant therein. The related transactions may be recorded as follows:[3]

1. To record the fair market value, per appraisal at date of donation:

[3] Some have argued, rather illogically, that the value recorded for assets donated by nonshareholders also should be credited to a special revenue account and reported on the current income statement, while donations by shareholders should be credited to contributed capital as illustrated. Present GAAP do not permit revenue recognition for the value of donated assets.

Plant building	8,000	
Plant land	4,000	
Contributed capital—donated plant		12,000

2. At date of transfer and payment of transfer costs:

Contributed capital—donated plant (basis: the fair market value already recognized implicitly includes this cost)	900	
Cash		900

3. To record depreciation for first year assuming a ten-year life and no residual value:

Depreciation expense	800	
Accumulated depreciation—plant building		800

If the donation is contingent upon the fulfillment in the future of some contractual obligation on the part of the recipient, most accountants agree that the asset should be treated as a contingent asset until such time that the contingent condition has been met. If the contractual obligation has not been undertaken or if there is some doubt that it will be fulfilled, the donated asset should be disclosed by a note to the financial statements. When the obligation is essentially met, or upon conditional transfer of ownership, the asset may be recognized in the accounts on a contingent basis. To illustrate, assume the city donated a plant site having a fair market value of $25,000 to a corporation subject to a provision that ownership would transfer one year after the beginning of operations. A conditional ownership transfer was executed. The transactions may be recorded as follows:

1. At date of agreement:

Contingent asset—donated plant site	25,000	
Contingent contributed capital—donated plant site		25,000

2. At date of transfer of ownership and incidental costs of $100:

Plant site	25,000	
Contingent contributed capital—donated plant site	25,000	
Contingent asset—donated plant site		25,000
Cash		100
Contributed capital—donated plant site		24,900

Depreciable assets received by donation should be depreciated in the normal manner on the basis of the fair market value recorded in the accounts. A contingent asset (as recorded in entry No. 1 above), if depreciable in nature, should be depreciated on the basis of the fair market value from date of initial recognition (or initial use, depending upon the circumstances) as a contingent asset.

Discovery Value

Property owned by a company may increase in value substantially as a result of the *discovery* of valuable mineral or other natural resources. In such cases the original cost of the property may not provide a suitable basis for accountability. In the case of discovery value the accounting profession recognizes another exception to the cost principle. The fair market value of the property, in consideration of the valuable natural resource, should be realistically estimated, usually by appraisal, and recorded in the accounts. The resulting credit should be to Unrealized Capital Increment—Discovery Value. Depletion should be recognized on the basis of the increased value. To illustrate, assume a tract of land was purchased in 1954 for $2,000 and that in 1976 a valuable gravel deposit (that will be commercially exploited) was discovered on it. Related entries are:

1. To record purchase in 1954:

Land	2,000	
Cash		2,000

2. To record discovery value (estimated total quantity exploitable, 100,000 tons; appraised at $25,000 exclusive of residual land value) in 1976:[4]

Land—appraisal increment (gravel deposit)	25,000	
Unrealized capital increment (gravel deposit)		25,000

3. To record depletion for first year based on depletion rate of $.25 per ton; 10,000 tons mined during first year:

Depletion expense	2,500	
Land—appraisal increment (gravel deposit)		2,500

WRITE-DOWN OF OPERATIONAL ASSETS BASED ON DECREASED USE VALUE

If an operational asset loses its operational value by a *material amount,* it should be written down or written off as the circumstances warrant. Thus, for example, a plant may become idle due to factors such as continuing decline in demand, the obsolescence of its products, or inadequate transportation facilities, so that it has little or no resale value and its decreased value, if any, can only be realized as salvage. In such cases, accounting standards *require* an immediate write-down to net realizable value and recognition of the related loss for the period. Normally the write-down should be accomplished through a credit to the accumulated depreciation account (in recognition of obsolescence) and a debit to a nonrecurring loss. The loss would be extraordinary if it is *(a)* unusual and *(b)* occurs infrequently *(APB Opinion No. 30).* As a general principle it can be said that operational assets should not be carried at a book value in excess of their fair market value in use.

OUTLAYS SUBSEQUENT TO ACQUISITION BUT PRIOR TO USE

Outlays subsequent to acquisition but prior to operational use of a fixed asset, made to improve the asset and to bring it up to operational condition, should be capitalized as a part of the cost of the asset.

[4] The accounting profession has sanctioned, but not required, this procedure.

Prior to operational use, a secondhand asset frequently will require considerable outlays for repairs, reconditioning, remodeling, and installation, all of which should be capitalized. Reinstallation and rearrangement costs of machinery, rearrangement of partitions, renovation of buildings, and similar outlays on operational assets purchased in a used condition should be capitalized as a part of the cost. Overhead items such as insurance, taxes, supervisory salaries, and similar incidental expenditures directly related to the asset during a period of renovation also should be capitalized. Depreciation should not be recorded prior to the period of use.

LUMP-SUM PURCHASES OF ASSETS

It is not unusual for a business to acquire several dissimilar assets for a lump sum. This type of acquisition, frequently referred to as a basket purchase, poses the problem of apportioning the lump-sum cost to the several assets acquired, some of which may be depreciable and others nondepreciable. The apportionment should be based upon some realistic indicator of the relative values of the several assets involved, such as appraised values, tax assessment, cost savings, or the present value of estimated future earnings.

To illustrate, assume that $90,000 was paid for property that included land, a building, and some machinery. Assume further that an independent appraisal showed appraised values of land, $30,000; building, $50,000; and machinery, $20,000. The cost apportionment and entry to record the transaction are shown below.

Asset	*Appraised Value*	*Multiplier**	*Apportioned Cost*
Land	$ 30,000	.9	$27,000
Building	50,000	.9	45,000
Machinery	20,000	.9	18,000
Total	$100,000		$90,000

* Multiplier – $90,000 ÷ $100,000 = .9

Entry to record the purchase:

Land	27,000	
Building	45,000	
Machinery	18,000	
Cash		90,000

ASSETS CONSTRUCTED FOR OWN USE

Companies may construct buildings, plants, equipment, furniture, and fixtures on occasion for their own use. Operational assets may be constructed rather than acquired from the outside in order to utilize idle facilities and personnel, to effect an expected cost saving, or to satisfy a need that outsiders cannot meet in the desired time. In the case of assets constructed for a company's own use, several problems arise relative to measurement of the amount that should be capitalized as the cost of the asset. Obviously, all material, labor, and overhead costs *directly* identifiable with the construction should be capitalized. Capitalizable costs during the construction period also should include charges for licenses, permits and fees, taxes, insurance, and similar charges relating to the assets being constructed. Aside from the directly identifiable costs of construction that should be capitalized, there are two problems that require further consideration, viz:

1. General company overhead as a cost of assets constructed for own use.
2. Excess costs on assets constructed for own use.

General Overhead as a Cost of Construction

Assets may be constructed by a company for its own use under two different operating circumstances.

First, there is the case where for all practical purposes the plant is operating at capacity in producing goods for sale and the management decides to construct some asset to be used rather than sold. Management might make such a decision when the item otherwise is unavailable at the time required. In this case production of regular goods for sale is reduced. Clearly, in this situation the asset should be charged for all direct costs incurred in construction including *(a) additional* overhead costs caused by the construction, and *(b)* a fair share of *general factory overhead* allocated on the same basis as that applied to goods manufactured for sale.

Second, there is the instance where the plant is operating at less than capacity in producing regular goods for sale. In this case idle plant capacity, or a part of such capacity, is utilized in manufacturing an asset for own use and production of goods for sale is unaffected. In this case the asset should be charged with all direct costs incurred in such construction including *additional* overhead costs caused by the construction. At this point the question arises as to whether any of the *general factory overhead* also should be allocated to the asset constructed for own use. On this specific point some accountants take the position that the general factory overhead should be apportioned to the asset on the same basis as it is apportioned to the production for sale; others take the opposite position that none of the general factory overhead should be assigned to the asset constructed.

When idle plant capacity is used, it is argued in support of assigning a ratable portion of general factory overhead to the asset being constructed that *(a)* such assets should be accorded the same treatment as regular products; *(b)* the full cost of the asset should include general factory overhead (otherwise loss from idle capacity is overstated); *(c)* a future benefit is involved, hence such costs should be deferred; *(d)* no special favor should be accorded such assets; *(e)* normal operations should not be penalized by carrying such overhead costs; and *(f)* in conformance with the cost principle, an allocation is essential if the true cost of both the asset being constructed and the concurrent production for sale is to be assigned.

On the other hand, it is argued in support of not assigning a portion of the general factory overhead to the asset being constructed that *(a)* such allocation would be reflected as an increase in income due to construction rather than as a result of production and sale of goods; *(b)* the full cost of the asset should not include overhead that would be incurred even in the absence of such construction; *(c)* the cost of production for sale should not be influenced by such construction; and *(d)* management should not consider the general factory overhead in making the decision to construct the fixed asset.

Although there are persuasive arguments for both positions, the authors are of the opinion that in theory it is preferable to capitalize a portion of general factory overhead when idle plant capacity is used in the construction of assets for a firm's own use.

When assets are diverted from inventory and put into use as property, plant, and equipment, the carrying values they had as inventory should be transferred to the plant account.

Excess Costs of Construction

Ordinarily when management has made a decision to construct assets for own use, the full cost should be capitalized on the basis that the alternative cost of outside producers is not now available as an alternative. However, when construction costs of such assets are materially in excess of their fair value, the excess cost should be recorded as a period loss, as opposed to a capitalization. Construction costs materially in excess of those of an independent producer may be an indication that the full construction cost is an unwarranted charge to future operations through capitalization.

INTEREST DURING CONSTRUCTION PERIOD

Traditionally, public utilities have capitalized interest costs during construction on funds used to finance construction of fixed assets as part of the cost of those assets. Governmental regulatory agencies responsible for regulating the rates charged by utilities have allowed (but not required) interest during construction as a cost of the asset rather than as a current expense. This has the effect of deferring the impact of interest cost on utility rates to the period of usage of the fixed assets. The future impact will be greater because the utility rate base is higher by the amount of interest capitalized.

Historically, interest has been viewed as a cost of borrowing funds rather than a cost of the asset acquired with those funds. Therefore, capitalization of interest during the construction period generally has been viewed as not theoretically sound from the accounting point of view. Obviously, if interest during construction is capitalized, any premium or discount related to the borrowing should be accorded the same treatment.

Capitalization of interest during construction outside the public utility industry was not a widespread practice but became a growing one in the early 1970s. However, its spread has been halted, temporarily at least for most companies, by issuance of SEC *Accounting Series Release No. 163.* Under provisions of this release (after June 21, 1974), only electric, gas, water, and telephone utilities plus, in certain situations, those companies covered by provisions of two AICPA industry guides can capitalize interest.[5] In addition, companies that, prior to June 21, 1974, had publicly disclosed an accounting policy of capitalizing interest may continue interest capitalization but may not extend it to new types of assets. On all financial statements filed after January 1, 1975, the amount of interest capitalized must be reported. In the case of nonutility companies, the basis for capitalizing interest and the method of determining capitalized interest must be disclosed.

The issue is under serious study by the FASB, SEC, and the accounting profession because it poses some critical theoretical and practical questions, such as:

1. Should interest on all funds, or only borrowed funds, be capitalized?
2. On what basis are internally generated and borrowed funds separately identified?
3. What rate of interest should be used? Typically, there are several borrowing rates. What rate should be used on general funds used?
4. What assets should qualify for capitalization of interest?
5. What should be the credit entry to offset the debit to the asset for interest capitalized? Should interest on borrowed or internally generated funds be permitted to increase net income during the construction period? For example, some utilities have experienced their highest earnings during construction and a significant drop when the plant goes on stream.

ACQUISITION COSTS OF SPECIFIC PROPERTY

In determining the acquisition cost of an operational asset, the general principles discussed heretofore are applicable; however, certain items of property give rise to special problems in applying the general principles. These special problems are considered in the immediately succeeding paragraphs.

Land

The acquisition cost of land should be recorded in an account captioned Land or Real Estate. Some of the specific elements of land cost include the following:

---

[5] *Audits of Savings and Loan Associations,* an AICPA industry audit guide (1973); and *Accounting for Retail Land Sales,* an AICPA industry accounting guide (1973).

1. Original contract price.
2. Brokers' commissions.
3. Legal fees for examining and recording ownership.
4. Cost of ownership guarantee insurance policies.
5. Cost of real estate surveys.
6. Cost of an option when it is exercised.
7. Special paving assessments.
8. Cost of razing an old building (net of any salvage).
9. Cost of cancellation of an unexpired lease.
10. Payment of noncurrent taxes accrued on the land at date of purchase if payable by the purchaser.

On the other hand, the cost of land does not include: fees for surveying, ownership searches, geological opinions, legal and other expert services on land not purchased, expenditures in connection with disposal of refuse, costs of easements or rights of way which are limited as to time, assessments for repairs to roads and sidewalks, and repairs to other improvements.[6]

Costs incurred subsequent to acquisition to *permanently* improve the land for the purpose acquired, such as draining, clearing, landscaping, grading, and subdividing costs, are proper additions to the capitalized cost of the land.

A special problem arises concerning the treatment of taxes and carrying charges in respect to real estate held for investment or for future use. From a conservative point of view such charges should be recorded as current expenses. However, accounting theory tends to hold that in view of the fact that the asset is not producing income against which the charges may be offset, the carrying charges should be capitalized, particularly when the fair market value of the property is increasing. If the real estate is producing income, through rent for example, or is declining in value, there are sound reasons for treating the carrying costs as a current expense. Such charges may be either capitalized or expensed for income tax purposes.

Buildings

Specific cost elements of buildings include:

1. Original contract price or cost of construction.
2. Expenses incurred in remodeling, reconditioning, or altering a purchased building to make it available for the purpose for which it was acquired.
3. Cost of excavation or grading or filling of land for the specific building.
4. Expenses incurred for the preparation of plans, specifications, blueprints, and so on.
5. Cost of building permits.

---

[6] *Fixed Asset Accounting: The Capitalization of Costs* (New York: NAA, 1972), pp. 9–10.

6. Payment of noncurrent taxes accrued on the building at date of purchase if payable by purchaser.
7. Architects' and engineers' fees for design and supervision.
8. Other costs, such as temporary buildings used during the construction period.
9. Unanticipated expenditures such as rock blasting, piling, or relocation of the channel of an underground stream.

On the other hand, the cost of building should not include: extraordinary costs incidental to the erection of a building, such as those due to a strike, flood, fire, or other casualty, and the cost of abandoned construction.[7]

Removable building equipment may have a shorter life than the building and may be subject to replacement without impairment of the integrity of the building, in which case it should be separately recorded as building equipment and be separately depreciated. Razing costs of a building that has been used by an entity should be identified with the retirement of the old building.

Machinery, Furniture, Fixtures, and Equipment

Specific cost elements of machinery, furniture, fixtures, and equipment include:

1. Original contract or invoice cost.
2. Freight- and drayage-in, cartage, import duties, handling and storage costs.
3. Specific in-transit insurance charges.
4. Sales, use, and other taxes imposed on the acquisition.
5. Costs of preparation of foundations, protective apparatus, and other costs in connection with making a proper situs for the asset.
6. Installation charges including company overhead on the same basis as it is charged to inventory.
7. Charges for testing and preparation for use.
8. Costs for reconditioning used items when purchased.[8]

Since machine and hand tools are relatively low in cost per unit, are frequently lost or broken, and thus have a short service life, they normally are not accorded the same treatment as other tangible fixed assets; rather they are accounted for in one of three ways, viz:

1. Capitalized at date of purchase, periodically inventoried, and the asset account adjusted to the inventory value, thereby charging the losses due to breakage, theft, or disappearance to current expense.
2. Capitalized as an asset at a conservative valuation for the ordinary or normal stock; all subsequent tool purchases are then charged to current expense.
3. Expensed as acquired (see Chapter 13).

---

[7] Ibid., pp. 10–11.

[8] Ibid.

Patterns and Dies

Patterns and dies are used in the fabrication of many manufactured items such as automobile bodies. Patterns and dies used for regular production over a period of time should be recorded in a fixed asset account, Patterns and Dies, and depreciated over their estimated service life. Patterns and dies that are purchased or constructed for a particular job or order should be charged directly to the cost of that job.

Returnable Containers

Products are frequently sold in containers that have a relatively high value, hence are returnable for reuse. Gas cylinders, oil drums, and steel tanks generally can be returned by the purchaser for value. In some cases the purchaser is charged a deposit for the container and will receive a credit or refund when it is returned. In such cases, until returned, the containers should be carried in the vendor's accounts as a fixed asset and depreciated over their estimated useful life. Containers not returned within a reasonable time are accounted for as retired by sale; the deposit becomes the sales price. In contrast some companies do not bill the customer for the container, although the customer is expected to hold the container available for pickup. In such cases the vendor may account for the containers as operating supplies rather than as fixed assets and the loss determined by inventory similar to the procedure described for tools.

Leasehold Improvements

Improvements on *leased* property such as buildings, walks, landscaping, and certain types of permanent equipment, unless specifically exempted in the lease agreement, revert to the owner of the property upon termination of the lease. Improvements on leased property of this nature are referred to as *leasehold improvements.* The cost of such improvements should be capitalized by the lessee in a tangible fixed asset account entitled Leasehold Improvements (considered by some to be an intangible asset). The cost of the leasehold improvements should be depreciated over the term of the lease or the service life of the improvement, whichever is the shorter. Renewal provisions in the lease agreement normally are disregarded in depreciating leasehold improvements.

COST OUTLAYS SUBSEQUENT TO ACQUISITION

REPAIRS AND MAINTENANCE

After acquisition cost has been measured and recorded, numerous costs related to *utilization* of plant and equipment assets are incurred such as repairs, maintenance, betterments, and replacements. What outlays should be charged to an asset account, to the accumulated depreciation account, to Retained Earnings, to expense, or to some combination of these accounts? The problem is particularly critical as a result of the difficulty in distinguishing between the several classifications of outlay, such as ordinary repairs as opposed to extraordinary repairs, each of which requires different treatment in the accounts and financial reports.

Maintenance costs are those costs, such as lubrication, cleaning, adjustment, and painting, which are incurred to keep equipment in normal usable condition. *Ordinary repairs* (as distinguished from major repairs) are outlays for parts, labor, and other related costs which are necessary to keep the equipment in normal operating condition but do not add materially to the use value of the asset, nor prolong its life appreciably. Ordinary repairs are recurring and normally involve relatively small expenditures. Examples of ordinary repairs are fixing a broken chain or electrical circuit, and replacing spark plugs. Since maintenance costs and ordinary repairs are similar in many respects and accounted for in the same way, they usually are combined for accounting purposes.

Ordinary Repairs and Maintenance

Maintenance and ordinary repair costs may be accounted for using either of two approaches:

1. As revenue expenditures—an appropriate expense account is debited for each outlay as incurred. The effect of this procedure is to recognize expenses when the repairs and maintenance actually happen. Since use precedes repairs, it is sometimes argued that the matching principle is not adequately implemented. However, materiality and the short-term gap involved are compensating factors.
2. Allowance procedure—in the case of a new asset, the maintenance and repair costs initially will be low, increasing in amount each year as the asset is utilized. Repair costs also follow use and tend to vary during the year. Rather than charging operating expense as the repairs are incurred, it is sometimes preferable to use the allowance procedure. The allowance procedure requires an estimate of the total cost of ordinary repairs and maintenance during *(a)* the life of the asset, or *(b)* during the year, depending on the choice of period over which apportionment is desired. The amount of estimated repairs is allocated to each interim period on the basis of time (an equal amount each month or year as the case may be) or on the basis of production or output. Repair and Maintenance Expense is debited, and an allowance account is credited for the estimated amount. Actual expenditures for maintenance and ordinary repairs are then debited to the allowance account when incurred. To illustrate, assume ordinary repairs and maintenance for the year have been estimated at $1,800 and that this amount is to be apportioned on a time basis (an equal amount each month). Assume that the actual repairs and maintenance costs incurred for the first month amounted to $110. The entries would be:

1. To record the estimated maintenance and ordinary repair cost for the month:

Repairs and maintenance expense	150	
Allowance for maintenance and repairs		150

2. To record actual outlays for the month for ordinary repairs and maintenance:

Allowance for maintenance and repairs	110	
Cash or payables		110

The income statement would report repairs and maintenance expense of $150 for the month. The $40 credit balance in the allowance account would be reported on the interim balance sheet as a current liability because it reflects a future demand on current assets. In this example, at the end of the year any balance in the allowance account would be closed to the related repair expense account.

The allowance procedure for maintenance and ordinary repairs has been accorded general acceptability by the accounting profession. The procedure is justifiable for apportioning an expense where there is a sound basis for doing so; it is not acceptable simply as a means of equalizing profits as between several periods. It is used on either an annual basis, or to cover the entire life of the asset. In the latter case, the ending balance in the allowance account, each year, is reported on the balance sheet as a special liability (a claim against future assets) or as a contra to the related asset account similar to accumulated depreciation. The allowance method is not acceptable for federal income tax purposes.

EXTRAORDINARY REPAIRS

Extraordinary or major repairs involve relatively large amounts, are not recurring in nature, and tend to increase the *use value* (efficiency and use utility) or the service life of the asset beyond what it was originally. There are two acceptable alternative approaches in accounting for extraordinary repairs:

1. Capitalize – If the expenditure serves primarily to increase the use value, the cost is debited to the related asset account.
2. Reduce accumulated depreciation – If the expenditure serves primarily to increase the service life of the asset (and perhaps the residual value), the cost is debited to the related accumulated depreciation account.

Examples of extraordinary repairs are major overhauls, major improvements in the electrical system, and strengthening the foundation of a building.

Because of the difficulty in making a realistic distinction between increase in utility and increase in useful life as a result of extraordinary repairs, and because the two methods give the same net results (with the same set of facts) both are widely used. Often the depreciation rate must be revised.

REPLACEMENTS AND BETTERMENTS

Replacements involve the removal of a major part or component of plant or equipment and the substitution of a new part or component of essentially the *same type and performance capabilities.* Replacement may involve specific subunits or a number of major items similar in many respects to an extraordinary repair. In fact, the line between replacements and extraordinary repairs often is difficult to draw.

In contrast, *betterments,* or improvements, constitute the removal of a major part or component of plant or equipment and the substitution of a different part or component having significantly *improved and superior* performance capabilities. The result of the improved substitute serves to increase the overall efficiency and tends to increase the useful life of the primary asset. The replacing of an old shingle roof with a modern fireproof tile roof, installing a more powerful engine in a shrimp boat, and replacement of an improved electrical system in a building, are illustrations of betterments.

Because of the difference in circumstances in which replacements and betterments are made, three different approaches are used, viz:

1. Capitalize–The cost of the replacement or betterment is debited to the primary asset in conformance with the cost principle. The primary asset is improved as to performance and perhaps remaining life. In this approach, the cost and accumulated depreciation on the unit replaced are not removed from the accounts because they are not realistically determinable. Often the depreciation rate must be revised. This approach is used when the old costs and related accumulated depreciation amounts are not known and when the primary effect is to increase efficiency (rather than to lengthen the life of the basic asset). Because of the difficulty in making this distinction in practice, this approach and the next one are generally viewed as full-fledged alternatives.
2. Reduce accumulated depreciation–The cost of the replacement or betterment is debited to the related accumulated depreciation account on the basis that it is a recovery of past depreciation and that the life of the primary asset is lengthened. This approach is recommended when the primary effect is to lengthen the remaining life of the related asset; however, it is used as a full-fledged alternative to capitalization in the asset account. Often the depreciation rate must be revised.
3. Substitution–Conceptually this method assumes that there has been a disposal of the old unit and acquisition of a new unit. Therefore, these two separate events are recorded as follows:
   a. The cost of the old unit replaced is removed from the asset account, the accumulated depreciation on the old unit is removed, and a gain or loss on disposal recognized.
   b. The new replacement unit is debited to the asset account.

To illustrate, assume the old shingle roof on Plant A, original cost $20,000, 80% depreciated, is replaced with a new fireproof tile roof that cost $60,000. The two entries (which could be combined) are:

a. To remove old roof from the accounts:

Accumulated depreciation, old roof ($20,000 × 80%)	16,000	
Loss on disposal of plant assets	4,000	
Plant assets (old roof)		20,000

b. To record acquisition of new roof:

Plant assets (new roof)	60,000	
Cash		60,000

Theoretically, the third method is sound in every respect. However, it can be applied only when the cost of the old subunit, and the related accumulated depreciation, are known or can be realistically estimated. The loss would not be extraordinary as prescribed by *APB Opinion No. 30* ("Reporting the Results of Operations").[9]

ADDITIONS

Additions are extensions, enlargements, or expansions made to an existing asset. An extra wing or room added to a building and the addition of a production unit to an existing machine are examples of additions. An addition represents a capital expenditure and should be recorded in the fixed asset accounts at the full acquisition cost determined under the principles discussed above for acquisition cost of the original asset. Work done on the existing structure such as the shoring up of the foundation to accommodate the addition or the cutting of an entranceway through an existing wall should be regarded as a part of the cost of the addition and capitalized. The cost of an addition, less any estimated residual value, normally should be depreciated over its own service life or the remaining life of the original asset of which it is a part, whichever period is the shorter.

Pollution control devices have recently been added or are now being added by large numbers of entities either voluntarily or in compliance with laws or court or administrative orders. Sometimes, either because the original assets (which are the source of the pollution) were acquired when prices were low or because of stringency of the control regulations, the antipollution devices are quite costly in relation to the original assets. The devices themselves are capitalizable as plant additions. A question arises as to the accounting dispostion of fines, damages, or penalties which are sometimes assessed in connection with pollution which has been caused. Some have argued such costs should be charged to the current period; others believe that the proper treatment is a prior period adjustment; still others contend the costs should be capitalized and amortized over future periods. The authors prefer the first of the three alternatives. Whatever case can be made for the second alternative would have to rest on the notion that the penalty was assessed to correct damage resulting from production of prior periods and thus the costs of

---

[9] Some accountants believe that this is a change in estimate (*APB Opinion No. 20,* "Accounting Changes"); therefore, the loss should not be separately recognized but should be debited to accumulated depreciation and thereby spread prospectively, over the remaining life of the primary asset.

those periods was understated; some of the criteria for a prior period adjustment may well be met. Accounting for the costs as a capitalizable item to be amortized in the future has to rest on the notion that if the assessment is not paid, the entity will not get to operate in the future; therefore, there is a measurable future benefit.

REARRANGEMENT OF ASSETS

The cost of reinstallation, rerouting, or rearrangement of factory machinery for the purpose of securing greater efficiency in production or reduced production costs in the future should be capitalized if material in amount and if the benefits of the rearrangement definitely will extend beyond the current accounting period. Such costs should be capitalized as a deferred charge and amortized over the ensuing periods benefiting from the rearrangement.

RETIREMENT OF OPERATIONAL ASSETS

Operational assets may be retired voluntarily through disposal by sale, trade, or abandonment—or involuntarily lost as a result of casualty such as fire or storm. Irrespective of the cause of retirement, if the asset is subject to depreciation, it should be depreciated to date of such retirement. Likewise, taxes, insurance premium costs, and similar costs should be accrued up to the date of retirement. At date of retirement the cost of the asset and its related accumulated depreciation should be removed from the accounts. To illustrate, assume a truck costing $3,200 on February 1, 1972, is sold on July 1, 1976, for $650. Straight-line depreciation has been recorded on the basis of an estimated service life of five years and an estimated residual value of $200. The company closes its books on December 31 of each year. The entries at date of sale would be as follows:

1. Depreciation expense	300	
Accumulated depreciation—equipment		300
To record 6 months' depreciation for 1976 at $50 per month computed as follows:		
Amount to be depreciated ($3,200 − $200) ... $3,000		
Service life—5 years or 60 months.		
Monthly depreciation ($3,000/60 months)...... $ 50		
2. Cash	650	
Accumulated depreciation—equipment	2,650	
Delivery equipment		3,200
Gain on sale of equipment*		100
To record retirement of old truck by sale.		

* Sales price			$650
Less book value of asset sold:			
Original cost		$3,200	
Accumulated depreciation:			
1972–11 months	$550		
1973–12 months	600		
1974–12 months	600		
1975–12 months	600		
1976– 6 months	300	2,650	550
Gain on Sale			$100

The gain on sale of equipment is closed to the Income Summary account.

The accounting entries for an exchange were discussed and illustrated earlier in the chapter. In case an operational asset is abandoned or disposed of because it has no value, the cost and accumulated depreciation amounts should be removed from the accounts and any loss on abandonment, including costs of disposal, recognized.

Outlays made to restore and repair uninsured assets damaged through fire, storm, or other casualty should be recorded as losses and closed to the Income Summary account. Outlays made where the properties are improved beyond their approximate operating condition prior to the casualty should be apportioned between losses and the asset.[10] Damaged assets not restored should be reduced to a carrying value consistent with the decrease in going-concern utility. Accounting for *insured* casualty losses is discussed in Chapter 14.

QUESTIONS

1. Operational assets used in day-to-day business operations can be classed as tangible or intangible; distinguish between the two, giving examples. Under what balance sheet caption are tangible operational assets reported? Give at least one synonym for whatever title you specify.
2. Distinguish between capital and revenue expenditures. What accounting implications are involved?
3. Relate the *cost principle* to the acquisition of operational assets. Relate the *matching principle* to operational asset accounting.
4. How is asset acquisition cost determined when the consideration given is securities?
5. Define book value with respect to *(a)* assets having no limited service life, and *(b)* assets having a limited service life.
6. Explain the relationship between book value and fair market value of an operational asset.
7. In determining the cost of an operational asset how should the following items be treated: *(a)* invoice price, *(b)* freight, *(c)* discounts, *(d)* ownership costs, *(e)* installation costs, *(f)* breaking-in costs, and *(g)* cost of major overhaul before operational use?
8. A machine is purchased on the following terms: cash, $10,000, plus ten semiannual payments of $3,000 each. How should the acquisition cost of the machine be recorded? Explain.
9. Basically, how are assets acquired recorded when payment includes the trading in of an old asset (refer to *APB Opinion No. 29*)?
10. Where several assets are bought for a single lump-sum consideration, a cost apportionment procedure is usually employed. Explain the procedure. Why is apportionment necessary?

---

[10] In instances where the casualty loss is both *(a)* unusual and *(b)* occurs infrequently, as defined in *APB Opinion No. 30*, it must be reported as an extraordinary item.

11. Some businesses self-construct plant assets. What costs should be capitalized? In connection with self-construction of assets, explain what to do with (*a*) general company overhead, and (*b*) any excess costs incurred.

12. Capitalization of interest during the period operational assets were under construction has been a widespread practice in one industry. Identify the industry; explain why interest capitalization was practiced.

13. Distinguish between maintenance, ordinary repairs, and extraordinary repairs.

14. Explain the accounting for (*a*) extraordinary repairs, (*b*) replacements and renewals, and (*c*) betterments and improvements.

15. The XY Corporation added a new wing at a cost of $50,000, plus $1,000 spent in making passageways through the walls of an old structure to the existing plant. The plant was 10 years old and was being depreciated an equal amount each year over a 30-year life. Discuss the implications in determining the depreciation of the new wing.

16. What are leasehold improvements? How should they be accounted for?

17. Outline the accounting steps related to the disposition of an operational asset.

DECISION CASE 12–1

One of your clients, a savings bank with several local branches, recently acquired ownership to a lot and building located in a historical part of the city. The building was in a dilapidated condition, unsuitable for human habitation. The bank, at the time, thought it was, in essence, acquiring a site for a new branch. Although a firm of architects recommended demolition, the city council, in whose discretion such activity rests, refused consent in view of the building's historical and architectural value.

In order to comply with safety requirements and to make the building suitable for use as a branch location, the bank spent $125,000 restoring and altering the old building. It had paid $25,000 for the building and lot and had contemplated spending $80,000 on a new building after demolishing the old structure. Somewhat similar old buildings in less run-down condition could have been bought in the same area for about the same $25,000 price. It is possible, even likely, that some of these which were not so old could have been demolished without governmental intervention, and the bank could have carried out its original plan.

Now that the restoration has been completed and the bank is making final plans to open its newest branch in the restored building, the bank has been informed by the State Historical Commission that the building qualifies for and will receive a plaque designating it as a historical site. This designation will be of some value in attracting traffic to the site, will probably result in the building being pointed out when tours of the city visit the area, and so on. Under present laws, receipt of the designation may well mean that the bank can never demolish the structure as long as it is the owner and has obligations to preserve it even if the property is later vacated.

Required:

a. Discuss the pros and cons of capitalizing the entire $125,000 spent on restoration of the building.

b. How should the $25,000 original expenditure be treated? What would have been the cost of the site if the bank had been able to carry out its original plans?

c. Sooner or later, your client is likely to seek advice as to proper accounting of subsequent costs—repairs, depreciation, possible improvements, and so on. What advice will you give?

DECISION CASE 12–2

Elmo Company operates several plants at which limestone is processed into quicklime and hydrated lime. The Bland plant, where most of the equipment was installed many years ago, continually deposits a dusty white substance over the surrounding countryside. Citing the unsanitary condition of the neighboring community of Adeltown, the pollution of the Adel River, and the high incidence of lung disease among workers at Bland, the state's Pollution Control Agency has ordered the installation of air pollution control equipment. Also, the Agency has assessed a substantial penalty, which will be used to clean up Adeltown. After considering the costs involved (which could not have been reasonably estimated prior to the Agency's action), Elmo decides to comply with the Agency's orders, the alternative being to cease operations at Bland at the end of the current year. The officers of Elmo agree that the air pollution control equipment should be capitalized and depreciated over its useful life, but they disagree over the period(s) to which the penalty should be charged.

Required:

Discuss the conceptual merits and reporting requirements of accounting for the penalty as a—

a. Charge to the current period.
b. Correction of prior periods.
c. Capitalizable item to be amortized over future periods.

(AICPA adapted)

EXERCISES

Exercise 12–1

When examining the accounts of a new corporate client, you encounter the following items:

Identity	*Description or Added Data*	*Valuation Data*
a. Franchise	Acquired as perpetual franchise.	Cost, $12,000
b. Land	Purchased last year for future plant site.	Cost, $ 6,000
c. Building	Purchased 12 years ago for warehouse. (Being depreciated over 45-year life by straight-line method; no salvage value.)	Cost, $90,000
d. Patent	Purchased three years ago. (Half of useful life has elapsed and is reflected by amortization recorded.)	Cost, $15,000
e. Fixtures	Purchased at start of current year.	Cost, $30,000
f. Returnable Containers	Bought three years ago. (Being depreciated on basis of ten-year life by straight-line method; 20% are expected not to be returned.)	Cost, $30,000
g. Goodwill	Arose when business acquired a division in 1971 which has since been merged in as integral part of client corporation.	Remaining unamortized balance $9,000
h. Land	Bought for speculative purposes last year.	Cost, $25,000
i. Hand tools	Bought at various times.	Remaining balance is value at date of examination, $8,000.

Required:

Indicate the balance sheet classification and amount for each of the foregoing items.

Exercise 12–2

What is the proper cost to use for recording the land in each of the following independent cases? Give reasons in support of your answer.

Case A – Issued 15,000 shares (par value per share $1) par value capital stock with a "market value" of $1.50 per share (based upon a recent sale of ten shares) for the land. The land was recently appraised at $17,000 by competent appraisers.

Case B – Rejected an offer two years ago by the vendor to sell the land for $7,500 cash. Issued 1,000 shares of capital stock for the land (market value of the stock based on several recent transactions, $7 average volume, sold 2,000 shares).

Case C – At the middle of the current year gave a check for $5,000 for the land and assumed the liability for unpaid taxes: taxes in arrears last year, $100; assessed for current year, $80.

Case D – Issued 1,000 shares of capital stock for the land. The par value of the stock was $50 per share; the market value (stock sells daily with an average daily volume of 5,000 shares) was $63 per share at time of purchase of land. Vendor offered to sell the land for $62,000 cash. Competent appraisers valued the land at $64,000.

Exercise 12–3

a. Delivery equipment was purchased having a list price of $6,000; terms were 2/10, n/30. Payment was made within the discount period.

b. Delivery equipment was purchased having a list price of $4,000; terms were 2/10, n/30. Payment was made after the discount period.

c. Delivery equipment listed at $10,000 was purchased and invoiced at 2/10, n/30. In order to take advantage of the discount, the company borrowed $8,000 of the purchase price by issuance of a 60-day, 9% note which was repaid with interest at maturity.

Required:

Give entries in each separate situation for costs, borrowing, and any expenses involved.

Exercise 12–4

Franklin Company purchased a machine, having an estimated ten-year useful life, on a time payment plan. The cash price of the machine was $28,771. Terms were $3,000 cash down payment plus three equal annual payments to include interest on the unpaid balance at 8% per annum.

Required:

(Round to even dollars).

a. Give entry to reflect the purchase.

b. Give entry for depreciation at the end of one year assuming straight-line depreciation and no residual value.

c. Compute the amount of the annual payments.
d. Prepare a table to reflect the accounting entries for each of the four payments.

Exercise 12–5

For each of the following numbered items, indicate, by using one of the five lettered choices listed below, which accounting treatment is correct. Explain questionable items and assumptions you make. Each cost, identified as a numbered item, was incurred by a corporation incident to acquisition of a new machine.

Lettered Choices:

a. Increases or decreases Machinery account.
b. Debit an expense account for current period.
c. Debit Prepaid Expense or Deferred Charge and amortize separately from machinery.
d. Debit Plant, Property, and Equipment account other than machinery.
e. An accounting treatment other than the four choices above. Explain.

1. Invoice price of the machinery, before discount.
2. Cash discount for prompt payment of foregoing invoice, not taken.
3. Cost of moving machinery into place.
4. Cost of removing old machine which this machinery replaced.
5. Sales tax based on purchase price of new machinery.
6. Special electrical wiring required to connect new machine.
7. Enlargement of electrical system of plant to accommodate new machine and provide for some expected future needs.
8. Service contract paid in full covering first two years' operation of the machine.
9. Cost of materials used while testing new machine.
10. Payment to technicians who assisted with break-in of new machine.
11. Cost of training three of our employees who will operate machine.
12. Charge to machine which was offset by credit to "Miscellaneous Revenue" amounting to anticipated first years' savings from use of new machine.
13. Insurance premium paid covering first year of protection of new machine against hazards to which it will be exposed.
14. Repair charges incurred during first year of operations.
15. Cost of installing sound insulation so new machine will not disturb those who work near it.

Exercise 12–6

Strong Company purchased a tract of land on which was located a warehouse and an office building. The cash purchase price was $128,650 plus $350 fees in connection with the purchase. The following data were collected concerning the property:

	Tax Assessment	*Vendor's Book Value*	*Original Cost*
Land	$10,000	$10,000	$10,000
Warehouse	20,000	15,000	30,000
Office building	30,000	25,000	60,000

Required:

Journalize the purchase; show computations.

Exercise 12–7

Marshal Company bought a machine on a time payment plan. The cash purchase price was $23,936. Terms were $7,000 cash down payment plus four equal annual payments of $5,000 which includes interest on the unpaid balance at 7% per annum.

Required:

1. Give entry to record the purchase. Show computations (round to even dollars).
2. Give entry to record depreciation at the end of the first full year assuming straight-line depreciation, an eight-year life and no residual value.
3. Prepare a table to reflect the accounting entries for each of the four installment payments.

Exercise 12–8

Charmaine Company manufactured a new machine for its own use. The ledger account below reflects charges and credits made during the year to the Machinery account incidental to the project.

Machinery (new)

Cost of dismantling old machine replaced	1,200	Cash proceeds from sale of old machine	300
Labor charges	22,000		
Raw materials used	24,000		
Installation charges	3,000		
Materials spoiled	800		
Profit on construction	5,000		
Spare parts	4,500		
Auxiliary tools	3,000		

Your investigation revealed the following additional facts:

1. The old machine that was removed had originally cost $30,000; accumulated depreciation was $29,600.
2. The manufacturing overhead account balance is $200,000; you determine that 96% of this relates to ordinary manufacture and the rest to the self-construction.
3. Cash discounts average 2% on all raw material purchases; the entire amount of discounts taken was recorded as Purchase Discounts.
4. The installation charges represent a payment to outsiders for technical assistance during the break-in period of the machine.
5. Materials spoiled represent the cost of materials used during the testing and break-in period.
6. Profit on construction was credited to an account of that title. Charmaine Company estimates it saved at least $5,000 by self-constructing the machinery instead of purchasing it.
7. The charge for spare parts represents the cost of parts purchased and set aside to cover breakdowns and maintenance during the first two years of normal use of the machine.

8. Auxiliary tools are items used in conjunction with the machine which have an estimated useful life of five years. The machine is expected to last from 10 to 12 years.

Required:

Prepare journal entries to correct the machinery account and other accounts of Charmaine Company. Insofar as possible, key your entries to the numbers identifying data above.

Exercise 12–9

Select the best answer for each of the following. Briefly justify your choice for each item.

1. If the present value of a note issued in exchange for a plant asset is less than its face amount, the difference should be–
   a. Included in the cost of the asset.
   b. Amortized as interest expense over the life of the note.
   c. Amortized as interest expense over the life of the asset.
   d. Included in interest expense in the year of issuance.
2. When a closely held corporation issues preferred stock for land, the land should be recorded at the–
   a. Total par value of the stock issued.
   b. Total book value of the stock issued.
   c. Appraised value of the land.
   d. Total liquidating value of the stock issued.
3. The debit for a sales tax levied and paid on the purchase of machinery preferably would be a charge to–
   a. The Machinery account.
   b. A separate Deferred Charge account.
   c. Miscellaneous Tax Expense (which includes all taxes other than those on income).
   d. Accumulated Depreciation–Machinery.
4. The Wise Corporation purchased a new machine on October 31, 19A. A $250 down payment was made, and three monthly installments of $800 each are to be made beginning on November 30, 19A. The cash price would have been $2,500. Wise paid no installation charges under the monthly payment plan but a $50 installation charge would have been incurred with a cash purchase. The amount to be capitalized as the cost of the machine during 19A would be–
   a. $2,700.
   b. $2,650.
   c. $2,550.
   d. $1,850.
   e. None of the above.
5. If a corporation purchased a lot and building and subsequently demolished the building and now uses the property as a parking lot, the accounting treatment of the cost of the building at acquisition would depend on–
   a. The significance of the cost allocated to the building in relation to the combined cost of the lot and building.
   b. The length of time for which the building was held prior to its demolition.
   c. The contemplated future use of the parking lot.
   d. The intention of management for the property when the building was acquired.

6. Property, plant, and equipment may properly include:
   a. Cash paid on machinery purchased but not yet received.
   b. Idle equipment awaiting sale.
   c. Property held for investment purposes.
   d. Land held for possible future plant site.
   e. None of the above.

(AICPA adapted)

Exercise 12–10

Morris Company has some old equipment that cost $11,500; accumulated depreciation, $7,200. This equipment was traded in on a new machine that had a list price of $14,000; however, it could be purchased without a trade-in for $13,700 cash. The difference is to be paid as cash boot.

Required:

Give the entry to record the acquisition of the new machine under each of the following independent cases:

Case A–The new machine was purchased for cash with no trade-in.
Case B–The equipment and the machine are dissimilar. The old machine is traded in and $9,000 cash boot is paid.
Case C–Same as Case B except that the equipment and the machine are similar.

Exercise 12–11

Frank Company operates two separate plants. In Plant A, the accounting policy is to consider all ordinary (minor) repairs as revenue expenditures when incurred. In contrast, in Plant B, the accounting policy is to use the allowance procedure that charges repairs equally each period. Selected data for 19A are:

	Plant A	*Plant B*
Estimated repair costs budgeted for the year	$3,000	$3,600
Actual repair costs incurred and paid:		
First quarter	150	400
Second quarter	1,400	700
Third quarter	900	2,100
Fourth quarter	550	500

Required:

1. Give the entries in parallel columns for each plant for each of the four quarters.
2. Would you recommend any changes in the accounting policies? Explain and justify your response.

Exercise 12–12

Steele Company operates one plant which is adjacent to its relatively modest office building. The plant building is old and demands continuous maintenance and repairs. The accounts reflect the cost of the plant building to be $125,000, and accumulated depreciation is $100,000. During the current year, the following expenditures relating to the plant building were made:

a. Continuing, frequent, and low-cost repairs	$13,000
b. Complete overhaul of the plumbing system (old costs not known)	8,500
c. Added a new storage shed attached to the building, estimated physical life of eight years	24,000
d. Removed the original roof, original cost, $16,000, and replaced it with a new modern roof that was guaranteed	30,000
e. Unusual, infrequent, and costly repairs	4,000

Required:

Give the journal entry to record each of the above items. Explain the basis for your treatment of each item.

PROBLEMS

Problem 12–1

An examination of the Property, Plant, and Equipment account of Phillips Company disclosed the following transactions:

a. Bought a delivery truck for which the list price was $4,500; paid cash $1,500 and gave a one-year noninterest-bearing note payable for the balance. The current interest rate for this type of note was 7%.

b. Contracted for a building at a price of $400,000. Settlement was effected with the contractor by transferring $400,000, 20-year, 8% company bonds payable, at which time financial consultants advised that the bonds would sell at 96.

c. Purchased a new machine having a list price of $20,000. Failed to take a 1% cash discount available upon full payment of the invoice within ten days. Shipping costs paid by the vendor amounted to $100. Installation costs amounted to $250, including $100 which represented 10% of the monthly salary of the factory superintendent (installation period two days). A wall was torn out and replaced (moved two feet) at a cost of $500 to make room for the machine.

d. Purchased an automatic counter to be attached to a machine in use. The counter cost $560. The estimated useful life of the counter was seven years, whereas the estimated life of the machine was ten years.

e. During the first month of operations the machine became inoperative due to a defect in manufacture. The vendor repaired the machine at no cost; however, the specially trained operator was idle during the two weeks the machine was inoperative. The operator was paid the regular wages ($540) during the period, although the only work performed was to observe the repair by the factory representative.

f. After one year of use, exchanged the electric motor on the machine for a heavier motor at an exchange cost of $400. The new motor had a list price of $1,250. The parts list indicated a list price for the original motor of $900.

Required:

Prepare entries to record each of the above transactions. Explain and justify your decision on questionable items.

Problem 12–2

Kraus Construction Company entered into a contract to buy five Master Loaders, agreeing to make five equal annual payments of $6,800 each at the end of each of the next five years. Master Loaders have a list price of $5,576 each, an estimated service life of eight years, and zero salvage value.

Required:

(Round to nearest dollar.)

1. Determine the implied interest rate of the contract and give appropriate entries to record the transaction at the date of the contract.
2. Assuming the first payment date coincides with the close of Kraus' fiscal year, make all appropriate entries if the payment is made.
3. Give entries for the fifth year.

Problem 12–3

Murphy Corporation bought equipment on July 1, 19A, for which its entries throughout the first year and one half of ownership were as below:

	Debit	Credit
July 1, 19A:		
Equipment	25,000	
Installment note payable		25,000
December 31, 19A:		
Depreciation expense (1/2 year)	1,250	
Accumulated depreciation		1,250
July 1, 19B:		
Installment note payable	5,000	
Cash		5,000
December 31, 19B:		
Depreciation expense	2,500	
Accumulated depreciation		2,500

As can be inferred from the foregoing, the equipment is being depreciated on a straight-line basis with an assumed ten-year life and zero salvage value. The $25,000 installment note is payable in five equal annual installments which includes interest. Assume 8% is a reasonable interest rate to impute.

Required:

1. Prepare a table to reflect the entries for the note. The present value of an annuity of 1 for five periods at 8% is 3.99271.
2. Give the journal entry or entries to correct Murphy Corporation's books as of December 31, 19B, on the basis that the books are still open as of that date.

Problem 12–4

MW Corporation acquired a new machine by trading in an old machine and paying $35,000 cash. The old machine originally cost $40,000 and had accumulated depreciation at the date of exchange of $30,000. This transaction could be recorded by either of the two following methods:

	Method 1		Method 2	
Machinery (new)	42,500		45,000	
Accumulated depreciation (old)	30,000		30,000	
Loss on disposal of machinery	2,500			
Cash		35,000		35,000
Machinery (old)		40,000		40,000

Required:

1. Identify and discuss the reasons for recording the above transaction using Method 1.
2. Identify and discuss the reasons for recording the above transaction using Method 2.
3. Suppose the fair value of the used machine traded in was $18,000 at the time of the exchange, how would the exchange be recorded in accordance with today's accounting principles? (Assume the same amount of cash boot as above, $35,000.)

(AICPA adapted)

Problem 12–5

The city of Rockdale entered into an agreement with Watt Manufacturing Company whereby the city would donate to Watt Company a tract of land near the city on which was located a vacant building suitable for manufacturing operations. The agreement provided that ownership would transfer to the company at the end of five years (from January 1, 19A) if a plant was put in operation for not less than three years and that the company would employ on the average of 300 or more employees. Watt Company entered into the agreement on January 1, 19A, and started operations on November 1, 19A, on a reduced scale; by the end of 19B the plant was in full production and 325 persons were on the payroll.

Just prior to signing the agreement the city had hired a competent appraiser to appraise the property with the following results: plant site, $30,000; and building, $85,000. The appraiser estimated the remaining useful life for the building at 20 years. Watt Company spent $150 in connection with the ownership of the site and $23,000 on renovating the building.

Required:

1. Give entries to record the donation, incidental costs, renovating costs, depreciation for 19A and 19B (if any), and to record the transfer of ownership. Disregard residual values.
2. Give entries assuming that Watt Company did not complete the agreement and abandoned the plant in January 19C.

Problem 12–6

Max Company utilized its own facilities to construct a small addition to their office building. Construction began on March 1 and was completed on June 30 of the same year. Prior to the decision to construct the asset with its own facilities, the company accepted bids from outside contracts; the lowest bid was $240,000. Detailed costs accumulated during the construction period are summarized as follows:

Materials used (including $120,000 for normal production)	$180,000
Direct labor (including $300,000 for normal production)	450,000
General supplies used on construction	8,000
Rent paid on construction machinery	3,000
Insurance premiums on construction	700
Supervisory salary on construction	5,000
Total general administrative overhead for the year	115,000
Total factory overhead for the year:	
Fixed ($10,000 due to construction)	100,000
Variable	60,000
Direct labor hours (including 100,000 for normal production)	150,000

The company allocates factory overhead to normal production on the basis of direct labor cost.

Required:

Compute the amounts that might be capitalized–

a. Assuming the plant capacity to be 150,000 direct labor hours and that the construction displaced production for sale to the extent indicated.

b. Assuming the plant capacity to be 200,000 direct labor hours and that idle capacity was utilized for the construction.

Hint: Use overhead rates for factory overhead.

Problem 12–7

Prepare journal entries to record the following transactions related to the acquisition of fixed assets. Justify your position on doubtful items.

a. Purchased a tract of land for $20,000, assumed taxes already assessed amounting to $180. Paid title fees, $50, and attorney fees of $300 in connection with the purchase. Payments were in cash.

b. Purchased property which included land and buildings for $78,900 cash. The purchase price included an offset of $300 for unpaid taxes. Purchaser borrowed $30,000 at 7% interest (principal and interest due one year from date) from the bank to help make the cash payment. The property was appraised for taxes as follows: land, $22,000; and building, $44,000.

c. Prior to use of the property purchased in *(b)* above the following expenditures were made:

Repair and renovation of building	$7,000
Installation of 220-volt electrical wiring	4,000
Removal of separate shed of no use (sold scrap lumber for $50)	300
Construction of a new driveway	1,000
Repair of existing driveways	600
Deposits with utilities for connections	50
Painting the company name on two sides of the building	400
Installation of wire fence around property	2,500

d. The land purchased in *(a)* above was leveled and two retaining walls built to stop erosion that had created two rather large gulleys across the property. Total cash cost of the work was $4,500. The property is being held as a future plant site.

e. Purchased a used machine at a cash cost of $12,500. Subsequent to purchase the following expenditures were made:

General overhaul prior to use	$1,500
Installation of machine	500
Cost of moving the machine	150
Cost of removing two small machines to make way for the larger machine purchased	100
Cost of reinforcing the floor prior to installation	140
Testing costs prior to operation	60
Cost of tool kit (new) essential to adjustment of machine for various types of work	170

Problem 12–8

The books of Braley Manufacturing Company had never been audited prior to 1976. In auditing the books for the year ended December 31, 1976, the auditor found the following account for the plant:

Plant and Equipment

Debits		Credits	
1973		1973	
Plant purchased	90,000	Sale of scrap	300
Repairs	5,300	Depreciation (5%)	5,000
Legal	600	1974	
Title fees	50	Depreciation (5%)	6,700
Insurance	3,000		
Taxes	1,200	1975	
1974		Cash proceeds from old machine	1,150
Addition to plant	15,000	Depreciation (5%)	6,800
Write-up	20,000		
Interest expense	1,500	1976	
Repairs	500	Depreciation (5%)	7,100
Machinery for new addition	2,000		
1975			
New machine	3,000		
Installation	600		
1976			
Machinery overhaul	1,350		
Replaced roof	900		
Fence	3,400		

(Balance $121,350)

Additional data relating to plant and equipment developed during the audit follow:

a. The plant was purchased during January 1973. At that time the tax assessment listed the plant as follows: plant site at $10,000, the building at $20,000, and the machinery therein at $30,000. The estimated life of the plant and machinery was 20 years.

b. During the first six months of 1973 the company expended the amounts listed in the account for the year in getting the plant ready for operation; operations began July 1. The repairs pertain to both the building and machinery. No breakdown was available. The legal fees were incurred in connection with the plant purchase and applied to all components of it. The $3,000 insurance premium represented a one-year policy on the plant and equipment, dated January 10, 1973 ($1,000 of the premium applied to the machinery). The property tax rate for the year was 2%. The scrap was accumulated during the "repair period."

c. In 1974 a plant addition was completed costing $15,000, at which time the company was paying 10% on some funds borrowed. The addition was under construction for four months. During the year $1,500 was spent for ordinary repairs, of which one third was capitalized. Machine costing $2,000 was purchased. The asset account was written up by $20,000 to bring it in line with the bank's security allowance on loans (Paid-In Surplus credited).

d. During 1975 a new machine was purchased (July 1) for $3,000 plus installation costs of $600; an old machine costing an estimated $2,100 was sold for $1,150. The old machine was acquired when the plant was acquired.

e. During 1976 several items of equipment were completely reconditioned at a cost of $1,350. Minor repairs were charged to expense during the year. The roof was replaced on one wing of the plant. A fence was constructed around the plant to keep unauthorized personnel out; it is estimated that the fence will have the same remaining life as the plant.

Required:

1. Set up a worksheet to compute the correct balances for the following accounts: (suggested top captions) Land, Buildings, Machinery, Land Improvements, and Accumulated Depreciation (assume 5% straight-line depreciation on ending balances; disregard residual value and round to even dollars.) Suggested side captions: list each item by year. Justify any assumptions that you make.
2. Give entry to correct the accounts assuming the books are closed for 1976.

Problem 12–9

Ellford Corporation received a $400,000 low bid from a reputable manufacturer for the construction of special production equipment needed by Ellford in an expansion program. Because the company's own plant was not operating at capacity, Ellford decided to construct the equipment there and recorded the following production costs related to the construction:

Services of consulting engineer	$ 10,000
Work subcontracted	20,000
Materials	200,000
Plant labor normally assigned to production	65,000
Plant labor normally assigned to maintenance	100,000
Total	$395,000

Management prefers to record the cost of the equipment under the incremental cost method. Approximately 40% of the corporation is devoted to government supply contracts which are all based in some way on cost. The contracts require that any self-constructed equipment be allocated its full share of all costs related to the construction.

The following information is also available:

a. The above production labor was for partial fabrication of the equipment in the plant. Skilled personnel were required and were assigned from other projects.

The maintenance labor would have been idle time of nonproduction plant employees who would have been retained on the payroll whether or not their services were utilized.

b. Payroll taxes and employee fringe benefits are approximately 30% of labor cost and are included in manufacturing overhead cost. Total manufacturing overhead for the year was $5,630,000.

c. Manufacturing overhead is approximately 50% variable and is applied on the basis of production labor cost. Production labor cost for the corporation's normal products totaled $6,810,000.

d. General and administrative expenses include $22,500 of executive salary cost and $10,500 of postage, telephone, supplies, and miscellaneous expenses identifiable with this equipment construction.

Required:

1. Prepare a schedule computing the amount which should be reported as the full cost of the constructed equipment to meet the requirements of the government contracts. Any supporting computations should be in good form.
2. Prepare a schedule computing the incremental cost of the constructed equipment.
3. What is the greatest amount that should be capitalized as the cost of the equipment? Why?

(AICPA adapted)

Problem 12–10

Valley Manufacturing Company was incorporated on January 2, 19A, but was unable to begin manufacturing activities until July 1, 19A, because new factory facilities were not completed until that date.

The Land and Building account at December 31, 19A, was as follows:

Date	*Item*	*Amount*
Jan. 31, 19A	Land and building	$ 98,000
Feb. 28, 19A	Cost of removal of building	1,500
May 1, 19A	Partial payment of new construction	35,000
May 1, 19A	Legal fees paid	2,000
June 1, 19A	Second payment on new construction	30,000
June 1, 19A	Insurance premium	1,800
June 1, 19A	Special tax assessment	2,500
June 30, 19A	General expenses	12,000
July 1, 19A	Final payment on new construction	35,000
Dec. 31, 19A	Asset write-up	12,500
		$230,300
Dec. 31, 19A	Depreciation – 19A at 1%	2,300
	Account balance	$228,000

The following additional information is to be considered:

a. To acquire land and building the company paid $48,000 cash and 500 shares of its 5% cumulative preferred stock, par value $100 per share.

b. Cost of removal of old buildings amounted to $1,500 with the demolition company retaining all materials of the building.

c. Legal fees covered the following:

Cost of organization	$ 500
Examination of title covering purchase of land	1,000
Legal work in connection with construction work	500
	$2,000

d. Insurance premium covered premiums for three-year term beginning May 1, 19A.

e. General expenses covered the following for the period from January 2, 19A, to June 30, 19A:

President's salary	$ 6,000
Plant superintendent covering supervision on new building	5,000
Office salaries	1,000
	$12,000

f. The special tax assessment covered street improvements.

g. Because of a general increase in construction costs after entering into the building contract, the board of directors increased the value of the building $12,500, believing such increase justified to reflect current market at the time the building was completed. Retained Earnings was credited for this amount.

h. Estimated life of building – 50 years.
Write-off for 19A – 1% of asset value (1% of $230,300 = $2,300).

Required:

1. Prepare entries to reflect correct land, and building and depreciation allowance accounts at December 31, 19A.
2. Show the proper presentation of land, building and depreciation allowance on the balance sheet at December 31, 19A.

(AICPA adapted)

Problem 12–11

Equipment which cost $12,800 on January 1, 19A, was sold for $4,000 on June 30, 19F. It had been depreciated over a ten-year life by the straight-line method on the assumption its salvage value would be $800.

A warehouse that cost $110,000, residual value $5,000, was being depreciated over 35 years by the straight-line method. When the structure was 20 years old, an additional wing was constructed at a cost of $36,000. The estimated life of the wing considered separately was 25 years, and its residual value is $1,000. The accounting period ends December 31.

Required:

1. Give entries (and show computations) to record:
   a. The sale of the equipment. Accrue current depreciation in the sale entry.
   b. The addition; cash was paid.
   c. Depreciation for the warehouse and its addition after the latter has been in use for one year.
2. Show how the structures would be reported on a balance sheet prepared immediately after entry (*c*).

Problem 12–12

Sampler Company, a manufacturer, operates three plants in different locations. This problem focuses on Plant No. 1. The plant asset records reflected the following at the beginning of the current year, January 1, 19A:

Plant building (residual value, $20,000; estimated useful life, 30 years)	$120,000
Accumulated depreciation	75,000
Machinery (residual value, $35,000; estimated useful life, 15 years)	200,000
Accumulated depreciation	110,000

During the current year ending December 31, 19A, the following transactions (summarized) relating to the above accounts were completed:

a. Expenditures for nonrecurring, relatively large repairs that tend to increase the use value of the assets:	
Plant building	$32,000
Machinery	19,000
b. Replacement of the original electrical wiring system of the plant building (original cost, $21,000)	42,000
c. Additions:	
Plant building—added a small wing to the plant building to accommodate new equipment acquired. The wing has a useful life of 15 years and no residual value	45,000
Machinery—added special protection devices to ten machines. These devices are attached to the machines and will have to be replaced every five years (no residual value)	2,000
d. Outlays for maintenance parts, labor, and so on to keep the assets in normal working condition:	

Quarter	*Plant Building*	*Machinery*
1	1,700	2,000
2	1,500	6,000
3	1,800	1,000
4	2,000	10,000

Required:

1. Give appropriate entries to record transactions (*a*) through (*c*). Explain the basis underlying your decisions.
2. Give appropriate entries by quarter, in parallel columns, for transaction (*d*) assuming: (*a*) the accounting policy is to record all ordinary repairs incurred as revenue expenditures, and (*b*) to use an allowance procedure. The annual budgeted amounts for this item were: plant building, $7,500; machinery, $18,000.
3. Which method used in Requirement 2 do you prefer? Explain.

Problem 12–13

On July 15, 19E, Joseph Doan, your client, sold his apartment house to John Ames. The escrow statement follows:

	Joseph Doan, Seller		John Ames, Buyer	
	Charges	Credits	Charges	Credits
Sales price		$250,000	$250,000	
Paid directly to seller	$ 10,000			$ 10,000
First mortgage assumed by buyer	106,000			106,000
Purchase money mortgage	84,000			84,000
Prorations:				
Real estate taxes		250	250	
Insurance adjustment		200	200	
Interest		300	300	
Fees:				
Escrow	100		100	
Title insurance			790	
Recording	5		10	
Attorney	35		50	
Revenue stamps			550	
Funds deposited in escrow account: July 14, 19E				52,250
Items paid from escrow account:				
Commission to Lion Reality Company	15,000			
Remit:				
Joseph Doan	35,610			
	$250,750	$250,750	$252,250	$252,250

Doan's accounting records are maintained on the cash basis method. When you undertake the September 30, 19E, quarterly audit for your client, the following information is available to you:

1. A "Suspense" account was opened for money received in connection with the sale of the property.
2. The apartment building and land were purchased on July 1, 19A, for $225,000. The building was being depreciated over a 40-year life by the straight-line method for the purposes of both reporting and income taxes. Accumulated depreciation at December 31, 19D, was $17,500. A half year's depreciation has been consistently recorded on Doan's books for assets purchased or sold during the year. No depreciation has been recorded on the books for 19E.
3. The contract of sale stated that the price for the land on which the building was built was $25,000; the cost recorded on Doan's books.
4. The purchase money mortgage payments are $1,000 per month plus accrued interest. The first payment was due on August 1, 19E.

Required:

Prepare the adjusting journal entries to record the sale on Doan's books.

(AICPA adapted)

Problem 12–14

You are the accountant for the White Corporation and receive a telephone call from their bookkeeper informing you that the corporation has sold a storage building and land. You have submitted a list of annual adjusting entries for this client as of December 31 each year. The sale of the property took place as of June 30, 19D, and the bookkeeper requests that you advise her how to record the transaction. You advise her to open an account called "Sale of Property" and credit the account with the proceeds and charge same with expenses paid in connection with the sale, if any, and you will complete the recording when you make your next audit.

The escrow statements were as follows:

Seller's Statement

Selling price			$34,000.00
Cash due from—			
Bank	$14,740.27		
Buyer	6,725.75	$21,466.02	
Purchase money from second mortgage		12,000.00	
Balance 19C taxes to be paid by bank		166.53	
Tax adjustment for 19D:			
Credit to buyer—6 months		354.75	
Revenue stamps		35.20	
Insurance adjustment—credit to seller			22.50
		$34,022.50	$34,022.50

Buyer's Statement

Purchase price	$34,000.00	
Cash due to seller		$ 6,725.75
Insurance adjustment	22.50	
Title fee and recording	58.00	
Tax adjustment for 19D		354.75
First mortgage to bank		15,000.00
Purchase money for second mortgage		12,000.00
	$34,080.50	$34,080.50

Note: The bank will deduct from the $15,000 (first mortgage) the following items:

		$ 15,000.00
19C taxes	$ 166.53	
Revenue stamps	35.20	
Title fee and recording	58.00	259.73
Net due from bank		14,740.27
Net due from buyer		6,725.75
Total Due Seller		$21,466.02

Property taxes are assessed on December 31 of each year and are payable either in full the following September or the first of four quarterly installments is due on that date. Included in the accrued tax account are:

1. The balance of the 19C taxes	$166.53
2. One half of the 19D assessment	354.75*
Total	$521.28

* This represents the estimated tax expense applicable to the first six months of 19D.

During your subsequent quarterly audit, you find the following facts:

a. The property was purchased January 1, 19A, at a total cost of $32,000, $30,000 for the building and $2,000 for the land.

b. Depreciation is booked annually at 2½%, and the accumulated depreciation at December 31, 19C, is $2,250.

c. The account, Sale of Property, contains a credit of $21,466.02 (funds received from sale) and a debit of $500 which is a commission paid to an individual who obtained the buyer.

Required:

1. Give journal entries to complete the recording of the transaction on White Corporation's books.
2. Prepare a schedule showing the gain or loss.

(AICPA adapted)

Problem 12–15

Part 1–Company X had an old machine that originally cost $10,000 and has depreciation to date of $7,500. The old machine was exchanged for a new similar machine that had a firm cash price of $4,500. Two independent cases are assumed:

Case A–There was a direct exchange (no cash difference was paid or received).

Case B–Company X exchanged the old machine for the new machine and paid a cash difference of $2,100.

Part 2–Company Y had an old machine that originally cost $12,000 and has accumulated depreciation to date of $8,000. The old machine was exchanged for a new similar machine that had a firm cash price of $3,000. Two independent cases are assumed:

Case C–There was a direct exchange (no cash difference was paid or received).

Case D–Company Y exchanged the old machine for the new machine and received a cash difference of $500.

Required:

1. Give the entries to record the exchange of similar assets in Cases A, B, C and D.
2. Give the entries for each case assuming the assets were dissimilar.

Problem 12–16

Two dissimilar operational assets were exchanged when the accounts of the two companies involved reflected the following:

Account	Company A (designate as Asset A)	Company B (designate as Asset B)
Operational asset	$5,000	$8,000
Accumulated depreciation	3,000	5,300

The fair market value of Asset A was realistically determined to be $2,500; no realistic estimate could be made for Asset B.

Required:

1. Give the exchange entry for each company assuming no cash difference was involved.
2. Give the exchange entry for both companies assuming a cash difference of $100 was paid by Company A to Company B.

Problem 12–17

Two similar operational assets were exchanged when the accounts of the two companies involved reflected the following:

Account	*Company A (designate as Asset A)*	*Company B (designate as Asset B)*
Operational asset	$5,000	$8,000
Accumulated depreciation	3,000	5,300

The fair market value of Asset A was realistically determined to be $2,500; no realistic estimate could be made for Asset B.

Required:

1. Give the exchange entry for each company assuming no cash difference is involved.
2. Give the exchange entry for each company assuming a cash difference of $500 was paid by Company A to Company B.

Chapter 13

Property, Plant, and Equipment—Depreciation and Depletion

At the outset of the preceding chapter we defined the several classes of assets acquired for operational purposes rather than for sale; that is, they are acquired and utilized because of their *future* revenue-generating potentials to the enterprise. Thus, they can be viewed by the enterprise as comprising a store of economic-service values that will expire as they are utilized in the revenue-generating process. Therefore, as these economic-service values are utilized in generating revenue, a portion of their total cost periodically must be matched with (allocated against) the period revenues generated in order to fulfill the requirements of income measurement. The process of periodically allocating a portion of the total cost of property, plant, and equipment against the revenue generated must be applied to most operational assets (land is an exception). This entails application of allocation procedures to three distinct classes of assets; the accounting terminology commonly utilized in this respect is:

1. Depreciation. The accounting process of allocating against periodic revenue the cost expiration of *tangible* property, plant, and equipment.
2. Depletion. The accounting process of allocating against periodic revenue the cost expiration of an asset represented by a *natural resource* such as mineral deposits, gravel deposits, and timber stands.
3. Amortization. The accounting process of allocating against periodic revenue the cost expiration of *intangibles* represented by *special rights* or benefits such as patents, copyrights, and leaseholds.

This chapter discusses depreciation and depletion; Chapter 14 considers the amortization of intangibles.

Clearly, the three processes just described are similar conceptually; each focuses on a different class of assets. Conceptually they represent the process of cost allocation as opposed to asset valuation. They constitute an application of the *matching principle*.

In a sense, the cost of property, plant, and equipment may be compared with a prepaid expense; the cost is prepaid (in advance of utilization of the asset), hence is recorded as an asset; as the economic service life of the asset expires with the passage of time and through use, the cost thereof must be systematically allocated to operations as a current cost. Operational assets, like goods and services represented by current expenditures for operating costs, contribute measurable future benefits to the enterprise.

In accounting for operational assets the underlying principles are: *(a)* at acquisition, the assets are recorded at cost on the basis of the *cost principle; (b)* subsequent to acquisition, those assets that have a determinable limited life are reported at the cost recognized at acquisition less the accumulated allocations of such costs (depreciation amortization and depletion); and *(c)* periodic allocations of acquisition cost, made on a systematic and rational basis, are recognized as current expense in conformance with the *matching principle.*

DEPRECIATION

Now let's turn our attention specifically to depreciation as defined above. In order to understand fully the nature of depreciation accounting it is necessary to examine its effects on *(a)* the income statement, *(b)* retained earnings and dividends, *(c)* cash flow, and *(d)* balance sheet presentation.

Depreciation is recognized on the income statement as selling, administrative, or manufacturing expenses, depending upon the nature and use of the assets involved. The periodic depreciation charge may affect the income statement in two ways. That portion of the depreciation charge in a period classified as selling expense and administrative expense directly reduces pretax income by the amount involved. That part of the depreciation charge classified as factory cost is reported as a part of the cost of goods manufactured. The goods sold during the current period carry to cost of goods sold a portion of the depreciation charge allocated to manufacturing cost. Such depreciation costs likewise decrease reported income where the goods are sold. On the other hand, that portion of depreciation charge remaining in the valuation of goods on hand at the end of the period is reported as an *asset* (inventory) and deferred until the goods are sold. It follows that income of a given period is reduced by depreciation initially charged to inventory only to the extent that such goods are sold during that period.

Depreciation and Dividends

Since the depreciation charge reduces reported pretax income, the amount of retained earnings is likewise reduced. This effect reduces the reported amount of retained earnings available for dividends; consequently, over the life of the operational asset an amount equivalent to the cost of the tangible fixed asset recognized at acquisition (less any residual value) is "held back" from retained earnings and dividend availability. Thus one of the results of depreciation accounting is to prevent the impairment of capital through dividends based upon overstated earnings. Failure to recognize depreciation causes overstatement of income with an attendant possible dissipation of capital through liquidating dividends.

Depreciation and Cash Flow

Depreciation accounting attempts to measure a cost and to charge it against income. Where revenue is sufficient, depreciation like other expenses is recovered. It should be apparent, however, that the mere booking of depreciation can have no effect upon the amount of assets coming into the business through sales of product. But if a business can sell its product for enough to cover all operating costs including depreciation, the assets received from customers (cash and receivables) will exceed other expense outlays by at least the amount of the depreciation. Since dividends normally are paid only out of net income, net assets equal to the amount of the depreciation charged off will be retained in the business which operates at a profit or merely at break even.[1]

In view of the above discussion it is important to realize that although the depreciation provision does hold back assets from dividends equivalent to the provision, it does not provide or "hold back" cash specifically. The relationship of depreciation and cash flow is simply that although most costs and expenses require cash when incurred, the depreciation charge is a noncash reduction of net income; the cash was disbursed when the fixed asset was acquired. Therefore, the *cash generated by net income is greater* than reported net income by the amount of noncash expenses (less noncash revenues) reported on the income statement. Obviously, the fact that depreciation has been recognized does not mean that cash (or even other assets) necessarily will be available to replace the assets when their service life expires. The assets retained as a result of deducting from income a provision for depreciation before making the dividend distribution are not automatically segregated into a fund for replacements. On the contrary, the retained funds will probably find uses in paying off liabilities and in purchasing of new and different types of assets; therefore, such funds seldom are available for actual replacements when old assets reach the end of their service life. Any specific fund for replacement must be the result of planned appropriation of cash or other liquid assets from period to period.

Depreciation Is an Estimate

The importance of depreciation as an expense may be seen readily upon examination of the operating statements of any business with a

---

[1] Different methods of depreciation have different effects on cash flow. For example, accelerated depreciation in the early years will give a higher depreciation expense amount than will straight line; consequently, income taxes would be lower. This would result in a saving of cash paid for income taxes during the early periods. See Chapter 21 for discussion of cash flows.

relatively large investment in property, plant, and equipment. The importance of depreciation varies with the nature of the business and the degree of mechanization or automation involved. Significantly, reported net income is no more accurate than the estimate of the periodic depreciation figure. Since periodic depreciation expense as well as certain other expenses are estimates, reported net income reflects such estimates. In view of these considerations any attempt to compute and report the depreciation provision to even pennies, for example, implies a degree of accuracy that does not exist. With respect to accounting, rounding of the periodic charge should be consistent with the probable margin of error involved in the estimate.

DEPRECIATION DISCLOSURES

Because of the significant effects of the depreciation methods used, on both financial position and the results of operations, the APB in *Opinion No. 12* reaffirmed an earlier ARB that the following disclosures should be made in the financial statements or accompanying notes:

a. Depreciation expense for the period.
b. Balances of major classes of depreciable assets, by nature or function, at the balance sheet date.
c. Accumulated depreciation, either by major classes of depreciable assets or in total, at the balance sheet date.
d. A general description of the methods used in computing depreciation on major classes of depreciable assets.

This was augmented in *APB Opinion No. 22*, "Disclosure of Accounting Policies" (April 1973), where depreciation methods and amortization policies were cited as examples of disclosure which would be commonly required.

CAUSES OF DEPRECIATION

The causes of depreciation may be classified as follows:

Physical Factors	*Functional Factors*
1. Wear and tear from operation.	1. Inadequacy.
2. Action of time and other elements	2. Supersession and obsolescence.
3. Deterioration and decay.	

Significantly, a *change in market value* is not recognized as one of the causes of depreciation in the accounting sense.[2] The three physical factors, as they affect the service life of a tangible fixed asset, are self-explanatory. Inadequacy is brought about by expansion of a business,

[2] Depreciation is not caused by changes in the market value of an operational asset; however, when the carrying value is significantly above the use value to the entity, in terms of fair value (such as an idle plant), the asset must be written down to reflect the loss (this is not depreciation expense). See Chapter 12.

the fixed asset becoming unequal to the increased service required, although still in good condition and quite capable of the service originally expected of it. Supersession results when an asset is superseded by another asset which operates more efficiently. Supersession is brought about when inventions give rise to new assets which may be operated more cheaply in rendering the same or an improved service. In such cases it may be desirable to discard the old asset. Obsolescence may arise from inadequacy, supersession, and other causes. Obsolescence of an operational asset may arise as a result of the outmoding of the product being produced or the service being rendered.

Depreciation accounting takes into account all predictable factors that tend to limit the economic usefulness of an operational asset to the enterprise. The periodic apportionment of cost through depreciation must be based upon both the physical and functional causes of depreciation. Generally those factors that operate more or less continuously are given recognition in depreciation accounting, whereas sudden and unexpected factors such as storms, floods, sudden change in demand, and radical outmoding of the asset must be accorded special treatment with respect to the fixed assets involved. One of these special treatments, for example, might result in the immediate removal of an asset from the accounts and the related recording of a loss.

The useful life of an operational asset generally is influenced directly by the repair and maintenance policies of the firm. Low standards of maintenance and repairs may reduce costs temporarily; however, the useful life of the asset will be shortened considerably thereby increasing the periodic depreciation expense. Although some have contended that depreciation should include both amortization of the original cost and current repair costs, accountants have viewed repairs and depreciation (as previously defined) as separate cost elements.

In the case of facilities temporarily idle or being held for possible future use, depreciation should continue since the physical and functional causes, which tend to reduce the ultimate economic usefulness of the asset to the firm, continue. Operational assets that will not be returned to service should be reduced to their fair market value in anticipation of disposal. Special accounts normally should be established in accounting for idle facilities.

FACTORS IN DETERMINING THE DEPRECIATION CHARGE

The periodic depreciation expense should represent the allocation of the original cost (less the estimated residual value) of the asset to operations in proportion to the economic benefit received from the asset. The factors which must be considered in calculating the periodic depreciation charge are:

1. Actual cost (as defined in the preceding chapter).
2. Estimated residual (scrap) value.
3. Estimated service life.

Clearly, determination of depreciation is based on one "actual" and two "estimated" factors. The residual value is the estimated amount which may be recovered through sale, trade-in allowance, or by other means when the asset is finally retired from service. In estimating the residual value, allowance must be made for the costs of dismantling and disposal of the retired asset. For example, assume it is estimated that upon retirement the asset can be sold for $250 and that the costs of dismantling and selling are estimated at $50. In this case the residual value would be $200. In practice, recovery value and dismantling and selling costs are frequently disregarded entirely—a procedure which is acceptable when the recovery and disposal costs may offset, when the amounts involved are immaterial, or when the estimates involve a wide margin of error.

In estimating the service life of an asset for accounting purposes it is important to realize that service life implies *(a)* use of the asset by the owner, *(b)* use of the asset for the purpose for which acquired, and *(c)* a definite repair and maintenance policy over the life of the asset. Allocation of depreciation charges should be representative of the expiration of the "economic-service values" of the asset to the enterprise. Thus, the service life should be measured in terms that are most representative of the expiration of such values. Accordingly, service life may be measured in terms of *(a)* definite time periods such as months or years, *(b)* units of output, or *(c)* hours of operating time. Selection of the appropriate measure of service life should depend upon the nature of the asset involved and the primary causes of depreciation.

RECORDING DEPRECIATION

The periodic depreciation amount is recorded as a debit to an expense account or a cost of manufacturing account (factory overhead) and a credit to an asset contra account entitled Accumulated Depreciation. Rather than a direct credit to the related asset account, a special contra account traditionally has been credited in order to maintain a separation of the original cost and the amount of that cost expired through depreciation. The contra account should not be labeled as a "reserve" for depreciation, but as Accumulated Depreciation.

In the subsidiary asset records, the periodic depreciation charges and accumulated depreciation are recorded for each individual asset or group of assets.

METHODS OF DEPRECIATION

Methods of depreciation focus on computation of the amount of depreciation expense that should be recorded each period. A number of methods have been developed, each of which provides a somewhat different pattern of depreciation charges over the life of the tangible asset. The methods may be classified as follows:

a. Based on time:
   1. Straight line.

b. Based on output:
   2. Service hours.
   3. Units of output.

c. Reducing depreciation charge:
   4. Sum-of-the-years' digits.
   5. Fixed percentage on declining base amount.
   6. Declining rate on cost.
   7. Double-declining balance.

d. Based on investment and interest concepts (discussed in Chapter 6):
   8. Annuity.
   9. Sinking fund.

To illustrate these methods the following symbols and simplified amounts are used:

Item	*Symbol*	*Illustrative Figures*
Acquisition cost	*C*	$ 100
Scrap or residual value	*S*	10
Estimated service life	*n*	
Years		3
Service hours		6,000
Productive output in units		9,000
Depreciation rate (per year, per service hour, or per unit of productive output)	*r*	
Dollar amount of depreciation per period	*D*	

Straight-Line Method

The straight-line method has been used widely because of its simplicity. This method relates depreciation directly to the passage of time rather than to specific use. It is called straight line because it results in an equal charge for depreciation in each of the periods of the service life of the asset; thus, when graphed against time, both the accumulated depreciation and the undepreciated asset cost are indicated by straight lines. The use of the formula for computing the periodic depreciation charge (annual in this case) is illustrated below.

$$D = \frac{C - S}{n} \quad \text{or} \quad D = \frac{\$100 - \$10}{3} = \$30 \text{ per period}$$

Depreciation frequently is expressed as a *rate*. For the illustrative figures that the periodic (annual) rate *(r)* may be expressed as either *(a)* 33⅓% on net depreciable value ($90 × 33⅓% = $30) or *(b)* 30% on cost ($100 × 30%)[3]; the percent on cost generally is used.

Exhibit 13–1 illustrates application of straight-line depreciation over the life of the illustrative asset and the accounting entries involved.

---

[3] Many accountants prefer to express the rate as a percent of depreciable value, viz, $30 ÷ ($100 − $10) = 33⅓%. In this case, to compute the periodic charge, the "net to be depreciated" is multiplied by the rate.

EXHIBIT 13–1
Depreciation Table and Entries, Straight-Line Method (life three years)

Year	Depreciation Expense (debit)	Accumulated Depreciation (credit)	Balance Accumulated Depreciation	Undepreciated Asset Balance (book value)
0............				$100
1............	$30	$30	$30	70
2............	30	30	60	40
3............	30	30	90	10 (residual value)
	$90	$90		

The straight-line method is simple, easy to understand, and is widely used. It meets the criterion of being "systematic and rational" (*ARB No. 44*, revised, par. 2). It is theoretically acceptable when the following conditions prevail:

1. The decline in economic-service potential of the asset is approximately the same each period.
2. The decline in economic-service potential of the asset is related to the passage of time rather than to use.
3. Use of the asset is consistent from period to period.
4. Repairs and maintenance are essentially the same each period.

Straight-line depreciation is deficient in that *(a)* depreciation is considered a function of time rather than a function of use, which often is not the case; *(b)* it may not effectively match expense with revenue; and *(c)* it causes a distortion in certain rate of return computations.

The latter effect occurs because depreciation expense remains constant each period (and affects the rate of return, numerator, net income, in this way) whereas the asset (and total assets, the denominator) reduces each year. Of course, similar effects occur for all depreciation methods except in the case where depreciation expense changes each period inversely and in proportion to changes in the carrying value of the depreciable assets.

Service-Hours Method

The service-hours method is based upon the assumption that the decrease in service life is conditioned primarily by the actual running time of the asset rather than by the mere passage of time. Rather than an equal periodic charge for depreciation, this method results in a periodic charge which correlates with the amount of time the asset operated. If a machine is operated twice as much in the current period as in the prior period, the depreciation charge for the current period will be twice as much as that of the last period. In utilizing this method the service life of the asset must be estimated in terms of total probable service or working hours prior to retirement; then a rate per service hour is computed.

Assuming a 6,000-hour estimated useful life, the formula for the depreciation rate would be:

$$r = \frac{C - S}{n} \quad \text{or} \quad r = \frac{\$100 - \$10}{6{,}000} = \$.015 \text{ per service hour}$$

Assuming 3,000 actual hours of running time the first year, depreciation expense would be:

$$D = r \times \text{Service Hours Current Period}$$

or

$$D = \$.015 \times 3{,}000 = \$45$$

Exhibit 13–2 illustrates application of the service-hours method over the life of the illustrative asset.

EXHIBIT 13–2
Depreciation Table and Entries, Service-Hours Method (life 6,000 hours)

Year	*Service Hours Worked**	*Depreciation Expense (debit)*		*Accumulated Depreciation (credit)*	*Balance Accumulated Depreciation*	*Undepreciated Asset Balance (book value)*
0............						$100
1............	3,000	(3,000 × $.015)	$45	$45	$45	55
2............	2,000	(2,000 × $.015)	30	30	75	25
3............	1,000	(1,000 × $.015)	15	15	90	10 (residual value)
	6,000		$90	$90		

* It is assumed that the asset was actually used in this manner and that the original estimate of useful life was confirmed.

The service-hours method satisfies the criterion of "rational and systematic" and would tend to insure a logical matching of cost and revenue on the assumption that the asset loses service potential on the basis of running time. Under this method the amount of cost allocated would tend to vary with the productive output of the asset. However, to the extent that there was running time without productive output, this relationship would not prevail. Where obsolescence is not a primary factor and where the economic-service potentials of the asset to the company are used up primarily by running time, the service-hours method would seem appropriate. Also wide variations in use from period to period would suggest application of the service-hours method. Obviously, relative to many assets, such as buildings, furniture, and typewriters, it would be impracticable, if not impossible, to apply the service-hours method. In contrast, it would be appropriate for vehicles.

Productive-Output Method

Under this method the service life of the asset is estimated in terms of the number of *units* of output. A proportionate part of the total cost to be depreciated (cost less scrap value) is charged to each unit of output as a cost of production; consequently, depreciation charges fluctuate periodically with changes in the volume of production or output. Each unit of output is charged with a constant amount of depreciation, in contrast to the straight-line method where each unit of output will be charged with a different amount of depreciation if output varies from period to period.

The cost to be depreciated over the life of the asset is divided by the service life in units to derive a depreciation rate per unit of output; multiplication of this rate times the output for the period gives the periodic depreciation charge. Thus computation of the rate, assuming an estimated productive life of 9,000 units of output, would be:

$$r = \frac{C - S}{n}$$

or

$$r = \frac{\$100 - \$10}{9{,}000} = \$.01 \text{ per unit of output}$$

Assuming 4,000 units of actual output during the first year, the depreciation charge would be:

$$D = r \times \text{Units of Output Current Period}$$

or

$$D = \$.01 \times 4{,}000 = \$40$$

Exhibit 13–3 illustrates an application of the productive-output method over the life of the asset.

EXHIBIT 13–3
Depreciation Table and Entries, Productive-Output Method (life 9,000 units)

Year	*Units of Output**	*Depreciation Expense (debit)*		*Accumulated Depreciation (credit)*	*Balance Accumulated Depreciation*	*Undepreciated Asset Balance (book value)*
0............						$100
1............	4,000	(4,000 × $.01)	$40	$40	$40	60
2............	3,000	(3,000 × $.01)	30	30	70	30
3............	2,000	(2,000 × $.01)	20	20	90	10 (residual value)
	9,000		$90	$90		

* It is assumed that the asset was actually used in this manner.

The productive-output method and the service-hours method both recognize the fact that some assets, such as trucks and machinery, depreciate more rapidly with higher usage than with lower usage. These methods relate more closely the benefit derived from the use of the asset and the depreciation cost allocated than do other methods. The productive-output method is particularly appropriate where obsolescence is not a major factor, where actual output can be realistically measured, and where the service life in units of output can be reasonably estimated.

The differences between the periodic depreciation in the service-hours method and the productive-output method in the illustrative problem are due to a change in the efficiency of operations—the asset was used more efficiently in some periods than others. This observation would lead to the conclusion that in situations where either method could be applied, the productive-output method generally would be preferable.

It is important to recognize the effect the different methods have on *total cost of products* and on *unit product cost.* The straight-line method reports depreciation as a *fixed cost in total,* but *variable per unit* of output. In contrast, the service-hours method and productive-output method reports depreciation as *variable in total,* but *fixed per unit of output.* To illustrate assume an asset costing $600 (no residual value) with an estimated life of five years or 500 units of output. Assume further that output was: Year 1—90; Year 2—100; Year 3—110; Year 4—120; and Year 5—80. The comparative depreciation charges and unit cost figures for the straight-line and output methods are compared below:

		Output Depreciation		*Straight-Line Depreciation*	
Year	*Units of Output*	*Amount*	*Unit Cost*	*Amount*	*Unit Cost*
1............	90	$108	$1.20	$120	$1.33
2............	100	120	1.20	120	1.20
3............	110	132	1.20	120	1.09
4............	120	144	1.20	120	1.00
5............	80	96	1.20	120	1.50
	500	$600		$600	

These distinctions are particularly important in cost analyses for managerial pricing, control, and decision-making considerations. These relative effects should be considered carefully in selecting a method of depreciation.

Reducing-Charge Methods

The reducing-charge methods are designed to allocate the cost to be depreciated in such a manner that periodic depreciation expense charges are higher in the early years and lower in the later years of the life of the operational asset. The reducing-charge methods are based upon the theory that new assets are more efficient than old assets; therefore, the economic-service potentials rendered by the asset are greater during the early life of the asset. If the cost of these greater values being consumed through utilization of the asset is to be matched with the resulting revenue, some form of reducing-charge depreciation (frequently referred to as accelerated depreciation) is theoretically desirable. The reducing-charge methods are also defended on the grounds that the annual depreciation charge should decrease as repair costs on the asset increase, thus resulting in a more equitable charge to the operating periods for the use of the operational asset.

Numerous procedures have been proposed for computing a reducing depreciation charge from period to period over the life of an asset; however, the principal methods currently being used are:

1. Sum-of-the-years'-digits.
2. Fixed-percentage-on-declining-base.
3. Declining rate on cost.
4. Double-declining balance.

Sum-of-the-Years'-Digits Method

This method (usually referred to as the SYD method) applies to a decreasing fraction each succeeding period during the life of the asset to the cost to be depreciated. The fractions are determined by using as the denominator the sum-of-the-years'-digits for the life of the asset. The numerator, which changes each period, is the years' digits in inverse order (same as the remaining life including the current period). For example, the asset in the illustration, having an estimated service life of three years, would be depreciated as follows:

Denominator:	Sum-of-the-years'-digits; $1 + 2 + 3 = 6$.
Numerators:	Digits in inverse order; 3, 2, and 1.
Fractions:	First period, $^3/_6$.
	Second period, $^2/_6$.
	Third period, $^1/_6$.

Exhibit 13–4 illustrates an application of the method for the illustrative asset.

EXHIBIT 13–4
Depreciation Table and Entries—Sum-of-the-Years'-Digits Method (life three years)

Year		*Depreciation Expense (debit)*	*Accumulated Depreciation (credit)*	*Balance Accumulated Depreciation*	*Undepreciated Asset Balance (book value)*
0............					$100
1............	($^3/_6 \times$ $90)	$45	$45	$45	55
2............	($^2/_6 \times$ $90)	30	30	75	25
3............	($^1/_6 \times$ $90)	15	15	90	10 (residual value)
		$90	$90		

Note that the reducing fraction is multiplied by the cost to be depreciated (cost less residual value) in each period. When the life of the asset is relatively long, the denominator (sum of the digits) can be readily computed by using the following formula and a 25-year assumed life:

$$\text{SYD} = n\left(\frac{n+1}{2}\right) \quad \text{or} \quad \text{SYD} = 25\left(\frac{25+1}{2}\right) = 325$$

Fixed-Percentage-on-Declining-Base Method

To apply this method the book value of the asset (undepreciated asset balance) is multiplied by a constant percentage rate. Since a constant rate is applied to a *declining base,* each subsequent periodic depreciation charge will be less. The rate must be computed taking into account the cost, estimated life, and residual value; consequently, the rate will automatically provide for the residual value at the end of the service life of the asset. The depreciation rate (the fixed percentage) and its application is illustrated below:

$$r = 1 - \sqrt[n]{\frac{S}{C}} \quad \text{or} \quad r = 1 - \sqrt[3]{\frac{\$10}{\$100}} = .536, \text{ or } 53.6\%$$

Calculation of $\sqrt[n]{\frac{S}{C}}$ is readily achieved by use of logarithms or some pocket calculators.

EXHIBIT 13–5
Depreciation Table and Entries—Fixed-Percentage-on-Declining-Base Method

Year	*Depreciation Expense (debit)*		*Accumulated Depreciation (credit)*	*Balance Accumulated Depreciation*	*Undepreciated Asset Balance (book value)*
0..............					$100.00
1..............	(53.6% × $100)	$53.60	$53.60	$53.60	46.40
2..............	(53.6% × $46.40)	24.87	24.87	78.47	21.53
3..............	(53.6% × $21.53)	11.53	11.53	90.00	10.00 (residual value)
		$90.00	$90.00		

Observe in Exhibit 13–5 that the book value at the end of the service life is precisely the estimated scrap value. It should be pointed out that where the asset has no scrap value the formula given above for calculation of the depreciation percentage or rate cannot be used unless a nominal scrap value of, say, $1, is assumed. As a matter of practical application it is usually desirable to round the rate to an even percentage.

Declining-Rate-on-Cost Method. This method is not based on a particular formula; the depreciation rate is different each period, since it is selected arbitrarily for each period. A series of decreasing percentages are selected to provide the desired reduction in the periodic depreciation charge. The residual or scrap value, as a percent of cost, is provided for by excluding it from the periodic rates. The total of the periodic rates plus the scrap percent must total 100%. Application of the declining-rate-on-cost method is shown in Exhibit 13–6, assuming the declining rates selected are those indicated in the second column.

EXHIBIT 13–6
Depreciation Table and Entries—Declining-Rate-on-Cost Method (estimated life three years)

Year	Declining Rates	Depreciation Expense (debit)		Allowance for Depreciation (credit)	Balance Accumulated Depreciation	Undepreciated Asset Balance (book value)
0						$100
1	55%	(55% × $100)	$55	$55	$55	45
2	25	(25% × $100)	25	25	80	20
3	10	(10% × $100)	10	10	90	10 (residual value)
	90%		$90	$90		
Scrap %	10					
	100%					

A primary weakness of the declining-rate-on-cost method is that the periodic rates, being *arbitrarily* selected, lack objectivity and may not be representative of the actual expiration of service values throughout the life of the asset. The method also has a serious flaw in that it cannot be classed as "rational and systematic," and therefore is not in accordance with GAAP.

Double-Declining-Balance Method

Reducing-charge depreciation is acceptable for federal income tax purposes, except the regulations provide that the amount of depreciation must not be more than double the amount that would result under the straight-line method when the residual value is ignored.[4] This provision gave rise to the double-declining-balance method. Under this method the fixed percentage used is simply double the straight-line rate; residual value is ignored. This rate is multiplied each year by the declining book value. Based on the above data the rate would be 67% (i.e., 33⅓% × 2). The depreciation would be:

---

[4] For income tax purposes there are numerous restrictions on the double-declining-balance method. Double the straight-line rate may be used only on certain types of new property acquired within certain range dates. Used property, certain types of new property, and property acquired before 1954 may be depreciated at 150% of the straight-line rate. Although residual is ignored, an asset may not be depreciated below a reasonable residual value.

Double-Declining-Balance Depreciation

Year	*Book Value*		*Rate*		*Depreciation**
1	$100	×	67%	=	$ 67
2	33	×	67	=	22
3	11	×	67	=	1
					90
Implicit residual value					10
					$100

* Illustrative only—the present time double-declining depreciation may be used for tax purposes only when the life is three years or more.

The reducing-charge methods discussed above can be classed as rational and systematic, except for the declining rate on cost. They are not difficult to apply. For all practical purposes the sum-of-the-years'-digits and double-declining-balance methods are the only reducing-charge methods used. The important criterion to apply is whether they properly match periodic depreciation expense with periodic revenue.

With respect to acceptability of the reducing-charge approach, the Committee on Accounting Procedure of the AICPA stated in *Accounting Research Bulletin No. 44* that

> The declining-balance method is one of those which meets the requirements of being "systematic and rational." In those cases where the expected productivity or revenue-earning power of the asset is relatively greater during the earlier years of its life, or where maintenance charges tend to increase during the later years, the declining-balance method may well provide the most satisfactory allocation of cost. The conclusions of this bulletin also apply to other methods, including the "sum-of-the-years'-digits" method, which produce substantially similar results.

DEPRECIATION BASED ON INVESTMENT CONCEPTS

The preceding paragraphs discussed depreciation approaches that provided: (1) a *constant* depreciation charge (expense) per period, (2) a *decreasing* depreciation charge per period, or (3) a *varying* depreciation charge per period (output methods). The *compound interest methods* represent a distinctly different approach since they provide an *increasing periodic* expense effect. The other approaches to depreciation have been criticized because, among other things, they ignore the investment characteristics of the ownership of property, plant, and equipment. Depreciation based on investment concepts view an investment in property, plant, and equipment, and the return on that investment, in the same manner as if an annuity investment was made. Implicit is the concept that the subsequent periodic returns received over the life of the annuity comprises both principal and interest. Therefore, the total depreciation expense amount each period would be offset by two credits: (1) the recovery of principal is credited to accumulated depreciation, and (2) the remainder is credited to an account for *imputed interest revenue*. The effect of this entry each period, since the principal amount increases each period and the interest amount decreases, is an increasing reduction in net income because of depreciation. Currently, generally accepted accounting standards do not accept these methods except in a very few limited situations. The two methods—annuity and sinking fund—give the same net effect on income; they are briefly illustrated in the Appendix to this chapter.

FRACTIONAL YEAR DEPRECIATION

Implicit in the preceding illustrations has been the assumption that the asset year and the company's fiscal year coincide; however, assets seldom are purchased on the first day of a fiscal period and are seldom retired at the end of the fiscal year. Therefore, depreciation often must be computed for fractional parts of the year. An accounting policy should be established so that consistent and realistic amounts of depreciation are recorded for fractional parts of the year. Most companies do not count days because depreciation is an estimate and such precision would be irrelevant. Policies widely used are:

1. Compute depreciation on the basis of even months.
2. Depreciate from the first of the month all assets acquired on or before the 15th of the month; if acquired after the 15th, do not depreciate for the partial month. Assets disposed of on or before the 15th of the month are not depreciated for the partial month; if disposed after the 15th, record a full month's depreciation.
3. To determinc the monthly depreciation amount, divide the annual amount by $\frac{1}{12}$ regardless of the method of depreciation used.
4. For methods other than straight-line depreciation, when the asset year and the fiscal year do not coincide, compute partial depreciation on the basis of the months for each of the partial years of the asset life and sum the results.

To illustrate implementation of the latter policy, assume the asset used in the preceding illustration was acquired on May 5, Year 1, and was retired on April 25, Year 4. The fiscal year ends on December 31. Using sum-of-the-years'-digits depreciation, as given in Exhibit 13–4, the computations and results would be as follows:

Year	*Annual Depreciation (Exhibit 13–4)*	*Months*	*Computation*	*Depreciation Expense*
1............	$45	8	($45 × $\frac{8}{12}$)	$30
2............	30	12	($45 × $\frac{4}{12}$) + ($30 × $\frac{8}{12}$)	35
3............	15	12	($30 × $\frac{4}{12}$) + ($15 × $\frac{8}{12}$)	20
4............		4	($15 × $\frac{4}{12}$)	5
	$90	36		$90

Other viable alternatives include (1) depreciation computed on the balance in the asset account at the beginning of the year; (2) depreciation computed on the balance in the asset account at the end of the year; (3) depreciation computed only on assets acquired during the first half of the year, and no depreciation on assets disposed of during the first half of the year; and (4) depreciation computed on a semiannual basis.

SPECIAL DEPRECIATION SYSTEMS

Special problems confronting the firm, due to both internal and external factors, frequently require adaptations of the *depreciation methods* of cost allocation discussed above. The primary adaptations, generally referred to as "systems," are discussed in this section under the captions:

1. Inventory (or appraisal) system.
2. Retirement system.
3. Replacement system.
4. Composite life system.
5. Group system.

Inventory System

Under this system, sometimes referred to as the appraisal system, purchases of depreciable assets are debited to an appropriate asset account in the usual manner, and allocations of cost representing depreciation are credited to the same account. The amount recorded as depreciation for the period is determined by estimating the "value" of the asset on hand in its present condition; the asset account then is reduced to this amount and depreciation expense is charged. Salvage recovery serves to reduce depreciation expense for the period. The value of the asset on hand is determined by inventory procedures and an estimate of its cost, taking into account its present condition.

To illustrate, assume the Hand Tools account showed a balance of $680; an inventory of the tools on hand at the end of the period, valued at cost and adjusted for present condition, indicated a value of $560. The broken and obsolete tools were sold for $10. The entry to record the periodic depreciation is:

Cash	10	
Depreciation expense – hand tools ($120 – $10)	110	
Hand tools ($680 – $560)..........		120

The inventory system should be used only in situations where the asset account represents numerous asset items of a small unit cost, such as hand tools, machine tools, patterns, and dies. Even in these cases the system should be used only when the usual methods are impractical with respect to the specific asset.

In applying the inventory system care must be exercised to exclude changes in value due to changes in the price level or other market fluctuations, otherwise the depreciation charge will include noncost elements such as unrealized (holding) market gains and losses. A conventional matching of expired cost and periodic revenues requires that the items be valued at original cost adjusted for present condition.

Retirement and Replacement Systems

The retirement and replacement systems of depreciation frequently are used by public utilities because of the peculiar problems often encountered with respect to certain assets such as poles and other line items. They are also used in accounting for low-cost items such as hand tools. Under both systems, no periodic entry is made for depreciation in the normal manner; instead depreciation is recognized at the *time of replacement* of the asset. The basic distinction between them is that under the *retirement* system, the cost of the *old* asset (less its residual value) is charged to depreciation expense when it is replaced, whereas under the *replacement* system the cost of the *new* asset (less residual value of the *old* asset) is charged to depreciation expense when it replaces the old asset. To illustrate both systems assume the Hi-Power Utility Company replaced ten utility poles at a cost of $100 each. The old poles replaced originally cost $50 each and have a salvage value of $10 each.

Retirement System

1. To record the retirement of the old poles:

Depreciation expense	400	
Salvage inventory (residual value, old poles)	100	
Plant assets (cost of old poles)		500

2. To record the new asset:

Plant asset (cost of new poles)	1,000	
Cash (or inventory)		1,000

Replacement System

Depreciation expense	900	
Salvage inventory (residual value, old poles)	100	
Cash (cost of new poles)		1,000

From this example it should be clear that the retirement system represents a *Fifo* approach whereas the replacement system represents a *Lifo* system in allocating the asset cost to depreciation. The retirement system provides depreciation charges based on older costs and reports the operational asset at newer costs, whereas the replacement system provides depreciation charges based on newer costs and reports the operational asset at the older cost. Neither system adequately matches cost with revenue particularly in the early and late life of the business, inasmuch as depreciation is recognized when assets are being replaced. Once the company has reached a relatively stable level of growth and replacement, the resulting periodic depreciation charges may approximate cost depreciation. Neither of these systems provides a "systematic and rational" allocation of operational asset costs. The systems have been used in the utility field because of the practical difficulty in depreciating large numbers of relatively low-cost items such as poles, crossmembers, brackets, and conduits at many locations. In such situations the distinction between ordinary repairs and capitalizable replacements is difficult to establish and apply on a practical basis. Although lacking theoretical justification, the retirement system in particular has practical justification under certain conditions.

Group and Composite-Life Systems

The discussions up to this point have assumed that each item of property will be depreciated as a separate unit. In actual practice, many companies group certain fixed assets for depreciation purposes. For example, all of the one-ton trucks may be grouped, or an entire operating assembly such as a refinery may be depreciated as a single unit. In such cases an *average depreciation* rate is applied to the group or assembly. Where an average rate of depreciation is applied to a number of *homogeneous* assets having similar characteristics and service lives, such as the trucks mentioned above, the procedure is referred to as *group depreciation*. Where an average rate of depreciation is applied to a number of *heterogeneous* assets having dissimilar characteristics and service lives, such as the refinery mentioned above, the procedure is referred to as *composite depreciation*. Many accountants view composite depreciation as a special variation of group depreciation. It is difficult to draw a definite distinction between the two on the basis of characteristics and service lives. From the accounting standpoint there is no difference in mechanical application of the average rate nor in the resulting journal entries as between the two systems.[5]

Under the group system, all of the assets in the group are recorded in one asset account, and one accumulated depreciation account is established for the entire group; consequently, it would be incorrect to consider that any one item in the group has a "book value"—the book value appearing in the account applies to the entire group and not to individual items. Subsequent acquisitions of items belonging to the group are similarly charged to the group asset account at cost. Depreciation is computed by multiplying an *average depreciation rate* times the balance in the group asset account regardless of the age of the individual assets represented therein. The rate may be computed and applied to cost or cost less salvage value, as desired. The depreciation entry is made by charging Depreciation Expense and crediting Accumulated Depreciation for the periodic amount of depreciation thus computed. Upon retirement of a unit which is a part of the group, the group asset account is credited for the *original cost* of the item and the Accumulated Depreciation account is debited for the *same amount less*

---

[5] Eugene L. Grant and Paul T. Norton, Jr., *Depreciation* (New York: The Ronald Press Co., 1955), chap. vii.

any salvage recovery. The system, therefore, does not recognize "losses or gains" on retirement of group assets.[6]

To illustrate the group system, assume the Derden Wholesale Corporation purchased ten panel trucks for delivery purposes, each costing $2,400. Each truck has an estimated residual value of $400 at the end of the estimated service life of five years. The company desires to depreciate the trucks on a group basis. Assuming depreciation is recognized on the ending balance in the asset account, typical entries under the group system are indicated below:

1. To record the initial purchase of ten trucks at $2,400 each:

Trucks	24,000	
Cash		24,000

2. To record group depreciation at the end of the first year:

Depreciation expense ($24,000 × 16⅔%)	4,000	
Accumulated depreciation		4,000

Computation:

Cost	$24,000
Estimated residual value	4,000
To be depreciated over 5 years	$20,000
Depreciation per year ($20,000 ÷ 5)	$ 4,000
Depreciation rate on asset balance ($4,000 ÷ $24,000)	16⅔%

3. To record retirement of one truck at the end of the second year due to wreck; amount received from insurance, $1,500:

Cash	1,500	
Accumulated depreciation (cost less residual recovery)	900	
Trucks		2,400

4. To record purchase of two additional trucks at $2,500 each:

Trucks	5,000	
Cash		5,000

5. To record the retirement of a truck that has been used for 5½ years, and then sold to a salvage yard for $150, original cost, $2,400:

Cash	150	
Accumulated depreciation	2,250	
Trucks		2,400

In applying the group system it may be necessary to approximate the "book value" of a specific unit that is a part of the group. For example, when a unit is transferred from one group account to another group account, as might be done when the asset is moved from one organizational division of the company to another, it is desirable that the original acquisition cost and accumulated depreciation to date be transferred in the accounts. In such cases the accumulated depreciation under the group system may be approximated as follows:

$$\frac{\text{Present Age}}{\text{Service Life}} \times (\text{Acquisition Cost} - \text{Residual Value})$$

[6] Ibid.

To illustrate, assume a machine is being transferred from Plant A to Plant B; the machine originally cost $5,300 and has been in operation six years. Its estimated service life is 15 years, and the estimated salvage value, $300. The machine has been depreciated on a group basis, the *average* group rate being used is 8%. The entry to record the transfer might be:

Machinery—Plant B	5,300	
Accumulated depreciation—machinery—Plant A*	2,000	
Machinery—Plant A		5,300
Accumulated depreciation—machinery—Plant B*		2,000

* Computation: $\frac{6}{15} \times (\$5,300 - \$300) = \$2,000$

Under the *composite system* the units making up the operating unit or assembly may have a fairly wide range of service lives. Because of this condition, composite-life depreciation is subject to theoretical objections. In establishing the average rate under composite depreciation, both the *composite life* and *composite rate* may be computed. Composite life is the average life of the various units which go to make up an operating unit or assembly, and the composite rate is the ratio of the periodic depreciation to the acquisition cost of all components of the operating unit, as illustrated in Exhibit 13–7.

EXHIBIT 13–7
Composite Depreciation—Operating Assembly XY

Component Item	*Original Cost*	*Residual Value*	*Amount to Be Depreciated*	*Estimated Service Life (years)*	*Annual Depreciation*
A	$50,000	$5,000	$45,000	15	$3,000
B	20,000	4,000	16,000	10	1,600
C	7,000	600	6,400	8	800
D	3,000	-0-	3,000	3	1,000
	$80,000	$9,600	$70,400		$6,400*

* Composite life: $70,400 ÷ $6,400 = 11 years.
Composite depreciation rate:
$6,400 ÷ $80,000 = 8% on cost.

Depreciation first period:

Depreciation expense ($80,000 × 8%)	6,400	
Accumulated depreciation		6,400

If there are no changes in the asset account, the assembly will be depreciated to the residual value (at the end of the 11th year in the above example). However, when replacements of component parts are made, the debit to the asset account for the replacement and the credit to the asset account for the cost of the old component (the compensating entry is a debit to Accumulated Depreciation for this same amount, less any salvage recovery) would tend to spread the total cost of utilizing the asset over the actual service life. This service life would be determined in large part by the repair and replacement policy.

The group and composite methods are easier to apply than the unit method and would therefore result in savings on recordkeeping costs for many entities. Of course, for those entities using computers this factor likely becomes insignificant. Group and composite methods recognize that depreciation estimates are based on averages and that gains or losses on disposition of single assets are of minor significance.

The chief disadvantage of the group and composite methods is that it is possible for them to conceal faulty estimates for long periods; and through their failure to recognize gains or losses, not correct for changes in asset usage or for other errors. Unit methods are simple and theoretically they facilitate computation of gains or losses on retirements of particular assets. In case portions of the assets should become idle, depreciation on those could be more readily isolated under unit methods.

DEPRECIATION POLICY

With the possible exception of inventories, no single area of accounting offers as much potential variety of practice or choice as does depreciation accounting. About the only "constant" is the starting point, which usually is historical cost; there are not many variables in the calculation of cost, though such matters as capitalizing or not capitalizing interest during construction, determining fair values in some cases, and treatment of overhead on self-construction afford examples of how identical assets acquired at the same time can begin with different costs. During the life of an asset there are often many judgmental decisions on whether a related expenditure is to be capitalized or expensed. As to capitalized balances (original cost plus post acquisition expenditures), we have seen there are many patterns and formulas which can be adopted for depreciation expense. It is necessary to determine in advance such uncertain elements as life in years, output or hours of use, and rate of return. It is also usually necessary to estimate salvage value; sometimes it is necessary to anticipate costs of dismantling or of restoration incident to retirement of a plant asset. Small wonder, then, that great variability attends depreciation accounting.

For larger companies, it is easier to report their depreciation practices than to assess whether these practices conform to theoretical ideals. To judge whether a particular company's depreciation policies are rational requires an intimate knowledge of maintenance policies, particulars about obsolescence, plans for replacement, and financial considerations, among other things. Only a limited segment of the management of most entities is privy to such data or sophisticated enough to appreciate its implications. The financial statement reader, even if knowledgeable is probably able to make only limited judgments about what is reported concerning depreciation.

Accounting Trends and Techniques, 1975, the AICPA annual survey of practices of 600 large industrial corporations, indicates that in annual reports, the straight-line method is used more than the other methods accounting for 70% of the total, and its popularity is growing.

Accelerated depreciation account for almost 25% of the total, while unit of production methods accounted for almost 5%.[7] Details from the 1975 survey covering the four preceding years are set out in Exhibit 13-8.

EXHIBIT 13-8
Depreciation and Depletion Policy*

	1974	*1973*	*1972*	*1971*
Method used:				
Straight line	563	568	565	545
Declining balance	71	74	73	77
Sum-of-the-years' digits	45	47	52	51
Accelerated method – not specified	74	76	80	74
Unit of production	35	40	38	36
Other methods	1	1	1	1
Total Disclosures	789	806	809	784

* AICPA, *Accounting Trends and Techniques, 1975* (New York, 1975), p. 287.

The same study indicates that approximately 83% of the companies used different depreciation methods on their income tax returns than they did for financial reporting purposes. For the most part, accelerated methods were used for tax purposes while straight line was used for financial reporting. This, of course, would require interperiod income tax allocation. In a substantial number of instances, the use of different depreciation methods was disclosed but the nature of the differences was not.

The effects of inflation on depreciation is a critical problem facing the accounting profession. Chapter 25 discusses this problem and illustrates certain price-level adjustments.

CHANGES AND CORRECTION OF DEPRECIATION

Occasionally a business will change the method of depreciation used, change estimates of service life or residual value, or locate prior errors. *APB Opinion No. 20*, "Accounting Changes" (July 1971), carefully specifies how each of these three different situations should be accounted for and reported. The provisions of the *Opinion*, as they relate to depreciation, may be summarized as follows:

1. Changes in accounting principle – A change from one generally accepted method to another generally accepted method (such as from SYD to straight line). Changes of this type require an adjustment for the differences in accumulated depreciation to date between the old

[7] The depreciation practices of small companies for financial reporting companies are known only on a piecemeal basis. Those public accountants who have large numbers of small clients and those banks which receive large numbers of reports from small customers can tell what *their* clientele's practices are, but overall data on small business at large are woefully inadequate.

and new methods. This difference is recorded as a depreciation adjustment which is reported on the income statement for the period of change between the captions "extraordinary items" and "net income."

To illustrate, assume XY Corporation has a machine that cost $150,000, having an estimated life of five years and no residual value. After the end of Year 2, the company decided to change from SYD to straight-line depreciation. Computation of the adjustment, the change entry, and reporting on the income statement are illustrated below:

a. Computation of adjustment:

	Prior Method–SYD			
Year	*SYD*	*Amount*	*New Method–Straight Line*	*Difference to Date*
1	5/15	$50,000	$30,000	$20,000
2	4/15	40,000	30,000	10,000
Total..............		$90,000	$60,000	$30,000

b. Change entry at start of Year 3:

Accumulated depreciation	30,000	
Depreciation adjustment, change in accounting method		30,000

c. Reporting on the current income statement:

Income before extraordinary items	$60,000
Extraordinary items (detailed)	(10,000)
Adjustment due to accounting charge (depreciation)	30,000*
Net Income	$80,000

* Appropriate footnote.

This treatment is theoretically sound since it does not permit the adjustment to be reflected as an operating item, documents the item, does not permit it to "bypass" the income statement, and establishes better values for future financial reports.

2. Change in estimate–A change in either, or both, the estimated useful life and residual value. Changes of this type are made prospectively. This means that the undepreciated balance is apportioned to the new remaining life taking into account the new residual value (if changed).

   To illustrate, assume XY Corporation has another machine that cost $160,000, with an estimated useful life of five years, no residual value, and straight-line depreciation. At the start of the fourth year, it is decided that an eight-year estimated life would be more realistic with no change in the residual value. Computation of annual depreciation for the remaining life of five years and the adjusting entry for the fourth year follows:

a. Computation of depreciation expense:

Undepreciated balance: $160,000 × 2/5 = $64,000.
Annual depreciation, straight line: $64,000 ÷ 5 years = $12,800.

b. Adjusting entry for depreciation expense end of fourth year:

Depreciation expense	12,800	
Accumulated depreciation		12,800

3. Accounting error – Errors in depreciation recorded in prior years should be corrected when found. A correcting entry is required which reflects a *prior period adjustment* (reported on the statement of retained earnings) for the net effect of the error. To illustrate, assume that a machine that cost $10,000, estimated service life of five years, no residual value, was incorrectly debited to expense when acquired. The error was discovered at the end of the third year after acquisition. The correcting and adjusting entries for the third year follow:

a. Correcting entry at end of third year:

Machine	10,000	
Accumulated depreciation ($10,000 × 2/5)		4,000
Prior period adjustment – error correction		6,000

b. Adjusting entry for depreciation expense, end of third year:

Depreciation expense ($10,000 ÷ 5)	2,000	
Accumulated depreciation		2,000

Accounting changes, as prescribed in *APB Opinion No. 20,* are discussed more comprehensively in Chapter 20.

THE INVESTMENT TAX CREDIT

From time to time Congress has included in the income tax laws provisions designed to encourage certain kinds of investments. The *investment tax credit* which relates to investment in productive facilities is such a provision. Details concerning the investment credit have changed from time to time.[8] The most recent changes provide that taxpayers who acquire qualified property after January 21, 1975, and place it in service before January 1, 1977, receive a 10% investment credit. The tax effect of the investment credit is to reduce by the amount of the credit the amount of taxes that would otherwise have to be paid. To illustrate the essential nature of the investment credit, assume data pertaining to X Corporation for 1976 as follows:

[8] The first investment credit was provided by the Revenue Act of 1962; it was revised by the 1964 Act, suspended in 1966, and restored in 1967. The Tax Reform Act of 1969 again repealed the credit, but its provisions remained effective for property bought as late as 1975. When effective prior to 1975, the rate was 7% for most entities; it is now 10%.

a. Equipment bought early in 1976 that qualified for the investment credit (ten-year life, zero salvage value)	$200,000
b. Straight-line depreciation on equipment for 1976	20,000
c. Income subject to tax for 1976 (after deducting $20,000 depreciation on equipment)	60,000
d. Income tax before investment credit	24,000*

* Assuming a flat 40% rate for illustrative purposes.

The effect of the investment credit would be as follows:

Income taxes for 1976 before investment credit	$24,000
Less investment credit (10% of $200,000)	20,000
Amount of tax to be paid	$4,000

In the above example the significant reduction in income taxes, as a result of the investment credit, obviously would be viewed with considerable interest by the taxpayer and surely would influence some of his or her investment decisions. With respect to proper accounting, the question is posed as to how the $20,000 tax credit should be recorded and reported. Fundamentally, two distinctly different accounting approaches have been vigorously debated by the accounting profession. In these discussions the nature of the investment credit has been viewed as:

a. A reduction in income taxes. The proponents of this view feel that since the investment credit was made available by the Revenue Act, it is in substance a selective reduction in taxes related to the taxable income of the year in which the credit arises. They feel that it is a "tax item"; to view it as a reduction of the cost of the asset would permit identical items purchased from the same supplier, at the same cost, to be recorded at different costs depending on the respective tax problems of several purchasers and not upon the conditions existing between the buyer and seller of the equipment. They note that various tax consequences as well as the investment credit affect a whole host of managerial decisions. They feel that the investment credit, as an adjustment to income taxes, should affect the net income (after taxes) only in the year in which the tax credit arises. This frequently is referred to as the "flow-through" method.

b. Cost reduction or deferral method. Proponents for this position argue that it is the *use*, not the *purchase*, of the asset that gives rise to the benefits to be received from the investment credit. Strong support for this argument is found in the fact that if the property which gave rise to the credit is not retained, part or all of the credit will be lost. It can also be noted that shorter lived property receives a smaller credit. The original tax provision, although later revised, required that the credit be treated for tax purposes as a reduction of asset cost.

The effects of these two diverse positions may now be emphasized by comparing the accounting entries that would result from the illustrative data given above. Entries in 1976 would be as follows:

Investment Credit Treated as a Reduction in Income Taxes (flow-through method)			*Investment Credit Treated as a Cost Reduction (deferral)*		
a. To record purchase of equipment early in 1976 for $200,000:					
Equipment	200,000		Equipment........................	200,000	
Cash		200,000	Cash		200,000
b. To record income taxes for 1976:					
Income tax expense	4,000		Income tax expense	24,000	
Income tax payable ...		4,000	Income tax payable ...		4,000
			Deferred investment credit		20,000
			Deferred investment credit	2,000	
			Income tax expense (1/10 of $20,000)		2,000
c. Depreciation on equipment for 1976 (ten-year life):					
Depreciation expense	20,000		Depreciation expense	20,000	
Accumulated depreciation		20,000	Accumulated depreciation		20,000

The above tabulation of entries clearly reveals that when the investment credit is treated as a reduction in income taxes, its effects flow through the income statement and balance sheet in a single year. In contrast, under the deferral method, with a ten-year asset only one tenth of the benefit is recognized in the first year and similarly (assuming the asset is retained) in each subsequent year another one tenth of the tax reduction benefit increases net income. The credit balance in the Deferred Investment Credit account is a contra account on the balance sheet to the related asset account; however, it is sometimes illogically reported as a liability.

Either procedure may be followed at the present time under generally accepted accounting principles as specified in *APB Opinion Nos. 2* and *4*. This not altogether ideal state of affairs is the result of some early indecision on the part of the Accounting Principles Board. To the Board's credit, however, it should be pointed out that it moved to correct the situation in 1971 by issuing an exposure draft of an *Opinion* which would have allowed only the deferral method. The Board lost the battle in the political arena when business executives pressured Congress to insert a provision in the Revenue Act of 1971 which legally permitted choice of either method of accounting for the investment credit. Whichever method is adopted it must be used consistently and disclosed.

DEPLETION

Nature of Depletion

Depletion in the accounting sense represents allocation against revenue of the cost of a natural resource (wasting asset) that is being exploited. Examples of such resources are ore, oil, coal, timber, and gravel. In accounting for such assets, the original cost is recorded in harmony with the *cost principle* and subsequently amortized over the total production economically available. Allocation between periods, consistent with the *matching principle,* usually is accomplished by dividing the cost of the asset (less any residual value) by the estimated number of units that can be withdrawn economically; the *unit depletion rate* thus computed is multiplied by the actual units withdrawn during the period to determine the depletion charge for the period. As with other tangible assets, three factors are involved: (1) cost, including all development costs that can be related to the resource, (2) estimated residual value of the property upon exhaustion of the natural resource, and (3) the estimated production over the life of the resource. To illustrate, assume that it is estimated by competent reserve geologists that a given mineral lease has a potential production of two million units, and that the total cost of the lease, including development costs, is $160,000 with no residual value. The depletion rate per unit of mineral produced and its application would be computed as follows:

Depletion rate: $160,000 ÷ 2,000,000 = $.08 per unit
Production for period: 10,000 units
Depletion charge for period: 10,000 × $.08 = $800

This method generally is used for financial and cost accounting purposes. For federal income tax purposes, other depletion methods may be employed in accordance with the Internal Revenue Code. For example, the Code permits the taxpayer to elect *statutory* or *percentage depletion* rather than cost depletion illustrated above. Under statutory depletion a stated percentage of gross income may be taken as the depletion deduction on the tax return. The percentage varies from 5% on some deposits to 22% on others. Some of the more common depletion percentages follow:

Sulphur and uranium; and, if from deposits in the United States, asbestos, lead, zinc, nickel, and certain others	22%
Oil and gas*	22%
Gold, silver, copper, iron ore, and oil shale	15%
Coal and sodium chloride	10%
Clay and shale used for certain purposes	7½%
Other clay	5%
Most other minerals and metallic ores	14%

* For many years the percentage rate on oil and gas was 27½%; it was cut to 22%. Recently it was eliminated for larger oil producers but still has applicability on a greatly reduced scale.

Under the Code the sum of the statutory depletion charges allowed may (and in practice frequently does) exceed the original cost of the resource.

Original acquisition costs, development costs, and tangible property costs associated with a natural resource should be set up in separate accounts. If any of such facilities is likely to have a shorter life than the natural resource, its cost should be amortized over the shorter period. When buildings and similar improvements are constructed in connection with the exploitation of the specific resource, their lives may be limited by the duration of the resource. In such cases costs should be amortized on the same basis as the other costs related to the resource.

In view of the difficulties in estimating underground deposits of minerals, the evaluation of additional information derived through further developmental work and the additional costs incident thereto, the depletion rate must be changed from time to time. The new rate is determined by dividing the unamortized cost plus any additional development costs by the *remaining* estimated reserves. Past depletion charges are not revised.

Dividends sometimes are paid by companies exploiting natural resources equivalent to accumulated net income plus the accumulated depletion charge. State laws generally permit such dividends. This practice is common where there are no plans to replace the natural resource in kind and operations are to cease upon exhaustion of the deposit. In such cases, the stockholders should be informed of the portion of each dividend that represents a return of capital (i.e., the depletion charge). To illustrate, assume the Tex Oil Company accounts showed the following (summarized):

Assets	$1,000,000
Accumulated depreciation	(200,000)
Allowance for depletion	(100,000)
	$ 700,000
Liabilities	$ 150,000
Capital stock	500,000
Retained earnings	50,000
	$ 700,000

The board of directors could declare a dividend of $150,000 which would be recorded as follows:

Retained earnings	50,000	
Return of capital to stockholders	100,000	
Cash		150,000

The return of capital to stockholders would be reported as a deduction in the owners' equity section of the balance sheet.

Appendix. Annuity and Sinking Fund Methods of Depreciation

The annuity and sinking fund methods of depreciation are based on the same concepts that underlie an annuity investment. In this situation an investment is made and subsequently returns are received, usually each period. Each return is viewed as comprising two elements:

(*a*) a return of principal, and (*b*) investment revenue. Each period, assuming a constant amount received, the principal element is larger (this represents depreciation) and the interest element is smaller. The annuity and sinking fund methods derive the same overall effect on the income statement and balance sheet; their differences relate to depreciation expense and imputed interest revenue reported on the income statement.

To illustrate the annuity and sinking fund methods of depreciation, assume the following simplified data:

Investment in plant item at cost at beginning of Year 1	$100
Residual or scrap value estimated at end of Year 3	$ 10
Estimated useful life of the plant item..	3 years
Average cost of capital..	5%
Present value of 1 for 3 periods at 5% (from Table 6–2)	.863838
Present value of annuity of 1 for 3 periods at 5% (from Table 6–4)...	2.723248

ANNUITY METHOD OF DEPRECIATION

To apply this method the annual depreciation charge is computed on an annuity basis. The amount of the annual return on the investment is assumed to represent depreciation expense; accumulated depreciation is credited for the portion that represents return of principal, and the difference is credited to imputed interest revenue.

To illustrate, the periodic charge to depreciation expense would be computed as follows:

$$\text{Depreciation Expense} = \frac{CV-(SV\times p)}{P} = \frac{\$100-(\$10\times .863838)}{2.723248} = \$33.55$$

With this value we can construct a depreciation table reflecting the entries for depreciation and the periodic carrying value of the asset from acquisition to retirement. The table would be as follows:

Depreciation Table and Journal Entries – Annuity Method

Year	*Depreciation Expense Dr.* *(a)*	*Accumulated Depreciation Cr.* *(b)*	*Interest Revenue Cr.* *(c)*	*Unamortized Asset Balance* *(d)*
0	–	–	–	$100.00
1	$ 33.55	$28.55	$ 5.00	71.45
2	33.55	29.98	3.57	41.47
3	33.55	31.47	2.08	10.00
	$100.65	$90.00	$10.65	

(*a*) Constant amount from formula as computed above.
(*b*) (*a*) minus (*c*).
(*c*) Previous unamortized asset balance times .05.
(*d*) Previous balance minus current (*b*).

Observe that the above table is identical with an annuity amortization table (Chapter 6) except for the column captions. Also observe the following characteristics of the annuity method, as revealed by the entries in the above table, viz:

1. Depreciation Expense is debited each period for a *constant* amount.
2. Accumulated Depreciation is credited for an *increasing* amount each period.
3. Interest Revenue (this is imputed interest) is credited for a *decreasing* amount each period.
4. Because of the net effect of Depreciation Expense and Interest Revenue, there is an *increasing expense* effect on the income statement. It is the same as the credit to accumulated depreciation each period.
5. The carrying value of the asset decreases each period by a continuously increasing amount.

SINKING FUND METHOD OF DEPRECIATION

The sinking fund and annuity methods are closely akin. Their chief difference is that under the sinking fund method interest is reflected in the periodic depreciation charge but is not separately recorded and reported, while under the annuity method imputed interest is accorded separate recognition. It should be pointed out that while a sinking fund to replace the asset being depreciated might be maintained, most companies would prefer to invest in other productive assets and that formal sinking funds (asset replacement funds) are quite rare. The journal entries, assuming depreciation only and no sinking fund, for the two methods are as follows:

Annuity and Sinking Fund Depreciation Methods Compared

	Annuity Method		*Sinking Fund Method*	
Year 1:				
Depreciation expense	33.55		28.55	
Accumulated depreciation		28.55		28.55
Interest revenue		5.00		
Year 2:				
Depreciation expense	33.55		29.98	
Accumulated depreciation		29.98		29.98
Interest revenue		3.57		
Year 3:				
Depreciation expense	33.55		31.47	
Accumulated depreciation		31.47		31.47
Interest revenue		2.08		

Observe in the illustration that the sum of the three annual amounts of depreciation under the sinking fund method is $90 (enough to replace the asset if its replacement cost does not rise and if the $10 estimated salvage value is realized). Also observe that if a series of three payments of $28.55 were made to a sinking fund earning 5%, $90 would accumulate at the end of three years. The above entries reveal the basic difference between the two methods; the sinking fund method does not report imputed interest revenue; otherwise, we see the same effects on the income statement and balance sheet.

The compound interest methods have been criticized on several counts. Some claim that they are not "rational" since an increasing charge for depreciation over the life of the asset is inconsistent with the fact that ownership costs based on value tend to decrease in later years. Also a part of the depreciation charge under the *annuity method* is for imputed or theoretical interest; the offsetting credit for this element is made to Interest Revenue and therefore affects the income or loss of the period in which the depreciation is recorded. If the assets being depreciated are used in the production of goods for inventory, the consequence may be that an element of imputed interest will be found in an asset balance rather than in an expense balance at the close of the period.

For a combination of reasons the compound interest methods have been used relatively little in practice. Many entities, for reasons already cited, prefer to adopt depreciation methods which result in a somewhat opposite pattern of depreciation charges. The complexity and extra calculation effort of the compound interest methods may also be a deterrent to their adoption. The limited extent to which the methods have been used seems to be confined largely to public utilities. There is some theoretical justification for their use by regulated businesses where a precalculated rate of return on investment is contemplated and revenues and rates are theoretically set on the basis of rate of return on invested capital.

QUESTIONS

1. Distinguish between amortization, depletion, and depreciation.
2. Explain the effects of depreciation on *(a)* the income statement, and *(b)* the balance sheet.
3. Explain the relationship of depreciation to *(a)* cash flow, and *(b)* assets.
4. What is the relationship of depreciation to replacement of the assets being depreciated?
5. What are the primary causes of depreciation? What effect do changes in the market value of the asset being depreciated have on the depreciation estimates?
6. List and briefly explain the three factors which must be considered in allocating the cost of an operational asset.
7. What is meant by reducing-charge methods of depreciation? Under what circumstances would these methods generally be appropriate?
8. What accounting policy problems arise when the entity's fiscal year and the

asset year do not coincide? In other words, if a company closes books on June 30 but has bought a depreciable asset on January 1.

9. Briefly explain the inventory system of depreciation. Under what circumstances is such a system appropriate?

10. Compare the retirement and replacement depreciation systems.

11. Wherein are composite-life depreciation and group depreciation similar? Explain.

12. There are three categories in respect to change and correction of depreciation. Briefly explain each and outline the accounting involved as specified in *APB Opinion No. 20*.

13. What is the investment credit? What are the accepted ways of accounting for it?

14. Define depletion. How is depletion generally computed for financial and cost accounting purposes?

DECISION CASE 13–1

Two symbols of modern technology which comprise costly, if not principal, depreciable assets owned by some companies are computers and jet airplanes. They pose interesting depreciation problems. Consider the following items abstracted from news stories in *The Wall Street Journal*.

Part A—Computers. In computer circles, Gordon Berg is fondly known as "the king of the IBM 7074." Mr. Berg, who buys computers for Pacific Telephone & Telegraph Company, has, in recent years, accumulated 13 of the six-foot tall International Business Machines Corporations computers to tabulate customer bills. "On a cost-performance basis, they (IBM 7074s) can't be beat," he says. That's because Mr. Berg buys them used. Four 7074's he purchased last year cost Pacific Telephone something under $20,000 each—a nifty savings over the nearly $1 million IBM charged until it stopped making 7074's four years ago. Nor does Mr. Berg just buy used 7074's. A quarter of all Pacific Telephone's dozens of computers were purchased used (February 7, 1974).

And adapted from the same issue, another story—Dearborn-Storm Corporation said it agreed in principle to sell its System 360 computers for $17 million in cash to a group of private investors here. The company said it expects the transaction to be closed within 30 days. The effect of the sale will be reflected in the company's results for the fiscal year ended October 31, 1973, and will result in a loss, including phase-out costs, of about $9 million after tax benefits of about $4.2 million. For the nine months ended last July 31, the company reported a loss of $315,000 after a new charge of $4.5 million for additional depreciation on the leased computers. This compared with a profit of $3.6 million, or $1.32 per share, in the year-earlier period.

Part B—Jet Airplanes. In late 1974 and early 1975, several items appeared in *The Wall Street Journal* detailing how various airlines were dealing with their surplus jet capacity during the energy crisis and a period when passenger demand was well below their ability to transport passengers. Excerpts adapted from this story, dated February 3, 1975, are representative.

Trans World Airlines announced the near conclusion of arrangements to sell six 747 jumbo jets to Iran for $99 million. At $16.5 million per plane, TWA was in a position to underbid Pan Am (which had also been interested in selling off surplus 747's). At this price, TWA was selling below its book value, said to average $17 to $18 million (exact figures would vary with the age of each plane). Pan Am was barred by conditions of its debt arrangements from selling aircraft at less than book value; TWA was aware of this restriction and took advantage of the restriction in setting its price.

On the other hand, consider the following excerpts adapted from the February 27, 1975, issue concerning another type of plane – the DC3. Douglas Aircraft division of McDonnell Douglas Corporation began producing the DC3 in 1935, subsequently turned out 10,928 military and commercial versions of the plane. Douglas estimates 2,500 to 3,000 DC3's are still flying. Some 159 commercial companies owned or operated 512 of the venerable workhorses as recently as last June. Douglas continues to make money from the DC3, selling something on the order of $50,000 of parts a year. But International Engine Parts, Incorporated, does better, selling about $100,000 annually to repair shops and foreign governments. "This business will continue on for another ten years or so," says Verne Morand, sales manager. "It's a phenomenally good aircraft." "What's a DC3 worth?" says one New York aircraft dealer, "I suppose you could buy one for $25,000 to $30,000."

Added information (not from *The Wall Street Journal*): For income tax purposes, depreciable lives used for new computers appear to range from five to seven years and for aircraft, from four to six years. Although the stories cited deal with three specific situations, Pacific Telephone, Dearborn-Storm, and TWA and a widespread phenomena (the DC3), other similar evidence to bolster what was cited could be adduced.

Required:

1. Discuss the problems of properly depreciating and valuing computers and aircraft when purchased new in the light of what was recited.
2. Do buyers of used assets, of the types cited at bargain prices, have special problems in respect to depreciation? Discuss.

EXERCISES

Exercise 13–1

In order to demonstrate the mechanical computations involved in several methods of depreciation the following simplified situation is presented:

Acquisition cost	$ 6,400
Scrap or residual value	$ 400
Estimated service life:	
Years	4
Service hours	10,000
Productive output	24,000

Required:

Compute the annual depreciation under each of the following situations (show computations and round to even dollars):

1. Straight-line depreciation; compute the depreciation charge and rate for each year.
2. Service-hours method; compute the depreciation rate and charge for the first year assuming 3,000 service hours of actual operation.

3. Productive-output method of depreciation; compute the depreciation rate and charge for the first year assuming 7,000 units of output.
4. Sum-of-the-years'-digits method; compute the depreciation charge for each year.
5. Double-declining-balance method; compute the depreciation charge for each year.

Exercise 13–2

Equipment which cost Davis Company $12,000 will be depreciated on the assumption it will last eight years and have an $800 residual value. Several possible methods of depreciation are under consideration.

Required:

1. Prepare a schedule which shows annual depreciation expense, accumulated depreciation, and book values for the *first two* years assuming (show computations and round to even dollars):
   a. Fixed percentage on declining base method. The eighth root of .06667 is .71283.
   b. Productive output method. Estimated output is a total of 84,000 units, of which 9,000 will be produced the first year; 12,000 for each of the next three years; 15,000 the fourth year; 9,000 the fifth, sixth, and seventh years; and 6,000 the final year.
   c. Sum-of-the-years'-digits method.
2. What criteria would you consider in selecting a method?

Exercise 13–3

A depreciable asset acquired by Ute Company cost $4,800 and is estimated to have a useful life of four years and a residual value of $400.

Required:

1. Prepare a depreciation table covering the life of the asset assuming (show computations and round to even dollars):
   a. Straight-line method.
   b. Sum-of-the-years'-digits method.
   c. Double-declining-balance method.
2. What criteria should be considered in selecting a method?

Exercise 13–4

A machine is to be depreciated which cost $8,000, has an estimated service life of four years, and a residual value of $600.

Required:

1. Prepare a depreciation table covering the life of the machine assuming (show computations and round to even dollars):
   a. Sum-of-the-years'-digits method.
   b. Productive output method. Total output is estimated at 36,000 units. Actual output from start to end, in order, was 11,000, 8,000, 7,000, and 10,000 units.
   c. Double-declining-balance method.

2. Facts are the same as requirement 1(*a*) except that in the fourth year, after ten months, the machine was sold for $600. Give the entry to record the sale.
3. What criteria should be considered in selecting a method?

Exercise 13–5

Ellen Company bought equipment on January 1, 19A, for $22,000 for which the expected life is ten years and residual value is $2,000. Under three popular depreciation methods, the annual depreciation expense and cumulative balance of accumulated depreciation at the end of 19A and 19B are shown below:

	Method A		*Method B*		*Method C*	
Year	*Annual Expense*	*Accumulated Amount*	*Annual Expense*	*Accumulated Amount*	*Annual Expense*	*Accumulated Amount*
19A	$4,400	$4,400	$2,000	$2,000	$3,636	$3,636
19B	3,520	7,920	2,000	4,000	3,272	6,908

Required:

1. Identify the depreciation method used in each instance.
2. Project continued use of the same method through years 19C and 19D and determine the annual depreciation expense and accumulated depreciation amount for each year under each method.

Exercise 13–6

Taylor Utility Company purchased 500 poles at $120 per pole; the debit being to the Inventory–Poles P-113 account. Subsequent to the purchase, 100 of the new poles were used to replace an equal number of old poles (Poles M-101) which were carried in the tangible fixed asset account, Poles–Austin Line. The old poles originally cost $30 each and had an estimated salvage value of $10 per pole.

Required:

1. Give all indicated entries (*a*) assuming the retirement system is employed, and (*b*) assuming the replacement system is used.
2. Compare the effect on the periodic depreciation charge and the asset accounts as between the two systems.

Exercise 13–7

Milton Company owned a power plant which consisted of the following, all acquired on January 1, 1973:

	Cost	*Estimated Scrap Value*	*Estimated Life (years)*
Building	$450,000	None	15
Machinery, etc.	180,000	$18,000	10
Other equipment	150,000	10,000	5

Required:

1. Compute the total straight-line depreciation for 1976 on all items combined.
2. Compute the composite depreciation rate on the plant.
3. Determine the composite life of the plant.

Exercise 13–8

Mannix Company depreciates its spot welders on a straight-line basis. Transactions relative to spot welders in Plant A were:

a. January 2, 19A: Bought six spot welders for an aggregate price of $16,500, paying cash.
b. December 31, 19A: On the assumption the salvage value of the group would total 10% of original cost and their useful life was five years, recorded depreciation at year-end.
c. Recorded depreciation at year-end, December 31, 19B.
d. January 2, 19C: One unit which performed unsatisfactorily was sold for $1,250 cash.
e. Two additional spot welders were bought January 10, 19C, at the same unit price as the original elements of the group and added to the group.
f. Recorded depreciation at December 31, 19C, for full year for all units in group.
g. Transferred one spot welder to Plant C on January 2, 19D.

Required:

Give entries for each transaction in general journal form. Show computations; closing entries are not required.

Exercise 13–9

Clara Company's records show the following property acquisitions and retirements during the first two years of operations:

			Sales or Retirements	
Year	*Cost of Property Acquired*	*Estimated Useful Life (years)*	*Year of Acquisition*	*Amount*
19A..............	$50,000	10	–	–
19B..............	20,000	10	19A	$7,000

Property is depreciated one half in the year of acquisition. Retired property is to be depreciated for the full year in its year of retirement. Assume zero salvage values.

Required:

Determine depreciation expense for 19A and for 19B and the balances of the Property account and related Accumulated Depreciation at the end of each year under the following depreciation methods (show computations and round to even dollars):

a. Straight-line method.
b. Sum-of-the-years'-digits method.

(AICPA adapted)

Exercise 13–10

Downs Company owned ten warehouses of a similar type except for varying size. The group system is applied to the ten warehouses, the rate being 8% per year on cost. At the end of the tenth year the asset account Warehouses showed a balance of $530,000 (residual value $30,000), and the Accumulated Depreciation account showed a balance of $240,000. Shortly after the end of the tenth year, Warehouse No. 65, costing $60,000, was retired and demolished. Materials of $5,000 were sold, and $1,500 was spent in demolition.

Required:

Give entries to record *(a)* depreciation for the 10th year, *(b)* retirement of the warehouse, and *(c)* depreciation for the 11th year.

Exercise 13–11

Brown Corporation purchased a machine (which qualified for the 10% investment credit) on January 1, 19A, at a cost of $60,000; having an estimated useful life of 12 years and no residual value. The company uses straight-line depreciation and has an average tax rate of 35%. Income (after deducting depreciation expense) subject to tax was: 19A, $40,000; and 19B, $45,000.

Required:

Give the entries for income taxes and depreciation at December 31, 19A, and December 31, 19B, end of the fiscal period, assuming the–

a. Flow-through method.
b. Deferral method.

Exercise 13–12

XT Company's investment in a gravel quarry amounted to $400,000, of which $40,000 could be ascribed to land value after the gravel has been removed. Geologists were engaged to estimate the economically removable gravel reported originally that three million cubic yards (units) could be extracted. In the first year 600,000 units were extracted and 550,000 units were sold. In the second year 400,000 units were extracted and sales were 450,000 units.

At the start of the third year management of XT Company had the quarry examined again, at which time it was determined the remaining economically removable gravel was 1.5 million units. Production and sales for the third year amounted to 300,000 units. In the fourth year production was 500,000 units while sales amounted to 150,000 units.

Required:

1. Calculate the depletion deduction to be reported on XT's income statement for each of the four years. Show supporting computations.
2. Show how the gravel deposit would be reported on XT's balance sheet at the end of the fourth year. Assume an accumulated account is used.

Exercise 13–13

Rankin Minerals, Inc., paid $1,700,000 for property with removable ore estimated at 2,000,000 tons. The property has an estimated value of $100,000 after the ore has been extracted. Before any ore could be removed it was necessary to incur $400,000 of developmental costs. In the first year 200,000 tons were removed and 175,000 tons of ore were sold; in the second year 300,000 tons were removed and 325,000 tons were sold. In the course of the second year's production, discoveries were made which indicated that if an added $300,000 is spent on developmental costs, future removable ore will total 2,700,000 tons. After incurring these added costs, production and sales for the third year amount to 540,000 tons.

Required:

1. Calculate the depletion deduction to be reported on Rankin's income statement for each of the three years. Show supporting computations.
2. Show how the resource would be reported on Rankin's balance sheet at the end of the third year. Assume an accumulated account is used.
3. Give the journal entry to record depletion expense at the end of the first year.

PROBLEMS

Problem 13–1

Depreciation continues to be one of the most controversial, difficult, and important problem areas in accounting.

Required:

1. *a.* Explain the conventional accounting concept of depreciation accounting.
   b. Discuss its conceptual merit with respect to *(a)* the value of the asset, *(b)* the charge(s) to expense, and *(c)* the discretion of management in selecting the method.
2. *a.* Explain the factors that should be considered when applying the conventional concept of depreciation to the determination of how the value of a newly acquired computer system should be assigned to expense for financial reporting purposes. (Ignore income tax considerations.)
   b. What depreciation methods might be used for the computer system?

(AICPA adapted)

Problem 13–2

Scott Company purchased a special machine at a cost of $45,500. It was estimated that the machine would have a net resale value at the end of its useful life for the company of $3,500. Statistics relating to the machine over its service life were as follows:

Estimated service life:	
Years	5
Output, units	6,000

Actual operations:

Year	*Units of Output*
1	1,400
2	1,300
3	1,000
4	1,100
5	1,200

Required:

Prepare a depreciation table for each assumption below indicating entries for the asset over the useful life under the following methods: (*a*) straight line, (*b*) output, (*c*) sum-of-the-years'-digits, (*d*) fixed percentage of 40% on declining base, and (*e*) double-declining balance. Show computations and round to even dollars.

Problem 13–3

Royal Company purchased a piece of special factory equipment on January 1, 19A, costing $51,000. In view of pending technological developments it is estimated that the machine will have a resale value upon disposal in four years of $15,500 and that disposal cost will be $4,500.

Data relating to the equipment follows:

Estimated service life:	
Years	4
Service hours	20,000

Actual operations:

Calendar Year	*Service Hours*
19A	5,500
19B	5,000
19C	4,800
19D	4,600

Required:

(Round to even dollars and show computations):

1. Prepare a depreciation table for the service-hours method assuming the books are closed each December 31.
2. Compute depreciation expense for the first and second years assuming: (*a*) straight line, (*b*) sum-of-the-years'-digits, (*c*) fixed percent on declining base (30% rate), and (*d*) double-declining balance.

Problem 13–4

Machinery which cost Karen Corporation $10,000 is expected to last ten years and have a $500 residual value. Several depreciation methods in common use were applied to these data. The results in terms of annual charges covering the Year 2 and Year 3 are set out below:

Year	*Method A*	*Method B*	*Method C*	*Method D*
1	?	?	?	?
2	$1,924	$1,600	$1,555	$950
3	1,424	1,280	1,382	950

Required:

1. Identify the method used to get the results for each method; show computations to support your response. Round to even dollars.

2. In connection with Methods C and D, suppose that after the completion of Year 3, it is determined the total remaining life of the machinery is five instead of seven years. Determine the annual charge and the balance of Accumulated Depreciation at the end of Year 4 and Year 5.

Problem 13–5

BK Manufacturing Company utilizes a number of small machine tools in their operations. Although there are numerous variations in the tools, they cost approximately the same and have similar useful lives. The company carries a Machine Tools account in the records; the account showed a balance of $1,600 (200 tools) at the end of 19A. Acquisitions, retirements, and other data for a period of two years are given below:

	19B	*19C*
Acquisitions	100 @ $7.50	120 @ $7.75
Retirements:		
Number	150	80
Salvage proceeds	$ 40	$ 20
Inventory	150 @ $5.20	190 @ $5.40

Required:

1. Give entries for each of the two years assuming (round to even dollars and show computations):
   a. The inventory system is used.
   b. The retirement system is used.
   c. The replacement system is used.
2. Prepare a tabulation covering the two years to present for the annual depreciation charge and the balance in the Machine Tools account under each system.

Problem 13–6

Davis Company utilizes a large number of identical small tools in operations. On January 1, 19A, the first year of operations, 1,000 of these tools were purchased at a cost of $4 each. On December 31, 19A, 200 of the tools were scrapped, the estimated salvage value being $40 ($.20 each). During the year the 200 were replaced at a cost of $4.20 each. On December 31, 19B, 300 of the tools were scrapped, having an estimated salvage value of $.25 each and replaced at a cost of $4.50 each. On December 31, 19C, 140 of the tools were scrapped (salvage value $.25 each) each being replaced at a cost of $3.60.

Required:

1. Compute the annual depreciation charge for 19A, 19B, and 19C and the balance at the end of each year in the Tools account, assuming the company employed the *(a)* retirement system, and *(b)* the replacement system.
2. Compare the results.

Problem 13–7

One set of plant assets depreciated by Sonntag Company on a composite basis is identified as Group No. 16, components of which are as follows:

Component	Cost	Estimated Residual Value	Estimated Life (years)
A...............	$29,800	$1,800	10
B...............	14,000	0	7
C...............	38,000	8,000	15
D...............	6,200	200	5
E...............	12,000	2,000	5

Required:

1. Calculate the composite life and annual composite depreciation for Group No. 16. Record depreciation after one full year of use.
2. During the second year it became necessary to replace component B which was sold for $8,000. The replacement component cost $16,000 and has an estimated salvage value of $2,600 at the end of its estimated six-year useful life. Record the retirement and substitution which was a cash acquisition.
3. Record depreciation at the end of the second full year.

Problem 13–8

The accounts for Trucks and Accumulated Depreciation on the books of Dacy Hardware Store are as shown below:

Trucks

1/1/19A	Trucks No. 1 and 2	7,200	1/1/19C	Truck No. 1 scrapped	3,600
1/1/19C	Truck No. 3	3,780	1/1/19D	Truck No. 2 scrapped	3,600
1/1/19D	Truck No. 4	3,840			
7/1/19D	New tires, Truck 3	600			

Accumulated Depreciation

1/1/19C	Truck No. 1 scrapped ($1,500 received as salvage)	2,400	12/31/19A	Depreciation	2,400
			12/31/19B	Depreciation	2,400
			12/31/19C	Depreciation	2,460
1/1/19D	Truck No. 2 scrapped ($300 received as salvage)	3,300	12/31/19D	Depreciation	2,460
			12/31/19E	Depreciation	1,905

Required:

1. Prepare a depreciation schedule showing correct account balances and depreciation by year, assuming the estimated lives of Trucks No. 3 and No. 4 were changed from three to four years on January 1, 19E. Suggested captions: Date, Truck No., Trucks (debit-credit*), Correct Depreciation by Year (five columns), and Accumulated Depreciation (debit-credit*).
2. Journal entry or entries to correct the books as of December 31, 19E, assuming they were not yet closed for 19E. The schedule prepared for Requirement 1 should provide the data needed.

Problem 13–9

The Machinery account as of December 31, 19F, on the books of the Darwin Company was as follows:

Machinery

1/1/A Purchase	$50,000	12/31/A Depreciation	$ 5,000
7/1/B Purchase	10,000	9/ 1/B Machinery sold......	2,000
11/1/C Purchase	30,000	12/31/C Depreciation	6,200
		12/31/D Depreciation	7,200
		7/ 1/E Machinery sold......	1,000
		12/31/E Depreciation	7,200
		12/31/F Depreciation	8,700

Additional data:

Machinery sold September 1, 19B, cost $3,600 on January 1, 19A; machinery sold July 1, 19E, cost $2,500 on January 1, 19A. Machinery costing $2,000, which was purchased on July 1, 19B, was destroyed on July 1, 19F and was a total loss.

Required:

1. A depreciation schedule showing correct annual depreciation and account balances. Assume ten-year life on all items, straight line and no residual value. Suggested captions: Date, Machinery (debit-credit*), Correct Depreciation by Year (six columns), and Accumulated Depreciation (debit-credit*).
2. Journal entry or entries to correct the books on December 31, 19F, assuming the books are not closed for 19F.

Problem 13–10

Thompson Corporation, a manufacturer of steel products, began operations on October 1, 19A. The accounting department of Thompson has started the fixed asset and depreciation schedule presented on page 585. You have been asked to assist in completing this schedule. In addition to ascertaining that the data already on the schedule are correct, you have obtained the following information from the company's records and personnel:

a. Depreciation is computed from the first of the month of acquisition to the first of the month of disposition.

b. Land A and Building A were acquired from a predecessor corporation. Thompson paid $812,500 for the land and building together. At the time of acquisition, the land had an appraised value of $72,000 and the building had an appraised value of $828,000.

c. Land B was acquired on October 2, 19A, in exchange for 3,000 newly issued shares of Thompson's common stock. At the date of acquisition, the stock had a par value of $5 per share and a fair value of $25 per share. During October 19A, Thompson paid $10,400 to demolish an existing building on this land so it could construct a new building.

d. Construction of Building B on the newly acquired land began on October 1, 19B. By September 30, 19C, Thompson had paid $210,000 of the estimated total construction costs of $300,000. Estimated completion and occupancy date is July 19D.

e. Certain equipment was donated to the corporation by a local university. An independent appraisal of the equipment when donated placed the fair value at $16,000 and the salvage value at $2,000.

f. Machinery A's total cost of $110,000 includes installation expense of $550 and normal repairs and maintenance of $11,000. Salvage value is estimated as $5,500. Machinery A was sold on February 1, 19C.

THOMPSON CORPORATION
Fixed Asset and Depreciation Schedule
For Fiscal Years Ended September 30, 19B, and September 30, 19C

Assets	*Acquisition Date*	*Cost*	*Salvage*	*Depreciation Method*	*Estimated Life in Years*	*Depreciation Expense Year Ended September 30,*	
						19B	*19C*
Land A	October 1, 19A	$ (1)	N/A	N/A	N/A	N/A	N/A
Building A	October 1, 19A	(2)	$47,500	Straight line	(3)	$14,000	$ (4)
Land B	October 2, 19A	(5)	N/A	N/A	N/A	N/A	N/A
Building B	Under construction	210,000 to date	–	Straight line	Thirty	–	(6)
Donated equipment	October 2, 19A	(7)	2,000	150% declining balance	Ten	(8)	(9)
Machinery A	October 2, 19A	(10)	5,500	Sum-of-the-years'-digits	Ten	(11)	(12)
Machinery B	October 1, 19B	(13)	–	Straight line	Fifteen	–	(14)

N/A—Not applicable.

g. On October 1, 19B, Machinery B was acquired with a down payment of $4,000 and the remaining payments to be made in ten annual installments of $4,000 each beginning October 1, 19C. The prevailing interest rate was 8%. The following data were abstracted from present-value tables:

Present Value of $1 at 8%		*Present Value of Annuity of $1 in Arrears at 8%*	
10 years...............	.463	10 years...............	6.710
11 years...............	.429	11 years...............	7.139
15 years...............	.315	15 years...............	8.559

Required:

Number your answer sheet from 1 to 14. For each numbered item on the preceding schedule, supply the correct amount next to the corresponding number on your answer sheet. Round each answer to the nearest dollar. *Do not recopy the schedule*. Show supporting computations in good form.

(AICPA adapted)

Problem 13–11

Hotstrike Minerals Company bought mineral-bearing land for $90,000 which engineers say will yield 200,000 tons of economically removable ore; the land will have a value of $20,000 after the ore is removed.

To work the property, the company built structures and sheds on the site which cost $30,000; these will last 12 years and, because their use is confined to mining and it would be expensive to dismantle and move them, they will have no salvage value. Machinery which cost $30,000 was installed at the mine and added cost for installation was $6,000. This machinery should last 15 years; like the structures, usefulness of the machinery is confined to mines. Dismantling and removal costs when the property has been fully worked will approximately equal the value of the machinery at that time.

In the first year, Hotstrike removed only 10,000 tons of ore; however, production was doubled in the second year. It is expected that all of the removable ore will be extracted within eight years from the start of operations.

Required:

1. Prepare a schedule showing unit and total depletion and depreciation and book value for the first and second year of operation.
2. On the assumption that in the first year 90% of production was sold, and in the second year, the inventory carried over from the first year plus 90% of the second year's production was sold, give entries to record accumulated depreciation and depletion. To show the affect of these costs, make the offsetting debits to goods sold and inventory. Use accumulated accounts.

Problem 13–12 (reviews Chapters 12 and 13)

For each of the following situations, *(a)* select the best response from those given, and *(b)* explain the basis for your choice showing computations where appropriate.

On July 1, 19A, Miller Mining, a calendar-year corporation, purchased the rights to a copper mine. Of the total purchase price, $2,800,000 was allocable to the copper. Estimated reserves were 800,000 tons of copper. Miller expects to extract and sell 10,000 tons of copper each month. Production began immediately.

The selling price is $25 per ton. Miller uses percentage depletion (15%) for tax purposes.

To aid production, Miller also purchased some new equipment on July 1, 19A. The equipment cost $76,000 and had an estimated useful life of eight years. However, after all the copper is removed from this mine, the equipment will be of no use to Miller and will be sold for an estimated $4,000. Use straight line depreciation.

1. If sales and production conform to expectations, what is Miller's depletion expense on this mine for financial accounting purposes for the calendar year, 19A?
   a. $105,000. *c.* $225,000.
   b. $210,000. *d.* $420,000.
2. If sales and production conform to expectations, what is Miller's depreciation expense on the new equipment for financial accounting purposes for the calendar year 19A?
   a. $4,500. *c.* $9,000.
   b. $5,400. *d.* $10,800.
3. Willard, Inc., purchased some equipment on January 2, 19A, for $24,000 (no salvage). Willard used straight-line depreciation based on a ten-year estimated life. During 19D, Willard decided that this equipment would be used only three more years and then replaced with a technologically superior model. What entry, if any, should Willard make as of January 1, 19D, to reflect this change?
   a. No entry.
   b. Debit an extraordinary item for $4,800 and credit accumulated depreciation for $4,800.
   c. Debit a prior period adjustment for $4,800 and credit accumulated depreciation for $4,800.
   d. Debit depreciation expense for $4,800 and credit accumulated depreciation for $4,800.
4. Gorch Company sold an item of plant equipment. Gorch received a noninterest-bearing note to be paid $1,000 per year for ten years. A fair rate of interest for this transaction is 8%. What discount should Gorch reflect on this transaction?
   a. Zero. *c.* $4,630.
   b. $3,290. *d.* $6,710.
5. Blacker Company exchanged a business car for a new car. The old car had an original cost of $3,500, an undepreciated cost of $1,600, and a market value of $2,000 when exchanged. In addition, Blacker paid $2,200 cash for the new car. The list price of the new car was $4,300. At what amount should the new car be recorded for financial accounting purposes?
   a. $3,500. *c.* $4,200.
   b. $3,800. *d.* $4,300.

Items 6 and 7 are based on the following information: On January 2, 19A, Kirk Manufacturing Company acquired some equipment from Quarter Corporation. The sale contract requires Kirk to make annual payments of $10,800 at the start of each year. The first payment was made on January 2, 19A, and no deposit was required. The equipment has an estimated useful life of 12 years with no anticipated salvage value. The prevailing interest rate for Kirk in similar financing arrangements is 8%.

6. At what amount should Kirk have capitalized this equipment?
   a. $77,100. *c.* $103,720.
   b. $81,390. *d.* $106,040.

7. If the equipment was capitalized at $80,000 and all other facts remain as originally stated, how much interest expense should Kirk have recorded in 19A?
   a. Zero.
   b. $6,400.
   c. $7,200.
   d. $9,600.

(AICPA adapted)

Problem 13–13

Rocky Gravel Company mines and processes rock and gravel. It started in business on January 1, 19A, when it purchased the assets of another company. You have examined its financial statements at December 31, 19A, and have been requested to assist in planning and projecting operations for 19B. The company also wants to know the maximum amount by which notes payable to officers can be reduced at December 31, 19B.

The adjusted trial balance on December 31, 19A, was:

Cash	$ 17,000	
Accounts receivable	24,000	
Mining properties	60,000	
Accumulated depletion		$ 3,000
Equipment	150,000	
Accumulated depreciation		10,000
Organization expense	5,000	
Accumulated amortization		1,000
Accounts payable		12,000
Federal income taxes payable		22,000
Notes payable to officers		40,000
Capital stock		100,000
Premium on capital stock		34,000
Sales		300,000
Production costs (including depreciation and depletion)	184,000	
Administrative expense (including amortization and interest)	60,000	
Provision for federal income taxes	22,000	
	$522,000	$522,000

You are able to develop the following information:

1. The total yards of material sold is expected to increase 10% in 19B, and the average sales price per cubic yard will be increased from $1.50 to $1.60.
2. The estimated recoverable reserves of rock and gravel were 4,000,000 cubic yards when the properties were purchased.
3. Production costs include direct labor of $110,000 of which $10,000 was attributed to inefficiencies in the early stages of operation. The union contract calls for 5% increases in hourly rates effective January 1, 19B. Production costs, other than depreciation, depletion and direct labor, will increase 4% in 19B.
4. Administrative expense, other than amortization and interest, will increase $8,000 in 19B.
5. The company has contracted for additional movable equipment costing $60,000 to be in production on July 1, 19B. This equipment will result in a direct labor hour savings of 8% as compared with the last half of 19A. The

new equipment will have a life of 20 years. All depreciation is computed on the straight-line method. The old equipment will continue in use.

6. The new equipment will be financed by a 20% down payment and a 6% three-year chattel mortgage. Interest and principal payments are due semiannually on June 30 and December 31, beginning December 31, 19B. The notes payable to officers are demand notes dated January 1, 19A, on which 6% interest is provided for and was paid on December 31, 19A.
7. Accounts receivable will increase in proportion to sales. No bad debts are anticipated. Accounts payable will remain substantially the same.
8. Percentage depletion allowable on rock and gravel is to be computed at 5% of gross income and is limited to 50% of net income before depletion.
9. It is customary in the rock and gravel business not to place any value on stock-piles of processed material which are awaiting sale.
10. Assume an income tax rate of 50%.
11. The company has decided to maintain a minimum cash balance of $20,000.
12. The client understands that the ethical considerations involved in preparing the following statements will be taken care of by your letter accompanying the statements. (Do not prepare the letter.)

Required:

1. Prepare a statement showing the net income projection for 19B.
2. Prepare a statement which will show cash flow projection for 19B and will indicate the amount that notes payable to officers can be reduced at December 31, 19B.

   Note: Round all amounts to the nearest $100. If the amount to be rounded is exactly $50, round to the next highest $100.

(AICPA adapted)

Problem 13–14 (based on Appendix)

Equipment costing $100,000 has an estimated five-year life and $20,000 salvage value.

Required:

Using an 8% rate, prepare a depreciation table covering the entire life of the equipment assuming:

1. Annuity method.
2. Sinking fund method.

Problem 13–15 (based on Appendix)

Machinery with an estimated life of ten years and a salvage value of 15% was acquired for $10,000. Using a 7% rate, what depreciation entries would be made at the end of each of the first two years assuming *(a)* the annuity method, and *(b)* the sinking fund method.

Chapter 14

Intangible Assets

In the broad sense, intangible assets are those properties, *without physical substance*, which are useful to an entity because of the special *rights* their ownership confers. The accounting classification of assets reports some intangibles as *(a)* current assets, such as cash, receivables, short-term investments and prepaid insurance; *(b)* funds and investments, such as bond sinking funds; bond investments, and equity securities; *(c)* other assets, such as noncurrent claims to cash; *(d)* operational or fixed assets, such as patents, franchises, and goodwill; and *(e)* deferred charges (i.e., long-term expense prepayments).

Since a number of different kinds of intangibles have been discussed in prior chapters, this chapter focuses on three different kinds of intangible assets, viz: (1) intangible operational assets, (2) deferred charges, and (3) cash surrender value of insurance and premium prepayments. Each will be considered separately.

The intangibles used in operating a business are generally classified for accounting purposes as *intangible* assets; other titles used are intangible fixed assets, intangible operational assets, or simply, intangibles. This classification includes intangible long-lived assets such as patents, copyrights, franchises, trademarks, trade names, secret processes, and goodwill. The primary characteristics of these intangible assets are *(a)* they are purchased from external sources or developed internally, *(b)* their ownership confers some exclusive rights, *(c)* they provide future benefits to operations, and *(d)* they are relatively long-lived. For example, a company that owns a patent used in making one of its products has a valuable intangible asset.[1]

Intangible assets may be further classified on the basis of—

1. Identifiability—separate indentifiability, such as a patent, or unidentifiability, such as goodwill.
2. Manner of acquisition—acquired from external sources by purchase,

[1] A patent held for speculative rather than for operational purposes would be classified as a noncurrent investment or other asset.

such as the purchase of a patent, or internally created, such as the development of a patent by the company research department.
3. Expected period of benefit—limited by law, contract, or economic factors, such as the 17-year legal life of a patent or indeterminate life, such as company goodwill.
4. Separability from the entire enterprise—salable without title, such as a trademark, or inseparable from the entity, such as goodwill.[2]

ACCOUNTING FOR INTANGIBLE ASSETS

Accounting for intangible assets involves essentially the same problems, accounting principles, and procedures as for tangible property, plant, and equipment (discussed in Chapters 12 and 13); that is:

1. At acquisition—measuring and recording acquisition cost.
2. During period of use—measuring, recording, and reporting for expiration of the acquisition cost over the period of benefit. This process is usually referred to as *amortization.* In contrast, the process when applied to property, plant, and equipment is called depreciation; and when applied to natural resources, it is called depletion.
3. At disposition—recording and reporting disposition at sale, exchange, or end of economic useful life.

Accounting and reporting for intangible assets acquired after October 1970 is prescribed by *APB Opinion No. 17,* "Intangible Assets." Accounting for intangible assets acquired on or before October 30, 1970, may be accounted for in accordance with *APB Opinion No. 17* or *ARB No. 43,* Chapter 5 (otherwise this *ARB* was superseded by the *Opinion*).

Prior to *APB Opinion No. 17,* intangible assets were accounted for on the basis of *life expectancy.* Intangible assets having limited lives were identified as *Type A;* they were amortized over their estimated period of future use. Intangible assets having indeterminate lives were identified as *Type B;* and were not amortized until a realistic determination of useful life could be made. Often this determination was never made; hence, many Type B intangibles were carried indefinitely as assets. *Opinion No. 17,* among other things, stopped this practice by providing that:

> . . . the value of intangible assets at any one date eventually disappears and that the recorded costs of intangible assets should be amortized by systematic charges to income over the periods estimated to be benefited. . . . The cost of each type of intangible should be amortized on the basis of the estimated life of that specific asset. . . . The period of amortization should not, however, exceed 40 years.

MEASURING AND RECORDING INTANGIBLE ASSETS AT ACQUISITION

Intangible assets should be recorded at acquisition at their cash equivalent cost in conformity with the cost principle. When an intangible

---

[2] AICPA, "Intangible Assets," *APB Opinion No. 17* (New York, 1970), par. 10.

asset is acquired for some consideration other than cash, cost is determined by either the market value of the consideration given or by the fair market value of the right acquired, whichever is the more clearly evident. For example, if a patent is acquired by the issuance of capital stock, the cost of the patent may be determined as the fair market value of the shares of stock issued; or if the shares issued do not have an established market value consistent with the volume issued, then evidence of the fair market value of the patent should be sought as the measurement of cost in the transaction. If there is evidence of a definite cash offer to sell the patent, this offering price might be acceptable as a measure of the cost of the intangible asset. Supporting evidence of fair market value should be rather conclusive if the cost measured thereby is to be accepted as valid.

Classification of the Cost of Intangible Assets

With intangibles, as in the case of property, plant, and equipment, costs must be carefully classified in the accounts to facilitate subsequent accounting. Proper accounting for cost requires that where two or more intangible assets are acquired at a single lump-sum purchase price, an allocation of the joint cost should be made to determine the cost basis of each intangible involved. Allocation of the cost of intangibles acquired in a "basket purchase" may be made by using the methods described for tangible assets, such as the relative sales value method.

AMORTIZATION OF THE COST OF INTANGIBLE ASSETS

The cost of intangible assets should be *amortized* by systematic charges to expense over the estimated periods of useful life, just as the cost of tangible assets having a limited period of usefulness is depreciated. Capricious and arbitrary determination of the amount to be charged as expense from period to period distorts income and violates the *matching principle*. Neither is it desirable from the standpoint of income determination to accelerate the amortization process and write off the cost of intangibles substantially before the end of their usefulness. In the past, overconservatism frequently resulted in inappropriate accounting in these respects. Intangible assets normally are amortized by a direct credit to the asset account and a debit to expense.

In estimating the future useful life of an intangible asset the following factors should be considered:[3]

a. Legal, regulatory, or contractual provisions may limit the maximum useful life.

b. Provisions for renewal or extension may alter a specified limit on useful life.

---

[3] AICPA, "Intangible Assets," *APB Opinion No. 17* (New York, 1970), par. 27.

c. Effects of obsolescence, demand, competition, and other economic factors may reduce a useful life.
d. A useful life may parallel the service life expectancies of individuals or groups of employees.
e. Expected actions of competitors and others may restrict present competitive advantages.
f. An apparently unlimited useful life may in fact be indefinite and benefits cannot be reasonably projected.
g. An intangible asset may be a composite of many individual factors with varying effective lives.

The method of amortization should be systematic and should reflect over time the decline in economic service value of the intangible. Thus, straight-line, declining-balance charges, or increasing balance charges, may be appropriate. Perhaps reflecting precedent rather than economic realities, *APB Opinion No. 17* states that "the straight-line method of amortization—equal annual amounts—should be applied unless a company demonstrates that another systematic method is more appropriate." The *Opinion* also states that changes in amortization rates should be *prospective;* that is, the remaining unamortized cost should be amortized over the remaining life, but not to exceed 40 years after acquisition. Intangibles seldom, if ever, have a residual value.

DISPOSITION OF INTANGIBLE ASSETS

When an intangible asset is sold, exchanged, or otherwise retired, the unamortized cost (or cost and accumulated amortization if separately recorded) must be removed from the accounts and a loss or gain recorded.

Because analysts often viewed intangibles as of questionable asset value and because of overconservatism, accounting practice in the past tended to encourage their arbitrary write-down to a nominal amount, either by lump sum in one period or over an unrealistically short estimated life. Contemporary accounting principles and practice do not support this arbitrary practice because it misstates net income and financial position. On this point, *APB Opinion No. 17* states that intangible assets "should not be written off in the period of acquisition" and "analysis of all factors should result in a reasonable estimate of the useful life. . . ."

On the other hand, in common with all assets, during the period of use, an estimate of value and future benefits of an intangible asset may indicate that the unamortized cost is above current fair value. Therefore, the unamortized cost should be significantly reduced in determining net income. In these unusual circumstances, an intangible asset should be written down to a realistic value and that value amortized over the estimated remaining useful life, not to exceed 40 years from date of acquisition (see *APB Opinion No. 17*, par. 31). Full disclosure is required by a note to the financial statement.

IDENTIFIABLE INTANGIBLE ASSETS

Identifiable intangible assets are so designated because they can be specifically and separately identified from the enterprise itself. Examples are patents, copyrights, franchises, and trademarks (but not goodwill). They may be *(a)* acquired by purchase, or *(b)* developed internally. In either instance, they are recorded initially at cost, in conformance with the cost principle and amortized, as used, in conformance with the matching principle.

Because of the wide range of intangible assets, the procedures tend to vary somewhat in applying the foregoing principles and guidelines. In the next few paragraphs, we will discuss the specifically identifiable intangible assets commonly encountered in accounting.

Patents

A patent is an exclusive grant by the U.S. Patent Office that enables the holder to use, manufacture, sell, and control the patent without interference or infringement by others. In reality the registration of the patent with the Patent Office is no guarantee of protection. Therefore, the patent is not conclusive until it has been successfully defended in court. For this reason it is generally held that the cost of *successful* court tests should be capitalized as a part of the cost of the patent.

The cost of a patent acquired by purchase is determined according to the *cost principle,* that is, cost is the cash or cash-equivalent value of the consideration given. Where the patent is produced in the company's own experimental laboratory, it must be accounted for as specified by FASB *Statement No.* 2 as discussed on page 603.

Patents are granted for a period of 17 years. The useful life of most patents is for a shorter period due to new patents, improved models, substitutes, and general technological progress. Patent costs should be amortized over the useful life or legal life, whichever is shorter.

Patent amortizations may be credited directly to the Patent account or to an Accumulated Patent Amortization account; the former is the more common practice.

Copyrights

A copyright is an exclusive right granted by the federal government to reproduce, publish, sell, and control a literary product or artistic work. The right is for a term of 28 years with provision for renewal for another 28 years. Many copyrights have value for a much shorter term, and their costs should be amortized over the shorter period. Often these costs are nominal and are written off in the period of expenditure.

Franchises

A common type of franchise is a grant by some governmental unit for the use of public properties (or a monopoly to furnish services such as the telephone company) in a manner beneficial to the public. Franchises normally involve rights for a specified period; therefore, the cost of acquiring them should be amortized over that period.

In recent years another type of franchise has become rather common; that is, the granting of a right, by one company to another entity, to utilize a specific designation (such as Colonel Sanders Fried Chicken) subject to certain obligations agreed to by each party. The consideration paid for such a franchise should be recorded by the franchisee as an intangible asset and amortized over its expected useful life. When the era of franchising was in its heyday and fast food chains, motels, and similar franchised type businesses were expanding rapidly, there were some rather optimistic accounting practices adopted by some franchisors (i.e., grantors of franchises) to recognize revenue. Due to action by the practicing profession and the issuance of an AICPA publication, the abuses have been substantially curbed.[4]

TRADEMARKS

Trademarks can be registered with the federal patent office to help prove ownership. Thus, names, symbols, or other devices providing distinctive identity for a product are afforded a degree of legal protection. Amounts paid or incurred directly in the acquisition, protection, expansion, registration, or defense of a trademark or trade name should be capitalized. Such capitalized balances are subject to amortization. Since they are amortizable for income tax purposes over periods of not less than five years, it is likely that many entities will use a similar amortization period for financial accounting purposes.

UNIDENTIFIABLE INTANGIBLE ASSETS

Unidentifiable intangible assets are so designated because they result from a number of economic factors and cannot be separately identified from the enterprise. Examples are goodwill and going value. Unidentifiable intangible assets can be *(a)* purchased externally through the acquisition of a going business (not purchased singly), or *(b)* developed internally by excellent business practices, providing superior goods and services, promotion, and so on, all of which builds long-range customer appeal.

In contrast to identifiable intangible assets, unidentifiable intangibles are recorded and reported *only when acquired by purchase*. In this situation, the cost of unidentifiable intangibles usually can be realistically measured. *APB Opinion No. 17* states:

> The cost of unidentifiable intangible assets is measured by the difference between the cost of the group of assets or enterprise acquired and the sum of the assigned costs of individual tangible and identifiable intangible assets acquired less liabilities assumed.

---

[4] AICPA, *Accounting for Franchise Fee Revenue* (New York, 1973).

To illustrate, assume X Company purchased Y Company with the following results:

Purchase price		$900,000
Assets acquired from Y Company (at fair market value):		
Tangible assets	$890,000	
Identifiable intangibles:		
Patent	14,000	
Franchise	16,000	
Total	920,000	
Less: Liabilities of Y Company assumed	120,000	
Net tangible fair market values acquired		800,000
Difference—unidentifiable intangibles (i.e., goodwill) ...		$100,000

In contrast, unidentifiable intangibles developed internally by the company are *not* capitalized under generally accepted accounting principles because the efforts and continuing expenditures (i.e., promotion, cost of superior service, etc.) ordinarily are not distinguishable from the current expenses of operations. *APB Opinion No. 17* states that the costs of developing, maintaining, or restoring unidentifiable intangible assets "inherent in a continuing business and related to the enterprise as a whole—such as goodwill—should be deducted from income when incurred."

Goodwill

Goodwill represents the potential of a business to earn above "normal" profits. Goodwill arises as a result of such factors as customer acceptance, efficiency of operation, reputation for dependability, quality of products, location, internal competences, and financial standing. The cost of goodwill represents a valuation placed upon the *above-normal earning capacity* of the firm. Conceptually, goodwill is the *present value* of the expected future excess earnings. Above-normal or excess earning capacity is the earning power of a firm above what is considered normal for the industry. For example, a firm consistently earning, say, 15% on total assets in an industry averaging a 10% return would have an excess earning capacity of 5%. The basic principle in accounting for goodwill initially is that it should be recorded at cost in conformance with the cost principle. In implementing this principle, goodwill should be recognized only when *actually paid for* in an arm's-length transaction. Consequently, goodwill should be recorded only when a business is purchased (or part of the business is purchased, as in the admission of a new partner) and the price paid exceeds the fair market value of all other tangible and identifiable intangible assets acquired less any debts assumed. Goodwill is recognized in the accounts only under these limited conditions so that an objective accounting will result and misrepresentation in financial statements will not occur. In the normal process of building up a business over time, an element of goodwill is developed.

This is frequently referred to as "internally developed goodwill," and in contrast to purchased goodwill is not properly reflected as an asset for two fundamental reasons: (1) directly there has been no disbursement of assets for it as is the case of other assets such as equipment; and (2) to the extent that expenses have been incurred that may have indirectly contributed to goodwill (such as promotion expenditures), they have been reflected in past income statements as expenses and any attempt to separate them out would be quite arbitrary.

Amortization of Goodwill. Accounting for purchased goodwill is controversial. One view is that it should not be amortized but should be reported as an intangible asset until there is definite evidence of its demise (such as failure to earn profits). Another view is that it should be deducted in full from capital at date of acquisition. Still another view is that it should be amortized over a realistic period during which the above-normal or superior earnings contemplated in the purchase decision are being realized.[5]

Some argue that there should be no amortization so long as profits are high since it is a permanent asset that has resale value. It is also argued that future profits and earnings per share should not be "penalized" because of a "good deal"; to amortize would penalize the excess profits which justified recording the goodwill in the first instance. The logical extension of this argument would be *(a)* to write it off directly to capital, or *(b)* to amortize goodwill only when profits fail to materialize.

The argument in favor of amortization is that purchased goodwill, like any other fixed asset, was acquired to generate earnings and, like other assets, should be amortized against those earnings. Thus, the conclusion is that goodwill should be amortized when the superior earnings are being realized. The argument continues that the purchase decision contemplated a specific amount of goodwill at the date of purchase which had already been developed. The purchaser envisioned a particularly profitable period in the future for which a price would be paid; that is, the cost of the *original goodwill purchased.* Acquired goodwill should be amortized over the approximate period of excess earnings contemplated in the purchase decision. Obviously, a competent management will continue to build *new* layers of internally generated goodwill the cost of which will flow through the income statements as current operating expenses. Thus, there is the concept that purchased goodwill

[5] It is sometimes alleged that goodwill can be negative. Cases cited are when the book value of assets purchased are in excess of the purchase price, or alternatively where the fair market value of the individual assets is in excess of the purchase price. In the opinion of the authors this reasoning flies in the face of both reality and concept. In the first instance book value has no relationship to market value, and in the second instance the fair value of a package of assets is the cash consideration given (or its equivalent). It is difficult to perceive, as a practical matter, an informed seller disposing of a group of assets for an amount substantially less than he could derive for them piecemeal. The instances cited usually make an absurd assumption or there is an obvious breakdown in the measurement process. There are situations where a credit may emerge; however, it should be identified for what it is and not carelessly labeled "negative goodwill." *APB Opinion No. 17* requires revaluation of the tangible and intangible identifiable assets acquired so that no negative goodwill will be recognized.

represents an established layer; the purchase cost of it should be allocated to the revenues generated by that particular layer.

These arguments were resolved, as far as current practice is concerned, by *APB Opinion No. 17*. It requires that goodwill be amortized by systematic charges each period, using the straight-line method, "unless a company demonstrates that another systematic method is more appropriate." The amortization period must be the estimated useful life, but not more than 40 years from date of purchase.

Amortization of goodwill is not permitted for income tax purposes—it does not cause a tax timing difference; therefore, allocation of income taxes is inappropriate.

Estimating Goodwill. In negotiations relating to the purchase or sale of a business the accountant may be requested to assist in valuing goodwill. *However, in such circumstances goodwill obviously is the result of bargaining between the purchaser and seller.* Computations based upon an analysis of asset values and income potentials frequently are useful in such negotiations since goodwill relates to the excess earning capacity of the business. In such analyses it must be emphasized that *future earning potentials* rather than past earnings are significant. Past earnings, properly adjusted, may provide a sound basis for estimating future potentials. In estimating future earnings, the earnings history of the firm should be studied. As a basis for estimating future earnings the following steps may be suggested:

1. Select for study a series of past years' earnings which appears to be most representative of usual operations and indicative of future expectations. A period of five years frequently is used. The period of years should be long enough to reveal the pattern of earnings fluctuations experienced by the company.
2. Adjust these past earnings *(a)* by eliminating all extraneous and nonrecurring gains and losses; *(b)* for changes in accounting, such as depreciation estimates and methods; *(c)* for changes which are expected to occur in salaries; and *(d)* for any other changes in costs, expenses, and revenue which are expected to occur in the future.
3. Analyze the trend and uniformity of past earnings. Even though past earnings have been above normal, any observed downward trend in the immediate past may indicate the disappearance of above-normal earning capacity. Such a downward trend would largely negate any basis for goodwill value.
4. On the basis of the above analysis project the future earnings and assets.

Within the above framework several approaches in *estimating* the value of goodwill are discussed below. To illustrate, assume that on January 1, 1977, it is desired to estimate the goodwill for Company X and that the data in Exhibit 14–1 are available.

Assume after careful analysis of the data in Exhibit 14–1, appraisal of the assets, and other pertinent factors the following estimates are derived:

EXHIBIT 14–1
Estimation of Goodwill

Year	Net Income (adjusted for nonrecurring items)	Book Values: Total Assets	Liabilities	Owners' Equity
1972	$18,000	$162,000	$ 82,000	$ 80,000
1973	17,000	172,000	90,000	82,000
1974	19,000	190,000	105,000	85,000
1975	19,000	187,000	90,000	97,000
1976	21,000	200,000	98,000	102,000
Total	$94,000	$911,000	$465,000	$446,000
Five-year average	$18,800	$182,200	$ 93,000	$ 89,200

Average annual earnings expected	$ 20,000
Estimated average future value of net assets (exclusive of goodwill) at appraised values less liabilities to be assumed	100,000

We will illustrate four rather unsophisticated methods followed by a conceptually sound one.

CAPITALIZATION OF EARNINGS. The expected earnings may be capitalized at a "normal" rate of return for the industry in order to estimate the total asset value. The difference between this value (total asset value implied) and the average assets expected (exclusive of goodwill) may be considered as an unsophisticated representation of goodwill. To illustrate, assuming a "normal" rate of return of 12%, goodwill for Company X may be computed as follows:

Average annual earnings expected	$20,000	
Normal rate of return for the industry	12%	
Total asset value implied ($20,000 ÷ 12%)		$166,667
Average assets expected (exclusive of goodwill)		100,000
Estimated goodwill		$ 66,667
Total Valuation Including Goodwill ($100,000 + $66,667)		$166,667

CAPITALIZATION OF EXCESS EARNINGS. The preceding method may be deficient in that it does not recognize excess earnings as a special factor. Capitalization of excess earnings requires the selection of a special rate to be applied to such earnings. The special capitalization rate should represent the planned annual rate of recovery of investment in the intangible as a result of excess earnings. The special rate should be higher than the normal rate because of the greater risk of not earning above the "normal" rate. Obviously, the greater the risk the higher the rate should be.

To illustrate the computation for Company X, assume a normal rate on assets of 12% and a capitalization rate for the excess earnings of 20%.

Average annual earnings expected	$20,000	
Return on average assets expected (exclusive of goodwill) at the normal rate ($100,000 × 12%)	12,000	
Excess earnings	$ 8,000	
Goodwill: Excess earnings capitalized at 20% ($8,000 ÷ 20%)		$ 40,000
Total Valuation Including Goodwill ($100,000 + $40,000)		$140,000

Year's Purchase of Average Excess Earnings. The goodwill may be estimated more directly by multiplying the estimated excess earnings by the number of years over which the investor expects to recover his or her investment in goodwill from the above-normal earnings of the business. To illustrate, assume the expected period of recovery is six years:

Excess earnings (computed above)	$ 8,000
Expected period of recovery	6 years
Estimated goodwill	$ 48,000
Total Valuation Including Goodwill ($100,000 + $48,000)	$148,000

Obviously, there is implicit in this method an amortization period for goodwill of six years.

Other Unsophisticated Methods of Estimating Goodwill Value. Other methods are used in estimating goodwill value. Generally, any method which does not take into account the expectation of above-normal earnings is not recommended. For example, the following method is sometimes used:

Years' Purchase of Average Earnings

Average annual earnings expected	$ 20,000
Four years' purchase (multiply by 4)	× 4
Estimated goodwill	$ 80,000
Total Valuation Including Goodwill ($100,000 + $80,000)	$180,000

Under this method some goodwill would be estimated even though below-normal earnings were experienced. For example, if average annual earnings expected were $7,000, an estimated goodwill of $28,000 would result despite the fact that annual earnings were $5,000 *below* normal.

Present Value Estimation of Goodwill

A conceptually sound approach to estimating (and amortizing) goodwill is to determine the *present value of the future excess earnings purchased.* To illustrate, assume for the above example that the negotiations implied the purchase of future excess earnings for ten years in addition to the identifiable assets and that the expected earnings rate was 8%. Computation of the implied goodwill would be as follows:

Average annual expected earnings purchased (estimated for ten years)	$20,000	
Average assets expected (at fair value)		$100,000
Normal expected annual earnings expected ($100,000 × 8%)	8,000	
Excess annual earnings for ten years	$12,000	
Goodwill:		
Present value of future earnings for $n = 10$, $i = 8\%$:		
$12,000 × $P_{n=10,i=8}$ (from Table 6–4)		
$12,000 × 6,7101 =		80,521
Total Valuation Including Goodwill		$180,521

The *purchase* at $180,521 would be recorded as follows:

Identifiable assets (detailed)	100,000*	
Goodwill	80,521	
Cash (or other consideration)		180,521

* At fair value.

Conceptually, the goodwill would then be amortized over the ten years as shown in Exhibit 14–2.

Of course, straight-line amortization over the ten-year period could be utilized; however, the present value approach as illustrated above conceptually is in harmony with the nature of goodwill.

The recording and reporting of purchased goodwill and its amortization is a central issue in mergers and consolidations; a topic discussed in Chapter 18.

EXHIBIT 14–2
Goodwill Amortized on Present Value Basis

Year	*Annual Excess Earnings (a)*	*(8%) Return on Goodwill Investment (b)*	*Goodwill Amortization* Expense (dr) (c)	*Goodwill Amortization* Goodwill (cr) (d)	*Goodwill Investment Carrying Value (e)*
Start					$80,521
1	$12,000	$6,442	$ 5,558	$ 5,558	74,963
2	12,000	5,997	6,003	6,003	68,960
3	12,000	5,517	6,483	6,483	62,477
4	12,000	4,998	7,002	7,002	55,475
5	12,000	4,438	7,562	7,562	47,913
6	12,000	3,833	8,167	8,167	39,746
7	12,000	3,180	8,820	8,820	30,926
8	12,000	2,474	9,526	9,526	21,400
9	12,000	1,712	10,288	10,288	11,112
10	12,000	888*	11,112	11,112	-0-

* Rounding error—$1.
(a) Projected annual excess earnings.
(b) 8% of previous goodwill balance ($80,521 × 8% = $6,440, etc.).
(c) and *(d)* Column *(a)* minus column *(b)*.
(e) Previous balance minus column *(d)*.

GOING VALUE

Going value (also known as going-concern value) is closely akin to goodwill but does not appear as such on the financial records of businesses.[6] It has greater importance in the income tax field than in financial reporting. Despite the fact that it does not appear on the financial statement, it constitutes a substantial asset that should be considered in negotiating the price of a business to be bought or sold. Going value's chief distinction from goodwill is that the latter is associated with unusual profitability, whereas going value is associated with the value of the effort and cost to start a business. An ordinary profitable business (or even one temporarily reporting losses) may have going value.

Like goodwill, going value is an intangible asset. It may be reflected in the financial statements as part of a lump-sum amount representing the excess of a purchase price over the values of the underlying tangible and intangible assets acquired (i.e., as a part designated as goodwill). As an alternative to buying a going business, persons planning to enter a line of activity have the alternative of starting a new entity from scratch, thus incurring numerous start-up costs. Leading authorities on engineering valuation have presented methods of estimating going value based on (1) revenues, costs, and net operating losses; and (2) return on investment foregone during a representative start-up period. These costs and economic losses would be required to bring the same or a similar new business from start-up status to a stage where the business would earn the same rate of return as the industry average.

Several recent court decisions have taken cognizance of going value; one held that the buyer of a going business must recognize the element of going value as an intangible asset and assign to it a portion of the lump-sum purchase price. The Tax Court allowed a deduction for the loss of the tax basis for going-concern value at the time that one plant was closed and manufacturing operations were transferred to another plant.

DEFERRED CHARGES

Deferred charges are intangibles and are closely related to intangible assets as defined in the preceding section of this chapter. Whereas intangible assets derive value based on *rights*, deferred charges derive asset value because they are long-term prepayments of expenses that will contribute to the production of future revenues. Also, deferred charges are akin to prepaid expenses (a short-term intangible reported as a current asset). Examples of deferred charges are bond issue costs, organization costs, machinery rearrangement costs, long-term prepaid insurance premiums, and prepaid leasehold costs.

A special item, debit balances, arising from interperiod income tax allocation are reported under this classification.

Deferred charges are amortized over the future period that they will

---

[6] See the subsequent discussion of organization costs which is a related issue.

contribute to the generation of future revenues. The 40-year rule, specified in *APB Opinion No. 17*, does not apply to deferred charges; however, they seldom, if ever, have lives that long.

In the next few paragraphs we will discuss the deferred charges usually encountered in accounting.

Research and Development Costs

Research and development costs, commonly called R & D, have become an increasingly important factor in modern industry. R & D departments are responsible for the development of new products, improvement of present products, testing of competitors' products, development of new or improved manufacturing methods, and similar functions.

Accounting practice for to R & D costs became quite varied over the years. Some businesses expensed all R & D expenditures in the period they were incurred. At an opposite extreme, others capitalized practically all R & D expenditures, followed by their amortization. In between were various practices, including selective capitalization of costs related to successful projects with subsequent amortization at varying rates. This hodge-podge practice received the early attention of the Financial Accounting Standards Board and resulted in the issuance of FASB *Statement No.* 2 (October 1974), titled "Accounting for Research and Development Costs."

The main provisions of this *Statement* are as follows:

1. All R & D costs covered by the statement shall be charged to expense when incurred.[7] Stated another way, R & D expenditures (except for item 3 below) must not be capitalized.
2. Financial statements must disclose *total* R & D costs charged to expense in each period for which an income statement is presented.
3. It does not apply to R & D costs where work is done for others under contract. Also, exceptions were made for certain government-regulated entities. In other words, in these areas, R & D costs can be charged to an asset account when incurred.
4. The *Statement* became effective for fiscal years beginning on or after January 1, 1975. Those entities who had capitalized R & D costs on that date are to clear their books by means of prior period adjustments.

The statement represents a practical solution to a critical problem.

[7] In the context of the standard, *research* is planned activities aimed at discovery of new knowledge with the hope it will be useful in developing new products, processes, or services, or in bringing about significant improvement to existing products or processes. *Development* is the translation of research findings into a plan or design for a new product or process or for a significant improvement to an existing one, whether intended for sale or use. It includes conceptual formulation, design, and testing of product alternatives, construction of prototypes, and operation of pilot plants. It excludes routine or periodic alterations to existing products, manufacturing processes, and other on-going operations, even though these alterations may represent improvements. It also excludes market research and testing activities.

Careful study indicated that it was difficult to establish criteria for deferment of R & D costs and that companies were reporting their R & D expenditures in a variety of ways (the majority expensing them).[8]

One of the chief aims of the FASB and its predecessors and of the SEC is to reduce the variety of ways in which essentially similar factual situations can be reported. By mandating that all R & D costs be expensed when incurred, the FASB swept away the wide range of alternatives in this area. From an income statement standpoint, long-run implementation of the standard sometimes makes little difference. The amount of R & D expense will be about the same whether there is immediate expensing or temporary deferment of some costs and subsequent amortization of them.

Critics of the standard argue that while its long-run income statement effects are often minimal, from a balance sheet standpoint it is hard to defend. In essence the standard requires companies to report that none of their R & D expenditures has future benefit since no intangible asset related to R & D costs can appear on the balance sheet. For successful companies operating in high-technology industries such as electronics, chemicals, and aero-space, to name but a few, this means that some of their most valuable assets (from an intrinsic if not from a cost standpoint) are not even reported. Whether this could be corrected, since the assets do not appear on the basic statements, if current value statements were to be prepared is a good question. Defenders of the standard rejoin that informed analysts and others are well aware that successful, high-technology companies have assets resulting from R & D and that the standard was not aimed at such companies; it was aimed at companies inclined to exaggerate the value of assets associated with their R & D efforts. Regardless of who has the better side of the argument, the standard is operational and seemingly has the strong support of the practicing profession.

Organization Costs

Expenditures incurred in the original incorporation and promotion of a business enterprise, such as legal fees, state incorporation fees, stock certificate costs, stamp taxes, reasonable underwriting costs, and office expenses incident to organizing, are capitalized as organization costs on the theory that such costs benefit each succeeding year; hence, to charge them off as a cost in the first year of operation would result in an incorrect matching of cost and revenue. Since the life of a corporation generally is indefinite, the length of the period which will receive the benefits of this cost is usually indeterminate. For this reason, and because the recognition of organization costs as a business asset depends entirely upon intangible values presumably attached to the corporate form of organization for the particular business, organization expenses generally are amortized over an arbitrarily selected short period. This practice

---

[8] Oscar S. Gellein and Maurice S. Newman, "Accounting for R & D Expenditures" *Accounting Research Study No. 14* (New York: AICPA, 1973).

is encouraged by the tax rules which permit the corporation to amortize most organization costs ratably over such period as the company desires as long as that period is not less than five years.

A troublesome problem is posed in respect to *stock issue costs;* that is, the costs of printing stock certificates, attorney fees related directly to the issue, commissions paid for sale, and accountants' fees (such as the cost of filing with the SEC). Three approaches in accounting for these particular costs are found in practice:

1. *Charge such costs to organization costs.* Although this is a fairly common practice, many accountants feel that it is conceptually deficient.
2. *Offset such costs against the sales price of the stock.* Under this practice they would be included in the determination of stock discount or premium. In this alternative such costs would not be amortized against revenue. It is conceptually deficient since it may create a recorded discount on stock that does not agree with the amount paid in by the shareholder. This approach appears to be the most widely used primarily because *(a)* frequently the costs are not separable from the issue transaction, and *(b)* such costs benefit the entire life of the corporation.
3. *Charge such costs to a deferred charge and amortize them similar to organization costs.* This approach is conceptually sound providing such costs are amortized over the useful life of the "asset." As a practical matter they generally are amortized over a short period similar to organization costs.

Leaseholds

The right of a lessee to use real property under the terms of a lease agreement is known as a *leasehold.*[9] A lease agreement calls for periodic rent and may require, in addition, the down payment of a lump sum. The lump sum is a deferred charge (leasehold) which should be amortized over the life of the lease. Amortization may be *(a)* on a straight-line basis or preferably *(b)* on a present value basis. The amortization period is the life of the lease; options to renew the lease are usually disregarded in determining the amortization period. Procedurally, the down payment should be debited to a deferred charge account labeled Leaseholds; the amortization is recorded as a credit to this account and as a debit to Rental Expense.

To illustrate, assume a property owner is leasing a building for $8,000 per year payable at the start of each year. As a result of bargaining between the lessor (owner) and lessee (tenant), instead of annual rentals, a lump-sum payment at the start of the upcoming year of $40,801.60 would constitute the total rent for six years. This arrangement could be accounted for by each party on a *straight-line* amortization basis as follows:

---

[9] These discussions assume operating leases; other types of leases are discussed in Chapter 23.

	Lessor			*Lessee*	
1. At date of prepayment:					
Cash	40,801.60		Prepaid rent expense (or leasehold)	40,801.60	
Prepaid rent revenue		40,801.60	Cash........................		40,801.60
2. Amortization each year for six years (straight line):					
Prepaid rent revenue	6,800.27		Rent expense	6,800.27	
Rent revenue		6,800.27	Prepaid rent expense		6,800.27
($40,801.60 ÷ 6 = $6,800.27)					

The straight-line approach does not consider the time value of money; hence, the rent revenue (or expense) is misstated and interest as a factor is not recognized. Theoretically, the leasehold and the amortization (on both sets of books) should be accounted for on a present value basis. The advance payment represents the present value of an annuity of $8,000 for six periods. Since the first payment (rent) is due immediately there is an *annuity due* which may be schematically demonstrated as follows:

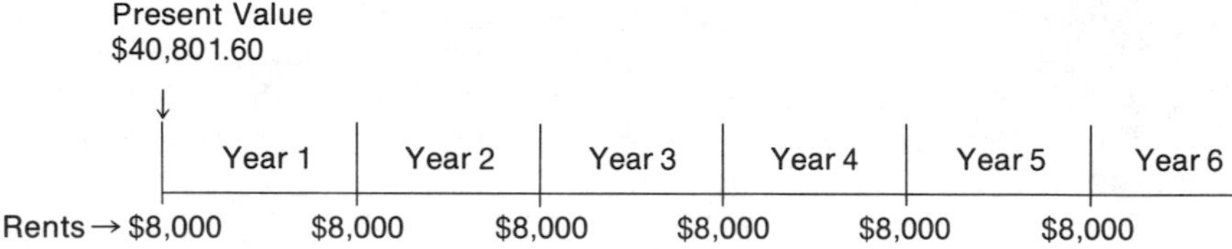

The agreed rate of interest between the parties was 7%; therefore, the advance payment was computed as follows:

Present value of annuity due for six rents at 7%: That is, an annuity due is equivalent to the (n − 1 rents) + 1 value for an ordinary annuity Table 6–4, 7%, 5 rents = 4.1002 + 1 =	5.1002
Multiply by annual rental	× $8,000
Lump-Sum Payment, (if made now)	$40,801.60

Determination of (1) the periodic amortization using the present value approach, and (2) the related accounting entries are best accomplished for either the lessor or lessee by development of an amortization table as shown in Exhibit 14–3. Since the annual rent is due at the beginning of each period, you should observe that there would be no interest in the sixth year as reflected in the above schematic for the annuity due.

The interest computations in Exhibit 14–3 reflect the characteristics of an annuity due, that is, the *rents* are assumed to be paid at the beginning of each period.

Amortization entries for the lessor and lessee for the first, second, and

EXHIBIT 14–3
Leasehold Amortization Table (present value basis) at $8,000 Annual Rental*

Year-End	Rent	Computation of Interest		Leasehold Amortization	Leasehold Balance
					$40,801.60†
1	$8,000	$(40,801.60−$8,000)7% =	$2,296.11	$5,703.89‡	35,097.71§
2	8,000	(35,097.71− 8,000)7% =	1,896.84	6,103.16	28,994.55
3	8,000	(28,994.55− 8,000)7% =	1,469.62	6,530.38	22,464.17
4	8,000	(22,464.17− 8,000)7% =	1,012.49	6,987.51	15,476.66
5	8,000	(15,476.66− 8,000)7% =	523.34	7,476.66	8,000.00
6	8,000			8,000.00	-0-

† Present value of future rents as computed above.
‡ $8,000.00 − $2,296.11 = $5,703.89.
§ $40.801.60 − $5,703.89 = $35,097.71.
* Alternatively the table could have been started as follows with the same results:

Period	Rent	Interest	Amortization	Balance
Balance				$40,801.60
Start	8,000			32,801.60
1....................................	8,000	$32,801.60 × 7% = $2,296.11	$5,703.89	27,097.71
2....................................	8,000	27,097.71 × 7% = 1,896.84	6,103.16	20,994.55
Etc.				

sixth years are shown in the tabulation below assuming the fiscal and lease years coincide. Entries for the years not shown would be made in accordance with the amortization table shown in Exhibit 14–3.

Lessor			Lessee		
Year 1:					
At start of lease:					
Cash..................	40,801.60		Leasehold	40,801.60	
Deferred rent revenue ...		40,801.60	Cash..................		40,801.60
At end of first year:					
Deferred rent revenue	5,703.89		Rent expense	8,000.00*	
Interest expense	2,296.11*		Interest revenue		2,296.11*
Rent revenue ...		8,000.00*	Leasehold		5,703.89
Year 2:					
Deferred rent revenue	6,103.16		Rent expense	8,000.00	
Interest expense	1,896.84		Interest revenue		1,896.84
Rent revenue ...		8,000.00	Leasehold		6,103.16
Year 6:					
Deferred rent revenue	8,000.00		Rent expense	8,000.00	
Interest expense	-0-		Interest revenue		-0-
Rent revenue ...		8,000.00	Leasehold		8,000.00

* These two amounts generally are offset for practical reasons.

Clearly the present value (scientific) approach provides more realistic values for the balance sheet and the income statement than does the straight-line approach. The present value approach derives rental and interest values that represent the economic essence of the lease contract. Obviously, the difference between the present value of $40,801.60 and the $48,000.00 that would have been paid is due to the time value of money agreed to by the two parties.

DEVELOPMENT STAGE COMPANIES

The subject of accounting for companies in the development stage is closely akin to deferred charges because such companies in the past deferred a wide range of costs. This was done because, during the development stage, they incur high start-up costs and generally have little or no revenues against which they can be matched.

Because of the lack of guidelines and the wide variety of practices, the FASB issued *Statement of Financial Accounting Standards No. 7*, "Accounting and Reporting by Development Stage Companies" (June 1975).

The *Statement* defines development stage companies essentially as follows:

> An enterprise shall be considered to be in the development stage if it is devoting substantially all of its efforts to establishing a new business and either of the following conditions exists: (a) planned principal operations have not commenced, or (b) planned principal operations have commenced but there has been no significant revenue therefrom. A development stage enterprise will typically be devoting most of its efforts to activities such as financial planning; raising capital; exploring for natural resources; developing natural resources; research and development; establishing sources of supply; acquiring property, plant, or other operating assets, such as mineral rights; recruiting and training personnel; developing markets; and starting up production.

Prior to the issuance of *Statement No. 7*, the accounting practices of development stage companies included the following which many accountants felt did not accord with generally accepted accounting principles: *(a)* deferral of various types of costs without regard to their recoverability; *(b)* issuance of special types of statements, including statements of assets and unrecovered preoperating costs; and *(c)* other practices, in the view of many far outside the purview of generally accepted accounting principles.

To correct these abuses, *Statement No. 7* requires development stage companies to present financial statements prepared on the same basis as other businesses; special reporting formats are unacceptable. Capitalization and deferral of costs is subject to the same assessment of future benefit and recoverability applicable to established businesses. Thus, the statement specifies that a development stage company is required to prepare basic statements and provide additional disclosure as follows:

a. A balance sheet, including any cumulative net losses reported with a descriptive caption such as "deficit accumulated during the development stage" in the owners' equity section.

b. An income statement, showing amounts of revenue and expenses for each period covered by the income statement and, in addition, cumulative amounts from the enterprise's inception.
c. A statement of changes in financial position, showing the sources and uses of financial resources for each period for which an income statement is presented and, in addition, cumulative amounts from the enterprise's inception.
d. A statement of stockholders' equity, showing from the enterprise's inception for each issuance:
   1. date and number of shares issued for cash or other consideration.
   2. dollar amounts (per share or other equity unit) assigned to consideration received for securities.
   3. where there is noncash consideration, its nature and the basis of determining amounts.[10]

The *Statement* also requires that the financial statements be *specifically identified* as those of a development stage enterprise and include a description of the nature of the development stage in which the enterprise is engaged.

INSURANCE

Practically all businesses carry one or more kinds of insurance. Insurance requires prepayment of the premium, at which time an asset having intangible characteristics is created. Depending on the type and length of time covered, the prepaid premium may represent *(a)* a current asset (i.e., short-term prepayments), *(b)* a long-term investment (i.e., cash surrender value of life insurance policies), or *(c)* a deferred charge (i.e., long-term prepayments).

Although there are many different kinds of insurance, the usual kinds carried by businesses include *(a)* liability insurance, *(b)* casualty insurance, and *(c)* life insurance on key executives.

Liability Insurance

Liability insurance involves a contract whereby the insurance company, in consideration of a specified premium, assumes an obligation to assume liabilities to third parties that arise from specified events such as damages sought by a customer for injuries in an accident on company premises. The premium typically is paid in advance for periods of one to five years—the longer the period, the less the prorated premium. Prepaid premiums represent an intangible asset. To illustrate, assume on January 1, 19A, that Company B paid a $2,500 five-year premium for a liability insurance contract. The accounting and reporting for 19A would be as follows:

---

[10] Adapted from FASB *Statement of Financial Accounting Standards No. 7*, "Accounting and Reporting by Development Stage Enterprises" (Stanford, Conn.: FASB, June 1975), par. 11.

Entries:

January 1, 19A – insurance premium paid:

Prepaid insurance	2,500	
Cash		2,500

December 31, 19A – adjusting entry:

Insurance expense	500	
Prepaid insurance		500

Reporting at December 31, 19A:

Income Statement:	
Insurance expense	500
Balance Sheet:	
Current Assets:	
Prepaid insurance	500
Deferred Charges:	
Prepaid insurance, long term	1,500

Casualty Insurance

Casualty insurance involves a contract whereby the insurance company in consideration for a premium payment assumes an obligation under certain circumstances to reimburse the policyholder an amount not exceeding the *fair market value* (at date of loss) of the property lost due to storm, fire, and so on, as specified in the policy. The indemnity in no case exceeds the amount stipulated in the contract, that is, the *face* of the policy.

The great diversity in the forms of policies and the legal status of their provisions in the past caused most states to adopt a standard policy. The companies are allowed a certain degree of flexibility in varying the terms of the standard policy by attaching "riders" (standardized paragraphs).

The premium, a charge per $100 of insurance carried, is usually computed on a standard basis, depending upon the nature of the asset insured. For example, in the case of insurance on a building, the premium is adjusted for such things as type of construction, kind of roof, types of flues, occupancy by owner or tenant, space rented, office in the building, and location.

When a policy is canceled at the request of the insurance company, the insured is entitled to a refund of a pro rata portion of the premium, which covers the unexpired time. If the cancellation is requested by the insured, the premium to be returned is computed by reference to a short-rate table which refunds less than the pro rata portion of the premium. For example, one state's schedule provides that the insured who pays 2½ times the annual rate for a three-year policy may recover 60% of the premium if he or she has the policy canceled at the end of one year.

Coinsurance

To encourage adequate insurance coverage many policies carry a *coinsurance clause* which provides that if the property is insured for less than a stated percentage (often 80%) of its fair market value at the time of a loss, the insured is a *coinsurer* with the insurance company. As a coinsurer the insured must stand a share of any loss. The share of a loss, when there is a coinsurance clause, is determined by application of the policy provision that the insurance company will pay the *lower* of the three following amounts:

1. Face of the policy.
2. Fair market value of the loss.
3. Coinsurance indemnity (determined by formula).

To illustrate the effect of a coinsurance clause, assume the following for Company C:

1. Policy on casualties—face, $7,000; coinsurance clause, 80%.
2. Casualty—fire, fair market value of the loss at date of fire (there was a partial loss of the property), $5,680.
3. Fair market value of the property immediately prior to the fire, $10,000.

Computation of the coinsurance indemnity (by formula):

$$\frac{\text{Face of Policy}}{.80 \times \text{Fair Market Value of Property at Date of Casualty}} \times \text{Fair market Value of the Loss} = \text{Coinsurance Indemnity}$$

$$\frac{\$7,000}{.80 \times \$10,000} \times \$5,680 = \$4,970$$

Thus, the insurance company would reimburse the insured for $4,970 because it is lower than either the face of the policy ($7,000) and the amount of the loss ($5,680).

Application of this rule is further illustrated by the cases shown in Exhibit 14–4 (assuming in each case that the policy contains an 80% coinsurance clause).

EXHIBIT 14–4
Indemnity under Coinsurance

	Case 1 (when formula is lowest)	*Case 2 (when loss is lowest)*	*Case 3 (when policy is lowest)*
Fair market value of property at date of loss	$10,000	$10,000	$10,000
Face of policy carried by insured	7,000	8,800	6,000
Fair market value of loss	5,680	6,000	10,000
Maximum indemnity (formula)	4,970*	6,600†	7,500‡
Actual indemnity payable	4,970	6,000	6,000

* Computed above.

† $\frac{8,800}{.80 \times \$10,000} \times \$6,000 = \$6,600.$

‡ $\frac{\$6,000}{.80 \times \$10,000} \times \$10,000 = \$7,500.$

Blanket Policy

When a company takes out a fire insurance policy covering several items of property (frequently called a blanket policy), the policy usually includes an "average" clause, which provides that the protection shall attach to each item of property in such proportion as each property bears to the entire value (fair market value at time of loss) of the property insured. For example, assume that a blanket policy for $9,000, containing the 80% coinsurance clause, insured two buildings—A having a fair market value at the date of the fire of $10,000 and B of $5,000. The face of the policy would be allocated as $6,000 on A and $3,000 on B. If a fire loss of $2,000 occurred in B, the maximum indemnity would be:

$$\frac{\$3,000}{.80 \times \$5,000} \times \$2,000 = \$1,500$$

Since $1,500 is less than either the loss ($2,000) or the effective policy ($3,000), the actual indemnity would be $1,500, the maximum set by the formula.

Accounting for a Casualty Loss

When there is a casualty loss, prepaid insurance must be adjusted accordingly. To illustrate the nature of the adjustment we will utilize a *fire loss*. When a fire has occurred, an orderly accounting procedure is essential for *separately reporting the loss* and for proper matching of operating expense and revenue. In accounting for a fire loss, certain procedures should be followed, viz:

1. Determine to what extent the accounting records have been damaged or destroyed. Take steps to supplement damaged records, or to reconstruct them if they have been destroyed.
2. Adjust the books to the date of the fire for all operating items affected by the fire. Make all necessary adjusting entries for depreciation, amortization, accrued and prepaid expense, and income items affected by the fire.
3. Determine the *book value* of all assets destroyed by the fire.
4. Open a Fire Loss account in the general ledger and transfer to it the book value of all assets destroyed. Charge the Fire Loss account with any unexpired insurance premium on that portion of the policy which is paid by the insurance company as a result of the casualty, and with any expenses incurred in connection with the fire and the settlement. When a policy is paid in full, the entire adjusted unexpired premium should be charged to Fire Loss. If 60% of the potential indemnity were collected, 60% of the adjusted unexpired premium should be changed to Fire Loss. The remainder of the policy amount could be continued in force as insurance on what was not damaged or, if the policy is cancelled, could become the basis of a refund. These provisions tend to vary according to the policy provisions.
5. Determine the amounts recoverable (this determination is made through negotiations with the adjuster appointed by the insurance

company) under the insurance policies in force. Credit the Fire Loss account with these amounts, and with any proceeds from the sale of damaged assets or merchandise whose cost has been charged to Fire Loss.

6. Close the balance of the Fire Loss account to Income Summary. It is advisable to close the books as at year-end when the fire is of major proportions.

In determining the book value of assets destroyed, cognizance must be taken not only of the estimated depreciation recorded for past periods but also of the depreciation to be accrued for the elapsed portion of the present period to date of loss. The portion of the insurance premium to be charged to the Fire Loss account is the unexpired portion at the date of the fire if the full amount of the policy is paid. If only a portion of the policy is paid, then the amount of the payment is endorsed on the policy and the remainder continues in force. In this case, that portion of the unexpired premium which the endorsement bears to the face of the policy is taken out of Prepaid Insurance and charged to Fire Loss. If the policy is continued, the remainder is left in the Prepaid Insurance account; if canceled, this remainder is a cash refund.[11]

If a perpetual inventory system is used, and if the records are not destroyed, the amount of the merchandise on hand at the time of the fire can be determined from the records. In the absence of such records, the amount of the inventory may be estimated by the "gross margin" method as described in Chapter 10.

Accounting for Fire Loss Illustrated. Assume the Fire Alarm Company suffered a fire loss on July 1 of the current year; the relevant values were:

a. Fair market values at date of the fire (July 1):	
Inventory (same as cost), 100% loss	$ 3,000
Furniture and equipment, 100% loss	1,000
Building—total fair market value	26,250
Building—amount of loss at fair market value, ⅔ loss	17,500
b. Insurance coverage:	
Inventory—none.	
Furniture and equipment, insured—face of policy $2,400 (no coinsurance clause). Unexpired insurance on January 1 of current year (30 months unexpired)	50
Building, insured—face of policy $16,800 (includes an 80% coinsurance clause). Unexpired insurance on January 1 of current year (24 months unexpired)	320
c. Account balances January 1 of current year:	
Prepaid insurance ($50 + $320)	370
Inventory (at cost)	1,500
Furniture and equipment (at cost)	2,400
Accumulated depreciation, furniture and equipment (depreciation rate, 25% on cost)	1,200
Building (at cost)	30,000
Accumulated depreciation, building (depreciation rate, 3⅓% on cost)	10,000

[11] These tend to vary depending upon the specific provisions of the insurance contract.

The entries to adjust the books to the date of the fire, to record the fire loss, and to record the settlement with the insurance company follow with explanations and computations.

1. Entries to adjust the books to the date of the fire for operating items affected:

Fire loss (goods destroyed)	3,000	
Goods burned (inventory destroyed)		3,000
To set up inventory of unsold merchandise destroyed by fire. (Note: Goods Burned is closed to Income Summary at regular closing. This amount offsets the charges to regular income from the beginning inventory and purchases, part of which was burned).*		

* An alternative treatment would be to credit the beginning inventory and purchases to the extent of the loss and to debit the Fire Loss account.

Depreciation on furniture and equipment	300	
Accumulated depreciation on furniture and equipment		300
To record depreciation, at a rate of 25% per year, from January 1 to July 1 ($2,400 × 25% × 6/12).		
Depreciation on building	500	
Accumulated depreciation on building		500
To record depreciation, from January 1 to July 1 ($30,000 × 3 1/3% × 6/12 = $500.		
Insurance expense	90	
Prepaid insurance		90
To record the expired insurance premium from January 1 to July 1, as follows:		
Furniture and equipment ($50 × 6/30) ... 10		
Building ($320 × 6/24) ... 80		

2. Entries to close the book value of assets destroyed to the Fire Loss account:

Fire loss	900	
Accumulated depreciation on furniture and equipment	1,500	
Furniture and equipment		2,400
To close the accumulated depreciation and the asset account into the Fire Loss account.		
Fire loss	13,000	
Accumulated depreciation on building	7,000	
Building		20,000
To close two thirds of the accumulated depreciation and of the asset account into the Fire Loss account ($10,000 + $500) × 2/3 = $7,000.		

3. Entry to record the settlement with the insurance company:

Cash	15,000	
Fire loss		15,000
To record the payment received from the insurance company, computed as follows: furniture and equipment,		

$1,000 (full settlement): building, per formula [$16,800 ÷ ($26,250 × 80%)] × $17,500 = $14,000 (which is less than face of policy or fair market value of the loss). No insurance or inventory loss.

4. To adjust balance in Prepaid Insurance:

If Policies Continued

Fire loss	217	
Prepaid insurance..............		217

If Policies Not Continued

Fire loss	217	
Cash	63	
Prepaid insurance..............		280

Analysis of prepaid insurance:

	Furniture and Fixtures	Building	Total
Unexpired January 1	$50	$320	$370
Amortized to July 1	10	80	90
Unexpired July 1..	40	240	280
Amount related to indemnity:			
$1,000/$2,400 × $40 =	17		17
$14,000/$16,800 × $240 =		200	200
Unexpired after fire loss (or cash refund)	$23	$ 40	$ 63

The Fire Loss account is closed to Income Summary.

Life Insurance

Life insurance companies sell insurance contracts that call for a stipulated payment (indemnity) in case of death, receiving in return compensation in the form of premiums. In an *ordinary life* policy, the premiums are paid until the death of the insured at which time the stipulated benefit is paid to the beneficiary. During the period the policy is in force it has both a cash surrender value and a loan value. In a *limited payment* policy, the premiums are paid for a stated number of periods or until the death of the insured (if prior to the end of the stipulated period) and the benefit is paid at death or after a stipulated date as an endowment. As with the ordinary life policy there is a cash surrender value and a loan value. In *term insurance,* the premium payments are made for a stated number of periods or until death (if prior to the end of the stipulated period); the benefit is paid only if death occurs within the stated number of periods. In term insurance, there is no cash surrender or loan values and the policy must be renewed at the end of the stipulated period; otherwise it lapses. At renewal, a new premium scale is effective based on the advanced age. As most of the characteristics are involved in ordinary life policies, the discussion to follow will be limited to this type.

The law and insurance companies have long recognized that a company has an insurable interest in certain of its *executives*. Thus, it is not uncommon for a company to insure the life of certain key executives; the proceeds are payable to the company to compensate for the loss incurred in replacing a deceased executive.

In accounting for a life insurance contract of this type, premiums paid (cash paid less any dividends) and the related asset (intangible) must be recorded and reported.

Cash Surrender and Loan Value. The cash surrender value of a policy is the sum payable upon the cancellation of the policy at the request of the insured. The loan value of a policy is the sum the insurance company will loan on a policy maintained in force. The cash surrender value is computed as of the end of the year; the loan value is computed as of the beginning of the year. Each policy carries a table that indicates the cash surrender value and the loan value for specific policy years. At any given time the loan value is somewhat less than the cash surrender value. Since the policy could be canceled and a portion of the premiums which have been paid out be returned in the form of the cash surrender value, not all of the premiums paid constitute an expense but only the excess of the total premiums paid over the cash surrender value.[12]

The portion of premiums paid equal to the cash surrender value is an asset and should be shown as such on the balance sheet under the caption Investments and Funds.

To illustrate one sequence of entries, assume the following data taken from an insurance policy having an indemnity of $25,000.

Year	*Premium (beginning of year)*	*Cash Surrender Value (end of year)*
1	$720	-0-
2	720	-0-
3	720	$1,140
4	720	1,480
5	(Etc., as specified in the policy)	

Indicated entries:

Year 1:	Life insurance expense	720	
	Cash		720
Year 2:	Life insurance expense	720	
	Cash		720

[12] In mutual companies the stated premium is reduced by a dividend credit.

		Debit	Credit
Year 3:	Life insurance expense	720	
	Cash		720
	At year-end:		
	Cash surrender value of life insurance	1,140	
	Life insurance expense (1/3 × $1,140)		380
	Nonrecurring adjustment – prior year (2/3 × $1,140)		760*
Year 4:	Life insurance expense	720	
	Cash		720
	At year-end:		
	Cash surrender value of life insurance ($1,480 − $1,140)	340	
	Life insurance expense		340

* Another alternative would be to "allocate" the third-year cash surrender value to the first three years on some basis (say, equally) at the time the annual entry for premium is made.

Each year thereafter the Cash surrender value of life insurance account would be debited for the increase in the cash surrender value as shown by the table in the policy. The above example was simplified by assuming the policy year and the accounting year coincided. If they do not coincide, as is the normal case, an adjusting entry at the end of each accounting period would be required for the prepaid amount of insurance expense.

The following entry would be made when the face of policy is paid at the death of the president, assuming the cash surrender value of the policy at date of death was $3,500 and that three months' premium is to be refunded in accordance with the insurance contract whereby premiums paid beyond date of death are refunded.

	Debit	Credit
Cash [$25,000 + (3/12 × $720)]	25,180	
Life insurance expense (3/12 × $720)		180
Cash surrender value of life insurance		3,500
Gain on settlement of life insurance indemnity		21,500

The gain normally would be extraordinary.

REPORTING INTANGIBLES

Noncurrent assets that characteristically are properly classified as intangibles are variously reported under the balance sheet captions (or similar captions): "Intangibles," "Deferred charges," and "Other assets." Although reasonably precise definitions have been provided in this chapter, in the practical world of accounting, there are no comparable authoritative distinctions between the three captions. Therefore, considerable variation between companies can be observed in the balance sheet reporting of noncurrent intangibles. Usually each intangible is descriptively titled in the statement and then noted so that the statement user will not be misled.

QUESTIONS

1. What distinguishes intangibles from other assets traditionally reported outside the current asset category? How are intangibles reported on the balance sheet?
2. What factors should determine whether or not an intangible asset is amortized and over what span of time?
3. What outlays are properly considered part of the cost of an intangible asset?
4. Explain the conceptual nature of goodwill and the basis on which goodwill is amortized.
5. What is the proper role of the accountant in valuation of goodwill?
6. Briefly describe going value. How can it be distinguished from goodwill?
7. What is the nature of a franchise? Of a trademark?
8. There are different kinds of deferred charges. What are they? Give one or more examples of the different kinds.
9. Define a deferred charge. Is it an intangible?
10. How are deferred charges distinguished from prepaid expenses? Give examples of each.
11. What are the chief provisions of the FASB accounting statement on accounting for research and development costs?
12. What items are properly chargeable to organization costs? Should organization costs be amortized? Explain.
13. What is a leasehold? What are the primary accounting aspects of a leasehold?
14. Some casualty policies have coinsurance clauses. What is the purpose of such a clause? Does its presence in a policy affect the indemnity which the insured can collect if the insured property is totally destroyed?
15. When a casualty occurs for which insurance is in force, certain accounting steps should be taken. What are these accounting measures?
16. What is the relationship between cash surrender value and loan value of a life insurance policy? Which one affects accounting entries? How?
17. For what reasons do some companies insure the lives of executives and name the companies as beneficiaries?

DECISION CASE 14–1

A new corporation was organized in 19A with a capital of $10,000,000 to manufacture a new type of sports car.

In 19A and 19B, it invested $4,000,000 in a plant, machinery, and tools and expended $2,000,000 for materials, labor, advertising, and overhead expenses in connection with perfecting a first experimental model. There was no income from sales or other sources in those years. Management charged the expenses of $2,000,000 to a Development and Experimental Expense account which appeared among "Deferred charges" on the December 31, 19A balance sheet.

In January 19C its model was pronounced a success and its factory was ready to produce at the ratc of 100 cars per year, to be sold for $10,000 per car. However, because of labor, material, and other problems, only five cars were produced and only three cars were sold. In 19C its total sales were $30,000; purchases of material and supplies were $200,000; factory labor was $80,000; and advertising, clerical, and overhead costs were $150,000. Management charged the net loss for the year 19C to Developmental and Experimental Expense which was reported on the balance sheet under "Deferred charges."

During 19D, management forecast the production and sale of 100 units. However, 80 were produced and only 20 were sold. The net operating loss for the year was $400,000, which management suggests deferring.

Required:

1. If 19A through 19D were years shortly before 1975 and you were the auditor of the company, discuss the acceptability of the accounting treatment, the disclosures, if any, you would make and the opinion you wound render as of—
   a. December 31, 19B.
   b. December 31, 19C.
   c. December 31, 19D.
2. If instead the years 19C and 19D were calendar years 1976 and 1977 (or later), what about the acceptability of the accounting treatment, disclosures, and so on, as of—
   a. December 31, 19C.
   b. December 31, 19D.

(AICPA adapted)

EXERCISES

Exercise 14–1

The data below pertain to two separate intangible assets:

	Asset X	*Asset Y*
Cost	$7,200	$8,400
Estimated economic life	Indefinite	14 years

Required:

1. Give annual entry for amortization, if any, for each asset. (Assume both were acquired in 1971 or later.)
2. If after Asset Y has been in use for eight full years, it is determined at the start of the ninth year that its remaining life will be four years, make any entry then that is appropriate. Give the amortization entry for Asset Y at the end of its ninth year.

Exercise 14–2

Check the best answer in each of the following and indicate the basis for your choice.

1. On January 15, 19A, a corporation was granted a patent on a product. On January 2, 19J, to protect its patent, the corporation purchased a patent on a competing product that originally was issued on January 10, 19F. Because of its

unique plant, the corporation does not feel the competing patent can be used in producing a product. The cost of the competing patent should be–

a. Amortized over a maximum period of 17 years.
b. Amortized over a maximum period of 13 years.
c. Amortized over a maximum period of 8 years.
d. Expensed in 19J.

2. Goodwill should be written off–
   a. As soon as possible against retained earnings.
   b. As soon as possible as an extraordinary item.
   c. By systematic charges against retained earnings over the period benefited, but not more than 40 years.
   d. By systematic charges to expense over the period benefited, but not more than 40 years.
3. A large publicly held company has developed and registered a trademark during 19A. How should the cost of developing and registering the trademark be accounted for?
   a. Charged to an asset account that should not be amortized.
   b. Expensed as incurred.
   c. Amortized over 25 years if in accordance with management's evaluation.
   d. Amortized over its useful life or 17 years, whichever is shorter.
4. A deferred charge should be–
   a. Expensed as incurred.
   b. Capitalized and not amortized until it clearly has no value.
   c. Capitalized and amortized over the estimated future benefited.
   d. Capitalized and amortized over the estimated period benefited but not exceeding 40 years.
5. The cost of purchasing patent rights for a product that might otherwise have seriously competed with one of the purchaser's patented products should be–
   a. Charged off in the current period.
   b. Amortized over the legal life of the purchased patent.
   c. Added to factory overhead and allocated to production of the purchaser's product.
   d. Amortized over the remaining estimated life of the patent for the product whose market would have been impaired by competition from the newly patented product.
6. Research and development costs incurred after 1975 should be–
   a. Capitalized on a selective basis, then amortized.
   b. Capitalized, then amortized over 40 years.
   c. Expensed in the year in which they are incurred.
   d. Charged directly to retained earnings.
7. Goodwill is most closely akin to–
   a. Going value.
   b. Franchises.
   c. Trademarks.
   d. Copyrights.

(Items 1–3, 5 AICPA adapted)

Exercise 14–3

For the past five years, the total assets of Day Brothers Store have averaged $700,000 while average liabilities amounted to $150,000. Cumulative total earnings for the five-year period have been $280,000. Included in the latter figure are extraordinary gains of $45,000 and nonrecurring losses of $30,000. An 8% return on investment is considered normal for the industry. In calculating goodwill where a transfer of the business to new interests is contemplated, the parties agree that excess earnings should be capitalized at 15%.

Required:

In the light of the foregoing, calculate the implied goodwill. Show computations.

Exercise 14–4

A quarry which is available for purchase can be expected to produce for the next three years; it will be exhausted at that time and have a zero salvage value due to restoration cost obligations. Best estimates place its net receipts at $35,000 for the first year; thereafter, there will be an annual $10,000 drop in net receipts.

Required:

Using an assumed 9% return rate and assuming net receipts occur at year-end, calculate the goodwill implicit in an offer of $67,750 for the property. Round calculations to the nearest dollar.

Exercise 14–5

The following projections were developed as a basis for estimating goodwill:

Budgeted average annual expected earnings	$ 9,000
Budgeted average future value of assets (excluding goodwill)	66,000

Required:

Estimate goodwill under each independent approach below:

a. Goodwill equal to earnings capitalized at 12½% (normal rate for industry) over budgeted average assets.
b. Goodwill equal to excess earnings capitalized at 20%; normal rate for industry, 10%.
c. Goodwill equal to six years of excess earnings; normal earnings rate for industry, 10%.
d. Goodwill based on present value of excess earnings as computed in *b* at an 8% expected earnings rate for five years. Prove your answer.

Exercise 14–6

New Corporation is negotiating with the Old Company with a view to purchasing the entire assets and liabilities of the latter. You have been asked to help evaluate the "goodwill on the basis of the latest concepts." Accordingly, you decide to utilize the present value approach. The following data have been assembled on Old Company:

	Fair Market Value	*Book Value*
Total identifiable assets (exclusive of goodwill)	$8,000,000	$5,000,000
Liabilities	3,000,000	3,000,000
Average annual earnings expected (next five years)	520,000	

Required:

(Round to even dollars.)

1. Compute goodwill assuming a 9% expected earnings rate.
2. Assume the deal is consummated; New's offer, as accepted, was cash equal to the fair market value of the net identifiable assets plus the goodwill computed in (1). Give entry on New's books to record the transaction.
3. Prepare an amortization table that is conceptually consistent with your computations in (1).

Exercise 14–7

Sanders Company signed a contract on January 1 whereby the company was to pay $6,000 cash plus $600 per month rent for an office building. The contract covered a ten-year period and was renewable at the end of that time for an additional ten years at a rental not to exceed 10% of that specified for the prior period. The management has no definite ideas as to whether the renewal option will be exercised.

Prior to occupancy the Sanders Company spent $2,000 in renovation costs. In addition, a large garage was built upon the property costing $15,000. It is estimated that the garage has a 15-year life with no significant residual value. Give all entries on Sanders' books for the first year of the lease; assume straight-line accounting procedures.

Exercise 14–8

In lieu of paying six $7,000 rentals at six-month intervals with each payment due in advance, a lessor and lessee agree upon a single lump-sum advance payment of $38,162.74 which covers the entire lease period. This reflects recognition of interest at an annual rate of 8% throughout the lease period.

Required:

1. Show how the lump-sum figure was calculated and prepare an amortization table covering the entire term of the lease.
2. Give the entry by the lessee to record the initial payment under the lease and the entries at end of the first year assuming the lease year and the lessee's fiscal year coincide.

Exercise 14–9

After extended negotiations, a lessor and lessee agree that instead of paying $6,000 annual rental over a four-year term with each rental payable in advance, a single lump-sum payment of $21,187.74 at the start of the lease should be paid. This amount was arrived at through use of a 9% interest rate.

Required:

1. Show how the initial amount was calculated.
2. Prepare an appropriate leasehold amortization schedule using the 9% rate. Make journal entries for the first year for both the lessor and lessee, assuming their fiscal years and the lease year coincide.

Exercise 14–10

Select the best answer in each of the following and indicate the basis for your choice (show computations if appropriate).

1. Inger Company bought a patent in January 19A for $6,800. For the first four years, it was amortized on the assumption that the total useful life would be eight years. At the start of the fifth year, it was determined six years would be the probable total life. Amortization at the end of the fifth year should be—
   a. $1,133.
   b. $1,700.
   c. $850.
   d. None of the foregoing.
2. XY Company has a lease on a site which does not expire for 25 years. With the land owner's permission, XY erected a building on the site which will last 50 years. XY should recognize expense in connection with the building's cost—
   a. One fortieth each year.
   b. One twenty-fifth each year.
   c. In totality as soon as it is completed.
   d. One fiftieth each year.
3. Where there is an 80% coinsurance clause, the fair value of the insured property is $30,000 and the amount of loss and of the face of the policy are respectively $15,000 and $12,000, indemnity collectible would be—
   a. $7,500.
   b. $12,000.
   c. $15,000.
   d. $30,000.
4. Where the policy has an 80% coinsurance clause, if the fair value of the property is $10,000, the amount of loss is $8,500, and insurance carried is $7,000, the indemnity collectible would be—
   a. $10,000.
   b. $8,500.
   c. $8,000.
   d. $7,000.
   e. None of the foregoing.
5. Suppose the facts are as in 4 above except that the amount of the loss is $7,000, then the indemnity collectible would be—
   a. $10,000.
   b. $8,000.
   c. $7,000.
   d. $6,000.
   e. None of the foregoing.
6. Which of the following is not properly reported as a deferred charge?
   a. Bond issue costs.
   b. Discount on bonds payable.
   c. Organization costs.
   d. Deferred income taxes.
7. Prepaid expenses and deferred charges are alike in that they are both—
   a. Reported as current assets on a classified balance sheet.
   b. Destined to be charged to expense in some subsequent period in harmony with the matching principle.
   c. Reported as other assets.
   d. Applicable to the fiscal period immediately following the balance sheet on which they appear.

Exercise 14–11

Assuming that all policies contain an 80% coinsurance clause, show what the insurance company would pay under each of the following cases:

	Case A	*Case B*	*Case C*
Fair market value of property	$25,000	$15,000	$10,000
Amount of loss	24,000	3,000	3,200
Face of policy	22,500	12,500	2,500

Exercise 14–12

On January 1, a store had $120 unexpired premiums on an 80% coinsurance fire policy, which ran one year, for $15,000 on its merchandise. On January 1, the inventory was $20,000. January purchases were $44,000, and January sales were $60,000. A fire on February 1 destroyed the entire stock on hand. The insurance policy is canceled upon payment of the indemnity, and any unexpired premium after the fire was refunded.

Required:

Give journal entries to record the estimated inventory and the fire loss assuming a 30% gross margin rate on sales.

Exercise 14–13

ABC Company sustained a fire loss on February 28. The following data were available (fiscal year ends December 31):

a. Sixty percent of the inventory burned; cost and fair market value of loss was $1,800 (assume periodic inventory procedures).
b. Furniture and fixtures: depreciation $20 per month; fair market value of the item burned, $3,600 (original cost, $3,000; accumulated depreciation to January 1, $480).
c. Insurance premium $60 per year paid on last January 1 for one year; payment of the indemnity canceled the policy and the unexpired premium after the fire was refunded in cash.
d. Settled with insurance company; face of policy, $5,000, 90% coinsurance clause; fair market value of property insured, $7,500. Close Fire Loss account.

Required:

Give indicated journal entries.

Exercise 14–14

On January 1, Wilkins Company purchased a $100,000 ordinary life insurance policy on its president. The following data relate to the first five years:

Year	Annual Advance Premium	Cash Surrender Value (Year-End)	
		Increase	Cumulative
1	$2,000	-0-	-0-
2	2,000	-0-	-0-
3	2,000	$2,100	$2,100
4	2,000	720	2,820
5	2,000	750	3,570
6	Etc.	Etc.	Etc.

Required:

1. Give all entries indicated up to death of the president on July 2 of the fifth year.
2. Give entry to record insurance settlement upon death of the president. The premium unexpired was refunded. Assume the policy year and accounting year agree; also there are no dividends since the company is not a mutual.

PROBLEMS

Problem 14–1

Case A. One of your corporate clients bought all of the assets of another company whose operations were compatible with those of the client and continued to operate the business of the acquired entity as a separate division. The purchase price paid included an excess consideration for such items as cutomers' lists, going concern value, and goodwill, aside from what was paid for identifiable tangibles and intangibles. Under terms of the original contract, if the division (i.e., the acquired unit) proves sufficiently profitable, an added payment will become due. This added payment is almost certain to materialize and will approximately equal what was already paid for customer lists, going concern value, and goodwill. These intangibles have been amortized since acquisition over a more or less arbitrary eight-year total life. The client has inquired whether the added payment, which is clearly related, can be amortized over 12 years from the date the payment is to be made. If this were to be done, vestiges of the balance related to the new payment would remain on the books as much as seven years after the last of the first payment had been fully amortized.

Case B. Another corporate client is in a regulated industry and has franchise rights granted by a federal commission. The rights are worth considerably more than the cost of obtaining them; they can be transferred with the permission of the commission (which usually is not difficult to obtain). The rights do not lapse as long as the client is a going concern, although they could be revoked. Revocation of such rights has rarely occurred. The client's management contends there is no need to amortize the franchise rights over 40 years, much less a shorter period. Indeed, some of the managers feel they should be written up in value.

Required:

Draft memoranda setting forth your recommendations concerning the above situations. Support whatever positions you take.

Problem 14–2

The Tiger Corporation, a retail farm implements dealer, has increased its annual sales volume to a level three times greater than the annual sales of a dealer purchased eight years ago in order to begin operations.

The board of directors of Tiger Corporation recently received an offer to negotiate the sale of Tiger Corporation to a large competitor. As a result, the majority of the board wants to increase the stated value of goodwill on the balance sheet to reflect the larger sales volume developed through intensive promotion and the current market prices of the company's products. However, a few of the company's board members would prefer to eliminate goodwill altogether from the balance sheet in order to prevent "possible misinterpretations." Goodwill was properly recorded when the business was acquired eight years ago.

Required:

1. *a.* Discuss the meaning of the term "goodwill." Do not discuss goodwill arising from consolidated statements or the conditions under which goodwill is recorded.
   b. List the techniques used to calculate the tentative value of goodwill in negotiations to purchase a going concern.

2. Why are the book and market values of the goodwill of Tiger Corporation different?
3. Discuss the propriety of—
   a. Increasing the stated value of goodwill prior to the negotiations.
   b. Eliminating goodwill completely from the balance sheet prior to negotiations.

(AICPA adapted)

Problem 14–3

After considerable analysis the following projections were derived as a basis for estimating the potential value of goodwill in anticipation of negotiations for the sale of the business:

Average annual earnings projected	$ 40,000
Average fair value of net assets expected..................................	350,000
"Normal" rate of return for the industry, 8½%.	
Rate of return expected on excess profits, 10%.	
Expected recovery period for excess earnings, five years.	
Years' purchase of average annual earnings, three.	

Estimate the value of goodwill under five different approaches (including a present value determination at 8½%). Present value amounts for five periods at 8½% annually: PV of 1 is .665045; PV of annuity of 1 is 3.940642.

Problem 14–4

On June 30, 19A your client, Vandiver Corporation, was granted two patents covering plastic cartons that it has been producing and marketing profitably for the past three years. One patent covers the manufacturing process, and the other covers the related products.

Vandiver executives tell you that these patents represent the most significant breakthrough in the industry in the past 30 years. The products have been marketed under the registered trademarks Safetainer, Duratainer and Sealrite. Licenses under the patents have already been granted by your client to other manufacturers in the United States and abroad and are producing substantial royalties.

On July 1, Vandiver commenced patent infringement actions against several companies whose names you recognize as those of substantial and prominent competitors. Vandiver's management is optimistic that these suits will result in a permanent injunction against the manufacture and sale of the infringing products and collection of damages for loss of profits caused by the alleged infringement.

The financial vice president has suggested that the patents be recorded at the discounted value of expected net royalty receipts.

Required:

1. What is an intangible asset? Explain.
2. *a.* What is the meaning of "discounted value of expected net receipts?" Explain.
   b. How would such a value be calculated for net royalty receipts?
3. What basis of valuation for Vandiver's patents would be generally accepted in accounting? Give supporting reasons for this basis.

4. *a.* Assuming no practical problems of implementation and ignoring generally accepted accounting principles, what is the preferable basis of evaluation for patents? Explain.
   b. What would be the preferable theoretical basis of amortization? Explain.
5. What recognition, if any, should be made of the infringement litigation in the financial statements for the year ending September 30, 19A? Discuss.

(AICPA adapted)

Problem 14–5

Your new client, PQR Company, is being audited for the first time. In the course of your examination, you encounter in the ledger, an account titled "Intangibles" which is essentially as below:

Intangibles

June 30, 19A	Goodwill	5,000	Dec. 31, 19B	Amortization	480
Dec. 31, 19A	R & D	10,700	Dec. 31, 19C	Amortization	1,200
Apr. 1, 19B	Goodwill	11,400			
June 30, 19B	Patent	9,600			
Dec. 31, 19B	R & D	13,900			
June 1, 19C	Goodwill	16,500			
July 1, 19C	Bond discount	4,800			
Dec. 31, 19C	R & D	17,100			

By tracing entries to the journal and other supporting documents, you ascertain the following facts:

a. The June 30, 19A, entry was made when, somewhat surprisingly, the first six months' operations were profitable; a loss had been anticipated. At the direction of the company president, and with the approval of the board of directors, an entry was made charging Intangibles and crediting Retained earnings for $5,000.

b. All debit entries dated December 31 pertaining to R & D arise from the fact that the company has continuously engaged in an extensive research and development program to keep its products competitive and to develop new products. The charges represent half of the costs of the R & D program transferred at year-end from the R & D expense account.

c. The April 1, 19B, entry was made after an extensive advertising campaign had seemingly proved particularly successful. Sales rose 8% after the campaign and never dropped again to within 4% increase over their former level. The charge represents the cost of the campaign.

d. The $9,600 charge on June 30, 19B represents the purchase price of a patent bought because the company feared if it fell into other hands, it would damage the company's products competitively.

e. The June 1, 19C, charge was made after PQR acquired a division of another profitable company. The price represented an excess payment of $16,500 over the fair values of identifiable assets acquired and was based on an expectation of continued high profitability.

f. The July 1, 19C, charge for $4,800 represents discount on a ten-year $100,000 bond issue marketed by the company on that date. (Since the amount is relatively immaterial, use of straight-line amortization need not be changed.)

g. The credits to the intangibles account represent an attempt by the company bookkeeper to amortize the year-end balances 10% each year (subject to the policy described below). When you question the bookkeeper and company officials, you learn the company's policy is to amortize those intangibles it regards as having limited lives over ten years. For this purpose, acquisitions and retirements are accounted for in terms of the most proximate quarter in which they entered or were removed from the books. All items are regarded as amortizable except R & D and Goodwill. You concur with the judgment as to the ten-year life of those intangibles properly subject to amortization.

Required:

Make journal entries to correct PQR's books as of December 31, 19C, on the assumption the books have been adjusted but not closed for the year as of that date. (Although years such as 19A and 19B have not been specifically identified as particular calendar years, for purposes of your solution, assume all events of the problem have occurred recently and that the current pronouncements of authoritative bodies reflected in the text apply to the various items.)

It is suggested you key your entries to the letter, identifying the items in the problem. Explain each correcting entry. For the most part, compound entries should be avoided unless elements of the entry are closely related.

Problem 14–6

During an examination of the financial statements of the Fendo Company, your assistant calls attention to significant costs incurred in the development of EDP programs (i.e., software) for major segments of the sales and production scheduling systems.

The EDP program development costs will benefit future periods to the extent that the systems change slowly and the program instructions are compatible with new equipment acquired at three- to six-year intervals. The service value of the EDP programs is affected almost entirely by changes in the technology of systems and EDP equipment and does not decline with the number of times the program is used. Since many system changes are minor, program instructions frequently can be modified with only minor losses in program efficiency. The frequency of such changes tends to increase with the passage of time.

Required:

1. Discuss the propriety of classifying the unamortized EDP program development costs as—
   a. A prepaid expense.
   b. An intangible fixed asset with limited life.
   c. An operational asset.
2. Numerous methods are available for amortizing assets that benefit future periods. Each method (like a model) presumes that certain conditions exist and, hence, is most appropriate under those conditions. Discuss the propriety of amortizing the EDP program development costs with—
   a. The straight-line method.
   b. An increasing-charge method (e.g., the annuity method).
   c. A decreasing-charge method (e.g., the sum-of-the-years'-digits method).
   d. A variable-charge method (e.g., the units-of-production method).

(AICPA adapted)

Problem 14–7

On January 1, 19A, Charmes Company negotiated a five-year lease with Box Realty Company whereby in lieu of payment of annual rents (at the beginning of the year) of $10,000, the lessor and lessee agreed upon a single lump-sum payment discounted at 8% per annum.

Required:

1. Determine the amount of the lump-sum payment per the agreement.
2. Box Realty Company (lessor) closes the books on December 31 and intends to utilize present value accounting for the lease. Develop an amortization table and give entries for the first two, and the last, years.
3. The tenant (lessee) also closed the books on December 31 but had adopted straight-line accounting procedures for the lease. Give entries for the first two, and the last, years.
4. Which party has adopted the more realistic approach? Explain.

Problem 14–8

Marsalles Mercantile Company operates retail branches in various cities. Branches in four cities are served out of Warehouse No. 16 which sustained fire damage on April 10.

Between January 1 and April 10 recorded shipments from Warehouse No. 16 to its four stores were as below:

Branch	*Shipments*
W	$80,500
X	92,000
Y	69,000
X	23,000

Shipments to branches are marked up 15% above cost as reflected in the foregoing amounts. The January 1 inventory at Warehouse No. 16 was $43,100; purchases between January 1 and April 10 totaled $220,100; freight-in was $7,300; purchase returns were $4,700.

To arrive at the April 10 inventory for insurance settlement purposes it was agreed to deduct 5% for goods shopworn and damaged prior to the fire as goods are determined based on the foregoing data.

A compromise agreement between the insurance adjuster and Marsalles Company management set the amount of inventory lost in the fire at $20,950.

Required:

1. Estimate the amount of inventory in the warehouse at April 10.
2. Determine the indemnity claim if the warehouse contents were insured by a single $20,000 policy having an 80% coinsurance clause. Calculate to nearest dollar.

Problem 14–9

The records of Company X showed at date of fire (all merchandise destroyed): sales, $240,000; initial inventory, $15,000; purchases, $205,000; insurance (one-year policy for $12,000 with 80% coinsurance clause) premium, $200; salespersons' salaries, $15,000; and general expense, $13,000. The fire occurred six months after the premium was paid; payment of the indemnity canceled the insurance policy, hence any unexpired insurance premium was refunded. It was agreed that the gross margin percentage based on sales was 16⅔%.

Required:

1. Compute the indemnity to be received from the insurance company.
2. Give entries relating to the fire loss.
3. Prepare a classified income statement for the period ending on a date immediately following the fire.

Problem 14–10

Estimate the amount of insurance collectible on each of the following assets assuming the policies include an 80% coinsurance clause:

Asset	*Fair Market Value*	*Loss Suffered*	*Insurance Carried*
Buildings	$80,000	$40,000	$65,000
Furniture	20,000	18,000	15,000
Delivery equipment	9,000	4,000	5,000
Merchandise	?	60%	10,000

To find the value of the merchandise destroyed, the following facts are submitted from which to select the significant data:

The gross margin averages 30% of sales.
The fair market value of the inventory is the same as its cost.

Purchases for the period	$60,000
Beginning inventory	23,400
Return purchases	2,000
Salespersons' commission and advertising	8,000
Interest revenue	200
Postage and stationery	1,000
Sales	84,000
Credit department expense	700
Sales returns	2,000

Problem 14–11

Prince Company operates in a leased building; it adjusts and closes books each December 31. On April 30 a fire seriously damaged its inventory and fixtures. Inventory was totally destroyed; fixtures were half destroyed. Different insurance policies cover the assets, but both have a common feature providing they are canceled for future or remaining coverage to whatever extent a portion of the total potential indemnity is collected.

The company uses a periodic inventory system, and the accounting records were saved; these reveal that in the past three years gross margin has averaged 38% of sales price. The January 1 inventory was $73,280. Between January 1 and April 30 purchases and sales were respectively $116,320 and $206,500. Inventory was insured by a $65,000 policy with no coinsurance clause. The latest premium payment covering a one-year period from September 1 of last year amounted to $720.

When the books were closed last December 31, the fixtures were two and one-half years old. Accounts related to the fixtures and their insurance policy are set forth below.

Fixtures		**Accumulated Depreciation**		**Prepaid Insurance**	
Balance 20,000			Year 1 900	Policy A 42	
			Year 2 1,800	Policy B 480	
			Year 3 1,800		

Policy A expired February 28 of the current year. Policy B was immediately put in force to replace it and covers a two-year period. It is for $10,000 maximum coverage, provides for indemnity on the basis of market value of any loss, and has an 80% coinsurance clause. It is determined that the fair value of the fixtures when the fire occurred was $15,000 and that the damage amounted to a loss of half their value.

Required:

1. Adjust the books to April 30 and reflect the inventory as of that date.
2. Open a Fire Loss account; set up the indemnities collectible as a receivable due from the Insurance Company.
3. Transfer the net balance in Fire Loss to Income Summary.

Problem 14–12

On April 1, 19A, Clara Company insured the life of its president, Ray Cox, for $60,000, naming itself as beneficiary. Annual premiums paid each April 1 are $2,400. As a result of the third premium payment and at the end of the third year, the policy has a cash surrender value of $1,200. One year later this will increase to $1,620. It is decided to "anticipate" recognition of the cash surrender value and subsequent increments by recording the amounts at the time the premium payments are made which assure the values will materialize.

Clara Company adjusts and closes its books on December 31 and charges premium payments to Prepaid Insurance. All premiums are paid when due. Mr. Cox died July 1, 19D. No refund of unexpired premiums as of date of death is provided for in the policy.

Required:

Make all entries related to the policy through July 1, 19D, including adjusting and closing entries at the end of each year the policy is in force.

Problem 14–13

One of your corporate clients is somewhat "insurance minded" and maintains in force, several life insurance policies which have a cash surrender value feature on which the corporation is beneficiary. Several questions have arisen concerning the accounting presentation or treatment of these policies and their cash surrender value aspects.

a. One policy is on the life of the company president (who is not a stockholder). A substantially high proportion of what could be borrowed against this policy has been borrowed; the loan amounts to 88% of the cash surrender value at balance sheet date. One reason for borrowing this way is that the interest rate is about half the rate at which other loans could be obtained. You are asked for advice as to how to report the loan on the company's balance sheet and whether the fact that there may be a current liability against the policy changes the classification of cash surrender value.

b. Most of the stock of the corporation is held by a few large stockholders. To retain control within a limited group, your client has bought policies on the lives of these principal stockholders which will provide for repurchase of their stock in the event of a stockholder's death. The cash surrender value of these policies has been reported on the balance sheet. You are asked whether further disclosure is necessary.

c. Looking to the future and possible repayment of the loan on the policy mentioned, especially if interest rates should fall, a hypothetical question is posed.

Assuming the loan is repaid, would it be mandatory to report cash surrender value on this policy since the insurance is carried to cover the loss it is anticipated would be sustained as the result of the death of a key official?

d. For a time, another officer of the corporation (who also is not a stockholder) personally owned and paid premiums on a substantial life insurance policy on which his wife was beneficiary. For business reasons, your client bought the policy from him at a price equal to his past premium payments ($80,000). The corporation became beneficiary of the policy and beneficial owner of its cash surrender value ($45,000); the latter amount was recorded on the accounts as an asset. The $35,000 difference is being amortized over the life expectancy of the insured as disclosed on a mortality table. You are asked for your concurrence or disagreement with this accounting treatment.

Required:

Draft a reply responding to the above questions. Give reasons to support whatever positions you take.

Chapter 15

Corporations—Formation and Contributed Capital

The corporate form of business organization has become a dominant one in the United States. This particular form gained widespread use primarily as a result of the legal foundations upon which it is built. A corporation is, in the eyes of the law, an entity separate and apart from the owners. Limited liability of corporate owners, provision for succession of ownership, facility for capital accumulation, separation of management from ownership, and the legal right to act in the same capacity as an individual in the transaction of authorized business are five important factors contributing to the growth of the corporate form of business. In view of the unique features of the corporate form and its extensive use, accountants have considerable concern with respect to the special accounting problems encountered. This chapter and the next two consider these special accounting problems.

Unique problems are encountered in accounting for a corporation in respect to the *owners' equity*. In other respects the accounting treatment of transactions is largely unaffected by the form of business organization. At the outset it is well to realize that there is not complete agreement in the accounting profession on a number of the issues related to accounting for owners' equity. In a sole proprietorship, owners' equity usually is represented by a single equity account and in a partnership by separate equity accounts for each partner. In contrast, accounting for a corporation generally requires a number of owners' equity accounts.

In accounting for corporate proprietary equities, accountants adhere to the concept of *source of capital*. In order to apply this concept, owners' equity accounts are established so that the *sources* of the capital used in the enterprise are clearly segregated. In accounting by *source*, aside from the funds supplied by creditors (liabilities), the primary sources of corporate capital are *(a)* contributions by the owners, and *(b)* earnings retained in the business. The term capital has long been used to refer to the resources provided by owners; that is, the shareholders. It includes contributions by owners plus retained earnings. In recent years it has been more often called shareholders' or stockholders' equity. The accountant should be familiar with the four following classes of equities and capital:

1. *Total equity (enterprise capital).* Total equity represents the total interests of all lenders and owners of a particular corporation in the properties of that business; it is the sum of the creditors' equity and the owners' equity.
2. *Proprietary equity (owners' equity).* Proprietary equity represents the total equity at a given time of the legal owners of the enterprise; it is the total of contributed capital and all subsequent accretions in the form of additional contributions and retained earnings.
3. *Contributed capital.* Contributed capital is the investment made by the owners; in a corporation it is the total amount paid in by all parties other than creditors. It does not include retained earnings.
4. *Legal or stated capital.* Legal capital is that portion of corporate capital that is required by statute to be retained in the business for the protection of creditors.

CLASSIFICATIONS OF CORPORATIONS

The laws of each state provide for the formation and operation of corporations. Although state laws relating to corporations vary in many respects, there is much similarity in basic provisions. The statutes of all states provide for the existence of a separate entity and for the basic capital structure (capital stock). Corporations are brought into legal existence by submitting an application (articles of incorporation) for a charter to the secretary of state; if approved, a charter is issued which specifies the detailed conditions under which the corporation may operate such as what business activities are permitted, types of capital stock to be issued, and the method of electing officers. The charter is supplemented with bylaws which are adopted by the stockholders.

Corporations may be classified as follows:

By Ownership:

1. Public corporations, when they relate to governmental units or business operations owned by governmental units.
2. Private corporations, when they are privately owned. Such corporations may be nonstock (nonprofit organizations such as colleges and churches) or stock (usually organized for profit making).

By Nationality:

3. Domestic corporations, when operating in the state in which incorporated.
4. Foreign corporations, when operating in states other than the one in which incorporated.

By Availability of Ownership Interests:

5. Open corporations, when the stock is available for purchase. The stock is usually widely held.
6. Closed corporations, when the stock is not available for purchase and is generally held by a few shareholders.

NATURE OF CAPITAL STOCK

Shares of capital stock, represented by stock certificates, evidence ownership in a corporation. Shares may be transferred freely by shareholders unless there is an enforceable agreement not to do so. Ownership of shares entitles the holder to certain basic rights. These rights are:

1. The right to participate in the *management* of the corporation through participating and voting in stockholder meetings.
2. The right to participate in the *profits* of the corporation through dividends declared by the board of directors.
3. The right to share in the distribution of *assets* of the corporation at liquidation or through liquidating dividends.
4. The right to purchase shares of stock on a *pro rata basis* in the corporation when such shares represent additional capital stock issues. This right is designed to protect the proportional interests of each shareholder in the ownership.

These rights are shared equitably and proportionately by all stockholders unless the charter or bylaws (and stock certificates) specifically provide otherwise. In the case of one class of stock, all holders enjoy equal rights; in the case of two or more classes of stock, the holders of one class of stock may have rights that have been withheld from the others.

In order to comprehend clearly the nature of capital stock, and to account for it correctly, the accountant must understand the following terms:

1. Authorized capital stock – the number of shares of stock that can be issued legally as specified in the charter.
2. Issued capital stock – the number of shares of authorized stock that have been issued to date.
3. Unissued capital stock – the number of shares of authorized capital stock that have *never* been issued.
4. Outstanding capital stock – the number of shares of stock that have been issued and are being held by shareholders at a given date.
5. Treasury stock – those shares once issued and later reacquired by the corporation, that is, the difference between issued shares and outstanding shares.
6. Subscribed stock – unissued shares of stock set aside to meet subscription contracts. Subscribed stock usually is not issued until the subscription price is paid in full.

In accounting for stockholders' equity descriptive terms have been evolved by the accounting profession. Although in practice there is some variation in such categories and in terminology, the following appears to represent current trends:[1]

1. Contributed capital (sometimes referred to as paid-in capital):
   a. Capital stock:
      (1) Preferred stock.
      (2) Common stock.
   b. Other contributed capital (an obsolete term, capital surplus, is sometimes used):
      (1) From owners:
         Contributed capital in excess of par or stated value (sometimes called premium on capital stock).
      (2) From outsiders:
         Donation of assets.
2. Retained earnings (an obsolete term, earned surplus, is sometimes used).
   a. Appropriated (frequently referred to as reserves).
   b. Unappropriated.
3. Unrealized capital increment.

The above classifications of stockholders' equity are used in well-designed balance sheets. To illustrate, the stockholders' equity section of a balance sheet may be reported as shown in Exhibit 15–1.

Although in practice one frequently observes different terms and arrangements of the various subclassifications of stockholders' equity shown in Exhibit 15–1, emphasis should be on *source, clarity of presentation,* and *avoidance of needless technical terminology.*

CLASSES OF CAPITAL STOCK

Corporations tend to use several different types of capital stock, which give the respective shareholders various privileges, restrictions, and responsibilities. Some of these restrictions may result from provisions of state statutes, the charter, or the bylaws of the corporation, and are made operative by contract between the corporation and the shareholders. The two primary classifications of capital stock are *(a)* par-value and nopar-value stock, and *(b)* common and preferred stock.

Par-Value Stock

The laws of each state provide for the issuance of par-value stock; that is, shares of stock with a designated dollar "value" per share as provided for in the articles of incorporation and as printed on the face

---

[1] In AICPA *Accounting Terminology Bulletin No. 1,* "Review and Résumé," the Committee on Terminology recommended: "The use of the term *surplus* (whether standing alone or in such combination as *capital surplus, paid-in surplus, earned surplus, appraisal surplus,* etc.) be discontinued."

EXHIBIT 15–1
Stockholders' Equity Section of a Balance Sheet

Stockholders' Equity		
Contributed Capital:		
Capital stock:		
Preferred stock, 6%, par $10, cumulative and nonparticipating, 20,000 shares authorized, 15,000 issued ...	$150,000	
Preferred stock subscribed, 100 shares	1,000	
Total	151,000	
Common stock, nopar value, authorized 10,000 shares, issued and outstanding 8,000 shares, stated value, $5	40,000	$191,000
Other Contributed Capital:		
In excess of par value, preferred stock	12,000	
In excess of stated value, common stock	3,000	
Donation of plant site	5,000	20,000
Total Contributed Capital		211,000
Retained Earnings:		
Appropriated:		
Reserve for bond sinking fund	50,000	
Unappropriated	70,000	
Total Retained Earnings		120,000
Unrealized increment, discovery value of natural resource		50,000
Total Stockholders' Equity		$381,000

of the stock certificates. Par-value stock may be either common or preferred. In the early history of corporations in the United States, only par-value stock was authorized. Since the owners of a corporation were not liable to creditors (beyond the assets of the corporation), statutes provided for a par value to afford some measure of protection to creditors. In this respect the courts tended to hold that shareholders who had paid *less* than par value for their stock could be assessed for an amount equal to the discount to satisfy creditors' claims. Par-value stock sold initially at less than par is said to have been issued at a discount, whereas par-value stock sold above par is said to have been issued at a premium. Today the issuance of stock at a discount is illegal in most, if not all, states. Subsequent to issue, par value has no particular relationship to market value. Today par value has significance in most states in that (1) it represents the minimum amount that must be paid in at initial sale of the stock, (2) it establishes the maximum liability of a holder of a share of stock in case of insolvency or liquidation, and (3) it establishes the minimum amount of owners' equity that must be maintained.

In order to avoid a real or implied discount, most new corporations, and those distributing new issues, use a very low par value, such as $1, and offer the stock at a much higher price such as $10, $20, or even $100 per share.

Nopar-Value Stock

True nopar stock does not carry a designated or assigned value per share—nor is such provided for in the articles of incorporation. However, the laws of most states authorize the issuance of nopar stock with a *stated* or *assigned* value. The stated or assigned value is established by the corporate directors or the bylaws of the corporation. Nopar stock with a stated or assigned value is encountered more frequently than is true nopar stock. The use of an assigned or stated value serves to place the nopar stock on practically the same basis as par-value stock for accounting purposes. Both common and preferred stock may be represented by nopar shares. Nopar stock was first permitted by statute in New York in 1912; since that date the authorization of stock without par value has become so generally accepted that today practically all states permit its issuance. The chief advantages claimed for this type of stock are as follows:

1. It avoids a contingent liability of stockholders to creditors for stock discount.
2. It places the investor on guard to determine the true value of the stock rather than blindly to assume it to be worth the par value.
3. It facilitates the accounting for capital in that the total amount paid in generally is credited to the capital stock account.
4. It does away with the dubious expediency, frequently encountered in par-value stock, of overvaluing assets received for stock in order to report such stock fully paid. The use of nopar stock is particularly advantageous in connection with issuance for property such as patents, leaseholds, manufacturing rights, goodwill, and other intangibles, the true worth of which has not been proved.

The disadvantages of nopar stock result from excessive franchise and other taxes levied by some jurisdictions and the opportunity to manipulate part of the proceeds of the issue to give the appearance of excessive paid-in capital upon organization. Conversely, in some jurisdictions there is less tax on nopar shares.

Legal Capital

The distinction between par and nopar capital stock may be more fully appreciated by a consideration of legal capital. The total proprietary equity in a corporation is represented by capital contributed by owners, capital contributed by outsiders, retained earnings, and unrealized capital increments. *Legal capital* is defined by the laws of each state somewhat differently. Recall that the stockholders in a corporation have limited liability; that is, they cannot be held legally liable for the debts of the corporation. In order to afford some measure of protection to creditors, state laws designate some minimum investment in the corporation to be identified specifically as legal capital. This legal capital usually cannot be returned to the owners through dividends or by purchase of shares held by them, unless creditor claims are first satisfied.

When par-value stock is issued, most states specify that the par value of all outstanding shares constitutes legal capital. In the case of nopar stock the legal capital generally is regarded as the stated or assigned value per share. In the case of true nopar stock most states require that the full proceeds from the sale of nopar stock be treated as legal capital. In case the legal capital is impaired through dividend payments or purchase of the corporation's own shares (treasury stock), the courts generally have held that creditors may obtain payment from the shareholders for claims to the extent of such impairment.

The concept of legal capital is particularly important in accounting for corporate ownership equities. The capital accounts should be maintained so that sources are known, thereby providing appropriate data for determination of legal capital in conformance with the statutes of the particular state in which incorporated. Since state statutes define legal capital and there is considerable variation as between states, careful accounting for corporate capital is essential.

The amount of legal capital should be entered in the capital stock account, and investments in excess of legal capital should be recorded in other appropriately designated capital accounts.

Common Stock

Common stock represents the basic issue of shares and normally carries all of the basic rights listed in a preceding paragraph. When there is only one class of stock all of the shares are common stock.

Preferred Stock

Preferred stock is so designated because it has some preference or priority over the common stock. The preference or priority may relate to:

1. Dividends.
   a. Cumulative or noncumulative.
   b. Fully participating, partially participating, or nonparticipating.
2. Assets.
3. Redemption.
4. Convertibility.

Since the right to vote is a basic right, preferred shareholders have full voting rights unless specifically prohibited in the charter. Likewise, all the other basic rights listed in a preceding paragraph apply to preferred stock unless specifically stated otherwise in the charter.

Preferred stock is usually par-value stock, in which case the dividend preference is expressed as a percentage. For example, 6% preferred stock would carry a dividend preference of 6% of the *par value* of each share. In the case of nopar preferred stock a dividend preference is expressed as a specific dollar *amount* per share. Occasionally a corporation may issue two or more classes of preferred stock each having different preferences.

In order to identify correctly the preferences relating to preferred stock, corporations must indicate on the stock certificate the exact nature of the preferences; that is, whether the stock is cumulative, participating, callable, or convertible.[2]

Cumulative Preferences on Preferred Stock

Noncumulative preferred stock provides that dividends not declared (i.e., dividends passed or in arrears) for any year or series of years are lost permanently as far as the preferred shareholder is concerned. As a result the noncumulative restriction generally is viewed as an undesirable feature by potential investors.

Cumulative preferred stock provides that dividends in arrears for any year or series of years accumulate and must be paid to the preferred shareholders when dividends are declared, before the common stockholders may receive a dividend. If only a part of the preference is met for any one year, then the balance of the preference is in arrears. Cumulative preferred stock does not carry the right, in liquidation of the corporation, to dividends in arrears if there are no retained earnings. However, express provisions may be made in the charter and stock specifications concerning dividends in arrears in such situations. At common law, where the charter is silent as to the cumulative feature, preferred stock is considered to be cumulative.

APB Opinion No. 9, paragraph 35, requires disclosure on the financial statements of "the aggregate and per share amounts of arrearages in cumulative preferred dividends."

Participating Preferences on Preferred Stock

Preferred stock is *fully* participating when the preferred shareholders are entitled to extra dividends on a pro rata basis (based on par or stated value) with the holders of common stock. In this case the preference relates to a prior claim to dividends up to a stated percent of par (the preferential rate), after which both classes of stock share ratably (including the preference).

Preferred stock is nonparticipating when the dividends on such stock for any one year are limited in the charter to a specified preferential rate. *Partially* participating preferred stock provides that the shareholders thereof participate above the preferential rate with the common stockholders, but only up to an additional rate which is specified in the charter and on the stock certificate. For example, a corporation may issue 6% preferred stock, with participation up to a total of 8%, in which case participation privileges with the common shareholders would be limited to an additional 2%.

---

[2] In some cases the distinction between common and preferred stock represents restrictions or negative features. For example, noncumulative, nonparticipating, and nonvoting are negative features.

In the absence of an expressed stipulation most courts have taken the view that preferred stock has no right to participate with the common stock, unless this preference is stated expressly in the preferred stock specifications in the charter.

Since accountants frequently are called upon to advise management with respect to dividend declarations, it is important that computation of dividends be clearly understood. To illustrate dividend computations, assume the following:

Preferred stock, 5% ($100 par value per share—1,000 shares) ...	$100,000
Common stock ($100 par value per share—2,000 shares)	200,000

	Preferred	*Common*
Illustration No. 1: Preferred stock is cumulative, nonparticipating; dividends two years in arrears; dividends declared, $28,000.		
Step 1—Preferred in arrears	$10,000	
Step 2—Preferred, current (at 5%)	5,000	
Step 3—Common (balance)		$13,000
	$15,000	$13,000
Illustration No. 2: Preferred stock is cumulative, fully participating; dividends two years in arrears; dividends declared, $28,000.		
Step 1—Preferred in arrears	$10,000	
Step 2—Preferred, current (at 5%)	5,000	
Step 3—Common, current (to match preferred at 5%)		$10,000
Step 4—Balance (ratably with par)	1,000	2,000
	$16,000	$12,000
Illustration No. 3: Preferred stock is noncumulative, partially participating up to 7%; dividends declared, $28,000.		
Step 1—Preferred, current (at 5%)	$ 5,000	
Step 2—Common, current (to match preferred at 5%) ...		$10,000
Step 3—Preferred, partial participation, additional 2% ...	2,000	
Step 4—Common (balance)		11,000
	$ 7,000	$21,000
Illustration No. 4: Preferred stock is noncumulative; partially participating up to 7%; dividends declared, $16,000.		
Step 1—Preferred, current at 5%	$ 5,000	
Step 2—Common, current (to match preferred at 5%) ...		$10,000
Step 3—Preferred, partial participation	333	
Step 3—Common		667
	$ 5,333	$10,667

Preferred stock that is *preferred as to assets* (i.e., a liquidation preference) provides that the holders, in case of corporate dissolution, have a priority up to par value or other stated amount per share over common shareholders. Once the priority for the preferred is satisfied, the remainder of the assets are distributed to the common shareholders.

APB Opinion No. 10, paragraph 10, states that "the liquidation preference of the preferred stock be disclosed in the equity section of the balance sheet in the aggregate, either parenthetically or 'in short' rather than on a per share basis or by disclosure in notes."

Preferred stock having *redemption* privileges (redeemable stock), provides that the shareholder, at his or her option, may, under the conditions specified, turn in the shares owned to the corporation at a specified price per share.

Preferred stock may carry a provision of *convertibility* (convertible stock), at the option of the holder, for other securities such as common stock. Conversion privileges frequently turn out to be particularly valuable and, hence, are favored by investors.

Preferred stock may be *callable;* that is, the corporation may, at its option, call the stock (purchase it) for cancellation under specified conditions of time and price.

APB Opinion No. 10, paragraph 11, states that there should be disclosure "on the face of the balance sheet or in notes pertaining thereto: the aggregate or per share amounts at which preferred shares may be called or subject to redemption through sinking fund operations or otherwise."

ACCOUNTING FOR ISSUANCE OF PAR-VALUE STOCK

In accounting for stockholders' equity, recall that *source* is particularly important; accordingly, if a corporation has more than one class of stock, separate accounts must be maintained for each class. In case there is only one class of stock, an account "Capital Stock" is usually employed. In cases where there are two or more classes of stock, titles such as "Common Stock," "Preferred Stock, 5%," and "Common Stock, Nopar" are appropriate. The complete sequence of transactions related to issuance of stock is *(a)* authorization of shares, *(b)* subscriptions, *(c)* collections on subscriptions, and *(d)* issuance of the shares.

Authorization

The authorization in the charter to issue a specified number of shares may be recorded *(a)* by notation or *(b)* by a formal journal entry. To illustrate, under the first method the notation for the journal and the ledger account heading may be as follows:

Common Stock—Par Value $100 per Share
(authorized 5,000 shares)

In case a formal journal entry is made, it would be as follows:

Unissued common stock	500,000	
Common stock (5,000 shares, par $100)		500,000
To record authorization of 5,000 shares of common stock, par value $100 per share.		

Observe that these two accounts are offsetting. The notation approach is preferred by most accountants.

Stock Issued for Cash

In most situations capital stock is sold and issued for cash rather than on a subscription basis. Using the above example and assuming the sale of 1,000 shares at $102 per share, the issue entry would be:

1. Notation method:

Cash	102,000	
Common stock (1,000 shares, par $100)		100,000
Contributed capital in excess of par, common		2,000

2. Unissued capital stock method:

Cash	102,000	
Unissued common stock (1,000 shares, par $100)		100,000
Contributed capital in excess of par, common		2,000

The capital stock account is credited for the par value of the stock times the number of shares issued, and the excess over par is credited to a descriptively named contributed capital account to record *source* in detail.

ACCOUNTING FOR NOPAR CAPITAL STOCK

Because the statutes in many states permit two types of nopar stock—true nopar stock and stated value nopar stock—there is some variation in accounting. Nopar-value stock with a stated value is accounted for as discussed above for par-value stock since the stated value places the nopar stock on practically the same basis as par-value stock. Amounts received in excess of stated value should be credited to an account with a descriptive title such as Contributed Capital in Excess of Stated Value, Nopar Common Stock.

In the case of *true* nopar stock, no entry can be made for the authorization; instead, notation may be made in the journal and in the ledger account heading such as:

Common Stock—Nopar Value
(authorized 10,000 shares)

With respect to nopar stock, most states require that the total number of shares authorized, as well as the number of shares represented by the individual stock certificate, be shown on the face of each such certificate. It is important to note that entries to record true nopar stock should indicate the *number of shares* as well as the dollar amounts. In the case of true nopar stock the accounting treatment should follow the applicable legal requirements. If the statutes provide that all proceeds represent legal capital, then the capital stock account should be credited for the full amount received so that no "excess" amount need be recorded separately. If the statutes establish a minimum amount per share, then at least this amount should be credited to the capital stock account. In the absence of legal requirements, the total amount received normally should be credited to the capital stock account.

EXHIBIT 15–2
Entries for Nopar Stock

	Stated Value Method		*True Nopar Value Method*	
1. To record authorization of nopar stock:				
Notation – 10,000 shares of nopar common stock authorized.	(Stated value, $5)*		(No stated value)	
2. To record sale of 5,000 shares @ $6:				
Cash	30,000		30,000	
Common stock, nopar, stated value $5		25,000		
Common stock, nopar				30,000
Contributed capital in excess of stated value, nopar common stock		5,000		
3. To record sale of 5,000 shares @ $6; 20% paid in cash:				
Cash	6,000		6,000	
Subscriptions receivable – nopar common stock	24,000		24,000	
Nopar common stock subscribed (5,000 shares)		25,000		30,000
Contributed capital in excess of stated value, nopar common stock		5,000		
4. To record collection of subscription and issuance of stock:				
Cash	24,000		24,000	
Subscriptions receivable – nopar common stock		24,000		24,000
Nopar common stock subscribed	25,000		30,000	
Common stock, nopar, stated value $5 (5,000 shares)		25,000		
Common stock, nopar (5,000 shares)				30,000

* Note: This could take the form of a journal entry as illustrated above for par-value stock.

The entries in Exhibit 15–2 show the accounting for nopar stock, assuming that the corporation is authorized to issue 10,000 shares of nopar common stock.

Subscriptions

Prospective stockholders may sign a contract to purchase a specified number of shares with payment to be made at one or more stated dates in the future. Such a contract is known as a *stock subscription*. Since a legal contract is involved, accounting recognition must be given to this transaction. The purchase price is debited to Stock Subscriptions Receivable, Common Stock Subscribed is credited for the par, stated, or assigned amount per share, and the difference is credited to Contributed Capital in Excess of Par (or Stated Value).

To illustrate, assume 1,000 are subscribed for at $102; the entry would be:

Stock subscriptions receivable—common stock	102,000	
Common stock subscribed (1,000 shares).................		100,000
Contributed capital in excess of par, common...........		2,000

Observe that the premium is recorded when the subscription is recorded rather than later when the cash is collected. The Common Stock Subscribed account recognizes the corporation's obligation to issue the 1,000 shares upon fulfillment of the terms of the agreement by the subscribers. This account is reported on the balance sheet in a manner similar to the related capital stock account (see Exhibit 15–1). Subscriptions receivable is classified as a current asset if the corporation expects current collection. If there are no plans for collection, subscriptions receivable cannot be considered a realizable asset and therefore should be offset against capital stock subscribed in the owners' equity section of the balance sheet. In some cases subscription contracts call for installment payments. In such cases separate "call" accounts may be set up for each installment. If there are a number of subscriptions it is usually desirable to maintain a *subscribers' ledger* as a subsidiary record to the subscriptions receivable account in a manner similar to that maintained for regular accounts receivable.

Collections on stock subscriptions may be in cash, property, or services. The appropriate account is debited, and subscriptions receivable is credited. If a service or property is received, the *amount* recorded would result from an agreement between the individual and the corporate officials as to the value of the property or services.

Stock certificates usually are not issued until the subscription price is paid in full.[3] Therefore, the last collection often requires two entries. To illustrate, assume the last collection on the above subscription (for $102,000) was $25,000; the entries would be:

To record collection:

Cash	25,000	
Stock subscriptions receivable—common stock		25,000

To record issuance of the stock:

Common stock subscribed	100,000	
Common stock (1,000 shares)		100,000

Accounting for nopar stock, including stock subscriptions is illustrated in Exhibit 15–2.

In order to issue the stock, a *stock certificate* is prepared for each shareholder specifying the number of shares represented. An entry for each shareholder would be made in the *stockholder ledger* which is a subsidiary ledger to the capital stock account.

When a subscriber *defaults* after fulfilling a part of the subscription contract, certain complexities arise. In case of default, the corporation simply may decide to (1) return to the subscriber all payments made, or

[3] Although the shares are not issued, the subscriber is accorded all the privileges of a stockholder unless the subscription contract specifies otherwise.

(2) issue shares equivalent to the number paid for in full, rather than the total number contracted. These two options obviously involve no disadvantage to the subscriber, although the corporation may incur a resultant loss. The laws of most states cover the contingency where the corporation does not elect either of these alternatives. Such laws vary considerably; two contrasting provisions follow–

a. The stock is *forfeited,* and all payments made by the defaulting subscriber are lost to the subscriber; hence, they become a source of contributed capital to the corporation. Further, the corporation is free to sell the shares again. Obviously, provisions of this type favor the corporation.

b. The stock is forfeited, and the corporation must resell the stock under a *lien,* whereby the original subscriber must be reimbursed for the amount that the total receipts for the stock (his or her payments plus the later sale proceeds), less the costs incurred by the corporation in making the second sale, exceed the original subscription price. The reimbursement to the defaulting subscriber cannot exceed the amount paid by the subscriber to the date of default.

ACCOUNTING FOR STOCK PREMIUM AND DISCOUNT

In the preceding discussions and illustrations, amounts received in excess of par value were credited to an appropriately designated stock premium account. Similarly, amounts received less than par are debited to an appropriately titled stock discount account. Premium constitutes an increase in total corporate capital, whereas stock discount serves to reduce total corporate capital. In view of the advent of nopar stock and the passage of laws in many states forbidding the sale of stock at a discount, accountants seldom encounter the problem of stock discount.

Contributed capital in excess of par value is classified as contributed or paid-in capital and should remain in the accounts until retirement of the stock. Upon retirement of the stock the related premium should be removed from the accounts. Some states allow such contributed capital to be used for stock dividends; a few allow charges to such accounts for cash dividends as well. When state laws allow these charges, the shareholders receiving the dividends should be informed that they represent a return of original investment (i.e., a liquidating dividend) rather than a distribution of earnings.

Separate premium and discount accounts should be established for each class of stock. Premium and discount should not be offset against each other. Discount can be disposed of by additional collections (stock assessments) from shareholders or through retirement of the related stock. Discount is reported on the balance sheet *(a)* preferably as a negative item directly under the particular class of stock to which it relates, or *(b)* secondarily as a negative item under the "other contributed" capital. See Chapter 14 for a discussion of stock issue costs.

SPECIAL SALES OF STOCK

A corporation may sell each class of stock separately as assumed in the preceding discussions or it may sell two or more classes of securities for one lump sum. Further, a corporation may sell stock for services or property rather than for cash. Each of these situations presents special accounting problems.

In the situation where two or more classes of securities are sold for a single lump sum, the proceeds must be allocated between the several classes of securities on some logical basis. Two methods available for such situations are *(a)* the proportional method, where the lump sum received is allocated proportionally between the classes of stock such as on the relative fair market value of each security related to the units involved, and *(b)* the incremental method, where the market value of one security is used as a basis for that security and the remainder of the lump sum is allocated to the other class of security. Selection of an appropriate method should depend upon the information available. To illustrate several situations, assume 100 shares of common stock (par value $100 per share) and 50 shares of preferred stock (par value $80 per share) are sold for a lump sum of $15,000.

Assumption 1: The common stock is selling at 104, and the preferred stock at 101 – apportionment on basis of relative fair market values.

Cash	15,000	
Common stock (100 shares, par $100)		10,000
Preferred stock (50 shares, par $80)		4,000
Contributed capital in excess of par, common		100
Contributed capital in excess of par, preferred		900

Computations (rounded):

Common: $\frac{\$10,400}{\$15,450} \times \$15,000 = \$10,100$ $\quad \$10,100 - \$10,000 = \$100$

Preferred: $\frac{\$5,050}{\$15,450} \times \$15,000 = \underline{4,900}$ $\quad \$4,900 - \$4,000 = \$900$

$\underline{\underline{\$15,000}}$

Assumption 2: The common stock is selling at 104; no market has been established for the preferred stock – apportionment on basis of fair market value of one class of shares.

Cash	15,000	
Common stock (100 shares, par $100)		10,000
Preferred stock (50 shares, par $80)		4,000
Contributed capital in excess of par, common ($4 per share)		400
Contributed capital in excess of par, preferred		600

Assumption 3: No current market value is determinable for either class of stock. In this case an arbitrary allocation is the only alternative. In the absence of any other logical basis, a temporary allocation may be made on the basis of relative par values. Should a market value be estab-

lished for one of the securities in the relatively near future, a correcting entry based on such value would be appropriate. The entry to record the arbitary allocation would be:

Cash	15,000	
Common stock (100 shares, par $100)		10,000
Preferred stock (50 shares, par $80)		4,000
Contributed capital in excess of par, common		714
Contributed capital in excess of par, preferred		286

Computations:

$\frac{\$10,000}{\$14,000} \times \$15,000 = \$10,714$ $\quad \$10,714 - \$10,000 = \$714$

$\frac{\$4,000}{\$14,000} \times \$15,000 = \$\ 4,286$ $\quad \$\ 4,286 - \$\ 4,000 = \$286$

Noncash Sale of Stock

When a corporation issues stock as payment for assets or services, the question of stock valuation for accounting purposes arises. The values to apply in this situation, in determination of the proceeds, are as follows, in order of preference:

1. Current fair market value of the assets or services.
2. Current fair market value of the stock issued.
3. Appraised value of the assets or services.
4. Valuation of the assets or services established by the board of directors.

The exchange of noncash assets for stock has given rise to many abuses over the years through improper valuation of the assets received. Overvalued assets create an overstatement of corporate capital–a condition frequently referred to as *watered stock*. On the other hand, undervaluation of assets creates an understatement of corporate capital giving rise to what is frequently referred to as *secret reserves*. Secret reserves also may be created by depreciating or amortizing assets over a period substantially less than their useful life.

UNREALIZED CAPITAL INCREMENT

Unrealized capital increment, as a category of stockholders' equity, is not widely used in practice. It arises when assets are written up above cost; thus, it violates the cost principle. Because of adherence to the cost principle and the concept of conservatism, assets rarely are written up from cost to fair market value (sometimes called appraisal increases). The most common example of such write-ups involve *discovery value* of natural resources. Other examples are to be found in a few industries such as the insurance industry. Typically, in the insurance and mutual fund industries the investment portfolio is adjusted to fair market value at the end of each period. An adjustment upward of the asset account requires an offsetting credit to either revenue or unrealized capital increment. There are a number of unsettled issues such as *(a)* measurement of fair market value, *(b)* classification of the credit, and *(c)* adequate disclosure. As the profession moves toward "fair value accounting" these issues will necessarily come into greater focus and demand definitive solutions.

The write-up of fixed assets to appraisal value was briefly discussed in Chapter 13. Other examples are briefly discussed in subsequent chapters. However, except in limited situations, current GAAP does not permit the write-up of assets to fair market value. However, when the fair market value of an asset has dropped significantly below its carrying value in the accounts, it is written down and a loss recognized. Examples are lower of cost or market for inventories and short-term investments, and idle plants.

FASB *Statement No. 12,* "Accounting for Certain Marketable Securities," (December, 1975) requires the recording of an "Unrealized Loss on Long-term Investments in Equity Securities." This *negative* unrealized capital item is discussed in Chapter 18, Part A.

ASSESSMENTS ON SHAREHOLDERS

Some states permit the issuance of *assessable stock,* providing the charter includes such a provision. Also in some states, under certain conditions, stockholders may be assessed a certain amount per share, although the stock held is not identified as assessable stock. A stock assessment involves the collection of cash from the stockholders in proportion to the shares held without the issuance of additional stock. Stock assessments are used only when the corporation is in dire need of cash or when the stock originally was issued at a discount. If the stock was issued originally at a discount, the assessment (up to the amount of the discount) is credited to the discount account. If no stock discount is carried in the accounts, the credit is to a contributed capital account with an appropriate title such as Contributed Capital, Stock Assessments.

INCORPORATION OF A GOING BUSINESS

The owner, or owners, of a sole proprietorship or partnership may decide to incorporate, or a corporation may acquire another business in exchange for shares of stock.[4] Certain accounting problems arise in such situations, particularly with respect to *(a)* the values to be placed on the assets received for shares of stock, and *(b)* the entries to record the exchange.

In accounting for assets in the situation where an unincorporated business is selling its assets, the cost principle requires that the assets be recorded by the acquirer at their fair market value as of the date of the exchange. If this is not determinable, the fair market value of the stock issued for the assets should be used. In many situations neither of these values can be determined; in such cases the responsible parties

---

[4] See Chapter 18 on business combinations.

involved must be relied upon to establish a realistic estimate of fair market value. It is not unusual, in the case of a going business, for the parties to agree to an exchange value in excess of the total fair market value of the tangible assets acquired because of the recognition of goodwill. In cases where goodwill is paid for, it should be recorded as an intangible asset at the purchased price.

In situations where the only change is in the form of organization; that is, the ownership and management is continuous, as where a partnership is simply incorporated, a case can be made for carrying forward the book values and no recognition of goodwill.

The entries to record the exchange of a going business for shares of stock will depend upon whether the original books of the acquired business will be continued or whether new books will be opened for the corporation, and any adjustments to fair market values.

If the *original books* are retained, two basic steps are required assuming the cost principle applies:

1. Entries must be made to revalue the assets (and any other items agreed upon) in accordance with the cost principle.
2. Entries must be made to close out the old owners' equity accounts, and to replace them with corporate capital accounts.

If *new books* are to be started the old books must be closed and new books for the corporation opened. Entries should be made on the *old books* to–

1. Revalue the assets (and any other items agreed upon) in accordance with the cost principle.
2. Record the transfer of the assets.
3. Record receipt of the stock and its distribution.

Entries must be made on the *new books* to–

1. Record the stock authorization.
2. Record the receipt of the assets.
3. Record issuance of the stock.

To illustrate each situation, assume the books for the AB Partnership showed the following:

Cash	$ 2,000	Accounts payable	$ 5,000
Accounts receivable	10,000	Notes payable	2,000
Allowance for doubtful accounts	(1,000)	A, capital	30,000
Inventory	21,000	B, capital	20,000
Fixed assets	40,000		
Accumulated depreciation	(15,000)		
	$57,000		$57,000

The XYZ Corporation is formed with 20,000 shares of common stock authorized (par value $5 per share); 12,000 of the shares are issued in exchange for the assets, except the cash; the liabilities are assumed by the corporation. It was agreed that the inventory should be written down to $16,000 and that the accumulated depreciation should be $14,000. The book value of the remaining assets essentially represented fair market value at the time of transfer to XYZ Corporation. The 12,000 shares and the $2,000 cash are to be divided between A and B according to their capital balances after the above adjustments. The partners had divided profits and losses equally. The remaining 8,000 shares were sold to the public at $5.10 per share.

Assumption 1: The old books are to be retained.

1. To record the adjustments:

Accumulated depreciation	1,000	
Adjustment account	4,000	
Inventory		5,000

2. To record goodwill:[5]

Goodwill*	17,200	
Adjustment account		17,200

* Computation:

Value of shares exchanged (12,000 at $5.10)	$61,200
Value of net assets (after adjustment and excluding cash)	44,000
Goodwill	$17,200

3. To close Adjustment account to partners' capital accounts:

Adjustment account	13,200	
A, capital		6,600
B, capital		6,600

4. Notation: Capital stock authorized, 20,000 shares, par $5 per share.
5. To record distribution of $2,000 cash and issuance of 12,000 shares of stock to the partners for the other assets (net):

A, capital ($30,000 + $6,600)	36,600	
B, capital ($20,000 + $6,600)	26,600	
Cash		2,000
Common stock (12,000 shares, par $5)		60,000
Contributed capital in excess of par		1,200

6. To record sale of 8,000 shares at $5.10 per share:

Cash	40,800	
Common stock (8,000 shares, par $5)		40,000
Contributed capital in excess of par		800

Assumption 2: New books are opened and the old books closed. See Exhibit 15–3.

For tax purposes, if control is continued by the original owners (at least 80% of the voting stock), no loss or gain is recognized and the valuation basis for tax purposes remains unchanged.

---

[5] See Chapter 14 for discussion of amortization of goodwill.

EXHIBIT 15–3
Incorporation of a Partnership

Entries on New Books			*Entries on Old Books*		
1. To record authorization of capital stock:					
Notation: Common stock authorized, 20,000 shares, $5. par value per share.					
2. To record adjustments agreed upon:					
			Accumulated depreciation	1,000	
			Adjustment account	4,000	
			Inventory		5,000
3. To record goodwill (as computed in Assumption 1):					
			Goodwill	17,200	
			Adjustment account		17,200
4. To close Adjustment account to capital accounts:					
			Adjustment account	13,200	
			A, capital		6,600
			B, capital		6,600
5. To record transfer of assets and liabilities as adjusted:					
Accounts receivable	10,000		Allowance for doubtful accounts	1,000	
Inventory	16,000		Accumulated depreciation	14,000	
Fixed assets	40,000		Accounts payable	5,000	
Goodwill	17,200		Notes payable	2,000	
Allowance for doubtful accounts		1,000	Receivable from XY Corporation	61,200	
Accumulated depreciation		14,000	Accounts receivable		10,000
Accounts payable		5,000	Inventory		16,000
Notes payable		2,000	Fixed assets		40,000
Payable to AB partnership		61,200	Goodwill		17,200
6. To record transfer of stock:					
Payable to AB Partnership	61,200		Stock in XY Corporation	61,200	
Common stock		60,000	Receivable from XY Corporation		61,200
Contributed capital in excess of par		1,200			
7. Distribution of stock and cash:					
			A, capital	36,600	
			B, capital	26,600	
			Stock in XY Corporation		61,200
			Cash		2,000
8. To record sale of 8,000 shares at $5.10 per share:					
Cash	40,800				
Common stock		40,000			
Contributed capital in excess of par		800			

QUESTIONS

1. Explain the meaning of each of the following: total equity, contributed capital, proprietary equity, and legal capital.

2. Distinguish between public, private, domestic, foreign, open, and closed corporations.

3. What are the four basic rights of shareholders? How may one or more of these rights be withheld from the shareholder?

4. Explain each of the following: authorized capital stock, issued capital stock, unissued capital stock, outstanding capital stock, subscribed stock, and treasury stock.

5. In accounting for corporate capital why is *source* particularly important?

6. Distinguish between par and nopar stock.

7. Distinguish between common and preferred stock.

8. Explain the difference between cumulative and noncumulative stock.

9. Explain the difference between nonparticipating, partially participating, and fully participating stock.

10. Under what circumstances should stock subscriptions receivable be reported *(a)* as a current asset, *(b)* as a noncurrent asset, and *(c)* as a deduction in the corporate capital section of the balance sheet?

11. What is a liquidating dividend? Why is it important that a liquidating dividend be identified separately?

12. Explain and illustrate "secret reserves" and "watered stock."

13. How should premium and discount on capital stock be accounted for and reported?

14. Indicate the priorities for stock valuation when assets other than cash are received in payment thereof.

15. What is a stock assessment?

DECISION CASE 15–1

C. Banfield, an engineer, developed a special device to be installed in backyard swimming pools that would set off an alarm should anything fall into the water. Over a two-year period Banfield's spare time was spent developing and testing the device. After receiving a patent, three of Banfield's friends, including a lawyer, considered plans to market the device. Accordingly, a charter was obtained which authorized 25,000 shares of $10 par-value stock. Each of the four organizers contributed $1,000, and each received in return 100 shares of stock. They agreed that each would receive 500 additional shares. The remaining shares were to be held as unissued stock. Each organizer made a proposal as to how the additional 500 shares would be paid for. These individual proposals were made independently; then the group considered them as a package. The four proposals were:

BANFIELD: The patent would be turned over to the corporation as payment for the 500 shares.

LAWYER: One hundred shares to be received for legal fees already rendered during organization, 100 shares to be received as advance payment for legal retainer fees for the next three years, and the balance to be paid for in cash at par.

FRIEND NO. 3: A small building, suitable for operations, would be turned over to the corporation plus $750 cash, in payment for 500 shares. It was estimated that $750 would be needed for renovation. The owner estimates that the fair value of the property is $25,000 and there is an $18,000 loan on it to be assumed by the corporation.

FRIEND NO. 4: To pay $1,000 cash on the stock and to give a noninterest-bearing note for $4,000 to be paid out of dividends over the next five years.

Required:

You have been engaged as an independent CPA to advise the group. Specifically, you have been asked the following questions:

1. How would the above proposals be recorded in the accounts? Criticize the valuation basis for each.
2. What are your recommendations for an agreement that would be equitable to each organizer; explain the basis for such recommendations?

EXERCISES

Exercise 15–1

Burke Corporation received a charter authorizing 50,000 shares of stock, par value $10 per share. During the course of the first year, 30,000 shares were sold at $15 per share. One hundred additional shares were issued in payment for legal fees. At the end of the first year, reported net income was $20,000. Dividends of $6,000 were paid as of the last day of the year. Liabilities at the year-end amounted to $10,000.

Required:

Complete the following tabulation (show calculations):

Item	*Amount*	*Assumptions*
a. Total equities	$	
b. Owners' equity	$	
c. Contributed capital	$	
d. Legal capital	$	
e. Issued capital stock	$	
f. Outstanding capital stock	$	
g. Unissued capital stock	$	
h. Treasury stock	$	

Exercise 15–2

Texas Corporation charter authorized 50,000 shares of common stock, nopar value, and 20,000 shares of 6%, cumulative and nonparticipating preferred stock, par value, $10 per share. Stock issued to date: 30,000 shares of common sold at $150,000 and 10,000 shares of preferred stock sold at $18 per share. Subscriptions for 1,000 shares of preferred have been taken, and 30% of the purchase price of $18 has been collected. The stock will be issued upon collection in full. The Retained earnings balance is $60,000.

Required:

Prepare the stockholders' equity section of the balance sheet in good form.

Exercise 15–3

Prepare, in good form, the stockholders' equity section of the balance sheet for AB Manufacturing Company.

Retained earnings	$ 60,000
Premium on common stock	32,000
Preferred stock subscribed (1,000 shares)	10,000
Preferred stock, 6%, par $10, authorized 25,000 shares	140,000 (issued)
Common stock, par $20, authorized 50,000 shares	160,000 (issued)
Stock subscriptions receivable, preferred	4,000
Donation of plant site	12,000
Premium on preferred stock	30,000

Exercise 15–4

The following data were provided by the accounts of Askew Corporation at December 31, 19A:

Subscriptions receivable	$ 4,000
Retained earnings	150,000
Capital stock, par ?, authorized 100,000 shares	600,000
Future site for office donated	15,000
Capital stock subscribed, 1,000 shares (to be issued upon collection in full)	10,000
Premium on capital stock	315,000
Subscriptions receivable, capital stock (due in three months)	2,000
Bonds payable	100,000
Net income for 19A (included in retained earnings above)	120,000

Required:

1. Respond to the following (state any assumptions made):

a. Total retained earnings is	$________
b. Retained earnings on January 1, 19A was	$________
c. The number of shares outstanding is	________ shares
d. Legal capital is	$________
e. Total stockholders' equity is	$________
f. Earnings per share for 19A was	$________
g. Number of shares issued is	________ shares
h. The selling price per share was	$________
i. The number of shares sold was	________ shares
j. The par value per share is	$________

2. Prepare the stockholders' equity section of the balance sheet at December 31, 19A. Use good form and complete with respect to details.

Exercise 15–5

Troy Corporation has the following stock outstanding:
Common, $50 par value – 6,000 shares
Preferred, 6%, $100 par value – 1,000 shares

Required:

Compute the amount of dividends payable in total and per share on the common and preferred for each separate case:

Case A – Preferred is noncumulative and nonparticipating; dividends declared, $15,000.

Case B—Preferred is cumulative and nonparticipating; three years in arrears; dividends declared, \$36,000.

Case C—Preferred is noncumulative and fully participating; dividends declared, \$24,000.

Case D—Preferred is noncumulative and fully participating; dividends declared, \$33,000.

Case E—Preferred is cumulative and participating up to an additional 3%; three years in arrears; dividends declared, \$60,000.

Case F—Preferred is cumulative and fully participating; three years in arrears; dividends declared, \$60,000.

Exercise 15–6

Baker Corporation reported net income during four successive years as follows: \$1,000; \$2,000; \$1,000; and \$20,000.

The capital stock consisted of \$70,000 common (par \$20 per share) and \$30,000 of 5% preferred (par \$10 per share).

Required:

If net income in full were declared and paid as dividends each year, determine the amount to be paid on each class of stock for each of the four years assuming:

Case A—Preferred is noncumulative and nonparticipating.
Case B—Preferred is cumulative and nonparticipating.
Case C—Preferred is noncumulative and fully participating.
Case D—Preferred is cumulative and fully participating.

Exercise 15–7

Tavis Corporation received a charter authorizing the issuance of 100,000 shares of common stock. Give the journal entries in parallel columns for the following transactions during the first year assuming: Case A—par value of \$5 per share; and Case B—true nopar stock.

a. To record authorization.
b. Sold 50,000 shares at \$6; collected in full and issued shares.
c. Received subscriptions for 10,000 shares at \$6 per share; collected 60% of the subscription price. The stock will not be issued until collection in full.
d. Issued 100 shares to attorney in payment for legal fees.
e. Issued 8,000 shares and paid cash \$50,000 in payment for a building.
f. Collected balance on subscriptions receivable in *(c)*.

State and justify any assumptions you made.

Exercise 15–8

Story Manufacturing Company's charter authorized the issuance of 50,000 shares of nopar common stock. Give journal entries for the following transactions assuming: Case A—the board of directors set a stated value of \$6 per share; Case B—the stock is true nopar. Set up two columns so that Case A is to the left and Case B is to the right. Explain and justify any assumptions you make.

a. Authorization recognized.
b. Sold 30,000 shares at \$7 and collected in full; shares were issued.
c. Received subscriptions for 10,000 shares at \$7 per share; collected 40% of the subscription price. The shares will be issued upon collection in full.

d. Issued 100 shares for legal services.
e. Issued 2,000 shares and paid $10,000 cash for some used machinery.
f. Collected balance of subscriptions in (*c*).

Exercise 15–9

Morley Corporation charter authorized 100,000 shares of $10 par-value stock. A. B. Cook subscribed to 500 shares at $25 per share, paying $2,500 down, the balance to be paid $1,000 per month. The stock will not be issued until collection in full. After paying for three months, Cook defaulted. Subsequently, the corporation sold the stock for $30 per share and at that time made a full refund to Cook.

Required:

Give all entries relative to the 500 shares originally subscribed for by Cook. State and justify any assumptions you made.

Exercise 15–10

The charter for Kork Manufacturing Company authorized 50,000 shares of common stock ($100 par value) and 10,000 shares of preferred stock ($50 par value). The company issued 100 shares of common and 50 shares of preferred for used machinery.

Required:

For each separate situation, give the entry to record the purchase of the machinery assuming: Case A—the common stock currently is selling at $120 and the preferred at $60; Case B—the common stock has been selling at $120 and there have been no recent sales of the preferred stock; Case C—there is no current market price for either class of stock, however, the machinery has been appraised at $14,000.

State and justify any assumptions made.

Exercise 15–11

RT Corporation charter authorized 10,000 shares of $20 par value common stock and 10,000 shares of $10 preferred stock. The following transactions were completed. Assume each is completely independent.

a. Sold 200 shares of common and 100 shares of preferred for a lump sum amounting to $6,000. The common had been selling at $25 and the preferred at $12.
b. Issued 40 shares of common stock for some used equipment. The equipment had been appraised at $1,100; the book value shown by the seller was $600.
c. A 10% assessment on par was voted on both the common and preferred when 6,000 shares of common and 4,000 shares of preferred were outstanding. The assessment was collected in full.
d. Sold 300 shares of common and 200 shares of preferred to one person for a total cash price of $10,000. The common recently had been selling at $26; there were no recent sales of the preferred.

Required:

Give the journal entries for each transaction. State and justify any assumptions you made.

Exercise 15–12

Model Corporation was incorporated with 250 shares of capital stock, par $100; 210 of the shares were issued for the equity in the Brown and Black partnership. The remaining 40 shares were sold at par. The balance in the accounts for the partnership were as follows:

Cash	$ 1,000	Accounts payable	$10,000
Notes receivable	3,000	Allowance for doubtful	
Accounts receivable	7,000	accounts	1,000
Inventory	6,000	Accumulated depreciation	2,000
Fixed assets	15,000	Brown, capital	10,000
		Black, capital	9,000
	$32,000		$32,000

The following adjustments were to be made prior to the exchange: decrease inventory to $4,000 and increase accumulated depreciation to $3,000. The partners shared profits equally.

Required:

Give entries assuming the old books are to be continued (compute goodwill assuming the fair market value of the stock issued was $100 per share).

PROBLEMS

Problem 15–1

Using appropriate data from the information given below, prepare, in good form, the stockholders' equity section of a balance sheet for the Miller Corporation.

Stock subscriptions receivable, preferred stock	$ 8,000
Reserve for bond sinking fund	60,000
Unrealized capital increment per appraisal of natural resources (discovery value)	45,000
Preferred stock, 6%, authorized 1,000 shares, par $100 per share, cumulative and participating	60,000
Bonds payable, 7%	125,000
Common stock, nopar, 5,000 shares authorized and outstanding	250,000
Donation of future plant site	6,000
Premium on preferred stock	12,000
Discount on bonds payable	1,000
Retained earnings, unappropriated	50,000
Preferred stock subscribed (to be issued upon collection in full)	10,000

Problem 15–2

Moore Corporation was granted a charter authorizing 10,000 shares of 6% preferred stock, par value $10 per share, and 50,000 shares of common stock, nopar value. No stated or assigned value was identified with the common stock. During the first year, the following transactions occurred:

a. 20,000 shares of common stock were sold for cash at $5 per share.
b. 1,000 shares of preferred stock sold for cash at $15 per share.
c. Subscriptions were received for 1,000 shares of preferred stock at $15 per share;

40% was received as a down payment, and the balance in two equal installments. The shares will be issued upon collection in full.

d. 5,000 shares of common stock, 500 shares of preferred stock, and $15,500 cash were given as payment for a small plant that the company needed. This plant originally cost $40,000 and had a depreciated value on the books of the selling company of $20,000.

e. The first installment on the preferred subscriptions was collected.

Required:

1. Give journal entries to record the above transactions. State and justify any assumptions you made.
2. Prepare the stockholders' equity section of the balance sheet at year-end. Retained earnings at the end of the year amounted to $17,000.

Problem 15–3

Fisher Corporation received a charter to conduct a manufacturing business. It was authorized to issue common stock 50,000 shares, nopar value; and 6% preferred stock 10,000 shares, cumulative and nonparticipating and par value per share of $10. During the first year, the following transactions occurred:

a. Each of the six incorporators subscribed to 1,000 shares of the common at $15 per share and 500 shares of the preferred, at par. One half of the subscription price was paid and one half of the subscribed shares issued.

b. Another individual purchased 500 shares of common and 100 shares of preferred stock paying $9,010 cash.

c. One of the incorporators purchased a used machine for $40,000 and immediately transferred to the Fisher Corporation for 2,000 shares of common stock, 200 shares of preferred stock, and a one year interest-bearing note for $8,000.

d. The investors paid the subscriptions, and the remaining stock was issued.

Required:

1. Give all entries indicated for the Fisher Corporation.
2. Prepare the stockholders' equity section of the balance sheet. Assume Retained earnings of $23,000 at year-end.

Problem 15–4

Grayson Corporation received a charter that authorized 100,000 shares of capital stock. During the first year, the following transactions affecting stockholders' equity were completed:

a. Sold 60,000 shares at $25 per share for cash.

b. Received a subscription for 1,000 shares at $25 per share, collected 60% cash, balance due within one year. The stock will be issued upon collection in full.

c. Issued 500 shares for a used machine that would be used in operations. The machine had cost $20,000 new and was carried by the seller at a book value of $11,000. It was recently appraised at $13,000.

d. Collected one half of the unpaid subscriptions in *(b)*.

Required:

1. Give entries for each of the above transactions, assuming: Case A – the stock has a par value of $10 per share; Case B – the stock is true nopar value; Case C – the stock is nopar; however, it is assigned a stated value of $5 per share.

Set up parallel columns for each case. State and justify any assumptions you make.

2. Prepare the stockholders' equity section of the balance sheet at the end of the first year for each case. Use good form. Assume a balance in Retained earnings of $124,000.

Problem 15–5

The charter for Jackson Corporation authorized 500,000 shares of capital stock. During the first year of operations, the following transactions were completed that affected stockholders' equity:

a. Sold 400,000 shares of capital stock at $10 per share; collected cash.
b. Sold 10,000 shares of capital stock to one individual at $10 per share. Collected 40% of the subscription and the balance is due at the end of one year. The shares will be issued upon collection in full.
c. Exchanged 6,000 shares of capital stock for a plant site. The site was carried on the books of the seller at $25,000, and it had been appraised within the past year at $65,000.
d. Collected $12,000 on the subscription in (*b*).

Required:

1. Give entries for the above transactions assuming:

   Case A—Par-value stock; $2 par value per share.
   Case B—True nopar-value stock.
   Case C—Nopar-value stock with a stated value of $1 per share.

   Set up parallel columns for each case. State and justify any assumptions you make.
2. Prepare the stockholders' equity section of the balance sheet at the end of the first year for each case. Use good form. Assume a $119,000 ending balance in Retained earnings and, in addition, a reserve for bond sinking fund of $10,000.

Problem 15–6

The charter of Peerless Corporation authorized the issuance of 20,000 shares of 6% cumulative, nonparticipating preferred stock, par $10 per share, and 100,000 shares of common stock, nopar value. During the first year of operations, the following transactions affecting stockholders' equity were completed:

a. The promoters sold 9,000 shares of the preferred stock at par; the stock was issued.
b. Subscriptions were received for an additional 1,000 shares of preferred stock at $10.50 per share; 20% was collected, the balance is to be paid in three equal installments, at which time the stock will be issued.
c. Each of the three promoters was issued 1,000 shares of common stock (only the common stock carried voting privileges) at $20 per share, each paid one fifth in cash, the remainder was considered to be reimbursement for promotional activities; the shares were issued. Debit Organization expense.
d. An individual purchased 100 shares of preferred and 100 shares of common stock and paid a single sum of $3,300. The stock was issued. Assume a current market price of $20 for the preferred stock and no current market for the common.
e. Collected cash from the promoters (*b* above) for 10% of the receivable.

f. Issued 5,000 shares of common stock for a used plant. The plant had been appraised during the past month at $110,000 and was carried by the seller at a book value of $60,000.

Required:

1. Prepare journal entries to record the foregoing transactions. State and justify any assumptions you make.
2. Prepare the stockholders' equity section of the balance sheet assuming retained earnings at year-end of $131,000.

Problem 15–7

The stockholders' equity section of the balance sheet for the Day Metals Corporation at the end of its first fiscal year was reported as follows:

Stockholders' Equity

Contributed Capital:		
Capital stock:		
Preferred 6% cumulative, $100 par value, redeemable at $125 per share, authorized 5,000 shares, issued and outstanding 4,185	$ 418,500	
Preferred stock subscribed, 465 shares	46,500	$ 465,000
Common stock, stated value $8 per share, authorized 1,500,000 shares, issued and outstanding 954,000 shares	7,632,000	
Common stock subscribed, 106,000 shares	848,000	8,480,000
Other contributed capital:		
Excess of par, preferred stock	15,000	
In excess of stated value, common stock	21,200	36,200
Retained earnings		110,000
Total Stockholders' Equity		$9,091,200

Required:

Prepare journal entries during the first year as indicated by the above report. Use unissued stock accounts and assume that all stock was purchased through subscriptions under terms of 60% down and 40% six months later. Also assume that 90% of the subscriptions were collected in full by year-end. The shares are issued upon collection in full.

Problem 15–8

Tobias Corporation reported net income during five successive years as follows: $20,000; $30,000; $9,000; $5,000; and $60,000. The capital stock consisted of $300,000, $20 par value common and $200,000, $10 par value, 6% preferred.

Required:

For each separate case, prepare a computation showing the amount each class of stock would receive in dividends (1) if the entire net income was distributed each year, and (2) if 60% of the earnings were distributed each year.

Case A – Preferred stock is noncumulative and nonparticipating.
Case B – Preferred stock is cumulative and nonparticipating.
Case C – Preferred stock is cumulative and fully participating.

Problem 15–9

The charter for Hillary Corporation authorized 5,000 shares of 6% preferred stock, par value $20 per share, and 8,000 shares of common stock, par value of $50 per share, all of which have been issued. In a five-year period, total dividends paid were $4,000; $40,000; $32,000; $5,000; and $40,000.

Required:

Compute the amount of dividends paid to each class of stock for each year under the following separate cases:

Case A – Preferred stock is noncumulative and nonparticipating.
Case B – Preferred stock is cumulative and nonparticipating.
Case C – Preferred stock is noncumulative and fully participating.
Case D – Preferred stock is cumulative and fully participating.
Case E – Preferred stock is cumulative and partially participating up to an additional 2%.

Problem 15–10

Town Corporation was formed with 5,000 shares of capital stock authorized. The shares were to be issued as follows:

a. 400 shares for $40,800 cash.
b. 800 shares for the equity in the RT Partnership which reported the following balance sheet at "appraised fair market value."

Accounts receivable	$ 13,000	Notes payable	$ 20,000
Inventory	22,000	R, capital	40,000
Fixed assets	65,000	T, capital	40,000
	$100,000		$100,000

Required:

Give entries for the acquisition of the partnership on (1) the partnership books and (2) the corporation books (new books are opened) in each separate case below, assuming profits are divided equally:

Case A – The capital stock has a par value of $50, and the implied goodwill is recognized.
Case B – The capital stock is nopar value with a stated value of $40 per share. The goodwill is to be recognized.
Case C – The capital stock is nopar value and is to be recorded on a consideration-received basis. The goodwill is to be recognized.

Hint: Set up six columns across the top; that is, a debit and credit column for each case. List entries down the left side. Do not use unissued and subscription accounts. State and justify any assumptions you make.

Problem 15–11

National Corporation was formed to take over the partnership of Brown and Smith. The charter authorized 10,000 shares of capital stock, par value $100 per share. The balance sheet as of June 30 for Brown and Smith was as follows (at book value):

BROWN & SMITH PARTNERSHIP

Assets		*Liabilities and Proprietorship*	
Cash	$ 10,000	Accounts payable	$ 29,000
Accounts receivable	13,000	Accrued expenses	4,000
Allowance for doubtful accounts	(1,000)	Brown, proprietorship	60,000
Prepaid expenses	1,000	Smith, proprietorship	40,000
Buildings	90,000		
Accumulated depreciation	(20,000)		
Equipment	60,000		
Accumulated depreciation	(30,000)		
Land	10,000		
	$133,000		$133,000

The partnership profits and losses were divided 70% to Brown and 30% to Smith. Incorporators were Brown, Smith, Franks, Box, and Cane. The latter three purchased 2,000 shares each at $102. According to the agreement, 1,500 shares will be issued to Brown and Smith, based upon their capital balances, in payment for the business (including the liabilities), except for cash $10,000 which will be distributed 60% to Brown and 40% to Smith (i.e., in their capital ratios prior to adjustment). The following adjustments to the appraised fair market value, prior to the exchange, were agreed upon:

a. Allowance for doubtful accounts increased to $3,000.
b. Accumulated depreciation, buildings decreased to $7,000.
c. Land revalued to $20,000.
d. Goodwill recognition based on the "appraised fair market values."

Required:

1. Prepare entries for National Corporation assuming the old partnership books are to be continued by the corporation. The partnership will go out of existence.
2. Prepare an unclassified balance sheet immediately after the above entries.

Chapter 16

Corporations—Retained Earnings and Dividends

In Chapter 15, the three major categories of corporate capital were identified as contributed capital, retained earnings, and unrealized capital increment. Contributed capital was discussed there; this chapter focuses on retained earnings and dividends.

Retained earnings represent the accumulated gains and losses of a corporation to date reduced by dividend distributions to shareholders and amounts transferred to permanent capital accounts. *Gains* and *losses* may come from regular operations, nonrecurring or unusual transactions, extraordinary items, and prior period adjustments. If the accumulated losses and distributions of retained earnings exceed the accumulated gains, a *deficit* in retained earnings exists and must be reported.

Some variation in terminology with respect to retained earnings may be noted in practice. In prior years the term *earned surplus* was commonly used to denote what has been defined above as retained earnings. More descriptive terminology is much preferred since the basic concept involved is strongly implied, whereas the older term is quite inappropriate since there is no "surplus." On this point the AICPA Committee on Terminology recommended:

> The use of the term *surplus* (whether standing alone or in such combinations as *capital surplus, paid-in surplus, earned surplus, appraisal surplus,* etc.) be discontinued. . . .
>
> The term *earned surplus* be replaced by terms which will indicate source, such as *retained income, retained earnings, accumulated earnings* or *earnings retained for use in the business.*[1]

In accounting for stockholders' equity careful distinction is maintained between contributed capital (comprised of the capital stock and other contributed capital accounts) and retained earnings.

[1] AICPA, "Review and Résumé," *Accounting Terminology Bulletin No. 1* (New York, 1961), pp. 30–31.

It is reemphasized that in accounting for retained earnings, as with other elements of corporate capital, reporting in terms of *source* is paramount.

In accounting for *total* retained earnings, often more than one account is involved. Total retained earnings at a given date may be represented in two categories of accounts. The Retained Earnings account (undesignated otherwise) represents that portion of retained earnings not appropriated or set aside by the management for specific purposes. The second category is often called appropriated retained earnings, and the accounts comprising it are given special designations such as Retained Earnings Appropriated for Bond Sinking Fund (or, Reserve for Bond Sinking Fund). This category is discussed in a subsequent section. The usual debits and credits to the Retained Earnings account are as follows:

Retained Earnings

Debits	*Credits*
Net losses (including extraordinary losses)	Net income (including extraordinary gains)
Prior period adjustments	Prior period adjustments
Cash dividends	
Stock dividends	

Particularly observe that no debits or credits are included that occur as a result of the sale, issuance, purchase (as treasury stock), or exchanges of capital stock. These items are accounted for as elements of contributed capital.

DIVIDENDS

Dividends consist of distributions to the corporation's stockholders in proportion to the number of shares of each class of stock held. In most cases such distributions take place at regular intervals; however, on occasion, extraordinary dividends may be distributed. The term *dividends* used alone usually refers to cash dividends. When dividends in a form other than cash are distributed, they should be labeled according to the form of disbursement. The following types of dividends are encountered with some frequency by accountants:

1. Cash dividends.
2. Property dividends.
3. Liability or scrip dividends.
4. Liquidating dividends.
5. Stock dividends.

Distributions to stockholders may involve:

1. The distribution of corporate assets and a decrease in *total* corporate capital as in the case of cash, property, or liquidating dividends.
2. The creation of a liability and a decrease in *total* corporate capital

as in the case of liability dividends or a cash dividend declared but not yet paid.

3. No change in assets, liabilities, or *total* corporate capital, but only a change in the internal categories of corporate capital as in the case of a stock dividend.

The question always arises on the "use" of retained earnings for dividends. Obviously, dividends are not *paid* with retained earnings but are paid with cash or some other asset (except in the case of a stock dividend). More appropriately, dividends generally reduce both retained earnings and assets. Cash or property dividends cannot be paid without this dual effect. As noted above, assets other than cash, and even liabilities, may be involved in dividend distributions. Similarly other elements of corporate capital may be affected rather than retained earnings. The laws of all states allow retained earnings to be used as a basis for dividends, although some states place restrictions even here, such as a provision that dividends in any one year may not exceed the earnings for the preceding year. Some states permit debits to certain contributed capital accounts, such as stock premium, as a basis for cash dividends, providing creditor interests are not jeopardized.[2] Generally statutes are much more liberal with respect to stock dividends since no assets are disbursed. The statutes of the particular state are controlling; however, in the absence of any statement or information to the contrary one should assume a debit to Retained Earnings when dividend distributions are recorded.

In accounting for dividends three dates are important: (1) date of declaration, (2) date of record, and (3) date of payment. Prior to payment, dividends must be formally *declared* by the board of directors of the corporation. Stockholders normally cannot force a dividend declaration; the courts have consistently held that dividend declaration is a matter of prudent management to be decided upon by the duly elected board of directors. Of course, the board must meet all statutory, charter, and bylaw requirements, act in good faith, and protect the interests of all parties involved. In deciding whether to declare a dividend (and of what type), the board of directors should consider the financial impact on the company, including the adequacy of cash and retained earnings, and financial expectations for the future including corporate growth and expansion needs.

On the *date of declaration* the board formally announces the dividend declaration. In the case of a cash or property dividend, the declaration is recorded on this date by debiting Retained Earnings and crediting Dividends Payable. In the absence of fraud or illegality,[3] the courts have held that formal announcement of the declaration of a cash, property, or liability dividend constitutes an enforceable contract (i.e., a nonrevocable declaration) between the corporation and the shareholders. In view of the irrevocability of this action, the liability is recorded on

---

[2] A liquidating dividend may be involved; see subsequent section on liquidating dividends.

[3] Questions of legality should be referred to an attorney.

declaration date. In the case of *stock dividends,* no assets are involved, directly or indirectly, as far as the corporation is concerned; therefore, the courts generally have held that a stock dividend declaration is revocable. Consequently, no formal entry is made on declaration date in the case of a stock dividend.[4]

The *date of record* is selected by the board and is stated in the announcement of the declaration. The date of record is the date on which the list of stockholders of record is prepared. Individuals holding stock at this date receive the dividend, regardless of sales or purchases of stock after this date. No formal dividend entry is made in the records on this date.

The *date of payment* is also determined by the board and generally is stated in the announcement of the declaration. At the date of payment, in the case of cash or property dividends, the liability recorded at date of declaration is debited, and the appropriate asset account is credited. A stock dividend distribution is recorded on this date as illustrated in a subsequent section.

Dividends on par-value stock may be stated as a certain percent of the par value, but dividends on nopar stock must be stated as a dollar amount per share.

Cash Dividends

The usual form of distributions to stockholders involves cash dividends. The declaration must meet the preferences of the preferred stockholders and then may extend to the common stockholders. In declaring a cash dividend the board of directors should be careful that the cash position for the coming months is not jeopardized and the retained earnings balance is sufficient. The cash problem may be met, in part, by careful selection of the *payment* date.

To illustrate a cash dividend, assume the following announcement is made: The board of directors of the Bass Company, at their meeting on January 20, 19A, declared a dividend of $.50 per share, payable March 20, 19A, to shareholders of record as of March 1, 19A. Assume further that 10,000 shares of stock, par value $10 per share, are outstanding.

At date of declaration (January 20, 19A):[5]

Retained earnings (or dividends paid)	5,000	
Cash dividends payable		5,000

At date of record (March 1, 19A):

No entry. The stockholders' record is "closed," and the list of dividend recipients is prepared.

---

[4] A few accountants prefer to make a formal entry at this date. See subsequent section on stock dividends. Also, in the case of cash dividends, if the declaration date and payment date are in the same accounting period there would be no reason to make an entry in the accounts on the declaration date.

[5] Sometimes a temporary account, Dividends Paid, is debited at this date and subsequently closed to Retained Earnings.

At date of payment (March 20, 19A):

Cash dividends payable	5,000	
Cash		5,000

Cash Dividends Payable is reported on the balance sheet as a current liability.

Property Dividends

Corporations occasionally pay dividends in a form of assets other than cash. Such dividends are known as property dividends. The property may be in the form of securities of other companies held by the corporation, real estate, merchandise, or any other asset designated by the board of directors. Property received by the stockholder as a dividend is subject to income tax at its fair market value.

A property dividend should be recorded at the fair market value of the assets transferred. On this point *APB Opinion No. 29* (May 1973), "Accounting for Nonmonetary Transactions," states:

> A transfer of a nonmonetary asset to a stockholder or to another entity in a nonreciprocal transfer should be recorded at the fair value of the asset transferred, and a gain or loss should be recognized on disposition of the asset.

Most property dividends are paid with the securities of other companies. Among other advantages, this avoids the problem of indivisibility of units as would be the case with most assets other than cash.

To illustrate a sequence of entries for a property dividend, assume a $10,000 balance in the account "Investment in X Company Stock (at cost)" and a fair market value of $15,000. Assume further that a $15,000 property dividend is declared and that this stock is to be used for payment. The transactions would be recorded as follows:

1. Investment in X Company stock	5,000	
Gain on disposal of stock investment		5,000
2. Retained earnings	15,000	
Property dividends payable (stock of X Company)		15,000
3. Property dividends payable (stock of X Company)	15,000	
Investment in X Company stock		15,000

Liability Dividends

Strictly speaking, any dividend involving the distribution of assets is a liability dividend between the declaration date and the date of payment. Nevertheless, liability or *scrip* dividends refer to instances where the board of directors declares a dividend and issues promissory notes, bonds, or scrip to the stockholders. In most cases scrip dividends are declared when a corporation has sufficient retained earnings to serve as a basis for dividends but is short of cash The stockholder may hold the scrip until due date and collect the dividend or possibly may discount it to obtain immediate cash. When bonds or notes are involved, the due date and rate of interest are specified. Scrip may or may not be interest bearing and is usually payable at a specified date; however, in some cases the maturity date is indefinite, being left to the option of the issuing corporation. The immediate effect of a scrip or liability dividend is a charge to Retained Earnings and a credit to a liability account such as Scrip Dividends Payable or Notes Payable to Stockholders. Upon payment, Cash is credited and the liability account debited. A liability dividend is in effect a cash dividend with a considerable time lapsing between declaration date and payment date. Since interest paid on a liability dividend is not a part of the dividend itself, such payments should be charged to interest expense.

Liquidating Dividends

Distributions that constitute a *return of capital* rather than earnings are known as liquidating dividends. Liquidating dividends may be either intentional or unintentional. Intentional liquidating dividends occur when the board of directors knowingly declares dividends which will, in effect, represent a return of investment to the shareholders, as in the case when a corporation is discontinuing operations or when there is excessive capitalization.

Mining companies may pay dividends on the basis of earnings prior to a deduction for depletion. In such cases there is an intentional liquidating dividend equal to the depletion not deducted. Stockholders should be informed of the portion of any dividend that represents a return of capital. Such dividends are not taxable to the shareholder as income but serve to reduce the cost basis of his or her stock.

In accounting for liquidating dividends, contributed capital rather than retained earnings should be charged since a portion of stockholder investment is returned. Rather than debiting the capital stock accounts, as would be done if shares were being retired, other contributed capital accounts such as premium accounts may be charged. In some cases it may be desirable to set up a special account, Capital Repayment, which would be treated as a deduction in the corporate capital section of the balance sheet.

Unintentional liquidating dividends may occur when net income, and hence retained earnings, is overstated because of errors and inappropriate accounting. The omission or understatement of depreciation charges, amortizations, and depletion charges would cause retained earnings to be overstated. In such cases if reported retained earnings (prior to correction) were used in full as a basis for dividends, part of the resulting dividend would represent a return of contributed capital.

Stock Dividends

A stock dividend is a distribution of additional shares, without cost, to the shareholders in proportion to their prior stock holdings. A stock dividend may be in the form of treasury stock or unissued stock; and common or preferred shares may be issued. When the stock dividend is of the same class as that held by the recipients, there is an *ordinary* stock dividend; on the other hand, when a different class of stock is issued, it is a *special* stock dividend. It was noted in a preceding section that state laws vary as to the availability of various classes of corporate capital for stock dividends. Some states permit the use of certain *contributed* capital, such as stock premium and unrealized capital increment. All states permit retained earnings to be used as a basis for stock dividends. In the absence of information to the contrary it should be assumed that the charge is to Retained Earnings. The entry to record a stock dividend should be made on the date of issuance (not date of declaration); the credit is to the respective contributed capital accounts for the shares issued.

There are a number of circumstances and reasons that might make a stock dividend advisable. The principal reasons are:

1. To permanently retain profits in the business by *capitalizing* a portion of the retained earnings. The effect of a stock dividend, through a charge to Retained Earnings and an offsetting credit to permanent capital, is to raise the contributed (and legal) capital.
2. To continue dividends without distributing assets needed for expansion and working capital. This action may be motivated by a desire to pacify stockholders, since many shareholders are willing to accept a stock dividend representing accumulated profits almost as readily as a cash dividend. Ordinary stock dividends are not subject to income tax; they serve instead to reduce the cost per share to the holder.
3. To increase the number of shares outstanding, thus reducing the market price per share. An indirect effect of a stock dividend may cause increased trading of the shares in the market.

It is especially important that the exact nature of a stock dividend be understood and that it be clearly differentiated from a *stock split*. A stock dividend does not require the distribution of assets or the creation of a liability. It does not change *total* corporate capital. Rather, a stock dividend is no more than an interequity transaction. Normally, the only effect on the issuing corporation's balance sheet is a transfer of part of the retained earnings to contributed capital and an increase in the number of shares outstanding. A stock dividend does not affect the par value per share. Thus, a stock dividend does not affect the assets, liabilities, or total capital, but only the internal content of corporate capital.

In contrast, a *stock split* increases the number of shares and at the same time it involves a *pro rata reduction in the par value per share.* A stock split is accomplished by replacing the old shares with a greater number of new shares which have a smaller par value per share; total par value outstanding remains the same after a stock split. A stock split does not cause a transfer of retained earnings to contributed capital; neither is changed. In the case of stock split only the content (number of shares, but not the dollar amount) of contributed capital is changed, whereas in a stock dividend the dollar amount of contributed capital is changed. To illustrate, assume X Corporation had authorized 40,000 shares of common stock, par $100, of which 10,000 shares were sold at par, and $1,600,000 in retained earnings. The effects of a 100% stock dividend versus a stock split may be summarized as follows:

	Prior to Change	*After Stock Dividend*	*After Stock Split*
Stock outstanding:			
10,000 shares, par $100	$1,000,000		
20,000 shares, par $100		$2,000,000	
20,000 shares, par $50			$1,000,000
Retained earnings	1,600,000	600,000	1,600,000
Total Capital........................	$2,600,000	$2,600,000	$2,600,000

Since a stock dividend requires capitalization of retained earnings, the question arises as to the amount of retained earnings to be capitalized (transferred to contributed capital) for the additional shares issued. The *statutory minimum* in most states is par value.[6] In the case of preferred stock it may be the liquidating value. However, the amount transferred from retained earnings to contributed capital should not necessarily be limited to the statutory minimum. The Committee on Accounting Procedure of the AICPA has stated a definite position on this matter. The committee recognized two distinct situations and indicated a different accounting procedure for each, viz:

Situation 1—A Small Stock Dividend: The proportion of additional shares is *small* in relation to the total shares previously outstanding. In this situation the *fair market value* of the additional shares should be capitalized. The committee stated:

> ...many recipients of stock dividends look upon them as distributions of corporate earnings and usually in an amount equivalent to the fair value of the additional shares received. Furthermore, it is to be presumed that such views of recipients are materially strengthened in those instances, which are by far the most numerous, where the issuances are so small in comparison with the shares previously outstanding that they do not have any apparent effect upon the share market price and, consequently, the market value of the shares previously held remains substantially unchanged. The committee therefore believes that where these circumstances exist the corporation should in the public interest account for the transaction by transferring from retained earnings to the category of permanent capitalization . . . an amount equal to the fair value of the additional shares issued (i.e., the fair market value immediately after issuance.).[7]

This position is further buttressed by the fact that the market price per share, in the case of a small stock dividend, does not drop proportionately to the increased number of shares outstanding after the dividend. Thus, the shareholders received a real value increase in their holdings.

[6] Most of the states specify as the legal minimum either the par value, stated value, or average price per share originally paid in.

[7] AICPA, "Restatement and Revision of Accounting Research Bulletins," *Accounting Research Bulletin No. 43* (New York, 1961), p. 51. (Words in parentheses supplied.)

Situation 2—A Large Stock Dividend: The proportion of additional shares is *large* in relation to the total shares previously outstanding. In this situation the legal minimum (generally par value) should be capitalized, as the committee stated:

> Where the number of additional shares issued as a stock dividend is so great that it has, or may reasonably be expected to have, the effect of materially reducing the share market value, the committee believes that the implications and possible constructions discussed in the preceding paragraph are not likely to exist. . . . Consequently, the committee considers that under such circumstances there is no need to capitalize earned surplus (retained earnings), other than to the extent occasioned by legal requirements.[8]

The dividing line between the two situations described above (a small versus a large stock dividend) is often difficult to draw. The significant distinction is the effect of the additional shares on the market price rather than the exact proportion between the new and old shares. The market price per share will depend upon a number of factors such as the economic characteristics of the company, the vagaries of the market, the general condition of the economy, and the number of additional shares issued. In considering this problem the committee further stated: "It would appear that there would be few instances involving the issuance of additional shares of less than, say, 20% or 25% of the number previously outstanding where the effect would not be such as to call for the procedure" for a small stock dividend outlined above as *Situation 1.*

As explained, there is a minimum amount per share (the legal amount required) that should be capitalized in some situations and a preferred higher amount per share (fair market value) that should be capitalized in other situations. In the past many corporate managements have elected to capitalize an amount between these two extremes, frequently using the *average* contributed capital per share on the old shares. It may be noted further that the above discussions are particularly applicable to *ordinary* stock dividends. In the case of special stock dividends, such as a stock dividend in preferred stock issued to common shareholders, theoretical considerations would suggest that fair market value be capitalized in all cases.

In order to illustrate several situations involving stock dividends, assume the following for Z Corporation:

Preferred stock, par value $20, 10,000 shares authorized, 5,000 shares outstanding	$100,000	
Common stock, par value $10, 20,000 shares authorized, 10,000 shares outstanding	100,000	
Contributed capital in excess of par, preferred stock	10,000	
Contributed capital in excess of par, common stock	15,000	
Retained earnings	150,000	
Total Stockholders' Equity		$375,000
Market price per share immediately after issuance:		
Preferred	$25	
Common	11	

[8] Ibid., p. 52.

Illustration 1—A Small Stock Dividend: A 10% common stock dividend (i.e., one additional share is issued for each ten shares held) is declared on the common stock.

At date of issuance:[9]

Retained earnings (1,000 shares at market $11)	11,000	
Common stock (1,000 shares)		10,000
Contributed capital in excess of par, common stock		1,000

Illustration 2—A Large Stock Dividend: A 50% common stock dividend (i.e., one additional share for each two shares held) is declared. The market value per share drops to $7.50.

At issue date:

Retained earnings (5,000 shares at par, $10)	50,000	
Common stock (5,000 shares)		50,000

Situation 3—A Large Stock Dividend: A 50% common stock dividend is declared. The market value drops to $7.50 per share. Management decides to capitalize on the basis of the average paid in.

At issue date:

Retained earnings (5,000 shares at $11.50)	57,500	
Common stock (5,000 shares)		50,000
Contributed capital in excess of par, common stock		7,500

Computation: ($100,000 + $15,000) ÷ 10,000 shares = $11.50.

Situation 4—A Small Stock Dividend: A 20% common stock dividend (i.e., one additional share for each five shares held) is issued to both common and preferred shareholders. The market price per share does not change appreciably.

At issue date:

Retained earnings (3,000 shares at $11)	33,000	
Common stock (3,000 shares)		30,000
Contributed capital in excess of par, common stock		3,000

Computation: (10,000 + 5,000) × .20 = 3,000 shares.

ACCUMULATED DIVIDENDS ON PREFERRED STOCK

Dividends in arrears on *cumulative* preferred stock, prior to formal declaration of such dividends, do not constitute a liability to the corporation. However, full disclosure requires that cumulative dividends in

---

[9] A few accountants prefer to make an entry on declaration date and another entry on issue date by using a temporary contributed capital account entitled Stock Dividend Distributable. The two entries would be:

Declaration date:

Retained earnings	11,000	
Stock dividends distributable		10,000
Contributed capital in excess of par, common stock		1,000

Payment date:

Stock dividends distributable	10,000	
Common stock		10,000

arrears be reported. Preferably a footnote should be used to indicate the years and amounts of dividends in arrears. An alternative method is to report the years and amount of dividends in arrears separately from the unappropriated retained earnings figure. For example, retained earnings may be reported as follows:[10]

Retained earnings:		
Amount equal to preferred dividends in arrears	$10,000	
Unappropriated balance	20,000	$30,000

Fractional Share Warrants

Stock warrants, often called stock rights, are agreements issued to shareholders that entitles them to purchase a particular class of stock from the corporation under specified conditions. Usually warrants provide for purchase of stock under favorable conditions compared to purchase in the open market. Subject to the conditions, one or more warrants may be required as a basis for acquiring one share of stock.

When a stock dividend is issued (except when it is 100%; i.e., one for one), *fractional share warrants* often must be issued. For example, if a one for five (i.e., 20%) stock dividend is declared, a holder of 13 shares of stock would receive two additional shares and three fractional share warrants. To get another share the shareholder must obtain two additional fractional share warrants in the marketplace. Soon after issuance, stock warrants generally are freely traded on the market (also see Chapter 17).

To illustrate the accounting for fractional share warrants, assume Z Corporation (page 672) declared a 20% stock dividend whereby each shareholder receives one share of common stock, par $10, for each five shares held. Assume further that 1,730 shares of common stock and 1,350 fractional share warrants were issued to various shareholders calling for 270 shares (1,350 ÷ 5). Each fractional share warrant qualifies for one fifth of a share of stock. In order to obtain a share, five such warrants have to be presented. The resulting entries would be:

1. At date of issuance (assumed to be a small stock dividend):

Retained earnings (2,000 shares at market, $11)	22,000	
Common stock (1,730 shares at par)		17,300
Stock warrants outstanding, common (1,350 warrants requiring 270 shares of common stock)		2,700
Contributed capital in excess of par, common (2,000 shares at $1)		2,000

2. Receipt of the 1,350 stock warrants:

Stock warrants outstanding, common (1,350)..................	2,700	
Common stock (270 shares at par)..........................		2,700

---

[10] *APB Opinion No. 10* states that "the liquidation preference of the stock be disclosed in the equity section of the balance sheet in the aggregate, either parenthetically or 'in short' rather than on a per share basis or by disclosure in notes"; and *APB Opinion No. 9*, par. 35, specifies that amounts in arrearages in cumulative preferred also should be disclosed.

3. Alternatively, assume 90% of the warrants are turned in and the remainder lapse:

Stock warrants outstanding, common (1,350)	2,700	
Common stock (243 shares at par)		2,430
Contributed capital, lapse of stock warrants (for 27 shares)*		270

* An alternative would be to reverse that portion of the entry that relates to 27 shares.

If a balance sheet for Z Corporation is prepared between the date of the issuance of the stock warrants and their receipt later, the outstanding warrants would be reported as follows:

Z CORPORATION
Stockholders' Equity

Contributed Capital:		
Capital stock:		
Preferred stock, $20 par value, 10,000 shares authorized, 5,000 shares outstanding		$100,000
Common stock, $10 par value, 20,000 shares authorized, 11,730 shares outstanding	$117,300	
Common stock warrants outstanding (for 270 shares)	2,700	120,000
Total Capital Stock		220,000
Other contributed capital:		
Contributed capital in excess of par, preferred	10,000	
Contributed capital in excess of par, common	17,000	27,000
Total Contributed Capital		247,000
Retained Earnings:		
Unappropriated		128,000
Total Stockholders' Equity		$375,000

Observe that stock warrants outstanding are reported next to the related stock account. This reports the obligation to issue the requisite number of shares.

Dividends and Treasury Stock

Dividends are not paid on treasury stock. However, treasury stock occasionally is used to pay a stock dividend. If treasury stock is used for this purpose, it should be recorded as having been issued at its fair market value (also see discussion of treasury stock in Chapter 17).

To illustrate a stock dividend from treasury stock, assume a corporation issued 6,000 shares of $20 par-value common stock at $22 per share of which 5,000 shares are currently outstanding and 1,000 shares are held as treasury stock acquired (and recorded) at $21 per share. The board of directors declared a stock dividend whereby one share of treasury stock would be transferred for each five shares of stock held. The current market value per share remained essentially unchanged at

$23 per share. The indicated entry assuming a small stock dividend is:

Retained earnings (1,000 shares at market of $23)	23,000	
Treasury stock (1,000 shares at cost of $21)		21,000
Contributed capital, treasury stock transactions		2,000

LEGALITY OF DIVIDENDS

The availability of retained earnings and certain elements of contributed capital as a basis for dividends was mentioned in the first section of this chapter. To attempt to define just what elements of corporate capital are available as a basis for cash, property, and stock dividends would require a minute and detailed study of the laws of each state. Manifestly, such a study is beyond the scope of this text; further, questions of law rather than accounting are involved. There are at least two limitations which appear uniform, namely, that dividends may not be paid from *legal capital* (usually represented by the capital stock accounts) and that unappropriated retained earnings are available for dividends.[11] Between these two limits there are numerous variations, depending upon the respective state statutes, such as:

1. All contributed capital, other than legal capital, is available for dividends.
2. Specified items of contributed capital, other than legal capital, are available for dividends.
3. Contributed capital, other than legal capital, is available for dividends on preferred stock but not on common stock.
4. Unrealized capital increment is not available for dividends.
5. Unrealized capital increment is available for stock dividends only.
6. Capital losses and deficits must be restored before payment of any dividends.
7. Dividends from retained earnings must not reduce the retained earnings balance below the cost of treasury stock held.

The accountant has a responsibility in circumstances where the propriety and legality of dividends are at issue to *(a)* insure that such matters are referred to an attorney, and *(b)* ascertain that the financial statements fully disclose all known and material facts concerning such dividends.

APPROPRIATIONS OF RETAINED EARNINGS

Income and losses from operations and extraordinary gains and losses are transferred to the Retained Earnings account. This account is also charged for dividends in the manner explained previously. From time to time *appropriations* of retained earnings may be made as a result of management action, by contract, or by law. Appropriations of

[11] Some states permit the payment of dividends from current earnings even though the corporation has an accumulated deficit in retained earnings.

retained earnings constitute a *restriction* on a specified portion of accumulated earnings for specific purposes. Such specific appropriations nevertheless represent a part of *total* retained earnings. Thus, retained earnings is comprised of two subcategories: (1) appropriated retained earnings, and (2) unappropriated retained earnings.

Although retained earnings fundamentally may be appropriated to indicate that such amounts are not available as a basis for dividends, thereby protecting the working capital position of the corporation, such restrictions arise from a number of situations, the primary reasons are:

1. To fulfill a *legal requirement,* as in the case of a restriction on retained earnings equivalent to the cost of treasury stock held as required by the law of the specific state.
2. To fulfill a *contractual agreement,* as in the case of a bond issue where the bond indenture requires a sinking fund and carries a stipulation providing for a restriction on retained earnings. Such agreements have been used less in recent years.
3. To record formally a discretionary action by the board of directors to restrict a portion of retained earnings as an aspect of *financial planning.*
4. To record formally a discretionary action by the board of directors to restrict a portion of retained earnings in anticipation of *possible future losses.*

Since item (1) in the above list will be discussed in Chapter 17, the remaining items will be discussed below. Preliminary to the discussions to follow, observe that the appropriation of retained earnings fundamentally has no direct effect upon the composition of the assets. The appropriation is a "clerical" identification and does not set aside specific assets; this latter effect would occur only if a separate fund, such as a Bond Sinking Fund, also is set aside.

Appropriations of retained earnings may be accounted for and reported using either of two approaches, viz:

1. Make no formal entries in the accounts. Report the appropriations or restrictions either parenthetically on the balance sheet (or statement of retained earnings) or by footnote to the statements.
2. Make formal entries in the accounts and report the appropriations as a subclassification of retained earnings.

Some years ago the second approach was used almost exclusively; however, in recent years the first approach has been used by an increasing number of companies. Both approaches will be discussed in the paragraphs to follow. Sometimes it is desirable to supplement the reporting under the second approach with footnote disclosure.

When an appropriation ceases, as a result of either management action or by time expiration, the restriction is no longer reported; and prior entries recording the restriction (if the second approach is used) are reversed.

When the second approach is used, the restriction is formally entered in the accounts as a debit to the Retained Earnings account (i.e., unappropriated retained earnings) and as a credit to an appropriately designated appropriated account, such as Retained Earnings Appropriated for Bond Sinking Fund, or simply, Reserve for Bond Sinking Fund.[12] Under this approach the basic principle is that an appropriation account is *never* debited for a loss, or for any other reason, except to return the balance to the original source; that is the Retained Earnings account. Even in the case of a stock dividend (which requires a debit to Retained Earnings) or when a new appropriation is established as the consequence of closing another such account, balances of any appropriated Retained Earnings accounts should be returned first to the regular Retained Earnings account, and the new restriction should be recorded in the normal manner. On this point FASB *Statement No. 5* states:

> Some enterprises have classified a portion of retained earnings as "appropriated" for loss contingencies. In some cases, the appropriation has been shown outside the stockholders' equity section of the balance sheet. Appropriation of retained earnings is not prohibited by this Statement provided that it is shown within the stockholders' equity section of the balance sheet and is clearly identified as appropriation of retained earnings. Costs or losses shall not be charged to an appropriation of retained earnings, and no part of the appropriation shall be transferred to income.[13]

Exhibit 16–1 illustrates the second approach used in reporting appropriations of retained earnings.

APPROPRIATION RELATED TO A CONTRACTUAL AGREEMENT

To offer more security to purchasers of a bond issue, the bond indenture may include various provisions favorable to the bondholders (also see Chapter 19). One such provision, generally referred to as a bond sinking or redemption fund, might call for the periodic deposit of a specified amount of cash in a fund, held by a trustee, to be used to pay the bonds at maturity. A second provision might also call for the periodic *appropriation* of a specific amount of retained earnings. The amount to be appropriated may or may not be the same as the cash contributed to the fund. Or in some cases there may be an appropriation agreement without a fund provision. This situation is frequently true for serial bonds. The appropriation of retained earnings related to a bond sinking fund has two purposes: (1) to inform statement users of the planned use of assets (derived from earnings) to retire the fixed liability, and (2) to assure creditors (bondholders) that assets received from revenue are being held back to meet the drain occasioned by the bond liability requirement.

To illustrate, assume a $1 million bond issue, sold at par, with the provisions that *(a)* $100,000 per year for ten years shall be deposited in a

---

[12] Recall the discussion of *reserves* in Chapter 5. The term reserve should be limited in usage to appropriations of retained earnings (AICPA, "Review and Résumé," *Accounting Terminology Bulletin No. 1* (New York, 1961), p. 27.

[13] FASB, "Accounting for Contingencies," *Statement of Financial Accounting Standards No. 5* (March 1975), par. 15.

special fund, and *(b)* that an equal amount shall be set aside as an appropriation of retained earnings. Assuming the appropriation is to be recorded in the accounts (the second approach above), the entries would be:

1. At date of sale of bonds:

Cash	1,000,000	
Bonds payable		1,000,000

2. At end of each of the ten years:[14]

Bond redemption fund (or bond sinking fund)	100,000	
Cash		100,000
Retained earnings	100,000	
Retained earnings appropriated for bond redemption fund (or reserve for bond sinking fund)		100,000

3. At date of maturity:

Bonds payable	1,000,000	
Bond redemption fund		1,000,000
Retained earnings appropriated for bond redemption fund	1,000,000	
Retained earnings		1,000,000

Since the original proceeds of the bond issue may have been used to acquire fixed assets, upon payment of the bonds the management may desire to reappropriate the $1,000,000 or to "capitalize" it through a stock dividend. To illustrate each situation:

1. The board of directors voted that $1,000,000 be reappropriated in view of investment in plant:

Retained earnings	1,000,000	
Retained earnings appropriated for investment in plant		1,000,000

2. The board of directors declared and issued a $1,000,000 stock dividend (to be capitalized at par value):

Retained earnings	1,000,000	
Capital stock		1,000,000

Similar contractual appropriations may relate to agreements such as the purchase of specific assets, retirement of preferred stock and payment of various obligations.

If the appropriation is not recorded in the accounts (approach 1), a footnote is used to report the restriction. However, under any event the entries relating to the *fund* (but not to the appropriation) would be necessary.

---

[14] Interest revenue on the fund balance is revenue disregarded in this example. Interest normally is recorded as a credit to interest revenue and a debit to the sinking fund. This serves to reduce the amount of cash transferred to the sinking fund each year (see Chapters 11 and 19).

APPROPRIATIONS AS AN ASPECT OF FINANCIAL PLANNING

Many corporations began with a small initial capital investment and have grown large through earnings; that is, a good portion of the earnings have been retained in the business in order to expand, purchase fixed assets, and increase working capital. In such circumstances a portion of accumulated earnings may be permanently capitalized through stock dividends (or increases in par values); or instead, the management, at least temporarily, may set aside a portion of accumulated earnings in one or more appropriation accounts such as the following:

Retained Earnings Appropriated for Investment in Plant
Retained Earnings Appropriated for Working Capital
Retained Earnings Invested in Fixed Assets

Appropriations of this type serve only to inform statement users that *(a)* the retained earnings, in part, are represented in the asset structure as more or less permanent committments, and *(b)* there is a limitation on retained earnings for dividend availability.

These appropriated accounts are established through a debit to the regular Retained Earnings account (unappropriated) and are returned to this account when the purpose has been served. Obviously, they represent only a restriction on retained earnings and do not relate to *specific* earnings or assets since accounting does not identify assets with specific items of corporate capital or vice versa. In many cases upon return of the appropriation to the regular Retained Earnings account (unappropriated), a stock dividend for the same amount is declared and issued as was illustrated above for the bond transactions.

APPROPRIATION FOR POSSIBLE FUTURE LOSSES

In anticipation of possible future losses often the board of directors will direct that a portion of accumulated earnings be appropriated and specifically identified with titles such as the following:

Retained Earnings Appropriated for Contingencies
Retained Earnings Appropriated for Possible Storm Damage
Retained Earnings Appropriated for Possible Future Inventory Cost Declines
Retained Earnings Appropriated for Possible Loss in Pending Lawsuit
Retained Earnings Appropriated for Self-insurance

Appropriations of this type are reported on the financial statements, or by footnote, and often are recorded in the accounts. When recorded in the accounts they are established through a debit to the Unappropriated Retained Earnings account and are subsequently returned to this same account. As stated earlier, even though the anticipated contingency does materialize, any actual loss arising therefrom should be charged to operations or to the regular Retained Earnings account as would be done when there is no related appropriation account; such losses are not properly charged to the appropriation account. If the balance of an appropriation account needs adjustment, such changes should directly involve the Unappropriated Retained Earnings account.

An appropriation for possible future inventory cost decline is not the same account discussed in Chapter 8 which related to the valuation of inventory at lower of cost or market (Allowance to Reduce Inventory to Lower of Cost or Market). That account was related to a cost decline that had *already* materialized, whereas the appropriation account relates to a possible cost decline in the future, that is, one that has not yet materialized and may not ever materialize but the possibility does exist.

The use of this type of appropriation is subject to specific constraints given in FASB *Statement No. 5*, "Accounting for Contingencies." This FASB *Statement* is discussed in detail in Chapter 20.

REPORTING RETAINED EARNINGS

The statement of retained earnings was discussed in Chapter 4; illustrative examples were given in Chapters 4 and 5. Within recent years there has been considerable diversity of views as to what should be reported on the income statement versus the statement of retained earnings. The issue tended to focus on reporting extraordinary items and prior period adjustments. *APB Opinion Nos. 9, 12,* and *30* largely resolved these issues. Those *Opinions* require that extraordinary items be reported on the income statement and prior period adjustments on the statement of retained earnings.

APB Opinion No. 30 revised the definition of extraordinary items previously given in *Opinion No. 9. APB Opinion No. 30* is much more restrictive; it specifies that extraordinary items must meet two criteria: *(a)* unusual in nature, and *(b)* infrequent in occurrence (see Chapter 4). Extraordinary items are not permitted on the statement of retained earnings.

APB Opinion No. 9 carefully defines prior period adjustments which are reported on the statement of retained earnings as follows:

> Adjustments related to prior periods—and thus excluded in the determination of net income for the current period—are limited to those material adjustments which (a) can be specifically identified with and directly related to the business activities of particular prior periods, and (b) are not attributable to economic events occurring subsequent to the date of the financial statements for the prior period, and (c) depend primarily on determinations by persons other than management and (d) were not susceptible of reasonable estimation prior to such determination. Such adjustments are rare in modern financial accounting. . . .

Thus, to be accounted for and reported as a prior period adjustment, all four criteria listed in the above definition must be met. In recording prior period adjustments in the accounts, specially designated accounts are used which are closed directly to the Retained Earnings account. A typical example would be: Prior Period Adjustment, Damages Paid from Lawsuit.

APB Opinion No. 9 also specifies a full-disclosure requirement for prior period adjustments as follows:

> When financial statements for a single period only are presented, this disclosure should indicate the effects of such restatement on the balance of retained earnings at the beginning of the period. When financial statements for more than one period are presented, which is ordinarily the preferable procedure, the disclosure should include the effects for each of the periods included in the statements. Such disclosures should include the amounts of income tax applicable to the prior period adjustments.

Under generally accepted accounting principles, as specified in these and other pronouncements, the statement of retained earnings should report the following:

1. Beginning balance.
2. Prior period adjustments.
3. Net income or loss for the period.
4. Dividends.
5. Appropriations of retained earnings.
6. Adjustments made pursuant to a quasi-reorganization.
7. Ending balance.

To illustrate the reporting of retained earnings, the following data from the records of Model Stores, Incorporated, are used:

For Year Ended December 31, 1976

Sales		$520,000
Cost of goods sold		300,000
Expenses		120,000
Income taxes on ordinary income		52,000
Extraordinary gain		25,000
Extraordinary loss		15,000
Income taxes on extraordinary items		6,000
Balance in retained earnings, January 1, 1976:		
Unappropriated	$120,000	
Appropriation for bond sinking fund	40,000	
Appropriation for plant expansion	60,000	220,000
Refund from overpayment of 1974 income taxes		27,000
Damages from 1973 lawsuit (paid this year)	15,000	
Less: Related income tax adjustment	7,000	8,000
Dividends for current year		30,000
Appropriation of retained earnings for bond sinking fund for current year		10,000

The income statement and statement of retained earnings for Model Stores are shown in Exhibit 16–1.

When the statement of retained earnings is not complex it is sometimes included with the income statement in a combined income and

EXHIBIT 16–1
Income Statement and Statement of Retained Earnings Illustrated

MODEL STORES, INCORPORATED
Income Statement
For the Year Ended December 31, 1976

Sales		$520,000
Less: Cost of goods sold		300,000
Gross margin		220,000
Less: Expenses	$120,000	
Income taxes	52,000	172,000
Income before extraordinary items		48,000
Extraordinary items:		
Gain (designated)	25,000	
Loss (designated)	(15,000)	
	10,000	
Less: Applicable income tax	6,000	
Total Extraordinary Items		4,000
Net Income		$ 52,000

Earnings per share (not illustrated)

MODEL STORES, INCORPORATED
Statement of Retained Earnings
For the Year Ended December 31, 1976

Unappropriated Retained Earnings:				
Unappropriated balance, January 1, 1976			$120,000	
Adjustments applicable to prior periods:				
Refund of 1974 income taxes		$27,000		
Damages paid from lawsuit (1973)	$15,000			
Less: Tax adjustment	7,000	8,000	19,000	
Corrected balance			139,000	
Add: Net income for current year			52,000	
			191,000	
Deductions and appropriations:				
Dividends		30,000		
Appropriation to reserve for bond sinking fund		10,000	40,000	
Unappropriated balance, December 31, 1976				$151,000
Appropriated Retained Earnings:				
Reserve for bond sinking fund, balance January 1, 1970		40,000		
Addition for current year		10,000		
Reserve for bond sinking fund, balance December 31, 1976			50,000	
Appropriation for plant expansion			60,000	
Appropriated balance, December 31, 1976				110,000
Total Appropriated and Unappropriated, Balance December 31, 1976				$261,000

retained earnings statement. In complex situations, full disclosure will necessitate the use of notes to the statement of retained earnings.

APB Opinion No. 12 ("Omnibus Opinion," 1967) also has had an impact on the reporting of retained earnings; paragraph 10 of the *Opinion* states:

> When both financial position and results of operations are presented, disclosure of changes in the separate accounts comprising stockholders' equity (in addition to retained earnings) and of the changes in the number of shares of equity securities during at least the most recent annual fiscal period and any subsequent interim period presented is required to make the financial statements sufficiently informative. Disclosure of such changes may take the form of separate statements or may be made in the basic financial statements or notes thereto.

Consequently, in recent years there has been widespread use of comprehensive supplementary statements of all changes in owners' equity similar to that illustrated in Chapter 5, Exhibit 5–3.

QUASI-REORGANIZATIONS

When a corporation has sustained heavy losses over a period of time so that there is a significant deficit in Retained Earnings and a related *overstatement* of the carrying value of certain assets, a quasi-reorganization may be desirable from the prudent management and the accounting points of view.

A quasi-reorganization refers to a procedure whereby a corporation may, without formal court proceedings of dissolution, establish a new basis for accounting for assets and corporate capital. In effect, a quasi-reorganization is an accounting reorganization in which a "fresh start" is effected in the accounts with respect to certain assets, legal capital, and retained earnings.

The Committee on Accounting Procedure of the AICPA recognized the procedure, provided it is properly safeguarded.[15] The Securities and Exchange Commission listed certain safeguards or conditions with respect to a quasi-reorganization. These conditions are summarized below:

1. Retained earnings after the quasi-reorganization must be zero.
2. Upon completion of the quasi-reorganization no deficit shall remain in any corporate capital account.
3. The effects of the whole procedure shall be made known to all stockholders entitled to vote and appropriate approval in advance obtained from them.
4. A fair and conservative balance sheet shall be presented as of the date of the reorganization and the readjustment of values should be reasonably complete, in order to obviate as far as possible future readjustments of like nature.[16]

Characteristics of a quasi-reorganization are: (*a*) the recorded values

[15] *Accounting Research Bulletin No. 43*, pp. 45–47.

[16] Securities and Exchange Commission, *Accounting Series Release No. 25*.

relating to appropriately selected assets are restated downward; (*b*) the capital accounts are restated, and the Retained Earnings account is restated to a zero balance; (*c*) the Retained Earnings account is "dated" for a period of time (five to ten years) following the reorganization (illustrated below); (*d*) full disclosure of the procedure and the effects thereof are reported on the financial statements; and (*e*) the corporate entity is unchanged.[17]

To illustrate the accounting for a quasi-reorganization, assume the following simplified balance sheet at January 1, 19A:

Current assets	$ 200,000	Capital stock	$1,500,000
		Premium on stock	100,000
Fixed assets	1,000,000	Retained earnings	(400,000)
	$1,200,000		$1,200,000

Assume that it is determined that the inventories are overvalued by $50,000 and that the fixed asset carrying value should be reduced by $250,000 if a realistic accounting is to be made in the future.

Under these conditions the company would consider two alternatives. First, the corporation may be dissolved and a new corporation formed. The new corporation would receive the assets, record them at $900,000, and report the same amount as corporate capital. Second, the corporation may undergo a quasi-reorganization (without dissolution) which would be less cumbersome and less expensive than legal reorganization. By complying with the conditions set forth above, including stockholder approval, the quasi-reorganization may be effected through the following entries, assuming capital stock is to be reduced to $900,000:

1. To write down assets:

Clearance—quasi-reorganization	300,000	
Current assets (inventories)		50,000
Fixed assets		250,000

2. To eliminate the deficit in retained earnings:

Clearance—quasi-reorganization	400,000	
Retained earnings		400,000

3. To write off premium:

Premium on stock	100,000	
Clearance—quasi-reorganization		100,000

4. To reduce legal capital from $1,500,000 to $900,000:

Capital stock	600,000	
Clearance—quasi-reorganization		600,000

The balance sheet, including the dating of retained earnings, after the quasi-reorganization would be:

---

[17] For a detailed treatment of quasi-reorganization see: James S. Schindler, *Quasi-Reorganization* (Michigan Business Studies, vol. XIII, no. 5) (Ann Arbor: Bureau of Business Research, University of Michigan, 1958).

Current assets	$150,000	Capital stock	$900,000
Fixed assets	750,000	Retained earnings (Note 1)	—
	$900,000		$900,000

Note 1. Retained earnings represents accumulations since January 1, 19A, at which time a $400,000 deficit was eliminated as the result of a quasi-reorganization.

In general, a quasi-reorganization is justified when *(a)* a large deficit from operations exists, *(b)* it is approved by the stockholders and creditors, *(c)* the cost basis of accounting for fixed assets becomes unrealistic in terms of going-concern values, *(d)* a break in continuity of the historical cost basis is clearly needed so that realistic financial reporting is possible, *(e)* the retained earnings balances are totally inadequate to absorb an obvious decrease in going-concern asset values, and *(f)* a "fresh start," in the accounting sense, appears to be desirable or advantageous to all parties properly concerned with the corporation.

QUESTIONS

1. What are the principal sources and dispositions of retained earnings?
2. Differentiate between total retained earnings and the balance of the Retained Earnings account.
3. What is the position of the accounting profession on use of the word *surplus*? What is the basis for this position?
4. What are the three important dates relative to accounting for dividends? Explain the importance of each.
5. Distinguish between cash dividends, property dividends, and liability dividends.
6. What is a liquidating dividend? What are the responsibilities of the accountant with respect to such dividends?
7. Explain the difference between intentional and unintentional liquidating dividends.
8. Basically what is the difference between a cash or property dividend and a stock dividend?
9. Distinguish between a stock dividend and a stock split.
10. What are the reasons for appropriations of retained earnings?
11. Explain the distinction between *(a)* a bond sinking fund and *(b)* an appropriation of retained earnings for bond sinking fund.
12. What items are properly reported on the statement of retained earnings?
13. Is the following statement correct? "Retained earnings was reduced by $10,000 appropriated for plant expansion." Explain.
14. What is a quasi-reorganization? Under what conditions is it acceptable?

DECISION CASE 16–1

Bland Plastics, Incorporated, was formed in 1969 to manufacture a wide range of plastic products from three basic components. The company was originally owned by 23 shareholders; however, five years after formation the capital structure was expanded considerably at which time preferred stock was issued for the first time. At the present time there are over 250 holders of preferred and common stock. The preferred is nonvoting, cumulative, 6% stock. The company had experienced a substantial growth in business over the years. This growth was due to two principal factors: *(a)* the dynamic management, and *(b)* geographical location. The firm served a rapidly expanding area with relatively few regionally situated competitors.

The last audited balance sheet showed the following (summarized):

Balance Sheet, December 31, 1976

Cash	$ 11,000
Other current assets	76,000
Investment in K Company stock (at cost)	30,000
Plant and equipment (net)	310,000
Intangible assets	15,000
Other assets	8,000
	$450,000
Current liabilities	$ 38,000
Long-term loans	60,000
Preferred stock, par value $100*	50,000
Common stock, $15 par value (10,000 shares)*	150,000
Premium on preferred stock	2,000
Retained earnings	25,000
Profits invested in plant	125,000
	$450,000

* Authorized shares—preferred, 2,000, common, 20,000.

The board of directors had not declared a dividend since organization; instead, the profits were used to expand the company. This decision was based on the facts that the original capital was small and there was a decision to limit the number of shareholders. At the present time the common stock is held by slightly fewer than 50 individuals. Each of these individuals also owns preferred shares; their total holdings approximate 46% of the outstanding preferred. The preferred was issued at the time of the expansion of capital.

The board of directors had been planning to declare a dividend during the early part of 1977, payable June 30. However, the cash position as shown by the balance sheet had raised serious doubts as to the advisability of a dividend in 1977. The president had explained that most of the cash was temporarily tied up in inventory and plant.

The company has a chief accountant, but no controller. The board relies on an outside CPA for advice concerning financial management. The CPA was asked to advise about the contemplated dividend declaration. Four of the seven members of the board felt very strongly that some kind of dividend must be declared so that all shareholders will get something.

Required:

You have been asked to analyze the situation and make whatever dividend proposals that appear to be worthy of consideration by the board. Present figures to support your recommendations in a form suitable for consideration by the board in reaching a decision. Provide the basis for your proposals and indicate any preferences that you may have.

EXERCISES

Exercise 16–1

Ace Corporation's books on January 1 showed the following balances (summarized):

Cash	$ 25,000	Current liabilities	$ 20,000
Other current assets	25,000	Long-term liabilities	60,000
Fixed assets (net)	250,000	Capital stock 2,000 shares	200,000
Other assets	50,000	Premium on stock	10,000
		Retained earnings	60,000
	$350,000		$350,000

The board of directors is considering a cash dividend, and you have been requested to provide certain assistance as the independent CPA. The following matters have been referred to you:

1. What is the maximum amount of dividends that can be paid? Explain.
2. What amount of dividends would you recommend based upon the data from the accounts? Explain.
3. What entries would be made assuming a $15,000 cash dividend is declared with the following dates specified: *(a)* declaration date; *(b)* date of record; and *(c)* date of payment.
4. Assuming a balance sheet is prepared between declaration date and payment date, how would the dividend declaration be reported?

Exercise 16–2

White Manufacturing Corporation had outstanding 12,000 shares of capital stock, par value $10 per share. The shares were held by ten stockholders, each having an equal number of shares. The Retained Earnings account showed a balance of $60,000, although the company was short of cash. The company owned 1,000 shares of stock in AB Company that had been purchased for $7,000. The current market value is $15 per share. The board of directors of White Corporation declared a dividend of $2 per share "to be paid with AB stock within 30 days after declaration date and scrip to be issued for the difference. The scrip will be payable at the end of 12 months from issue date and will earn 6% interest per annum."

Required:

1. Give all entries indicated through date of payment of the scrip.
2. What items related to the dividend declaration would be reported on the balance sheet prior to payment of the scrip?

Exercise 16–3

The board of directors of GT Mining Company declared a maximum dividend. There were 60 stockholders, each holding 200 shares of stock having a par value of $5 per share. The laws of the state provide that "dividends may be paid equal to accumulated profits prior to depletion charges." The Retained Earnings account showed a balance of $8,000; accumulated depletion charges amounted to $10,000. The dividend was payable within 60 days of declaration date.

Required:

1. What entries are indicated?
2. What special notification, if any, should be given the shareholders?
3. What items related to the dividend declaration would be reported on the balance sheet between declaration date and payment date?

Exercise 16–4

The records of Mason Corporation showed the following balances on November 1, 19A:

Capital stock authorized, par $10	$500,000
Capital stock unissued	225,000
Contributed capital in excess of par	82,500
Retained earnings	95,000

On November 5, 19A, the board of directors declared a stock dividend (from unissued stock) of one additional share for each five shares outstanding; issue date January 10, 19B. The market value of the stock immediately after the declaration was $18 per share.

Required:

1. Give entries in parallcl columns for the stock dividend assuming (*a*) fair market value is capitalized, (*b*) par value is capitalized, and (*c*) average paid in is capitalized.
2. Explain when each should be used.
3. What should be reported on the balance sheet at December 31, 19A assuming no intervening transactions?

Exercise 16–5

The records of Aiken Corporation showed the following:

Preferred stock, 6% cumulative, nonparticipating, par $20	$200,000
Common stock, nopar value, 50,000 shares issued	240,000
Contributed capital in excess of par, preferred	30,000
Retained earnings	125,000
Investment in stock of X Corporation (500 shares at cost)	10,000

The preferred stock has dividends in arrears for the past two years. The board of directors has just passed the following resolution: "The current year dividend shall be 6% on the preferred and $.90 per share on the common; the dividends in arrears are to be paid by issuing a property dividend using the requisite amount of X Corporation stock." Currently the stock of X Corporation is selling at $60 per share.

Required:

1. Compute the amount of the dividends to be paid to each class of shareholders, including the number of shares of X Corporation stock required and the amount of cash.
2. Give journal entries to record all aspects of the dividend declaration and payment at a later date.

Exercise 16–6

Owens Manufacturing Company's books carried an account entitled "Reserve for Profits Invested in Fixed Assets, $450,000" and another account entitled "Reserve for General Contingencies, $80,000." Capital stock outstanding, par value $20, amounted to $400,000.

The company also had bonds outstanding of $200,000. The following accounts were carried also: Bond Sinking Fund, $90,000; Bond Sinking Fund Reserve, $90,000.

The board of directors voted a 50% stock dividend and directed that the fair market value of the stock, $30 per share, be capitalized using as a basis "the general reserves" to the extent possible.

Required:

Give entries for the following using preferable titles:

a. To originally establish the reserves related to fixed assets and general contingencies.
b. To record the issuance of the stock dividend.
c. To originally establish the bond sinking fund.
d. To originally establish the reserve for bond sinking fund.
e. To record payment of the bonds assuming the bond sinking fund and the reserve each have a $160,000 balance at retirement date.

Exercise 16–7

Using the simplified data below construct (1) a single-step income statement, and (2) a statement of retained earnings. Assume all amounts are material and annual data:

Current items:	
a. Sales revenue	$400,000
b. Cost of goods sold	160,000
c. Expenses	120,000
d. Extraordinary loss	20,000
e. Prior period adjustment—Damages paid (arising from lawsuit instituted in prior year)	4,000
f. Appropriation to reserve for bond sinking fund	10,000
g. Dividends paid	40,000
Balances—beginning of period:	
h. Retained earnings	110,000
i. Reserve for bond sinking fund	60,000

Income taxes—assume a 40% average rate on all items including extraordinary items and prior period adjustments.

Exercise 16–8

Using the simplified data below construct comparative statements of (1) income (single step), and (2) retained earnings for 19A and 19B. Assume all amounts are material, annual data, and an average tax rate of 40% on all items.

Current items:	*19A*	*19B*
a. Sales	$110,000	$120,000
b. Cost of goods sold	45,000	50,000
c. Expenses	25,000	29,000
d. Extraordinary gain	3,000	
e. Extraordinary loss		6,000
f. Dividends paid	12,000	10,000
g. Appropriation for profits invested in fixed assets	40,000	
h. Prior period adjustment—Prior to 19A the corporation was sued for $10,000 damages; the suit was settled in 19A requiring the payment of $4,000 damages; this caused a reduction in income taxes.		
i. Prior period adjustment—Correction of accounting error made in prior period (no tax effect)		2,000 (credit)
Beginning balances:		
Unappropriated retained earnings	$130,000	?
Appropriation for profits invested in fixed assets	-0-	?

Exercise 16–9

AB Company had experienced a net loss for a number of years. Recently a new president was hired. The board of directors agreed to a quasi-reorganization and to restate certain items in the accounts as outlined by the new president, subject to stockholder approval. Prior to the restatement the balance sheet reported the following (summarized at July 1, 19A):

Cash and receivables	$ 21,000	Current liabilities	$ 50,000
Inventories	210,000	Fixed liabilities	85,000
Fixed assets (net)	560,000	Capital stock (8,000 shares)	800,000
Other assets	44,000	Premium on stock	40,000
		Retained earnings	(150,000)
		Reserve for contingencies	10,000
	$835,000		$835,000

The stockholders approved the quasi-reorganization which carried the following provisions:

a. The inventories to be reduced to a lower-of-cost-or-market value of $140,000.
b. Receivables of $3,000 to be written off as worthless.
c. The fixed assets to be reduced to a net carrying value of $400,000.

d. The capital structure to be adjusted so that the deficit will be eliminated and the capital reduced by the net adjustment made to assets.

Required:

1. Give entries to record the quasi-reorganization as approved by the stockholders.
2. Prepare a balance sheet after the quasi-reorganization.

PROBLEMS

Problem 16–1

The balance sheet for Ward Manufacturing Company is shown below in summary:

Cash	$ 28,000	Current liabilities	$ 26,000
Receivables	36,000	Bonds payable	50,000
Inventory	110,000	Preferred stock	20,000
Investments–4,000 shares of Taylor stock at cost	6,000	Common stock (5,000 shares, nopar	100,000
Fixed assets (net)	80,000	Premium on preferred	5,000
Other assets	10,000	Retained earnings	69,000
	$270,000		$270,000

The preferred stock is 6%, $100 par value and cumulative. Dividends are three years in arrears (excluding the current year).

The investment in stock of Taylor Company has been held for a number of years; that stock is now selling for $5 per share.

On October 1, 19A the board of directors of Ward declared dividends as follows:

a. Preferred stock, all dividends in arrears plus current year dividend; payment to be made by transferring the requisite number of shares of Taylor stock at $5 per share.

b. Common stock, $4 per share for the current year, payment to be made by transferring the remainder of the Taylor stock and issuing a scrip dividend for the balance. The scrip will earn 8% annual interest and will be paid at the end of six months from date of declaration.

Required:

1. Compute the amount of dividends payable to each class of shareholder, indicate the amount of the scrip dividend.
2. Give entries to record the transfer of the Taylor stock and the issuance of the scrip dividend (assume declaration and payment date are the same). Make separate entries for the common and preferred stock.
3. Give the adjusting entry at December 31, 19A, for the interest on the scrip dividend.
4. Give the entry to record payment of the scrip dividend and interest on March 31, 19B.
5. Prepare the stockholders' equity section of the balance sheet as of December 31, 19A. Assume reported net income of $20,000 for 19A (including the interest on the scrip dividend).

Problem 16–2

Bay Corporation's board of directors declared a stock dividend whereby each holder of common stock is to receive one share of common for each five shares held and a cash dividend on the preferred stock for the one year in arrears and for the current year. The average originally paid in per share of common will be capitalized for the stock dividend. At this date the records of the corporation showed:

Preferred stock, 6%, $10 par value, authorized 20,000 shares, 10,000 outstanding	$100,000
Common stock, nopar, stated value $5, authorized 50,000, issued 30,000 shares	150,000
Contributed capital—excess over stated value, preferred	20,000
Contributed capital—excess over stated value, common	30,000
Retained earnings	160,000

Upon issuance of the stock dividend, stock warrants were distributed for 1,000 shares of stock; subsequently warrants for 900 of the shares were exercised. The remaining warrants are outstanding to date.

Required:

1. Give entries to record the issuance of the stock dividend and payment of the cash dividend.
2. Prepare the stockholders' equity section of the balance sheet after giving effect to the entries in (1) above.

Problem 16–3

The accounts for Scott Corporation showed the following balances:

Stockholders' Equity

Preferred stock, 6%, par value $25, 10,000 shares authorized, 8,000 shares outstanding	$200,000
Common stock, nopar value, assigned value $10, authorized 20,000 shares, issued 12,000 shares	120,000
Contributed capital in excess of par, preferred	15,000
Contributed capital in excess of assigned value, common	30,000
Retained earnings	175,000

During the subsequent year the following sequential transactions were recorded relating to the capital accounts:

a. A stock dividend was issued whereby each holder of ten preferred shares received one share of common stock, and each holder of six shares of common stock received one share of common. The board directed that the "average originally paid in per share of common" be capitalized. In issuing the stock dividend, warrants were issued for 100 shares.

b. All of the warrants were redeemed except those for ten shares which remained outstanding.

c. A 6% cash dividend on the preferred shares and $.50 per share on the common shares were declared and paid.

d. Reported net income was $60,000.

Required:

1. Prepare journal entries for the above transactions.
2. Prepare the stockholders' equity section of the balance sheet.

Problem 16–4

The records for Jones Corporation showed the following balances at the end of 19A:

Current assets	$ 165,000	Current liabilities	$ 60,000
Fixed assets	960,000	Long-term liabilities	100,000
Other assets	300,000	Preferred stock	300,000
Investment in X Corporation stock (5,000 shares at cost)	5,000	Common stock, 100,000 shares	800,000
		Premium on preferred	12,000
		Retained earnings	158,000
	$1,430,000		$1,430,000

To date 3,000 shares of preferred stock (6%, $100 par value, cumulative) have been issued. Authorized shares were: common, 200,000; and preferred, 3,000. No dividends were declared for the preceding year. During the subsequent two years the following transactions affected stockholders' equity:

19B:

a. Declared and immediately issued one share of X Corporation stock to each shareholder of preferred stock as a property dividend. The current market value of $2 per share is to be recognized in the dividend. In addition, a cash dividend was paid to complete payment of the dividends in arrears.

b. Declared and immediately issued scrip dividends amounting to 6% on the preferred and $.80 per share on the common stock. Interest on the scrip is 7% per year.

c. Reported net income $150,000 including any effects of the above transactions.

19C:

d. Paid the scrip dividends including 7% per annum interest for 12 months.

e. Declared and issued a stock dividend, payable in common stock to holders of both preferred and common stock. The preferred holders to receive "value" equivalent to 6%, and the common holders to receive one share for each five shares held. The value and the amount capitalized per share shall be the fair market value. The current price per share on the common stock is $1.50.

Issued the stock dividend except for 500 shares for which stock warrants were issued; of these, 100 warrants related to the preferred.

f. Warrants for 300 shares were honored. The remaining warrants are outstanding.

g. Reported net income $87,000 including any effects of the above transactions.

Required:

1. Prepare journal entries for each of the foregoing transactions (round amounts to even dollars).
2. Prepare the stockholders' equity section of the balance sheet after giving recognition to the foregoing transactions.

Problem 16–5

Stone Manufacturing Company was organized with an authorization for 50,000 shares of $10 par-value stock. During the first five years of operations the following transactions affected stockholders' equity. Assume they occurred in the order given.

19A:

a. Received subscriptions for 20,000 shares of stock at $15 per share; 50% was collected from each subscriber as a down payment; the stock is not issued until fully paid.
b. Balance was collected on all shares except 1,500.
c. Reported net income was $5,000.

19B:

d. The balance was collected on 1,400 of the subscribed shares. Subscriptions for the other 100 shares were defaulted. The subscriber was refunded the amount paid in less 20% of the purchase price per agreement. Issued the 1,400 shares.
e. Reported net income was $7,000.

19C:

f. Declared and paid cash dividend amounting to $.50 per share on the shares outstanding.
g. Reported net income was $18,000.

19D:

h. Sold 5,000 shares of stock at $18; collected cash and issued stock.
i. Reported net income, $20,000.

19E:

j. Declared a 10% stock dividend on the shares outstanding. The board of directors voted that the "average paid in to date per share" be capitalized. Immediately issued the stock dividend and stock warrants for 200 of the shares.
k. Stock warrants for 190 shares received and stock issued; the balance lapsed.
l. Declared a $.50 per share dividend—one half payable in cash, balance in scrip payable in six months with interest at 7% per annum.
m. Accrued two months' interest on the scrip dividends.
n. Reported net income $18,000 (includes the interest on the scrip).

Required:

1. Prepare entries for the foregoing transactions.
2. Prepare the stockholders' equity section of the balance sheet after giving effect to the foregoing entries.

Problem 16–6

The following annual data were taken from the records of Barstow Corporation at the end of the current year (assume all amounts material; the items in parentheses are credit balances):

Current items:

a. Sales	$(400,000)
b. Cost of goods sold	230,000
c. Expenses	85,000
d. Extraordinary loss	20,000
e. An expense incorrectly charged to a nondepreciable asset in a prior year	3,000
f. Stock dividend issued	40,000
g. Cash dividend paid	9,000
h. Prior period adjustment—income tax renegotiation (refund of prior year taxes)	(12,000)
i. Prior period adjustment—damages paid from lawsuit (pending for past three years)	10,000
j. Current appropriation to reserve for bond sinking fund	10,000
k. Current appropriation to reserve for plant expansion	40,000

Income taxes:

Assume an average tax rate of 40% on all items including extraordinary items and prior period adjustments.

Beginning balances:

l. Unappropriated retained earnings	(80,000)
m. Reserve for bond sinking fund	(50,000)
n. Reserve for plant expansion	(60,000)

Required:

1. Prepare a single-step income statement.
2. Prepare a statement of retained earnings.

Problem 16–7

Cooper Corporation records provided the following annual data for the years 19A and 19B. (Assume all amounts to be material):

Current items:

	19A	*19B*
a. Sales	$240,000	$260,000
b. Cost of goods sold	134,000	143,000
c. Expenses	71,000	77,000
d. Extraordinary loss	7,000	2,000
e. Cash dividend paid	20,000	
f. Stock dividend issued		30,000
g. Appropriation to reserve for bond sinking fund	10,000	10,000
h. Increase in bond sinking fund	10,000	10,000
i. Prior period adjustment—error correction (debit)	6,000	
j. Income taxes—assume an average rate of 46% on all items including extraordinary items and prior period adjustments.		

Beginning balances:

k. Reserve for bond sinking fund	70,000	?
l. Unappropriated retained earnings	160,000	?
m. Reserve for plant expansion	100,000	?
n. Bond sinking fund	70,000	
o. Bonds payable	100,000	

Required:

1. Prepare a single-step comparative income statement for the years 19A and 19B.

2. Prepare comparative statements of retained earnings, in good form.

Problem 16–8

King Corporation records provided the following unclassified data at year-end:

a. Appropriation during the year of retained earnings for reserve for bond sinking fund, $15,000; the prior balance was $75,000.
b. Balance in Retained Earnings, Unappropriated, account per books at end of prior year, $90,000.
c. Dividends declared on preferred stock December 31 of the year just ended, payable the following January 15 amounting to $10,000.
d. Declared and issued a small stock dividend on common stock July 1 of year just ended; par, $20,000, and fair market value, $30,000.
e. Preferred stock sold during year just ended 200 shares, par, $100, and market, $130.
f. Income statement data for current year: sales, $340,000; cost of goods sold, $160,000; expenses, $80,000.
g. Additional assessment during year just ended by Internal Revenue Service for prior years' income taxes, $4,000 (a prior period adjustment).
h. Damages paid on prior year lawsuit, $8,000 (a prior period adjustment).
i. Income taxes—assume an average rate of 45% on all items including extraordinary items and the damages paid (item *h*).

Required:

1. Prepare a single-step income statement.
2. Prepare a statement of retained earnings.

Problem 16–9

Jackson Corporation is undergoing an audit. The books show an account entitled Surplus which is reproduced below covering a five-year period, January 1, 1972, to December 31, 1976.

Credits

1972–75	Net income carried to surplus	$ 800,000
1972	By debit to goodwill—authorized by board	50,000
12/31/73	Premium on capital stock sold	6,000
1/1/74	Correction of prior accounting error	2,000
1/1/74	Donation to company—fixed asset	5,000
12/31/74	Refund of prior years' income taxes	9,000
7/1/75	Reduction in capital stock from par value $100 to par value $50 with no change in the number of shares outstanding (10,000); approved by shareholders	500,000
12/31/76	Net income, 1976	70,000
		$1,442,000

Debits

1972–76	Cash dividends paid	$ 600,000
1/1/72	To reserve for bond sinking fund (annually)	20,000
12/31/74	Reserve for bond sinking fund	20,000
12/31/75	Reserve for bond sinking fund	20,000
9/1/76	Fifty percent stock dividend	250,000
		$ 910,000

Assume the net income amounts are correct.

Required:

1. The above account is to be closed and replaced with appropriate accounts. Complete a worksheet analysis of the above account to reflect the correct account balances and the corrections needed. It is suggested that the worksheet carry the following columns: *(a)* surplus account per books, *(b)* corrected net income, 1976, *(c)* unappropriated retained earnings, and *(d)* columns for any other specific accounts needed.
2. Give the appropriate entry or entries to close this account and to set up appropriate accounts in its place.

Problem 16–10

During the last five years, Hanson Corporation has experienced severe losses. A new president has been tentatively employed who is confident the company can be saved from going into bankruptcy (and dissolution). Working with an independent CPA, the new president has proposed a quasi-reorganization with the condition that it must be approved by the stockholders before the position is accepted. The board approved the proposal and submitted it to a vote of the stockholders.

Prior to reorganization, the balance sheet (summarized) reflected the following:

Cash	$ 20,000	Current liabilities	$150,000
Accounts receivable	94,000	Long-term liabilities	240,000
Allowance for doubtful accounts	(4,000)	Common stock, par $50	500,000
Inventory	150,000	Preferred stock, par $100	100,000
Fixed assets	800,000	Premium on preferred stock	30,000
Accumulated depreciation	(300,000)	Retained earnings	(220,000)
Deferred charges	40,000		
	$800,000		$800,000

The reorganization proposal, as approved by the stockholders, provided the following:

a. To adequately provide for probable losses on accounts receivable, increase the allowance by $6,000.
b. Write down the inventory to $100,000 because of obsolete and damaged goods.
c. Reduce the book value of the fixed assets to $400,000 by increasing accumulated depreciation.
d. By agreement of the creditors, reduce all liabilities by 5%.
e. Reduce the par value of the preferred shares to $60.
f. Change the common stock to nopar and reduce the balance to leave a zero balance in retained earnings.
g. Close all capital balances, other than the preferred and common stock accounts.

Required:

1. Give a separate entry for each of the above changes.
2. Prepare a balance sheet immediately after the quasi-reorganization.

Problem 16–11

Weston Corporation, a medium-sized manufacturer, has experienced losses for the past five years. Although operations for the year ended resulted in a loss, several important changes resulted in a profitable fourth quarter; and as a result, future operations of the company are expected to be profitable.

The treasurer suggested a quasi-reorganization to *(a)* eliminate the accumulated deficit of $423,620, *(b)* write up the $493,100 cost of operating land and buildings to their fair value, and *(c)* set up an asset of $203,337 representing the estimated future tax benefit of the losses accumulated to date.

Required:

1. What are the characteristics of a quasi-reorganization? That is, of what does it consist?
2. List the conditions under which a quasi-reorganization generally would be justified.
3. Discuss the propriety of the treasurer's proposals to:
   a. Eliminate the deficit of $423,620.
   b. Write up the value of the operating land and buildings of $493,100 to their fair value.
   c. Set up an asset of $203,337 representing the future tax benefit of the losses accumulated to date.

(AICPA adapted)

Chapter 17

Corporations—Contraction and Expansion of Corporate Capital after Formation; and Earnings per Share

Once the corporate charter is granted and the bylaws are approved, provisions governing corporate capital are established; however, this does not mean that such provisions may not be changed. Aside from the sale of unissued shares already authorized, a corporation may obtain authorization for additional classes of stock, expansion of the number of shares of currently authorized stock, or change the par or stated values. Or it may contract and expand corporate capital by purchasing and selling its own shares in the marketplace. Callable and redeemable shares may be acquired and convertible shares exchanged. The corporation may undergo a corporate reorganization involving a significant change in the entire capital structure; or it may combine with other entities. These changes are controlled in various manners: by state laws, by charter and bylaw provisions, or by the shareholders themselves. Obviously, upon approval of the shareholders the bylaws may be changed and even a new or amended charter obtained. In the long-term the primary source of expansion of stockholders' equity is net income not distributed as cash or property dividends.

Retained earnings frequently is capitalized by means of stock dividends (see Chapter 16) or through certain other forms of capital changes.

This chapter focuses on changes after initial formation, particularly treasury stock, stock conversion, expansion of legal and contributed capital, and stock rights. Earnings per share of common stock also is discussed.

In accounting and reporting changes in corporate capital, other than as a result of net income and prior period adjustments, five basic principles have general applicability, viz:

1. Sources of capital are separately recorded and reported.
2. Information must be accumulated and reported to meet the requirements of the accounting profession and the prevailing laws.
3. A corporation cannot recognize, as income or as increases in retained earnings, gains that result from capital transactions between itself and its owners; accounting recognition of increases resulting from transactions relating to the corporation's own stock are recorded as changes in contributed capital rather than as gains.
4. Increases in authorized shares, authorized legal capital, changes in par or stated values, or exchanges of its own equity shares (such as its own preferred shares for its own common shares) do not create income, losses, or retained earnings.
5. Certain payments (of assets) by a corporation for its own shares above the contributed capital per share may be considered to be a form of cash (or property) dividends which would be charged to retained earnings.

TREASURY STOCK

Expansion and contraction in contributed capital after formation frequently arise as a result of treasury stock transactions. The statutes of most states permit a corporation to purchase its own stock subject to certain limitations. *Treasury stock* is a corporation's own stock (preferred or common) that *(a)* has been issued; *(b)* is subsequently reacquired by the issuing corporation; and *(c)* after acquisition has not been sold or formally retired. Treasury shares may be subsequently sold and reclassified as outstanding shares. The courts generally have held that a discount liability does not apply to treasury stock resold (see Chapter 15), assuming the second purchaser did not have knowledge of any prior discount liability. The purchase of a corporation's own stock serves to contract both assets and corporate capital, whereas a sale of treasury stock serves to expand both assets and corporate capital. Treasury shares may be obtained by purchase, by settlement of an obligation, or through donation. Obviously, treasury stock does not carry voting, dividend, or liquidation privileges. Although the acquisition of treasury stock involves the disbursement of assets, or the cancellation of an obligation, it is not an asset since a corporation cannot own itself. Also treasury stock is generally viewed as similar to unissued stock, which by no stretch of the imagination can be viewed as an asset; it must be sold before any assets arise.

In contrast to treasury stock, a corporation may reacquire its own shares because they were issued as either callable or redeemable shares (see Chapter 15). Callable or redeemable shares received are not classified as treasury stock since their acquisition usually entails their immediate cancellation and they are not available for subsequent resale.

Treasury stock may be acquired for the following reasons: (1) the corporation has ready cash and the stock is considered to be unrealistically underpriced; (2) to use for employee stock options, bonus plans, and direct sale to employees; (3) to use in exchange for other securities or assets; (4) to pay a stock dividend; (5) to settle debts; (6) to increase earnings per share; (7) to buy out one or more particular stockholders; and (8) to support the market price of the stock.

RECORDING AND REPORTING TREASURY STOCK TRANSACTIONS

There are several prevailing views as to the approach that should be used in accounting for treasury stock. These views may be grouped broadly under two methods, viz:

1. Cost method (one-transaction concept).
2. Par-value method (dual-transaction concept).

Both of these methods are generally accepted; however, they derive different results for certain individual items in the stockholders' equity section of the balance sheet. Total stockholders' equity is the same under both methods.

Cost Method

This method sometimes is referred to as the one-transaction concept because the purchase and subsequent sale of treasury stock is viewed as one transaction rather than two. At acquisition, the *cost* of the treasury stock is debited to a "holding" account called Treasury Stock. Under this concept the cost is "held" until subsequent sale at which time the effect of the various components of stockholders' equity can be determined and recorded. Thus, at date of subsequent sale, any difference between cost and resale price is accounted for in the appropriate manner.

Separate treasury stock accounts should be established for each class of stock. Where treasury shares have been acquired at different costs, specific shares should be identified; otherwise a *Fifo* or average cost per share must be used to credit the Treasury Stock account at resale date.

Under the cost method the balance in the Treasury Stock account at the end of the accounting period is viewed as an *unallocated reduction* of total stockholders' equity (illustrated subsequently).

The following entries illustrate the accounting for treasury stock assuming the *cost method* is used:

Recording Treasury Stock—Cost Method

1. To record the initial sale and issuance of 10,000 shares of capital stock, par $25, at $26 per share:

Cash	260,000	
Contributed capital in excess of par		10,000
Capital stock (10,000 shares, par $25)		250,000

2. To record a purchase of 2,000 shares of treasury stock at cost ($28):

Treasury stock (by type of stock)	56,000	
Cash		56,000

3*a*. To record a sale of 500 of the shares of treasury stock at $28 per share (same as the purchase price):

Cash	14,000	
Treasury stock (500 shares @ $28)		14,000

b. Now assume instead a sale of the 500 shares at $30 per share (i.e., $2 per share above the purchase price):

Cash (500 shares @ $30)	15,000	
Contributed capital, from sale of treasury stock (500 shares @ $2)		1,000
Treasury stock (500 shares @ $28)		14,000

4. To record a sale of another 500 shares at $22 per share (i.e., $6 per share below the purchase price; also below par):

Cash	11,000	
Contributed capital, from sale of treasury stock	1,000	
Retained earnings	2,000	
Treasury stock (500 shares @ $28)		14,000

Under the cost method when treasury stock is sold at a price in excess of its cost, the "gain" should be recorded as contributed capital, as in transaction 3*b* above, and not as a credit to Income or Retained Earnings.

Alternatively, when treasury stock is sold at less than cost, the "loss" should be charged to contributed capital "to the extent that previous net 'gains' from the sales or retirements of the same class of stock are included therein, otherwise to retained earnings."[1] For example, in transaction 4 above, had there been no balance in the account, Contributed Capital from Sale of Treasury Stock, the entire $3,000 would have been debited to Retained Earnings; alternatively had the balance in the contributed account been in excess of $3,000, there would have been no charge to Retained Earnings. The debit to Retained Earnings may be viewed as a "dividend" to the stockholder from whom the shares were purchased, or, alternatively, as the capitalization of a portion of retained earnings.[2]

When the cost method is used, treasury stock is reported as an *unallocated reduction* of stockholders' equity reported as follows (assuming transaction 3*a* and a beginning balance in retained earnings of $40,000):

---

[1] AICPA, "Status of Accounting Research Bulletins," *APB Opinion No. 6* (New York, 1965), par. 12.

[2] A minor variation of the above method of recording the "loss" charges contributed capital with a pro rata amount per share of any premium that was recorded when that class of stock was originally sold; any remaining amount is charged to Retained Earnings. For example, transaction 4 illustrated above would be recorded as follows:

Cash	11,000	
Contributed capital in excess of par ($1 per share)	500	
Retained earnings	2,500	
Treasury stock		14,000

Stockholders' Equity
(cost method for treasury stock)

Contributed capital:	
Capital stock, par $25, authorized 50,000 shares, issued 10,000 shares of which 1,000 are held as treasury stock	$250,000
Contributed capital in excess of par	10,000
Total Contributed Capital	260,000
Retained earnings	38,000
Total Contributed Capital and Retained Earnings	298,000
Less: Treasury stock, 1,000 shares at cost	28,000
Total Stockholders' Equity	$270,000

The cost method is frequently used because of its simplicity. It may avoid the necessity of developing specific data concerning the original premiums, discounts, and so on, relating to the specific stock involved. It can be defended largely on practical grounds; theoretical justification is difficult even if no "gain" or "loss" is involved. The primary objection from the point of view of theory is that the *sources* of the various components of capital are not maintained. Under this procedure the actual capital contributed (after the treasury stock transactions are recorded) for the outstanding stock is not specifically identified in the accounts.

Par-Value Method

This method is sometimes referred to as the dual-transaction concept because it views the purchase and sale of treasury stock as completely independent and unrelated. The objectives of the par-value method are:

1. At date of purchase of treasury stock—to make a final accounting with the retiring stockholder and to adjust the capital accounts accordingly.
2. At date of sale of treasury stock—to record it in the same way as the sale and issuance of unissued stock.

To accomplish these purposes the Treasury Stock account is carried at the par or stated value per share; hence, the designation par-value method.

The final accounting with the retiring stockholder (at date of purchase of the treasury shares) involves comparing the amount withdrawn (price paid for the treasury shares) with the amount originally invested by the stockholder (computed on an average basis for all shares issued). If the amount withdrawn exceeds the original investment, the excess is charged to Retained Earnings as a form of dividend to the retiring stockholder. If the original investment exceeds the amount withdrawn, the difference is credited to an appropriately designated contributed capital account.

When the treasury stock is sold, the entire proceeds are viewed as an investment by the new stockholder. The Treasury Stock account is credited for par, and any excess over par or stated value is credited to Contributed Capital in Excess of Par (or Stated Value) in the same manner as for unissued shares. If, as rarely occurs, the treasury stock is sold for less than par (or stated value) the difference between the selling price and par should be debited to Retained Earnings since no discount liability is associated with treasury stock sold at less than par.

The preceding example is used to illustrate the accounting for treasury stock assuming the *par-value method* is used:

Recording Treasury Stock—Par-Value Method

1. To record the initial sale and issuance of 10,000 shares of capital stock, par $25, at $26 per share:

Cash	260,000	
Capital stock (10,000 shares, par $25)		250,000
Contributed capital in excess of par		10,000

2. To record a purchase of 2,000 shares of treasury stock at $28 per share:

Treasury stock (2,000 shares at par)	50,000	
Contributed capital in excess of par	2,000	
Retained earnings	4,000	
Cash		56,000

3*a*. To record a sale of 500 shares of treasury stock at $28 per share (same as the purchase price; $3 above par):

Cash	14,000	
Treasury stock (500 shares at par)		12,500
Contributed capital in excess of par, from treasury stock transactions*		1,500

* The separate designation "from treasury stock transactions" often is not used.

b. Now assume instead a sale of 500 shares of treasury stock at $30 per share ($5 per share above par):

Cash (500 shares @ $30)	15,000	
Treasury stock (500 shares at par)		12,500
Contributed capital in excess of par, from treasury stock transactions*		2,500

* The separate designation "from treasury stock transactions" often is not used.

4. To record a sale of another 500 shares at $22 per share ($3 per share below par):

Cash (500 shares @ $22)	11,000	
Retained earnings ($25 − $22) × 500 shares	1,500*	
Treasury stock (500 shares at par, $25)		12,500

* Discount on stock is not debited since a discount liability is not created.

When the par-value method is used, treasury stock is reported as a deduction, at its par or stated value, from the capital stock to which it relates. Stockholders' equity, using the above illustrative data would be reported as follows:

Stockholders' Equity (par-value method for treasury stock)	
Contributed capital:	
Capital stock, par $25, authorized 50,000 shares, issued 10,000 shares	$250,000
Less: Treasury stock, 1,000 shares at par	25,000
Total Capital Stock Outstanding, 9,000 Shares	225,000
Contributed capital in excess of par	10,500
Total Contributed Capital	235,500
Retained earnings	34,500
Total Stockholders' Equity	$270,000

Observe that total stockholders' equity reported under the cost method and par-value method is the same; the basic difference between the two methods is reflected in the capital stock and retained earnings subclassifications.

The dual-transaction concept, (i.e., the par-value method) theoretically is sound in that the *sources* of capital are maintained intact. An exact record of capital received on all outstanding stock is maintained. The principal disadvantage is the problem of identifying the various components of contributed capital with the specific shares involved.

In overall perspective the par-value method is considered to be theoretically preferable, and it is consistent with the concept of accounting and reporting by source. However, because of its simplicity the cost method is widely used.

ACCOUNTING FOR NOPAR TREASURY STOCK

Nopar stock having a *stated* or *assigned* value per share when purchased, is accounted for in exactly the same manner as illustrated above for par-value treasury stock under the two methods. The stated or assigned value per share is treated as if it were par value in all of the entries. However, if *true* nopar stock is purchased as treasury stock (no stated or assigned value per share), the transactions would be recorded somewhat differently as illustrated below.

If the cost method (i.e., the one-transaction concept) is used, the Treasury Stock account reflects the cost per share in the same manner as illustrated above for par-value stock. If the dual-transaction concept is used the Treasury Stock account reflects the average original issue price per share (i.e., the average amount per share credited to the Capital Stock account). To illustrate the accounting entries for true nopar stock, we will adapt the preceding example by assuming that the Nopar Capital Stock account was credited for the issue price originally.

Recording Treasury Stock – True Nopar Stock

	Cost Method		Par-Value Method	
1. To record sale and issuance of 10,000 shares of nopar capital stock at $26 per share:				
Cash	260,000		260,000	
Capital stock, nopar (10,000 shares @ $26)		260,000		260,000
2. To record purchase of 2,000 shares of treasury stock at $28 per share:				
Treasury stock (2,000 shares @ $28)	56,000			
Treasury stock (2,000 shares @ $26)			52,000	
Retained earnings			4,000	
Cash		56,000		56,000
3. To record the sale of 500 shares of treasury stock at $30 per share:				
Cash	15,000		15,000	
Treasury stock (500 shares @ $28)		14,000		
Treasury stock (500 shares @ $26)				13,000
Contributed capital, from treasury stock transactions		1,000		2,000
4. To record sale of 500 shares of treasury stock at $22 per share:				
Cash	11,000		11,000	
Contributed capital, from treasury stock transactions	1,000		2,000	
Retained earnings	2,000			
Treasury stock		14,000		13,000

TREASURY STOCK RECEIVED THROUGH DONATIONS

Shareholders may donate shares of stock back to the corporation. Such donations may *(a)* be to raise needed working capital through resale of donated stock, *(b)* represent the return of the stock in recognition of an overvaluation of assets originally given in exchange for the stock. Stock received by donation is classified as treasury stock. Neither total assets nor *total* equity is changed by the donation of treasury stock. Three methods have been employed in recording the receipt of donated treasury stock, viz:

1. When the donated stock is received, charge the Treasury Stock account with the fair market value of the stock and credit Contributed Capital, Donated Treasury Stock for the same amount. Upon subsequent sale any "gains" or "losses" would be accounted for as illustrated above for the cost method.
2. When the donated stock is received, charge the Treasury Stock ac-

count with the par, stated or, in the case of true nopar stock, average paid in and credit an appropriately designated donated capital account. Subsequent sale would be recorded as illustrated above for the par-value method.

3. When the donated stock is received, a memorandum entry is made on the basis that there was no cost. Subsequent sales would be credited to contributed capital for the full sales price.[3]

The first approach is theoretically preferable and is consistent with the thrust of *APB Opinion No. 29,* "Accounting for Nonmonetary Transactions" (however, the *Opinion* does not specifically cover this transaction). When the cost method is used this approach should be applied.

The second approach is internally consistent and is generally used with the par-value method. The third approach has very little merit; and although used in earlier years, it appears to be seldom used at the present time.[4]

RETIREMENT OF TREASURY STOCK

Subject to stockholder approval (in most jurisdictions) and in conformance with all legal requirements, including the protection of creditors, a corporation may decide to formally retire treasury shares and have them revert to unissued status. When treasury stock is retired in this manner, all capital account balances related to the treasury shares are closed out on a proportional basis and the net effect is charged to contributed capital (if a credit) or to retained earnings (if a debit).

To illustrate, we will continue the preceding example assuming par value stock. Recall that the capital balances, after the illustrative entries reflected the following (refer to the balance sheet examples):

	Cost Method	*Par-Value Method*
Capital stock, par $25, 10,000 shares issued ...	$250,000	$250,000
Contributed capital in excess of par	10,000	10,500
Treasury stock (1,000 shares):		
At cost	(28,000)	
At par value		(25,000)
Retained earnings, unappropriated..............	38,000	34,500
Total Stockholders' Equity.................	$270,000	$270,000

[3] In some cases donated stock may involve a "treasury stock subterfuge." This situation involves a collusive agreement to issue an excess number of shares for properties (when valued at fair market value) followed by a donation back to the corporation of a part of such shares. In some jurisdictions the donated shares have then been sold at a discount with no assumed discount liability since such liability normally attaches only to the *first* issuance. Recent court decisions have tended to hold this to be illegal; and because par values tend to be set very low, it rarely occurs today.

[4] At the present time the FASB has the topic of corporate capital on its agenda. It is anticipated that this and related issues will be definitively treated and the array of alternatives narrowed.

The entry to record retirement of the 1,000 shares of treasury stock would be:

	Cost Method		Par-Value Method	
Capital stock (1,000 shares × $25 par)	25,000		25,000	
Contributed capital in excess of par:				
($10,000 ÷ 10,000 shares) × 1,000 shares..........	1,000			
($10,500 ÷ 10,000 shares) × 1,000 shares..........			1,050	
Retained earnings	2,000			
Treasury stock:				
At cost		28,000		
At par..........				25,000
Contributed capital, from retirement of treasury shares				1,050

Had there been a balance in Contributed Capital from Treasury Stock Transactions it would have also been closed out in the above entry.

RESTRICTION OF RETAINED EARNINGS FOR TREASURY STOCK

In Chapter 15 legal capital was discussed and the point was made that the laws frequently attempt to protect creditor interests through the maintenance of legal capital requirements and restriction of dividends. When treasury stock is purchased, assets of the corporation are disbursed to the owners of the shares purchased. Should a corporation have a completely free hand in this matter, it is not difficult to perceive how creditor interests (or the interests of another class of shareholders) may be jeopardized through the distribution of corporate assets via treasury stock purchases, even though legal capital may be "reported intact." To prevent this situation many states have laws limiting the amount of treasury stock that may be held at any one time to some amount such as the total retained earnings. This provision has the effect of *(a)* requiring restriction of retained earnings equivalent to the cost of treasury stock, and *(b)* reducing the amount of retained earnings that may be used for dividends until the treasury shares are resold.[5] To illustrate, assume a corporation reports the following stockholders' equity:

Capital stock, par $25, 10,000 shares issued..............	$250,000
Contributed capital in excess of par..........................	10,000
Retained earnings, unappropriated	38,000

[5] In most states the restriction applies to retained earnings; on the other hand, some states permit the purchase of treasury stock equivalent in cost to other capital items such as premium. Throughout these discussions we will assume that the cost of treasury stock held cannot exceed the balance of retained earnings.

Assuming a statutory limitation that the cost of treasury stock held cannot exceed the balance of retained earnings, the corporation could purchase treasury stock costing $38,000; if it did, no dividends could be declared. Should the corporation purchase treasury stock with a cost of $30,000, dividends up to $8,000 could be declared. The restriction on retained earnings would be removed *(a)* by sale of the treasury shares, or *(b)* by their formal retirement. The restriction on retained earnings is reported either as a line item on the balance sheet or as a footnote as explained and illustrated in Chapter 16.

RETIREMENT OF CALLABLE STOCK

Corporations frequently issue callable preferred stock that provides that the corporation, at its option after a certain date, can call in the shares at a specified price for retirement. The call price is at or above the par value and is usually above the original issuance price.[6] Thus, callable shares are not classified as treasury stock.

When callable stock is acquired and immediately retired, all capital balances relating to the specific shares are removed from the accounts, any "loss" is charged to Retained Earnings as a form of dividends and any "gain" is recorded in a contributed capital account appropriately designated. If the stock is cumulative preferred and there are dividends in arrears, such dividends are paid and charged to Retained Earnings in the normal manner. To illustrate several typical situations, assume a corporation had 2,500 shares of callable preferred stock (par value $100) outstanding, $250,000; contributed capital in excess of par, preferred stock, $10,000; contributed capital from other sources, $5,000; and retained earnings, $45,000. Now assume the corporation called and retired 1,000 shares of the preferred stock. Three different assumptions as to the call and retirement are illustrated below:

Assumption 1: The preferred stock is callable at the original issue price of $104 per share.

Preferred stock (1,000 shares at par)	100,000	
Contributed capital in excess of par ($4 per share)	4,000	
Cash		104,000

Assumption 2: The preferred stock is callable at $110 per share—$6 per share above the original issue price of $104.

Preferred stock (1,000 shares at par)	100,000	
Contributed capital in excess of par ($4 per share)	4,000	
Retained earnings	6,000	
Cash		110,000

Assumption 3: The preferred stock is 5% cumulative; three years'

[6] *APB Opinion No. 10* recommends that "the liquidation preference of the stock be disclosed in the equity section of the balance sheet in the aggregate, either parenthetically or 'in short' rather than on a per share basis or by disclosure in notes." Amounts of arrearages on cumulative preferred dividends also should be disclosed.

dividends are in arrears. The stock is callable at 101 plus the dividends in arrears.

Retained earnings ($100,000 × 5% × 3 years)	15,000	
Cash		15,000

Note: The remaining preferred shares are not considered in this entry; cumulative dividends on them also would be paid and recorded at this time.

Preferred stock (1,000 shares at par)	100,000	
Contributed capital in excess of par ($4 per share)	4,000	
Contributed capital from retirement of preferred stock		3,000
Cash		101,000

If true nopar stock is retired, the average price per share originally credited to the stock account is removed and the "loss" or "gain" is accounted for as illustrated above. If nopar stock with a stated or assigned value is retired, the procedures illustrated above for par-value stock are appropriate.

CONVERTIBLE STOCK

Corporations frequently issue *convertible* stock which give the shareholder an option, within a specified time period, to exchange convertible shares currently held for other classes of capital stock (or bonds) at a specified rate. The convertible shares then are usually retired when received by the corporation. Conversion privileges require the issuing corporation to set aside a sufficient number of shares to fulfill the conversion rights until they are exercised or expire.

At date of conversion, all account balances related to the convertible shares are removed and the new shares issued are recorded at their par or stated value; any difference, if a credit, is recorded in an appropriately designated contributed capital account; if a debit, Retained Earnings is charged. To illustrate three typical situations, assume the following data:

Preferred convertible stock, par $2, 100,000 shares outstanding	$200,000
Contributed capital in excess of par, preferred stock	20,000
Common stock, par $1, 500,000 shares authorized, 150,000 shares outstanding	150,000
Contributed capital in excess of par, common stock	50,000

Situation 1: The conversion privilege specifies one share of common stock for each share of preferred stock converted. Shareholders turn in 10,000 shares of preferred stock for conversion.

Preferred stock (10,000 shares at par)	20,000	
Contributed capital in excess of par, preferred stock ($.20 per share)	2,000	
Common stock (10,000 shares at par)		10,000
Contributed capital from conversion of preferred stock		12,000

Situation 2: The conversion privilege specifies two shares of common stock for each share of preferred stock converted. Shareholders turn in 10,000 shares of preferred stock for conversion.

Preferred stock (10,000 shares at par)	20,000	
Contributed capital in excess of par, preferred stock	2,000	
Common stock (20,000 shares)		20,000
Contributed capital from conversion of preferred stock		2,000

Situation 3: The conversion privilege specifies three shares of common stock for each share of preferred stock converted. Shareholders turn in 10,000 shares of preferred stock for conversion.

Preferred stock (10,000 shares)	20,000	
Contributed capital in excess of par, preferred stock	2,000	
Retained earnings	8,000	
Common stock (30,000 shares)		30,000

Conversion of bonds for capital stock is discussed in Chapters 11 and 19.

CHANGING PAR VALUE

A corporation, if it conforms with the applicable state laws, may amend the charter and bylaws to change the par value of one or more classes of authorized stock. Par-value stock may be called in and replaced with nopar stock or stock of a different par value; conversely, nopar stock may be replaced with par-value stock.[7]

The entries to record changes in par value follow the principles enunciated at the beginning of this chapter and illustrated in the preceding paragraphs. To illustrate several typical situations, assume the following data:

Capital stock, par $2, 50,000 shares outstanding	$100,000
Contributed capital in excess of par	20,000
Retained earnings	30,000

Situation 1: The shares are changed from par value to an equal number of true nopar shares.

Capital stock, par $2 (50,000 shares)	100,000	
Contributed capital in excess of par	20,000	
Capital stock, nopar, (50,000 shares)		120,000

Situation 2: The shares are changed from par value to an equal number of nopar shares with a stated value of $1 per share.

[7] Stock splits are discussed in Chapter 16. In a stock split the par value is reduced and the number of shares outstanding is increased proportionately; therefore, the balance in the capital stock account is unchanged. Only a memorandum entry in the original stock account is needed to reflect the new par value per share and the number of shares outstanding after the split.

Capital stock, par $2 (50,000 shares)	100,000	
Contributed capital in excess of par	20,000	
Capital stock, nopar, stated value $1 (50,000 shares)		50,000
Contributed capital from change to nopar stock		70,000

Situation 3: The shares are changed from par value to an equal number of nopar shares with a stated value of $2.50 per share.

Capital stock, par $2 (50,000 shares)	100,000	
Contributed capital in excess of par	20,000	
Retained earnings	5,000	
Capital stock, nopar, stated value $2.50 (50,000 shares)		125,000

Situation 4: The original shares were true nopar, and the capital stock account reflected a credit balance of $120,000. The true nopar shares are changed to an equal number of shares with a par value of $2.

Capital stock, nopar (50,000 shares)	120,000	
Capital stock, par $2 (50,000 shares)		100,000
Contributed capital from conversion of nopar shares		20,000

STOCK RIGHTS

A corporation may extend rights to acquire shares of stock under specified conditions. A certificate, known as a *stock warrant,* is issued by the corporation which conveys to the holder one or more *stock rights;* such warrants allow the holder to acquire shares of a specified stock issued by the corporation when certain conditions are met. A warrant specifies *(a)* the option price for the specified security, *(b)* the number of rights required to obtain each share of the specified security, *(c)* the expiration date of the right, and *(d)* instructions for exercise of the right.

Each stock right is a privilege extended by the corporation to acquire a fractional share or a specified number of shares of its capital stock. For example, X Corporation issued to the holder of each share of its common stock one stock right. According to the specified conditions a share of new preferred stock could be purchased for $40 upon the presentation of five of the stock rights within a specified time period. The warrants would have value to the extent that the $40 per share option price is below the expected future price of the new shares during the option period. In the absence of a restriction, stock rights may be bought and sold on the market similar to shares of stock. The market value of a stock right at issuance will approximate the difference between the then current market price of the stock ex rights (i.e., without rights) and the option price specified on the stock warrant, divided by the number of rights needed to purchase one share of stock. For example, if the market price of X Corporation preferred stock was $45 on the date the rights were issued, they would have an approximate market value immediately of [($45 − $40) ÷ 5 rights] = $1 per right.

Situations where stock rights often are issued include:

1. A special concession to present shareholders to encourage them to purchase additional shares that are to be sold to raise additional capital.
2. As a means of handling fractional shares needed when a stock dividend is declared and issued (see Chapter 16).
3. As a means of enhancing the marketability of other securities issued by the corporation, such as bonds payable and preferred stock.
4. As compensation to outsiders (such as underwriters, promoters, and professionals) for rendering services to the corporation.
5. As additional compensation to corporate officers and other employees. In this situation, the stock rights are generally referred to as *stock options*.

The issuance of stock rights pose accounting problems for both the recipient and the issuing corporation. Accounting for stock rights received by an investor is discussed in Chapter 18.

In respect to the *issuing corporation,* at least a memorandum entry must be made at date of issuance of stock rights because the balance sheet, or notes to the statements, must disclose the number of stock rights outstanding by class of stock. However, accounting entries usually are made in the accounts for the last four situations listed above. Fractional share warrants with stock dividends are illustrated in Chapter 16, and the issuance of bonds payable with detachable stock warrants is illustrated in Chapter 19. In the case of items 4 and 5 above, the compensation must be recorded at the fair market value of the compensation or the fair market value of the stock rights, whichever is the more clearly determinable.

For example, if 500 stock rights are issued to an attorney for legal services when the rights are selling at $1 on the market, the entry by the issuing corporation, assuming five rights and $40 will acquire one share of stock, would be:

Expenses—legal services	500	
Stock rights outstanding (for 100 shares of stock)		500

When the rights are exercised, the Stock Rights Outstanding account is debited. During the period the rights are outstanding, the account is reported along with the capital stock account to which it relates.

ACCOUNTING FOR STOCK ISSUED TO EMPLOYEES

Corporations often establish plans whereby shares of stock in the company are issued to employees. The purposes of stock plans are quite varied, ranging from a desire to encourage ownership in the company by the employees, to raising equity capital, and to provide additional compensation to one or more employees. Often stock rights are given because shares are to be issued to the employees or a particular group of employees (such as top executives) at some future date. Consequently, stock warrants, or stock options, are often issued when an employee meets the certain specified conditions. In these instances, the stock rights generally are specified as *nontransferable;* the shares received, through exercise of the rights, are *transferable.*

Plans for the issuance of stock to employees are designated with a variety of terms, none of which has been accorded a uniform definition. Typical terms used are: stock purchase plans, stock option plans, stock bonus plans, stock award plans, stock thrift plans, and stock savings plans. One must carefully examine the specifications of a plan in order to determine the rights and obligations of the issuing corporation (sometimes called the grantor) and of the recipient of the shares (sometimes called the grantee). It is important that the accountant carefully examine the specifications of a plan to issue stock to employees because those specifications determine the appropriate accounting, reporting, and disclosures.

Fundamentally, there are two basic characteristics of a stock issue plan that the accountant must consider, viz:

1. Cost to the corporation – In some stock plans, such as a stock purchase plan, the corporation sets up a purchase plan (often by payroll deduction) whereby employees, at their option, can purchase shares directly from the company and thereby save certain marketing costs. These plans involve no cost to the company (and no additional compensation to the employee). In other stock plans, the company pays a part of the cost of the shares purchased. In these situations, there is a cost to the company for their part of the purchase price, and some additional compensation to the employee.

   In still other cases, the stock is given to the employee without cost when certain specified conditions are met. This is the case with many executive stock options; such stock serves as additional compensation to the employee. A stock plan is said to be *compensatory* if additional compensation is involved and *noncompensatory* if no additional compensation is involved.
2. Income tax effects – There are two income tax effects that are important: the tax implications for the company and for the employee. These are related because, as a general proposition, the tax laws permit a tax deduction for the corporation (when there is additional compensation to the employee) only when the employee (the grantee) is subject to income taxes on the options or shares received. In this regard, a plan is said to be a *qualified plan* if there is no tax to the recipient initially, and the shares, when sold, qualify as a long-term capital gain; if such is not the case, and the options are taxed as income to the employee, the plan is said to be a *nonqualified plan.*

The income tax requirements and effects may be summarized in general terms as follows:

Feature	*Qualified Plan*	*Nonqualified Plan*
1. Option price.	Not less than the fair market value of the stock at date of grant.	Can be set at any price.
2. Holding period by grantee.	Shares received must be held at least three years from issue date to qualify as a long-term capital gain.	No special constraints.
3. Expiration period for stock rights.	Options (rights) must expire within five years from date of grant.	Can be effective for any number of years.
4. Option granting period.	Options must be granted within ten years of approval of plan by the stockholders.	No limit on granting period.
5. Tax effects: *a.* Grantee.	Long-term capital gain when stock is sold; no tax at date of grant.	Taxable as earned income when option is granted.
b. Issuer.	Additional compensation expense not deductible for tax purposes.	Additional compensation expense (equivalent to amount taxed to grantee) deductible for tax purposes.

Fundamentally, the accounting, reporting, and disclosure requirements for all plans whereby stock is, or will be, issued to employees is determined by whether the plan is compensatory or noncompensatory. Within these two broad categories, certain accounting differences, though less fundamental, exist. Because of the numerous differences between plans, this discussion will focus only on the broad issues.

The accounting, reporting, and disclosure requirements, with respect to plans for the issuance of stock directly to employees, must be in conformity with *Accounting Research Bulletin (ARB) No. 43*, Chapter 13B, as amended and supplemented by *APB Opinion No. 25*, "Accounting for Stock Issued to Employees" (October 1972). The discussions to follow conform to these two pronouncements.

Theoretical Considerations

Historically, and continuing to date, there has been considerable controversy over the appropriate accounting for *compensatory plans*. There is a theoretical answer, upon which most informed accountants tend to agree, and a practical answer (provided by *ARB No. 43* and *APB Opinion*

No. 25) designed to cope with the real-world complexities caused by the wide variations in plans and the problems of measurement. The basic issues can best be pinpointed by illustration. For this purpose, assume the following continuing situation:

1. AB Corporation—executive stock option plan:
   Options approved for each designated top executive:
   a. Five thousand shares of common stock, par $5.
   b. Nontransferable, exercisable three years after grant and prior to expiration date (five years from date of grant) providing continuing employment.
   c. Option price, $20 per share.
2. On January 1, 1976, Executive Z was granted an option for 5,000 shares:
   a. For services rendered 1976 through 1980 (approximately equal each year).
   b. At January 1, 1976, the quoted market price was $30 per share.
   c. The option was exercised by Executive Z in December 1980 when the quoted market price per share was $70.

The fundamental question for the accountant is to determine the appropriate accounting, reporting, and disclosure procedures during the period 1976 through 1980. To answer this question, the detailed specifications of the plan must be carefully examined in light of the two aforementioned pronouncements. The following questions must be answered:

1. Is the plan compensatory?
   a. If no, there are no unique accounting problems.
   b. If yes, then:
2. At what date should the compensation be measured?
3. What is the total amount of the compensation?
4. To what accounting periods should the compensation, as measured, be assigned?

The theoretical response to these questions is not complicated. The issuance of stock to employees at less than cost, or no cost, (other than for services to be rendered) involves a cost to the corporation; therefore this constitutes a compensatory plan. The compensation should be measured *at the date the grant is made to the employee;* that is, the point when the corporation foregoes the principal alternative use of the shares. This is usually identified as the date on which the option is granted to a specific individual. The total amount of the compensation should be measured as the *fair market value* of the *stock rights* (not the shares themselves) at the date of the grant to the specific individual. The total amount of compensation, thus measured, should be assigned to the accounting periods in which the services are rendered. This serves to match the additional compensation expense with the related revenues in conformity with the matching principle.

Practical Considerations

The accounting profession, despite continued efforts, has not been able to attain the theoretical positions to the satisfaction of many accountants. The primary problem is one of measurement. Let's review the practical guidelines provided by *ARB No. 43* and *APB Opinion No. 25*. We will consider each of the questions listed above separately.

Is the plan compensatory? Because the decision on this point fundamentally affects the accounting, reporting, and disclosure procedures to be followed, and because the precise lines of distinction are not obvious in many plans, *APB Opinion No. 25*, paragraph 7, carefully defines a *noncompensatory* plan as follows:

> . . . at least four characteristics are essential in a noncompensatory plan: (a) substantially all full-time employees meeting limited employment qualifications may participate (employees owning a specified percent of the outstanding stock and executives may be excluded), (b) stock is offered to eligible employees equally or based on a uniform percentage of salary or wages (the plan may limit the number of shares of stock that an employee may purchase through the plan), (c) the time permitted for exercise of an option or purchase right is limited to a reasonable period, and (d) the discount from the market price of the stock is no greater than would be reasonable in an offer of stock to stockholders or others. An example of a noncompensatory plan is the "statutory" employee stock purchase plan that qualifies under Section 423 of the Internal Revenue Code.

All other plans are classified as compensatory.

Accounting for Noncompensatory Plans

Since noncompensatory plans do not involve compensation expense and are stock purchase plans, there are no unique accounting problems involved. To illustrate, assume Company Y has a stock purchase plan whereby employees may acquire stock from the company either by direct purchase or through payroll deduction. The price of the stock is 10% below the quoted market price. Assuming payroll deductions, typical entries would be:

1. To record the monthly payroll and related deductions:

Salary and wage expense	90,000	
Income taxes withheld		5,500
Payroll taxes withheld (F.I.C.A., F.U.T.A., etc.)		1,500
Union dues		440
Liability—employee stock purchase plan*		7,560
Cash (or salary and wages payable)		75,000

* Per payroll deductions authorized by employees.

2. To record issuance of shares to employees (market price, $12):

Liability—employee stock purchase plan	7,560	
Capital stock, par $10 (700 shares)		7,000
Contributed capital in excess of par		560

($7,560 ÷ .90) ÷ $12 = 700 shares.

Accounting for Compensatory Plans

Since accounting for compensatory plans involves measurement of the amount of *additional compensation*, and its recognition in appropriate periods, the complexities are significantly increased. To discuss these complexities, we will proceed to the remaining questions posed above and, for illustrative purposes, return to the data given above for AB Corporation.

When Should the Compensation Be Measured? In a compensatory plan, the amount of additional compensation is measured at a *measurement date* specified in *APB Opinion No.* 25, paragraph 10, as follows:

> The *measurement date* for determining compensation cost in stock option, purchase, and award plans is the first date on which are known both (1) the number of shares that an individual employee is entitled to receive and (2) the option or purchase price, if any.

The measurement date may be either:

a. At the date the option is granted to the individual employee. This is the usual case because both the number of shares and the purchase price generally are set at that date.
b. At a date subsequent to date of the grant; that is, the earliest subsequent date when both the number of shares and the purchase price are known. This situation occurs, for example, when either the number of shares or the purchase price are contingent upon future earnings of the company or upon future prices of the stock. Acceptance of this later date, rather than the date of the grant, is a concession to the measurement problem – additional compensation must be measured when both the purchase price and the number of shares to which the employee is entitled are known.

In respect to AB Corporation, the measurement date is the date of grant because, in this case, both the (*a*) number of shares, and (*b*) purchase or option price are known at that date.

What Is the Total Amount of the Compensation? On this measurement problem, the *Opinion* states that the total additional compensation:

> . . . for services that a corporation receives as consideration for stock issued through employee stock option, purchase, and award plan should be measured by the quoted market price of the stock at the measurement date less the amount, if any, that the employee is required to pay.

The difference between the quoted market price of the stock at measurement date and the option price is used as a surrogate for *fair market value* of the rights. The *Opinion* also states that "If a quoted market price is unavailable, the best estimate of the market value of the stock should be used to measure compensation."

In respect to the plan outlined above for AB Corporation, total additional compensation, which is measurable in this instance on the date of the grant, January 1, 1976, is $30 – $20 = $10 per share, or $50,000 for Executive Z. This particular measurement rule is subject to severe and justified criticism because it does not measure the fair market value of the stock rights involved; that is, fair market value cannot be determined because there will be no established market (since the rights are nontransferable). Typically, companies set the option price at the current market price of the shares in which case the total additional compensation would be measured, under this rule, as zero. Recall that a *qualified* plan does not permit an option price less than the current market price of the stock.[8]

When the measurement date is at a date subsequent to the date of the grant, the number of shares, the option price, and market price generally must be *estimated* for the measurement of the compensation because *accruals* of estimated annual compensation expense must be recorded between the date of grant and the measurement date (when the dates are different). Total *actual* compensation expense then is measured and recorded as a deferred expense on measurement date. Annual compensation expense is recorded for the remaining periods prior to expiration or exercise date.[9]

To What Accounting Periods Should the Measured Compensation Be Assigned? The total amount of additional compensation expense must be assigned to the periods in which the services are rendered so that compensation expense is matched with the related revenues. This generally requires accrual, and/or deferral, of the additional compensation expense. On this point, *APB Opinion No. 25* states (italics added):

> 12. *Accruing Compensation Cost.* Compensation cost in stock option, purchase, and award plans should be recognized as an expense of one or more periods in which an employee performs services and also as part or all of the consideration received for stock issued to the employee through a plan. The grant or award may specify the period or periods during which the employee performs services, or the period or periods may be inferred from the terms or from the past pattern of grants or awards (ARB No. 43, Chapter 13B, paragraph 14; APB Opinion No. 12, *Omnibus Opinion-1967*, paragraph 6).
>
> 13. An employee may perform services in several periods before an employer corporation issues stock to him for those services. The employer corporation should *accrue* compensation expense in each period in which the services are performed. If the measurement date is later than the date of grant or award, an employer corporation should record the compensation expense *each period from date of grant or award to date of measurement based on the quoted market price of the stock at the end of each period.*
>
> 14. If stock is issued in a plan before some or all of the services are performed, part of the consideration recorded for the stock issued is unearned compensation and should be shown as a *separate reduction of stockholders' equity*. The unearned compensation should be accounted for as expense of the period or periods in which the employee performs service.

---

[8] Some accountants believe that sophisticated measurement models are currently available that can cope effectively with this measurement problem.

[9] If the grantee exercises the option prior to the end of the expiration date, the amount of total compensation not assigned to specific periods usually is assigned to the period in which exercise occurs.

15. Accruing compensation expense may require estimates, and adjustment of those estimates in later periods may be necessary (APB Opinion No. 20, *Accounting Changes*, paragraphs 31 to 33). For example, if a stock option is not exercised (or awarded stock is returned to the corporation) because an employee fails to fulfill an obligation, the estimate of compensation expense recorded in previous periods should be adjusted by decreasing compensation expense in the period of forfeiture.

Thus, the *Opinion* specifies precise guidelines for accrual and deferral of total additional compensation when the measurement date is (*a*) at the date of grant, or (*b*) at a date subsequent to the date of grant. Observe that the phrase in italics in paragraph 13 is significant because it excludes service in *prior* periods.

With respect to AB Corporation, the total compensation expense of $50,000 should be assigned equally to the five-year period, 1976–80.

Illustrative Entries, Compensatory Plan, Measurement Date on Date of Grant

Using the example for AB Corporation, we have determined (in accordance with *ARB No. 43*, Chapter 13B, and *APB Opinion No. 25*) that:

1. The company plan is compensatory.
2. The measurement date is the date of the grant, January 1, 1976.
3. The total additional compensation for Executive Z is $50,000.
4. The total additional compensation expense should be assigned equally to the five years 1976 through 1980 (date of retirement or expiration).

Therefore, the employer, AB Corporation, should make the following entries with respect to participation by Executive Z in the executive stock option plan:

a. January 1, 1976 – date of grant; to record total deferred compensation expense and stock rights outstanding:

Deferred compensation expense	50,000	
Executive stock options outstanding (for 5,000 shares of common stock)		50,000

($30 – $20) × 5,000 shares = $50,000.

b. December 31, 1976, through 1980 – to record annual apportionment of compensation expense:

Executive compensation expense	10,000	
Deferred compensation expense		10,000

$50,000 ÷ 5 years = $10,000 per year.

c. December 31, 1980 – exercise date, to record the stock warrants tendered by Executive Z and issuance of the shares:

Cash (5,000 shares @ $20 option price)	100,000	
Executive stock options outstanding (for 5,000 shares)	50,000	
Common stock, par $5 (5,000 shares)		25,000
Contributed capital in excess of par		125,000

Compensation expense ($10,000) is reported on the income statement each period as a normal operating expense. Stock options outstanding and deferred compensation are reported on the balance sheet (December 31, 1976) as follows:

Stockholders' Equity

Contributed Capital:		
Common stock, par $5, authorized 500,000 shares, outstanding 200,000 shares		$1,000,000
Executive stock options outstanding (for 5,000 shares)..	$50,000	
Less: Deferred compensation expense..............	40,000	10,000
Other contributed capital (etc.)	(not illustrated)	

In addition, *ARB No. 43*, Chapter 13, paragraph 15, requires disclosure of—

a. The status of the option plan at the end of the period.
b. The number of shares under option.
c. The option price.
d. The number of shares to which options were exercisable.
e. The number of shares exercised during the period and the option price thereof.

Illustrative Entries, Compensatory Plan, Measurement Date Subsequent to Date of Grant

When the measurement date is subsequent to date of grant, because both the number of shares and option price are unknown, the entries are slightly more complex. To illustrate, the data for AB Corporation are adapted as follows:

1. The number of shares and option price are not known on the date of grant, January 1, 1976, since the plan defers their determination to the end of 1978 (the measurement date).
2. The number of shares and option price are based on the increase in net income from the date of grant to the *third* year following date of grant.
3. Estimated and actual data:

	Estimate Made on January 1, 1976 of What the Amount Will Be on December 31, 1978	*Actual Amount on December 31, 1978*
Number of shares optioned	5,000	5,000
Option price	$23	$22
Market price per share (a relatively steady increase each year)	$34	$32.50

Entries:

a. January 1, 1976—date of grant:

No entry—measurement and recording of total compensation cost occurs on subsequent measurement date.

b. December 31, 1976, and 1977—end of period; to record accrual of *estimated* annual compensation expense:

	1976		*1977*	
Compensation expense	11,000		11,000	
Accrued compensation expense (stock options)		11,000		11,000

Computations:
Total estimated compensation expense: ($34 − $23) × 5,000 shares = $55,000.
Assignment to periods: $55,000 ÷ 5 years = $11,000.

c. December 31, 1978—measurement date; to record actual total compensation cost:

Accrued compensation expense ($11,000 × 2)	22,000	
Deferred compensation expense ($52,500 − $22,000) ...	30,500	
Executive stock options outstanding (for 5,000 shares)		52,500

Computation of total compensation expense:
($32.50 − $22) × 5,000 shares = $52,500.

d. December 31, 1978, 1979, and 1980—end of period; to record annual compensation expense:

Compensation expense	10,167	
Deferred compensation expense..........................		10,167

$30,500 ÷ 3 years = $10,167.

e. December, 1980—exercise date; to record issuance of the 5,000 shares:

Cash ($23 × 5,000 shares)	115,000	
Executive stock options outstanding (for 5,000 shares) ...	52,500	
Common stock, par $5 (5,000 shares)		25,000
Contributed capital in excess of par		142,500

A decision tree is shown in Exhibit 17-1 which summarizes the decisions and sequence of entries for:

1. Noncompensatory plans.
2. Compensatory plans:
   a. Measurement date on date of grant.
   b. Measurement date subsequent to date of grant.

EARNINGS PER SHARE

Earnings per share was briefly discussed in Chapter 4. The comments and illustrations in that section should be reviewed at this point. Earnings per share is computed and reported as prescribed in *APB Opinion No. 15*, "Earnings Per Share" (May 1969). It is a complex opinion that

EXHIBIT 17–1
Decision Tree—Stock Issued to Employees

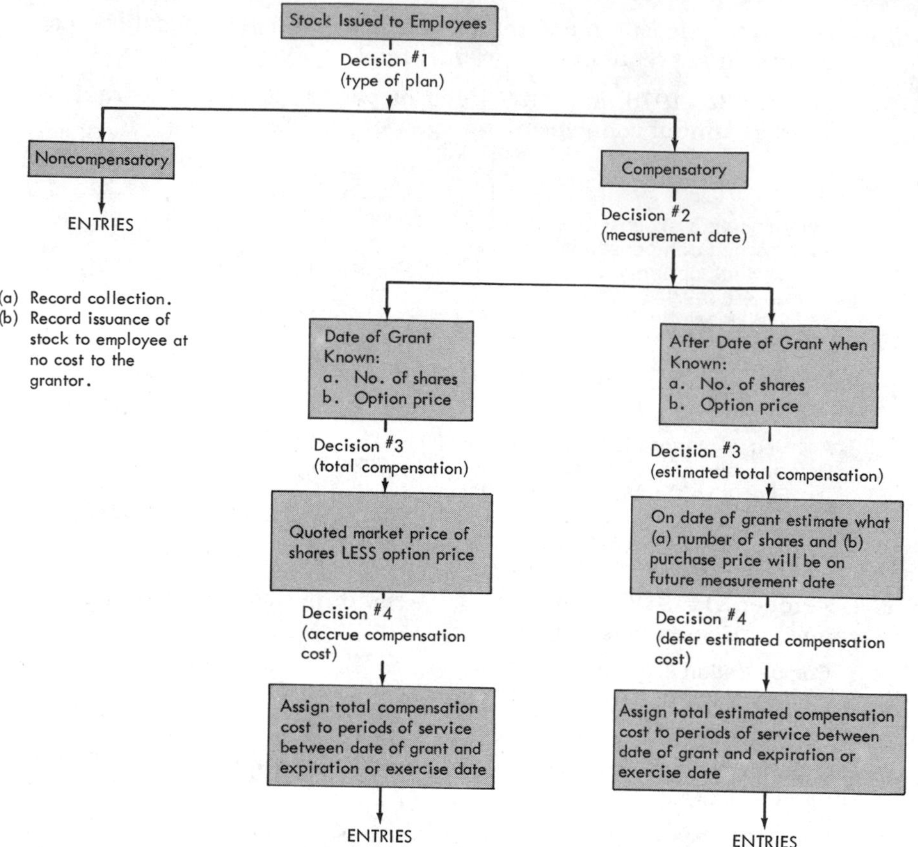
Stock Issued to Employees
Decision #1
(type of plan)
Noncompensatory
ENTRIES
(a) Record collection.
(b) Record issuance of stock to employee at no cost to the grantor.
Compensatory
Decision #2
(measurement date)
Date of Grant Known:
a. No. of shares
b. Option price
After Date of Grant when Known:
a. No. of shares
b. Option price
Decision #3
(total compensation)
Decision #3
(estimated total compensation)
Quoted market price of shares LESS option price
On date of grant estimate what (a) number of shares and (b) purchase price will be on future measurement date
Decision #4
(accrue compensation cost)
Decision #4
(defer estimated compensation cost)
Assign total compensation cost to periods of service between date of grant and expiration or exercise date
Assign total estimated compensation cost to periods of service between date of grant and expiration or exercise date

ENTRIES

a. Date of grant—Record accrued compensation cost and issuance of stock rights.
b. Each year—Assign portion of total compensation cost to year.
c. Exercise date—Record issuance of shares and cancellation of stock rights outstanding

ENTRIES

a. Date of grant—No entry; measurement and recording of total compensation will be on subsequent measurement date.
b. Each year from date of grant to measurement date —Accrue annual compensation expense based on estimates of number of shares, option price and market price per share.
c. Measurement date—Record total compensation expense and close accrued compensation expense from prior periods.
d. Each year from measurement date to expiration date—Record annual apportionment of compensation expense.
e. Exercise date—Record issuance of shares and cancellation of stock rights outstanding.

was supplemented with an interpretation of 186 pages.[10] It would be totally unrealistic to attempt to discuss all of the complexities in this book. Therefore, this discussion is intended to explain and illustrate, in a general way, only the major concepts involved in computing EPS.

Reporting Earnings per Share

APB Opinion No. 15 requires that earnings per share amounts (for common stock only) be reported on the income statement for each year financial information is presented. Computation of EPS and the reporting requirements depend on the capital structure of the corporation, viz:

1. Simple capital structure—the case where the stockholders' equity either consists of only common stock or it does not include convertible securities, stock warrants, or other rights convertible to common stock.[11] In the case of a simple capital structure, a single presentation of the basic EPS amounts for common stock is required. In Chapter 4, several cases were presented that illustrated EPS with simple capital structures. We will add one more example, a simple capital structure where there is *nonconvertible* preferred stock. Assume the following data for MW Corporation:

Common stock, par $10, authorized 200,000 shares:	
Outstanding at beginning of year, 90,000 shares	$900,000
Issued during the year, on May 1, 6,000 shares	96,000
Preferred stock, par $20, 6% nonconvertible, authorized 5,000 shares, outstanding at end of the year, 2,500 shares	50,000
Income before extraordinary items	120,000
Extraordinary loss (net of 45% tax rate)	(10,000)
Net income	110,000

To compute earnings per share in this situation (a simple capital structure), two preliminary computations must be made because (*a*) income, the numerator, must be reduced by the dividend claim of the preferred stock; and (*b*) the denominator must be the *average* shares outstanding during the year, viz:

a. Portion of net income (dividend claim) applicable to preferred stock (whether declared or not):

$$\$50,000 \times .06 = \underline{\underline{\$3,000}}$$

---

[10] J. T. Ball, *Computing Earnings per Share—Unofficial Accounting Interpretations of APB Opinion No. 15*, (New York, AICPA, 1970).

[11] Convertible securities that do not affect EPS by more than 3% may be disregarded on the basis of materiality. Also, a simple capital structure may include preferred stock if it is not convertible to common stock.

b. Average shares outstanding during the year:[12]

	Months	No. of Shares	Product
January 1 to April 30	4	90,000	360,000
May 1 to December 31	8	96,000	768,000
Totals	12		1,128,000

Average shares outstanding: 1,128,000 ÷ 12 = 94,000 shares

Earnings per share on common stock:

Income before extraordinary items ($120,000 − $3,000) ÷ 94,000 shares =	$1.25
Extraordinary loss $10,000 ÷ 94,000 shares =	(.11)
Net Income ($110,000 − $3,000) ÷ 94,000 shares =	$1.14

2. Complex capital structure – Capital that do not qualify as simple structures are classified as complex by *APB Opinion No. 15*. Such capital structures include securities such as convertible bonds, convertible preferred stock warrants, stock options, and stock rights. In the case of a complex capital structure, two sets of EPS amounts must be presented, viz:
   a. Primary EPS – Based on common stock plus common stock equivalents (defined below).[13]
   b. Fully diluted EPS – Based on common stock outstanding plus common stock equivalents and any other shares of common stock that would be issued assuming *all* stock purchase contracts and convertible securities are converted to common stock. This represents maximum dilution of EPS. Fully diluted EPS amounts will be less than (or equal to) primary EPS amounts because of convertible securities (i.e., convertible debt and preferred stock) that do not qualify as common stock equivalents.

The discussions and illustrations to follow will focus only on complex capital structures.

Computing EPS with Complex Capital Structures

Fundamentally, the difference between primary and fully diluted EPS is determination of whether or not the various convertible securities

[12] In computing the average, reacquired shares are included in the weighted average only for the time they were outstanding. Stock dividends and stock splits are always assumed to be at year-end; that is, the average is computed and then the additional shares are added.

[13] Primary EPS amounts in a complex capital structure would be identical with the basic EPS amount in a simple capital structure when there are no common stock equivalents.

and stock options outstanding represent common stock equivalents, viz:

a. Primary EPS—Based on the average number of common shares outstanding during the period *plus all common stock equivalents.*

b. Fully diluted EPS—Based on the average number of common shares outstanding during the period plus all common stock equivalents and *plus all other shares of common stock that potentially may be issued because of conversion privileges.*

Thus, the definition and identification of common stock equivalents are critical.

A *common stock equivalent* is defined in *Opinion No. 15* as: "A security which, because of its terms or the circumstances under which it was issued, is in substance equivalent to common stock." In form, it is not common stock; however, it enables its holder to acquire common stock under specified conditions.

Neither conversion nor the imminence of conversion is necessary to classify a security as a common stock equivalent for EPS purposes. Classification of a convertible security that is convertible to common stock, as to whether it is a common stock equivalent should be made "only at time of issuance and should not be changed thereafter so long as the security remains outstanding."

In determining when a security is a common stock equivalent and in computing *number of equivalent* shares for EPS computation, separate consideration must be given to *(a)* stock options, warrants, rights, and other stock purchase contracts; and *(b)* convertible securities composed of bonds and preferred stock convertible to common stock. These two categories must be considered separately because they have different characteristics; therefore, the computations are quite different. Each will be discussed and illustrated separately.

Stock Options, Warrants, Rights, and Other Stock Purchase Contracts. These items, although not designated as convertible securities, when exercised cause the issuance of common stock. Thus, they compose one category of common stock equivalents. Since exercise would cause a cash inflow, which would earn a return, some method of reflecting this "as if" situation is needed. *APB Opinion No. 15* prescribes the *treasury stock method* for this purpose. Basically, the method computes common stock equivalents as the number of shares that would be issued upon exercise of the stock rights (at the option price) less the number of those shares that could be bought back as treasury stock (at the average market price for the period). Thus, the method assumes that any cash proceeds from the issuance of common shares, should the options, warrants, rights, or other contracts be exercised, will be used immediately to purchase treasury stock.[14]

---

[14] If the number of common shares issuable exceeds 20% of the number of common shares outstanding at the end of the period, the treasury stock method, as illustrated above, must be modified to include both repurchase of stock and to reduce debt. Also the market price used for treasury stock calculations for fully diluted EPS is at the end of the current period (rather than the average price used for primary EPS).

Application of the treasury stock method to compute the number of equivalent shares may be illustrated as follows:

Basic data (MW Corporation):		
Common stock warrants outstanding....................	2,000 (for 2,000 shares)	
Option or exercise price per share	$20	
Average market price of the shares for the period of issuance of the warrants	$25	
Computation of common stock equivalents:		*Shares*
Shares that would be issued upon exercise of the warrants		2,000
Cash proceeds that would be realized, $20 × 2,000 shares = $40,000		
Treasury stock that could be purchased, $40,000 ÷ $25 =		1,600
Difference—common stock equivalents (i.e., incremental shares that would be outstanding)..		400

Thus, to complete both primary and fully diluted EPS the 400 common stock equivalents (not the 2,000 shares) would be added to the average number of common shares actually outstanding during the year.[15]

Convertible Securities. Bonds payable and preferred stock which are convertible to common stock are referred to as convertible securities. They may or may not represent a second category of common stock equivalents. Determination of whether a convertible security represents common stock equivalents depends upon the relationship between their *cash yield* rate (stated interest or dividend rate) and "normal" *interest rates* at the time of issuance. The *Opinion* states: "convertible securities should be considered common stock equivalents if the cash yield to the holder at time of issuance is significantly below what would be a comparable rate for a similar security of the issuer without the conversions option." The *Opinion* sets up an arbitrary *prime rate test* (as the "normal" rate) to make this distinction: "a convertible security should be considered as a common stock equivalent at the time of issuance if, based on its market price, it has a cash yield less that 66⅔% of the then current bank prime interest rate."[16] If this test is met, such dilutive common stock warrants are included in the computation of primary EPS. Alternatively, they are included in fully diluted EPS computations even though they do not meet this test.

From a realistic point of view, a security bought to yield less than two thirds of the prime rate obviously was acquired for potential appreciation and not for current yield; therefore, its conversion feature was an important element in the total consideration paid for it. Consequently, a test, such as this one, was necessary for primary EPS calculations be-

[15] An opposite effect occurs when the option price is greater than the current market price. In this case, the security would be antidilutive and the common stock equivalents excluded; see subsequent discussion of this concept.

[16] The current bank prime interest rate is the rate the banks locally are charging on short-term loans to borrowers with the best credit risk.

cause convertible securities may never be converted because of the relative earnings compared with the common stock. The prime rate test is an arbitrary method of determining whether, in fact, convertible securities are substantially common stock equivalents.

Application of the prime rate test may be illustrated as follows:

Basic data (MW Corporation):
- Convertible bonds payable, 6%, $100,000
- Conversion rate: Each $1,000 bond is convertible to 40 shares of common stock.
- Annual interest expense, net of tax: $6,000 × (1.00 − .45) = $3,300
- At issuance date: Bond price, 120
  Prime bank interest rate, 7%

Prime rate test:
- Shares issuable at conversion ($100,000 ÷ $1,000) × 40 = 4,000 shares
- Comparison of rates:

$$\frac{\text{Cash Yield (Interest) per Year}}{\text{Market Price at Issuance}} = \frac{\$6{,}000}{\$120{,}000} = 5.00\%\ \text{Cash Yield Rate}$$

Bond prime rate: 7% × 66⅔% = 4.67% adjusted prime rate

Interpretation: Since the cash yield rate is greater than the adjusted prime rate, the convertible bonds representing 4,000 shares of common stock would *not* be classified as common stock equivalents for primary EPS computations. They would be included in computing fully diluted EPS.

Computation of Earnings per Share, Complex Capital Structure

When there is a complex capital structure, primary and fully diluted EPS amounts are computed for (1) income before extraordinary items, (2) extraordinary items (optional), and (3) net income. The computation of each amount may be summarized as follows.[17]

Primary Earnings per Share*

Numerator	Denominator
1. Income before extraordinary items: Income before extraordinary items minus claims of nonconvertible preferred stock and plus interest (net of tax) on convertible debt classified as common stock equivalents.	Weighted average number of shares outstanding plus common stock equivalents.
2. Extraordinary items: Extraordinary gain or loss (net of tax).	Same.
3. Net income: Same as (1) plus or minus extraordinary items.	Same.

[17] This summary does not specify the numerous exceptions and certain detailed computations which would serve to confuse the broader issues. It is not feasible to cover all of the complexities, and memorization of them would be fruitless. As stated earlier our objective is to focus on the broad issues.

Fully Diluted Earnings per Share*

Numerator	Denominator
1. Income before extraordinary items: Income before extraordinary items minus claims of nonconvertible preferred stock plus interest expense (net of tax) on convertible debt.	Weighted average number of shares outstanding plus common stock equivalents and plus all *other common shares that would be issued on convertible securities.*
2. Extraordinary items: Extraordinary gain or loss (net of tax).	Same.
3. Net income: Same as (1) plus or minus extraordinary items.	Same.

* Excluding all antidilutive securities.

Computation of earnings per share, assuming a complex capital structure, is illustrated below for MW Corporation (adapted) and the prior illustrations of common stock equivalents and convertible debt.

Primary earnings per share (include common stock equivalents):

Income before extraordinary items: $\frac{\$120{,}000 - \$3{,}000}{94{,}000 + 400^{*}} = \$1.24$

Extraordinary loss: $\frac{\$10{,}000}{94{,}400} = (.11)$

Net income: $\frac{\$110{,}000 - \$3{,}000}{94{,}400} = \$1.13$

* See page 728.

Fully diluted earnings per share (include all potential issuances):

Income before extraordinary items: $\frac{\$120{,}000 - \$3{,}000 + \$3{,}300^{*}}{94{,}000 + 400 + 4{,}000^{*}} = \$1.22$

Extraordinary loss: $\frac{\$10{,}000}{98{,}400} = (.10)$

Net income: $\frac{\$110{,}000 - \$3{,}000 + \$3{,}300}{98{,}400} = \$1.12$

* See page 729.

In the case of a complex capital structure, *Opinion No. 15* requires additional disclosures: "a description, in summary form, sufficient to explain the pertinent rights and privileges of the various securities outstanding."

Antidilution

A reduction in earnings per share amounts resulting from common stock equivalents, and convertible securities that do not represent common stock equivalents, is known as *dilution,* and the stock purchase contracts and convertible securities that cause this effect are called *dilutive securities.*

Antidilution, caused by *antidilutive* stock purchase contracts and convertible securities, is the opposite effect. Antidilution causes an increase in earnings per share amounts above the amounts that would otherwise be reported. To attain the maximum dilutive effect on EPS (because of conservatism), all antidilutive securities are excluded in computing both primary and fully diluted earnings per share amounts. To repeat, antidilution may arise from either stock purchase contracts (options, warrants, rights, etc.) or convertible securities (convertible debt or preferred stock). For example, if the option price on common stock warrants outstanding is greater than the market price, those common stock equivalents would increase EPS; hence, they would be antidilutive and thus are excluded from the computations. Similarly, if the conversion of bonds payable in the above illustration had been 20 shares of stock per $1,000 bond (instead of 40 shares), the convertible bonds would have been antidilutive; in this case they would have been excluded from the computation of EPS amounts.

Antidilutive effects can be illustrated as follows:

1. Stock rights, warrants, options, and other stock purchase contracts: Was the option or exercise price *above* the average market price of the optioned stock? If yes, the common stock equivalents would be antidilutive and would not be included in the EPS calculations (see footnote 14).

   Illustration for WZ Corporation:

   a. Dilutive—option price *below* market price:

   As illustrated above—option price $20; market price $25.

   Computation: 2,000 shares − ($40,000 ÷ $25) = +400, positive common stock equivalents. Clearly, this positive amount in the denominator would cause it to increase, which would serve to *decrease* all of the EPS amounts below what they would be without the rights, warrants, and options. Thus, they are *dilutive*.

   b. Antidilutive—option price *above* market price:

   Assumption—option price $20; market price $18.

   Computation: 2,000 shares − ($40,000 ÷ $18) = −222, negative common stock equivalents. Clearly, this negative amount would decrease the denominator, which would serve to *increase* all of the EPS amounts above what they would be without the rights, warrants, and options. Thus, they are *antidilutive*.

2. Convertible debt and convertible preferred stock:

   Does the interest (or preferred dividends) added to the numerator, divided by the shares added to the denominator, exceed the EPS amounts that would be reported excluding the conversion assumptions? If yes, the common stock equivalents would be antidilutive and would not be included in the EPS calculations.

   Illustration for WZ Corporation:

   a. Dilutive—EPS amounts *decreased* because of conversion:

   Assumption—Conversion ratio 20 shares per bond (as illustrated above).

$$\text{EPS without Conversion} = \frac{\$120{,}000 - \$3{,}000}{94{,}000 + 400} = \$1.24$$

$$\text{EPS with Conversion} = \frac{\$120{,}000 - \$3{,}000 + \$3{,}300}{94{,}000 + 400 + 4{,}000} = \$1.22$$

Since the conversion feature *decreased* EPS, it was dilutive and would be included in the EPS computations.

b. Antidilutive – EPS amounts *increased* because of conversion: Assumption – conversion ratio 40 shares per bond.

$$\text{EPS without Conversion} = \frac{\$120{,}000 - \$3{,}000}{94{,}000 + 400} = \$1.24$$

$$\text{EPS with Conversion} = \frac{\$120{,}000 - \$3{,}000 + \$3{,}300}{94{,}000 + 400 + 2{,}000} = \$1.25$$

Since the conversion feature *increased* EPS, it was antidilutive and would not be included in the EPS computations.

QUESTIONS

1. Define treasury stock.
2. Explain the basic difference in theory between the one-transaction concept and the dual-transaction concept in accounting for treasury stock.
3. In comparing the recording of treasury stock at cost with recording at par "total capital is unaffected, however subdivisions thereof are affected." Explain this statement.
4. Why have many states limited purchases of treasury stock to the amount reported as retained earnings? How may the restriction on retained earnings be removed?
5. In recording treasury stock transactions why are "gains" recorded in a contributed capital account, whereas "losses" debited to retained earnings?
6. How is treasury stock reported on the balance sheet *(a)* under the cost method, and *(b)* under the par-value method?
7. How is the restriction on retained earnings, equal to the cost of treasury stock held, reported on the balance sheet?
8. How is stock donated back to the corporation recorded? Indicate any preference.
9. What are stock rights? In what situations are stock warrants frequently issued?
10. Distinguish between a compensatory and a noncompensatory stock option plan.
11. What is meant by the measurement date? When is it later than the date of grant?
12. Theoretically what is the amount of total compensation in a stock bonus plan?

13. Why are estimates necessary when the measurement date is later than the date of the grant of a stock option that is compensatory?

14. What is the basic impact on earnings per share computations and reporting as between a simple capital structure and a complex capital structure?

15. What is a common stock equivalent? How do common stock equivalents affect earning per share computations?

16. Contrast primary earnings per share and fully diluted earnings per share.

17. What is the difference between a dilutive security and an antidilutive security? Why is the distinction important in earnings per share considerations?

DECISION CASE 17–1

The Unknown Corporation purchased $144,000 of equipment in 1976 for $90,000 cash and a promise to deliver an indeterminate number of treasury shares of its $5 par common stock, with a market value of $15,000 on January 1 of each year for the next four years. Hence $60,000 in "market value" of treasury shares will be required to discharge the $54,000 balance due on the equipment.

The corporation then acquired 5,000 shares of its own stock in the expectation that the market value of the stock would increase substantially before the delivery dates.

Required:

1. Discuss the propriety of recording the equipment at—
   a. $90,000 (the cash payment).
   b. $144,000 (the cash price of the equipment).
   c. $150,000 (the $90,000 cash payment + the $60,000 market value of treasury stock that must be transferred to the vendor in order to settle the obligation according to the terms of the agreement).
2. Discuss the arguments *for* treating the balance due as—
   a. A liability.
   b. Treasury stock subscribed.
3. Assuming that legal requirements do not affect the decision, discuss the arguments *for* treating the corporation's treasury shares as—
   a. An asset awaiting ultimate disposition.
   b. A capital element awaiting ultimate disposition.

(AICPA adapted)

EXERCISES

Exercise 17–1

Young Corporation had 5,000 shares of $20 par-value common stock outstanding, originally sold at $50 per share. On January 15, Young purchased 20 shares of its own stock at $55 per share. On March 1, 12 of the treasury shares were sold at $58. The balance in retained earnings was $25,000 prior to these transactions.

Required:

1. Give all entries indicated in parallel columns, assuming *(a)* the cost method, and *(b)* the par-value method.

2. What would be the resulting balances in the stockholders' equity accounts for each method?

Exercise 17–2

Kyle Corporation had the following stock outstanding:

Common stock, nopar, 10,000 shares sold at $15	$150,000
Preferred stock, par $10, 5,000 shares sold at $25..............	50,000

The following treasury stock transactions were completed:

a. Purchased 20 shares of the common stock at $17 per share.
b. Purchased ten shares of the preferred stock at $27.
c. Sold 15 shares of the common stock at $14.
d. Sold five shares of the preferred stock at $30.

Required:

1. Give entries for all of the above stock transactions, assume the par-value method is used.
2. Give resulting balances in the stockholders' equity accounts; assume a starting balance in retained earnings of $20,000.

Exercise 17–3

Baker Corporation had outstanding 5,000 shares of preferred stock, par value $10, and 10,000 shares of nopar common stock sold initially for $20 per share. Contributed capital in excess of par on the preferred stock amounted to $25,000; and retained earnings balance is $30,000. The corporation purchased 200 shares of preferred at $18 per share and 300 shares of common stock at $24 per share. Subsequently, 100 shares of the common treasury stock was sold for $19 per share.

Required:

1. Give entries to record the treasury stock transactions assuming the cost method is used.
2. Prepare the resulting stockholders' equity section of the balance sheet.

Exercise 17–4

At January 1, 19A, the records of Adams Corporation showed the following:

Capital stock, par $10, 50,000 shares outstanding..............	$500,000
Contributed capital in excess of par	250,000
Retained earnings	150,000

During the year, the following transactions affecting stockholders' equity were recorded:

a. Purchased 500 shares of treasury stock at $20 per share.
b. Purchased 500 shares of treasury stock at $22 per share.
c. Sold 600 shares of treasury stock at $25.
d. Net income was $40,000.

The state law places a restriction on retained earnings equal to the cost of treasury stock held.

Required:

1. Give entries for the above transactions, in parallel columns, assuming *(a)* the cost method, and *(b)* the par-value method. Establish an appropriation of retained earnings.
2. Prepare the stockholders' section of the balance sheet for each method. Include any required disclosure related to the treasury stock.

Exercise 17–5

The balance sheet for Allison Corporation at December 31, 19A, showed the following:

Assets	$126,000
Liabilities	20,000
Stockholders' equity:	
Capital stock, par $10, 7,000 shares	70,000
Treasury stock, 1,000 shares (at cost)	17,000
Contributed capital in excess of par	14,000
Retained earnings	39,000

Required:

Prepare a balance sheet for the corporation with special emphasis on the stockholders' equity section assuming the state law places a restriction on retained earnings equal to the cost of treasury stock held. Assume *(a)* the cost method, and *(b)* the par-value method. Include all required disclosures related to the treasury stock.

Exercise 17–6

AB Corporation had 30,000 shares of $10 par-value capital stock authorized, of which 20,000 shares were issued three years ago at $15 per share. During the current year, the corporation received 500 shares of the capital stock as a bequest from a deceased shareholder; in addition, 1,000 shares were purchased at $14 per share. State law places a restriction on retained earnings equal to the cost of treasury stock held. At the end of the year, a cash dividend of $.50 per share was paid; prior to the dividend, retained earnings amounted to $40,000.

Required:

1. Prepare entries to record all of the transactions assuming the cost method for recording treasury stock is used. Record the donated stock at its fair market value.
2. Prepare the stockholders' equity section of the balance sheet at year-end and include all required disclosures related to the treasury stock.

Exercise 17–7

The records for XY Corporation reflected the following data on stockholders' equity:

a. Preferred stock, par $50, issued 2,000 shares.

b. Preferred treasury stock, 200 shares (cost $54 per share).
c. Premium on preferred stock at original issue was $1 per share.
d. Common stock, par $100, issued 3,000 shares.
e. Common treasury stock, 300 shares (cost $98 per share).
f. Premium on common stock at original issue was $2 per share.
g. Retained earnings, unappropriated, $110,000.
h. Retained earnings appropriated for cost of treasury stock, $40,200. The state law places a restriction on retained earnings equal to the cost of treasury stock held.

The shareholders voted to retire all of the treasury stock forthwith and another 400 shares of common stock that could be purchased immediately at $101 per share.

Required:

Give the following entries, in parallel columns, assuming the *(a)* cost method, and *(b)* par-value method:

1. Purchase of the 400 additional treasury shares for retirement.
2. To retire all of the treasury shares. Give separate entries for the preferred and common.

Exercise 17–8

The records of Erwin Corporation reflected the following:

Preferred stock, 1,000 shares outstanding, par $100	$100,000
Common stock, 1,000 shares outstanding, par $50	50,000
Contributed capital in excess of par, preferred stock	5,000
Contributed capital in excess of par, common stock	2,000
Retained earnings	50,000

The preferred stock is convertible into common stock. Give entry, or entries, required in each of the following cases:

Case A – The preferred shares are converted to common stock on a par-for-par basis; that is, two shares of common are issued for each share of preferred.

Case B – The preferred shares are converted to common share for share.

Case C – The preferred shares are converted to common stock on a one-for-three basis; that is, three shares of common are issued for each share of preferred.

Case D – The preferred shares are converted for a new class of stock known as Common Class B, nopar share for share.

Exercise 17–9

Swisher Corporation has a stock savings plan with the following provisions:

Each full-time employee, with a minimum of one year's service, may acquire common stock, par $5, in the company through payroll deductions at 4% below the market price on the date selected by the employee for stock purchase.

Employee Jones signed a payroll deduction form on January 1, 1976, for $40 per month. At that date, the market price of the stock was $27. Assume a monthly salary of $1,000 and other payroll deductions in the aggregate of 12%. At the end of 1976, Jones requested that stock be purchased equal to the amount accumulated to his credit. At that date, the market price of the stock was $25.

Required:

1. Is this a compensatory plan? Explain.
2. What is the total additional compensation to Jones? Explain.
3. How many shares is Jones entitled to? Show computations.
4. Give entries to record *(a)* the monthly payroll, and *(b)* issuance of the shares.

Exercise 17–10

Stiger Corporation is authorized to issue 300,000 shares of common stock, par $1; to date 140,000 shares have been issued. The corporation initiated a stock bonus plan during 1976 for designated managers. Each manager will receive stock rights to purchase 1,000 shares of common stock; if still employed by the company, any time after two years from the date of the grant, January 1, 1976. The rights are nontransferable and expire on December 31, 1980. The option price is $15 per share; the market price on date of grant was $20. The services will be rendered approximately equally over the five-year period.

Required:

1. Is this a noncompensatory plan? Explain.
2. What is the measurement date? Explain.
3. What is the amount of total compensation for each manager?
4. Over what period should this compensation expense be assigned? How much should be assigned to 1976? To 1977? Explain.
5. What entry should be made on the date of the grant (for one manager)?
6. What entry should be made on December 31, 1976?

Exercise 17–11

The records for Voss Corporation, at year-end, reflected the following:

Stockholders' Equity:	
Common stock, nopar, authorized shares 500,000:	
Outstanding at beginning of year, 100,000 shares	$175,000
Issued during the year, September 1, 3,000 shares	6,000
Preferred stock, 6%, par $10, nonconvertible, authorized 20,000 shares:	
Outstanding during the year, 6,000 shares	60,000
Contributed capital in excess of par, preferred stock	3,000
Retained earnings	50,000
Liabilities:	
Bonds payable, 6½%, nonconvertible	100,000
Income before extraordinary items	90,000
Extraordinary loss (net of tax)	(20,000)
Net income	70,000

Required:

1. Is this a simple or complex capital structure? Explain.
2. What kinds of EPS presentation is required? Explain.
3. Compute the required EPS amounts (show all computations).

Exercise 17–12

The records of Sterling Corporation provided the following data; assuming a complex capital structure; at year-end (assume all amounts are correct):

Average common shares outstanding during the year, 50,000 shares, par $2	$100,000
Preferred stock, 6½, par $5 nonconvertible, shares outstanding during the year, 3,000 ...	15,000
Common stock equivalents (based on stock warrants outstanding), 10,000 shares	
Additional shares that would be issued assuming full dilution, 5,000 shares (based on $30,000, 6% convertible bonds outstanding).	
Retained earnings	40,000
Income before extraordinary items	60,000
Extraordinary loss (net of tax)........................	(8,000)
Net income	52,000

Required:

1. What characteristics of the capital structure supports the assumption of a complex capital structure?
2. What kind of EPS presentation is required? Explain.
3. Compute the required EPS amounts (show all computations). Assume a 40% tax rate.

Exercise 17–13

Fisher Corporation is computing the EPS amounts at December 31, 19A. It is complicated because the capital structure is properly classified as complex. Two problems are yet to be resolved, viz:

a. Average common shares outstanding:
  Relevant data available:

Common stock, nopar, shares outstanding at beginning of year	75,000
Shares sold and issued on April 1, 19A	10,000
Shares acquired as treasury stock on October 1, 19A............	3,000

b. Common stock equivalents:
  Common stock options outstanding for 1,500 shares.
  Average market price of the common stock, $18 per share.
  Option price, $15 per share.

Required:

1. What kind of EPS presentation is required? Explain.
2. Compute the average number of shares outstanding (show computations).
3. Are there any common stock equivalents? Provide computations to support your response.
4. Under what conditions would the common stock options outstanding be omitted from the EPS computations?

Exercise 17–14

Jackson Corporation has a complex capital structure. At the end of 19A, the EPS presentation is to be developed. At issue is the proper treatment of the outstanding bonds, viz:

Bonds payable, 8%, convertible	$150,000
Conversion ratio: 30 shares of common stock for each $1,000 bond.	
Bond issuance price: 112.	
Prime bank interest rate: 7½%.	

Required:

1. Present an analysis to determine whether the bonds represent common stock equivalents (show computations).
2. How many additional shares, because of the bonds, should be included in the computation of the *(a)* primary EPS amount, and *(b)* fully diluted EPS amount? Explain.
3. Under what circumstances would the effect of the bonds payable be omitted from the EPS computations?

PROBLEMS

Problem 17–1

Martin Corporation reported the following summarized data:

Assets	$655,000	Stockholders' Equity:	
Less: Liabilities	100,000	Preferred stock, $10 par	$300,000
		Common stock, $5 par value, 30,000 shares	150,000
		Contributed capital in excess of par, preferred	30,000
		Retained earnings	75,000
	$555,000		$555,000

The state law places a restriction on retained earnings equal to the cost of treasury stock held.

The following transactions affecting stockholders' equity were recorded:

a. Purchased preferred treasury stock, 500 shares at $14.
b. Purchased common treasury stock, 1,000 shares at $20.
c. Sold preferred treasury stock, 100 shares at $15.
d. Sold common treasury stock, 400 shares at $18.

Required:

1. Give entries in parallel columns for the treasury stock transactions assuming *(a)* the cost method, and *(b)* the par-value method is used.
2. Prepare the resulting balance sheet (unclassified) for each method.

Problem 17–2

Sadler Corporation reported the following data:

Common stock, $5 par value, 50,000 shares outstanding	$250,000
Preferred stock, 6%, $10 par value, 10,000 shares authorized, 6,000 issued	60,000
Contributed capital in excess of par, common stock	62,500
Contributed capital in excess of par, preferred stock	6,000
Retained earnings	200,000

Subsequent to this date, the following transactions affecting stockholders' equity were recorded:

a. Purchased 2,000 shares of common treasury stock at $20 per share.
b. Purchased 1,000 shares of preferred treasury stock at $10.50 per share.
c. Sold 1,000 shares of the common treasury stock for $22 per share.
d. Transferred 20 shares of preferred treasury stock to A. K. Jones in payment for professional services rendered the corporation.

The state law places a restriction on retained earnings equal to the cost of treasury stock held.

Required:

1. Give the entries, in parallel columns, for the treasury stock transactions assuming *(a)* the cost method, and *(b)* the par-value method.
2. Prepare the resulting stockholders' equity section of the balance sheet for each method. Give all required disclosures with respect to the treasury stock.

Problem 17–3

Sala Corporation had authorized and outstanding 5,000 shares of common stock, par value $50 per share. The stockholders approved the recall of the old stock and the exchange for each share of old stock two shares of new common stock. The new authorization was for 15,000 shares of stock.

Required:

Prepare entries to record the change under each of the following separate cases (assume a sufficient balance in retained earnings):

Case A – The old stock originally was sold at a premium of $2 per share and the new stock was $25 par-value common stock.
Case B – The old stock was sold at a premium of $3 per share, and the new stock was nopar-value stock with no stated or assigned value.
Case C – The old stock was sold at a premium of $1 per share, and the new stock was nopar-value stock with no stated or assigned value.
Case D – The old stock was sold at par, and the new stock was nopar-value stock with no stated or assigned value.
Case E – The old stock was sold at a premium of $2 per share, and the new stock was nopar-value stock with a stated value of $20 per share.
Case F – The old stock was sold at a premium of $5 per share, and the new stock was nopar-value stock with a stated value of $30 per share.
Case G – The old stock was sold at par, and the new stock was nopar-value stock with a stated value of $27.50 per share.

Problem 17–4

The following account balances were shown on the books of SW Corporation at December 31:

Cumulative preferred stock, par $100, 6% 2,000 shares	$200,000
Common stock, par $50, 5,000 shares	250,000
Retained earnings (deficit)	(45,000)

At a stockholders' meeting (including holders of preferred shares) the following quasi-reorganization was decided on:

a. That an amendment to the charter be obtained authorizing a total issue of 5,000 shares of noncumulative 8% preferred, par $100 per share, and 40,000 shares of nopar common stock.

b. That all outstanding stock be returned in exchange for new stock as follows:
   (1) For each share of old preferred, one share of new preferred. Purchased for cash at par 20 shares of old preferred stock from a dissatisfied stockholder.
   (2) For each share of old common, two shares of new common; the credit to the nopar stock account shall be at an amount, in contributed capital from conversion, sufficient to exactly provide for the deficit in retained earnings.

c. That the past operating deficit be written off against the credit created by the conversion of the common stock.

During the ensuing year the following transactions were effected:

d. Sold 200 shares of the new preferred stock at $105 per share.

e. The company issued 1,200 shares of nopar common in payment for a patent tentatively valued by the seller at $20,000. (The market value of a share was $15).

f. The company sold 50 shares of nopar common at $19 per share, receiving cash, and at the same time issued 100, $1,000 bonds at 102; one share of common stock, as a bonus, was given with each bond.

g. At the end of the year the board of directors met and was informed that the net income before deductions for bonuses to officers was $100,000. The directors took the following actions:
   (1) Ordered that 500 shares of nopar common stock (from authorized but unissued shares) be issued to officers as a bonus. The market price of a nopar common share on this date was $16.
   (2) Declared and paid dividends (for one year) on the preferred stock outstanding.

Required:

1. Prepare journal entries to record the above transactions.
2. Prepare the stockholders' equity section of the balance sheet after giving effect to the above transactions.

Problem 17-5 (a review problem)

The following condensed trial balance was taken from the books of the LaRue Corporation at December 31:

Assets	$584,000	
Liabilities		$ 60,000
Common stock, $10 par value (100,000 shares authorized; 40,000 shares issued)		400,000
Contributed capital in excess of par		4,000
Retained earnings		120,000
	$584,000	$584,000

During the year the following transactions were completed:

a. Subscriptions were received for 10,000 shares of common stock at $11 per share; 40% of the subscription price was collected. The shares will not be issued until the full price is collected.

b. A patent was acquired in exchange for 5,000 shares of common stock. The owner valued the patent at $60,000. Common stock was selling at $11.

c. An original stockholder desired to get money back from the corporation for 1,000 shares purchased at $10.10 per share. The corporation purchased the shares paying $10.50 per share. The par-value method is used for treasury stock.

d. The balance on subscriptions (*a*) was collected; the stock was issued.

e. Machinery costing $34,000 was purchased; 50% was paid down, the balance due in one year.

f. The charter was amended authorizing 200,000 shares of nopar common stock (to replace the par-value common stock) and 5,000 shares of preferred stock, par $100.

g. The old common stock (54,000 shares outstanding) was exchanged for the new nopar stock; two shares of the new stock were issued for each share of old stock. The 1,000 shares of old treasury stock were canceled.

h. 1,000 shares of the preferred stock were sold at $105.

i. 200 shares of common were reacquired as treasury stock at $12; and 100 shares of preferred at $105.

j. Net income for the period was $40,000 (debit assets).

k. A 3% dividend was declared on the preferred, and $.50 per share was declared on the common stock.

Required:

1. Set up a worksheet with debit and credit columns for (*a*) starting balances, (*b*) interim entries, and (*c*) ending balances (six money columns). Enter the beginning balances as given, record the transactions, and compute the ending balances. Key the entries. Do not detail assets and liabilities; set up one account for assets and one for liabilities. Since the problem focuses on stockholders' equity it should be detailed.
2. Prepare the resulting balance sheet that reflects appropriate detail in the stockholders' section. Include all disclosures relating to treasury stock. Assume the state law places a restriction on retained earnings equal to the cost of treasury stock held.

Problem 17–6

You have just commenced your audit of Shaky Company for the year ended December 31, 19B. The president advises you that the company is insolvent and must declare bankruptcy unless a large loan can be obtained immediately. A lender who is willing to advance $450,000 to the company has been located, but will only make the loan subject to the following conditions:

1. A $450,000, 8% mortgage payable over 15 years on the land and buildings will be given as security on a new loan (cash received $450,000).
2. A new issue of 500 shares of $100 par-value, 5%, noncumulative, nonparticipating preferred stock will replace 500 outstanding shares of $100 par-value, 7%, cumulative, participating preferred stock. Preferred stockholders will repudiate all claims to $21,000 of dividends in arrears. The company has never formally declared the dividends.
3. A new issue of 600 shares of $50 par-value, class A common stock will replace 600 outstanding shares of $100 par-value, class A common stock.

4. A new issue of 650 shares of $40 par-value, class B common stock will replace 650 outstanding shares of $100 par-value, class B common stock.
5. A $600,000, 6% mortgage payable on the company's land and buildings held by a major stockholder will be canceled along with four months' accrued interest already recorded. The mortgage will be replaced by 5,000 shares of $100 par-value, 6%, cumulative if earned, nonparticipating preferred stock.
6. On May 1, 19A, the company's trade creditors had accepted $360,000 in notes payable on demand at 6% interest in settlement of all past-due accounts. No payment has been made to date on the accrued interest or principal. The company will offer to settle these liabilities at $.75 per $1 owed or to replace the notes payable on demand with new notes payable for full indebtedness over five years at 6% interest. It is estimated that $200,000 of the demand notes and the accrued interest thereon will be exchanged for the longer term notes and that the balance will accept the offer of a reduced cash settlement.

The president of the Shaky Company requests that you determine the effect of the foregoing on the company and furnishes the following condensed account balances (incomplete), which you believe are correct:

Bank overdraft	$ 15,000
Other current assets	410,000
Fixed assets	840,000
Trade accounts payable	235,000
Other current liabilities	85,000
Contributed capital in excess of par value	125,000
Retained earnings deficit	345,000

Required:

1. Prepare pro forma journal entries that you would suggest to give effect to the foregoing as of January 1, 19C. Entries should be keyed to numbered information in order.
2. Prepare a pro forma balance sheet for the Shaky Company at January 1, 19C, as if the recapitalization had been consummated.

(AICPA adapted)

Problem 17–7

Coulson Corporation is authorized to issue 100,000 shares of common stock, par $25; of which 60,000 is outstanding. During 1976, the company initiated a stock bonus plan for certain top managers. The plan provides for each qualified executive to receive an option for 1,000 shares of the common stock. Subject to continued employment, the option is exercisable at any time after three years and, prior to expiration, five years from the date of grant. The option is nontransferable and the specified option price is $60 per share. The option is considered to be additional compensation, prorated equally, for the year of the grant and the following four years. On January 1, 1976, E. R. Smalley, the company president, was granted an option under the plan when the market price of the stock was $66. Assume Smalley exercised the grant during the latter part of 1980 when the market price of the stock was $90 per share.

Required:

1. Is this a compensatory plan? Explain.
2. What is the measurement date? Explain.
3. What is the amount of the total compensation?

4. Over what period should this compensation be assigned as expense? How much should be assigned to 1976? to 1977? Explain.
5. Give appropriate entries on the following dates (if none, explain why):
   a. Date of grant.
   b. Measurement date.
   c. End of each year, starting on December 31, 1976.
   d. Exercise date.
6. Illustrate how the option would affect the income statement and balance sheet at the end of 1976 and 1977.

Problem 17–8

Foster Corporation has a stock option plan for the top managers that includes the following provisions:

a. Each manager that qualifies will receive an option to acquire 10,000 shares of Foster common stock, par $1, at an option price of $10 per share.
b. The option is nontransferable and, if not exercised, expires five years from date of grant.
c. The option cannot be exercised prior to the end of two years from date of grant and requires continued employment in a covered position.
d. The stock option is for additional compensation for the year of the grant and the following four years; approximately equal each year.

An option was granted to the top executive on January 1, 1976, at which time the common stock was selling at $16 per share. Assume the option is exercised on December 31, 1980, when the stock is quoted at $30 per share.

At January 1, 1976, common stock, par $1, authorized was 150,000 shares of which 90,000 was outstanding.

Required:

1. Is this a compensatory plan? Explain.
2. What is the measurement date? Explain.
3. Compute the total compensation expense.
4. Over what period of time should this total compensation be assigned as expense? Explain.
5. Give appropriate entries for the following dates (if none, explain why):
   a. Date of grant.
   b. Measurement date.
   c. End of each year, starting on December 31, 1976.
   d. Exercise date.
6. Illustrate how the option would affect the income statement and balance sheet at the end of 1976 and 1977.

Problem 17–9

Goodson Corporation has 100,000 shares of common stock, par $20, authorized, of which 40,000 shares are outstanding. The company has a stock option plan that provides the following:

a. Each qualified manager shall receive on January 1, a computed number of shares of common stock at a computed option price per share. The computation of each amount shall be made two years after the option is granted and will be related to the percentage increase in net income over that period.

b. The options are nontransferable and must be exercised, not earlier than two years and not later than five years, from date of grant. Affiliation with the company is required to the exercise date.

On January 1, 1976, an option was granted to A. B. Cox, the controller. At that date, the common stock was quoted on the market at $50 per share. Assume Cox exercised the option near the end of 1980.

	Estimates Made on January 1, 1976, of What the Amount Would Be on December 31, 1977	*Actual Amount on December 31, 1977*
Number of shares optioned	500	510
Option price	$60	$62
Market price per share (a relatively steady increase each year)	$70	$73

Required:

1. Is this a compensatory plan? Explain.
2. When is the measurement date? Explain.
3. Over what period should total compensation expense be assigned?
4. Give appropriate entries for the following dates (if none, explain why):
   a. Date of grant.
   b. End of 1976 and 1977.
   c. Measurement date.
   d. End of 1978, 1979, and 1980.
   e. Exercise date.

Problem 17–10

Frost Corporation is authorized to issue 200,000 shares of common stock, par $10; to date 75,000 shares have been issued. During 1976, the corporation initiated a stock option plan for the three top managers. The plan provides that each manager will receive an option to purchase, two years from date of grant, 2,000 shares of the common stock at a base option price of $48, adjusted for changes in earnings per share, and providing continued employment. The option price is to be established on December 31, 1977, and will be based on changes in earnings per share. EPS for 1975 was $2. The option price will be established at the end of 1977 as follows:

> The option price per share will be the base option price of $48 adjusted proportionately upward or downward in inverse relationship to changes in EPS from 1975 to 1977.

The options are nontransferable and expire five years from date of grant. The stock was quoted at $45 per share on the market on January 1, 1976. The management has made, what they consider to be, realistic estimates that earnings per share would increase steadily to $3.20 at December 31, 1977, and that the stock would increase steadily to $46 per share on that date. EPS on December 31, 1977, actually turned out to be $3, and the market price, $50.

The president received the options with the option price unknown at January

1, 1976. Assume the president exercised the option, the last day possible, on January 1, 1981.

Required:

1. Is this a compensatory plan? Explain.
2. What is the measurement date? Explain.
3. Over what period should this total compensation expense be assigned?
4. Give appropriate entries on the following dates (if none, explain why):
   a. Date of grant.
   b. End of 1976 and 1977.
   c. Measurement date.
   d. End of 1978, 1979, and 1980.
   e. Exercise date.

Problem 17-11

Beame Corporation is developing the EPS presentation at December 31, 19A. The records of the company provide the following information:

Liabilities:	
Convertible bonds payable, 7% (each $1,000 bond is convertible to 20 shares of common stock)	$200,000
Stockholders' Equity:	
Common stock, nopar, authorized 100,000 shares:	
Outstanding January 1, 19A, 59,000 shares	300,000
Issued 10,000 shares on April 1, 19A	60,000
Common stock warrants outstanding (for 4,000 shares of common stock)	16,000
Preferred stock, 6%, par $10, nonconvertible, authorized 20,000 shares, outstanding during 19A, 5,000 shares	50,000
Contributed capital in excess of par, preferred stock	10,000
Retained earnings	80,000
Income before extraordinary items	150,000
Extraordinary loss (net of tax)	(20,000)
Net income	130,000

Other data:

a. Stock warrants—option price $4 per share; market price of the common stock at date of issuance of the warrants, $6.
b. Convertible bonds—issue price, 115; prime interest rate at date of issuance was 8%.
c. Average income tax rate of 45%.

Required:

1. Is this a simple, or a complex, capital structure? Explain.
2. What kind of EPS presentation is required? Explain.
3. Prepare the required EPS presentation for 19A. Show all computations.
4. Were there any antidilutive securities? How was this determined?
5. How should antidilutive securities be treated in the computations of EPS? Why?

Problem 17–12

The records of Indus Corporation reflected the following data at the end of 19A:

Liabilities:	
Bonds payable, 7½%, convertible (each $1,000 bond is converted to 30 shares of common stock)	$150,000
Stockholders' Equity:	
Common stock, par $2, authorized 300,000 shares:	
Outstanding January 1, 19A, 150,000 shares	300,000
Issued on October 1, 19A, 20,000 shares	40,000
Common stock warrants outstanding (for 6,000 shares)	18,000
Preferred stock, 6%, par $5, authorized 100,000 shares, outstanding during 19A, 20,000 shares	100,000
Contributed capital in excess of par, common	340,000
Contributed capital in excess of par, preferred	60,000
Retained earnings	110,000
Income before extraordinary items	170,000
Extraordinary loss (net of tax)	(20,000)
Net income	150,000

Other data:

a. Stock warrants – option price, $3 per share; market price of common stock, $3.60 per share.
b. Convertible bonds – issue price, 125; prime interest rate at date of issuance of the bonds was 8½%.
c. Average income tax rate of 40%.

Required:

1. Is this a simple, or a complex, capital structure? Explain.
2. What kind of EPS presentation is required? Explain.
3. Prepare the required EPS presentation for 19A. Show all computations.
4. Were there any antidilutive securities? How was this determined?
5. How should antidilutive securities be treated in EPS computations? Why?

Chapter 18

Long-Term Investments in Equity Securities

A company may invest in another company by acquiring either *(a)* debt securities (i.e., notes, mortgages, and bonds) or *(b)* equity securities (i.e., common and preferred stock). The investments may be acquired with the intention of holding them on a short-term or long-term basis. Short-term investments (also called temporary investments) were discussed in Chapter 7. Investments are classified as current assets when they meet the dual test of (1) ready *marketability* and (2) a clear *intention* by management to convert them to cash during the upcoming year or normal operating cycle, whichever is the longer. All investments not clearly meeting both of these criteria are classified as noncurrent assets on the balance sheet under the caption "Investments and Funds" (see Chapter 5). Investments classified under this category are referred to as long-term or permanent investments. They include both debt and equity securities and may or may not meet the test of ready marketability; however, the intention of management must be to retain them in the long-term.

The purpose of this chapter is to discuss the measuring, accounting, and reporting of long-term investments in equity securities. Long-term investments in debt securities are discussed in Chapter 19. To accomplish this purpose, the chapter is divided into two parts: Part A–Cost, Equity, and Market Value Methods; and Part B–Consolidated Statements. There is a general discussion at the start of the chapter, and Part B is followed by a discussion of some special problems.[1]

[1] Subdivision of the chapter provides flexibility should consideration of consolidated statements be deferred to a more advanced course. Alternatively, this topic is included because surveys have consistently indicated that a good percentage of accounting majors do not take an advanced course in consolidations and mergers.

RECORDING LONG-TERM INVESTMENTS AT DATE OF ACQUISITION

At date of acquisition of a long-term investment, an appropriately designated investment account is debited with the full cost, in accordance with the cost principle. Shares of stock may be acquired on various security markets. At date of purchase, full cost includes the basic cost of the security plus brokerage fees, excise taxes, and any other transfer costs incurred by the purchaser. Stocks may be purchased for cash, "on margin," or on a subscription basis. When stock is acquired on margin, only part of the purchase price is paid initially, and the balance is borrowed. The stock should be recorded at its full cost, and the liability to the lender recognized. A stock subscription or agreement to buy the stock of another corporation creates an asset represented by the stock investment and a liability for the amount to be paid. Interest paid on a subscription contract, or on funds borrowed to purchase the investment, should be recorded as interest expense and not capitalized as part of the cost of the investment.

When noncash considerations (property or services) are given for long-term investments, the cost assigned to the securities should be (1) the fair market value of the consideration given or (2) the fair market value of the securities received, whichever is more definitely determinable. Determination of either value in the case of unlisted or closely held securities being exchanged for property for which no established market value exists may force resort to appraisals or estimates.

Securities frequently are purchased between regular interest or dividend dates. Under generally accepted accounting principles, interest is accrued on debt securities but dividends are rarely accrued. In the case of a purchase of cumulative preferred stock on which the issuing corporation has been regularly paying dividends, the correct treatment is debatable. The authors would not accrue dividends (even in this case) because dividends legally do not accrue.[2]

To illustrate, assume that on October 1, 1976, X Corporation purchased 500 shares of the common stock of Y Corporation, par $5, at $20 per share. Dividends are paid regularly around July 1 of each year; the last dividend was $.50 per share. The investment would be recorded as follows:

Long-term investment, Y Corporation common stock		
(500 shares)	10,000	
Cash		10,000

(Note: No dividends are accrued.)

Alternatively, assume that on October 1, 1976, X Corporation pur-

---

[2] Theoretically, dividends should be recognized when stock is purchased between the declaration date and record date (ex-dividend date).

The price of a listed stock (especially preferred) tends to rise as the regular dividend date approaches and to decline by approximately the amount of the dividend as soon as the stock goes "ex dividends." Prices of stocks are, however, subject to many variables which may obscure these pre- and post-dividend movements.

chased a $10,000, 6% bond (interest payable each July 1) of Y Corporation for $10,000 plus accrued interest. The acquisition of this long-term investment in *debt securities* would be recorded as follows:

Long-term investment, Y Corporation bond (at cost)	10,000	
Accrued investment revenue ($10,000 × .06 × 3/12)	150	
Cash		10,150

(Note: Interest accrued to date of purchase—discussed in detail in the next chapter.)

Special Cost Problems

A purchase of two or more classes of securities for a single lump sum (sometimes called a basket purchase) necessitates allocation of the total cost to each class of securities based upon their relative fair market value. For example, if a block of Security A purchased alone would cost $1,000 and a block of Security B purchased separately would cost $2,000, one third of the total lump-sum cost would be allocated to A and two thirds to B whether the combined cost was $3,000 or some other amount. In case one class of securities has a known market value and the other does not, the known market value is used for that class and the remainder of the lump-sum price is allocated to the others. If neither has a known market value it is better to defer any apportionment until evidence of at least one value becomes sufficiently clear.

Securities sometimes are acquired in exchange for other securities. The securities acquired should be recorded at their fair market value or at the fair market value of those given up at the time of the exchange, whichever is more clearly determinable. To illustrate an exchange of securities, assume that each holder of a share of $100 par value preferred stock in AB Corporation becomes entitled to receive in exchange five shares of nopar common stock of the company. An investor who had paid $6,000 for 50 shares of preferred stock makes the exchange. At the time of the exchange the nopar common shares were selling at $27. The exchange would be recorded as follows:[3]

Investment in nopar common stock of AB Corporation ($27 × 250 shares)	6,750	
Investment in preferred stock of AB Corporation		6,000
Gain on conversion of stock investment		750

In accounting for investments, generally, it is necessary to maintain an identification of each security acquired. Usually, this can be done by using the stock or bond certificate number. In effect, this requires the maintenance of inventory records with respect to securities in order that they may be "costed out" upon disposition. For example, if 10 shares of X Corporation stock are purchased at $150 per share and later an additional 30 shares are purchased at $200 per share, the subsequent sale of 5 shares at $180 per share would pose a cost identification problem. If the five shares can be identified by certificate number as a part of the

[3] A more extended discussion of the exchange of securities is presented in Chapter 19; an alternate treatment whereby no gain or loss is recognized also is presented. The authors are of the opinion that the treatment illustrated here is preferable, assuming materiality.

first purchase, a gain of $30 per share should be recognized. Alternatively, if they are identified with the second purchase, a loss of $20 per share should be recognized. If an averaging procedure were applied, the result would be a loss of $7.50 per share computed as follows:

First purchase	10 shares @ $150 =	$1,500
Second purchase	30 shares @ $200 =	6,000
Total	40	$7,500

Average cost per share $7,500 ÷ 40 shares =	$187.50
Sales price per share =	180.00
Loss per Share	$ 7.50

Identification of shares sold ordinarily is not difficult. However, where blocks of shares have been transferred through an estate, or where the issuing corporation has exchanged substitute securities for those originally purchased, an identification problem can arise. Federal tax laws require use of "first-in, first-out" where specific identification cannot be made. Use of either *Fifo* or an *average cost* procedure is acceptable from the standpoint of accounting theory.

ACCOUNTING AND REPORTING FOR STOCK INVESTMENTS SUBSEQUENT TO ACQUISITION

In accounting for long-term investments in stock subsequent to acquisition date, a careful distinction is maintained between *(a)* voting common stock and nonvoting stock, such as nonvoting preferred stock; and *(b)* the proportion of voting shares owned to the total shares outstanding (i.e., the level of ownership of the voting shares).[4]

Fundamentally, there are three different methods of accounting and reporting stock investments, viz: (1) cost method, (2) equity method, and (3) fair market value method. Each of these methods is used under certain specified conditions. In addition, when one company owns a controlling interest in the voting stock of another company, the controlling company must prepare *consolidated financial statements* (discussed in Part B of this chapter).

In accounting for long-term investments, a careful distinction must be maintained between *voting common stock* and nonvoting stock because the former permits the owner to exercise some influence or control through voting on the operating and financial policies of the other company. The degree of influence or control depends upon the proportion of voting shares owned as an investment (usually the common stock) to the total of such shares outstanding. Therefore, in accounting and reporting for long-term investments in the voting capital stock of

[4] Level of ownership refers to the proportion of shares owned to the total shares outstanding. To illustrate, assume Company X purchased 20,000 shares of common stock of Company Y when there were 100,000 total shares outstanding. The level of ownership by Company X in Company Y would be: 20,000 ÷ 100,000 = 20%. Ownership of exactly 50% of the voting shares may fit the "significant influence" category or the controlling interest category depending on other factors.

another company, *APB Opinion No. 18,* "Equity Method for Investments in Common Stock" (March 1971), defined two important concepts, "significant influence" and "control," as follows:

1. Significant influence—the ability of the investor company to affect, in an important degree, the operating and financing policies of another company because of ownership of a sufficient number of shares of its voting stock. Ability to exercise significant influence also may be indicated in several other ways, such as representation on the board of directors, participation in policy making processes, material intercompany transactions, interchange of managerial personnel, or technological dependency. In order to achieve a reasonable degree of uniformity, the APB provided an operational rule that an investment of 20% or more of the voting stock should lead to the presumption that in the absence of evidence to the contrary, an investor has the ability to exercise significant influence over the other company.
2. Controlling interest—a controlling interest exists when the investing company owns enough of the voting stock of the other company to effectively control its operating and financing policies. Ownership of over 50% of the outstanding voting stock usually would assure control; however, there are situations where this may not be the case (discussed in Part B). On the other hand, circumstances sometimes exist where ownership of something less than 50% may create a controlling interest. Factors such as number of shares outstanding, number of shareholders, and shareholder participation in voting bear on the point at which a controlling interest is attained. The accounting profession has found it very difficult to develop an operational definition of control based on 50% or less of the voting stock. As a consequence, the presumption is that a controlling interest is represented by over 50% of the voting stock.

The issuance of *APB Opinion No. 18* had a significant impact on the accounting for long-term investments in capital stock. In accordance with certain prior pronouncements and *Opinion No. 18,* accounting for long-term investments in stock may be outlined as follows:

Accounting for Long-Term Equity Investments

Investment Characteristics	*Level of Ownership*	*Reporting Method*
A. No significant influence or control:		
1. Nonvoting stock owned.	All levels	Cost
2. Voting stock owned.	Less than 20%	Cost
B. Significant influence but not control:		
3. Voting stock owned.	20% up to 50%	Equity
C. Controlling interest:		
4. Voting stock owned, but for special reasons not appropriate to consolidate.	Over 50%	Equity
5. Voting stock owned, appropriate to consolidate.	Over 50%	Consolidated statement basis

Part A of this chapter will discuss and illustrate categories (1) through (4); Part B will discuss the accounting and reporting where there is a controlling interest and when *consolidated statements* are required, that is, category (5).

PART A—COST, EQUITY, AND MARKET VALUE METHODS

COST METHOD

Under the cost method, a long-term investment in equity securities is recorded in the accounts at cost. Subsequently, it is reflected in the accounts and reported on the balance sheet at lower of cost or market. On this point, FASB *Statement No. 12* (December 31, 1975) states:

> The carrying value of a marketable equity securities portfolio shall be the lower of its aggregate cost or market value, determined at the balance sheet date. The amount by which aggregate cost of the portfolio exceeds market value shall be accounted for as the valuation allowance.
>
> Marketable equity securities owned by an entity shall, in the case of a classified balance sheet, be grouped into separate portfolios according to the current or noncurrent classification of the securities for the purpose of comparing aggregate cost and market value to determine carrying amount. In the case of an unclassified balance sheet, marketable equity securities shall for the purposes of this Statement be considered as noncurrent assets.

Equity securities, as used in *Statement No. 12,* encompasses all capital stock (including warrants, rights, and stock options) except preferred stock that by its terms either must be redeemed by the issuing enterprise or is redeemable at the option of the investor. Treasury stock and convertible bonds are excluded.

To apply the lower-of-cost-or-market concept, *Statement No. 12* defines *cost* after acquisition as the original cost of the equity security except when a *new cost basis* is established after acquisition; *(a)* when a marketable equity security is transferred between current and noncurrent classification and *(b)* when an individual marketable security (rather than the portfolio) has been written down to cost to reflect a permanent, as opposed to a temporary, decline in market value. These two situations are discussed later.

Statement No. 12 makes a careful distinction between realized and unrealized losses and gains on marketable equity securities. A *realized* loss or gain represents the difference between the net proceeds received and the investment cost of an equity security at date of sale. In contrast, an *unrealized* gain or loss on a marketable equity security represents the difference between the aggregate market value and aggregate cost of the long-term investment portfolio on a given date. Realized gains and losses on a marketable equity security are recognized only when securities are sold (or written down because of a permanent decline) whereas, unrealized gains and losses are recognized only at the end of the accounting period when the adjusting entry is made to apply the lower-of-cost-or-market concept to the portfolio.

In the adjusting entry, an allowance account (an asset contra account) is used to record the difference between cost and market, and an unrealized loss or gain account is used for the other side of the entry. On the balance sheet, the allowance account balance is subtracted from the cost of the portfolio and the accumulated unrealized loss amount is reported under the owners' equity caption as unrealized capital. In contrast, recall from Chapter 7 that, for marketable securities classified as *current assets,* both the unrealized and realized gains and losses are reported on the income statement. Under no circumstances can the cumulative unrealized gain exceed the unrealized losses on the long-term portfolio of equity securities.

Under the cost method, cash dividends received are recorded as investment revenue. Dividends are usually recorded as revenue when the cash is received; however if the accounting period ends between the declaration date and payment date, they should be recorded in the period of declaration. A cash dividend would be recorded as follows:

Cash	7,500	
Investment revenue		7,500

Occasionally, an investor receives a dividend that is entirely, or in part, a *liquidating dividend* (see Chapter 16). Dividends received in excess of earnings accumulated since the acquisition date are considered liquidating dividends. In such instances, the investor should reduce the investment account for the amount of the liquidating dividend. Dividends received in noncash assets should be recorded at the fair market value of the assets received.

To illustrate application of the cost method for long-term investments in equity securities, the following series of transactions and entries for X Corporation are presented:

January 5, 19A—Purchased the following equity securities as a long-term investment (less than 20% of the outstanding shares in each case):

Y Corporation, common stock (par $5), 5,000 shares at $12
Z Corporation, preferred stock (par $10, nonredeemable), 4,000 shares at $20

Long-term investments in equity securities	140,000	
Cash (5,000 × $12) + (4,000 × $20)		140,000

December 31, 19A—Adjusting entry to lower of cost or market; Market value: Y stock, $10; Z stock, $21.

Unrealized loss on long-term investments in equity securities...	6,000	
Allowance to reduce long-term investments in equity securities to market		6,000

Computation:

Security	Shares	Cost	Market	Unrealized Gain (Loss)
Y	5,000	@ $12 = $ 60,000	@ $10 = $ 50,000	($10,000)
Z	4,000	@ $20 = 80,000	@ $21 = 84,000	4,000
Total		$140,000	$134,000	($ 6,000)

August 10, 19B—Unexpectedly sold 1,000 shares of the Z Corporation stock at $24.

Cash (1,000 × $24)	24,000	
Long-term investments in equity securities (1,000 × $20)		20,000
Realized gain on sale of long-term investments*		4,000

* Closed to income summary

December 31, 19B—Adjusting entry to lower of cost or market; Market value: Y stock, $10.50; Z stock, $21.50.

Allowance to reduce long-term investment in equity securities to market	3,000	
Unrealized gain on long-term investment in equity securities		3,000

Computation:

Security	*Shares*	*Cost*	*Market*	*Unrealized Gain (Loss)*
Y	5,000	@ $12 = $ 60,000	@ $10.50 = $ 52,500	($7,500)
Z	3,000	@ $20 = 60,000	@ $21.50 = 64,500	4,500
Total		$120,000	$117,000	($3,000)

Balance in allowance account	$6,000
Balance needed in allowance account	3,000
Adjustment needed (debit)	$3,000

The financial statements for X Corporation would reflect the following:

	19A		*19B*	
Income Statement:				
Realized gain on long-term investment	$ 4,000			
Balance Sheet:				
Funds & Investments:				
Investments in equity securities, at cost	$140,000		$120,000	
Less: Allowance to reduce equity investments to market	6,000		3,000	
Investment portfolio at lower of cost or market		$134,000		$117,000
Stockholders' Equity:				
Unrealized capital:				
Unrealized loss on investment in equity securities		(6,000)		(3,000)

In the case of a *permanent decline* (as opposed to a temporary decline) in the value of a long-term marketable equity security, the *individual* security (separate from the portfolio) must be written down to market. This reduced valuation thereafter is considered to be *cost;* the amount of the writedown is accounted for as a *realized* loss and is reported on the current income statement.

To illustrate, refer to the above example. Assume Y Corporation stock was selling at $5.00 per share at the end of 19B and that the drop in value was clearly not temporary. This situation would be recorded as follows:

December 31, 19B – To record permanent decline in value of Y Corporation common stock.

Realized loss, permanent decline in valuation of equity security	35,000	
Long-term investment in equity securities [5,000 × ($12 − $5)]		35,000

In the case of a change in *classification* between short-term (current) and long-term (noncurrent) of an individual security, the security must be transferred at the lower-of-cost-or-market value at date of transfer. This value than becomes cost for subsequent periods. If market is below cost, the difference must be accounted for as a realized loss and reported on the income statement.

To illustrate, refer to the example above. Assume Y Corporation stock was reclassified at the end of 19B when the market value was $10.50 (cost was $12). This change in classification would be recorded as follows:

December 31, 19B – To record reclassification of Y Corporation stock.

Short-term investment in equity securities (at market)	52,500	
Realized loss on marketable equity securities*	7,500	
Long-term investment in equity securities (at cost)		60,000

* Closed to income summary

The cost method is relatively simple and limits the recognition of revenue to the receipt of dividends since the investor is presumed to have no ability to significantly influence or control the other company. Disclosure requirements are given in Chapter 7.

EQUITY METHOD

The equity method is more complex and is significantly different from the cost method. It is based on the presumption that the investor owns a sufficient number of the outstanding voting shares of the other company (usually called the investee company) to exercise significant influence (although not control) over the operating and financial policies of the other company. An important element is influence over the *dividend policy* of the investee. This presumption changes the basis for recognition of *investment revenue* from that used in the cost method.

APB Opinion No. 18 states that investors should use the equity method in accounting for "investments in common stock of all unconsolidated subsidiaries (foreign as well as domestic)" and also for all investments in common stock where the "investment in voting stock gives it the ability to exercise significant influence over operating and financial policies of an investee even though the investor holds 50% or less of the voting stock." The *Opinion* also states that "an investment (direct or indirect) of 20% or more of the voting stock of an investee should lead to a presumption that in absence of evidence to the contrary an investor has the ability to exercise significant influence over an investee."[5] *Opinion No. 18* sets forth procedures for applying the equity method; among them are the following:

a. Intercompany profits and losses should be eliminated until realized by the investor or investee as if a subsidiary, corporate joint venture or investee company were consolidated.
b. A difference between the cost of an investment and the amount of underlying equity in net assets of an investee should be accounted for as if the investee were a consolidated subsidiary.
c. The investment(s) in common stock should be shown in the balance sheet of an investor as a single amount, and the investor's share of earnings or losses of an investee(s) should ordinarily be shown in the income statement as a single amount except for the extraordinary items as specified in (d) below.
d. The investor's share of extraordinary items and its share of prior-period adjustments reported in the financial statements of the investee in accordance with *APB Opinions Nos. 9* and *30* should be classified in a similar manner unless they are immaterial in the income statement of the investor.
e. A transaction of an investee of a capital nature that affects the investor's share of stockholders' equity of the investee should be accounted for as if the investee were a consolidated subsidiary.
f. Sales of stock of an investee by an investor should be accounted for as gains or losses equal to the difference at the time of sale between selling price and carrying amount of the stock sold.

Thus, under the equity method the accounting procedure may be outlined as follows:

1. At acquisition of the investment, the investor records the stock purchase at cost.
2. Subsequent to acquisition, each period the investor—
   a. Records the proportionate share of the investee's reported profits by debiting the investment account and crediting Investment Revenue. For a loss the investment account would be credited and Investment Loss debited.
   b. Records the proportionate share of dividends received as a debit to Cash and a credit to the investment account.
   c. Records *depreciation* on any increase in the depreciable assets for the proportionate share of the difference between their fair market value at date of acquisition of the investment and the carrying value reported by the investee. The depreciation amount is debited to Investment Revenue and credited to the investment account.

---

[5] The equity method gives the same net results on the financial statements as would consolidation procedures discussed in Part B; as a consequence it is frequently referred to as "one-line consolidation." Recognition and amortization of goodwill as well as intercompany transactions must be accounted for. Explanations and illustrations of the equity method often assume that the stock was purchased at its book value. This oversimplification rarely occurs and gives misleading knowledge of the concept and essence of the equity method.

d. Records amortization of any *purchased goodwill* resulting from the acquisition transaction. Investment Revenue is debited and the investment account is credited.

3. If all or a part of the investment is subsequently sold, a gain or loss is reported for the difference between the sales price and the then carrying value of the investment (as reflected in the investment account).

Since the equity method is based upon the concept of *significant influence*, *(a)* the investment account is adjusted each period to reflect the proportionate increase or decrease in the ownership of the investee company, and *(b)* investment revenue is recognized by the investor on the basis of the proportionate share of the earnings of the investee (adjusted for additional depreciation and goodwill amortization based on market values).

To illustrate application of the equity method in a relatively simple situation, assume that on January 1, 19A, Company R (the investor) purchased 1,800 shares (representing 20%) of the outstanding voting common stock of Company E (the investee company) for $300,000 cash. Assume on date of acquisition the following values relating to Company E were assembled by Company R:

		Data on Company E	
		Book Values Reported by Co. E	*Fair Market Values*
Assets not subject to depreciation		$ 550,000	$ 570,000
Assets subject to depreciation (net of accumulated depreciation; remaining life, ten years)		500,000	700,000
Total Assets		$1,050,000	$1,270,000
Liabilities		$ 50,000	
Common stock (9,000 shares, par $100)	$900,000		
Retained earnings	100,000	1,000,000	
Total Liabilities and Shareholders' Equity		$1,050,000	

The *equity method* must be applied in this situation because Company R owns 20% of the outstanding stock of Company E as a long-term investment. The purchase of this investment would be recorded by Company R, the investor, as follows:

a. January 1, 19A—Purchase of 1,800 shares of Company E stock (20% ownership) as a long-term investment:

Investment, Company E common stock (1,800 shares)	300,000	
Cash		300,000

Assume further that at the end of 19A Company E reported the following:

1. Income before extraordinary items	$ 80,000
Extraordinary gain (net of tax)	30,000
Net Income	$110,000
2. Total Cash Dividends Declared and Paid	$ 50,000

To apply the equity method, the first step is to compute the *goodwill purchased,* which is the difference between the purchase price and the identifiable net assets of the investee company valued at *fair market value,* viz:[6]

Computation of Purchased Goodwill

Purchase price (for 20% ownership interest)		$300,000
Purchased book value ($1,000,000 × .20)		200,000
Excess of purchase price over book value purchased		100,000
Adjustments to market values:		
Increase on assets not subject to depreciation ($570,000 − $550,000) × .20	$ 4,000	
Increase on assets subject to depreciation ($700,000 − $500,000) × .20	40,000	44,000
Difference—Goodwill Purchased		$ 56,000

The entries to reflect the effects in the accounts of investor Company R at the end of 19A would be as follows:

b. End of 19A—To recognize revenue and an increase in the investment account, based on the proportionate share of net income reported by Company E.

Investment, Company E common stock	22,000	
Investment revenue (ordinary)		16,000
Extraordinary gain (on stock investment)		6,000

Computations:
Ordinary: $80,000 × .20 = $16,000
Extraordinary: 30,000 × .20 = 6,000

c. End of 19A—To record cash dividend received on Company E stock.

Cash	10,000	
Investment, Company E common stock		10,000

Computation: $50,000 × .20 = $10,000.
(Note: A cash dividend, under the equity method, is viewed as a "collection" of a part of the investment since revenue is recognized on net income of the investee and not on dividends.)

d. End of 19A—To record depreciation on the $40,000 *increase* in depreciable assets implicit in the purchase.

[6] Recall the discussion of goodwill in Chapter 14. Purchased goodwill is the difference between the total purchase price of a business and the fair market value of the net assets of that business. The net assets must be reduced to agree with the proportionate share of the business purchased. Under generally accepted accounting principles, goodwill is recorded only when purchased. *APB Opinion No. 17* requires that all intangibles, including goodwill, be amortized over a reasonable period not exceeding 40 years.

Investment revenue (ordinary)	4,000	
Investment, Company E common stock		4,000

Computation: $40,000 ÷ 10 years = $4,000.
(Note: This amount of depreciation is, in effect, a decrease in the revenue recognized in entry *(b)* above since it is additional expense above that included in the computation of net income reported by Company E.)

e. End of 19A – To record periodic amortization of the $56,000 goodwill purchased (as computed above). Assume straight-line amortization over 40 years (maximum permitted by *APB Opinion No. 17*):

Investment revenue (ordinary)	1,400	
Investment, Company E common stock		1,400

Computation: $56,000 ÷ 40 years = $1,400.
(Note: This entry is made for the same reason as the prior entry. It represents a decrease in the revenue recognized in entry *(b)* because it is an additional expense that was not included in the computation of net income reported by Company E.)

Careful study of the above illustration will emphasize the concepts of the equity method. They may be summarized as follows:

1. Investment amount – Record original acquisition at cost in the investment account. Subsequently, increase the investment account for the proportionate share of the income of the investee company; decrease the investment account for dividends paid, additional depreciation, and additional amortization of goodwill. Thus, the investment account in the above illustration was as follows:

Investment, Company E Common Stock (2,000 Shares; 20%)

a. Acquisition (cost)	300,000	*c.* Dividends received	10,000
b. Proportionate share of income of investee	22,000	*d.* Additional depreciation	4,000
		e. Amortization of goodwill	1,400

(Ending debit balance – $306,600)

The ending balance represents the 20% ownership interest of the investor, Company R, in the net assets of the investee, Company E.

2. Revenue recognition – Recognize revenue based upon a proportionate share of net income reported by the investee company, Company E. Reduce the revenue recognized by additional expenses – depreciation and amortization of goodwill. Separately record ordinary and extraordinary gains and losses. Thus, the two revenue accounts in the above illustration were as follows:

Investment Revenue (Ordinary)

d. Depreciation	4,000	*b.* Reported income	16,000
e. Amortization	1,400		

(Ending credit balance to income summary, $10,600)

Extraordinary Gain (Stock Investment)

		b. Reported gain	6,000

(Ending credit balance to income summary, $6,000)

For the investor, the equity method has significant conceptual and measurement differences from the cost method because it is based upon different concepts of (1) investment valuation, and (2) revenue recognition. To illustrate the differences:

		Amount	*Difference*
Investment valuation:			
Cost method (remains at original cost) ...		$300,000	
Equity method (adjusted to proportionate share of net assets)		306,600	$6,600
Revenue recognition:			
Cost method (limited to dividends received):			
Ordinary...		10,000	
Equity method (proportionate share of net income, adjusted):			
Ordinary...	$10,600		
Extraordinary	6,000	16,600	6,600

The two differences ($6,600) are the same because, under the equity method, the investment account is adjusted from the cost basis to the parent's share of the net income of the subsidiary, less dividends received. Similarly, investment revenue is different by the proportionate share of the income of the subsidiary after taking into account that dividends received were recognized as revenue under the cost method but not under the equity method.

MARKET VALUE METHOD

The market value method of accounting for, and reporting, long-term investments is based upon a fundamental concept that is entirely different from those underlying the other methods. The market value method is based upon the concept of *fair value accounting;* that is, the investment should be revalued at each balance sheet date to the then current market price of the stocks held. Thus, *investment valuation* is at current market value and *investment revenue* for the period is comprised of dividends received plus or minus the change in the market value of the securities held during the period.

Many accountants believe strongly that all marketable securities, whether short term or long term, should be accounted for using the market value method because the results *(a)* meet more closely the objective of reporting the economic consequences of holding the investment, and *(b)* are more useful to decision-makers in projecting future economic potentials and cash flows.

At the present time, the market value method is not in accordance with generally accepted accounting principles. However, the method is currently used in special circumstances.[7] Its use in special circumstances is permitted under the modifying principle–industry peculiari-

[7] AICPA, *APB Opinion No. 18,* March 1971, par. 9. Also see Chapter 25.

ties (see Chapter 2, page 26). The market value method is widely used today by insurance companies and mutual funds in accounting for their portfolios. The method is applied in those situations only to marketable securities (i.e., those readily marketable); other methods are used for "nonmarketable" securities. The market value method may be outlined as follows:

1. At date of acquisition, investments are recorded at full cost in accordance with the cost principle.
2. Subsequent to acquisition, the investment account periodically is adjusted to the then current market value of the securities held. The adjusted amount then becomes the "carrying value" for subsequent accounting.
3. Revenue recognized each period includes:
   a. All cash or property dividends received during the period.
   b. The increase (or decrease) in the market value of the portfolio during the period. This is often referred to as the *market* or *holding gain or loss.*
4. At disposition of the investment, the difference between carrying value and sales price is recognized as a gain or loss.

To illustrate the market value method, assume Company A purchased 3,000 shares (10%) of the outstanding common stock of Company B for $50 per share. The events and related journal entries for Company A, for a three-year period, are given below for the *market value method:*

a. Year 1 – purchased 3,000 shares of common stock of Company B at $50 per share.

Investment in Company B, common stock (3,000 shares)	150,000	
Cash		150,000

b. End of Year 1 – Company B reported net income, $20,000.

No entry on books of Company A.

c. End of Year 1 – market price per share on Company B common stock, $55.

Investment in Company B, common stock	15,000	
Investment revenue (holding gain on stock investment)		15,000

($55 – $50) × 3,000 shares = $15,000.

d. End of Year 2 – Company B reported net income, $22,000.

No entry on books of Company A.

e. End of Year 2 – Company B paid a cash dividend of $.25 per share.

Cash (3,000 shares × $.25)	750	
Investment revenue (dividends)		750

f. End of Year 2 – market price of Company B common stock, $55.

No entry on books of Company A since market price is unchanged.

g. Year 3 – sold 1,000 shares of the Company B stock at $54 per share.

Cash	54,000	
Loss on sale of stock investment	1,000	
Investment in Company B (1,000 shares × $55)		55,000

The market value method poses several critical problems in application; among them are the following:

1. Determination of fair market value. In the case of a thin market, a large block of stock may be overvalued if the price per share prevailing at a given time is simply multiplied by the number of shares held. Additionally, many accountants seriously question the realism of using a price per share on a given day (last day of the period). Strong arguments have been made for use of some form of average price per share.

2. Reporting the market gain or loss. Many take the position that the market gain or loss should be viewed as "unrealized" and reported as an unrealized increment (or decrease) in owners' equity. The gain or loss would later be reported through the income statement as "realized" upon disposal of the investment. In contrast, logic and theory suggest that market gains and losses should be reported on the income statement in the period in which they occur. In the illustration immediately above, this position was assumed. In contrast, if the market changes are accounted for as unrealized, the above entries would be changed as follows:

Entry *(c)*:

Investment in Company B, common stock	15,000	
Unrealized market gain on investments (owners' equity)		15,000

Entry *(g)*:

Cash	54,000	
Unrealized market gain on investments	5,000	
Investment in Company B, common stock		55,000
Gain on sale of stock investment		4,000

Numerous arguments have been advanced in favor of and against the valuation of marketable securities at fair market value. The principal arguments cited against it are: *(a)* it violates the cost principle and places on the balance sheet questionable and transitory values that tend to mislead the user, *(b)* it introduces another variance between book and tax amounts, *(c)* it violates the realization principle since revenue is recognized on market changes rather than on sale, and *(d)* because of the typical vagaries of stock prices it introduces a possible "Yo-Yo" effect on net income. In contrast, the proponents disagree with the first two points and argue that *(a)* market values are much more relevant information for decision making by the user; *(b)* it avoids "managed" earnings through the sale of selected securities held that have a low original cost and a high current market value; *(c)* stock yield including both dividends and holding gains and losses should be reported on the income statement each period since that best reflects what is happening to the investment; and *(d)* investors make decisions on the basis of present and future values and cash flows as opposed to historical costs.

PART B—CONSOLIDATED STATEMENTS

PURPOSE OF PART B

The purpose of Part B is to present the fundamental concepts underlying consolidated statements. Therefore, the numerous complexities involved are deferred to more advanced books.

CONCEPT OF A CONTROLLING INTEREST

When an investor company owns over 50% of the outstanding voting stock of another company, in the absence of overriding constraints, a controlling interest is deemed to exist. The investor company is often designated as the *parent* company, and the other company is known as a *subsidiary*. In a parent-subsidiary relationship, both corporations continue as separate legal entities; consequently, they are separate accounting entities (refer to separate-entity assumption, Chapter 2, page 17). As separate entities, they have separate accounting systems and separate financial statements. Because of their special ownership relationship, the *parent company* (but not the subsidiary) is required to prepare *consolidated financial statements* which view the parent and the subsidiary (or subsidiaries) as a single economic entity. To accomplish consolidation, the separate financial statements of the parent and the subsidiary are combined each period by the parent company into one overall set of financial statements as if they were one single entity. The income statement, balance sheet, and statement of changes in financial position are consolidated in this manner.

Consolidated financial statements are not always prepared when over 50% of the stock of another corporation is owned because certain constraints may preclude the exercise of a controlling interest. To qualify for consolidation as a single economic entity, two basic elements must exist, viz:

1. Control of voting rights—this is presumed to exist when over 50% of the outstanding voting stock of another entity is owned by the investor. Nonvoting stock is excluded because it does not provide an avenue for control by vote. However, control may not exist even though over 50% of the voting stock is owned as in the case of a foreign subsidiary where the restrictions imposed by the foreign country are such that effective control cannot be exercised by the parent company. In such situations, the subsidiary would not qualify for consolidation. These are commonly called *unconsolidated subsidiaries* and must be accounted for under the equity method.
2. Economic compatibility—this means that the operations of the parent and the subsidiary are complementary (i.e., they are related operationally and possess similar economic characteristics). For example,

a parent company manufacturing a major product and a subsidiary manufacturing a component part for that product would have economic compatibility. In contrast, a manufacturing company and a bank would lack economic compatibility. In the latter case, the statements would not be consolidated; the subsidiary would be accounted for as an unconsolidated subsidiary.

In applying these two basic elements, the criteria for including a subsidiary in consolidated statements generally are stated as follows:[8]

1. The parent corporation must have the ability to govern, or effectively regulate, the subsidiary corporation's managerial decisions.
2. The parent must be so related to the subsidiary that the economic results of the subsidiary will accrue to the parent (allowing for allocations to the minority shareholders of the subsidiary).
3. The expectation of continuity of control.
4. The degree of existing restrictions upon the availability of earnings of the subsidiary to the parent (frequently a problem with foreign subsidiaries).
5. The general coincidence of accounting periods.
6. The degree of heterogeneity in the operations of the parent and the subsidiary.

Although each affiliate (parent and subsidiaries) keeps separate books and prepares separate financial statements, these individualized statements do not present a comprehensive report of the *economic unit* as a whole. Since the entire economic unit is under one management (and one group of stockholders), a financial report for that unit is essential to meet the needs of owners, creditors, and management. When a subsidiary is less than 100% owned, there is a group of minority shareholders (minority interest) to be recognized in the consolidated financial statements.

ACQUIRING A CONTROLLING INTEREST

There are often a number of economic, legal, and operational advantages to a parent-subsidiary relationship. One company may acquire a controlling interest in the voting stock of another in two basic ways, viz:

1. Pooling of interests. The voting stock of an existing corporation is acquired by the parent by exchanging shares of its own capital stock for the acquired shares of the subsidiary. In this situation, the parent disburses no cash or other resources.
2. Purchase. The voting stock of an existing corporation is acquired by the parent with cash, noncash assets, or debt, for the acquired shares of the subsidiary. In this situation, the parent disburses a significant amount of resources.

---

[8] Adapted from: Charles H. Griffin, Thomas H. Williams, and Kermit D. Larson, *Advanced Accounting*, rev. ed. (Homewood, Ill.: Richard D. Irwin, Inc., 1971).

ACCOUNTING AND REPORTING PROBLEMS

Generally accepted accounting principles require that each subsidiary prepare its own financial statements in the usual manner. However, the parent company is required to prepare *consolidated* financial statements which include all subsidiaries, except those designated unconsolidated subsidiaries as described above. In consolidated financial statements, there is an item by item combination (aggregation) of the parent and subsidiary statements. For example, the amount of cash shown on a consolidated statement would be the sum of the amounts of cash shown on the separate statements of the parent and the subsidiaries.

Emphasis in accounting for a controlling interest is on the consolidated financial statements. Either the cost or equity method may be used by the parent company in its accounts; however, the resulting consolidated financial statements must be the same irrespective of the accounting method used in the accounts.[9] Therefore, this part of the chapter will focus on the *preparation* of consolidated financial statements.

In preparing consolidated financial statements, the method of acquistion—pooling of interests versus purchase—has a significant impact both on the parent company and the resultant consolidated statements.

Consolidated financial statements are prepared by means of a worksheet, and the results are not entered in the accounts. In practically all situations, a special worksheet approach is essential. The essential steps on a worksheet can be summarized as follows:[10]

1. The assets and liabilities of the subsidiary are substituted for the investment account as reflected on the books of the parent. This is accomplished by "eliminating" the owner equity accounts of the subsidiary against the investment account of the parent.
2. Elimination of intercompany receivables and payables.
3. Elimination of intercompany revenues, expenses, gains, and losses.
4. Elimination of other intercompany items.
5. Adjustments on the worksheet are made to reflect certain acquisition effects that differ from the book values.

---

[9] In the case of a controlling interest, the investment account may be carried on either the cost or equity basis. The cost basis is often used because the parent company does not desire to formally enter into its accounts the income, dividend offset, depreciation, amortization, and so on, required by the equity method. Also, the accounting periods may be different, and changes in percentage of ownership complicate the formal approach. Not infrequently, a company, when it moves from the equity approach range (i.e., 20%–50%) to a controlling interest range (over 50%), will adjust the accounts from the equity basis to the cost basis for these reasons. Since consolidation is a *reporting* approach, as opposed to an accounts approach, a worksheet is used, and the accounts of the parent are unaffected by the consolidation procedures. Under either method, the consolidation procedures are adapted on the worksheet so that the consolidated results are precisely the same whether the cost or equity method is used in the accounts. The cost method is used in the discussions in this chapter primarily for instructional convenience. When a parent company prepares unconsolidated statements for special purposes, all subsidiaries and other stock investments that qualify must be reported on the equity basis.

[10] It is important to realize that these steps refer to worksheet entries and to the resultant financial statements and not to the books of accounts of the respective entities which are continued as the records of separate legal entities.

6. The remaining revenues and expenses of the parent and subsidiary are combined to derive a consolidated income statement.
7. The assets and liabilities of the parent and subsidiary are combined to derive a consolidated balance sheet.
8. Utilize similar procedures to develop other desired financial statements on a consolidated basis.

Consolidated financial statements are commonly prepared *(a)* at the date of acquisition of a controlling interest (balance sheet only), and *(b)* for each accounting period subsequent to acquisition (income statement, balance sheet, and statement of changes in financial position).

COMBINATION BY POOLING OF INTERESTS

The acquisition of a controlling interest by one company (the parent company) in the stock of another company (the subsidiary company) by an exchange of shares of stock often occurs because the combination can be effected without the disbursement of cash or other resources by the parent company. The exchange of shares is viewed as the *uniting of ownership interests* and not as a purchase/sale transaction between two companies and their shareholders. As a consequence, the recorded assets, liabilities, revenues, expenses, and so forth, for both entities are combined for consolidated statement purposes, at their *recorded* or book amounts. The net income of the parent and its subsidiaries are combined and restated as consolidated net income. Since a purchase/sale transaction is not presumed for the exchange, fair market values of the assets of the subsidary are not considered in consolidation.

APB Opinion No. 16 specifies that "The combining of existing voting common stock interests by the exchange of stock is the essence of a business combination accounted for by the pooling of interests method." However, the *Opinion* specifies 12 conditions that must be met in order to apply the method; and if they are met, the pooling of interests method *must be used.* All combinations not meeting all of these twelve specifications *must* use the purchase method. Not all stock exchanges will meet the criteria for pooling of interests.

The general characteristics of the pooling of interests method of preparing consolidated statements may be summarized as follows:

1. The assets and liabilities of the combining companies are reported at the previously established *book values* of each. Although adjustments may be made to reflect consistent applications of accounting principles, the current fair values at the time of the combination are not used as a substitute for the book values at that date.
2. No goodwill results from the combination.
3. The retained earnings balances of the combining companies are added to determine the retained earnings balance of the combined companies at date of acquisition.
4. After combination, financial statements which pertain to precombination periods must be restated to reflect the data that would have

been reported had the firms been combined throughout the pre-combination periods being reflected.

We stated earlier that at date of acquisition, a consolidated balance sheet usually is prepared by the parent company; and at the end of each subsequent period, a consolidated income statement, balance sheet, and a statement of changes in financial position are prepared. At this point, we will illustrate preparation of a consolidated balance sheet at date of acquisition, *pooling of interests basis.*

Assume that Company P (parent) acquired 90% of the outstanding voting stock of Company S (subsidiary); therefore, minority shareholders own the remaining 10%. Prior to the exchange, their respective balance sheets reflected the following:

Amounts Immediately Prior to Acquisition

		Company S	
	Company P Book Value	*Book Value*	*Fair Value (appraised)*
Cash	$610,000	$ 20,000	$ 20,000
Inventories	20,000	30,000	25,000
Accounts receivable (net)	10,000*	40,000	40,000
Plant and equipment (net)	200,000	110,000	151,000
Patents (net)	20,000	10,000	14,000
	$860,000	$210,000	$250,000
Current liabilities	$ 10,000	$ 20,000*	
Long-term liabilities	50,000	40,000	
Common stock (par $100)	600,000	100,000	
Retained earnings	200,000	50,000	
	$860,000	$210,000	

* At date of acquisition, Company S owed Company P $5,000 accounts payable.

Company P issued 900 shares of its $100 par common stock to the shareholders of Company S for 900 shares of the outstanding $100 par common stock of Company S. This is an exchange of shares (a continuity of ownership), and we will assume that it meets the 12 criteria for pooling of interests (one of the criteria requires at least 90% ownership). Company S will continue as a separate legal entity, and as a 90% subsidiary of Company P. The exchange would not affect the books of Company S; however, Company P would make the following entry at date of acquisition:[11]

[11] Since this entry is not considered under the pooling of interests concept to be a purchase/sale transaction, it is generally recorded at par value of the stock issued or the proportionate share acquired of the subsidiary's contributed capital. Some accountants prefer to use average contributed capital per share; others prefer market value of the stock issued. This is an unsettled issue; however, in any case, the elimination entry is adapted to attain the pooling of interests result. Par value equal to the proportionate share of the subsidiary's contributed capital is used in this discussion because of its instructional convenience. Consideration of the broader issue is beyond the objective of this chapter (refer to *Advanced Accounting* of this series).

Investment in Company S, common stock (90% ownership)... 90,000
Common stock (900 shares at $100 par) 90,000

Now, assume that Company P prepares a consolidated balance sheet immediately after the acquisition; the worksheet used, on a pooling of interests basis, is shown in Exhibit 18–1.

EXHIBIT 18–1

Consolidation Worksheet to Develop Balance Sheet (at date of acquisition)
Company P and Its Subsidiary, Company S (90% interest)
Pooling of Interests Basis

	Balance Sheet per Books		*Eliminations*		*Consolidated Balance Sheet*
	Company P	*Company S*	*Debit*	*Credit*	
Cash	610,000	20,000			630,000
Inventories	20,000	30,000			50,000
Accounts receivable	10,000	40,000		(b) 5,000	45,000
Investment in Company S	90,000*			(a) 90,000	
Plant and equipment	200,000	110,000			310,000
Patents	20,000	10,000			30,000
	950,000	210,000			1,065,000
Current liabilities	10,000	20,000	(b) 5,000		25,000
Long-term liabilities	50,000	40,000			90,000
Common stock (par $100):					
Parent	690,000*				690,000
Subsidiary		100,000	(a) 90,000		10,000M
Retained earnings:					
Parent	200,000				200,000
Subsidiary		50,000			40,000 10,000M
	950,000	210,000			1,065,000

M—minority shareholders' 10% interest in Company S.
* Includes effects of acquisition entry.
Eliminations:
(a) To eliminate the investment account balance against the stockholders' equity (90%) of the subsidiary.
(b) To eliminate the intercompany debt of $5,000.

The worksheet is started by entering the two separate balance sheets, using *book values* for each company immediately *after* the acquisition entry. Observe, that two accounts on Company *P* balance sheet have been changed to reflect the above acquisition entry. The worksheet is designed to provide an orderly procedure for combining the two separate statements into a consolidated statement (the last column). The pair of columns for *eliminations* is used to prevent double counting of reciprocal items (i.e., items that are strictly between the two companies). In this instance, there are two such items that must be eliminated, viz:

a. The investment account balance reflected on the balance sheet of Company P ($90,000) must be eliminated because in its place the various assets and liabilities of Company S will be added to those of the parent. Similarly, 90% of the common stock reflected by Company S must be offset because it is owned now by the parent. Thus, entry *(a)* on the worksheet offsets the investment account balance on the balance sheet of the parent against the stock account reflected on the balance sheet of the subsidiary.

b. Intercompany debt—Included in current liabilities of Company S is a $5,000 debt owed to Company P; therefore, accounts receivable on the balance sheet of Company P also includes this amount. When the two balance sheets are combined, this intercompany debt must be eliminated since there is no debt or receivable involving the combined entity and outsiders. Entry *(b)* on the worksheet effects this offset.

After the elimination entries for all intercompany items are recorded on the worksheet, the two balance sheets are aggregated horizontally line by line. The 10% interest of the *minority shareholders* of Company S represented by their proportionate share of the owners' equity is set out separately (denoted as M). The last column provides all the data needed to prepare a formal consolidated balance sheet. Note that the *book value* of Company S is added to the book values of Company P; the fair market values given in the data above do not affect a combination by pooling of interests.

COMBINATION BY PURCHASE

The acquisition of a controlling interest by purchase occurs when the combination does not meet all of the criteria for a pooling of interests. Typically, an acquisition by purchase occurs when the parent company acquires a controlling interest in the subsidiary company by purchasing the voting stock with cash or other resources. This situation is viewed as a purchase/sale exchange transaction and the *fair market values* related to the subsidiary must be introduced into the consolidation procedures in accordance with the cost principle. *APB Opinion No. 16* states: "Accounting for a business combination by the purchase method follows the principles normally applicable under historical cost accounting to recording acquisitions of assets and issuances of stock and to accounting for assets and liabilities after acquisition." This means that the parent company must debit the investment account for the fair market value of the shares of the subsidiary acquired. The significant implication of this requirement is that in preparing consolidated statements, the assets of the subsidiary (including any purchased goodwill) must be valued at their *fair market value at date of acquisition* before being aggregated with the *book values* of the assets of the parent company. Recall that in a pooling of interests, book values rather than fair market values of the subsidiary are used in consolidation.

Although there are numerous complexities in application of the purchase method, the general characteristics may be outlined as follows:

1. The assets and liabilities of the subsidiary are reported by the parent

company at cost at date of acquisition in conformity with the cost principle. Cost is the price paid for the stock of the subsidiary (cash equivalent cost) and is the *fair market value* at that date.
2. Individual assets of the subsidiary are reported at their individual fair values at date of acquisition. This includes all identifiable tangible and intangible assets (land, equipment, patents, etc.). Liabilities of the subsidiary are reported at their present "debt" value.
3. The difference between the total purchase cost and the fair value of the identifiable assets acquired (less the liabilities acquired) is reported as "goodwill from acquisition."[12] Goodwill from acquisition is subsequently amortized as an income statement charge.
4. At date of combination, the retained earnings balance of the combined entity is defined as the retained earnings balance of the parent company; that is, the retained earnings balance of the subsidiary is eliminated (not carried forward).
5. After the combination, financial statements which pertain to precombination periods must depict the historical data of the parent company only.

To illustrate preparation of a consolidated balance sheet immediately after acquisition *by purchase*, we will again use the data given for Company P and Company S on page 768. Assume Company P purchases, in the open market, 90% of the 1,000 shares of outstanding stock of Company S for $211,000 cash. Company S will not make an entry to recognize this sale of stock by its stockholders; however, Company P will record the purchase, at cost, as follows:

Investment in Company S, common stock, 900 shares (90% ownership, at cost)	211,000	
Cash		211,000

Assume that Company P prepares a consolidated balance sheet immediately after acquisition and the purchase method must be used. The first step is to determine the amount of *goodwill purchased* in consideration of the fair market values as follows:

Purchase price for an 90% interest in Company S		$211,000
Book value of Company S purchased ($150,000 × .90)		135,000
Differential		76,000
Adjustments to fair market value (see page 768):		
Inventories ($25,000 − $30,000) × .90	$ (4,500)	
Plant and equipment ($151,000 − $110,000) × .90	36,900	
Patents ($14,000 − $10,000) × .90	3,600	
Total Adjustments		36,000
Difference—Goodwill Purchased		$ 40,000

The purchase basis worksheet shown in Exhibit 18–2 is used to de-

[12] If total purchase cost is less than the summed fair market values of individual assets and liabilities, the difference is applied to reduce the valuations of the identifiable tangible and intangible assets.

EXHIBIT 18–2

Consolidation Worksheet to Develop Balance Sheet (at date of acquisition)
Company P and Its Subsidiary, Company S (90% ownership)
Purchase Basis

	Balance Sheet per Books		*Eliminations and Adjustments*		*Consolidated Balance Sheet*
	Company P	*Company S*	*Debit*	*Credit*	
Cash	399,000*	20,000			419,000
Inventories	20,000	30,000		*(b)* 4,500	45,500
Accounts receivable	10,000	40,000		*(c)* 5,000	45,000
Investment in Company S	211,000*			*(a)* 211,000	
Plant and equipment (net)	200,000	110,000	*(b)* 36,900		346,900
Patents	20,000	10,000	*(b)* 3,600		33,600
Goodwill			*(b)* 40,000		40,000
	860,000	210,000			930,000
Differential			*(a)* 76,000	*(b)* 76,000	
Current liabilities	10,000	20,000	*(c)* 5,000		25,000
Long-term liabilities	50,000	40,000			90,000
Common stock:					
Company P	600,000				600,000
Company S		100,000	*(a)* 90,000		10,000M
Retained earnings:					
Company P	200,000				200,000
Company S		50,000	*(a)* 45,000		5,000M
	860,000	210,000			930,000

M—minority shareholders' 10% interest in Company S.

* Includes effects of the acquisition entry.

Adjustments and eliminations:

(a) To eliminate investment account balance against stockholders' equity (90% ownership) and to enter the differential of $76,000 (see prior computation of goodwill).

(b) To apportion the differential and to convert the assets of Company S from book value to fair market value (see prior computation of goodwill).

(c) To eliminate the intercompany debt.

velop the consolidated balance sheet. The worksheet is started by entering the two balance sheets, using amounts immediately after the acquisition entry. Observe that two accounts (i.e., cash and investments) on Company P balance sheets have been changed to reflect the acquisition entry. Also, the middle pair of columns are headed "eliminations and adjustments" because *(a)* the eliminating entries must be made, and *(b)* the assets of Company S must be *adjusted* from book value to fair market value. In respect to the latter, the above computation of goodwill reflects that inventories must be reduced by $4,500, plant and equipment increased by $36,900, patents increased by $3,600, and goodwill recorded as $40,000. These eliminations and adjustments are explained below the worksheet. The worksheet is completed by extending each item horizontally, taking into consideration the eliminations and adjustments. The last column provides all of the data needed to prepare a formal consolidated balance sheet, on the purchase basis.

In summary, a comparison of Exhibit 18–1 with Exhibit 18–2 reflects the following underlying conceptual difference: in pooling of interests the book values of the subsidiary are added to the book values of the parent, whereas in a purchase the market values of the subsidiary at acquisition are added to the book values of the parent. In the illustrations of consolidation to follow, this basic difference will be maintained in the combined statements for subsequent periods.

PREPARING CONSOLIDATED STATEMENTS SUBSEQUENT TO ACQUISITION

At the end of each accounting period subsequent to acquisition of a controlling interest in another company, the parent company must prepare consolidated statements of income, balance sheet, and changes in financial position. The worksheet illustrated above can be expanded to develop a consolidated balance sheet and income statement. A separate worksheet usually is needed to develop a consolidated statement of changes in financial position.

In this section, an expanded worksheet to develop a consolidated balance sheet and income statement subsequent to acquisition will be illustrated assuming *(a)* pooling of interests, and *(b)* purchase. The same data will be used for both illustrations. The section will conclude with an illustration of the formal consolidated statements (purchase basis).

Pooling of Interests Basis

For illustrative purposes, assume that Company P acquired a 90% interest in Company S on January 1, 19A. Company P issued 9,000 shares of its own common stock (par $10) in exchange for 9,000 shares of Company S stock (par $10) which represented 90% of the 10,000 shares outstanding. Assume this acquisition meets the 12 criteria for pooling of interests. Consequently, at acquisition date, Company P recorded the acquisition on a pooling of interests basis as follows:

January 1, 19A:

Investment in Company S, common stock (9,000 shares; 90% interest)	90,000	
Common stock (9,000 shares)		90,000

Assume one year later, at December 31, 19A, the separate income statements and balance sheets prepared by Companies P and S reflected the following:

	At December 31, 19A	
	Company P	Company S
Income Statement:		
Sales	$520,000	$105,000[(a)]
Cost of goods sold	300,000[(a)]	53,000
Depreciation	20,000	4,000
Other expenses	140,000	36,000
Total	460,000	93,000
Net Income	$ 60,000	$ 12,000
Balance Sheet:		
Current assets	$387,000[(b)]	$ 86,000
Investment in Company S (90%)	80,000[(c)]	
Fixed assets, net	480,000	76,000
Total	$947,000	$162,000
Liabilities	$ 97,000	$ 40,000[(b)]
Common stock	680,000 (par $10)	100,000 (par $10)
Retained earnings	170,000[(d)]	22,000[(d)]
Total	$947,000	$162,000

(a) Includes intercompany sales of $7,000 (transferred at cost).
(b) Includes intercompany debt of $3,000.
(c) Pooling of interests basis.
(d) Retained earnings balance at date of acquisition: Company P, $110,000; Company S, $10,000.

The expanded consolidation worksheet is shown in Exhibit 18–3 (on a pooling of interests basis). Note that it is the same as the worksheet shown in Exhibit 18–1 (consolidated balance sheet at acquisition) with the addition of the income statement. The reported amounts from the separate statements are entered directly on the worksheet. For worksheet convenience, and to facilitate understanding, common stock, retained earnings at date of acquisition, and income since acquisition are set out separately. The worksheet involves only one item not previously discussed—the $7,000 intercompany sales. During the year, Company S transferred to Company P goods with a cost of $7,000. Company S recorded this as a sale, and Company P recorded it as a purchase (cost of goods sold). This is an intercompany item that must be eliminated to prevent double counting—when Company P sold the goods to outsiders, a sale was recorded at that time.[13] The eliminations are explained at the bottom of the worksheet. Since the consolidated statements are prepared on a pooling of interests basis, the *book values* of the two companies are aggregated item by item. Note that consolidated income is the sum of the net income amounts reported by the companies separately; the same is true with respect to consolidated retained earnings.

[13] The elimination of intercompany sales of $7,000 assumed the goods were transferred at cost. If *(a)* the transfer price included an element of profit for the selling entity, and *(b)* the goods were still held by the purchasing entity, the profit residue (unrealized intercompany inventory profit) would be eliminated by debiting Sales for the sales price, crediting Cost of Goods Sold for the cost price, and crediting Ending Inventory for the markup.

EXHIBIT 18–3

Worksheet to Develop Consolidated Income Statement and Balance Sheet
Company P and Its Subsidiary, Company S (90% ownership) at December 31, 19A
Pooling of Interests Basis

	Reported Amounts		*Eliminations*		*Consolidated Statements*
	Company P	*Company S*	*Debit*	*Credit*	
Income Statement:					
Sales	520,000	105,000	*(c)* 7,000		618,000
Cost of goods sold	300,000	53,000		*(c)* 7,000	346,000
Depreciation	20,000	4,000			24,000
Other expenses	140,000	36,000			176,000
Total	460,000	93,000			546,000
Income (carried down)	60,000	12,000			72,000
Apportioned for consolidation:					
Minority interest (.10 × $12,000)					1,200M
Parent interest					70,800
Balance Sheet:					
Current assets	387,000	86,000		*(b)* 3,000	470,000
Investment in Company S	90,000*			*(a)* 90,000	
Fixed assets (net)	480,000	76,000			556,000
Total	957,000	162,000			1,026,000
Liabilities:	97,000	40,000	*(b)* 3,000		134,000
Common stock:					
Company P (par $10)	690,000*				690,000
Company S (par $10)		100,000	*(a)* 90,000		10,000M
Retained earnings (at acquisition):					
Company P	110,000				110,000
Company S		10,000			9,000 1,000M
Income (from above)	60,000	12,000			70,800 1,200M
Total	957,000	162,000			1,026,000

M—minority interests' share in Company S (10%).

* Includes effects of the acquisition entry.

Eliminations:

(a) To eliminate investment account balance against stockholders' equity (90% ownership) of the subsidiary.
(b) To eliminate intercompany debt, $3,000.
(c) To eliminate intercompany sales, $7,000 (at cost).

Purchase Basis

Assume the same facts for Company P and Company S as given on page 768 except that the acquisition was effected by purchase. Assume at date of acquisition, that Company P purchased 90% of the outstanding stock of Company S for $124,000 cash. Also assume that the fixed assets of Company S had a *fair market value* of $10,000 greater than their then book value (as reflected on the books of Company S at acquisition date); the current assets of Company S essentially reflect fair market value. On date of acquisition, Company P recorded the purchase of the 90% interest as follows:[14]

January 1, 19A:

Investment in Company S, common stock (9,000 shares, at cost)	124,000	
Cash		124,000

The analysis of the purchase to determine purchased goodwill at acquisition date:

Purchase price for 90% interest in Company S	$124,000
Book value of Company S purchased ($110,000 × 90)	99,000
Differential	25,000
Adjustments to fair market value:	
Fixed assets ($10,000 × .90)	9,000
Difference—Goodwill Purchased	$ 16,000

Assume the fixed assets have a 10-year remaining life (straight-line depreciation) and that goodwill will be amortized over 40 years.

The expanded consolidation worksheet is shown in Exhibit 18–4 on the purchase basis. Note that it follows the format shown in Exhibit 18–2 (consolidated balance sheet at date of acquisition) with the addition of the income statement. Recall that on the worksheet (Exhibit 18–2) there are *(a)* adjustments of the assets of Company S to fair market value, and *(b)* eliminations of intercompany reciprocal items. Exhibit 18–4 includes one additional concept not previously discussed; that is, the write-up of Company S assets, including goodwill, necessitates *adjustments* for additional depreciation and the amortization of goodwill for the period (adjustment [*c*]). The eliminations and adjustments are explained below the worksheet.

The consolidated income statement and balance sheet for Company P are shown in Exhibit 18–5. Note in particular the presentation of the 10% interest in Company S owned by the minority shareholders; alternatively it may be shown as a separate caption in shareholders' equity. Also, the balance sheet uses a more appropriate title for goodwill, cost of investment in excess of fair value of identifiable net assets of subsidiary.

---

[14] This entry changes two amounts on the balance sheet of Company P, viz:

Investment account (at cost)	$124,000
Current assets (i.e., cash) $387,000 – $124,000	263,000

EXHIBIT 18–4

Worksheet to Develop Consolidated Income Statement and Balance Sheet
Company P and Its Subsidiary, Company S (90% ownership), at December 31, 19A
Purchase Basis

	Reported Amounts		*Eliminations*		*Consolidated Statements*
	Company P	*Company S*	*Debit*	*Credit*	
Income Statement:					
Sales	520,000	105,000	(*d*) 7,000		618,000
Cost of goods sold	300,000	53,000		(*d*) 7,000	346,000
Depreciation	20,000	4,000	(*c*) 900		24,900
Other expenses	140,000	36,000			176,000
Amortization goodwill			(*c*) 400		400
Total	460,000	93,000			547,300
Income (carried down)	60,000	12,000			70,700
Minority interest (.10 × $12,000)					1,200M
Parent interest					69,500
Differential			(*a*) 25,000	(*b*) 25,000	
Balance Sheet:					
Current assets	263,000*	86,000		(*e*) 3,000	346,000
Investment in Company S	124,000*			(*a*) 124,000	
Fixed assets (net)	480,000	76,000	(*b*) 9,000	(*c*) 900	564,100
Goodwill			(*b*) 16,000	(*c*) 400	15,600
Total	867,000	162,000			925,700
Liabilities	97,000	40,000	(*e*) 3,000		134,000
Common stock:					
Company P (par $10)	600,000				600,000
Company S (par $10)		100,000	(*a*) 90,000		10,000M
Retained earnings at acquisition):					
Company P	110,000				110,000
Company S		10,000	(*a*) 9,000		1,000M
Income (from above)	60,000	12,000			1,200M
					69,500
Total	867,000	162,000			925,700

M—minority interest share in Company S (10%).

* Includes effects of acquisition entry (purchase basis).

Adjustments and eliminations:

(*a*) Elimination of investment account balance against stockholders' equity of Company S (90%) and to enter the differential of $25,000 (see prior computation of goodwill).
(*b*) To apportion the differential as an adjustment of the fixed assets of Company S to their fair market value at date of acquisition (see prior computation of goodwill).
(*c*) To record additional depreciation on fixed assets and amortization of goodwill for one year.
(*d*) To eliminate intercompany sales, $7,000 (at cost).
(*e*) To eliminate intercompany debt outstanding at December 31, 19A, $3,000.

EXHIBIT 18–5

COMPANY P AND SUBSIDIARY, COMPANY S
Consolidated Income Statement (unclassified)
For the Year Ended December 31, 19A

Sales		$618,000
Expenses:		
Cost of goods sold	$346,000	
Depreciation	24,900	
Other expenses	176,000	
Amortization of goodwill	400	547,300
Consolidated net income		70,700
Minority interest in net income (10%)		1,200
Controlling Interest in Net Income		$ 69,500

Consolidated Balance Sheet (unclassified), December 31, 19A

Assets

Current assets		$346,000
Fixed assets (net)		564,100
Cost of investment in subsidiary in excess of fair value of identifiable net assets of subsidiary (goodwill)		15,600
Total Assets		$925,700

Liabilities and Shareholders' Equity

Liabilities		$134,000
Minority interest in Company S (10%):		
Common stock	$ 10,000	
Retained earnings	2,200	12,200
Shareholders' Equity:		
Common stock, par $10, 60,000 shares outstanding	600,000	
Retained earnings	179,500	779,500
Total Liabilities and Shareholders' Equity		$925,700

Most *published* financial statements are consolidated statements involving one or a number of subsidiaries. Full disclosure on consolidated statements normally requires extensive use of notes to the statements as illustrated in the Appendixes to Chapters 4 and 5.

In summary, we can compare the results of pooling of interests with purchase as reflected in the common situation used in Exhibits 18–3 and 18–4, viz:

	Basis		*Difference—Pooling over Purchase*
	Pooling	*Purchase*	
Net income:			
Parent interest	$ 70,800	$ 69,500	$ 1,300
Minority interest	1,200	1,200	-0-
Current assets (i.e., cash)	470,000	346,000	124,000
Fixed assets (net)	556,000	564,100	(8,100)
Goodwill	-0-	15,600	(15,600)
Liabilities	134,000	134,000	-0-
Capital stock	690,000	600,000	90,000
Retained earnings:			
Parent interest	189,800	179,500	10,300
Minority interest	2,200	2,200	-0-

Net income is lower under the purchase basis because that approach requires that the assets of the subsidiary be adjusted to fair market value and that goodwill be recognized, each of which must be allocated on an annual basis to expense ($900 + $400 = $1,300). Cash and capital stock are lower under the purchase basis because, at acquisition, cash rather than capital stock is used to acquire the controlling interest. Purchase basis requires recognition of fair market values (for subsidiary assets) and purchased goodwill which caused the $15,600 difference. Retained earnings are higher under pooling of interests because it is the sum of the parent and subsidiary amounts, whereas when the purchase method is used, retained earnings of the subsidiary is eliminated. The minority interest in net income and retained earnings is the same under both methods.

Principally because of the *(a)* effect on cash and *(b)* accounting effects on net income and retained earnings, companies prefer pooling of interests. On the other hand, the stockholders of the acquired company often prefer cash to stock in the parent company. In respect to the accounting aspects, and the opportunity to manipulate reported earnings, the APB in *Opinion No. 16* placed severe restrictions (12 in number) on use of the pooling of interests approach. Also, in conformity with the full-disclosure concept, *Opinion No. 16,* paragraphs 64 and 95, specifies a number of items that must be explained in the notes to the consolidated financial statements; these vary somewhat between pooling of interests and purchase.

SOME SPECIAL PROBLEMS IN ACCOUNTING FOR STOCK INVESTMENTS

Several problems relating to the acquisition, holding, and sale of stock investments are discussed in the remaining paragraphs.

Stock Dividends on Investment Shares

In order to conserve cash and yet make a distribution to shareholders, a corporation may issue a dividend using its own shares of stock as payment. Such a dividend is referred to as a stock dividend. When a stock dividend is issued, the distributing corporation debits Retained Earnings and credits the appropriate capital stock accounts (see Chapter 16). The effect of a stock dividend as far as the issuing corporation is concerned is to "capitalize" a part of retained earnings; significantly, a stock dividend does not decrease the assets of the issuing corporation.

From the investor's point of view, the nature of a stock dividend is suggested by the effect on the issuing corporation. In effect, the investor does not receive assets or revenue from the corporation; neither does he or she own more of the issuing corporation. The investor does have more shares to represent the same prior proportional ownership. Thus, the receipt of a stock dividend in the same class of shares as already owned results, from the standpoint of the investor's records, in more shares but no increase in the cost (carrying value) of the holdings. Since such a dividend involves no distribution of corporate assets and does not affect the proportional interest of the stockholder in the assets of the corporation whose stock is held, the investor should make no entry for revenue nor change the investment account other than to record a memorandum entry for the number of shares received. In case of a sale of any of the shares, a new cost per share is computed by adding the new shares to the old and dividing this sum into the carrying value. To illustrate, assume X purchased 100 shares of stock at $90 and subsequently received a 50% dividend payable in identical stock, and later sold 20 shares at $85. A schedule showing the gain or loss on the sale and the balance remaining in the investment account (cost method) follows:[15]

	Shares	*Cost per Share*	*Total Cost Price*	*Sales Price*	*Gain (Loss)*
Purchase	100	$90	$9,000		
Stock dividend	50		0		
Total	150	60	9,000		
Sold	20	60	1,200	$1,700	$500
Ending Balance	130	60	$7,800		

If the stock dividend is of a different class of stock than that on which the dividend is declared, such as preferred stock received as a dividend on common stock, three methods of accounting for the dividend have been suggested:

1. Record the new stock in terms of shares only, and when it is sold recognize the total sales price as a gain.
2. Record the new stock at an amount determined by apportioning the carrying value of the old stock between the new stock and the old stock on the basis of the fair market value of the different classes of stock *after* issuance of the dividend.
3. Do not change the carrying value of the old stock but record the new stock on the books at its market value upon receipt with an offsetting credit to dividend revenue. This method is predicated on the assumption that stock of a different class received as a dividend is no different from a property dividend.

Of these three methods the first is the most conservative, the second is theoretically sound and more in keeping with generally accepted accounting principles, while the third is the least logical. To illustrate the second method, assume an investor purchased 50 shares of X Company common stock for $7,500. When the market value of the common stock was $10,000 the industry received a stock dividend of 20 shares of

[15] Under the Internal Revenue Code stock dividends are exempt from taxation except (*a*) where the shareholder can elect to take cash rather than stock for the dividend, and (*b*) when stock dividends satisfy dividend preference requirements.

X preferred stock having a fair market value of $2,500. Using the relative sales value method the cost may be apportioned as follows:

$$\text{Apportioned Cost—Common} = \$7{,}500 \times \frac{\$10{,}000}{\$12{,}500} = \$6{,}000$$

$$\text{Apportioned Cost—Preferred} = \$7{,}500 \times \frac{\$2{,}500}{\$12{,}500} = \underline{1{,}500}$$

$$\underline{\underline{\$7{,}500}}$$

Indicated entry:

Investment in preferred stock of X Company	1,500	
Investment in common stock of X Company		1,500

Stock Split of Investment Shares

A stock split is effected when a corporation issues new or additional shares without "capitalizing" (debiting) retained earnings or otherwise adding to the dollar amount of *legal capital.* In a stock split the number of shares outstanding is increased, accompanied by a proportionate decrease in the par or stated value per share of stock (refer to Chapters 16 and 17). Thus, a stock split is essentially different from a stock dividend from the point of view of the issuer but very similar from the point of view of the investor. To the latter a stock dividend is not income. A two-for-one stock split means, for example, that the holder of shares at the date of the split will receive two shares in place of each old share held; concurrently, the par or stated value per share of stock is halved. To the investor this merely means that he or she has twice as many shares after the split to represent the same total cost as was had before. The accounting for investment shares where there is a stock split simply involves a memorandum entry for the number of shares received; the resulting "cost per share" is reduced proportionately.

Convertible Securities

In recent years there has been a significant increase in the use of convertible securities. An enterprise may invest in preferred stock or bonds that are convertible into common stock under specified conditions. An accounting measurement problem arises at the time of conversion since the cost or book value of the convertible securities generally is different from the market value of the common stock received at the time of conversion. Two alternative views are held on this point:

1. At date of conversion record the book value of the convertible security given up as the cost of the new security received, thus no gain or loss upon conversion would be recognized. This position is supported by the arguments that *(a)* the original transaction is continuing to materialize; prearranged conversion does not constitute a distinct exchange transaction, *(b)* conversion usually is at the option of the investor, and *(c)* most conversions do not give rise to a taxable gain or loss.

2. At date of conversion record the new security received at its fair market value and recognize a gain or loss on conversion. This position is supported by the arguments that *(a)* a distinct and separate exchange transaction has occurred, *(b)* market value is objective evidence of the "value received," and *(c)* this is similar to the exchange of any other asset and should be accounted for accordingly.

The former view tends to prevail in practice although the latter appears to be theoretically preferable. Also see Chapter 19.

Stock Rights on Investment Shares

The privilege accorded stockholders (investors) of purchasing additional shares of stock from the issuing corporation at a specific price and by a specified future date commonly is known as a *stock right*. The term *stock right* is usually interpreted to mean the right related to *each share of old stock*. Therefore, a holder of ten shares of stock who receives the rights to subscribe for five new shares is said to own ten stock rights rather than five; that is, there is one right per old share irrespective of the "new" share arrangement. Rights have value when the holder can buy added shares through *exercise* of his or her rights at a lower price per share than can persons buying similar shares on the market without rights. As the spread between the privileged subscription price and the market price of shares bought without rights changes subsequent to issuance of the rights, the value of the rights will change.

When the intention to issue stock rights is declared, obviously the stock will start selling in the market "rights on"; that is, purchasers have time to "register" newly bought shares in their names so as to secure the rights when issued. Therefore, the market price of the share sold "rights on" is the price of a share and a right. After the rights are issued the shares will sell in the market "ex rights." After issuance, rights usually will have as ready a market as the related stock and thus will be quoted at a specific market price.

The accounting problems surrounding stock rights are important since some stockholders prefer to sell their rights rather than to exercise them, in which event any gain on rights sold must be determined and entries made to reflect allocation of the cost of the old shares between the rights and the stock. After rights are received the investor has shares of stock and stock rights, both arising out of the single original cost commitment. To determine the gain or loss on the sale of either stock or rights, it is necessary to apportion the total cost of the investment between the stock and the rights. This is done by the use of the relative sales value method; that is, the total cost of the old shares is divided between the old stock and the rights in proportion to their respective market values at the time that the rights are issued.

Illustrative Problem

A comprehensive illustration is presented to indicate the entries which would be made in the case of stock rights. Assume an investor purchased 500 shares of stock in the XY Corporation at $93 per share, and later by reason of the ownership of such stock received 500 stock rights entitling the investor to subscribe to 100 additional shares at $100 per share. Upon the issuance of the rights, each share of stock on which the rights were issued had a fair market value of $120 (ex rights), and the rights had a fair market value of $4 each when issued.

Case A—Assume that instead of subscribing for the additional shares, the investor later sold the rights at $4.50 each.

Case B—Assume the investor exercised his or her rights to subscribe to the additional shares and later sold one of the new shares for $140.

Solution:

Case A—Investor's Entries

	Debit	Credit
a. Investment—stock of XY Corporation	46,500	
Cash		46,500
For purchase of 500 shares at $93 = $46,500.		
b. Investment—stock rights XY Corporation*	1,500	
Investment—stock of XY Corporation		1,500

Allocation:

Shares: $\frac{\$120}{\$124} \times \$46,500 = \$45,000$

Rights: $\frac{\$4}{\$124} \times \$46,500 = \quad 1,500$

Total Cost $46,500

	Debit	Credit
c. Cash	2,250	
Investment—stock rights XY Corporation		1,500
Gain on sale of stock rights		750
For sale of the 500 stock rights at $4.50 each.		

Case B—Investor's Entries

	Debit	Credit
a. Investment—stock of XY Corporation—first purchase	46,500	
Cash		46,500
To record purchase of 500 shares at $93 = $46,500.		
b. Investment—stock rights XY Corporation	1,500	
Investment stock of XY Corporation—first purchase		1,500
To allocate cost of 500 rights as computed in Case A.		
c. Investment—stock of XY Corporation—second purchase	11,500	
Investment—stock rights XY Corporation		1,500
Cash		10,000
To record exercise of rights and receipt of 100 new shares of stock.		
d. Cash	140	
Investment—stock of XY Corporation—second purchase		115
Gain on sale of stock investment		25
To record sale of one new share; cost, $11,500 ÷ 100 = $115.		

In the unlikely event the rights are not sold or exercised, they will lapse. In this situation, theoretically a loss equivalent to the allocated cost of the rights should be recognized. However, as a practical matter, the allocation entry usually is simply reversed.

SPECIAL-PURPOSE FUNDS

Companies often set aside cash, and sometimes other assets, in special funds to be used in the future for a specific purpose. Funds may be set aside by contract, as in the case of a bond sinking fund, or voluntarily, as in the case of a plant expansion fund. Special-purpose funds may be either a current asset, as in the case of short-term investments, or a noncurrent asset, when they are not directly related to current operations. The latter are classified under the caption "Long-term Investments and Funds" (see Chapter 5). Typical long-term funds are:

1. Funds set aside to retire a specific long-term liability, such as bonds payable, mortgages payable, long-term notes payable (see Chapters 6 and 11).
2. Funds set aside to retire preferred stock (see Chapter 6).
3. Funds set aside to purchase major assets, such as land, buildings, and plant (see Chapters 6 and 13).

Typically, special-purpose funds are deposited with a *trustee,* such as a financial institution. In this situation, arrangements usually are agreed to whereby a specific rate of interest will be earned each period on the balance in the fund. Usually, the return earned on the fund each period is added to the fund balance. Depending upon the agreement, a fund increases *(a)* on a compound interest basis at an agreed rate, or *(b)* by the actual amount earned on the fund.

A special-purpose fund may be created *(a)* by making a single contribution at the start (an amount of 1 situation), or *(b)* by making equal periodic contributions (an annuity of 1 situation). The concepts, fund accumulation tables, and related accounting entries were comprehensively discussed and illustrated in Chapter 6. Liability funds were discussed in Chapter 11, and future asset acquisition funds in Chapter 13.

QUESTIONS

1. Distinguish between debt and equity securities; also between short-term and long-term investments.

2. What accounting principle is applied in recording the acquisition of an investment? Explain its applications in cash and noncash acquisitions.

3. Explain why interest revenue is accrued on investments but dividend revenue is not accrued.

4. In accounting under the cost method, no distinction is made between voting and nonvoting stock, alternatively, the distinction is important with respect to the equity and consolidation approaches. Explain.

5. Briefly define and distinguish between *(a)* controlling interest, *(b)* significant influence but not control, and *(c)* neither control nor significant influence. Briefly explain the effect of each situation on accounting for long-term investments.

6. Explain when the cost method of accounting for equity investments is applicable.

7. Explain the application of the lower-of-cost-or-market concept to long-term investments to equity securities.

8. Explain the basic features of the equity method of accounting for long-term investments. When is it applicable? In an overall perspective, what method is it most closely related to (cost, market value, pooling of interests, purchase)? Explain.

9. Assume Company R acquired, as a long-term investment, 30% of the outstanding voting common stock of Company S at a cash cost of $100,000. At date of acquisition, the balance sheet of Company S showed total shareholders' equity of $250,000. The fair market value of the assets of Company S was $20,000 greater than their book value at date of acquisition. Compute goodwill purchased. What accounting method should be used? Explain why.

10. Assume the same facts as given in Question 9, with the additional data that the net assets have a remaining estimated life of 10 years and goodwill will be amortized over 20 years (assume no residual values and straight line). How much additional depreciation and amortization expense should be reflected by the investor, Company R, each year in accounting for this long-term investment?

11. The equity method of accounting for a long-term investment usually will reflect a larger amount of investment revenue than would the cost method under the same circumstances. Explain why.

12. Explain the basic features of the market value method of accounting for investments. Is it a generally accepted method? Explain the basis for your response.

13. How would the market value method of accounting for investments, in contrast to the cost method, tend to prevent "managed" earnings?

14. When does a parent/subsidiary relationship exist? Identify and briefly explain the two basic elements that must be present as a basis for preparing consolidated financial statements.

15. Outline the characteristics of an acquisition transaction of a long-term investment that would generally indicate *(a)* a pooling of interests, and *(b)* a purchase situation.

16. Contrast the primary effects on the balance sheet and income statement of a pooling of interests versus a purchase. Why are the effects different?

17. Explain why fair market values are used in the purchase method but not in the pooling of interests method.

18. Explain why goodwill is recognized in a purchase but not in a pooling of interests.

19. What are intercompany items? Why must they be eliminated in preparing consolidated financial statements?

20. What is meant by minority interest in consolidated statements? How is this interest reported on *(a)* the income statement, and *(b)* the balance sheet?

21. Explain the basic reasons why many companies, other things being equal, would prefer the pooling of interests method over the purchase method of accounting for parent/subsidiary relationships.

22. Fundamentally, the investor accounts for a stock dividend and a stock split in the same way. Briefly, explain the accounting that should be followed by the investor in these situations.

23. What is a convertible security? Assume an investor has a convertible security with a book value of $200,000 which is turned in to the issuer for conversion. The investor receives, in conformance with the conversion, common stock with a current fair market value of $225,000. Explain how the investor should account for the conversion of this long-term investment.

24. What is a stock right (or warrant)? If they have a market value, briefly how would the investor account for the receipt of stock rights?

DECISION CASE 18–1

May Corporation is currently negotiating a combination with Nott Corporation, a successful enterprise that would complement the operations of May. An important factor in the negotiations has been the potential effects of the merger on May's financial statements. Accordingly, May management has requested that pro forma (i.e., as if) financial statements be prepared under two assumptions.

The balance sheets for the two corporations for the year just ended (prior to combination) is shown in the following table:

		Nott Corporation	
	May Corporation	*Book Value*	*Appraised Value*
Balance Sheet:			
Cash	$ 485,000	$ 15,000	
Receivables (net)	30,000	65,000	$ 50,000
Inventories	85,000	70,000	70,000
Land	50,000		
Plant	600,000	100,000	230,000
Patents	10,000	30,000	40,000
	$1,260,000	$ 280,000	
Current liabilities	$ 40,000	$ 15,000	
Long-term liabilities	110,000	25,000	
Common stock (par $100)	1,000,000	200,000	
Retained earnings	110,000	40,000	
	$1,260,000	$ 280,000	
Income Statement:			
Sales	$6,000,000	$1,000,000	
Costs and expenses (excluding depreciation and amortization)	5,754,000	967,000	
Depreciation	65,000	10,000	
Amortization of patents	1,000	3,000	
Income	180,000	20,000	

At year-end Nott Corporation owed a $10,000 current liability to May Corporation. For case purposes, assume that all depreciable assets and intangible assets have a remaining useful life of ten years from date of combination.

Required:

1. Assume that May will purchase all of the outstanding stock of Nott for a cash consideration of $460,000.
   a. Give the pro forma entry for the investment.
   b. Prepare a pro forma balance sheet on a purchase basis (or if you prefer, present a pro forma consolidation worksheet).
2. Assume instead that May obtained all of the outstanding shares of Nott by exchanging stock on a share for share basis.
   a. Give the pro forma entry for the exchange.
   b. Prepare a pro forma balance sheet (or worksheet) on a pooling of interests basis.
3. Identify the amounts on the two balance sheets that will be different between (1) and (2) above and explain the reasons for each. Identify and explain the amounts that would be different on the income statements for the next period as between (1) and (2).
4. Which alternative would you recommend to the management of May Corporation? Why?

EXERCISES

Exercise 18–1

On September 1, 1976, Thomas Company acquired, on a cash basis, the two securities listed below as long-term investments:

a. Bond payable of Dawson Company, maturity value, $20,000, 6% interest payable each August 31; purchased at par value.
b. Preferred stock of Castor Company, par $20, shares purchased, 1,000 at par. The preferred is 6% cumulative; and in the past, annual dividends have been paid during the latter part of August.

Required:

1. Give the entry to record each investment.
2. Assume it is December 31, 1976, end of the accounting period. Give any adjusting entries that should be made in respect to the two investments. Explain the basis for your response for each investment and show any computations.

Exercise 18–2

During 19A Franklin Company purchased shares in two corporations, as indicated below, with the intention of holding them as long-term investments; purchases were in the following order:

a. Purchased 100 shares of the 10,000 shares outstanding of common stock of M Corporation at $31 per share plus a 5% brokerage fee and transfer cost of $45.
b. Purchased 200 shares of preferred stock (nonvoting) of N Corporation at $78 per share plus a 3% brokerage fee and transfer costs of $42.

c. Purchased 20 shares of common stock of M Corporation at $35 per share plus a 5% brokerage fee and transfer costs of $5.

d. Received $.20 per share cash dividend on the N Corporation stock (out of earnings since acquisition).

Required:

1. Give the indicated entries in the accounts of Franklin Company for transactions (*a*), (*b*), (*c*), and (*d*). Assume the cost method is appropriate.
2. The market value of the shares held at the end of 19A were: M stock, $34; N stock, $75. Give the appropriate adjusting entry for Franklin Company; show computations.
3. The market value of the shares held at the end of 19B were: M stock, $36; N stock, $77. Give the appropriate adjusting entry with computations.
4. Show how the income statement and balance sheet for Franklin Company would reflect the long-term investments for 19A and 19B.

Exercise 18–3

Adams Company purchased common stock (par value $50) of the Baker Corporation as a long-term investment. Transactions related to this investment were as follows and in the order given.

a. Purchased 500 shares of the common stock at $90 per share (designated as lot No. 1).

b. Purchased 2,000 shares of the common stock at $95 per share (designated as lot No. 2).

c. At the end of the first year, Baker Corporation reported a net income of $52,000.

d. Baker Corporation paid a cash dividend on the common stock of $2 per share.

e. After reporting a net income of $5,000 for the second year, Baker Corporation issued a stock dividend whereby each stockholder received one additional share for each two shares owned. At the time of the stock dividend the stock was selling at $85.

f. Baker Corporation revised its charter to provide for a stock split. The par value was reduced to $25. The "old" common stock was turned in, and the holders received in exchange two shares of the new stock for each old share owned.

Required:

Give the entries for each transaction as they should be made in the accounts of Adams Company. Show computations. Assume the cost method and less than 20% ownership throughout.

Exercise 18–4

On January 1, 1975, Smith Company purchased 300 of the 1,000 outstanding shares of common stock of Rankin Corporation for $23,200. At that date, the balance sheet of Rankin showed the following book values:

Assets not subject to depreciation	$40,000
Assets subject to depreciation (net)	26,000*
Liabilities	6,000
Common stock (par $50)	50,000
Retained earnings	10,000

* Fair market value, $30,000; the assets have a ten-year remaining life (straight-line depreciation).

Required:

1. Assuming the equity method is appropriate, give the entry by Smith to record the acquisition at a cost of $23,200. Assume a long-term investment.
2. Show the computation of goodwill purchased at acquisition.
3. Assume at December 31, 1975 (end of the accounting period), Rankin Corporation reported a net income of $12,000. Assume goodwill amortization over a ten-year period. Give all entries indicated on the records of Smith Company.
4. In February 1976, Rankin Corporation paid a $2 cash dividend. Give the necessary entry.

Exercise 18–5

On January 1, 1975, Kyle Corporation purchased 2,000 of the 8,000 outstanding shares of common stock of Low Corporation for $20,000 cash. At that date, Low's balance sheet reflected the following book values:

Assets not subject to depreciation	$35,000
Assets subject to depreciation (net)..............	30,000*
Liabilities	5,000
Common stock (par $5)	40,000
Retained earnings	10,000

* Fair market value, $38,000; estimated remaining life of ten years (straight-line depreciation).

Required:

1. Assuming the equity method is appropriate, show the computation of goodwill purchased at acquisition.
2. At the end of 1975, Low reported income before extraordinary items, $19,000, extraordinary loss, $2,000, and net income, $17,000. In March 1976, Low Corporation paid a $1 per share cash dividend. Reconstruct the following accounts (use T-account format) for Kyle Corporation: Cash, Investment in Low Corporation Stock, Investment Revenue—Ordinary, Investment Revenue—Extraordinary. Assume the equity method is appropriate and straight-line amortization of goodwill is over a ten-year period. Date and identify all amounts entered in the accounts.

Exercise 18–6

On January 3, 1975, Bloomington Company purchased 2,000 shares of the 10,000 outstanding shares of common stock of Kokomo Corporation for $14,600 cash. At that date, the balance sheet of Kokomo reflected total shareholders' equity of $60,000. In addition, the fair market value of the assets, subject to depreciation, was $3,000 in excess of their book value reported on the balance sheet. Assume a ten-year remaining life (straight-line depreciation) and amortization of goodwill over ten years.

Required:

Set up captions as follows and enter the indicated information (show computations):

Information—Bloomington Accounts	*Assuming Cost Method Appropriate*	*Assuming Equity Method Appropriate*
a. Entry at date of acquisition.		
b. Goodwill purchased–computation only.		
c. Entry on December 31, 1975, to record $15,000 net income reported by Kokomo.		
d. Entry on December 31, 1975, for additional depreciation expense.		
e. Entry on December 31, 1975, for amortization of goodwill.		
f. Entry on March 3, 1976, for a cash dividend of $1 per share paid by Kokomo.		

Exercise 18–7

On January 10, 19A, Company X purchased as a long-term investment 12% of the 10,000 shares of the outstanding common stock of Company Y (par value $40 per share) at $50 per share. During 19A, 19B, and 19C the following additional data were available:

	19A	*19B*
Reported net income by Company Y at year-end	$30,000	$35,000
Cash dividends by Company Y at year-end	10,000	15,000
Quoted market price per share of Company Y stock at year-end	57	55

On January 2, 19C, Company X sold 100 shares of the Company Y shares at $56 per share.

Required:

1. Assuming the market value method is used, give all entries indicated in the accounts of Company X assuming market changes are considered as "realized."
2. Prepare a tabulation to show the investment revenue of Company X and the balance in the investment account for the years 19A, 19B, and 19C.

Exercise 18–8

On January 1, 19A, Company R purchased, as a long-term investment, 6% of the 50,000 (par $10) shares of the outstanding common stock of Company S at $11 per share. During the years 19A, 19B, and 19C the following additional data were available:

	Company S
End of 19A:	
Reported net income	$30,000
Cash dividends paid	20,000
Market value per share	15
End of 19B:	
Reported net income	25,000
Cash dividends paid	15,000
Market value per share	14
January 10, 19C:	
Company R sold 200 shares of the Company S stock at $17.50 per share.	

Required:

1. Assuming the market value method is used, give all entries related to the investment for Company R assuming:
   a. Market changes are considered "realized."
   b. Market changes are considered "unrealized."
2. In parallel columns for each assumption, show the *(a)* balance of the investment account at each year-end, *(b)* the balance in the "unrealized" account at each year-end, and *(c)* revenue from the investment for each period.

Exercise 18–9

During January 19A, Company A purchased 20% of the 5,000 shares of outstanding common stock of Company B at $20 per share. At that date, the following data were available:

	Company B	
	At Book Value	*Market Value per Appraisal*
Assets not subject to depreciation	$ 60,000	$63,000
Assets subject to depreciation (ten-year remaining life)	40,000	45,000
	$100,000	
Liabilities	$ 20,000	20,000
Common stock (par value $10)	50,000	
Retained earnings	30,000	
	$100,000	

At the end of 19A, Company B reported a net income of $15,000 and paid cash dividends of $5,000. At the end of 19A, Company B common stock was quoted on the market at $22 per share.

In January 19B, Company A sold 100 of the shares of Company B at $23 per share.

Required:

In parallel columns prepare entries for the accounts of Company A from the date of the purchase of the long-term investment through date of sale of the 100 shares assuming: Case A – the cost method is used; Case B – the equity method is used; and Case C – the market value method is used (market changes are treated as realized). Assume goodwill is amortized over a 20-year period.

Exercise 18–10

On January 1, 19A, Company P acquired all of the outstanding shares of Company S common stock by exchanging, on a share for share basis, 4,000 shares of its own stock. The balance sheets reflected the following summarized data:

	Company P	Company S
Assets not subject to depreciation	$180,000	$40,000*
Assets subject to depreciation (ten-year remaining life)	120,000	25,000
	$300,000	$65,000
Liabilities	$ 20,000*	$ 5,000
Common stock (par $10)	200,000	40,000
Retained earnings	80,000	20,000
	$300,000	$65,000

* Includes a $4,000 debt owed by Company P to Company S.

Required:

1. Give entry in the accounts of Company P for the acquisition of this long-term investment on a pooling of interests basis.
2. Prepare a consolidation worksheet at date of acquisition (assume the pooling of interests method).

Exercise 18–11

Refer to the balance sheets at the date of acquisition for Companies P and S as given in Exercise 18–10.

Assume the same requirements and facts except that Company P exchanged, on a share for share basis, 3,600 shares of its own stock for a 90% interest in Company S.

Exercise 18–12

In January 19A, Company P purchased, for $149,000 cash, all of the 10,000 outstanding voting shares of the common stock of Company S. At that date, the following additional summarized data were available:

		Company S	
	Company P Book Value	Book Value	Fair Value (appraised)
Assets not subject to depreciation	$410,000	$ 80,000*	$ 85,000
Assets subject to depreciation	200,000	60,000	67,000†
Total	$610,000	$140,000	$152,000
Liabilities	$ 40,000	$ 10,000	
Common stock (par $10)	500,000	100,000	
Retained earnings	70,000	30,000	
Total	$610,000	$140,000	

* Includes a $12,000 debt owed by Company P to Company S.
† Estimated remaining life, ten years (straight-line depreciation).

Required:

1. Give entry in the accounts of Company P to record acquisition of this long-term investment assuming the purchase method.
2. Compute the amount of goodwill purchased.
3. Prepare a consolidation worksheet at date of acquisition using the purchase method.
4. How much additional depreciation expense and goodwill amortization (assume a 20-year amortization period) will be reflected on the consolidated income statement each year after the acquisition?

Exercise 18–13

Refer to the balance sheets at date of acquisition for Companies P and S given in Exercise 18–12. Assume the same facts except that Company P purchased 60% of the outstanding shares of Company S for $146,200 cash.

Required:

1. Give entry in the accounts of Company P to record acquisition of this long-term investment assuming the purchase method.
2. Compute the amount of goodwill purchased.
3. Prepare a consolidated worksheet at acquisition using the purchase method.
4. How much additional depreciation expense and goodwill amortization (assume a 20-year amortization period) will be reflected on the consolidated income statement each year after the acquisition?

Exercise 18–14

On January 1, 19A, Par Company purchased a 80% interest in Sub Company for $116,400. At date of acquisition, the goodwill purchased was computed as follows:

Purchase price for 80% interest in Sub Company	$116,400
Book value of Sub Company purchased ($128,000 × .80)	102,400
Differential	14,000
Adjustments to market value:	
Increase fixed assets to fair market value ($104,000 − $99,000) × .80	4,000
Difference—goodwill purchased	$ 10,000

At the end of 19A, the financial statements reflected the following (summarized):

	Reported at End of Year 19A	
	Par Company	Sub Company
Income Statement:		
Sales	$360,000	$ 80,000
Interest revenue		400
	360,000	80,400
Cost of goods sold	150,000	42,000
Other operating expenses	109,600	26,300
Interest expense	400	100
	260,000	68,400
Net Income	$100,000	$ 12,000
Balance Sheet:		
Current assets	$172,000	$ 80,000
Investment in Sub Company	116,400	
Fixed assets (net)	400,000	90,000
	$688,400	$170,000
Current liabilities	$ 50,000	$ 30,000
Common stock	500,000	100,000
Retained earnings	138,400	40,000*
	$688,400	$170,000

* At acquisition, the balance was $28,000.

Intercompany items at year-end were:

a. Par Company sold Sub Company goods (at cost) during the year amounting to $5,000.
b. Par Company paid Sub Company $400 interest during the year.
c. Par Company owed Sub Company $3,000 at the end of the year.

Required:

Prepare a worksheet to develop a consolidated income statement and balance sheet at the end of 19A assuming the purchase method. Assume the fixed assets have a 10-year remaining life and goodwill will be amortized over 20 years.

Exercise 18–15

On January 1, 19A, X Company purchased 80% of the outstanding common stock of Y Company at a cost of $137,200. At date of acquisition, the goodwill purchased was computed as follows:

Purchase price for 80% interest in Y Company	$137,200
Book value of Y Company purchased ($159,000 × .80)	127,200
Differential	10,000
Adjustments to fair market value:	
Current assets ($1,250 × .80)	(1,000)
Fixed assets ($6,250 × .80)	(5,000)
Difference—goodwill purchased	$ 4,000

After one year of operations, each company prepared a balance sheet and income statement as follows (summarized):

	Reported at End of Year 19A	
	X Company	Y Company
Income Statement:		
Sales	$340,000	$ 90,000
Cost of goods sold	190,000	46,000
Depreciation	32,000	15,000
Other operating expenses	72,000	17,000
Interest expense	2,000	1,000
Total	296,000	79,000
Net Income	$ 44,000	$ 11,000
Balance Sheet:		
Current assets	$170,800	$ 40,000
Investment in Y Company	137,200	
Fixed assets (net)	330,000	160,000
	$638,000	$200,000
Liabilities	$138,000	$ 30,000
Common stock	400,000	150,000
Retained earnings	100,000	20,000*
	$638,000	$200,000

* Balance at date of acquisition, $9,000.

Intercompany items at year-end were determined to be:

a. Sales of X Company to Y Company during the year were $15,000 (at cost).
b. Depreciation on fixed assets; assume a ten-year remaining life.
c. Amortization of any goodwill; assume a 20-year amortization period.

Required:

Prepare a worksheet to develop a consolidated income statement and balance sheet at the end of 19A assuming the purchase method.

Exercise 18–16

Brown Company purchased, for a lump sum of $104,070, the three different stocks listed below:

Company and Stock	*Number of Shares*
X Corporation, common stock, par $10	200
Y Corporation, preferred stock, par $100	400
Z Corporation, common stock, no par	500

In addition, Brown paid transfer fees and other costs related to the acquisition amounting to $790. At the time of purchase, the stocks were quoted on the local market at the following prices per share: X common, $70; Y preferred, $120; and Z common, $90.

Required:

Give entry to record the purchase of these long-term investments and payment of the transfer fees. Show computations. Record each stock in a separate account.

Exercise 18–17

Each of the following situations are completely independent; however, both of them relate to the receipt of a stock dividend by an investor.

Case A: Corporation K had 20,000 shares of $50 par value stock outstanding at which time the board of directors voted to issue a 25% stock dividend (i.e., one additional share for each four [4] shares owned).

Required:

Company L owns 2,000 shares of the Corporation K stock (a long-term investment) acquired at a cost of $65 per share. After receiving the stock dividend, Company L sold 200 of the additional stock received at $70 per share. Give the entries for Company L to record (1) acquisition of the 2,000 shares, (2) receipt of the stock dividend, and (3) sale of the 200 shares. Assume the cost method.

Case B: During the course of an audit, you find accounts as follows:

Investments—Stock in A Company ($100 par per share)

Debits	
Jan. 1 Cost of 100 shares	$17,500
Feb. 1 50 shares received as a stock dividend (at par)...............	5,000
Credits	
July 1 25 shares of dividend stock sold at 125	3,125

Income Summary

	Credits
Feb. 1 Stock dividend on A Company stock	$ 5,000
July 1 Cash dividend on A Company stock	3,000

Required:

Assuming the cost method, restate these accounts on a correct basis. Give reasons for each change.

Exercise 18–18

Box Corporation issued one stock right for each share of common stock owned by investors. The rights provided that for each six rights held a share of new preferred stock could be purchased for $100 cash (par of the preferred was $80 per share). When the rights were issued they had a market value of $7 each and the common stock was selling at $142 per share (ex rights). Roy Company owned 300 shares of Box common stock, acquired as a long-term investment at a cost of $22,350. Assume the cost method.

Required:

1. How many rights did Roy Company receive?
2. Determine the cost of the stock rights to Roy Company and give any entry that should be made upon receipt of the rights.
3. Assume Roy Company exercised the rights, determine the cost of the new stock and give the entry to record the exercise of the rights.
4. Assuming that Roy Company sold its rights for $7.40 each. Give entry to record the sale.

Exercise 18–19

Give entries in the accounts of XY Corporation under the cost method for the following transactions which occurred over a period of time and in the chronological order shown:

a. XY Corporation purchased 100 shares of Bell Corporation common stock at $99 per share as a long-term investment.
b. Bell Corporation issued a 10% stock dividend in additional common shares.
c. Bell Corporation issued rights to present common stockholders entitling each holder of five old shares to buy one additional share of new common stock at 95. At the time the rights sold for $4 per right and the shares outstanding sold for $116 each (ex rights). Make an allocation to the rights.
d. XY Corporation exercised its rights and bought new shares.
e. XY Corporation sold 120 shares of Bell stock for $12,000 failing to identify the specific shares disposed of. (Use *Fifo* procedures.)

Exercise 18–20

Clay Company purchased 100 shares of X Corporation's common stock paying $90 per share. Shortly thereafter, Clay Company received stock rights entitling it to purchase one additional share of stock for $65 for each ten rights tendered. At the time the rights were issued, the common stock was selling at $115 per share (ex rights) and the rights were selling at $5 each.

Required:

1. Give entry to record the purchase of the investment assuming the cost method.
2. Give the entry to record the receipt of the rights by Clay Company (make an allocation).
3. Give entry assuming the investor sold 20 rights at $5.50 each.
4. Give entry assuming the investor exercised the remaining rights.

PROBLEMS

Problem 18–1

On January 1, 19A, Freeze Company purchased 4,000 shares of the 20,000 shares outstanding of common stock (par $10) of Gray Corporation for $64,000 cash and 3,000 shares of the 100,000 shares outstanding of common stock (nopar) of Hobbs Corporation for $14,000 cash as a long-term investment. The accounting periods for the companies end on December 31.

Subsequent information was as follows:

	Freeze	*Hobbs*
December 31, 19A:		
Income reported for 19A	$40,000	$20,000
Cash dividend per share paid at the end of 19A	$1.50	None
Market price per share of stock	$12	$8
October 20, 19B:		
Sold 1,000 shares of the Hobbs stock at $10 per share.		
December 31, 19B:		
Income reported for 19B	$50,000	$26,000
Cash dividends per share paid at the end of 19B	$1.00	$.50
Market price per share of stock	$14	$11
Reclassified Hobbs stock as a current asset (short-term investment).		

Required:

1. Assuming the cost method, give all entries indicated for Freeze Company for 19A and 19B.
2. Show how the investments in equity securities would be reported on the financial statements of Freeze Company at the end of each year.

Problem 18–2

On January 1, 19B, Abel Company purchased 3,000 shares of the 15,000 outstanding shares of common stock of Briggs Corporation for $80,000 cash as a long-term investment. At that date, the balance sheet of Briggs Company showed the following book values (summarized):

Assets not subject to depreciation	$140,000[a]
Assets subject to depreciation (net)	100,000[b]
Liabilities	40,000
Common stock (par $10)	150,000
Retained earnings	50,000

[a] Fair market value, $150,000.

[b] Fair market value, $140,000, estimated remaining life, ten years. Assume straight-line depreciation and amortization of goodwill over 20 years.

Additional subsequent data on Briggs Corporation:

	19B	*19C*
Income before extraordinary items	$25,000	$26,000
Extraordinary item – gain		5,000
Cash dividends paid	10,000	12,000
Market value per share	25	26

Required:

1. Set up captions as follows and enter the indicated information (show computations):

Information (Abel's accounts)	*Assuming Cost Method Is Appropriate*	*Assuming Equity Method Is Appropriate*
a. Entry at date of acquisition.		
b. Amount of goodwill purchased.		
c. Entries at December 31, 19B.		
(1) Investment revenue and dividends.		
(2) Additional depreciation expense.		
(3) Amortization of goodwill.		
d. Entries at December 31, 19C.		
(1) Investment revenue and dividends.		
(2) Additional depreciation expense.		
(3) Amortization of goodwill.		

2. Reconstruct the investment account for each assumption; also include the "allowance" and "unrealized" accounts.
3. Explain why the investment account balance is different between the cost and equity methods.

Problem 18–3

During January 19A, Riley Company purchased 1,000 shares of the 10,000 shares of the outstanding common stock (par $20) of Swanson Corporation for $36,000 cash, as a long-term investment. During 19A, 19B, and 19C, the following additional data were available:

	19A	19B
Net income reported by Swanson at year-end...............	$15,000	$20,000
Cash dividends paid by Swanson at year-end...............	10,000	12,000
Market price per share	40	37

On January 2, 19C, Riley sold 100 shares of the Swanson stock at $38 per share.

Required:

(Suggestion – Set up a three-column tabulation for Requirements 1–3.)

1. Give all entries indicated in the accounts of Riley Company assuming the cost method is used.
2. Give all entries indicated in the accounts of Riley Company assuming the market value method is used and that market value changes are considered "realized."
3. Give all entries indicated in the accounts of Riley Company assuming the market value is used and that market changes are considered "unrealized."
4. Explain why the investment account balance is different between Requirements 1 and 2.
5. Assuming you could make the choice, which of the three methods would you prefer? Explain the basis of your choice and why you rejected the other two methods.

Problem 18–4

In January 19A, Bricker Company purchased 10% of the 100,000 outstanding common shares of Core Company at $6 per share as a long-term investment. During the years 19A and 19B, the following additional data were available:

	Core Company
End 19A:	
Reported net income	$30,000
Cash dividends paid...............	15,000
Market value per share	9
End 19B:	
Reported net income	$ (8,000) loss
Cash dividends paid...............	10,000
Market value per share	7

Required:

(Suggestion: Set up a three-column tabulation for Requirements 1–3.)

1. Give all entries indicated in the accounts of Bricker Company assuming the cost method is used.
2. Give all entries indicated assuming that the market value method is used and that market changes are considered as "realized."
3. Give all entries indicated assuming that the market value method is used and that market changes are considered as "unrealized."
4. Prepare a tabulation to reflect by years, for each of the above requirements, (*a*) the balance in the investment account at each year-end, (*b*) the balance in any "unrealized" accounts, and (*c*) investment revenue for Bricker Company.
5. Give entry assuming 1,000 of the shares of Core Company were sold by Bricker early in 19C at $8 per share.

Problem 18–5

During January, 19A, Company P purchased 20% of the 30,000 outstanding common shares of Company S at $16 per share as a long-term investment. At date of acquisition of the shares, the following data in respect to Company S had been assembled by Company P:

	Company S	
	At Book Value	*At Estimated Value*
Assets not subject to depreciation	$250,000	$260,000
Assets subject to depreciation (ten-year remaining life; straight line)	200,000	220,000
	$450,000	
Liabilities	$ 50,000	
Common stock (par $10)................................	300,000	
Retained earnings..	100,000	
	$450,000	

Selected data available at year-end:

	19A	*19B*
Reported net income, Company S:		
Income before extraordinary items	$20,000	$(10,000) loss
Extraordinary items	10,000	
Cash dividends paid:		
Company S..	8,000	5,000
Quoted market price per share, Company S	21	15

Required:

1. In parallel columns, prepare all entries for Company P in respect to the investment assuming *(a)* the cost method is appropriate, *(b)* the equity method is appropriate (amortize any goodwill over 20 years straight line), and *(c)* the market value method is used, market value changes are considered as "realized."
2. Prepare a tabulation for each assumption in Requirement 1 to reflect *(a)* the balance in the investment account at each year-end, *(b)* investment revenue for each period, and *(c)* the allowance accounts.

Problem 18–6

In January, 19A, Company P acquired, as a long-term investment, 9,000 of the 10,000 outstanding common stock shares of Company S (par $20) by issuing 18,000 shares of its own common stock (par $10). Just prior to acquisition, the balance sheets reflected the following (summarized):

	Company P	Company S	
	Book Value	Book Value	Fair Market Value (appraisal)
Cash	$290,000	$ 70,000	$ 70,000
Inventories	237,000	170,000	160,000
Receivables (net)	63,000†	36,000	33,000
Fixed assets (net)	260,000	100,000	150,000*
Patents (net)		14,000	10,000*
Total	$850,000	$390,000	$423,000
Current liabilities	$ 60,000	$ 10,000†	
Long-term liabilities	150,000	140,000	
Common stock	514,000	200,000	
Retained earnings	126,000	40,000	
Total	$850,000	$390,000	

* Estimated useful life: fixed assets, ten years; patent, five years. Assume purchased goodwill recognized will be amortized over 20 years.

† Includes a $4,000 debt owed by Company S to Company P.

Required:

1. Assume the acquisition meets all of the criteria for the pooling of interests method.
   a. Give the entry to record the stock exchange in the accounts of Company P at date of acquisition.
   b. Prepare a consolidation worksheet for the balance sheet immediately after acquisition.
2. Assume the same facts as above except that, instead of the exchange of shares, Company P paid $286,700 cash for the 9,000 shares of Company S. Also assume the acquisition qualifies as a purchase.
   a. Give the entry to record the acquisition in the accounts of Company P.
   b. Compute the amount of goodwill purchased (show computations).
   c. Prepare a consolidation worksheet for the balance sheet immediately after acquisition.
3. To compare the two methods, pooling of interests versus purchase, complete the tabulation as follows:

Item (consolidated)	Consolidated Amounts the Same	Explanation of Reasons
1. Current assets		
2. Investment account balances		
3. Liabilities		
4. Common stock balance		
5. Retained earnings balance		
6. Minority interest amount		
7. Future net income		

Problem 18–7

On January 1, 19A, P Company acquired 90% of the common stock of S Company by issuing 13,500 shares of its own common stock to the shareholders of S Company for an equal number of S Company shares. After one year of operations, each company prepared an income statement and balance sheet as follows (summarized):

	Reported at End of Year 19A	
	P Company	*S Company*
Income Statement:		
Sales	$620,000	$140,000
Interest revenue	700	
Total	620,700	140,000
Cost of goods sold	370,000	75,000
Depreciation expense	40,000	15,000
Other operating expenses	132,700	36,300
Interest expense	1,000	700
Total	543,700	127,000
Net Income	$ 77,000	$ 13,000
Balance Sheet:		
Current assets	$335,000	$101,000
Investment in S Company	135,000	
Fixed assets (net—remaining life, ten years)	330,000	149,000
Total	$800,000	$250,000
Liabilities	$ 80,000	$ 40,000
Common stock (par $10)	600,000	150,000
Retained earnings	120,000	60,000*
Total	$800,000	$250,000

* Balance at acquisition date, $47,000.

Intercompany items and adjustments for 19A:

a. S Company sold $17,000 worth of goods (at cost) to P Company during the year.
b. S Company paid P Company $700 interest during the year.
c. At the end of 19A, S Company owed P Company $20,000.

Required:

1. Prepare a worksheet for 19A to develop a consolidated income statement and balance sheet. Use the pooling of interests basis. Assume straight-line depreciation.
2. Prepare a classified income statement and balance sheet clearly identifying the minority interest.

Problem 18–8

Refer to the balance sheets for Companies P and S given in Problem 18–7. Assume the same facts except that Company P purchased 13,500 shares (90%) of the common stock of Company S at a cash cost of $226,000. At date of acquisition, the fixed assets, at fair market value, were $43,000 above book value.

The purchase method changes the trial balance for Company P given in Problem 18–7 as follows (new balances):

Current assets	$109,000
Investment account (at cost)	226,000
Common stock (par $10)	465,000

Required:

1. Compute the purchased goodwill at date of acquisition. Show computations.
2. Prepare a worksheet for 19A to develop a consolidated balance sheet and income statement. Use the purchase basis. Use straight-line depreciation and amortize goodwill over 20 years.

Problem 18–9

On January 1, 19A, Company A purchased for cash, in the market, 80% of the outstanding common stock of Company B at a cost of $188,000. At date of acquisition, based upon an appraisal of Company B assets for consolidation purposes, the fixed assets had a fair market value of $10,000 above their book value and the current assets had a fair market value of $7,500 less than their book value.

After one year of operations, each company prepared an income statement and balance sheet as follows (summarized):

	Reported at End of Year 19A	
	Company A	*Company B*
Income Statement:		
Sales	$630,000	$180,000
Interest revenue	1,000	
Total	631,000	180,000
Cost of goods sold	370,000	98,000
Depreciation expense	37,000	16,000
Other operating expenses	140,000	45,000
Interest expense	4,000	1,000
Total	551,000	160,000
Net Income	$ 80,000	$ 20,000
Balance Sheet:		
Current assets	$372,000	$110,000
Investment in Company B (at cost)	188,000	
Fixed assets (net)	360,000	160,000
Total	$920,000	$270,000
Current liabilities	$ 70,000	$ 30,000
Common stock (par $10)	760,000	200,000
Retained earnings	90,000	40,000*
Total	$920,000	$270,000

* Balance at date of acquisition, $20,000.

Data relating to 19A eliminations and adjustments:

a. During the year, Company A sold merchandise to Company B for $35,000 (at cost).
b. During 19A, Company B paid Company A $1,000 interest on loans.
c. At the end of 19A, Company B owed Company A $20,000.
d. The assets of Company B have an estimated remaining life of ten years (no residual value, straight-line depreciation).
e. Goodwill is to be amortized over a 20-year life.

Required:

1. Compute the goodwill purchased at date of acquisition; show computations.
2. Prepare a worksheet to develop a consolidated income statement and balance sheet on the purchase basis.

Problem 18–10

Refer to the balance sheets for Companies A and B given in Problem 18–9. Assume the same facts except that Company A acquired the 90% interest in Company B by exchanging 18,000 shares of its own common stock for an equal number of shares in Company B.

The pooling of interests method changes the trial balance given for Company A in Problem 18–9 as follows:

Current assets	$560,000
Investment account	180,000
Common stock (par $10)...............	940,000

Required:

1. Prepare a worksheet for 19A to develop a consolidated income statement and balance sheet. Use the pooling of interest basis.
2. Prepare an unclassified income statement and balance sheet clearly identifying the minority interest.

Problem 18–11

Foster Corporation completed the following transactions, in the order given, relative to their portfolio of stocks held as long-term investments:

a. Purchased 200 shares of common stock (par value $50) of M Corporation at $70 per share plus a brokerage commission of 4% and transfer costs of $20.
b. Purchased, for a lump sum of $96,000, the following stocks of N Corporation:

Stocks	*Number of Shares*	*Market Price at Date of Purchase*
Class A, common, par value $100	200	$ 50
Preferred, par value $50	300	100
Class B, nopar value stock (stated value, $100) ...	400	150

c. Purchased 300 shares of common stock of M Corporation common at $80 per share plus a brokerage commission of 4% and transfer costs of $60.
d. Received a stock dividend on the M Corporation stock; for each share held, an additional share was received.
e. Sold 100 shares of M Corporation stock at $45 per share (from Lot 1).
f. Received a two-for-one stock split on the Class A common stock of the N Corporation (the number of shares doubled).
g. Received cash dividends as follows:

M Corporation common stock – $5 per share
N, Class A, common stock – $3 per share
N preferred – 6%
N, Class B, nopar value stock – $1.50 per share.

Required:

1. Give entries for Foster Corporation for the above transactions assuming the cost method is appropriate. Show calculations and assume *Fifo* order when shares are sold.
2. Prepare an inventory of the long-term investment portfolio; include number of shares and balance sheet valuations after giving effect to the above transactions.

Problem 18–12

Hay Company owns the following long-term investments:

a. 100 shares of Ajax Corporation common stock acquired in 1954 at $100 per share. No dividends have ever been received. In recent years, the stock has been selling around $6 per share.

b. 600 shares of Preston Mines, Inc., stock acquired in 1955 at $7 per share. In recent years a portion of each dividend has been designated as a liquidating dividend. Dividends have been received as follows:

	Revenue	*Return of Capital*	*Total*
1973..............	$3.00	$4.00	$7.00
1974..............	2.00	3.00	5.00
1975..............	2.00	1.00	3.00
1976..............	1.00		1.00

c. 2,000 shares of Brown, Inc., common stock acquired in 1968 at $150 per share; the current market price recently has been $210 per share. The stock regularly pays dividends. A two-for-one stock split has just been issued (the number of shares doubled).

d. 200 shares of common stock (par $30) and 400 shares of preferred stock (par $75) of the Sky Corporation. These shares were purchased as a package in 1975 at a lump sum of $48,500; at the time they were selling at common, $50, and preferred, $100, per share. During 1976, one-for-one stock dividend was received on the common shares (the number of shares doubled).

Required:

For Hay Company give *all* entries indicated since 1954; show computations with respect to each lot of shares. Explain any assumptions made. Also compute the carrying value and cost per share of each lot of shares at the end of 1976. Use the cost method.

Problem 18–13

Foster Corporation has long-range plans to build a new plant on the West Coast in approximately five years. To provide some of the funds, Foster management has decided to establish a future plant expansion fund. The funds will be deposited with a trustee and will earn 6% annual compound interest. The interest accumulations each year will be added to the fund balance.

Case A—Assume Foster makes only one contribution of $500,000 on January 1, 19A.

a. Compute the balance that will be in the fund at the end of the fifth year. Show computations.

b. Prepare a fund accumulation table for the five years. (*Hint:* Refer to Chapters 6 and 13.)

c. Prepare journal entries for Foster through January 1, 19B.

Case B—Assume instead that Foster decides to make five equal annual contributions of $100,000 on each January 1, starting January 1, 19A.

a. Compute the balance that will be in the fund immediately after the fifth and last contribution. Show computations.

b. Prepare a fund accumulation table for the five contributions. (*Hint:* Refer to Chapters 6 and 13.)

c. Give entries for Foster through January 1, 19B.

Explain why there is a different balance in the fund between the two cases at the end.

Chapter 19

Accounting for Bonds as Long-Term Liabilities and Investments

The preceding chapter discussed long-term investments in equity securities (i.e., capital stock), and Chapter 11 discussed short-term and long-term liabilities. Because of their unique characteristics, discussion of bonds was deferred to this chapter. This chapter analyzes bonds from the viewpoints of *(a)* the issuer (i.e., the borrower) and *(b)* the investor (i.e., the lender). This dual approach is logical because the accounting and reporting concepts and procedures for the issuer and the investor are essentially the same. Bonds represent a long-term liability for the issuer and usually a long-term investment for the lender.[1] The usual time from issuance date to maturity date of bonds is 10 to 20 years.

The chapter is divided into three parts: Part A – Accounting for the Issuer and Investor Compared; Part B – Special Problems in Accounting for Bonds; and Part C – Serial Bonds.

NATURE OF BONDS

Bonds, evidenced by outstanding bond certificates, are contractual representations that a debt is owed by one party, the issuer, to one or more other parties, the investors. A bond certificate indicates the principal amount, specified interest dates (usually semiannual), the nominal rate of interest based upon the principal amount, and any other special agreements. Thus, a bond may be defined as a formal (i.e., written) promise to pay a specified principal at a designated date in the future

---

[1] Bonds are sometimes held as short-term investments, in which case they are accounted for in the manner discussed in Chapter 7. They are recorded at cost, and subsequently, at lower of cost or market. Any premium or discount generally is not amortized in view of the short holding period (i.e., the operating cycle or one year, whichever is the longer). This chapter focuses on long-term investments in bonds.

and, in addition, periodic interest on the principal at a specified rate per period.

Bonds are used to borrow a large amount from the investment community, including individuals, by dividing the total long-term debt into a number of small units, usually in denominations of $10,000 and $1,000 (sometimes $100). The total amount to be borrowed, evidenced by the bond certificates, is usually referred to as a *bond issue*. A bond issue requires the preparation of a *bond indenture,* which is the basic contract between the borrower and the investors who acquire the bonds. The bond indenture usually includes provision for an outside *independent trustee* who is given the authority to protect the rights of both the investors and the lender. A bond indenture specifies the following information which is particularly important in accounting and reporting (1) the liability for the issuer and (2) the investment for the investor:

1. Maturity date.
2. Interest payments—dates and nominal rate of interest.
3. Denominations of principal.
4. Call and/or conversion provisions.
5. Security (i.e., whether supported by pledged assets or not).
6. The trustee, including certification of the bonds.
7. Repayment plans, such as a bond sinking fund.
8. Special provisions such as restrictions on retained earnings of the issuer and the maintenance of certain minimum ratios (such as the rate of debt to owners' equity).

CLASSES OF BONDS

Bonds are classified in various ways as follows:

1. Character of issuing corporation. The borrower may be a private corporation issuing *industrial* bonds or a public entity issuing *municipal* or *government* bonds.

2. Character of security. Secured bonds are supported by a lien, or mortgage, on specific assets, whereas unsecured bonds have no such support. Unsecured bonds are frequently called *debenture bonds*. *Guaranty security bonds* are those which, in case of default, will be paid as to principal and interest by the guarantor. For example, a parent corporation may guarantee payment of the bonds issued by its subsidiary companies. *Lien security bonds* are secured by a lien on property consisting of securities (collateral trust bonds), rolling stock (car trust and equipment bonds), or a lien on realty (real estate bonds).

3. Purpose of issue. *Purchase money bonds* are issued in full or part payment for property. *Refunding bonds* are issued to retire current obligations and may have the same security as the redeemed debt. *Consolidated bonds* replace several prior issues and unite the securities for the retired issues.

4. Payment of interest. *Income bonds* differ from ordinary bonds in

that the payment of interest each period on income bonds depends on the earning of net income by the issuer. *Participating bonds* have a specified minimum rate of interest plus a stated participation in the income of the issuer; they may have a specified limited participation or an unlimited participation.

Registered bonds are recorded in the name of the investor, and the periodic interest payments are sent only to that person; therefore, a sale or transfer by the investor must be reported to the issuer, trustee, or other party designated for this purpose. In contrast, *coupon bonds* have a coupon attached for each periodic interest payment. At each coupon due date, the holder of the bond simply detaches the appropriate coupon, signs it, and cashes it as if it were a check. The sale of a coupon bond does not require registration of title transfer.

5. Maturity of principal. Bonds maturing at a specified date are called *straight* (or ordinary) *bonds;* that is, the entire bond issue matures at a single date. Bonds maturing at stated installment dates, say one fifth each year, are called *serial bonds* (see Part C). *Callable bonds* give the *issuer* the option to retire them at a stated price before the obligatory maturity date. *Redeemable bonds* give the *investor* the option to turn them in for a stated redemption price prior to maturity. *Convertible bonds* give the *investor* the option to turn them in and to receive, in exchange, other specified securities of the borrower (usually common stock).

FINANCIAL AND MARKETING CONDITIONS

In going to the money market, a borrower needing a large amount of funds must make the fundamental decision as whether to use debt or capital stock, or a combination. This decision depends on a number of factors, some peculiar to the company and some based on the vagaries of the money market. Long-term debt has the advantage that interest payments are deductible as an expense for income tax purposes; thus, an 8% interest rate and a 45% tax bracket reduces the net interest rate (i.e., after tax) to 4.4%. In contrast, dividends paid on funds acquired from the sale of capital stock are not deductible for tax purposes. The periodic interest payments are fixed legal obligations that must be paid in cash each interest period. In contrast, dividends on capital stock are paid only when there are sufficient earnings (and cash). Debt has a fixed maturity date, whereas most capital stock does not.

From the *investor's* point of view, the guaranteed fixed interest rate and maturity amount must be balanced against the potential for dividends (that tend to vary with the earnings of the company) and accretion in the value of the stock. Generally speaking, equity investments are considered to be a better hedge against inflation than debt investments. Both interest revenue (except for tax-free municipal bonds) and dividend revenue are subject to income tax to the investor.

Bonds may be marketed initially by the borrower several ways. Typically, an entire bond issue is sold to one or more investment bankers who *underwrite* them at a specified price and then market them at a higher price to individual investors (and thus realize underwriter's compensation). Alternatively, the investment banker may agree to act as a selling agent for the borrower for an agreed commission; the selling price less the costs of selling is remitted to the issuer. Occasionally, the issuer may sell the bonds privately to financial institutions and individual investors.

Often, where there is no underwriter, the issuer may choose not to sell the entire bond issue if the bonds do not have sufficient appeal in the market. In these situations, unissued bonds should be disclosed in the financial statements, either parenthetically, or by note.

PART A—ACCOUNTING FOR THE BORROWER AND THE INVESTOR COMPARED

ILLUSTRATIVE DATA FOR BONDS

For convenience in illustration in Part A, a common set of facts will be used. Typically, bonds specify a long term from date of issuance to date of maturity (i.e., 10, 20, or more years), fractional interest rates, and semiannual interest payments. However, to simplify and shorten the illustrations at the outset, we will use a five-year term, even interest rates and annual rather than semiannual interest. These simplifications will not affect the basic concepts and accounting procedures.[2] The common set of facts used in this section are:

Issuer (i.e., the borrower):	X Corporation
Investor (i.e., the lender):	Y Corporation

Terms of the bond indenture:

a. Maturity amount of the bonds.	\$100,000 (in \$10,000 and \$1,000 denominations).
b. Date of the bonds.	January 1, 1976.
c. Maturity date.	December 31, 1980 (term, five years).
d. Stated interest rate.	7% per year.
e. Interest payments (cash).	Annually each December 31 (amount, \$100,000 × .07 = \$7,000).
f. Date sold.	January 1, 1976 (unless otherwise stated).
g. Price or effective interest rate.	As specified in the examples to follow.

End of the accounting period—December 31 for both companies (unless otherwise specified).

---

[2] Subsequent to the introductory illustrations, semiannual interest is assumed in the chapter.

To facilitate study, analysis, and problem solving, it is often quite helpful to prepare a *time scale* of a bond issue (or investment) that details important data such as issue date, interest dates, maturity date, period outstanding, and interest rates. A time scale for the above bond issue would appear as follows:

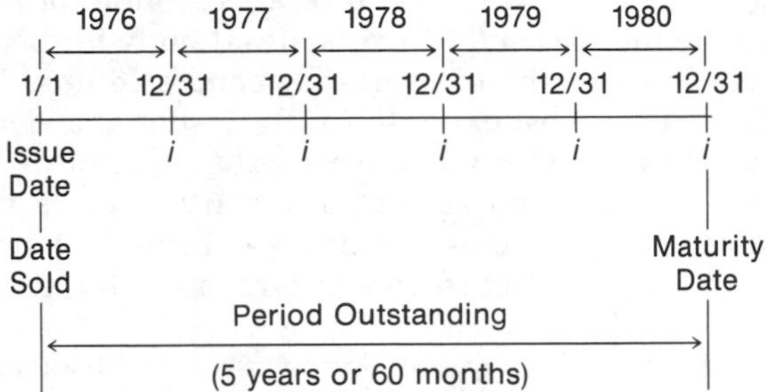

BOND INTEREST AND PRICES

Because bonds have fixed maturity values, definite maturity dates, and specified interest payments, they tend to fluctuate less in price than do stocks. As a class of securities, the market price of bonds fluctuates inversely with changes in the market interest rates. When the market rate of interest rises, the market price of outstanding bonds falls; when the market rate of interest falls, the market price of bonds rises. These market fluctuations adjust the fixed-dollar interest return specified on the bonds to the prevailing *yield rate* in the particular market. The price of individual bonds tends to move with the interest market; however, the price also is influenced by changes in the issuer's financial standing and the approach of maturity (when the market value and maturity amount normally will coincide).

The bond indenture, and the face of each bond certificate, will always specify a *nominal*[3] interest rate which is applied to the principal amount of the bond to determine the amount of *cash interest* that will be paid each period. For example, each bond certificate of X Corporation (see data above) will specify a nominal rate of 7% per year. Thus, each of the $10,000 bonds will always pay $700 cash interest each annual interest period (December 31), and a $1,000 denomination bond will always pay $70 cash, regardless of its issue price. In the case of semiannual interest payments, the bonds of X Corporation, would pay 3.5% nominal interest each six months (refer to Chapter 6 for discussion of interest calculations).

[3] The nominal rate also is often referred to as the contract, stated, or coupon rate of interest. The principal also often is referred to as the face, maturity, or par amount.

In contrast to the nominal rate of interest, the *yield* or *effective* rate is the true rate of interest paid by the issuer and earned by the investor after taking into account the issue (or purchase) price of the bond.[4] Because the money market may establish a rate of interest on the bonds different than the nominal rate, bonds may sell at more or less than their face or par amount.

A bond sold at *par* will incur interest expense for the issuer at the stated rate of interest and will earn interest revenue for the investor at the same rate of interest. Only in this situation, will the nominal and the yield rates of interest be the same. A bond sold at a *discount* (less than par) will incur interest expense for the issuer at a yield rate higher than the nominal rate, and it will earn for the investor the higher effective rate. Conversely, a bond sold at a *premium* (more than par) will incur interest expense for the issuer at a yield rate which is lower than the nominal rate and will earn interest revenue for the investor the lower yield rate.[5]

Investment houses often quote bonds on a yield basis. A 7% bond quoted at 7–50 can be bought at a price that will yield 7.5% on the price of the bond each year from date of sale to maturity date. Thus, a $1,000 bond with a nominal rate of 7%, payable 3.5% semiannually, sold on a 7.50% basis (yield rate) five years before maturity date would have a price of $979.47. The $20.53 discount is an adjustment of the nominal interest rate to the higher yield rate. Sometimes bonds are quoted in relation to their par or maturity amount. For example, a $1,000 bond quoted at 100 is selling for $1,000 (i.e., at par); if quoted at 97, it is selling at $970 (i.e., at a discount of $30); and if quoted at 103, it is selling at $1,030 (i.e., at a premium of $30).

Determination of Bond Prices

When bonds are marketed, investors make purchase offers tending to establish the yield rate of interest. Given the provisions of the bond indenture and the yield rate of interest, the price of a bond can be readily computed. Of course, if the yield rate is the same as the nominal rate, the price of the bond is par; that is, the face or maturity amount. Alternatively, when the yield rate established is different than the nominal rate, the *bond price* (sometimes called the bond valuation) is the *present value* of the future cash flows (i.e., principal plus all interest payments) at the yield rate of interest.

The *bond price* may be determined by either of two ways:

1. Compute the present value of *(a)* the future cash principal due (i.e.,

---

[4] The effective rate is also called the yield, true, or market rate.

[5] This discussion assumes that the issuer sells the bonds direct to the investors with no bond issue costs. Bond issue costs will be discussed in a later section.

the face amount) plus *(b)* the present value of the future *cash* interest payments.

To illustrate, assume the $100,000, 7% (annual interest payments), five-year bonds were sold by X Corporation to Y Corporation at an effective rate of 8% (see page 810).

Computation of the bond price:	
Present value of the future principal:	
$100,000 × $p_{n=5;i=8\%}$ (Table 6–2) = $100,000 × .68058 =	$68,058
Present value of future annual interest payments:	
$7,000 × $P_{n=5;i=8\%}$ (Table 6–4) = $7,000 × 3.99271 =	27,949
Bond price	$96,007

Since the yield rate (8%) was higher than the nominal rate (7%), the bond issue was sold at a *discount* of $100,000 − $96,007 = $3,993.

To illustrate a premium, assume instead that the bonds were sold at a yield rate of 6%.

Computation of the bond price:	
$100,000 × $p_{n=5;i=6\%}$ (Table 6–2) = $100,000 × .74726 =	$ 74,726
$7,000 × $P_{n=5;i=6\%}$ (Table 6–4) = $7,000 × 4.21236 =	29,486
Bond price	$104,212

Amount of premium: $104,212 − $100,000 = $4,212.

2. Refer to a *bond table* that gives bond prices for various nominal rates, yield rates, and time to maturity date. Exhibit 19–1 shows excerpts from three typical bond tables. The bond prices computed above can be verified by referring to Exhibit 19–1, Table A.

ACCOUNTING FOR, AND REPORTING, BONDS (BORROWER AND INVESTOR)

The cost principle governs the initial recording of a bond in the accounts. The issuer records the cash amount received for a bond and the present value of the liability (i.e., the maturity amount minus or plus any discount or premium). Similarly, the investor records the cash amount paid for the bond investment. It is important to note that a bond sold (or purchased) at par has a present value identical to the par or maturity amount. In contrast, a bond sold (or purchased) at a discount has a present value *less* than par or maturity amount (by the amount of the discount); a bond sold (or purchased) at a premium has a present value *higher* than par or maturity amount (by the amount of the premium).

To illustrate these three situations, the above data for X and Y Corporations and the computations of bond prices are used. Assume the entire issue, $100,000, was sold by X Corporation to Y Corporation on January 1, 1976 (date of the bonds):

EXHIBIT 19–1
Excerpts from Three Typical Bond Tables

Table A—Face of Bond $100,000; Nominal Interest 7% Payable Annually

Yield	*3 Years*	*4 Years*	*5 Years*
6.00	102,673.01	103,465.11	104,212.37
6.50	101,324.24	101,712.90	102,077.84
7.00	100,000.00	100,000.00	100,000.00
7.50	98,699.74	98,325.33	97,977.05
8.00	97,422.90	96,687.88	96,007.29

Table B—Face of Bond $100,000; Nominal Interest 7% Payable Semiannually

Yield	*3 Years*	*3½ Years*	*4 Years*	*4½ Years*	*5 Years*
6.00	102,708.60	103,115.14	103,508.92	103,893.11	104,265.00
6.50	101,343.17	101,543.00	101,736.56	101,924.03	102,105.58
7.00	100,000.00	100,000.00	100,000.00	100,000.00	100,000.00
7.50	98,678.75	98,486.55	98,299.29	98,119.78	97,946.76
8.00	97,378.93	96,998.97	96,633.63	96,282.33	95,944.57

Table C—Face of Bond $100; Nominal Interest 8% Payable Semiannually*

Time to Maturity		*Yield Rates*				
Years	*+ Months*	*7%*	*7.5%*	*8.0%*	*8.5%*	*9.0%*
2	Even	101.836540	100.912846	100.000000	99.097848	98.206237
2	1	101.899336	100.938290	100.000000	99.050970	98.124359
2	2	101.959145	100.964777	100.000000	99.013029	98.055281
2	3	102.028761	100.997959	100.000000	98.975859	97.984160
2	4	102.099515	101.033906	100.000000	98.944696	97.920657
2	5	102.176104	101.074992	100.000000	98.917427	97.860498
2	6	102.253567	101.118541	100.000000	98.895778	97.807526
2	7	102.314867	101.143701	100.000000	98.851452	97.729809
2	8	102.378644	101.171736	100.000000	98.810866	97.656296
2	9	102.443779	101.202734	100.000000	98.776419	97.590496
2	10	102.514595	101.238737	100.000000	98.745780	97.527980
2	11	102.586503	101.277397	100.000000	98.720893	97.472743
3	Even	102.664277	101.321268	100.000000	98.700065	97.421064
3	1	102.722250	101.344166	100.000000	98.655990	97.345035
3	2	102.777727	101.368367	100.000000	98.620563	97.281201
3	3	102.842574	101.399033	100.000000	98.586158	97.215846
3	4	102.908739	101.432560	100.000000	98.557652	97.157883
3	5	102.980613	101.471160	100.000000	98.533110	97.103406
3	6	103.053539	101.512319	100.000000	98.514082	97.055892
3	7	103.110178	101.535025	100.000000	98.472445	96.983774
3	8	103.169321	101.560621	100.000000	98.434528	96.915819
3	9	103.229997	101.589273	100.000000	98.402648	96.855356
3	10	103.296232	101.622865	100.000000	98.374642	96.798317
3	11	103.363732	101.659208	100.000000	98.352286	96.748341
4	Even	103.436978	101.700699	100.000000	98.334055	96.702057
4	6	103.800321	101.878147	100.000000	98.162873	96.367598
5	Even	104.158303	102.053197	100.000000	97.997278	96.043641

* This table is more precise than the traditional one established in the 1800s because when the bond is priced between interest dates the actual number of days in the month is used in the calculation instead of the traditional one that assumes 30 days in each month. The first month is January; in certain other situations a slight difference beyond the third decimal point may exist. This is close enough for instructional purposes.

Borrower's Books—X Corporation			*Investor's Books—Y Corporation*		
Case A—The bond issue was sold (and purchased) at par, $100,000:					
Cash	100,000		Bond investment (at cost)	100,000	
Bonds payable		100,000	Cash		100,000
Case B—The bond issue was sold (and purchased) at a discount, $96,007:					
Cash	96,007		Bond investment	100,000	
Discount on bonds payable	3,993		Discount on bonds investment		3,993
Bonds payable		100,000	Cash		96,007
Case C—The bond issue was sold (and purchased) at a premium, $104,212:*					
Cash	104,212		Bond investment	100,000	
Premium on bonds payable		4,212	Premium on bond investment	4,212	
Bonds payable		100,000	Cash		104,212

* Some accountants do not record the discount and premium in separate contra accounts. Under this approach, the entries would be:

Case B:

Borrower			*Investor*		
Cash	96,007		Bond investment	96,007	
Bonds payable		96,007	Cash		96,007

Case C:

Cash	104,212		Bond investment	104,212	
Bonds payable		104,212	Cash		104,212

This approach records the liability and the investment at the net amount that would be reported on the balance sheet. It also simplifies the amortization of premium and discount since the periodic amortization entries are made directly to the liability and investment accounts so that at maturity date, they both reflect the maturity amount. Either approach derives precisely the same results on the periodic financial statements.

Amortization of Discount and Premium

Bond discount or premium affects the amounts of interest expense for the issuer and interest revenue for the investor. For example, the interest effects in each of the three cases given above can be summarized as follows:

	Case A (sold at par)	*Case B (sold at discount)*	*Case C (sold at premium)*
Price of the bonds (cash)	$100,000	$ 96,007	$104,212
Payment of principal at maturity (cash)	(100,000)	(100,000)	(100,000)
Payment of periodic interest ($7,000 × 5)	(35,000)	(35,000)	(35,000)
Difference—Total interest	$ 35,000	$ 38,993	$ 30,788
Average interest per period (÷ 5)	$ 7,000	$ 7,799	$ 6,158

When sold at par, the total interest expense of $35,000 reflects both a nominal and yield rate of 7%. In contrast, the total interest in Case B is greater than $35,000 by the amount of the discount ($3,993), since the price reflects a yield rate of 8%; in Case C, the total interest is less than $35,000 by the amount of the premium ($4,212), since the price reflects a yield rate of 6%. Thus, we see that bond discount and premium affect *(a)* balance sheet investment or liability amounts, and *(b)* interest revenue or expense on the income statement. To record and report these effects in accordance with the matching principle, bond discount and premium must be *amortized* as interest over the *period outstanding; that is, the period from date of sale to maturity date.* The two amortization methods used are (1) the *straight-line* method, and (2) the *interest* method.

Straight-Line Amortization. Under this method, an *equal dollar amount* of the discount or premium is amortized each period over the life of the bonds. To illustrate for Cases B and C above, the amortization each period for the five-year life of the bonds would be recorded as follows:

Borrower's Books—X Corporation | *Investor's Books—Y Corporation*

December 31, annual interest and amortization (each year for five years):

Case B—bonds sold at a discount (straight-line amortization):

Borrower's Books			Investor's Books		
Bond interest expense	7,799*		Cash	7,000	
Discount on bonds payable		799	Discount on bond investment	799	
Cash		7,000	Bond interest revenue		7,799

Case C—bonds sold at a premium (straight-line amortization):

Borrower's Books			Investor's Books		
Bond interest expense	6,158		Cash	7,000	
Premium on bonds payable	842†		Premium on bond investment		842
Cash		7,000	Bond interest revenue		6,158

Computations:
* Cash: $100,000 × .07 = $7,000.
Amortization: $3,993 ÷ 5 yrs. = $799.
† Amortization: $4,212 ÷ 5 yrs. = $842.

The straight-line method of amortization, illustrated above, gives a constant *amount* of interest each period rather than a constant *rate* each period. It can be used under generally accepted accounting principles *only* when the results obtained are not material in comparison with the interest method results (refer to modifying principle, materiality, Chapter 2, page 26). This has been the case since the issuance of *APB Opinion No. 21* (August, 1971), which reads:

> . . . the difference between the present value and the face amount should be treated as discount or premium and amortized as interest expense or income over the life of the note in such a way as to result in a constant rate of interest when applied to the amount outstanding at the beginning of any given period. This is the "interest" method. . . . However, other methods of amortization may be used if the results obtained are not materially different from those which would result from the "interest" method.

When the results are not materially different from the interest method, straight-line amortization may be used because of its simplicity. It is a practical approach, although not theoretically sound.

Interest Method of Amortization. The interest method is also called present value amortization. As explained in the preceding paragraph, it is required by *APB Opinion No. 21* (unless the results of another approach used are not materially different). The interest method is based upon the concept of an annuity (see Chapter 6) because *(a)* changes in both interest and carrying value are recognized each period, and *(b)* periodic interest expense (i.e., the effective interest amount) is computed as a *constant rate* applied to the book value or carrying amount of the bonds. The constant rate is the yield rate of interest as illustrated in Exhibits 19–2 (8%) and 19–3 (6%). Because Exhibit 19–2 is based on a *discount,* the effective interest amount (column [*b*]) *increases* each period because the carrying value in column (*e*) is increasing. In contrast, since Exhibit 19–3 is based on a *premium,* the effective interest amount (column [*b*]) *decreases* each period, because the carrying value in column (*e*) is decreasing.

EXHIBIT 19–2
Bond Interest and Discount Amortization Interest Method—Annual Interest Payments (face amount—$100,000)

Date	Cash Interest (7% annual)	Effective Interest (8% annual)	Discount Amortization	Balance Unamortized Discount	Carrying Value of Bonds
1/1/76 starting date				3,993	96,007
12/31/76	7,000(*a*)	7,681(*b*)	681(*c*)	3,312(*d*)	96,688(*e*)
12/31/77	7,000	7,735	735	2,577	97,423
12/31/78	7,000	7,794	794	1,783	98,217
12/31/79	7,000	7,857	857	926	99,074
12/31/80	7,000	7,926	926	-0-	100,000

(*a*) $100,000 × .07 = $7,000 (based on nominal rate).
(*b*) $96,007 × .08 = $7,681 (based on yield rate of interest).
(*c*) $7,681 − $7,000 = $681.
(*d*) $3,993 − $681 = $3,312.
(*e*) $96,007 + $681 = $96,688 (or $100,000 − $3,312 = $96,688).

EXHIBIT 19–3
Bond Interest and Premium Amortization Interest Method—Annual Interest Payments (face amount—$100,000)

Date	Cash Interest (7% annual)	Effective Interest (6% annual)	Premium Amortization	Balance Unamortized Premium	Carrying Value of Bonds
1/1/76 starting date				4,212	104,212
12/31/76	7,000(*a*)	6,253(*b*)	747(*c*)	3,465(*d*)	103,465(*e*)
12/31/77	7,000	6,208	792	2,673	102,673
12/31/78	7,000	6,160	840	1,833	101,833
12/31/79	7,000	6,110	890	943	100,943
12/31/80	7,000	6,057	943	-0-	100,000

(*a*) $100,000 × .07 = $7,000 (based on nominal rate).
(*b*) $104,212 × .06 = $6,253 (based on yield rate of interest).
(*c*) $7,000 − $6,253 = $747.
(*d*) $4,212 − $747 = $3,465.
(*e*) $104,212 − $747 = $103,465 (or $100,000 + $3,465 = $103,465).

When the interest method is used, it is convenient to prepare an *amortization schedule* such as those illustrated in Exhibits 19–2 and 19–3. The entries for both the issuer and the investor, for the periodic interest and amortization of premium or discount, can be taken directly from the schedule. To illustrate, the entries at the end of the first year would be:

Borrower's Books—X Corporation			*Investor's Books—Y Corporation*		

December 31, 1976, annual interest and amortization:

Case B—Bonds sold at a discount (interest method amortization):

Bond interest expense	7,681		Cash	7,000	
Discount on bonds payable		681	Discount on bond investment ...	681	
Cash		7,000	Bond interest revenue		7,681

Computations: Exhibit 19–2.

Case C—Bonds sold at a premium (interest method amortization):

Bond interest expense	6,253		Cash	7,000	
Premium on bonds payable...	747		Premium on bond investment........................		747
Cash		7,000	Bond interest revenue		6,253

Computations: Exhibit 19–3.

A comparison of the results of straight-line amortization (page 816) and the interest method (Exhibits 19–2 and 3) clearly demonstrates the conceptual and practical differences between the two methods.[6]

REPORTING BONDS ON THE FINANCIAL STATEMENTS

If the unamortized bond discount or premium is separately recorded, as illustrated above, it should be reported as a direct deduction from or addition to the basic account balance.

Reporting by the Borrower

Bonds payable should be reported under the balance sheet caption Long-term Liabilities. The issuer should deduct unamortized bonds discount (a debit balance) from the face amount of the related bonds payable whereas unamortized bond premium (a credit balance) should be added to the face amount of the bonds. *APB Opinion No. 21* specifically states that bond discount or premium "should not be classified as a deferred charge or deferred credit." To assure full disclosure, the *Opinion* also states that the face of the note (i.e., the principal) and the yield rate of interest should be disclosed in the financial statements or in the notes to the statements.[7] To illustrate, the long-term liability for bonds payable should be reported essentially as follows (refer to Exhibit 19–2):

X CORPORATION
Balance Sheet (partial)
At December 31, 1976

Long-Term Liabilities:		
Bonds payable, maturity amount (due December 31, 1980, 7% interest, payable annually)	$100,000	
Less unamortized discount (based on 8% effective interest)	3,312	
Bonds payable less unamortized discount		$96,688

[6] If separate accounts are not used to record discount or premium, the amortization entry would be made directly to the respective liability or investment accounts. See footnote* to the tabulation of entries on page 815.

[7] *APB Opinion No. 21*, August 1971, Appendix, par. 19. Observe that the provisions of FASB *Statement No. 12* do not apply to long-term investments in debt securities and that the lower-of-cost-or-market concept is not applied to them.

Reporting by the Investor

Long-term investments in bonds should be reported under the balance sheet caption, Investments and Funds. The amount reported should include cost, plus or minus any unamortized discount or premium. In addition, the current market value, if determinable and materially different from the carrying value, and the yield rate of interest used for amortization purposes, should be reported to assure full disclosure. For example, the long-term investment analyzed in Exhibit 19–2 would be reported as follows:

Y CORPORATION
Balance Sheet (partial)
At December 31, 1976

Investments and Funds:	
Investment in 6% bonds of X Corporation (amortized cost based on 8% effective interest, due December 31, 1980)	$96,688

The maturity amount ($100,000), the unamortized discount ($3,312), and the difference ($96,688) could be shown separately; however, as a matter of practice, this is seldom done.

ACCOUNTING FOR SEMIANNUAL INTEREST PAYMENTS

Most bonds specify an annual interest rate with semiannual interest payments. In this situation, the semiannual rate used is one half the annual rate and the number of interest periods is double the number of years (see Chapter 6).

To illustrate the accounting process when interest is paid semiannually, assume the bonds issued on January 1, 19A, by X Corporation specified semiannual interest payments on June 30 and December 31. The *nominal* semiannual interest rate would be 3.5%, the number of semiannual *interest periods* would be 10; if sold at an effective annual rate of 8%, the semiannual *effective rate* would be 4%. The price of this bond issue on January 1, 1976, would be computed as follows:

Present value of future principal:	
$100,000 × $p_{n=10;i=4\%}$ (Table 6–2) = $100,000 × .67556 =	$67,556
Present value of future semiannual interest payments:	
$3,500 × $P_{n=10;i=4\%}$ (Table 6–4) = $3,500 × 8.11089 =	28,388
Bond Price (semiannual interest payments assumed)........................	$95,944*

* In Exhibit 19–1, Table A, this shown to be $95,944.57; the difference is due to table rounding.

The bond amortization table for this situation is presented in Exhibit 19–4. The entries for the issuer and the investor for this example are the same as previously illustrated except that *(a)* an interest entry must be made for each semiannual interest date, and *(b)* the amounts of cash, interest, and discount amortization will be as reflected in Exhibit 19–4.

EXHIBIT 19–4
Bond Interest and Discount Amortization Interest Method—Semiannual Interest Payments (face amount—$100,000)

Date	Cash Interest (3½% semi-annual)	Effective Interest (4% semi-annual)	Discount Amortization	Balance Unamortized Discount	Carrying Value of Bonds
1/1/76 starting date				4,056	95,944
6/30/76	3,500*(a)*	3,838*(b)*	338*(c)*	3,718*(d)*	96,282*(e)*
12/31/76	3,500	3,851	351	3,367	96,633
6/30/77	3,500	3,865	365	3,002	96,998
12/31/77	3,500	3,880	380	2,622	97,378
6/30/78	3,500	3,895	395	2,227	97,773
12/31/78	3,500	3,911	411	1,816	98,184
6/30/79	3,500	3,927	427	1,389	98,611
12/31/79	3,500	3,944	444	945	99,055
6/30/80	3,500	3,962	462	483	99,517
12/31/80	3,500	3,983	483	-0-	100,000

(a) $100,000 × .035 = $3,500 (based on nominal interest rate).
(b) $95,944 × .04 = $3,838 (based on effective rate).
(c) $3,838 − $3,500 = $338.
(d) $4,056 − $338 = $3,718.
(e) $95,944 + $338 = $96,282 (or $100,000 − $3,718 = $96,282).

PART B—SPECIAL PROBLEMS IN ACCOUNTING FOR BONDS

In Part A, certain complexities were excluded in order to provide a sound understanding of the fundamentals in accounting for and reporting bonds for both the issuer and the investor. A number of special problems often occur in accounting for and reporting bonds; however, they do not change the fundamentals discussed in Part A. These special problems will be discussed in this part of the chapter.

For illustrative purposes, a different fact situation will be used. Semiannual interest payments will be assumed; and an early maturity and even interest rates again will be used to shorten the illustrations. The common set of facts are:

Issuer: Cox Corporation
Investor: Day Corporation

Terms of the bond indenture:

a. Maturity amount of the bonds.	$200,000 ($10,000 and $1,000 denominations).
b. Date of the bonds.	January 1, 1976.
c. Maturity date.	December 31, 1978 (3 years).
d. Nominal interest rate.	8%, payable 4% semiannually.
e. Interest payments (cash).	$8,000 each June 30 and December 31.
f. Date sold.	As specified in each example to follow.
g. Yield interest rate and bond price.	7% (3½% semiannually); price, $205,329.
h. Amortization schedule (interest method):	

Date	Cash Interest (4% semi-annual)	Effective Interest (3½% semi-annual)	Premium Amortization	Balance Unamortized Premium	Carrying Value of Bonds
1/1/76 starting date ...				5,329	205,329
6/30/76	8,000*(a)*	7,186*(b)*	814*(c)*	4,515*(d)*	204,515*(e)*
12/31/76	8,000	7,158	842	3,673	203,673
6/30/77	8,000	7,129	871	2,802	202,802
12/31/77	8,000	7,098	902	1,900	201,900
6/30/78	8,000	7,066	934	966	200,966
12/31/78	8,000	7,034	966	-0-	200,000

(a) \$200,000 × .04 = \$8,000 (based on nominal rate).
(b) \$205,329 × .035 = \$7,186 (based on effective rate).
(c) \$8,000 − \$7,186 = \$814.
(d) \$5,329 − \$814 = \$4,515.
(e) \$200,000 + \$4,515 = \$204,515 (or \$205,329 − \$814 = \$204,515).

BONDS SOLD, AND PURCHASED, BETWEEN INTEREST DATES

Bonds often are sold and purchased at dates other than an interest date specified on the bonds. This situation necessitates recognition, in the accounts, of accrued interest from the *last interest date* to the date of the transaction. The amount of cash is increased by the amount of the accrued interest for the same period. Accrued interest arises because of a particular characteristic of bonds. That is, the *full amount* of the specified periodic *nominal interest* on a bond will be paid in cash on each interest date after sale, regardless of its sale date. Therefore, when a bond is sold between interest dates, the amount paid by the investor will be *(a)* the price of the bond plus *(b)* any accrued interest from the last interest date.

Bonds Sold between Interest Dates at Par

To illustrate when bonds are sold at par between interest dates, assume Cox Corporation sold the \$200,000, 8% bonds, dated January 1, 1976, to Day Corporation on November 1, 1976, at par plus the four months accrued interest. This situation can be reflected on a time scale as follows:

TIME SCALE

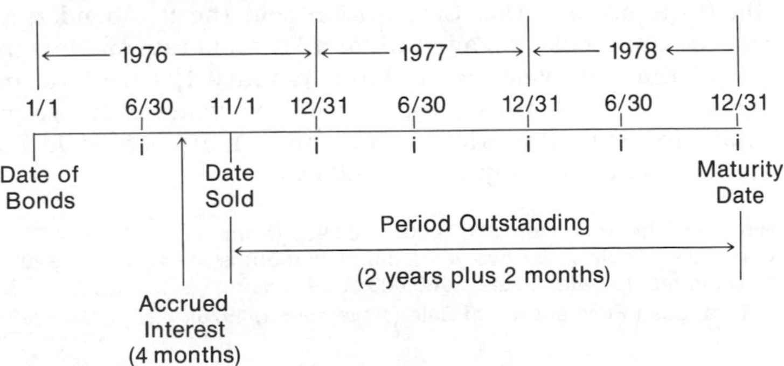

The amount of cash flowing from the investor to the issuer can be computed as follows:

Sales price of the bond issue on 11/1/76 (at par)	$200,000
Add: Accrued interest since last interest date (June 30 to November 1—$200,000 × .04 × 4/6)	5,333
Total Cash Paid on Date of Sale/Purchase Transaction	$205,333

The borrower and the investor would make the following entries in 1976:

Cox Corporation—Borrower			*Day Corporation—Investor*		
November 1, 1976—To record sale and purchase of the bonds (including four months accrued interest):					
Cash	205,333		Investment in bonds	200,000	
Bonds payable.........		200,000	Bond interest revenue	5,333	
Bond interest expense...............		5,333	Cash		205,333
December 31, 1976—To record payment of nominal semiannual interest:					
Bond interest expense ...	8,000		Cash	8,000	
Cash ($200,000 × .04)		8,000	Bond interest revenue.		8,000

If the purchase/sale transaction date is in one accounting period and the next interest date is in the following accounting period, most accountants use accrued interest expense and accrued interest revenue, respectively, in these two entries. Both approaches derive the same ultimate net effect. See Exhibits 19–6 and 19–7.

After posting both entries, the respective interest expense and interest revenue accounts will stand at $2,667 (i.e., $8,000 – $5,333) which represents interest for the two months outstanding ($200,000 × .04 × 2/6 = $2,667). Similarly, bond transactions between *individual investors,* when not on an interest date, necessitates recognition of accrued interest by both parties.

Bonds Sold between Interest Dates at a Discount or Premium

When a bond is sold or purchased between interest dates at a *discount* or *premium,* the accounting illustrated immediately above is followed except that the discount or premium must be recorded and amortized over the *period outstanding;* that is, *the period from the date of sale (not the date of the bond) to the maturity date.*

To illustrate, assume Cox Corporation sold the 8% bond issue, reflected on the time scale on page 821, at a 7% yield rate on November 1, 1976. Recall that the bonds were dated January 1, 1976, and mature on December 31, 1978; thus they are sold two years plus two months before maturity. The sales price on November 1, 1976, to yield 7%, and the cash flow would be computed as follows:

Sales price of the 8% bonds: $200,000 × 101.959 (from Exhibit 19–1, Table C, for two years plus two months at 7%) = ...	$203,918
Accrued interest to date of sale: $200,000 × .04 × 4/6 = ...	5,333
Total Cash Flow at Date of Sale (November 1, 1976)	$209,251

The borrower and investor would record the transaction as follows:

Borrower			*Investor*		
November 1, 1976 – to record sale/purchase of bond issue:					
Cash	209,251		Bond investment	200,000	
Bond interest expense		5,333	Bond interest revenue	5,333	
Premium on bonds payable		3,918	Premium on bond investment	3,918	
Bonds payable		200,000	Cash		209,251

The premium must be amortized over the total period outstanding (26 months); therefore, assuming the amortization amounts are not material, the straight-line method can be used. On the next interest date, the nominal interest (cash) for the full six months and amortization of premium for the two months since date of sale would be recorded as follows:[8]

Borrower			*Investor*		
December 31, 1976 – to record semiannual interest payment using straight-line amortization:					
Bond interest expense	7,698		Cash	8,000	
Premium on bonds payable	302		Premium on bond investment		302
Cash ($200,000 × .04)		8,000	Bond interest revenue		7,698

Amortization: $3,918 ÷ 26 (total months outstanding) = $151 per month (rounded)
$151 × 2 (months outstanding this period) = $302

After the above entries are posted, the respective interest expense and revenue accounts will reflect net interest amounts for two months (i.e., the period outstanding since the date of sale).

Alternatively, amortization based on the *interest method* would be as reflected in Exhibit 19–5. When the transaction is between interest dates, as in this illustration (two months before next interest date), the amortization amount at the first interest date after acquisition must be uniquely determined. It is computed as the difference between the sales price at transaction date (November 1, 1976, in the example) and the sales price at the next interest date (i.e., December 31, 1976). This computation is shown in Exhibit 19–5. Entries to reflect the semiannual interest and premium amortization also are reflected in that exhibit. This is an important example because typically bonds are bought and sold between interest dates, at a discount or premium, and the interest method should be used.

---

[8] These entries assume amortization on interest dates; amortization often is delayed until the end of the accounting period; see Exhibits 19–7 and 19–8. These entries also assume discount and premium are recorded in separate accounts. If the approach shown in footnote* to the tabulation of entries on page 815 is followed, the amount amortized would be recorded directly in the liability and investment accounts respectively.

EXHIBIT 19–5
Bond Interest and Discount Amortization between Interest Dates—Interest Method (semiannual interest payments)

Date	Cash Interest (4% semiannual)	Effective Interest (3½% semiannual)	Premium Amortization	Balance Unamortized Premium	Carrying Value of Bonds
11/1/76 starting date ...				3,918	203,918
12/31/76	8,000(b)	7,755(b)	245(a)	3,673	203,673
6/30/77	8,000	7,129	871	2,802	202,802
12/31/77	8,000	7,098	902	1,900	201,900
6/30/78	8,000	7,066	934	966	200,966
12/31/78	8,000	7,034	966	-0-	200,000

Computations:

(a) Bond price at date of sale (November 1, 1976), Exhibit 19–1, Table C, for two years plus two months at 7%; $200,000 × 101.959 = ...	$203,918
Bond price at next interest date (December 31, 1976), Exhibit 19–1, Table C, for two years even at 7%; $200,000 × 101.83654 = ...	203,673
Difference—Amortization for First Interest Period (two months)	$ 245
(b) Semiannual cash interest on December 31, 1976, $200,000 × .04 = ...	$ 8,000
Premium amortization first period as above	245
Effective Interest (before accrual of interest at acquisition)	$ 7,755
Net interest expense for 1976:	
Effective interest as computed above	$ 7,755
Less accrued interest at date of bond transaction (see issue transaction on November 1, 1976, given on page 823)	5,333
Net Interest Cost for the Two-Month Holding Period during 1976	$ 2,422

Alternatively: ($200,000 × .04 × 2/6) − $245 = $2,422.

ACCOUNTING WHEN THE INTEREST DATE AND END OF THE ACCOUNTING PERIOD DO NOT COINCIDE

Typically, the interest date on bonds (and other debt securities) does not coincide with the end of the accounting period. In this situation, a borrower must *accrue* interest expense on the debt from the last interest date to the end of the accounting period. Similarly, an investor must accrue interest revenue on the bond investment.

In respect to bonds sold (or purchased) at a discount or premium, there must be an accrual at the end of the accounting period of a portion of the unamortized amount. Each year the amount of discount or premium amortized must be equivalent to the portion of the year the bonds were outstanding (or held as an investment).

To illustrate, assume (for this example only) that the accounting periods for Cox Corporation and Day Corporation ends on March 31 and that the bonds were sold on January 1, 1976. At the end of the accounting period, the following adjusting entries would be made:[9]

[9] These entries assume amortization on interest dates; amortization often is delayed until the end of the accounting period; see Exhibits 19–7 and 19–8. These entries also assume discount and premium are recorded in separate accounts. If the approach shown in footnote* to the tabulation of entries on page 815 is followed, the amount amortized would be recorded directly in the liability and investment accounts respectively.

March 31, 1976—Adjusting entry for accrued bond interest and premium amortization for the three months, January–March (computations based on data from the amortization schedule shown on page 821):

Borrower—Cox Corporation:

Bond interest expense ($7,186 × 3/6)	3,593	
Premium on bonds payable ($814 × 3/6)	407	
Accrued bond interest payable ($200,000 × .04 × 3/6)		4,000

(Note: Assuming the straight-line method, the amortization would be $5,329 × 3/36 = $444).

Investor—Day Corporation:

Accrued bond interest receivable	4,000	
Premium on bond investment		407
Bond interest revenue		3,593

These entries are candidates for reversing entries (see Chapter 3). If reversed, the entry on the next entry date would be affected; whether reversed or not, the net results would be the same (see Exhibits 19–7 and 19–8 for a complete sequence of entries including reversing entries).

BOND ISSUE COSTS

There are numerous material expenditures incurred in preparing and selling a bond issue. Bond issue costs include legal, accounting, other professional fees, commissions, engraving, printing, registration, and promotion costs. Generally accepted accounting principles treat these expenditures collectively as a *deferred charge* rather than as an element of bond discount or premium.[10] As a deferred charge, the total amount should be amortized (usually on a straight-line basis) over the period outstanding between the sale date and the maturity date, because it is assumed that there will be related future revenue benefits flowing from the proceeds of the financing. Theoretically, bond issue costs should be amortized using the interest method; however, the straight-line method often is used because they are not material in amount. In some situations, these costs are immaterial in amount; in other cases where an underwriter handles the planning, issue, and sale of the bonds, it may be difficult to distinguish issue costs from the discount or premium.

To illustrate, assume W Corporation sold $100,000, 7½%, ten-year bonds at 101 on January 1, 19A (also date of the bonds). Bond issue costs were $300, and the bond interest is payable annually each December 31.

a. January 1, 19A—to record sale:

Cash	100,700	
Bond issue costs deferred	300	
Premium on bonds payable		1,000
Bonds payable		100,000

[10] *APB Opinion No. 21,* August 1971, par. 16.

b. December 31, 19A – to record interest and amortization of premium and bond issue costs (straight-line basis):

Bond interest expense	7,430	
Premium on bonds payable ($1,000 ÷ 10 years)...........	100	
Bond issue costs deferred ($300 ÷ 10 years)		30
Cash		7,500

COMPREHENSIVE ILLUSTRATION – AMORTIZATION AT YEAR-END VERSUS AT INTEREST DATES

The preceding discussion and illustrations focused on specific concepts and problems. At this point, a comprehensive illustration is presented to tie together the various elements of accounting for bonds. Additionally, bond discount or premium may be amortized either *(a)* at year-end only, or *(b)* at each interest date. Both approaches give the same results, and it is largely a matter of personal choice between them.

To provide a comprehensive illustration from date of sale to maturity date, assume the following facts:

Issuer: Z Corporation.
Maturity amount of the bonds: $10,000 (in $1,000 denominations).
Date of the bonds: April 1, 1975.
Issue date (date sold): April 1, 1975.
Maturity date: April 1, 1977 (two-year term).
Stated interest rate: 7%, payable 3½% semiannually.
Interest dates (cash): $350 each April 1 and October 1.
Price: $10,185.85 (i.e., a premium of $185.85).
Yield rate of interest: 6%.
Accounting period ends on December 31.

Exhibits 19–6, 19–7, and 19–8 illustrate entries for sale, interest payments, adjustments, reversals, closing entries, and debt payment at maturity.

An amortization table, using the interest method, is shown in Exhibit 19–6. Amortization on each *interest date* is illustrated in Exhibit 19–7. In contrast, amortization only at *year-end* is illustrated in Exhibit 19–8.

EXHIBIT 19–6
Amortization Bond Premium – Interest Method

Date	Cash Cr.	Bond Interest Expense Dr.	Bond Premium Dr.	Balance Unamortized Premium	Liability Carrying Value
4/1/75	(issuance)			185.85	10,185.85
10/1/75	350.00*(a)*	305.58*(b)*	44.42*(c)*	141.43*(d)*	10,141.43*(e)*
4/1/76	350.00	304.24	45.76	95.67	10,095.67
10/1/76	350.00	302.87	47.13	48.54	10,048.54
4/1/77	350.00	301.46	48.54	-0-	10,000.00

(a) $10,000 × .07 × 6/12 = $350.00 (at nominal rate, 7%).
(b) $10,185.85 × .06 × 6/12 = $305.58 (at effective rate, 6%).
(c) Column *(a)* minus column *(b)*.
(d) $185.85 − $44.42 = $141.43.
(e) $10,185.85 − $44.42 = $10,141.43.

EXHIBIT 19–7
Bonds Payable, Semiannual Interest—Amortization on Interest Dates (interest method)

Date	Explanation	Cash Dr., Cr.*	Bonds Payable Dr., Cr.*	Bond Interest Expense Dr., Cr.*	Accrued Bond Interest Dr., Cr.*	Income Summary Dr., Cr.*	Bond Premium Dr., Cr.*
4/1/75	Sale of bonds	10,185.85	10,000.00*				185.85*
10/1/75	Interest payment and amortization	350.00*		305.58			44.42
12/31/75	Adjusting entry			152.12	175.00*		22.88[(a)]
12/31/75	Closing entry			457.70*		457.70	
1/1/76	Reversing entry			152.12*	175.00		22.88*
4/1/76	Interest payment and amortization	350.00*		304.24			45.76
10/1/76	Interest payment and amortization	350.00*		302.87			47.13
12/31/76	Adjusting entry			150.73	175.00*		24.27[(b)]
12/31/76	Closing entry			605.72*		605.72	
1/1/77	Reversing entry			150.73*	175.00		24.27*
4/1/77	Interest payment and amortization	350.00*		301.46			48.54
4/1/77	Payment of bonds	10,000.00*	10,000.00				
12/31/77	Closing entry			150.73*		150.73	
		1,214.15				1,214.15	

Refer to Exhibit 19–6:
(a) $45.76 × 3/6 = $22.88
(b) $48.54 × 3/6 = $24.27

EXHIBIT 19–8

Bonds Payable, Semiannual Interest—Amortization Only at Year-End (interest method)

Date	Explanation	Cash Dr., Cr.*	Bonds Payable Dr., Cr.*	Bond Interest Expense Dr., Cr.*	Accrued Bond Interest Dr., Cr.*	Income Summary Dr., Cr.*	Bond Premium Dr., Cr.*
4/1/75..............	Sale of bonds	10,185.85	10,000.00*				185.85*
10/1/75..............	Interest payment	350.00*		350.00			
12/31/75..............	Adjusting entry			175.00	175.00*		
12/31/75..............	Premium amortization			67.30*			67.30[a]
12/31/75..............	Closing entry			457.70*		457.70	
1/1/76..............	Reversing of accrued interest			175.00*	175.00		
4/1/76..............	Interest payment	350.00*		350.00			
10/1/76..............	Interest payment	350.00*		350.00			
12/31/76..............	Adjusting entry			175.00	175.00*		
12/31/76..............	Premium amortization			94.28*			94.28[b]
12/31/76..............	Closing entry			605.72*		605.72	
1/1/77..............	Reversing of accrued interest			175.00*	175.00		
4/1/77..............	Interest payment	350.00*		350.00			
4/1/77..............	Payment of bonds	10,000.00*	10,000.00				
12/31/77..............	Premium amortization			24.27*			24.27[c]
12/31/77..............	Closing entry			150.73*		150.73	
		1,214.15				1,214.15	

Refer to Exhibit 19–7:

(a) \$44.42 + (\$45.76 × 3/6) = \$67.30.

(b) (\$45.76 × 3/6) + \$47.13 + (\$48.54 × 3/6) = \$94.28.

(c) (\$48.54 × 3/6) = \$24.27.

Observe in particular computations of the amortization amounts for the adjusting entries. The net results are the same in both exhibits as reflected in *(a)* the amount of interest expense each period (compare the closing entries), and *(b)* the carrying value of the bonds (face amount plus the unamortized premium) at the end of each accounting period.

EARLY EXTINGUISHMENT OF DEBT

Bonds and certain other debt instruments frequently carry a *call provision* stating that at the option of the *borrower*, the debt may be called for payment prior to the obligatory maturity date. Call provisions, including time limits and the call or reacquisition price, are specified in the bond indenture and are printed on each bond certificate. Obviously, bonds without a call provision may be reacquired by purchase in the market. Early extinguishment by exercise of a call normally is made on an interest date, in which case the amortization of any discount or premium and bond issue costs will be up-to-date; thus there will be no accrued interest. Early extinguishment by purchase in the market often is not at an interest date in which case accruals must be brought up to date prior to recording the extinguishment transaction.

In early extinguishment of debt, the difference between *reacquisition price* and *net carrying amount* of the debt is a "gain or loss on early extinguishment of debt." The net carrying amount is the net of the par, unamortized discount, premium and bond issue costs, related to the debt paid off.

APB Opinion No. 26, "Early Extinguishment of Debt" (October 1972), specifies the appropriate accounting for early extinguishment of debt. Prior to that opinion, four different alternatives were used to account for the gain or loss on early extinguishment of debt: it was (1) amortized over what would have been the remaining life of the old debt; (2) recorded as an *ordinary* item on the income statement in the year of recall; (3) reported as an *extraordinary* item on the income statement in the year of recall; and (4) amortized over the life of any new debt that was created to obtain funds to pay off the old debt. To attain uniformity and realistic reporting on the income statement, *Opinion No. 26* states: "A difference between the reacquisition price and the net carrying amount of the extinguished debt should be recognized currently in income of the period of extinguishment as losses or gains and identified as a separate item." Under the restrictive criteria given in *APB Opinion No. 30* (June 1973) for extraordinary items (see page 126), the gain or loss was reported as an ordinary item. Because early extinguishment was quickly used to generate a large credit (an ordinary gain) on the income statement, the FASB in *Statement No. 4* specified that the gain or loss on early extinguishment of debt be reported on the *income statement as an extraordinary item.*[11]

To illustrate early extinguishment of debt, assume the bonds issued by X Corporation (data on page 810A) had a call provision that they could

---

[11] FASB, *Statement of Financial Accounting Standards No. 4,* March 1975, par. 8.

be called at a reacquisition price of 102 at any time on or after December 31, 1978. At that date, assume the accounts of X Corporation reflected the balances shown in Exhibit 19–2 and, in addition, unamortized bond issue costs were $400. If all of the bonds are recalled, the reacquisition entry (after the entry to record interest and discount amortization on that date) would be:

December 31, 1978:

Bonds payable	100,000	
Extraordinary loss—early extinguishment of bonds	4,183	
Discount on bonds payable (unamortized)		1,783
Bond issue costs (unamortized)		400
Cash (at 102)		102,000

Refunding Bonds Payable

When debt (usually an old bond issue) is extinguished early and the necessary cash is obtained by issuing a new bond series, it is usually referred to as *refunding.* Refunding generally is advantageous *(a)* when the new series has a lower interest rate than the old series, or *(b)* when the old series can be reacquired in the market at a "deep" discount. The issuing corporation must consider factors before making a refunding decision, such as future interest costs including present value effects. The basic question should be: Can future costs be reduced by refunding? For example, in view of the current high interest rates, one company with an old $50,000,000, 4.75% bond issue outstanding could extinguish that issue by purchasing them at 82 in the market (i.e., for $41,000,000). The result would be a $9,000,000 gain in the year of extinguishment. In most situations, a large portion of the cash would be obtained by a *refunding issue* at interest rates about 8%. Several factors, in addition to present value analysis, entered into the decisions; such as the immediate effect of the $9,000,000 gain on the income statement. Accounting for refunding situations is the same as illustrated in the preceding paragraph.

Because of inappropriate *balance sheet reporting* practices, FASB *Statement No. 6*, "Classification of Short-Term Obligations Expected to Be Refunded," was issued in 1975. This statement affirms prior GAAP that "short-term obligations arising from transactions in the normal course of business that are due in customary terms shall be classified as current liabilities." The statement permits the exclusion from *current liabilities,* currently maturing debt that the enterprise intends to *refinance on a long-term basis.* The intention must be supported either by *(a)* long-term refinancing prior to issuance of the financial statements, or *(b)* an enforceable long-term financing agreement.

CONVERTIBLE BONDS

A convertible bond is a debt security which may be converted to capital stock (usually common stock) of the issuer, at the option of the *holder*, under specified conditions. Typically, convertible securities also are *callable* at a specified redemption or call price at the option of the *issuer* and are subordinated to nonconvertible debt. Subordinated means a lower class; that is, the convertible debt ranks below nonconvertible debt as a claim against assets. In case of insolvency, the nonconvertible debt would be paid first. Generally, convertible bonds can be sold at an interest rate lower than it would be for nonconvertible bonds because investors impute a value to the conversion privilege. Convertible securities also have a conversion ratio and a conversion price specified in the bond indenture. The *conversion ratio* is the number of shares of common stock the holder of a convertible bond will receive when tendered for conversion. In contrast, the *conversion price* is the relationship between the face amount of the convertible bond and the number of shares of common stock to be received upon conversion.

To illustrate, assume AB Corporation issued $1,000 convertible bonds, each of which could be converted, at the option of the holder at any time after the second year from issuance, for ten shares of AB Corporation common stock. The conversion ratio for each bond would be 10 (shares of stock) to 1 (bond); the conversion price would be $1,000 ÷ 10 shares = $100.

Convertible bonds offer certain advantages to both the issuer and the investor. The primary advantages to the issuer are *(a)* a lower rate of interest, and *(b)* a means of securing equity (stockholder) financing in the long run (after conversion, this is the net effect since the debt is not paid in cash). The call option usually is used by the issuer to force conversion when the aggregate price of the stock to be received on conversion is greater than the call price; in this case, only a foolish investor would take cash in lieu of the stock.

The primary advantages of convertible bonds to the investor are *(a)* an option to receive either the face of the bond at maturity or common stock of the issuer, *(b)* a guaranteed rate of interest up to conversion date or maturity, and *(c)* benefits of appreciation in the price of the common stock of the issuer.

Accounting for the Issuance of Convertible Bonds

Since convertible bonds specify a lower rate of interest than would nonconvertible debt for the same company, and since they can be converted to common stock, there is the basic question upon issuance as to what portion of the sales price should relate to *debt* and what portion should be allocated to *equity* (stockholders' equity). To illustrate the problem, assume AB Corporation issued $100,000, 7%, ten-year *nonconvertible* bonds payable which were sold for $96,000. The transaction would be recorded as follows:

Cash	96,000	
Discount on bonds payable	4,000	
Bonds payable, 7% (nonconvertible)		100,000

Now assume instead, that each $1,000 bond (without detachable stock warrants) was convertible after the second year, at the option of the holder, to ten shares of common stock (par $75) of AB Corporation. Because of this feature, the bonds specified an interest rate of 5% (as opposed to the prior 7% rate) and would sell for $106,000. How should this transaction be recorded? There are two alternatives:

Alternative 1 – View the transaction as debt only:

Cash	106,000	
Premium on bonds payable		6,000
Bonds payable, 5% (convertible)		100,000

Alternative 2 – View the transaction as part debt and part equity:

Cash	106,000	
Discount on bonds payable ($106,000 – $96,000)	10,000	
Bonds payable, 5% (convertible)		100,000
Contributed capital – bond conversion option		16,000

Reflecting the differing views and implementation problems, *APB Opinion No. 10* (1966) required the second alternative; the following year, *APB Opinion No. 12* (1967) suspended this requirement. Finally, *APB Opinion No. 14* (1969) specified the *current requirement* to be *Alternative 1*, except when there are detachable stock warrants (discussed below). The principal reasons for selecting Alternative 1 when the bonds do not have detachable stock warrants are *(a)* the inseparability of the debt and the conversion option, and *(b)* difficulty in implementation–in the absence of separate transferability for the two portions the amounts that should be assigned separately to debt and equity cannot be derived from the market. Therefore, because an objective assignment of separate values to debt and equity is impossible, Alternative 1, although not conceptually preferable, was considered more realistic.

The *investor* would record a $1,000 convertible bond of AB Corporation acquired as a long-term investment as follows:

Bond investment (convertible bonds)	1,000	
Premium on bond investment	60	
Cash		1,060

Accounting for Conversion by the Borrower

When convertible bonds are tendered by the investor to the issuer for conversion to common stock in accordance with the conversion privilege, the carrying value of the bonds must be removed from the accounts and issuance of the common stock recorded. Prior to recording the conversion transaction, all account balances related to the bonds should be brought up to the current status. If the conversion is made on an interest date, these items will be on a current basis; if not, bond discount or premium and accrued interest from the last interest date to date of conversion must be recorded.

In recording the conversion transaction, an accounting issue arises as to whether *(a)* market value of the bonds or the stock, whichever is the more clearly determinable, or *(b)* book value of the bonds should prevail. To illustrate, refer to AB Corporation, Alternative 1 above. Assume an AB Corporation bondholder tenders a $1,000 bond for conversion (to ten shares of common stock, par $75) when the bond accounts reflected the following:

Bonds payable, 5% (convertible)	$100,000
Bond premium (unamortized)	3,000

Assume further that at date of conversion, AB common stock was selling at $95 per share. There are two alternatives for recording conversion of the $1,000 bond:

Alternative 1 – Use market value:

Bonds payable, 5% (convertible)	1,000	
Premium on bonds payable	30	
Common stock (ten shares @ $75 par)		750
Contributed capital in excess of par (ten shares @ $20)		200
Gain on redemption of convertible bonds		80

Alternative 2 – Use book value of the bonds:

Bonds payable, 5% (convertible)	1,000	
Bond premium	30	
Common stock (ten shares @ $75)		750
Contributed capital in excess of par		280

Alternative 1, market value, is generally viewed as theoretically preferable on the basis that the exchange completes the transaction cycle for the bonds and starts a new cycle for the stock. Additionally, market value is theoretically preferable because it recognizes changes in market valuations which have been occurring and it subordinates a consideration determined some time in the past when the bonds were issued.

Despite this theoretical argument, *current practice* generally uses Alternative 2 because *(a)* in some situations, the market value of the stock or the bonds is not determinable; *(b)* the transaction is viewed merely as an exchange of two securities that have some characteristics in common; *(c)* there is no "earning process"; and *(d)* transactions in a corporation's own stock should not cause recognition of gains and losses.

The *investor* would record the conversion on an interest date of a $1,000 bond of AB Corporation, acquired as a long-term investment (see page 832) as follows (assuming the same rate of amortization as the issuer):

Investment in common stock (ten shares, AB Corporation)	1,030	
Bond investment		1,000
Premium on bond investment (unamortized)		30

Convertible bonds that are reacquired by exercise of the *call provision,* rather than by conversion, should be accounted for under the provisions of *APB Opinion No. 26,* and reported in accordance with FASB *Statement No. 4,* "Reporting Gains and Losses from Early Extinguishment of Debt," and FASB *Statement No. 6* as discussed and illustrated on page 829.

DEBT WITH DETACHABLE STOCK WARRANTS

Debt securities, usually bonds, sometimes are issued with *stock warrants* attached. A stock warrant gives the holder the option, within a specified time period, to purchase from the issuer a specified number of shares of common stock at a specified price per share. Detachable stock warrants are often "attached" to bonds to enhance the marketability of the bonds. As with convertible bonds, the bonds usually carry a lower interest rate and tend to sell for a higher market price on the market. Detachable warrants can be separated from the bonds and traded on the market; that is, they are *equity* instruments that are *separable* from the debt instrument. Because of this separability, *APB Opinion No. 14* states that: "the portion of the proceeds of debt securities issued with detachable stock purchase warrants which is allocable to the warrants should be accounted for as paid-in capital. The allocation should be based on the relative fair values of the two securities at time of issuance." When no fair market value can be determined, the fair market value of either of the elements must be used. To illustrate, assume AB Corporation issued $100,000, 5%, ten-year, *nonconvertible bonds with detachable stock warrants.* Each $1,000 bond carried ten detachable warrants; each warrant was for one share of common stock, par $10, at a specified option price of $15 per share. The bonds, including the warrants, sold at $105,000; and shortly after issuance, the warrants were quoted on the market for $4 each. No market value can be determined for the bonds above. The bond issuance would be recorded as follows:

Borrower:

Cash	105,000	
Bonds payable, 5% (with detachable stock warrants)...		100,000
Premium on bonds payable		1,000
Detachable stock warrants outstanding (1,000 warrants @ $4)		4,000

Investor:

Bond investment..	100,000	
Premium on bond investment................................	1,000	
Investment—detachable stock warrants (1,000 warrants @ $4)	4,000	
Cash		105,000

Subsequently, tender of the 1,000 detachable stock warrants would be recorded as follows:

Borrower:

Cash (1,000 × $15)	15,000	
Detachable stock warrants outstanding	4,000	
Common stock, 1,000 shares, par $10		10,000
Contributed capital in excess of par........................		9,000

Investor:

Investment in common stock, 1,000 shares	19,000	
Investment—detachable stock warrants		4,000
Cash (1,000 × $15)		15,000

PART C—SERIAL BONDS

CHARACTERISTICS OF SERIAL BONDS

An issue of bonds with provision for repayment of principal in a series of *installments* is called a serial bond issue. Serial bond issue are especially attractive since they avoid the need for a sinking fund. Serial bonds are well adapted for use by school districts and other taxing authorities which borrow money upon agreement that a special tax will be levied to pay off the obligation. As the taxes are collected, the money so raised can best be utilized by paying off a part of the indebtedness. This may be done by having a part of the bond issue mature each year.

DETERMINING SELLING PRICE OF SERIAL BONDS

The selling price of serial bonds may be derived by computing the selling price for each series separately in the same way that a straight bond issue is valued and then totaling the prices of the several series. For example, assume that serial bonds carrying 7% interest payable 3½% semiannually are sold to yield 5% with the following maturity dates: $10,000 at end of 12 months, $20,000 at end of 18 months, and $30,000 at end of 24 months. The selling price of each of the three series, as well as that of the whole issue, may be *(a)* derived from a bond table (similar to Exhibit 19-1) or *(b)* computed as follows (see page 814)[12]

	Bond Price	*Premium*
Series No. 1 (due in 12 months—2 interest periods):		
Principal: $10,000 × .9518144*	$ 9,518.14	
Interest payments: $350 × 1.9274242†	674.60	
	10,192.74	$ 192.74
Series No. 2 (due in 18 months—3 interest periods):		
Principal: $20,000 × .9285994	18,571.99	
Interest payments: $700 × 2.8560236	1,999.21	
	20,571.20	571.20
Series No. 3 (due in 24 months—4 interest periods):		
Principal: $30,000 × .9059506	27,178.52	
Interest payments: $1,050 × 3.7619742	3,950.07	
	31,128.59	1,128.59
Total Price of All Series	$61,892.53	
Total Premium on All Series		$1,892.53

* Table 6-2—$p_{\substack{n=2 \\ i=2\frac{1}{2}\%}}$

† Table 6-4—$P_{\substack{n=2 \\ i=2\frac{1}{2}\%}}$

[12] Although not realistic, a short time span is used to simplify the computations.

EXHIBIT 19–9
Amortization of Premium on Serial Bonds—Straight Line

Serial No. (a)	Months Outstanding (b)	Par Value (c)	Sales Price (d)	Total Premium to Be Amortized (e)	Amortization of Premium—Straight Line: At End of 6 Months (f)	At End of 12 Months (g)	At End of 18 Months (h)	At End of 24 Months (i)
1	12	$10,000	$10,192.74	$ 192.74	$ 96.37	$ 96.37		
2	18	20,000	20,571.20	571.20	190.40	190.40	$190.40	
3	24	30,000	31,128.59	1,128.59	282.15	282.15	282.15	$282.14
Total Amortization per Period				$1,892.53	$568.92	$568.92	$472.55	$282.14

AMORTIZATION OF PREMIUM AND DISCOUNT ON SERIAL BONDS

Amortization of premium or discount on serial bonds is identical with that on ordinary bonds; however, the computations involve more arithmetic. When the results are *not* materially different from the interest method, the straight-line method may be used; otherwise, the interest method must be used. In both methods, the amount of periodic amortization must be related to the amount of bonds *outstanding* during the period. Therefore the amount of periodic amortization of premium or discount will decrease as each serial is paid off at its maturity date.

Straight-line amortization of the $1,892.53 premium from the above example is computed for each period in Exhibit 19–9. Observe that the premium on each serial is simply apportioned to the number of periods it is outstanding.[13]

The entries for the foregoing example are given below, with the added assumption that $5,000 par of the Serial No. 3 bonds, which were to mature at the end of 24 months, were purchased for $5,100 and retired at the end of 12 months.

1. To record sale of the bonds:

Cash	61,892.53	
Premium on bonds payable		1,892.53
Bonds payable		60,000.00

2. To record payment of interest and straight-line amortization of premium at the end of six months:

Bond interest expense	1,531.08	
Premium on bonds payable	568.92	
Cash		2,100.00

3. To record payment of interest and amortization of premium at end of 12 months:

Bond interest expense	1,531.08	
Premium on bonds payable	568.92	
Cash		2,100.00

[13] Occasionally problems are given that do not provide a basis for determining the amount of premium or discount applicable to each series. In this situation, an approximation, known as the dollar-periods allocation, is used. It is appropriate only for the straight-line method. To illustrate, the $1,892.53 total premium could be allocated as follows:

Serial	*Par*	*Periods Outstanding (semiannual)*	*Dollar Periods*	*Allocation Fraction*	*Allocation to Serials*
1	$10,000	2	$ 20,000	20/200	× $1,892.53 = $ 189.25
2	20,000	3	60,000	60/200	× $1,892.53 = 567.76
3	30,000	4	120,000	120/200	× $1,892.53 = 1,135.52
			$200,000		$1,892.53

The amounts in the last column are then allocated to each period on a straight-line basis as illustrated in Exhibit 19–9.

4. To record payment of Serial No. 1 bonds at the end of 12 months:

Bonds payable (Serial No. 1)	10,000.00	
Cash		10,000.00

5. To record retirement of $5,000 of Serial No. 3 bonds at end of 12 months for $5,100 cash:

Bonds payable	5,000.00	
Bond premium	94.05*	
Loss on bonds retired	5.95	
Cash		5,100.00

*($5,000/$30,000) × ($282.15 + $282.14) = $94.05.

6. To pay interest, amortize premium, and pay off Serial No. 2 bonds at end of 18 months:

Bond interest	1,149.47	
Bond premium [$190.40 + (5/6 × $282.15)]	425.53	
Cash		1,575.00
Bonds payable	20,000.00	
Cash		20,000.00

7. To pay interest, amortize premium, and pay off Serial No. 3 bonds at end of 24 months:

Bond interest	639.88	
Bond premium (5/6 × $282.14)	235.12	
Cash		875.00
Bonds payable	25,000.00	
Cash		25,000.00

Interest method amortization, used when the amounts are material, requires that the yield rate of interest and the selling price must be known. When serial bonds are involved, an amortization table should be prepared in the same manner as the amortization table for ordinary (nonserial) bonds, except that the maturity values of each installment must be deducted from the "carrying value" figures when the installments are paid. An amortization table showing present value amortization of the premium and payment of the three serial installments on the serial bond issue illustrated in the preceding section is given in Exhibit 19–10. In that example, it will be recalled that the sales price was $61,892.53 and the yield rate was 2½% semiannually. In Exhibit 19–10, observe that the computations are identical to those previously illustrated for nonserial bonds (Exhibit 19–3) except for the payments on principal as each serial matures.

When the interest method is used and some portion of a serial is retired before maturity, the carrying value at the date of early extinguishment must be reduced by the present value of the portion retired. To illustrate, assume $5,000 par of Serial No. 3 bonds are purchased for retirement at the end of 12 months (i.e., two interest periods before maturity date); the reduction in carrying value would be:

Principal: \$5,000 × .951814 (i.e., $p_{\substack{n=2\\i=.025}}$ – Table 6–2) = \$4,759.07

Interest payments: \$175 × 1.927424 (i.e., $P_{\substack{n=2\\i=.025}}$ – Table 6–4) = 337.30

Present value retired (including premium retired, \$96.37) \$5,096.37

The retirement, using the present value computed above, is reflected in Exhibit 19–11, which is a continuation of Exhibit 19–10 starting with line 4. Observe that the first line of Exhibit 19–11 reflects the entry for early extinguishment. The loss, if material in amount, would be reported as an extraordinary item in conformance with FASB *Statement No. 4* (see page 829).

The straight-line method appears to be used much less than in prior years in view of the APB and FASB pronouncements and the ease with which the interest method calculations can be made on the computer (pocket or otherwise).

EXHIBIT 19–10
Serial Bond Entries Tabulated—Interest Method Amortization

Date	*Cash Cr.*	*Bond Interest Expense Dr.*	*Bond Premium Dr.*	*Bonds Payable Dr.*	*Carrying Value*
At issue	—	—	—	—	61,892.53
End 6 months	2,100.00	1,547.31*	552.69	—	61,339.84
End 12 months	2,100.00	1,533.50	566.50	—	60,773.34
End 12 months	10,000.00	—	—	10,000.00	50,773.34
End 18 months	1,750.00	1,269.33	480.67	—	50,292.67
End 18 months	20,000.00	—	—	20,000.00	30,292.67
End 24 months	1,050.00	757.33	292.67	—	30,000.00
End 24 months	30,000.00	—	—	30,000.00	—
	67,000.00	5,107.47	1,892.53	60,000.00	

* \$61,892.53 × .025 = \$1,547.31.

EXHIBIT 19–11
Serial Bond Entries Tabulated—Interest Method Amortization

Date	*Cash Cr.*	*Bond Interest Expense Dr.*	*Bond Premium Dr.*	*Bonds Payable Dr.*	*Loss on Retirement Dr.*	*Carrying Value*
Balance end 12 months	—	—	—	—	—	50,773.34*
End 12 months......	5,100.00	—	96.37	5,000.00	3.63	45,676.97
End 18 months......	1,575.00	1,141.92	433.08	—	—	45,243.89
End 18 months......	20,000.00	—	—	20,000.00	—	25,243.89
End 24 months......	875.00	631.11	243.89	—	—	25,000.00
End 24 months......	25,000.00	—	—	25,000.00	—	—

* From Exhibit 19–10, line 4.

QUESTIONS

1. What are the primary characteristics of a bond? What distinguishes it from capital stock?
2. Distinguish between each of the following classes of bonds: *(a)* industrial versus governmental, *(b)* secured versus unsecured, *(c)* ordinary versus income, *(d)* ordinary versus serial, *(e)* callable versus convertible, and *(f)* registered versus coupon.
3. What are the principal advantages, and disadvantages, of bonds versus common stock for *(a)* the borrower, and *(b)* the investor?
4. Explain the nominal and effective (or yield) rates of interest on a bond. What causes them to be different on a particular bond?
5. Distinguish between the face amount and the price of a bond. When are they the same? When different? Explain.
6. Explain the significance of bond discount and bond premium to *(a)* the borrower, and *(b)* the investor.
7. Assume a $1,000, 6%, payable semiannually, ten-year bond is sold at an effective rate of 8%. Explain two approaches for determining the sales price.
8. Conceptually, in terms of cash flows and interest rates, what is the current price of a bond?
9. What accounting principle governs in recording a bond sale/purchase transaction for *(a)* the borrower, and *(b)* the investor? Briefly, explain the application for each party.
10. Explain why, and how, bond discount and bond premium affects *(a)* the balance sheet of the borrower and the investor, and *(b)* the income statement of each.
11. Conceptually, what is the basic difference between the straight-line and interest methods of amortizing bond discount and premium?
12. Under generally accepted accounting principles, when is it appropriate to use *(a)* straight-line, and *(b)* interest method amortization for bond discount or premium?
13. When the end of the accounting period of the borrower (or the investor) is not on the bond interest date, adjusting entries must be made for *(a)* accrued interest, and *(b)* discount or premium amortization. Explain in general terms, the amount for each.
14. When bonds are sold (or purchased) between interest dates, accrued interest must be recognized. Explain why.
15. Bond discount or premium can be amortized either *(a)* at each interest date, or *(b)* at year-end. Which would you generally prefer? Why?
16. What is meant by early extinguishment of debt? How should any resultant gain or loss be reported?
17. What is meant by refunding? When would it generally be advantageous to the issuer?

18. What is a convertible bond? What are the primary reasons for their use?
19. Why is the accounting different for convertible bonds with detachable stock warrants and those without detachable stock warrants?

EXERCISES

PART A: EXERCISES 1–5

Exercise 19–1

BA Corporation has just issued $500,000, 8% (payable 4% semiannually) ten-year bonds payable. The bonds were dated January 1, 19A; interest dates are June 30 and December 31.

Assume four different cases with respect to the sale of the bonds:

Case A – Sold on January 1, 19A, at par.
Case B – Sold on January 1, 19A, at 102.
Case C – Sold on January 1, 19A, at 98.
Case D – Sold on March 1, 19A, at par.

Required:

1. For each case, what amount of interest (cash) will be paid on the first interest date, June 30, 19A?
2. In what cases is the nominal rate of interest not 4% each semiannual period?
3. In what cases will the effective rate of interest be *(a)* the same, *(b)* higher, or *(c)* lower than the nominal rate?
4. After sale of the bonds, in what cases will the carrying or book value of the bonds (as reported on the balance sheet) be *(a)* the same, *(b)* higher, or *(c)* lower than the maturity or face amount?
5. After the sale of the bonds, in Cases A, B, and C, which case will report bond interest expense (as reported on the income statement) *(a)* the same, *(b)* higher, or *(c)* lower than the amount of interest paid (in cash)?

Exercise 19–2

A $10,000 bond, 8% (payable 4% semiannually), ten-year (remaining period outstanding), was sold by A to B, on an interest date, at an effective rate of 10%. The bond price was computed as follows: $3,769 + $4,985 = $8,754.

Required:

Explain in detail, using values for "*i*" and "*n*" how each of the two dollar amounts was computed. Explain why the computation correctly derives the bond price.

Exercise 19–3

Determine the bond price for each of the following situations:

a. A ten-year $1,000 bond; annual interest at 7% (payable 3½% semiannually) purchased to yield 6% effective interest.
b. An eight-year $1,000 bond; annual interest at 6% (payable annually) purchased to yield 7% effective interest.

c. A 12-year $1,000 bond; annual interest at 8% (payable 4% semiannually) purchased to yield 7% effective interest. Present value amounts for 24 periods at 3½% interest per semiannual period: PV of 1, .43795; PV of annuity of 1, 16.058367.

Exercise 19–4

B Corporation sold to C Corporation a $20,000, 8% (payable 4% semiannually on June 30 and December 31) ten-year bond dated and sold on January 1, 19A. Assumptions: Case A – sold at par; Case B – sold at 103; and Case C – sold at 97.

Required:

In parallel columns for the issuer and the investor (as a long-term investment) for each case, give the appropriate journal entries on (1) January 1, 19A, and (2) June 30, 19A. Assume the amortization amount is not material, therefore, use straight line.

Exercise 19–5

Foster Corporation sold to Gray Corporation a $10,000, 8% (payable 4% semiannually on June 30 and December 31) ten-year bond, dated and sold on January 1, 19A. The bond was sold at a 6% effective rate (3% semiannually).

Required:

1. Compute the price of the bond.
2. In parallel columns for the issuer and the investor (as a long-term investment), give the appropriate journal entries on *(a)* January 1, 19A, and *(b)* June 30, 19A. Assume the amortization amount is material, therefore, use the interest method.

PART B: EXERCISES 6–15

Exercise 19–6

On September 1, 19A Royal Company sold Suber Company $30,000, five-year, 9% (payable 4½% semiannually) bonds for $32,320 plus accrued interest. The bonds were dated July 1, 19A, and interest is payable each June 30 and December 31. The accounting period for each company ends on December 31.

Required:

In parallel columns, give entries on the books of the borrower and investor (as a long-term investment) for the following dates: September 1, 19A, December 31, 19A, January 1, 19B, and June 30, 19B. Assume the amortization amounts are not material; and use straight-line amortization.

Exercise 19–7

XY Corporation sold $150,000, three-year, 8% (payable 4% semiannually) bonds payable for $156,400 plus accrued interest. Interest is payable each February 28 and August 31. The bonds were dated March 1, 19A, and were sold on July 1, 19A. The accounting period ends on December 31.

Required:

1. How much accrued interest should be recognized at date of sale?
2. How long is the amortization period?
3. Give entries for XY Corporation through February, 19B. Use straight-line method of amortization.
4. Would the above accounts also be recorded by the investor? Explain.

Exercise 19–8

Boston Corporation sold Charles Corporation (as a long-term investment) $50,000, four-year, 8% bonds on September 1, 1976. Interest is payable (4% semi-annually) on August 31 and February 28. The bonds mature on August 31, 1980, and were sold to yield 7% effective interest. The accounting period for both companies ends on December 31. Present value amounts for 8 periods at 3½% per semiannual period: PV of 1, .75941; PV of annuity of 1, 6.87396.

Required:

1. Compute the price of the bond (show computations).
2. In parallel columns, give all entries required through February 1977 in the accounts of the borrower and the investor. Assume the amortization amounts are not material; therefore use straight-line amortization.

Exercise 19–9

Assume the same fact situation and requirements in Exercise 19–8, except that the amortization amounts are material. Therefore, use the interest method of amortization.

Exercise 19–10

Goodson Company sold Hobson Company $30,000, three-year, 8% bonds dated June 1, 19A. Interest is payable 4% semiannually on May 31 and November 30. The bonds were sold on September 1, 19A, for $29,277 plus accrued interest. The accounting period ends on December 31 for both companies. The effective interest rate was 9%.

Required:

In parallel columns, give the entries for the borrower and the investor (as a long-term investment) for the following dates: September 1, 19A, November 30, 19A, January 1, 19B, and May 31, 19B. Use straight-line amortization.

Exercise 19–11

Assume the same facts and requirements as in Exercise 19–10 except that the amortization amounts are material; therefore, the interest method must be used. Refer to Exhibit 19–1 for appropriate value.

Exercise 19–12

XY Corporation, on January 1, 1971, issued $400,000, 6%, ten-year bonds payable at 103. The bonds are callable at the option of the issuer at 104. Since the amortization amounts are not material, the company uses the straight-line method of amortization.

On December 31, 1976, the bonds were selling at 92 because of the rise in interest rates. Since XY had available cash, they purchased $100,000 of the bonds in the open market at 92.

Required:

1. Give the entry by XY Corporation to record the issuance of the bonds on January 1, 1971.
2. Give the entry by XY Corporation to record the reacquisition on December 31, 1976.
3. Explain how any loss or gain on the reacquisition should be reported in the financial statements for 1976 and thereafter.

Exercise 19–13

Capps Corporation issued $200,000, 4½%, ten-year bonds on January 1, 1972. The issuer could call them at any time after 1975 at 104. The bonds were originally sold at 98. The amortization amounts are not material; therefore, straight-line amortization is used.

Due to a significant increase in interest rates, the bonds were being sold during 1976 at 90. In view of this situation, Capps decided to issue a new series of bonds (a refunding issue) in the amount of $150,000 (8½%, ten-year) on December 31, 1976. They have cash on hand sufficient for the remaining cost of retirement of the old bonds.

Required:

1. Give the entry to record the sale and issuance on January 1, 1972.
2. Assume the refunding issue is sold at par; give the required entry for Capps.
3. Assume the old bonds are purchased in the open market at 90 on December 31, 1976; give the required entry for Capps.
4. Explain how any loss or gain on retirement of the old bonds should be reported in the financial statements for 1976 and thereafter. What *APB Opinion* is controlling?

Exercise 19–14

Walters Corporation issued $40,000, 5%, ten-year convertible bonds (without detachable stock warrants). Each $1,000 bond was *(a)* callable at 103, and *(b)* convertible to ten shares of common stock (par $50) of Walters Corporation three years after issuance. At date of issuance of the bonds, the common stock was selling at $60 per share. The bonds were sold at 105 to Young Corporation as a long-term investment.

Required:

1. Give entry for the borrower and investor at the date of issuance.
2. Give entries for the borrower and investor assuming the call privilege is subsequently exercised by Walters Corporation on an interest date. Assume 10% of any premium or discount has been amortized.
3. Give entries for the borrower and investor assuming instead that the conversion privilege is subsequently exercised by Young Corporation. Assume 10% of any premium or discount has been amortized and that at date of conversion, the common stock was selling at $125 per share.

Exercise 19–15

Yates Corporation issued $150,000, 6%, ten-year bonds (nonconvertible) with detachable stock warrants. Each $1,000 bond carried 20 detachable warrants, each of which was for one share of Yates common stock, par $20, with a specified option price of $60. The bonds sold at 102 and at date of issuance, the common stock was selling at $40 per share and the warrants for $4.

The entire issue was acquired by Zinn Company as a long-term investment.

Required:

1. Give entries for the borrower and the investor at date of acquisition of the bonds.
2. Give entry for the investor assuming subsequent sale of all of the warrants to another investor at $5.50 each.
3. Give entries for the borrower and investor assuming subsequent tender of all of the warrants by the investor for exercise at the specified option price. At this date the stock was selling at $75 per share.

PART C: EXERCISES 16–17

Exercise 19–16

A serial bond issue was dated and sold on January 1, 1976, with the following maturities: December 31, 1976, $10,000; December 31, 1977, $15,000; and December 31, 1978, $25,000. The bonds carried a nominal interest rate of 7%, payable 3½% each June 30 and December 31. They were sold to yield 8% (4% semiannually). Compute the price on the bond issue on January 1, 1976; show computations.

Exercise 19–17

Stone Corporation sold a small bond issue that carried a 8% annual interest rate, payable annually, with a total maturity value of $60,000. The bonds were sold for $54,000 on the date of the indenture. The bonds were to be paid as follows:

Serial	*At End of Year*	*Maturity Value*
A	2	$10,000
B	3	20,000
C	4	30,000

Required:

1. Set up an amortization table using straight-line amortization to show the amortization by serial, by year. Assume the discount for each serial is as follows: A, $600; B, $1,800; and C, $3,600 (allocation on dollar-periods method).
2. Give entry to pay off one third of Serial C, at par, assuming it is paid one year before maturity, that is, at the end of the third year.

PROBLEMS

PART A: PROBLEMS 1–4

Problem 19–1

X Corporation needs $500,000 cash to implement current expansion plans. Two alternatives are under consideration: Alternative A, issue ten-year, 8% (payable 4% semiannually) bonds; and Alternative B, issue 20,000 shares of common stock (par $10) expected to sell at $25 per share. Average common stock data for the past three years: 30,000 shares outstanding; earnings per share, $2.60; dividends per share, $1.00.

Required:

Based on the data given, which alternative would you recommend? Explain the basis for your recommendation. Assume an income tax rate of 48% and that the bonds would probably sell at 98.

Problem 19–2

Able Corporation sold Baker Corporation (as a long-term investment) a $20,000, 7%, ten-year bond. The bond was dated January 1, 19A, and interest is payable annually each December 31. Assume the accounting periods end December 31. Assume four different cases in respect to the sale of the bond:

Case A – sold on January 1, 19A, at 7% yield.
Case B – sold on January 1, 19A, at 6% yield.
Case C – sold on January 1, 19A, at 8% yield.
Case D – sold on March 31, 19A, at 6% yield.

Required:

1. For each case, compute the amount of interest that will be paid (i.e., cash) on the first interest date, December 31, 19A.
2. Identify what cases sold at *(a)* par, *(b)* a discount, and *(c)* a premium.
3. For each case, indicate *(a)* the nominal interest rate, and *(b)* the effective rate of interest.
4. Excluding Case D, identify those cases where the amount of cash paid and received for the bond was *(a)* the same as par, *(b)* greater than par, and *(c)* less than par.
5. Subsequent to the transaction, in what cases will the respective balance sheets report the bonds at *(a)* par, *(b)* more than par, and *(c)* less than par?
6. Subsequent to the transaction, in Cases A, B, and C, which will report interest expense and interest revenue (on the respective income statements) at more or less than the amount of interest paid in cash?
7. Identify those cases where the book or carrying value of the bond liability (or bond investment) will be *(a)* the same, *(b)* higher, or *(c)* lower than the maturity amount.
8. Can straight-line amortization be used in each case? Explain.
9. Can the interest method of amortization be used in each case? Explain.
10. What is the effect of periodic amortization of bond premium and discount on *(a)* interest expense (as reported on the income statement), and *(b)* bond carrying value (as reported on the balance sheet).

Problem 19–3

Franklin Corporation sold Golden Corporation $200,000, 8% (payable 4% semiannually on June 30 and December 31), three-year bonds. The bonds were dated and sold on January 1, 19A, at an effective rate of 9%. The accounting period for each company ends on December 31. Present value amounts for six periods at 4½% per semiannual period: PV of 1, .76789; PV of annuity of 1, 5.15787.

Required:

1. Compute the price of the bonds.
2. Prepare an amortization table for the life of the bonds assuming the amounts involved are material.
3. Prepare in parallel columns, entries for the borrower and the investor (as a long-term investment) through June 30, 19B.
4. Show how the issuer and the investor would report the bonds on their respective balance sheets at December 31, 19A.
5. What would be reported on the income statement for each party for the year ended December 31, 19A?

Problem 19–4

Park Corporation sold to King Corporation, $40,000, 7% (payable 3½% semiannually on June 30 and December 31) four-year bonds dated January 1, 19A. The bonds were sold on January 1, 19A, at an effective rate of 6%.

Required:

1. Compute the price of the bonds.
2. Prepare an amortization table over the life of the bonds assuming material amounts.
3. In parallel columns for the issuer and investor (as a long-term investment) give all journal entries from issuance to retirement. Assume the accounting period for each company ends on December 31.
4. Show how the issuer and the investor should report the bonds on their respective balance sheets on December 31, 19A.
5. What would be reported on the income statement for each party for the year ended December 31, 19A?

PART B: PROBLEMS 5–17

Problem 19–5

Jackson Company sold King Company $50,000 bonds on June 1, 1976, for $51,320 plus accrued interest. The bond indenture provided the following information:

Maturity amount	$50,000
Date of bonds	April 1, 1976
Maturity date	March 31, 1978 (2 years)
Nominal interest rate	6½%, payable 3¼% semiannually
Interest payments	$1,625 each March 31 and September 30

Required:

1. In parallel columns, give entries for the borrower and investor (as a long-term investment) from date of sale to maturity. Assume the amortization amounts

are not material; therefore, use straight-line amortization. Also assume the accounting period ends December 31.
2. Show how the bonds would be reported on the balance sheet of the two companies at December 31, 1976.
3. What would be reported on the income statement for each party for the year ended December 31, 1976?

Problem 19–6

Mason Corporation has completed all arrangements for a bond issue with the following provisions:

Maturity amount	\$300,000 (\$1,000 denominations)
Date of bonds	June 1, 1976
Maturity date	May 31, 1979 (3 years)
Nominal interest rate	7½%, payable 3¾% semiannually
Interest payments (cash)	\$11,250 each May 31 and November 30

On September 1, 1976, Nash Corporation purchased \$10,000 of the bonds from Mason for \$9,604 plus accrued interest (as a long-term investment).

Required:

1. In parallel columns, give entries for the borrower and investor through May 31, 1977. Assume the amortization amounts are not material; therefore, use straight-line amortization. The accounting period for each corporation ends on December 31.
2. Show how these bonds would be reported on the balance sheets of the two corporations at December 31, 1976.
3. What would be reported on the income statement for each party for the year ended December 31, 1976?

Problem 19–7

R Corporation sold to S Corporation bonds payable having a maturity value of \$120,000. The bonds were due in ten years from March 1, 1976, and carried a nominal interest rate of 7% payable 3½% each February 28 and August 31. S Corporation purchased the bonds on March 1, 1976, at an effective rate of 6½%. Present value amounts for 20 periods at 3¼% interest per semiannual period: PV of 1, .527471; PV of annuity of 1, 14.539346.

Required:

1. Compute the price of the bond issue.
2. Assuming straight-line amortization, give in parallel columns, entries for the borrower and the investor through March 1, 1977. Assume both parties close their books on December 31.
3. Show how the bonds should be reported on the balance sheets of the borrower and the investor at December 31, 1976.
4. What should be reported on the income statements for the year ended December 31, 1976, for the borrower and the investor?

Problem 19–8

Owens Corporation has completed all arrangements for a bond issue with the following provisions:

Maturity amount	\$80,000
Date of bonds	May 1, 1976
Maturity date	April 30, 1979 (3 years)
Nominal interest rate	$7\frac{1}{2}$%, payable $3\frac{3}{4}$% semiannually
Interest payments (cash)	\$3,000 each April 30 and October 31
Date sold	May 1, 1976
Effective interest rate	8% (semiannual basis)

Required:

1. Compute the price of the bonds.
2. Prepare an amortization schedule assuming the straight-line method.
3. In parallel columns, give entries for the borrower and the investor (as a long-term investment) through May 1, 1977. Assume the accounting period ends December 31.
4. Show how the bonds should be reported on the balance sheets of the borrower and investor at December 31, 1976.
5. What should be shown on the income statements for the borrower and the investor for the year ended December 31, 1976?

Problem 19–9

Use the data given in Problem 19–8 and complete the following requirements:

1. Compute the price of the bonds.
2. Prepare an amortization table assuming the interest method.
3. Prepare a tabulation of entries for the borrower similar to Exhibit 19–7 for the life of the bonds (amortization on interest dates).
4. Show how the bonds and the interest should be reported on the balance sheet and income statement for each party for the statements prepared at the end of 1976?

Problem 19–10

B Corporation issued bonds, face amount \$100,000, three-year, 8% (payable 4% semiannually on June 30 and December 31). The bonds were dated January 1, 1976, and were sold on November 1, 1976, to yield 9% interest. The bonds mature on December 31, 1978. The bonds were purchased as a long-term investment by I Corporation. Refer to Exhibit 19–1 for appropriate table values.

Required:

1. Construct a time scale that depicts the important dates for this bond issue.
2. Determine (*a*) the price of the bond issue on the date of sale, and (*b*) the total cash paid by I Corporation.
3. In parallel columns, give the entries at November 1, 1976, for the borrower and the investor.
4. Prepare a bond amortization table from date of sale to maturity date using the interest method.
5. In parallel columns, give the entries for interest and amortization at the interest date, December 31, 1976.
6. Determine and verify the balance in the interest accounts of the two parties to the transaction immediately after Requirement 5.
7. Assume the accounting period for each party ends on February 28. In parallel columns, give the adjusting entries for each party on February 28, 1977. Assume the interest method of amortization.

8. Compute the amount of amortization per month for each party assuming straight-line amortization is appropriate (i.e., amounts are not material).

Problem 19–11

Bliss Corporation issued $200,000, 8% (payable each February 28 and August 31), four-year bonds. The bonds were dated March 1, 1976, and mature on February 28, 1980. They were sold on August 1, 1976, to yield 8½% interest. The bonds were purchased by Ivy Corporation as a long-term investment. The accounting period for both companies ends on December 31. Refer to Exhibit 19–1 for appropriate table values.

Required:

1. Diagram a time scale depicting the important dates for this bond issue.
2. Determine *(a)* the price of the bond issue on the date of sale, and *(b)* the total cash paid by Ivy Corporation.
3. Prepare an amortization table from date of sale to the maturity date using the interest method of amortization.
4. In parallel columns, give entries for the borrower and the investor from date of sale through February 28, 1977. Base amortization on Requirement 3.
5. Compute the amount of amortization per month for each party assuming the straight-line method is appropriate (i.e., amounts are not material).

Problem 19–12

Anderson Corporation, on July 1, 1971, issued $500,000, 4¾%, ten-year bonds. Interest is paid each June 30 and December 31. The bonds are callable at the option of the issuer at 102. The bonds were issued at 97 and issue costs were $1,400. The amortization amounts are not material; therefore, straight-line amortization is used for both the discount and issue costs.

Due to the increase in interest costs, these bonds were selling in the market during 1976 at 90. Since the company had available cash, $100,000 of the bonds were purchased in the market at 90 on December 31, 1976. The accounting period ends December 31.

Required:

1. Give the entry by Anderson Corporation to record the issuance of the old bonds on July 1, 1971.
2. Give the entry to record the reacquisition on December 31, 1976.
3. Explain how any gain or loss on the acquisition should be reported on the financial statements for 1976 and thereafter. What *APB Opinion* and FASB *Statements* are controlling?

Problem 19–13

Assume the same fact situation as given in Problem 19–12 for Anderson Corporation except that Anderson Corporation is short of cash, needing funds, and issues a new series of bonds (a refunding) to obtain the needed cash. The new issue is $500,000, 8%, six-year bonds. They were sold (and dated) October 1, 1976, at par, and issue costs were $2,880 (assume no accrued interest).

Required:

1. Give the entry for Anderson Corporation to record the issuance of the old bonds on July 1, 1971.

2. Give the entry by Anderson Corporation to record the issuance of the new refunding bonds during October 1976.
3. Give the entry by Anderson Corporation to record the reacquisition of all of the old bonds at 90 on December 31, 1976.
4. Explain how any gain or loss on the acquisition should be reported on the financial statements for 1976 and thereafter. What *APB Opinion* and FASB *Statements* are controlling?

Problem 19–14

On January 1, 1974, Brown Corporation issued $50,000, 5%, five-year convertible/callable bonds with the provisions that *(a)* Brown could recall the bonds at any time after 1975 at 102 and *(b)* the holder of each $1,000 bond can tender it for conversion to 15 shares of Brown common stock, par $50, at any time after 1975. The Company estimated that nonconvertible bonds would have to carry an interest rate of 7½% to sell at par. The bonds were sold for $54,000. On July 1, 1976, the stock was selling at $110 per share. Assume straight-line amortization.

Required:

1. Assume the bonds do not have detachable stock warrants. Give the entries for Brown at–
   a. Date of issuance–January 1, 1974.
   b. Date of conversion–July 1, 1976, assuming all bonds were turned in for conversion.
2. Assume Cooper Corporation acquired all of the bonds. Give entries by Cooper at *(a)* date of acquisition, and *(b)* date of conversion.
3. Explain the basis for the value recognized at date of conversion.

Problem 19–15

Assume the same situation given in Problem 19–14 except that instead of being convertible, each $1,000 bond had 15 detachable stock warrants. Each warrant was for one share of common stock at a specified price of $60 per share. Immediately after issuance of the bonds on January 1, 1974, the warrants sold on the market at $2.

Required:

1. Give entry by Brown Corporation at date of issuance, January 1, 1974.
2. Give entries for Cooper Corporation at date of acquisition (as a long-term investment) on January 1, 1974.
3. Explain the basis for the values recognized in Requirements 1 and 2.
4. Assume 100 of the detachable stock warrants are tendered on July 1, 1976. At that date the stock was selling at $70 per share. Give entry for *(a)* Brown Corporation, and *(b)* Cooper Corporation.

Problem 19–16

Myers Corporation issued $500,000, 6%, nonconvertible bonds with detachable stock warrants. Each $1,000 bond carried 20 detachable stock warrants, each of which called for one share of Myers common stock, par $50, at a specified option price of $60 per share. The bonds sold at 106, and shortly thereafter the warrants were quoted at $1 each on the market.

Nabors Company purchased the entire issue as a long-term investment.

Required:

1. Give the following entries for Myers Corporation (the borrower):
   a. To record the issuance of the bonds.
   b. To record the subsequent exercise by investor of the 10,000 stock warrants.
2. Give the following entries for Nabors Company (the investor):
   a. Acquisition of the bonds (including the warrants).
   b. Subsequent sale to another investor of one half of the stock warrants at $1.50 each.
   c. Subsequent exercise of the remaining one half of the stock warrants (by tendering them to Myers Corporation.)

Problem 19–17

Zakin Company recently issued $1 million face value, 5%, 30-year subordinated convertible debentures (i.e., bonds) at 97. The debentures are also callable at 103 upon demand by the issuer at any date upon 30 days' notice ten years after the issue. The debentures are convertible into $10 par value common stock of the company at the conversion price of $12.50 per share for each $500 or multiple thereof of the principal amount of the debentures.

Required:

1. Explain how the conversion feature of convertible debt has a value to the *(a)* issuer, and *(b)* purchaser.
2. Management of Zakin Company has suggested that in recording the issuance of the debentures a portion of the proceeds should be assigned to the conversion feature.
   a. What are the arguments for according separate accounting recognition to the conversion feature of the debentures?
   b. What are the arguments supporting accounting for the convertible debentures as a single element?
3. Assume that no value is assigned to the conversion feature upon issue of the debentures. Assume further that five years after issue, debentures with a face value of $100,000 and book value of $97,500 are tendered for conversion on an interest payment date when the market price of the debentures is 104 and the common stock is selling at $14 per share and that the company records the conversion as follows:

Bonds payable	100,000	
Bond discount		2,500
Common stock		80,000
Premium on common stock		17,500

Discuss the propriety of the above accounting treatment.

(AICPA adapted)

PART C: PROBLEMS 18–19

Problem 19–18

A serial issue of $700,000 of bonds dated April 1, 1976, was sold on that date for $707,600. The interest rate is 8%, payable 4% semiannually on March 31 and September 30. Scheduled maturities are as follows:

Serial	Date Due	Amount
A..............	March 31, 1977	$100,000
B..............	March 31, 1978	200,000
C..............	March 31, 1979	200,000
D..............	March 31, 1980	200,000

Required:

1. Prepare an amortization table; use straight-line and dollars-period allocation.
2. Give all entries relating to the bonds including closing entries through March 31, 1977. The company adjusts and closes its books each December 31. Use straight-line amortization.

Problem 19–19

On January 1, 1976, ABC Corporation sold serial bonds (dated January 1, 1976) due as follows: Series A, $10,000, December 31, 1980; Series B, $15,000, December 31, 1981; and Series C, $25,000, December 31, 1982. The bonds carried a 3% coupon (nominal) interest rate per semiannual period (each June 30 and December 31) and were sold to yield 4% interest per semiannual period.

Required:

1. Compute the selling price of the bond issue.
2. Prepare a table of amortization for the life of the bond issue assuming the interest method is used.
3. Give entry to record retirement of one half of Series C at 99½ on June 30, 1982. Assume the accounting period ends December 31.

Chapter 20

Accounting Changes, Error Correction, and Incomplete Records

Whether in public practice or in industrial accounting, situations are frequently encountered where changes in accounting methods and estimates and error corrections must be made. Similarly, situations are encountered, particularly in very small businesses, where the records maintained are incomplete in many respects. In recognition of these two problems, this chapter is divided into two parts: Part A is concerned with accounting changes and error correction. Part B is concerned with the preparation of financial statements from single-entry and other incomplete records.

In view of the nature of the two problems considered in this chapter there are no new accounting principles and concepts introduced; rather, the chapter deals exclusively with guidelines and techniques designed for orderly resolution of the two specific types of problems. The techniques presented herein have been developed and tested over many years and have been found to be efficient for problem-solving purposes whether for the student, the independent CPA, or the accountant in government or private industry.

PART A—ACCOUNTING CHANGES AND ERROR CORRECTION

Current practices and procedures for accommodating accounting changes and errors evolved gradually, and no authoritative body such as the APB dealt with them comprehensively prior to *APB Opinion No. 20*, "Accounting Changes" (August 1971). As a consequence there existed a diverse range of accounting approaches for recording and reporting their effects. These approaches were conceptually inconsistent and lacking in forthright disclosures in some cases. Prior to *Opinion No. 20* it was not unusual for changes in accounting, depending on how they were recorded and reported, to result in a particular amount of revenue or expense over time *(a)* "passing through" the income statement twice (or even three times in a few cases), or *(b)* completely missing the income statement. Accounting changes were widely used for "doctoring" net income, or loss. *APB Opinion No. 20* significantly narrowed the alternatives available; more consistent application will benefit the statement user. Those familiar with the earlier practices in this area are quite aware of the importance of the new direction provided by the *Opinion*.

TYPES OF ACCOUNTING CHANGES AND ERRORS

Because of the diversity of accounting changes and errors, *Opinion No. 20*, as a basis for specifying the accounting and reporting requirements, provides the following classifications:

A. Accounting Changes
   1. Change in accounting principle. When the enterprise adopts a different generally accepted accounting principle or procedure from the one previously used. An example would be: A change from straight-line depreciation to double-declining-balance depreciation.
   2. Change in accounting estimate. As more current and improved data are obtained in respect to accounting determinations based on estimates, the prior estimate may be changed. An example would be: Based on new information it is decided to depreciate Asset X over 12 years rather than on the 10-year life currently being utilized.
   3. Change in reporting entity. Because of changes in the reporting entity, such as including or excluding financial statements of subsidiaries in consolidated statements, accounting applications may be affected.

B. Error Correction
   4. Correction due to discovery of an error. An error is defined as a misapplication (i.e., incorrect recording) of the facts existing at the time of the exchange transaction; the misapplication may have been unintentional or intentional. An example would be charging expense for the cost of an operational asset when acquired that should have been capitalized and depreciated over its useful life.

METHODS FOR RECORDING AND REPORTING ACCOUNTING CHANGES AND ERROR CORRECTIONS

APB Opinion No. 20 recognizes that there are three fundamental ways in which accounting changes and error corrections can be reflected in the accounts and reported on the financial statements. They are:

1. Retroactively—The cumulative effect of the accounting change or error correction is determined. The "adjustment" for this amount is recorded in the accounts, usually as a prior period adjustment, and is reported in the same manner on the financial statements.

2. Currently—The cumulative effect of the accounting change or error correction is determined. The "adjustment" for this amount is recorded in the accounts as a special item (similar to extraordinary items) and is reported in the same manner on the current financial statements.
3. Prospectively—The cumulative effect of the accounting change or error correction is not determined. No "adjustment" is recognized or reported; rather, the change effect is spread over the current and future periods.

Because of the different characteristics of the three accounting changes and error correction listed above, the *Opinion* relies on each of these fundamental approaches. Basically, the *Opinion* prescribes the following (with certain exceptions and adaptations explained later):

Type of Change	*Basic Method*
1. Change in accounting principle	Currently
2. Change in accounting estimate	Prospectively
3. Change in accounting entity	Retroactively
4. Error correction	Retroactively

These relationships may be diagrammed as follows:

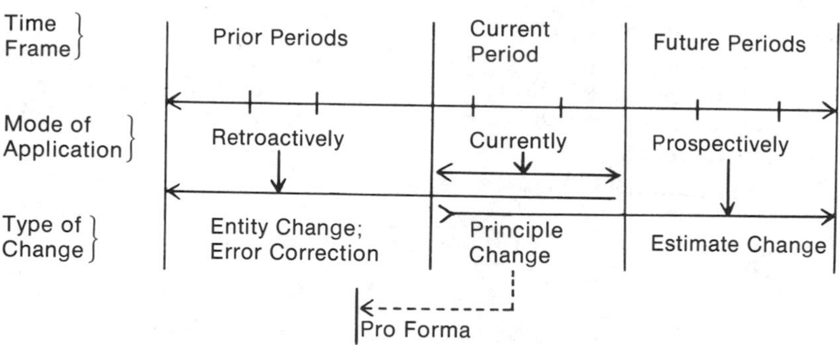

With these fundamentals in mind we can now proceed to a detailed discussion of each of the accounting changes and error correction. In the discussions to follow we will focus on (1) the appropriate entry in the accounts, and (2) appropriate reporting on the *comparative* financial statements affected.

CHANGE IN ACCOUNTING PRINCIPLE

A change in accounting principle occurs when a company adopts a generally accepted accounting principle different from a previously used one that *also* was generally accepted at the time adopted. The *Opinion* states that the term accounting principle includes "not only accounting principles and practices but also the methods of applying them." It excludes the adoption of a principle occasioned by events occurring for the first time or that were previously immaterial in their effect. Examples of a change in accounting principle are:

1. A change from straight line to some other acceptable method of depreciation.
2. A change in inventory cost flow such as *Fifo* to average.
3. A change in accounting for long-term construction contracts from completed contract basis to percentage of completion.

The *Opinion* states that *most* changes in accounting principle should be recognized by including the cumulative effect "in net income of the period of the change," but that a *few* specific changes in accounting principles "should be reported by restating the financial statements of prior periods" (i.e., retroactively). This latter quota is an exception to the basic rule; examples are (1) a change from *Lifo* inventory to another method, (2) a change in the method of accounting for long-term construction contracts, and (3) a change from "full cost" to another method in the extractive industries. These exceptions were deemed advisable to prevent income manipulation; observe that they generally give rise to credits (which would serve to increase net income materially in the year of change).

The cumulative effect is computed to the beginning of the period of change since the financial statements for the period of change must reflect the newly adopted principle. The amount of the cumulative effect should be shown separately between "income before extraordinary items" and "net income." The *Opinion* states that it is "not an extraordinary item but should be shown in a manner similar to an extraordinary item." Per share amounts should be shown for the cumulative amount reported.

The *Opinion* also requires that income before extraordinary items and net income be shown on a *pro forma* basis on the "face of the income statements for all periods presented as if the newly adopted accounting principle had been applied during all periods affected." This requirement is to satisfy the full-disclosure principle.[1]

To illustrate *a change in accounting principle*, assume Company M has been depreciating an asset for two years which cost $200,000, on a straight-line basis over ten years and no residual value. Starting in the third year the decision was made to adopt double-declining-balance depreciation.[2]

The accounting and reporting would be as follows:

---

[1] *Pro forma* is defined in *Webster's Dictionary* as "for the sake of or as a matter of form." Pro forma statements are "as if" statements; the "as if" assumptions should be clearly stated.

[2] This illustration disregards the tax effects; depending upon the circumstances deferred taxes should be taken into account.

a. **To compute the cumulative effect to beginning of year of change:**

Depreciation based on new method—double declining:		
Year 1—$200,000 × 20%	$40,000	
Year 2—($200,000 − $40,000) × 20%	32,000	
Amount that should be reflected in accumulated depreciation		$72,000
Depreciation recorded to date—straight-line method:		
Years 1 and 2 — $200,000 × 1/10 × 2		40,000
Cumulative effect of change (catch-up adjustment, increase in accumulated depreciation balance required)		$32,000

b. **Accounting—To record the catch-up adjustment in Year 3:**

Adjustment due to change in accounting principle (depreciation)	32,000	
Accumulated Depreciation		32,000

c. **Reporting—Comparative income statement presentation at end of Year 3:**

	Year 2	*Year 3*
Depreciation expense	$ 20,000	
($200,000 − $40,000 − $32,000) × 20% = $25,600		$ 25,600
Income before extraordinary items	$100,000	$110,000
Extraordinary item (loss)	(6,000)	10,000
Accounting change effect*		(32,000)
Net Income	$ 94,000	$ 88,000
Earnings per share (100,000 shares outstanding):		
Income before extraordinary items and changes	$1.00	$1.10
Extraordinary items	(.06)	.10
Change in accounting principle	–	(.32)
Net income	$ .94	$ .88
Pro forma net income, assuming retroactive application of accounting change‡	$ 82,000	$120,000
Pro forma EPS assuming retroactive application of accounting chage:†		
Income before extraordinary items‡	$ .88	$ 1.10
Net Income‡	.82	1.20

* Appropriate footnote.

† The pro forma share amounts represent what "would have been" had the new method been used from the beginning. *APB Opinion No. 15* recommends, but does not require, earnings per share amounts for the extraordinary items.

‡Computations:	*Year 2*	*Year 3*
Income before extraordinary items, as reported	$100,000	$110,000
Add back straight-line depreciation	20,000	
Deduct double-declining depreciation	(32,000)	(already deducted)
Income before extraordinary items	88,000	110,000
Extraordinary item	(6,000)	10,000
Net Income	$ 82,000	$120,000

Opinion No. 20 states that a change to another principle can be made only if the enterprise justifies the change "on the basis that it is preferable." The *Opinion* did not specify the criteria for determining when another principle is "preferable."

CHANGE IN ACCOUNTING ESTIMATE

Accounting necessarily requires the use of estimates because future developments and events cannot be perceived with certainty. For example, the periodic depreciation charge is the result of one known (cost) and two estimates (residual value and useful life). Estimates result from judgments which are based on specific assumptions and projections concerning future events. As the anticipated event, or events, approach reality in time, it is generally possible to improve on the accuracy of the estimates. As a consequence, the accountant is frequently faced with the problem of what to do about improved estimates. For example, during the first few years' life of a firm the estimated loss rate due to uncollectible accounts necessarily may have a relatively wide range of error due to the lack of historical experience on collections; as time progresses the rate is refined as a result of additional information. Thus, changes in accounting estimates are a *natural consequence* of the accounting process. A change in an accounting estimate is quite different in cause than is a change in accounting principle or an accounting error. Examples of changes in accounting estimates are:

1. Change in the residual value or estimated useful life of an asset subject to depreciation, amortization, or depletion.
2. Change in the estimated loss rate on receivables.
3. Change in the expected recovery of a deferred charge.
4. Change in the expected realization of a revenue collected in advance.
5. Change in the expected warranty cost on goods sold under guarantee.

When a change in an estimate has been decided upon, the accountant is faced with the dual problem of *(a)* how to reflect the change on the comparative financial statements, and *(b)* how to record the effect of the change of estimate in the accounts. The accountant presumes that a change in an accounting estimate will be made only when there are sound reasons for doing so as opposed to intent to manipulate reported net income.[3]

Generally accepted accounting principles tend to recognize that changes in estimates are occasioned primarily by uncertainties that are influenced by external conditions. As a consequence, changes in accounting estimates generally are accounted for *prospectively*. On this point *APB Opinion No. 20* states:

---

[3] This definition of a change in estimates assumes that the original estimate and the new estimate both represent realistic and good faith determinations based upon the information available at the time the respective estimates were made. Changes in estimates not meeting these criteria must be classified as an "accounting error" as defined and discussed in the next section of this chapter.

> The Board concludes that the effect of a change in accounting estimate should be recognized in (a) the period of change if the change affects that period only, or (b) the period of change and future periods if the change affects both.

Since there is no change or catch-up adjustment to be made, the only additional disclosure required by the *Opinion* is "The effect on income before extraordinary items, net income and related per share amounts of the current period should be disclosed."

In some situations a change in accounting principle and a change in estimate for the same item are made concurrently. When the effects of each can be separated, two changes should be reflected. However, when the two are indistinguishable, the one that is clearly dominant should be used; if neither is clearly dominant, a change in estimate should be reflected.

To illustrate a *change* in *estimate* assume assets that cost $120,000 (no residual value) are being depreciated over a 10-year life; on the basis of new information after 5 years' use, a 15-year life appears to be more realistic. The change in the depreciation estimate, starting in the sixth year, would be recognized as follows:

a. To compute annual depreciation for the current and subsequent years (no catch-up adjustment to be made):

Original cost	$120,000
Accumulated depreciation to date of change in estimate ($120,000 × 5/10)	60,000
Undepreciated balance at beginning of year of change in estimate	$ 60,000

Annual depreciation after change, $60,000 ÷ (15 − 5 years) = $6,000

b. Accounting—no catch-up adjustment.

To record depreciation for Year 6:

Depreciation expense	6,000	
Accumulated depreciation		6,000

c. Reporting—income statement for year of change, Year 6:

Depreciation expense	$6,000

Disclosure by note: Starting in Year 6 the company changed the estimated lives of certain tangible assets from 10 years to 15 years. This change in estimate increased net income by $3,600 (net of income taxes). Per share amounts were increased by $.036.

CHANGE IN REPORTING ENTITY

Changes in reporting entity are to be effected and reported through retroactive restatement; that is, "they should be reported by restating the financial statements of all prior periods presented in order to show financial information for the new reporting entity for all periods." *APB Opinion No. 20* also defines this type of accounting change as follows:

> One type of accounting change results in financial statements which, in effect, are those of a different reporting entity. This type is limited mainly to (a) presenting consolidated or combined statements in place of statements of individual companies, (b) changing specific subsidiaries comprising the group of companies for which consolidated statements are presented and (c) changing the companies included in combined financial statements. A different group of companies comprise the reporting entity after each change.

This type of change is discussed in detail in another book in this series.[4]

CORRECTION OF ERRORS

Accounting errors are of two basic types: (1) those that occur and are discovered in the same accounting period, and (2) those that occur in one accounting period and are discovered in a later accounting period. The accountant frequently must deal with these types of errors. When an accounting error is discovered it should be corrected immediately. The former type of error is not difficult to deal with since the accounts have not been closed and the financial statements have not been issued. This type of error can be readily corrected either *(a)* by reversing the incorrect entry and then entering the correct entry, or *(b)* by making a single correcting entry designed to directly correct the account balances.

APB Opinion No. 20 deals with the second type of error; those discovered in a subsequent period. Obviously, such errors must be corrected prior to issuance of the financial statements to which the CPA certifies. Seldom is an error discovered in statements on which the independent CPA has expressed an opinion. Accounting errors usually are inadvertent and reflect a lack of sophistication; at the same time, the auditor must be alert for intentional errors designed to manipulate income or financial position or to conceal fraud.

An accounting error is specifically defined as the *misapplication* of facts existing at the time the exchange transaction is recorded or when some other related effects are recorded or reported. The following are examples of accounting errors as distinguished from changes in accounting principle or changes in estimates:

a. Use of an inappropriate or unacceptable accounting principle. Thus a change from an unacceptable accounting principle to a generally accepted one would require the correction of an error (not a change in accounting principle).

b. Use of an unrealistic accounting estimate, that is, the misapplication of known information at the date of the decision in respect to the estimate. Thus, the adoption of a clearly unrealistic depreciation rate would require the correction of an error (not a change in accounting estimate).

---

[4] C. H. Griffin, T. H. William, and K. L. Larson, *Advanced Accounting* (Homewood, Ill.: Richard D. Irwin, Inc., 1971.

c. Misstatement of an accounting value, such as for inventory, a deferred charge or credit, liabilities, or owners' equity.
d. Failure to recognize accruals and deferrals.
e. Incorrect classification of an expenditure as between expense and asset.
f. Incorrect or unrealistic allocations of accounting values.
g. Failure to record a completed transaction.

Errors discovered in the current period that were made in a prior period require that all of the cumulative effects be computed and a correcting entry be made on a retroactive basis. The correcting entry should be made so as to correct all account balances affected; the amount of adjustment for correction of the total net incomes of the prior periods should be entered in an account Prior Period Adjustment–Correction of Accounting Error. This account is closed to Retained Earnings and serves to correct the balance of that account.

The prior period adjustment, in accordance with *APB Opinion No. 9* (par. 18), is reported on the statement of retained earnings as a retroactive adjustment of the beginning balance. As to disclosure, *Opinion No. 20* states: "The nature of an error in previously issued financial statements and the effect of its correction on income before extraordinary items, net income, and the related per share amounts should be disclosed in the period in which the error was discovered and corrected. Financial statements of subsequent periods need not repeat the disclosures."

To illustrate the correction of an accounting error, assume that a $6,000 expenditure for an asset, having a six-year estimated life (no residual value), was recorded in January 19A as an expense. Assume it is now 19C, and in the process of preparing the 19C year-end financial statement, the error was discovered. Net income originally reported in 19A was $14,000 and in 19B, $19,000. Accounting and reporting recognition of the error at the end of 19C, assuming straight-line depreciation and a 40% average income tax rate, would be as follows:

a. Accounting–at end of Year 19C:

To correct the accounts (assume no income tax adjustment):

Asset (designated)	6,000	
Accumulated depreciation ($6,000 × 2/6)		2,000
Prior period adjustment–correction of accounting error		4,000

To record depreciation for 19C:

Depreciation expense	1,000	
Accumulated depreciation		1,000

Closing entries at end of 19C:

Income summary	1,000	
Depreciation expense		1,000
Prior period adjustment–correction of accounting error	4,000	
Retained earnings		4,000

b. Reporting – at end of 19C (comparative statements):

	19B	*19C*
Balance Sheet:		
Asset	$ 6,000	$ 6,000
Less: Allowance for depreciation	2,000	3,000
	$ 4,000	$ 3,000
Income Statement:		
Depreciation expense........	$ 1,000	$ 1,000
Net income (Note 1)	18,000	21,000
Statement of Retained Earnings:		
Beginning balance	70,000	93,000
Prior period adjustment – depreciation correction (Note 1)	5,000	
Adjusted balance........	75,000	93,000
Net income	18,000	21,000
Ending Balance	$93,000	$114,000

Note 1. Appropriate explanation.

Observe that because these were comparative statements, the amounts are not the same as indicated in the above entries in two respects, viz: (1) net income for 19B was reduced from $19,000 to $18,000 which is the correct amount that would have been reported had the error not been made, and (2) the prior period adjustment is reflected as $5,000 instead of $4,000 since the beginning balance for 19B (rather than 19C) must be corrected in the comparative statement. Had the error been found during 19B the prior period adjustment would have been, $6,000 – $1,000 = $5,000.

The above illustration assumed that income tax expense each year was correct; however, this may well not be the case. If not, the above entries and reports would have to reflect net of tax effects. To illustrate, assume the error was carried to the income tax return each year and that a tax penalty of $352 is assessed. The correcting entry would be as follows:

Asset (designated)	6,000	
Accumulated depreciation		2,000
Taxes payable – prior years		1,952
Prior period adjustment – correction of accounting error ...		2,048

Computations:

Taxes payable:

19A – ($6,000 – $1,000) × .40 =	$2,000	
19B – $1,000 × .40 =	(400)	$1,600
Add penalty		352
Total		$1,952

Prior period adjustment:

Pretax – ($6,000 – $2,000)	$4,000	
Deduct tax plus penalty	1,952	$2,048

The remaining entries and the financial reports would reflect these net of tax amounts.

In overall perspective, we can observe that the four types of *changes* discussed are diverse in situation, characteristics, and accounting treatment. This is another area where the judgment and professional responsibility of the independent accountant is paramount. The distinctions discussed and illustrated in the preceding paragraphs focus on one central issue, that is, the distinction between changes occasioned by change in circumstances (change in principle, change in estimate, and change in entity) that provide a good faith and logical basis for change, and those occasioned either by lack of good faith or unsophistication (accounting errors). The accounting treatments that appear most appropriate are related to these circumstances and are designed to best serve the statement user through accuracy, full disclosure, and the absence of misleading inferences.

ANALYTICAL PROCEDURES FOR CORRECTING ERRORS

In many situations the accountant needs to use efficient analytical procedures for dealing with accounting changes whether they are due to principles, estimates, or errors. Changes and correcting entries must be determined, and previously prepared financial statements frequently must be revised. This section presents some analytical techniques that are useful for these purposes as well as for problem-solving purposes for students, CPA candidates, and others.

Errors may be classified according to which financial statements are affected. Some may affect only the balance sheet. For example, a credit to Retained Earnings instead of Contributed Capital would affect only the balance sheet. Correction would involve a transfer from one real account to another real account. In this case, balance sheets for future periods would be in error until correction of the respective account balances. Other changes affect only the income statement. For example, a credit to the Sales account instead of Interest Revenue would affect only the income statement. Correction of this error would involve a transfer from one nominal account to another nominal account. In this case financial reports of future periods would be unaffected whether or not the error is corrected.

A third type of error affects both the balance sheet and the income statement. This type may be further classified on the basis of the effect on the current and future financial statements as follows:

1. *Counterbalancing errors*. This kind of error results from failure to allocate properly an expense or revenue item between two consecutive accounting periods. There is no discernible effect upon the balance sheet at the end of the second period, since the total revenue and total expense to that date are correct; no error would be left in Retained Earnings or other balance sheet accounts. Examples of counterbalancing errors are:

a. Errors in adjusting for prepaid expenses, accrued expenses, prepaid revenues, or accrued (uncollected) revenues. Such errors cause an incorrect income statement in the period in which the error was made with an equal misstatement in the opposite direction on the income statement for the following period. To illustrate, assume accrued wages were not recognized in 19A. The effect of this error is as follows:

19A income statement – Wage expense understated
– Income overstated
19A balance sheet – Current liabilities understated
– Retained earnings overstated
19B income statement – Wage expense overstated
– Income understated
19B balance sheet – No misstatements

b. Errors in the merchandise inventory. Errors of this type are counterbalancing because the final inventory of the current period is the beginning inventory of the next period and the beginning and ending inventories have an opposite effect on income. To illustrate, assume the final inventory for 19A is understated. The effect of this error is as follows:

19A income statement – Ending inventory understated
– Cost of goods sold overstated
– Income understated
19A balance sheet – Assets (inventory) understated
– Retained earnings understated
19B income statement – Beginning inventory understated
– Cost of goods sold understated
– Income overstated
19B balance sheet – No misstatements

2. *Noncounterbalancing errors.* This kind of error continues to affect account balances until corrected; hence, one or more balance sheet accounts continue to be reported inaccurately. Examples of noncounterbalancing errors are:

a. Over- or understatement of the depreciation charge; the accumulated depreciation and retained earnings balances are in error until corrected or the asset is disposed of. The income statements are inaccurate for the periods in which the incorrect charges were recorded.

b. Recognition of a capital expenditure as an expense, or vice versa, results in incorrect asset balances, depreciation charges, and retained earnings.

Preparing Correcting Entries for Errors

Correcting entries will vary depending on whether the error is counterbalancing (i.e., self correcting) and the period of time lapsed since the error was made. To illustrate, the following situations involving both counterbalancing and noncounterbalancing errors are analyzed and corrected at two different points in time. Recall that when an error made in a prior period is corrected, the cumulative misstatement of prior years' net income is reflected in the period of correction as a *prior period adjustment.* Since prior period adjustments are closed to Retained Earnings, this serves to correct the balance of that account.

Situation 1: Error in merchandise inventory. Assume that the final inventory for 19A was understated by $1,000.

Case A—The error was found at the end of 19B (before books were closed).

Analysis: Net income for 19A was understated by $1,000; hence retained earnings at the start of 19B is understated by this amount. Beginning inventory for 19B is understated by $1,000.

Correcting entry in 19B:

Inventory, beginning	1,000	
Prior period adjustment, error correction		1,000

Case B—The error was found during 19C.

Analysis: Counterbalanced; net income for 19A was understated by $1,000 and 19B overstated by the same amount. No correcting entry is needed in 19C. Restate 19A and 19B financial statements for all subsequent reporting purposes.

Situation 2: Error in both purchases and inventory. Assume that a $2,000 purchase in 19A was not recorded until 19B and the goods were not included in the 19A ending inventory.

Case A—The two errors were discovered in 19B (before books were closed).

Analysis: In 19A both purchases and ending inventory were understated by the same amounts; therefore, since they have opposite effects on income, that amount for 19A was correct. However, on the balance sheet for 19A both inventory and payables were understated by $2,000. In 19B both inventory (beginning) and purchases are in error.

Correcting entry in 19B:

Inventory, beginning	2,000	
Purchases		2,000

Case B—The two errors were discovered in 19C.

Analysis: Both errors counterbalanced in 19B. No correcting entry is needed in 19C. Restate 19A and 19B financial statements for all subsequent reporting purposes.

Situation 3: Error in prepaid expense. Assume that a five-year fire insurance policy was acquired on January 1, 19A; the five-year premium of $500 was paid and charged to insurance expense in 19A.

Case A—The error was discovered at the end of 19B (before books were closed).

Analysis: In 19A insurance expense was overstated and income understated by $400. Also in 19A prepaid insurance and retained earnings were understated by $400. No insurance expense for 19B has been recorded.

Correcting entry in 19B:

Prepaid insurance	400	
Prior period adjustment, error correction		400

(An adjusting entry for $100 expired insurance must also be made for 19B.)

Case B – The error was discovered in 19C.

Correcting entry at end of 19C:

Prepaid insurance	300	
Prior period adjustment, error correction		300

(An adjusting entry for $100 expired insurance also must be made for 19C.)

Situation 4: Error in accrued expense. Assume accrued property taxes for $100 at the end of 19A were not recorded. They were paid early in 19B.

Case A – The error was found at the end of 19B (before books were closed).

Analysis: In 19A tax expense was understated and income overstated. Also liabilities were understated and retained earnings overstated by $100. Tax expense for 19B is overstated by $100 because of the payment entry.

Correcting entry at end of 19B:

Prior period adjustment, error correction	100	
Tax expense		100

Case B – The error was found during 19C.

Analysis: The error counterbalanced in 19B because 19A income was overstated and 19B income understated by $100. No correcting entry is needed for 19C. Restate 19A and 19B financial statements for all subsequent reporting purposes.

Situation 5: Error in revenue earned but not yet collected. Assume interest receivable of $75 at the end of 19A was not recorded. The interest was collected in 19B.

Case A – The error was found at the end of 19B (before books were closed).

Analysis: In 19A interest revenue was understated and income was understated. On the balance sheet receivables and retained earnings were understated. In 19B interest revenue is overstated because of the collection entry.

Correcting entry at end of 19B:

Interest revenue	75	
Prior period adjustment, error correction		75

Case B – The error was discovered during 19C.

Analysis: The error counterbalanced in 19B because 19A income was understated and 19B income overstated. No correcting entry is needed in 19C. Restate 19A and 19B financial statements for all subsequent reporting purposes.

Situation 6: Expense capitalized. Assume that on January 1, 19A, $500 was expended for ordinary repairs; the $500 was debited to the Machinery account which was being depreciated 10% per year.

Case A—The error was discovered at the end of 19B (before books were closed).

Analysis: For 19A repair expense was understated, depreciation expense overstated, and income incorrect by the difference. On the balance sheet assets were overstated and retained earnings overstated by $\$500 \times .90 = \$450$.

Correcting entry at end of 19B:

Accumulated depreciation (for 19A)	50	
Prior period adjustment, error correction	450	
Machinery		500

Case B—The error was discovered during 19C (before the adjustment for depreciation expense was made for 19C).

Correcting entry at end of 19C:

Accumulated depreciation (for 19A and 19B)	100	
Prior period adjustment, error correction	400	
Machinery		500

These illustrations should be sufficient to indicate the care that must be taken in analyzing and correcting errors. Fundamental to the analysis are the following: (1) a clear understanding of how the incorrect entry was made, (2) a determination of what the correct entry should have been, and (3) development of correcting entry to bring (1) in conformity with (2) by taking into account the effects between the date of the error and the date of the correction.

Worksheet Techniques for Correcting Errors

Usually errors can be analyzed and appropriate accounting developed without a worksheet. However, when errors are numerous and complicated a worksheet approach often is helpful. An efficient worksheet usually can be designed easily to meet the needs of the particular situation. Of necessity, the worksheet will be unique to the situation; therefore, the accountant should develop an ability to design efficient worksheets for specific problems when they arise.[5] In the remainder of this part two different worksheets often used will be presented.

---

[5] A reasonable skill in worksheet design often is quite helpful in tackling problems on the CPA examination.

Worksheet to Correct Net Income and Provide Correcting Entries

A type of problem sometimes encountered is where there have been a number of errors in income. Usually the situation requires *(a)* determination of correct income for a series of periods, and *(b)* preparation of a correcting entry (or entries) at the time the errors are discovered.

To illustrate, assume the following data have been developed for Company A:

	19A	*19B*	*19C*
Reported income (uncorrected)	$5,000	$7,000	$6,000
Errors made in the records and reports:			
a) Prepaid expenses not recognized	100	200	400
b) Prepaid revenue (collected in advance, not recognized)	300	500	100
c) Accrued expenses not recognized	600	800	500
d) Accrued revene (revenue earned but not yet collected, not recognized)	500	400	600
e) Depreciation understated	200	200	200

Required:

1. Determine correct income for each year.
2. Give the correcting entries needed assuming:

   Case A – the errors were discovered at the end of 19C (before the adjusting and closing entries were made).

   Case B – the errors were discovered during 19D (before the adjusting and closing entries were made).

A worksheet, designed to meet Requirement 1 is shown in Exhibit 20–1. Observe that the worksheet starts with the uncorrected amounts and *(a)* provides for correction of income for each year, and *(b)* identifies account balances that are incorrect at the end of 19C. To explain the mechanics of the worksheet, observe prepaid expenses. Since prepaid expenses of $100 were not recognized in 19A, expenses were overstated and income understated for that year by $100. In the following year the opposite effect occurred because of this item. Therefore, income for 19A is increased and for 19B decreased on the worksheet by $100. At the end of 19C the $400 prepaid expense has not counterbalanced; that amount should be reflected as a debit in prepaid expenses (to be reported on the 19C balance sheet). The remaining entries on the worksheet follow this pattern. You should carefully study each item on the worksheet.

Requirement 2, Case A – the errors were discovered at the end of 19C (books were not closed). Based on data provided in Exhibit 20–1.

a. Prepaid expense	400	
Expense, 19C ($400 – $200)		200
Prior period adjustment, error correction		200
b. Prior period adjustment, error correction	500	
Revenue, 19C ($500 – $100)		400
Revenue collected in advance (prepaid revenue)		100

	Debit	Credit
c. Prior period adjustment, error correction	800	
Expense, 19C ($800 – $500)		300
Accrued expenses payable		500
d. Revenue earned but not collected (accrued revenue)	600	
Revenue, 19C ($600 – $400)		200
Prior period adjustment, error correction		400
e. Depreciation expense, 19C	200	
Prior period adjustment, error correction	400	
Accumulated depreciation		600

Observe that each of the above entries could be made in two separate entries; for example, entry (*a*) could be as follows:

	Debit	Credit
a–1. Prepaid expense	400	
Expense, 19C		400
a–2. Expense, 19C	200	
Prior period adjustment, error correction		200

Requirement 2, Case B – the errors were discovered in 19D (prior to adjusting and closing entries). See Exhibit 20–1 for data.

	Debit	Credit
a. Prepaid expense	400	
Prior period adjustment, error correction		400
b. Prior period adjustment, error correction	100	
Revenue collected in advance (prepaid revenue)		100

EXHIBIT 20–1
Worksheet to Correct Income and Provide Data for Correcting Entry At End of Year 19C

Particulars		19A	19B	19C	Corrections	
					Amount	Account
Reported income (loss)		5,000	7,000	6,000	18,000*	Balancing
Corrections:						
a. Prepaid expenses	– 19A	100	100*			
(not recognized)	19B		200	200*		
	19C			400	400*	Prepaid expenses
b. Prepaid revenue	– 19A	300*	300			
(not recognized)	19B		500*	500		
	19C			100*	100	Prepaid revenue
c. Accrued expenses	– 19A	600*	600			
(not recognized)	19B		800*	800		
	19C			500*	500	Accrued expenses
d. Accrued revenue	– 19A	500	500*			
(not recognized)	19B		400	400*		
	19C			600	600*	Accrued revenue
e. Depreciation	– 19A	200*				
(understated)	19B		200*		600	Accumulated depreciation
	19C			200*		
Correct income (loss)		4,500	6,400	6,900	17,800*	Balancing

Note: As an arithmetic check note that the last line and last column sum to the same total.
* Denotes debit.

	Debit	Credit
c. Prior period adjustment, error correction	500	
Accrued expenses payable		500
d. Revenue earned but not collected (accrued revenue)	600	
Prior period adjustment, error correction		600
e. Prior period adjustment, error correction	600	
Accumulated depreciation		600

Worksheets to Recast Financial Statements

Another group of problems commonly require that the income statement, balance sheet, and statement of retained earnings be recast on a correct basis. To demonstrate adaptation of the *interim worksheet* to problems where an uncorrected trial balance is available and the requirement is to provide correct statements of income, retained earnings, and assets and equities, the following illustrative problem is presented. To simplify, income tax effects are disregarded.

ILLUSTRATIVE PROBLEM

1. Uncorrected and unadjusted trial balance at December 31, 19B – As shown in the first two columns of Exhibit 20–2.
2. Additional data:
   - *a.* Merchandise inventory December 31, 19A, overstated $4,000.
   - *b.* Prepaid advertising of $2,000 at December 31, 19B, not recorded.
   - *c.* Prepaid insurance of $2,000 at December 31, 19B, not recorded; the entire premium paid on June 1, 19B, was debited to general expense.
   - *d.* Accrued sales salaries of $1,000 at December 31, 19A, not recorded.
   - *e.* Accrued rent expense of $1,000 at December 31, 19B, not recorded; treated as general expense.
   - *f.* No provision was made for doubtful accounts. The following estimates have been made: 19A, $1,000; 19B, $3,000. Treated as general expense.
   - *g.* No provision was made for depreciation. The following amounts have been computed: prior to 19B, $15,000; 19B, $5,000. Treated as general expense.
   - *h.* Dividends paid and properly recorded in 19B, $8,000. (Note: Transactions occurring during the current year and affecting retained earnings may be entered on the worksheet so that the worksheet will provide detail concerning all changes in retained earnings.)
   - *i.* Cash shortage, $1,000 at end of 19B.
   - *j.* Correction for premium on capital stock (7,500 shares, par $10 per share).
   - *k.* The inventory was $32,000 at the end of 19B.

Required:

Complete a worksheet to provide corrected amounts for 19C income statement, statement of retained earnings, and balance sheet. Key all entries on the worksheet to the data given.

EXHIBIT 20–2
Worksheet to Correct Financial Statements—December 31, 19B

	Trial Balance		Entries		Income Summary		Retained Earnings		Balance Sheet	
	Debit	Credit	Debit	Credit	Debit	Credit	Debit	Credit	Debit	Credit
Cash	9,000			*(i)* 1,000					8,000	
Receivables	20,000								20,000	
Allowance for doubtful accounts				*(f)* 4,000						4,000
Inventory, beginning	30,000			*(a)* 4,000	26,000					
Equipment	60,000								60,000	
Accumulated depreciation				*(g)* 20,000						20,000
Accounts payable		5,000								5,000
Capital stock, par $10, 7,500 shares outstanding		76,000	*(j)* 1,000							75,000
Retained earnings		25,000		*(h)* 8,000				33,000		
Prior period adjustments:										
Inventory correction			*(a)* 4,000				4,000			
Salaries correction			*(d)* 1,000				1,000			
Bad debt correction			*(f)* 1,000				1,000			
Depreciation correction			*(g)* 15,000				15,000			
Sales		130,000				130,000				
Purchases	90,000				90,000					
Selling expenses	17,000			*(b)* 2,000	14,000					
				(d) 1,000						
General expenses	10,000		*(e)* 1,000	*(c)* 2,000	18,000					
			(f) 3,000							
			(g) 5,000							
			(i) 1,000							
	236,000	236,000								
Prepaid advertising			*(b)* 2,000						2,000	
Prepaid insurance			*(c)* 2,000						2,000	
Accrued rent expense				*(e)* 1,000						1,000
Dividends paid 19B			*(h)* 8,000				8,000			
Inventory, ending						32,000			32,000	
Premium on capital stock				*(j)* 1,000						1,000
Net income					14,000			14,000		
Retained earnings balance							18,000			18,000
			44,000	44,000	162,000	162,000	47,000	47,000	124,000	124,000

Exhibit 20–2 shows an efficient worksheet that meets all of the requirements of this situation. Observe that it is similar to the worksheets illustrated in Chapter 3. The entries include both *(a)* current adjusting entries, and *(b)* correcting entries. You should follow each item through the worksheet. The required financial statements, on a corrected basis, can be readily prepared from the worksheet.

This type of worksheet is especially important throughout accounting because (1) it can be adapted to many different problem situations, and (2) its built-in debit/credit feature assures a degree of accuracy and completeness not otherwise attainable.

PART B—STATEMENTS FROM SINGLE-ENTRY AND OTHER INCOMPLETE RECORDS

Most businesses maintain a reasonably complete record of all transactions directly affecting the firm. Usually complete records are best accomplished through a systematic model based on *(a)* the double-entry concept and *(b)* the accounting model. However, a small entity, especially if a sole proprietorship, may maintain only a single-entry system that records just the "bare essentials." The proprietor may maintain the records and may not be familiar with effective recordkeeping procedures nor appreciate the importance of good records to sound management.

Single-entry recordkeeping includes all those records, whether kept systematically or not, deemed necessary by the proprietor but which do not attempt to record the *dual effect* of each transaction on both assets and equities as expressed in the accounting model. In some cases only records of cash, accounts receivable, accounts payable, and taxes paid may be maintained. No record may be kept, except perhaps in memorandum form, of fixed assets, inventories, expenses, revenues, and other elements usually considered essential in an accounting system. However, the incomplete data, plus other information that often can be assembled, generally can be analyzed sufficiently to provide a reasonably accurate income statement and balance sheet.

Preparation of Balance Sheet from Single-Entry Records

Since single-entry records usually provide sparse information about assets other than cash and accounts receivable, preparation of the balance sheet involves inventorying, counting, and verification procedures to determine the nature and amount of most of the assets and liabilities. The cost of the fixed assets must be determined from such data as are available. Canceled checks, receipts, bills of sale, deeds, papers transferring title to real estate, and other similar records provide much of the needed data. Once the cost of the fixed assets is determined, depreciation can be computed. The amount of merchandise, supplies, and other inventories on hand are obtained by actual count. The original cost of these items must be determined in order to cost the inventory. If

EXHIBIT 20-3

A. A. BROWN COMPANY
Balance Sheet, At December 31, 19A

Assets		
Current Assets:		
Cash		$2,345
Accounts receivable		90
Notes receivable, trade		50
Merchandise inventory		1,550
Total Current Assets		4,035
Property and Equipment:		
Office and store fixtures	$500	
Less accumulated depreciation	25	475
Total Assets		$4,510
Liabilities		
Current Liabilities:		
Accounts payable		$ 240
Long-Term Liabilities		None
Total Liabilities		240
Owner's Equity		
A. A. Brown, proprietorship ($4,510 − $240)		4,270
Total Liabilities and Owner's Equity		$4,510

original cost cannot be obtained, merchandise and supplies can be priced at current replacement cost.

Similarly, notes payable and other liabilities (except accounts payable for which there is generally a record) must be obtained from memoranda, correspondence, and even by consultation with creditors. Usually in this manner a fairly reliable balance sheet can be developed.

To illustrate preparation of a balance sheet from single-entry records, assume the following data has been gathered for the sole proprietorship, A. A. Brown Company for 19A:

a. Cash on hand and on deposit, $2,345—from count of cash and bank statement.
b. Merchandise inventory, $1,550—Count made by Brown, costed at current replacement cost since purchase invoices were not available.
c. Store and office equipment acquired on January 1, 19A, $500—from invoice found in the files.
d. Brown agreed that a depreciation rate of 5% per annum, with no material amount of residual value, was reasonable.
e. Interest-bearing note, dated December 31, 19A, $50—This note, signed by a customer for goods purchased, was in the files.
f. Accounts receivable, $90—Brown maintained a "Charge Book" which listed four customers as owing a total of $90; Brown was positive that the bills were outstanding. You called the customers for verification.
g. Accounts payable, $240—The "unpaid invoices" file contained two

invoices that totaled to this amount; Brown assured you that they had not been paid.

A balance sheet prepared from the above data is shown in Exhibit 20–3. Owner's equity was determined by subtracting total liabilities from total assets.

Computation of Income

The computation of income where single-entry records are kept may be based on an analysis of the changes in owner's equity for the period. For example, if it is determined that the only change in owner's equity for Brown Company resulted from a gain or loss from operations, the summary income statement in Exhibit 20–4 may be prepared (proprietorship, January 1, 19A, taken from balance sheet for prior period).

If there had been additional investments or withdrawals during the period, these must be considered in the computation of income or loss. The following equation indicates the procedure when there have been investments or withdrawals during the period:

Income = Ending Owner's Equity − Beginning Owner's Equity + Withdrawals − Additional Investments

The two examples of the single-entry income statement computations shown in Exhibit 20–5 indicate the procedure when there have been investments and withdrawals during the period.

EXHIBIT 20–4

A. A. BROWN COMPANY
Computation of Net Loss
For the Year Ended December 31, 19A

Owner's equity, January 1, 19A	$4,500
Owner's equity, December 31, 19A	4,270
Net Loss for Period	$ 230

EXHIBIT 20–5
Income Determination – Single Entry

	Computation Where There Was–	
	An Income	*A Loss*
Owner's equity, end of period	$8,000	$5,500
Owner's equity, beginning of period	7,100	6,300
Change (increase)	900	
(decrease)		(800)
Add: Withdrawals during period	1,200	1,000
	2,100	200
Deduct: Additional investments during period	500	400
Income for Period	$1,600	
Loss for Period		$ (200)

PREPARATION OF A DETAILED INCOME STATEMENT FROM INCOMPLETE DATA

Computation of the amount of income or loss can be accomplished as shown in the preceding section. However, knowing only the amount of income or loss does not meet the internal needs of management for information about operations nor does it meet the needs of other interested parties. Banks and other credit grantors usually request a statement setting out the details of operations. The Internal Revenue Service requires a detailed statement of revenues and expenses for income tax purposes.

An itemized income statement in the conventional form may be prepared from single-entry records and supplemental data without converting the records to double-entry form. By analyzing the cash receipts and disbursements, much of the needed detail may be obtained. The preparation of an income statement from single-entry data may be simply illustrated as follows:

The following information was obtained from the single-entry records of John Mercer Company. Balance sheets as of January 1 and December 31 and an income statement for 19A are to be prepared:

	19A	
	January 1	*December 31*
Accounts and trade notes receivable (no doubtful accounts)	$35,000	$48,000
Inventory (per physical count)	6,900	8,700
Building and equipment (appraised at estimated cost less depreciation)	17,000	17,400
Prepaid expenses (per memoranda)	100	110
Accounts payable (per files)	8,100	9,200
Notes payable (for equipment per files)		500
Cash on hand (register)	60	110
Accrued expenses (per memoranda)	120	150
Salaries		7,000

An analysis of the bank statements indicated deposits and disbursements as follows:

Bank overdraft, January 1, 19A	$ 2,800
Deposits during year:	
Collections on account	42,000
Additional capital contributions by owner	10,000
Checks drawn during year:	
Purchases	26,000
Expenses	6,000
Salaries of employees	7,000
Withdrawals by owner	3,000
Purchase of equipment	340

Balance Sheet Preparation

In preparing the balance sheets, cash in the bank on December 31, 19A, must be computed; there was an overdraft on January 1, 19A. Total deposits of $52,000 less the January 1 overdraft of $2,800 and total checks drawn of $42,340 indicates a December 31, 19A, balance of $6,860. The balance sheets would be as shown in Exhibit 20–6.

EXHIBIT 20–6

JOHN MERCER COMPANY
Balance Sheets

	19A	
	January 1	*December 31*
Assets		
Cash in bank	$ –	$ 6,860
Cash in register	60	110
Accounts and notes receivable	35,000	48,000
Inventory	6,900	8,700
Prepaid expenses	100	110
Buildings and equipment	17,000	17,400
	$59,060	$81,180
Liabilities		
Notes payable	$ –	$ 500
Bank overdraft	2,800	–
Accounts payable	8,100	9,200
Accrued expenses payable	120	150
	11,020	9,850
Owner's Equity (difference)		
John Mercer, proprietorship	$48,040	$71,330

Computation of Net Income

Using the single-entry method, net income may be computed by analysis of the change in proprietorship as follows:

Owner's equity, December 31, 19A	$71,330
Owners' equity, January 1, 19A	48,040
Increase in owner's equity	23,290
Add withdrawals during year	3,000
	26,290
Deduct additional investments during year	10,000
Net Income, 19A	$16,290

Analysis of Revenue and Expenses. To prepare a detailed income statement, each item of revenue and expense to be included thereon must be determined. Such a determination may be made by summarizing all the transactions in debit and credit form, which in effect would involve conversion to double-entry procedures. This approach is subsequently illustrated (in worksheet form) in this chapter. Alternatively, the desired figures may be derived directly by analyzing the respective items as illustrated below.

Computation of Sales. Cash and credit sales combined may be determined by analyzing cash receipts and changes in accounts receivable and trade notes receivable as follows:

Schedule 1

Accounts and trade notes receivable, December 31, 19A	$48,000
Cash collected from customers and deposited	42,000
Increase in cash on hand	50
	90,050
Less: Accounts and trade notes receivable, January 1, 19A	35,000
Sales for the Period, 19A	$55,050

Alternatively, to determine the sales for the period, you may prefer simply to reconstruct the T-accounts for the *accounts receivable* and *sales* accounts as follows:

Accounts Receivable

Beg. bal. (Jan. 1)	35,000	Cash collections (deposited)	42,000
(A) Sales (amount necessary to complete account)	55,050	Cash collections (on hand)	50
		End balance (Dec. 31)	48,000
	90,050		90,050
Balance carried forward	48,000		

Sales

		(A)	55,050

Many people find the T-account approach preferable to the schedule in that the problem of whether to add or subtract a given amount is easily resolved by making the normal entries; also there is a built-in self-check. The items are simply entered in the account in the normal manner and the missing amount (sales in the above case) is the "plug" figure. Note that the *ending* balance is always entered on the "opposite side" for balancing purposes in reconstructing the account as is done in the normal year-end closing of accounts with balances to be carried forward.

Note that the increase of cash on hand is assumed to represent collections from customers. If there had been data relative to cash discounts on sales, returned sales, or accounts charged off as uncollectible, both the sales discounts and the bad debts written off should be added to the total in Schedule 1. In such cases if the T-account analysis is used, it would appear advisable to reconstruct the following accounts: Accounts Receivable, Allowance for Doubtful Accounts, Loss from Doubtful Accounts, Sales Discounts, Sales Returns, and Sales.

Computation of Purchases

The amount of purchases may be determined by the analysis of cash disbursements and changes in both accounts payable and trade notes payable.

Schedule 2

Accounts and trade notes payable, December 31, 19A	$ 9,200
Payments to creditors	26,000
	35,200
Less: Accounts and trade notes payable, January 1, 19A	8,100
Purchases for the Period, 19A	$27,100

It should be noted that cash discounts may have been taken. If this is the case, such discounts should be added in the schedule (or included in the T-account analysis) to derive gross purchases.

Computation of Depreciation

The building and equipment were valued at appraised cost less depreciation. The decrease in the net book value of the asset, taking into account additions and dispositions of equipment during the period, is the amount of depreciation for the period as computed below:

Schedule 3

Net balance of buildings and equipment, January 1, 19A	$17,000
Purchases of equipment during 19A:	
By issue of note payable	500
By cash payment	340
Balance before depreciation	17,840
Less: Net balance on December 31, 19A (after current depreciation)	17,400
Depreciation for the Period, 19A	$ 440

Computation of Expenses

The expenses paid in cash, determined from an analysis of cash disbursements, must be adjusted for prepaid and accrued items at the beginning and at the end of the period as follows:

Schedule 4

Expenses paid in cash during 19A		$6,000
Add: Expenses accrued on December 31, 19A		150
Prepaid expenses on January 1, 19A		100
		6,250
Deduct: Accrued expenses, January 1, 19A	$120	
Prepaid expenses, December 31, 19A	110	230
Expenses for the Period, 19A		$6,020

Again, you may find it easier to analyze the more involved situations, such as this one, by reconstructing the related accounts in the following manner:

Prepaid Expenses

Debit		Credit	
Beginning balance (Jan. 1)	100	(A) Transfer to expense	100
(C) To record final balance (Dec. 31)	110		

Accrued Expenses

Debit		Credit	
(B) Transfer to expense	120	Beginning balance (Jan. 1)	120
		(D) To record final balance (Dec. 31)	150

Expenses

Debit		Credit	
Paid in cash during 19A	6,000	(B) Transfer from accrued	120
(A) Transfer from prepaid	100	(C) Final balance prepaid	110
(D) Final balance accrued	150		

(Expenses for 19A—account balance, $6,020.)

Note again that the beginning balances are entered, then the "normal" accounting entries are made in the accounts.

The information does not reveal any adjustments to salary expense; therefore, that expense is $7,000 as given.

Preparation of the Income Statement

All information needed to prepare the income statement has now been determined. That statement would appear as shown in Exhibit 20–7.

EXHIBIT 20–7

JOHN MERCER COMPANY
Income Statement
For Year Ended December 31, 19A

Sales (Schedule 1)		$55,050
Cost of goods sold:		
Inventory, January 1, 19A (given)	$ 6,900	
Purchases (Schedule 2)	27,100	
Goods available for sale	34,000	
Less: Inventory, December 31, 19A (given)	8,700	
Cost of Goods Sold		25,300
Gross margin on sales		29,750
Less: Expenses:		
Depreciation (Schedule 3)	440	
Expenses (Schedule 4)	6,020	
Salaries. (given)	7,000	13,460
Net Income		$16,290

WORKSHEETS FOR PROBLEMS FROM SINGLE-ENTRY AND OTHER INCOMPLETE RECORDS

The preceding example, although simplified, demonstrates the need for a worksheet approach to reduce clerical work and minimize the possibility of errors and omissions. In problem-solving situations, whether in study or in practice, the *interim worksheet* again is particularly useful. The interim worksheet provides for several internal checks on accuracy and recognizes each group of transactions in their debit and credit effects. In order to provide a "track record" such worksheets should be accompanied by explanations and computations of the analyses involved.

The following illustrative problem is presented to demonstrate adaptation and use of the interim worksheet in solving problems involving incomplete data:

J. C. Main had been in business two years and had not maintained double-entry records. A financial statement was prepared by an accountant at the end of last year, 19A. This balance sheet (balances at January 1, 19B) and one developed at the end of the current year (dated December 31, 19B) are presented in Exhibit 20–8. They were developed by "inventorying" all assets and liabilities.

The following additional information for 19B was developed:

a. Main kept no record of cash receipts and disbursements, but an analysis of canceled checks showed the following payments: accounts payable, $71,000; expenses, $20,700; and purchase of equipment, $3,700. No checks appeared to be outstanding.

b. Main stated that $100 cash was withdrawn regularly each week from the cash register for personal use. No record was made of these personal withdrawals.

c. The bank loan was for one year, the note was discounted by the bank at 6% on July 1, 19B.

EXHIBIT 20–8

J. C. MAIN COMPANY
Balance Sheets

	19B	
	January 1	*December 31*
Cash	$ 10,000	$ 22,000
Notes receivable	5,000	3,000
Accounts receivable	61,000	68,000
Inventories	25,000	27,000
Prepaid expenses	500	200
Furniture and equipment (net)	10,600	12,400
	$112,100	$132,600
Bank loan	$ –	$ 5,000
Accounts payable	30,000	36,000
Accrued expenses	800	650
J. C. Main, proprietorship	81,300	90,950
	$112,100	$132,600

EXHIBIT 20–9

J. C. MAIN COMPANY
Worksheet for Year Ended December 31, 19B

	Beginning Balances January 1, 19B	Interim Entries Debit	Interim Entries Credit	Income Statement	Ending Balances December 31, 19B
Debit accounts:					
Cash	10,000	(c) 4,700	(a) 95,400		22,000
		(d) 620	(b) 5,200		
		(e) 4,000			
		(h) 103,280			
Notes receivable	5,000	(g) 2,400	(e) 4,000		3,000
			(f) 400		
Accounts receivable	61,000	(i) 112,680	(g) 2,400		68,000
			(h) 103,280		
Inventories	25,000	(j) 27,000	(j) 25,000		27,000
Prepaid expenses	500	(c) 150	(k) 500		200
		(k) 50			
Furniture and equipment (net)	10,600	(a) 3,700	(d) 900		12,400
			(l) 1,000		
Expenses		(a) 20,700	(k) 50	21,000	
		(k) 500	(n) 800		
		(n) 650			
Interest expense		(c) 150		150	
Loss on sale of equipment		(d) 280		280	
Loss on worthless note		(f) 400		400	
Depreciation		(l) 1,000		1,000	
Purchases		(m) 77,000		77,000	
Net income		(o) 14,850		14,850	
	112,100			114,680	132,600
Credit accounts:					
Bank loan			(c) 5,000		5,000
Accounts payable	30,000	(a) 71,000	(m) 77,000		36,000
Accrued expenses	800	(n) 800	(n) 650		650
J. C. Main, proprietorship	81,300	(b) 5,200	(o) 14,850		90,950
Sales			(i) 112,680	112,680	
Income summary (inventory change)		(j) 25,000	(j) 27,000	2,000	
	112,100	476,110	476,110	114,680	132,600

d. Main stated that equipment listed in the January 1 balance sheet at $900 was sold for $620 cash.
e. The bank reported that it had credited Main with $4,000 during the year for customers' notes left for collection.
f. One $400 note on hand December 31, 19B, was past due and appeared to be worthless. Therefore, this note was not included in the $3,000 notes receivable listed in the December 31 balance sheet. Assume no allowance for doubtful accounts; bad debts are written off directly to expense because of immateriality.

Main needs a detailed income statement for the current year, 19B.

Solution. An eight-column or five-column interim worksheet may be adapted for this problem. A five-colum worksheet is shown in Exhibit 20–9. Note that a five-column worksheet is achieved by placing "debits over credits." Columns are set up for beginning balances, interim entries (debit and credit), income statement, and ending balances.

The beginning and ending balances, taken from the two balance sheets, are entered directly on the worksheet as illustrated with sufficient line spacing for the anticipated entries. Next the interim entries for all transactions are reconstructed (as explained below) to account for all changes in each account during the period. Last, all items not listed in the column "ending balances" are carried as debits or credits to the column headed "Income Statement." At this point in the solution the *net income* (or loss) is the difference between the debits and credits in the Income Statement column. Particular attention should be called to the fact that considerable data needed for reconstruction of the entries are missing; therefore, care must be exercised as to sequence of developing the entries. Note that all of the data available are used first (entries [*a*] through [*f*]) then subsequent entries are developed by computing the "missing data" as illustrated in entry (*g*) and following. Problems such as this one are frequently referred to as missing data problems.

Explanation of Entries on the Worksheet:

a. To record payments shown by analysis of canceled checks.
b. To record Main's cash withdrawals of $100 per week for 52 weeks.
c. To record bank loan of $5,000 less $300 interest of which $150 was prepaid as of December 31, 19B.
d. To record sale of equipment, cost less depreciation, $900, for $620 cash.
e. To record $4,000 notes receivable collected by bank.
f. To record charge-off of bad note, $400.
g. To record notes from customers, computed as follows (data taken directly from worksheet):

Notes collected	$4,000
Note written off	400
Notes on hand December 31, 19B	3,000
	7,400
Less: Notes on hand January 1, 19B	5,000
New Notes Receivable	$2,400

h. Cash collected from customers (observe that it does not matter whether the collection was at time of sale or on account) is computed as follows from data shown in the Cash account on the worksheet:

Cash paid out ($95,400 + $5,200)	$100,600
Cash balance, December 31, 19B	22,000
	122,600
Cash collected from all sources other than from customers: ($4,700 + $620 + $4,000)	9,320
	113,280
Less: Cash balance, January 1, 19B	10,000
Cash Collected from Customers	$103,280

i. Sales are computed by finding the only entry missing on the worksheet in accounts receivable, which entry is for sales on account. (Balance in notes receivable has been already reconciled on the worksheet.)

Notes received on account	$ 2,400
Cash collected from customers	103,280
Final balance of accounts receivable	68,000
Total credits and balance	173,680
Less: January 1 balance	61,000
Total Debits for the Year (Sales)	$112,680

j. To close the January 1 inventory and to record the December 31 inventory (to income summary).

k. To close the January 1 balance of prepaid expenses and to increase the prepaid expense balance as of December 31 to $200 as given.

l. To set up the depreciation allowance for the period. All entries have been made in the Furniture and Equipment accounts on the worksheet except the depreciation credit. Depreciation is computed as follows:

Furniture and equipment, January 1, 19B	$10,600
Equipment purchased	3,700
	14,300
Less: Equipment sold	900
	13,400
Less: Balance of furniture and equipment, December 31, 19B	12,400
Depreciation for the Period	$ 1,000

m. Purchases are computed by finding the missing entry in accounts payable on the worksheet as follows:

Payments on accounts payable	$ 71,000
Balance of accounts payable, December 31, 19B	36,000
	107,000
Less: Accounts payable, January 1, 19B	30,000
Purchases for the Period	$ 77,000

n. To close the January 1 balance of accrued expenses and to record accrued expenses as of December 31.

o. To close net income to proprietorship. The net income may be computed by analyzing the changes in capital from January 1 to December 31, 19B, as illustrated previously or by extending nominal accounts balances to the column "Income Statement" and then computing the difference between the debits and credits. Obviously, one computation would serve as a check on the other.

The resulting income statement taken directly from the worksheet is shown in Exhibit 20–10.

EXHIBIT 20–10

J. C. MAIN COMPANY
Income Statement
For Year Ended December 31, 19B

Revenues:		
Sales		$112,680
Costs and expenses:		
Cost of goods sold:		
Beginning inventory, January 1, 19B	$ 25,000	
Purchases	77,000	
Total Goods Available for Sale	102,000	
Less: Final inventory, December 31, 19B	27,000	75,000
Gross margin on sales		37,680
Less: Expenses:		
Expenses	21,000	
Depreciation	1,000	
Loss on worthless note	400	22,400
Operating income		15,280
Less: Other costs and losses:		
Interest expense	150	
Loss on sale of equipment	280	430
Net Income		$ 14,850

LIMITATIONS OF SINGLE-ENTRY RECORDKEEPING

Single-entry recordkeeping is employed by a large number of particularly small businesses, by nonprofit organizations, by persons acting in a fiduciary capacity as administrators or executors of estates, and by many individuals relative to their personal affairs. Even some regular systems of recordkeeping recommended for retail outlets by trade associations and by manufacturers are based on single entry. For example, one such system is used by a large number of small retail druggists. Single-entry systems are used in the interest of simplicity and generally are less expensive to maintain than double-entry records since they do not require the services of a trained person. In fact, more often than not, single-entry records are maintained by the proprietor or someone closely associated with the activities being recorded.

Single-entry recordkeeping is generally inadequate except where operations are especially simple and the volume of activity is small. Some of the more important disadvantages of single-entry systems are:

1. Data are not available to the management for effectively planning and controlling the business.
2. Lack of systematic and precise recordkeeping may lead to inefficiency in administration and control over the affairs of the business.
3. They do not provide a check against clerical errors, as does a double-entry system. This is one of the most serious of the defects of single entry.
4. They seldom make provision for recording all transactions. Many internal transactions (i.e., those normally reflected through adjusting entries) in particular are not recorded.
5. Since no accounts are provided for many of the items appearing in both the balance sheet and income statement, omission of important data is always a possibility.
6. In the absence of detailed records of all assets, lax administration of those assets is quite likely.
7. Theft and other losses are less likely to be known.

QUESTIONS

1. Briefly distinguish between the following: *(a)* change in principle, *(b)* change in estimate, *(c)* change in entity, and *(d)* accounting error.

2. What are the three basic alternatives for reflecting the effects of accounting changes and error corrections?

3. Complete the following matrix:

	*Method of Reflecting the Effect**		
	(1)______	(2)______	(3)______
a. Change in estimate	____	____	____
b. Change in principle	____	____	____
c. Correction of error	____	____	____

* Identify these three captions; then enter appropriate check on each line.

4. What is a pro forma statement? Why are they used in respect to some accounting changes?

5. What is the difference between a counterbalancing and a noncounterbalancing error? Basically, why is the distinction significant in the analysis of errors?

6. Complete the following matrix by entering a plus to indicate overstatement and a minus to indicate understatement:

	Effect of Error on–			
	Net Income	Assets	Liabilities	Owners' Equity
a. Ending inventory for 19A understated:				
19A financial statements	____	____	____	____
19B financial statements	____	____	____	____
b. Ending inventory for 19B overstated:				
19A financial statements	____	____	____	____
19B financial statements	____	____	____	____
c. Failed to record depreciation in 19A:				
19A financial statements	____	____	____	____
19B financial statements	____	____	____	____
d. Failed to record revenue collected in advance at end of 19A:				
19A financial statements	____	____	____	____
19B financial statements	____	____	____	____

7. Give two examples of each of the following types of errors:
   a. Affects income statement only.
   b. Affects balance sheet only.
   c. Affects both income statement and balance sheet.
8. Briefly explain the differences between a double-entry and a single-entry system.
9. What are the primary shortcomings of a single-entry system? What are the advantages?

EXERCISES

PART A: EXERCISES 1–7

Exercise 20–1

Lyle Corporation has been depreciating Machine A over a ten-year life on sum-of-the-years'-digits basis. The machine cost $68,000 and has an estimated residual value of $13,000. On the basis of an engineering study of its economic potential to the company, completed during the fifth year (19B), the management decided to change to straight-line depreciation with no change in the estimated useful life or the residual value. The annual financial statements are prepared on a comparative basis (two years presented). Net incomes (no extraordinary items) prior to giving effect to this change (i.e., on the old basis) were: 19A, $50,000; 19B, $51,000. Shares of stock outstanding, 100,000. Disregard income tax considerations.

Required:

1. Identify the type of accounting change involved and analyze the effects of the change.
2. Prepare the entry, or entries, to appropriately reflect the change in the accounts in 19B (fifth year), the year of the change.
3. Illustrate how the change should be reflected on the 19B financial statement which includes 19A results for comparative purposes.

Exercise 20–2

Lyle Corporation has been depreciating Machine B over a ten-year life on a straight-line basis. The machine cost $24,000 and has an estimated residual value of $6,000. On the basis of experience since acquisition (four years prior to 19B) the management has decided to depreciate it over a total life of 14 years instead of 10, and no change in the estimated residual value. The annual financial statements are prepared on a comparative basis (two years presented). Net incomes (no extraordinary items) on the old basis were: 19A, $50,000; 19B, $51,000. Shares of stock outstanding, 100,000. Disregard income tax considerations.

Required:

1. Identify the type of accounting change involved and analyze the effects of the change.
2. Prepare entry, or entries, to appropriately reflect the change in the accounts for 19B (fifth year), the year of the change.
3. Illustrate how the change should be reflected on the 19B financial statement which includes 19A results for comparative purposes.

Exercise 20–3

AB Corporation has never had an audit prior to 19D, the current year. Prior to the arrival of the auditor the company accountant had prepared a comparative financial statement with 19C and 19D shown thereon for comparative purposes. The books for 19D have not been closed. During the audit it was discovered that an invoice dated January 19A for $9,000 (paid in cash at that time) was debited to operating expenses, although it was for the purchase of Machine X. Machine X has an estimated useful life of ten years and no residual value.

Reported income reflected on the comparative financial statement prepared by the company auditor (prior to discovery of the error) was: 19C, $30,000; 19D, $33,000. Shares of stock outstanding, 100,000. Disregard income tax considerations.

Required:

1. Identify the type of accounting change involved and analyze the effects of the change.
2. Prepare entry, or entries, to appropriately reflect the change in the accounts for 19D, the year of the change.
3. Illustrate how the change should be reflected on the 19D financial statement which includes 19C results for comparative purposes.

Exercise 20–4

Give journal entries to correct the accounts, and the subsequent adjusting entry, for each of the errors listed below assuming (1) the errors were discovered on December 31, 19B, before the books were adjusted and closed, and (2) the errors were discovered in January 19C (after the books for 19B were adjusted and closed). Assume each item is material. Disregard income tax considerations.

a. Merchandise costing $6,000 was received on December 28, 19A, and was included in the final inventory of 19A, but the purchase was not recorded in the purchases journal until January 3, 19B.

b. An entry was made on December 30, 19B, for write-off of organization expense as follows (assume only one year's amortization was justified through 19B; amortization per year $1,000):

General expense	5,000	
Deferred organization expense		5,000

c. Discount of $3,300 on a long-term bond investment purchased on May 1, 19A, was written off to retained earnings on that date. These bonds mature on July 1, 19J. Use straight-line amortization.
d. Machinery costing $900 was purchased and charged to repair expense on June 30, 19A. The depreciation rate on machinery is 10% per year.

Exercise 20–5

You are in the process of auditing the accounts of Zero Manufacturing Corporation for the year ended December 31, 19B. You discover that the adjustments made on the previous audit for the year 19A were not entered in the accounts; therefore, the accounts are not in agreement with the audited amounts as of December 31, 19A. The following adjustments were included in the 19A audit report:

a. Invoices for merchandise purchased in December 19A, not entered on the books until January 19B and not included in the December 31, 19A inventory, $6,000.
b. Invoices for merchandise received in December 19A were not recorded in the accounts; the goods were included in the 19A ending inventory, $9,000.
c. Provision for doubtful accounts for 19A understated by $1,000.
d. Factory expense for 19A not entered in the accounts until January 19B, $2,500.
e. Accrued payroll at December 31, 19A, not recorded at that date, $2,000.
f. Prepaid insurance at December 31, 19A, $300 not recorded.
g. Property taxes for year ended December 31, 19A, not entered in the accounts until January 19B, $1,200.
h. Depreciation not recorded prior to January 19A, $3,000; for year ended December 31, 19A, $1,500.

Required:

Assume you have the uncorrected and unadjusted trial balance dated December 31, 19B. Give the journal entry for each of the above items that should be made to the trial balance before using it for further audit purposes. Show computations. Disregard income tax implications.

Exercise 20–6

Dawson Company has made several accounting changes with a view to improving the matching of expenses with revenue. Assume it is at the end of 19C and that the accounting period ends on December 31. The books have not been adjusted and closed at the end of 19C. Among the changes were the following:

a. Machinery that cost $25,000, estimated useful life ten years, residual value $3,000. The company has been using sum-of-the-years'-digits depreciation. Early in the eighth year (19C), it was decided to change to straight-line depreciation (with no change in residual value or estimated life).
b. A patent that cost $8,500 is being depreciated over the legal life of 17 years. Early in the 6th year (19C), it was decided that the economic benefits would not last longer than 13 years from date of acquisition.
c. During 19A and 19B all repair expenditures have been debited to the Machinery account. The repair expenditures capitalized amounted to $7,000 and $11,000 during the two years respectively. The machinery was being depreciated 12% per year on cost. It is now the third year (19C), and the error has been discovered.

Required:

1. For each of the above situations, identify the type of accounting change or error that was involved and briefly explain how it should be accounted for.
2. Give the appropriate entry to reflect the change and the 19C adjusting entry in each instance. Show computations and disregard income tax considerations. If no entry is required in a particular instance, explain why.

Exercise 20–7

RB Company failed to recognize accruals and prepayments since organization three years previously. The net income, accruals, and prepayments at year-end are given below:

	19A	*19B*	*19C*
Reported income	$4,000	$1,000*	$5,000
Items not recognized at year-end:			
a. Prepaid expenses	200	280	109
b. Accrued expenses	250	225	247
c. Revenue collected in advance	325	360	293
d. Revenue earned but not yet collected	275	230	196

* Net loss.

Required:

1. Compute the correct net income for each year (disregard income tax effects).
2. Give entry to correct each item assuming the errors were discovered at year-end 19C (books were not closed).
3. Give entry to correct each item assuming the errors were discovered during 19D prior to the 19D adjusting and closing entries.

PART B: EXERCISES 8–13

Exercise 20–8

During the year ended December 31, 19A, M. Lane, a retail merchant who had started a business January 2, 19A, paid trade creditors $49,062 in cash, and final inventory per count (*Fifo* basis) was $9,563. Balances available on December 31, 19A, were the following: accounts payable, $16,125; expenses, $2,450; capital (representing total investment in cash January 2, 19A), $45,000; accounts receivable, $13,188; and sales, $50,000. There were no withdrawals. All sales and purchases were on credit.

Required:

1. Develop a worksheet and complete it to provide information for a corrected income statement and balance sheet. *Hint:* Set up columns for interim entries, income statement, and balance sheet.
2. Prepare a statement of cash inflows and outflows for the year ended December 31, 19A.

Exercise 20–9

On January 1, 19A, A. B. Cline invested $5,000 cash in a television repair shop. Memoranda revealed that $50 per week was withdrawn for living expenses. Cline's personal automobile, having a fair market value of $2,500 at that time, was invested in the business for use as a service car. The shop then paid $500 for body changes on the car to make it suitable for its needs; this amount was capitalized. On January 1, 19A, F. Frye also invested as a partner. Frye invested equipment valued at $3,000 and $1,000 cash. It was agreed that the partners would share profits equally after January 1, 19A. Frye withdrew $800 cash during the year.

On December 31, 19A, the following assets and liabilities were determined from memoranda and incomplete records: cash, $4,810; equipment (less depreciation), $4,600; receivables, $1,200; car-truck (less depreciation), $2,250; notes payable, $1,000.

Required:

Prepare a balance sheet showing capital balances for each partner and a separate computation of net income.

Exercise 20–10

Make the computations needed for the 19B income statement from the following data (each item is independent):

a. Wages: amount paid, $15,000; accrued on December 31, 19A, $1,000; accrued on December 31, 19B, $2,000.
b. Rent revenue: amount collected, $8,000; prepaid $500 on December 31, 19A, and $300 on December 31, 19B; accrued rental, $200 on December 31, 19A, and $600 on December 31, 19B.
c. Total sales: Cash account, balance, December 31, 19A, $26,000; balance, December 31, 19B, $33,000; total disbursements for 19B, $39,000. All cash receipts were from customers. Accounts receivable: balance, December 31, 19A, $40,160; balance, December 31, 19B, $59,000. Accounts written off during 19B as uncollectible, $960.
d. Purchases (before discounts): accounts payable balance on December 31, 19A, $28,320, and on December 31, 19B, $33,000; payments made on accounts during 19B, $46,000; cash discounts taken, $820.

Exercise 20–11

Give the journal entry to account for the missing amount in each of the following situations:

a. Prepaid Insurance: starting balance, $1,400; final balance, $1,900; amount expired, $1,200.
b. Allowance for Doubtful Accounts: starting balance, $5,000; final balance, $6,000; bad debts written off, $2,700.
c. Sinking Fund: starting balance, $90,000; final balance, $102,000; current payment to sinking fund, $20,000.
d. Premium on Bonds Payable: starting balance, $6,000; final balance, $4,500.
e. Capital Stock: starting balance, $200,000; final balance, $250,000; stock sold at par during the year, $30,000.
f. Retained Earnings: starting balance, $34,000 (credit); appropriation to reserve for bond sinking fund, $10,000; charge for stock dividend, $20,000; net income, $42,000; final balance, $36,000 (credit).
g. Accounts Receivable: starting balance, $25,000; collections on accounts, $27,000; bad accounts written off, $1,200; sales returns on account, $900; notes received on accounts, $3,000; final balance, $25,900.
h. Accounts Payable: starting balance, $17,300; cash paid on accounts, $30,200; cash discounts taken, $600; final balance, $15,500.

Exercise 20–12

For each account indicate the amount that should be reported on the income statement. Show computations.

			Beginning of Period	End of Period
a.	Deferred (prepaid) interest revenue		$ 50	$ 75
	Uncollected interest revenue earned		65	20
	Interest collected during period, $200.			
	Interest revenue should be reported as $____.			
b.	Accrued wages		$ 1,000	$ 1,800
	Prepaid wages		400	200
	Wages paid during period, $12,000.			
	Wages should be reported as $____.			
c.	Accounts receivable		$10,000	$14,000
	Notes receivable		2,000	1,000
	Cash sales	$120,000		
	Collections on accounts	40,000		
	Return sales (on account)	2,000		
	Collection on trade notes	5,000		
	Accounts written off as bad	500		
	Discounts given (on account)	600		
	Gross sales should be reported as $____.			
d.	Accounts payable		$ 5,000	$ 7,000
	Notes payable (trade)		10,000	6,000
	Payments on accounts	$ 40,000		
	Cash purchases	100,000		
	Discounts taken on credit purchases	1,000		
	Purchase returns (on account)	1,500		
	Payments on trade notes	8,000		
	Gross purchases should be reported as $____.			

Exercise 20–13

M. F. Sharp operated a hat shop but had not kept careful business records. The following data were secured from various memoranda and records:

An analysis of canceled checks revealed the following cash expenditures: expenses, $4,800; accounts payable, $9,200. Sharp stated that money was withdrawn from time to time from the cash register for personal living expenses. These withdrawals were estimated to total $3,600. All other receipts were deposited in the bank.

A list of assets and liabilities that was developed follows:

	Jan. 1, 19A	Dec. 31, 19A
Cash	$ 1,200	$ 900
Accounts receivable	1,000	1,500
Inventories	3,900	4,600
Prepaid expenses	100	60
Equipment (net)	4,200	3,800
	10,400	10,860
Accounts payable	1,100	1,300
Proprietorship	$ 9,300	$ 9,560

Required:

Prepare a worksheet to develop the income statement and balance sheet.

PROBLEMS

PART A: PROBLEMS 1–6

Problem 20–1

Franklin Corporation initiated several accounting changes during the year and discovered some errors. The changes and errors are given below. Assume the current year is 19C and that the accounting period ends December 31. The books have not been adjusted or closed at the end of 19C. Disregard income tax considerations.

a. The merchandise inventory at December 31, 19B, was overstated by $10,000.
b. During January 19A, extraordinary repairs on machinery was debited to repair expense; the $15,000 should have been debited to machinery which is being depreciated 15% per year on cost (no residual value).
c. A patent that cost $9,350 has been amortized for the past 7 years (excluding 19C) over its legal life of 17 years. It is now clear that its economic life will not be more than 12 years from acquisition date.
d. At the end of 19B revenue collected in advance of $3,000 was included in revenue. It is earned in 19C.
e. A machine that cost $8,000, acquired during January 19A was debited to Operating Expense. It has an estimated life of five years and a residual value of $3,000. Assume straight-line depreciation.
f. The rate for bad debts used has been ½ of 1% which has proven to be too low; therefore, for 19C and thereafter the rate is to be 1% of credit sales. The amount of the adjustment under the old rate was: 19A, $800; 19B, $1,000; and 19C, $1,100 (the amount for 19C has not been entered in the accounts since the adjusting entries have not been made).
g. During January 19A, a five-year insurance premium of $750 was paid which was debited to Insurance Expense.
h. At the end of 19B, accrued wages payable of $1,800 were not recorded; they were paid early in 19C.

Required:

1. For each of the above situations, identify the type of accounting change or error that was involved and briefly explain how each should be accounted for.
2. Give the appropriate entry to record the change and any subsequent adjusting entry in each instance at the end of 19C. Show computations. If no entry is needed, explain why.

Problem 20–2

On January 3, 19A, Cooper Company purchased a machine that cost $15,000. Although the machine has an estimated useful life of ten years and estimated residual value of $3,000, it was debited to expense when acquired. It is now December 19D, and the error was discovered. The average income tax rate is 45% and straight-line depreciation is used.

Required:

1. Give the entry to correct the accounts at the end of 19D and a second entry for depreciation for 19D. Assume the income tax return was correct; therefore, disregard income taxes.
2. Assume instead that the income tax return also was incorrect because of this error; therefore, additional taxes will have to be paid including an 8% penalty

per annum (for three years) on the amount of the tax underpayments. Give the entry to correct the accounts at the end of 19D and a second entry for depreciation for 19D.

Problem 20–3

The accounting department of Virginia Corporation had completed the comparative financial reports for the period ending 19C prior to the initiation of the first audit by an outside certified public accountant. This problem relates specifically to two changes recommended by the CPA after the statements were prepared by the company.

The statements have been summarized for problem purposes; details are provided only in respect to the recommended changes; the statements were:

	19A	19B	19C
Balance Sheet:			
Assets:			
Machinery	$ 300,000	$ 300,000	$ 300,000
Accumulated depreciation	(80,000)	(100,000)	(120,000)
Remaining assets	2,280,000	2,290,000	2,420,000
Total	$2,500,000	$2,490,000	$2,600,000
Liabilities	$ 373,000	$ 349,000	$ 410,000
Capital stock (200,000 shares)	2,000,000	2,000,000	2,000,000
Retained earnings	127,000	141,000	190,000
Total	$2,500,000	$2,490,000	$2,600,000
Income Statement:			
Sales (all on credit)	$1,000,000	$1,100,000	$1,200,000
Cost of goods sold	600,000	650,000	700,000
Gross margin	400,000	450,000	500,000
Operating expenses	300,000	330,000	360,000
Income taxes (assume 50%)	50,000	60,000	70,000
Income before extraordinary items	50,000	60,000	70,000
Extraordinary items	10,000	(20,000)	14,000
Less income tax effect	(3,000)	4,000	(5,000)
Net Income	$ 57,000	$ 44,000	$ 79,000
Earnings per share data:			
Income before extraordinary items	.250	.300	.350
Net income	.285	.220	.395
Statement of Retained Earnings:			
Beginning balance	$ 100,000	$ 127,000	$ 141,000
Net income	57,000	44,000	79,000
Dividends	(30,000)	(30,000)	(30,000)
Ending Balance	$ 127,000	$ 141,000	$ 190,000

On the basis of the examination the auditor insisted on the following changes:

1. Starting with 19C, change the loss experience rate on credit sales from one half of 1% to one fourth of 1%. This change was dictated by collection experi-

ence and losses during the past two years. These analyses indicate a drop in expected losses due to bad debts. The company has initiated a tight control on credit granting and stepped up collection efforts.

2. On January 1, 19A, a machine costing $20,000 (ten-year life, no residual value) was inadvertently debited to Operating Expense at that time. The error was discovered by the CPA at the end of 19C; the machine has seven more years of useful life (after 19C). Assume a 6% per annum tax penalty on net tax deficiencies for 19A and 19B only.

Required:

a. Analyze the nature of each of the changes.

b. Determine the effects on the financial statements assuming they are to be reported on comparative statements covering the three years.

c. Give the entry to effect the change including the correction of 19C entries. The books for 19C have been adjusted but not closed.

d. Compute the correct amounts for those items that would be affected for each of the three years.

Problem 20–4

Landon Company failed to recognize accruals and deferrals in the accounts. In addition, numerous other errors were made in computing net income. The net incomes for the past three years are given below along with a list of the items that were not recognized in the recordkeeping.

You are to set up a worksheet to correct net income for each year. Set up columns for the following: particulars, 19A, 19B, 19C, and accounts to be corrected. Key and briefly identify the errors under the "particulars" column and enter amounts under the respective years as plus or minus so that the last line will report corrected net income. Maintain equality of balances in the worksheet. Assume that all items are material. Disregard income tax effects.

	19A	*19B*	*19C*
a. Reported income	$4,000	$(3,500)	$10,000
Items not recognized at each year-end:			
b. Accrued expenses	400	250	300
c. Revenue collected in advance	100		200
d. Prepaid expenses	320	410	120
e. Revenue earned but not collected	170	140	
f. Annual depreciation overstated (not cumulative)		1,000	1,200
g. Annual provision for doubtful accounts understated	170	200	190
h. Goods purchased on December 31, included in ending inventory; not recorded until following year	460	210	150
i. Sales on December 31 not recorded until following year; the goods were not included in final inventory	290	770	390
j. Ending inventory overstated	130	240	290
k. Checks written and mailed on December 31 as payment on accounts payable; not recorded until next year	1,100	1,500	1,400
l. Bad debts not written off to allowance for doubtful accounts by year-end	800	950	1,170

Problem 20–5

R. Waters established a retail business in 19A. Early in 19D Waters entered into negotiations with J. Jones with a view to forming a partnership. You have been asked by Waters and Jones to check Waters' books for the past three years and to compute correct net income for each year.

The profits per clients' statements were as follows:

	Year Ending 12/31		
	19A	*19B*	*19C*
Net Income..............	$9,000	$10,109	$8,840

During the audit, you found the following:

		Year Ending 12/31		
		19A	*19B*	*19C*
	Omissions from the books:			
Item				
A	Accrued expenses at end of year	$2,160	$2,094	$4,624
B	Accrued (uncollected) revenue at end of year	200	–	–
C	Prepaid expenses at end of year	902	1,210	1,406
D	Deferred revenue at end of year	–	610	–
	Goods in transit at end of year omitted from inventory:			
E	For which purchase entry had been made	–	2,610	–
F	For which purchase entry had not been made......	–	–	1,710
	Other points requiring consideration:			
G	Depreciation on equipment had been recorded monthly by a charge to expense and a credit to an allowance for depreciation account at a blanket rate of 1% of end-of-month balances of equipment accounts. However, the sale during December 19B of certain equipment was entered as a debit to Cash and a credit to the asset account for the sale price of..	–	5,000	–
	(This equipment was purchased in July 19A at a cost of $6,000.)			
H	No allowance had been set up for uncollectible accounts. It is decided to set up one for the estimated probable losses as of December 31, 19C, for:			
	19B accounts	–	–	700
	19C accounts	–	–	1,500
	and to correct the charge against each year so that it will show the losses (actual and estimated) relating to that year's sales.			
	Accounts had been written off to expense as follows:			
	19A accounts	1,000	1,200	–
	19B accounts	–	400	2,000
	19C accounts	–	–	1,600

(AICPA adapted)

Problem 20–6

The records of AB Corporation have never been audited. At the end of 19C, the company prepared the following financial statements (summarized):

Income Statement:	
Sales and service revenue	$600,000
Expenses:	
Cost of goods sold	(350,000)
Distribution expenses	(120,000)
Administrative expenses	(60,000)
Pretax income	70,000
Income taxes	21,500
Net Income	$ 48,500
Balance Sheet:	
Assets:	
Cash	$ 23,000
Accounts receivable (net)	40,000
Inventory (periodic system)	110,000
Property, plant, and equipment (net)	160,000
Patent	8,000
Other assets	9,000
Total Assets	$350,000
Liabilities:	
Accounts payable	$ 80,000
Income taxes payable	15,000
Notes payable, long term (8%)	40,000
Total Liabilities	135,000
Stockholders' Equity:	
Common stock, par $10 (12,000 shares)	145,000
Retained earnings	80,000
Dividends paid	(10,000)
Total Stockholders' Equity	215,000
Total Liabilities and Stockholders' Equity	$350,000

The company is in the process of negotiating a large loan for expansion purposes. The bank has requested that an audit be performed. During the course of the audit, the following facts were determined:

a. The inventory at December 31, 19B, was overstated by $10,000.
b. The inventory at December 31, 19C, was overstated by $20,000.
c. The property, plant, and equipment was underdepreciated in 19B by $9,000 and in 19C by $12,000.
d. A three-year insurance premium of $900 paid on January 3, 19B, was debited to expense at that time.
e. Accrued wages were not recorded as follows: 19B, $800; 19C, $1,000.
f. The patent which originally cost $17,000 has been amortized to administrative expense over a 17-year life (including 19C). Evidence clearly indicates that its economic life will approximate 14 years from date of acquisition.
g. Service revenue earned but not yet collected were not recognized as follows: 19B, $5,000; 19C, $7,500.
h. A special delivery truck purchased January 19C at a cost of $13,000, was

debited to Distribution Expense at that time. The truck has an estimated useful life of ten years and an estimated residual value of $2,000. The company uses straight-line depreciation.

i. Bad debts amounting to $7,500 have not been written off.

Required:

1. Set up a worksheet to develop corrected amounts for the income statement and balance sheet. Complete the worksheet and key your entries. Assume the income tax expense amount is correct despite the above items.
2. Prepare a corrected income statement and balance sheet.

PART B: PROBLEMS 7–10

Problem 20–7

Cooper Hat Shop maintained incomplete records. After investigation you found the following assets and liabilities:

	Jan. 1, 19A	Dec. 31, 19A
Assets		
Cash on hand	$ 90	$ 160
Cash in bank	1,250	870
Accounts receivable	6,700	6,830
Inventory	3,100	3,800
Equipment (net of depreciation)	5,200	5,600
Prepaid insurance	120	60
	16,460	17,320
Liabilities		
Accounts payable	1,000	2,200
Bank loan		3,000
Accrued expenses payable	90	50
	1,090	5,250
Owner's Equity	$15,370	$12,070

An analysis of bank deposits and disbursements showed:

Deposits:	
Collections from customers	$8,900
Proceeds of bank loan	3,000
Additional investment by proprietor	1,200
Checks and charges:	
Payments to creditors	6,100
Expenses	4,500
Refunds on sales (allowances)	350
Proprietor's withdrawals	1,500
Interest on bank loan	30
Purchase of equipment	1,000

Required:

1. Compute the net income or loss by analyzing the changes in proprietorship.

2. Prepare a detailed income schedule including computation schedules.

Problem 20–8

Harper Company has maintained incomplete records. In applying for a loan that was very important to the company, a financial statement was needed. An analysis of the records provided the following data:

Cash receipts:	
Cash sales	$130,000
Collections on credit sales	43,000
Collections on trade notes	1,000
Purchase allowances	1,500
Miscellaneous	250
Cash payments:	
Cash purchases	84,500
Payments to trade creditors	34,100
Payment on mortgage plus annual interest	4,020
Sales commissions	7,200
Rent expense	2,400
General expenses	14,590
Other operating expenses	29,800
Sales returns ($3,000 of which $1,000 was cash)	1,000
Insurance (renewal three-year premium, April 1)	468
Fixed assets purchased	1,500

	Balances	
	Jan. 1, 19A	*Dec. 31, 19A*
Cash	$14,100	$10,172
Accounts receivable	13,000	18,000
Trade notes receivable	2,000	1,500
Inventory	10,000	18,400
Unexpired insurance	39	?
Prepaid interest expense	600	510
Trade accounts payable	26,500	23,800
Income taxes payable		1,984
Accrued operating expenses	600	400
Fixed assets (net)	35,400	33,290
Other assets	11,861	11,861
Capital stock	40,000	40,000
Mortgage payable (6% dated July 1)	20,000	?

No fixed assets were sold during the year.

Required:

Prepare a worksheet that will provide data for a detailed income statement for the year and a balance sheet for 19A. Show computations.

Problem 20–9

The following data were taken from the incomplete records of Baker's Sporting Goods Store:

	Balances	
	Jan. 1, 19A	Dec. 31, 19A
Accounts receivable	$ 2,300	$ 3,900
Notes receivable (trade)	1,500	2,000
Accrued interest on notes receivable	90	70
Prepaid interest on notes payable	75	60
Inventory	9,255	10,400
Prepaid expenses (operating)	100	130
Store equipment (net)	8,500	8,600
Other assets	–	500
Accounts payable	1,700	1,900
Notes payable (trade)	11,000	11,500
Notes payable (equipment)	–	500
Accrued interest payable	40	30
Accrued expenses (operating)	170	210
Prepaid interest revenue	30	40

An analysis of the checkbook, canceled checks, deposit slips, and bank statements provided the following summary for the year:

Balance, January 1, 19A		$4,200
Cash receipts:		
Cash sales	$23,000	
On accounts receivable	7,600	
On notes receivable	1,000	
Interest revenue	160	
Cash disbursements:		
Cash purchases	11,800	
On accounts payable	2,400	
On notes payable (trade)	500	
Interest expense	560	
Operating expenses	14,130	
Miscellaneous nonoperating expenses	970	
Other assets purchased	500	
Withdrawals by H. Baker	2,400	
Balance, December 31, 19A		$2,700

Required:

1. Compute the net income by analyzing the changes in the capital account.
2. Prepare a detailed income statement with supporting schedules; show computations.

Problem 20–10

Kelley-Thomas Company is a partnership that has not maintained adequate accounting records because it has been unable to employ a competent bookkeeper. The company sells hardware items to the retail trade and also wholesales to builders and contractors. As the company's CPA, you have been asked to prepare the company's financial statements as of June 30, 19B.

Your work papers provide the following post-closing trial balance at December 31, 19A:

Post-Closing Trial Balance
December 31, 19A

	Debit	Credit
Cash	$10,000	
Accounts receivable	8,000	
Allowance for bad debts		$ 600
Merchandise inventory	35,000	
Prepaid insurance	150	
Automobiles	7,800	
Accumulated depreciation—automobiles		4,250
Furniture and fixtures	2,200	
Accumulated depreciation—furniture and fixtures		650
Accounts payable		13,800
Bank loan payable		8,000
Accrued expenses		200
Kelley, capital		17,500
Thomas, capital		18,150
Total	$63,150	$63,150

You are able to collect the following information at June 30, 19B:

a. Your analysis of cash transactions, derived from the company's bank statements and checkbook stubs, is as follows:

Deposits:	
Cash receipts from customers	$65,000
($40,000 of this amount represents collections on receivables including deposited protested checks totaling $600)	
Bank loan, 1/2/19B (due 5/1/19B, 5%, face $8,000)	7,867
Bank loan, 5/1/19B (due 9/1/19B, 5%, face $9,000)	8,850
Sale of old automobile used by the business	20
Total Deposits	$81,737
Disbursements:	
Payments to merchandise creditors	$45,000
Payment to Internal Revenue Service on Thomas' 19B declaration of estimated income taxes	3,000
General expenses	7,000
Bank loan, 1/2/19B	8,000
Bank loan, 5/2/19B	8,000
Payment for new automobile for the business	2,400
Protested checks	900
Kelley withdrawals	5,000
Thomas withdrawals	2,500
Total Disbursements	$81,800

b. The protested checks, amounting to $900, include customers' checks totaling $600 that were redeposited and a $300 check from an employee that is still on hand.

c. Accounts receivable from customers for merchandise sales amounts to $18,000 on June 30, 19B, and includes accounts totaling $800 that have been placed with an attorney for collection. Correspondence with the client's attorney reveals that one of the accounts for $175 is uncollectible. Experience indicates that 1% of credit sales will prove uncollectible.

d. On April 1, 19B a new automobile was purchased. The list price of the automobile was $2,700, and $300 was allowed for the trade-in of an old automobile, even though the dealer stated that its condition was so poor that it could not be used. The old automobile cost $1,800 and was fully depreciated at December 31, 19A.

e. Depreciation is recorded by the straight-line method and is computed on acquisitions to the nearest full month. The estimated life for furniture and fixtures is ten years and for automobiles three years. [Salvage value is to be ignored in computing depreciation. No asset other than the car in item *(d)* was fully depreciated prior to June 30, 19B.]

f. Other data as of June 30, 19B, include the following:

Merchandise inventory..............	$37,500
Prepaid insurance.....................	80
Accrued expenses.....................	166

g. Accounts payable to merchandise vendors total $18,750 on June 30, 19B. There is on hand a $750 credit memorandum from a merchandise vendor for returned merchandise; the company will apply the credit to July merchandise purchases. Neither the credit memorandum nor the return of the merchandise had been recorded on the books nor included in the June 30 inventory.

h. Profits and losses are divided equally between the partners.

Required:

Prepare a worksheet that provides, on the accrual basis, information regarding transactions for the six months ended June 30, 19B, the results of the partnership operations for the period, and the financial position of the partnership at June 30, 19B. (No need to prepare formal financial statements or formal journal entries.)

(AICPA adapted)

Chapter 21

The Statement of Changes in Financial Position

Throughout the preceding chapters, references have been made to the statement of changes in financial position. Since the issuance of *APB Opinion No. 19,* "Reporting Changes in Financial Position" (March 1971), this statement has been required along with the income statement and balance sheet. The APB made it mandatory in the following terms:

> The Board concludes that information concerning the financing and investing activities of a business enterprise and the changes in its financial position for a period is essential for financial statement users, particularly owners and creditors, in making economic decisions. When financial statements purporting to present both financial position (balance sheet) and results of operations (statement of income and retained earnings) are issued, a statement summarizing changes in financial position should also be presented as a basic financial statement for each period for which an income statement is presented. These conclusions apply to all profit-oriented business entities, whether or not the reporting entity normally classifies its assets and liabilities as current and noncurrent.

Opinion No. 19 is particularly noteworthy in that it *(a)* made the statement mandatory, *(b)* required that it be developed on an *all-resources* basis, and *(c)* strongly recommended the title, statement of changes in financial position. This title is now used almost exclusively. The significance of the statement, as prescribed by *Opinion No. 19,* is that it requires the reporting of comprehensive information on the financing and investing activities of the business. The *financing activities* result in inflows of resources, and the *investing activities* result in outflows of resources.

The words "changes in financial position" are descriptive of the report because the inflows and outflows of resources are reflected in the changes in the asset, liability, and owners' equity accounts during the period. The statement focuses on reporting these changes.

The balance sheet reports the financial position at a *specific point in time;* consequently, it is not a change statement. In contrast, the income statement is a change statement; it reports the change in retained earnings *during* a specified period due to operations and extraordinary items. The details on the income statement serve to explain comprehensively specific factors that underlie net income. Similarly, the statement of retained earnings is a change statement; it explains, in detail, all of the changes in retained earnings *during* the specified period. Observe, that neither of these two change statements report the *causes* of the changes in assets, liabilities, and owners' equity (other than retained earnings). The statement of changes in financial position has the objective of filling this gap by reporting the other changes *during* the specified period. To do this, it reports changes in asset, liability, and owners' equity accounts measured in terms of *funds flow.*

This chapter discusses and illustrates development of the statement of changes in financial position in conformity with *APB Opinion No. 19.*

BASIC CHARACTERISTICS OF THE STATEMENT OF CHANGES IN FINANCIAL POSITION

The statement of changes in financial position measures the changes in assets, liabilities, and owners' equity during a specified period in terms of the inflows and outflows of funds. The key concept is that assets, liabilities, and owners' equity increase and decrease during a period only because funds are generated and used. For example, the disposition of an asset or incurrence of a liability generates an inflow of funds, and the acquisition of an asset or the payment of a liability causes an outflow or use of funds. The generation or inflows of resources is called *financing activities,* and the use or outflow of resources is called *investing activities.*

The statement of changes in financial position, as prescribed in *APB Opinion No. 19,* must be based on an *all-resources concept,* viz: "... the statement summarizing changes in financial position should be based on a broad concept embracing all changes in financial position" and "each reporting entity should disclose all important aspects of its financial and investing activities regardless of whether cash or other elements of working capital are directly affected." This means that the statement also must include all direct exchanges of nonfund items; that is, those transactions that involve neither the direct inflow or outflow of funds. For example, if a business acquires a machine (an asset acquisition) and pays for it in full by issuing its own capital stock to the vendor, there has been no inflow or outflow of funds. Under *Opinion No. 19,* transactions of this type must be reported as *(a)* an inflow of funds (from the issuance of the stock), and *(b)* an outflow of funds (due to acquisition of the asset).[1] This means that the statement must report:

1. The inflows of all funds during the period and an identification of these inflows with changes in assets, liabilities, and owners' equity.
2. The outflows of all funds during the period and an identification of these outflows with changes in assets, liabilities, and owners' equity.
3. The net increase or decrease in funds during the period.

In the preceding paragraphs, the terms "funds" and "resources" have been used interchangeably. The inflows and outflows reported on the statement of changes in financial position are measured in dollars of "funds." For measurement purposes, we must be precise in defining what is meant by "funds." This general term is used throughout financial and accounting literature with diverse meanings.[2] Because of this diversity, and the need for precise measurement, *APB Opinion No. 19* stated:

> The Statement may be in balanced form or in a form expressing the changes in financial position in terms of cash, or cash and temporary investments combined, of all quick assets, or of working capital.

Basically, this means that the inflows and outflows of funds may be measured in terms of *either:*

1. Cash (or cash plus near-cash items), or
2. Working capital (i.e., current assets minus current liabilities).

In elaboration of these two bases for measurement, the *Opinion* states:

> a. If the format shows the flow of cash, changes in other elements of working capital (e.g., in receivables, inventories, and payables) constitute sources and uses of cash and should accordingly be disclosed in appropriate detail in the body of the statement.
> b. If the format shows the flow of working capital and two-year comparative balance sheets are presented, the changes in each element of working capital for the current period (but not for earlier periods) can be computed by the user of the statements. Nevertheless, the Board believes that the objectives of the Statement usually require that the net change in working capital be analyzed in appropriate detail in a tabulation accompanying the Statement, and accordingly this detail should be furnished.

Because of these specifications, the statement of changes in financial position takes the following general formats:

---

[1] Prior to *APB Opinion No. 19*, these types of transactions were not reported on the old "funds flow statements." This was a significant improvement in meeting the requirements of the full-disclosure principle.

[2] Funds is a particularly troublesome term because of the wide diversity of use. It is sometimes viewed as cash only, cash plus near-cash items (such as short-term investments), working capital (i.e., current assets minus current liabilities), assets set aside for a specific purpose (such as a bond sinking fund), and it has yet another special meaning in governmental accounting.

(a) *Funds Measured on Cash, or Cash plus Near-Cash Basis*	*(b)* *Funds Measured on Working Capital Basis**
1. Sources of cash, or cash plus near-cash items (inflows).	*Part A*—Sources and Uses of Working Capital
2. Uses of cash, or cash plus near-cash items (outflows).	1. Sources of working capital (inflows).
3. Net increase or decrease in cash, or cash plus near-cash items.	2. Uses of working capital (outflows).
	3. Net increase or decrease in working capital.
	Part B—Changes in Working Capital Accounts
	4. Net Change in current asset accounts.
	5. Net change in current liability accounts.
	6. Net increase or decrease in working capital.

* The designations "Part A and Part B" are not specifically reflected on the statement; they are used here to facilitate explanation.

The *Opinion* permits the use of either approach; however, the specific basis used must be clearly disclosed; for example, "Cash Provided from Operations" or "Working Capital Provided from Operations."[3]

In order to establish a clear-cut delineation between the two approaches to measure "funds" and to facilitate discussion, this chapter discusses, separately, changes in financial position, working capital basis; and, changes in financial position, cash (or cash plus near-cash) basis.

Illustration of Cash Flows versus Working Capital Flows

The statement of changes in financial position reports significant differences in results when the flow of funds is measured on a cash flow basis rather than a working capital basis. The distinction between the cash flow and working capital bases is important in understanding the analyses and discussions in this chapter.

Exhibits 21–1 and 21–2 present analyses of a series of situations to illustrate the distinction between the cash and working capital bases. The resulting statement of changes in financial position is summarized in Exhibit 21–3. These exhibits should be studied carefully.

In Exhibit 21–1, observe that more cash than working capital was generated in each of the four situations. In item *(d)*, note that total sales caused an increase in working capital, whereas only cash sales caused an increase in cash. Expenses, whether paid or accrued as a current liability, caused a decrease in working capital, whereas only

---

[3] Since cash flows are generally viewed as more critical than working capital flows, and the latter often are larger in amount, there have been cases where an entity, by vague terminology, has led users to believe working capital amounts to be cash flow. The *Opinion* recognized this problem by stating: "Terms referring to 'cash' should not be used to describe amounts provided from operations unless all non-cash items have been appropriately adjusted."

cash expenses caused a decrease in cash. Depreciation expense does not affect either working capital or cash flow.

In transactions (*a*), (*b*), and (*c*), the differences between working capital and cash flows resulted from the short-term (current) receivables and payables; long-term receivables and payables have the same affect on both cash and working capital flows.

In transactions (*b*) and (*d*), the $2,000 gain on sale of plant assets did not generate cash or working capital; rather cash was increased by the amount of the sales price collected during the period and working capital was increased by the amount of the sales price "collected" in cash plus the short-term receivable recorded during the period. These situations will be discussed in detail subsequently.

Criteria for the Statement of Changes in Financial Position

In view of the wide diversity in the old funds statements, *APB Opinion No. 19* specifies certain criteria that should be satisfied in developing a statement of changes in financial position; these criteria may be summarized as follows:

1. The statement should be presented as a basic financial statement for each period in which an income statement is prepared.
2. The statement applies to all profit-oriented business entities whether or not there is a classification of assets and liabilities between current and noncurrent.
3. The statement should be based on a broad concept embracing all changes in financial position (not limited to working capital or cash). The statement should disclose all important changes in financial position for the period.
4. The statement should begin with the income or loss before extraordinary items, if any, and add back (or deduct) items recognized in determining income (or loss) which did not use (or provide) working capital or cash during the period.[4]
5. The items to be added back (or deleted) in 4 above should be clearly presented to avoid the interpretation that they provided funds (e.g., "Add – Expenses not requiring outlay of working capital in the current period.")
6. The effects of extraordinary items should be reported separately from the effects of normal operating items.
7. The effects of all financing and investing activities, as well as working capital or cash, should be *individually* disclosed.
8. If the format shows the flow of working capital and two-year comparative balance sheets are presented, the detailed changes in working capital accounts nevertheless must be presented.

[4] An acceptable alternative procedure, which gives the same result, starts with revenues that generated working capital or cash during the period and deducts therefrom operating expenses that required the outflow of working capital or cash. This approach has the advantage of not suggesting that "adjustments" to net income, such as depreciation, generated working capital or cash.

EXHIBIT 21–1
Inflows of Cash and Working Capital Compared

Transaction			*Cash Generated*	*Working Capital Generated*
a. Sold 1,000 shares of common stock during the period resulting in the following entry:				
Cash	3,000		$ 3,000	$ 3,000
Special receivable (current)	4,000			4,000
Special receivable (noncurrent)	5,000			
Common stock (par $10)		10,000		
Contributed capital in excess of par		2,000		
Total Generated			3,000	7,000
Observe that working capital was generated by the amount of current assets received and not by the selling price, the par value of the stock, or the noncurrent receivable.				
b. Sold a plant asset during the period resulting in the following entry:				
Cash	4,000		4,000	4,000
Notes receivable, short term	5,000			5,000
Mortgage receivable, long term	14,000			
Accumulated depreciation	10,000			
Plant asset		31,000		
Gain on sale of plant asset		2,000		
Total Generated			4,000	9,000
Observe that working capital generated was the sum of cash and current receivables recognized and not the amount of the sales price, the gain recognized on the sale, or the noncurrent receivable.				
c. Borrowed from the bank resulting in the following entry:				
Cash	30,000		30,000	+30,000
Notes payable, short term		20,000		−20,000
Notes payable, long term		10,000		
Total Generated			30,000	10,000
Observe that, although there was an inflow of cash of $30,000, working capital increased by only $10,000. This was because the increase in current liabilities for the short-term debt "offset" $20,000 of the inflow. Thus, working capital was increased by the amount of the increase in long-term debt.				
d. Net income for the period was as follows:				
Sales: Cash	$40,000		+40,000	+40,000
On account	10,000	$50,000		+10,000
Cost of goods sold:				
Goods purchased for cash	18,000		−18,000	−18,000
Goods purchased on account	7,000			− 7,000
Reduction in inventory	3,000	28,000		− 3,000
Gross margin		22,000		
Expenses:				
Paid in cash	10,000		−10,000	−10,000
Accrued (liability)	2,000			− 2,000
Depreciation	4,000	16,000		
Income from operations		6,000		
Gain on sale of plant asset		2,000		
Net Income		$ 8,000		
Total Generated from Operations*			12,000	10,000
Total Generated for the Period (all transactions)			$49,000	$36,000

* The results of this analysis are: *(a)* Net income on accrual basis of $8,000 converted to a working capital basis is $10,000, and *(b)* Net income on accrual basis of $8,000 converted to a cash basis is $12,000.

EXHIBIT 21–2
Outflows of Cash and Working Capital Compared

Transaction			Cash Applied	Working Capital Applied
a. Purchased a plant asset during the period resulting in the following entry:				
Plant asset	30,000			
Cash		3,000	$ 3,000	$ 3,000
Note payable, short term ...		7,000		7,000
Mortgage payable, long term		20,000		
Total Applied			3,000	10,000
Observe that working capital applied was the sum of the cash paid plus the current liability recognized, not the purchase price or the long-term debt incurred.				
b. Cash dividends declared, or paid, resulted in the following entry:				
Retained earnings	12,000			
Cash		8,000	8,000	8,000
Dividends payable (current)		4,000		4,000
Total Applied			8,000	12,000
c. Payments on debts during the period resulted in the following entry:				
Accounts payable	15,000			−15,000
Notes payable, long term.........	25,000			
Cash		40,000	40,000	+40,000
Total Applied			40,000	25,000
Observe that although $40,000 cash (and working capital) was disbursed, the decrease in net working capital was only $25,000. This was because the $15,000 paid on a working capital debt constituted an "offset." Thus the working capital applied was equivalent to the decrease in long-term debt only.				
d. Treasury stock purchased during the period resulted in the following entry:				
Treasury stock (at cost)	8,000			
Cash		5,000	5,000	5,000
Special payable, short term		3,000		3,000
Total Applied			5,000	8,000
Total Applied for the Period (all transactions)			$56,000	$55,000

EXHIBIT 21–3

Statement of Changes in Financial Position (summarized)*
For the Year Ended December 31, 19XX

	Cash Basis	Working Capital Basis
Resources generated (inflows):		
From operations	$12,000	$ 10,000
Sale of common stock.......................	3,000	7,000
Sale of plant assets	4,000	9,000
Borrowing	30,000	10,000
Total Resources Generated	49,000	36,000
Resources applied (outflows):		
Purchase of plant assets.....................	3,000	10,000
Dividends..	8,000	12,000
Debt retirement	40,000	25,000
Acquisition of treasury stock..............	5,000	8,000
Total Resources Applied...............	56,000	55,000
Net increase (decrease) in resources during period:		
Cash	$ (7,000)	
Working Capital..........................		$(19,000)

* This summarized statement omits some details required for full disclosure. It is summarized in this manner for instructional purposes; detailed statements will be presented subsequently.

9. Working capital or cash provided from (or used) should be appropriately described.
10. If the format shows the flow of cash, detailed changes in other working capital accounts should be disclosed in the body of the statement.
11. Terms referring to cash should not be used unless all noncash items have been appropriately adjusted.
12. There should be flexibility in form, content, and terminology in the statement; flexibility should be used to develop the presentation that is most informative in the circumstances.
13. It is strongly recommended that isolated statistics of working capital and cash, especially on a per-share basis, not be presented.

Next we discuss and illustrate the development of the statement of changes in financial position on the working capital basis in Part A and on the cash basis in Part B.

PART A—STATEMENT OF CHANGES IN FINANCIAL POSITION, WORKING CAPITAL BASIS

Working capital is composed of positive current items (cash, short-term investments, short-term receivables, inventories, prepaid expenses, etc.) and a series of negative current items (accounts payable, short-term notes payable, accrued liabilities, etc.); the difference represents a "liquid pool" of net working resources. In a transaction where there is a net increase in working capital, it is said that working capital has been generated, or provided; where there is a net decrease in working capital, it is said that working capital has been applied or used. Thus, transactions such as the payment of a current liability, the collection of a current receivable, or the purchase of inventory for cash will neither generate or use working capital; they merely rearrange the internal *content* of working capital. In contrast, certain other transactions, such as the purchase of a noncurrent asset for cash or the payment of a long-term debt, will cause both the *content* and the *amount* of net working capital to change.

A statement of changes in financial position, working capital basis, necessitates considerable analysis, except in very simple situations because the accounts do not directly provide the required data. Recall from the discussions above that the inflows and outflows of working capital are the result of changes in assets, liabilities, and owners' equity. Thus, the key to developing the statement of changes in financial position is an analysis of the transactions that affected these three groups of accounts. Clearly, in most situations, this will involve a rigorous analytical process. Since the statement summarizes the changes in assets, liabilities, and owners' equity *during* the period, the basic data needed for analytical purposes can be taken from the comparative balance sheets, the income statement, the statement of retained earnings, and other records concerning certain transactions.

On page 906, the statement of changes in financial position, working capital basis, was outlined; two distinct parts were identified: Part A—sources and uses of working capital and Part B—changes in working capital accounts. A statement for the Adamson Company detailed in this way is shown in Exhibit 21–5. This statement was developed from the comparative balance sheets and other data given in Exhibit 21–4.

The statement for Adamson Company (Exhibit 21–5) has four sig-

EXHIBIT 21–4

ADAMSON COMPANY
Summarized Data for the Year Ended December 31, 1976

	Dec. 31, 1976	*Dec. 31, 1975*
1. Balance Sheet:		
Cash	$ 45,000	$ 30,000
Accounts receivable (net)	38,000	40,000
Inventory	67,000	60,000
Long-term investments	162,000	200,000
Land	128,000	100,000
Building (net)	98,000	
Total	$538,000	$430,000
Accounts payable	$ 36,000	$ 40,000
Notes payable, short term (nontrade)	24,000	30,000
Bonds payable	35,000	50,000
Mortgage payable	100,000	
Common stock	295,000	270,000
Retained earnings	48,000	40,000
Total	$538,000	$430,000
2. Income Statement:		
Sales	$100,000	
Cost of goods sold	51,000	
Expenses (including interest and taxes)	16,000	
Total	67,000	
Net Income	$ 33,000	

3. Summary of transactions for 1976:
   a. Net income, $33,000.
   b. Purchases, $58,000, on account.
   c. Increase in inventory, $7,000.
   d. All sales were on credit.
   e. Expenses, $14,000, cash.
   f. Collection on accounts receivable, $102,000.
   g. Paid on accounts payable, $62,000.
   h. Sold bonds payable, $10,000, for cash at par value.
   i. Purchased land, $28,000 cash.
   j. Paid cash dividend, $25,000.
   k. Paid short-term notes payable, $6,000 (nontrade).
   l. Sold long-term investment for cash, $38,000 (sold at book value). Assume this is an extraordinary item for illustrative purposes.
   m. Retired $25,000 bonds payable by issuing common stock. The bonds retired were equivalent to the market value of the $25,000 stock issued.
   n. A new building was completed on the land in January 1976 at a cost of $100,000; gave an interest-bearing mortgage for the full amount. The building had an estimated life of 50 years and no residual value; straight-line depreciation.
   o. Depreciation expense, $2,000.

nificant captions, viz: (1) working capital generated (inflows of working capital), (2) working capital applied (outflows of working capital), (3) financing and investing activities that did not affect (flow through) working capital, and (4) a detailed report of changes in the internal content of working capital. This statement was designed to meet the *minimum* criteria specified in *APB Opinion No. 19*.

THE WORKSHEET APPROACH

In simple situations, such as the hypothetical Adamson Company, it would be possible to develop the statement of changes in financial position by inspection of the data or in a more rational way by using the elementary T-account approach. However, for more complex and typical situations, one would find the use of a worksheet more convenient if not essential. Practically, a worksheet is necessary to handle the large quantities of data and the complex transactions found in extensive problems frequently encountered by students and in real-life situations. Exhibit 21–6 presents an efficient worksheet that has been designed for analysis of the *nonworking capital accounts* and to sort out the data needed for each major classification on the statement of changes in financial position. In contrast to some worksheets (which involve complex reversing and reclassifying entries), this one simply requires summary restatement of the former entries without change of format or direction. The interim entries are keyed to the list of transactions given in Exhibit 21–4.

It is significant to observe that this worksheet is built around the fact that the *causes* of the changes in working capital and nonworking capital financing and investing activities can be found only in an analysis of the *nonworking capital accounts*. In contrast, an analysis of *only* the working capital accounts will divulge only changes in the *content* of working capital; observe that the worksheet does not deal with the content of working capital.

The worksheet is set up with four amount columns and five major side captions. The first column (beginning balance) and last column (ending balance) are taken from the two consecutive balance sheets; the two interim columns (debit and credit) are provided for "reconciling through analysis" the beginning and ending balances for each account listed. The five side captions may be explained as follows.

Basic Data:

1. Working Capital. This is the net working capital at the beginning and ending dates; it is entered on the worksheet only for balancing purposes since the worksheet does not deal with an analysis of the content of working capital accounts themselves.
2. Nonworking Capital Accounts. These are the accounts to be analyzed in detail; they are grouped by debit and credit balances only for convenience. The amounts are taken directly from the two consecutive balance sheets; sufficient space should be provided for accounts that may have had high activity during the period.

Data to be Elicited and Grouped from the Analysis:

3. Working Capital Generated. This section, paralleling the statement to be developed, provides for listing the various sources of working capital inflow. The amounts under this section normally will be reflected on the worksheet as debits.
4. Working Capital Applied. This section parallels the statement to be developed and the amounts normally will be reflected as credits.
5. Financing and Investing Activities Not Affecting Working Capital. This section parallels the statement and will reflect each direct exchange as both a debit and credit. This effect is due to the fact that the direct exchanges analyzed in this section, represent simultaneous financing and investing activities.

Completion of the worksheet involves an analysis of the transactions that affected a *nonworking capital account* (transactions that affect working capital *only* are not entered on the worksheet) and entering them on the worksheet in the debit-credit format used when they were originally recorded in the accounts; all debits and credits to working capital accounts (such accounts are not on the worksheet) are reflected under the third and fourth captions on the worksheet. Transactions that did not directly affect (flow through) working capital result in debits and credits under the fifth caption (financing and investing activities not affecting working capital). The following is a step-by-step approach to be used in completing the worksheet (Exhibit 21–6) for Adamson Company.

Step 1: Set up the four amount columns and the five major side captions.

Step 2: Enter the original data from the beginning and ending balance sheets for *(a)* working capital and *(b)* each nonworking capital account.

Step 3: Analyze each account; enter on the worksheet under "analysis of interim entries" only those transactions that affected one or more *nonworking capital accounts* so that all differences between the beginning and ending balances are finally accounted for. The analysis may be explained as follows (the entries are keyed to the transactions listed in Exhibit 21–4).

	Original Entry		*Worksheet Entry*	
a. Net income for the period:				
Income summary	33,000			
Working capital generated, net income			33,000	
Retained earnings		33,000		33,000

Analysis: Net income for the period *(a)* generated working capital, and *(b)* affected a noncurrent account (Retained Earnings). The worksheet entry repeats the original entry except for the debit; on the worksheet this debit reflects the generation of working capital.

EXHIBIT 21–5

ADAMSON COMPANY
Statement of Changes in Financial Position, Working Capital Basis
For the Year Ended December 31, 1976

Part A—Sources and Uses of Working Capital

Working Capital Generated:		
From operations:		
Net income before extraordinary items	$33,000	
Add expenses not requiring working capital in the current period:		
Depreciation	2,000	
Total working capital generated by operations (exclusive of extraordinary items)		$ 35,000
Extraordinary items generating working capital:		
Long-term investments sold		38,000
Other sources of working capital:		
Bonds payable issued		10,000
Total Working Capital Generated		83,000
Working Capital Applied:		
Land purchased	$28,000	
Cash dividends paid	25,000	
Total Working Capital Applied		53,000
Net Increase in Working Capital during the Period		$ 30,000
Financing and Investing Activities Not Affecting Working Capital:		
Bonds retired by issuing common stock		$ 25,000
Building acquired in exchange for long-term mortgage payable		100,000
Total		$125,000

Part B—Changes in Working Capital Accounts

	Balances December 31		
	1976	*1975*	*Working Capital Increase (decrease)*
Current Assets:			
Cash	$ 45,000	$ 30,000	$15,000
Accounts receivable (net)	38,000	40,000	(2,000)
Inventory	67,000	60,000	7,000
Total Current Assets	150,000	130,000	
Current Liabilities:			
Accounts payable	$ 36,000	$ 40,000	4,000
Notes payable—short term (nontrade)	24,000	30,000	6,000
Total Current Liabilities	60,000	70,000	
Working Capital	$ 90,000	$ 60,000	$30,000

EXHIBIT 21–6

ADAMSON COMPANY
Worksheet to Develop Statement of Changes in Financial Position, Working Capital Basis
For the Year Ended December 31, 1976

Debits	Beginning Balance Dec. 31, 1975	Analysis of Interim Entries		Ending Balance Dec. 31, 1976
		Debit	Credit	
1. Working Capital	60,000	(*p*) 30,000		90,000
2. Nonworking Capital Accounts:				
Long-term investments	200,000		(*l*) $ 38,000	162,000
Land	100,000	(*i*) 28,000		128,000
Building (net)		(*n* – 1) 100,000	(*o*) 2,000	98,000
	360,000			478,000
Credits				
Bonds payable	50,000	(*m* – 1) 25,000	(*h*) 10,000	35,000
Mortgage payable			(*n* – 2) 100,000	100,000
Common stock	270,000		(*m* – 2) 25,000	295,000
Retained earnings	40,000	(*j*) 25,000	(*a*) 33,000	48,000
	360,000	208,000	208,000	478,000
3. Working Capital Generated:				
From operations:				
Net income		(*a*) 33,000		
Adjustments for nonworking capital items:				
Depreciation		(*o*) 2,000		
Extraordinary items generating working capital:				
Long-term investments sold		(*l*) 38,000		
Other sources of working capital:				
Bonds payable issued		(*h*) 10,000		
4. Working Capital Applied:				
Land purchased			(*i*) 28,000	
Cash dividends paid			(*j*) 25,000	
5. Financing and Investing Activities not Affecting Working Capital:				
Bonds retired by issuing common stock		(*m* – 2) 25,000	(*m* – 1) 25,000	
Building purchased; gave long-term mortgage		(*n* – 2) 100,000	(*n* – 1) 100,000	
Increase in net working capital for the period			(*p*) 30,000	
		208,000	208,000	

Source of data: Exhibit 21–4.

The following transactions are not entered on the worksheet since each one did not affect a noncurrent account: *(b)* purchases on account; *(c)* inventory increase; *(d)* sales on account; *(e)* expenses paid in cash; *(f)* collection on accounts receivable; *(g)* payment on accounts payable; and *(k)* payment on short-term notes payable.

	Original Entry		*Worksheet Entry*	
h. Sold bonds payable for cash:				
Cash	10,000			
Working capital generated, Other sources			10,000	
Bonds payable		10,000		10,000

Analysis: This worksheet entry corresponds to the original entry except that the original debit to a working capital account (Cash) is reflected in the lower part of the worksheet as a debit to Working Capital Generated, Other Sources. The original debit to Cash (a working capital account) cannot be entered as such on the worksheet since no working capital accounts are listed; this is a built-in safety feature.

i. Purchased land for cash:				
Land	28,000		28,000	
Cash		28,000		
Working capital applied				28,000

Analysis: This transaction used working capital; a nonworking capital account, Land, was affected. This worksheet entry corresponds to the original entry except for the original credit to working capital (Cash); on the worksheet this is reflected as a credit under Working Capital Applied.

j. Paid cash dividend:				
Retained earnings	25,000		25,000	
Cash		25,000		
Working capital applied				25,000

Analysis: This transaction used working capital; a noncurrent account, Retained Earnings, was affected. The worksheet entry reflects the original credit to Cash as a credit under Working Capital Applied.

k. Paid short-term notes payable: Not entered on the worksheet since noncurrent accounts were not affected.

l. Sold long-term investment for cash:				
Cash	38,000			
Working capital generated, Other sources			38,000	
Long-term investments		38,000		38,000

Analysis: This transaction generated working capital; a noncurrent account, Long-Term Investments, was affected. Since the investment was sold at book value there was no gain or loss. The worksheet entry reflects the original debit (to Cash) under working capital generated as a debit.

	Original Entry		Worksheet Entry	
m. Retired bonds payable by issuing common stock:				
Bonds payable	25,000		25,000 ($m-1$)	
Common stock		25,000		25,000 ($m-2$)
Financing and investing activities not affecting working capital			25,000 ($m-2$)	25,000 ($m-1$)

Analysis: This transaction is a *direct exchange*, and as such it (1) did not affect working capital, and (2) affected only noncurrent accounts, yet it constituted both a financing and an investing activity. It must be reflected on the statement of changes in financial position; therefore, it must be entered on the worksheet under the caption Financing and Investing Activities Not Affecting Working Capital. Obviously, if one were to simply repeat the original entry on the worksheet this aspect would be omitted. As a consequence, it is desirable to reflect on the worksheet two interrelated and concurrent entries as shown above. The view is that entry ($m-1$) reflects payment of a debt (the debit) and an outflow for that purpose (the credit), and entry ($m-2$) reflects the issuance of common stock (the credit) and an inflow from that source (the debit). This is what is sometimes called an "in and out" item of financing and investing. At this point you should follow this entry through the worksheet and back to the statement (Exhibit 21-5).

	Original Entry		Worksheet Entry	
n. Purchased new building; gave long-term mortgage note for purchase price:				
Building	100,000		100,000 ($n-1$)	
Mortgage payable...............		100,000		100,000 ($n-2$)
Financing and investing activities not affecting working capital			100,000 ($n-2$)	100,000 ($n-1$)

Analysis: This transaction is a direct exchange; it is the same type as analyzed in *(m)* above. This transaction (1) did not affect working capital, and (2) affected only noncurrent accounts; yet it constituted a financing and investing activity. It is reflected on the worksheet as an "in and out" item as explained immediately above.

	Original Entry		Worksheet Entry	
o. Depreciation expense for the period:				
Expenses, depreciation	2,000			
Working capital generated, net income (adjustment).........			2,000	
Accumulated depreciation ...		2,000		2,000

Analysis: This transaction did not generate working capital, yet it affected a noncurrent account—Accumulated Depreciation. Since depreciation is an expense it was deducted from net income; however, it did not require the use of working capital in the period of recognition, in contrast to other expenses that are either paid in the period or recognized as a current liability (accrual). Significantly, we see an item that reduced net income but did not require working capital; as a consequence, to determine the amount of working capital generated from operations, depreciation must be added back. The worksheet entry (a debit to Working Capital Generated, Net Income) reflects this effect. At this point you should follow this item through the worksheet and back to the statement.

p. Entry *(p)* does not represent a transaction; it is an optional entry that may be made simply to balance the worksheet. After this entry is made, two internal checks for accuracy and completeness can be made, viz:

1. Check each line on the worksheet horizontally to be sure that the interim entries clear out all differences between the beginning and ending balances.
2. Total the debit and credit columns under "Analysis of Interim Entries" at two levels on the worksheet as illustrated; the worksheet debits and credits in these columns must balance at these two levels.

One of the special features of this worksheet is that the formal statement of changes in financial position (Exhibit 21–5) can be copied directly from the lower portion of the worksheet, adding thereto the last section wherein the *content* of the working capital accounts is presented. The last section (Part B in Exhibit 21–5) is copied directly from the balance sheet.[5]

For examination and problem-solving purposes by students, this worksheet generally will suffice without the added clerical burden of preparing a formal statement of changes in financial position.

Some Special Problems

In developing the worksheet the following special situations may require careful attention.

1. Transactions that affect only owners' equity accounts. Generally, such changes (e.g., a common stock dividend on common stock) are not reported on the statement of changes in financial position. However, *APB Opinion No. 19* specifies that the statement should disclose: "Conversion of long-term debt or preferred to common stock." This is interpreted to mean that basic changes in owners' equity should be reported. The exchange of preferred stock for common stock would be reflected on the worksheet and on the statement as an "in and out" item similar to that previously illustrated for the exchange of debt for stock.

2. Amortization of long-term items. Long-term (noncurrent) amortizations (either debits or credits) reduce or increase reported net income, although they do not require or provide working capital during the current period. Examples of this type of item are discount and premium on bonds. To illustrate, assume $1,000 discount on bonds payable is being amortized over a ten-year period on a straight-line basis. The annual amortization of $100 would appear on the income statement as

[5] For this reason some accountants consider Part B to be redundant; however, it is required by *APB Opinion No. 19*.

an increase in bond interest expense, although it would not require the application of working capital during the current period. Therefore, the worksheet entry would be a debit to "Net Income–Adjustment" similar to depreciation and a credit to Discount on Bonds Payable.

3. Reclassification of a long-term liability. When a long-term liability is payable within the upcoming year it is usually reclassified as a current liability. The reclassification has the effect of decreasing working capital; therefore, there should be recognition on the worksheet and in the statement of a working capital application. The entry on the worksheet would be a debit to Long-Term Liabilities and a credit to Working Capital Applied.

COMPREHENSIVE ILLUSTRATION

The comprehensive illustration that follows for F. P. Corporation presents a situation where the data are more complex and the analysis more involved than those shown in the previous example. The illustration includes the following:

Exhibit 21–7–Basic data for illustration
Exhibit 21–8–Worksheet to develop statement of changes in financial position, working capital basis
Exhibit 21–9–Statement of changes in financial position, working capital basis

The analysis of transactions and the related entries on the worksheet (Exhibit 21–8) are explained below; the discussions and entries are keyed to the basic data given in Exhibit 21–7. Only those transactions that represent situations different from those explained above for Adamson Company are discussed.

	Original Entry		*Worksheet Entry*	
h. Common stock dividend issued:				
Retained earnings	10,000		10,000	
Common stock		10,000		10,000

Analysis: This transaction *(a)* did not affect working capital and *(b)* did not represent a financing or investing activity, although two noncurrent accounts were affected. It merely represents a transfer of one equity account to another and is generally considered not to be encompassed in the provisions of *APB Opinion No. 19.* The worksheet entry, identical to the original entry, must be made for clearing purposes.

	Original Entry		*Worksheet Entry*	
j. Sold land for cash at a gain:				
Cash	53,000			
Working capital generated, extraordinary item			53,000	
Land		35,000		35,000
Gain on sale of land (assumed to be an extraordinary item)		18,000		
Working capital generated, net income (adjustment)				18,000

EXHIBIT 21–7

F. P. CORPORATION
Basic Data for Illustration

Comparative Balance Sheet Data:

	Amounts Reported at–	
Debits	*12/31/19A*	*12/31/19B*
Cash	$ 30,000	$ 84,000
Short-term investments (X Company stock)	10,000	8,000
Accounts receivable (net)	50,000	80,000
Inventory	20,000	30,000
Prepaid expenses		2,000
Land	60,000	25,000
Machinery	80,000	90,000
Accumulated depreciation	(20,000)	(27,900)
Other assets	29,000	39,000
Discount on bonds payable	1,000	900
Total debits	$260,000	$331,000
Credits		
Accounts payable	$ 40,000	$ 55,000
Dividends payable		15,000
Bonds payable	70,000	55,000
Common stock, nopar	100,000	131,000
Preferred stock, nopar	20,000	30,000
Retained earnings	30,000	45,000
Total Credits	$260,000	$331,000

Income Statement Data:

	12/31/19B
Sales	$180,000
Cost of goods sold	90,000
Expenses	55,000
Depreciation	7,900
Amortization of discount on bonds payable	100
Total Expenses	153,000
Income before extraordinary items	27,000
Extraordinary items:	
Gain on special sale of land (net of tax)	18,000
Loss on bond retirement	(1,000)
Net Income	$ 44,000

Additional data; summary of selected transactions for the year:

a. Sales (on account), $180,000.
b. Purchases (on account), $100,000.
c. Inventory increase, $10,000.
d. Expenses, $55,000 (including income taxes).
e. Depreciation, $7,900.
f. Prepaid expenses increased $2,000 during the year.
g. Cash dividend declared, $15,000.
h. Common stock dividend issued; retained earnings debited for $10,000.
i. Issued bonds payable for cash, $5,000.
j. Sold land for $53,000 cash; book value, $35,000 (net of tax); for illustrative purposes, assumed to be an extraordinary item.
k. Purchased machinery for $10,000 cash.
l. Purchased short-term investments, $2,000 cash.
m. Paid dividend on preferred stock with short-term investments, $4,000.
n. Retired $20,000 bonds payable by issuing common stock; the common stock had a fair market value of $21,000 (assumed to be extraordinary for illustrative purposes).
o. Collected cash on accounts receivables, $150,000.
p. Paid cash on accounts payable, $85,000.
q. Acquired other assets for $10,000 by issuing preferred stock.
r. Amortization of discount on bonds payable, $100.

Analysis: This transaction generated working capital by the amount of cash received ($53,000) rather than by the amount of the gain ($18,000). Since net income included the gain, it must be *removed from the net income amount* through an adjustment (credit on the worksheet). This has the effect of restoring net income to the amount de-

EXHIBIT 21–8

F. P. CORPORATION
Worksheet to Develop Statement of Changes in Financial Position, Working Capital Basis
For the Year Ended December 31, 19B

Debits	Balance Dec. 31, 19A	Analysis of Interim Entries: Debit		Analysis of Interim Entries: Credit		Balance Dec. 31, 19B
Working Capital	70,000	(s)	64,000			134,000
Nonworking Capital Accounts:						
Land	60,000			(j)	35,000	25,000
Machinery	80,000	(k)	10,000			90,000
Other assets	29,000	(q − 1)	10,000			39,000
Discount on bonds payable	1,000			(r)	100	900
Total	240,000					288,900
Credits						
Accumulated depreciation	20,000			(e)	7,900	27,900
Bonds payable	70,000	(n − 2)	20,000	(i)	5,000	55,000
Common stock	100,000			(h)	10,000	131,000
				(n − 1)	21,000	
Preferred stock	20,000			(q − 2)	10,000	30,000
Retained earnings	30,000	(g)	15,000	(a)	44,000	45,000
		(h)	10,000			
		(m)	4,000			
Total	240,000		133,000		133,000	288,900
Working Capital Generated:						
Net income		(a)	44,000			
To remove gain on land				(j)	18,000	
To remove loss on bonds		(n − 2)	1,000			
Adjustments:						
Depreciation expense		(e)	7,900			
Amortization of bond discount		(r)	100			
Extraordinary items:						
Land sold		(j)	53,000			
Other sources of working capital:						
Bonds payable sold		(i)	5,000			
*Nonworking capital resources generated:						
Common stock issued to retire bonds		(n − 1)	21,000			
Preferred stock issued for other assets		(q − 2)	10,000			
Working Capital Applied:						
Dividends declared				(g)	15,000	
Machinery purchased				(k)	10,000	
Dividends on preferred stock, paid with short-term investments				(m)	4,000	
*Nonworking capital resources applied:						
Bonds payable retired by issuing common stock				(n − 2)	21,000	
Other assets acquired by issuing preferred stock				(q − 1)	10,000	
Increase in net working capital for the period				(s)	64,000	
			142,000		142,000	

*On this worksheet these two captions are illustrative of a variation in format; observe that these two captions were combined in Exhibit 21–6.

sired—income before extraordinary items. This transaction should be traced through the worksheet and then to the statement of changes in financial position.

	Original Entry		Worksheet Entry	
m. Paid dividends with short-term investments (X Company stock):				
Retained earnings	4,000		4,000	
Investments, short term		4,000		
Working capital applied				4,000

Analysis: This transaction used working capital (short-term investments) and affected a nonworking capital account.

	Original Entry		Worksheet Entry	
n. Retired bonds payable by issuing common stock:				
Bonds payable	20,000		20,000 (n − 2)	
Extraordinary loss on bond retirement	1,000		1,000 (n − 2)	
Common stock		21,000		21,000 (n − 1)
Financing and investing activities not affecting working capital			21,000 (n − 1)	21,000 (n − 2)

Analysis: This transaction was a direct exchange that affected two nonworking capital accounts but did not affect working capital; it is an in and out item that must be reported on the statement (see prior discussion). Since common stock with a market value of $21,000 was issued to retire bonds payable with a carrying value of $20,000, a $1,000 loss on retirement was recognized (as required by *APB Opinion No. 29*) and classified as an extraordinary item (as required by FASB *Statement No. 4*).[6]

	Original Entry		Worksheet Entry	
q. Acquired other assets by issuing preferred stock:				
Other assets	10,000		10,000 (q − 1)	
Preferred stock		10,000		10,000 (q − 2)
Financing and investing activities not affecting working capital			10,000 (q − 2)	10,000 (q − 1)

Analysis: This transaction is a direct exchange that did not affect working capital; it affected two nonworking capital accounts. It is an "in and out" item that represents a financing and investing activity; hence it must be recognized on the worksheet (see prior discussion of direct exchanges).

	Original Entry		Worksheet Entry	
r. Amortization of discount on bonds payable:				
Expenses, amortization of bond discount	100			
Working capital generated, net income (adjustment)			100	
Discount on bonds payable		100		100

Analysis: This transaction did not affect working capital; it affected

[6] *APB Opinion No. 29*, "Accounting for Nonmonetary Transactions" (May 1973), specifies with certain exceptions that direct exchanges shall be recorded to recognize fair market value. FASB *Statement of Financial Accounting Standards No. 4* (March 1975) specifies that loss or gain on early extinguishment of debt shall be reported as an extraordinary item (if material in amount), net of tax. The above amounts are assumed to be net of tax.

a nonworking capital account—Discount on Bonds Payable—and reported net income. Since it was deducted from net income, but did not affect working capital, it must be *added back to net income as a nonworking capital charge*. This item is similar in effect to depreciation expense for the period previously discussed.

The following transactions were not entered on the worksheet since they affected only working capital accounts: *(a)*, *(b)*, *(c)*, *(d)*, *(f)*, *(l)*, *(o)*, and *(p)*. Entry *(s)* is an optional balancing entry on the worksheet.

STATEMENT FORMAT

APB Opinion No. 19 stated that "Provided that these guides are met, the statement may take whatever form gives the most useful portrayal of the financing and investing activities and the changes in financial position of the reporting entity." In the light of this statement there is a range of variation in the forms developed by industry. Clearly, numerous variations of form can meet the criteria specified in *Opinion No. 19* (see list of criteria on page 907).

In Exhibit 21–5, and at the end of Chapters 4, 5, and 24, various statement formats are illustrated. A statement of changes in financial position for F. P. Corporation is presented in Exhibit 21–9 that maximizes explanation and disclosure, and uses some variation in terminology. Note in particular the manner of reporting the direct-exchange transactions. In Exhibit 21–9 for F. P. Corporation, the effects of direct exchanges are reported twice, under working capital generated and under working capital used. In contrast, direct exchanges in Exhibit 21–4 for Adamson Company are reported once under a separate caption. These are mere reporting differences and do not suggest substantive differences in the concept of analyzing and reporting direct exchanges.

PART B—STATEMENT OF CHANGES IN FINANCIAL POSITION, CASH BASIS (AND CASH PLUS NEAR CASH)

The critical problems of cash planning and cash control create a serious need by internal management for meaningful statements of cash inflows and outflows coupled with the other financing and investing activities. Similarly, in decision making the external investor has a critical need for relevant information on the ability of the enterprise to generate cash inflows, the cash requirements, and the related noncash financing and investing activities. Although a statement of changes in financial position prepared on a working capital basis, as discussed in the first part of this chapter, serves useful purposes, similar statements prepared on a cash flow basis are more relevant both for internal management and the investor. Clearly, cash, as opposed to the concept of working capital, is understood by the investor. Also, working capital problems tend to be reflected first in the cash position. A statement of changes in financial position prepared on the cash basis would preclude the need for a similar statement on the working capital basis, although the opposite is not the case.

In view of the greater relevance of cash-based statements, one may

EXHIBIT 21–9

F. P. CORPORATION
Statement of Changes in Financial Position, Working Capital Basis
For the Year Ended December 31, 19B

Financial Resources Generated:		
Working capital generated:		
Income before extraordinary items ($44,000 – $18,000) ...	$26,000	
Add: Expenses not requiring working capital in the current period:		
Loss on bonds ...	1,000	
Depreciation expense ...	7,900	
Amortization of bond discount ...	100	
Working capital generated by operations exclusive of extraordinary items ...		$ 35,000
Extraordinary items:		
Land sold ...		53,000
Other sources of working capital:		
Bonds payable sold ...		5,000
Total Working Capital Generated ...		93,000
Financial resources generated not affecting working capital:		
Common stock issued to retire bonds payable ...	21,000	
Preferred stock issued to acquire other assets ...	10,000	
Total ...		31,000
Total Financial Resources Generated ...		$124,000
Financial Resources Applied:		
Working capital applied:		
Cash dividends declared ...	$15,000	
Machinery purchased ...	10,000	
Dividends paid on preferred stock with short-term investments ...	4,000	
Total Working Capital Applied ...		$ 29,000
Financial resources applied not affecting working capital:		
Bonds payable retired by issuing common stock ...	21,000	
Other assets acquired by issuing preferred stock ...	10,000	
Total ...		31,000
Increase in net working capital during the period ...		64,000
Total Financial Resources Applied ...		$124,000

Changes in Working Capital Accounts:

	Account Balances		*Working Capital Increase (decrease)*
	12/31/19B	*12/31/19A*	
Current Assets:			
Cash ...	$ 84,000	$ 30,000	$54,000
Short-term investments ...	8,000	10,000	(2,000)
Accounts receivable (net) ...	80,000	50,000	30,000
Inventory ...	30,000	20,000	10,000
Prepaid expenses ...	2,000		2,000
Total Current Assets ...	204,000	110,000	
Current Liabilities:			
Accounts payable ...	55,000	40,000	(15,000)
Dividends payable ...	15,000		(15,000)
Total Current Liabilities ...	70,000	40,000	
Working Capital ...	$134,000	$ 70,000	$64,000

ask the question as to why working-capital-based statements have tended to dominate in published financial statements (although not in internal managerial accounting reports). The answer probably lies in the facts that working capital based statements *(a)* developed first in external reports, *(b)* are easier to prepare, *(c)* divulge less about the critical financing strengths and weakness of the enterprise, *(d)* have been given more attention in textbooks on financial accounting, and *(e)* represent precedent (which is difficult to change). In *Opinion No. 19* the APB specified that the statement of changes in financial position could be presented either on a working capital or cash basis. Unfortunately the APB did not specifically recognize the greater relevance of the cash flow approach.[7] However, a major concession to the cash flow approach is evidenced in the *Opinion* by the requirement, under the working capital approach, that: "Whether or not working capital flow is presented in the Statement, net changes in each element of working capital (as customarily defined) should be appropriately disclosed for at least the current period, either in the Statement or in a related tabulation." In contrast, in respect to the cash flow approach the *Opinion* states: "If the format shows the flow of cash, changes in other elements of working capital (e.g., in receivables, inventories, and payables) constitute sources and uses of cash and should accordingly be disclosed in appropriate detail in the *body* of the Statement" (italics supplied). The difference in reporting on a cash basis versus a working capital basis can be observed by comparing the illustrations in this chapter in Parts A and B since identical data (for Adamson Company and F. P. Corporation) are used in both parts.

Changing from the working capital basis to the cash basis is not difficult; the latter simply requires the additional analysis of the noncash working capital items. Thus, more transactions must be analyzed and reported. In respect to the cash basis statement, a separate schedule of the changes in working capital accounts (Part B of the statement illustrated in Exhibit 21–5) is not required because the cash flow analysis incorporates these data in the basic report.

The statement of changes in financial position on a cash basis can be developed by measuring funds as *(a)* cash only, or *(b)* cash plus near-cash items. The total of cash plus short-term investments is generally used because this is consistent with the definition of short-term marketable securities. Cash only will be illustrated for the Adamson Company, and cash plus short-term investments for the F. P. Corporation.[8]

---

[7] There are a few situations where the cash basis is required, such as in the land development industry and for companies that do not classify assets and liabilities as current (primarily financial institutions). The Trueblood Committee Report on the objectives of financial statements took a strong stand for cash flow reports on the grounds that users are more concerned with cash flows.

[8] It is sometimes suggested that either a summary of the Cash account, or a conversion of the income statement to a cash basis, adequately reports cash flows for the period. Both of these approaches are superficial, incomplete, and are apt to be misleading. In contrast, a statement of changes in financial position, cash basis, focuses on the changes in assets, liabilities, and owners' equity, on an all-resources basis, that is measured in terms of cash. Conceptually, it is the same as the working capital basis except that funds are measured as cash rather than as working capital.

In Exhibits 21–1 and 21–2, a series of transactions were analyzed to compare the cash flow and working capital effects. The resulting statement of changes in financial position (summarized) for each basis were presented in Exhibit 21–3. You should return to those illustrations and the related discussions for restudy at this point. Observe that cash generated *from net income* was $12,000. Alternatively, this amount could have been derived by starting with reported net income and adding and deducting the noncash items that are reflected either directly or indirectly on the income statement. In effect, this would convert accrual basis, net income as reported on the income statement, to a cash flow basis. Using the data in Exhibit 21–1, the alternative computation is:

Net income reported (accrual basis)	$ 8,000
Add (deduct) noncash items affecting the income statement:	
Trade receivables increase	(10,000)
Trade payables increase	7,000
Inventory decrease	3,000
Depreciation expense	4,000
Accrued expense increase	2,000
Gain on sale of fixed asset	(2,000)
Cash Generated from Operations	$12,000

In Exhibit 21–3, you can observe the fundamental distinctions between a statement developed on a cash basis versus a working capital basis. With these concepts and distinctions in mind, we can proceed directly to the development of the statement of changes in financial position on a cash basis and a cash plus near-cash basis in more complex situations.

WORKSHEET TO DEVELOP STATEMENT OF CHANGES IN FINANCIAL POSITION, CASH BASIS

Development of a statement of changes in financial position, cash basis, except in the simplest of situations, requires an organized approach to analyzing the transactions for the period. For complex situations and those involving a large number of transactions, the worksheet approach is necessary. Since the general format of the statement of changes in financial position is the same under either the working capital or cash approaches, we can utilize the same worksheet approach for each. In order to simplify the illustrations in this part of the chapter we have decided to parallel the worksheet format shown in Exhibit 21–8 with a few changes in terminology (essentially from the words *working capital to cash*). For the first example, we will utilize the data for Adamson Company given in Exhibit 21–4. The cash basis worksheet for these data is shown in Exhibit 21–10. In preparing the worksheet the summarized transactions are analyzed and entered in debit-credit format under the pair of columns headed "Analysis of Interim Entries." Observe that similar to the working capital basis, the original entries are repeated with adaptation and entry at the bottom of the worksheet for the original debits and credits to Cash. Fundamentally the worksheet reflects the following major side captions:

Cash–Entered on the worksheet simply as a balancing feature.

Noncash Accounts–All of the noncash accounts from the beginning and ending balance sheets are entered on the worksheet for analysis and reconciliation. It is in the analysis of the noncash accounts that we find the sources and applications of cash; or to state it another way, to identify the *causes* of the changes in cash during the period. As with the working capital approach, we are also able to identify and "pull out" the effects of the "in and out" items. Recall that these are noncash investing and financing activities that did not affect (flow through) cash.

Cash Generated–This major caption is subdivided for net income, extraordinary items, other sources of cash, and finally for the noncash financing activities.

Cash Used or Applied–This major caption is subdivided for cash applied for nonoperating items and for noncash resources applied.

Net Increase (Decrease) in Cash for the Period.

In developing the worksheet (and the related statement) on a working capital basis, *net income* and other amounts are converted from an accrual basis amount to a working capital basis (i.e., working capital generated by operations exclusive of extraordinary items). This concept is carried over to the cash basis worksheet (and the related statement); that is, net income, and other amounts, on an accrual basis are converted to a *cash basis* (i.e., cash generated by operations exclusive of extraordinary items). Therefore, in Exhibit 21–10, cash basis worksheet, and Exhibit 21–11, cash basis statement, you will observe that the "adjustments" to net income are for all *noncash charges and credits* reported on the income statement.[9]

In studying the worksheet for Adamson Company you are urged to compare it with the respective worksheet under the working capital basis shown in Exhibit 21–6. The interim entries reflected on the cash basis worksheet are identical with those entered on the working capital basis worksheet, except for the following:

	Original Entry		*Worksheet Entry*	
c. Inventory increase of $7,000:				
Inventory	7,000		7,000	
Cost of goods sold		7,000		
Cash generated, net income (adjustment)				7,000

[9] General practice is to start with net income and add (or deduct) the noncash items to derive the cash or working capital generated from operations. Alternatively, many accountants prefer to use a gross rather than a net approach. This approach gives precisely the same cash or working capital generated by operations. On this point *APB Opinion No. 19* states: "An acceptable alternative procedure, which gives the same result, is to begin with total revenue that provided working capital or cash during the period and deduct operating costs and expenses that required the outlay of working capital or cash during the period. In either case the resulting amount of working capital or cash should be appropriately described, e.g., 'Working capital provided from [used in] operations for the period, exclusive of extraordinary items.' This total should be immediately followed by working capital or cash provided or used by income or loss from extraordinary items, if any; extraordinary income or loss should be similarly adjusted for items recognized that did not provide or use working capital or cash during the period."

Analysis: This change in a noncash account must be reconciled. Cash Generated, Net Income account is credited as an adjustment to net income since this item represents a noncash credit to cost of goods sold through the inventory increase.

	Original Entry		Worksheet Entry	
b & g. Decrease in accounts payable, $4,000:				
Accounts payable	4,000		4,000	
Cash		4,000		
Cash generated, net income (adjustment)				4,000

EXHIBIT 21–10

ADAMSON COMPANY
Worksheet to Develop Statement of Changes in Financial Position, Cash Basis
For the Year Ended December 31, 1976

Debits	Balance Dec. 31, 1975	Analysis of Interim Entries Debit		Credit		Balance Dec. 31, 1976
Cash	30,000	(*p*)	15,000			45,000
Noncash Accounts:						
Accounts receivable (net)	40,000			(*d & f*)	2,000	38,000
Inventory	60,000	(*c*)	7,000			67,000
Long-term investments	200,000			(*l*)	38,000	162,000
Land	100,000	(*i*)	28,000			128,000
Building (net)		(*n* – 1)	100,000	(*o*)	2,000	98,000
Total	430,000					538,000
Credits						
Accounts payable	40,000	(*b & g*)	4,000			36,000
Notes payable, short term (nontrade)	30,000	(*k*)	6,000			24,000
Bonds payable	50,000	(*m* – 1)	25,000	(*h*)	10,000	35,000
Mortgage payable				(*n* – 2)	100,000	100,000
Common stock	270,000			(*m* – 2)	25,000	295,000
Retained earnings	40,000	(*j*)	25,000	(*a*)	33,000	48,000
Total	430,000		210,000		210,000	538,000
Cash Generated:						
Net income		(*a*)	33,000			
Adjustments for noncash items:						
Inventory increase				(*c*)	7,000	
Accounts payable decrease				(*b & g*)	4,000	
Accounts receivable decrease		(*d & f*)	2,000			
Depreciation expense		(*o*)	2,000			
Extraordinary items generating cash:						
Long-term investment sold		(*l*)	38,000			
Cash from other sources:						
Bonds payable sold		(*h*)	10,000			
Noncash financing activities:						
Common stock issued to retire bonds payable		(*m* – 2)	25,000			
Mortgage payable issued for building		(*n* – 2)	100,000			
Cash Applied:						
For nonoperating items:						
Land purchased				(*i*)	28,000	
Dividends paid				(*j*)	25,000	
Notes paid, short term (nontrade)				(*k*)	6,000	
Noncash resources applied:						
Bonds payable retired by issuing common stock				(*m* – 1)	25,000	
Building acquired, gave long-term mortgage				(*n* – 1)	100,000	
Net increase in cash for the period				(*p*)	15,000	
			210,000		210,000	

Analysis: This is the net effect of two entries: *(b)* purchases of goods on account, \$58,000, and *(g)* payment on accounts, \$62,000. They could be represented on the worksheet as two entries; however, it is convenient to combine them for the net effect. The decrease in accounts payable affects one noncash account that must be reconciled. Cash Generated, Net Income account is credited as an adjustment to net income since this item represents a noncash credit through cost of goods sold.

	Original Entry		*Worksheet Entry*	
d & f. Decrease in accounts receivable \$2,000:				
Cash	2,000			
Cash generated, net income (adjustment)			2,000	
Accounts receivable		2,000		2,000

Analysis: This is the net effect of two entries: *(d)* sales on account of \$100,000, and *(f)* collections on receivables, \$102,000. They could be represented on the worksheet as two entries; however, it is convenient to combine them for the net effect. Cash Generated, Net Income account is debited as an adjustment to net income since this item represents a noncash debit to income (sales).

EXHIBIT 21–11

ADAMSON COMPANY
Statement of Changes in Financial Position, Cash Basis
For the Year Ended December 31, 1976

Cash Generated:		
Income before extraordinary items	\$33,000	
Add (deduct) items not requiring, or generating, cash during the current period:		
Inventory increase	(7,000)	
Trade payables decrease	(4,000)	
Trade receivables decrease	2,000	
Depreciation expense	2,000	
Total Cash Generated by Operations Exclusive of Extraordinary Items		\$ 26,000
Extraordinary items generating cash:		
Long-term investment sold		38,000
Other sources of cash:		
Bonds payable sold		10,000
Total Cash Generated		74,000
Cash Applied:		
Land purchased	\$28,000	
Dividends paid	25,000	
Notes—short term (nontrade) paid	6,000	
Total Cash Applied		59,000
Increase in Cash for the Period		\$ 15,000
Financing and Investing Activities Not Affecting Cash:		
Bonds payable retired by issuing common stock		\$ 25,000
Building acquired, gave long-term mortgage payable		100,000
Total		\$125,000

EXHIBIT 21–12

F. P. CORPORATION
Worksheet to Develop a Statement of Changes in Financial Position, Cash Plus Near-Cash Basis
For the Year Ended December 31, 19B

Debits	Balance Dec. 31, 19A	Analysis of Interim Entries Debit	Credit	Balance Dec. 31, 19B
Cash plus short-term investments	40,000	(s) 52,000		92,000
Noncash Accounts:				
Accounts receivable (net)	50,000	(a & o) 30,000		80,000
Inventory	20,000	(c) 10,000		30,000
Prepaid expenses		(f) 2,000		2,000
Land	60,000		(j) 35,000	25,000
Machinery	80,000	(k) 10,000		90,000
Other assets	29,000	(q − 1) 10,000		39,000
Discount on bonds payable	1,000		(r) 100	900
Total	280,000			358,900
Credits				
Accumulated depreciation	20,000		(e) 7,900	27,900
Accounts payable	40,000		(b & p) 15,000	55,000
Dividends payable			(g − 2) 15,000	15,000
Bonds payable	70,000	(n − 2) 20,000		55,000
			(i) 5,000	
Common stock	100,000		(h) 10,000	131,000
			(n − 1) 21,000	
Preferred stock	20,000		(q − 2) 10,000	30,000
Retained earnings	30,000	(g) 15,000	(a) 44,000	45,000
		(h) 10,000		
		(m) 4,000		
	280,000	163,000	163,000	358,900
Financial Resources Generated:				
Cash generated:				
Net income		(a) 44,000		
To remove gain on land			(j) 18,000	
To remove loss on bonds		(n − 2) 1,000		
Adjustments for noncash items:				
Depreciation expense		(e) 7,900		
Amortization of bond discount		(r) 100		
Inventory increase			(c) 10,000	
Prepaid expenses increase			(f) 2,000	
Accounts receivable increase			(a & o) 30,000	
Accounts payable increase		(b & p) 15,000		
Extraordinary items generating cash:				
Land sold		(j) 53,000		
Cash from other sources:				
Bonds payable sold		(i) 5,000		
Noncash financing activities:				
Liability for dividends declared		(g − 2) 15,000		
Common stock issued to retire bonds		(n − 1) 21,000		
Preferred stock issued for other assets		(q − 2) 10,000		
Financial Resources Applied:				
Cash applied for nonoperating items:				
Machinery purchased			(k) 10,000	
Noncash resources applied:				
Dividends declared but not paid			(g − 1) 15,000	
Bonds retired by issuing common stock			(n − 2) 21,000	
Dividends on preferred stock paid with short-term investments			(m) 4,000	
Other assets acquired by issuing preferred stock			(q − 1) 10,000	
Net increase in cash during the period			(s) 52,000	
		172,000	172,000	

EXHIBIT 21–13

F. P. CORPORATION
Statement of Changes in Financial Position, Cash Plus Near-Cash Basis
For the Year Ended December 31, 19B

Financial Resources Generated:		
Cash generated:		
Net income before extraordinary items	$27,000	
Add (deduct) items not requiring, or generating, cash during the current period:		
Depreciation expense	7,900	
Amortization of discount on bonds payable	100	
Inventory increase	(10,000)	
Prepaid expenses increase	(2,000)	
Trade accounts receivable increase	(30,000)	
Trade accounts payable increase	15,000	
Total Cash Generated by Operations Exclusive of Extraordinary Items		$ 8,000
Extraordinary items generating cash:		
Land sold		53,000
Total Cash Generated by Operations		61,000
Other sources of cash:		
Bonds issued		5,000
Total Cash Generated		66,000
Financial resources generated not affecting cash:		
Liability for dividends declared but not paid	15,000	
Common stock issued to retire bonds payable	21,000	
Preferred stock issued for other assets	10,000	
Total		46,000
Total Financial Resources Generated		$112,000
Financial Resources Applied:		
Cash applied:		
Machinery purchased	10,000	
Dividends on preferred stock paid with short-term investments	4,000	
Total		14,000
Financial resources applied not affecting cash:		
Cash dividends declared but not paid	15,000	
Bonds payable retired by issuing common stock	21,000	
Other assets acquired by issuing preferred stock	10,000	
Total		46,000
Increase in cash during the period		52,000
Total Financial Resources Applied		$112,000

	Original Entry		Worksheet Entry	
k. Paid short-term notes payable (nontrade) $6,000:				
Notes payable—short term (nontrade)	6,000		6,000	
Cash		6,000		
Cash applied for nonoperating items				6,000

Analysis: This item affected a noncash account and represented the use of cash for an item not related to the income statement. Note—It did not appear on the working capital analysis since the transaction did not affect a nonworking capital account.

Since the worksheet involves an analysis of all noncash accounts, it is obvious that all transactions as summarized (except the rare cash to cash transaction) would be reflected on the worksheet. Entry *(p)* is an optional "balancing" entry. Observe, the arithmetic checks at two levels on the worksheet.

PREPARING THE STATEMENT OF CHANGES IN FINANCIAL POSITION (CASH BASIS)

The completed worksheet in Exhibit 21–10 provides all of the details needed to prepare the statement of changes in financial position on a cash basis in conformity with the criteria of *APB Opinion No. 19.* Observe on the cash basis statement, in contrast to the working capital basis statement, that it is not necessary to include a section comparable to "Changes in Working Capital Accounts." As was discussed in respect to the working capital basis, the statement on a cash basis may be prepared under flexible guidelines. The formal statement is illustrated in Exhibit 21–11.

COMPREHENSIVE ILLUSTRATION, CASH PLUS NEAR-CASH BASIS

The data for F. P. Corporation provided in Exhibit 21–7 are used to illustrate some of the complexities omitted from the previous illustration. The cash basis worksheet is reflected in Exhibit 21–12, and the resultant statement of changes in financial position, cash basis, is shown in Exhibit 21–13. You are urged to follow each transaction through the worksheet, remembering the principles and concepts previously discussed. In this respect it should be helpful to compare this worksheet and statement with those for the F. P. Corporation on a working capital basis as reflected in Exhibits 21–8 and 21–9.

A comparison of the statement of financial position, cash basis, for Adamson Company with that for F. P. Corporation, as well as those presented at the end of Chapters 4, 5, and 24, will reflect the flexibility in format and terminology permitted by *APB Opinion No. 19*. No single format can said to be the best because of the differing characteristics of each situation. However, reasonable uniformity as to terminology and format will better serve the statement users.

QUESTIONS

1. Briefly explain the objectives and significance of the statement of changes in financial position.
2. Distinguish between an investing activity and a financing activity.
3. Explain the all-resource concept as applied to the statement of changes in financial position.
4. Explain the basic measurement distinction between the cash basis and the working capital basis for the statement of changes in financial position.
5. Why is it necessary that the changes in the noncurrent accounts rather than the changes in the current accounts be analyzed in developing the statement of changes in financial position, working capital basis?
6. The income statement for X Company reported a net income of $10,000. The statement also showed a deduction for depreciation of $5,000 and an increase in accounts receivable of $8,000. Give the *(a)* cash and *(b)* working capital generated by operations and explain why each is different from net income.
7. The income statement for Y Company reported a net loss of $7,000. The statement also showed a deduction for depreciation of $6,000 and amortization of patents of $3,000. In addition, the statement showed amortization of premium on bonds payable of $1,000. Compute the working capital generated by operations and explain why it is different from the net loss.
8. There are two "parts" to the statement of changes in financial position, working capital basis, and only one part for the cash basis statement. Explain.
9. Give an example of working capital generated involving *(a)* noncurrent assets, *(b)* noncurrent liabilities, *(c)* capital stock, and *(d)* retained earnings.
10. Give an example of working capital applied involving *(a)* noncurrent assets, *(b)* noncurrent liabilities, *(c)* capital stock, and *(d)* retained earnings.
11. Assume the sale of a fixed asset that cost $50,000, one-half depreciated, for $5,000 cash plus a $15,000 one-year, interest-bearing note. How much cash was generated? How much working capital was generated? Explain why an adjustment to the net income for the loss or gain on this transaction is necessary to determine the amount of cash or working capital generated from operations.
12. Explain why net income is adjusted for the depreciation amount but not for the estimated bad debt amount in determining working capital generated. How do they affect cash flow?
13. Why is the cash basis often more relevant than the working capital basis for evaluating the financing and investing activities of an enterprise?

DECISION CASE 21–1

The following statement was prepared by the controller of the Clovis Company. The controller indicated that this statement was prepared under the "all financial resources" concept of funds, which is the broadest concept of funds and includes all financing and investing activities.

CLOVIS COMPANY
Statement of Source and Application of Funds
December 31, 19B

Funds were provided by:	
Contribution of plant site by the city of Camden (Note 1)	$115,000
Net income after extraordinary items per income statement (Note 2)	75,000
Issuance of note payable—due 19F	60,000
Depreciation and amortization	50,000
Deferred income taxes relating to accelerated depreciation	10,000
Sale of equipment—book value (Note 3)	5,000
Total Funds Provided	$315,000
Funds were applied to:	
Acquisition of future plant site (Note 1)	$250,000
Increase in working capital	30,000
Cash dividends declared but not paid	20,000
Acquisition of equipment	15,000
Total Funds Applied	$315,000

Notes to Financial Statement

1. The city of Camden donated a plant site to Clovis Company valued by the board of directors at $115,000. The company purchased adjoining property for $135,000.
2. Research and development expenditures of $25,000 incurred in 19B were expensed.
3. Equipment with a book value of $5,000 was sold for $8,000. The gain was included as an extraordinary item on the income statement.

Required:

1. Why is it considered desirable to present a statement similar to the above in the financial reports?
2. Define and discuss the relative merits of the following three concepts used in funds flow analysis in terms of their measurement accuracy and freedom from manipulation (window dressing) in one accounting period:
   a. Cash concept of funds.
   b. Net monetary assets (quick assets) concept of funds.
   c. Working capital concept of funds.
3. In view of *APB Opinion No. 19,* identify and discuss the weaknesses in presentation and disclosure in the above statement for Clovis Company. Your discussion should explain why you consider them to be weaknesses and what you consider the proper treatment of the items to be. Do not prepare a revised statement.

(AICPA adapted)

EXERCISES

Exercise 21–1

The balance sheets for TS Company showed the following information.

	December 31	
	19A	19B
Cash	$ 4,000	$17,000
Accounts receivable (net)	5,000	9,000
Inventory	10,000	12,000
Long-term investment	2,000	
Fixed assets	30,000	47,000
Total Debits	$51,000	$85,000
Accumulated depreciation	$ 5,000	$ 7,000
Accounts payable	3,000	5,000
Notes payable, short term (nontrade)	4,000	3,000
Long-term notes payable	10,000	18,000
Common stock	25,000	40,000
Retained earnings	4,000	12,000
Total Credits	$51,000	$85,000

Additional data concerning changes in the noncurrent accounts:

a. Net income for the year 19B, $26,000.
b. Depreciation on fixed assets for the year, $2,000.
c. Sold the long-term investment at cost.
d. Paid dividends of $7,000.
e. Purchased fixed assets costing $5,000; paid cash.
f. Purchased fixed assets and gave a $12,000 long-term note payable.
g. Paid a $4,000 long-term note payable by issuing common stock.
h. Issued a stock dividend; $11,000 debited to Retained Earnings and credited to Capital Stock.

Required:

1. Prepare a statement of changes in financial position, working capital basis, without the benefit of a worksheet.
2. Prepare a statement of changes in financial position, cash basis, without the benefit of a worksheet.

Exercise 21–2

During the year ended December 31, 19A, AC Corporation completed the following transactions:

a. Sold 2,000 shares of common stock, par $10, for $20 per share, collected cash.
b. Borrowed $10,000 on a one-year, 9%, interest-bearing note; the note was dated June 1.

c. On December 31, 19A, purchased machinery that cost $25,000; paid $5,000 cash and signed two notes: (1) a 60-day, 8%, interest-bearing note, face $15,000; and (2) a 1-year, 7%, interest-bearing note, face $5,000.

d. Purchased merchandise for resale at a cost of $40,000; paid $30,000 cash, balance credited to Accounts Payable.

e. Declared a cash dividend of $6,000; paid $2,000 in December 19A, the balance will be paid March 1, 19B.

f. Income statement:

Sales: Cash	$55,000	
On credit	20,000	$75,000
Cost of goods sold:		
Purchases *(d)* above	40,000	
Less: ending inventory	10,000	(30,000)
Expenses (including income taxes):		
Paid in cash	10,000	
Accrued (unpaid)	17,000	
Depreciation	2,000	(29,000)
Net Income		$16,000

Required:

1. Set up a tabulation to derive the fund flows for each item on a *(a)* cash basis, and *(b)* working capital basis. Use parallel columns.
2. Prepare a summarized statement of changes in financial position (similar to Exhibit 21–3).

Exercise 21–3

Use the data given below to compute *(a)* total cash generated by operations, and *(b)* total working capital generated by operations.

Transaction	*Cash Basis*	*Working Capital Basis*
Net income reported (accrual basis)*	$50,000	$50,000
Depreciation expense, $6,000	______	______
Increase in accrued wages payable, $1,000	______	______
Increase in trade accounts receivable, $1,800	______	______
Decrease in merchandise inventory, $2,300	______	______
Amortization of patent, $200	______	______
Decrease in long-term liabilities, $10,000	______	______
Sale of capital stock for cash, $25,000	______	______
Amortization of bond discount, $300	______	______
Total Cash Generated by Operations	______	
Total Working Capital Generated by Operations		______

* Revenues, $190,000; expenses, $140,000.

Exercise 21–4

The following worksheet has been set up; you are to complete it in every respect on a working capital basis:

DOLLEY CORPORATION
Worksheet, Statement of Changes in Financial Position, Working Capital Basis
For the Year Ended December 31, 19B

Debits	Balances Dec. 31, 19A	Analysis Debit	Analysis Credit	Balances Dec. 31, 19B
Working Capital	30,000			29,800
Nonworking Capital Accounts:				
Investments, long-term				10,000
Fixed assets (net)	60,000			59,000
Patent (net)	3,000			2,700
Other assets	7,000			7,000
	100,000			108,500
Credits				
Bonds payable	40,000			20,000
Capital stock, par $10	35,000			40,000
Contributed capital in excess of par				4,500
Retained earnings	25,000			44,000
	100,000			108,500
Sources of Working Capital:				
Uses of Working Capital:				
Change in Working Capital:				

Additional data:

a. Net income, $23,000 (after tax).
b. Payment on bonds payable (on principal), $20,000.
c. Amortization of patent, $300.
d. Purchased long-term investment, $10,000.
e. Purchased fixed asset, paid cash, $7,000.
f. Purchased short-term investment, $3,000.
g. Depreciation expense, $8,000.
h. Paid cash dividend, $4,000.
i. Sold unissued stock, 500 shares at $19 per share.

Exercise 21–5

The records of K Company reflected the following data.

Balance Sheet Data

	December 31	
	19A	*19B*
Cash	$ 34,000	$ 33,500
Accounts receivable (net)	12,000	17,000
Inventory	16,000	14,000
Long-term investments	6,000	
Fixed assets	80,000	98,000
Treasury stock		11,500
Total Debits	$148,000	$174,000
Accumulated depreciation	$ 48,000	$ 39,000
Accounts payable	19,000	12,000
Bonds payable	10,000	30,000
Common stock, nopar	50,000	65,000
Retained earnings	21,000	28,000
Total Credits	$148,000	$174,000

Additional data for the period January 1, 19B, through December 31, 19B:

a. Sales on account, $70,000.
b. Purchases on account, $40,000.
c. Depreciation, $5,000.
d. Expenses paid in cash, $18,000.
e. Decrease in inventory, $2,000.
f. Sold fixed assets for $6,000 cash; cost $21,000 and two-thirds depreciated (assume loss or gain is not an extraordinary item).
g. Purchased fixed assets for cash, $9,000.
h. Purchased fixed assets; exchanged unissued bonds payable of $30,000 in payment.
i. Sold the long-term investments for $9,000 cash (assume this is an extraordinary item).
j. Purchased treasury stock for cash, $11,500.
k. Retired bonds payable by issuing common stock, $10,000.
l. Collections on accounts receivable, $65,000.
m. Payments on accounts payable, $47,000.
n. Sold unissued common stock for cash, $5,000.

Required:

Prepare a worksheet to develop a statement of changes in financial position, working capital basis.

Exercise 21–6

The records of DK Company showed the following information relating to the balance sheet accounts.

Balance Sheet Data

	December 31	
Debits	*19A*	*19B*
Cash	$ 15,000	$ 20,000
Accounts receivable (net)	14,000	19,000
Inventory	53,000	51,000
Prepaid expenses	3,000	4,000
Long-term investments	10,000	
Buildings	90,000	120,000
Machinery	40,000	67,000
Patents	5,000	4,000
	$230,000	$285,000
Credits		
Accounts payable	$ 13,000	$ 9,000
Notes payable—short term (nontrade)	9,000	13,000
Accrued wages	3,000	2,000
Accumulated depreciation	40,000	38,000
Notes payable—long term	30,000	35,000
Common stock, nopar	120,000	155,000
Retained earnings	15,000	33,000
	$230,000	$285,000

Additional data relating to the noncurrent accounts:

a. Net income for the year was $28,000.
b. Depreciation recorded on fixed assets was $7,000.
c. Amortization of patents amounted to $1,000.
d. Purchased machinery costing $15,000; paid one third in cash and gave a five-year interest-bearing note for the balance.
e. Purchased machinery costing $30,000 which was paid for by issuing common stock.
f. Sold old machinery for $7,000 that originally cost $18,000 (one-half depreciated); loss (or gain) reported on income statement as ordinary item.
g. Made addition to building costing $30,000; paid cash.
h. Paid a $5,000 long-term note by issuing common stock.
i. Sold the long-term investments for $12,000 cash (assume this is an extraordinary item).
j. Paid cash dividends.
k. Sales of $120,000 on account.
l. Collections on accounts receivable, $115,000.

Required:

Prepare a worksheet to determine changes in financial position, working capital basis.

Exercise 21–7

The following worksheet has been set up; you are to complete it in every respect on a cash flow basis:

Debits	Balances Dec. 31, 19A	Analysis Debit	Analysis Credit	Balances Dec. 31, 19B
Cash plus short-term investments	19,500			32,200
Accounts receivable (net)	34,000			34,000
Merchandise inventory	78,000			85,000
Investments, long term				10,000
Fixed assets	168,500			180,500
	300,000			341,700
Credits				
Accumulated depreciation	44,000			34,000
Accounts payable	21,000			19,000
Accrued expenses	1,500			500
Income taxes payable	2,000			3,500
Bonds payable	100,000			100,000
Premium on bonds payable	4,000			3,700
Capital stock, nopar	120,000			155,500
Retained earnings	7,500			25,500
	300,000			341,700
Sources of Cash:				
Uses of Cash:				

Additional data:

a. Net income (after tax), $28,000.
b. Acquisition of fixed asset, $30,000; issued 1,000 shares of capital stock in full payment.
c. Depreciation expense, $6,000.
d. Increase in merchandise inventory, $7,000.
e. Decrease in accounts payable, $2,000.
f. Amortization of bond premium, $300.
g. Purchased long-term investment, $10,000.
h. Increase in income taxes payable, $1,500.
i. Decrease in accrued expenses, $1,000.
j. Declared and paid cash dividend, $10,000.
k. Sold fixed assets for $5,000 that cost $18,000; accumulated depreciation, $16,000 (not an extraordinary items).
l. Sold 500 shares of capital stock at $11 per share.

Exercise 21–8

Use the data given in Exercise 21–5 to prepare a worksheet to develop a statement of changes in financial position, cash basis.

Exercise 21–9

Use the data given in Exercise 21–6 to prepare a worksheet to develop a statement of changes in financial position, cash basis.

PROBLEMS

Problem 21–1

The following worksheet has been set up; you are to complete it in every respect on a working capital basis:

Debits	Balances Dec. 31, 19A	Analysis Debit	Analysis Credit	Balances Dec. 31, 19B
Cash plus short-term investments	40,000			44,900
Accounts receivable (net)	60,000			52,500
Merchandise inventory	180,000			141,600
Prepaid insurance	2,400			1,200
Investments, long term	30,000			
Land	10,000			38,400
Fixed assets	250,000			259,000
Patent (net)	1,600			1,400
Total Debits	574,000			539,000
Credits				
Accumulated depreciation	65,000			79,000
Accounts payable	50,000			53,000
Accrued wages payable	2,000			1,500
Income taxes payable	9,000			13,400
Bonds payable	100,000			50,000
Premium on bonds payable	5,000			1,700
Capital stock, par $10	300,000			306,000
Contributed capital in excess of par	15,000			18,000
Retained earnings	28,000			16,400
	574,000			539,000
Sources of Working Capital:				
Uses of Working Capital:				

Additional data:

a. Revenues, $400,000 – expenses (including income taxes), $375,000 = $25,000.
b. Depreciation expense, $14,000.
c. Cash dividends declared and paid, $30,000.
d. Increase in income taxes payable, $4,400.
e. Amortization of patent, $200.
f. Purchased fixed asset, cost $9,000; payment by issuing 600 shares of stock.
g. Decrease in accrued wages payable, $500.

h. Payment on bonds payable, principal, $50,000.
i. Sold the long-term investments for $40,000 after tax (assume this is an extraordinary item).
j. Decrease in accounts receivable (net), $7,500.
k. Decrease in prepaid insurance, $1,200.
i. Decrease in merchandise inventory, $38,400.
m. Increase in accounts payable, $3,000.
n. Amortization of bond premium, $3,300.
o. Payment of additional assessment on prior years' income taxes (a prior period adjustment), $6,600.
p. Purchased land, $28,400, paid cash.

Problem 21–2

The balance sheets of Murray Company provided the information shown below.

	December 31	
	19A	*19B*
Cash	$ 4,000	$ 11,000
Accounts receivable (net)	9,000	12,000
Inventory	8,000	5,000
Long-term investments	2,000	
Plant	30,000	30,000
Equipment	20,000	22,000
Land	10,000	40,000
Patents	8,000	7,000
	$91,000	$127,000
Accumulated depreciation—plant	$ 7,000	$ 10,000
Accumulated depreciation—equipment	10,000	8,000
Accounts payable	8,000	2,000
Accrued wages payable	1,000	
Notes payable, long term	10,000	19,000
Common stock, par $10	50,000	75,000
Retained earnings	5,000	13,000
	$91,000	$127,000

Additional data:

a. Net income for the year, $12,000.
b. Depreciation on plant for the year, $3,000.
c. Depreciation on equipment for the year, $2,000.
d. Amortization of patents for the year, $1,000.
e. Sales on account, $67,000.
f. Purchases on account, $35,000.
g. Expenses paid in cash (including accrued wages), $15,000.
h. At the end of the year sold equipment costing $8,000 (50% depreciated) for $3,000 cash (assume this was not an extraordinary item).
i. Purchased land costing $10,000; paid $2,000 cash, gave long-term note for the balance.
j. Paid $4,000 on long-term notes.
k. Sold $10,000 capital stock at par.
l. Purchased equipment costing $10,000; paid one-half cash, balance due in three years (interest-bearing note).

m. Issued 1,500 shares common stock (at par) for land that cost $20,000, balance in cash.
n. Collections on accounts receivable, $64,000.
o. Payment on accounts payable, $41,000.
p. Sold the long-term investments for $8,000 cash (assume this was an extraordinary item).
q. Paid dividends, $4,000.

Required:

1. Prepare a worksheet to develop a statement of changes in financial position, working capital basis, for 19B. Key your entries.
2. Prepare a statement of changes in financial position unless directed otherwise by your instructor.

Problem 21–3

The records of Mills Trading Company provided the following summaries and data:

1. Income statement for the month of April 19A:

Sales		$ 80,000
Less: Purchases	$ 40,000	
Increase in inventory	5,000	35,000
		45,000
Expenses:		
Depreciation	$ 5,000	
Allowance for doubtful accounts	1,000	
Insurance	1,000	
Interest expense	2,000	
Salaries and wages	12,000	
Other expenses (including income taxes)	16,000	
Loss on sale of fixed assets	2,000	
Total Expenses		39,000
Net Income		$ 6,000

2. Balance sheets (unclassified):

	March 31, 19A	*April 30, 19A*
Cash	$ 15,000	$ 31,000
Accounts receivable	30,000	28,500
Allowance for doubtful accounts	1,500*	2,000*
Inventory	10,000	15,000
Prepaid insurance	2,400	1,400
Fixed assets	80,000	81,000
Accumulated depreciation	20,000*	16,000*
Land	40,100	81,100
Total	$156,000	$220,000
Accounts payable	$ 10,000	$ 11,000
Wages payable	2,000	1,000
Accrued interest payable		1,000
Notes payable, long term	20,000	46,000
Common stock, nopar	100,000	136,000
Retained earnings	24,000	25,000
Total	$156,000	$220,000

* Deductions.

3. Cash account:

Debits		*Credits*	
Balance	$15,000	Purchases	$10,000
Sales	20,000	Salaries and wages	5,000
Fixed assets	4,000	Accounts payable	4,000
Sales	15,000	Salaries and wages	2,000
Notes payable	20,000	Purchases	5,000
Sales	15,000	Expenses	6,000
Accounts receivable	31,000	Dividends	5,000
Common stock	5,000	Purchases	5,000
		Expenses	10,000
		Accounts payable	6,000
	125000	Land	20,000
		Accounts payable	9,000
		Wages	6,000
		Interest	1,000
			85000

4. Retained Earnings account showed a debit for dividends, $5,000.
5. Wrote off $500 accounts receivable as uncollectible.
6. Acquired land for common stock issued.
7. Acquired fixed assets costing $16,000; gave three-year, interest-bearing note.
8. Paid a $10,000 long-term note by issuing the creditor common stock.

Required:

1. Prepare a worksheet to develop a statement of changes in financial position, working capital basis.
2. Prepare the statement of changes in financial position (unless directed otherwise by your instructor).

Problem 21–4

The comparative balance sheets for Hall Corporation reflected a significant increase in current assets, a relatively minor increase in current liabilities, and a low net income. The executive committee of the corporation has requested a report that shows the detailed financing and investing activities for the year 19B. You have been provided the incomplete data below.

Balance Sheet Data

	December 31	
	19A	*19B*
Cash	$ 2,000	$ 11,510
Investments, short term		2,000
Accounts receivable	7,000	8,300
Inventory	39,000	43,500
Prepaid property insurance	250	225
Office supplies inventory	75	80
Sinking fund		300
Delivery equipment	5,000	20,250
Office equipment	2,000	1,900
Organization expense (unamortized)	600	400
Discount on Series A bonds	100	
Patents	1,000	800
Cash surrender value of life insurance policies	1,000	1,100
Land		20,000
	$58,025	$110,365

	December 31	
	19A	19B
Notes payable, short term (nontrade)	$ 300	$ 250
Accounts payable	2,000	2,590
Cash dividends payable		1,500
Bonds payable, Series A	2,000	
Bonds payable, Series B		25,000
Premium on Series B bonds		700
Allowance for doubtful accounts	700	900
Accumulated depreciation—delivery equipment	2,500	3,050
Accumulated depreciation—office equipment	400	520
Preferred stock, par $10	3,500	
Common stock, par $20	40,000	46,000
Retained earnings	6,625	4,055
Contributed capital in excess of par, common		25,500
Reserve for bond sinking fund		300
	$58,025	$110,365

Selected additional data:

a. Net income for 19B was $7,040.
b. Preferred stock, par value $500, purchased at 110 and canceled. The premium paid was debited to Retained Earnings.
c. Sold 50 shares of common stock at $105 per share.
d. Office equipment costing $100, recorded depreciation $80, was sold for $15. The gain or loss was reported on income statement as an ordinary item.
e. Delivery equipment costing $500, recorded depreciation $450, sold for $30. The gain or loss was reported as ordinary item.
f. Depreciation for the year: delivery equipment, $1,000; office equipment, $200.
g. Discount on the Series A bonds was written off as follows: July 1 amortized $25 to interest expense; July 2 by recording the retirement of the issue before maturity by payment of $1,775 cash.
h. Amortized $200 organization expense.
i. Paid $100 legal costs in defense of the patent rights which was capitalized. Amortized $300 patent costs.
j. Paid cash dividends on preferred stock, $260.
k. Declared $1,500 cash dividends on common stock, payable January 15 next year.
l. Sold $5,000 of the Series B bonds at 115 on July 1 and amortized $50 of the premium to expense.
m. Paid premium on life insurance on certain executives, $500; the cash value increased $100.
n. Bad debts written off during the period totaled $1,000; bad debt expense recorded for the period was $1,200.
o. Office supplies of $250 costing were purchased during the year.
p. U.S. bonds were purchased on August 1 as a short-term investment, $2,000.
q. Property insurance premiums paid totaled $150; expired premiums totaled $175.
r. Retired the preferred stock (par $3,000) by issuing 100 shares of the common stock. The common stock was selling at $105.
s. Issued Series B bonds at par value for land, $20,000.
t. Acquired delivery equipment by issuing 150 shares of common stock. The common stock was selling at $105.

The Retained Earnings account reflected the following changes:

Balance December 31, 19A	$6,625
Net income	7,040
Preferred stock purchased	(50)
Dividends, preferred	(260)
Dividends, common	(1,500)
Preferred stock retired	(7,500)
Appropriated to bond sinking fund	(300)
Balance, December 31, 19B	$4,055

Required:

1. Prepare a worksheet to develop a statement of changes in financial position, working capital basis.
2. Unless directed otherwise by your instructor, prepare a formal statement of changes in financial position, working capital basis suitable for presentation to the executive committee.

Problem 21–5

Use the data given in Problem 21–1.

Required:

1. Prepare a worksheet to develop a statement of changes in financial position, cash basis.
2. Unless directed otherwise by your instructor, prepare a statement of changes in financial position, cash basis.

Problem 21–6

Use the data given in Problem 21–2.

Required:

1. Prepare a worksheet to develop a statement of changes in financial position, cash basis.
2. Unless directed otherwise by your instructor, prepare a statement of changes in financial position, cash basis.

Problem 21–7

Use the data given in Problem 21–3.

Required:

1. Prepare a worksheet to develop a statement of changes in financial position, cash basis.
2. Unless directed otherwise by your instructor, prepare a statement of changes in financial position, cash basis.

Problem 21–8

Use the data provided in Problem 21–4

Required:

1. Prepare a worksheet to develop a statement of changes in financial position, cash basis.
2. Unless directed otherwise by your instructor, prepare a statement of changes in financial position, cash basis for the executive committee.

Chapter 22

Accounting for Pension Costs

Pension plans sponsored by business enterprises have become quite pervasive and important, and the assets dedicated to pension purposes now account for a staggering sum of wealth. Half of today's work force in commerce and industry is now covered by some form of retirement plan other than social security, whereas 35 years ago, fewer than 20% of a much smaller work force was so covered.[1]

Not surprisingly, with so many persons affected and with vast amounts of wealth involved, the federal government is vitally interested in the subject. Late in 1974, comprehensive legislation regulating many aspects of employee pension plans was enacted. The law, officially known as The Employee Retirement Income Security Act of 1974 (ERISA) is often referred to as the Pension Reform Act of 1974. The full accounting impact of its lengthy, complex provisions is not yet altogether determined, but seemingly it is relatively slight.

PENSION PLAN FUNDAMENTALS

The primary purpose of pension plans is to provide retirement income to employees. This goal can be accomplished in various ways. Insofar as employers having large numbers of employees are concerned, the goal is attained by establishing a *defined benefit plan* which is funded either by purchase of investments whose income will hopefully provide wherewithal for the benefits, or by purchase of annuity contracts.

Defined benefit plans state the amount of benefits or the method of determining the benefits to be received by employees after retirement. In plans for hourly paid employees, the benefit is ordinarily a specified amount per month based upon years of credited service. In plans for

[1] *Journal of Accountancy*, February 1975, p. 52, citing in turn, *Life Insurance Fact Book 1973*. According to these sources, in 1940, assets of private plans were below $3 billion; they now exceed $150 billion and are expected to rise to $250 billion by the end of the decade. A source quoted in *The Wall Street Journal*, September 2, 1975, predicts pension plan assets of around $400 billion in 1980 (p. 23).

salaried employees, benefits are usually related to their compensation (for example, a percent of the highest five years' earnings). Other types of plans are not specific in this respect; rather they provide that whatever the accumulated contributions (plus interest earned) will purchase at the time of retirement will comprise the benefits.

A preponderance of pension benefits payable under defined benefit plans are related to length of service rendered by the employee who is to receive a pension. In general, it can be said that an hourly paid employee who worked in covered employment 20 years is likely to draw about twice as large periodic pension benefits as one who worked in covered employment only 10 years.

Because pension benefits are related to length of employment, a unique problem often arises in connection with pension plans. Most pension plans were adopted after substantial numbers of employees had already been on their employers' payrolls for some time. It would have been inequitable to put these experienced employees on the same footing with respect to their future pension benefits as employees who were hired at about the time or after the pension plan was adopted. If from the date a pension plan is adopted two employees, A and B, work 20 years for the same employer in the same kind of employment, then retire, but A has worked there 15 years before the plan was adopted but B did not, it is hardly fair to A that their pension benefits should be equal. Providing A benefits for the 15 years worked before adoption of the plan causes the employer to incur *past service costs.*

Most pension plans are formally established through a "retirement plan" that meets Internal Revenue Code qualifications so that:

1. Contributions paid by the employer are deductible for income tax purposes.
2. Earnings of the pension fund are not subject to income tax.
3. Employer contributions in behalf of employees are not taxable to the employees at the time the contributions are made.

Prior to passage of the 1974 Pension Reform Act, employers with defined benefit plans had the option of funding or not funding past service costs connected with their plans. Funding meant paying currently for the past service costs. Funding was accomplished by periodically remitting to a trustee (who administered the pension plan and its assets and payments in behalf of the employer and employees) a series of annual cash payments which would, with interest, cover the total lump sum past service cost liability "inherited" at the time a pension plan was adopted. Funding seldom was completed in less than ten years (partly because of income tax provisions) and sometimes was done even more slowly. As will be seen later in the chapter, some companies did not reduce their liability for past service costs but simply funded the accrued interest on the liability. The option to fund or not to fund past service costs no longer exists; the only option the law has left pertains to the date a defined benefit plan began. For plans which existed on January 1, 1974, the funding of past service cost must now be accomplished in 40 years or less. Past service liabilities which arise after January 1, 1974, must be funded in 30 years or less.

Similarly, prior to the 1974 Pension Reform Act, employers had the option of funding or not funding the normal pension costs and the vesting costs. The act now requires that these continuing pension costs also be funded.

A pension plan may be contributory, where the employees bear part of the cost, or noncontributory, where the employer bears the entire cost. An employee's right to receive a present or future pension benefit is said to *vest* when his or her right to eventually receive the benefit is no longer contingent upon remaining an employee of the company. Vesting occurs when the employee retires, but may occur prior to that date. For example, a benefit may vest after a specified number of years of service or at a specified age.[2]

Actuarial determinations and estimates are an integral part of pension plans since *pension costs* are related to a number of significant uncertainties concerning future events, such as: retirement age, mortality (the average life expectancy of employees both before and after retirement), employee turnover, interest rates, gains and losses of fund investments, administrative requirements, future salary levels, pension benefits, and vesting provisions.

A pension plan may be initiated under one of two quite different circumstances which would have significant effects on pension costs, funding requirements, and accounting, viz:

1. A pension plan may be initiated when the company is organized, in which case persons upon initial employment would qualify for the pension plan. Subsequent to inception of the plan only *normal pension costs* would be incurred (each year) by the company.

2. A pension plan may be initiated some years after the company was organized. In this case *present* employees, as well as new employees subsequently hired, would qualify for the plan. *Normal* pension costs would be incurred (each year) by the company for both groups of employees. However, in this case an additional pension cost also would be incurred at date of inception of the pension plan. All employees working for the enterprise at date of the inception of the pension plan generally are given past service credits under the plan for prior years' employment with the company. Thus, the company must bear a one-time pension cost (in addition to the normal pension cost incurred on a year-to-year basis) to provide for the "catch-up" for prior employees; this cost generally is referred to as *past service pension cost.*

---

[2] The 1974 act has imposed stringent safeguards in behalf of employees concerning their vesting rights. An employee must now be at least 25% vested in accrued benefits derived from employer contributions after five years of covered service. By the time an employee has 15 years of covered service, the vesting must have risen (according to a table in the law) to 100%. Under another provision an employee with five years of covered service must be at least 50% vested in the accrued benefit from employer contributions when the sum of the employee's age and years of covered service totals 45.

Past service cost (just defined) is often called *initial past service cost* because it is a cost that comes into existence at the date of adoption of a pension plan. In contrast, *prior service cost* arises when the pension plan is amended or assumptions relating to it are changed with the result that the liabilities related to the past are changed. Prior service cost sometimes is used in the broad sense to include the entire past cost; this includes *initial* past service cost plus the effect of the changes that relate to all service before the amendment date. Examples of these changes are fluctuations in earnings and values of securities held by the pension plan trustee, and changes in the benefits and rates of employee turnover which would affect the actuarial calculations of the fund requirements.[3]

PENSION PLAN ACCOUNTING

Since most pension plans are funded, accounting for pension plans focuses on *(a)* accounting for the costs of the plan to the employer, and *(b)* accounting for the funding. Most business prefer to keep these two phases in harmony to the extent possible.[4]

There are two basic types of pension costs that must be recorded each period (assuming past services are involved); they are:

1. Normal pension costs – the amount of expense, on an accrual basis, that should be assigned each period to the pension plan for current services by the employees. It is determined by actuarial calculations, for the service credits earned by the employees during the current period.
2. Prior (including past) service costs – the amount of expense, on an accrual basis, assigned for service credits earned by the employees of the entity *prior* to the inception of the pension plan. It includes initial past service cost plus prior service cost (as defined above). Thus, prior service cost exists when *(a)* an established company has instituted a pension plan which recognizes past service credits, and *(b)* when the pension plan or assumptions are changed which relate to past service credits.[5]

Each period these two costs are charged to *pension expense* which is reported on the income statement as an ordinary expense of the business.

The amount of pension expense recorded each period will be affected

---

[3] The distinction drawn here between past and prior service cost is one that has been made in authoritative accounting literature. The 1974 act refers to what accountants call *past service cost* as *initial past service cost* and to what they call *prior service cost* as *past service cost.*

[4] Ernest L. Hicks and René A. Miller, "Pension Cost" in Sidney Davidson, ed., *Handbook of Modern Accounting* (New York: McGraw-Hill Book Co., 1970), 25:17–22.

[5] Although the actuary normally computes the cost of a vesting provision separately, it usually is added to the normal and past service costs respectively for accounting purposes. Separate accounting for it would present no special problem.

by the extent to which the prior service costs have been funded, or are being funded during the current period.

APB Opinion No. 8, "Accounting for the Cost of Pension Plans" (December 1966), provides the current guidelines for accounting for pension plans. It was largely based on *Accounting Research Study No. 8*, "Accounting for the Cost of Pension Plans," published by the AICPA in 1965. The discussions to follow are consistent with *Opinion No. 8*.

In accounting for pension plans, all costs, including fund gains and losses, must be identified, recorded, and reported in a manner consistent with the long-term characteristics of a pension plan; on this point *APB Opinion No. 8* states:

> In the absence of convincing evidence that the company will reduce or discontinue the benefits called for in a pension plan, the cost of the plan should be accounted for on the assumption that the company will continue to provide such benefits. This assumption implies a long-term undertaking, the cost of which should be recognized annually whether or not funded. . . . The entire cost of benefit payments ultimately to be made should be charged against income subsequent to the adoption or amendment of a plan and that no portion of such cost should be charged directly against retained earnings.

In accounting for pension plans it is essential that a careful distinction be made between *pension costs* and *pension funding*. In the discussions and illustrations to follow, however, you will observe that they are intimately related.

In respect to *funding* a pension plan, the company must disburse cash for each of the two types of pension costs, viz:

1. For normal pension costs, the company disburses cash (to the fund trustee or funding agency) each period in an amount sufficient to satisfy the *normal* pension credits being earned currently by the employees.

2. For past service pension cost (a one-time cost), the company may elect to disburse cash at date of inception of the plan sufficient to satisfy this obligation, or, as is the usual case, to spread the payments over a selected number of periods in the future (say ten) from date of inception of the plan. The latter choice, obviously, is tantamount to paying a currently due debt on an installment basis which would give rise to an interest charge.

Past service pension costs represent a "catch-up" obligation and the question as to when it should be reflected in the accounts and the manner of reflecting it has been the concern of the accounting pronouncements mentioned above. Obviously, since it is a one-time and generally significant amount that relates to past service of the employees, this has caused it to be somewhat controversial. All accountants agree that it must be given recognition at date of inception of the plan; however, there is a difference of opinion as to whether past service cost should be reflected as (1) an adjustment to prior period earnings (retained earnings), (2) an extraordinary item on the income statement in the year of inception of the plan, or (3) spread over a selected number of years (as a current cost) in the future (after inception of the plan). The quotation above from *APB Opinion No. 8* clearly requires the latter. The details of the *Opinion* state, in effect, that past service cost must be amortized after date of inception of the plan as a part of total pension cost each year; the period of amortization is variable, being subject to the particular circumstances. The following quotation from *APB Opinion No. 8* applies:

> To be acceptable for determining cost for accounting purposes, an actuarial cost method should be rational and systematic and should be consistently applied so that it results in a reasonable measure of pension cost from year to year. Therefore, in applying an actuarial cost method that separately assigns a portion of cost as prior service cost, any amortization of such portion should be based on a rational and systematic plan and generally should result in reasonable stable annual amounts.

For analytical and problem-solving purposes it is sometimes helpful to diagram a pension plan along the following lines:

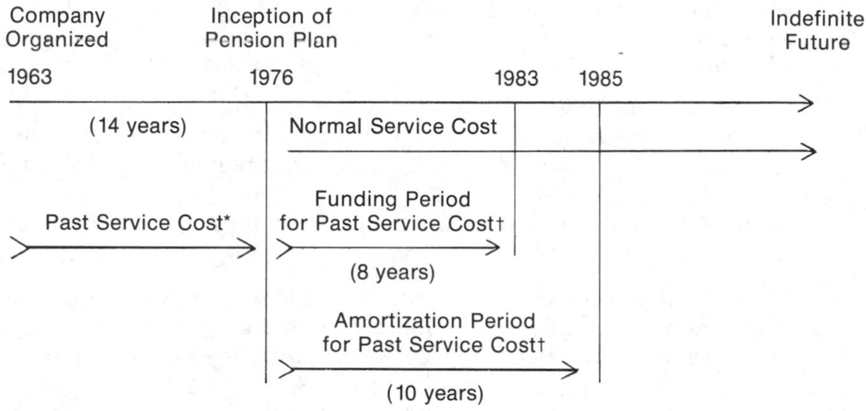

* $70,000 (present value)
† Must be on present value basis; see Case II pages 956–57.

The accounting entries for a pension plan are not complex; however computations of the amounts of *(a)* normal pension cost for the period, *(b)* prior service cost and its amortization, and *(c)* funding and its earnings, often are complex. *APB Opinion No. 8* specifies that actuarial determinations and the application of *present value* concepts are necessary both with respect to the amortization of prior pension cost and to the funding.

However, to introduce the entries we will first use a simple situation employing "straight-line" relationships and disregarding interest. Bear in mind that this is only for instructional purposes; present value applications will be introduced in the next illustration as required by the *Opinion*. Four separate cases will be presented.

Case A – A new company is formed and a pension plan is initiated immediately, hence there are no past service costs. The pension cost is fully funded each year.

To record the normal pension cost, and funding, appropriately determined at the end of the first two years:

	Year 1		*Year 2*	
Pension expense	10,000		12,000	
Cash (paid to trustee)		10,000		12,000

No entry would be made for subsequent payments to retired employees; payment would be made to the retired employees by the funding agency (trustee).

Case B – An established company initiates a funded pension plan. Past service costs are appropriately determined to be $70,000; normal pension costs as in Case A.

To record the normal pension cost, amortization of past service costs over a ten-year future period, and a ten-year funding period for the past service costs.

	Year 1		*Year 2*	
Pension expense	17,000		19,000	
Cash (paid to trustee)		17,000		19,000
	Cost	*Funding*	*Cost*	*Funding*
Computation:				
Normal pension cost	$10,000	$10,000	$12,000	$12,000
Past pension cost amortization (ten years)	7,000		7,000	
Annual funding (ten years)		7,000		7,000
Total	$17,000	$17,000	$19,000	$19,000

Case C – Same as Case B except that the funding is over a 15-year period for the past service costs. Therefore, the funding each year is: $70,000 ÷ 15 years = $4,667.

	Year 1		*Year 2*	
Pension expense	17,000		19,000	
Liability – pension costs in excess of funding		2,333		2,333
Cash (paid to trustee)		14,667		16,667
	Cost	*Funding*	*Cost*	*Funding*
Computation:				
Normal pension cost	$10,000	$10,000	$12,000	$12,000
Past pension cost amortization	7,000		7,000	
Annual funding (15 years)		4,667		4,667
Total	$17,000	$14,667	$19,000	$16,667

Case D – Same as Case B except that the funding is over an eight-year period for the past service costs. The funding each year is: $70,000 ÷ 8 years = $8,750.

	Year 1		*Year 2*	
Pension expense	17,000		19,000	
Deferred charge – funding in excess of pension costs	1,750		1,750	
Cash (paid to trustee)		18,750		20,750

Measuring the Amount of Pension Cost

The preceding illustrations and discussions emphasized that the critical aspects of accounting for pension plans are determination (estimation) of *(a)* the periodic pension cost for accounting purposes and *(b)* the funding required each period (in the case of funded plans). Accountants generally agree that pension costs should be accounted for on an accrual basis; however, there is not general agreement as to the precise nature of periodic pension costs (expense) in relationship to the future (prospective) benefits that will have to be paid. Clearly, interest earned on funds set aside many years before disbursement as benefits will significantly affect certain accounting values to be recorded. *Opinion No. 8*, as quoted above, clearly specifies that both "normal" and "past service" costs should be included in the periodic charge (pension cost). The board also stated in *Opinion No. 8* that the annual provision for pension cost should be based on an *accounting method* that uses an acceptable *"actuarial cost method"* (as defined below).[6]

The *actuarial cost methods* are approaches that have been developed primarily as funding techniques in that they provide the specific amounts for periodic payments to be made to the funding agency (funded plans) such as insurance companies or trustees (trust agreements). Since determination of the funding requirements explicitly requires estimation of the underlying pension costs for several of the actuarial cost methods they are also useful in determining pension costs for accounting purposes. Although these methods are alike in that they utilize present value concepts and rest on actuarial assumptions, they differ significantly in their approach and can produce quite different results for the same situation.

We noted above that, in accordance with *APB Opinion No. 8*, the *accounting method* utilized in accounting for pension plans must use an acceptable *actuarial cost method*. The *Opinion* states:

> (1) Accrued Benefit Cost Method (Unit Credit Method)—under the unit credit method, future service benefits are funded as they accrue—that is, each employee works out the service period involved. The past service cost is the present value at the plan's inception date of the units of future benefit credited to employees for service prior to inception of the plan. Thus, the annual contribution (and cost) comprises primarily *(a)* the normal cost and *(b)* the past service cost.
>
> (2) Projected Benefit Cost Methods—There are four methods in this group; entry age normal, individual level premium, aggregate, and attained age normal methods. The amount assigned (for funding) to the current year usually represents a level or constant amount that will provide for the estimated projected retirement benefits over the service lives of either the individual employees or the employee group, depending on the method selected. Pension cost projected under these methods tends to be stable or decline year by year, depending on the method selected.

---

[6] The minimum amortization period for past service costs is ten years; to minimize computations shorter periods are utilized in the chapter and in the exercises and problems. This simplification for instructional purposes does no violence to the concepts involved.

Although the APB, in *Opinion No. 8*, listed these methods as acceptable it recognized that other methods may be acceptable if they conform to the guidelines established in the *Opinion*. It is important to understand that the above methods are applied by the actuary that determines the appropriate funding requirements each year for the company. *They provide both the amounts needed by the accountant to record pension costs and funding requirements as illustrated below.*

ILLUSTRATION OF RECORDING OF PENSION COSTS AND FUNDING

Now that we have identified the basic approaches utilized by actuaries in determining funding requirements, normal pension costs, and past service costs, the essential steps leading to development of the periodic accounting entries may be listed as follows:

1. Determination of *past service cost* by the actuary. This involves a complicated actuarial estimate derived by applying an acceptable actuarial method taking into account factors such as those listed on page 949. The actuary develops the present obligation (present value) of the cost of credits for services prior to the inception of the pension plan.
2. Determination of normal pension cost for the period by the actuary. This involves a complicated determination based upon service credits for the current year. There must be a separate determination for each year as it occurs. Obviously, the number of employees, salaries, and terms of the plan must underlie this actuarial determination for each period.
3. When there are past service costs, develop a present value amortization schedule for the period of amortization (at an appropriate interest rate). Develop a funding schedule for the funding period (at an appropriate interest rate). The two schedules may be combined in one table as shown in Exhibit 22–1.
4. Based upon *(a)* the normal pension cost for the period, *(b)* the amortization schedule, and *(c)* the funding schedule, develop the accounting entries for the period.

To illustrate, assume the AB Corporation, having been in operation for 14 years, decided in 1976 to adopt a funded pension plan for its employees. A trust agreement has been entered into with a bank (trustee) whereby the required payments to the fund will be made each year. The pension plan provides for vesting after 20 years of service by each eligible employee; it is noncontributory. An actuary was engaged on a consultation basis to develop the normal and past service costs and fund contributions each period. The management decided to utilize the "unit credit method." After an extended analysis, and based upon certain actuarial assumptions, the actuary developed the following:

1. Normal pension cost for 1976, $10,000.
2. Present value of the past service cost at date of inception of the pension plan (January 1, 1976), $70,000.

The management, upon recommendation of the actuary, decided to assume a 4% interest rate and to amortize the past service costs over a ten-year period.[7]

Three cases will be illustrated in respect to *funding* of the past service costs (funding payments to be made at the end of each year):

Case I. Past service costs to be funded over a ten-year period (same as the amortization period).

Case II. Past service costs to be funded over an eight-year period (two years less than the amortization period; see diagram on page 952).

Case III. Past service costs to be funded over a 12-year period (two years more than the amortization period).

Case I. The next step is to compute the periodic *amortization* and *funding* for the *past service costs.* In this case the amortization and funding periods are identical; therefore, the two schedules (periodic amounts) are the same; that is, we have two questions and they have identical responses:

1. Assuming a present obligation of $70,000 to be paid in equal installments over ten years, at 4%, what is the periodic payment?
2. Assuming a $70,000 value (cost) to be amortized over ten equal periods (years) on a present value basis, at 4%, what is the periodic amortization?

Computation:

Periodic Funding Payment
(and amortization) = $70,000 ÷ Present Value of Annuity of 1 for Ten Rents at 4% (Table 6–4)
= $70,000 ÷ 8.11090
= $ 8,630.37

Indicated entries for the pension costs and funding at year-end:

1976:

Pension expense (normal)	10,000.00	
Pension expense (amortization of past service cost)*	8,630.37	
Cash (paid to trustee)		18,630.37

1977 (assuming normal pension cost of $12,000):

Pension expense (normal)	12,000.00	
Pension expense (amortization of past service cost)*	8,630.37	
Cash (paid to trustee)		20,630.37

* Observe that these amounts implicitly include an interest factor that decreases each period.

Clearly, after the tenth year the past service costs, and the related funding, would drop out and only the normal costs and normal funding would be recognized thereafter.

Case II. This case introduces another complexity; that is, the amor-

[7] This interest rate is net of all administration costs and charges by the trustee; hence, it represents a net return.

tization period is ten years whereas the funding period is eight years. Clearly, in this situation we must compute the amortization schedule on one basis and the funding schedule on another basis. Since funds will be disbursed at a greater rate than the cost accrual we also must adjust the *amortization* schedule for the interest differential. A special table is essential to this determination (Exhibit 22–1).

In respect to the distinctive features of Exhibit 22–1 you should observe the following:

1. This table relates only to past service costs (not normal pension costs).
2. The periodic amortization of past service costs (column [*a*]) is *reduced* by the interest on the funding paid in *excess* of the periodic amortization; this causes a decreasing periodic amortization (column [*c*]).
3. The periodic funding payments cease at the end of Year 8 (1983).
4. Payments to the fund are constant each year.
5. The amortization of past service costs terminates at the end of the tenth year (1985).

EXHIBIT 22–1
Schedule of Past Service Pension Costs and Related Funding†
(amortization period ten years; funding period eight years)

	Amortization of Past Service Cost—10 Years			*Funding—8 Years*	*Balance Sheet—Deferred Charge*	
Year	*10-Year Accrual Factor (a)*	*Reduction for Interest (b)*	*Past Pension Cost (Debit) (c)*	*Cash (Credit) (d)*	*Debit/Credit* (e)*	*Account Balance (f)*
1976	$8,630.37‡		$ 8,630.37	$10,396.95§	$1,766.58	$ 1,766.58
1977	8,630.37	$ 70.66	8,559.71	10,396.95	1,837.24	3,603.82
1978	8,630.37	144.15	8,486.22	10,396.95	1,910.73	5,514.55
1979	8,630.37	220.58	8,409.79	10,396.95	1,987.16	7,501.71
1980	8,630.37	300.07	8,330.30	10,396.95	2,066.65	9,568.36
1981	8,630.37	382.73	8,247.64	10,396.95	2,149.31	11,717.67
1982	8,630.37	468.71	8,161.66	10,396.95	2,235.29	13,952.96
1983	8,630.37	558.12	8,072.25	10,396.95	2,324.70	16,277.66
1984	8,630.37	651.11	7,979.26	-0-	7,979.26*	8,298.40
1985	8,630.37	331.97	8,298.40	-0-	8,298.40*	-0-
			$83,175.60	$83,175.60		

† It may be observed that this table assumes (1) amortization at end of the period (year), (2) the present value of the past service cost is at the beginning of the period, and (3) the funding payments are made at the end of each period. Other viable assumptions are possible.

‡ Amortization: (10 periods, @ 4%):
Periodic amortization = $70,000 ÷ 8.1109 (Table 6–4)
= $ 8,630.37 to column *(a)*

§ Funding: (8 periods, @ 4%):
Periodic payment = $70,000 ÷ 6.73274 (Table 6–4)
= $10,396.95 to column *(d)*

(a) Independently computed above.
(b) 4% of the preceding balance of column *(f)*.
(c) Column *(a)* less column *(b)*.
(d) Independently computed above.
(e) Column *(d)* minus column *(c)*.
(f) Preceding balance plus (or minus) column *(e)*.

6. Total past pension costs (column [*c*]) and total fund payments (column [*d*]) are equal ($83,175.60) although their timing is different.
7. The deferred charge (column [*f*]) to be reported on the balance sheet is due to the fact that funding payments exceed amortization; however, at the end of the amortization period the deferred charge balance is zero.
8. Total funding payments are comprised of two elements; principal (past service cost), $70,000, and interest (on unpaid principal), $13,175.60.
9. Accounting entries are indicated by the table but do not include normal pension costs.

Entries for pension costs and funding at year-end:

1976:

Pension expense (normal)	10,000.00	
Pension expense (amortization of past service cost)	8,630.37	
Deferred charge–funding in excess of pension costs	1,766.58	
Cash (paid to trustee)		20,396.95

1977:

Pension expense (normal)	12,000.00	
Pension expense (amortization of past service cost)	8,559.71	
Deferred charge–funding in excess of pension costs	1,837.24	
Cash (paid to trustee)		22,396.95

Case III. This is the same as Case II except that the amortization period for past service costs is two years less than the funding period. As a consequence, the Schedule of Past Pension Costs and Related Funding (as shown in Exhibit 22–1) obviously must be changed in two respects: (1) in the amortization portion the interest differential must be added (rather than deducted), and (2) in the balance sheet column a *liability* (rather than a deferred charge) must be reflected. Exhibit 22–2 reflects these differences.

The entries indicated in Exhibit 22–2 are:

1976:

Pension expense (normal)	10,000.00	
Pension expense (amortization of past service cost)	8,630.37	
Liability–pension cost in excess of funding		1,171.72
Cash (paid to trustee)		17,458.65

1977:

Pension expense (normal)	12,000.00	
Pension expense (amortization of past service cost)	8,677.24	
Liability–pension cost in excess of funding		1,218.59
Cash (paid to trustee)		19,458.65

For instructional purposes we have recorded normal and past service costs separately. In practice these two amounts usually are recorded in one expense account since there is no requirement that they be separately recorded and reported. Pension expense is classified as an ordinary business expense.

EXHIBIT 22–2
Schedule of Past Service Pension Costs and Related Funding (amortization period 10 years; funding period 12 years)

	Amortization of Past Service Cost—10 Years			*Funding—12 Years*	*Balance Sheet—Liability*	
Year	*10-Year Accrual Factor (a)*	*Addition for Interest (b)*	*Past Pension Cost (Debit) (c)*	*Cash (Credit) (d)*	*Credit Debit* (e)*	*Account Balance (f)*
1976	$8,630.37†		$ 8,630.37	$ 7,458.65‡	$1,171.72	$1,171.72
1977	8,630.37	$ 46.87	8,677.24	7,458.65	1,218.59	2,390.31
1978	8,630.37	95.61	8,725.98	7,458.65	1,267.33	3,657.64
1979	8,630.37	146.31	8,776.68	7,458.65	1,318.03	4,975.67
1980	8,630.37	199.03	8,829.40	7,458.65	1,370.75	6,346.42
1981	8,630.37	253.86	8,884.23	7,458.65	1,425.58	7,772.00
1982	8,630.37	310.88	8,941.25	7,458.65	1,482.60	9,254.60
1983	8,630.37	370.18	9,000.55	7,458.65	1,541.90	10,796.50
1984	8,630.37	431.86	9,062.23	7,458.65	1,603.58	12,400.08
1985	8,630.37	496.00	9,126.37	7,458.65	1,667.72	14,067.80
1986	-0-	562.71	562.71	7,458.65	6,895.94*	7,171.86
1987	-0-	286.79	286.79	7,458.65	7,171.86*	-0-
			$89,503.80	$89,503.80		

† Periodic amortization = $70,000 ÷ 8.11090 (Table 6–4)
= $ 8,630.37 To column *(a)*

‡ Periodic funding = $70,000 ÷ 9.38507 (Table 6–4)
= $ 7,458.65 To column *(d)*

(a) Independently computed above.
(b) 4% of the preceding balance of column *(f)*.
(c) Column *(a)* plus column *(b)*.
(d) Independently computed above.
(e) Column *(c)* less column *(d)*.
(f) Preceding balance plus (or minus) column *(e)*.

MAXIMUM AND MINIMUM PROVISION FOR PAST SERVICE COSTS

Recall from the prior discussion and illustrations that the periodic debit to pension expense is comprised of *(a)* normal pension cost plus *(b)* an amortized amount of prior pension cost. Recall also that the funding provisions affect the determination of the amount of past service cost amortized for the period (because of the interest effect); the accounting does not affect the funding provision.

APB *Opinion No. 8* specifies a maximum and minimum provision for pension expense; this means that the debit to pension expense for the period should not be less than the minimum nor more than the maximum. The maximum and minimum for pension expense is different only because of the amortization of prior service cost and the interest effect of any unfunded past service cost. The maximum and minimum provisions specified in *Opinion No. 8* essentially read as follows:

Minimum. The provision for pension cost should not be less than the *total* of:

1. Normal cost.
2. An amount equivalent to interest on any unfunded prior service cost.
3. If indicated – a provision for vested benefits.

Maximum. The annual provision for pension cost should not be greater than the *total* of:

1. Normal cost.
2. Ten percent of the past service cost (i.e., at least a ten year amortization period).
3. Ten percent of the amounts of any increases or decreases in prior service costs arising on amendments of the plan (until fully amortized); in effect, a ten-year minimum period.
4. Interest equivalents on the difference between provisions (pension costs) and amounts funded.

The maximum provision includes normal service cost for the period plus the amortization of past service cost including the effect of interest on any unfunded past service cost. In contrast, the minimum provision includes normal service cost for the period plus interest only on any unfunded prior service cost. Clearly, the minimum provision is very difficult to justify.

The accounting illustrated above, Exhibits 22–1 and 22–2, reflect *maximum* pension expense since amortization of past service cost and the interest effect is included. Application of the maximum and minimum provisions for these two situations is shown in Exhibit 22–3 (for the first two years only).

Significantly, the maximum and minimum provisions are no longer important since the 1974 Pension Reform Act, for all practical purposes, requires that the maximum amount be used for pension expense.[8]

EXHIBIT 22–3
Application of Maximum and Minimum Limits on Pension Expense

	Normal Cost (a)	*Ten Percent Unamortized Prior Service Cost* (b)*	*Vested Cost (c)*	*Interest on Unfunded Past Service† (d)*	*Total Pension Expense Maximum (a + b + c)*	*Total Pension Expense Minimum (a + c + d)*
Exhibit 22–1:						
1976	$10,000	$8,630.37	-0-	$ -0-	$18,630.37	$10,000.00
1977	12,000	8,559.71	-0-	70.66	20,559.71	12,070.66
Exhibit 22–2:						
1976	10,000	8,630.37	-0-	-0-	18,630.37	10,000.00
1977	12,000	8,677.24	-0-	46.87	20,677.24	12,046.87

* From Column *(c)* on prior exhibits.
† From Column *(b)* on prior exhibits; assuming funding.

---

[8] As this is being written the FASB has revision of *Opinion No. 8* on its agenda. It will undoubtedly be made to conform to the requirements of the new act in all respects.

EXPERIENCE GAINS AND LOSSES

Recall that the entries presented in Cases I, II, and III presumed that the interest rate (4% net) materialized and that the determinations of past service cost would not change over time. Obviously, actuaries must deal with many uncertainties in making such estimates. Regardless of the degree of competence, it is likely that some of these determinations will subsequently have to be revised. The effects on actuarially calculated pension costs of *(a)* changes in the underlying assumptions, and *(b)* deviations between planned and actual results have, in the past, been called actuarial gains and losses. The Pension Reform Act of 1974 refers to such deviations as *experience gains and losses*—terminology which is considerably more descriptive. Adjustments for experience gains and losses may be needed annually to reflect actual experience or from time to time to reflect a revision in the underlying assumptions. There are two related questions: *(a)* determination of the experience gain or loss, and *(b)* timing of its recognition in the accounts. In practice three methods are to be found: immediate recognition, spreading on a prospective basis, and averaging. On this point *Opinion No. 8* states:

> Actuarial gains and losses, including realized investment gains and losses, should be given effect in the provision for pension cost in a consistent manner that reflects the long-range nature of pension cost. . . . Accordingly, (with certain exceptions) actuarial gains and losses should be spread over the current year and future years or recognized on the basis of an average.

The Pension Reform Act of 1974 provides that under the required funding rules, *experience losses* are to be amortized over a period of not more than 15 years from the time that an experience deficiency is determined. Similarly, *experience gains* are to be amortized over a period of up to 15 years. The losses would increase amounts employers must contribute to meet funding requirements, while the gains would decrease such amounts.

DISCLOSURE

According to *APB Opinion No. 8*, the following disclosures should be made in financial statements or their notes:

1. A statement that such plans exist, identifying or describing the employee groups covered.
2. A statement of the company's accounting and funding policies.
3. The provision for pension cost for the period.
4. The excess, if any, of the actuarially computed value of vested benefits over the total of the pension fund and any balance sheet pension accruals, less any pension repayments or deferred charges.
5. Nature and effect of significant matters affecting comparability for all periods presented, such as changes in accounting methods (actuarial cost method, amortization of past and prior service cost, treatment of actuarial gains and losses, etc.), changes in circumstances (actuarial assumptions, etc.), or adoption or amendment of a plan.

PENSION PLAN DISCLOSURE REQUIREMENTS OF 1974 ACT

The 1974 act has imposed disclosure requirements for pension plans which treat the plans as separate entities. Plan administrators must publish a comprehensive plan description and a summary plan description; the latter must be so written that participants can understand it. Both of these descriptions must be filed with the Secretary of Labor.

Plan administrators must publish annual reports on plans within 210 days after the close of the plan year in accordance with forms prescribed by the Secretary of Labor. These annual reports must contain:

1. Statements of the pension plan assets and liabilities.
2. Statements of changes in net assets available for plan benefits which shall include details of revenues and expenses and other changes aggregated by general source and application.
3. Schedules of investment assets.
4. Schedules of transactions involving known "parties in interest" (e.g., officer, fiduciary, or counsel of the plan).
5. Schedules of loans in default or uncollectible and other loans exceeding 3% of the value of the plan as well as loans to "parties in interest."
6. When fund assets are held in a common trust or separate trust by a bank or similar institution, a statement of the assets and liabilities of that trustee must be filed.
7. Schedules of each transaction involving amounts exceeding 3% of the value of the fund.
8. Detailed statements of salaries, fees, and commissions charged to the plan.
9. Identity of each plan fiduciary and an indication of his or her relationship to the employer or employee organization and any position held with "parties in interest."
10. Number of employees covered by the plan.
11. An actuarial report. (A full actuarial report is required only every third plan year.)
12. Information concerning items 8, 9, and 10 plus an explanation of any changes of trustee, actuary, independent accountant, administrator, investment manager, custodian, or insurance carrier.
13. If any benefits are purchased from an insurance carrier, a statement from the carrier enumerating premiums and benefits paid, administrative expense charged, commissions, and amount held to pay future benefits.

The act requires plan administrators to engage qualified independent public accountants to conduct examinations of plan financial statements of sufficient scope as the accountants deem necessary to express an opinion on the items enumerated above.[9]

[9] Under certain circumstances, item 6 is an exception.

FUTURE DEVELOPMENTS

Further developments in the realm of pension accounting and reporting can be expected as the FASB and their task forces progress with studies which have been launched, as experience is gained under the 1974 act, and as federal administrators issue detailed regulations for implementation of the act. Meanwhile, the FASB has issued one interpretation as an outgrowth of the 1974 act.[10] Some principal provisions of that interpretation are summarized below.

1. No change in the minimum and maximum limits for the annual provision for pension cost set forth in *APB Opinion No. 8* is required as a result of the 1974 act.[11]

2. If, prior to the date a plan becomes subject to the act's participation, vesting, and funding requirements, it appears likely that compliance will have a significant effect in the future on the entity's *(a)* periodic pension expense, *(b)* periodic pension funding, or *(c)* unfunded vested benefits, this fact and an estimate of the effect shall be disclosed in notes to the financial statements.

3. With but two exceptions, the FASB does not believe that the act creates legal obligations for unfunded pension costs that warrant accounting recognition as a liability. *(a)* There are minimum funding requirements (unless a waiver is obtained); in the absence of a waiver, the amount currently required to be funded shall be recognized as a liability by a charge to pension expense for the period, by a deferred charge, or by a combination of the two as appropriate. *(b)* In the event of termination of a pension plan, the act imposes a liability on an enterprise. In the face of strong evidence a plan will be terminated and that the liability on termination will exceed fund assets and related prior accruals, the excess liability shall be accrued. Where the amount cannot be reasonably determined, disclosure of the circumstances and an estimate of the possible range of the liability shall appear in notes to the financial statements.[12]

---

[10] FASB *Interpretation No. 3*, "An Interpretation of APB Opinion No. 8" (High Ridge, Conn.: FASB, 1974).

[11] The interpretation points out, however, that *APB Opinion No. 8* requires that "the entire cost of benefit payments ultimate to be made should be charged against income subsequent to the adoption or amendment of a plan." Consistent with that requirement, and within the minimum and maximum provisions of the *Opinion*, any change in pension cost resulting from compliance with the act shall enter into determination of periodic provisions for pension expense *subsequent* to the date a plan becomes subject to the act's participation, vesting, and funding requirements. That date will be determined either by dates prescribed by the act or by an election of earlier compliance with its provisions.

[12] "A Flood of Pension Plan Terminations," *Business Week*, September 1, 1975 (p. 42). Although the legislation is still quite new and there has been very little time for companies to decide whether or not to terminate their pension plans under the option provided in the 1974 act, early experience indicates a very brisk rate of terminations. In its first five months of existence the newly created federal Pension Benefit Guaranty Corporation received notifications of termination of 4,000 plans—four times as many as had been expected. Most terminated plans have been small and relatively new; most of the assets that have come in to PBGC have come from large plans that have failed.

QUESTIONS

1. What does the acronym ERISA stand for? By what other identification is the same thing known? Thus far has accounting been greatly affected by it?
2. What is vesting?
3. In connection with pension plans, explain the meaning of *(a)* normal service cost, *(b)* past service cost, and *(c)* prior service cost.
4. Under *APB Opinion No. 8* certain guidelines as to the *minimum* and *maximum* annual provision for pension cost are set out. What are they?
5. In respect to pension plans, what are actuarial gains and losses? By what term are these referred to in the 1974 act?
6. Under *APB Opinion No. 8* guidelines for pension plan accounting, what disclosures should be made in financial statements or their related notes?
7. If accounting charges for past service costs exceed funding payments, what kind of account arises and how should it be reported in financial statements? Suppose the reverse is true, that is, payments exceed charges, what then?
8. What statements and schedules of a financial character are required to be included in the annual report of a pension plan filed annually with the Secretary of Labor?
9. What are the principal provisions of the FASB *Interpretation* issued in connection with pension plan accounting?

EXERCISES

Exercise 22–1

Welzee Company initiated a pension plan on a funded, noncontributory basis several years after the company began operations. Its consulting actuary determined that at inception of the plan the past service cost amounted to $338,721.

Required:

1. Using a 7% interest table, prepare a schedule that reflects amortization of the past service cost over a four-year period and funding over a three-year period. Round to nearest dollar.
2. Give journal entries relating to the pension plan covering its first two years of operations based upon funding in accordance with the table developed in compliance with Requirement 1 and on the assumptions that the plan year and the fiscal year coincided and normal costs for the first two years were Year 1, $50,000, and Year 2, $53,000.

Exercise 22–2

The independent actuary engaged by Martin Company determined that should it adopt the type of pension plan contemplated, its unfunded past service cost would amount to $331,213.

Required:

1. Prepare a schedule that reflects amortization of the past service cost over a four-year period and funding over a six-year period based on 8% annual interest rates. Round to nearest dollar.
2. Assuming the actuary determined the normal pension cost to be Year 1, $120,000, and Year 2, $132,000, journalize pension expense for both years.
3. Indicate what would be reported on Martin Company's income statement and balance sheet for each of the two years.

Exercise 22–3

Cisco Corporation initiated a funded pension plan and gave employees credit for past service. The actuary estimated the past service cost at inception at $50,000.

Required:

(Round calculations to the nearest dollar.)

1. Using a 5% annual rate calculate the periodic amortization factor and periodic funding payment assuming:
   Case A – Funding and amortization are over three years.
   Case B – Funding is over four years; amortization is over three.
   Case C – Funding is over two years; amortization is over three.
2. Prepare an amortization and funding schedule for the past service cost for Case C.
3. Give entries for four years for Case C if the normal costs for the years are respectively: $12,000, $14,000, $18,000, and $22,000.
4. Indicate the amounts that would be reflected on the income statement and the balance sheet under Case C for the four years.

Exercise 22–4

Check the best answer in each of the following and explain the basis for your choice.

1. When pension plan costs are presented in a statement of income and retained earnings, past and current service costs–
   a. Must be shown separately in computing income before extraordinary items.
   b. Must be separated so that past service costs can be treated as a prior period adjustment.
   c. Must be separated so that past service costs can be treated as an extraordinary item.
   d. May be either combined or shown separately in computing income before extraordinary items.
2. In accounting for a pension plan any difference between the pension cost charged to expense and payments into the found should be reported as–
   a. An offset to the liability for past service cost.
   b. Accrued or prepaid pension cost.
   c. An operating expense in this period.
   d. An accrued actuarial liability.
3. A company in accounting properly for pension cost–
   a. Allocates total pension costs systematically and rationally.

b. Records fluctuating gains and losses on pension fund investments as they occur.
c. Gives recognition to all pension costs for which legal liability exists.
d. Establishes a positive relationship between contributions to the fund and the recorded provision.

4. Benefits under a pension plan that are not contingent upon an employee's continuing service are—
a. Granted under a plan of defined contribution.
b. Based upon terminal funding.
c. Actuarially unsound.
d. Vested.

5. When an established company adopts a pension plan, the costs related to past services of employees should be charged to—
a. Operations of current and future periods.
b. Operations of prior periods.
c. Operations of the current period.
d. Retained earnings.

(AICPA adapted)

Exercise 22–5

Set forth below is an amortization table of a company which adopted a pension plan at a time when its past service cost amounted to $1,000,000. This past service cost is being funded in a lesser number of years than it is being amortized.

(a)	*(b)*	*(c)*	*(d)*	*(e)*	*(f)*	*(g)*
1......	$123,290.94	—	$123,290.94	$148,527.83	$ 25,236.89	$ 25,236.89
2......	123,290.94	$1,009.48	122,281.46	148,527.83	26,246.37	51,483.26
3......	123,290.94	2,059.33	121,231.61	148,527.83	27,296.22	78,779.48
4......	123,290.94	3,151.18	120,139.76	148,527.83	28,338.07	107,167.55
5......	123,290.94	4,286.70	119,004.24	148,527.83	29,523.59	136,691.14
6......	123,290.94	5,467.65	117,823.29	148,527.83	30,704.54	167,395.68
7......	123,290.94	6,695.83	116,595.11	148,527.83	31,932.72	199,328.40
8......	123,290.94	7,973.14	115,317.80	148,527.83	33,210.03	232,538.43
9......	123,290.94	9,301.54	113,989.40	—	113,989.40*	118,549.03
10......	123,290.94	4,741.91*	118,549.03	—	118,549.03*	—

* Reflects rounding.

Required:

1. What interest rate was assumed in making the amortization and funding calculations? Show how you arrived at your results.
2. Supply appropriate titles for columns *(a)* through *(g)* of the table.
3. If the normal costs in Years 1, 2, and 3 were respectively $90,000, $100,000, and $110,000, what were *(a)* total disbursements for pensions for these three years, and *(b)* total pension plan expenses for these three years?
4. What balance sheet amounts would be shown by this company in respect to its pension plan at the end of Years 7, 8, and 9 and what is the nature of the account under which the amounts would be reported?

PROBLEMS

Problem 22–1

After having been in business a number of years without a pension plan, Dean Corporation adopted a funded, noncontributory plan. For simplicity, the number of periods dealt with will be limited and the first year of the pension plan will be designated as 19A. Amounts will be kept small. Past service costs as of January 1, 19A, amounted to $60,000. Normal costs for 19A were $9,000; in the four succeeding years they were $9,500, $10,000, $10,400, and $10,900.

Required:

1. Using 8% interest rate and assuming year-end funding, prepare schedules of amortization and funding for each of the following sets of assumptions as to years over which amortization and funding of past service is to occur:

	Periods	
	Amortization	*Funding*
Case A.	4	4
Case B.	3	4
Case C.	4	3
Case D.	4	1

2. Give journal entries related to pension costs and cash payments for 19A, 19D, and 19E (round all computations to nearest dollar). Use present value, not straight line.
3. Indicate amounts that would be reported on the income statement and balance sheet for 19A, 19D, and 19E concerning the pension plan.

Problem 22–2

Mannix Company initiated a funded, noncontributory pension plan effective January 1, 1976. This was several years after the company began operations so there was an initial past service cost of $30,000. Because the company has an excess of investable cash it was decided to fund the past service cost fully as of year-end, 1976, and to amortize the cost over a four-year term. In connection with the latter, a 7% rate will be assumed. Payments will be made to an independent pension fund trustee.

Required:

1. Prepare a schedule of amortization and funding of the past service cost. Round all amounts to the nearest dollar.
2. Assuming that normal costs are as follows: 1976, $9,000; 1977, $9,400; 1978, $10,000; and 1979, $10,500, give journal entries related to pension costs and cash payments for each year.
3. Suppose the first eligible employee retired late in 1978 and was paid first benefits amounting to $500 late that year. Give any entries indicated. Explain.
4. Indicate amounts that would be reported on the income statement and balance sheet for 1976, 1977, and 1978.

Schedule of Amortization of Past Service Costs and Related Funding

	Amortization Past Pension Cost—10 Years				Balance Sheet—Liability	
Year	10-Year Accrual Factor	Addition for 6% Interest	Past Pension Cost (a) + (b)	12-Year Funding	Credit Debit*	Account Balance
1	$135,867.96[(a)]	—	$135,867.96[(b)]	$119,277.03	$ 16,590.93[(c)]	$ 16,590.93
2	135,867.96	$ 995.46[(d)]	136,863.42	119,277.03	17,586.39	34,177.32
3	135,867.96	2,050.64	137,918.60	119,277.03	18,641.57	52,818.89
4	135,867.96	3,169.13	139,037.09	119,277.03	19,760.06	72,578.95
5	135,867.96	4,354.74	140,222.70	119,277.03	20,945.67	93,524.62
6	135,867.96	5,611.48	141,479.44	119,277.03	22,202.41	115,727.03
7	135,867.96	6,943.62	142,811.58	119,277.03	23,534.55	139,261.58
8	135,867.96	8,355.69	144,223.65	119,277.03	24,946.62	164,208.20
9	135,867.96	9,852.49	145,720.45	119,277.03	26,443.42	190,651.62
10	135,867.96	11,439.10	147,307.06	119,277.03	28,030.03	218,681.65
11	—	13,120.90	13,120.90	119,277.03	106,156.13*	112,525.52
12	—	6,751.51†	6,751.51	119,277.03	112,525.52*	—

† Reflects rounding of 2 cents.

Computations:

(a) Amortization (10 years, 6%):
$1,000,000 ÷ 7.3600871 = $135,867.96.

(b) Funding (12 years, 6%):
$1,000,000 ÷ 8.3838439 = $119,277.03.

(c) $135,867.96 − $119,277.03 = $16,590.93.

(d) $16,590.93 × 6% = $995.46.

Problem 22–3

Set forth opposite is an amortization and funding table for a company whose past service cost was determined to be $1,000,000 when its pension plan was adopted. If the company were to amortize this amount of past service cost over a 10-year period and to fund it over a 12-year period, using a 6% rate the table would apply.

Required:

(Make all computations and entries rounded to nearest dollar.)

1. If the company's normal cost for pensions for Years 1 and 2 respectively amounted to $140,000 and $148,000 and the management had decided initially to postpone funding of the past service cost rather than to implement, what is the *minimum* pension expense the company could report under provisions of *APB Opinion No. 8*? Show computations. (Assume there are no vesting requirements.)
2. If the company instead decided to implement the funding and amortization as reflected on the foregoing table, what is the *maximum* pension expense the company could report for Years 1 and 2 if normal costs are as given in Requirement 1?
3. Again assume the normal costs for the first two years are the same as in Requirement 1. In this instance the company management decides to amortize the $100,000 past service cost over ten years but to fund it in eight years and to use a 5% annual rate in connection with past service cost. Calculate the ten-year accrual factor and the eight-year funding factor; prepare a partial table (through the first two years) and indicate the *maximum* allowed pension expense under provisions of *APB Opinion No. 8*.

Problem 22–4

The TP Company decided to initiate a funded pension plan and to give employees credit for prior employment. The plan is noncontributory, and the benefits vest at age 60. The actuary estimated the past service cost at date of inception of the plan to be $50,000. To keep the problem short assume the past service cost is to be amortized over three years and that the interest rate is 5%.

Required:

1. Compute the periodic amortization *factor* and the periodic funding payment assuming:

   Case A – Funding is over a three-year period.
   Case B – Funding is over a four-year period.
   Case C – Funding is over a two-year period.

2. Prepare an amortization and funding schedule for the past service cost for Case C.
3. Give entries for the four years for Case C assuming the actuarially determined normal pension costs to be: Year 1, $15,000; Year 2, $18,000; Year 3, $20,000; and Year 4, $24,000.
4. Indicate the amounts that would be reflected on the income statement and the balance sheet under Case C for the four years.

Problem 22–5

Simpson Company was organized in 1964. The decision was made to initiate a funded, noncontributory pension plan starting January 1, 1976. The First Security Bank will be the funding agency. The actuary determined the past service cost at date of inception of the plan (as of January 1, 1976) to be $30,000 and the normal pension cost for the year 1976 to be $10,000. Since the company had an excess of ready cash, it was decided to completely fund the past pension cost at the end of 1976. Past pension cost will be amortized over four years; a 6% rate of interest will be assumed.

Required:

1. Prepare a schedule of funding and amortization of past service costs.
2. Give all entries indicated for 1976.
3. Give entries for 1977–81 assuming the following normal pension costs: 1977, $11,000; 1978, $12,000; 1979, $13,000; 1980, $14,000; and 1981, $15,000.
4. Assume a long-time employee retired during 1981 and was paid a first monthly pension benefit of $300. Give any entries indicated. Explain.
5. What would be reported on the income statement and balance sheet for each period 1976–81 inclusive?

Problem 22–6

Rake Corporation has been in business for approximately 25 years. Recently the management made a decision to institute a funded, noncontributory pension plan. A trustee has been selected to receive and disburse the pension funds in accordance with the plan. To shorten this problem the amounts are relatively small and the number of periods limited. Assume that the program started on January 1, 1976, and that estimates through 1980 made by the actuary were:

1. Past service costs at the beginning of 1976, $60,000.
2. Normal service costs: 1976, $8,000; 1977, $8,400; 1978, $9,000; 1979, $9,500; and 1980, $10,200.
3. Interest rate, 5%.

In respect to amortization of past service costs and their funding there are four separate cases:

	Periods	
Case	*Amortization*	*Funding*
A	4	4
B	3	4
C	4	3
D	4	1

Required:

For each case, show computations.

1. Schedule of amortization and funding (assume funding at year-end).
2. Journal entries for years 1976, 1979, and 1980.
3. Balances to be reported on financial statements for 1976, 1979, and 1980.

Problem 22–7

Sims Distributing Company began operations a number of years ago. Recently its management decided to add pensions as a fringe benefit for the employees. The actuary employed determined that as of the year the pension plan was to begin, past service costs amounted to $800,000. A decision was made to amortize these costs over eight years and to fund them over six years. Star Trust Company will serve as trustee of the noncontributory pension trust; a 7% interest rate has been assumed.

Required:

1. Prepare a schedule of amortization and funding for the past service cost. Round all calculations to the nearest dollar.
2. Give journal entries for Years 1, 3, 6, and 7 if normal costs paid for these years are, respectively, $80,000, $85,000, $95,000, and $110,000, and other payments are in accordance with the table developed in Requirement 1.
3. Give any necessary entry to record payments in Year 6 to long-time employee Smith who retired in that year and who drew pension benefits that year amounting to $1,300. Explain.
4. What would be reflected on the income statement and balance sheet of Sims Distributing Company for Years 1, 3, 6, and 7 in respect to its pension plan?

Problem 22–8

The Tudor Corporation adopted a qualified profit-sharing plan for its employees on January 1, 1966. The trust agreement contains the following provisions:

1. For each year in which the amount of eligible net earnings equals or exceeds the profit-sharing base for that year, the corporation shall remit to the trustee an amount equal to 5% of the profit-sharing base for the year plus 10% of any eligible net earnings for the year in excess of the base.
2. "Eligible net earnings" with respect to any year shall be net income for the year after deducting the payment to the trustee and the provision for federal income taxes.
3. An employee shall be eligible to participate in the plan on January 1 of the year following the completion of one full year of employment.
4. The annual payment to the trustee shall be allocated to the interests of the participants according to the following unit system:
   a. For each full calendar year of employment under the plan each participant shall be entitled to eight units.
   b. For each $10 of average weekly pay earned in the current year, based on a 52-week year, the employee shall be entitled to one unit.
5. Ten percent of a participant's total interest is vested for each full year of his participation in the plan.
6. Forfeitures and investment income will be distributed to the remaining participants at the end of each year in proportion to their interests in the plan at the beginning of the year.

In the course of your audit of Tudor Corporation as of December 31, 1975, you find that the trustee has submitted the trial balance below but that the corporation's 1975 contribution to the trust has not been computed and allocated to the participants.

PROFIT-SHARING TRUST
Trial Balance
December 31, 1975

	Debit	Credit
Cash	$ 500	
Investment, 1/1/75	26,000	
R. Johnson's interest, 1/1/75..............		$ 6,512
K. Kegler's interest, 1/1/75..................		5,984
J. Wright's interest, 1/1/75..................		7,500
M. Penny's interest, 1/1/75..................		5,104
Investment income for 1975		1,400
	$26,500	$26,500

The following information also is available.

Employee	Date Employed	Date Terminated	1975 Salary
R. Johnson	12/8/65		$ 8,320
K. Kegler	7/1/66		7,280
J. Wright	11/20/66	8/1/75	6,200
M. Penny	9/15/71		5,200
J. Rawlings	8/20/74	12/26/75	800
A. Morris	5/5/74		1,100
			$28,900

The 1975 net income for Tudor Corporation before deducting the payment to the trustee and the provision for federal income taxes is $88,500.

Required:

a. Assume that the profit-sharing base for 1975 is $30,000 and the income tax rate is 50%. Compute the corporation's 1975 contribution to the trust.

b. Assume that the answer to Requirement *(a)* is $4,000. Prepare a schedule allocating the 1975 contribution to the various participants.

c. Prepare a schedule allocating the amount of any forfeitures and investment income to the remaining participants.

(AICPA adapted)

Problem 22–9

C & L Printers, Inc., was organized over a decade ago. Four years ago the company established a formal pension plan to provide retirement benefits for all employments. The plan is noncontributory and funded through a trustee, X Bank, which pays all benefits as they become due. Original past service cost of $110,000 is being amortized over 15 years and funded over 10 years. C & L also funds an amount equal to current normal cost net of actuarial gains and losses. There have been no plan amendments since inception. Portions of the independent actuary's report covering the latest year appear below.

I. Current Year's Funding and Pension Cost:		
Normal cost (before adjustment for actuarial gains) computed under the entry-age-normal method		$34,150
Actuarial gains:		
Investment gains (losses):		
Excess of expected dividend income over actual dividend income		(350)
Gain on sale of investments		4,050
Gains in actuarial assumptions for:		
Mortality		3,400
Employee turnover		5,050
Reduction in pension cost from closing of plant		8,000
Net actuarial gains		20,150
Normal cost (funded currently)	$ 14,000	14,000
Past service costs:		
Funding	14,245	
Amortization		10,597
Total Funded	$ 28,245	
Total Pension Cost for Financial-Statement Purposes		$24,597
II. Fund Assets:		
Cash	$ 4,200	
Dividends receivable	1,525	
Investment in common stocks, at cost (market value, $177,800)	162,750	
	$168,475	

Required:

1. Comment on *(a)* treatment of actuarial gains and losses, and *(b)* computation of pension cost for financial-statement purposes on the basis of requirements for accounting for pension plan costs.
2. What interest rate is being used in connection with the past service cost amortization and funding? Support your findings.

(AICPA adapted)

Chapter 23

Accounting for Leases

Lease accounting can best be described as "state of the art" accounting. It has been evolving since 1949 when *Accounting Research Bulletin No. 38* appeared.[1] The highlights of what is regarded currently as proper lease accounting and reporting will be discussed. It is safe to predict that new forms of lease contracts will emerge and that new accounting principles and procedures will be developed as a result.

Some material in this chapter is based upon provisions of an exposure draft of an FASB *Statement on Lease Accounting* which was to have become effective January 1, 1976. Shortly before the statement was to become operational it was withdrawn for further study. Since that exposure draft represents the latest authoritative expression of what lease accounting should be (even though it has not become effective in March, 1976) we have chosen to present it as a model of modern lease accounting.

A lease is a contract between an owner (the lessor) and another party (the lessee) which conveys to the lessee the right to use the lessor's property in return for a consideration, usually periodic rental payments. Broadly, there are two principal types of leases—operating leases and financing or capital leases.

Under an *operating lease*, the lessor, while giving the lessee use of the leased property, retains practically all of the risks and rewards of ownership (e.g., early obsolescence and appreciation of value). Operating leases characteristically are of shorter duration than financing leases. Rentals of apartments, space in shopping centers, and automobiles typify operating leases.

In contrast, *financing leases* almost invariably are long term; they transfer most of the ownership risks and rewards to the lessee, usually are noncancellable, and obligate the lessee to pay taxes, insurance, and maintenance on the property.[2] Often the lessee has the option to buy the

---

[1] AICPA, "Disclosure of Long-Term Leases in Financial Statements of Lessees," *ARB No. 38* (New York, 1949).

[2] The same lease identified as a *financing lease* by a lessor is called a *capital lease* by the lessee.

property for a nominal sum when the financing lease expires. The lessor is primarily interested in a rate of return on his or her investment in the property, not in its appreciation or longevity. The distinctions between an operating and a financing lease may be summarized as follows:

Usual Lease Characteristics	*Type of Lease*	
	Operating	*Financing*
a. Duration of lease	Short term	Long term
b. Cancellation of lease prior to termination date	Cancellable or noncancellable	Noncancellable
c. Composition of periodic rental payments	Includes return on investment and most ownership costs (maintenance, taxes, depreciation, obsolescence, casualty losses, etc.)	Includes return on investment but little or no ownership costs
d. Termination options	None	Asset may be acquired at no cost or a nominal cost
e. Special property rights	None transferred	Substantially transferred
f. Financing characteristics	Short term, and lessor does not tend to assume role of financial institution.	Substantial and usually long term. Lessor tends to assume role of financing institution.

Some contracts are called leases when in fact they are nothing more than long-term installment sales contracts; in these cases, the accountant has to look beyond the form and account for the substance of the transaction. A fairly recent development is the three-party or *leverage lease*.[3]

Before studying the details of lease accounting the different situations, it may be helpful to study Exhibit 23–1 which presents an overview of current accounting for leases.

ACCOUNTING FOR OPERATING LEASES

The two broad classifications of leases defined above (operating leases and financing leases) have influenced the development of accounting concepts and procedures for lease agreements. In the discussions to follow operating leases will be accounted for under the following methods:[4]

[3] Leveraged leases are discussed in the Appendix to the chapter.

[4] John H. Meyers, "Reporting Leases in Financial Statements," *Accounting Research Study No. 4* (New York: AICPA, 1962). FASB Exposure Draft, "Accounting for Leases, Financial Accounting Standards Board" (Stamford, Conn., 1975).

EXHIBIT 23–1
Accounting for Leases Summarized

	Lessor Accounting	*Lessee Accounting*
Operating Leases:		
1. Accounting method	Operating (or rental) method	Noncapitalization (or expense) method
2. Conceptual basis	Ownership of leased property not transferred	Ownership of leased property not acquired
3. Leased asset	Accounted for as a *tangible* asset	Not accounted for as an asset
4. Debt	No receivable for the rent contract recorded	No liability for the rent contract recorded
5. Depreciation	Recorded in normal manner	Not recorded
6. Maintenance costs	Recorded in normal manner	Not paid or recorded
7. Rental payments	Recorded as revenue	Recorded as expense
Financing Leases:		
1. Accounting method	Financing (sale) method	Financing (capitalization or purchase) method
2. Conceptual basis	Ownership of leased property is transferred (as a sale)	Ownership of leased property is acquired (as a purchase)
3. Leased asset	Cost removed from the tangible asset accounts (as in a sale)	Cost recorded in a capitalized lease asset account (an intangible asset)
4. Debt	Record present value of lease payments as a receivable	Record present value of lease payments as a liability
5. Depreciation	Not recorded	No depreciation; however, amortize the intangible asset
6. Maintenance costs	Not paid or recorded	Paid and recorded as expense
7. Rental payments	Collection on receivable (plus interest revenue)	Payment on liability (plus interest expense)

Lessor – operating (or rental) method
Lessee – noncapitalization (or expense) method

These methods are consistent in that both sides of the lease agreement, as represented by the lessor and the lessee, recognize revenue, expense, and amortization on the same conceptual basis. Both methods focus on determination of net income by recognizing revenues and expenses on an accrual basis; they ignore *future* rights, obligations, and commitments (because such rights normally do not exist in an operating lease situation).

An example of a simple operating lease situation is presented in Exhibit 23–2. A owns a small office building, part of which is rented to B for an annual rental of $1,200 payable in advance each January 1. It is assumed that the fiscal period of each party ends October 31. This is an operating lease since the lessor retains all the normal risks of ownership and the lessee gains no special property or purchase rights, but only temporary and cancellable occupancy rights.

EXHIBIT 23–2
Simple Operating Lease Situation – Accounting by Lessor and Lessee

Lessor A (operating method)			*Lessee B (noncapitalization method)*		
January 1, 19A:					
To record annual rental payments:					
Cash	1,200		Rent expense	1,200	
Rent revenue.........		1,200	Cash		1,200
October 10, 19A:					
To record payment of property taxes:					
Expense	60		No entry.		
Cash		60			
October 13, 19A:					
To report payment of monthly telephone bill:					
No entry.			Expense................................	15	
			Cash		15
October 31, 19A:					
To record adjusting entry (two months' rent unexpired):					
Rent revenue..............	200		Prepaid rent expense...............	200	
Unearned rent revenue		200	Rent expense		200

Prepaid Rent

An operating lease becomes slightly more complex when, in addition to the annual rental, there is a payment made in advance (a downpayment). In this situation the additional payment must be allocated (amortized) over the life of the lease on a realistic basis. Two amortization methods are commonly used, viz:

1. Straight-line method – a constant *dollar amount* of the prepayment is allocated to each period covered by the lease.[5]
2. Present value (or interest) method – a constant *rate* of allocation is utilized as determined by application of the annuity concept to the prepayment. This method necessitates utilization of the present value of an annuity (Table 6–4).

This type of situation, including both methods of amortization of the prepayment, is presented in Exhibit 23–3. This illustration is identical with the preceding one, Exhibit 23–2, with the additional provision that *(a)* there is a three-year lease agreement, *(b)* there is an advance payment of $3,000 (in addition to the $1,200 annual rental), and *(c)* the fiscal year for both parties ends on December 31. A 6% annual interest rate is assumed.

As the unamortized balance of Leasehold or Prepaid Rent diminishes, so also does periodic rent revenue or expense.

In summary, we may observe that the lessor under the operating method did not recognize any transfers of rights or property, or any "purchase" agreements. The lessor recognized the prepayment of a revenue and then amortized it to derive a periodic credit to revenue. The lessee, under the noncapitalization method, did not capitalize any property rights or recognize any "purchase" agreements. The prepayment was capitalized as an intangible asset which was then amortized to derive a periodic charge to expense.

EVOLUTION OF ACCOUNTING FOR FINANCING LEASES

For many years practically all leases were accounted for as operating leases. However, accounting theorists contended that long-term leases that reflected primarily the characteristics of a financing transaction (and hence were called financing leases) should be recorded by the lessor as a sale involving recognition of a long-term receivable. Consistent accounting for the lessee conceptually would require capitalization of the leased asset and recognition of a long-term liability. While many thought this was conceptually sound, relatively few entities accounted for leases in this way, and it was not required by generally accepted accounting principles. An increasing amount of footnote disclosure about lease terms and obligations occurred during this period.

Because of the rapid increase in leasing and the wide array of accounting alternatives used by both the lessee and lessor, the APB issued *Opinion No. 5*, "Reporting of Leases in Financial Statements of Lessee" (September 1964), and *Opinion No. 7*, "Accounting for Leases in Financial Statements of Lessors" (May 1966). Each of these opinions specified conditions under which a lease should be accounted for as a financing

[5] The FASB has expressed a preference for use of the straight-line method by lessees on operating leases. The FASB Exposure Draft, "Accounting for Leases," states: "Normally, rent on an operating lease shall be charged to expense over the lease term as it becomes payable. If rental payments are not made on a straight-line basis, rental expense nevertheless shall be recognized on a straight-line basis unless another systematic and rational basis is justified by the circumstances."

EXHIBIT 23–3
Operating Lease with Amortization—Accounting by Lessor and Lessee

	Lessor A (operating method)			*Lessee B (noncapitalization method)*		
January 1, 19A:						
To record prepayment of rent:						
	Cash	3,000		Leasehold (prepaid rent) expense	3,000	
	Prepaid rent revenue		3,000	Cash		3,000
To record annual rental:						
	Cash	1,200		Rent expense	1,200	
	Rent revenue		1,200	Cash		1,200
December 31, 19A:						
To record amortization of advance rental payment (for 12 months):						
Case A—Straight-line method:						
	Prepaid rent revenue	1,000		Rent expense	1,000	
	Rent revenue		1,000	Leasehold		1,000
	* Computation: $3,000 \times {}^{12}/_{36} = \$1,000$					
Case B—Present value method (see computations below):						
	Prepaid rent revenue	942.33		Rent expense	1,122.33	
	Interest expense	180.00		Interest revenue		180.00
	Rent revenue		1,122.33	Leasehold		942.33
December 31, 19A:						
Closing entry (Case B):						
	Rent revenue	2,322.33		Income summary	2,142.33	
	Interest expense		180.00	Interest revenue	180.00	
	Income summary		2,142.33	Rent expense		2,322.33

Computations:

Schedule of Amortization (see note)

Period	*Periodic Rent*	*Interest (6%)*	*Amortization of Prepayment*	*Unamortized Balance*
1-1-19A				$3,000.00
12-31-19A	$1,122.33*	$180.00†	$ 942.33‡	2,057.67§
12-31-19B	1,122.33	123.46	998.87	1,058.80
12-31-19C	1,122.33	63.53	1,058.80	-0-

* Implied periodic rent = $3,000 ÷ Present value of ordinary annuity (3 rents, 6%)
= $3,000 ÷ 2.6730120 (Table 6–4)
= $1,122.33

† $3,000 × 6% = $180.00

‡ $1,122.33 − $180.00 = $942.33

§ $3,000.00 − $942.33 = $2,057.67

Note: An ordinary annuity is assumed; that is, that the advance payment represents the present value of three equal year-end amounts of $1,122.33 each. Alternatively, an annuity due could have been assumed; that is, that the three payments would be at the *beginning* of each period. In this case the Table 6–4 value would be $(n - 1) + 1$. An annuity due for advance rentals was illustrated in Chapter 14, under the caption "Leaseholds."

lease; all leases not classifiable as financing leases were accounted for as operating leases. These two *Opinions* were inconsistent in that different criteria for identifying financing leases were specified for the lessee and the lessor. *APB Opinion No. 27*, "Accounting for Lease Transactions by Manufacturer or Dealer Lessors (November 1972), was issued in response to questions concerning a special type of lease involving "manufacturer's or dealer's profit" and "third party" leases. To enhance full disclosure, *APB Opinion No. 31*, "Disclosure of Lease Commitments by Lessees" (June 1973), was issued. These *Opinions* represented a significant move in the direction of theoretical correctness in accounting for leases. However, for a variety of reasons they still presented a number of theoretical and practical problems.

The latest step in the development of lease accounting and reporting is the issuance of an FASB Exposure Draft of a proposed Statement, "Accounting for Leases." This statement is planned to supercede the four APB *Opinions* cited above *(Nos. 5, 7, 27,* and *31)* and establish new criteria and reporting requirements for both the lessee and the lessor. Leases meeting the criteria must be accounted for as financing leases, and all other must be accounted for as operating leases.

CRITERIA FOR IDENTIFYING TYPES OF LEASES

The FASB Exposure Draft has provided two sets of criteria for distinguishing different types of leases. From the standpoint of the *lessee*, if a lease meets any one of the five criteria set out in Column A below, it shall be classed as a *capital* (synonymous with "financing") *lease;* otherwise, it shall be classed as an *operating lease.* From the standpoint of the *lessor*, if a lease meets any one of the five criteria from Column A and *both* of the criteria in Column B, it shall be classed as a *financing lease;* otherwise, it shall be classed as an operating lease.

Criteria for Classifying Leases

Column A	*Column B*
1. Transfers title to property to lessee by end of lease term.	1. Collectibility of payments required from the lessee is reasonably predictable.
2. Contains a bargain purchase option.*	2. No important uncertainties surround the amount of costs yet to be incurred by the lessor under the lease.
3. Lease term is equal to 75% or more of the estimated economic life of the property.	
4. Estimated residual value of leased property is less than 25% of property's fair value at inception of lease.	
5. Leased property as a whole is specially designed for the needs of the lessee.	

* A bargain purchase option is a provision which allows the lessee, at his or her option, to buy the leased property for a price that at the inception of the lease is expected to be substantially less than the fair value of the property when the option becomes exercisable.

The FASB proposed statement identifies two types of financing leases for the lessor and one type for the lessee, viz:

Lessor:

1. Direct financing leases—leases that do not give rise to manufacturer's or dealer's profit (or loss) to the lessor that meets one or more of the criteria in Column A above and both of the criteria in Column B above.
2. Sales-type leases—leases that give rise to manufacturer's or dealer's profit (or loss) to the lessor that meets one or more of the criteria in Column A above and both of the criteria in Column B above.

Lessee:

1. Capital leases—leases that meet one or more of the criteria in Column A above. Thus, both types of financing leases for the lessor qualify as capital leases to the lessee.

Clearly, the key distinction for the lessor between a direct financing lease and a sales-type lease is whether there is a manufacturer's or dealer's profit (or loss). Manufacturer's profit relates to the situation where the lessor is a manufacturer, and dealer's profit relates to the situation where the lessor is not a manufacturer. Manufacturer's or dealer's profit arises when the sum of the future lease payments required by the lease (selling price) is greater than the cost of the leased equipment. In contrast, there is no manufacturer's or dealer's profit when the present value of the future lease payments are equal to the cost of the leased equipment. To illustrate—

	Type of Financing Lease—Lessor Company		
	Direct Financing	*Sales Type*	
Sum of the required lease payments ($47,479.28 × 5)	$237,396.40		$237,396.40
Present value of the rental payments (page 983)	200,000.00		
Sales price:			
Cost (assumed)		$180,000	
Manufacturer's or dealer's profit ...		20,000	200,000.00
Lease Revenue (interest)	$ 37,396.40		$ 37,396.40

ACCOUNTING FOR FINANCING LEASES

The discussions to follow will relate to much more complex lease arrangements than operating leases. Financing leases have become rather common in recent years, and they represent a fairly wide range of contractual specifications. They are commonly referred to as financing leases in view of their dominant characteristic as a form of major financing; the lessor primarily is in the business of providing financing and the lessee is using the lease as a source of financing.

Frequently, the primary business activities of the lessor-owner are providing financing by lending money and by leasing assets such as equipment and buildings. Basically, the lessor-owner has money to invest for a return and may choose to invest it in property acquired for rental purposes and thus gain a return on the investments through rents. In these circumstances the lessor-owner may offer lease contracts that give rise to *special property rights* for the lessee. On the other side, by renting under these conditions, the lessee basically is using this approach as one means of major financing of the business. The lessor provides the capital through the assets leased and the lessee makes "installment" payments in the form of rent. These payments include both principal and interest; generally they are deductible for tax purposes by the lessee. Thus, in accounting for leases of this type the underlying concept is that the *special* property rights and related liabilities (and receivables) should be measured, accounted for, and reported in the financial statements of the two parties to the transaction.

The underlying accounting concept for *financing leases* as they relate to the lessor-owner and the lessee as outlined in Exhibit 23–1 may be detailed as follows:

Party	*Accounting Method*	*Characteristics*
Lessor	Financing (sale) method	Underlying concept—in essence the lessor is providing financing for the lessee by purchasing assets which are conveyed to the lessee, and the latter assumes the risks of ownership without a formal transfer of title. Accounting—recognizes *(a)* a receivable from the lessee for the life of the lease; *(b)* a "sale" of the leased asset; and *(c)* an unearned lease and/or interest revenue. The receivable and unearned revenue, recognized at inception of the lease, should be amortized over the life of the lease on a present value (interest) basis as the periodic rentals are collected.
Lessee	Financing (capitalization or purchase) method	Underlying concept—in essence the lessee is obtaining major financing by contracting for *special* property rights on a noncancellable basis. As a consequence, over the life of the property rented, the rental payments to the lessor constitute a payment of principal plus interest. The ordinary costs of ownership will be paid by the lessee; hence they must be recognized as current expenses as paid (or accrued). Accounting—recognizes *(a)* an intangible asset "leaserights" for the life of the lease; *(b)* a payable "lease obligation" to the lessor extending over the life of the lease; *(c)* rental payments as reductions of the payable to the lessor; *(d)* the interest should be amortized over the life of the lease on a present value (interest) basis; and *(e)* amortization of the intangible asset over the life of the lease (or if acquired finally, over its useful life).

Accounting by the lessor and lessee using the financing method will now be illustrated separately with a common set of facts.

Illustration of Financing Method (Lessor)

There is one difference in accounting for a direct financing lease and a sales-type lease; that is, whether there is manufacturer's or dealer's profit. First we will discuss and illustrate direct financing leases.

Direct Financing Leases. Recall that this type of lease does not involve a manufacturer's or dealer's profit. The gain to the lessor is composed only of *interest* on the investment in the asset leased. To illustrate accounting for direct financing leases by the *lessor*, assume that the Lessor Company is primarily engaged in leasing out heavy construction equipment. Among the equipment that the company has available for leasing is a newly acquired package of machines that cost $200,000 with an estimated useful life of five years and no residual value. Lessor Company has been negotiating with Lessee Company in respect to the capital needs of the latter. As a result of these negotiations a lease agreement was signed on January 1, 19A, by the two parties with the essential provisions that: *(a)* Lessor Company would provide a package of new machines on a five-year contract; *(b)* Lessee Company would pay an equal annual rent at the *end* of each year amounting to $47,479.28; *(c)* the contract is noncancellable; *(d)* Lessee Company would assume (pay directly in addition to the rent) all of the normal ownership costs such as taxes, maintenance, and insurance; and *(e)* at the termination of the lease the equipment reverts to the lessor unless the lessee elects to pay $1,000 for it. These conditions meet the criteria for a *direct financing* lease, and there is no manufacturer's or dealer's profit (see page 981). On January 1, 19A, the effective date of the agreement, the equipment was turned over to Lessee Company. Using these data we will illustrate accounting by the lessor; the next section will consider accounting by the lessee.

Lessor Company established the annual rental amount quoted to Lessee Company (and incorporated in the lease agreement) on the basis that it had an investment with a present value of $200,000 and expected a 6% return on that investment. The resultant computations were:

Annual Rent = $200,000 ÷ Present Value of an Ordinary Annuity (5 periods @ 6%) (Table 6–4)
= $200,000 ÷ 4.2123638
= $ 47,479.28

The following amortization schedule for the life of the lease (investment) was developed as a basis for the accounting entries for the lessor:

Lessor—Schedule of Lease Amortization and Related Accounting Entries (direct financing method)

Date	Annual Rental (a)	Interest on Unrecovered Investment (b)	Investment Recovery (c)	Unrecovered Investment (d)
Jan. 1, 19A				$200,000.00
Dec. 31, 19A	$ 47,479.28	$12,000.00	$ 35,479.28	164,520.72
Dec. 31, 19B	47,479.28	9,871.24	37,608.04	126,912.68
Dec. 31, 19C	47,479.28	7,614.76	39,864.52	87,048.16
Dec. 31, 19D	47,479.28	5,222.89	42,256.39	44,791.77
Dec. 31, 19E	47,479.28	2,687.51	44,791.77	-0-
	$237,396.40	$37,396.40	$200,000.00	-0-

(a) Computed directly per above.
(b) Preceding balance in columns *(d)* times 6%.
(c) Column *(a)* minus column *(b)*.
(d) Preceding balance minus column *(c)*.

Based on the amortization schedule, the lessor would make the following accounting entries under the financing method:

January 1, 19A:

To record the inception of the lease by recognizing the receivable, the "constructive" sale of the asset, and the unearned lease (interest) revenue:

Receivables—lease contracts	237,396.40*	
Equipment..		200,000.00
Unearned interest revenue		37,396.40*

* Obviously, these two amounts could be recorded "net" in the receivables account, thus the balance in the receivables account would accord with column *(d)* in the above tabulation from period to period. The net effect on the financial statements would be the same.

December 31, 19A:

To record first rental collection and to recognize the interest revenue earned (per above schedule):

Cash	47,479.28	
Receivables—lease contracts		47,479.28
Unearned interest revenue	12,000.00	
Interest earned (or lease revenue)....................		12,000.00

December 31, 19B:

To record second rental and to recognize revenue earned:

Cash	47,479.28	
Receivables—lease contracts		47,479.28
Unearned interest revenue	9,871.24	
Interest earned..		9,871.24

Entries for the remaining periods of the lease would follow the pattern established above. Obviously, after the December 31, 19E entries, each account established in the initial entry on January 1, 19A, would have a zero balance and the Cash account of the lessor would have been increased by the investment ($200,000) plus the interest earned ($37,396.40); and if not purchased by the lessee for the $1,000 nominal amount, the lessor would reclaim the worn-out equipment which has little value. Alternatively, should the lessor sell the worn-out equipment, say as scrap, at an amount in excess of the cost of disposal, a "gain on sale of scrap" would be recorded. You should note that the lessor recorded no depreciation on the machinery; the recovery of principal was included in the rental collections which served to reduce the receivable from the lessor.

In respect to reporting and disclosure on the periodic financial statements, during the life of the lease the lease revenue earned would be reported as an operating revenue by the Lessor Company. On the balance sheet the debit balance in the receivables account would be reduced by the credit balance in the Unearned Lease Revenue account. The current portion would be reported as a current asset and the remainder under a noncurrent receivable or "other" asset caption. To illustrate, the Lessor Company would report at December 31, 19B, as follows (refer to the above amortization schedule for source of amounts):

December 31, 19B*

Income Statement:		
Interest revenue	$ 9,871.24	
Balance Sheet:		
Current Assets:		
Receivables—lease contracts	47,479.28	
Less: Unearned interest revenue	7,614.76	$39,864.52
Other Assets:		
Receivables—lease contracts	94,958.56	
Less: Unearned interest revenue	7,910.40	87,048.16

Appropriate footnote.

* Alternatively, some accountants believe that the balance sheet amounts should be:

Current Assets:		
Receivables—lease contracts	$47,479.28	
Less: Unearned interest revenue	2,687.51	$44,791.77
Other Assets:		
Receivables—lease contracts	94,958.56	
Less: Unearned interest revenue	12,837.65	82,120.91

Sales-Type Financing Leases. Recall that this type of financing lease, for the *lessor*, includes a manufacturer's or dealer's profit. The profit is the difference between the sum of the required lease payments and the sum of the cost of the leased equipment plus the required interest payments (see computation on page 981).

In the case of sales-type financing leases, the manufacturer's or dealer's profit is recognized in the period of the sale (i.e., period in which the lease is signed). Accounting for interest revenue and lease rental payments is the same as illustrated above for direct financing leases.

To illustrate, a sales-type financing lease we will adopt the above example for Lessor and Lessee Companies. Assume the following change in the basic data for Lessor Company:

Cost of equipment	$180,000
Manufacturer's or dealer's normal profit	20,000
Normal Sales Price of the Equipment	$200,000

The lease rental payments and the amortization table would be based on the $200,000 normal sales price since this is the amount Lessor Company expects from the transaction *plus* interest on the long-term receivable. The lessor would make the following entries:

January 1, 19A:

Receivables—lease contracts	237,396.40	
Equipment (cost or carrying value)		180,000.00
Revenue (manufacturer's profit) interest		20,000.00
Unearned interest revenue (see page 981)		37,396.40
To record the lease including manufacturer's or dealer's profit and unearned interest revenue (often called unearned lease revenue).		

December 31 and subsequent entries would be as those shown on page 984. The lessee's entries would be unaffected; they would be as shown on page 988.

In respect to disclosure by the lessor, the FASB Exposure Draft calls for presentation of the following information in the lessor's financial statements or footnotes thereto:

1. For direct financing and sales-type leases:
   a. Minimum rents receivable as of the date of the latest balance sheet presented, in the aggregate and for each of the succeeding five fiscal years, with separate deductions for—
      (1) Unearned interest and lease revenue.
      (2) Accumulated allowance for uncollectible rentals.
      (3) Amounts representing executory expenses included in the minimum rentals (these include taxes, maintenance, and insurance to be paid by lessor).
   b. Minimum rents receivable and estimated residual values, separately, by major property categories as of the date of the latest balance sheet presented.
   c. Total contingent rentals included in income for each period for which an income statement is presented.
2. For operating leases:
   a. Cost of property on lease (included in 3 below).
   b. Minimum future rents on noncancellable leases in the aggregate and for each of the give succeeding years.
   c. Total contingent rentals included in income for each period for which an income statement is presented.
3. Cost of property on operating leases and cost of that held for leasing purposes by major property categories as of the date of the latest

balance sheet presented. Amounts of accumulated depreciation shall also be disclosed by major property categories.

4. A general description of the lessor's leasing arrangements.

The proposed FASB statement illustrates the balance sheet presentation by the lessor as follows:

Lessor's Disclosure (other than for leveraged leases)

COMPANY X
Balance Sheet

	December 31,	
Assets	*1975*	*1974*
Current Receivables:		
Receivables under sales-type leases and direct financing leases (net of accumulated allowance for uncollectibles of $XXX and $XXX and unearned income of $XXX and $XXX for 1975 and 1974, respectively) (Note 2)	XXX	XXX
Long-Term Receivables:		
Receivables under sales-type leases and direct financing leases (net of accumulated allowance for uncollectibles of $XXX and $XXX and unearned income of $XXX and $XXX for 1975 and 1974, respectively) (Note 2)	XXX	XXX
Property, Plant, and Equipment:		
Property on operating leases (net of accumulated depreciation of $XXX and $XXX for 1975 and 1974, respectively) (Note 4)	XXX	XXX
Property held for lease (net of accumulated depreciation of $XXX and $XXX for 1975 and 1974, respectively) (Note 4)	XXX	XXX
Estimated residual values of leased property (Note 3)	XXX	XXX

(Appropriate disclosure notes, not illustrated)

Illustration of Financing Method (Lessee)

For this purpose we will utilize the preceding example with no changes thus enabling you to compare the two methods. You should observe that they are internally consistent conceptually. Upon signing the five-year lease, which called for five equal rentals of $47,479.28, payable annually at *year-end,* Lessee Company should debit an asset account for the *present value* of the special property rights accruing under the lease agreement and credit a liability to Lessor Company for the total amount of the obligation—the difference is the interest factor. To determine the capitalizable value of the special rights the Lessor Company would make the following computation:

Present Value of the Special Property Rights = $ 47,479.28 × Present Value of an Ordinary Annuity (5 periods @ 6%) (Table 6–4)

= 47,479.28 × 4.2123638

= $200,000

The Lessee Company would then develop the following schedule of amortization and related entries for the period covered by the lease:

Lessee—Schedule of Lease or Amortization and Related Accounting Entries (financing or capital lease method)

Date	*Annual Rental (a)*	*Interest on Unpaid Liability (b)*	*Payment on Principal (c)*	*Unpaid Principal (d)*
Jan. 1, 19A......				$200,000.00
Dec. 31, 19A......	$ 47,479.28	$12,000.00	$ 35,479.28	164,520.72
Dec. 31, 19B......	47,479.28	9,871.24	37,608.04	126,912.68
Dec. 31, 19C......	47,479.28	7,614.76	39,864.52	87,048.16
Dec. 31, 19D......	47,479.28	5,222.89	42,256.39	44,791.77
Dec. 31, 19E......	47,479.28	2,687.51	44,791.77	-0-
	$237,396.40	$37,396.40	$200,000.00	-0-

(*a*) Annual payment per lease contract.
(*b*) Preceding balance in column (*d*) times 6%.
(*c*) Column (*a*) minus column (*b*).
(*d*) Preceding balance minus column (*c*).

Based on the amortization schedule, the lessee would make the following accounting entries under the capital lease method:

January 1, 19A:

To record the inception of the lease by capitalizing the present value of the special property rights; to recognize the liability and the interest:

Asset—leasehold rights (equipment)........................	200,000.00	
Discount on lease contracts	37,396.40*	
Liability—lease contracts		237,396.40*

* Obviously these two amounts could be recorded "net" in the liability account, thus the balance therein from period to period would accord with column (*d*) of the above tabulation. The net effect on the financial statements would be the same.

December 31, 19A:

To record payment of the first rental (per above schedule):

Liability—lease contracts	47,479.28	
Cash		47,479.28

To record interest expense (per above schedule):

Interest expense (or lease expense)	12,000.00	
Discount on lease contracts		12,000.00

To record amortization of asset—leasehold rights (straight line):

Expense—amortization of property rights (equipment)	40,000.00	
Asset—leasehold rights (equipment)..................		40,000.00

Note: Frequently the interest expense and amortization expense is reported on the income statement as one expense item; also these three entries generally are combined.

October 15, 19B:

To pay a cost of ownership such as repairs:

Repair expense	600.00	
Cash		600.00

December 31, 19B:

To record payment of the second rental:

Liability—lease contracts	47,479.28	
Cash		47,479.28

To record interest expense (per above schedule):

Interest expense	9,871.24	
Discount on lease contracts		9,871.24

To record amortization of asset—leasehold rights (straight line):

Expense—amortization of property rights (equipment)	40,000.00	
Asset—leasehold rights (equipment)		40,000.00

Observe in the above tabulation that two distinctly separate series of entries are involved, viz:

1. Recording the equal annual payments on the liability; each rental constitutes in part a payment on the principal and in part a payment of interest for the period. Since the principal is reduced each period by a progressively greater amount, the interest is less each period. This reflects the economic essence of installment payments on debt.[6]

2. Recording periodic amortization (or depreciation) of the asset, leasehold rights. The FASB Exposure Draft states that "the asset shall be amortized in a manner consistent with the lessee's normal depreciation policy." The lessee should amortize the asset following conventional approaches: straight line, decreasing charge, and so on. Alternatively, a strong conceptual argument can be made for amortizing leasehold rights on a present value basis in view of the financing characteristics of the leasing arrangement. In this instance the periodic amortization would accord with column *(c)* in the above schedule; this approach would be comparable to depreciation by the sinking fund method discussed in a prior chapter. Obviously, the lessee has no residual value to consider.

Entries for the remaining periods would follow the pattern established above. Obviously, after the December 31, 19E, entries, the balances in the asset, liability, and discount accounts, established at the inception of the lease, would be zero. If not purchased, the worn-out equipment would be returned to the lessor and no further entries would be needed. Note that the lessee, by virtue of the lease agreement, received $200,000 financing which was repaid over a five-year period plus 6% interest (total interest expense, $37,396.40).

---

[6] Although conceptually unsound in every respect a few have argued for "straight-line" recognition of the interest expense.

In respect to reporting and disclosure on the periodic financial statements, during the life of the lease, the expense (amortization and interest) would be reflected as an operating item by the Lessee Company. On the balance sheet the asset "Leasehold rights" would be reported as an intangible asset; the payable, less the unamortized discount, would be reported under liabilities appropriately classified as to current and noncurrent. To illustrate, the balance sheet for Lessee Company on December 31, 19B, should reflect the following (refer to above amortization schedule for source of amounts; also see footnote * to table on page 988):

Intangible Assets:		
Leasehold rights capitalized ($200,000–$80,000)	$120,000.00	
Current Liabilities:		
Liability—lease contracts	47,479.28	
Less: Unamortized discount*	7,614.76	$39,864.52
Long-Term Liabilities:		
Liability—lease contracts	94,958.56	
Less: Unamortized discount*	7,910.40	87,048.16

* A less desirable alternative would be to report this as a deferred charge; also some accountants prefer to report the leasehold rights under fixed assets.

LEASE DISCLOSURES BY THE LESSEE

The following information with respect to leases shall be disclosed in the lessee's financial statements or related footnotes:

1. For capital leases:
   a. The gross amount of assets recorded under capital leases with separate identification of lease-related assets. Amounts of additions for major categories such as real estate, office equipment, trucks, and so on, between balance sheet dates. The amount of accumulated amortization shall be disclosed in total.
   b. Minimum future payments required as of the date of the latest balance sheet presented, in the aggregate and for each of the succeeding five fiscal years.
   c. The range of rates used to reduce the net minimum future payments in *(b)* above to present value and the weighted average of those rates.
   d. The total of minimum sublease rents due in the future under noncancellable subleases as of the date of the latest balance sheet.
   e. Total contingent rents actually incurred for each period for which an income statement is presented.
2. For operating leases (where the initial or remaining noncancellable terms exceeds one year):
   a. Minimum future rents in the aggregate and for each of the five succeeding fiscal years, with a deduction from the total for imputed interest to reduce the rents to present value.

   b. The range of rates used in (*a*) above and the weighted average of those rates.
   c. The present value of minimum future rents by major property categories.
   d. The total of minimum rents due in the future under noncancellable subleases as of the date of the latest balance sheet presented.
3. For all operating leases:
   a. Rental expense for each period for which an income statement is presented, with separate amounts for minimum rentals, contingent rentals, and sublease rentals.

In addition, there shall be a description of the lessee's leasing arrangements including, but not limited to, the following: (1) basis on which contingent rents are determined; (2) existence and terms of renewal or purchase options and escalation clauses; and (3) restrictions imposed by lease agreements (e.g., on dividends, additional debt, etc.).

The FASB Exposure Draft illustrates the balance sheet presentation by the lessee as follows:

Lessee's Disclosure

COMPANY X
Balance Sheet

	December 31,			December 31,	
Assets	*1975*	*1974*	*Liabilities*	*1975*	*1974*
Leased property:			Current:		
Capital leases, less accumulated amortization (Note 2)	XXX	XXX	Obligations under capital leases (Note 2)	XXX	XXX
			Long term:		
Operating leases ($XXX and $XXX for 1975 and 1974, respectively) (Note 3)			Obligations under capital leases (Note 2)	XXX	XXX
			Commitments under operating leases ($XXX and $XXX for 1975 and 1974, respectively) (Note 3)		

(Appropriate notes, not illustrated)

SALE AND LEASEBACK

A typical sale and leaseback arrangement involves the sale of real estate or other long-lived property to a financial institution and immediately leasing it back from that institution. Such a contract can provide important tax advantages. Ownership of the property would have entitled its original owner to a deduction for depreciation, but under the sale and leaseback contract the entire rental payments can be deducted.

Since the latter will include interest and amortization of the cost of both *the land* and the building, a substantially larger tax deduction results, expecially if the building had already been partly depreciated.

When the lease contract meets the criteria for treatment as a capital lease (see Column A, page 980), the seller-lessee should account for the lease as a capital lease as previously described. Any profit on the sale must be deferred and then amortized over the lease term in proportion to the amortization of the leased asset. Whereas any deferred profit must be deducted in the balance sheet from the asset reported under the capital leases, any loss on the sale shall be recognized in full at the time of the transaction. Suppose property with a book value of $250,000 is sold for $285,000 under a sale and leaseback contract which meets the criteria for treatment as a capital lease. Immediately after the sale and before it was subject to any form of amortization it would be reported on the balance sheet as follows:

Right to use property transferred under sale leaseback contract	$285,000	
Less: Deferred profit on contract	35,000	$250,000

Instead, if the same property had been sold for $220,000, it would be reported at that amount and the $30,000 loss would be recognized in the period of sale.

In case the lease contract does not meet the criteria for treatment as a capital lease and the sales price of the asset exceeds its cost to the seller-lessee, a fair rental value for the property shall be determined. If this fair rental value for the lease term equals or exceeds the amount of the rental called for under the lease, the seller-lessee shall recognize the excess of the sales price over cost as income at the time of the sale. On the other hand, if the fair rental value is less than the amount of the rental called for under the lease, the seller-lessee shall record, as an obligation, the amount of the difference, calculated over the lease term, not to be greater than the excess of the sales price over cost. Any excess remaining after deducting the obligation shall be recognized as income at the time of the sale. A proportionate share of each rent must be recorded as a reduction of the obligation over the lease term. The remainder of each rental payment shall be recognized as rent expense.

When the lease fails to meet the criteria for treatment as a capital lease and the cost of the asset to the seller-lessee is in excess of sales price, the difference shall be recognized as a loss at the time of sale. When the lease meets the criteria for treatment as a direct financing lease, the purchaser-lessor must record the transaction as a purchase and a direct financing lease; otherwise, the transaction should be recorded as a purchase and an operating lease.

Appendix. Leveraged Leases

The leveraged lease is a relative newcomer to the field of leasing. It is a three-party lease involving a *lender* in addition to the usual lessor and lessee. The lender typically is a financial institution who supplies from 50% to 80% of the purchase price of the leased asset.[7] A dominant characteristic of the leveraged lease is the unique pattern of cash flows to the lessor. After making the initial investment in the asset (for the portion not financed by the long-term creditor), the lessor ordinarily receives an early substantial net cash inflow consisting of lease rentals, an investment tax credit based on the total cost of the property, plus other income tax benefits such as depreciation on the total cost of the property (often on an accelerated basis), interest expense on the debt, and possibly others.

A leveraged lease is designated in this way because loans coupled with income tax advantages are used to provide a particularly favorable return on the *equity participation* by the lessor. Analysis of the merits of a leveraged lease is made on a cash flow basis.

ILLUSTRATION OF LEVERAGED LEASE ACCOUNTING

The essential characteristics of a leveraged lease can be illustrated with a simple example. While the periodic cash flows might occur more frequently than in the example, and while the useful life of the asset and the lease would often be longer, nothing would be gained in illustrating the concepts and procedures by having a vast array of figures.

Data: Assume the lessor has an average income tax rate of 40% over the lease term, and that the investment credit and accelerated depreciation are acceptable for income tax purposes. At the start of Year 1, the lessor acquired property costing $1,000,000 and immediately leased it for $216,315 annually payable at the end of each of the next six years (the interest rate is 8%). At the end of the sixth year, the property will be fully depreciated and the residual value, zero. The lessor provides $200,000 (called the equity participation) of the purchase price of the property and finances the remainder by borrowing $800,000 (called the leverage) at 9% interest; the loan is to be repaid in six equal annual installments, at the end of each year, of $178,336 (i.e., $800,000 principal plus $270,015 interest). For income tax purposes, the property will be depreciated by the lessor over a four-year term using the double-declin-

[7] Ordinarily the loan is nonrecourse to the general credit of the lessor and is secured by a mortgage on the leased property plus an assignment of the lease and lease payments; the lessee may also guarantee the debt. If the property is realty, the percentage of the loan may exceed 80% of the total cost.

EXHIBIT 23–4

Leveraged Lease—Cash Flow Analysis by Years for the Lessor

Year	(1) Cash Lease Rentals (as given)	(2) Depreciation (double-declining for tax purposes) (a)	(3) Cash Interest Payments (b)	(4) Taxable Income (loss) (Cols. 1 − 2 − 3)	(5) Income Tax Credits (charges) (Col. 4 × 40%)	(6) Cash Payments on Loan Principal (b)	(7) Annual Cash Flow (Cols. 1 − 3 + 5 − 6)	(8) Cumulative Cash Flow
Initial investment by lessor							(200,000)	(200,000)
Investment tax credit							70,000	(130,000)
1 ...	216,315	500,000	72,000	(355,685)	142,274	106,336	180,253	50,253
2 ...	216,315	250,000	62,430	(96,115)	38,446	115,906	76,425	126,678
3 ...	216,315	125,000	51,998	39,317	(15,727)	126,338	22,252	148,930
4 ...	216,315	125,000	40,628	50,687	(20,275)	137,708	17,704	166,634
5 ...	216,315	–	28,234	188,081	(75,232)	150,102	(37,253)	129,381
6 ...	216,317	–	14,275	201,592	(80,637)	163,610	(42,655)	86,726
	1,297,892	1,000,000	270,015	27,877	(11,151)	800,000	86,726	

(a) $1,000,000 × 50% = $500,000 (etc.)

(b) Equal period payment on bank loan $178,336
Interest payment on unpaid principal,
$800,000 × 9%... 72,000
Payment on Loan Principal........................ $106,336 (etc.)

EXHIBIT 23–5
Leveraged Lease—Income Statement Reporting by Lessor Financing Lease

Year	(1) Unrecovered Investment (a)	(2) Lease Revenue (Col. 1 × 8%)	(3) Interest Expense (b)	(4) Income before Tax (Col. 2 − 3)	(5) Income after 40% Taxes (Col. 4 × 60%)	(6) Investment Credit (c)	(7) Net Income (Col. 5 + 6)
1	1,000,000	80,000	72,000	8,000	4,800	18,798	23,598
2	863,685	69,095	62,430	6,665	3,999	16,236	20,235
3	716,465	57,317	51,998	5,319	3,191	13,469	16,660
6	557,467	44,597	40,628	3,969	2,381	10,480	12,861
5	385,749	30,860	28,234	2,626	1,576	7,252	8,828
6	200,294	16,023	14,725	1,298	779	3,765	4,544
		297,892	270,015	27,877	16,726	70,000	86,726

Computations:

(a)

Prior unrecorded balance		$1,000,000
Less: Lease rental	$216,315	
Deduct Column 2 amount	80,000	
Recovery of investment		136,315
New Balance		$ 863,685 (etc.)

(b) Interest on unpaid principal on bank loan, $800,000 × 9% = $72,000 (etc.)

(c) Proration on basis of Column 1: $70,000 × $80,000/$297,892 = $18,798 (etc.)

ing-balance method.[8] At the time the property was acquired, the investment credit was 7%; this was recognized by the lessor for tax purposes in the year of acquisition but was deferred for financial accounting purposes.

The *lessor's* cash flow analysis is set out in Exhibit 23–4. All amounts have been rounded to the nearest dollar. Column 2, Depreciation, reflects double-declining-balance depreciation of a $1,000,000 asset over a four-year life. Column 3, Cash Interest Payments, reflects interest at 9% on the unpaid debt principal for any given year. For each period, the loan principal payment (Column 6) is the difference between the $178,336 equal periodic payments on the loan and the period interest.

Exhibit 23–5 summarizes the income statement for each year of the lease assuming the lease agreement qualifies as a *financing lease*. Recall that the annual rent of $216,315, for a $1,000,000 cost, indicates an annual interest rate or return of 8%; that is, $1,000,000 ÷ 4.62288 (from Table 6–4, n=6, i=8%) = $216,315. This ignores the investment credit because it is realized immediately and will be separately considered (Exhibit 23–5, Column 6).

On Exhibit 23–5, the investment of $1,000,000 is recovered on an annuity basis as reflected in the computation below the table. The investment credit, although realized in Year 1 as a cash inflow (i.e., a reduction in income taxes payable), is prorated or amortized on a rational basis each year; the basis used is lease revenue (Column 2) as indicated in the computations below the table in Exhibit 23–5. The remaining computations are indicated on the exhibit.

The underlying concepts may be better understood by studying the entries that would be made by the lessor for the first year. Two cases will be assumed:

Case A—The lease transaction qualifies as a financing lease.
Case B—The lease transaction qualifies as an operating lease.

Case A—Year 1 entries assuming financing lease:

a. January 1—asset acquired:

Asset—property	1,000,000	
Cash		200,000
Liability—bank loan, 9%		800,000

b. January 1—lease contract (financing lease):

Receivable, lease contract	1,297,892	
Asset—property		1,000,000
Unearned lease revenue		297,892

c. January 1—investment credit deferred:

Income taxes payable (debit balance)	70,000	
Investment credit deferred (unamortized)		70,000

[8] Because of flexible tax provisions, the lessor is permitted to depreciate property for tax purposes, although it is a financing lease.

d. December 31 – payment on bank loan:

Liability – bank loan, 9% (Exhibit 23–5, Column 6) ...	106,336	
Interest expense (Exhibit 23–5, Column 3)	72,000	
Cash (per loan agreement)		178,336

e. December 31 – collection of rental:

Cash (per lease agreement)	216,315	
Receivable, lease contract		216,315

f. December 31 – lease revenue earned:

Unearned lease revenue	80,000	
Lease revenue (Exhibit 23–5, Column 2)		80,000

g. December 31 – amortize investment credit:

Investment credit deferred (unamortized)	18,798	
Investment credit realized, revenue (Exhibit 23–5, Column 6)		18,798

h. December 31 – income taxes:

Income tax expense ($8,000 × .40)	3,200	
Income taxes payable		3,200

The resultant unclassified balance sheet relating solely to the leverage(lease would be:

Cash		$ 37,979
Taxes payable (debit balance)		66,800
Receivable, lease contracts	$1,081,577	
Less: Unearned lease revenue	217,892	863,685
Total Assets		$968,464
Liability – bank loan, 9%		$693,664
Investment credit, deferred		51,202
Capital (original investment)		200,000
Retained earnings (Year 1 net income)		23,598
Total Liabilities and Stockholders' Equity		$968,464

Case B – Year 1 entries assuming an operating lease:

a. January 1 – asset acquired:

Asset – property	1,000,000	
Cash		200,000
Liability – bank loan		800,000

b. January 1 – investment credit:

Income taxes payable	70,000	
Income tax expense		70,000

c. December 31 – annual depreciation (double declining, Exhibit 23–5):

Depreciation expense	500,000	
Accumulated depreciation		500,000

d. December 31 – payment on loan:

Liability – bank loan	106,336	
Interest expense	72,000	
Cash		178,336

e. December 31 – collection of annual rent:

Cash	216,315	
Lease revenue		216,315

f. December 31 – income taxes:

Income tax expense	3,200	
Income taxes payable		3,200

The economics of a typical leveraged lease are reflected in Exhibits 23–4 and 23–5. The cash flows and net income results are significantly different; however, at the termination of the lease, they total to the same amount ($86,726). The cumulative cash flow and cumulative net income are shown graphically in Exhibit 23–6. The graph shows that the

EXHIBIT 23–6
Leveraged Lease – Graph of Lessor's Cash Flow and Net Income Compared

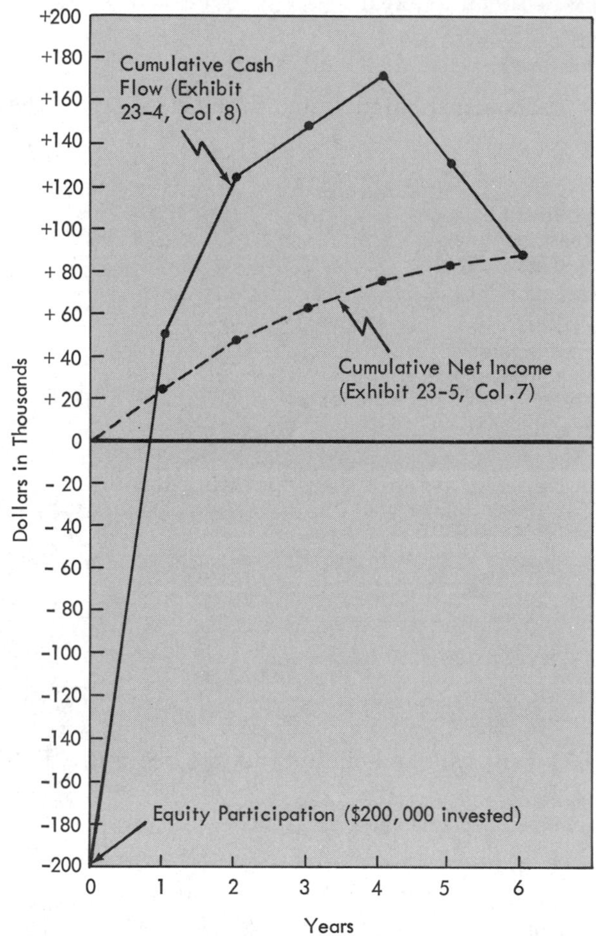

cumulative cash received by the lessor during the positive cash inflow period exceeded both the total net income and the equity participation ($200,000). The excess cash inflow rises quickly but reverses slowly. The reversal is due to the termination of the tax advantage of depreciation expense at the end of the fourth year. In leveraged leases, a relatively small equity investment, 20% in this case, and a high leverage loan, 80% in this case, provides a significant tax advantage. The tax advantages in respect to (1) interest on the loan is a tax deductible expense, and (2) high depreciation at an accelerated rate, on the total investment, makes leveraged leases excellent investments for those in a high tax bracket. The graph shown in Exhibit 23–6 reflects these advantages and also the importance of cash flow analysis as well as accrual accounting analysis.

The lease illustrated above is typical, except that the time span has been capsuled to a shorter period than normal for a typical leveraged lease, also the cash flow is somewhat accelerated. Typically, the equity participation is recovered in the first or second year. These simplifications do not alter the analytical and accounting approaches.

QUESTIONS

1. Match the numbered items below with the lettered items at the right.

1. Lessor.	*a.* Comparatively new type of contract in which owner puts up relatively small portion of cost of the property to be leased.
2. Leveraged lease.	*b.* Lender in a lease contract transaction.
3. Operating lease.	*c.* Tenant in a lease contract transaction.
4. Lessee.	*d.* Property owner in a lease contract transaction.
	e. Type of lease which transfers most of risks of ownership to the tenant.
	f. Type of lease in which owner retains most of usual rewards and risks of ownership.

2. Distinguish between operating leases and financing leases.

3. Give highlights of generally accepted accounting methods for *(a)* operating leases, and *(b)* financing leases.

4. Often advance rental payments are received under operating lease contracts which extend well beyond a single fiscal year. Outline possible accounting procedures to be followed in respect to such payments.

5. By what criteria can financing or capital leases be distinguished from operating leases according to the FASB?

6. In some sale and leaseback transactions the seller-leasee realizes a profit on sale of the asset; in others, a loss is realized. Briefly describe proper accounting treatment of gains and losses related to sale and leaseback transactions.

7. XYZ Company operates retail stores in numerous cities; for the most part leased locations are used. Most of the leases are noncancelable; their average life is 9 years (some run as long as 16 years). Quite a number of the leases are

in shopping centers in which part of the rent may be dependent on the volume of business transacted. Some of the leases contain renewal option clauses; virtually none give XYZ an option to buy the properties involved, nor do they involve the company in guarantees, dividend restrictions, and so on. What disclosures should XYZ make in its current financial statements in respect to the leases?

8. What distinguishes a leveraged lease from other leases? What pattern of cash flow usually attends a leveraged lease insofar as the lessor is concerned?

DECISION CASE 23–1

The practice of obtaining the right to use property by noncancellable leases is becoming more prevalent.

Required:

1. Assets acquired under noncancellable leases that are in substance installment purchases should be capitalized in the accounts of the lessee in order to show the facts properly. List the defects in the lessee's balance sheet and income statement that would result from *not* recording assets acquired under such contracts.
2. Other noncancellable leases that give the lessee essentially all the rights and obligations of ownership are not installment purchases in substance.
   a. Discuss the case *against* recording assets acquired by such leases.
   b. The case for recording assets acquired by such leases rests primarily on the belief that the opportunity to exercise the right of use creates an asset that should be recognized in the accounts with its related liability. Discuss the arguments that *support* this belief.

(AICPA adapted)

EXERCISES

Exercise 23–1

Lessors engage in leasing activies for diverse reasons.

Required:

1. What factors should a lessor consider in choosing a method of assigning revenues and expenses to lease periods?
2. For what types of leasing activities should lessors utilize the—
   a. Financing method?
   b. Operating (or rental) method?
3. Under the operating method, lessors report gross rentals as revenues over the life of the lease.
   a. How should the investment be classified?
   b. What should be disclosed?

(AICPA adapted)

Exercise 23–2

Margo Company paid $7,000 on January 1, 19A, to Dexter Properties as a lease bonus to secure a three-year lease on premises it will occupy starting from that date. Additionally, $6,000 per annum paid on each December 31 throughout the term of the lease will be paid as rent. There is no specific renewal agreement. Margo adjusts and closes its books each December 31. Dexter will maintain the property, pay taxes, and other ownership costs.

Required:

1. What type of lease contract is involved?
2. What are Margo's alternatives as to treatment of the $7,000? Develop an amortization table using an 8% rate.
3. What is Margo's total occupancy cost for 19B under each alternative given in your response to Requirement 2?
4. What should Margo's financial statements reflect as of December 31, 19A, if the amortization table developed in Requirement 2 is used?

Exercise 23–3

Delta Leasing Company agreed with Wilson Corporation to provide the latter equipment under lease for a four-year period. The equipment cost Delta $18,500 and will have no salvage value when the lease term ends. Wilson has agreed to pay all normal ownership costs throughout the lease period including taxes, maintenance, and insurance. On January 1, 19A, the equipment was delivered. Delta expects a 9% return; the four equal annual rents are payable in advance starting January 1, 19A.

Required:

1. Assuming this is a financing lease, for both parties, prepare an amortization table suitable for use by either party.
2. On the assumption both companies adjust and close books each December 31, give journal entries relating to the lease for both companies through December 31, 19A, based on data derived in the amortization table. Assume straight-line amortization.

Exercise 23–4

Select the best answer in each of the following and give your basis for selecting it.

1. Where the balance sheet for the lessor indicates that a portion of property, plant, and equipment and of the related accumulated depreciation pertains to equipment leased to customers, it is evident that the–
   a. Operating method of accounting is used for these leases.
   b. Financing method of accounting is used for these leases.
   c. Lessor has violated generally accepted accounting principles.
   d. Lessor is using the income tax method of accounting for these leases.
2. Under the provisions of authoritative pronouncements, when leases are treated as installment purchases, the method of amortization used by the lessee should be appropriate to the nature and use of the asset and should be chosen–
   a. To result in a level annual pattern of charges to expense over the useful life of the property.
   b. To result in a level annual rate of return on the capitalized amount over the useful life of the property.
   c. To result in an annual pattern of charges to expense based on the annual change in the present value of the related obligation.

d. Without reference to the period over which the related obligation is discharged.

3. Iden Company leased a warehouse from Jarrold, Inc., on January 2, 19A, for five years for a fixed annual rental payment. On April 1, 19A, Iden subleased the same warehouse to Walter Company for a substantially larger yearly rental for the four years and nine months remaining on the lease. Walter is a well-established company with an excellent credit rating and earnings history. How should Iden disclose the lease and sublease on its financial statements at December 31, 19A?
   a. By means of a footnote to the financial statements only.
   b. No disclosure is needed in the balance sheet or in the footnotes because Iden's earnings statement should show rental revenue received from Walter and rental expense paid to Jarrold.
   c. Iden should capitalize the lease payments to be made to Jarrold and amortize the balance over the five years of the lease. No disclosure needs to be made for the sublease.
   d. Iden's statement of financial position should include an asset and a liability each for the present value of the difference between the amount to be received from the sublease and the amount to be paid for the lease.
4. On June 30, 19A, the Ingalls Corporation sold equipment for $420,000 which had a net book value of $400,000 and a remaining life of ten years. That same day, the equipment was leased back at $1,000 per month for five years with no option to renew the lease or repurchase the equipment. Ingall's rent expense for this equipment for the six months ended December 31, 19A, would be—
   a. $5,000. *c.* $6,000.
   b. $4,000. *d.* ($14,000).
5. Property under construction to be sold and leased back for operating use under a leasing arrangement, which in substance is a purchase, should be reported by the lessee on a classified balance sheet under the caption—
   a. Long-term investments.
   b. Deferred charges.
   c. Property, plant, and equipment.
   d. Short-term investment.
6. Material gains resulting from sale-and-leaseback transactions usually should be accounted for—
   a. As an ordinary gain in the period of the transaction.
   b. As an extraordinary gain in the period of the transaction.
   c. By amortizing the gain over the life of the lease.
   d. By crediting the gain to the cost of the related property.
7. Manufacturers and dealer lessors sometimes sell or assign leases to third parties, usually independent financing companies. Where such a lease sale or assignment has occurred—
   a. The lease cannot qualify for treatment as a sale even though it would have met the criteria for sale accounting treatment if only the lessor and the lessee had been involved.
   b. Involvement of the independent financing company does not disqualify the lease from sale accounting treatment if it otherwise qualifies for this treatment.
   c. The operating method of accounting for lease transactions becomes mandatory.
   d. The financing method of accounting for lease transactions becomes mandatory.

(Items 4 through 7 AICPA adapted)

Exercise 23–5

Select the best answer in each of the following and explain the basis for your choice.

1. In accounting for a lease, the account(s) that should appear on the balance sheet of a lessor using the financing method but not using the operating method would be the–
   a. Investment in Leased Property account.
   b. Property, Plant, and Equipment account.
   c. Receivable–Equipment Rentals and Property, Plant, and Equipment accounts.
   d. Receivable–Equipment Rentals account.
2. Under the financing method of accounting for leases, the excess of the present value of the aggregate rentals over the cost of leased property should be recognized as revenue by the lessor–
   a. In increasing amounts during the term of the lease.
   b. In constant amounts during the term of the lease.
   c. In decreasing amounts during the term of the lease.
   d. After the cost of the leased property has been fully recovered through rentals.
3. A company sold property at a price which exceeded book value and then leased back the property for ten years. The gain resulting from the sale should be recognized by the company–
   a. In the year of sale.
   b. At the end of the ten-year period or termination of the lease, whichever is earlier.
   c. Over the term of the lease.
   d. As a prior period adjustment.
4. When measuring the present value of future rentals to be capitalized as part of the purchase price in a lease that is to be accounted for as a financing lease, identifiable payments to be made by the lessee to cover taxes, insurance, and maintenance should be–
   a. Included with the future rentals to be capitalized.
   b. Excluded from future rentals to be capitalized.
   c. Capitalized but at a different discount rate and recorded in a different account than future rental payments.
   d. Capitalized but at a different discount rate and for a relevant period that tends to be different than for the future rental payments.
5. On January 1, 19A, Ramos Company signed a ten-year noncancelable lease for certain machinery. The terms of the lease call for payments of $10,000 per year to be made by Ramos for ten years. The machinery has a 20-year life and no salvage value. Ramos uses the straight-line depreciation method on all depreciable assets.

   Assume that, in substance, this lease is an installment purchase of the machinery by Ramos, and accordingly should be capitalized (i.e., a financing lease). Assuming a 10% discount rate, the lease payments have a present value of $61,440.

   Relative to the capitalized lease described above, Ramos' 19A income statement should include–
   a. Interest expense of $10,000 and depreciation expense of $3,072.
   b. Interest expense of $10,000 only.
   c. Interest expense of $6,144 and depreciation expense of $3,072.
   d. Interest expense of $6,298 and depreciation expense of $3,072.

6. On December 31, 19A T Company entered into an agreement to lease a piece of machinery from Y Company. Lease payments are $1,000 per month for ten years. The lease is in substance an installment purchase of the machinery by T Company, and so the machinery and related lease obligations must be capitalized (i.e., a financing lease). This means that on T Company's balance sheet as of December 31, 19A, the leased machinery will be carried at—
   a. Some amount greater than $120,000.
   b. Some amount less than $120,000.
   c. Cannot determine whether the amount should be more or less than $120,000 from the information given.
   d. Exactly $120,000.

(AICPA adapted)

Exercise 23–6

Case A: XYZ Company leases computers to various lessees and uses the financing method. The average length of its lease contracts is 42 months. For balance sheet purposes, describe how its receivables should be classified, valued, and characterized.

Case B: Your client, DEF Corporation, recently concluded an arm's-length sale and leaseback of all of its plant, property, and equipment. The transaction resulted in a gain of $600,000 in terms of book value which the client wants to pick up as extraordinary gain in financial statements of the current year. Can you, as DEF's independent CPA, accept this proposal? If not, what alternatives can you offer?

Case C: Another client (a lessee) intends to lease a material amount of machinery under terms of a lease which calls for the client to be responsible for and pay directly (not included in the rental) maintenance, taxes, insurance, and other expenses related to the property while used by the lessee. At the termination of the noncancellable lease, your client would have the option to buy the machinery at a nominal salvage value. The duration of the lease and expected life of the machinery are about the same. How would you advise your client to account for this lease transaction and its related payments?

Exercise 23–7 (based on the Appendix)

LR Company leased from LE Leasing Company, for a four-year period, equipment with an estimated four-year life and zero salvage value. The equipment cost the LE Company $125,000. LE Company paid $25,000 cash and borrowed the remainder at 9% interest under a loan which provided for repayment by four equal annual installments of $30,867 payable at the end of each of the four years.

LR agreed to pay the lessor four equal annual rents of $39,434. On this basis, the lessor will earn 10% before taxes (aside from the investment credit) since the rents are due at the end of each of the four years. Assume the equipment will be depreciated by the sum-of-the-years'-digits method and that a 7% investment credit can be fully realized in the year the equipment is acquired; assume also that the investor will remain in a 40% income tax bracket throughout the term of the lease, and that the lease transaction qualifies as a financing lease.

Required:

Prepare for the lessor an anticipated cash flow schedule covering the entire four-year lease period similar to Exhibit 23–4. Round all amounts to the nearest dollar.

Exercise 23–8 (based on the Appendix)

Brand Company leased to Neville, Inc., for a four-year period, equipment which cost Brand $600,000. Brand obtained the equipment by paying $100,000 cash and signing a note calling for four equal annual payments at the end of the four years $150,960 (due to rounding, raise the last payment by $1). On this basis, the $500,000 loan bears interest at 8%.

Neville agreed to pay Brand four equal annual rents of $189,282 at the end of each of the four years. The leased property has an estimated zero value at the termination of the lease. It will qualify for a 7% investment credit. Brand will depreciate the property by the sum-of-the-years'-digits method. The rents will yield the lessor 10% return before taxes ignoring the investment credit. Assume the transaction qualifies as a financing lease.

Required:

Prepare for Brand an anticipated cash flow schedule covering the entire four-year lease period similar to Exhibit 23–4. Assume Brand's income will be taxed throughout the period at 40%. Round all amounts to the nearest dollar.

PROBLEMS

Problem 23–1

Dix Corporation leased some space to Menn Company under a three-year contract starting January 1, 19A. Terms of the contract required an annual rental of $8,000 starting January 1, 19A, plus an advance payment of $6,000 on January 1, 19A. There is no provision for renewal; and Dix is to pay insurance, taxes, and maintenance expenses. Both companies adjust and close books annually on December 31.

Required:

1. Indicate the type of lease involved and explain. What accounting approach should be used by each company? Indicate any alternatives.
2. Develop an amortization table (interest method) suitable for use by either party using 7% interest.
3. What would be the annual amortization assuming the straight-line method is adopted?
4. Give all entries related to the lease contract for 19A and 19B for the lessor and lessee in parallel columns using present value (interest) amortization.
5. What should be reflected on the income statement and balance sheet of both parties at December 31, 19A, and December 31, 19B?

Problem 23–2

On January 1, 19A, Company A rented an office to Company B for an annual rental of $1,200 payable each January 1. In addition, an advance payment of $3,000 was required. The lease was for three-year period. The advance payment represented three annual rentals that would have been payable each January 1;

the $3,000 was somewhat less than the sum of the three annual payments that would have been made in addition to the normal rent of $1,200. This is an operating lease as to both parties.

Required:

1. Give all entries, including closing entries, for both the lessor and lessee assuming *(a)* both parties' fiscal year ends December 31, and *(b)* a 6% interest rate for amortization purposes. Utilize present value amortization and present the two sets of entries in parallel columns. Show all computations.
2. Show amounts that would be reported on the income statement and balance sheet for each year for both the lessor and lessee.

Problem 23–3

During 19A, Amx Finance Company began leasing equipment to small manufacturers. Information regarding leasing arrangements follows:

a. Amx Finance Company leases equipment with terms from three to five years depending upon the useful life of the equipment. At the expiration of the lease, the equipment will be sold to the lessee at 10% of the lessor's cost, the expected salvage value of the equipment.

b. The amount of the lessee's monthly payment is computed by multiplying the lessor's cost of the equipment by the payment factor applicable to the term of the lease.

Term of Lease	*Payment Factor*
Three years..............	3.32%
Four years	2.63
Five years	2.22

c. The excess of the gross contract receivable for equipment rentals over the cost (reduced by the estimated salvage value at the termination of the lease) is recognized as revenue over the term of the lease under the sum-of-the-years'-digits method computed on a monthly basis.

d. The following leases were entered into during 19A:

Machine	*Dates of Lease*	*Period of Lease*	*Machine Cost*
Die	7/1/19A–6/30/19E	4 years	$45,000
Press	9/1/19A–8/31/19D	3 years	30,000

Required:

1. Prepare a schedule of gross contracts receivable for equipment rentals at the dates of the lease for the die and press machines.
2. Prepare a schedule of unearned lease revenue at December 31, 19A, for each machine lease.
3. Prepare a schedule computing the present value of contracts receivable for equipment rentals at December 31, 19A. (The present value of the "contracts receivable for equipment rentals" is the outstanding amount of the gross contracts receivable less the unearned lease income included therein.) Without prejudice to your solution to Requirement 2, assume that the unearned lease revenue at December 31, 19A, was $14,500.

(AICPA adapted)

Problem 23–4

Stokes Leasing Corporation is a newly formed dealer lessor. Stokes will be engaged in leasing a basic machine that costs $50,000 each and has a six-year life and no residual value at the end of its useful life. Stokes started operations with ten of the machines; its equities consist of a $150,000 note due in three years which bears 5% interest payable each December 31 and $350,000 capital stock. The fiscal year ends on December 31. The machines will be rented under six-year contracts whereby annual rentals are paid at year-end; 6% return on the investment is expected. The lessee assumes all risks and costs of normal ownership, and the lease is noncancellable. The machines revert to the lessor at the termination of the lease. Assume a financing lease for both the lessor and lessee.

Required:

1. Show how the lessor would compute the annual rent on a machine.
2. Show how the lessee would compute the present value of the special property rights.
3. Prepare an amortization table that would be suitable for either the lessor or lessee.
4. Give journal entries for the lessor for the following transactions; you may use abbreviated account titles.

   Jan. 1, 19A–Concluded leases on all ten machines with various lessors.
   Dec. 31, 19A–Collected lease rentals due; paid salaries and other expenses, $20,000; paid interest due on the note.
   Dec. 31, 19A–Adjust the lease accounts and accrue income taxes at 20%; closing entries not required.

5. Prepare a classified balance sheet for the lessor as of December 31, 19A.
6. Give journal entries for a lessee who leased one of the machines on January 1, 19A, for the following: *(a)* to record the lease, and *(b)* to record payment of first rental and adjustment of lease accounts (present value amortization of the asset).

Problem 23–5

Lessor Company and Lessee Company entered into a financing type of lease on January 1, 19A. The lease was for new construction equipment which cost the Lessor Company $200,000 (useful life five years, no residual value). Lessor Company expects 6% return over the five-year period of the lease. The lease calls for five annual rentals payable each January 1, that is, at the *beginning* of each year starting on January 1, 19A. Lessee Company is to assume all the risks and normal costs of ownership and the machines revert to the lessor at the termination of the lease.

Required:

1. Show how the Lessor Company would compute the annual rental amount. How would the Lessee Company compute the present value of the lease rights?
2. Prepare an amortization table that would be suitable for each party (straight-line amortization).
3. Give the entries for both the lessor and lessee, in parallel columns, for the years 19A and 19B. You may use abbreviated account titles.
4. Show the items and amounts that would be reported on the income statement and balance sheet at the end of 19B for both the lessor and lessee.

Problem 23–6

James Leasing Company rented a new machine to Conway Contractors that cost $18,000; having a four-year life and no residual value at that time. The lease was signed on January 1, 19A, and the lessee was to assume all normal risks and costs of ownership; the lease was noncancellable. The James Company computed the rent on the basis of a 7% return and the lessee utilized this same rate for accounting for the lease. The property will revert to the lessor at termination of the lease.

Required:

1. Assuming the annual rentals are payable at the end of each year complete the following: *(a)* lessor computation of periodic rental payments; *(b)* lessee computation of the present value of the special property rights under the lease; and *(c)* an amortization table that would be suitable for both the lessor and lessee.
2. Assuming the annual rentals are payable at the start of each year complete the same three items required in Requirement 1.
3. Give the entries for the lessor and lessee, in parallel columns, for Requirement 2 throughout 19A. You may utilize abbreviated account titles (straight-line amortization).
4. Indicate the asset and liability amounts that would be reported on the balance sheets at December 31, 19A, by the lessor and lessee.

Problem 23–7 (based on the Appendix)

Barnes Company, needing a new special trailer, seeks one under lease. Kandu Corporation, a company which specializes in providing such equipment, agreed to furnish a trailer to Barnes' specifications. Kandu acquired the $100,000 trailer by paying $25,000 from its own funds and borrowed the remaining $75,000 on a loan which requires seven equal annual loan payments of $14,902 (due to rounding, the last payment is $2 less). The interest rate is 9%, and the payments are due at the end of each year.

The lease term is for seven years, and Barnes is to pay Kandu $18,555 at the end of each year. The trailer is expected to have a residual value of $6,000 at the end of the seven years; it is to be depreciated initially by the double-declining-balance method for both tax and book purposes; however, in the last two years, straight-line depreciation is to be applied to the remaining book value.* The asset qualifies for the 7% investment credit which is recognized in the first year. Assume that Kandu is subject to an income tax rate of 40% throughout the term of the lease and that the company has other taxable income of substantial amounts.

Required:

1. Develop for Kandu a schedule showing annual and cumulative cash flow effects of this lease contract for the seven years. Round all amounts to the nearest dollar. Assume the $6,000 residual value of the property is realized as cash when the lease is terminated.
2. Prepare journal entries for Kandu's books to reflect the lease transactions for the first and second years. This includes acquisition of the leased property, the loan, closing entries, and so on. Assume the operating method of accounting for the lease is used.

* *Hint:* Use .28571 as the depreciation rate.

Problem 23–8 (based on the Appendix)

Refer to the data in Problem 23–8. Although figures were not given, Kandu's yield rate on the lease, if it were treated as a financing lease (before income taxes and ignoring the investment credit), is 7%.

Required:

1. Prepare a schedule to reflect net income for each year (similar to Exhibit 23–5).
2. Prepare journal entries for Kandu's books for all transactions relating to the leased property and the lease for the first two years if the lease were treated as a financing lease. Round all computations to the nearest dollar.

Problem 23–9 (based on the Appendix)

Lessor Company leased a large machine to Lessee Company for a five-year period, starting on January 1, 19A. Lessor Company acquired the machine especially for Lessee Company at a cost of $250,000, paying cash, $50,000, and borrowing the difference from a bank on a 8% note which provides for four equal annual year-end payments starting on December 31, 19A.

Lessee Company is required to pay five equal annual rental payments determined on the basis of a 9% return to the lessor, not considering the investment credit. The rental payments are to be made each December 31. The lease essentially transfers all of the risks and rewards of ownership to Lessee Company; therefore, it is a financing lease for both parties. However, for tax purposes, the Lessor will realize the 10% investment credit and depreciation over a five-year estimated life, on a straight-line basis with no residual value. Lessor Company has extensive income from other leases; therefore, its average tax rate for the life of this lease is 45%.

Required:

(Round all amounts to the nearest dollar.)

1. Compute the amount of the equal annual payments to be made by Lessor Company on the bank loan and prepare a loan amortization schedule.
2. Compute the amount of the equal annual rental payments to be made by Lessee Company.
3. Prepare an estimated cash flow schedule for the Lessor Company covering the life of the lease.
4. Prepare a five-year summary of the income statement effects of this lease for Lessor Company.
5. Prepare the journal entries for 19A to reflect the amounts shown in the income statement prepared in Requirement 4.
6. Prepare an unclassified balance sheet giving the effects of this single lease.

Chapter 24

Analysis of Financial Statements

Throughout this book, the focus is on financial reporting to external parties—stockholders, potential investors, financial analysts, creditors, other interested individuals and groups, and the public at large. External financial reports are designed to serve a wide range of users with quite different levels of financial sophistication. In contrast, the management of an enterprise has access to a variety of detailed and summary internal reports—daily, weekly, monthly, quarterly, and annually—to serve their diverse and continuing decision-making needs. Basically, the external reports are not designed to meet the decision-making needs of the management of the enterprise.

Because of the diversity of external users of financial statements, analytical techniques are important. They can be applied to help meet the particular needs of external decision-makers. The accountant is often involved in the analysis, interpretation, and evaluation of financial statements, as well as in the process of their development.

The purpose of this chapter is to discuss and illustrate analytical approaches by which accounting information may be better understood, interpreted, and evaluated for decision-making purposes. However, no single approach can be devised that would be wholly appropriate for all situations.

To add a practical focus an Appendix to the chapter is included which presents a specially selected actual case for study.

CHARACTERISTICS OF THE ANALYSIS OF FINANCIAL STATEMENTS

Analysis of financial statements focuses on the data reported plus supplementary information from other sources such as the company management, investment advisors, business periodicals, and other materials distributed by the company. These latter sources are often particularly important because many of the strengths and weaknesses of a company may not be reflected directly in the financial statements. For example, the most important element in evaluating the future potentials of a company often is the quality of the management. This kind of information obviously is very difficult to obtain; hence, as an indirect measure of management quality, one is forced to rely largely on the past track record of earnings, financial position, and funds flow as reported in the financial statements. A particularly important aspect of the analysis of financial statements is to identify *major changes* (i.e., turning points) in trends, amounts, and relationships and then to investigate the reasons underlying those changes. Often a *turning point* may provide an early warning of a significant change in the future success or failure of the business.

In analyzing and interpreting financial statements, one should recognize that financial statements necessarily are *organized summaries* of an extensive mass of detailed financial information. For example, the published financial statements of a large corporation, such as General Motors, Exxon, or IBM, usually fills from five to ten printed pages including the supporting notes. It is difficult to imagine the number of transactions, the critical accounting decisions, and the mass of detail summarized in these few pages. It is also difficult to imagine, although it is often true, that amounts of $5 million or more may be immaterial because it is less than 5% of the total base amount of which it is a part. Summarization presents serious communication problems. On the other hand, excessive detail has been found to be undesirable because most statement users experience such constraints as time, motivation, or understanding.

ANALYTICAL APPROACHES AND TECHNIQUES

The analysis of financial statements is much broader than the mere computation of a few ratios. More importantly, it involves an organized approach to glean from the totality of the statements the maximum amount of interpretative and evaluative information. Often investors look at the net income, EPS, and total asset amounts and then sign off. Important steps in the interpretation and evaluation of financial statements are:

1. Examine the auditors' report.
2. Analyze the statement of accounting policies.
3. Examine the overall financial statements, including notes and supporting schedules.
4. Apply analytical techniques:
   a. Comparative statements.
   b. Horizontal and vertical percentage analyses.
   c. Proportionate (or ratio) analyses.
5. Search for important supplemental information not provided by the financial statements.

EXAMINE THE AUDITORS' REPORT

Expert financial analysts consistently report that in evaluating a financial statement, the first basic step is careful examination of the auditors' report (often called the accountants' report). Of course, this presumes that the financial statements are audited – if they are not, one should usually give very little, if any, credibility to them. The auditors' report is important because it provides the analyst with information concerning the "fairness" of the representations in the financial statements and calls attention to all major concerns of the auditor that came to light as a result of the auditor's intensive examination.

The auditors' report was discussed in Chapter 5 and it would be advisable to restudy those discussions. Examples of unqualified auditors' opinions were given there and at the end of Chapter 4. Also the Appendix presents an auditors' report and the statements to which it relates. Of particular importance is the possibility that instead of an *unqualified opinion*, the auditor may give *(a)* a qualified opinion, *(b)* an adverse opinion, or *(c)* a disclaimer of opinion. Each of these unfavorable opinions must include an explanation by the auditor of the underlying factors. These serve to alert the statement user to major problem areas that should be carefully investigated. Throughout the process of statement analysis, these problem areas should be kept to the forefront. Often they are so significant that the company will go to great lengths to satisfy the requirements for an unqualified opinion. An unfavorable auditors' opinion generally causes an immediate and significant adverse impact on the market price of the company's stock, on the credit standing, and perhaps even on their general reputation – depending of course on the nature and magnitude of the problem cited.

Below is a qualified opinion (and related matters) illustrating the kind of information frequently cited by an auditor.[1] Observe in this situation that the qualification is related to an expropriation by a foreign government, an action over which the management of the company had no control. Nevertheless, the action will have a significant adverse affect on the earnings and financial position of the company for a number of years, although this is not reflected in the historical financial information, up to an including the financial statements to which this opinion relates. Clearly, this is the single most important bit of information in the financial statements for this particular situation.

To the Board of Directors and Shareholders
The Anaconda Company

We have examined the consolidated balance sheets of The Anaconda Company as of December 31, 1973 and 1972 and the related statements of consolidated income and retained earnings and of changes in consolidated financial position for the years then ended. Our examinations were made

---

[1] Anaconda Company, Annual Report, 1973. Extracted from AICPA *Accounting Trends and Techniques*, 28th ed. (New York, 1975) pp. 411–12.

in accordance with generally accepted auditing standards and accordingly included such tests of the accounting records and such other auditing procedures as we considered necessary in the circumstances.

The current status of the company's efforts to obtain compensation for the 1971 loss, through expropriation, of its Chilean investments is reported on page 23 of this Annual Report. The net amount the company may realize as indemnification for its expropriated investments from Chile, Overseas Private Investment Corporation, or through court actions, is not subject to final determination at this time.

In our opinion, subject to the effect of the ultimate resolution of the uncertainties referred to in the preceding paragraph, the accompanying consolidated financial statements present fairly the consolidated financial position of The Anaconda Company and its consolidated subsidiaries at December 31, 1973 and 1972 and the results of their operations and the changes in financial position for the years then ended, in conformity with generally accepted accounting principles. These principles have been consistently applied during the period subsequent to the change, with which we concur, made as of January 1, 1972 in the method of translating foreign currency obligations as described on page 26 of this Annual Report. —*Report of Independent Accountants.*

Financial Review

Current Status of Chilean Expropriation Loss—During the year Anaconda continued its efforts to recover losses resulting from the expropriation of its investments in Chile by the Chilean government in 1971.

The government of President Allende, which expropriated the investments, was deposed by Chilean military forces on September 11, 1973 and was replaced by a military government. The new government is taking steps to restore the productivity of the mines and to reestablish credit relationships throughout the world.

Representatives of the new government have advised the company that they expect to initate negotiations on the issues of the payment of compensation for the expropriated investments and the possible role of Anaconda in the development and operation of Chile's copper properties. Anaconda has indicated its willingness to participate in such negotiations and preliminary meetings have been held. The government has publicly stated that the mines will not be returned to the former owners.

Anaconda is preserving its rights to pursue other remedies, including the following:

Ligitation is still pending in New York on suits brought against Corporacion del Cobre and Corporacion de Fomento de la Produccion, Chilean public corporations, for unpaid principal and interest due on promissory notes issued at the end of 1969 in connection with the sale of a 51% interest in Anaconda's major properties in Chile.

Included in the Consolidated Balance Sheet at December 31, 1973 and 1972 is the aggregate amount of the claims pending against Overseas Private Investment Corporation (OPIC) as a result of the expropriation of investments in the Chuquicamata and El Salvador properties. In 1972 OPIC formally rejected these claims. The company continues to believe that it is entitled to payment, and has submitted the claims to binding arbitration as provided in the OPIC insurance contracts. Proceedings before the arbitration panel are expected to take place in 1974.

ANALYZE THE STATEMENT OF ACCOUNTING POLICIES

Accounting is man-made and must accommodate a wide variety of circumstances. Although accounting principles and their implementation are largely prescribed by the *ARBs*, *APB Opinions*, FASB *Statements*, and by precedent, there is considerable room for judgment by the reporting entity and by the independent accountant. Also, in numerous areas of accounting, several alternatives are acceptable, such as the completed-contract and percentage-of-completion methods of recognizing revenue on long-term construction contracts (see Chapter 11). The range of judgments and alternatives permitted place the statement user in a literal "no-man's land" if the major judgments made and alternatives used by the company are not clearly communicated.

In response to the *full-disclosure* principle, *APB Opinion No.* 22 (April 1972) states that "information about the accounting policies adopted by a reporting entity is essential for financial statement users." Accounting policies are the specific accounting principles and methods of application that have been adopted by a company for preparation of its financial statements. The *Opinion* requires that a statement of these policies be clearly enunciated either in the notes, or preferably "in a separate *Summary of Significant Accounting Policies* preceding the notes to the financial statements or as the initial note." The statement must disclose all important accounting policies including *(a)* selections from acceptable alternatives, *(b)* accounting policies used that are peculiar to the industry, and *(c)* unusual or innovative applications of generally accepted accounting principles. Examples include the basis for consolidated statements, depreciation and amortization methods, inventory pricing, translation of foreign currencies, revenue recognition on long-term construction contracts, franchising, and leasing.

An comprehensive statement of accounting policies for a well-known company follows:

> SHELL OIL COMPANY (DEC)
>
> *Accounting Policies*
>
> This summary of the major accounting policies of Shell Oil Company and its consolidated subsidiaries (hereinafter referred to as "Shell") is presented to assist the reader in evaluating Shell's financial statements and other data contained in this report. In all material respects, Shell has consistently followed these policies for the ten year period covered by this annual report and originally reported net income has not been revised or restated. As noted below, in 1973 Shell changed its method of valuing inventories of oils and chemicals.
>
> *Principles of Consolidation*—The financial statements include the accounts of Shell Oil Company (hereinafter referred to as "Company") and all of its wholly owned subsidiaries. All companies acquired have consistently been accounted for as purchases; goodwill, if any, is amortized over a period of benefit which has not exceeded ten years.
>
> The only subsidiary of Shell not wholly owned is Butte Pipe Line Company (51% owned), and the investment therein, plus the investments in less than majority owned companies in which Shell has a voting stock interest of 20% or more, are carried at equity in underlying net assets. Investments

in less than 20% owned companies are carried at cost with dividends recorded in income as received.

Short Term Securities—Short term securities are carried at cost which approximates market. Interest is accrued and reflected in dividends, interest and other income.

Inventories—In 1973 the Company adopted as its cost basis the last-in-first-out method of valuing inventories of oils and chemicals. Prior to 1973 inventories of oils and chemicals were carried at the lower of market or of the average cost resulting from charging to costs the highest of inventory carrying value, current cost of production or purchases. Materials and supplies inventories are carried at average cost or less, as in the past.

The new method, which was adopted to achieve a better matching of current costs against current income and to conform more closely to U.S. petroleum industry practice, had no material effect on 1973 net income.

Mineral Leasehold Costs—Direct cost of acquiring undeveloped acreage, generally called lease bonus, is capitalized. Amortization from date of acquisition is based upon experience of the Company in order to fully amortize over the holding period those leases that may be unproductive. The cost of leases which become productive is transferred to a producing property account.

Exploratory Costs—Exploratory expenses, including geological and geophysical expenses, annual delay rentals on oil and gas leases and all exploratory and development dry hole costs are charged to income as incurred.

Research—Expenditures for research, except for land, buildings and standard items of equipment which extend beyond the immediate life of a project, are expensed when incurred.

Depreciation, Depletion and Amortization—Depreciation, depletion and amortization of the capital cost of producing properties, both tangible and intangible, are provided for on a unit of production basis. Developed reserves are used in computing unit rates for tangible and intangible development costs and proved reserves for depletion of leasehold costs. In all cases the unit determination is by field. Other plant and equipment are depreciated on a straight line basis over their estimated useful lives. On a cycle basis asset lives are reviewed for propriety of estimated useful life. Changes in depreciation rates, if any, are prospective only. Differing rates or deductions are used for tax purposes.

Maintenance, Repairs and Retirement of Properties—Major renewals and betterments are charged to the property accounts while minor replacements, maintenance and repairs which do not improve or extend life are expensed currently. At the time properties are retired or otherwise disposed of in the normal course of business, the cost is charged against the accumulated provision; however, if the retirement relates to a casualty or material obsolescence, the loss or gain is reflected in current income.

Office Relocation, Employee Relocation and Severance Costs—The cost directly related to relocating operating and executive offices from New York was amortized over a four year period ending in September, 1973. The cost of consolidating research facilities is being amortized over a four year period commencing in January, 1972. All other office relocation, employee relocation or severance costs are charged to expense when incurred.

Non-Mineral Leases—Obligations under noncancellable leases and other contractual commitments are reflected in the Notes to Financial Statements.

> *Income Taxes*—Items of income or income deductions are often recognized for payment of income taxes and for book purposes in different time periods; however, tax allocation accounting as prescribed by Accounting Principles Board Opinion No. 11 adjusts book income to eliminate the effect of all material book/tax timing differences.
>
> For those differences pertaining to capital extinguishments, including intangible drilling and development costs deducted currently for tax purposes, tax deferment is computed by applying the current tax rates to the current difference in deduction. The net cumulative effect is reflected in Deferred Credits—Federal Income Taxes in the Balance Sheet.
>
> For other timing differences tax deferment is computed by setting up initial differences at current tax rates and reversing these amounts in the appropriate subsequent period. The net cumulative effect of the latter is reflected in Receivables, Prepayments, Etc. in the Balance Sheet.
>
> Investment tax credits are applied to reduce federal income taxes in the year realized.[2]

The information in the statement of accounting policies is fundamental to understanding, interpreting, and evaluating much of the significant information reported in the financial statements. It is particularly useful in evaluating the *credibility and quality of the reported earnings,* and in comparing data across companies and industries.

OVERALL EXAMINATION OF THE FINANCIAL STATEMENTS

Following the examination of the accountants' opinion and analysis of the summary of accounting policies used by the company, the interpretation and evaluation process should continue with a careful examination of the financial statements in their entirety. This phase of the analysis involves study of each statement in order to gain overall perspective and to identify major strengths, weaknesses, and unusual changes such as *turning points* in the trend of sales, earnings, asset structure, liabilities, and cash flow.

The overall examination should include careful study of all of the statements included and the *notes* referred to in those statements. Each note should be read and evaluated at the point in the statement where it is referenced. Consideration of the notes as a separate activity is not fruitful; a specific note is helpful primarily in the context of the specific statement item to which it is referenced.

Concurrent with, or subsequent to, the overall examination of the financial statements under review, application of the techniques of proportional analysis, discussed in the next section, are often quite helpful to the analyst.

APPLICATION OF ANALYTICAL TECHNIQUES

Several techniques are used to enhance communication by financial statements. Techniques commonly incorporated in the financial state-

---

[2] Shell Oil Company, Annual Report, 1973. Extracted from AICPA, *Accounting Trends and Techniques,* 28th ed. (New York, 1975) pp. 17–18.

ments themselves are earnings per share (EPS), subclassifications of information on the statements, comparative statements, and supplementary information in separate schedules and notes to the statements. In addition, numerous analytical techniques often are applied, external to the financial statements, to aid the particular external decision-maker in the evaluation process. Some of the techniques often used are discussed in the paragraphs to follow.

Comparative Statements

Comparative statements involve the presentation of financial information for the current and one or more past periods in a way that facilitates comparison by the statement user. Basically, comparative statements are of two types, viz:

1. Presentation of financial reports for *(a)* the current year, and *(b)* the immediately preceding year.
2. Presentation of selected financial information for a number of years past (usually five or ten years). These are often referred to as *financial* summaries.

Trends in the financial development of a business have particular significance to all users. The comparison of current results with those of one or more prior periods provides the reader wih an added perspective in evaluating the reasonableness of current performance; that is, the period results provide a sound basis for evaluating progress, improvement, or deterioration. In recognition of the importance of presenting comparative financial information, the AICPA Committee on Accounting Procedure, in *Bulletin No. 43*, Chapter 2, stated:

> 1. The presentation of comparative financial statements in annual and other reports enhances the usefulness of such reports and brings out more clearly the nature and trends of current changes affecting the enterprise. Such presentation emphasizes the fact that statements for a series of periods are far more significant than those for a single period and that the accounts for one period are but an installment of what is essentially a continous history.
>
> 2. In any one year it is ordinarily desirable that the balance sheet, the income statement, and the statement of retained earnings be given for one or more preceding years as well as for the current year. Footnotes, explanations, and accountants' qualifications which appeared on the statements for the preceding years should be repeated, or at least referred to, in the comparative statements to the extent that they continue to be of significance. If, because of reclassifications or for other reasons, changes have occurred in the manner of or basis for presenting corresponding items for two or more periods, information should be furnished which will explain the change. This procedure is in conformity with the well recognized principle that any change in practice which affects comparability should be disclosed.

As a result of this pronouncement, practically all published financial statements include comparative data for the current and prior year. The actual financial statements illustrated at the end of Chapters 4 and 5, and at the end of this chapter, are comparative.

For illustrative purposes, the financial statements for WZ Corporation are used throughout this chapter. Exhibits 24–1, 24–2, and 24–3 present the three comparative statements (condensed for discussion purposes). Observe the form: the current year results in the first column, and single underscores for subtotals to facilitate the presentation in a single column for each period. Placing the various items for the two periods in juxtaposition in the two columns is thought to be preferable to separation as would be necessary for the multiple column approach for each period.

The *long-term summaries* of selected financial information often included in the annual financial report are especially significant. An excellent example of such a summary is presented at the end of this chapter. Observe in particular the nature of the items selected for inclusion in the summary. These vital statistics of the long-term financial performance of the company are particularly relevant to practically all statement users. The annual financial statements for a particular

EXHIBIT 24–1

WZ CORPORATION
Comparative Income Statements
For the Years Ended December 31, 1975 and 1976

	1976		*1975*	
Revenues:	*Amount*	*Percent**	*Amount*	*Percent**
Sales	$400,000		$370,000	
Investment revenue	4,500		3,000	
Gain on disposal of investments	500			
Total Revenue	405,000	100	373,000	100
Expenses:				
Cost of goods sold	265,000	65	250,000	67
Distribution	67,000	17	61,200	16
General administrative	30,000	7	27,000	7
Interest	7,100	2	6,200	2
Total Expenses	369,100	91	344,400	92
Pretax operating income	35,900	9	28,600	8
Income tax expense	16,155	4	12,870	4
Income before extraordinary item	19,745	5		
Extraordinary loss (net of taxes, $3,600)	4,400	1		
Net Income	$ 15,345	4	$ 15,730	4
Earnings per share:				
Income before extraordinary item		$.40		
Extraordinary item		.11		
Net Income†		$.29		$.33

* For illustrative purposes; not usually included on published statements.

† ($15,345 − $2,500) ÷ 44,000 = $.29.
($15,730 − $2,500) ÷ 40,000 = $.33.

EXHIBIT 24–2

WZ CORPORATION
Comparative Balance Sheets
At December 31, 1975, and 1976

	1976		1975	
Assets	*Amount*	*Percent**	*Amount*	*Percent**
Current Assets:				
Cash	$ 55,000	12	$ 74,000	16
Investments, short term	4,000	1	10,000	2
Accounts receivable (net of allowance for doubtful accounts)	39,000	8	30,000	6
Inventory (*Fifo,* lower of cost or market)	95,000	20	80,000	17
Prepaid expenses	200		1,000	
Total Current Assets	193,200	41	195,000	41
Long-term investments	55,000	11	50,000	11
Land, plant, and equipment:				
Land	10,000	2	10,000	2
Plant and equipment	315,000	66	290,000	62
Less: Accumulated depreciation	(97,000)	(20)	(77,000)	(16)
Total	228,000	48	223,000	48
Intangible assets:				
Patent (less amortization)	1,800		2,000	
Total Assets	$478,000	100	$470,000	100
Liabilities				
Current Liabilities:				
Accounts payable	$ 40,000	8	$ 55,000	12
Notes payable, short term	5,000	1	8,000	2
Taxes payable	4,555	1	7,000	1
Total Current Liabilities	49,555	10	70,000	15
Long-Term Liabilities:				
Bonds payable (less unamortized discount)	99,100	21	99,000	21
Total Liabilities	148,655	31	169,000	36
Stockholders' Equity:				
Common stock, par $5, authorized 60,000 shares	220,000	46	200,000	42
Preferred stock, 5%, par $10, authorized 10,000 shares	50,000	10	50,000	11
Contributed capital in excess of par, common stock	14,000	3	12,000	3
Retained earnings	45,345	10	39,000	8
Total Stockholders' Equity	329,345	69	301,000	64
Total Liabilities and Stockholders' Equity	$478,000	100	$470,000	100

* For illustrative purposes; not usually included on published financial statements.

EXHIBIT 24–3

WZ CORPORATION
Comparative Statements of Changes in Financial Position, Working Capital Basis
For the Years Ended December 31, 1975 and 1976

	1976		*1975*	
	Amount	*Percent**	*Amount*	*Percent**
Sources of Working Capital:				
Income before extraordinary items...	$19,745		$15,730	
Add (deduct) items not requiring or generating working capital:				
Depreciation	20,000		18,000	
Amortization of bond discount	100		100	
Amortization of patent	200		200	
Working capital provided by operations	40,045	66	34,030	86
Extraordinary loss (net of tax)	(4,400)	(7)		
Total	35,645	59	34,030	86
Other sources:				
Sale of common stock	22,000	36	5,500	14
Tax refund (from 1974)	3,000	5		
Total from Other Sources	25,000	41	5,500	14
Total Funds Provided	$60,645	100	$39,530	100
Uses of Working Capital:				
Equipment acquired	$25,000	59		
Long-term investments	5,000	12	10,000	56
Cash dividends	12,000	29	8,000	44
Total Funds Used	$42,000	100	$18,000	100
Difference—Net Increase in Working Capital	$18,645		$21,530	
Summary of Changes in Components of Working Capital:				
Increase (decrease) in current assets:				
Cash	$(19,000)		$ (6,070)	
Investments, short term	(6,000)		10,000	
Accounts receivable (net)	9,000		11,000	
Inventory	15,000		12,000	
Prepaid expenses	(800)		600	
Total	(1,800)		27,530	
Increase (decrease) in current liabilities:				
Accounts payable	15,000		(2,000)	
Notes payable, short term	3,000		(3,000)	
Taxes payable	2,445		(1,000)	
Total	20,445		(6,000)	
Net Increase in Working Capital	$ 18,645		$21,530	

* For illustrative purposes; not usually included on published financial statements.

year present a very narrow view of the successes and failures of the company. In contrast, the long-term summary provides a broad overview of where the company has been (financially) and where it is apt to go in the future. Clearly, the results of one, or even two, years may give an overly optimistic or pessimistic view of the future potentials of the company. It is for these reasons that experienced analysts always take a careful look at the long-term summary. Its importance is suggested by the current discussions concerning the desirability of subjecting the summary to audit which is not now required.

PERCENTAGE ANALYSIS OF FINANCIAL STATEMENTS

Financial information expressed in absolute amounts is necessary for practically all purposes; nevertheless, there is a weakness in that proportionate relationships are not clearly revealed. Thus, the expression of relationships in terms of percentages significantly aids the interpretation of financial information. There are two common forms of percentage analyses used on financial statements—vertical analysis and horizontal analysis.

Vertical analysis involves the expression of each item on a particular financial statement as a percent of one specific item which is referred to as the base. For example, the component items on the income statement may be expressed as a percent of total revenue as shown in Exhibit 24–1. Note that the base amount representing 100% is divided into each component item to derive the component percentages, and that the percentages may then be summed. Alternatively, the relationships may be expressed as ratios, in which case net sales would represent 1.00 (rather than 100%) and the components likewise would be expressed in terms of this base.

In applying vertical analysis, an appropriate base amount must be selected for each statement. Observe on Exhibit 24–2 that the base amount for the balance sheet is total assets, and total liabilities plus stockholders' equity respectively; and in Exhibit 24–3 the base amounts for the statement of changes in financial position are total funds provided and total funds used respectively. Financial statements expressed in percentages only are referred to as *common-size* statements.

Horizontal analysis refers to the development of percentages indicating the proportionate change in the same item over *time*. The conversion of absolute amounts of change to percentages facilitates interpretation and evaluation of trends. For example, horizontal percentages shown on the income statements in Exhibit 24–4 serve to emphasize the trend of each component.

It should be noted in the examples relating to horizontal analysis that in computing the percent as well as the amounts of increase or decrease, the base year usually is the earlier period. The percents may not be added or subtracted as between lines since each separate component percentage has a different base. In this respect, attention should be called to the incorrectness of percentages of increase and decrease

EXHIBIT 24–4

WZ CORPORATION
Comparative Income Statements
For the Years Ended December 31, 1975 and 1976
(horizontal analysis)

	Year Ended December 31		*Increase or (decrease) 1976 over 1975*	
	1976	*1975*	*Amount*	*Percent*
Revenues:				
Sales	$400,000	$370,000	$30,000	8
Investment revenue	4,500	3,000	1,500	50
Gain on disposal of investments	500		500	
Total Revenue	405,000	373,000	32,000	9
Expenses:				
Cost of goods sold	265,000	250,000	15,000	6
Distribution	67,000	61,200	5,800	9
General administrative	30,000	27,000	3,000	11
Interest	7,100	6,200	900	15
Total Expenses	369,100	344,400	24,700	7
Pretax operating income	35,900	28,600	7,300	26
Income tax expense	16,155	12,870	3,285	26
Income before extraordinary item	19,745	15,730	4,015	26
Extraordinary loss (net of taxes)	4,400		4,400	
Net Income	$ 15,345	$ 15,730	$ (385)	(2)

which are computed from negative or zero base-year amounts. For example, assume a net loss in 19A of $5,000 and a net gain in 19B of $5,000. With an actual increase of $10,000 the ratio of increase appears to be a minus 200% (+10,000 ÷ −$5,000), a computation which may be misleading. Manifestly, percentage figures should not be computed for accounts which for the base year had no balance or a negative balance. The table in Exhibit 24–5 points out the correct procedure for computing percentages resulting from horizontal increases and decreases.

In considering percentage increases or decreases the analyst also should be aware of misleading inferences when the absolute amounts are small. For example, assume a particular expense in 19A was $10 and in 19B, $30. The percentage increase is 200% which appears significant despite the fact that there was only a $20 increase.

When the statements for more than two years are to be compared, the columns may be shown as in Exhibit 24–6. Note that the base year for 19B changes is 19A, while the base year for 19C changes is 19B.

Practically all users of financial statements will benefit significantly from comparative data and percentage analyses. In this respect a word of caution is in order; the accountant, whether industrial or public, should be discriminating in the selection of information to be presented to the several groups of users; for example, an income statement prepared for internal use should be quite different from one prepared for

EXHIBIT 24–5
Computing Differences – Horizontal Analysis

	December 31		*Increase (decrease)*	
	19B	*19A*	*Amount*	*Percent*
Positive amounts in the base year (19A):				
Item No. 1	$ (200)	$800	$(1,000)	(125)
2	–	800	(800)	(100)
3	200	800	(600)	(75)
4	1,200	800	400	50
Negative amounts in the base year (19A):				
Item No. 5	(1,000)	(800)	(200)	–
6	200	(800)	1,000	–
7	–	(800)	800	–
No amounts in the base year (19A):				
Item No. 8	200	–	200	–
9	(200)	–	(200)	–

external use. Frequently, the quantitative information presented is so voluminous that the user is confused rather than enlightened, or perhaps completely discouraged, thereby precluding serious consideration of the information. It should be realized that large volumes of complex tabulations dismay the average person. Discrimination must be exercised in selecting *(a)* information relevant to the normal problems of the intended users, and *(b)* appropriate analyses of data that will shed light on the situations generally confronting expected users.

In interpreting comparative data and the related percentage analyses, the accountant, as well as the user, should recognize unusual or nonrecurring items that are reflected in the data for each of the periods. Nonrecurring items should be omitted in projecting future potentials. In addition, changes in the general price level (value of the dollar) may have a significant monetary effect on financial data covering a long period. In such cases it may be desirable to express data for all periods in terms of dollars of current (or common) purchasing power (see Chapter 25).

EXHIBIT 24–6
Determination of Base Period

	December 31			*Increase–Decrease**		*Percent of Increase–Decrease**	
	19C	*19B*	*19A*	*During 19C*	*During 19B*	*During 19C*	*During 19B*
Item No. 1	$200	$400	$300	$200*	$100	50.0*	33.3
2	400	300	200	100	100	33.3	50.0
3	400	300	400	100	100*	33.3	25.0*

PROPORTIONATE (OR RATIO) ANALYSIS

The relationship between two amounts may be expressed as a fraction, a percent, or a decimal. The analysis of financial statements generally includes one or more forms of proportionate analysis (often called ratio analysis). It involves the selection of two amounts from one statement, such as the income statement, or from two statements, such as the income statement and balance sheet. The amounts may represent the balances of two different accounts, the balance of one account and a classification total (such as total assets), or two classification totals. Proportionate analysis, however expressed, is supplementary information for the decision-maker that often is particularly important in interpreting the information provided directly by the financial statements.

The mode of expression of proportionate analysis is quite varied. To illustrate, working capital has been discussed and referred to in a number of preceding chapters. The *current ratio* is the relationship between current assets and current liabilities. Assume the following:

Current assets	$5,000,000
Current liabilities	2,000,000
Difference—Working Capital	$3,000,000

The amount of working capital, $3,000,000, standing alone is a useful figure; however, proportionate analysis adds insight to this relationship, viz:

Current Ratio (or working capital ratio) = $5,000,000 ÷ $2,000,000 = 2.5

Alternatively, this ratio may be expressed as 250%; 2.5 to 1; or for each $2.50 of current assets there was $1 of current liabilities.

Proportionate analysis is significant only when the relationship between the selected factors, when expressed as a proportionate relationship, sheds additional light on the interpretation of the individual absolute amounts. In view of the large number of ratios that could be computed it is important that the accountant select for analysis only those related amounts that appear to have significance. In determining significance, consideration must be given to the purposes for which the ratios are to be used. Investors, managers, and creditors have essentially different interests and problems; consequently, they would have somewhat different needs with respect to ratio analyses. Since a complete study of proportionate analysis is outside the scope of this text, only representative ratios having general application are discussed. The analyses selected for discussion will be explained under the following general headings:

1. Proportionate measurements of current position.
2. Proportionate measurements of equity position.
3. Proportionate measurements of operating results.

PROPORTIONATE MEASUREMENTS OF CURRENT POSITION

The proportionate measurements in this category focus on working capital; they are supplementary to the statement of changes of financial position, working capital basis. The ratios relate to selected elements of working capital and are designed to help the statement user evaluate the short-term liquidity and the ability of the business to meet its maturing current liabilities. Seven measurements of current position are summarized in Exhibit 24–7. Observe that they are variously expressed as a percent, decimal, fraction, or turnover figure. The analysis of current position involves *(a)* tests of overall liquidity, and *(b)* movement of current assets (turnovers).[3]

Current Ratio

The current or working capital ratio has long been recognized as an index of short-term liquidity—the ability of the business to meet the maturing claims of the creditors plus the current operating costs. The amount of working capital and the related ratio have a direct impact on the amount of short-term credit that may be granted. Traditionally, as a rule of thumb, a working capital ratio of 2 to 1 has been considered to be adequate. However, analysts in recent years have tended to disavow simplistic decision rules such as this one in favor of a more enlightened approach. The working capital ratio tends to be unique to the industry in which the business operates and even to the business itself in the light of its operating and financial characteristics. For example, a ratio of 2 to 1 may be realistic in one situation, but it may be too low or too high in another situation. The peculiarities of the industry in which the firm operates and other factors, such as methods of operations and seasonal influences, also should be taken into account in evaluating the current ratio.

The working capital ratio is only one measure or index of solvency and ability to meet short-term obligations, and it has certain weaknesses. A high working capital ratio may be the result of overstocking of inventory; a business may have a high current ratio while at the same time it may have a cash deficit. In addition, an extremely high working capital ratio may indicate excess funds which should be invested or otherwise put to use. As with all ratios there is a delicate balance between a ratio that is too high and one that is too low. The determination of the most desirable ratio varies from firm to firm, and the determination of the optimum ratio for a particular firm is a complex problem.

[3] The reader should be cautioned that there is no single "generally accepted" method of computing specific ratios or of determining the values to be substituted in the formulas. Generally the precise computation should be determined by (1) the data available, and (2) the use and interpretation expected in the particular situation. The formulas given herein are indicative of the general approach.

Acid-Test Ratio

Cash, accounts receivable, short-term notes receivable, and short-term investments in marketable securities generally represent funds which may be made readily available for paying current obligations,

EXHIBIT 24–7
Ratios that Measure Current Position

Ratio	*Formula for Computation*	*Significance*
Ratios that measure short-term solvency:		
1. Current or working capital ratio.	Current Assets / Current Liabilities	Primary test of short-term liquidity indicates ability to meet current obligations from current assets as a going concern. Measure of adequacy of working capital.
2. Acid-test or quick ratio.	Quick Assets / Current Liabilities	A more severe test of immediate liquidity than the current ratio. Tests ability to meet sudden demands upon current assets.
3. Working capital to total assets.	Working Capital / Total Assets	Indicates relative liquidity of total assets and distribution of resources employed.
Ratios that measure movement of current assets(turnover):		
4. *a.* Receivable turnover.	Net Credit Sales / Average Receivables (Net)	Velocity of collection of trade accounts and notes. Test of efficiency of collection.
b. Age of receivables.	365 (Days) / Receivable Turnover (computed per [*a*] above)	Average number of days to collect receivables.
5. Inventory turnover.		
a. Merchandise turnover (retail firm).	Cost of Goods Sold / Average Merchandise Inventory	Indicates liquidity of inventory. Number of times inventory "turned over" or was sold on the average during the period. Will exhibit tendency to over- or under-stock.
b. Finished goods turnover (manufacturing firm).	Cost of Goods Sold / Average Finished Goods Inventory	Same as 5*(a).*
c. Raw material turnover.	Cost of Raw Materials Used / Average Raw Materials Inventory	Number of times raw material inventory was "used" on the average during the period.
d. Days' supply in inventory.	365 (Days) / Inventory Turnover (computed per [*a*], [*b*], or [*c*] above)	Average number of days' supply in the ending inventory. Indicates general condition of over- or understocking.
6. Working capital turnover.	Net Sales / Average Working Capital	Indicates adequacy and activity of working capital.
7. Percent of each current asset to total current assets.	Each Current Asset / Total Current Assets	Indicates relative investment in each current asset.

hence they are referred to as *quick assets*. Inventories, on the other hand, must be sold and collection made before cash is available for paying obligations. In many cases, particularly where there are raw materials and work in process inventories, the time element as well as marketability involve considerable uncertainty. In view of these considerations the quick ratio (quick assets divided by current liabilities) has come into general usage as a significant test of immediate solvency. Traditionally, an acid-test ratio of 1 to 1 (a rule-of-thumb standard) has been considered to be desirable. As with the current ratio, the acid-test ratio for a particular company must be evaluated in light of industry characteristics and other factors.

Working Capital to Total Assets

The ratio of working capital to total assets often is considered to be an important ratio in that it is a generalized expression of the distribution and liquidity of the assets employed after current liabilities have been deducted from the current assets. An excessively high ratio might indicate excess cash and/or overstocking of inventory, whereas a low ratio would indicate a definite weakness in the current position.

A related analysis involves a *vertical* percentage analysis of current assets employing *total current assets* as the base (100%). This analysis has particular significance in that *(a)* the relative composition of the current asset structure is revealed, and *(b)* when compared with similar data from prior periods, important trends may be revealed.

Evaluation of Movement of Current Assets

The usual operating cycle for a trading business is from cash to inventory to receivables and back to cash. The analysis of the movement of inventory and receivables is significant in that efficiency of use of these individual items of current assets has a direct bearing on the current position and the overall efficiency with which operations are conducted. Receivable turnover (collections) and inventory turnover are critical in respect to cash flow and funds invested.

Receivable Turnover

In some businesses cash sales predominate, whereas in others credit sales predominate. In either case the amount of trade receivables on the average should bear some relationship to the sales for the period and the terms of credit. The application of the receivable turnover in these respects may be illustrated by referring to WZ Corporation financial statements (Exhibits 24–1 and 24–2):

$$\text{Receivable Turnover} = \frac{\text{Credit Sales, \$345,000}}{\text{Average Receivables, } \dfrac{\$30,000 + \$39,000}{2}} = 10$$

$$\text{Age of Receivables} = \frac{\text{365 Days}}{10} = 36.5 \text{ (average number of days to collect)}$$

If we assume the terms of sale are 1/10, n/30, it appears that collections are lagging terms by six days or more on the average—a reflection of lack of care and inefficiencies with which *(a)* credit is granted, and *(b)* collections are made.

The above simplified illustration also points up several technical aspects of the computation, viz:

1. Should the total of cash and credit sales, or credit sales only, be used in the computation? A more stable and meaningful ratio will result if credit sales only are used; otherwise a shift in the proportion of cash to credit sales will affect the ratio although collection experience is unchanged. For internal use credit sales should be used (since the figure is available or may be reconstructed readily); however, for comparison with other firms the total of cash and credit sales generally must be used since published data seldom provide the credit sales figures for other businesses.
2. Should the ending balance of receivables or average receivables be used? The average *monthly* receivables balance generally should be used in order to smooth out seasonal influences. The average should be determined by adding the 13 monthly balances (January 1, January 31, and through December 31) of trade accounts and trade notes receivable, then dividing by 13. In the absence of monthly balances the average of the annual beginning and ending balance or only the ending balance may be used. For comparison with other firms the ending balance may, by necessity, have to be used.
3. Receivables should be net of the allowance for doubtful accounts.
4. Trade notes receivable should be included in averaging receivables.

Whether to express the receivable movement as a "turnover" or as "number of days to collect" is principally a matter of personal preference. It is appropriate to note that if the company uses a "natural" business year, the receivables reported on the balance sheet normally will be quite low which would cause the turnover to look better than is actually the case on the average.

Merchandise Turnover

Merchandise turnover is the ratio between the cost of goods sold (or used) and the average inventory balance. The procedures for determining the average inventory balance are similar to those discussed above for average receivables. For comparisons with other firms the analyst may have to use *sales* rather than cost of goods sold. Obviously, such a ratio would at best represent an approximation since the markup in the sales amount (but not in the inventory amount) would distort the ratio. This error may be minimized by restating the inventory to retail.

The merchandise inventory turnover may be expressed as a "turnover" or as "days' supply"; the latter appears more often in current usage.[4]

---

[4] Some analysts prefer to use 250 (5-day workweek) or 300 (6-day workweek) days, as the case may be, as an approximation of the number of business days in the year.

The turnover or days' supply figure has significance in that the amount of inventory on hand normally should bear a close relationship to cost of goods sold. The relationship necessarily will vary from industry to industry—a grocery store normally should expect a high inventory turnover, whereas an antique dealer may expect a comparatively low turnover. Also, the ratio represents an average—a generalization that does not reflect how fast particular items are moving, but rather how fast all items on the average are moving. For example, a grocer may have a turnover of 15, yet may have items on the shelves that have not turned over at all during the entire year.

Inventory turnover is directly related to profitability. To illustrate, assume that the inventory turnover is 12 (cost of goods sold, $1,200,000; average inventory, $100,000) and that the entrepreneur realizes a profit of $1,000 each time the $100,000 investment in inventory turns over. A $12,000 profit is indicated. Now assume another firm identical in every respect except that the inventory turnover is 6 indicating a $6,000 profit on a similar $100,000 inventory investment.

Work in process inventory turnover is computed by dividing cost of goods manufactured by the average work in process inventory. With respect to all inventories, turnover computations based on appropriate unit data, when practicable, will provide more reliable results than when based on dollar amount data.

PROPORTIONATE MEASUREMENT OF THE EQUITY POSITION

The balance sheet reports the two basic sources of funds used by the business: *(a)* owners' equity, and *(b)* creditors' equity. The relationships between these two distinct equities often are measured because they tend to reflect the financial strengths and weaknesses of the business; in other words, the long-term solvency of a business and its potential capacity to generate and obtain investment resources. Exhibit 24–8 summarizes eight ratios that are commonly used measures of equity position.

Equity Ratios

These three ratios reflect essentially the same relationship; that is, the proportion of total assets provided by *(a)* the owners, and *(b)* the creditors. The three equity ratios for WZ Corporation (Exhibit 24–2) for 1976 are:

1. $\dfrac{\text{Owners' Equity, \$329,345}}{\text{Total Assets, \$478,000}}$ = 69% of the assets were provided by owners

2. $\dfrac{\text{Creditors' Equity, \$148,655}}{\text{Total Assets, \$478,000}}$ = 31% of the assets were provided by creditors

   100% total assets provided

3. $\dfrac{\text{Creditors' Equity, \$148,655}}{\text{Owners' Equity, \$329,345}}$ = 45% —the creditors' equity is 45% of the owners' equity

EXHIBIT 24–8
Ratios that Measure Equity Position

Ratio	Formula for Computation	Significance
Equity ratios:		
1. Owners' equity total assets.	Owners' Equity / Total Assets	Proportion of assets provided by owners. Reflects financial strength and cushion for creditors.
2. Creditors' equity to total assets.	Total Liabilities / Total Assets	Proportion of assets provided by creditors. Extent of "trading on the equity."
3. Owners' equity to total liabilities. (Sometimes computed as total liabilities to owners' equity.)	Owners' Equity / Total Liabilities	Relative amounts of resources provided by owners and creditors. Reflects strengths and weaknesses in basic financing of operations.
Other ratios related to equity position:		
4. Fixed assets to long-term liabilities.	Operational Assets (Net) / Long-Term Liabilities	Reflects extent of resources from long-term debt. May suggest potential borrowing power. If the fixed assets are pledged—degree of security.
5. Fixed assets to owners' equity.	Fixed Assets (Net) / Owners' Equity	May suggest over- or under-investment by owners; also weakness or strength in "trading on the equity."
6. Fixed assets to total equities.	Fixed Assets (Net) / Total Liabilities and Owners' Equity	May suggest overexpansion of plant and equipment.
7. Sales to fixed assets (plant turnover).	Net Sales / Fixed Assets (Net)	Turnover index which tests roughly the efficiency of management in keeping plant properties employed.
8. Book value per share of common stock.	Common Stock Equity / Number of Outstanding Common Shares	Number of dollars of equity (at book value) per share of common stock.

Although the three equity ratios sometimes are computed, usually only one of the three is used because each one reflects the same relationship (but in a somewhat different way).

The balance between resources provided by debt versus owners' equity is considered critical by expert analysts; however, there is no rule of thumb that can be pointed to as a guide for evaluation. Clearly, a company that has 80% debt and 20% owners' equity usually would be considered to be in an overborrowed (overextended) position; interest payments must be made whether there are profits, and the debts must be paid at the fixed maturity dates. In contrast, if debt and owners' equity are 20% and 80%, respectively, the creditors' position is better and interest payments lower. However, owners' equity usually is more costly than debt capital, particularly since interest paid on debt is deductible for income tax purposes, whereas dividends are not. On the other hand, equity capital does not have maturity dates.

Debt financing also is an important avenue for most businesses because of a favorable effect known as *trading on the equity* or *financial leverage*. These are common terms that refer to the advantage to be gained for the stockholders' by borrowing funds, say at 8%, when the business is earning 12% on *total assets*. This topic is discussed later in the chapter in respect to return on investment.

In computing the equity ratios, it is important that all components, such as the appropriated retained earnings and unrealized capital, be included in owners' equity. Some analysts prefer to subtract the carrying value of intangible assets thereby using *tangible capital* for owners' equity. The authors see no basic reason for this approach since we assume the intangibles are accounted for properly and, as a consequence, are not carried at more than the appropriate value.

Three of the other ratios listed on Exhibit 24–8 (4 through 6) focus in general on measurement of the relationships of the long-term committments of resources to fixed assets and the sources of capital that provided them. They are viewed as rough measures of over- or underexpansion of fixed assets in relation to the sources of long-term capital. Because of their general nature, they are not widely used. The sales to fixed assets ratio, sometimes called the *plant turnover ratio*, attempts to measure over- or underexpansion of plant (i.e., fixed assets) in relation to sales. A high plant turnover rate is favorable because it reflects the effeciency of the plant to produce goods; however, it does not reflect the cost factors—the plant volume may be high, but the costs or production may be prohibitive.

Book Value per Share of Capital Stock

Although it is often computed, book value per share of capital stock has limited usefulness. It has little, if any, correspondence with the market value per share. Some investors are particularly impressed with stock that has a book value in excess of the market price because, under the cost, matching, and conservatism principles, the assets are apt to be carried at amounts significantly less than their fair market value; they should never be reflected in the accounts at more than their fair value (recall that a loss is recognized when it occurs even though there has been no transaction to measure it). Book value per share is also used for comparative purposes with other companies.

Book value per share is computed by dividing total common stockholders' equity by the number of common shares outstanding. When there is more than one class of stock outstanding, total stockholders' equity must be apportioned between the various classes in accordance with the legal and statutory claims that would be effective in case of liquidation of the company. Since additional classes of stock typically are preferred stock, the usual situation requires allocation based upon the preferential rights of the preferred stock. Liquidation, cumulative, and participating preferences must be in the computation.

To illustrate a typical allocation, assume the Stone Manufacturing Corporation balance sheet reflected the following at a specific date:

Stockholders' Equity:	
Preferred stock, 6%, cumulative, nonparticipating, par value $100 per share, 1,000 shares outstanding	$100,000
Common stock, $100 par value (2,000 shares issued)	200,000
Contributed capital in excess of par, preferred	10,000
Contributed capital in excess of par, common	15,000
Retained earnings	75,000
Treasury stock—common (100 shares at cost)	(17,000)
Total Stockholders' Equity	$383,000

Preferred preferences—liquidation value $105 per share—two years' dividends in arrears, this includes the year just ended.

Computation of book value per share:

Total stockholders' equity		$383,000
Allocation to preferred stock:		
Liquidation value—1,000 shares @ $105	$105,000	
Cumulative dividends—$100,000 × 6% × 2 (two years in arrears at 6% including current year just ended)	12,000	117,000
Allocation to common stock (1,900 shares outstanding)		$266,000

Book value per share of preferred:

$$\frac{\$117{,}000}{1{,}000} = \$117$$

Book value per share of common:

$$\frac{\$266{,}000}{1{,}900} = \$140$$

RATIOS MEASURING OPERATING RESULTS

In recent years increasing attention has been given to the ability of a business to earn a satisfactory income and return on investment, rather than to the value of the assets. Although ratios relating to income are perhaps of somewhat more interest to investors than to creditors, the latter are giving increasing attention to profitability. A creditor may be unwilling to make loans or grant merchandise credit if an unhealthy profit picture exists in the prospective borrower's business, even though adequate collateral is available. Management and investors are particularly concerned with evidences of the earnings potential of a business. The principal ratios that measure operating results are summarized in Exhibit 24-9.

EXHIBIT 24–9
Ratios that Measure Operating Results

Ratio	*Formula for Computation*	*Significance*
1. Profit margin.	Net Income / Net Sales	Indicates net profitability of each dollar of sales.
2. Return on investment: *a.* On total assets.	Net Income Plus Interest Expense* / Total Assets	Rate earned on *all resources* used. Measures earnings on all investments including both owners and creditors.
b. On owners' equity.	Net Income / Owners' Equity	Rate earned on resources provided by owners (excludes creditors). Measures earnings accruing to the owners.
3. Investment turnover.	Net Sales / Total Investment	Number of times total investment (total assets) turns. Indicative of efficiency with which total resources are utilized.
4. Earnings per share.	Income Accruing to Common Stock / Common Shares Outstanding	Profit earned on each share of common stock. Indicative of ability to pay dividends and to grow from within. See Chapter 17.
Market Tests		
5. Price-earnings ratio (the multiple).	Market Price per Share / Earnings per Share	Earnings rate based on cost of share of stock on the market. Indicates profitableness of firm related to market value of stockholders' equity.
6. Payout ratio.	Market Price per Share / Dividends per Share	Measures the length of the cash payout period for the investor.
7. Dividend ratio.	Dividends per Share / Earnings per Share	Measures the proportion of income (before extraordinary items) paid out in dividends on the average.

* Adjusted for tax savings.

Profit Margin

The ratio of net income to net sales, generally referred to as the *profit margin,* is widely used as an index of profitability; however, one significant factor related to profitability—investment—is given no consideration in the ratio. To illustrate, assume the accounts of the Conway Company showed the following data: net income, $20,000; net sales, $2,000,000; and total assets, $100,000. In this case the profit margin is 1% whereas the 20% return on total investment appears to be satisfactory. Thus, the profit margin appears inadequate as a measure of profitability. The profit margin has value primarily for evaluation of trends and for comparison with industry and competitor statistics.

Return on Investment

This ratio is considered by many accountants to be the single most important ratio because it incorporates the two basic factors that should be considered in measuring profitability: (1) earnings, and (2) investment. Fundamentally, return on investment is computed by dividing *income by investment*. Return on investment is referred to variously as capital yield, return on assets employed, return on capital, rate of return, or simply ROI. Return on investment has two important applications in business situations:

1. Evaluating proposed capital additions (not discussed herein).[5]
2. Measuring profitability in relation to investment.

As a measure of profitability, return on investment may be computed on the basis of either:

1. Owners' equity; that is, net income divided by owners' equity (ROI_o).
2. Total assets; that is, net income (adjusted for interest expense) divided by total assets (ROI_t).

Most analysts compute both ratios and compare them to measure the effect of *financial leverage* (i.e., trading on the equity). The following data are used to illustrate return on investment:

XY COMPANY

Balance Sheet Data:	
Total assets	$100,000
Total liabilities	40,000
Stockholders' equity	60,000
Total Equities	$100,000
Income Statement Data:	
Operating income	$ 20,000
Interest expense	3,200
Pretax income	16,800
Income taxes ($16,800 × 40%)	6,720
Net Income	$ 10,080

Return on investment for a business is computed as follows:

1. Return on owners' equity:

$$\frac{\text{Net Income}}{\text{Owners' Equity}} = ROI_o$$

XY Company (data above):

$$\frac{\$10,080}{\$60,000} = 16.8\%\ ROI_o$$

[5] For an excellent discussion, see Harold Bierman, Jr. and Seymour Smidt, *The Capital Budgeting Decision* (New York: The Macmillan Co., 1960).

2. Return on total assets (i.e., total investment):

$$\frac{\text{Net Income} + \text{Interest Expense, Net of Tax}}{\text{Total Assets}} = \text{ROI}_t$$

XY Company (data above):

$$\frac{\$10{,}080 + (\$3{,}200 - \$1{,}280)}{\$100{,}000} = \frac{\$12{,}000}{\$100{,}000} = \underline{12.0}\ \text{ROI}_t$$

Difference: Financial Leverage Factor...... $\underline{\underline{4.8\%}}$

In computing return on total investment, interest expense (net of income taxes) is added to net income because it is a part of the return earned on total assets which includes the liabilities on which the interest was paid. Interest expense (net of tax) was deducted in determining net income (as reported on the income statement). Also, the denominator includes the resources provided by both creditor and owners; therefore, the numerator must include the return to both sources (net income plus interest).

Return on total assets measures the profitability of the total resources available to the business. It indicates the efficiency with which management used the total resources available to them.

Return on owners' equity is used to measure the return that accrues to the stockholders *after* the interest payments to the creditors are deducted to derive net income. It does not measure the efficiency with which total resources were used, but rather the *residual* return to the owners on their total investment in the business (i.e., the original investment plus retained earnings).

Financial Leverage

In a prior paragraph, the concept of financial leverage, sometimes called trading on the equity, was briefly defined. More comprehensively, financial leverage is the effect on return on investment of borrowing versus investment by owners; it may be either positive or negative as regards the interest of the owners. If the interest rate on debt is lower than the rate earned on total assets, financial leverage will be positive; if the interest rate is higher, financial leverage will be negative. Financial leverage can be measured by subtracting return on total assets (ROI_t) from return on owners' equity (ROI_o).

For XY Company, the financial leverage effect was (+) 4.8% (positive) because the return on owners' equity was greater than the return on total assets. The 4.8% positive effect in favor of owners' equity was due to the fact that the company earned a greater rate of return on total assets than the rate of interest, net of tax, paid for borrowed resources. This can be demonstrated for XY Company, assuming interest expense averages 8% on the total debt, as follows:

Earnings on resources provided by debt ($40,000 × 12%*)...............	$4,800
Cost (net of tax) of resources provided by debt ($40,000 × .08 × .60)	1,920
Net Gain on Resources Provided by Debt............................	$2,880
Financial leverage factor ($2,880 ÷ $60,000)	4.8%

* The 12% ROI_t, as computed, is net of tax.

Obviously, had there been no debt, return on investment on total assets and return on owners' equity would be identical. In contrast, when there is debt, and the interest rate on the debt and the rate of return on total assets are different, there will be a financial leverage effect causing the two ROI percentages to be different.

The computations for XY Company, when compared, show three separate factors that cause financial leverage, viz.:

1. Investment differential—the difference in investment as between all investors and the owner-investor only. The denominator in computing ROI_o was $60,000 whereas the denominator in computing ROI_t was $100,000.
2. Rate differentials—the difference between the rate earned on total assets and the interest rate paid for debt capital.
3. Income tax differential—the cost of resources obtained by incurring debt (i.e., interest expense) is deductible by the company for income tax purposes whereas dividends paid to owners are not.

The cause and measurement of financial leverage may be diagrammed as follows:

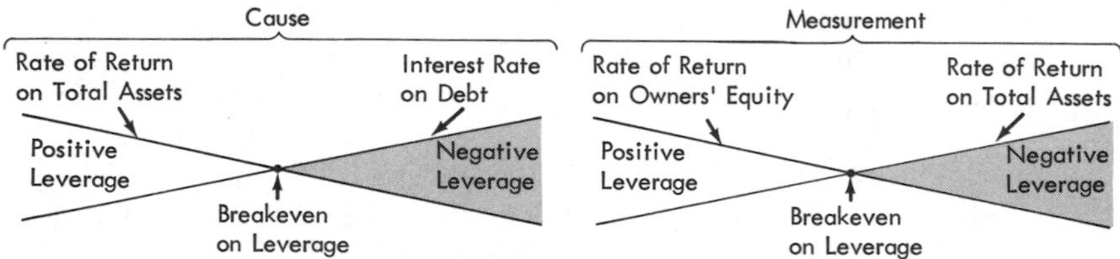

Financial leverage is an important aspect of financial planning in a business because of the greater returns (leverage) that can accrue to the owners. However, excessive debt has the disadvantages of (1) cash interest payments each period must be made whether or not earnings and cash flow are satisfactory, and (2) maturity payments on principal must be made on the specified dates.

The analysis of financial statements should always include *return on investment* and *financial leverage* evaluations. A comparison of the rates of return on owners' equity and total assets provides a particularly realiable measure of the degree and effect of financial leverage. Expert analysts look at this relationship very closely.

Return on investment has gained wide acceptance in the last few years as an important tool of managerial control. The measure has the distinct advantage of directing management attention clearly and forcefully to a combination of the three principal factors affecting profit—sales, expense, and total assets employed. Many accountants believe that the APB in *Opinion No. 15* (see Chapter 17) did not best reflect the long-range needs of the users in recognizing earnings per share as a fundamental measure of the success or failure of a business. Earnings per share, among other weaknesses, gives little attention to the total amount of investment (resources) used in the process of creating net income. Many accountants believe, because of its fundamental characteristics, that return on total investment and return on owners' equity should have been selected as the fundamental measures of profitability and financial leverage. They recognize that profitability fundamentally is the relationship between investment and earnings on that investment.

Investment Turnover

This ratio, also called the asset turnover, is computed by dividing net sales by average total assets for the year. It measures the effectiveness with which management used the total resources at their disposal. It is similar in concept to inventory turnover. Sales is considered the principal activity of the business, and the lower the amount of investment needed in relation to sales the greater earnings should be. However, this ratio does not include the effect of expenses. A company may have a high asset turnover, viewed as a favorable condition, in the face of a substantial net loss.

Market Tests

Several different market tests are often used by investors and analysts to measure the relationship between investment by the stockholders (i.e., the purchase price of the shares owned) and the return from the shares (i.e., dividends). Three market tests are listed in Exhibit 24–9. The price-earnings ratio, generally called the *multiple*, is a widely used market test of profitability because it relates the earnings of the business to the current market price of the stock. For this reason, it is of particular interest to the potential investor. Of course, this ratio changes each time the market price of the stock changes. Several years ago, multiples of 50 or more were not unusual; however, multiples in the range of 10 to 20 are more common currently. The multiple generally should be computed on the basis of earnings per share before extraordinary items. To illustrate, assuming the common stock of WZ Corporation is selling at $6.50 per share, on December 31, 1976, the multiple would be:

$$\frac{\text{Market Price per Share, \$6.50}}{\text{EPS (Exhibit 24–1), \$.40}} = 16 \text{ (i.e., the stock was selling at 16 times the earnings per share)}$$

The *payout ratio* is used as a rough measure of the length of time that it may take the investor to recover the cash investment. For example, if the dividends per share have been averaging $.65 per year and a market price of $6.50 per share, the payout period would be 10 years. This ratio is not given much weight because of its imprecision and theoretical weaknesses (tax effects and the interest factor for the investor are ignored).

The *dividend ratio* also is a rough measure of potential return to the investor. It is computed by dividing dividends per share by earnings per share. Preferably, averages covering the past several years should be used. It is a market test that investors consider along with other data; however, it is relatively insignificant in situations where dividends are unstable.

USE AND INTERPRETATION OF RATIO ANALYSES

In evaluating the financial position of a business, the relationships indicated by both the absolute amounts and the ratios, it is especially important that the limitations of the data be realized. Significantly, ratios represent average conditions; therefore, they must be interpreted broadly. In addition, changes in the accounting system and classification of data may significantly affect a ratio. One writer has suggested that the idea of their use may be conveyed by a comparison with the interpretation of a thermometer reading by a doctor—beyond a certain range the fever reading indicates *something* is wrong with the patient, but not exactly what it is. An unfavorable ratio can be thought of as a red flag—the matter should be investigated. Additionally, one ratio or even several ratios standing alone, whatever their values, may be insignificant. Consequently, a primary problem confronting both the analyst and the statement user relates to the evaluation of a specific ratio. For example, is it good or bad that the inventory turnover for a company is 12? In determining what constitutes an unfavorable or favorable ratio for a particular business the following comparisons are suggested:

1. Comparison of ratios for the current year with those of preceding years for the company. The trend of certain ratios may be highly significant.
2. Comparison of the company's ratios with those of leading competitors (when available from published financial statements).
3. Comparison with ratios of the industry within which the company operates. Industry statistics may be obtained from the following sources:
   a. Industry trade associations—practically all industries support one or more trade associations that generally collect and publish financial statistics (averages) relating to the industry. The National Retail Merchants Association is a good example.
   b. Bureaus of business research of universities—the University of Texas prepares comparative data on approximately 100 Texas retail stores, and other universities perform a similar function.
   c. U.S. Department of Commerce, Washington, D.C.

d. Publications of Robert Morris Associates.
e. Dun & Bradstreet, Inc., in the magazine *Modern Industry* and separate booklets.

4. Comparison with budgeted or standard ratios developed by the company.

Because differences in product lines, methods of operation, size, geography, accounting methods, and variations in the method of computing the ratios may significantly influence the results caution should be exercised in comparing ratios with those from other sources. When comparing ratios over a period of several years, price-level changes also assume considerable significance (see Chapter 25). Despite the shortcomings mentioned above, ratio analysis is a useful tool in interpreting financial statements and in evaluating the financial strength of a business. The accountant, both public and industrial, should employ this useful tool to the extent consistent with the situation and the needs of the statement users.

The presentation of ratio analyses is an important aspect of financial reporting. The accountant should report the results of the analyses in a manner that is consistent with the problem at hand. A special report involving a tabulation of specific data often is required for creditor purposes. External annual financial statement usually include a limited number of ratios, although it is fairly common to include some graphical representation based on ratios such as a pie chart indicating the "disposition" of the sales dollar; that is, a graphic representation of a vertical percentage analysis of the income statement.

THE SEARCH FOR ADDITIONAL INFORMATION

The serious investor should search for information to supplement that provided by the financial statements. Hearsay is hazardous; the investor should seek hard data on the company—its operations, policies, competitive position, the quality of the management, and other nonquantitative information. Brokerage firms and security analysts typically gather and disseminate relevant information. Periodic reports, by listed companies, to the SEC are available; and in some respects, they provide information not included in the published financial statements.

The financial media often is a rich source of information on companies and industries. In addition to news items; they generally carry special well-researched articles. Examples of financial publications include Fortune, Barrons, The Wall Street Journal, Business Week, Forbes, and various industry publications; such publications are available in most libraries on a current basis.

OVERVIEW

This chapter presented a wide range of techniques for analysis of financial statements. The purpose of these techniques is to glean from the statements particularly relevant information for the statement user.

We re-emphasize that each decision by the statement user tends to be unique and therefore has somewhat different information needs. Not all of the techniques (and specifics) are relevant to all decisions; the statement user must use sound judgment in deciding what information is relevant to the decision at hand.

However, for most important decisions, when the statement user has completed an analysis of the financial statements along the lines suggested in this chapter, a major input to most important decision models exists. Consideration of other relevant factors such as the trend of the industry, the global situation, and the impact of governmental regulation is essential. When such considerations are coupled with the results of the analysis of the financial statements sufficient basis usually exists to support a sound decision by the statement user.

The appendix to follow presents a complete set of actual statements for an interesting situation. Observe that the summary of financial results covers the entire life span of this company. This case is presented as a supplementary device for studying and applying the analytical techniques discussed in the chapter.

Appendix: Financial Statements, Earth Resources Company

HISTORICAL CORPORATE PROFILE

Development and marketing of mineral and energy resources of the earth to benefit its shareholders and the nation is the mission of Earth Resources Company. Major operations include a petroleum refinery at Memphis, Tennessee; retail gasoline stations throughout the mid-South, a copper mine in New Mexico, a marine transportation system on the Mississippi River, and a majority interest in a silver and gold mine being developed in Idaho. Through Energy Company of Alaska, a subsidiary, the company is also engaged in supplying roadbuilding and paving materials, and plans to build a petroleum refinery to serve the Alaskan Interior. The company also conducts an active mineral exploration program, and owns a coal mine in Alaska. Earth Resources Company common stock is traded on the American Stock Exchange and the Pacific Coast Stock Exchange, with the symbol **ERC**.

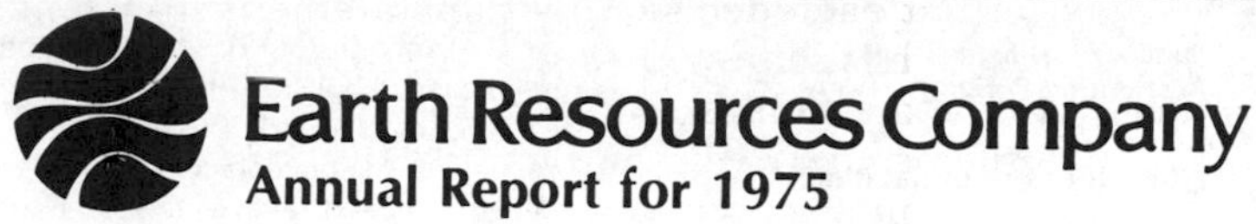

Financial Highlights

	1975	1974	% Increase
Revenues	**$230,859,000**	$141,874,000	63%
Income before taxes	**20,068,000**	14,366,000	40%
Net income	**10,380,000**	7,392,000	40%
Earnings per common and common equivalent share	**$2.31**	$1.68	38%
Cash flow (before exploration, interest and taxes on income)	**24,255,000**	19,387,000	25%
Dividends on common stock	**3,092,000**	1,843,000	68%
Dividends per share	**$ .70**	$ .42	67%
Total assets	**90,081,000**	70,850,000	27%
Shareholders' equity	**31,663,000**	24,286,000	30%

Corporate Profile

The diversified resource development activities of Earth Resources Company offer a broad scope of service to America's needs. Major operations include a 44,000 BPD petroleum refinery; retail gasoline operations throughout the mid-South; marine and surface transportation; silver, gold, and copper mining, and an active mineral exploration program. Energy Company of Alaska, a subsidiary, manufactures roadbuilding materials, provides contracting services, and plans to build the Alaskan Interior's first refinery, near Fairbanks. Earth Resources Company common stock is traded on the American Stock Exchange and the Pacific Stock Exchange with the symbol ERC.

Summary of Significant Accounting Policies
EARTH RESOURCES COMPANY AND SUBSIDIARIES

Principles of Consolidation:

The consolidated financial statements include the accounts of all subsidiaries. All intercompany balances and significant intercompany transactions have been eliminated. The cost of investments in subsidiaries has been assigned to the acquired assets based on the fair value of such assets.

Inventories:

Inventories are valued at the lower of cost or market. Effective September 1, 1974, cost of the petroleum products and crude oil of the company's refinery are determined on a last-in, first-out (LIFO) basis. The cost of other inventories is determined on a first-in, first-out basis.

Exploration, Research and Development Expenditures:

The company charges all exploration, research and development expenditures to income as incurred. Exploration costs previously expensed on properties on which commercial development is later undertaken are capitalized and assigned to the related mine investment.

Property, Plant and Equipment:

Property, plant and equipment is stated at cost. Depreciation other than for mining facilities is based on the straight-line method over estimated service lives from three to twenty years. Depreciation, depletion and amortization of mining facilities, including development costs, is based substantially on the units of production in relation to total estimated units of reserve.

Expenditures for general property maintenance and repairs are charged to earnings as incurred. The company capitalizes major replacements and betterments and relieves the asset and the related allowance for depreciation accounts of the cost and accumulated depreciation in respect to items replaced, retired or otherwise disposed of. The gain or loss on property, plant and equipment items sold or retired is included in current earnings.

Income Taxes:

Deferred income taxes are provided to the extent of the benefit received from timing differences between financial and taxable income. The timing differences relate primarily to mine development costs, depreciation methods and income recognition. The allowable investment tax credit is applied as a current reduction of income tax expense.

Pension Plans:

Pension costs are provided for and funded at amounts not less than actuarially determined estimates. Unfunded past service costs are being amortized over a thirty-year period.

Opinion Of Independent Accountants

The Board of Directors
Earth Resources Company
Dallas, Texas

We have examined the consolidated balance sheet of Earth Resources Company and Subsidiaries as of August 31, 1975 and the related consolidated statements of income and retained earnings and changes in financial position for the year then ended. Our examination was made in accordance with generally accepted auditing standards, and accordingly included such tests of the accounting records and such other auditing procedures as we considered necessary in the circumstances. We previously examined and reported upon the consolidated financial statements of the company for the year ended August 31, 1974.

In our opinion, the aforementioned financial statements present fairly the consolidated financial position of Earth Resources Company and Subsidiaries at August 31, 1975 and 1974 and the consolidated results of their operations and changes in financial position for the years then ended, in conformity with generally accepted accounting principles applied on a consistent basis, except for the change, with which we concur, to the last-in, first-out method of determining costs of certain inventories as discussed in Note 1 to the notes to consolidated financial statements.

Dallas, Texas
October 10, 1975

Coopers & Lybrand

Consolidated Statement of Income and Retained Earnings
EARTH RESOURCES COMPANY AND SUBSIDIARIES
For the years ended August 31, 1975 and 1974

	1975	1974
Net sales and other income	**$230,859,000**	$141,874,000
Costs and expenses:		
Cost of sales (Note 1)	**195,265,000**	114,568,000
Selling expenses	**8,140,000**	5,866,000
Exploration, research and development expenses (Note 3)	**596,000**	740,000
General and administrative expenses	**5,868,000**	5,562,000
Interest expense	**922,000**	772,000
	210,791,000	127,508,000
Income before income taxes	**20,068,000**	14,366,000
Provision for federal and state income taxes (Note 7):		
Current	**8,483,000**	7,739,000
Deferred	**1,205,000**	(765,000)
	9,688,000	6,974,000
Net income	**10,380,000**	7,392,000
Retained earnings, beginning of year	**9,204,000**	3,655,000
Dividends declared on common stock (Note 6)	**(3,092,000)**	(1,843,000)
Retained earnings, end of year	**$ 16,492,000**	$ 9,204,000
Earnings per common and common equivalent share (Note 8)	**$2.31**	$1.68
Dividends declared per share of common stock	**$ .70**	$ .42

The accompanying summary of significant accounting policies and notes are an integral part of the financial statements.

Consolidated Balance Sheet
EARTH RESOURCES COMPANY AND SUBSIDIARIES
August 31, 1975 and 1974

ASSETS	**1975**	1974
Current assets:		
Cash	**$ 9,357,000**	$ 4,158,000
Temporary cash investments	**15,175,000**	15,550,000
Accounts receivable, trade	**11,455,000**	9,398,000
Other accounts and notes receivable	**1,525,000**	1,826,000
Inventories, primarily crude oil and petroleum products (Note 1)	**9,526,000**	8,563,000
Prepaid expenses	**825,000**	670,000
Future income tax benefits		434,000
Total current assets	**47,863,000**	40,599,000
Property, plant and equipment:		
Land and mineral leases	**6,939,000**	6,973,000
Refinery facilities	**22,288,000**	16,896,000
Mining facilities and development costs	**12,357,000**	12,413,000
Other property and equipment	**17,760,000**	11,147,000
	59,344,000	47,429,000
Less allowance for depreciation, depletion and amortization	**21,279,000**	19,311,000
	38,065,000	28,118,000
Other assets	**4,153,000**	2,133,000
	$90,081,000	$70,850,000
LIABILITIES AND CAPITAL		
Current liabilities:		
Current portion of long-term debt (Note 4)	**$ 1,515,000**	$ 1,602,000
Accounts payable, trade	**19,513,000**	16,179,000
Accrued expenses	**14,028,000**	11,903,000
Federal and state income tax payable (Note 7)	**2,586,000**	7,442,000
Total current liabilities	**37,642,000**	37,126,000
Long-term debt (Note 4):		
Banks	**12,284,000**	1,945,000
Other	**4,726,000**	5,964,000
	17,010,000	7,909,000
Less current portion	**1,515,000**	1,602,000
	15,495,000	6,307,000
Deferred federal and state income taxes (Note 7)	**4,973,000**	3,014,000
Minority interest in consolidated subsidiary	**308,000**	117,000
Commitments and contingencies (Note 5)		
Capital (Notes 4 and 6):		
Common stock, no par value	**14,992,000**	14,904,000
Paid-in capital	**290,000**	289,000
Retained earnings	**16,492,000**	9,204,000
Less 7,407 common shares in treasury, at cost	**(111,000)**	(111,000)
	31,663,000	24,286,000
	$90,081,000	$70,850,000

The accompanying summary of significant accounting policies and notes are an integral part of the financial statements.

Consolidated Statement of Changes in Financial Position
EARTH RESOURCES COMPANY AND SUBSIDIARIES
For the years ended August 31, 1975 and 1974

	1975	1974
Working capital provided:		
From operations:		
Net income	**$10,380,000**	$ 7,392,000
Items not affecting working capital in the current period:		
Depreciation, depletion and amortization	**2,669,000**	3,509,000
Noncurrent portion of deferred income taxes (credit)	**771,000**	(331,000)
Other, net	**236,000**	11,000
Working capital provided from operations	**14,056,000**	10,581,000
Issuance of long-term debt	**11,000,000**	7,868,000
Noncurrent income tax payable	**1,188,000**	
Proceeds from disposal of property, plant and equipment	**791,000**	664,000
Proceeds from issuance of common stock	**88,000**	447,000
Other	**270,000**	304,000
	27,393,000	19,864,000
Working capital applied:		
Additions to property, plant and equipment	**13,644,000**	6,489,000
Property, plant and equipment of company acquired		4,458,000
Reductions of long-term debt	**1,812,000**	8,624,000
Dividends declared on common stock	**3,092,000**	1,843,000
Increase in other assets	**2,097,000**	943,000
Other		97,000
	20,645,000	22,454,000
Increase (decrease) in working capital	**$ 6,748,000**	($ 2,590,000)
Changes in components of working capital:		
Increase (decrease) in current assets:		
Cash and temporary cash investments	**$ 4,824,000**	$ 9,881,000
Receivables	**1,756,000**	6,144,000
Inventories	**963,000**	4,473,000
Prepaid expenses	**155,000**	271,000
Future income tax benefits	**(434,000)**	434,000
	7,264,000	21,203,000
Increase (decrease) in current liabilities:		
Current portion of long-term debt	**(87,000)**	(627,000)
Accounts payable and accrued expenses	**5,459,000**	17,861,000
Federal and state income taxes payable	**(4,856,000)**	6,559,000
	516,000	23,793,000
Increase (decrease) in working capital	**$ 6,748,000**	($ 2,590,000)

The accompanying summary of significant accounting policies and notes are an integral part of the financial statements.

Notes to Consolidated Financial Statements
EARTH RESOURCES COMPANY AND SUBSIDIARIES

1. Inventories:

Prior to 1975, petroleum products and crude oil costs for the company's refinery had been determined on the latest three-month average cost method. As of September 1, 1974, the company adopted the LIFO method of determining cost for these inventories. The new method is considered preferable because it more closely matches current costs with current revenues in periods of price level changes. This change had the effect of reducing inventory by $1,802,000 and net income for the year ended August 31, 1975 by $881,000 or $.20 per share. There is no cumulative effect on retained earnings as of August 31, 1974 for this type of accounting change.

2. Company Acquired:

On October 16, 1973, the company's majority-owned subsidiary, Energy Company of Alaska ("ECA"), acquired all of the outstanding capital stock of Rogers & Babler, Inc., of Anchorage, Alaska for the purchase price of $6,000,000. The acquisition was accounted for by the "purchase method." The results of operations of Rogers & Babler, Inc., have been included in the consolidated statement of income of the company since the date of acquisition. The pro forma effect on the 1974 consolidated statement of income prior to the date of acquisition is not material.

3. Mining Operations:

The company has entered into an operating joint venture with others providing for the commercial development of the DeLamar Silver Mine. The company has a 52½% interest and is manager of the joint venture. Under the terms of the agreement the company will provide up to $9,700,000 as its share of the estimated costs required to place the mine and mill in operation. At August 31, 1975, the company's investment is $1,115,000 including prior year's exploration costs of $369,000 capitalized during the year.

In February 1975, the company suspended operations at its Nacimiento Copper Mine since the United States producer price for copper did not permit an adequate return of investment. At August 31, 1975, Nacimiento Copper Mine total assets were $10,393,000. Management is of the opinion that the mine's potential remains undiminished and there has been no diminution in the carrying value of the assets. Management intends to resume operations when the price the company will receive for its copper concentrate will yield a sufficient rate of return after deducting operating and other costs.

4. Long-Term Debt and Credit Agreements:

During 1974 and 1975, the company entered into long-term credit agreements which provide up to $12,500,000. As of August 31, 1975, $12,053,000 was outstanding under these agreements which amount bears interest at rates ranging from ½ of 1% over bank prime rate (7¾% at August 31, 1975) to 9¾%. The notes have various maturities through 1980.

In connection with the acquisition of Rogers & Babler, Inc., ECA issued notes payable to the selling stockholders of which $3,408,000 was outstanding at August 31, 1975. The notes are payable in four equal annual installments bearing interest at bank prime rate (7¾% at August 31, 1975) with the final payment due in October 1978. During 1974, ECA entered into a 9¾% bank loan agreement of which $1,213,000 was outstanding at August 31, 1975. The bank notes are due in quarterly installments through 1979. The company has guaranteed these ECA notes.

Other long-term debt aggregating $336,000 at August 31, 1975 bears interest at rates ranging from 5% to 9¼% and are payable in installments to 1986.

Maturities of long-term debt are scheduled as follows:

Years ending August 31:	
1976	$ 1,515,000
1977	7,545,000
1978	3,578,000
1979	3,144,000
1980	1,026,000
After 1980	202,000
	$17,010,000

The terms of certain long-term loan agreements contain covenants, the most significant of which requires the maintenance of certain working capital amounts, limits future borrowings and prohibits "unreasonable" dividend rates. Retained earnings of $12,837,000 were available for the payment of dividends at August 31, 1975.

The company has short-term bank lines of credit of $6,500,000 which stipulate compensating balances of $650,000 on the loan commitments and increasing amounts when funds are drawn. The compensating balances are not legally restricted and are available for the company's use on a temporary basis. No amounts were outstanding at August 31, 1975.

The company has received approval of a $30,000,000, 15-year loan from two insurance companies. The terms of the loan include an average interest rate of 11-3/8% and warrants to purchase 200,000 shares of the company's common stock at a price of $14 per share. Notes payable to banks totaling $12,213,000 at August 31, 1975 will be repaid from the proceeds of the loan. The funds will become available to the company upon conclusion of a satisfactory loan agreement.

5. Commitments and Contingencies:

The board of directors of the company has approved a capital expenditure program estimated at $45,000,000 largely for the construction of a refinery and development of the DeLamar Silver Mine of which approximately $21,000,000 is expected to be expended during 1976.

The company is obligated under long-term lease agreements primarily for land used in petroleum product marketing. Minimum lease rental payments total approximately $6,773,000 over the lives of the leases and are due as follows:

Years ending August 31:	
1976	$ 675,000
1977	638,000
1978	618,000
1979	593,000
1980	574,000
Five-year periods thereafter:	
1981 to 1985	2,151,000
1986 to 1990	956,000
1991 to 1995	351,000
After 1995	217,000

These leases extend for varying periods of time, generally 10-15 years and in most cases contain renewal options equal to the original term of the lease. There are no material noncapitalized financing lease agreements.

The company has several pension plans covering substantially all employees. Such plans provide retirement benefits through investments, insurance and trust funds. The expense of the pension plans for 1975 and 1974 was approximately $404,000 and $290,000, respectively. The impact of the Employees Retirement Income Security Act of 1974 (ERISA) on future provisions for pension expense and funding pension costs has not been determined at this time. In management's opinion no significant liability will result from complying with ERISA.

Certain sales made by the company are subject to the Renegotiation Act of 1951, as amended. The company's reports have been filed through 1974 and accepted through 1972. Management is of the opinion that refunds, if any, would not result in any material adjustment of net income as reported.

The company has a stock redemption agreement, presently fully funded with life insurance, with the president and another stockholder of the company in the event of one or both of their deaths. The terms of the agreement provide that the funds necessary to effect such redemption must be provided from insurance, for which the cost is not material.

6. Capital:

The company's charter authorizes 5,000,000 shares of $10 par value preferred stock, none of which has been issued. During 1975, the charter was amended increasing the authorized common stock from 5,000,000 to 8,000,000 shares. A summary of common stock activity for the two years ended August 31, 1975 follows:

	Common Stock	
	Shares	Amount
Balance, August 31, 1973	4,313,476	$14,457,000
Issued on exercise of employee stock option and stock purchase agreements (plan terminated in 1974)	100,597	447,000
Balance, August 31, 1974	4,414,073	14,904,000
Issued on exercise of employee stock options	17,224	88,000
Balance, August 31, 1975	4,431,297	$14,992,000

The company has qualified and nonqualified stock option plans. The plans cover 550,000 shares of common stock which includes an increase of 200,000 shares under the nonqualified plan approved by the board of directors in 1975, subject to stockholders' approval. The plans provide that option prices for the qualified and nonqualified stock options shall be not less than 100% and 85% of market value at the date of grant, respectively. Options for the purchase of 178,428 shares were available for grant under the plans at August 31, 1975. Options to purchase 185,754 shares, at prices ranging from $4.04 to $10.94 per share, were outstanding at August 31, 1975, of which 101,804 shares were exercisable. The company makes no charges to income in connection with the stock option plans.

The company's equity in the capital of ECA in excess of its cost therein has been credited to paid-in capital.

On September 15, 1975, the board of directors declared a $.25 per share cash dividend totaling approximately $1,100,000 on the company's common stock payable October 10, 1975 to stockholders of record on September 30, 1975.

7. Income Taxes:

Deferred federal and state income taxes include $1,188,000 representing taxes not currently payable related to a change in the tax basis of valuing inventory. The provision for federal and state income taxes is summarized as follows:

	1975	1974
Current:		
Federal	**$7,321,000**	$6,889,000
State	**1,162,000**	850,000
	$8,483,000	$7,739,000
Deferred:		
Federal	**$1,011,000**	($ 767,000)
State	**194,000**	2,000
	$1,205,000	($ 765,000)

The federal provisions for 1975 and 1974 have been reduced by investment tax credits of $1,160,000 and $66,000, respectively.

The provision for deferred federal and state income taxes for the years ended August 31, 1975 and 1974 relates to timing differences between financial and tax reporting as follows:

	1975	1974
Depreciation	**$ 478,000**	$ 59,000
Inventory pricing	**(1,386,000)**	1,126,000
Income recognition	**1,689,000**	(1,736,000)
Mine development costs	**595,000**	(232,000)
Other	**(171,000)**	18,000
	$1,205,000	($ 765,000)

Following is a reconciliation of the statutory federal income tax rate with the effective income tax rate for the years ended August 31, 1975 and 1974:

	1975	1974
Statutory income tax rate	**48%**	48%
State income taxes, net of federal income taxes	**3**	3
Investment tax credit	**(6)**	
Statutory depletion		(3)
Other	**3**	1
Effective income tax rate	**48%**	49%

8. Earnings Per Share:

Earnings per common and common equivalent share have been computed on the basis of the weighted average number of common and common equivalent shares outstanding during the year, 4,495,520 shares in 1975 and 4,411,027 shares in 1974. Options to purchase common stock have been considered to be common stock equivalents.

Management's Discussion and Analysis of the Summary of Operations

Fiscal 1975 Compared with 1974

Financial results benefited from increased refinery processing of 10,500 BPD. Refinery sales volume increased 55%. Higher crude costs of 30% were offset by refinery price increases of 26%. The number of retail gasoline stations in operation was increased by 37. Gasoline costs and related selling expense increased 15% and 39% respectively. However, these increases were offset by volume gains of 37% and price increases of 8%. During the year, the U.S. producer price of copper declined 27%, and mining operations were suspended pending an increase in prices.

Fiscal 1974 Compared with 1973

Crude oil and other raw material costs increased 72% and refinery expenses by 14%. Prices for petroleum products escalated by 70% offsetting the higher costs and expenses. Retail gasoline operations are included in the financial results for a full year in 1974 — 8½ months in 1973. Forty stations were also added during the year. Higher gasoline selling prices of 33% and a sales volume gain of 44% offset increased costs of operation. Record high copper prices prevailed throughout a large part of fiscal 1974 and were reflected in an increase in mining revenues of 33%. General and administrative expenses were up over the prior year due to G&A costs associated with new operations such as retail gasoline, paving materials and general corporate expenses.

Summary of Operations Years Ended August 31 (In thousands of dollars except per share amounts)

	1975	1974	1973	1972	1971
Net sales and other income	**230,859**	141,874	88,203	66,587	57,295
Costs and expenses:					
Cost of sales and operating expenses	**209,273**	125,996	81,429	63,438	54,986
Exploration expense	**596**	740	846	719	1,167
Interest expense	**922**	772	875	1,014	242
	210,791	127,508	83,150	65,171	56,395
Income before taxes	**20,068**	14,366	5,053	1,416	900
Provision for federal and state income taxes	**9,688**	6,974	2,625	747	501
Net income	**10,380**	7,392	2,428	669	399*
Earnings per common and common equivalent share	**$2.31**	$1.68	$.61	$.20	$.12*
Dividends per share	**$.70**	$.42	$.06		
Weighted average common and common equivalent shares (000 omitted)	**4,496**	4,411	4,007	3,384	3,376

Summary of Financial Data August 31

	1975	1974	1973	1972	1971
Working capital	**10,221**	3,473	6,062	2,557	545
Capital expenditures	**14,390**	10,947	3,776	2,204	8,263
Total assets	**90,081**	70,850	42,206	32,107	31,503
Long-term debt	**15,495**	6,307	7,063	9,146	8,577
Shareholders' equity	**31,663**	24,286	18,311	13,849	13,039
Book value per share	**$7.16**	$5.51	$4.25	$4.09	$3.87

*1971 net income is before $147,000 and $.04 per share reduction for an extraordinary item.

Lines of Business

The following information summarizes the approximate contributions to sales and income of ERC's lines of business for the five years ended August 31, 1975:

	1975	1974	1973	1972	1971
Sales:					
Petroleum Refining	**78%**	65%	65%	94%	99%
Retail Petroleum Operations	**46%**	51%	34%		
All Others (1)	**5%**	9%	8%	9%	4%
Intercompany sales eliminated	**(29%)**	(25%)	(7%)	(3%)	(3%)
	100%	100%	100%	100%	100%
Income (2):					
Petroleum Refining	**60%**	51%	65%	90%	82%
Retail Petroleum Operations	**23%**	34%	30%		
All Others (1)	**17%**	15%	5%	10%	18%
	100%	100%	100%	100%	100%

1 Includes marine transportation, paving materials, construction and copper mining. Each of the individual lines of business contributed less than 10% of sales and income during 1975 and 1974.
2 Income is before exploration, corporate administrative expenses, income taxes and extraordinary items.

Market and Dividend Information

ERC's common stock is traded on the American Stock Exchange. High and low sales prices and dividends per share of common stock for the years ended August 31, 1975 and 1974 are shown below:

	Sales Price of Common Stock				Dividends Per Share	
	1975		1974		1975	1974
	High	Low	High	Low		
1st Quarter	11 7/8	7 5/8	9 3/4	5 5/8	$.15	$.03
2nd Quarter	10 1/4	8 3/4	10 3/4	7	$.15	$.03
3rd Quarter	14 3/4	9 1/4	10 1/8	6 3/4	$.15	$.09
4th Quarter	16 1/2	12 1/8	9 1/4	6 7/8	$.25	$.27*

*Includes a special dividend of $.15 per share declared in August and paid in September 1974.

QUESTIONS

1. Why is the past financial track record of a company important to the investor? What is meant by a turning point?
2. Explain why expert financial analysts, in analyzing a set of financial statements, first examine the auditors' report and the summary of accounting policies.
3. Explain why the notes to the financial statement should be carefully read in the process of analyzing a set of financial statements. Why are long-term summaries considered to be particularly important to the statement user?
4. Distinguish between vertical and horizontal analyses. Briefly explain the importance of each.
5. What is meant by proportionate ratio analysis? Why is important in the analysis of financial statements?
6. Distinguish between the current ratio and the quick ratio. What purpose does each serve?
7. Current assets and current liabilities for two companies having the same amount of working capital are summarized below; evaluate their relative solvency.

	X Company	*Y Company*
Current assets	$200,000	$900,000
Current liabilities	100,000	800,000
Working capital	$100,000	$100,000

8. X Corporation has an accounts receivable turnover of 15; interpret this value. What would be the age of the receivables? What does it reveal?
9. Y Corporation has an inventory turnover of 9; interpret this value. What would be average number of days of supply?
10. Explain and illustrate trading on the equity.
11. Compute and explain the meaning of the book value per share of common stock of the Pride Manufacturing Company assuming the following data are available:

Preferred stock, 6%, cumulative, nonparticipating, 200 shares outstanding	$ 20,000
Common stock, par value $100, 1,000 shares outstanding	100,000
Retained earnings	7,000
(Three years dividends in arrears on preferred stock including current year.)	

12. Explain the circumstances where a company has debt financing and the leverage factor is *(a)* positive, *(b)* negative, and *(c)* zero.
13. Explain the ROI concept. Why is it a fundamental measure of profitability?
14. What is meant by "the multiple"? Why is it considered to be important?
15. What are the principal limitations in using ratios?

DECISION CASE 24–1

Scott Corporation needs additional funds for plant expansion. The board of directors is considering obtaining the funds by issuing additional short-term notes, long-term bonds, preferred stock, or common stock.

Required:

1. What primary factors should the board of directors consider in selecting the best method of financing plant expansion?
2. One member of the board of directors suggests that the corporation should maximize trading on equity, that is, using stockholders' equity as a basis for borrowing additional funds at a lower rate of interest than the expected earnings from the use of the borrowed funds.
   a. Explain how trading on equity affects earnings per share of common stock.
   b. Explain how a change in income tax rates affects trading on equity.
   c. Under what circumstances should a corporation seek to trade on equity to a substantial degree?
3. Two specific proposals under consideration by the board of directors are the issue of 7% subordinated income bonds (secured only by the general credit of the issuer with interest paid each year only if there is net income equal to the interest charge) or 7% cumulative, nonparticipating, nonvoting preferred stock, callable at par. In discussing the impact of the two alternatives on the debt to stockholders' equity ratio, one member of the board of directors stated that he felt the resulting debt-equity ratio would be the same under either alternative because the income bonds and preferred stock should be reported in the same balance sheet classification. What are the arguments *(a)* for and *(b)* against using the same balance sheet classification in reporting the income bonds and preferred stock?

(AICPA adapted)

EXERCISES

Exercise 24–1

Baker Trading Company income statements (condensed) for two quarters are shown below. Prepare a multiple-step comparative income statement including a vertical percentage analysis. (Round to even percents).

	First Quarter	*Second Quarter*
Gross sales	$221,000	$242,000
Returns and allowances	(1,000)	(2,000)
	220,000	240,000
Cost of goods sold	(110,000)	(130,000)
	110,000	110,000
Expenses:		
Selling expenses	(62,000)	(63,000)
Administrative expenses (including income taxes)	(30,000)	(31,000)
Financial expenses (net of financial revenue)	(3,000)	2,000
Net income before extraordinary items	15,000	18,000
Extraordinary items, net of tax	5,000	(3,000)
Net Income	$ 20,000	$ 15,000
Shares of common stock outstanding	10,000	10,000

Exercise 24–2

Prepare a single-step comparative income statement including horizontal percentage analysis for Baker Trading Company using the data given in Exercise 24–1. (Round to even percents.)

Exercise 24–3

The following data were taken from the financial statements of the Ralston Company. Based on these data compute *(a)* the working capital, *(b)* the current ratio, and *(c)* the acid-test ratio (carry to even percents). Evaluate each change.

Current Assets:	*19A*	*19B*
Cash	$ 30,000	$ 40,000
Short-term investments	10,000	10,000
Trade accounts receivable (net)	60,000	70,000
Notes receivable	6,000	2,000
Inventory	150,000	170,000
Prepaid expenses	4,000	2,000
Current Liabilities	90,000	120,000

Exercise 24–4

The condensed financial data given below were taken from the annual financial statements of Foster Corporation:

	19A	*19B*	*19C*
Current assets (including inventory)	$ 200,000	$ 250,000	$ 270,000
Current liabilities	150,000	180,000	130,000
Cash sales	800,000	780,000	820,000
Credit sales	200,000	280,000	250,000
Cost of goods sold	560,000	600,000	600,000
Inventory	120,000	140,000	100,000
Quick assets	80,000	90,000	85,000
Accounts receivable (net)	60,000	58,000	64,000
Total assets (net)	1,000,000	1,200,000	1,400,000

Required:

1. Based on the above data, calculate the following for 19B and 19C (round to even percents):
   a. Current ratio.
   b. Acid-test ratio.
   c. Working capital to total assets.
   d. Receivable turnover.
   e. Age of receivables.
   f. Merchandise turnover.
   g. Days' supply in inventory.
   h. Working capital turnover.
2. Evaluate the results of each computation including trends. Use 360 days for computation purposes.

Exercise 24–5

The following data were taken from the financial statements of the Action Company:

	19A	*19B*	*19C*
Sales—cash	$190,000	$200,000	$220,000
Sales—credit	100,000	120,000	130,000
Average receivables	25,000	34,000	50,000
Average inventory	60,000	70,000	80,000
Cost of goods sold	180,000	190,000	200,000

Required:

What conclusions may be made relative to (*a*) inventories and (*b*) receivables? (Use 300 business days in year; credit terms are 90 calendar days.)

Exercise 24–6

The balance sheet for two similar companies reflected the following:

	Company A	*Company B*
Current liabilities	$ 30,000	$100,000
Long-term liabilities	70,000	300,000
Stockholders' Equity:		
Common stock, par $5	220,000	46,000
Preferred stock, par $10	100,000	20,000
Contributed capital in excess of par	20,000	4,000
Retained earnings	60,000	30,000
Net Income (less taxes, 45%)	49,500	33,000

Required:

1. Compute the three equity ratios that measure equity position.
2. Interpret and evaluate each situation. The average interest rate is 10% (on total liabilities).

Exercise 24–7

Basey Manufacturing Corporation balance sheet showed the following as of December 31, 19A:

Preferred stock, 7%, par value, $50 per share	$200,000
Common stock, nopar, 30,000 shares outstanding	360,000
Contributed capital in excess of par, preferred stock	40,000
Retained earnings	80,000

Required:

Compute the book value per share of preferred and common stock assuming:

a. None of the preferred shares have been issued.
b. Preferred is noncumulative and nonparticipating.
c. Preferred is cumulative and nonparticipating (three years' dividends in arrears including current year).
d. Preferred has a liquidation value of $60 per share and is noncumulative and nonparticipating.
e. Preferred has a liquidation value of $60 per share and is noncumulative and nonparticipating, and the Retained Earnings account shows a *deficit* of $40,000.

Exercise 24–8

The financial statements for Weston Corporation for 19C reported complete comparative statements. The following data were taken therefrom:

	19A	*19B*	*19C*
Sales revenue	$12,000,000	$13,000,000	$14,000,000
Net income	100,000	120,000	100,000
Interest expense, net of tax	10,000	12,000	9,000
Stockholders' equity	1,400,000	1,450,000	1,460,000
Shares of common stock outstanding	20,000	20,000	24,000
Total assets	3,500,000	3,500,000	3,700,000
Market value per share	$66.00	$72.00	$70.00

Required:

1. Based on the above financial data, compute the following ratios for 19B and 19C: *(a)* profit margin; *(b)* return on investment, total assets; *(c)* return on investment, owners' equity; *(d)* the leverage factor; and *(e)* the earnings per share. (Carry computations to two decimal places.)
2. What ratios would you prefer as a measure of profitability? Why?
3. Explain any significant trends that appear to be developing.

Exercise 24–9

The following data relate to the Wallace Printing Company:

	19A	*19B*	*19C*	*19D*	*19E*
Net income	$ 12,000	$ 15,000	$ 25,000	$ 30,000	$ 40,000
Interest expense, net of tax	1,000	1,200	2,000	2,200	3,000
Sales	120,000	140,000	180,000	230,000	260,000
Total assets	50,000	72,000	110,000	160,000	190,000
Total liabilities	25,000	30,000	40,000	70,000	80,000

Required:

Evaluate the company in terms of the *(a)* profit margin, *(b)* ROI, and *(c)* leverage factor.

PROBLEMS

Problem 24–1

The following pretax data of Knox Corporation was provided by the accounts:

	For Year Ended December 31	
	19A	*19B*
Sales revenue	$400,000	$450,000
Return sales	(5,000)	(3,000)
Cost of goods sold	(236,000)	(265,000)
Selling expenses	(90,000)	(95,000)
Administrative expenses	(70,000)	(73,000)
Extraordinary items (loss)	2,000	(5,000)
Pretax net income	$ 1,000	$ 9,000
Shares of common stock outstanding	20,000	20,000

Required:

1. Prepare a single-step income statement including a vertical percentage analysis. Assume an income tax rate of 40% on all items. Round to even percent.
2. Prepare a multiple-step income statement including a horizontal percentage analysis (amounts and percents). Round to even percents.
3. Evaluate the results and pinpoint items that you think need further investigation. Explain what further investigation should be considered.

Problem 24–2

The following condensed data (rounded to even $1,000) for Royal Manufacturing Company financial position are available for two years:

	Year Ended December 31	
Assets	*19A*	*19B*
Cash	$ 476,000	$ 451,500
Trade receivables	184,000	220,000
Allowance for doubtful accounts	(8,400)	(8,800)
Inventories	640,000	682,000
Prepaid expenses	16,000	11,000
Bond sinking fund	320,000	120,000
Long-term investments		176,000
Land	48,000	48,000
Plant and equipment	400,000	673,000
Accumulated depreciation	(120,000)	(176,000)
Goodwill	40,000	
Deferred charges	4,400	3,300
Total	$2,000,000	$2,200,000
Liabilities and Stockholders' Equity		
Accounts payable	$ 300,000	$ 310,000
Income taxes payable	30,000	44,000
Accrued wages	10,000	15,400
Bonds payable	500,000	300,000
Capital stock	1,000,000	1,200,000
Retained earnings	160,000	210,600
Reserve for bond sinking fund		120,000
Total	$2,000,000	$2,200,000

Required:

1. Prepare a classified balance sheet including a vertical analysis. Round to even percents.
2. Prepare a classified balance sheet including a horizontal analysis (Note: Requirements 1 and 2 can be combined if you prefer). Round to even percents.
3. Evaluate the results and pinpoint items that you think need further investigation. Explain what areas warrant further investigation.

Problem 24–3

The following data were taken from the annual financial statements of Mason Corporation:

	19A	19B	19C
Current Assets:			
Cash	$ 10,000	$ 5,000	$ 8,000
Trade receivables	180,000	170,000	190,000
Less: Allowance for doubtful accounts	(5,000)	(6,000)	(8,000)
Notes receivable (nontrade)	110,000	125,000	100,000
Short-term investments	45,000	30,000	20,000
Inventories	298,000	355,000	387,000
Prepaid expenses	12,000	11,000	13,000
Total	$ 650,000	$ 690,000	$ 710,000
Current Liabilities:			
Trade payables	$ 70,000	$ 158,000	$ 196,000
Notes payable	90,000	72,000	60,000
Accrued wages payable	72,000	46,000	52,000
Income taxes payable	19,000	23,000	24,000
Deferred rent revenue	2,000	2,000	2,000
Accrued liabilities	17,000	19,000	16,000
Total	$ 270,000	$ 320,000	$ 350,000
Additional Data:			
Cash sales	$3,300,000	$3,500,000	$3,200,000
Credit sales	1,500,000	1,700,000	1,800,000
Cost of goods sold	2,500,000	2,900,000	2,800,000
Total assets (net)	6,600,000	7,200,000	7,200,000

Required:

1. Compute the ratios for each year that measure current position. Round to even percents.
2. Evaluate the current position as indicated by the statements and the ratios. What additional information would you need to buttress your evaluation?

Problem 24–4

The financial statements of Staley Manufacturing Company for a three-year period showed the following:

	19A	19B	19C
Total assets	$2,000,000	$2,040,000	$1,940,000
Total current assets	368,000	450,000	480,000
Total current liabilities	230,000	150,000	150,000
Fixed assets (net)	1,248,000	1,257,600	1,260,000
Total liabilities	1,090,000	1,110,000	900,000
Common stock (par value $100)	600,000	600,000	700,000
Retained earnings	310,000	330,000	340,000
Sales (net)	6,600,000	7,000,000	7,100,000
Net income (after tax)	50,000	70,000	40,000
Interest expense (net of tax)	34,000	38,000	30,000

Required:

1. Based on the above data, calculate the following ratios to measure the current

position for each year (round to even percents, or if a decimal, to two places):
a. Current ratio.
b. Working capital turnover.
Evaluate the current position. What additional significant information do you need to adequately evaluate the current position? Explain.

2. Based on the above data, calculate the following ratios to measure the equity position (round to even percents):
   a. Creditors' equity to total assets.
   b. Book value per share of common stock.
   Evaluate the equity position. What additional significant information do you need to adequately evaluate the equity position? Explain.
3. Based on the above data, calculate the following ratios to measure operating results (round to even percents):
   a. Profit margin.
   b. Return on investment on total assets.
   c. Return on investment on owners' equity.
   d. Earnings per share.
4. Evaluate the operating results. What additional significant information do you need to adequately evaluate operating results? Explain.
5. Evaluate the financial leverage factor.

Problem 24–5

The following annual data was taken from the records of Grant Trading Corporation:

	19A	*19B*	*19C*	*19D*	*19E*
Sales	$400,000	$420,000	$450,000	$440,000	$490,000
Net income	15,000	16,000	20,000	5,000	40,000
Total assets	200,000	220,000	230,000	240,000	250,000
Owners' equity	100,000	110,000	120,000	115,000	140,000
Market price per share	60	62	55	50	60
Dividends per share	4	4	4	1	5
Capital stock outstanding (shares)	4,000	4,000	4,000	3,900	3,800
Interest expense (net of tax)	4,000	4,500	4,600	5,000	4,100

Required:

1. Compute the ratios that measure operating results.
2. Compute the market test ratios.
3. Evaluate the profitability of the company; pinpoint indicated strengths and weaknesses. What additional significant information do you need? Explain.
4. Compute the financial leverage factor.

Problem 24–6

The following summarized data were taken from the published statements of two companies that are being compared:

	(in thousands)	
	Company A	*Company B*
Sales	$3,000	$ 9,000
Cost of goods sold	1,900	6,942
Operating expenses	400	1,600
Interest expense (net of tax)	8	108
Extraordinary items (loss), after tax	(22)	550
Income taxes (on income before extraordinary items)	240	300
Current assets	1,000	4,000
Fixed assets	5,000	19,000
Accumulated depreciation	2,000	7,000
Investments, long term	400	100
Other assets	600	7,900
Current liabilities	900	2,000
Long-term liabilities	100	1,800
Capital stock ($10 par value)	3,000	18,000
Retained earnings	1,000	2,200
Current market value per share	$16.75	$1.50

Compute the one ratio that would best answer each of the following questions (show computations). Justify your choice.

a. Which company probably has the best current position?
b. Which company has the best working capital turnover?
c. Which company is earning the best rate on total resources available to the management? On resources provided by the owners?
d. Which company has the advantage in "trading on the equity"?
e. Which company has the best profit margin?
f. Which company has the highest book value per share?
g. Which stock is the best buy?

Problem 24–7

Fulger Corporation is considering building a second plant at a cost of $600,000. The management is considering two alternatives to obtain the funds: *(a)* sell additional common stock or *(b)* issue $600,000, five-year bonds payable at 8% interest. The management believes that the bonds can be sold at par (for $600,000) and the stock at $30 per share.

The balance sheet (before the new financing) reflected the following:

Liabilities	None
Common stock, par $10	$200,000
Contributed capital in excess of par	100,000
Retained earnings	120,000
Average net income for past several years (net of tax)	30,000

The average income tax rate is 45%. Average dividends per share have been $.50 per share per year. Expected increase in pretax net income (excluding interest expense) from the new plant, $100,000 per year.

Required:

1. Prepare an analysis to show *(a)* expected net income after the addition and *(b)* cash flows for the new capital, and *(c)* the leverage advantage or disadvantage to the present shareholders of issuing the bonds to obtain the financing.

2. What are the principal arguments against issuing the bonds (as opposed to selling the common stock)?

Problem 24–8 (based on the Appendix)

This problem focuses on an actual set of financial statements. Assume you are a prospective investor and are in the process of analyzing several sets of financial statements with a tentative decision to invest $10,000 in common stocks.

Required:

1. Examine the auditors' report. Does it present any problems to you as a potential investor? Explain.
2. Examine the summary of accounting policies. Does it present any problems to you as a potential investor? What particular items does it pinpoint where you should be cognizant of the accounting policy? Explain.
3. Examine the financial statement in overall context, noting comparative amounts and percentage increases:
   a. Income statement—What is the amount of net income? Did it increase from last year? Do you observe any particular items that should be carefully watched during your analysis to follow? Explain.
   b. Balance sheet—What are the amounts of (1) cash, (2) total assets, (3) long-term liabilities, and (4) stockholders' equity? Do you observe any particular items that you should watch during your analysis to follow? Explain.
   c. Statement of changes in financial position—Is the statement on a cash or working capital basis? Did cash and working capital increase or decrease? What was the primary source of working capital? What was the primary use of working capital?
4. Examine the long-term financial review. What strengths and weaknesses do you observe? Explain.
5. Analytical—Develop ratios for 1974 and 1975 as follows:
   Measurements of current position:
   a. Current ratio.
   b. Quick ratio.
   Measurements of equity position:
   c. Creditors' equity to total assets.
   d. Book value per share.
   Measurements of operating results:
   e. Profit margin.
   f. Return on total assets.
   g. Return on owners' equity.
   h. Earnings per share (already computed).
   i. Leverage factor.
6. On the basis of your response to the above requirements:
   a. Evaluate the current position.
   b. Evaluate the equity position.
   c. Evaluate the profitability and leverage effect.
7. What specific additional information about this company, other than that reported in the financial statements and your analysis, would you urgently need prior to a decision to invest or not?

Problem 24–9 (based on the Appendix)

The chapter Appendix presents a complete set of financial statements for a medium-sized company. This problem focuses on those statements. The objective is to develop an analysis of them.

Required:

1. Examine the auditors' report. What significant information (favorable and unfavorable) is provided?
2. Examine the summary of significant accounting policies. What important information (favorable and unfavorable) is provided?
3. Examine the overall financial report:
   a. What titles are used for the three required statements?
   b. How many notes are included? What is the topic of each?
   c. Is there a statement of retained earnings? Explain.
   d. Is there a long-term financial summary? How many periods does it encompass?
   e. Income statement–What are the amounts for each year and the changes in net sales, net income, dividends, EPS, extraordinary items, and income tax expense? Did you observe any unusual items? Explain.
   f. Balance sheet–What are the amounts for each year and the changes for cash, inventory, current assets, fixed assets, total assets, current liabilities, long-term debt and stockholders' equity? Do you observe any unusual items other than those above? Explain.
   g. Statement of changes in financial position–On what basis was it prepared? What were the two largest sources of funds for each year? What were the two largest uses of funds each year? Did funds increase or decrease during each year? By how much? Did you observe any unusual items? Explain.
4. Explain the long-term financial summary. What strengths and weaknesses do you observe? Explain.
5. Analytical–Develop ratios for 1974 and 1975 as follows (show computations and carry to even percents, or if a decimal, to two places):
   Measurements of current position:
   a. Current ratio.
   b. Acid test ratio.
   c. Receivable turnover.
   d. Inventory turnover.
   Measurements of equity position:
   e. Creditors' equity to total assets.
   f. Plant turnover.
   g. Book value per share.
   Measurements of operating results:
   h. Profit margin.
   i. Return on total assets.
   j. Return on owners' equity.
   k. Earnings per share (already computed).
   l. Leverage factor.
6. On the basis of your responses to the above requirements:
   a. Evaluate the current position.
   b. Evaluate the equity position.
   c. Evaluate the profitability.
   d. Evaluate the leverage effect.
7. Assume you have $25,000 cash to invest and are interested in acquiring common stock. What specific information about this company, other than that reported in the financial statements and your analysis, would you urgently need prior to making a decision to invest, or not invest, in this company?

Chapter 25

Price-Level and Fair Value Accounting and Reporting

Each of us is aware, almost daily, that prices of most things we buy have been rising sharply. While this fact may have unpleasant personal consequences, the focus of this chapter is to analyze the accounting consequences and to describe various proposals designed to cope with them.

When the unit-of-measure assumption was discussed in Chapter 2, it was noted that the conventional accounting model, based on historical cost, either assumed a stable monetary unit or assumed that changes in the value of money were not material. At some eras in the history of the U.S. economy such assumptions were valid; and even today, for a limited category of entities, there may be some validity to the assumption that changes in the value of money are not significant.[1] For the vast majority of businesses and other entities, however, changing prices are quite important in accounting and financial reporting as will be shown in the section "The Impact of Inflation on Financial Statements."

PRICE CHANGES AND HOW THEY ARE MEASURED

Since the early years of the Great Depression of the 1930s, prices of virtually all goods and services in the United States (and in most of the world) have been rising almost without interruption. Stated another way, the general purchasing power of the dollar (and other monetary units) has been falling almost continuously. General purchasing power is the power of the monetary unit to purchase real goods and services. When there is a general increase in prices (i.e., the general purchasing power of the monetary unit decreases), the condition is referred to as

[1] For example, financial institutions, whose obligations consist primarily of debts, the dollar amount of which can be determined with precision and whose assets consist of cash, receivables, bonds, lease contracts and the like can be less seriously concerned with the effects of inflation.

inflation. When there is a general decline in prices (i.e., when the general purchasing power of the monetary unit rises), that condition is called *deflation.* Because inflation has been so pervasive, our discussions, illustrations, and assignment material will be primarily in the context of rising prices; however, the concepts discussed apply to deflation as well. It should be borne in mind, of course, that "purchasing power losses" which are reflected under conditions of inflation would become "purchasing power gains" should similar holdings prevail under conditions of deflation.

Because we use the dollar as the unit of measure or common denominator to express many diverse kinds of assets and claims and because each business entity is likely to own many kinds of assets and owe diverse types of claims and also because statement users are interested in making interfirm comparisons, it is both logical and necessary that measures be devised to express the degree of change in the prices of assets and the purchasing power represented by various claims. These measures of changes in prices are known as *index numbers.*

A price index has been defined as "a series of measurements, expressed as percentages, of the relationship between the average price of a group of goods and services at a succession of dates and the average price of a similar group of goods and services at a common date. The components of the series are price index numbers. A price index does not, however, measure the movement of the individual component prices, some of which move in one direction, and some in the opposite direction."[2] There are several index numbers which purport to measure changes in prices in the United States on a general basis. The three most widely known measures of general price changes in the United States are the Gross National Product Implicit Price Deflator (GNP Deflator), the Consumer Price Index, and the Wholesale Price Index. The GNP Deflator has been recommended in connection with the preparation of price-level adjusted financial statements successively in an AICPA *Research Study*, an *APB Statement* and in an FASB exposure draft.[3] It is accurate to say that the three indices move roughly in parallel. In other words when there is a sharp rise or persistent upward movement of prices, all will show increases, but not the same relative change. However when prices are comparatively stable, it is not uncommon for two of the indices to move in one direction while the other moves in an opposite direction.[4]

---

[2] AICPA, *Accounting Research Study No. 6*, "Reporting the Financial Effects of Price-Level Changes" (New York, 1963), p. 63.

[3] Successively, see footnote 2, also AICPA, "Financial Statements Restated for General Price Level Changes," *APB Statement No. 3* (New York, 1969); and "Financial Reporting in Units of General Purchasing Power" Exposure Draft (Stamford, Conn.: FASB, December 31, 1974).

[4] Reasons for preference of the GNP Deflator over the other measures are to be found in the following quotations in Appendix A of *Accounting Research Study No. 6*, "The only index currently compiled that is a measure of the general level of prices in the United States is the GNP Implicit Price Deflator. It is the only price index compiled in this country whose 'universe' encompasses the entire economy" (p. 111).

It is important to recognize that a price index is an average or composite; therefore, it measures the average trend of a group of prices over time. Not all of the prices in the group change at the same rate; in a period of inflation some will increase faster than others, and while the overall index is rising some prices included in the set may be falling.[5]

HOW MUCH HAVE PRICES CHANGED?

Because the GNP Deflator has been preferred by three authoritative studies as a basis for preparing price-level adjusted financial statements, it is pertinent to indicate the extent to which prices have changed according to this index. Currently, 1958 serves as base year and is assigned a value of 100. This index dates back to 1929 when the average value was 50.6; it fell steadily to an all-time low of 39.3 in the depression year of 1933, then rose continuously thereafter except for three years. The years in which it fell were 1938, 1939, and 1949; in none of these was the percent of decrease more than 1.6% from the level of the preceding year. "Double-digit" inflation was experienced in four years. The years and their rates of increase over the preceding year were: 1942, 12.3%; 1946, 11.7%; 1947, 11.8%; and from the first quarter of 1974 to the first quarter of 1975, 10.8%. By the first quarter of 1975 the index had risen to an all-time high of 181.4.

Stated one way, the price-level change implies that what would have cost $100 in 1929 cost more than $358 in early 1975, but this is not altogether a valid statement or comparison. In 1929 one could not buy TV sets (much less color sets), cars with automatic transmissions, air-conditioned homes, electronic computers, clothing made of synthetic fibers, open-heart surgery, and a host of other products and services accepted as fairly commonplace in 1975. Further, people were spending different proportions of their incomes for shelter, food, recreation, communication, and medical care in those days than they are today. These kinds of change present some of the major problems in constructing an index number and keeping it valid over an extended period of time—technological factors change, quality of goods and services improves, and the proportions of goods and services people buy do not remain constant.

IMPACT OF INFLATION ON FINANCIAL STATEMENTS

The impact of inflation on financial reports, prepared in accordance with the conventional accounting model, varies considerably from one entity to the next depending upon a number of factors. One factor is

[5] From 1965 to 1972, for example, wholesale prices of commodities in the United States generally rose over 23% (the index changed from 96.6 to 119.1). During this same period wholesale prices of the following items were showing these percentage drops: home electronic equipment, 10.1%; floor coverings, 6.7%; crude rubber, 6.0%; and plastic resins, 10.7%.

In the area of communications it is rather startling to note that most long-distance telephone calls are cheaper in 1975 than they were in 1951, while it costs eight times more to mail a postcard in the United States in 1975 than it did in 1951.

that by selecting from the array of alternative accounting procedures which comprise current GAAP, the impact of inflation on some elements of the financial report may be lessened or postponed. The financial statements of businesses which are *capital intensive* (i.e., they commit a relatively large proportion of their resources to investment in fixed assets) are likely to be affected by inflation more than those whose capital is largely committed to short-term assets. At the same time businesses which borrow heavily on a long-term basis (and this is likely to include the capital intensive ones) are in a better position to gain from inflation than those which do not. Also, some businesses can serve their customers with little or no investment in inventory, while others must make large investments in inventory which often have a low turnover. The latter type of businesses are affected by inflation more than the former, though they may be able to reduce the impact on financial statements by selecting *Lifo* rather than *Fifo* for inventory purposes.

During a period of inflation, the conventional accounting model reflects a matching of dollars of different "size" on the income statement. Revenues are usually expressed in current dollars, but many of the expenses matched against them frequently are not. For example, depreciation and similar cost expirations may reflect cost levels which prevailed years ago when the dollar had a vastly different purchasing power. Depending on the inventory flow method in use, *cost of goods sold* may represent an amount in current dollars or it may not. If there is a relatively high correspondence between the volume of purchases and the volume of sales, and if selling prices are based on current costs, use of *Lifo* will tend to give a reasonable matching of current costs against current revenues.[6] The conventional accounting model ignores the fact that an entity which maintains large balances of cash and receivables during periods of inflation loses purchasing power as a result, while one that is heavily in debt gains because it has borrowed dollars with greater *buying* power than the ones it is likely to repay. Conventional accounting defers all gains (or losses) from the holding of an asset until it is sold; no recognition is given to the price-level effect on that gain (or loss).

When there has been marked inflation and comparative statements for two or more successive periods are prepared on a conventional basis, they can be quite misleading. Suppose, for example, the sales amount on the current income statement is 15% higher than on the income statement of four years ago. If prices of the company's product and prices generally have risen 50% in the interval, there has been a material decline in *physical volume* of goods sold. On a common-dollar (i.e., price-level adjusted) basis the change in volume would have been evident. Conventional financial statements also obscure the comparability of financial statements of two or more entities whose accounts consist of items that were bought in different years.

---

[6] At the same time, use of *Lifo* during a period of sustained inflation will ultimately result in unrealistically low balance sheet valuation of inventories.

DEPRECIATION AND RISING REPLACEMENT COSTS

The purpose of depreciation accounting, as traditionally viewed, is to allocate the original cost of depreciable property over its economic useful life. Other things being equal, recording depreciation holds back an amount of assets equal to the investment in the depreciable property, thereby facilitating its replacement if the replacement cost remains constant (i.e., no inflation). Since depreciation is an expense that must be recovered, it is included in pricing decisions on products and services sold by the entity. Therefore, the management of an entity must be concerned with the adequacy of depreciation charges in *(a)* asset replacement, and *(b)* current pricing policy. Because present GAAP permits depreciation charges to be based only on historical cost, extensive attention is being accorded some form of price-level accounting or current-value accounting (both discussed later in this chapter) because under conditions of inflation they would afford means of recording depreciation charges that *(a)* in total can approximate replacement costs, and *(b)* are appropriate to realistic financing policy.

Illustrated simply, suppose Jones bought a new automobile in 1972 and put it in service as a taxi in a small town. Jones and a hired driver comprise the entire staff of the enterprise. All expenses except depreciation of the cab are incurred on a cash basis; as a consequence, except for depreciation, the excess of receipts over payments is regarded by Jones as pretax income. Because the cab cost $3,600 and is expected to trade in for $600 after five years of use, Jones decided to set aside $600 each year to replace the cab. The $600 depreciation expense is deducted on the tax return. Aside from the $600 set aside, Jones spends the remaining cash receipts from the business for living expenses and income taxes. By 1976 the cheapest comparably equipped car had risen in cost to $5,500, and it likely will cost $6,000 if Jones replaces the cab on schedule in 1977. Where will Jones get the extra $2,400 that will be needed? The $3,000 saved back plus the $600 trade-in allowance will not buy even the smallest comparably equipped compact car by 1977, besides such a vehicle would be obviously unsuited to use in the enterprise. Is it not logical to say Jones has overstated the income from the enterprise by $2,400? Has Jones paid income taxes on what amounts to both income and a return of capital? Has Jones priced the taxi services on the basis of economic reality if the additional cost of replacing the taxi when worn out was disregarded?

One may ask whether this example is relevant to a large corporation. The answer must be that it is relevant. Profitable corporations generally pay taxes at a rate of 48% on most of their income and, in addition, their shareholders pay another income tax on dividends received. Therefore, to the extent that what is taxed as income is really a return of capital, the problem exists. Corporations have essentially the same fixed asset replacement and pricing problems as sole proprietors. In an era of sustained inflation a hotel chain, a factory, or a local business which does not include in its pricing of products and services an amount sufficient to cover the future replacement cost of facilities now in use will be unable to maintain its present scope of operations when the existing facilities must be replaced unless it is willing and able *(a)* to incur added debt, or *(b)* obtain additional equity capital, and perhaps to dilute the equity of existing owners. Obviously, the adoption of either price-level or current-value accounting will not solve the capital replacement and pricing problems of an entity, but it may add more economic realism in financial reports on which these decisions, in part, are made.

PIECEMEAL ACCOUNTING APPROACHES UNDER CONDITIONS OF INFLATION

One piecemeal accounting approach focuses on *inventories*. The *Lifo* inventory method has been cited as a means of achieving a closer matching of current costs against current revenues when prices are changing. This is true, of course, only to the extent that there is some correspondence between the physical volume of goods purchased and sold during the period. Also, if prices have doubled after *Lifo* was adopted (as they have between 1955 and 1975), and physical volume remains constant, the inventory value reported on the balance sheet would be about one half its cost. Thus, this piecemeal solution is totally inadequate because *(a)* it does not attain effective reporting on the financial statements, and *(b)* it deals with only one problem area–inventories.

Another accounting approach focuses on *depreciation* and similar cost allocations. The use of accelerated depreciation in the accounts and reports has been cited as a means of solving the problem of *understatement* of depreciation during inflation. Accelerated depreciation is effective only when property, plant, and equipment items subject to depreciation are relatively new and also the compensating effect generally is during the first half of their useful lives. Over their total useful life, the aggregate amount of the depreciation charges cannot exceed what it would under straight-line or any other allowed alternative. This piecemeal solution is singularly deficient because *(a)* it deals only with the short run, *(b)* focuses only on one aspect of the problem–depreciable assets, and *(c)* tends to cause arbitrarily determined effects.

Still another piecemeal accounting approach which has some balance sheet impact, but does not affect reported net income, is the technique of appropriating retained earnings (i.e., replacement costs) for excess plant designed to notify statement users that the management is cognizant of inflationary effects on asset replacement and that dividends must be restricted. The implication is that there are no adequate means of coping with the problem within the purview of present GAAP. This piecemeal approach is deficient on all counts.

Another piecemeal approach, not accorded general acceptability, is the proposal that an extra expense charge be made in the income statement to compensate for the understatement of depreciation, cost of goods sold, and other expired costs likely to be too low because of inflation during the period. The proposal has a number of obvious difficulties. First, such a charge is likely to be arbitrarily estimated instead of being objectively and systematically measured; second, it does not consider the balance sheet impact; and, third, it does not deal with the broader problem of inflationary impacts.

The piecemeal approaches are subject to numerous objections. They ignore replacement costs. In some situations they may achieve a reasonably desirable short-run result (from a standpoint of counteracting the effects of inflation) on one financial statement but they either ignore or worsen the reporting on another statement. They make it unrealistic to attempt to compute meaningful rates of return for the entity (partly because of the lack of consistency between the balance sheet and income statement). They may lull many users of the financial statements into a false sense of security that the inflation problem is adequately accounted for and reported by the entity or that it is not serious enough to cause concern. Finally, they do not deal with the broad area of inflationary effects and as a result cause inconsistent measurements of assets, liabilities, and net income.

COMPREHENSIVE ACCOUNTING APPROACHES

Three of the four piecemeal approaches to cope with the major changes in the price level have serious deficiencies. Primarily, they do not comprehensively deal with the problem. The two major alternatives that deal with the price-level problem comprehensively are discussed and illustrated in the paragraphs to follow.

GENERAL PURCHASING POWER (INDEX NUMBER) APPROACH

Fundamentally, the general purchasing power or index number approach uses a selected index, such as the GNP Deflator, to restate on a *current basis* those elements of the financial statements which are out of date in terms of most recent price levels. This general explanation requires demonstration of its application. Therefore, after a review of the background of the index approach, the application steps will be explained. This will be followed by a simple example and then a more complex illustration.

Background

Dr. Henry W. Sweeney introduced the index approach in a series of *Accounting Review* articles in the 1920s and 1930s. The concept and its application were presented in his book *Stabilized Accounting* which first appeared in 1936 and was republished as an accounting classic in 1964. Sweeney's thinking was heavily influenced by experience and practice in Germany following World War I when that nation experienced drastic and ruinous inflation. Although academicians were aware of the techniques involved in the index approach (also called general purchasing power or price level approach), they were largely ignored by the world of accounting practice. The first significant attention by practitioners to the deficiencies of conventional accounting when prices change rapidly came in the late 1940s—not a surprising development in view of the fact that in 1946, 1947, and 1948 prices rose 11.7%, 11.8%, and 6.7%, respectively, as measured by the GNP Deflator.

AICPA and the Price-Level Problem

In December 1947 the AICPA's Committee on Accounting Procedure, in *ARB 43*, Chapter 9A, (which at the time had responsibility for determination of accounting principles) considered the problem, which they designated as "Depreciation and High Costs"; they concluded:

1. At that time it would not be satisfactory to increase depreciation charges against current income to reflect higher replacement costs of plant or to recognize such costs by recording appraisals.
2. In considering depreciation in connection with product costs, prices, and business policies, management must take into consideration the likelihood that replacement costs of plant assets then in use would greatly exceed their historical costs.
3. Periodic appropriation of net income or retained earnings in contemplation of replacement of plant at higher costs was a proper managerial action.

This basic position was reaffirmed by the same committee the next year in a letter addressed to the AICPA membership.

In 1953 the same committee again considered the problem and reaffirmed its earlier position. The vote was 14 to 6, whereas in 1947 it had been 20 to 0, with one member not voting and another voting favorably but with qualification.

The Committee on Accounting Procedure was replaced in 1959 by the Accounting Principles Board. Initially the APB commissioned research studies on six problem areas; one dealt with price-level accounting. *Accounting Research Study No. 6*, "Reporting the Effects of Price-Level Changes," was published in 1963. After considering reactions to this study the APB developed *Statement No. 3*, "Financial Statements Restated for General Price-Level Changes," published in 1969. In the process of developing the statement, the techniques recommended in it were experimentally applied over a two-year period to the financial records of 18 cooperating businesses. Results of this experiment were reported in the *Journal of Accountancy* (June 1969).

Timing of the issuance of *Statement No. 3* was fortunate in one sense, but unfortunate in another. The *Statement* was timely in that it appeared when prices were again rising sharply. Concurrently, though, business profits began to fall in 1969 and continued to decline in 1970. As a consequence, business managements were loath to adopt the recommended procedures of *Statement No. 3*. The statement recommended preparation of a set of supplemental statements to accompany the regularly prepared balance sheet, income statement, and retained earnings statement. The supplemental statements would reflect the application of a price index reflective of general price changes to specific statement items and amounts. Given the long inflation which preceded 1969 and the sharp acceleration of prices in that year and in 1970, and given the drop in reported profits as compared with 1968 and earlier, one can understand the reluctance of the typical company management to adopt on a voluntary basis an accounting procedure which may worsen their already deteriorating profit picture. As a consequence, almost no adoptions of supplementary price-level adjusted statements occurred and interest in the subject outside academic circles largely disappeared.

FASB and the Price-Level Problem

When the FASB was created early in 1973, it initially placed six topics on its agenda; none of them related to inflation accounting. This is understandable because up to that time it was the view of many that inflation was not a serious problem in this country. Throughout the 1960s the rate of inflation as measured by the GNP Deflator had been well below 3% per year. The rate began to accelerate in the late 1960s. By year-end 1973 it was found the highest rate of increase experienced for a quarter of a century had been attained; 1973 was 5.6% higher than 1972 in terms of average prices for the year. At the December 1973 meeting of the FASB's Advisory Council action was taken to get the subject on the Board's agenda. Thereafter, events unfolded swiftly; a Discussion Memorandum issued on February 15, 1974, led to a two-day public hearing in April 1974. By December 1974, based on testimony gathered at the hearing and from other sources, the FASB issued a proposed accounting standard on the subject. The Discussion Memorandum and the proposed accounting standard both relied heavily on earlier work done by the AICPA's research staff and the APB. The principal provisions of the proposed standard are summarized, and two illustrations show application of its provisions. The proposed standard uses index numbers and many of the techniques first introduced by Sweeney.

The preceding background review provides a sound basis for considering the two basic accounting approaches that depart significantly from the traditional, or conventional, historic cost model, viz:

1. Financial statements restated on purchasing power or price-level bases.
2. Current fair value accounting and reporting.

Each will be discussed and illustrated in this order.

APPLICATION OF THE INDEX NUMBER APPROACH TO RESTATE FINANCIAL STATEMENTS

Financial statements under current GAAP are prepared on the traditional historical cost basis. The historical cost basis amounts on the financial statements are restated in terms of *units of general purchasing power.* The FASB clearly does not view restatement by using index numbers as a departure from the historical cost basis; rather there is a change in the *measuring unit* but not in the attribute (i.e., the cost of the asset) being measured.[7]

The restatement of historical cost basis amounts on traditional financial statements to units of general purchasing power, by using index numbers, involves the following steps:

1. Obtain the complete set of financial statements prepared under current GAAP.
2. Select the appropriate index to use and obtain the index numbers for each period covering the life of the *oldest* item on the financial statements. The FASB stated that "The Gross National Product Implicit Price Deflator shall be the index of the general purchasing power of the dollar used in preparing general purchasing power financial information."
3. Each statement item is classified as monetary or nonmonetary. *Monetary items* are defined as cash and claims to cash that are fixed in terms of numbers of dollars regardless of change in prices. Thus, cash, receivables, and most liabilities are monetary items. All other items are classified as *nonmonetary* items. Thus inventories, fixed assets, and common stock equity are nonmonetary items. Exhibit 25–1 presents more details on the classification of items as monetary or nonmonetary.
4. Restate each nonmonetary item in terms of its current general purchasing power for financial statement purposes. This involves computation of a *conversion factor* which is the index number that prevailed when the nonmonetary item was originally recorded in the accounts divided into the current year index number. The cost of the item as reported on the traditionally prepared financial statement is multiplied by the conversion factor to derive the restated amount. Example: Land was acquired for $22,000 when the GNP Deflator figure was 110; and on the date statements are being prepared it is 132. The conversion factor is: 132 ÷ 110 = 1.20. On the general purchasing power adjusted statements, computation of the Land restated amount to be reported would be $22,000 × 1.20 = $26.400.[8] Significantly, the *monetary items are not restated* because the amount of dollars they will command (assets) or demand (liabilities) is fixed.[9]
5. Compute the *general purchasing power gain or loss* (sometimes called *price-level gain or loss*) on the monetary, but not the nonmonetary, items. Recall that purchasing power gains and losses occur *only* on monetary items because the number of dollars to satisfy them is fixed—they are constant in amount, although these dollars are changing in real value. The change in their real value is the purchasing power gain or loss. To compute the purchasing power

[7] An alternative procedure, *current value accounting* (discussed in the next section) is significantly different conceptually, procedurally, and as to results. *Fair value* accounting is a conceptual departure from the historical cost concept.

[8] Arithmetically this is $22,000 × $^{132}/_{110}$ = $26,400.

[9] FASB Exposure Drafts (see footnote 3).

EXHIBIT 25–1
Classification of Items as Monetary or Nonmonetary

	Monetary	*Nonmonetary*
Cash on hand and in banks[1]	x	
Foreign currency on hand and claims thereto		x
Marketable securities:		
Stocks (nonmonetary because prices can change)		x
Bonds (expected to be held to maturity)	x	
Bonds (expected to be sold before maturity)		x
Receivables	x	
Allowance for doubtful accounts	x	
Inventories[2]		x
Prepaid expenses		x
Property, plant, and equipment		x
Accumulated depreciation		x
Cash surrender value of life insurance	x	
Deferred charges (including income taxes)		x
Intangibles		x
Accounts and notes payable, accrued expenses	x	
Advances received on sales contracts[3]		x
Bonds payable and other long-term debt	x	
Unamortized premium or discount on debt	x	
Obligations under warranties		x
Deferred income tax credits (and debits)		x
Preferred stock[4]		x
Common stockholders' equity		x

[1] All claims are assumed to be payable in U.S. dollars unless specifically stated otherwise.

[2] An exception would be inventories produced under fixed price contracts accounted for at the contract price. Such inventories would be monetary.

[3] This obligation will be satisfied by delivery of goods or services that are nonmonetary because their prices can fluctuate.

[4] Preferred stock carried at an amount equal to its fixed liquidation or redemption price is monetary because the claim of the preferred shareholders on assets of the entity is in a fixed number of dollars. In other instances preferred stock would be nonmonetary.

gain or loss, the monetary items are restated in the computation, but not on the price-level financial statements. The restated amount is compared with the reported historical cost to determine the purchasing power gain or loss. In contrast, the nonmonetary items, by their characteristics, change in the number of dollars they will command. Thus, no purchasing power gain or loss is recognized on them in price-level accounting. Nonmonetary items are not included in the computation of purchasing power gains or losses; they are restated on the price-level adjusted statements.

The gain and loss effects of holding monetary items may be summarized as follows:

	General Price Level Rising		*General Price Level Falling*	
Item	*Gain*	*Loss*	*Gain*	*Loss*
Monetary assets		✓	✓	
Monetary liabilities	✓			✓

Computation of the purchasing power gain or loss on monetary items involves a series of sub steps, viz:

a. Determine excess of monetary assets over monetary liabilities (or vice versa) at the start of the period.

b. Restate the excess of the monetary items described in step *(a)* to its end-of-the-period purchasing power equivalent. Assume cash and payables (both monetary) at the start of the period were $20,000 and $8,000, respectively, and the starting and ending index numbers were 140 and 151.2. The excess of the monetary assets over monetary liabilities of $12,000 would be restated as: $12,000 × 151.2/140 = $12,960. Since there is an *asset excess* there is a potential purchasing power *loss* of $960 for the period.

c. Identify all transactions during the year which *increased monetary items;* restate them to the year-end basis and add the total restated amount to the restated balance derived in step *(b)*. Example: Sales for cash and on account occurred evenly throughout the year and amounted to $728,000. The average index value for the year is 145.6; the year-end value is 151.2. The increase in monetary items due to sales would be restated to $756,000 ($728,000 × 151.2/145.6) which would be added to *(b)*.

d. Identify transactions which *decreased monetary items;* restate them to the year-end basis and subtract the total restated amount from the sum of *(b)* + *(c)*. Examples: Purchases for cash and on account occurred evenly throughout the year and amounted to $436,800. The restatement of the decrease in monetary items due to *(a)* purchases, and *(b)* equipment would be computed as follows: $436,800 × 151.2/145.6 = $453,600. Equipment was bought at the start of the year for $28,000. The restatement would be $28,000 × 151.2/140 = $30,240.

e. Derive a total of the price-level adjusted net monetary items as above, and a total of the carrying value of the monetary items as of the end of the period; subtract the latter from the former to determine the *purchasing power gain or loss.* Using the foregoing figures we have the following:

	Monetary Items	
	Carrying Values (historical cost)	*Restated Amount (end-of-period purchasing power)*
From step *(b)*	$ 12,000	$ 12,960
From step *(c)*	728,000	756,000
Subtotal	740,000	768,960
From step *(d)*	464,800	483,840
Totals—per Step *(e)*	$275,200	285,120
Deduct historical carrying value		−275,200
Purchasing Power Gain (Loss)		$ (9,920)

The comprehensive procedures recommended by the FASB will now be illustrated; first with a simplified example, followed by a more complex and realistic example.

SIMPLIFIED ILLUSTRATION OF PRICE-LEVEL ACCOUNTING

To illustrate all aspects of the accounting process, including price-level restatement, this example will include the following:

1. Beginning trial balance (dated December 31, 19C) for XY Company (given in the first two columns of Exhibit 25–2).
2. Transactions for 19D including relevant price index data:
   a. Sold merchandise for cash and on credit, $400,000.
   b. Bought merchandise on credit, cost $290,000 (assume periodic inventory system).
   c. Payments on current liabilities, $340,000.
   d. Declared and paid a $12,000 cash dividend at year-end.
   e. Various expenses paid at an approximately uniform rate throughout the year, $55,000.
   f. Depreciation expense on fixtures recorded at year-end, $20,000. The fixtures, acquired on January 1, 19A, when the price index stood at 116, have an estimated ten-year life and zero residual value. The future plant site also was acquired on this date.
   g. Income tax expense of $20,000 was accrued uniformly throughout the year.
   h. Ending inventory, $105,000.
   i. Relevant price index data:

	Index Numbers	*Conversion Factor (%)*
January 1, 19A	116	159.5/116 = 137.5
December 31, 19C	145	159.5/145 = 110.0
December 31, 19D	159.5	159.5/159.5 = 100.0
Average for 19D	151.9	159.5/151.9 = 105.0

3. Worksheet for 19D to derive traditional cost basis income statement and balance sheet (Exhibit 25–2).
4. Application of conversion factors to convert traditional cost basis statements to purchasing power basis, that is, price-level conversion (Exhibit 25–3).

Application of Conversion Factors

The preceding summary of steps to develop price-level adjusted statements indicated that cost basis amounts are restated (by using the conversion factors) for two purposes, viz:

EXHIBIT 25–2

XY COMPANY
Worksheet to Develop Income Statement and Balance Sheet—Traditional Cost Basis
Year Ended December 31, 19D

	Balances December 31, 19C		19D Transactions and Adjustments		Income Summary—19D		Balance Sheet, December 31, 19D	
	Debit	Credit	Debit	Credit	Debit	Credit	Debit	Credit
Cash and receivables	145,000		(a) 400,000	(c) 340,000 (d) 12,000 (e) 55,000			138,000	
Inventory	90,000				90,000	105,000*	105,000	
Future plant site	50,000						50,000	
Fixtures	200,000						200,000	
Accumulated depreciation		60,000		(f) 20,000				80,000
Current payables including taxes		60,000	(c) 340,000	(b) 290,000 (g) 20,000				30,000
Long-term note payable		50,000						50,000
Capital stock, par $10		300,000						300,000
Retained earnings		15,000	(d) 12,000		30,000†			33,000
Sales				(a) 400,000		400,000		
Purchases			(b) 290,000		290,000			
Expenses (except depreciation and income taxes)			(e) 55,000		55,000			
Depreciation expense			(f) 20,000		20,000			
Income tax expense			(g) 20,000		20,000			
	485,000	485,000	1,137,000	1,137,000	505,000	505,000	493,000	493,000

* Ending inventory.

† Net income transferred to retained earnings.

1. To compute the purchasing power gain or loss on *monetary items*.
2. To develop price-level adjusted financial statements by restating the nonmonetary items.

Computation of the 19D Purchasing Power Gain or Loss

If this were the first year of operations for XY Company, the purchasing power gain or loss could be directly computed by applying the conversion factors to each monetary item. However, in subsequent periods the computation becomes more complex. Therefore, restatement steps 5*(a)*–*(e)* page 1073 must be completed for XY Company (as is the usual case). These restatement steps are reflected in Exhibit 25–3. Observe that first the beginning restated net amount of monetary items (i.e., carried over from 19C) is determined by using the 19C conversion factor of 110, viz: $35,000 × 110% = $38,500. The transactions during 19D that

EXHIBIT 25–3

XY COMPANY
Calculation of General Purchasing Power (Price-Level) Gain or Loss
Year Ended December 31, 19D

	Cost Basis Amount (per books)	*Conversion Factor*	*Restated at December 31, 19D*
Net monetary items at December 31, 19C:			
Cash and receivables	$145,000		
Current payables, including income taxes	(60,000)		
Long-term payable	(50,000)		
Net (assets)	35,000	110	$ 38,500
Add sources of net monetary items during 19D:			
Sales	400,000	105	420,000
Subtotal	435,000		458,500
Deduct uses of monetary items during 19D:			
Purchases	290,000	105	304,500
Operating expenses (except depreciation)	55,000	105	57,750
Income taxes	20,000	105	21,000
Dividends paid at year-end	12,000	100	12,000
Total Uses	377,000		395,250
Net monetary items restated at December 31, 19D ($458,500 − $395,250)			63,250
Net monetary items at December 31, 19D, not restated:			
Cash and receivables	138,000		
Current payables including taxes	(30,000)		
Mortgage payable	(50,000)		
Total	$ 58,000		58,000*
Purchasing Power Gain (Loss) in 19D on Monetary Basis			$ (5,250)

* This amount can be calculated directly as $435,000 − $377,000 = $58,000, or detailed as reflected here.

increased (i.e., sources) and decreased (i.e., uses) monetary items are identified and restated. Deduction of the 19D ending balances of the monetary items from the net of these amounts gives the purchasing power gain or loss. For XY Company there was a $5,250 loss because the losses on monetary assets held exceeded the gains on the monetary liabilities owed during 19D. This loss is reported on the restated income statement shown in Exhibit 25–5.

Restatement of Balance Sheet Amounts

When steps in the application of the index number approach were summarized, it was pointed out that *only nonmonetary items* are restated in terms of their current general purchasing power for financial statement purposes. As to balance sheet items, this means taking the end of the period index value as a numerator and the index value which prevailed, when the nonmonetary item was first recorded in the accounts, as a denominator and multiplying this fraction by the historical cost (book carrying amount) of each nonmonetary item. For example, as to Future Plant Site and Fixtures acquired on January 1, 19A, when the index was 116, for arriving at the purchasing power equivalent of those assets at the end of 19D when the index is at 159.5, one would multiply the book value of these items by the conversion factor of 137.5 (i.e., 159.5/116). As to ending inventory, under a *Fifo* flow assumption, the inventory came from purchases made during the period, so the inventory needs an upward adjustment only by the amount which pur-

EXHIBIT 25–4

XY COMPANY
Restatement of Balance Sheet—Price-Level Basis

Assets	*Cost Basis Amount*	*Conversion Factor*	*Restated Amount*
Cash and receivables	$138,000	100	$138,000
Inventory	105,000	105	110,250
Future plant site	50,000	137.5	68,750
Fixtures	200,000	137.5	275,000
Less: Accumulated depreciation	(80,000)	137.5	(110,000)
Total Assets	$413,000		$482,000
Liabilities			
Current payables, including taxes	$ 30,000	100	$ 30,000
Long-term payable	50,000	100	50,000
Total Liabilities	80,000		80,000
Stockholders' Equity			
Capital	300,000		
Retained earnings	33,000		
Total Stockholders' Equity	333,000		402,000*
Total Liabilities and Stockholders' Equity	$413,000		$482,000

* This is a balancing figure; Total Assets, $482,000 − Total Liabilities, $80,000 = Stockholders' Equity, $402,000.

chases lagged the end-of-the-period index value. Since purchases were assumed to have occurred evenly over the period and since the average index number for the period was 151.9 (as compared with the ending index number of 159.5), an upward adjustment for 19D of 5% (i.e., 159.5/151.5 = 1.05) is needed to restate the inventory. If the company had been using *Lifo* for some period of time the degree of inventory adjustment would have been much larger because the lag would be much longer.

Recall monetary items on the current statements *are not restated* on the price-level statements because the amounts of cash, receivables, and payables are fixed; they do not change in dollar amount because of a change in the price level. As to common stock equity, the FASB recommended that a lump-sum restated amount be shown because separate historical cost figures for capital stock, premium on capital stock, and retained earnings generally would not have much significance. The view is that attempting to preserve such a separation on price-level adjusted statements would be meaningless from a legal standpoint and involve far more effort than the benefit would warrant.

The restated 19D balance sheet for XY Company is shown in Exhibit 25–4.

Restatement of the Income Statement

The revenue and expense items on an essentially current basis (such as sales, purchases, and expenses, but not depreciation and similar items) require upward adjustment only to the extent average prices for

EXHIBIT 25–5

XY COMPANY
Restatement of Income Statement—Price-Level Basis

	Cost Basis Amount	*Conversion Factor*	*Restated Amount*
Sales	$400,000	105	$420,000
Inventory, January 1, 19D	90,000	110	99,000
Purchases	290,000	105	304,500
Goods available	380,000		403,500
Inventory, December 31, 19D	105,000	105	110,250
Cost of goods sold	275,000		293,250
Gross margin	125,000		126,750
Expenses*	55,000	105	57,750
Depreciation expense	20,000	137.5	27,500
Total Operating Expense	75,000		85,250
Income before taxes	50,000		41,500
Income taxes	20,000	105	21,000
Net Income	$ 30,000		20,500
Purchasing power loss			5,250
Net Income Restated			$ 15,250

* Excluding depreciation and income taxes.

the period lag the level of prices at the end of the period. In the example, as explained above, this requires an upward adjustment of 5% for 19D.

Depreciation expense is restated by relating it to the price-level restatement of the assets involved. To illustrate, in the example for XY Company the fixtures cost $200,000 and were depreciated on a cost basis of 10% or $20,000 for 19D. The $200,000 asset cost is restated to $275,000 by application of the 137.5 conversion factor. The restated depreciation expense is: $20,000 × 137.5 = $27,500.

Cost of goods sold is derived as beginning inventory plus purchases minus ending inventory. Restatement of this amount requires restatement of each of these three component amounts. To illustrate, for XY Company the beginning inventory was restated at the end of 19C when the price level was 145, hence it is subject to the conversion factor of 110 (i.e., 159.5/145). Both purchases and ending inventory are subject to the 105 conversion factor, (i.e., 159.5/151.9) as explained above.

The restated 19D income statement for XY Company is shown in Exhibit 25–5.

PREPARATION OF COMPARATIVE PRICE-LEVEL STATEMENTS

The preceding discussion and illustrations focused on the development of price-level adjusted statements for the current year (i.e., 19D for XY Company). An additional problem is posed when *comparative* price-level statements are needed, which is the usual situation. The problem is due to the fact that the price-level statements reported for the *prior* year are no longer appropriate; they must be restated again, but on the current year price-level basis. The restatement procedures are similar to those discussed above.

To illustrate, assume comparative statements are required at the end of 19D for XY Company. The balance sheet reported at December 31, 19C, on a price-level basis, was as follows:

XY COMPANY
Restated Balance Sheet – Price-Level Basis
At December 31, 19C

Cash and receivables	$145,000	Current payables	$ 60,000
Inventory	90,000	Long-term note payable	50,000
Future plant site	62,500	Stockholders' equity	362,500
Fixtures	250,000		
Accumulated depreciation	(75,000)		
	$472,500		$472,500

Since this balance sheet is no longer relevant at December 31, 19D, the 19C cost basis statement must again be restated using 19D conversion factors as reflected in Exhibit 25–6. The price-level adjusted amounts shown in Exhibits 25–4 and 25–6 would be reported in juxtaposition on the 19D comparative price-level balance sheets.

EXHIBIT 25–6

XY COMPANY
Data for Comparative Balance Sheet—Restatement of Prior Year, 19C
For Comparative Statement, 19C and 19D
(stated in terms of 19D price level)

Assets	*Cost Basis Amount*	*Conversion Factor*	*Restated Amount*
Cash and receivables	$145,000	110	$159,500
Inventory	90,000	110	99,000
Future plant site	50,000	137.5	68,750
Fixtures	200,000	137.5	275,000
Less: Accumulated depreciation	(60,000)	137.5	(82,500)
Total Assets	$425,000		$519,750
Liabilities			
Current payables, including taxes	$ 60,000	110	$ 66,000
Mortgage note payable	50,000	110	55,000
Total Liabilities	110,000		121,000
Stockholders' Equity			
Capital Stock	300,000		
Retained earnings	15,000		
Total Stockholders' Equity	315,000		398,750*
Total Liabilities and Stockholders' Equity	$425,000		$519,750

* This is a balancing figure:
Total Assets, $519,750 − Total Liabilities, $121,000 = Stockholders' Equity, $398,750.

Preparation of a comparative income statement would require the same approach. Since 19C revenue and expense data were not provided for XY Company, development of the comparative income statement is not illustrated at this point. However, the basic procedure which would be followed can easily be described. Assume sales for 19C on a historical cost basis were $340,000 and had been restated to $350,000 on the 19C price-level statement because the year-end index number was almost 3% higher than the average index value for 19C. Now assume the year-end index number for 19D is 10% higher than the year-end value prevailing at 19C year-end. Consequently, the original $350,000 sales amount would be raised to $385,000 (i.e., $350,000 × 159.5/145) when the 19C amounts are restated to 19D year-end equivalent purchasing power. Consider another item, depreciation expense. On the 19C price-level statement, this expense would have been $25,000 (i.e., $20,000 × 145/116). It would be again restated for the 19D comparative income statement to $27,500, which is the same amount as on the 19D price-level statement (because straight-line depreciation was used).

PROOF OF RESTATEMENT

When comparative balance sheets are prepared as illustrated above, a proof of the accuracy of the price-level adjustment process can be developed as follows:

December 31, 19C stockholders' equity at December 31, 19D price level (Exhibit 25–6)	$398,750
Add: Net income including purchasing power gain or loss (Exhibit 25–5)	15,250
Total	414,000
Deduct: Dividends adjusted to price-level basis (Exhibit 25–3)	12,000
December 31, 19D stockholders' equity at December 31, 19D, price level (Exhibit 25–4)	$402,000

COMPLEX ILLUSTRATION OF PRICE-LEVEL ACCOUNTING

This illustration is more realistic than the preceding one because revenue and expense data are given on a quarterly rather than on an annual basis. It also involves the acquisition of fixed assets and payment of a dividend during the year. Since GNP Deflator data are released on a quarterly basis, quarterly application is realistic. This illustration will focus on the development of price-level statements for AB Company for the year ended December 31, 19F. The assumed data are as follows:

1. Relevant price index numbers (see also transactions C and D):

	Index Number	*Conversion Factor*
December 31, 19E (when beginning inventory was acquired)	147	(159/147) = 108.2
End of–		
First quarter, 19F	150	(159/150) = 106.0
Second quarter, 19F	153	(159/153) = 103.9
Third quarter, 19F	156	(159/156) = 102.0
Fourth quarter, at December 31, 19F	159	(159/159) = 100.0

2. Trial balance, cost basis, December 31, 19E: As reflected on Exhibit 25–7.
3. Transactions for 19F: As reflected at the bottom of Exhibit 25–7.
4. Additional information: Assume a *Fifo* basis for inventory (therefore the ending inventory was from purchases made during the fourth quarter). Sales, purchases, general expenses, and income tax expense are restated from historical cost amounts to price-level amounts on a quarterly basis.

Based on these data, development of price-level statements for 19F is illustrated as follows:

1. *Exhibit 25–7.* Worksheet to develop traditional cost basis income statement and balance sheet for 19F.
2. *Exhibit 25–8.* Restatement of quarterly revenues and expenses. Completion of this schedule requires application of the 19D *quarterly* conversion factors to the cost basis amounts. The annual total for each revenue and expense is transferred to the restated annual income statement.
3. *Exhibit 25–9.* Calculation of purchasing power gain or loss. The purchasing power loss of $2,195 is carried to the income statement.

EXHIBIT 25–7

AB COMPANY
Worksheet to Develop Income Statement and Balance Sheet—Traditional Cost Basis
For Year Ended December 31, 19F

	Dec. 31, 19E Balances		19F Transactions and Adjustments		19F Income Summary		Dec. 31, 19F Balance Sheet	
Cash	36,000		(f) 115,000	(e) 12,000 (g) 80,000 (h) 10,000 (i) 20,000			29,000	
Receivables	24,000		(a) 120,000	(f) 115,000			29,000	
Inventory	20,000				20,000	25,000*	25,000	
Building	100,000						100,000	
Accumulated depreciation, building		20,000		(c) 4,000				24,000
Fixtures	40,000		(i) 20,000				60,000	
Accumulated depreciation, fixtures		20,000		(d) 4,000				24,000
Accounts payable		35,000	(g) 80,000	(b) 85,000				40,000
Income taxes payable				(j) 10,000				10,000
Capital stock		100,000						100,000
Retained earnings		45,000	(h) 10,000		10,000†			45,000
Sales				(a) 120,000		120,000		
Purchases			(b) 85,000		85,000			
Depreciation expense, building			(c) 4,000		4,000			
Depreciation expense, fixtures			(d) 4,000		4,000			
General expenses			(e) 12,000		12,000			
Income tax expense			(j) 10,000		10,000			
	220,000	220,000	460,000	460,000	145,000	145,000	243,000	243,000

* Ending inventory.

† Net income transferred to retained earnings.

Transactions during 19F (summarized):

(a) Sales of $30,000 were made each quarter (assume all on credit).
(b) Purchases of $20,000 were made each of the first three quarters and $25,000 the last quarter (assume all on credit).
(c) The building is depreciated 4% per year with no residual value; when bought in 19A, the price index was 127.
(d) Fixtures are depreciated 10% per year with no residual value; when the original fixtures were bought in 19B, the price index was 138.
(e) General expenses of $3,000 were paid each quarter.
(f) Collections on receivables, $115,000.
(g) Payments on accounts payable, $80,000.
(h) At mid-year, a $10,000 cash dividend was paid.
(i) New fixtures costing $10,000 were bought at year end.
(j) Income taxes in the amount of $2,500 were accrued each quarter.

EXHIBIT 25–8

AB COMPANY
Conversion Schedule of Quarterly Revenues and Expenses
For Year Ended December 31, 19F

	First Quarter	*Second Quarter*	*Third Quarter*	*Fourth Quarter*	*Year Total*
Conversion factor	106	103.9	102	100	
Sales	$30,000	$30,000	$30,000	$30,000	$120,000
Restated sales	31,800	31,170	30,600	30,000	123,570
Purchases	20,000	20,000	20,000	25,000	85,000
Restated purchases	21,200	20,780	20,400	25,000	87,380
General expenses	3,000	3,000	3,000	3,000	12,000
Restated general expenses	3,180	3,117	3,060	3,000	12,357
Income tax	2,500	2,500	2,500	2,500	10,000
Restated income tax	2,650	2,598	2,550	2,500	10,298

EXHIBIT 25–9

AB COMPANY
Calculation of Purchasing Power Gain or Loss
For Year Ended December 31, 19F

	Cost Basis Amount (per books)	*Conversion Factor*	*Restated at Dec. 31, 19F*
Net monetary items at December 31, 19E:			
Cash	$ 36,000		
Receivables	24,000		
Accounts payable	(35,000)		
Net	25,000	108.2	$ 27,050
Add: Sources of net monetary items during 19F:			
Sales	120,000	*	123,570
Subtotal	145,000		150,620
Deduct: Uses of net monetary items during 19F:			
Purchases	85,000	*	87,380
General expenses (except depreciation)	12,000	*	12,357
Income tax expense	10,000	*	10,298
Dividends paid at mid-year	10,000	103.9	10,390
Fixtures purchased	20,000	100	20,000
Total Uses	137,000		140,425
Net monetary items at December 31, 19F, restated ($150,620 – $140,425)			10,195
Net monetary items at December 31, 19F, not restated:			
Cash	29,000		
Receivables	29,000		
Accounts payable	(40,000)		
Taxes payable	(10,000)		
Total	$ 8,000		8,000
Purchasing power gain (loss) in 19F on monetary items			$ (2,195)

* See Exhibit 25–8.

EXHIBIT 25–10

AB COMPANY
Restatement of Balance Sheet—Price-Level Basis
At December 31, 19F

	Cost Basis Amount	*Conversion Factor*	*Restated Amount*
Cash	$ 29,000		$ 29,000
Receivables	29,000		29,000
Inventory	25,000	100(a)	25,000
Building	100,000	125.2	125,200
Accumulated depreciation, building	24,000	125.2	30,048
Fixtures	60,000	(b)	66,080
Accumulated depreciation, fixtures	24,000	115.2	27,648
	$195,000		$216,584
Accounts payable	40,000		40,000
Taxes payable	10,000		10,000
Capital stock	100,000		
Retained earnings	45,000		
Balancing amount			166,584
	$195,000		$216,584

(a) Since the ending inventory was entirely from purchases during the fourth quarter, no price-level adjustment on statement should be made.

(b) Old asset acquired for $40,000 in 19B when index was 138; therefore, restatement is:

$40,000 × 159/138 (i.e., 115.2) =	$46,080
New asset acquired for $20,000 on December 31, 19F; therefore, no restatement needed	20,000
Total Restated Amount	$66,080

EXHIBIT 25–11

AB COMPANY
Restatement of Income Statement—Price-Level Basis
For Year Ended December 31, 19F

	Cost Basis Amount	*Conversion Factor*	*Restated Amount*
Sales	$120,000	(b)	$123,570
Inventory, January 1, 19F	20,000	108.2	21,640
Purchases	85,000	(b)	87,380
Goods available for sale	105,000		109,020
Inventory, December 31, 19F	25,000	100	25,000
Cost of goods sold	80,000		84,020
Gross margin	40,000		39,550
General expenses	12,000		12,357
Depreciation expense, building	4,000	125.2(a)	5,008
Depreciation expense, fixtures	4,000	115.2(a)	4,608
Total Expenses	20,000		21,973
Income before taxes	20,000		17,577
Income tax	10,000	(b)	10,298
Purchasing power loss	—	(c)	2,195
Net Income	$ 10,000		$ 5,084

(a) See restated balance sheet, Exhibit 25–10.
(b) See Exhibit 25–8.
(c) See Exhibit 25–9.

4. *Exhibit 25–10.* Restatement of 19F balance sheet. Observe that only the nonmonetary amounts are restated and that restated stockholders' equity is a plug figure.
5. *Exhibit 25–11.* Restatement of 19F income statement.
6. *Exhibit 25–12.* Data for comparative balance sheet—restatement of 19E balance sheet at 19F price level.
7. *Exhibit 25–13.* Proof of restatement—December 31, 19F.

EXHIBIT 25–12

AB COMPANY
Data for Comparative Balance Sheet—Restatement of Prior Year (19E)
At December 31, 19E and 19F
(stated in terms of December 31, 19F, price level)

	Cost Basis Amount	*Conversion Factor*	*Restated Amount*
Cash	$ 36,000	108.2	$ 38,952
Receivables	24,000	108.2	25,968
Inventory	20,000	108.2	21,640
Building	100,000	125.2	125,200
Accumulated depreciation, building	(20,000)	125.2	(25,040)
Fixtures	40,000	115.2	46,080
Accumulated depreciation, fixtures	(20,000)	115.2	(23,040)
			$209,760
Accounts payable	35,000	108.2	$ 37,870
Stockholders' equity	145,000	*	171,890
			$209,760

* Balancing amount.

EXHIBIT 25–13

AB COMPANY
Proof of Restatement
December 31, 19F

December 31, 19E, stockholders' equity at December 31, 19F, price level (Exhibit 25–12)	$171,890
Add: Net income, including purchasing power gain or loss (Exhibit 25–11)	5,084
Total	176,974
Deduct: Dividends adjusted to price-level basis (Exhibit 25–9)	10,390
December 31, 19F, stockholders' equity at December 31, 19F, price level (Exhibit 25–10)	$166,584

Some brief explanation of the conversion of fixtures from the historical cost amount of $60,000 at December 31, 19F, to its price-level equivalent may be in order. Recall $20,000 of fixtures were added at year-end. For practical purposes, therefore, we are concerned only with conversion of $40,000 of fixtures held during an interval over which prices changed.

The $40,000 acquisition took place when the index was at 138; at December 31, 19F, it is at 159, so the adjustment applied to the $40,000 and to the related accumulated depreciation of $24,000 is 115.2 (159/138).

The discussions and illustrations of the development of financial statements restated on a price-level basis have focused on the underlying concepts and basic computational procedures. It encompasses the proposed FASB *Statement* and should provide an adequate understanding of the problems and their resolution. Price-level adjusted statements do not report "fair value" except by occasional coincidence. The next section will consider fair-value accounting.

HIGHLIGHTS OF THE FASB STATEMENT ON REPORTING IN TERMS OF GENERAL PURCHASING POWER

Now that the procedures for implementing price-level restatement of financial statements have been illustrated, it is appropriate to highlight the following salient points of the proposed FASB *Statement* on the subject.

1. Conventional financial statements prepared at the close of a fiscal year shall be accompanied by information stated in units of general purchasing power. The information shall be based upon comprehensive rather than piecemeal restatement of the financial statement items. General purchasing power information is not required to accompany financial statements for interim periods such as a month or a quarter.
2. The same accounting principles used for the conventional cost-basis statements shall be used in preparing the general purchasing power (price-level restated) information. Only the measuring unit is changed. The GNP Deflator shall be used for restatement purposes.
3. General purchasing power information shall be stated at the most recent statement date. The most recent quarterly GNP Deflator numbers will serve as an acceptable approximation of the general purchasing power at the balance sheet date.
4. The net gain or loss of general purchasing power from holding monetary assets and liabilities shall be included in determining income in units of general purchasing power; there shall be no deferrals to future periods.
5. The amount of income tax expense included in determining net income in units of general purchasing power shall be based on the amount of income tax expense included in determining net income in units of money. No added taxes shall be accrued for income taxes that may be paid in the future because of the nondeductibility for tax purposes of the excess amounts of nonmonetary assets revalued over their amounts as conventionally stated.
6. It is permissible to present less than a complete income statement;

but, at a minimum, the following elements must be presented in units of general purchasing power:

a. Total revenues.
b. Depreciation of property, plant, and equipment.
c. Net purchasing power gain or loss.
d. Income from continuing operations (includes *c* above).
e. Net income.
f. Net income per common share.
g. Cash dividends per common share.

7. It is permissible to present less than a complete balance sheet, but the following elements must be presented in units of general purchasing power:
   a. Inventories.
   b. Working capital.
   c. Total property, plant, and equipment (net of depreciation).
   d. Total assets.
   e. Total common stockholders' equity.
8. A "normal" presentation presumably should set out details of the computation of purchasing power gain or loss rather than Item 6(*c*) as one line.

CURRENT FAIR-VALUE ACCOUNTING

Current fair value (hereafter called current-value or fair-value accounting), although significantly different conceptually, is akin to price-level accounting in some respects. For example, it draws the same distinction between monetary and nonmonetary items. On the other hand, a major difference is that it substitutes fair or current dollar values for the general index restatement of nonmonetary items. Fair value accounting has not been definitely described, and no authoritative guidelines have been developed, much less agreed upon. There are numerous proponents of fair value accounting, and a variety of views of the basic concepts that should prevail. Proponents of current-value systems are less well agreed as to the implementation guidelines that should be followed. Significantly, there are numerous ways of arriving at fair values. Aside from this problem, some advocates of fair value accounting would also separately identify the effects of general price-level changes while others would not.

Measuring Current Values

Several ways of measuring current values have been proposed, and some have limited application under the historical-cost based accounting model. Means of measuring current values include:

Entry values:
1. Replacement cost
2. Reproduction cost

Exit values:
3. Realization value

Special:
4. Discounted cash inflows
5. Specific price-index numbers
6. Appraisals

Replacement cost is the estimated cost of acquiring new similar items at current prices after allowing for comparable physical and functional depreciation that has already occurred on the items being valued. If the property would serve the same function, it need not be identical.

Reproduction cost is the estimated cost of producing new essentially identical property in kind adjusted for physical and functional depreciation to date.

Realization value is the amount that could be realized from the current sale of the item assuming no forced or distress sale is implied. It is recognized that many of the assets of an entity are not ordinarily up for sale.

Discounted cash inflows are the present value of the future estimated net cash inflows, or cost savings, of an item being valued. The future cash inflows are discounted at a realistic rate of interest. The concepts discussed in Chapter 6 are used.

Specific price-index numbers are regularly developed and published for various types of construction, kinds of machinery, equipment, and vehicles, and for hundreds of commodity groups. Some larger companies have found it feasible to develop their own index numbers to value specific assets, such as plant assets. Specific index numbers are to be distinguished from general index numbers such as the GNP Deflator which measures changes in a broad range of prices. Whereas, general index numbers can be used, as discussed in the preceding section, to measure changes in general purchasing power, specific index numbers tend to measure the change in value of single or groups of similar items. Thus, specific index numbers are often viewed as a realistic way to measure fair value.

Appraisals are estimates developed by professionally competent and independent individuals of the current fair value of an item in its present condition.

Measurement of Current Fair-Value Costs of Specific Assets

The measurement of the current fair value of each kind of asset at each financial statement date presents complex inplementation solutions. Let's consider a few.

1. Inventories. Price lists or catalogs from suppliers adjusted for discounts and transportation and handling costs often would provide realistic fair values for purchased inventories. As to manufactured inventories, the cost accounting systems usually provide past unit cost amounts for material, labor, and overhead; and these can be modified, for known changes, to a current basis. Standard costs can be used, provided they are frequently revised. Some inventories are, of course, subject to quotations in established markets (e.g., commodities, precious metals).

2. Investments. Market quotations often can be used for marketable securities which would not be sold in such large quantities as to materially affect the quotations. If market quotations are not available, or if the blocks are apt to be too large, satisfaction of this criterion is much more difficult.

3. Property, plant, and equipment. The current fair value of some fixed assets can be measured on the basis of price data from supplier's catalogs. In some instances there is a well-established market for used property. Another approach is to determine the reproduction or replacement cost of new similar property and consider the remaining service life of the property being valued against the new cost as a starting point. In the case of land and buildings, it may be possible to determine recent sales prices for property with a similar location and function. Appraisals represent another approach particularly appropriate for fixed assets.

4. Natural resources. Valuation of natural resources on a current fair value basis often must be made by technical experts, such as geologists, forestry specialists, or engineers. Their valuations are based on careful estimates of what is economically recoverable and marketable from the resource. Realistic current sales prices of variable grades of the product are often available and can be used for future projection. If recoverable assets, future sales prices, and removal costs can be determined with reasonable accuracy, discounted cash flow techniques can be applied to measure the current fair value of the natural resource. There are often well publicized sales prices to leases and other mineral rights which may afford useful guidelines to the valuation of a natural resource.

COMPARATIVE EFFECTS OF ACCOUNTING ALTERNATIVES

Criticisms of traditional cost-basis accounting include (1) gains are recognized only in the periods in which a sale takes place, and (2) the amount of gain recognized is the difference between the original cost (carrying value) of the asset sold and its sale price.[10] Both price-level

[10] Except for the softening effect of allowing possible capital gains treatment, income tax laws tend to do the same thing. There are some tax exceptions, as for example when the disposition of the asset was an involuntary conversion and the gain is reinvested soon after the sale.

and fair-value accounting report gains differently as to both amount and timing than conventional cost-basis accounting. To illustrate, assume that in 19A an entity paid $4,000 for oil for resale when the general price level index number was 154. In 19B, the price index was 10% higher at 169.4, and the replacement cost of oil was $6,000. In 19C the oil was sold for $7,500. The gain (ignoring income taxes) would be reported under conventional cost basis accounting, price-level accounting, and current-value accounting for 19A, B, and C as follows:

	Profit Reported (before monetary gains and losses) Assuming—		
	Conventional Cost Basis	*Price-Level Basis*	*Current Fair Value Basis*
19A (period of purchase)	$ 0	$ 0	$ 0
19B (period of price change):			
Increase in income due to increased ending inventory valuation	0	400[(a)]	0
Fair-value adjustment ($6,000 − $4,000)			2,000
19C (period of sale):			
Increase due to sale:			
($7,500 − $4,000)	3,500		
($7,500 − $4,400)		3,100	
($7,500 − $6,000)			1,500

(a) The inventory is restated on the price-level basis to: $4,000 × 169.4/154 = $4,400.

In the case of the current fair-value example the $2,000 gain in 19B can be separated into two effects as follows:

Current replacement cost	$6,000
Deduct acquisition cost	4,000
Total gain	2,000
Price-level adjustment ($4,000 × 10%)	400
Holding gain	$1,600

A holding gain is viewed as a real value increase (i.e., the amount of the gain which exceeds inflation) which accrues to the entity by holding an asset while specific prices rise (i.e., the inventory price), as opposed to a rise in the general price level.

Sale of Fixed Assets

Similar differences result in respect to fixed assets. To illustrate, assume a business bought equipment for $20,000 when the price index was at 105. The equipment is depreciated on a straight-line basis with no residual value and a 20-year life. At the end of the eighth year, the general price-level index was 147 and the equipment had a current fair value of $14,000. Early in the ninth year, the equipment was sold for $15,000. The results would be as follows:

	Gain (Loss) Reported Assuming–		
	Conventional Cost Basis	*Price-Level Basis*	*Current Fair Value Basis*
First eight years:			
Depreciation expense	$(8,000)		
Price-level restatement		$(11,200)[(a)]	
Fair value adjustment ($20,000 − $14,000)			$(6,000)
Year of sale:			
$15,000 − ($20,000 − $8,000)	3,000		
$15,000 − ($28,000 − $11,200)		(1,800)	
$15,000 − $14,000			1,000

(a) The asset and accumulated depreciation, as nonmonetary assets, would be restated as follows:

	Restated Amount	*Change*
Equipment $20,000 × 147/105 =	$28,000	$8,000
Accumulated depreciation $8,000 × 147/105 =	(11,200)	(3,200)
Net effect*	$16,800	$4,800

* The $4,800 net restatement increase in this nonmonetary asset would not be reflected as a gain on the income statement, but rather it is reflected in the restatement of owners' equity.

Long-Term Capital Gains

The combined inflation and income tax effects of long-term gains are reported differently under conventional cost basis accounting, price-level account, and current fair value accounting. To illustrate, assume a taxpayer is subject to a long-term capital gain tax rate of 25%. The taxpayer bought land for $20,000 in 1946 when the GNP Deflator number was at 66.7. The land was sold in 1973 when the GNP Deflator was 156.7 (approximately 135% higher) for $56,000 when its fair value recorded in the fair-value accounts was $50,000. The reported gain or loss for 1973 would be as follows:

	Gain (Loss) Reported Assuming–		
	Conventional Cost Basis	*Price-Level Basis*	*Current Fair Value Basis*
Sales price (1973)	$56,000	$56,000	$56,000
Deduct carrying value	20,000	46,987[(a)]	50,000[(b)]
Gain before income tax	36,000	9,013	6,000
Deduct income taxes at 25% (per tax return)	9,000	9,000	9,000
Gain (loss) after tax	$27,000	$ 13	$ (3,000)

[(a)] $20,000 × 156.7/66.7 = $46,987. The price-level restatement does not create a gain; since this is a nonmonetary asset the restatement change is reflected in owners' equity.

[(b)] During the prior year a gain of $50,000 − $20,000 = $30,000 was recognized.

Regardless of the accounting basis, the taxpayer has $47,000 cash after paying income taxes and, therefore, has the same *purchasing power* in general price-level terms as when the original $20,000 investment was made in 1946. Under price-level accounting no gain would have been reported, but successive price-level adjusted balance sheets would have shown the land (and owners' equity) at increasingly higher amounts. On fair-value statements, as increments in fair value occurred, they would have been reflected both on balance sheets and on the income statements of the periods in which the increments were recorded for an aggregate increase in income of $30,000 over the 27-year period.

Situations and problems often are encountered where the required sales price (i.e., target proceeds) to stay abreast of inflation must be computed. In solving for *target proceeds* to enable an investor to stay abreast of inflation, the basic formula is as follows:

$$X = \text{Target Proceeds (i.e., necessary sales price)}$$

$$\text{Cost} \times \frac{\text{Index at Date of Sale}}{\text{Index at Date of Purchase}} = \text{Cost} + (1.0 - \text{Tax Rate}) \times (X - \text{Cost})$$

In the preceding example, substituting—

$$\$20{,}000 \times \frac{156.7}{66.7} = \$20{,}000 + .75\ (X - \$20{,}000)$$
$$\$47{,}000 = \$20{,}000 + .75X - \$15{,}000$$
$$X = \$56{,}000$$

Summary of Dollar Effects of Accounting Alternatives

In an era of inflation, what would be the comparative dollar effects that one could ordinarily expect the balance sheet and income statement to reflect under the various techniques? The tabulation below gives a general indication of the comparative effects using conventionally prepared statements as the base. Amounts on the conventional statements are designated "Base"; if these would be the same on statements prepared under either of the two alternative accounting approaches discussed in this chapter (i.e., price level, and fair value), "Base" is repeated. If the amount would be higher than base *a*, + appears; if it would likely be still higher under yet another alternative, ++ appears. If the amount would be lower than base *a*, – appears; if it would likely be still lower under yet another alternative, —– appears. In case an item is irrelevant to a particular alternative, a 0 appears.

In respect to the following summary, a qualifying comment is in order. It is likely that for most companies the replacement cost of plant and equipment, and hence the current fair value, will exceed a valuation derived by application of a general index such as the GNP Deflator. This assumption is reflected in respect to "property, plant, and equipment," "cost of goods sold," and "depreciation" in the tabulation above. In respect to net income, because such expenses as depreciation and cost of goods sold will be higher for most entities under each of the alternative techniques than under historical cost, a – sign was shown

	Inflationary Effect Assuming–		
	Conventional Historical Cost Basis	General Price-Level Basis	Current Fair-Value Basis
Balance Sheet:			
Cash and receivables	Base	Base	Base
Inventories	Base	+	+
Property, plant, and equipment	Base	+	++
Monetary liabilities	Base	Base	Base
Common stock equity	Base	+	++
Income Statement:			
Sales	Base	+	Base
Cost of goods sold (if manufacturing)	Base	+	++
Depreciation	Base	+	++
Purchasing power gain (or loss)	0	+	0
Increase in value of nonmonetary assets	0	0	+
Net income (assuming profits)	Base	–	–

for net income as compared to "Base." It should be pointed out, however, that the reduction occasioned by these foreseeable increases might be more than offset by purchasing power gains if the company were heavily in debt or by increases during the current period of the value of nonmonetary assets. If *Lifo* inventory is used, the adjustment of cost of goods sold would tend to be minimal compared with *Fifo* and average inventory techniques.

Usage of current replacement values for external reporting purposes received important official support in March, 1976. This impetus came with the issuance of Accounting Series Release No. 190 by the SEC requiring that specified replacement cost information be disclosed in the annual financial statements of certain listed corporations. All companies with inventories and gross plants aggregating more than $100 million and amounting to more than 10% of their total assets must disclose, either in footnote or in a separate section of their financial statements, the current costs of replacing inventories and productive plant, and the amount of cost of goods sold and depreciation as if these costs had been computed on the basis of current replacement costs. This disclosure requirement takes effect for fiscal years ending on or after December 25, 1976. (For mineral resource assets of registrants in the extractive industries and all assets located outside North America or the Common Market, the effective date is one year later.)

The replacement cost disclosures may be labeled "unaudited" although the auditor will be deemed to be associated with the information. It has been estimated these new rules may apply to the largest one thousand nonfinancial corporations in the nation. It is expected (not now required) that the affected companies will include the same information in annual reports to stockholders. The SEC expects the requirement to be extended to smaller companies in two or three years.

FUTURE TRENDS

For internal management uses, it is generally believed current fair-value accounting has more relevance than does price-level accounting. Fair-value accounting also is considered to be more relevant for external reporting purposes as well, assuming reasonably objective and consistent implementation is possible. In the view of many accountants, objectivity and realism in applying fair-value concepts is not possible. Therefore, its use would bring about such wide variation in valuation of virtually identical assets as to render attempts at comparison on a value basis almost meaningless. Price-level accounting, on the other hand, preserves whatever comparability now exists on traditional cost basis statements on an intercompany basis because it adjusts cost basis amounts by using a common set of index numbers.

Current fair-value accounting is relevant for internal reporting purposes for a number of reasons. One of the most significant reasons relates to capital preservation and asset replacement. A management concerned with asset replacement is interested in the cost of particular kinds of assets—those in need of replacement, not in how much the general price level had changed. If the price level had doubled since a major fixed asset was acquired and is now fully depreciated, but the cost of replacing that particular asset has trebled, management would have been better served by basing pricing decisions and financing plans on current-value rather than on price-level accounting information.

As we have seen, current value accounting may or may not be implemented in such a way as to reflect purchasing power (price-level) gains or losses. On the other hand, price-level accounting always reflects such gains but does not reflect holding gains and losses. Up to a point, it is "favorable" to be in debt when prices are rising; one retires debt with dollars of lower purchasing power. The most important thing, however, is to be able to pay maturing obligations when they fall due. The idea of running up debt to profit by doing so can be dangerous. It is, however, a fact that price-level accounting makes some of the least solvent companies look good because of the large gains based on excessive debt.

Abandonment of historical cost accounting, or the substitution of price-level accounting or current fair value accounting for it, in this country is not likely in the foreseeable future. It appears that for the foreseeable future the historical cost model will continue to survive and coexist with price level accounting. In time this may be followed by dual usage of historical cost and current fair-value accounting.

QUESTIONS

1. What is the price phenomenon known as *inflation*? What is the opposite condition called?

2. What indices measure changes in the general purchasing power of the U.S. dollar? What index has been preferred for preparation of price-level adjusted financial statements?

3. In general terms, how much have prices changed in the United States between 1933 and 1975? Why may it be inaccurate to say that prices have changed as much as the percentage of rise in the index between these dates?

4. "When prices are going up, they all go up; when they drop, they all drop." Comment on this statement.

5. As between sales, cost of goods sold, salaries, and depreciation expense, during an era of rapidly changing prices, which would be on the most current cost basis under conventional accounting procedures and which would be on a least current cost basis? Give reasons for your response.

6. When prices are changing rapidly, why are financial statements prepared on the conventional cost basis likely to be deficient in some respects?

7. When prices are rising and depreciation expense is computed in the conventional manner, what is likely to be true insofar as replacement of the depreciable assets is concerned?

8. Several "piecemeal" procedures have been employed or proposed to cope with the inadequacies of cost basis accounting under conditions of rapidly changing prices. Briefly describe them. Indicate which ones are acceptable in the framework of generally accepted accounting principles.

9. Under the index number approach, financial statement items are classified as monetary or nonmonetary. Briefly, by what criteria can these two categories be distinguished?

10. Indicate, with explanations where necessary, whether the following items are monetary or nonmonetary: *(a)* stocks held as investments; *(b)* bonds held as investments; *(c)* deposits in domestic banks; *(d)* deposits in foreign banks; *(e)* allowance for doubtful accounts; *(f)* machinery and equipment; *(g)* accounts payable; *(h)* preferred stock; *(i)* retained earnings; and *(j)* deferred credit related to income taxes.

11. During its most recent fiscal period, XY Company had a larger balance of cash and receivables than liabilities; prices rose steadily. Would this condition give rise to a purchasing power gain or a loss?

12. If prices rise steadily over an extended period of time, indicate whether the following items would give rise to a purchasing power gain, a purchasing power loss, or neither purchasing power gain nor loss:
    a. Maintaining a balance in a checking account.
    b. Owing bonds payable.
    c. Owning land.
    d. Amortizing goodwill.
    e. Holding common treasury stock.

13. If data are available on a quarterly basis rather than on an annual basis, how would this alter the preparation of price-level adjusted statements at the end of a year?

14. How would statements prepared on a restated price-level basis differ from those prepared on a current fair value basis? In what respects would they be similar?

DECISION CASE 25–1

In this situation, restated price-level statements, as supplements to the conventional cost basis statements are presented (inflation has been near double-digit rates). Knowing that you have accounting training, a friend, who owns common stock in several companies, drops their latest annual reports before you with a look that hovers between dismay and bewilderment.

Your friend begins, "I used to think that I understood a little about these reports, but now that the companies have all gone to this price-level accounting, the only things clear to me are the nice pictures of company employees and products!" Upon your inquiry, it develops that the following points bother your friend most of all:

a. Most of the companies reported higher net income on their conventional cost basis statements than on their price-level statements while at the same time, the latter statement showed the assets to be larger in amount.

b. Some of the companies reported purchasing power gains concurrent with operating gains; other reported purchasing power losses concurrent with operating gains; yet all of the companies were subject to the same degree of inflation.

c. The comparative statements, prepared on a restated price-level basis, showed that even the amount of cash reported for last year had changed. Your friend wonders whether the companies discovered overages or shortages of cash or are somehow "juggling the figures."

d. Your friend realizes that the prices of most things are rising and wonders whether the increased values of certain assets on the restated price-level statements represent what the items are worth. At the same time, your friend noticed that some assets are carried at identical amounts on both sets of statements.

Required:

1. Explain the specifics that are confusing your friend in such a way that a sophisticated layman (who is not an accountant) can understand them.
2. To cope with inflation (or deflation), aside from price-level statements, what alternative accounting techniques could be used? Describe them briefly and cite some of their pros and cons.
3. What is your assessment of the usefulness of price-level adjusted financial statements? Give reasons for your answer.

EXERCISES

Exercise 25–1

Select the best answer in each of the following. Items are independent of one another except where indicated to the contrary. Give the basis, including computations, for your choice.

The following information is applicable to items 1 through 4:

Equipment purchased for $120,000 on January 1, 19A, when the price index was 100, was sold on December 31, 19C, at a price of $85,000. The equipment originally was expected to last six years with no salvage value and was depreciated on a straight-line basis. The price index at the end of 19A was 125; 19B, 150; and 19C, 175.

1. Price-level financial statements prepared at the end of 19A would include:
   a. Equipment, $150,000; accumulated depreciation, $25,000; and a gain, $30,000.

b. Equipment, $150,000; accumulated depreciation, $25,000; and no gain or loss.
c. Equipment, $150,000; accumulated depreciation, $20,000; and a gain, $30,000.
d. Equipment, $120,000; accumulated depreciation, $20,000; and a gain, $30,000.
e. None of the above.

2. Price-level comparative statements prepared at the end of 19B would show the 19A financial statements' amount for equipment (net of accumulated depreciation) at:
a. $150,000.
b. $125,000.
c. $100,000.
d. $80,000.
e. None of the above.

3. Price-level financial statements prepared at the end of 19B should include depreciation expense of–
a. $35,000.
b. $30,000.
c. $25,000.
d. $20,000.
e. None of the above.

4. The general price-level income statement prepared at the end of 19C should include:
a. A gain of $35,000.
b. A gain of $25,000.
c. No gain or loss.
d. A loss of $5,000.
e. None of the above.

5. If land were purchased at a cost of $20,000 in January 19A when the general price-level index was 120 and sold in December 19F when the index was 150, the selling price that would result in no economic gain or loss would be:
a. $30,000.
b. $24,000.
c. $20,000.
d. $16,000.
e. None of the above.

6. If land were purchased in 19A for $100,000 when the general price-level index was 100 and sold at the end of 19G for $160,000 when the index was 170, the general price-level statement of income for 19G would show:
a. A price-level gain of $70,000 and a loss on sale of land of $10,000.
b. A gain on sale of land of $60,000.
c. A price-level loss of $10,000.
d. A loss on sale of land of $10,000.
e. None of the above.

7. If the base year is 19A (when the general price index = 100) and land is purchased for $50,000 in 19C when the general price index is 108.5, the cost of the land restated to 19A general purchasing power (rounded to the nearest whole dollar) would be:
a. $54,250.
b. $50,000.
c. $46,083.
d. $45,750.
e. None of the above.

8. Assume the same facts as in Item 7. The cost of the land restated to December 31, 19G, general purchasing power when the general price index was 119.2 (rounded to the nearest whole dollar) would be:
a. $59,600.
b. $54,931.
c. $46,083.
d. $45,512.
e. None of the above.

(AICPA adapted)

Exercise 25-2

Select the best answer in each of the following. Give the basis for your response.

1. In preparing price-level financial statements, a nonmonetary item would be:
   a. Accounts payable in cash.
   b. Long-term bonds payable.
   c. Accounts receivable.
   d. Allowance for doubtful accounts.
   e. None of the above.
2. In preparing price-level financial statements, monetary items consist of–
   a. Cash items plus all receivables with a fixed maturity date.
   b. Cash, other assets expected to be converted into cash and current liabilities.
   c. Assets and liabilities whose amounts are fixed by contract or otherwise in terms of dollars, regardless of price-level changes.
   d. Assets and liabilities classed as current on the balance sheet.
   e. None of the above.
3. An accountant who recommends the restatement of financial statements for price-level changes should not support this recommendation by stating that–
   a. Purchasing power gains and losses should be recognized.
   b. Historical dollars are not comparable to present-day dollars.
   c. The conversion of asset costs to a common-dollar basis is a useful extension of the original cost basis of asset valuation.
   d. Assets should be valued at their replacement cost.
4. When price-level balance sheets are prepared, they should be presented in terms of–
   a. The general purchasing power of the dollar at the latest balance sheet date.
   b. The general purchasing power of the dollar in the base period.
   c. The average general purchasing power of the dollar for the latest fiscal period.
   d. The general purchasing power of the dollar at the time the financial statements are issued.
   e. None of the above.
5. During a period of deflation, an entity usually would have the greatest gain in general purchasing power by holding–
   a. Cash.
   b. Plant and equipment.
   c. Accounts payable.
   d. Mortgages payable.
   e. None of the above.
6. The restatement of historical-dollar financial statements to reflect general price-level changes reports assets at–
   a. Lower cost or market.
   b. Current appraisal values.
   c. Costs adjusted for purchasing power changes.
   d. Current replacement cost.
   e. None of the above.
7. An unacceptable practice for reporting general price-level information is:
   a. The inclusion of general price-level gains and losses on monetary items in the price-level income statement.
   b. The inclusion of extraordinary gains and losses in the general price-level income statement.
   c. The use of charts, ratios, and narrative information.
   d. The use of specific price indices to restate inventories, plant, and equipment.
   e. None of the above.

(AICPA adapted)

Exercise 25–3

Whatley Company is preparing financial statements on the purchasing power basis. Selected data are as follows:

1. Price-index data:

January 1, 19A	95
December 31, 19A..............	100
June 30, 19B	105
December 31, 19D..............	140
Average for 19E..................	145
December 31, 19E..............	150

2. Property, plant, and equipment acquisition and depreciation data:
   a. Land acquired January 1, 19A, at a cost of $80,000.
   b. Building acquired December 31, 19A, at a cost of $120,000; by year-end, 19D and 19E respectively, accumulated depreciation on the building amounted to $44,000 and $48,000.
   c. Equipment costing $168,000 was acquired June 30, 19B; by December 31, 19D, accumulated depreciation amounted to $109,200; depreciation recorded for 19E was $8,400.
   d. New equipment added during 19E at a time when the index was at an average value for the year cost $58,000; depreciation recorded on this new equipment for 19E amounted to $4,350.
3. Monetary items:
   At the start of 19E, total monetary assets amounted to $112,000, while total monetary liabilities amounted to $180,000. At the end of 19E, total monetary assets amounted to $120,000 while total monetary liabilities were $190,000.

Required:

Use the numbers below for identification and compute the amounts for each numbered item. Round to nearest dollar.

A. On the price-level balance sheet as of December 31, 19E, carrying values for each would be:
   1. Land.
   2. Building (gross amount).
   3. Accumulated depreciation–building.
   4. Original equipment (gross amount).
   5. New equipment (gross amount).
   6. Accumulated depreciation–equipment (original).
   7. Accumulated depreciation–equipment (new).
   8. Total monetary assets.
   9. Total monetary liabilities.
B. On the price-level income statement for the year ended December 31, 19E, amounts reported would be:
   10. Depreciation expense (original equipment).
   11. Depreciation expense (new equipment).
   12. Depreciation expense (building).
   13. Sales (if sales of $290,000 were made evenly throughout 19E).
C. If, as of December 31, 19E, comparative balance sheets were being prepared on a price-level basis, and the amounts related to the December 31, 19D, balance sheet were being restated, the amounts would be:
   14. Land.
   15. Equipment (gross amount).
   16. Building (gross amount).
   17. Accumulated depreciation–building.
   18. Monetary assets.
   19. Monetary liabilities.

Exercise 25–4

Some items on conventional cost basis financial statements are expressed in current period dollars (or nearly so), while other items are normally expressed in dollars of prior periods.

Required:

1. Name the principal balance sheet items which likely would not be expressed in current period dollars. If any part of your answer depends on the accounting procedures employed, explain.
2. Name the principal items in the income statement which likely would not be expressed in current period dollars (or nearly so). If any part of your answer depends on the accounting procedures used, explain.
3. Name the principal items in the statement of changes in financial position which likely would not be expressed in current period dollars. If any part of your answer depends on the accounting procedures used, explain.

(AICPA adapted)

Exercise 25–5

DE Company is completing its fifth year of operations (19E). Comparative balance sheets (historical cost basis) at year-end 19D and 19E appear below.

	December 31	
	19D	*19E*
Cash and receivables	$250,000	$325,000
Inventories	187,500	162,500
Future plant site	62,500	62,500
Fixtures	210,000	270,000
Accumulated depreciation	(50,000)	(74,000)
	$660,000	$746,000
Current liabilities	$ 75,000	$137,500
Long-term liabilities	150,000	125,000
Capital stock	400,000	400,000
Retained earnings	35,000	83,500
	$660,000	$746,000

The income statement (historical cost basis) for the year ended December 31, 19E, follows.

Sales		$1,000,000
Cost of goods sold:		
Beginning inventory	$187,500	
Purchases	625,000	
Goods available	812,500	
Ending inventory	162,500	
Cost of goods sold		650,000
Gross margin		350,000
Expenses:		
Operating expenses except depreciation	120,000	
Depreciation	24,000	144,000
Income before taxes		206,000
Income taxes		87,500
Net Income		$ 118,500

A dividend of $70,000 was paid at year-end. In mid-year added fixtures costing $60,000 were bought. The annual rate of depreciation on fixtures is 10% of cost. Inventories are on a *Fifo* basis. When the original fixtures and the future plant site were acquired during the first year of operations the relevant price index was at 105. Other price index data and conversion factors are as follows:

	Index	*Conversion Factor*
December 31, 19E	136.5	100
December 31, 19D	125	109.2
Average for 19E	131.25	104

Assume the beginning inventory was acquired at 19D year-end prices. Purchases, sales, operating expenses, and income taxes occurred or accrued ratably throughout the year.

Required:

1. Prepared a price-level balance sheet as of December 31, 19E, and a price-level income statement for 19E. Determine the price-level (purchasing power) gain or loss and present a separate schedule detailing its computation.
2. Indicate the gross and net carrying values of the fixtures and of the future plant site for a price-level balance sheet as of December 31, 19D.

Exercise 25–6

The items reflected in the trial balance below were acquired when the relevant price index was 105.

Cash	$57,235	
Land	79,500	
Liability		$ 2,570
Capital stock		100,000
Retained earnings		34,165

The following transactions took place during the first quarter of the current fiscal year:

Date	*Index*	*Data*
Oct. 1	110	Purchased machinery costing $8,500 on account.
Oct. 15	120	Paid for machinery purchased on October 1.
Oct. 31	135	Billed customers for services rendered, $7,500.
Nov. 15	140	Paid $1,230 of the initial liability balance.
Nov. 30	145	Collected half of the billed revenue.
Dec. 10	150	Paid general expense of $5,700.
Dec. 31	160	Accrued three months' depreciation on machinery which has a five-year life with no scrap value.

Required:

1. Enter the initial balances, and then record the transactions for the first quarter directly in ledger accounts; also include, in parentheses, the index number values prevailing when each transaction occurred.

2. As of the close of the quarter, prepare both balance sheets and income statements on both conventional cost basis and price-level basis using the index number procedures illustrated in the chapter. Show calculation of the price-level (purchasing power) gain or loss. Since no average index value for the period is given, it will be necessary to apply to each transaction, a specific conversion factor. For example, if a $360 transaction occurred when the index was 120, in December 31 terms, this would convert to: $360 × 160/120 = $480. Round all calculations to the nearest dollar.

Exercise 25–7

An investor bought land for $60,000 in 19A when the index measuring general purchasing power of the dollar was 110. Assuming a gain on sale of the land is taxable at a capital gains rate of 25%, at what price would the land have to be sold on each of the following dates for the investor to maintain the equivalent purchasing power after taxes? In each instance the index number on the date of sale was:

Date of Sale	*Index*
a. October 1, 19B	121
b. May 1, 19C	129
c. July 1, 19D	143
d. December 1, 19E	154

Round answers to nearest dollar.

Exercise 25–8

The controller of the Robinson Company is discussing a comment you made in the course of presenting your audit report.

". . . and frankly," L. Fisher continued, "I agree that we, too, are responsible for finding ways to produce more relevant financial statements which are as reliable as the ones we now produce.

"For example, suppose the company acquired a finished item for inventory for $40 when the general price-level index was 110. And, later, the item was sold for $75 when the general price-level index was 121 and the current replacement cost was $54. We could calculate a 'holding gain.' "

Required:

1. Explain to what extent and how current replacement costs already are used *within* generally accepted accounting principles to value inventories.
2. Calculate in good form the amount of the holding gain in Fisher's example.
3. Why is the use of current replacement cost for *both* inventories and cost of goods sold preferred by some accounting authorities to the generally accepted use of *Fifo* or *Lifo*?

(AICPA adapted)

PROBLEMS

Problem 25–1

MR Company is preparing financial statements on the purchasing power basis. Selected data are as follows:

1. Price level numbers:

January 1, 19A	90
December 31, 19A	95
June 30, 19B	100
December 31, 19B	106
December 31, 19D	145
Average for 19E	150
December 31, 19E	155

2. From historical cost statements—property, plant, and equipment acquisition and depreciation data:
   a. Land acquired January 1, 19A, at a cost of $45,000.
   b. Building acquired December 31, 19A, at a cost of $380,000; by year-end 19D and 19E respectively, Accumulated Depreciation—Building account reflected balances of $22,800 and $30,400.
   c. Fixtures costing $77,000 were acquired June 30, 19B; on these accumulated depreciation recorded by year-end 19D and 19E amounted to $19,250 and $26,950.
   d. Additional fixtures were bought in mid-year 19E for $30,000 when the index was 150; by year-end depreciation recorded on the newest fixtures amounted to $2,250.
3. Monetary assets:
   At the start of 19E, total monetary assets were $87,000 and total monetary liabilities were $31,900. At the end of 19E, total monetary assets were $96,400, and total monetary liabilities were $33,800.

Required:

Use the numbers given below for identification and compute the amounts that would appear on price-level financial statements. Round to nearest dollar.

A. On the price-level balance sheet as of December 31, 19E, the carrying values would be:
   1. Land.
   2. Building (gross amount).
   3. Old fixtures (gross amount).
   4. New fixtures (gross amount).
   5. Accumulated depreciation—building.
   6. Accumulated depreciation—old fixtures.
   7. Accumulated depreciation—new fixtures.
   8. Total monetary assets.
   9. Total monetary liabilities.
B. On the price-level income statement for the year ended December 31, 19E, amounts reported would be:
   10. Depreciation expense (building).
   11. Depreciation expense (new fixtures).
   12. Depreciation expense (old fixtures).
   13. Purchases (assume purchases of $285,000 were made evenly throughout 19E).
   14. Price-level gain or loss (based solely on starting and ending monetary items).
C. If, as of December 31, 19E, comparative balance sheets were being prepared on a price-level basis and amounts related to the December 31, 19D, balance sheet were being restated, the restated amounts would be:
   15. Land.

16. Fixtures (gross amount).
17. Monetary assets.
18. Monetary liabilities.
19. Building (gross amount).
20. Accumulated depreciation–fixtures.

Problem 25–2

Barden Corporation, a manufacturer with large investments in plant and equipment, began operations in 1938. The company's history has been one of expansion in sales, production, and physical facilities. Recently, some concern has been expressed that the conventional financial statements do not provide sufficient information for decisions by investors. After consideration of proposals for various types of supplementary financial statements to be included in the 1976 annual report, management has decided to present a balance sheet as of December 31, 1976, and a statement of income and retained earnings for 1976, both restated for changes in the general price level.

Required:

1. On what basis can it be contended that Barden's conventional statements should be restated for changes in the general price level?
2. Distinguish between financial statements restated for general price-level changes and current-value financial statements.
3. Distinguish between monetary and nonmonetary assets and liabilities, as the terms are used in general price-level accounting. Give examples of each.
4. Outline the procedures Barden should follow in preparing the proposed supplementary statements.
5. Indicate the major similarities and differences between the proposed supplementary statements and the corresponding conventional statements.
6. Assuming that in the future Barden will want to present comparative supplementary statements, can the 1976 supplementary statements be presented in 1977 without adjustment? Explain.

(AICPA adapted)

Problem 25–3

CTZ Company prepared the following comparative balance sheets (historical cost basis) at the close of its fourth year of operations (19D).

	December 31	
	19C	*19D*
Cash	$ 29,000	$ 40,320
Receivables	75,000	100,000
Inventory	21,000	35,000
Land	100,000	100,000
Building	320,000	320,000
Accumulated depreciation–building	(38,400)	(51,200)
Fixtures	90,000	120,000
Accumulated depreciation–fixtures	(40,500)	(58,500)
Total	$556,100	$605,620

Current liabilities	$ 50,000	$ 75,000
Bonds payable	50,000	50,000
Common stock	250,000	250,000
Retained earnings	206,100	230,620
	$556,100	$605,620

The income statement (historical cost basis) for 19D was:

Sales		$950,000
Cost of goods sold:		
Beginning inventory	$ 21,000	
Purchases	584,000	
Goods available	605,000	
Ending inventory	35,000	
Cost of goods sold		570,000
Gross margin		380,000
Expenses:		
Operating expenses	125,000	
Depreciation – building	12,800	
Depreciation – fixtures	18,000	
Salaries	100,000	255,800
Income before taxes		124,200
Income tax		49,680
Net Income		$ 74,520

A $50,000 dividend was paid at year-end. Fixtures costing $30,000 were bought on January 2, 19D. Fixtures are depreciated 15% per annum on cost. Inventories are on a *Fifo* basis; the ending inventory can be assumed to have been acquired at the average level of prices prevailing during 19D. When the land, buildings, and original fixtures were acquired the price index was 103. Other price index data and conversion factors are:

	Index	*Conversion Factor*
December 31, 19D	127	100
December 31, 19C	119	106.7
Average for 19D	124	102.4

The beginning inventory can be assumed to have been acquired at 19C year-end prices. Purchases, sales, operating expenses (which include interest), salaries, and income taxes accrued evenly throughout 19D. The building is depreciated over a 25-year life; no residual value, straight-line basis.

Required:

1. Prepare a price-level balance sheet as of December 31, 19D, and a price-level income statement for 19D; show computation of the purchasing power gain or loss for the year.
2. Indicate the gross and net carrying values of fixtures and building for a price-level balance sheet as of December 31, 19C.

Problem 25–4

Dolphin Company prepared the comparative balance sheets (historical cost basis) which appear below at the close of its tenth year of operations (19J).

	December 31	
	19I	*19J*
Cash	$ 75,000	$101,000
Receivables	215,000	195,000
Inventory	135,000	127,000
Land	150,000	150,000
Building	240,000	240,000
Accumulated depreciation – building	(56,000)	(64,000)
Machinery	225,000	280,000
Accumulated depreciation – machinery	(115,000)	(137,500)
Total	$869,000	$891,500
Current liabilities	$124,000	$137,000
Long-term liabilities	75,000	81,000
Bonds payable	60,000	60,000
Common stock	350,000	350,000
Retained earnings	260,000	263,500
	$869,000	$891,500

The land was bought in 19A when the price index was 104. The building was acquired early in 19C when the index was 107; it has an estimated 30-year life and no salvage value and is depreciated on a straight-line basis. Machinery is depreciated 10% per annum on cost with no salvage value. The first machinery was bought in 19B when the price index was 106 at a cost of $50,000; a second machine was acquired for $100,000 in 19D when the index was 108.5; a third machine was bought in 19H when the index was 117. A full year's depreciation is taken in the year of acquisition unless the purchase is at year-end. At year-end 19J machinery costing $55,000 was acquired.

On January 2, 19J, an $85,000 dividend was declared and paid. The beginning inventory can be assumed to have been acquired when the index was 107; the ending inventory should be converted on the assumption the index was 125 when it was bought.

Sales, operating expenses, income taxes, and purchases accrued ratably during 19J. Relevant price index data (aside from that already given) are as follows:

	Index	*Conversion Factor*
December 31, 19J	127	100
December 31, 19I	121	104.96
Average for 19J	125	101.6

The income statement (historical cost basis) for the year 19J was as follows:

Sales		$1,275,000
Cost of goods sold:		
Inventory, January 1	$135,000	
Purchases	850,000	
Goods available	985,000	
Inventory, December 31	127,000	
Cost of goods sold		858,000
Gross margin		417,000
Expenses:		
Operating expenses	210,000	
Depreciation, building	8,000	
Depreciation, machinery	22,500	240,500
Income before taxes		176,500
Income tax		88,000
Net income		$ 88,500

Required:

1. Prepare an income statement for 19J and a balance sheet as of December 31, 19J on a price-level adjusted basis. Show computations of the purchasing power gain or loss.
2. Compute the gross and net carrying values of machinery and the building for the December 31, 19I price-level balance sheet.

Problem 25–5

When items in the following trial balance were acquired, the price index was 150.

Cash	$ 7,500	
Equipment	10,000	
Accumulated depreciation		$2,000
Liability		1,900
Capital stock		8,000
Retained earnings		5,600

Transactions during the first half of current fiscal year were as follows. Index values prevailing at the time are indicated parenthetically.

Jan. 10	A payment of $800 on the liability balance is made (160).
Feb. 15	Revenue for services is billed to customers, $2,500 (175).
Mar. 1	Four fifths of the revenue billed is collected (180).
Apr. 20	Land is purchased for $8,000 cash (190).
May 5	General expenses are paid, $500 (185).
June 30	Accrued six month's depreciation on the equipment which has a ten-year life and no scrap value (200).

The index at June 30 was 200.

Required:

1. Enter the initial balances, then record the six months' transactions directly in ledger accounts; also enter the date and the index number parenthetically.
2. At the close of the six-month period, prepare both a conventional and price-level balance sheet and income statement using index number procedures illustrated in the chapter. Calculate the purchasing power gain or loss. Since no average for the six-month period is given, it will be necessary to apply to each transaction and balance, a specific conversion factor. For example, if a $660 transaction occurred when the price index was 165, in June 30 terms (when the index was 200), the restatement would be calculated as: $660 × 200/165 = $800. Round all calculations to nearest dollar.

Problem 25–6

Published financial statements of United States companies are currently prepared on a stable-dollar assumption even though the general purchasing power of the dollar has declined considerably because of inflation in recent years. To account for this changing value of the dollar, many accountants suggest that financial statements should be adjusted for general price-level changes. Three independent, unrelated statements regarding general price-level adjusted financial statements follow. Each statement contains some fallacious reasoning.

Statement I

The accounting profession has not seriously considered price-level adjusted financial statements before because the rate of inflation usually has been so small from year-to-year that the adjustments would have been immaterial in amount. Price-level adjusted financial statements represent a departure from the historical-cost basis of accounting. Financial statements should be prepared from facts, not estimates.

Statement II

If financial statements were adjusted for general price-level changes, depreciation charges in the earnings statement would permit the recovery of dollars of current purchasing power and, thereby, equal the cost of new assets to replace the old ones. General price-level adjusted data would yield statement-of-financial-position amounts closely approximating current values. Furthermore, management can make better decisions if general price-level adjusted financial statements are published.

Statement III

When adjusting financial data for general price-level changes, a distinction must be made between monetary and nonmonetary assets and liabilities, which, under the historical-cost basis of accounting, have been identified as "current" and "noncurrent." When using the historical-cost basis of accounting, no purchasing-power gain or loss is recognized in the accounting process, but when financial statements are adjusted for general price-level changes, a purchasing-power gain or loss will be recognized on monetary and nonmonetary items.

Required:

Evaluate each of the independent statements and identify the areas of fallacious reasoning in each and explain why the reasoning is incorrect. Complete your discussion of each statement before proceeding to the next statement.

(AICPA adapted)

Problem 25–7

AB COMPANY
Balance Sheet
At December 31, 19E

Cash and receivables	$105,000	Current liabilities	$ 60,000
Inventory	75,000	Capital stock	250,000
Land	20,000	Retained earnings	93,000
Building	200,000		
Accumulated depreciation–building	(20,000)		
Fixtures	40,000		
Accumulated depreciation–fixtures	(17,000)		
	$403,000		$403,000

AB COMPANY
Income and Retained Earnings Statements
For Year Ended December 31, 19E

Sales		$850,000
Inventory, January 1	$ 90,000	
Purchases	640,000	
Goods available for sale	730,000	
Inventory, December 31	75,000	
Cost of goods sold		655,000
Gross margin		195,000
Operating expenses	136,000	
Depreciation–building	4,000	
Depreciation–fixtures	5,000	
Total Expenses		145,000
Income before taxes		50,000
Income tax expense (40%)		20,000
Net income		30,000
Retained earnings, January 1		83,000
Total		113,000
Dividend, paid at mid year		20,000
Retained Earnings, December 31		$ 93,000

The foregoing statements, prepared on the conventional historical cost basis, are for the most recent year. Land, buildings, and $30,000 of fixtures were acquired January 1, 19A, when AB Company was formed and began operations. Fixed assets are depreciated on a straight-line basis with assumed zero salvage values. The building is assumed to have a 50-year life and the original fixtures, a 10-year life. An added $10,000 of fixtures bought in January, 19E, have a five-year life.

Inventory is accounted for on a *Fifo* basis. Sales and purchases and expenses (including income tax) occurred or accrued uniformly throughout the year.

Relevant price index data are:

Date	*Value*	*Conversion Factor*
January 1, 19A	121.3	1.20
January 1, 19E	136	1.07*
Average for 19E..................	140	1.04
December 31, 19E..............	145.6	1.00

* Use this value to restate the beginning inventory.

Balances of working capital elements at January 1, 19E, were:

Cash and receivables...............	$100,000
Current liabilities.....................	79,000

Required:

1. Prepare a price-level balance sheet and an income statement as of December 31, 19E. Show computations of the purchasing power gain or loss.
2. Show computations of the gross and net carrying values of buildings and fixtures on the price-level statements dated January 1, 19E.

Problem 25–8

When the items reflected in the trial balance below were acquired, the relevant price index was 120.

Cash	$5,800	
Equipment	3,000	
Accumulated depreciation..............		$ 600
Liability		900
Capital stock		5,000
Retained earnings		2,300

Transactions during the first quarter of the current fiscal year were as follows. Index values prevailing at the time are indicated parenthetically.

Jan. 15 A payment of $480 on the liability balance is made (125).
Jan. 31 Revenue for services is billed to customers, $1,300 (130).
Feb. 15 Half of the revenue billed is collected (140).
Mar. 10 Land is purchased for $5,200 cash (130).
Mar. 20 General expenses are paid, $700 (140).
Mar. 31 Accrued three months' depreciation on the equipment which has a six-year life and no scrap value (150).

The index at March 31 was 150.

Required:

1. Enter the initial balances, then record the transactions directly in ledger accounts; also enter dates and the index number data (parenthetically).
2. As of the close of the quarter, prepare both conventional statements and price-level statements using the index number procedures described in the chapter. Show calculations of the purchasing power gain or loss. Since no average for the period is given, it will be necessary to apply to each transaction, a specific conversion factor. For example, if a $650 transaction occurred when the index

was 130, in March 31 terms, this would be restated as follows: $650 × 150/130 = $750. Round calculations to the nearest dollar.

Problem 25–9

Skadden, Inc., a retailer, was organized during 19A. Skadden's management has decided to supplement its December 31, 19D, historical dollar financial statements with general price-level financial statements. The following general ledger trial balance (historical dollar) and additional information have been furnished:

SKADDEN, INC.
Trial Balance
December 31, 19D

	Debit	Credit
Cash and receivables (net)	$ 540,000	
Marketable securities (common stock)	400,000	
Inventory	440,000	
Equipment	650,000	
Equipment—Accumulated depreciation		$ 164,000
Accounts payable		300,000
6% first mortgage bonds, due 19V		500,000
Common stock, $10 par		1,000,000
Retained earnings, December 31, 19C	46,000	
Sales		1,900,000
Cost of sales	1,508,000	
Depreciation	65,000	
Other operating expenses and interest	215,000	
	$3,864,000	$3,864,000

a. Monetary assets (cash and receivables) exceeded monetary liabilities (accounts payable and bonds payable) by $445,000 at December 31, 19C. The amounts of monetary items are fixed in terms of numbers of dollars regardless of changes in specific prices or in the general price level.

b. Purchases ($1,840,000 in 19D) and sales are made uniformly throughout the year.

c. Depreciation is computed on a straight-line basis, with a full year's depreciation being taken in the year of acquisition and none in the year of retirement. The depreciation rate is 10%, and no salvage value is anticipated. Acquisitions and retirements have been made fairly evenly over each year and the retirements in 19D consisted of assets purchased during 19B which were scrapped. An analysis of the equipment account reveals the following:

Year	Beginning Balance	Additions	Retirements	Ending Balance
19B	—	$550,000	—	$550,000
19C	$550,000	10,000	—	560,000
19D	560,000	150,000	$60,000	650,000

d. The bonds were issued in 19B and the marketable securities were purchased fairly evenly over 19D. Other operating expenses and interest are assumed to be incurred evenly throughout the year.

e. Assume that Gross National Product Implicit Price Deflators (1958 = 100) were as follows:

Annual Averages		*Index*	*Conversion Factors (19D 4th Qtr. = 1.000)*
19A		113.9	1.128
19B		116.8	1.100
19C		121.8	1.055
19D		126.7	1.014
Quarterly Averages			
19C	4th	123.5	1.040
19D	1st	124.9	1.029
	2nd	126.1	1.019
	3rd	127.3	1.009
	4th	128.5	1.000

Required:

1. Prepare a schedule to convert the Equipment account balance at December 31, 19D, from historical cost to general price-level adjusted dollars.
2. Prepare a schedule to analyze in historical dollars the Equipment–Accumulated Depreciation account for the year 19D.
3. Prepare a schedule to analyze in general price-level dollars the Equipment–Accumulated Depreciation account for the year 19D.
4. Prepare a schedule to compute Skadden, Inc.'s general price-level gain or loss on its net holdings of monetary assets for 19D (ignore income tax implications). The schedule should give consideration to appropriate items on or related to the balance sheet and the income statement.

(AICPA adapted)

Problem 25–10

The Melgar Company purchased a tract of land as an investment in 19D for $100,000; late in that year the company decided to construct a shopping center on the site. Construction began in 19E and was completed in 19G; one third of the construction was completed each year. Melgar originally estimated the costs of the project would be $1,200,000 for materials, $750,000 for labor, $150,000 for variable overhead, and $600,000 for depreciation.

Actual costs (excluding depreciation) incurred for construction were:

	19E	*19F*	*19G*
Materials	$418,950	$434,560	$462,000
Labor	236,250	274,400	282,000
Variable overhead..............	47,250	54,208	61,200

Shortly after construction began, Melgar sold the shopping center for $3,000,000 with payment to be made in full on completion in December 19G. One hundred and fifty thousand dollars of the sales price was allocated for the land.

The transaction was completed as scheduled, and now a controversy has developed between the two major stockholders of the company. One feels the company should have invested in land because a high rate of return was earned on the land. The other feels the original decision was sound and that changes in the price level which were not anticipated affected the original cost estimates.

You were engaged to furnish guidance to these stockholders in resolving their controversy. As an aid, you obtained the following information:

a. Using 19D as the base year, price-level indices for relevant years are: 19A = 90, 19B = 93, 19C = 96, 19D = 100, 19E = 105, 19F = 112, and 19G = 120.
b. The company allocated $200,000 per year for depreciation of fixed assets allocated to this construction project; of that amount $25,000 was for a building purchased in 19A and $175,000 was for equipment purchased in 19C.

Required:

1. Prepare a schedule to restate in base year (19D) costs the actual costs, including depreciation, incurred each year. Disregard income taxes and assume that each price-level index was valid for the entire year.
2. Prepare a schedule comparing the originally estimated costs of the project with the total actual costs for each element of cost (materials, labor, variable overhead, and depreciation) adjusted to the 19D price level.
3. Prepare a schedule to restate the amount received on the sale in terms of base year (19D) purchasing power. The gain or loss should be determined separately for the land and the building in terms of base year purchasing power and should exclude depreciation.

(AICPA adapted)

Appendix—List of Official Pronouncements

This appendix is included to help students *(a)* gain an overview of the official pronouncements, and *(b)* identify appropriate source documents for numerous accounting issues discussed in this book. Further study of these issues in the source documents often is desirable.

Accounting Research Bulletins (ARBs), Accounting Procedures Committee, AICPA (ARBs discontinued in 1959)

ARB No.	*Contents*	*Status, January 1, 1976*	*Chapter Citations in this Book*
43.	Restatement and Revisions of Accounting Research Bulletins Nos. 1–42, June, 1953	Continued in force by APB Opinion No. 6 (as amended)	1, 4, 5, 7, 8, 9, 11, 14, 16, 17, 24
	Chapter 1. Prior Opinions	Amended	
	Chapter 2. Form of Statements	Amended and partially superseded	5, 24
	Chapter 3. Working Capital	Amended and partially superseded	7
	Chapter 4. Inventory Pricing	Amended	8, 9
	Chapter 5. Intangible Assets	Amended and partially superseded	14
	Chapter 6. Contingency Reserves	Superseded by FASB Statement No. 5	
	Chapter 7. Capital Accounts	Amended and partially superseded	
	Chapter 8. Income and Earned Surplus	Superseded by APB Opinion No. 9	
	Chapter 9. Depreciation	Amended and partially superseded	25
	Chapter 10. Taxes	Amended and partially superseded	
	Chapter 11. Government Contracts	Amended	
	Chapter 12. Foreign Operations and Foreign Exchange	Amended	
	Chapter 13. Compensation (Pension Plans)	Amended and partially superseded	17
	Chapter 14. Disclosure of Long-Term Leases in Financial Statements	Superseded by APB Opinion No. 5	
	Chapter 15. Unamortized Discount, Issue Cost, and Redemption Premium on Bonds Refunded	Amended and partially superseded	
44.	Declining-Balance Depreciation; Revised July 1958	Amended	13
45.	Long-Term Construction-Type Contracts; October 1955	Unchanged	10
46.	Discontinuance of Dating Earned Surplus; February 1956	Unchanged	
47.	Accounting for Costs of Pension Plans; September 1956	Superseded by APB Opinion No. 8	
48.	Business Combinations; January 1957	Superseded by APB Opinion No. 16	
49.	Earnings per Share; April 1958	Superseded by APB Opinion No. 9	
50.	Contingencies; October 1958	Superseded by FASB Statement No. 5	
51.	Consolidated Financial Statements, August 1959	Amended and partially superseded	

Accounting Terminology Bulletins, Committee on Terminology, AICPA (Bulletins discontinued in 1959)

ATB No.	*Contents*	*Status January 1, 1976*	*Chapter Citations in this Book*
1.	Review and Resume (of the eight original terminology bulletins), June 1953	Partially superseded	1, 5, 10, 15, 16
2.	Proceeds, Revenue, Income, Profit, and Earnings	Amended	
3.	Book Value	Unchanged	
4.	Cost, Expense, and Loss	Amended	

Accounting Principles Board (APB) Opinions, AICPA (Opinions discontinued in 1973)

APB No.	*Contents*	*Status, January 1, 1976*	*Chapter Citations in this Book*
1.	New Depreciation Guidelines and Rules, November 1962	Unchanged	
2.	Accounting for the "Investment Credit," December 1962	Unchanged	13
	Addendum to Opinion No. 2—Accounting Principles for Regulated Industries, December 1962	Unchanged	
3.	The Statement of Source and Application of Funds, October 1963	Superseded by APB Opinion No. 9	
4.	Accounting for the "Investment Credit" (Amending No. 2), March 1964	Unchanged	13
5.	Reporting of Leases in Financial Statements of Lessee. September 1964	Partially superseded	23
6.	Status of Accounting Research Bulletins, October 1965	Amended and partially superseded	5, 17
7.	Accounting for Leases in Financial Statements of Lessors, May 1966	Partially superseded	23
8.	Accounting for the Cost of Pension Plans, November 1966	Unchanged	22
9.	Reporting the Results of Operations, December 1966	Partially superseded	4, 14, 15, 16, 18, 20
10.	Omnibus Opinion—1966, December 1966	Amended and partially superseded	4, 15, 16, 17
11.	Accounting for Income Taxes, December 1967	Amended and partially superseded	4, 11
12.	Omnibus Opinion—1967, December 1967	Amended and partially superseded	4, 5, 13, 16

13. Amending Paragraph 6 of APB Opinion No. 9, Application to Commercial Banks, March 1969	Amended	Beyond scope of this book
14. Accounting for Convertible Debt and Debt Issued with Stock Purchase Warrants, March 1969	Unchanged	
15. Earnings per Share, May 1969	Unchanged	4, 17
16. Business Combinations, August 1970	Amended	18
17. Intangible Assets, August 1970	Unchanged	14, 18
18. The Equity Method of Accounting for Investments in Common Stock, March 1971	Amended and partially superseded	18
19. Reporting Changes in Financial Position, March 1971	Unchanged	5, 21
20. Accounting Changes, July, 1971	Unchanged	2, 4, 7, 9, 11, 12, 13, 17, 20
21. Interest on Receivables and Payables, August 1971	Unchanged	2, 11, 19
22. Disclosure of Accounting Policies, April 1972	Unchanged	5, 13, 24
23. Accounting for Income Taxes—Special Areas, April, 1972	Amended	Beyond scope of this book
24. Accounting for Income Taxes—Equity Method Investments, April 1972	Unchanged	Beyond scope of this book
25. Accounting for Stock issued to Employees, October 1972	Unchanged	17
26. Early Extinguishment of Debt, October 1972	Unchanged	19
27. Accounting for Lease Transactions by Manufacturer or Dealer Lessors, November 1972	Unchanged	23
28. Interim Financial Reporting, May 1973	Partially superseded	2
29. Accounting for Nonmonetary Transactions, May 1973	Unchanged	12, 21
30. Reporting the Results of Operations, June 1973	Unchanged	4, 8, 12, 15, 18, 19
31. Disclosure of Lease Commitments by Lessees, June 1973	Unchanged	23

Financial Accounting Standards Board (FASB), Statements of Financial Accounting Standards (1973 to date)

FASB No.	*Contents*	*Status, January 1, 1976*	*Chapter Citations in this Book*
1.	Disclosure of Foreign Currency, December 1973	Unchanged	Beyond scope of this book
2.	Accounting for Research and Development Costs, October 1974	Unchanged	5, 14
3.	Reporting Accounting Changes in Interim Financial Statements, December 1974	Unchanged	20
4.	Reporting Gains and Losses from Extinguishment of Debt, March 1975	Unchanged	19, 21
5.	Accounting for Contingencies	Amended	8, 11, 16
6.	Classification of Short-Term Obligations Expected to be Refinanced, May 1975	Unchanged	5, 7, 11, 19
7.	Accounting and Reporting by Development Stage Enterprises, June 1975	Unchanged	14
8.	Accounting for the Translation of Foreign Currency Transactions and Foreign Currency Financial Statements, October 1975	Unchanged	Beyond scope of this book
9.	Accounting for Income Taxes—Oil and Gas Producing Companies (an Amendment of APB Opinions Nos. 11 and 23), October 1975	Unchanged	11
10.	Extension of "Grandfather" Provisions for Business Combinations (an Amendment of APB Opinion No. 16), October 1975	Unchanged	18
11.	Accounting for Contingencies—Transition Method (an Amendment of FASB Statement No. 5), December 1975	Unchanged	11
12.	Accounting for Certain Marketable Securities, December 1975	Unchanged	5, 7, 15, 18

Index

A

B

J

L

M

N

This book has been set in 9 and 8 point Primer, leaded 2 points. Chapter numbers are 18 and 36 point Helvetica italic and chapter titles are 16 point Helvetica. The size of the type page is 27 by 45½ picas.